The New York Times
HERITAGE COOKBOOK

The New York Times
HERITAGE COOKBOOK

BY JEAN HEWITT

Wings Books

New York • Avenel, New Jersey

To Marianne

Drawings by Ray Skibinski

This 1992 edition is published by Wings Books,
distributed by Random House Value Publishing, Inc.,
40 Engelhard Avenue, Avenel, New Jersey 07001,
by arrangement with G.P. Putnam's songs.

Random House
New York • Toronto • London • Sydney • Auckland

Printed and bound in the United States of America

Library of Congress Cataloging-in-Publication Data
Hewitt, Jean.
     The New York Times heritage cook book / by Jean
Hewitt.
         p.   cm.
     Originally published: New York : Putnam, 1972.
     Includes index.
     ISBN 0-517-30997-1
     1. Cookery, American.   I. New York times.   II. Title.
III. Title: Heritage cook book.
TX715.H4984   1992
641.5973—dc20   91-44089
                                                                CIP

18   17   16   15   14   13

Contents

Introduction... xv

1. Northeast

Appetizers and Soups 3

Fish and Shellfish 23

Meat, Poultry, Game and Other Main Dishes 44

Vegetables, Main Dish Accompaniments and Salads........... 73

Breads.. 96

Pies, Cakes, Desserts and Cookies......................... 106

Miscellaneous... 149

> Pickles, Relishes and Preserves, 149
>
> Sauces, 156
>
> Beverages, 158
>
> Candies, 159
>
> Dressings (Stuffings), 161
>
> Dumplings, 163

2. South

Appetizers and Soups 167

Fish and Shellfish 185

Meat, Poultry, Game and Other Main Dishes 208

Vegetables, Main Dish Accompaniments and Salads.......... 236

Breads... 255

Pies, Cakes, Desserts and Cookies. 264
Miscellaneous. 291

    Pickles, Relishes and Preserves, 291

    Sauces, 300

    Beverages, 306

    Candies, 309

3. Midwest

Appetizers and Soups 315
Fish and Shellfish 330
Meat, Poultry, Game and Other Main Dishes 338
Vegetables, Main Dish Accompaniments and Salads. 369
Breads. 390
Pies, Cakes, Desserts and Cookies. 408
Miscellaneous. 447

    Pickles, Relishes and Preserves, 447

    Sauces, 455

    Beverages, 459

    Candies, 461

    Dressings (Stuffings), 463

    Dumplings, 465

4. Mountain/Northern Plains

Appetizers and Soups 469
Fish. 474
Meat, Poultry and Game 477
Vegetables, Main Dish Accompaniments and Salads. 501
Breads. 513
Pies, Cakes, Desserts and Cookies. 524
Miscellaneous. 547

    Pickles, Relishes and Preserves, 547

    Sauces, 554

    Beverages, 555

    Candies, 556

    Dumplings, 557

5. Southwest

Appetizers and Soups 561
Fish and Shellfish 570
Meat, Poultry, Game and Other Main Dishes 575
Vegetables, Main Dish Accompaniments and Salads 603
Breads 623
Pies, Cakes, Desserts and Cookies 630
Miscellaneous 645

    Pickles, Relishes and Preserves, 645

    Sauces, 649

    Beverages, 651

    Candies, 652

6. Northwest

Appetizers and Soups 657
Fish and Shellfish 672
Meat, Poultry, Game and Other Main Dishes 693
Vegetables, Main Dish Accompaniments and Salads 713
Breads 728
Pies, Cakes, Desserts and Cookies 736
Miscellaneous 755

    Pickles, Relishes and Preserves, 755

    Sauces, 760

    Candies, 762

    Dressings (Stuffings), 763

Index 765

Acknowledgments

The publication of this book would not have been possible without the cooperation of many people throughout the United States who made their recipes available to *The New York Times.* Some contributed their recipes anonymously, and others received a credit line when their recipes appeared in *The New York Times.* I wish to thank them all for their generosity. The credited names are listed below in the order in which their recipes appear in these pages.

I also wish to acknowledge the cooperation and encouragement given by Craig Claiborne, formerly of *The New York Times,* during the preparation of this book.

Northeast

John E. Panck, *Deer Liver Pâté;* Mrs. David Black, *Pâté Maison;* John E. Panck, *Pickled Venison Heart;* Kathy Gidding, *Quiche à la Roma;* Kay Linz, *Curried Flan Appetizer;* Mrs. John G. Baker, Jr., *Cape Cod Clam Chowder;* Jerry Komarek, *Snapping Turtle and Vegetable Soup.*

Mrs. Raymond Eldridge, *Clam Pie;* Mrs. Isaac Taylor, *Chilmark Scallops;* Felice Chiapperini, *Fresh Tuna Fra Diavolo;* Sandra Capsis, *Tuna-Stuffed Peppers à la Sorda;* Mrs. Isaac Taylor, *Martha's Vineyard Stonewall Bouillabaisse.*

Mrs. Frederick Churchill, *Deviled Steak;* Vivienne Wilson, *Meat Balls;* George Bacalakis, *Greek Meat Balls;* Sandra Capsis, *Ravioli à la Romana;* Elaine Light, *Crumbed Butterflied Leg*

of Lamb; Kay Linz, *Leg of Lamb with Saffron-and-Caper Sauce;* Mrs. Donald Law, *Baked Lamb;* Mrs. Blake, *Connecticut Bean Pot;* Kay Linz, *Galatoise Polonaise;* Joan Owen, *Roast Veal with Plums;* Mrs. Frank Brinckerhoff, *Paprika Cream Schnitzel;* Captain Lindsay, *Pheasant Cacciatore.*

Mrs. August Midgett, *Samp 'n' Beans;* Lorraine Kennedy, *Dandelion Stems* and *Sautéed Dandelion Flowers;* Evelyn Sharpe, *Cabbage-Filled Peppers* and *Cucumber in Sour Cream;* George Bacalakis, *Greek Salad;* Mrs. McIntyre, *Salade de Champignons;* Kay Linz, *Poppy Seed Dressing.*

Mrs. Molenski, *Banana Bread;* Elaine Light, *Flaky Rolls;* Joan Owen, *Sour Dough White Bread;* Mrs. Sidney B. Klein, *Passover Crispy Sticks.*

Mrs. Arthur Morawski, *Cape Cod Cranberry Pie;* Mrs. Ploss, *Pecan-Maple Pie;* Elaine Light, *Chocolate Pie;* Mrs. John Lloyd, *Mince Pies;* Miss Karen Michaelis, *Sour Cream Pastry Turnovers;* Mrs. Raymond Schenck, *Pumpkin Cake;* Mrs. Charlotte Kelly, *Honey Chocolate Cake;* Evelyn Sharpe, *French Chocolate Cake;* Mrs. Feffer, *Seven-Layer Chocolate Cake for Passover;* Mrs. Howard Keyser, *Maple Sugar Cake;* Mrs. Buzell, *Velvet Lunch Cake;* Ann Mattison, *Fruitcake;* Laura B. Goodenough, *Christmas Cake;* Mrs. Sidney B. Klein, *Passover Apple Cake;* Mrs. John Kelemen, *Apricot Lattice Cake;* Dorothy Jewiss, *Coffeecake;* Laura Goodenough, *Apple Coffeecake;* Mrs. Ferris, *Sour Cream*

Coffeecake; Mrs. Sidney B. Klein, *Passover Cheesecake*; Evelyn Sharpe, *Evelyn's Cheesecake*; Mrs. Peter Duncan, *Plum Pudding*; Laura Goodenough, *Christmas Pudding*; Mrs. Groff, *Cracker Pudding*; Evelyn Patterson, *Orange Mousse*; Kathy Gidding, *Cider Apples*; Mrs. Nancy Mortensen, *Down-East Blueberry Cobbler*; Margaret Umberger, *Maple Lace Wafers*; Mrs. Amy German, *Maple Walnut Bars*; Mrs. David Mullen, *Jan Hagel*; Mrs. Sidney B. Klein, *Passover Brownies*.

Mrs. Frances Hulle, *Bread and Butter Pickles*; Mrs. James Clarke, *Green Tomato Mincemeat*; John E. Panck, *Venison Mincemeat*; Marion Johnson, *Vermont Mincemeat*; Ellen Clarke, *Piccalilli* and *Beet Relish*; Mrs. Burpee, *Apple Chutney*; Mrs. Hammerstein, *Bourbon "Brandied" Peaches* and *Lemon-Peach-Ginger Conserve*; Mildred Pack, *Tomato Marmalade*; Sandra Capsis, *Sandra's Tomato Sauce*; Captain Lindsay, *Game Sauce*; Mrs. August Midgett, *Slemp*; Mrs. David Black, *Hot Buttered Rum*; Wrede Smith, *Caramel Popcorn*; Mary Jane Burgess, *Blue Ribbon Maple Syrup Fudge*; Mrs. Feffer, *Fruit Candy for Passover, Candied Orange Peel* and *Candied Grapefruit Peel*; Mrs. Samuel Duerr, *Potato Stuffing or Filling*; Mrs. Feffer, *Marrow Bone Matzoh Balls*.

SOUTH

Enrique Ucan, *Conch Seviche*; Annie Rooney, *Shrimp Paste*; Alex Hawkes, *Conch Chowder*; Mrs. Wiley Hill, *She-Crab and Lobster Soup*; Paul E. Welsh, *Maryland Clam Chowder*; Mrs. Van Exem, *Tomato Soup*; Mrs. Lionel Legge, *Cream of Spinach Soup*.

Delton Harrison, *Crab Stew*; Ina Mae Heathman, *Deviled Oysters*; E. Lysle Aschaffenburg, *Pontchartrain Creole Gumbo*.

John Shinn, *Southern Fried Chicken III* and *Chicken Cream Gravy*; Mrs. Yohe, *Chicken Olivette*; Mary Randolph, *Chicken Pudding*; Ruby Craven, *Barbecued Chicken*; Mrs. Robert Murphy, *Seven Hearths Chicken*; Maida Heatter, *Poulet Floride*; Mrs. Van Exem, *Pressed Chicken*; Kathleen Claiborne, *Chicken Spa-*ghetti; Ruby Craven, *Chicken Bog*; Mrs. Robert Murphy, *Brunswick Stew*; J. Tunkie Saunders, *Pressed Duck*; Mrs. E. V. Lewis, *Fresh Quail with Grits and Gravy*; Mrs. Wiley Hill, *Baked Christmas Mushroom Omelet*; Mrs. John DeReamer, *Cheese Grits Casserole*.

Mrs. Jackson Porter Dick, Jr., *Green Beans, Southern Style*; Mrs. Robert Murphy, *Cabbage Casserole*; Celia Marks, *Celery with Egg and Lemon Sauce*; Bessie Bogan, *Stuffed Eggplant*; Mrs. Howell Newton, *Fried Hominy Grits*; Sarah Walker, *Sarah's Oando*; Miss Francille Killion, *Baked Hominy and Tomatoes* and *Southern-Style Turnip Greens*; James Sparks, *Steamboat Rice*; Mrs. John DeReamer, *Cauliflower Slaw*.

Miss Mae Creswell, *Spoon Bread*; Mrs. Morris Whitehurst, *Batter Bread*; Mrs. Jackson Porter Dick, Jr., *Crackling Bread Cakes* and *Lacy Hoe Cakes*; Mrs. Mescal Johnston, *Corn Meal Muffins*; Mrs. Van Exem, *Light Rolls*.

Mrs. Mescal Johnston, *Sweet Potato Pie*; Richard Hougen, *Chocolate-Butterscotch Pie* and *Kentucky Lemon Pie*; Mrs. Simon Waring, *Lemon Chiffon Pie*; Mrs. Mescal Johnston, *Peach Cobbler*; Hazel Detwiler, *Rum and Rhubarb Chess Pie*; Mae Butler, *Orange Cake*; Miriam Smith, *Butter Cake*; Mrs. Van Exem, *Poundcake I*; Mrs. Thomas Milford, *Poundcake II*; Celia Marks, *Sugar Plum Cake*; Mrs. Philip Licalzi, *Applesauce Fruitcake*; Mrs. Mescal Johnston, *Rice Custard with Lemon Sauce* and *Banana Pudding*; Maida Heatter, *Flan*; Mrs. Mescal Johnston, *Cooked Custard Ice Cream* and *Sugar Cookies*.

Mrs. Mescal Johnston, *Fig Preserves*; Martha Adams, *Louisiana Sauce Remoulade*; Pat DeReamer, *Pendennis Club Barbecue Sauce*; John Scott, *John's Eggnog*; Mrs. Robert Murphy, *Edenton Punch*; Augusta Claiborne Barnwell, *Chocolate Candy* and *Caramels*.

MIDWEST

Mrs. Harry N. Phillips, *Cheese-Olive Appetizers*; Mrs. Anne Weiskopf, *Oven-Barbecued Chicken Wings*; Mrs. Albert Weisheimer, *Vege-*

table Soup; Mrs. Harry N. Phillips, *Cold Vegetable Soup;* Mrs. Mae Blake, *Chicken Soup with Noodles* and *Potato Soup with Rivals;* Mrs. Willis Peterson, *Cream of Tomato Soup;* Mrs. Hugo Busche, *Duchess Soup;* Mrs. Craig Harbison, *Cold Buttermilk Soup.*

Ruth Ellen Church, *Shrimp à la Mann;* Mrs. Mae Blake, *Salmon Cakes.*

Mrs. Dean Karns, *Chicken Fried Round Steak with Cream Gravy;* Mrs. Arthur Johnson, *German Rolled Steak;* Mrs. Anne Weiskopf, *Anne's Hamburgers;* Mrs. Clinton Sage, *Camping Hamburgers;* Mrs. Harry Theusen, *Meat Balls III;* Mrs. Willis Peterson, *Barbecued Meat Balls;* Mrs. Harry N. Phillips, *One Dish Supper;* Mrs. Viola Lewis, *Savory Veal Cutlet;* Mrs. George Finch, *Scaloppine of Veal;* Mrs. Sylvia Malkasian, *Armenian Squash Dolma;* Mrs. Willis Peterson, *Apricot-Stuffed Pork Chops;* Mrs. James Holland, *Pork Chops and Potato Casserole;* Mrs. Willis Peterson, *Kraut, Pork and Apple;* Mrs. James Holland, *Braised Stuffed Pork Chops;* Mrs. Willis Peterson, *Pork Steaks and Apple Kraut;* Mrs. Anne Weiskopf, *Barbecued Spareribs;* Mrs. Ruth Archibald, *Head Cheese;* Mrs. W. H. Burlingame, *Pioneer Sausage;* Mrs. Clinton Sage, *Ham Loaf;* Mrs. George Finch, *Old-Fashioned Brunswick Stew, Michigan Style;* Mrs. Johnston, *Roast Young Capon with Wild Rice and Almond Stuffing;* Greta Bowers, *Iowa Fried Chicken;* Esther Helton, *Hot Chicken Salad;* J. L. McClellan, *Barbecued Venison;* Harold Bitzegaio, *Herbed Game Sauce;* J. L. McClellan, *Wild Burgers;* Tom Patrick, *Grilled Duck Breasts;* George Herter, *Doves Wyatt Earp.*

Mrs. W. H. Billings, *Missouri Country-Style Green Beans;* Mrs. Sylvester, *Baked Kidney Beans;* Alice Wessels Burlingame, *Cream Cabbage;* Mrs. Willis Peterson, *Corn with Chipped Beef* and *Scalloped Corn;* Ruth Archibald, *Homemade Noodles;* Edith Harrison, *Macaroni Deluxe;* Mrs. Dockstader, *Baked Wild Rice with Carrots;* Mrs. Harry Theusen, *Mixed Vegetables;* Betty Johnson, *Vegetable Bake;* Mrs. Dean Karns, *Whipped Cream Cole Slaw;* Greta Bowers, *Greta's Cabbage Salad;* Mrs. Dean Karns, *Cucumbers in Sour Cream* and *Hot Slaw;* W. W.

Jones, *Sauerkraut Salad;* Mrs. W. H. Burlingame, *Russian Salad Dressing.*

Mrs. James Weems, *Steamed Indian Bread;* Lizabeth Ellis, *Hot Water Corn Bread;* Benna Walton, *Harvest Corn Bread;* Mrs. John DeReamer, *Pumpkin Bread;* Mrs. J. G. Lundholm, *Fruit Bread;* Mrs. Russell Hinderer, *Banana Muffins;* Mrs. Claire Dahl, *Lefsa;* Mrs. Donald Demuth, *Large Yeast Bread Recipe;* Mrs. Dockstader, *Adobe Bread;* Mrs. J. G. Lundholm, *Swedish Rye Bread;* Mrs. Claire Dahl, *Quick Mixer Rolls;* Mrs. Lorraine Rice, *Filled Danish;* Mrs. Irma Estes, *German Apple Coffeecake;* Valborg Hansen, *Valborg's Coffeecake;* Ruth Turner, *Sour Cream Doughnuts;* Mrs. John Hopper, *Buttermilk Pancakes;* Mrs. Craig Harbison, *Aebleskiver.*

Donna Bohannon, *No-Fail Pie Crust;* Mrs. Gering, *'89er Lemon Pie;* May Chailland, *Amber Pie;* Lind Brown, *Poorman's Pie;* Mrs. Henry Shardelow, *Graham Cracker Pie;* Monte Sifers, *French Silk Chocolate Pie;* Mrs. Austin, *Strawberry Pie;* Mrs. Anne Weiskopf, *St. Louis Pumpkin Pie;* Greta Bowers, *Greta's Apple Pie;* Peggy Weems, *Cider Apple Pie;* Mrs. Dean Karns, *Mulberry Pie;* Mrs. J. G. Lundholm, *Danish Raspberry Pie;* Mrs. Sylvester, *Poundcake;* Mrs. James Weems, *Golden Cake;* Mary Jurik, *Slovak Prune and Apricot Upside-Down Cake;* Mrs. Anne Weiskopf, *Banana Fruitcake;* Mrs. Dymple Green, *Dymple's Fruitcake* and *Dymple's Sausage Cake;* Peggy Weems, *Buttermilk Glazed Pineapple Carrot Cake;* Mrs. Helen Goodyear, *Banana Chiffon Cake;* Greta Bowers, *Greta's Chocolate Cake;* Mrs. J. V. O'Donnell, *1870 Mahogany Cake;* Mrs. J. G. Lundholm, *Oatmeal Cake;* Mrs. James Weems, *Applesauce Cake;* Mrs. Kathryn Ashcraft, *Buckeye Maple Syrup Cake;* Ina Salmon, *Persimmon Upside-Down Cake;* Dymple Green, *Molasses Cake;* Bosiljka Marich, *Serbian Torte;* Mrs. Dean Karns, *Poppy Seed Cake;* Mrs. Lester Sunderman, *Homemade Ice Cream;* Greta Bowers, *Frozen Raspberry Dessert;* Mrs. James Holland, *Lemon Ice Cream;* Peggy Weems, *Vanilla Ice Cream;* Mrs. R. G. Surridge, *Floating Island;* Alice Wessels Burlingame, *Lemon Mousse;* Mrs. Tinkers, *Wild Grape*

Dumplings; Mrs. R. G. Surridge, *Royal Bread Pudding;* Howard Hewett, *Pioneer Popcorn Pudding;* Pat DeReamer, *Chocolate Puff Balls;* Mrs. J. G. Lundholm, *Raisin-Suet Pudding;* Lorraine Rice, *Date Pudding* and *White Sugar Sauce;* Clara Phillips, *Steamed Pudding;* Lorraine Rice, *Danish Pastry;* Alice Wessels Burlingame, *Refrigerator Cookies;* Alison Hayford, *Alison's Shortbread;* Kaisa Juntunen, *Finnish Christmas Cookies;* Mrs. Harry Shardelow, *Buttergebachtness;* Mrs. Claire Dahl, *Tea Biscuits;* Peggy Weems, *Chocolate "Macaroons";* Mrs. Claire Dahl, *Lemon Bonbons;* Mrs. J. G. Lundholm, *Sugar-Coated Banana Drops;* Edith Harrison, *Persimmon Cookies.*

Mrs. William Stockwell, *Easy Pickles;* Mrs. Thomas Hatch, *Special Dills;* Mrs. Ralph Carpenter, *Bread and Butter Pickles;* Sarah Templeton Roberts, *Best Ever Beet Pickles;* Mrs. Zenda Lazdin, *Latvian Pumpkin Pickle;* Mrs. Myrtle Mann, *Sweet Relish;* Peggy Weems, *Tomato Butter;* Mildred Pack, *Tomato Marmalade;* Mrs. Ruth S. Archibald, *Mincemeat;* Mrs. John Turner, *End-of-the-Garden Sauce* and *Quick and Easy Sauce;* Mrs. Mae Blake, *Mae's Tomato Gravy;* Peggy Weems, *Jefferson Davis Punch;* Alice Wessels Burlingame, *Dandelion Wine;* Mrs. Ruth S. Archibald, *Peanut Butter Fudge;* Mrs. Kochek, *Salami Sweetmeat;* Mrs. Harold Andersen, *Dressing for Fowl;* Mrs. James Holland, *Dumplings for Chicken Stew.*

MOUNTAIN/NORTHERN PLAINS

Mrs. Ester Stage, *Rullepolse;* Vern Bressler, *Mountain Fish Chowder;* Mrs. Emil Rezac, *Potato Dill Soup, Bohemian Oukrop* and *Fresh Vegetable Soup.*

Dani Lee, *Trout Meunière;* Jackie Hiller, *Baked Trout;* Theo Owen, *Baked Mackinaw.*

Mrs. Logan Ward, *Beef Cubes with Biscuits;* Renee Smelker, *Steak in a Sack;* Mrs. John Cressey, *Dakota Beef Loaf;* Clarence Jaeger, *Fleischkuechle;* Mrs. Emil Rezac, *Bohemian Spareribs* and *Pork Goulash;* Janece Reiman, *Chicken with Noodle Balls;* Mrs. Julius Mosley, *Wild Duck I;* Jackie Hiller, *Wild Duck II;* Syb

Gulickson, *Stuffed Snow Goose;* Margaret Barker, *Wild Goose with Stuffing;* Syb Gulickson, *Pheasant in Sour Cream;* Dona Brown, *Braised Pheasant;* Mrs. Roy Houck, *Buffalo Birds* and *Apple-Stuffed Buffalo Ribs;* Syb Gulickson, *Venison Ragout;* Joan Renner, *Venison Shish Kebabs;* Dani Lee, *Venison or Elk Fondue;* Barbara Barker, *Elk Carbonnades à la Flamande;* Betty Barker, *Elk Steak and Kidney Pie;* Patty Ewing, *Pickled Elk's Heart.*

Janece Reiman, *Lima Bean Bake;* Dona Brown, *Baked Cabbage;* Mrs. Gordon Babcock, *Cabbage and Potato;* Pru Schuler, *Baked Mushrooms;* Lou Breitenbach, *Deep-Dish Mushroom Pies;* Patty Estes, *Cabbage Slaw;* Mrs. Ethel Heising, *Cole Slaw with Bulghur;* Lois Restemayer, *Dilled Potato Salad;* Miss Brown, *Boiled Dressing;* Joan Renner, *Sour Cream Dressing.*

Mrs. John Coles, *Ranch Bread;* Ethel Flaten, *Ethel's Flat Bread;* Mrs. John Turner, *Salt-Rising Bread;* Mrs. Emil Rezac, *Yeast Fruit Dumplings* and *Czech Christmas Bread;* Syb Gulickson, *Julekage;* Mrs. Dorothy Collins, *Potato Doughnuts;* Dona Brown, *Banana Bread;* Mrs. Murie, *Sour Dough Pancakes.*

Mrs. Hazel Jorgenson, *Lard Pie Crust;* Lou Breitenbach, *Lou's Pie Crust;* Mrs. Sundquist, *Apple Strudel;* Dorothy Habel, *Pecan Tarts;* Mrs. G. Middaugh, *Juneberry Pie;* Mrs. Emil Rezac, *Raw Apple Cake;* Mrs. T. S. Kopseng, *Apple Cake;* Dona Brown, *Prune Cake;* Mrs. David Noell, *Sandbakkelse;* Mrs. Emil Rezac, *Rhubarb Cake;* Mrs. Hazel Jorgenson, *Old-Fashioned Christmas Pork Cake;* Dona Brown, *O-Apple Cake;* Mrs. S. G. Mason, *Devil's Food Cake;* Mrs. Luther M. Wells, *Cranberry Coffeecake;* Sabre Jorgensen, *Rose Hip Pudding;* Mrs. Ellen Fechner, *Apple Bread Pudding;* Mrs. Clarence Schlabsz, *Apple Cobbler;* Mrs. Amelia Fischer, *Apple Crunch;* Mrs. David Noell, *Berlinerkranser;* Mrs. Betty Bay, *Coconut Cookies;* Mrs. Miller, *Applesauce Bars;* Mrs. Mathilde Castonia, *Fattigman;* Mrs. Hazel Jorgenson, *Old-Style Ginger Cookies;* Dona Brown, *Dona's Cookies;* Syb Gulickson, *Spritz Cookies;* Mrs. Borgny Pettersen, *Krum Kake I.*

Janece Reiman, *Green Tomato Relish;* Mrs. Deloy Hendricks, *Uncooked Chili Sauce;* Dona Brown, *Kraut Relish;* Mrs. Burt, *Pioneer Wild Plum Butter;* Dona Brown, *Corncob Jelly;* Mrs. Ed Spencer, *Chokecherry and Buffalo Berry Jelly;* Mrs. Mardy Murie, *Spruce Tip Syrup;* Evelyn Refearn, *Rose Hip Syrup;* Mrs. Mosley, *Game Sauce;* Mrs. Sam Stoney, *Rum and Cherry Sauce;* Dona Brown, *Easy No-Cook Fudge;* Mrs. John Coles, *Beef Candy;* Syb Gulickson, *Raw Potato Dumplings;* Mrs. Emil Rezac, *Potato Dumplings* and *Bread Dumplings.*

SOUTHWEST

Robert Balzer, *Veal Tartar with Lemon;* Lucy Delgado, *Chili con Queso;* Robert Balzer, *Artichoke Hearts in Batter, Jicama Appetizer* and *Cheese Appetizers;* Mrs. Presnall, *Sausage Ball Appetizer;* Carmen Camarillo Jones, *Sopa de Albondigas;* Alan Hooker, *Herbed Fresh Pea Soup* and *Cream of Spinach Soup.*

Mrs. Field, *Texas Chili;* Nelson Waggener, *Nelson's Chili con Carne;* Maida Heatter, *Chili with Rice;* Alan Hooker, *Avocado Meat Loaf;* Wallace Seawell, *Meat Ball Stroganoff;* Dutchie Heselton, *Dutchie's Meat Balls;* Mrs. Roy Jones, *Gesado;* Philip Brown, *Pork Tenderloin en Croute;* Alan Hooker, *Lamb and Eggplant;* Lucy Delgado, *Posole;* Mrs. Roy Hodges, *Chicken Castillia;* Mrs. Cyril Heselton, *Chicken Almond;* Lucy Delgado, *Arroz con Pollo Nuevo Mexicano;* Mrs. John Ramirez, *Eggs Rancheros;* Mrs. Roy Jones, *Chili Sauce, Menudo à la California* and *Escabeche-Tongue Salad;* Cleto Hernandez, *Wild Duck Gumbo.*

Mrs. Presnall, *Eggplant Casserole;* Mrs. Millard J. Beemer, *Nopales or Nopalitos;* Alan Hooker, *Zucchini Torre;* Lucy Delgado, *Calabacitas;* G. P. Whitlock, *California Avocado Salad;* Mrs. Cyril Heselton, *Kidney Bean Salad;* Robert Balzer, *Fresh Mushroom Salad.*

Mrs. C. W. Henderson, *Wheat Germ Rolls;* Mrs. Cyril Heselton, *Two-Bite-Size Muffins* and *Avocado Pecan Bread;* Mrs. Millard Beemer, *Orange Nut Bread;* Lucy Delgado, *Sopaipillas.*

Robert Balzer, *Orange Cake;* Mrs. Downs, *Oatmeal Cake;* Jo Myers, *Walnut Cake;* Mrs. Gross, *Citrus Cake;* Mrs. Oscar Yerke, *Bavarian Fruit Ice Cream;* Jo Myers, *Orange Flambé;* Willa Holland, *Crisp Sugar Cookies;* Cherine Laner, *Fig Bar Cookies;* Lucy Delgado, *Biscochitos.*

Dr. Sydney Ruffner, *Pickled Peppers, Sweet Carrot Pickles* and *Pickled Beans;* Woodruff de Silva, *Mustard Pickles;* Mrs. Oscar Yerke, *Candied Walnuts;* Mrs. Cyril Heselton, *Toffee;* Dutchie Heselton, *Five Minute Fudge;* Mrs. William Byrne, *Perfect Divinity.*

NORTHWEST

Jamie Davies, *Parmesan Wafers;* Nellie Munson, *Sea Hag Clam Chowder.*

Bernice Manlove, *Clam Casserole;* Bertha Meier, *Bertha's Pickled Salmon;* Bob Perry, *Shrimp with Vermouth.*

Mrs. Sebastiani, *Mock Ravioli Casserole;* Ed Hicks, *Vine Maple Roast;* Chris Hair, *Hawaiian Short Ribs;* Ruby Nozaki, *Ruby's Teriyaki* and *Ruby's Sukiyaki;* Jim Hands, *Lamb Curry Baked in Coconuts;* Chuck Williams, *Osso Buco;* Ruby Nozaki, *Fried Chicken in Teriyaki Sauce;* Mrs. Adolph Mathisen, *Roast Venison.*

Ruby Nozaki, *Su-No-Mo-No;* Jamie Davies; *Vegetable Quiche;* Mrs. Sebastiani, *Malfatti;* Wallace Seawell, *Spinach Salad;* Agnes Kuhn, *Agnes' Oregon Slaw* and *Agnes' Wilted Lettuce;* Wayne Kuhn, *"Alfalfa";* Mrs. Sebastiani, *Potato Gnocchi* and *Zucchini in Batter;* Chuck Williams, *Risotto Milanese;* Mrs. Green, *Chicken Spaghetti Salad.*

Mrs. Henderson, *Cottage Cheese Biscuits;* David Eyre, *David's Pancake.*

Mrs. MacPherson, *Apple and Apricot Pie;* Mrs. Jones, *Rhubarb Cake Pudding;* Mrs. Sebastiani, *Italian Biscotti.*

Introduction

America is a land where cultures merge from one generation to the next, but in kitchens across the country, women continue to take pride in preserving the traditions of the past. These women follow handwritten recipes, in the yellowed pages of old notebooks, to prepare the dishes their grandmothers knew.

In five years of crisscrossing the country in search of regional foods, I've eaten wild persimmon pudding in Mitchell, Indiana, kolache in Oklahoma and Wisconsin, lamb's quarters and sour dough pancakes in California and Wyoming and enchiladas in a pink adobe house in New Mexico.

The influence of ancestors who came from Europe or the Middle East is quickly seen if one is lucky enough to be invited to dine at the family table. In rural areas, the abundant game, fish, berries and plants dictate many of the delicacies prepared by successive generations of fine cooks.

It is unfortunate that a foreign visitor can travel on our superhighways from coast to coast, Maine to Florida, and go away with the impression that Americans subsist largely on a diet of hot dogs, hamburgers and soggy French fries. Even a tour of a large supermarket in any one of the fifty states would reveal similar packaged convenience foods, suggesting a uniformity of eating patterns in homes across the land.

However, a determined search of homes, grange halls, festivals and fellowship rooms across the country turns up some excellent cooking.

But woe betide the neophyte in the kitchen who tries to follow Grandmother's recipe for rye bread or the directions for Abigail's pickles. Ingredient measurements were often approximate —"a pinch of this" and "enough flour to make a dough"—while preparation instructions were vague at best. Everyone knew how to cook.

This book offers a selection of heirloom recipes, in an easy-to-follow form. These recipes are America's culinary heritage. They were gathered during the course of many short and extended trips around the country over a period of many years. This book is an attempt to bring honesty back into cooking, not just invoke nostalgia, and share again the delights that loving cooks prepare in "old-fashioned" kitchens.

The earliest known North American cuisine, that of the American Indian, was based on wild game, fish, seeds, corn and berries and was as varied as the number of tribes and location of their hunting grounds. It was the Indians who cultivated corn, sweet potatoes, tomatoes, squash and peanuts and domesticated the wild turkey. Indians gathered the wild rice and tapped the maple tree.

They were the fishermen of the Pacific Northwest, the gardeners of the Southwest, the nomad hunters of the Plains, the planters of the South and the woodsmen of the Northeast. Today, in

Tahlequah, Oklahoma, and Warm Springs, Oregon, Indians still prepare such delicacies as squaw bread, connuche (a strange-tasting hickory nut soup) and boiled salmon heads.

In discussing regional food differences, it is convenient to divide the country into broad regions showing different terrain, climatic conditions and eating patterns. No two people agree on where those boundaries should be and, because of the fluidity of the population, there tends to be overlapping.

For instance, there are pockets of German culture in states from Pennsylvania to Oregon where women make the sauerbraten, sauerkraut and pigs' knuckles that their ancestors knew in the homeland. There are "Czech" villages in South Dakota, Oklahoma and Wisconsin, and the Scandinavian influence is found from Brooklyn to Seattle.

The six regions making up the separate sections in this book are the Northeast, stretching from Maine to the border of Maryland; the South; the Midwest; the Mountain States and Northern Plains; the Southwest, including Southern California, and the Northwest, including Hawaii and Alaska.

The Northeast's long shoreline and many fishing ports suggest the important part that sea food played in the diet of earlier generations and is reflected in old recipes for codfish balls, clam pie and chowders. An authentic shore dinner in Maine and a clambake in Rhode Island are experiences to savor and remember.

The best homemade pies, cakes, muffins and baked beans can be found at the small church fair or the fraternal organization's annual barbecue. On Saturday in many New England homes, there is a smell of beans baking all day long, to be served with a supper of ham and brown bread. Leftover beans are Sunday's breakfast and often Monday's midday sandwich filling.

The culinary influence of ethnic groups, such as the Irish, Greek, Portuguese and Jewish, in urban centers cannot be overlooked, although each warrants a book to itself.

Among the settlers who deserve special mention because of their style of cooking are the Pennsylvania Dutch who came from Germany and coined a new language, and a new style of cooking, in the new country.

Visitors to Lancaster, Pennsylvania, and the annual Kutztown Fair can sample schnitz un knepp (dried apples and dumplings served with ham), drechter or funnel cakes, and funeral and shoofly pies.

Moving into the South, one finds that there is tremendous diversity in food patterns, but in general, it is a corn- (that is, white corn and grits) and hog-based cookery. Every part of the pig, from the snout to the tail, is used, and every Southern cook knows that "fat" listed in a recipe means pork fat or lard.

Pot likker, to spoon over feather-light hot biscuits, is the bonus to cooking greens the Southern way by simmering with a piece of fatback for hours on end. Red-eye gravy to serve with a slice of fried country ham is another Southern treat that tempts the visitor. Enjoyment is enhanced by Southern-style hospitality and some of the country's most gracious hostesses.

From the oysters, crabs and rockfish of Chesapeake Bay to the "blues" of the Carolinas, the big game fish of Florida and the ubiquitous catfish, the fruits of the sea and inland waterways are an important ingredient in Southern cookery. Crawfish from the Louisiana bayous are essential to Creole, or Cajun, bisques and stews. This distinctive and delicious style of cooking shows the influence of Indian, French and Spanish settlers.

When fish and meat were scarce, the Southern family turned to hunting squirrels and coons for the stew pot and possum to go with 'taters. Today the South offers some of the best quail, dove, pheasant and wild duck hunting in America.

The traditional Hunt Breakfast, served, despite its name, at all hours of the day, gives a guest, who incidentally doesn't have to ride horseback, an excellent opportunity to sample a wide assortment of Southern delicacies. These might include Maryland stuffed ham, Georgia country captain (curried chicken) and Virginia scalloped Chincoteague oysters.

Almost every meal in the South is accompanied by a myriad variety of hot breads from tender buttermilk biscuits to lacy corn and crackling breads. And no section on Southern cooking would be complete without recipes for such delectable desserts as Lane cake, Lady Baltimore cake, chess tarts and Moravian sugar cake.

The culinary treasures of the Midwest are not so startling. However, people of German and Eastern European stock still make borscht, pirogs, dumplings and Viennese pastries. And the Scandinavian heritage of others is clear in the smorgasbords they set and cardamom-flavored breads they bake.

The annual Milwaukee, Wisconsin, Folk Festival, held just before the opening of the hunting season in October, brings together more than thirty ethnic groups from across the state to demonstrate and sell their food specialties. One can sample Danish liver paste, Scottish shortbread and Greek baklava or dine on hearty Bavarian sauerbraten, dumplings and red cabbage.

The Midwest is meat 'n' taters country and the meat is generally of high quality and the vegetables farm fresh. Women make chocolate pudding, strawberry ice cream and angel food cakes that don't taste synthetic.

These women bake with native hickory nuts, black walnuts, rhubarb and gooseberries. One ninety-year-old Iowa woman recalled that she must have been fifteen years old before her mother first used baking powder. There were always soured milk and cream on hand. The addition of baking soda was all it took to raise cakes, dumplings and doughnuts. Pickling, canning and jelly-making in the family kitchen were as inevitable as the changing seasons.

In Oklahoma, the culinary patterns and native dishes of the Plains Indians make a fascinating subject for study. Connuche, squaw bread, jerky (dried venison) and wild grape dumplings are still prepared by women of the Cherokee, Sioux and Osage tribes.

Indians who were friendly with the early settlers helped prevent starvation by giving them corn and demonstrating how to grow and cook it. The white man learned to make hominy with ash-lye and Indian shuck-bread from corn meal. The Quawpaw tribe was making pecan butter

long before peanut butter became an American staple.

Women in the sparsely settled Mountain and Northern Plains states are experts on cooking buffalo, moose, bear and venison. There are buffalo burgers on the menu in South Dakota's state parks. When the catch is from the lake or river, local cooks know how to capture the delicate flavor of perch, trout or pickerel. Forays into the wilderness provide the berries, wild mushrooms and greens for more regional delights.

Another distinctive group, from a culinary standpoint, are the Mormons, especially in Utah, where their numbers are greatest. Because of a church edict that encourages families to have at least a year's supply of food on hand at all times, cooking is done with basic staples. Homemaking is revered and Mormon women pickle, can and bake with tremendous enthusiasm. Some even grind their own flour from whole wheat berries and they favor whole wheat flour over white flour for biscuits, doughnuts and cakes.

The Southwest, including Texas, Arizona, New Mexico and Southern California, offers exciting food experiences reflecting the Spanish influence from across the border and the abundance of tropical and subtropical fruits and vegetables. From arroz con pollo, tamales, tacos and refried beans to Texas chili and barbecued beef or goat, there's infinite variety to shock and please the palate.

The Pacific Northwest from Monterey, California, to the Canadian border includes some of this country's most famous fishing grounds and scenic wonders. I remember particularly the tiny succulent Olympia oysters in Washington and the lingcod cooked over charcoal within an hour after being caught off Monterey.

And I remember trout from Oregon's Diamond Lake, the spectacular snow-capped, mountain-ringed body of blue water. The fish was corn-dipped and pan-fried for tender sweet goodness. For a tempting appetizer, extra rainbow trout were smoked in back of the boat shed.

A deep-sea fishing expedition off Depot Bay, Oregon, was the prelude to an Indian-style salmon bake. And although no two recipes for

San Francisco's cioppino are quite the same, the garlic-scented crab and sea bass stew is one of the West Coast's most famous dishes.

Wild blackberry tarts and pies, sold at every wayside snack-bar in Oregon, utilize just one of the fine-flavored wild, and cultivated, fruits available to the home baker. Oregon's Tillamook and California's Monterey Jack cheeses are listed among the ingredients in many West Coast recipes and the nearest, but not close, substitute is a sharp store Cheddar.

A collection of American regional specialties cannot ignore the diverse culinary contributions of Hawaii and Alaska, and for convenience these are included in the Northwest section. It is hoped that the relatively few recipes from these states will convince the reader to explore further. I would like to think that regional dishes prepared from the recipes in this book will encourage travelers to seek out the best food every area has to offer.

JEAN HEWITT

Author's Note: For information on high-altitude baking see notes on pages 513 and 524.

1. Northeast

Appetizers and Soups

Deer Liver Pâté

New York

½ cup diced salt pork
1 onion, sliced
2 tablespoons butter
1 deer liver
2 slices pumpernickel bread
  Milk
¼ teaspoon salt
¼ teaspoon freshly ground black pepper
⅛ teaspoon nutmeg
1 teaspoon grated lemon rind
½ cup diced lean bacon
2 eggs, beaten
8 slices lean bacon
  Hot pumpernickel toast triangles.

1. Cook the salt pork in a heavy skillet. Add the onion and cook until tender. Add the butter and half the deer liver. Cook quickly to brown. Cover and braise gently fifteen minutes, or until tender.

2. Preheat the oven to 350 degrees.

3. Soak the pumpernickel slices in milk; then squeeze dry. Grind with the braised liver and remaining liver half. Stir in salt, pepper, nutmeg, lemon rind, diced bacon and the eggs.

4. Line a loaf pan with the bacon slices. Pile in the liver mixture, cover with aluminum foil and bake one and one-half hours. Serve with hot pumpernickel toast.

Yield: Eighteen to two dozen servings.

Pâté Maison

Massachusetts

  Gizzards and hearts from six to eight chickens, ducks or geese
  Water or chicken broth
2 onions, finely chopped
⅓ cup butter, approximately
6 to eight chicken, duck or goose livers
2 tablespoons cognac
2 hard-cooked eggs, finely chopped
  Salt and freshly ground black pepper to taste
1 teaspoon thyme
½ teaspoon marjoram
  Toast triangles.

1. Cover the gizzards and hearts with water or broth. Bring to a boil, cover and simmer until tender, about twenty-five minutes. Drain. Chop finely or grind.

2. Sauté the onions in one-third cup butter in a heavy skillet until golden and add to the ground giblets. Fry the livers quickly in the skillet, adding more butter if necessary.

3. Chop finely and add to the giblet mixture.

4. Add the cognac, eggs, salt, pepper, thyme and marjoram. Mix well. Pile into a crock and chill well. Serve with toast triangles.

Yield: Ten servings.

Sweetbreads and Oyster Appetizer

New York

2 pounds sweetbreads
Cold water
Cider vinegar
Salt
Boiling salted water
5 tablespoons butter
3 tablespoons flour
1 cup milk
1 pint shucked oysters with liquor
1 teaspoon Worcestershire sauce
Freshly ground black pepper to taste
⅛ teaspoon cayenne pepper
¼ teaspoon paprika
¼ teaspoon nutmeg
Toast triangles or eight hot cooked puff
paste shells.

1. Early in the day, soak the sweetbreads about two hours in cold water to which one tablespoon vinegar and one teaspoon salt have been added. Change the water, adding more vinegar and salt, two or three times, removing membrane as it loosens.

2. Drain the sweetbreads, cover with boiling salted water and simmer gently twenty minutes, or until tender. Plunge immediately into cold water.

3. Remove remaining membrane and stems. Place the sweetbreads under weights for two hours to remove excess water, draining occasionally.

4. Close to serving time, melt three tablespoons of the butter in a heavy skillet and sauté the sweetbreads in it five minutes on each side. Remove sweetbreads and slice. Reserve in a warm place.

5. Add remaining butter to skillet. Blend in the flour and gradually stir in the milk. Bring to a boil, stirring.

6. Stir in the oysters with liquor, stirring constantly. Season with the Worcestershire, one-half teaspoon salt, the pepper, cayenne, paprika and nutmeg.

7. Return sweetbreads to mixture and heat through. Serve over toast or in patty shells.
Yield: Eight servings.

Pickled Venison Heart

New York

1 venison heart
4 quarts water
2 teaspoons salt
¼ teaspoon poppy seeds
¼ teaspoon celery seeds
¼ teaspoon black peppercorns
1 clove garlic, crushed
1 teaspoon thyme
½ teaspoon marjoram
1 bay leaf
1 bottle chianti
Horseradish
Jewish pumpernickel.

1. Cut a three-quarter-inch slice off the top of the heart. Mix two quarts of the water with one teaspoon of the salt. Soak heart two hours in mixture. Clean out all the blood. Drain.

2. Place heart in a saucepan with remaining water and add the poppy seeds, celery seeds, peppercorns, garlic, thyme, marjoram, bay leaf and remaining salt. Bring to a boil and simmer, covered, until heart is very tender. Cool and let stand in refrigerator two days.

3. Pour off top of broth, leaving about two cups in the bottom with most of the seasonings. Pour in the wine so that it covers the heart and let set in the refrigerator at least a week.

4. Slice very thinly and serve with horseradish and Jewish pumpernickel.
Yield: One dozen to two dozen servings.

Caviar Mousse

New York

3 envelopes unflavored gelatin
⅓ cup cold water
1 cup boiling water
1 teaspoon Worcestershire sauce

3 tablespoons lemon juice
1 teaspoon dry mustard
¼ cup mayonnaise
6 cups sour cream, preferably homemade (see note)
12 ounces caviar
Toast rounds.

1. Soften the gelatin in the cold water. Add the boiling water and stir to dissolve gelatin.
2. Add the Worcestershire, lemon juice and mustard. Cool slightly.
3. Blend the mayonnaise and sour cream together. Stir in the caviar and then the gelatin mixture. Pour into a shallow serving dish or lightly oiled mold. Chill until firm. Unmold and serve with toast rounds.

Yield: Eighteen servings.

Note: To prepare homemade sour cream, mix three tablespoons buttermilk with six cups heavy cream and leave at room temperature twenty-four hours, or until mixture thickens.

Baked Stuffed Clams   *New Jersey*

12 medium-size cherrystone clams, well scrubbed
2 tablespoons water
Rock salt (optional)
2 tablespoons butter
2 shallots, finely chopped
2 cloves garlic, finely chopped
2 cups soft bread crumbs
¼ cup finely chopped celery
2 tablespoons chopped parsley
½ teaspoon basil
½ teaspoon oregano
2 tablespoons freshly grated Parmesan cheese
1 tablespoon olive oil
1 tablespoon dry white wine
Freshly ground black pepper to taste
8 slices bacon, each cut into thirds.

1. Preheat the oven to 350 degrees.
2. Place the clams and water in a pan. Cover and steam until clams just open, about eight minutes. Reserve broth. Remove clams from shells and chop finely. Wash all shell halves and set in a shallow baking pan. Bury in rock salt if it is available.
3. Melt the butter in a skillet and sauté the shallots and garlic in it until tender but not browned. Stir in the bread crumbs, celery, parsley, basil, oregano, cheese, oil, wine and pepper. Mix well.
4. Stir in enough of the reserved clam broth to moisten the stuffing but not to make it soggy.
5. Distribute the chopped clams among the twenty-four shells. Top with bread crumb mixture and then a piece of bacon. Bake ten minutes and then brown under the broiler.

Yield: Four servings.

Baked Crab and Shrimp   *New Jersey*

1 medium-size onion, finely chopped
2 tablespoons butter
1 medium-size green pepper, finely chopped
1 cup chopped celery
1½ cups flaked crab meat
1½ cups roughly cut cooked and cleaned shrimp
½ teaspoon salt
⅛ teaspoon freshly ground black pepper
1 teaspoon Worcestershire sauce
1 cup mayonnaise
1 cup buttered soft bread crumbs.

1. Preheat the oven to 350 degrees.
2. Sauté the onion in the butter and combine with the other ingredients except the bread crumbs. Divide mixture among eight greased shells or ramekins and top with crumbs. Bake twenty-five minutes, or until bubbly hot.

Yield: Eight servings.

Lobster Canapés *Rhode Island*

3 tablespoons butter
½ cup freshly grated Parmesan cheese
1 egg yolk
3 tablespoons dry sherry
⅛ teaspoon cayenne pepper
½ teaspoon Worcestershire sauce
1½ cups cooked lobster meat, finely chopped
48 one-and-one-half-inch to two-inch rounds toasted bread.

1. Preheat the oven to 425 degrees.
2. Cream the butter and cheese together. Stir in the egg yolk, sherry, cayenne and Worcestershire. Add the lobster and mix well.
3. Place a spoonful of the lobster mixture on each toast round. Place on a baking sheet and bake five minutes.
Yield: Four dozen.

Pickled Mackerel *Rhode Island*

4 small mackerel, cleaned
4 cups water
½ cup cider vinegar
½ cup salt
4 bay leaves
12 peppercorns
1 small hot red pepper
Lemon wedges
Buttered thinly sliced brown bread.

1. Preheat the oven to 250 degrees.
2. Place the mackerel in a shallow baking dish.
3. Combine the remaining ingredients and pour over fish. Bake forty-five minutes. Allow to cool in the liquid.
4. To serve, remove fish from bones and skin. Serve fish with lemon wedges and brown bread.
Yield: Eight servings.

Oysters in Cream *New York*

24 oysters
Rock salt
1 cup heavy cream
1 cup freshly grated Parmesan cheese
½ cup melted butter.

1. Open the oysters and remove from shell. Wash twenty-four half shells and place an oyster in each. Set in a shallow baking pan filled with rock salt.
2. Pour two teaspoons cream over each oyster. Sprinkle each with two teaspoons cheese and one teaspoon melted butter. Broil under a preheated broiler just until the oyster edges curl and the cheese is lightly browned.
Yield: Six servings.

Marinated Maine Sardines

3 three-and-three-quarter-ounce to four-ounce cans sardines
¾ cup sour cream
¼ cup light cream
¼ cup tarragon vinegar
2 tablespoons lemon juice
2 tablespoons dry white wine
1 clove garlic, crushed
½ teaspoon horseradish
½ teaspoon salt
½ cup onion, thinly sliced, separated into rings
1 cup thinly sliced peeled cucumber
Boston lettuce cups.

1. Day before, drain the sardines and arrange in a single layer in a shallow baking dish. Combine the sour cream, light cream, vinegar, lemon juice, wine, garlic, horseradish and salt.
2. Mix together cream mixture, the onion and cucumber and spread over sardines. Chill overnight. Next day, arrange in lettuce cups.
Yield: Six servings.

Scallops Mayonnaise *Massachusetts*

1 pound scallops
Salt to taste
¾ cup mayonnaise
½ cup sour cream
1 tablespoon horseradish, or to taste
1 teaspoon mustard, preferably Dijon or Düsseldorf
3 tablespoons finely chopped scallions, including green part
2 tablespoons finely chopped stuffed green olives
Tabasco sauce to taste.

1. If bay scallops are used, leave them whole; if sea scallops are used, cut them in half. Place in a saucepan with water to barely cover. Add salt. Bring to a boil and simmer three to five minutes. Do not overcook or scallops will toughen. Drain and chill well.

2. Combine the remaining ingredients. Serve scallops with mayonnaise dressing.

Yield: Four servings.

Crevettes Paula *New York*

1 cup homemade mayonnaise
1 teaspoon finely grated onion
1 clove garlic, crushed
1 tablespoon catchup
1 tablespoon cognac
1 cup cooked, shelled and deveined shrimp
Lettuce cups.

Combine the mayonnaise, onion, garlic, catchup and cognac in a bowl. Add the shrimp, toss and chill. Serve in lettuce cups.

Yield: Three servings.

Savory Soufflé Roll *New York*

4 tablespoons butter
½ cup flour

½ teaspoon salt
⅛ teaspoon white pepper
2 cups milk
5 eggs, separated
Ham and spinach filling (recipe below).

1. Preheat the oven to 400 degrees.

2. Grease, line with wax paper and grease again a 15½-by-10½-by-1-inch jellyroll pan. Dust lightly with flour.

3. Melt the butter in a saucepan and blend in the flour, salt and pepper. Gradually stir in the milk. Bring to a boil, stirring, and cook one minute.

4. Beat the egg yolks just to mix. Add a little of the hot sauce while beating. Return all to the pan and cook over medium heat one minute longer, stirring. Do not allow to boil. Set aside. Cool to room temperature, stirring occasionally.

5. Beat the egg whites until stiff but not dry and fold into the cooled sauce. Pour into the prepared pan and spread to form an even layer.

6. Bake twenty-five to thirty minutes, or until well puffed and browned. Turn immediately onto a clean towel. Spread with warm filling. Roll, with the aid of the towel, and slide, seam side down, onto a serving platter or board.

Yield: Ten appetizer servings or six luncheon-supper servings.

Ham and Spinach Filling *New York*

2 tablespoons butter
4 shallots, finely chopped
4 medium-size mushrooms, chopped
1 cup cooked, well-drained chopped spinach
1 cup finely chopped or ground cooked ham
1 tablespoon Dijon mustard
¼ teaspoon nutmeg
2 three-ounce packages cream cheese, softened
Salt and freshly ground black pepper to taste.

1. Melt the butter in a skillet and sauté the

shallots in it until they are tender. Add the mushrooms and cook until they give up their moisture and it evaporates, about three minutes.

2. Add the spinach, ham, mustard and nutmeg and heat while stirring. Stir in the cream cheese and season with salt and pepper.

Yield: About two cups.

Felafel   *New York*

½ pound dried chick-peas
2 cloves garlic
½ teaspoon paprika
  Salt and pepper to taste
¼ teaspoon baking soda
½ tablespoon dry bread crumbs
1 teaspoon chopped parsley
  Oil or fat for deep-frying.

1. Soak the chick-peas overnight in water to cover.

2. Next day, drain, rinse and grind the chick-peas. Grind again with the garlic, paprika, salt, pepper, baking soda and bread crumbs.

3. Mix in one-quarter cup water and the parsley and form into tiny balls.

4. Fry the balls in oil or fat heated to 360 degrees. Do not burn. Drain and serve hot.

Yield: Six servings.

Anchovy-Stuffed Cherry Tomatoes
New York

18 to twenty-four cherry tomatoes
6 hard-cooked egg yolks, mashed
12 flat anchovy fillets, chopped
1 tablespoon drained chopped capers
  Freshly ground black pepper to taste
1 tablespoon finely chopped parsley.

1. Cut a small piece off the end (away from the stem) of each tomato. Scoop out the pulp and discard. Place tomatoes upside down to drain.

2. Combine the egg yolks, anchovies, capers, pepper and parsley and use to fill the tomatoes. Chill.

Yield: Ten servings.

Zucchini Appetizer   *New York*

1 large zucchini
2 tablespoons olive oil
1 medium-size onion, finely chopped
½ clove garlic, finely chopped
½ tablespoon wine vinegar
  Salt and freshly ground black pepper to taste
½ teaspoon chervil
½ teaspoon tarragon
1 tablespoon chopped parsley
  Toast triangles.

1. Halve the zucchini lengthwise and scoop out the flesh, leaving a one-quarter-inch shell. Chop the flesh.

2. Heat the oil and sauté the onion, garlic and chopped zucchini in it until tender. Increase heat to evaporate any excess moisture.

3. Add the vinegar, salt, pepper, chervil, tarragon and parsley. Pile into zucchini shells and serve warm or cold, with toast triangles.

Yield: About four servings.

Quiche à la Roma   *New York*

2 eggs, lightly beaten
  Salt and freshly ground black pepper to taste
½ teaspoon Dijon mustard
¼ cup finely chopped onion
1 cup (packed) grated Cheddar cheese
1 unbaked eight-inch to nine-inch pie shell
1 tomato, thinly sliced
1 green pepper, cut into thin strips
¼ pound thinly sliced salami
1 tablespoon oregano.

1. Preheat the oven to 350 degrees.

2. Combine the eggs, salt, pepper, mustard, onion and cheese and spread in the bottom of the pie shell.

3. Arrange the slices of tomato, green pepper and salami on top of the egg mixture and sprinkle with the oregano.

4. Bake thirty to forty minutes, or until pastry is cooked and egg mixture is set.

Yield: Six servings.

Note: This is not a custard-type quiche.

Tiropetes (Cheese Pastries)   *New York*

 3 tablespoons butter
 3 tablespoons flour
1½ cups hot milk
 2 eggs
 1 egg yolk
⅛ teaspoon freshly ground black pepper
¾ pound feta cheese, finely crumbled
½ pound phyllo pastry sheets (see note)
½ pound butter, melted.

1. In a saucepan, melt the three tablespoons butter. Add the flour and cook, stirring, until well blended. Remove from heat and add the milk. Mix with a wire whisk until blended. Return to heat and cook, stirring with whisk, until sauce is smooth and thickened.

2. Beat the eggs and egg yolk with a little of the hot sauce, stir into remaining sauce and cook over low heat, whisking constantly, two minutes. Remove from heat and stir in the pepper and cheese.

3. Preheat the oven to 425 degrees.

4. Cut the phyllo pastry sheets into long strips two inches wide. Brush one strip at a time with the melted butter. (Keep phyllo not being used covered at all times with wax paper and lightly dampened towel.) For each appetizer, put one teaspoon of the cheese mixture at one end of one strip and fold over and over into a small triangle. With each fold, make sure that the bottom edge

is parallel with alternate edge. Arrange triangles on baking sheets and brush with butter.

5. Bake pastries ten to fifteen minutes, or until golden. Serve hot.

Yield: Four dozen.

Note: To prepare another easy filling, combine one-half pound each pot cheese and crumbled feta cheese, one egg, one egg yolk, two tablespoons chopped fresh dill and one-quarter teaspoon freshly ground black pepper.

Phyllo pastry sheets are available frozen in many specialty food stores and fresh at Kassos Brothers, 570 Ninth Avenue, New York City, Poseidon Pastry Shop, 629 Ninth Avenue, New York City.

Cheese-Stuffed Mushrooms   *Pennsylvania*

½ cup white bread cubes
12 large mushrooms
 2 cloves garlic, finely minced
 2 tablespoons chopped parsley
   Salt and freshly ground black pepper to taste
 2 eggs
½ cup ricotta cheese
¼ cup olive oil
¼ cup freshly grated Parmesan cheese.

1. Preheat the oven to 400 degrees.

2. Soak the bread cubes in water; then squeeze dry. Shred into a mixing bowl.

3. Chop the mushroom stems and add to bread crumbs along with the garlic, parsley, salt, pepper, eggs and ricotta cheese. Blend well. Stuff mushrooms with filling and arrange them, cap side down, on a dish rubbed lightly with a little of the oil. Sprinkle with remaining oil and the Parmesan. Bake twenty minutes.

Yield: Six servings.

Mushroom Quiche   *Pennsylvania*

¾ pound mushrooms
4 tablespoons butter
1 unbaked nine-inch pie shell
¾ cup finely chopped onions
4 eggs, lightly beaten
2 cups heavy cream or one cup each milk
and cream
¼ teaspoon nutmeg
Cayenne pepper to taste
Salt and freshly ground black pepper to
taste.

1. Chop the mushrooms until they are very fine. Melt two tablespoons of the butter, add the mushrooms and cook, stirring, until wilted. Cover and simmer slowly about thirty minutes. Let cool slightly.
2. Preheat the oven to 450 degrees.
3. Bake the pie shell five minutes.
4. Meanwhile, melt the remaining butter, add the onions and cook until wilted but not browned.
5. Combine the eggs, cream, nutmeg, cayenne, salt and pepper. Stir in the mushrooms and onions and pour all into the partly baked pie shell.
6. Bake fifteen minutes, reduce the oven temperature to 350 degrees and bake about ten minutes longer, or until a knife inserted one inch from the pastry edge comes out clean. Serve hot.
Yield: Six to ten servings.

Three Drops   *New York*

Filling:
¼ cup oil
1 cup finely chopped onions
2 cloves garlic, finely chopped
½ teaspoon salt
¼ teaspoon freshly ground black pepper
1 can sliced mushrooms (eight ounces
drained weight)
2 tablespoons tomato paste
2 eggs
36 small stuffed olives.

Dough:
2 eggs
1¼ cups milk
⅓ cup oil
3 tablespoons freshly grated Parmesan
cheese
1¼ cups flour
½ teaspoon salt
1 teaspoon baking powder.

1. Preheat the oven to 450 degrees.
2. To prepare filling, heat the oil in a skillet and add the onions, garlic, salt and pepper. Sauté until onions are tender. Add the mushrooms, tomato paste and eggs. Stir until the eggs are cooked. Cool. Reserve the olives.
3. Put the dough ingredients into an electric blender and blend until smooth.
4. Drop one teaspoon dough into each of thirty-six greased one-and-three-quarter-inch (two-bite size) muffin tins. Add one teaspoon filling, top with one stuffed olive and cover with one teaspoon dough. Bake about ten minutes.
Yield: Three dozen muffins.

Curried Flan Appetizer   *Connecticut*

½ onion, finely chopped
1 rib celery, finely chopped
1½ tablespoons butter
2 to three teaspoons curry powder, or to
taste
5 teaspoons unflavored gelatin
2¼ cups chicken broth
1 cup mayonnaise
4 hard-cooked eggs, chopped
¼ cup chopped salted almonds (optional)
2 tablespoons chopped parsley (optional)
Pumpernickel or crackers.

1. Sauté the onion and celery in the butter until tender. Sprinkle with the curry powder and cook, stirring, one minute.
2. Soak the gelatin in one-quarter cup of the broth. Heat the remaining broth to boiling, add

softened gelatin and stir into the curry mixture. Bring to a boil, stirring.

3. Cool and chill the mixture until it begins to thicken. Blend in the mayonnaise, eggs, almonds and parsley if desired. Pour mixture into a cold wet mold and chill until firm. Unmold and serve as spread with pumpernickel or crackers.

Yield: About one dozen to twenty servings.

Cape Cod Clam Chowder *Massachusetts*

¼ pound bacon, finely diced
2 medium-size onions, finely chopped
3 cups diced potatoes
2 teaspoons salt
½ teaspoon oregano
¼ teaspoon basil
2 cups boiling water
24 chowder clams (preferably large quahogs), ground, liquor and all, through medium blade of food grinder.

1. Sauté the bacon and onions in a large kettle until onions are tender and golden. Pour off excess fat.

2. To the kettle, add the potatoes, salt, oregano, basil and water and let simmer until potatoes are tender, about fifteen minutes.

3. Add the clams. This is the base. (See note to prepare chowder.)

Yield: About one quart of base.

Note: Next day, add to base one quart of milk, two tablespoons butter and salt and freshly ground black pepper to taste. Heat.

Old-Fashioned Clam Chowder

Massachusetts

60 to 72 chowder clams, scrubbed until water runs clear
½ pound salt pork, diced
6 large onions, sliced
4 to six leeks, cleaned and sliced
3 tomatoes, peeled and chopped
2 cups canned tomatoes

3 ribs celery, diced
1 tablespoon chopped parsley
1 teaspoon thyme
1 bay leaf
3 large potatoes, peeled and diced
  Salt and freshly ground black pepper to taste
2 tablespoons flour
2 tablespoons butter
2 large pilot crackers, crumbled
1 teaspoon Worcestershire sauce
2 to four drops Tabasco sauce.

1. Place the clams in a large kettle or clam steamer with one-half cup water. Steam the clams until they open, about ten minutes, depending on the size.

2. Reserve the broth. Remove clams from shells and remove the long necks and coarse membrane. Chop half the clams, leaving remaining clams whole. Reserve.

3. Cook salt pork in a heavy kettle until golden. Add onions and leeks and sauté until tender.

4. Measure the reserved broth and add water to make up to two quarts and add to the kettle. Add the chopped tomatoes, canned tomatoes, celery, parsley, thyme, bay leaf, potatoes, salt and pepper. Bring to a boil and simmer, covered, about thirty to forty minutes.

5. Blend the flour with the butter and, while stirring, add a little at a time to the hot soup. Add the crackers, Worcestershire, Tabasco and reserved clams. Reheat and test for seasoning.

Yield: About five quarts; fifteen to twenty servings.

Down-East Haddock Chowder *Maine*

⅓ cup diced salt pork
1 onion, finely chopped
3 potatoes, peeled and cubed
2 pounds haddock fillets, cut into strips or cubes
1 quart water

1 rib celery with leaves, chopped
  Salt and freshly ground black pepper to
  taste
⅛ teaspoon mace
3 cups milk
3 large pilot crackers, crumbled.

1. Cook the salt pork in a kettle until crisp. Remove the pieces and reserve.

2. In the fat remaining in the kettle, sauté the onion until tender but not browned. Add the potatoes, fish, water, celery, salt, pepper and mace. Bring to a boil, cover and simmer gently until potatoes are tender, about fifteen minutes.

3. Stir in the milk, crackers and reserved pork pieces and heat to boiling.

Yield: About six servings.

Note: This chowder can be made with smoked haddock or smoked cod fillets provided three tablespoons of butter is substituted for the salt pork.

Cape Cod Lobster Soup   *Massachusetts*

2 one-pound to one-and-one-half-pound live
  lobsters
5 tablespoons butter
3 large ship biscuits or pilot crackers
4 cups milk, scalded
  Salt and freshly ground black pepper to taste
1 cup diced cooked lobster meat.

1. Plunge a knife into the thorax of the lobsters where body and head join, to kill them. Discard head and thorax, but retain tomalley and coral. With a cleaver or large chef's knife, cut tail and claws into small sections.

2. Heat two tablespoons of the butter in a heavy sauté pan. Add lobster sections and cook, stirring, until pieces turn pink.

3. Crush the biscuits or crackers and mix to a paste with remaining butter. Mix in the milk and pour over the lobster in the pan. Season with salt and pepper. Bring to a boil, stirring. Grate in the coral and add tomalley.

4. Add the cooked lobster meat and serve.

Yield: Four servings.

Oyster Stew   *New York*

2 cups oysters
4 cups milk, scalded
¼ cup butter
1½ teaspoons salt
¼ teaspoon freshly ground black pepper.

1. Strain the liquor from the oysters through cheesecloth into a saucepan. Pick over the oysters for shell or grit and clean if necessary.

2. Bring the oyster liquor to a boil. Add the oysters, bring to a boil and simmer just until the edges curl, about four minutes. With a slotted spoon, remove the oysters. If they are very large, quarter them.

3. Add the milk and butter to oyster liquor. Season with the salt and pepper and return oysters. Reheat and serve immediately.

Yield: Four servings.

Scallop Stew   *Massachusetts*

¼ cup butter
4 cups sea scallops
1 tablespoon flour
4 cups milk
½ teaspoon salt
⅛ teaspoon freshly ground white pepper.

1. Melt two tablespoons of the butter in a skillet. Add the scallops and sauté three minutes.

2. In a small saucepan, melt remaining butter and blend in the flour. Gradually stir in the milk and bring to a boil, stirring.

3. Add the salt and pepper. Add scallop-and-butter mixture.

4. Transfer the stew to the top of a double boiler set over low heat to keep water in bottom

of boiler hot but not boiling. Let stew set about ten minutes.

Yield: Four servings.

How to Prepare a Snapping Turtle for Soup   *New Jersey*

1. Snapping turtles for soup may range in size from about ten pounds to thirty-six pounds. To kill the turtle, place a wooden object in its mouth and pull to extend the neck away from the shell. Keep fingers clear of the turtle's mouth. Hold the neck over a solid chopping block in the open and sever the neck quickly with a hatchet. Tie a small rope around the turtle's tail and hang the turtle, neck side down, in the open air to bleed. Let the turtle hang twenty-four hours.

2. Bring three gallons water to a boil in a container large enough to hold the turtle. Plunge the turtle, shell side down, into the hot water and let stand one minute. Do not let the turtle remain for long in the water or turtle will start to cook and toughen. Using the fingers, peel off the tough outer coating of the turtle. Use a knife to loosen the outer coating of the upper shell. It may be necessary to dip parts of the turtle into the hot water once or twice more if the outer coating is hard to pull off. When all the outer coating of the turtle is removed, you will find that the turtle looks clean and gray. Do not cut away the skin of the turtle. Once cooked, the skin is edible.

3. Lift up one leg of the turtle at a time and plunge a sharp knife where the skin joins the shell. Cut all around one leg joint to sever it. Set aside and continue until all legs are separated. Cut around and under the white cross bone that covers the underside of the turtle, leaving the red meat attached. Cut off the neck and throat. Cut off the tail. If the turtle is male, cut off and discard the organ under the tail. With a knife, snip off the claws of the legs. Discard all inner parts of the turtle (the digestive organs, heart, gall bladder and so on).

4. Generously sprinkle all parts of the turtle and the under part of the shell with coarse salt

and refrigerate several hours. Cover with cold water and let stand in the refrigerator twenty-four hours, changing the water several times. Drain and rinse well. The turtle is now ready to be cooked.

How to Cook Turtle for Soups
New Jersey

1 eighteen-pound turtle, cleaned and ready to cook (if a smaller or larger turtle is used, increase or decrease quantities of other ingredients accordingly)
3 ribs celery with leaves, broken
6 sprigs parsley
2 bay leaves
1 teaspoon thyme
  Salt to taste
15 peppercorns
3 carrots, quartered
2 medium-size onions, each studded with two whole cloves.

1. Place the turtle legs, neck, tail, breast or cross bone and all the edible parts in a large kettle and add water to cover. Add the remaining ingredients. The mouth of the kettle should be large enough so that the turtle pieces may be covered with the turtle shell. This is important because the underside of this shell contains meat and must cook or steam while the remaining parts simmer.

2. Place the lid on the kettle and simmer about one and one-half hours, or until the meat is fork-tender. Pull off all meat and skin from the bones and cut into small cubes, each about one-half inch. Remember, there is much meat on the underside of the large shell. Strain the broth.

Yield: About four quarts meat and skin and one and one-half gallons broth.

Note: Leftover meat and skin may be packed in jars, covered with leftover broth and frozen for future use.

Snapping Turtle and Vegetable Soup

New Jersey

2 cups chopped well-rinsed leeks
4 cups cubed potatoes
2 cups chopped onions
8 shallots, finely chopped
3 cloves garlic, finely chopped
2 carrots, coarsely chopped
24 green beans, cut into one-inch lengths
   Salt to taste
1 ham bone
1 ten-ounce package frozen cut okra
3 quarts canned tomatoes
1 teaspoon peppercorns
2 bay leaves
1 teaspoon paprika
2 sprigs marjoram, chopped
½ teaspoon dried savory
1 teaspoon dried sweet basil
5 quarts to six quarts turtle broth (page 13)
   Turtle meat from one cooked turtle (page 13).

Combine all ingredients in a large kettle and simmer one to two hours.

Yield: Eight quarts to twelve quarts.

Note: Leftover soup may be frozen.

A-Snapper-Soup-More-or-Less-in-the-Style-of-Bookbinder's

Pennsylvania

4 tablespoons butter
1 two-and-one-half-pound to three-pound veal shank
   Salt and freshly ground black pepper to taste
3 cups chopped onions
2 cups chopped carrots
1 cup chopped celery
½ teaspoon dried thyme
½ teaspoon dried marjoram
3 whole cloves
1 bay leaf
1 cup flour
1 quart fresh or canned tomatoes
4 quarts turtle broth (page 13)
4 cups cooked turtle meat and skin, cut into one-half-inch cubes (page 13)
2 to six cloves, crushed in a mortar and pestle
   Tabasco sauce to taste (the soup should be a bit spicy)
3 lemon slices
2 hard-cooked eggs, coarsely chopped
   Dry sherry.

1. Preheat the oven to 350 degrees.

2. On top of stove, heat the butter in a small heavy roasting pan. Sprinkle the veal shank with salt and pepper and add. Cook shank, turning to brown it lightly all over. Scatter the onions, carrots, celery, thyme, marjoram, whole cloves and bay leaf around shank. Cook about five minutes, occasionally turning the shank and stirring the vegetables.

3. Place the pan in the oven and roast thirty minutes, stirring occasionally so that the vegetables and meat do not stick or burn.

4. Sprinkle the vegetables with the flour and stir until will coated. Bake thirty minutes longer. Scrape all this into a large soup kettle and add the tomatoes and turtle broth, stirring constantly. Bring to a boil and simmer about two hours, stirring frequently all over the bottom to make certain the soup does not stick. (If it sticks, it will burn or scorch.)

5. Add the turtle meat and skin, crushed cloves, Tabasco and lemon slices. Simmer about fifteen minutes longer. Add salt and pepper. Stir in the eggs. Serve with a decanter of sherry on the table so that guests may add their own according to taste.

Yield: About one gallon.

Montauk Whiting Chowder

New York

4 one-pound whiting
1 bay leaf
2 sprigs parsley

Salt and freshly ground black pepper to
taste
½ cup diced salt pork
1 onion, chopped
4 potatoes, peeled and diced
4 cups milk, scalded.

1. Wash the whiting and place in a kettle with
water barely to cover. Add the bay leaf, parsley,
salt and pepper. Bring to a boil, cover and simmer
gently about ten minutes, or until fish flakes easily.
2. When whiting are cool enough to handle,
skin and bone them and cut into chunks. Strain
the stock in which the fish was cooked and reserve.
3. Cook the salt pork until crisp, remove
pieces and reserve. In fat remaining, sauté the
onion until tender. Add the potatoes, salt, pepper
and reserved fish stock and pork bits. Simmer
fifteen minutes.
4. Add fish pieces and the milk. Reheat, but do
not boil.
Yield: Four servings.

Rhode Island Fish Chowder

1 pound salt pork, cut into strips, soaked in
  boiling water five minutes and drained
4 pounds cod or sea bass fillets, cut into
  four-inch squares
3 cups finely chopped onions
1 tablespoon chopped fresh summer savory or
  one teaspoon dried savory
3 tablespoons chopped parsley
⅛ teaspoon cayenne pepper
  Split pilot crackers, cream crackers or ship
  biscuits or any plain, unsalted crackers that
  have not been oil-dipped
3 tablespoons butter
1 tablespoon flour.

1. Make a layer of the salt pork in the bottom
of a chowder kettle. Top with layer of the fish,
then the onions and season with some of the savory, parsley and cayenne.
2. Make a layer of the crackers. Repeat layers
until all ingredients are used, ending with crackers that have been spread with two tablespoons of
the butter.
3. Pour water down the side of the kettle until
water almost covers top layer of crackers. Bring
to a boil, cover and simmer one hour. Replenish
water level with boiling water if level sinks too
low.
4. Decant the liquid into a saucepan. Blend
together the remaining butter and the flour and
gradually whisk the mixture into the simmering
liquid.
5. Transfer solid part of chowder to a tureen
or soup bowls and pour thickened liquid over.
Yield: Eight to ten servings.

Philadelphia Pepper Pot   *Pennsylvania*

1 pound honeycomb tripe
½ cup diced salt pork
½ cup chopped onion
1 green pepper, cored, seeded and chopped
½ cup chopped celery
½ cup chopped carrot
2 cloves garlic, finely minced
1 small hot green pepper pod, trimmed and
  chopped, or more to taste
12 cups water
5 pounds veal knuckles
  Salt and freshly ground black pepper to
  taste
1 bay leaf
1 sprig fresh thyme or one-half teaspoon
  dried thyme
1 cup diced potatoes
1 teaspoon paprika
2 tablespoons butter
2 tablespoons flour
½ cup heavy cream
  Dumplings for soup (page 163) (optional).

1. Rinse the tripe under cold running water. Drain.

2. Place the tripe on a flat surface and cut tripe into thin shreds. Chop the shreds into one-inch lengths. Set aside.

3. Heat the salt pork in a kettle. When salt pork is rendered of fat, add the onion. Cook, stirring, until onion is wilted. Add the tripe, green pepper, celery, carrot and garlic and cook briefly. Stir in the hot pepper and water and add the knuckles, salt, pepper, bay leaf and thyme. Bring to a boil and simmer three hours.

4. Add the potatoes and continue to cook about one hour longer, or until the tripe is thoroughly tender. It should not be chewy. Sprinkle with the paprika.

5. Blend the butter with the flour and stir, bit by bit, into the soup. When the mixture is thickened slightly and boiling, stir in the cream. If dumplings are desired, drop the batter by tablespoons into the soup. Cover and cook fifteen minutes longer.

Yield: About three quarts.

Beef and Barley Soup   *Maine*

1 pound beef shin or soup beef, cubed
1 tablespoon bacon drippings
1 large cracked beef or veal knuckle bone
8 cups cold water
1½ teaspoons salt
1 teaspoon freshly ground black pepper
3 sprigs parsley
1 onion, sliced
1 bay leaf
¼ cup pearl barley
¼ cup brown rice
½ cup chopped celery
2 cups stewed tomatoes
2 tablespoons chopped parsley.

1. Day before, sauté the meat cubes in the bacon drippings until sealed but not browned. Add the bone, water, salt, pepper, parsley sprigs, onion and bay leaf. Bring to a boil and boil vigor-

ously while skimming the surface of scum. Cover and cook gently two hours.

2. Add the barley and rice and cook one hour longer.

3. Cool and chill overnight. Next day, remove surface fat, bones and parsley sprigs. Add the remaining ingredients. Check seasoning and simmer forty-five minutes.

Yield: Eight servings.

Stock Pot Soup   *New York*

4 pounds, more or less, fresh or cooked chicken carcasses, beef bones or veal bones
3 pounds chicken wings
1 veal knuckle
2 beef marrow bones
2 large onions, each studded with four whole cloves
3 cloves garlic
6 carrots
4 leeks, trimmed, split in half and well washed
3 white turnips, peeled
3 bay leaves
2 cups dry white wine
6 tablespoons coarse salt
16 peppercorns
6 sprigs parsley
Top leaves and outside ribs of six celery stalks
3 pounds brisket of beef
1 four-pound to five-pound chicken.

1. Place the carcasses, wings, veal knuckle, marrow bones, onions, garlic, carrots, leeks, turnips, bay leaves, wine, salt, peppercorns, parsley and celery in an eight-quart to ten-quart kettle. Add cold water to within two inches of the kettle rim. Bring slowly to a boil and skim frequently as necessary. Let simmer so that the broth barely bubbles four to five hours.

2. One hour before the broth is to be removed from the stove, add beef brisket and chicken. Cook until brisket and chicken are cooked and

tender. Remove the chicken and brisket, which may be served at this point, using as much broth as necessary.

3. Strain all the broth and store in pint and quart containers. Refrigerate overnight. Skim off all fat; then freeze the stock.

Yield: Five quarts to six quarts strained broth.

Cream of Chicken Soup   *New York*

1 three-and-one-half-pound chicken, cut into serving pieces
6 cups water
2 ribs celery with leaves, diced
1 bay leaf
2 sprigs parsley
1¾ teaspoons salt
½ teaspoon freshly ground black pepper
¼ cup butter
2 onions, thinly sliced
4 baking potatoes, peeled and thinly sliced or diced
¼ teaspoon saffron
1 cup light cream
¼ cup chopped parsley.

1. Place the chicken pieces in a heavy casserole or kettle. Add the water, celery, bay leaf, parsley sprigs, one teaspoon of the salt and one-quarter teaspoon of the pepper. Bring to a boil, cover and simmer gently until chicken is tender, about fifty minutes. Remove chicken pieces from the broth. Strain the broth into a kettle and remove surface fat.

2. Take the chicken meat from the bones and skin and cut meat into large slivers. Set aside.

3. Heat the butter in a skillet and sauté the onions in it until transparent but not browned. Add the potatoes, toss and cook two to three minutes without browning.

4. Add vegetables to the broth in the kettle. Add the saffron and remaining salt and pepper. Cover, bring to a boil and simmer forty-five minutes, or until the potatoes are very tender.

5. Pass the mixture through a sieve or puree in

an electric blender. Return to the kettle. Stir in the cream and reserved chicken. Reheat, but do not boil. Serve garnished with chopped parsley.

Yield: Eight servings.

Chicken and Corn Soup   *Pennsylvania*

1 five-pound chicken, cut into serving pieces
Salt to taste
12 peppercorns
2 ribs celery, chopped
2 carrots, quartered
1 onion
6 ears corn on the cob
2 hard-cooked eggs, chopped
1 tablespoon finely chopped parsley
1 cup cubed cooked ham

1. Place the chicken in a kettle. Add water to cover, salt, peppercorns, celery, carrots and onion. Simmer until the chicken is thoroughly tender.

2. Strain the broth and pour it into a clean kettle. Simmer while preparing the remaining ingredients.

3. Remove the chicken from the bones and skin and cut the chicken meat into bite-size pieces.

4. Shuck the corn and drop it into the kettle. Bring just to a boil. Scrape the kernels from the cobs into the soup. Add the chicken and remaining ingredients. Serve piping hot.

Yield: Eight to one dozen servings.

Corn Chowder   *New Jersey*

½ pound salt pork
Boiling water
1 large onion, thinly sliced
2 potatoes, cubed
2 cups chicken broth
1½ cups corn kernels freshly cut from the cob
1 teaspoon salt

½ teaspoon freshly ground white pepper
2 cups light cream.

1. Place the salt pork in a bowl and pour boiling water over. Let stand five minutes. Drain. Cut pork into 1-by-¼-inch strips.
2. Cook the pork strips in a kettle until crisp. Remove bits and reserve. In the fat remaining, sauté the onion until it is tender.
3. Add the potatoes and broth. Cover and simmer until potatoes are barely tender, about fifteen minutes. Add the corn, salt and pepper and cook two minutes longer.
4. Stir in the cream and heat to boiling. Sprinkle top with reserved pork bits before serving.
Yield: Four to six servings.

Escarole Soup   *New York*

    5 pounds soup bones with marrow
    1 six-ounce can tomato paste
    8 cups water
 3¼ teaspoons salt
    ¾ pound ground chuck
    ¼ teaspoon finely chopped garlic
    1 egg, lightly beaten
    ¼ teaspoon freshly ground black pepper
    3 tablespoons grated Parmesan cheese
    1 pound chopped escarole
    1 cup diced onions
    1 cup diced celery
    1 cup diced potatoes
    2 tablespoons chopped fresh parsley.

1. Place the soup bones, tomato paste, water and two and one-half teaspoons of the salt in a four-quart saucepan. Cover and simmer one hour.
2. Combine the chuck, garlic, egg, pepper, cheese and remaining salt. Shape into three-quarter-inch balls. Add to hot soup and simmer ten minutes longer. Add the vegetables and simmer thirty minutes, or until vegetables are tender. Remove bones and serve soup hot with chopped parsley sprinkled over the top.
Yield: Eight servings.

Parsnip Soup   *Massachusetts*

    ½ cup diced salt pork
    1 onion, finely chopped
    2 cups peeled, cubed parsnips
    2 cups peeled, cubed potatoes
    2 cups water
      Salt and freshly ground black pepper to taste
    4 cups half and half, scalded
    2 tablespoons flour
    ¼ cup butter
    2 tablespoons chopped parsley.

1. Cook the salt pork until it is crisp. Remove pieces and reserve. In the fat remaining, sauté the onion until tender but not browned. Add the parsnips, potatoes, water, salt and pepper.
2. Simmer, covered, until vegetables are tender, about twenty minutes. Stir in half and half.
3. Blend together the flour and butter and whisk, bit by bit, into the simmering soup. Sprinkle with the parsley and reserved pork pieces.
Yield: Eight servings.

Midsummer Eve Soup of Fresh Green Peas   *Connecticut*

 1½ cups fresh peas and a few tender young pods broken into bits
      Boiling salted water
      Chopped fresh tarragon
      Chopped fresh mint
 2½ cups well-seasoned, concentrated, boiling chicken broth
    1 tablespoon butter
    1 tablespoon flour
    ½ cup heavy cream
    1 cup champagne.

1. Cook the peas and pods in boiling salted

water until just tender. Drain and place in an electric blender.

2. Add three-quarters teaspoon each tarragon and mint, the broth, butter and flour and blend one minute. Pour into a saucepan, bring to a boil and simmer five minutes or until thick. Chill.

3. Just before serving, stir in the cream and champagne. Garnish with additional mint and tarragon.

Yield: Four servings.

Mushroom Soup   *Pennsylvania*

1 pound mushrooms
4 cups fresh or canned chicken broth
¼ cup butter
2 tablespoons flour
    Salt and freshly ground black pepper to taste
¼ cup dry sherry
½ cup heavy cream.

1. Remove the stems from the mushrooms and chop the stems coarsely. Reserve the caps.

2. Place the chopped stems in a saucepan and add the broth. Bring to a boil and simmer twenty minutes. Strain the broth and reserve.

3. Slice the mushroom caps. Heat the butter in a saucepan and add the caps. Cook, stirring, until lightly browned. Sprinkle with the flour and add salt and pepper. Using a wire whisk, stir in the broth and bring to a boil. Simmer five minutes and add the sherry and cream. Heat thoroughly and serve hot.

Yield: Four to six servings.

Pumpkin Soup   *Massachusetts*

1 onion, finely chopped
1 bunch scallions with some of the green part, finely chopped
¼ cup plus three tablespoons butter
1 two-pound-thirteen-ounce can pumpkin puree

8 cups chicken broth
    Salt and freshly ground black pepper to taste
3 tablespoons flour
2 cups light cream
2 cups crisp croutons.

1. Sauté the onion and scallions in one-quarter cup of the butter until tender but not browned.

2. Add the pumpkin puree and cook gently five minutes.

3. Stir in the broth and cook, stirring, ten minutes. Season with salt and pepper.

4. Blend together the remaining butter and the flour and whisk into the simmering soup. Stir in the cream and reheat just before serving. Serve sprinkled with the croutons.

Yield: About eight to ten servings.

Hot Clam and Tomato Broth   *New York*

1½ cups fresh or bottled clam broth
1½ cups tomato juice
    Juice of half a lemon
    Freshly ground black pepper to taste
1 teaspoon Worcestershire sauce
4 tablespoons whipped cream
2 teaspoons chopped fresh parsley or chives.

1. Combine the broth and tomato juice in a saucepan and bring just to a simmer. Add the lemon juice, pepper and Worcestershire.

2. Pour the broth into four hot cups and top each serving with whipped cream. Garnish the cream with the parsley or chives.

Yield: Four servings.

Fresh Tomato Soup   *Delaware*

¾ cup butter
2 tablespoons olive oil
1 large onion, thinly sliced
2 teaspoons chopped fresh thyme or one-half teaspoon dried thyme

2 tablespoons chopped fresh basil or one teaspoon dried basil
Salt and freshly ground black pepper to taste
3 pounds ripe tomatoes, cored and quartered
3 tablespoons tomato paste
¼ cup flour
4 cups chicken broth
1 teaspoon sugar
1 cup heavy cream.

1. Heat one-half cup of the butter and the oil in a heavy kettle. Add the onion and cook until tender but not browned.

2. Add the thyme, basil, salt, pepper, tomatoes and tomato paste. Simmer ten minutes.

3. Mix the flour with six tablespoons of the broth and stir into the tomato mixture. Add remaining broth and cook thirty minutes, stirring frequently.

4. Pass mixture through the finest blade of a food mill or through a fine sieve. Reheat and stir in the sugar and cream. Do not boil. Swirl in remaining butter.

Yield: About eight servings.

Water Cress Soup   *Delaware*

¼ cup diced salt pork
1 small onion, finely chopped
1 large potato, diced
2 cups water
6 cups water cress with stems, coarsely cut
1 cup cooked peas
4 eggs.

1. Cook the salt pork until pieces are crisp.

2. Add the onion and cook until tender but not browned.

3. Add the potato and water. Simmer, covered, until potato is tender, about fifteen minutes.

4. Add the water cress, bring to a boil and boil two minutes.

5. Add the peas and bring to a boil again.

6. Add the eggs and poach gently three to four minutes. Serve immediately.

Yield: Four servings.

Chilled Asparagus Soup   *New Jersey*

2 ripe tomatoes, peeled, seeded and quartered
1 cucumber, peeled, seeded and chopped
4 scallions, including green part, chopped
1½ cups cooked asparagus tips and stalks
2 teaspoons salt
½ teaspoon freshly ground black pepper
1 teaspoon oregano
2 tablespoons olive oil
2 tablespoons wine vinegar
½ teaspoon sugar
2½ cups tomato juice.

1. Mix together the tomatoes, cucumber and scallions. Chop the asparagus stalks and add. Reserve the tips.

2. Stir the salt, pepper, oregano, oil, vinegar and sugar into the vegetable mixture. Blend in an electric blender, in two or three batches, until smooth, using some of the tomato juice if needed.

3. Stir in remaining juice and chill well. Garnish with asparagus tips.

Yield: Six servings.

Chilled Beer and Cucumber Soup
                            Pennsylvania

½ cup sour cream
1 twelve-ounce bottle light beer
2 cucumbers
1 teaspoon salt
¼ teaspoon freshly ground black pepper
½ teaspoon sugar
1 tablespoon freshly snipped dill weed.

1. Combine the sour cream and beer.

2. Cut three or four slices from one cucumber and reserve. Peel cucumbers, halve lengthwise

and remove seeds. Chop cucumbers and add to the beer mixture. Add the salt, pepper and sugar.

3. In two or three batches, pass the mixture through an electric blender and blend until smooth. Stir in the dill and chill.

4. Serve in chilled soup bowls, garnished with reserved cucumber slices.

Yield: Three or four servings.

Yankee Bean Chowder *Massachusetts*

1 cup dried pea beans or navy beans
1 onion, finely chopped
1 cup diced carrots
1 green pepper, diced
1½ cups canned tomatoes
1 teaspoon salt
½ teaspoon freshly ground black pepper
1 cup diced potatoes
2 cups milk.

1. Day before, pick over and wash the beans. Cover with cold water and let soak overnight.

2. Next day, drain the beans and place in a kettle with one and one-half quarts fresh cold water.

3. Add the onion and bring to a boil. Cover and simmer until beans are barely tender, about thirty minutes. Add the carrots, green pepper, tomatoes, salt and black pepper and cook ten minutes. If desired, soup can be put through an electric blender or food mill at this point.

4. Add the potatoes and milk and cook fifteen minutes longer, or until the potatoes are tender. Check seasoning.

Yield: Six servings.

Baked Bean Soup *Massachusetts*

2 cups cold baked beans
2 medium-size onions, minced
½ clove garlic, finely chopped

4 cups cold water
2 cups canned tomatoes
2 tablespoons flour
2 tablespoons butter
Salt and freshly ground black pepper to taste.

1. Place the beans, onions, garlic and water in a saucepan and simmer about thirty minutes.

2. Heat the tomatoes, put through an electric blender or food mill and add to the bean mixture.

3. Mix the flour and butter together and add a little of the hot soup. Return all to the pan and cook, stirring, until soup thickens. Season with salt and pepper.

Yield: Six servings.

Split Pea Soup *New Hampshire*

2 cups dried yellow split peas
Cold water
1 ham bone
2 ribs celery, chopped
1 onion, studded with two whole cloves
1 carrot, quartered
Salt and freshly ground black pepper to taste
1 large potato, diced
Boiling water, if necessary.

1. Day before, pick over and wash the peas. Cover with cold water and let soak overnight.

2. Next day, drain the peas and place in a kettle with fresh water to cover. Add the ham bone, celery, onion studded with cloves, carrot, salt and pepper. Bring to a boil, cover and simmer two hours, or until peas are tender. Add the potato and cook thirty minutes longer.

3. Rub the soup through a sieve or pass through an electric blender. Adjust consistency with boiling water if·soup is too thick. Check seasoning.

Yield: Eight servings.

Rivel Soup   *Pennsylvania*

1 cup flour
¼ teaspoon salt
1 egg yolk
8 cups boiling chicken broth
1 cup corn kernels freshly cut from cob
Salt and freshly ground black pepper to taste.

1. Place the flour and salt in a bowl. Add the egg yolk and with the fingers work together until mixture is crumbly.
2. Add the crumbs, a few at a time, to the boiling broth. Add the corn, salt and pepper and boil ten minutes.
Yield: Six servings.

Egg Chowder   *Maine*

¾ cup diced salt pork
1 onion, thinly sliced
3 potatoes, sliced
4 cups milk, scalded
Freshly ground black pepper to taste
4 eggs
Pilot crackers.

1. Cook the salt pork until it releases some of the fat, but do not allow to become crisp.

2. Add the onion and potatoes and cook, stirring occasionally, ten minutes. Add the milk and pepper and cook gently until potatoes are tender.
3. Break eggs into simmering mixture and cook three minutes. Serve with crackers.
Yield: Four servings.

Cheese Soup   *Vermont*

2 tablespoons butter
1 onion, finely chopped
2 tablespoons flour
¾ cup chicken broth
4 cups milk, scalded
¾ pound finely grated sharp Cheddar cheese
⅛ teaspoon dry mustard
½ teaspoon celery salt
½ teaspoon Worcestershire sauce
⅛ teaspoon freshly ground black pepper.

1. Melt the butter in a heavy saucepan and sauté the onion in it until tender. Sprinkle the flour over all and cook two minutes.
2. Gradually stir in the broth and milk. Bring to a boil.
3. Add the cheese, mustard, celery salt, Worcestershire and pepper and stir until cheese is melted. Remove from the heat and serve immediately.
Yield: Six servings.

Fish and Shellfish

Clam Pie
New York

2¼ cups flour
1 teaspoon salt
¾ cup shortening
6 tablespoons water, approximately
3 cups ground clams, preferably quahogs
½ cup finely chopped onion
¾ cup fresh cracker crumbs, preferably made from pilot crackers
Freshly ground black pepper to taste
¼ teaspoon thyme
¾ cup light cream.

1. Preheat the oven to 375 degrees.
2. In a mixing bowl, combine the flour and salt. With a pastry blender or two knives, cut in the shortening until mixture looks like coarse corn meal.
3. Sprinkle the water over the mixture, one tablespoon at a time, and mix lightly with a fork until all flour is moist.
4. With the hands, gather the dough into a ball and divide it in half. On a lightly floured board, roll out each half in a circle one-eighth-inch thick and about one and one-half inches larger in diameter than the pie plate used. Line a nine-inch pie plate with one circle of dough, leaving one-half inch overhanging.
5. Combine the clams, onion, crumbs, pepper, thyme and all but one tablespoon of the cream in a mixing bowl. Pour the filling into the pie plate. Cover with remaining circle of dough and neatly trim the edges. Fold the edge of the top pastry under the edge of the lower pastry and seal by pressing together. Flute the edges, if desired. Brush the top of the pie with the remaining cream, prick the top of the pie and bake forty minutes, or until golden brown and baked through.
Yield: Six to eight servings.

Cape Cod Deep-Dish Clam Pie
Massachusetts

8 cups soft-shelled clams
2 cups cold water
2 cups cubed potatoes
1 onion, finely chopped
1 cup salted water
1 teaspoon sugar
Freshly ground black pepper to taste
3 tablespoons butter
3 tablespoons flour
1 cup milk
Pastry made from one and one-half cups flour.

1. Wash the clams in several changes of lukewarm water.
2. Drain the clams and place in a kettle. Add the cold water and bring slowly to a boil. When the clams have opened, remove from the heat.

Strain the clam broth through a double thickness of cheesecloth. Reserve broth.

3. Remove clams from shells. Dip each clam into the broth. Snip off and discard the dark heads. Strain the broth again. Chop the clams to any size desired.

4. Preheat the oven to 400 degrees.

5. Place the potato cubes and onion in a saucepan and add the salted water. Bring to a boil, cover and simmer until potatoes are tender. Add the sugar, pepper, chopped clams and the strained clam broth. Bring to a boil.

6. Blend the butter and flour, using the fingers. Stir, bit by bit, into the simmering stew. Bring the milk to a boil and add it to the stew. Remove from the heat.

7. Butter a one-and-one-half-quart pie dish or casserole generously and pour in the clam mixture. Cover with rolled-out pastry and prick the top with a fork or make small slashes with a knife. Bake thirty minutes, or until pastry is golden brown. Serve piping hot.

Yield: Six to eight servings.

Clam Pie   *Massachusetts*

4 cups ground clams with their liquor
1 egg, lightly beaten
1 cup cracker crumbs
⅛ teaspoon marjoram
⅛ teaspoon thyme
  Salt and freshly ground black pepper to taste
½ cup milk
  Pastry for a two-crust ten-inch pie
2 tablespoons butter.

1. Preheat the oven to 425 degrees.

2. In a bowl, mix together the clams, egg, crumbs, marjoram, thyme, salt, pepper and milk.

3. Line a ten-inch pie plate with the pastry. Pour in the clam filling, dot with the butter and top with remaining pastry. Make a steam hole and bake fifteen minutes. Reduce oven heat to

350 degrees and continue baking forty-five minutes longer.

Yield: Six servings.

Clam Soufflé   *Massachusetts*

6 tablespoons butter
6 tablespoons flour
1 cup clam juice
1 cup heavy cream
1½ cups minced canned clams
8 egg yolks
¼ cup freshly chopped parsley
  Salt and freshly ground white pepper to taste
  Grated nutmeg to taste
12 egg whites.

1. Preheat the oven to 375 degrees.

2. Melt the butter and blend in the flour. Mix the clam juice and cream and slowly add to the butter-flour mixture, stirring constantly. Cook, stirring, until thickened. Add the minced clams and remove from the heat to cool slightly.

3. Beat the egg yolks thoroughly and add to the sauce. Stir in the parsley and season with salt, pepper and nutmeg.

4. Beat the egg whites until firm. Fold them thoroughly into the sauce. Pour into two buttered two-quart soufflé dishes and bake thirty-five minutes.

Yield: Ten to one dozen servings.

Baked Clams   *New York*

24 fresh cherrystone or littleneck clams (see note)
¼ cup water
3 slices bacon, cut into small cubes
½ pound mushrooms, caps and all, finely minced
1½ tablespoons finely chopped shallots
⅛ pound Gruyère cheese, Swiss cheese or Fontina cheese

2 tablespoons finely chopped parsley
1 small clove garlic, finely minced
¾ cup fine soft bread crumbs
½ cup finely minced heart of celery
3 tablespoons dry white wine
1 egg yolk
   Salt and freshly ground black pepper to
   taste
½ cup freshly grated Parmesan cheese.

1. Preheat the oven to 400 degrees.
2. Wash the clams well and place in a kettle. Add the water, cover and steam until clams open. Remove the clams and let them cool. Take the clams from the shells and chop on a flat surface. There should be about two-thirds cup chopped clams. Set aside. Reserve twenty-four shells for filling.
3. Cook the bacon in a large saucepan until bits are crisp. Do not burn. Remove the bacon bits and reserve. Pour off all but two tablespoons of fat from the saucepan. Add the mushrooms to the fat in the saucepan. Add the shallots and cook, stirring, until mushrooms are wilted. Let cool.
4. Chop the Gruyère, Swiss or Fontina cheese into tiny cubes. Add with the parsley, garlic, bread crumbs, celery, wine and egg yolk to the mushroom mixture. Add salt, pepper and the reserved clams.
5. Fill the reserved clam shells with the mixture and sprinkle with the Parmesan cheese and reserved bacon bits. Bake ten minutes or longer, or until filling is bubbly and golden brown. Serve hot.
   Yield: Six servings.
   Note: Canned clams may also be used in this recipe. To do this, drain the clams and measure out approximately two-thirds cup. Proceed with the recipe, starting with step 3. In lieu of the reserved clam shells, spoon the mixture into scallop shells or small ramekins and bake.

Clam Cakes *Massachusetts*

2 tablespoons butter
2 tablespoons finely minced shallot
1¼ cups soft bread crumbs
2 eggs, lightly beaten
½ cup heavy cream
2 seven-ounce cans minced clams, drained
½ cup finely minced celery
1 tablespoon lemon juice
2 tablespoons chopped parsley
½ teaspoon salt
⅛ teaspoon white pepper
1 egg, beaten and diluted with one
   tablespoon water
   Fat for deep-frying.

1. Melt the butter in a saucepan and sauté the shallot in the butter until soft but not browned.
2. Add one-half cup of the bread crumbs, the lightly beaten eggs, the cream, clams, celery, lemon juice, parsley, salt and pepper. Chill the mixture at least two hours.
3. Shape into eight two-inch cakes. Dip the cakes into the remaining crumbs and then into the remaining egg. Coat the cakes with crumbs a second time. Allow the cakes to dry out for fifteen minutes.
4. Fry the cakes, a few at a time, until golden brown in deep fat heated to 375 degrees. Drain.
   Yield: Four servings.

Spaghetti with Clam Sauce *New Jersey*

⅓ cup olive oil
2 cloves garlic, halved and flattened
1 quart cherrystone clams, shucked, chopped,
   and liquor reserved
   Bottled clam juice
3 tablespoons chopped Italian parsley
   Salt and freshly ground black pepper to
   taste
½ teaspoon oregano
1 pound spaghetti, cooked al dente, drained.

1. Heat the oil in a heavy saucepan and sauté the garlic in it until lightly browned. Remove the garlic.

2. Measure the reserved clam liquor and make up to one cup with bottled clam juice. Add with chopped clams and the parsley to the oil, bring to a simmer and cook about two minutes.

3. Season with salt and pepper and add the oregano. Pour over the spaghetti.

Yield: Four servings.

Rhode Island Steamer Clambake

6 cups water
  Seaweed or wet celery, lettuce and/or spinach
3 broiler-fryer chickens, split
6 unpeeled medium-size baking potatoes
6 unpeeled medium-size onions
6 ears corn in husks, soaked in salted water one hour
48 small clams
4 to six one-pound lobsters
  Melted butter.

1. Place the water in bottom of a twenty-quart steamer. Cover with upper section and place a generous layer of wet, well-rinsed seaweed or greens in the bottom.

2. Wrap the chicken pieces in cheesecloth, tie corners and place on top of seaweed or greens. Wrap five of the potatoes similarly and place on chicken. Wrap the onions and place on chicken.

3. Wrap the ears of corn in cheesecloth and place on top of potatoes, and then the clams wrapped in four bundles of a dozen each, and last, the lobsters in cheesecloth.

4. Top ingredients with more seaweed or wet greens. Place remaining potato in middle and cover.

5. Steam until potato on top is cooked, about one and one-half hours; that means the bake is ready to pull. Serve with melted butter.

Yield: Six servings.

Fried Clams   *Massachusetts*

1 egg, separated
½ cup milk
1 tablespoon butter
¼ teaspoon salt
½ cup flour
24 clams, shucked and drained of liquor
  Fat or oil for deep-frying.

1. Beat the egg yolk with one-quarter cup of the milk. Stir in the butter, salt and flour and beat until smooth. Gradually beat in remaining milk.

2. Beat the egg white until stiff but not dry. Fold into the batter. Dip each clam into the batter. Fry clams, a few at a time, in fat or oil heated to 375 degrees. Drain on paper towels.

Yield: Three or four servings.

Clam Fritters   *Rhode Island*

2 cups clams
1¾ cups flour
1 tablespoon baking powder
½ teaspoon nutmeg
1½ teaspoons salt
2 eggs, lightly beaten
1 cup milk
2 teaspoons grated onion
1 tablespoon butter, melted
  Fat or oil for deep-frying.

1. Drain the clams and chop them.

2. Place the flour, baking powder, nutmeg and salt in a bowl. In a second bowl, mix together the eggs, milk, onion, butter and clams. Pour clam mixture into dry ingredients and stir until smooth.

3. Drop batter by teaspoonfuls into fat or oil heated to 360 degrees. Fry until golden. Drain on paper towels.

Yield: Four servings.

Rhode Island Clam Cakes

2 eggs, lightly beaten
1 cup clams, drained and chopped
1 teaspoon salt
⅛ teaspoon freshly ground black pepper
1 cup milk
2 cups flour
3 teaspoons baking powder
  Fat or oil for deep-frying.

1. Combine the eggs, clams, salt, pepper, milk, flour and baking powder.

2. Form into small cakes and fry, a few at a time, in a frying basket in fat or oil heated to 360 degrees. Drain on paper towels.

Yield: Four servings.

Crab Stew   *New Jersey*

2 tablespoons butter
2 tablespoons finely chopped shallots or scallions, including green part
4 white mushrooms, thinly sliced
  Juice of half a lemon
2 ripe tomatoes, peeled, seeded and cubed
1 pound lump crab meat, picked over to remove bits of shell and cartilage
2 tablespoons chopped parsley
2 tablespoons finely chopped chives
1¼ cups heavy cream
  Tabasco sauce to taste
  Salt and freshly ground black pepper to taste
2 tablespoons warm cognac
  Cooked rice.

1. Heat the butter in a skillet or chafing dish and add the shallots or scallions. Cook about three minutes and add the mushrooms. Sprinkle with the lemon juice and cook briefly, stirring. Add the tomatoes and simmer five minutes.

2. Add the crab meat, but treat it gently so as not to break up the lumps. Add the parsley and chives and simmer five minutes. Stir in the cream

and Tabasco and add salt and pepper. Add the cognac and ignite it. Serve stew immediately, with rice.

Yield: Four to six servings.

Crab Bake   *New Jersey*

2 pounds flaked crab meat, picked over to remove bits of shell and cartilage
1 cup sour cream
⅓ cup freshly grated Parmesan cheese
1 tablespoon lemon juice
1 tablespoon grated onion
½ teaspoon salt
  Few drops Tabasco sauce
¾ cup buttered soft bread crumbs.

1. Preheat the oven to 350 degrees.

2. Place the crab meat in a bowl. Combine the sour cream, cheese, lemon juice, onion, salt and Tabasco and pour over crab meat. Toss to mix.

3. Turn into six lightly greased individual shells or ramekins. Top with the bread crumbs and bake twenty-five minutes, or until lightly browned.

Yield: Six servings.

Baked Lobster   *New York*

1 one-and-one-half-pound live lobster
  Salt and freshly ground black pepper to taste
¼ cup butter
  Lemon wedges
  Melted butter (optional).

1. Preheat the oven to 350 degrees.

2. Plunge a heavy butcher knife into the thorax or center of the lobster where the body and tail meet, to kill the lobster. Quickly cut the body in half lengthwise. Break the lobster in half and remove the tough "sac."

3. Sprinkle the lobster with salt and pepper and dot the cut portions generously with the but-

ter. Place, cut side up, on a baking dish and bake exactly twenty minutes.

4. Serve with lemon wedges and, if desired, melted butter.

Yield: One or two servings.

Note: This method for baking lobster is better than broiled. The lobster is more moist and tender.

Steamed Lobster   *New York*

Use a kettle large enough to hold all the lobsters to be cooked. Add one inch of water to the bottom of the kettle and bring to a rolling boil. Add the lobsters, head down, and cover closely. Cook twelve minutes for one-and-one-quarter-pound to one-and-one-half-pound lobsters; fifteen minutes for two-pound lobsters; twenty minutes for three-pound lobsters, and so on.

Cape Cod Lobster Roll   *Massachusetts*

8 frankfurter buns
¼ cup butter, melted
3 cups (about one and one-half pounds to two pounds) cooked lobster meat, cut into bite-size pieces
1 cup mayonnaise
½ cup minced heart of celery
1 small clove garlic, finely minced
2 tablespoons chopped fresh basil or one-half teaspoon dried basil
1 tablespoon finely chopped parsley
¼ cup finely chopped scallions, including green part
Tabasco sauce to taste
Lemon juice to taste
Salt and freshly ground black pepper to taste
Stuffed olives, parsley sprigs or lobster claws for garnish.

1. Preheat the oven to 400 degrees.
2. Split the buns and arrange them, split side up, on a baking dish. Brush them with the butter and bake until lightly browned. Remove from the oven and set aside.

3. Combine the lobster, mayonnaise, celery, garlic, basil, parsley, scallions, Tabasco, lemon juice, salt and pepper. Blend well.

4. Spoon equal parts of the filling onto each of the split buns and serve garnished with stuffed olives, parsley sprigs or lobster claws.

Yield: Eight servings.

Lobster Alexander   *Massachusetts*

1 large or two small lobsters, steamed and chilled
½ teaspoon finely chopped fresh tarragon
½ teaspoon finely chopped fresh parsley
½ teaspoon finely chopped fresh chives
½ teaspoon finely chopped fresh chervil (optional)
2 hard-cooked egg yolks
Salt and freshly ground black pepper to taste
1 teaspoon Dijon mustard
1 tablespoon wine vinegar
¼ teaspoon Worcestershire sauce, or more to taste
½ cup olive oil
½ teaspoon Madeira wine.

1. Remove the lobster meat from the tail and claws. Slice the tail meat and arrange it on a platter. Add the claw meat left whole.

2. Blend the tarragon, parsley, chives and chervil if desired in a mixing bowl. Add the egg yolks and mash them thoroughly with a fork. Add salt, pepper, the mustard, vinegar and Worcestershire. Blend thoroughly with a wire whisk.

3. While beating with a whisk, gradually add the oil to sauce. Stir constantly until sauce is like a mayonnaise. Add the Madeira and spoon a little sauce onto each piece of lobster.

Yield: Four to six servings.

Creamed Lobster   *Maine*

    5 one-and-one-half-pound lobsters
   12 tablespoons butter
       Salt and freshly ground black pepper to
       taste
    1 teaspoon paprika
   ¾ cup chopped onions
    1 cup finely diced carrots
    1 cup chopped celery
    1 teaspoon thyme
    1 bay leaf
   ¼ cup chopped shallots
    1 cup dry sherry
    2 cups finely chopped mushrooms
    4 cups heavy cream, scalded
    2 tablespoons flour
       Boiled rice.

1. Plunge a knife into the thorax or center portion of each lobster where the body and tail meet, to kill the lobster.

2. For each lobster, break off the large claws and sever body and tail. Crack the claws and cut the tail section in two crosswise. Split the body lengthwise and remove and discard the tough "sac" near the eyes. Remove the coral and tomalley or liver.

3. Place all corals and livers in a mixing bowl and add three tablespoons of the butter. Set aside.

4. Melt three tablespoons of the remaining butter in each of two heavy skillets large enough to accommodate the lobster pieces and claws (can be done in one pan if a large enough one is available). Dividing the ingredients between the pans, sprinkle lobster with salt, pepper and the paprika and stir. Add the onions, carrots, celery, thyme, bay leaf and shallots and cook, stirring, over relatively high heat until lobster turns pink.

5. Add the sherry, stirring. Add the mushrooms. Simmer, covered, ten minutes.

6. Add two cups of the cream to each of the pans.

7. Remove the lobster from the skillets. Discard body pieces. If desired, the lobster meat may be removed from the shell. Or the meat may be served in the shell. In any event, keep the lobster covered and warm until ready to serve.

8. Combine the two pans of sauce and simmer, uncovered, fifteen minutes. Strain and press as much liquid from the solids as possible.

9. Using the fingers, blend the butter with the livers and corals. Turn off heat from sauce and stir in the mixture. Knead the remaining butter with the flour to make a beurre manie and with a wire whisk incorporate into the sauce. Heat to thicken and add the lobster. Cook without boiling until lobster is heated through. Serve piping hot, with boiled rice.

Yield: Six servings.

Lobster Thermidor   *Maine*

   ¼ cup butter
    2 cups cubed cooked lobster meat
    2 tablespoons cognac
    3 tablespoons dry sherry
    1 cup heavy cream, scalded
    3 egg yolks, beaten
       Salt and freshly ground black pepper to taste
   ⅛ teaspoon cayenne pepper.

1. Melt the butter, add the lobster meat and cook three minutes. Shake the pan or stir while cooking.

2. Add the cognac and sherry.

3. Pour the cream over the egg yolks and add to lobster mixture. Reheat, stirring, until mixture thickens, but do not allow to boil.

4. Season with salt, pepper and cayenne.

Yield: Two servings.

Broiled Live Maine Lobster

    1 two-pound to two-and-one-half-pound
       lobster
   ½ cup cracker crumbs

Salt and freshly ground black pepper to taste

¼ cup melted butter.

1. Plunge a knife into the thorax or center of lobster between the head and tail, to kill the lobster. Cut the entire length of lobster from between the eyes to end of the tail.

2. Remove the tomalley or liver and mix with the cracker crumbs, salt, pepper and butter.

3. Broil lobster, shell side up, six minutes. Turn, spread with the cracker mixture and broil six minutes on flesh side.

Yield: One serving.

Broiled Stuffed Lobster   *Connecticut*

Oyster stuffing:
¼ cup butter
½ cup chopped onion
½ cup chopped celery
4 mushrooms, chopped
1 pint oysters with liquor
4 cups dry bread crumbs
2 tablespoons chopped parsley
1 teaspoon salt
¼ teaspoon freshly ground black pepper
½ teaspoon thyme
¼ teaspoon marjoram.
Lobsters:
4 one-pound to one-and-one-half-pound lobsters
Melted butter
Lemon wedges.

1. To prepare stuffing, melt the butter in a skillet and sauté the onion and celery in it until tender. Add the mushrooms and cook two minutes longer.

2. Drain the oysters, reserving liquor. Chop the oysters and add to the mushroom mixture.

3. Add the bread crumbs, parsley, salt, pepper, thyme, marjoram and enough of the reserved oyster liquor to moisten.

4. Split the lobsters lengthwise and remove the

dark vein down the center and the "sac" behind the eyes. Crack the claws.

5. Place the lobsters shell side up over hot coals on a barbecue grill or shell side down under a preheated broiler and broil five minutes.

6. Fill the body cavity with the oyster stuffing and wrap in heavy-duty aluminum foil to grill shell side down on charcoal grill or shell side up under a broiler. Broil about fifteen minutes. Serve with melted butter and lemon wedges.

Yield: Four servings.

Steamed Mussels   *New York*

24 mussels, well scrubbed and beards removed
½ cup dry white wine
1 bay leaf
¼ teaspoon thyme
½ onion, chopped
1 clove garlic, chopped
  Salt and freshly ground black pepper to taste
2 tablespoons chopped parsley.

1. Place the mussels in a kettle with remaining ingredients. Cover tightly and bring to a boil.

2. Cook about eight minutes, or until mussels open. Serve with broth.

Yield: Four servings.

Fried Oysters   *New York*

2 twelve-ounce containers oysters with liquor, or about 36 shucked, fresh oysters with liquor
1½ cups dry bread crumbs
1½ cups flour
¼ cup milk
2 eggs, lightly beaten
1 teaspoon salt
⅛ teaspoon freshly ground black pepper
  Fat or oil for deep-frying
  Lemon wedges or tartar sauce (page 157).

1. Drain the oysters.
2. Combine the bread crumbs and flour.
3. Combine the milk, eggs, salt and pepper.
4. Roll oysters in crumb mixture, then in egg mixture and again in the crumb mixture.
5. Fry, a few at a time, two to three minutes, or until they are golden, in a fry basket, in fat or oil heated to 350 degrees. Drain on paper towels. Serve with lemon wedges or tartar sauce.

Yield: Six servings.

Chilmark Scallops   *Massachusetts*

2 pounds bay scallops
½ cup flour
¼ cup soft bread crumbs
 Cayenne pepper to taste
½ teaspoon paprika
 Salt and freshly ground black pepper to taste
 Juice of one lemon
¼ pound butter, melted.

1. Preheat the broiler.
2. Drain the scallops and set aside.
3. Combine the flour, bread crumbs, cayenne, paprika, salt and pepper. Dredge scallops lightly in the mixture and arrange them in one layer in a baking dish. Sprinkle the lemon juice over all and then pour the butter over.
4. Broil until golden on one side; then turn and cook until golden on the other. Do not overcook. Serve hot.

Yield: Four servings.

Baked Fresh Shrimp with Feta Cheese
New York

12 shrimp, shelled and deveined
2 tablespoons butter
1 egg
¼ cup heavy cream
¼ cup finely crumbled feta cheese
 Tabasco sauce to taste

1 large tomato, peeled and sliced
 Juice of half a lemon
1 tablespoon chopped parsley
 Freshly ground black pepper to taste.

1. Preheat the oven to 400 degrees.
2. Cook the shrimp in the butter on both sides just until shrimp turn pink. Transfer them to a small baking dish and discard the butter.
3. Combine the egg and cream and beat with a fork until blended. Add the cheese and continue mixing. Add the Tabasco and pour the mixture over the shrimp. Arrange the tomato slices on top and bake until cheese mixture starts to bubble, about ten minutes.
4. Sprinkle the lemon juice on top and sprinkle with the parsley. Serve immediately, with pepper.

Yield: Three or four servings.

Shrimp à la Perea   *New York*

4 tablespoons olive oil
2 pounds large shrimp, shelled and deveined with the tails left on
2 tablespoons finely chopped shallots
1 large clove garlic, finely chopped
2 ten-ounce packages frozen artichoke hearts, cooked until just thawed, then drained
½ pound mushrooms, sliced
 Salt and freshly ground black pepper to taste
½ teaspoon thyme
1 tablespoon chopped parsley
2 to three tablespoons lemon juice, or to taste.

1. Heat the oil in a large heavy skillet. Add the shrimp and sauté quickly, stirring frequently, until pink.
2. Add the shallots and garlic and cook two minutes.
3. Add the artichoke hearts, mushrooms, salt, pepper, thyme, parsley and lemon juice. Cook,

stirring, until mushrooms and shrimp are tender, about three minutes.

Yield: Six servings.

Striped Bass with Minced Clam Stuffing
Massachusetts

1 four-pound to six-pound striped bass, cleaned
  Salt and freshly ground black pepper to taste
2 five-ounce cans minced clams
¼ cup chopped onion
¼ cup chopped celery
½ cup butter, melted
4 cups soft bread crumbs
2 tablespoons lemon juice.

1. Preheat the oven to 400 degrees.
2. Wipe the fish with a damp paper towel. Sprinkle cavity with salt and pepper. Drain the clams, reserving the liquor.
3. Cook the onion and celery in half the butter until tender. Stir in the bread crumbs until butter is absorbed. Toss crumbs until they brown slightly. Stir in the lemon juice, clams and enough clam liquor to moisten. Season with salt and pepper.
4. Spoon stuffing into cavity of fish. Close with skewers or lace with string. Brush fish with remaining butter. Bake in pan lined with aluminum foil fifty to seventy minutes, or until fish flakes easily when tested with a fork.

Yield: Six to eight servings.

Baked Striped Bass
New York

1 four-pound striped bass
¼ cup diced salt pork or butter
2 tablespoons finely chopped shallots
½ cup sliced mushrooms
1 pound shrimp, shelled, deveined and roughly chopped
½ cup fine soft bread crumbs

1 tablespoon chopped parsley
¼ teaspoon thyme
  Salt and freshly ground black pepper to taste
2 tablespoons melted butter
2 tablespoons lemon juice.

1. Clean the fish, but leave the head on.
2. Preheat the oven to 400 degrees.
3. Cook the salt pork, if used, in a skillet until the bits are crisp. Remove salt pork bits and reserve. Add the shallots to the drippings or to the butter, if used, and cook until tender but not browned.
4. Add the mushrooms and shrimp and cook quickly until shrimp turn pink and mushrooms wilt, about five minutes. Add the bread crumbs, parsley, thyme, salt, pepper and reserved pork bits. Stuff the fish with the mixture and secure with skewers or sew to close.
5. Place the fish in a greased baking dish. Brush with the melted butter, season with salt and pepper and sprinkle the lemon juice over all.
6. Bake about thirty-five minutes, or until fish flakes easily.

Yield: Four servings.

Baked Bluefish with Rosemary
New Jersey

1 four-pound bluefish
  Salt and freshly ground black pepper
1 teaspoon chopped fresh rosemary
½ cup butter
1 tablespoon wine vinegar
  Lemon slices
  Boiled potatoes.

1. Preheat the oven to 400 degrees.
2. Thoroughly clean and scale the fish, but leave the head and tail intact. Rinse the fish under cold water and pat dry with paper towels. Sprinkle the fish inside and outside with salt and pepper.
3. Place the fish in a baking dish and sprinkle

the rosemary around the fish. Dot fish generously with the butter.

4. Bake the fish about thirty minutes, basting every five minutes or so. When fish flakes easily, transfer to a hot serving platter.

5. Add the vinegar to the baking dish, heat thoroughly and pour pan drippings over the fish. Garnish with lemon slices and serve with boiled potatoes.

Yield: Six servings.

Baked Stuffed Bluefish *Massachusetts*

1 four-pound bluefish
1½ teaspoons salt
1 recipe oyster stuffing (see "Broiled Stuffed Lobster," page 30)
3 small strips salt pork
2 tablespoons melted butter
1 tablespoon lemon juice.

1. Preheat the oven to 350 degrees.
2. Wash and dry the fish and sprinkle with salt inside and outside. Stuff the cavity loosely with the oyster stuffing and close by sewing or with skewers.
3. Make three diagonal slashes in the flesh of the fish and insert the salt pork. Place fish in a greased baking dish.
4. Pour the butter and lemon juice over fish and bake about forty minutes, or until the fish flakes easily.

Yield: Six servings.

Boston Bluefish Florentine *Massachusetts*

1½ pounds spinach, washed and chopped
¼ cup butter
2 shallots, finely chopped
¼ cup flour
1½ cups milk or light cream
   Salt and freshly ground black pepper to taste
¼ teaspoon nutmeg

1 teaspoon Worcestershire sauce
⅓ cup grated Gruyère cheese
2 pounds Boston bluefish (American pollock) fillets, skinned and cut into six serving pieces
¼ cup freshly grated Parmesan cheese.

1. Preheat the oven to 350 degrees.
2. In a large pan, put the spinach with just the water that clings to it. Cover tightly and cook until spinach wilts. Drain well in a sieve, pressing out excess moisture.
3. Melt the butter and sauté the shallots in it until tender. Stir in the flour; then gradually stir in the milk or cream.
4. Bring the sauce to a boil, stirring, and simmer two minutes. Season with salt and pepper. Add the nutmeg, Worcestershire and Gruyère cheese. Stir until cheese has melted.
5. Mix drained spinach with half the sauce and spread in the bottom of a shallow heatproof dish. Arrange the fish fillet pieces over the top.
6. Pour remaining sauce over all, sprinkle with the Parmesan and bake about twenty minutes, or until fish flakes easily. Dish can be glazed under the broiler if desired.

Yield: Six servings.

Poached Pollock with Crab Sauce
Massachusetts

2 pounds pollock fillets, cut into six serving pieces
6 tablespoons butter
2 tablespoons lemon juice
   Salt and freshly ground black pepper to taste
2 tablespoons chopped scallions, including green part
¼ cup flour
½ cup fish stock or light cream
1 cup milk
2 tablespoons dry sherry
   Few drops Tabasco sauce, or to taste

½ pound flaked and picked-over crab meat, preferably fresh
¼ cup buttered soft bread crumbs.

1. Preheat the oven to 350 degrees.
2. Place the fillets in a single layer in a buttered baking dish. Melt two tablespoons of the butter and mix with the lemon juice, salt and pepper and pour over the fish. Bake until it flakes easily, about twenty minutes.
3. Meanwhile, melt the remaining butter and sauté the scallions in it until tender. Stir in the flour; then gradually stir in the fish stock or cream and the milk. Bring to a boil, stirring, and cook two minutes.
4. Stir in the sherry, Tabasco and crab meat. Season with salt and pepper.
5. Pour crab sauce over the cooked fish. Sprinkle with the bread crumbs and glaze under the broiler.

Yield: Six servings.

Fresh Cod Maître d'Hôtel   *Massachusetts*

1 six-pound codfish, boned and skinned
1 clove garlic, thinly sliced
3 sprigs fresh thyme or one-half teaspoon dried thyme
1 onion, sliced
15 peppercorns
½ bay leaf
2 sprigs parsley
  Salt to taste
6 medium-size unpeeled potatoes
5 tablespoons butter
¼ cup flour
1 cup heavy cream
1 tablespoon finely chopped parsley
¼ teaspoon cayenne pepper
1 tablespoon finely chopped chives
  Coarse salt (Maldon or kosher salt)
  Freshly ground black pepper.

1. It is best to have the fish boned and skinned

by the fish man. Be certain, however, to remove all small bones he may have overlooked.
2. Place the filleted fish in one layer in a large skillet. Add the garlic, thyme, onion, peppercorns, bay leaf, parsley sprigs, salt and water to cover. Bring to a boil and simmer ten minutes. Turn off heat and let fish stand in stock until ready to serve.
3. Meanwhile, place the potatoes in a large saucepan and add salt and water to cover. Cook until tender.
4. Melt three tablespoons of the butter and stir in the flour, using a wire whisk. Carefully pour off and strain two cups fish stock and add it, stirring. When the mixture is thickened and smooth, simmer twenty minutes, stirring occasionally. Add the cream and simmer twenty minutes longer, stirring occasionally. Add the chopped parsley, cayenne and chives. Remove the sauce from the heat and swirl in the remaining butter.
5. Carefully transfer the fish from the stock to a warm serving platter. Peel the potatoes and slice them around the fish. Pour the hot sauce over all and serve immediately. Serve with coarse salt and black pepper on the side.

Yield: Six servings.

Codfish Pie   *Massachusetts*

½ pound salt codfish, cut into pieces
¼ pound salt pork, diced
1 medium-size onion, finely chopped
3 tablespoons flour
⅛ teaspoon freshly ground black pepper
2½ cups milk
1 cup diced cooked potatoes
  Biscuit dough made from one and one-half cups flour (page 261).

1. Soak the codfish two hours in water to cover, changing the water three times. Drain codfish and place in a kettle with fresh water to cover. Bring to a boil and simmer, covered, until tender, about ten minutes. Drain and flake the fish.

2. Preheat the oven to 450 degrees.

3. Cook the salt pork in a skillet until pieces are crisp. Remove salt pork pieces and reserve. Remove all but three tablespoons fat from the skillet.

4. Sauté the onion in the fat in the skillet until tender. Blend in the flour and pepper. Gradually stir in the milk and cook, stirring, until mixture thickens. Stir in codfish, reserved pork pieces and the potatoes.

5. Turn into a deep baking dish. Drop the biscuit dough mixture on top of the hot cod mixture and bake fifteen minutes, or until biscuit topping is browned and cooked.

Yield: Four servings.

Creamed Cod   *New Hampshire*

1½ pounds salt codfish
½ cup butter
1½ tablespoons flour
 2 cups light cream
 2 eggs, lightly beaten
   Boiled potatoes
   Pickled beets.

1. Soak the codfish several hours in water to cover, changing the water frequently. Drain codfish and place in a saucepan with fresh water to cover. Bring to a boil and simmer gently ten minutes. Drain and flake the fish.

2. Melt the butter and blend in the flour. Gradually stir in the cream and bring to a boil, stirring until mixture thickens. Cook three minutes. Add the codfish and cook five minutes longer.

3. Add a little hot sauce to the eggs, return all to the pan and reheat, but do not boil. Serve with boiled potatoes and pickled beets.

Yield: Six servings.

Broiled Scrod   *Massachusetts*

2 pounds scrod fillets (small cod or haddock)
  Salt and freshly ground black pepper
½ cup butter, melted
2 cups fine soft bread crumbs
¼ cup chopped green pepper
¼ cup finely chopped onion
1 tablespoon Dijon or Düsseldorf mustard
1 teaspoon Worcestershire sauce
  Few drops Tabasco sauce
3 tablespoons lemon juice
2 tablespoons freshly grated Parmesan cheese.

1. Cut the fish into four portions. Season with salt and pepper.

2. Combine one-third cup of the butter, the bread crumbs, green pepper, onion, mustard, Worcestershire, Tabasco and lemon juice.

3. Place the fish on a broiler tray. Brush with remaining butter and broil five minutes. Turn fish pieces. Top with bread crumb mixture and sprinkle with the Parmesan. Broil about seven minutes, or until fish flakes easily and surface is lightly browned.

Yield: Four servings.

Herb's Crab-Stuffed Whole Flounder
                                New Jersey

⅓ cup plus three-quarters cup butter
½ cup chopped onion
⅓ cup chopped celery
⅓ cup chopped green pepper
1 clove garlic, finely chopped
2 cups soft bread crumbs
3 eggs, lightly beaten
1 tablespoon chopped parsley
  Salt
½ teaspoon freshly ground black pepper
1 pound crab meat, picked over to remove
  bits of shell and cartilage
6 whole flounder, each weighing
  three-quarters pound to one pound
⅓ cup lemon juice.

1. Preheat the oven to 350 degrees.

2. Melt one-third cup of the butter in a skillet and sauté the onion, celery, green pepper and garlic in it until tender.

3. Add the bread crumbs, eggs, parsley, two teaspoons salt, the pepper and crab meat.

4. Wash and dry flounder and make a pocket for the stuffing by laying fish, light side down, on a board. Cut down the center of the fish along the backbone from tail to about one inch from the head end. Turn knife flat and loosen flesh from the backbone and ribs on each side, making two flaps.

5. Stuff fish loosely with crab meat mixture.

6. Melt remaining butter and mix with the lemon juice and salt to taste.

7. Spread two tablespoons butter mixture on each of six eighteen-inch square pieces heavy-duty aluminum foil. Place a fish on top and spoon another tablespoon butter mixture over fish. Close foil with tight drugstore wrap. Place in shallow baking pan and bake thirty minutes, or until fish flakes easily.

Yield: Six servings.

Note: The foil packages can be cooked on a grill over moderately hot coals if desired.

Abigail's Biscuit-Topped Haddock Pie
Massachusetts

4 boiled potatoes, sliced
3 onions, thinly sliced
3 cups cooked haddock, roughly flaked
4 hard-cooked eggs, sliced
  Salt and freshly ground black pepper to taste
¼ cup fish stock or potato water
1 teaspoon catchup
1 teaspoon prepared mustard
2 tablespoons butter
1 recipe biscuit dough (page 261).

1. Preheat the oven to 450 degrees.

2. In a buttered shallow baking dish, make alternate layers of the potatoes, onions, fish and eggs, seasoning each layer with salt and pepper.

3. Combine the stock or potato water, catchup and mustard and pour over. Dot with the butter and top with the biscuits. Bake twenty minutes, or until biscuits are done and mixture is bubbling hot.

Yield: Six servings.

Note: Cooked cod may be substituted for the cooked haddock.

Smoked Haddock Flan
Maine

Pastry shell:
  1 cup flour
  ¼ teaspoon salt
  ⅓ cup butter or shortening
  1 egg yolk
  Ice water.

Fish:
1½ pounds smoked haddock with bones (see note), if salty, soaked thirty minutes in cold water
1 cup milk, approximately.

Filling:
  2 tablespoons butter
  ½ cup finely chopped leeks
  2 tablespoons chopped parsley
  Freshly ground black pepper to taste
  2 hard-cooked eggs, halved.

Sauce:
  2 tablespoons butter
  2 tablespoons flour
  Salt and freshly ground black pepper to taste.

Potato mixture:
  3 medium-size baking potatoes, boiled, peeled and riced or sieved
  2 egg yolks
  Salt and freshly ground black pepper to taste
  6 tablespoons finely grated Gruyère cheese.

1. To prepare pastry, place the flour and salt in a bowl. With the finger tips or a pastry blender,

blend in the butter or shortening until mixture resembles coarse oatmeal. With a fork, stir in the egg yolk and enough ice water to make a dough.

2. Roll out the dough on a lightly floured board or pastry cloth and use to line an eight-inch or nine-inch scalloped pie pan or pie plate. Chill well.

3. Preheat the oven to 425 degrees.

4. Line the chilled shell with aluminum foil and fill with dried beans or uncooked rice. Bake eight minutes, or until shell is set. Remove foil and beans or rice and bake shell three to five minutes longer, or until done and lightly browned.

5. Meanwhile, place the fish in a large skillet. Pour in milk until fish is three-quarters submerged.

6. Bring to a simmer, cover and simmer eight to ten minutes, or until the fish flakes easily. Remove the fish, strain the liquid and reserve one cup for the sauce. Remove the skin and bones from the fish and flake it. There should be about two cups. Reserve.

7. To prepare filling, melt the butter in a skillet and sauté the leeks in it until tender but not browned. Stir in the reserved fish and the parsley, season with pepper and keep warm. Reserve the hard-cooked egg halves.

8. To prepare sauce, melt the butter in a small pan, blend in the flour and gradually stir in the reserved cup fish stock. Season with salt and pepper.

9. Bring to a boil, stirring until sauce thickens. Hold over hot water until needed.

10. To prepare potato mixture, place the hot riced or sieved potatoes in a bowl and beat in the egg yolks, salt, pepper and four tablespoons of the cheese.

11. Place the filling in the bottom of the baked pie shell and embed the hard-cooked egg pieces in the filling in a pattern like spokes in a wheel. Pour the sauce over all.

12. Fit a pastry bag with a star tube. Pipe the potato mixture through the pastry bag around the flan and make a wheel pattern.

13. Sprinkle with the remaining cheese and brown under the broiler.

Yield: Four servings.

Note: Any good fish store can order smoked haddock.

This recipe may be made ahead through step 12 and held refrigerated. Reheat in a preheated 375-degree oven until bubbly, about twenty to thirty minutes. Proceed with step 13.

One pound boneless smoked cod may be substituted for the haddock. If salty, it too should be soaked thirty minutes in cold water.

Baked Haddock   *Maine*

    4 thin slices salt pork
    1 onion, sliced
 2½ pounds haddock fillets (see note)
    3 tablespoons melted butter
    2 tablespoons flour
    1 cup milk
    1 bay leaf
       Salt and freshly ground black pepper to
       taste
  ¼ cup lemon juice.
Sauce:
    2 egg yolks
  ½ cup heavy cream
  ¼ teaspoon salt
  ½ cup boiling water
    2 tablespoons lemon juice
  ½ cup finely chopped cooked lobster meat or
       cooked shrimp.

1. Preheat the oven to 350 degrees.

2. Place the salt pork in the bottom of a shallow baking dish.

3. Sprinkle with half the onion slices. Arrange the fish fillets over the onion and salt pork. Sprinkle with remainder of the onion slices.

4. Spoon the butter over all and sprinkle with the flour. Pour the milk over the fish. Add the bay leaf, salt, pepper and lemon juice. Cover and bake twenty minutes. Remove cover and bake twenty minutes longer.

5. Meanwhile, prepare the sauce. Combine the egg yolks and cream and beat very well. Beat in the salt and boiling water and place in the top of a double boiler over hot water. Cook, stirring, three minutes, or until thickened. Add the lemon juice and lobster or shrimp. Serve separately with the fish.

Yield: Six servings.

Note: Cod fillets may be substituted for the haddock fillets.

Fish Steaks Atlantic Avenue Style
New York

¼ cup olive oil
1 cup finely chopped onions
1 green pepper, cored, seeded and chopped
4 individual fish steaks such as salmon; small fish fillets such as flounder; or small whole fish
  Salt and freshly ground black pepper to taste
  Cayenne pepper to taste
  Juice of one lemon
2 tomatoes, cored, peeled and chopped (about one and one-half cups)
½ cup fish stock (see note)
3 tablespoons taheeni (sesame paste, see note)
¼ cup dry white wine
2 egg yolks, lightly beaten
2 tablespoons finely chopped parsley
8 stuffed olives
4 slices white bread
  Oil for frying
1 clove garlic.

1. Heat half the olive oil in a large aluminum or enamelware skillet and cook the onions and green pepper in it until wilted.

2. In another skillet, heat remaining olive oil, add the fish and cook, first on one side and then on the other, until lightly browned. Transfer fish in one layer to skillet with onion mixture. Sprinkle with salt, pepper, cayenne and half the lemon juice. Spoon the tomatoes over fish and add the stock. Cover with aluminum foil or parchment paper and cook over very low heat ten to fifteen minutes. Do not overcook.

3. Combine the taheeni and remaining lemon juice in a small mixing bowl. Start beating with a wire whisk and add salt and pepper. Beat in the wine. Carefully pour liquid from cooked fish into taheeni mixture and beat well. Beat in the egg yolks and parsley and spoon mixture over fish. Run fish under broiler until there is a brown glaze. Scatter the olives over fish.

4. Meanwhile, fry the bread in the oil and rub lightly with garlic. Serve fish and toast while hot.

Yield: Four servings.

Note: Fish stock is the simplest of stocks to make. Simply cover a few very fresh broken fish bones with water. Add one small onion, chopped; salt and freshly ground black pepper to taste; half a bay leaf and three sprigs parsley and simmer twenty minutes. Strain.

Taheeni or sesame paste is available in New York City at Kassos Brothers, 570 Ninth Avenue (10036), and Trinacria Importing Company, 415 Third Avenue (10016), health food stores and stores selling Middle Eastern foods.

Fourth of July Boiled Salmon, Peas and Egg Sauce
Maine

Salmon:
2 tablespoons butter
1 small onion, chopped
1 rib celery, chopped
2 sprigs parsley
1 tablespoon salt
1 bay leaf
3 whole cloves
2 cups dry white wine
2 quarts boiling water
1 four-pound to six-pound piece fresh salmon.
Sauce:
½ cup butter
2 tablespoons flour
½ teaspoon salt
¼ teaspoon freshly ground black pepper

2 hard-cooked eggs, chopped
3 cups cooked fresh peas.

1. To prepare salmon, melt the butter and sauté the onion and celery in it until tender. Add the parsley, salt, bay leaf, cloves, wine and water. Simmer ten minutes.

2. Wrap the salmon in double thickness of muslin and lower into the simmering stock. Cover and simmer very gently about thirty-five to forty-five minutes, or until fish flakes easily.

3. Remove fish by lifting muslin and unwrap onto a warm platter. Remove skin and keep fish warm. Strain fish stock and reserve two cups.

4. To prepare sauce, melt one-quarter cup of the butter in a saucepan and blend in the flour. Gradually stir in the reserved fish stock, the salt and pepper. Bring to a boil, stirring until mixture thickens.

5. Stir in the eggs and remaining butter.

6. Arrange the peas around the salmon and pour the egg sauce over the fish.

Yield: Eight to ten servings.

Broiled Shad Roe   *Connecticut*

1 pair shad roe
4 slices bacon
2 tablespoons melted butter
  Lemon wedges.

1. Wrap the roe in the bacon slices and broil five minutes on each side, or until bacon and roe are done. Do not overcook.

2. Pour the butter over and serve with lemon wedges.

Yield: One serving.

Smelts with Anchovy Spaghetti

                                          Maine

1 cup dry bread crumbs
½ cup freshly grated Parmesan cheese
½ teaspoon salt

2 pounds pan-dressed smelts
2 eggs, lightly beaten
  Vegetable oil for frying
12 anchovy fillets
1 clove garlic, crushed
¼ cup soft butter
2 tablespoons olive oil
⅛ teaspoon cayenne pepper
8 ounces spaghetti, cooked al dente, drained.

1. Combine the bread crumbs, cheese and salt. Wash and dry fish. Dip into the eggs and then into bread crumb mixture. Set fish on a rack and let stand about fifteen minutes to allow coating to dry.

2. Pour the vegetable oil into a heavy skillet to a depth of one and one-half inches. Heat to about 360 degrees. Add the smelts and fry four to five minutes on each side, or until fish flakes easily. Drain on paper towels.

3. Mash the anchovies and garlic together with a fork. Gradually work in the butter, olive oil and cayenne. Add to the hot cooked spaghetti and toss. Serve the smelts with the spaghetti.

Yield: Four servings.

Fresh Tuna Fra Diavolo   *New York*

2 pounds fresh tuna fish
  Cold salted water
¼ cup olive oil
½ cup finely chopped onion
½ cup finely diced carrot
½ cup finely diced celery
1 cup sliced mushrooms
6 anchovy fillets, finely chopped
8 cherrystone clams, well scrubbed
¼ cup tomato sauce
¼ teaspoon oregano
¼ teaspoon thyme
1 bay leaf
  Salt and freshly ground black pepper to taste
¾ cup dry white wine
¼ cup fish stock or clam juice

2 egg yolks
Juice of one lemon
Chopped parsley.

1. Soak the tuna overnight in cold salted water, draining and replacing the water as often as practical.

2. Next day, heat the oil in a large heavy saucepan and sauté the onion, carrot, celery and mushrooms in it until lightly browned. Beat in the anchovies until well blended.

3. Towel-dry the tuna and brown on both sides in the pan.

4. Add the clams in their shells, the tomato sauce, oregano, thyme, bay leaf, salt and pepper. Stir. Add the wine and stock or clam juice.

5. Bring to a boil, cover and simmer slowly about fifteen minutes, or until fish flakes easily. Remove the fish to a warm platter. Strain the stock remaining and return to the pan.

6. Mix the egg yolks with the lemon juice. Add a little of the hot stock to the mixture, return to the pan and stir until sauce thickens slightly. Do not boil. Pour over fish. Garnish with chopped parsley.

Yield: Four servings.

Tuna-Stuffed Peppers à la Sarda

Connecticut

  8 large green peppers
  4 cloves garlic
    Olive oil
  1 can anchovy fillets, chopped
1½ cups soft bread crumbs
  2 seven-ounce cans tuna fish, flaked
  1 cup peeled, seeded, chopped tomatoes
½ cup capers, drained
¼ cup finely chopped parsley
  1 teaspoon chopped fresh basil
¼ cup pignoli (pine nuts)
½ cup currants.

1. Preheat the oven to 375 degrees.
2. Cut a slice off the stem end of each pepper

and remove core and seeds. Set peppers in a baking dish.

3. Sauté the garlic in one-half cup oil until brown. Remove garlic and discard.

4. Add the anchovies and bread crumbs to the oil and sauté briefly.

5. Add the remaining ingredients. Mix well and use to fill peppers. Spoon a little oil over each one. Bake, uncovered, about one hour, or until tender.

Yield: Four servings.

Fish Stew

New York

  3 cloves garlic, finely minced
  3 shallots, finely minced
½ cup olive oil
½ teaspoon chopped thyme
¼ cup chopped parsley
  1 bay leaf
1½ cups dry white wine
  3 ripe tomatoes, peeled, cored and coarsely chopped (two and one-half cups to three cups)
    Salt and freshly ground black pepper to taste
  1 large or two small cleaned squid
1½ pounds cod fillets
1½ pounds striped bass fillets
 12 littleneck clams, scrubbed and rinsed under cold water.

1. In a Dutch oven, cook the garlic and shallots in the oil briefly without browning. Add the thyme, parsley, bay leaf and wine and bring to a boil. Simmer, partially covered, about ten minutes. Add the tomatoes, salt and pepper and simmer ten minutes longer, stirring occasionally.

2. Lay the squid lengthwise on the sauce; then add the cod and bass fillets. Sprinkle with salt and pepper. Cover and simmer ten minutes. Add the clams and cover. Simmer just until the clams open and give up their juices. Serve piping hot.

Yield: Six servings.

New England Fish Stew   *Massachusetts*

⅓ cup butter
¾ cup finely chopped onions
1 clove garlic, finely chopped
¾ cup diced celery
2 cups fresh or bottled clam juice
1 cup water
2 one-pound cans tomatoes
½ teaspoon thyme
1 bay leaf, crumbled
¼ teaspoon saffron
   Salt and freshly ground black pepper to taste
1 pound whiting fillets, cut into two-inch slices
1 pound cod fillets, cut into two-inch pieces
1 pound scallops, halved if large
2 small cooked lobsters or two cups cooked lobster meat.

1. Melt the butter and sauté the onions and garlic in it until tender.

2. Add the celery, clam juice, water, tomatoes, thyme, bay leaf, saffron, salt and pepper. Bring to a boil and simmer ten minutes.

3. Add the whiting, cod and scallops and cook eight minutes, or until fish flakes easily. Remove the lobster meat from cooked lobsters, if used. Add lobster meat to stew.

Yield: Eight servings.

Martha's Vineyard Stonewall Bouillabaisse   *Massachusetts*

3 pounds fresh fluke or flounder with bones, heads and tails
3 pounds black bass, sea bass or striped bass with bones, heads and tails
2 pounds scrod with bones, heads and tails
1 whole eel
80 mussels, scrubbed and cleaned
80 littleneck or cherrystone clams, the smaller the better
   Salted water

½ cup olive oil
2 medium-size onions, finely chopped
6 shallots, finely minced
2 cloves garlic, finely minced
1 bay leaf
¼ teaspoon chopped fresh thyme or dried thyme
¼ teaspoon crushed fennel seeds
   Salt to taste
½ teaspoon freshly ground black pepper
¼ teaspoon leaf saffron, crushed
   Cayenne pepper to taste
1 two-inch piece fresh orange rind
½ gallon dry white wine
3 cups heavy cream
6 one-pound to one-and-one-half-pound lobsters, steamed (page 28)
   Crusty French bread
   Chilled white wine.

1. Have the fluke, black bass, scrod or whatever fish are used cut into fillets. but reserve the bones, heads and tails. Cut the fillets into serving pieces and set aside.

2. Have the eel skinned and cleaned. Set aside.

3. Toss the mussels and clams into separate basins of plain water to which salt has been added. Drain and set aside.

4. Heat the oil in a large steamer or kettle and cook the onions, shallots and garlic in it, stirring, until onions are wilted. Add the bay leaf, thyme, fennel seeds, salt, black pepper, saffron, cayenne, orange rind and wine. Add the reserved eel and the fish bones, heads and tails. Cover and simmer, stirring occasionally, about twenty minutes. Drain in a colander, pressing with a wooden spoon to extract most of the liquid. Rinse out the kettle. Discard the solids in the colander.

5. Add the liquid to the kettle. Bring to a boil and add the reserved pieces of fish fillets. Cook gently five minutes, or until fish flakes easily. Do not overcook. Using a slotted spoon or other skimmer, carefully remove the fish from the kettle. Cover fish with aluminum foil or plastic wrap to keep warm.

6. Add the mussels and clams to the kettle and

cover. Simmer until shells open, eight to ten minutes. Add the cream and bring just to a boil, but do not boil. If desired, add salt and pepper to taste.

7. Pour the contents of the kettle into a very large, hot serving bowl. Add the reserved fish fillets. Garnish the bowl with the lobster meat and lobster claws stuck upright into the mussels and clams. Serve immediately in hot soup bowls, with crusty French bread and a chilled white wine.

Yield: Fourteen servings.

Gefilte Fish   *New York*

2 pounds whitefish
2 pounds pike
2 pounds carp
4 medium-size onions
4 teaspoons salt
1½ teaspoons freshly ground black pepper
3 eggs
¾ cup ice water
½ teaspoon sugar
3 tablespoons matzoh meal, cracker meal or dry bread crumbs
3 carrots, sliced
 Grated horseradish or tiny beets hollowed out and filled with horseradish.

1. Have the fish filleted and reserve the heads, skin and bones.

2. Place one quart water in a saucepan. Add the fish trimmings, three of the onions, two teaspoons of the salt and three-quarters teaspoon of the pepper. Simmer about twenty minutes.

3. Grind the fish fillets with the remaining onion. Place in a chopping bowl and chop until very fine. Add the eggs, ice water, sugar, meal or crumbs and remaining salt and pepper and beat until thoroughly blended. Moisten the hands and shape the mixture into balls.

4. Bring the stock to a boil. Drop the fish balls gently into boiling stock and add the carrots. Cover and simmer over low heat one hour. If stock cooks down too much, it may be necessary to add a little water. Remove the cover and simmer thirty minutes longer. Adjust seasonings, if necessary.

5. Cool the fish balls slightly in the pan. Remove the fish balls to a bowl, strain the stock over them and garnish with the carrot slices. Chill. Serve with grated horseradish or tiny beets hollowed out and filled with horseradish.

Yield: One dozen servings.

Baked Gefilte Fish   *New York*

2 pounds whitefish, filleted
2 pounds pike, filleted
2 pounds carp, filleted
1 onion
3 eggs
¾ cup ice water
½ teaspoon sugar
3 tablespoons matzoh meal
2 teaspoons salt
¾ teaspoon freshly ground black pepper
 Toasted almonds
 Grated horseradish or horseradish-filled beets.

1. Preheat the oven to 350 degrees.

2. Grind the fish fillets with the onion and place in a chopping bowl. Chop until very fine. Add the eggs, ice water, sugar, meal, salt and pepper and beat until thoroughly blended.

3. Turn mixture into a narrow loaf pan and cover lightly with aluminum foil. Bake one hour.

4. Serve hot or cold. To serve, slice the loaf and garnish slices with toasted almonds. Serve with grated horseradish or horseradish-filled beets.

Yield: Six to eight servings.

Sister Lisset's Shaker Fish Balls

Massachusetts

2 cups leftover cooked fish, bones removed
  and fish flaked
4 cups chopped cooked potatoes
2 egg yolks, beaten
1 tablespoon minced parsley
  Salt and freshly ground black pepper to
  taste
  Lard or fat for deep-frying
  Salt pork-and-milk gravy (next recipe).

1. Put the fish in a wooden chopping bowl and add the potatoes. Chop together until very fine.

2. Add the egg yolks, parsley, salt and pepper. Form into balls the size of a goose egg. Deep-fry in lard or fat until golden brown. Serve with gravy.

Yield: Six servings.

Hancock Shaker Village Salt Pork-and-Milk Gravy

Massachusetts

¼ pound salt pork, cut into cubes
¼ cup flour
 3 cups milk
  Salt and freshly ground black pepper to
  taste.

1. Place the salt pork cubes in a saucepan and cook, stirring, until they start to become crisp. Remove cubes from the saucepan and set aside.

2. Add the flour to saucepan and cook briefly, stirring, without burning. Add the milk, stirring rapidly. When mixture thickens and is smooth, add salt and pepper. Simmer ten minutes, stirring.

3. Chop salt pork cubes and add to sauce. Serve with fish balls.

Yield: Three cups.

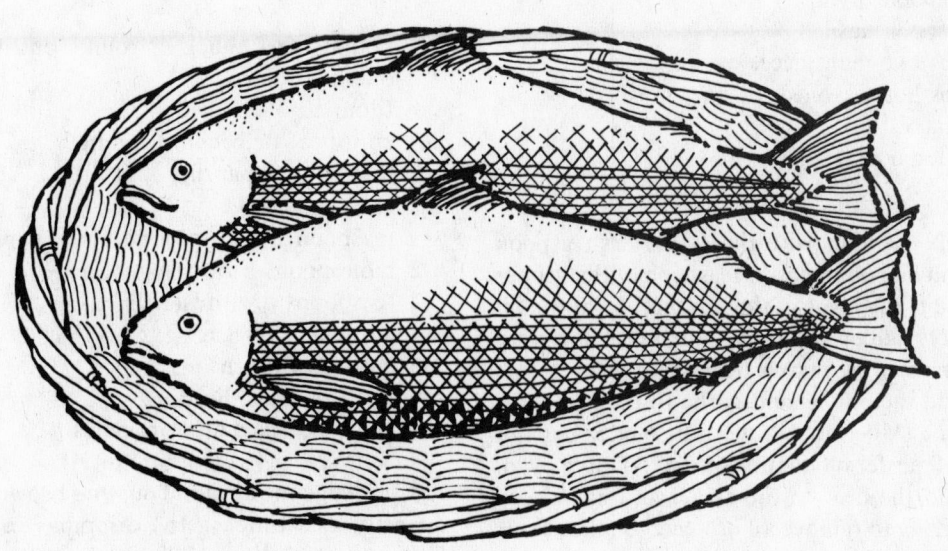

Meat, Poultry, Game and Other Main Dishes

Beef Pudding   *Vermont*

½ cup flour
1¼ teaspoons salt
½ teaspoon freshly ground black pepper
2 pounds boneless beef chuck, cubed
6 tablespoons oil
5 medium-size onions, chopped
2 cloves garlic, finely chopped
1¼ cups beer
1 bay leaf
½ teaspoon thyme
¼ teaspoon basil
2 cups two-inch pieces carrots
4 cups hot seasoned, creamy mashed potatoes
2 tablespoons butter.

1. Mix the flour with three-quarters teaspoon of the salt and one-quarter teaspoon of the pepper and dredge the meat in the mixture. Heat the oil in a heavy skillet and brown the meat in it very well. Transfer meat to a heavy Dutch oven.

2. Add the onions and garlic to the drippings left in the skillet and sauté until tender but not brown. Transfer onions and garlic to Dutch oven.

3. Add the beer to the skillet and bring to a boil, stirring to remove all browned-on bits. Pour into Dutch oven and add remaining salt and pepper, the thyme and basil. Bring to a boil, cover and simmer one and one-half hours, or until ten-

der. Add the carrots and cook twenty minutes longer.

4. Preheat the oven to 400 degrees.

5. Transfer meat mixture to an oblong casserole and top with potatoes. Swirl a fork, or the bowl of a spoon, over the potato mixture to make a decorative pattern. Dot with the butter and bake until lightly browned, about fifteen minutes.
    Yield: Eight servings.

Deviled Steak   *New York*

4 pounds beef chuck or round, cut into one-inch cubes
   Flour
¼ cup meat or bacon drippings
2 tablespoons paprika
2 teaspoons salt
½ teaspoon freshly ground black pepper
2 tablespoons brown sugar
2 teaspoons dry mustard
½ cup cider vinegar
1⅓ cups beef broth
8 large onions, sliced
   Buttered spaetzle or noodles.

1. Dredge the meat in flour and brown, a small quantity at a time, in the drippings in a heavy Dutch oven or large skillet.

2. Return all meat to skillet. Add the paprika, salt, pepper, sugar, mustard, vinegar, one cup of

the beef broth and the onions. Bring to a boil, cover and simmer two hours, or until meat is tender.

3. Measure the liquid in meat mixture. For every cup liquid, measure out one and one-half tablespoons flour and add to remaining beef broth. Add to meat mixture and cook, stirring, until gravy thickens. Check seasoning and serve over hot buttered spaetzle or noodles.

Yield: Eight servings.

Monday's Bean Pot Stew   *Connecticut*

2 tablespoons bacon drippings
1 pound top round beef, cut into cubes
2 onions, sliced
3 carrots, sliced
1 white turnip, diced
¼ yellow turnip, diced
2 ribs celery, diced
  Salt and freshly ground black pepper to taste
¼ cup old-fashioned oats
  Boiling water
3 potatoes, cubed.

1. Preheat the oven to 350 degrees.
2. Heat the bacon drippings in a skillet, add the beef cubes and brown on all sides. Add the onions, carrots, white turnip, yellow turnip, celery, salt and pepper. Turn into a bean pot.
3. Stir in the oats and enough boiling water barely to cover. Bake two hours, replenishing water as needed. Add the potatoes and cook one hour longer.

Yield: Four servings.

Spicy New England Pot Roast
New Hampshire

3 tablespoons flour
2 teaspoons salt
¼ teaspoon freshly ground black pepper

1 four-pound boned and rolled beef arm or blade or bottom round pot roast of beef
3 tablespoons bacon drippings or oil
½ cup freshly grated horseradish or prepared drained horseradish (four-ounce jar, see note)
1 cup whole cranberry sauce
1 stick cinnamon, broken in two
4 whole cloves
1 cup beef broth
16 small white onions
1 bunch carrots, cut into three-inch lengths.

1. Mix the flour with the salt and pepper and dredge the meat in the mixture. Rub the mixture into all the surfaces.
2. Heat the bacon drippings or oil in a heavy Dutch oven or casserole and brown the meat in it on all sides very well over high heat. Pour off the drippings into a skillet and reserve.
3. Mix together the horseradish, cranberry sauce, cinnamon, cloves and broth and add to the meat.
4. Bring the mixture to a boil, cover tightly and simmer gently about two hours, or until the meat is barely tender.
5. Meanwhile, brown the onions in the reserved drippings in the skillet. Add the carrots and cook two minutes longer. Drain from the fat and add to the meat broth. Cover and cook about twenty-five minutes longer, or until vegetables and meat are tender.

Yield: Eight servings.
Note: The quantity of horseradish is correct—it loses its pungency as it cooks.

The gravy is delicious over noodles.

Meat Balls   *New York*

3 pounds ground beef chuck
2 cups soft bread crumbs
2 teaspoons salt
½ teaspoon freshly ground black pepper
2 tablespoons oregano
⅓ cup freshly grated Parmesan cheese

3 Italian hot sausages, ground
2 onions, ground
1 clove garlic, ground
1 green pepper, ground
2 eggs
  Milk
4 cups homemade tomato sauce (page 52).

1. Mix all ingredients together except the milk and tomato sauce. Add enough milk to make a stiff mixture that can be molded into meat balls.

2. Form into one-inch balls and simmer in tomato sauce thirty minutes.

Yield: Ten servings.

Note: The meat mixture can be shaped into hamburgers or cooked as meat loaf.

Polenta Ring with Meat Sauce

Connecticut

  1 cup yellow corn meal
3½ cups water
  2 teaspoons salt
  1 cup grated sharp Cheddar cheese
  2 tablespoons peanut oil
  1 cup finely chopped onions
  1 clove garlic, finely minced
  ¼ cup chopped green pepper
  ½ pound ground round steak
2½ cups Italian plum tomatoes
  ½ teaspoon thyme
  ½ bay leaf

1. Blend the corn meal with one cup of the water.

2. Add one teaspoon of the salt to remaining water and bring to a boil. Add the corn meal mixture, stirring constantly. Cook, stirring frequently, until thickened. Continue cooking over low heat ten minutes, stirring frequently. Add the cheese and stir until melted. Grease an eight-inch ring mold and add the polenta mixture. Keep warm while preparing meat sauce.

3. Heat the oil in a skillet and add the onions, garlic and green pepper. Cook until onions are wilted. Add the ground round steak. Stir to break up the meat and continue cooking until meat loses its red color. Add the tomatoes, thyme, bay leaf and remaining salt and simmer about thirty minutes.

4. Unmold the polenta ring onto a serving dish and pour the sauce in the center. Serve immediately.

Yield: Six to eight servings.

Papa's Maltese Baked Rice   *New York*

1½ cups uncooked rice
  3 tablespoons olive oil
  1 bay leaf, crumbled
  ¾ pound ground beef round
  ¼ pound Italian sausage, diced
  1 small onion, finely chopped
  1 clove garlic, finely chopped
  1 small green pepper, finely chopped
  ½ rib celery, finely chopped
2½ cups water, beef broth or chicken broth
  1 eight-ounce can tomato sauce
  3 medium-size or two extra-large eggs, lightly beaten
  2 tablespoons tomato paste
  3 tablespoons grated Romano cheese
  2 teaspoons salt
  ½ teaspoon freshly ground black pepper
  ½ teaspoon sugar
  6 slices mozzarella cheese (optional).

1. Soak the rice fifteen minutes in water to cover. Drain rice and place in a one-and-three-quarters-quart casserole.

2. Place the oil, bay leaf, ground beef, sausage, onion, garlic, green pepper and celery in a skillet and cook until meat loses its redness and vegetables are tender. Cool ten minutes.

3. Preheat the oven to 350 degrees.

4. To the rice, add the water or broth, the tomato sauce, eggs and tomato paste and mix well. Add the cooled meat mixture, grated cheese, salt, black pepper and sugar. Stir to mix well. Bake two hours, or until rice is tender.

5. Place the mozzarella cheese, if desired, on top during the last ten minutes of cooking.
Yield: Four servings.

Greek Meat Balls   *New York*

½ pound stale white, Italian or French bread slices
1½ pounds ground lean chuck
1½ pounds ground lean lamb
2 large onions, finely chopped
½ cup finely chopped fresh mint leaves
2 eggs, lightly beaten
2 tablespoons grated Romano cheese
1 tomato, peeled and chopped
Salt and freshly ground black pepper to taste
Flour
Oil and melted butter for frying.

1. Pull the bread into pieces and place in a bowl. Cover with water and let stand five minutes. Squeeze out excess moisture from the bread.

2. Put the chuck and lamb in a large bowl and add the bread. Add the onions, mint, eggs, cheese, tomato, salt and pepper. Mix well with the hands. If the mixture is too stiff, add a little water. Let mixture stand several hours to blend flavors before shaping.

3. Shape the meat into two-inch balls for luncheon size or one-inch balls for appetizers and flatten slightly on the top. Dredge well in flour to give a good coating.

4. Heat enough oil and melted butter in a large heavy skillet just to cover the bottom depth of one-eighth inch. Add the meat balls and fry on all sides over medium heat until browned. The meat balls should have a crusty brown outside.

Yield: Ten luncheon servings or two dozen appetizer servings.

Paula's Surprise Meat Loaf with Mushroom Tomato Sauce   *New York*

Mushroom tomato sauce:
2 tablespoons olive oil
1 tablespoon butter
1 medium-size onion, finely chopped
1 clove garlic, finely chopped
2 cups mushrooms, sliced
1 one-pound-twelve-ounce can Italian plum tomatoes packed in puree
1 six-ounce can tomato paste
1½ cups water
1½ teaspoons salt or one bay leaf, if salt cannot be used
½ teaspoon freshly ground black pepper
1 teaspoon basil, pulverized
¼ cup to one-third cup dry red wine.
Meat loaf:
2 pounds ground lean beef chuck
2 eggs
1 small green pepper, diced
⅓ cup chopped parsley
1 onion, finely chopped
3 slices stale bread, soaked in water and then excess moisture squeezed out
½ teaspoon salt
½ teaspoon freshly ground black pepper
¾ cup Italian plum tomatoes.
Filling:
3 hard-cooked eggs, chopped
½ cup julienne strips Genoa salami
¼ cup freshly grated Romano and/or Parmesan cheese
⅓ cup julienne strips pimento
½ cup finely chopped parsley
½ cup soft bread crumbs
1 tablespoon mayonnaise
½ teaspoon thyme
Freshly ground black pepper to taste.

1. To prepare mushroom tomato sauce, heat the oil and butter in a heavy three-quart to four-quart saucepan. Add the onion and garlic and sauté until tender. Add the mushrooms and cook three minutes longer.

2. Add the tomatoes, tomato paste, water, salt and pepper. Stir to mix and bring to a boil, stirring.

3. Simmer the sauce, partially covered with a lid, thirty to thirty-five minutes (the lid prevents spattering but allows some evaporation), stirring occasionally to prevent sticking. Stir in the basil and wine and cook five minutes longer.

4. Meanwhile, combine the meat loaf ingredients in a large bowl and mix thoroughly with the hands.

5. Preheat the oven to 375 degrees.

6. Combine the filling ingredients in another bowl and mix well.

7. On a double thickness of aluminum foil, pat out the meat loaf mixture into a rectangle about 12 by 9 inches. Place the filling in a long sausage shape atop meat about two inches from a long side.

8. Gradually roll the meat loaf mixture around the filling like a jellyroll, using the foil as a guide to the rolling. Remove the foil and place the stuffed meat roll in a baking pan. Bake forty-five minutes, or until done. Serve in slices, with the sauce served separately.

Yield: Eight to ten servings.

Fruit-Stuffed Meat Loaf   *Pennsylvania*

Meat loaf:
1½ pounds ground beef chuck
 ½ pound ground lean pork
 2 eggs, lightly beaten
 1 cup soft bread crumbs
1½ teaspoons salt
 ¼ teaspoon freshly ground black pepper.
Filling:
 ¼ cup raisins
 ¼ cup dried apricots, chopped
 ¼ cup chopped parsley
 ½ cup chopped onion
 ½ teaspoon sage
 ¼ teaspoon thyme
 ½ cup beef broth.

1. Preheat the oven to 350 degrees.

2. Combine the meat loaf ingredients in a bowl and mix well. Spread the mixture in a rectangle about one-half-inch thick on large piece of heavy-duty aluminum foil.

3. Combine the filling ingredients and mix thoroughly. Spread over meat loaf mixture and then roll up meat and filling like a jellyroll. Bring foil up around the roll and make a drugstore wrap to seal.

4. Place the package on a baking sheet and bake one hour. Open up the foil to allow surface to brown and bake thirty minutes longer.

Yield: Six servings.

Meat Balls with Brown Beans   *Vermont*

Brown beans:
 2 cups dried pinto beans
2½ quarts water
 ¼ cup cider vinegar
 2 teaspoons salt
 ¼ cup maple syrup.
Meat balls:
 1 cup fine dry bread crumbs
 1 cup milk
 3 tablespoons bacon drippings
 ¼ cup chopped onion
 1 pound ground beef chuck
 1 pound ground lean pork
 3 eggs, lightly beaten
 2 teaspoons salt
 ½ teaspoon freshly ground black pepper
 ½ teaspoon ground allspice
 1 teaspoon nutmeg
 1 cup water, approximately.

1. To prepare brown beans, wash the pinto beans and soak in the water overnight. Next day, place beans and soaking liquid in a kettle and bring to a boil. Cover and simmer until tender, about one and one-half hours. Add the vinegar, salt and syrup and mix well. Cook thirty minutes longer.

2. To prepare meat balls, soak the bread

crumbs in the milk for fifteen minutes. Melt two tablespoons of the drippings and sauté the onion in them until tender.

3. Combine soaked bread crumbs, the onion, beef, pork, eggs, salt, pepper, allspice and nutmeg. Mix well. Shape into one-inch balls.

4. Melt remaining bacon drippings in a heavy skillet. Add the meat balls and brown on all sides. Add one-third cup of the water and simmer, covered, until meat balls are tender and cooked through, about forty-five minutes. Add more of the water as necessary during cooking.

5. Serve the meat balls over, or in the middle of a circle of, the brown beans.

Yield: Six to eight servings.

Ravioli à la Romana   *Connecticut*

1 large Bermuda onion, finely chopped
3 tablespoons olive oil
2 pounds fresh spinach, chopped, or two
  packages frozen chopped spinach
½ cup pignoli (pine nuts) (optional)
½ pound ricotta cheese
1 egg
  Freshly grated Parmesan cheese
1 three-pound beef pot roast, braised with
  onion and red wine, put through the finest
  blade of a meat grinder
  Salt and freshly ground black pepper to
  taste
1 recipe pasta (recipe below), thinly rolled
  Boiling salted water
4 cups homemade tomato sauce (page 52).

1. Sauté the onion in the oil until tender and golden. Add the spinach and cook until spinach is cooked and mixture is dry. Pass through the finest blade of the meat grinder, with nuts if used.

2. Mix together the ricotta, egg and one-quarter cup Parmesan. In a large bowl, combine the meat, spinach mixture and cheese mixture and mix well. Season with salt and pepper. Form into tiny one-inch balls.

3. Line a ravioli tin with pasta dough. Place a meat ball in each depression. Cover with dough, roll to cut and set ravioli to dry. Repeat until all dough and filling are used.

4. Preheat the oven to 375 degrees.

5. Cook the ravioli, in small batches, in large kettle of boiling salted water about ten minutes. Drain and arrange in a shallow casserole. Spoon the sauce over. If desired, sprinkle with three-quarters cup Parmesan. Bake about fifteen minutes.

Yield: Six dozen ravioli; nine to ten servings.

Note: The uncooked ravioli can be frozen after thirty minutes' drying time.

Pasta   *Connecticut*

6 cups flour
1 tablespoon salt
6 eggs.

1. Place the flour and salt in a bowl. Make a well in the center and add the eggs. Beat with a wooden spoon, gradually incorporating the flour.

2. Add water to make a fairly stiff dough. Knead the dough until it is elastic and smooth, about ten minutes.

3. Pass one-sixth of the dough through pasta machine at the widest setting several times, folding dough in thirds as it lengthens for successive rollings. Set the machine at number two or three for the final rolling to make ravioli.

Yield: Enough for six dozen ravioli.

Vermont Boiled Dinner

4 pounds corned beef
3 large yellow turnips, peeled and cut into
  one-half-inch slices
6 large carrots or about twenty small carrots
6 medium-size potatoes, peeled and halved
10 to twelve beets, freshly cooked and peeled
2 to four heads cabbage, quartered and
  freshly cooked
  Melted butter

Chopped parsley
Mustard (optional)
Horseradish (optional).

1. Place the corned beef in a large kettle and add water to cover. Simmer three hours, or until tender when pierced with a fork. Meanwhile, one hour before meat is done, add the turnips. Thirty minutes before meat is done, add the carrots and potatoes.

2. When meat and vegetables are tender, slice the meat and place it on a warm large serving platter. Surround the meat with turnip slices, carrots, potatoes, the beets and cabbage. Pour melted butter over the vegetables and sprinkle potatoes with parsley.

3. Serve with mustard and horseradish if desired.

Yield: Ten to one dozen servings.

Reuben Sandwich   *New York*

3 pounds corned beef
1 one-pound-eleven-ounce can sauerkraut
20 to twenty-four slices rye bread with
    caraway seeds
    Butter
1 pound sliced imported Swiss cheese.

1. Place the corned beef in a deep kettle or casserole and cover with cold water. Bring to a boil, cover and simmer gently about fifty minutes a pound, or until tender. Thirty minutes before cooking is scheduled to be finished, pile the sauerkraut on top of the meat.

2. Slice the corned beef and drain the sauerkraut.

3. For each sandwich, toast two slices of rye bread. Butter each slice on one side. Place one piece buttered side up, top with several slices of hot corned beef and spoon hot drained sauerkraut over corned beef. Arrange slices of Swiss cheese over the sauerkraut and broil until the cheese

melts. Top with remaining piece of toast, buttered side down.

Yield: Ten to one dozen sandwiches.

Red Flannel Hash   *Vermont*

2 cups chopped cooked corned beef
3 cups diced cooked potatoes
1½ cups diced cooked beets
2 tablespoons grated onion
1 teaspoon Worcestershire sauce
  Salt to taste
¼ teaspoon freshly ground black pepper
2 tablespoons bacon drippings.

1. In a bowl, combine the corned beef, potatoes, beets, onion, Worcestershire, salt and pepper.

2. Heat the bacon drippings in a heavy skillet and spread the corned beef mixture over bottom of skillet. Cook over medium-high heat until underside of hash is browned. Turn and brown the other side.

Yield: Four servings.

Corned Beef Hash   *Massachusetts*

3 cups finely diced cooked corned beef
2 cups finely diced cooked potatoes
3 tablespoons butter
¾ cup finely chopped onions
1 tablespoon Worcestershire sauce
  Salt and freshly ground black pepper to
  taste
  Peanut oil
  Catchup (optional).

1. Combine the corned beef and potatoes in a mixing bowl.

2. Melt the butter and cook the onions in it until thoroughly wilted. Add onions to the corned beef mixture. Add the Worcestershire, salt and pepper and blend lightly.

3. Brush a skillet with oil and spoon the

corned beef mixture into the skillet, pressing down to cover the bottom fully. Cook over moderate heat until well browned on the bottom.

4. Serve with catchup if desired.

Yield: About four servings.

Ham Mousse   *Massachusetts*

3½ cups finely ground cooked ham (see step 1)
1⅓ cups chicken broth
1 envelope unflavored gelatin
¼ cup cold water
2 eggs, separated
1 cup heavy cream
¼ cup dry sherry.

1. The ham must be ground as fine as possible. Refrigerate.

2. Bring the broth to a boil.

3. Soak the gelatin in the water and stir into the hot broth. Stir to dissolve gelatin.

4. Beat the egg yolks lightly; add a little of the hot mixture to the yolks; then add yolks to the broth, stirring constantly. Cook over low heat, stirring with a wooden spoon, just until sauce coats the spoon. Do not overcook or sauce may curdle. Cool sauce, but do not chill.

5. Beat the egg whites until stiff. Beat the cream until stiff. Blend the two; then fold in the sauce, ham and sherry. Pour the mixture into a one-and-one-half-quart mold and chill. Unmold onto a platter before serving.

Yield: Six servings.

Glazed Vermont Ham

1 twelve-pound Vermont ham
½ cup Vermont apple jelly
½ cup apple syrup

1. Preheat the oven to 325 degrees.

2. Place a whole Vermont ham, uncovered, on a rack in a shallow roasting pan. Bake the ham twenty-five minutes to the pound, or, if a meat thermometer is used, until it registers 160 degrees. Just before the ham is to be done, remove it from the oven and trim off most of the rind, leaving a collar of rind around the shank. Score the fat side of the ham in diamond shapes. Combine the apple jelly and syrup and spread on ham.

3. Increase the oven heat to 450 degrees. Return ham to oven and bake until glazed, five to fifteen minutes.

Yield: Sixteen to eighteen servings.

Schnitz un Knepp (Apples and Dumplings)
Pennsylvania

2 cups dried apples
1 two-pound smoked ham (a picnic shoulder or boned butt is ideal)
2 tablespoons brown sugar.
Dumplings:
2 cups flour
4 teaspoons baking powder
½ teaspoon salt
1 egg, lightly beaten
2 tablespoons butter, melted
½ cup milk, approximately.

1. Day before, cover the apples with water and let soak overnight.

2. Next day, place the ham in a kettle, cover with cold water, bring to a boil and simmer, covered, about two hours. Add apples, soaking water and brown sugar and cook one hour longer.

3. To prepare dumplings, combine the flour, baking powder and salt. Stir in the egg, butter and enough milk to make a fairly stiff batter.

4. Drop the batter by spoonfuls into the simmering apple and ham mixture. Cover and let cook thirty minutes.

Yield: Six to eight servings.

Helen's Eggplant and Macaroni Casserole
New York

⅓ cup olive oil
1 large eggplant, peeled and cubed (about two quarts)
½ cup diced celery
8 ounces elbow macaroni, cooked al dente, drained
1 pound ground lamb
Salt and freshly ground black pepper to taste
1 teaspoon oregano
¼ teaspoon cinnamon
1 recipe tomato sauce (recipe below)
8 ounces mozzarella cheese, thickly sliced.

1. Preheat the oven to 375 degrees.
2. Heat the oil in a large skillet. Add the eggplant and sauté until lightly browned. Combine the eggplant, celery and macaroni in a large bowl.
3. Cook the lamb in a skillet until lightly browned, breaking up the lumps as meat cooks. Season with salt, pepper, oregano and cinnamon. Add to macaroni mixture.
4. Stir in the tomato sauce and check the seasoning. Turn into a two-and-one-half-quart to three-quart deep casserole. Top with the mozzarella and bake thirty minutes, or until the casserole is bubbly hot and cheese is melted and lightly browned.
Yield: Four servings.

Tomato Sauce
New York

¼ cup olive oil
1 large onion, finely chopped
1 clove garlic, finely chopped
1 two-pound-thirteen-ounce can Italian plum tomatoes or one quart peeled, seeded and chopped fresh tomatoes
1 six-ounce can tomato paste
Salt and freshly ground black pepper to taste
1 bay leaf

1 teaspoon basil
½ teaspoon thyme
½ teaspoon oregano.

1. Heat the oil in a large saucepan. Sauté the onion and garlic in the oil until tender but not browned.
2. Add the tomatoes, tomato paste, salt, pepper, bay leaf and basil. Bring to a boil and let simmer twenty minutes.
3. Add the thyme and oregano and let simmer five minutes longer.
Yield: About one quart.

Eggplant-Stuffed Crown Roast of Lamb
New York

¼ cup soft bread crumbs
½ recipe eggplant and macaroni casserole (recipe above), using only enough tomato sauce to moisten and omitting the mozzarella cheese
1 crown roast of lamb, made from sixteen rib chops
2 tablespoons lemon juice
Salt and freshly ground black pepper to taste
3 tablespoons freshly grated Parmesan cheese.

1. Preheat the oven to 350 degrees.
2. Mix the bread crumbs into the casserole mixture.
3. Rub the crown roast all over with the lemon juice and season with salt and pepper. Stuff with the eggplant mixture, piling it up and placing any extra in a small baking dish. Sprinkle with the cheese.
4. Place the roast on a rack in a shallow pan and roast one hour and twenty minutes, or until roast reaches desired degree of doneness. Cook the extra dish of stuffing for the last twenty minutes of roasting time.
Yield: Eight servings.

Crumbed Butterflied Leg of Lamb

Pennsylvania

1 five-pound to six-pound leg of lamb, boned
2 cloves garlic, mashed
1 teaspoon salt
  Freshly ground black pepper to taste
1 teaspoon oregano
  Juice of one lemon
  Olive oil
2 shallots, minced
1 tablespoon butter
1 cup soft bread crumbs
1 tablespoon chopped parsley
¼ cup freshly grated Parmesan cheese.

1. Split the lamb lengthwise and spread flat like a thick steak. Combine the garlic, salt, pepper, oregano and lemon juice and mix into a paste. Rub this into the boned lamb on both sides. Let stand at room temperature one hour.

2. Preheat the oven to 450 degrees.

3. If the lamb is lean, sprinkle the surface with two teaspoons oil. Place in a shallow roasting pan and roast, uncovered, twenty minutes, or until well browned.

4. Reduce the oven heat to 325 degrees. Roast a total of about ten to fifteen minutes a pound, or until lamb reaches the desired degree of doneness. Lamb should be pink in the middle.

5. Meanwhile, sauté the shallots in the butter and one tablespoon oil until tender. Stir in the bread crumbs, parsley and cheese. Spread the mixture over the lamb ten minutes before it is done.

Yield: Six servings.

Baked Lamb Ring with Mashed Potatoes

Vermont

2 tablespoons oil
2 tablespoons chopped onion
1 clove garlic, finely chopped
4 mushrooms, finely chopped
2 pounds ground lean lamb
2 eggs, lightly beaten
½ cup chopped green pepper
1½ cups soft bread crumbs
1 teaspoon salt
¼ teaspoon freshly ground black pepper
1 tablespoon chopped parsley
1 teaspoon rosemary
12 piped rosettes made from three cups seasoned mashed potatoes mixed with two egg yolks
2 tablespoons melted butter.

1. Preheat the oven to 350 degrees.

2. Heat the oil in a small skillet and sauté the onion and garlic in it until lightly browned. Add the mushrooms and cook until the extra liquid has been evaporated.

3. Place the onion mixture in a bowl and mix with the lamb, eggs, green pepper, bread crumbs, salt, pepper, parsley and rosemary. Pack into a greased eight-inch ring mold.

4. Bake one hour. Set in a warm place.

5. Increase the oven heat to 375 degrees. Place the potato rosettes on a greased baking sheet, sprinkle with the butter and bake until lightly browned, about ten minutes.

6. Unmold the lamb ring onto a hot platter and pile the rosettes in the middle or around.

Yield: Six servings.

Lamb on a Spit

Connecticut

½ cup plus two tablespoons olive oil
1 large carrot, finely chopped
1 large onion, finely chopped
2 shallots, finely minced
½ cup finely minced celery
  Salt
½ teaspoon peppercorns
4 bay leaves
6 sprigs parsley
2 whole cloves
1 clove garlic, crushed
6 cups dry red wine or dry white wine
2 cups wine vinegar

2 teaspoons thyme
1 six-pound leg of lamb, boned and tied
  Freshly ground black pepper.

1. Heat one-half cup of the oil and add the carrot, onion, shallots and celery. Cook, stirring, until onion is wilted.

2. Add one tablespoon salt, the peppercorns, bay leaves, parsley, cloves, garlic, wine, wine vinegar and one teaspoon of the thyme. Simmer slowly thirty minutes. Cool thoroughly.

3. Pour the marinade over the meat. Let stand three days in refrigerator, turning occasionally.

4. When ready to roast, drain the meat one hour before cooking, reserving marinade. Rub meat with remaining oil, remaining thyme and salt and pepper to taste.

5. If the spit is used, roast the lamb to the desired degree of doneness, basting occasionally with a little of the marinade. The time will depend on the intensity of the heat and proximity to the fire. If the meat is to be roasted in the oven, preheat the oven to 350 degrees. Place the lamb in a roasting pan and roast, basting occasionally with a little of the marinade, fifteen to twenty minutes a pound.

6. When the meat is cooked, a sauce may be made with the drippings. To do this, pour off the fat and stir into the drippings, bit by bit, butter kneaded with equal parts of flour. The sauce should be thin.

Yield: Ten servings.

Leg of Lamb with Saffron-and-Caper Sauce   *Connecticut*

6 tablespoons butter
2 cloves garlic, mashed
1 teaspoon monosodium glutamate (optional)
1 teaspoon salt
1 teaspoon cayenne pepper
1 five-pound to six-pound leg of spring lamb, boned and tied, with bones reserved
1 tablespoon cornstarch
½ cup heavy cream

¾ teaspoon leaf saffron
1 bottle capers, drained.

1. Night before, cream together the butter, garlic, monosodium glutamate if desired, salt and cayenne and spread all over the roast. Double-wrap the lamb and bones in heavy-duty aluminum foil and refrigerate overnight.

2. Next day, remove meat package from refrigerator two hours before cooking.

3. Preheat the oven to 375 degrees.

4. Place the meat package in a roasting pan and roast thirty-five minutes a pound for medium degree of doneness and forty-five minutes a pound for well done.

5. Combine the cornstarch and three tablespoons water. Open the foil and pour off the juices from the roast. Add to the juices the cornstarch mixture, cream and saffron. Measure liquid. It should measure two and one-half cups. Add water to make up quantity if necessary.

6. Bring the mixture to a boil, stirring, and cook five minutes. Sauce should be the consistency of light cream. Add water if necessary. Add the capers.

7. Discard the bones and carve the roast. Serve hot with the sauce served separately. Or, to serve cold, arrange lamb slices in a serving dish, pour sauce over and chill.

Yield: About ten servings.

Baked Lamb   *New York*

3 pounds breast of lamb, cut into two-inch pieces
  Salt and freshly ground black pepper to taste
1 cup dry red wine
¼ cup water
¼ cup currant jelly
2 tablespoons chopped parsley
1 teaspoon marjoram.

1. Preheat the oven to 375 degrees.

2. Place the meat, fat side down, in a large

open roasting pan. Season with salt and pepper. Bake one hour, or until barely tender.

3. Combine the remaining ingredients in a small saucepan and bring to a boil.

4. Pour off the accumulated drippings and fat from the roasting pan. Pour the wine mixture over lamb and bake, basting frequently, thirty minutes longer, or until lamb is glazed and tender.

Yield: Six servings.

Nicole's Lamb Ragout   *New York*

2 links pork sausage
¼ cup olive oil
2 or three cloves garlic, finely minced
2 pounds lamb, cut into one-inch cubes
2 carrots, diced
3 ribs celery, finely chopped
½ teaspoon ground rosemary
1 teaspoon paprika
  Salt and freshly ground black pepper to taste
1½ cups fresh or canned beef broth
1½ cups homemade or canned tomato sauce
  Cooked rice or noodles.

1. Place the sausage in a skillet and cook until done. Drain the sausage; then cut into thin slices.

2. Heat the oil and add the garlic. Cook over moderate heat until garlic starts to brown; then remove garlic and discard. Brown the lamb in the oil remaining in pan. Add the vegetables, sausage and seasonings.

3. Add the broth and tomato sauce and bring to a boil. Simmer one and one-half hours, or until meat is fork-tender. Serve with rice or noodles.

Yield: Four to six servings.

Lamb with Dill   *New York*

3 pounds breast of lamb
  Salt and freshly ground black pepper to taste

1 large carrot, sliced
1 medium-size onion, diced
½ cup diced celery
1 to two tablespoons flour, depending on desired thickness of sauce
1 tablespoon cider vinegar
1 teaspoon sugar
½ cup heavy cream
2 egg yolks
¾ cup freshly snipped dill weed, or more to taste
  Boiled potatoes
  Cucumber salad.

1. Trim the lamb of excess fat. Cut the meat into two-inch cubes. Sprinkle with salt and pepper. Place in a deep kettle. Add the carrot, onion, celery and water to cover. Simmer, covered, over low heat about one to one and one-quarter hours, or until meat is tender, skimming as necessary and stirring occasionally.

2. Drain the cooking liquid into a saucepan and cook down to one and one-half cups. Mix the flour with a little water and stir into liquid. Cook, stirring constantly, until smooth and thickened. Stir in the vinegar and sugar.

3. Beat together the cream and egg yolks. Stir into sauce. Pour sauce over meat and heat thoroughly. Sprinkle with the dill before serving. Serve with boiled potatoes and cucumber salad.

Yield: Four to six servings.

Scrapple   *Pennsylvania*

4 large or six small pigs' knuckles
1 pound lean pork
3 quarts water
1 tablespoon salt
1 hot red pepper or two teaspoons hot red pepper flakes
½ teaspoon freshly ground black pepper
1 teaspoon leaf sage, rubbed between the fingers
2¾ cups yellow corn meal

Flour
Melted butter or meat drippings.

1. Place the knuckles, pork, water, salt and red pepper in a large kettle. Bring to a boil and simmer gently about two hours, or until meat is tender.

2. Remove the meat from the knuckles and grind meat along with the pork.

3. Skim off the fat from the top of the broth. Measure the broth and return two quarts to the kettle. Reserve remaining broth. Add ground meat, the black pepper and sage to kettle. Bring to a rapid boil.

4. Cool one quart reserved broth to lukewarm. Combine with the corn meal and add to boiling meat mixture. Cook, stirring, until thickened.

5. Place the kettle over an asbestos mat and continue to cook slowly, stirring, thirty minutes.

6. Adjust the seasonings. Turn mixture into two lightly oiled 9-by-5-by-3-inch loaf pans. Cover and chill.

7. To serve, cut loaves into one-half-inch-thick slices. Coat lightly with flour and brown in melted butter or drippings.
Yield: One dozen servings.

Connecticut Bean Pot

1 pound Italian hot sausages, sliced
1 pound Italian sweet sausages, sliced
1 kielbasa (polish sausage), sliced
3 onions, sliced and separated into rings
½ teaspoon thyme
½ teaspoon basil
2 bay leaves
¾ cup dry sherry
3 one-pound cans pork and beans
1 eight-ounce can tomato sauce
Whole or sliced frankfurters (optional).

1. Preheat the oven to 350 degrees.
2. Place the sausages and onions in a heavy Dutch oven or casserole and cook gently until sausages are done.

3. Add the remaining ingredients and bring to a boil. Cover and bake one and one-half hours. If desired, frankfurters, whole or sliced, may be added during the last twenty minutes of baking.
Yield: Ten to one dozen servings.

Mustard Pork Chops   *New York*

¼ cup bacon drippings
1 to two cloves garlic, finely minced
6 thick pork chops
2 teaspoons dry mustard
Salt and freshly ground black pepper
¾ cup dry white wine
¾ cup freshly squeezed orange juice
1½ cups thinly sliced onions
2 green peppers, cored, seeded and cut into strips
Cooked rice.

1. Heat the bacon drippings and add the garlic. Cook, stirring, but do not brown.

2. Smear the pork chops with the mustard and sprinkle with the salt and pepper. Brown on both sides in the bacon drippings and add the wine and orange juice. Cook over low heat until sauce is slightly reduced. Add the onions and green peppers. Cover the pan.

3. Continue cooking over low heat until chops are tender, one to one and one-half hours. If desired, add more salt and pepper to taste and serve hot with rice.
Yield: Six servings.

Baked Pork Steaks   *Pennsylvania*

6 shoulder pork chops (about one and one-half pounds to two pounds)
2 tablespoons shortening
Salt and freshly ground black pepper
½ cup finely chopped leeks
1 cup uncooked rice
2½ cups chicken broth
1 cup drained canned tomatoes

½ teaspoon thyme
½ teaspoon sage
¼ teaspoon marjoram
2 tablespoons chopped parsley
1 bay leaf.

1. Preheat the oven to 350 degrees.
2. In a large skillet, brown the chops on both sides in the shortening. Remove chops, season lightly with salt and pepper and keep warm. Add the leeks to the fat remaining in the skillet and sauté slowly until tender.
3. Add the rice and cook, stirring, five minutes. Add the broth, tomatoes, thyme, sage, marjoram, parsley, bay leaf, one and one-half teaspoons salt and one-quarter teaspoon pepper and bring to a boil.
4. Place the rice mixture in the bottom of a heavy three-quart casserole. Top with the chops. Cover and bake one hour. Remove the bay leaf before serving.
Yield: Six servings.

Cranberry Pork Chops   *Massachusetts*

6 rib or loin pork chops, each three-quarters-inch to one-inch thick
1 tablespoon butter
1 teaspoon salt
⅛ teaspoon freshly ground black pepper
1 cup fresh cranberries
¼ cup brown sugar
2 teaspoons cornstarch
⅔ cup water
1 large orange, peeled and cut into one-quarter inch slices.

1. Brown the chops on both sides in the butter in a heavy skillet or Dutch oven. Pour off excess drippings. Season chops with the salt and pepper.
2. Add the cranberries and brown sugar, cover tightly and simmer forty-five minutes, or until the chops are thoroughly cooked.
3. Remove the chops to a heated platter. Combine the cornstarch with the water and add to the

liquid in skillet. Cook, stirring, until the sauce is thickened. Add the orange slices and reheat. Pour the sauce over the chops.
Yield: Six servings.

Galatoise Polonaise   *Connecticut*

½ pound thin-sliced lean bacon, cooked until crisp
1 pound fresh lean boneless pork, cut into thin slices
½ pound cooked smoked ham, sliced
½ pound frankfurters, sliced
1 pound mushrooms, sliced
1 eight-ounce bottle pitted stuffed green olives, sliced
3 to four tomatoes, peeled and sliced
1½ teaspoons sugar
1 pound sauerkraut, rinsed and drained
2 juicy apples, peeled, cored and sliced
4 white onions, thinly sliced
1 small head cabbage, sliced, parboiled in salt water five minutes
  Salt and freshly ground black pepper to taste
2 bay leaves, crumbled
2 cups tomato juice
½ cup butter.

1. Preheat the oven to 375 degrees.
2. Make an assembly line of the following ingredients: the bacon, pork, ham, frankfurters, mushrooms, olives, tomatoes, sugar, sauerkraut, apples, onions and cabbage. Starting with one-third of the bacon slices, make alternate layers of the ingredients in a four-quart to five-quart baking dish, leaving plenty of cabbage and tomato slices for the next-to-last layer and a few bacon slices to top everything. As galatoise is being assembled, season each layer lightly with salt and pepper and sprinkle with bits of crumbled bay leaves.
3. Pour the tomato juice over all, dot with the butter, cover dish and bake one and three-quarters hours. Remove the cover, to brown galatoise

lightly, and bake fifteen minutes longer. Serve topped with sour cream-and-mustard sauce (recipe below).

Yield: About one dozen servings.

Sour Cream-and-Mustard Sauce
Connecticut

6 cups sour cream
9 to twelve tablespoons Dijon or Düsseldorf mustard
¼ cup chopped chives.

Stir the sour cream and mustard together and sprinkle with the chives.

Yield: About one and one-half quarts.

Pork Roast with Herbs   *Pennsylvania*

1 four-pound to five-pound rib end of pork
1 clove garlic, finely minced
1 teaspoon finely minced rosemary
Salt and freshly ground black pepper to taste
2 cups brown sugar
1 cup cider vinegar.

1. Preheat the oven to 450 degrees.
2. Rub the pork with garlic, rosemary, salt and pepper. Place roast, fat side up, in a Dutch oven. Bake, uncovered, fifteen minutes.
3. Meanwhile, put the brown sugar in a skillet. Cook over very low heat until sugar melts and starts to caramelize, but do not let the sugar burn. Stir in the vinegar.
4. Reduce the oven temperature to 300 degrees. Pour off the fat that has accumulated from the pork. Baste the meat with the vinegar-sugar mixture. Bake, covered, basting frequently, two hours or longer, until pork is fork-tender.
5. Serve the pork sliced. Pour off excess fat from the liquid in the Dutch oven and serve the remaining sauce separately.

Yield: Four to six servings.

Pork Chops with Apricot-Apple Stuffing
Pennsylvania

1 cup diced dried apricots
½ cup boiling water
1 tablespoon sugar
¼ cup flour
Salt and freshly ground black pepper to taste
6 one-inch-thick rib pork chops
3 tablespoons shortening
4 tablespoons butter
½ cup diced celery
½ cup finely chopped onion
4 cups one-quarter-inch stale white, French or Italian bread cubes
1 large tart apple, peeled, cored and diced
2 tablespoons chopped parsley
½ teaspoon thyme
¼ teaspoon marjoram.

1. Preheat the oven to 325 degrees.
2. Place the apricots in a bowl and add the boiling water and sugar.
3. Combine the flour, salt and pepper. Trim excess fat from the chops and coat chops with the flour mixture. Melt the shortening in a skillet. Add chops, brown on both sides, remove and set aside.
4. Add the butter to the skillet. Add the celery and onion and sauté until tender but not browned.
5. Combine the bread cubes, apple, parsley, thyme and marjoram and add cooked vegetables. Add the apricots. Season with salt and pepper.
6. Place stuffing in the bottom of a shallow baking dish or casserole and place the chops on top of stuffing. Cover and bake one and one-half hours, or until chops are thoroughly cooked.

Yield: Six servings.

Pork Chops with Spinach   *Connecticut*

¼ cup flour
¾ teaspoon salt

4 large pork chops, trimmed
2 tablespoons olive oil
1 clove garlic, minced
2 tablespoons minced parsley
1 tablespoon chopped onion
¼ cup dry white wine
½ teaspoon prepared mustard, preferably
    Dijon or Düsseldorf
1 pound fresh spinach, well washed and
    chopped, or one package frozen chopped
    spinach, partially defrosted
½ cup croutons, fried in oil.

1. Combine the flour and one-half teaspoon of the salt and rub mixture into pork chops. Brown chops in the oil. Cover and cook ten minutes over low heat. Transfer chops to a shallow casserole.

2. Preheat the oven to 375 degrees.

3. Add the garlic, parsley and onion to skillet and cook until onion is wilted. Add the wine, mustard, spinach and remaining salt.

4. Cook, covered, four minutes. Drain off excess liquid. Puree the spinach mixture in an electric blender or force through sieve. Pile spinach over chops.

5. Top with the crisp croutons. Cover casserole and bake twenty to twenty-five minutes.

Yield: Four servings.

Roast Veal with Plums   *New York*

1 three-and-one-half-pound rolled boned leg
    of veal, tied (reserve bones)
    Salt and freshly ground black pepper to
    taste
1 clove garlic, crushed
4 slices lean bacon
1 one-pound can dark plums in heavy syrup
1 onion, sliced
2 carrots, quartered
2 ribs celery, quartered
1 bunch fresh dill weed, pulled into small
    twigs
1 cup Rhine wine.

1. Preheat the oven to 400 degrees.

2. Season the roast with salt and pepper and rub with the garlic. Lay the bacon over the top and secure with string. Place the roast, seam side up, in a shallow roasting pan.

3. Drain the plums, reserving the syrup. Place the plums, veal bones, onion, carrots, celery and dill around the roast.

4. Combine the plum syrup and wine. Roast the meat, uncovered, thirty minutes, basting frequently with the plum-wine syrup.

5. Turn the meat, seam side down, and continue roasting and basting well about two hours longer, covering with an aluminum foil tent if roast begins to brown too much.

6. Remove the roast to a warm platter. Strain the juices. Pass the vegetables and plums through a sieve or food mill and add to the strained juices. Heat, season with salt and pepper and serve with roast.

Yield: Four to six servings.

Shoulder Veal Roast   *New Jersey*

1 three-pound rolled shoulder of veal
3 cloves garlic, finely chopped
4 tablespoons butter
1 tablespoon paprika
2 teaspoons rosemary, crushed
    Salt
2 tablespoons chopped shallots
1 bay leaf
1¼ cups chicken broth, approximately
1 tablespoon flour
2 tomatoes, peeled, seeded and chopped
1 green pepper, cored, seeded and diced
    Freshly ground black pepper
⅓ cup sour cream.

1. Preheat the oven to 375 degrees.

2. With a sharp knife, make one-half-inch-deep incisions over the top of the roast.

3. Blend the garlic, two tablespoons of the butter, the paprika, rosemary and one-half teaspoon salt into a paste with a pestle and mortar. With

the tip of a knife, push paste down into the incisions in the roast. Smear the remainder over the top and sides of the roast.

4. Melt the remaining butter in a roasting pan and place the veal roast in it. Sprinkle with the shallots and add the bay leaf and one and one-quarter cups of the broth.

5. Roast, uncovered, about one and one-half to two hours, basting at least four times, until meat is tender.

6. Transfer the meat to a warm serving dish and carve into one-quarter-inch slices.

7. Reduce the oven temperature to 300 degrees.

8. Strain the cooking liquid and remove surface fat. Measure liquid and make up to one and one-quarter cups with more broth, or water, that has been mixed with the flour.

9. Transfer to a saucepan and bring to a boil, stirring. Add the tomatoes, green pepper and salt and pepper to taste. Simmer four minutes and spoon over the meat.

10. Spoon the sour cream in three bands across the meat and roast five minutes.

Yield: Six servings.

Note: This dish can be prepared ahead the day before or early in the day up to and including step 5. The roast should be reheated slowly in a covered casserole on top of the stove before continuing with steps 6 through 10.

Creamed Veal *Connecticut*

4 tablespoons butter
1 one-pound untrimmed veal steak, cut as for schnitzel
  Salt and freshly ground black pepper to taste
3 cups heavy cream
  Toast.

1. Heat two tablespoons of the butter in a skillet and add the veal steak. Sprinkle with salt and pepper and brown on both sides over high heat. Remove the skillet from the heat.

2. Trim the meat. Remove and discard the bone. Cut the meat into one-inch pieces.

3. Add the remaining butter to the skillet and cook the cubed veal once more until browned. Add the cream, partially cover and cook, stirring occasionally, thirty to forty minutes. Serve with toast.

Yield: Two servings.

Veal Lorraine *New York*

1 pound boneless veal cutlet, cut one-third-inch to one-half-inch thick
  Salt and freshly ground black pepper to taste
¼ cup butter
3 shallots, finely chopped
¼ pound mushrooms, sliced
1 thin slice baked ham, finely chopped
2 tablespoons finely chopped parsley
1 cup dry white wine
1 teaspoon lemon juice
½ cup fine buttered soft bread crumbs.

1. Preheat the oven to 350 degrees.

2. Cut the veal into strips about one-half-inch wide and season with salt and pepper.

3. Melt the butter in a heavy skillet and sauté the shallots in it until tender but not browned. Add the mushrooms, ham and parsley and cook, stirring occasionally, three minutes.

4. Add the veal strips and cook, stirring constantly, two minutes longer.

5. Add the wine and lemon juice. Bring to a boil, stirring, and simmer, covered, five minutes. Transfer to a shallow baking dish. Top with the bread crumbs and bake, uncovered, fifteen to twenty minutes, or until veal is tender.

Yield: Four servings.

Paprika Cream Schnitzel   *New York*

4 slices bacon
1½ pounds veal cutlet, one-half-inch thick and cut into serving pieces
2 tablespoons chopped onion
1 teaspoon sweet Hungarian paprika
Salt to taste
1 cup sour cream
½ cup tomato sauce, preferably homemade.

1. Cook the bacon until crisp. Remove from skillet, crumble and reserve.
2. Brown the veal pieces on all sides in the bacon drippings. Add the onion and cook until lightly browned.
3. Season with the paprika and salt. Stir in the sour cream and tomato sauce. Cover and simmer, but do not boil, twenty minutes, or until the veal is tender. Serve topped with reserved bacon bits.
Yield: Four servings.

Veal Scallops with Cheese   *Connecticut*

2 eggs, lightly beaten
Salt and freshly ground black pepper to taste
6 veal scaloppine (about three-quarters pound), pounded lightly until thin
½ cup strained lemon juice
1 cup fine soft bread crumbs
3 tablespoons butter
3 tablespoons oil
12 wafer-thin slices lemon
6 thin slices Gruyère or Swiss cheese
1 cup half and half or heavy cream.

1. Preheat the oven to 400 degrees.
2. Season the eggs with salt and pepper. Dip the scaloppine into the eggs, then into the lemon juice and finally into the bread crumbs.
3. Heat the butter and oil in a heavy skillet, add the scaloppine and brown on one side only. Remove the scaloppine and place, cooked side down, in a single layer in a baking dish.

4. Cover each scallop with two lemon slices and one cheese slice. Sprinkle with salt and pepper. Pour the cream over all and bake ten to fifteen minutes, or until the cheese melts and cream bubbles slightly. Do not overcook.
Yield: Six servings.

Veal Rollatine   *New York*

6 veal scaloppine (about one and one-quarter pounds), lightly pounded
Salt and freshly ground black pepper to taste
5 tablespoons butter
¾ cup soft bread crumbs
1 clove garlic, finely minced
1 tablespoon freshly grated Parmesan cheese
¼ cup finely chopped parsley
Grated rind of one lemon
½ teaspoon chopped fresh thyme or one-quarter teaspoon dried thyme
½ teaspoon chopped fresh basil or one-quarter teaspoon dried basil
3 tablespoons heavy cream
1 tablespoon flour
1 cup fresh or canned chicken broth
1 tablespoon lemon juice.

1. Preheat the oven to 350 degrees.
2. Place the scaloppine on a flat surface and sprinkle with salt and pepper.
3. Melt two tablespoons of the butter. Combine with the bread crumbs, garlic, cheese, parsley, lemon rind, thyme, basil, cream, salt and pepper. Spread equal portions of this mixture on the veal slices. Roll each slice like a jellyroll and secure with toothpicks or string.
4. Melt remaining butter in a skillet, add veal rolls and brown on all sides. Transfer veal rolls to a casserole.
5. Sprinkle the flour over the fat remaining in the skillet and cook briefly. Add the broth and stir with a wooden spoon to dissolve the brown particles that cling to the bottom and sides of the skillet. Pour mixture over the veal and sprinkle

with salt and pepper. Add the lemon juice and bring to a boil. Cover and bake forty-five minutes.

Yield: Four to six servings.

Swiss Veal   *New York*

6 tablespoons butter
2 pounds veal scaloppine, cut into thin strips
1 tablespoon chopped shallots
½ cup dry white wine
1 cup heavy cream
⅓ teaspoon grated nutmeg
  Salt and freshly ground black pepper to taste
¼ cup brown sauce or canned beef gravy
2 tablespoons chopped parsley.

1. Heat the butter in a large skillet and add the veal. Cook, stirring just until all veal changes from pink to white. Using a slotted spoon, transfer veal to a warm dish and keep warm.

2. Add the shallots to skillet and cook briefly without browning. Add the wine and cook until it is almost totally reduced.

3. Return veal to skillet and add the cream, nutmeg, salt and pepper. Bring to a boil and simmer briefly. Stir in brown sauce or beef gravy and bring to a boil. Serve sprinkled with the chopped parsley.

Yield: Six servings.

Veal Shanks à la Grecque   *Massachusetts*

4 veal shanks
  Salt and freshly ground black pepper to taste
  Flour
½ cup olive oil
4 cups tomatoes, preferably Italian plum style
1 teaspoon oregano
1 clove garlic, finely minced
1 eggplant
4 cups fresh or canned chicken broth, approximately.

1. Preheat the oven to 450 degrees.

2. Wipe the veal shanks with a damp cloth and sprinkle them with salt and pepper. Dredge in flour.

3. Pour half the oil into a heavy casserole or Dutch oven large enough to hold the shanks. Add the shanks. Bake, basting frequently with the oil, about twenty minutes, or until meat is golden brown.

4. Pour off the fat from the casserole or Dutch oven and reduce the oven heat to 350 degrees.

5. Pour the tomatoes around the shanks and add the oregano, garlic and remaining oil. Return to the oven and continue baking and basting fifteen minutes.

6. Pare off the ends of the eggplant, but leave the skin on. Cut the eggplant into cubes and scatter these around the meat. Add one cup of the broth and continue baking and basting. Add more broth as the original broth boils away and continue baking and basting. The total cooking time for this dish is about one and one-half to two hours, depending on the size and tenderness of the veal.

Yield: Four servings.

Jelled Veal   *New Hampshire*

4 veal shanks, split
1 veal knuckle bone, cracked
1 onion, sliced
2 carrots, sliced
2 ribs celery, diced
4 sprigs parsley
1 bay leaf
1 teaspoon salt
6 peppercorns, crushed
1 teaspoon chervil, if available
2 tablespoons chopped parsley
2 tablespoons chopped green pepper.

1. Place the shanks, knuckle bone, onion, carrots, celery, parsley sprigs, bay leaf, salt, peppercorns and chervil in a kettle. Add water almost to cover.

2. Bring to a boil and boil vigorously, skimming off scum, five minutes. Cover and simmer gently three hours, or until meat is very tender. Leave shanks in broth until cool enough to handle.

3. Remove and discard knuckle bone. Remove meat from shanks. Dice meat and place in a one and one-half-quart to two-quart bowl or ring mold. Add the chopped parsley and green pepper and toss.

4. Strain the cooking broth into a saucepan and reduce by boiling until liquid measures two cups. Pour over the meat mixture. Cool and chill until firm.

5. Unmold and serve as lunchon or buffet dish or as sandwich filling.

Yield: Six to eight servings.

Veal and Ham Picnic Loaf   *Connecticut*

3 pounds ground veal
2 teaspoons salt
½ teaspoon freshly ground black pepper
2 teaspoons dried sage
½ teaspoon ground allspice
2 eggs, lightly beaten
2 tablespoons cognac
1 pound baked ham, cut into
  one-quarter-inch cubes
3 hard-cooked eggs
24 anchovy-stuffed cherry tomatoes (page 174).

1. Preheat the oven to 350 degrees.
2. Mix together the veal, salt, pepper, sage, allspice, beaten eggs, cognac and ham. Pack half the mixture into a greased 9-by-5-by-3-inch loaf pan. Arrange the hard-cooked eggs down the middle.
3. Pack remaining meat mixture around and over the eggs. Place on a baking sheet (to catch drips) and bake one and one-half hours. Cool and then chill in the pan.
4. To unmold loaf, set in a bowl of warm water

for a moment or two; then turn out onto serving platter. Garnish the platter with tomatoes.
Yield: Ten servings

Veal-Sour Cream Meat Loaf
New Hampshire

1½ pounds ground veal
½ pound ground pork
2 tablespoons grated onion
2 carrots, finely grated or ground
½ teaspoon rubbed leaf sage or one teaspoon
  chopped fresh sage
1½ teaspoons salt
¼ teaspoon freshly ground black pepper
½ teaspoon grated lemon rind
½ cup sour cream.

1. Preheat the oven to 350 degrees.
2. Mix all ingredients together and pack into a 9-by-5-by-3-inch loaf pan. Bake one and one-half hours.
Yield: Six servings.

Manicotti with Veal and Ham   *New York*

½ pound ground veal
½ pound ground cooked ham
1 tablespoon finely chopped onion
3 tablespoons olive oil
½ teaspoon salt
¼ teaspoon freshly ground black pepper
¼ teaspoon rosemary
⅛ teaspoon nutmeg
1 egg, lightly beaten
2 tablespoons Marsala wine
1 cup soft bread crumbs
1 cup freshly grated Parmesan cheese
8 four-inch pieces manicotti
6 quarts boiling salted water
3 to four cups tomato sauce, preferably
  homemade marinara style.

1. Preheat the oven to 375 degrees.

2. Sauté the veal, ham and onion in one table-spoon of the oil until lightly browned.

3. In a bowl, combine the meat mixture, salt, pepper, rosemary, nutmeg, egg, Marsala, bread crumbs and two tablespoons of the cheese.

4. Cook the manicotti in the boiling salted water until half done, about twelve minutes. Drain and rinse in cold water. Add remaining oil.

5. Cover the bottom of a shallow baking dish with half the sauce. Fill the manicotti with the meat mixture and arrange in a single layer on top of the sauce.

6. Cover with remaining sauce, sprinkle with remaining cheese and bake about thirty minutes, or until tender and bubbly hot.

Yield: Four servings.

Oxtail Stew   *New York*

4 oxtails, skinned and cut into sections
¼ cup oil
¼ cup butter
2 cups finely chopped celery
¼ cup finely chopped parsley
2 cloves garlic, finely minced
1 bay leaf
2 carrots, chopped
2 tablespoons flour
1 cup fresh or canned beef broth
1 cup dry red wine
3 tablespoons cognac
1 pound ripe tomatoes, peeled, seeded and chopped, or one one-pound can Italian plum tomatoes, drained and chopped
Salt and freshly ground black pepper to taste
Juice of half a lemon
¼ teaspoon nutmeg
1 cup Madeira wine
Additional chopped parsley (optional)
Boiled potatoes or noodles.

1. Preheat the oven to 350 degrees.

2. In a large skillet, brown the oxtails well in the oil and butter.

3. Line a buttered casserole with the celery, parsley, garlic and bay leaf. Transfer the oxtails to the casserole.

4. Add the carrots to the skillet and cook, stirring, until lightly browned. Sprinkle with flour and, when it starts to brown, add a little broth. Stir to dissolve brown particles. Scrape this mixture into the casserole.

5. Add the remaining broth to the casserole. Add the red wine, cognac, tomatoes, salt and pepper. Cover and bake two and one-half to three hours. Transfer the oxtails to a hot serving dish.

6. Strain the gravy, but press as much of the cooked vegetable mixture as possible through the sieve. Bring strained liquid to a boil and add the lemon juice, nutmeg and Madeira. Simmer five minutes and pour the sauce over the oxtails. Serve sprinkled with additional chopped parsley if desired. Serve with boiled potatoes or noodles.

Yield: Eight servings.

Boston Tripe   *Massachusetts*

2 pounds honeycomb tripe
1 onion, studded with two whole cloves
2 sprigs fresh thyme or one-half teaspoon dried thyme
1 bay leaf
1 carrot, quartered
Salt to taste
12 peppercorns
Freshly ground black pepper to taste
1½ tablespoons prepared mustard, preferably Dijon or Düsseldorf
3 tablespoons peanut oil or vegetable oil
1 teaspoon Worcestershire sauce
1 tablespoon wine vinegar
¼ teaspoon Tabasco sauce
2 cups soft bread crumbs.

1. Cut the tripe into large squares measuring about 4 by 4 inches.

2. Place the tripe in a kettle and add water to reach about one inch above the top of the tripe. Add the onion, thyme, bay leaf, carrot, salt and

peppercorns. Bring to a boil and simmer until the tripe is thoroughly tender, two to three hours. Drain tripe. When cool enough to handle, pat dry with paper towels.

3. Preheat the oven to 425 degrees.

4. Sprinkle the tripe with salt and pepper.

5. Combine the mustard, oil, Worcestershire, vinegar and Tabasco. Dip the tripe, piece by piece, into the mixture; then dip each piece into the bread crumbs until thoroughly coated.

6. Generously oil a baking pan and arrange the tripe pieces in it. Bake thirty to forty-five minutes, or until crumbs are crisp and well browned. Serve with Dijon or Düsseldorf mustard on the side.

Yield: Four to six servings.

Baked Chicken   *Delaware*

1 one-pound loaf firm white bread
¾ cup freshly grated Parmesan cheese
¼ cup finely chopped parsley
1 clove garlic, chopped
2 teaspoons salt
   Freshly ground black pepper (use a generous amount)
1 four-pound chicken, cut into serving pieces
½ cup melted butter.

1. Preheat the oven to 350 degrees.

2. Trim the crusts from the bread and grate it by hand or cut into cubes and blend a handful at a time in an electric blender.

3. Combine the crumbs, cheese, parsley, garlic, salt and pepper.

4. Dip each chicken piece into the butter and then into crumb mixture. Arrange the chicken pieces, so they do not touch each other, on a large baking pan. Pour a little of the remaining butter over the chicken and bake one hour, or until fork-tender.

Yield: Six servings.

Pennsylvania Chicken Pot Pie

1 five-pound chicken, cut into serving pieces
   Water
   Salt
12 peppercorns
2 ribs celery, chopped
2 carrots, quartered
1 onion
2 cups flour
4 egg yolks
4 to six tablespoons hot water.

1. Place the chicken in a kettle. Add water to cover, salt to taste, the peppercorns, celery, carrots and onion. Simmer until chicken is thoroughly tender, about one and one-quarter hours.

2. Strain the broth and pour it into a clean kettle. Simmer while preparing the remaining ingredients.

3. Remove the chicken from the bones. Discard the bones and skin. Cut the chicken into bite-size pieces.

4. Sift the flour and one-half teaspoon salt together onto a board. Make a well in the center and put the egg yolks in it. Gradually work the egg yolks into the flour until a stiff dough is formed, adding the hot water as necessary. Knead until smooth, about five minutes.

5. Cut the dough in half and roll each half until paper thin. Cut the dough into noodles about one-inch wide.

6. Add the chicken to the simmering broth and add the noodles, a few at a time. Continue boiling until noodles are done, about five minutes.

Yield: Eight to one dozen servings.

Chicken Livers with Sage   *Delaware*

1 pound chicken livers
¼ cup butter
   Salt and freshly ground black pepper to taste
1 teaspoon rubbed sage

2 wafer-thin slices ham, preferably prosciutto
8 ounces noodles, cooked, drained and buttered
¼ cup Madeira wine or Marsala wine.

1. Pick over the livers and cut each in half.

2. Melt the butter and add the livers. Sprinkle with salt, pepper and the sage. Cook, stirring gently, until livers are cooked on all sides. Do not overcook.

3. Add the ham and toss until heated through.

4. Place the buttered noodles on a hot serving dish and pour the livers into the center.

5. Add the wine to the skillet in which livers cooked. Simmer, stirring with a wooden spoon to scrape up brown particles that cling to bottom and sides of skillet. When wine is slightly reduced, pour it over livers and serve immediately.

Yield: Four servings.

Eggplant and Chicken Liver Casserole
Pennsylvania

2 medium-size eggplants
  Boiling salted water
5 tablespoons butter
½ pound chicken livers
  Salt and freshly ground black pepper to taste
½ pound mushrooms, thinly sliced
2 eggs, lightly beaten
¼ cup finely chopped parsley
½ cup heavy cream
¼ teaspoon freshly grated nutmeg, or to taste
  Cayenne pepper to taste
¾ cup soft bread crumbs
½ cup freshly grated Parmesan cheese.

1. Trim off and discard the ends of the eggplants. Cut the eggplants into one-inch cubes. Barely cover with boiling salted water and simmer until tender, about ten minutes. Drain in a colander. Empty the eggplant into a mixing bowl and mash with a fork.

2. Preheat the oven to 350 degrees.

3. Heat two tablespoons of the butter in a skillet. Add the chicken livers and sprinkle with salt and pepper. Cook livers until brown on all sides; then chop livers in the skillet. Add them to the eggplant.

4. Heat two tablespoons of the remaining butter in the same skillet. Add the mushrooms, sprinkle with salt and pepper and cook until mushrooms are wilted. Add them to the eggplant mixture.

5. Stir in the eggs, beating thoroughly. Add the parsley, cream, nutmeg, cayenne and all but two tablespoons of the bread crumbs. Add all but two tablespoons of the cheese. Mix well and pour the mixture into a one-quart casserole.

6. Sprinkle with the remaining bread crumbs and cheese and dot with the remaining butter. Bake twenty-five to thirty minutes.

Yield: Six to eight servings.

Elegant Chicken Pie
Massachusetts

1 three-pound chicken, trussed (reserve giblets)
  Salt and freshly ground black pepper
¼ teaspoon nutmeg
¼ teaspoon cloves
¼ teaspoon cinnamon
6 tablespoons butter
1 carrot, sliced
2 small white onions
1 pair sweetbreads
  Salted water
½ cup diced cooked ham
¼ pound mushrooms, sliced
  Juice of half a lemon
3 tablespoons cognac
3 tablespoons port wine
2 cups heavy cream
1 tablespoon foie gras
  Rich pie pastry for one 10-inch crust.

1. Preheat the oven to 450 degrees.

2. Sprinkle the chicken inside and outside with

salt and pepper. Add the nutmeg, cloves and cinnamon to the inside of the chicken.

3. Heat half of the butter in a large open ovenproof skillet. Add the chicken and turn to coat on all sides in the butter. Let the chicken rest on one side. Add the giblets, carrot and onions and roast fifteen minutes, basting often with a large spoon. Turn chicken to the other side and roast fifteen minutes, basting. Turn chicken on its back and continue roasting and basting about thirty minutes, or until done. Leave chicken in the skillet while completing the dish.

4. Meanwhile, soak the sweetbreads one hour and drain. Place sweetbreads in a saucepan and add salted water to cover. Bring to a boil. Simmer five minutes and drain. Rinse under cold running water. Trim or pare away the skin and tubes of the sweetbreads. Slice the sweetbreads.

5. Heat remaining butter in another skillet and add sweetbread slices. Cook, turning occasionally, about two minutes. Add the ham, mushrooms and lemon juice. Cook, stirring gently once in a while, about five minutes.

6. Cut chicken into serving pieces and place in the bottom of a deep baking dish. Add the cognac and port wine to the juices in the skillet in which chicken cooked. Bring to a boil and stir to dissolve. Add salt to taste and all but two tablespoons of cream. Strain this into a saucepan and add sweetbread mixture. Simmer three to four minutes.

7. Blend remaining cream with the foie gras and add to the saucepan. Pour this sauce over chicken and cover the dish with rolled-out pastry. Bake fifteen minutes, or until the crust is a rich golden brown.

Yield: Six servings.

Hancock Shaker Village's Sister Clymena's Chicken Pie   *Massachusetts*

2 three-pound chickens, quartered
2 cups water
3 eggs, well beaten
2 cups heavy cream

½ small onion, minced
4 sprigs parsley, minced
4 sprigs chervil, minced
  Salt and freshly ground black pepper to taste
  Pastry for a deep two-crust ten-inch pie.

1. Place the chickens in a kettle and add the water. Cover, bring to a boil and simmer thirty minutes. Remove meat from bones, but leave in large pieces. Discard bones and skin. Reserve chicken liquid. Place chicken meat in a bowl.

2. Preheat the oven to 425 degrees.

3. Combine the eggs and cream. Add the onion, parsley, chervil, salt and pepper. Add enough hot chicken liquid to cream and egg mixture to cover chicken pieces. Combine chicken and sauce.

4. Butter a deep ten-inch pie dish well and line bottom and sides with rolled-out pastry. Fill with chicken mixture and cover with top crust, cutting small vents for steam. Bake one-half hour.

Yield: Four to six servings

Parsley-Stuffed Chickens   *Delaware*

2 two-pound chickens
1 lemon, cut in half
  Salt and freshly ground black pepper to taste
1 cup plus one tablespoon butter
2 cups finely chopped onions
  Juice of half a lemon
2 cups chopped parsley
1 cup hot chicken broth, approximately.

1. Rub the chickens inside and outside with the lemon halves, salt and pepper.

2. Heat one tablespoon of the butter, add the onions and cook until wilted. Sprinkle with salt, pepper and the lemon juice. Stir in the parsley and one-half cup of the remaining butter. Use this mixture to stuff the chickens.

3. Melt the remaining butter in a large pot or Dutch oven. Add the chickens and brown on all

sides, turning with a wooden spoon so as not to tear the skin. Reduce heat and add one-quarter cup of the hot broth.

4. Cover pot with aluminum foil; then partly cover with a lid. Cook chickens slowly until done, basting occasionally and add remaining broth as necessary, about forty minutes.

5. Before serving, run the chickens under the broiler to crisp the surface. Strain the broth and serve separately.

Yield: Four to six servings.

Chicken with Eggplant   *New Jersey*

2 medium-size eggplants, approximately
  Boiling water
½ pound skinned boneless breast of chicken
1 tablespoon cornstarch
2 tablespoons soy sauce
1 tablespoon dry sherry
2 fresh hot green peppers, or to taste, or
  dried red pepper flakes to taste
¼ cup peanut oil
1 small clove garlic, finely minced
1 tablespoon freshly grated ginger
½ cup fresh or canned chicken broth.

1. Peel the eggplants and, using a sharp knife, slice them into one-quarter-inch rounds. Slice each round into very thin, matchlike strips. There should be about four cups of thin strips. Pour boiling water over eggplant strips and let stand five minutes. Drain well in a colander.

2. Cut the chicken into thin slices; then cut each slice into thin, matchlike strips. Place the chicken strips in a mixing bowl and add the cornstarch, soy sauce and sherry.

3. Split the peppers in half and discard the seeds and stem of each. Cut the peppers into thin shreds.

4. Heat the oil, add the peppers and cook until they start to color. With a slotted spoon, remove the peppers and reserve. Add the chicken to the oil and cook, stirring briskly, until the flesh turns white. Add the eggplant strips, garlic, ginger,

chicken broth and reserved peppers. Cook just until the mixture boils and is slightly thickened.

Yield: Six servings.

Chicken Paprika   *Delaware*

2 tablespoons shortening or butter
2 medium-size onions, finely chopped
2 teaspoons salt, or more to taste
1 to two tablespoons Hungarian sweet
  paprika (the quantity used will depend on
  the strength of the spice)
4 whole chicken breasts, halved
2 cups chicken broth or water
2 teaspoons flour
2 cups sour cream
  Cooked rice.

1. Heat the shortening or butter in a heavy pot and cook the onions in it until golden. Sprinkle with the salt and paprika and add the chicken. Cook briefly, turning; then add the broth or water. Cover and simmer until tender, about forty-five minutes.

2. Take the chicken from the pot and, when cool enough to handle, carefully remove and discard skin and bones. Combine the flour and sour cream and stir mixture into the drippings in the pot. Stir rapidly with a wire whisk. Put the sauce through a sieve and add the chicken. Heat thoroughly just to the boiling point, but do not boil. Serve immediately, with rice.

Yield: Four or more servings.

Chicken and Zucchini   *Delaware*

2 tablespoons oil
1 large whole chicken breast, skinned, boned
  and cut into one-inch pieces
3 to four zucchini, cut into one-quarter-inch
  slices
1 onion, chopped
1 small clove garlic, finely minced
1 small bay leaf

1 rib celery with leaves, chopped
1 large potato, peeled and cut into six wedges
¾ cup chicken broth
½ teaspoon salt
⅛ teaspoon freshly ground black pepper
1 cup sliced mushrooms
1 tablespoon lemon juice
2 tablespoons finely chopped parsley.

1. Heat the oil in a heavy skillet. Add the chicken pieces and cook quickly on all sides until the chicken turns white.

2. Add two of the zucchini, the onion, garlic, bay leaf, celery, potato, one-half cup of the broth, the salt and pepper. Stir and cook fifteen minutes, but with a slotted spoon, remove the potato wedges as soon as they are done.

3. Add the remaining broth. If the potatoes have not already been removed, remove them with a slotted spoon. Pile potato wedges in the middle of a warm serving dish.

4. Push the chicken pieces to one side of the skillet and gently mash the vegetables in skillet into the liquid. Add the remaining zucchini and the mushrooms. Cook, stirring, four to five minutes. The zucchini just added should remain crisp-tender and green.

5. Stir in the lemon juice and arrange the mixture around the mound of potatoes. Sprinkle potatoes with the parsley.

Yield: Two servings.

Cold Chicken Breasts   *New Jersey*

3 whole chicken breasts, halved
1 carrot, diced
1 rib celery, diced
  Salt
10 peppercorns
1 bay leaf
3 sprigs parsley
1 onion, chopped
½ teaspoon thyme
  Freshly ground black pepper

2 egg yolks
1 tablespoon tarragon vinegar
1 tablespoon lemon juice
¼ teaspoon dry mustard
  Cayenne pepper
½ cup olive oil
½ cup vegetable oil
1 envelope unflavored gelatin
¼ cup heavy cream, approximately
  Ripe olives or truffles
  Pimentos
  Green leek leaves
4 tomatoes, peeled and sliced
1 red onion, sliced and separated into rings
⅓ cup French dressing
  Water cress.

1. Day before, place the chicken breasts in a large skillet with the carrot, celery, one teaspoon salt, the peppercorns, bay leaf, parsley, onion and thyme. Add water to three-quarters cover the breasts.

2. Bring to a boil, cover and simmer very gently ten to fifteen minutes, or until chicken is tender. Chill overnight, still in the broth.

3. Next day, remove skin and bones from breasts, but keep meat in whole pieces. Season with salt and pepper.

4. Place the egg yolks, vinegar, lemon juice, mustard and salt and cayenne to taste in an electric blender with one-quarter cup of the olive oil. Blend at high speed, gradually adding remaining olive oil and the vegetable oil in a continuous stream.

5. Soak the gelatin in one-quarter cup water and dissolve while stirring over gentle heat. Add gelatin to mayonnaise in blender and continue blending while adding enough cream to give a spreading consistency.

6. With a spatula or spoon, coat chicken pieces with mayonnaise and decorate immediately with olives or truffles, pimentoes and leek greens. Chill.

7. Combine the tomatoes and onion rings. Pour the dressing over and chill.

8. To serve, place tomato mixture on a platter

and top with chicken breasts. Garnish with water cress.

Yield: Six servings.

Crab-Stuffed Chicken   *Delaware*

Chicken:
¼ cup plus two tablespoons butter
1 teaspoon salt
¼ teaspoon freshly ground black pepper
2 teaspoons Hungarian sweet paprika
2 two-and-one-half-pound to three-pound chickens, split
½ pound mushrooms, sliced
¼ cup dry sherry
¼ cup catchup
1 tablespoon chopped parsley.

Stuffing:
3 slices stale white bread, cut into very small cubes
5 tablespoons heavy cream
12 ounces crab meat, picked over to remove bits of shell and cartilage
¼ cup melted butter
⅛ teaspoon cayenne pepper
1 teaspoon salt
1 teaspoon prepared mustard
½ teaspoon thyme
¼ teaspoon marjoram
¼ teaspoon sage.

1. Preheat the oven to 350 degrees.
2. To prepare chicken, mix two tablespoons of the butter with the salt, pepper and paprika. Rub the chicken pieces with the mixture and place, skin side up, wings tucked under, in a single layer in a baking dish. Bake thirty-five minutes.
3. Heat remaining butter and sauté the mushrooms in it. Add the sherry, catchup and parsley. Spoon one tablespoon butter mixture over each chicken half and bake ten minutes longer.
4. Meanwhile, to prepare stuffing, combine the ingredients in a bowl.
5. Turn chicken pieces over and stuff with crab

stuffing. Spoon remaining butter-mushroom mixture over all and bake thirty minutes longer, or until chicken is tender.

Yield: Four servings.

Turkey and Oysters in Patty Shells
Massachusetts

3 tablespoons butter
1 tablespoon chopped shallots
½ pound mushrooms, sliced
3 tablespoons flour
½ cup dry white wine
1½ cups light cream
   Salt and freshly ground black pepper to taste
¼ teaspoon nutmeg
½ teaspoon thyme
2 to three cups diced cooked white turkey meat
1 cup cooked or thawed frozen peas
2 teaspoons lemon juice
2 egg yolks
1 cup heavy cream
2 pimentos, diced
2 cups oysters with their liquor
6 to eight homemade or purchased patty shells, warmed.

1. Melt the butter in a large skillet and sauté the shallots in it until tender. Add the mushrooms and cook two minutes.
2. Sprinkle with the flour and stir. Cook one minute.
3. Stir in the wine and light cream and bring to a boil, stirring. Season with salt, pepper, the nutmeg and thyme. Cook two minutes.
4. Add the turkey, peas and lemon juice and reheat. Beat the egg yolks with the heavy cream, add a little of the hot sauce and return all to the pan. Heat, stirring, until mixture thickens a little, but do not boil.
5. Add the pimentos and oysters and maintain low heat without boiling until the edges of the

oysters just curl, about three minutes. Test the seasoning. Spoon into and over the patty shells.
Yield: Six to eight servings.

Roast Goose   *New York*

1 seven-pound to nine-pound goose (reserve giblets)
  Salt and freshly ground black pepper to taste
1 recipe oyster stuffing (page 162) or fruit stuffing (page 162)
1 onion
1 bay leaf
1 rib celery with leaves
3 tablespoons flour
  Gravy coloring and flavoring (optional)
  Crab apples or orange slices.

1. Preheat the oven to 450 degrees.
2. Wash and clean the goose inside and outside. Wipe dry. Burn off any hairs that remain. Season the cavity with salt and pepper.
3. Using the desired stuffing, stuff the cavity three-quarters full. Put any leftover stuffing under the neck skin. Truss the bird and place on a rack in a shallow roasting pan. Roast ten minutes.
4. Reduce the oven heat to 325 degrees and continue to roast twenty to twenty-five minutes a pound, removing fat as it accumulates.
5. Meanwhile, wash the gizzard, neck and heart (the liver goes into the stuffing or is sautéed and seasoned as a delicacy) and place in a saucepan with the onion, bay leaf, celery, salt, pepper and water to cover. Bring to a boil and simmer several hours.
6. Strain liquid. If desired, chop some of giblet meat.
7. Transfer the cooked goose to a warm platter. Pour off all but three tablespoons goose fat from the roasting pan. Sprinkle fat in pan with the flour. Cook, stirring, two minutes. Stir in three to four cups strained liquid and the chopped giblet meat. Cook, stirring, until gravy thickens. Season with salt and pepper and add gravy coloring and flavoring (Kitchen Bouquet) if desired.

8. Garnish goose platter with crab apples or orange slices. Serve gravy separately.
Yield: Six servings.

Pheasant Cacciatore   *Connecticut*

1 brace of pheasant, plucked, cleaned and tail feathers reserved
1 tablespoon juniper berries
2 tablespoons salt
1 teaspoon cayenne pepper
2 teaspoons chopped chives
1 tablespoon chopped fresh rosemary or one teaspoon dried rosemary
2 tablespoons chopped fresh parsley
1 teaspoon olive oil
4 thick slices bacon
  Cognac
  Game sauce (page 158)
  Bulghur or wild rice.

1. Preheat the oven to 450 degrees.
2. Wash out the body cavity of the birds (discard liver, heart, etc. if birds have been hung) and dry with paper towels.
3. If juniper berries are soft, chop on a board; if they are dry, pound well in a mortar. Combine berries with the salt, cayenne, chives, rosemary and parsley.
4. Divide two-thirds of the mixture between the two body cavities and shake the birds to coat the walls. Place the birds, breast side up, in a roasting pan lined with oiled aluminum foil.
5. Pat the oil over the surface of the birds and then sprinkle remaining herb-spice mixture over all the surface. Cover the birds with the bacon slices, securing with toothpicks if necessary.
6. Roast twenty minutes. Reduce oven heat to 325 degrees and roast about one hour longer, or until birds are done.
7. Place pheasants on a warm platter. Sprinkle a little cognac over the birds and decorate with the reserved tail feathers. Serve game sauce and bulghur or wild rice separately.
Yield: Four servings.

Venison Supreme

New York

2 cups flour
2 eggs, beaten
½ teaspoon salt
½ cup water
6 thick slices bacon
1 two-inch-thick cut, boned top round
   venison, beaten well with a mallet to
   tenderize
   Currant jelly.

1. Combine the flour, eggs, salt and water to make a paste.

2. Preheat the oven to 425 degrees.

3. Roll out flour mixture until thin. Cover with the bacon slices.

4. Place the venison on top of bacon. Moisten edges of flour mixture, draw around meat and pinch to seal. Wrap in heavy-duty aluminum foil, set on a baking sheet and bake fifty minutes a pound.

5. Fifteen minutes before meat is due to be done, open up the foil, increase oven heat to 450 degrees and bake to brown. Serve with currant jelly.

Yield: About eight servings.

Vegetables, Main Dish Accompaniments and Salads

Baked Asparagus with Cheese Sauce
New Jersey

2 pounds asparagus
  Boiling salted water
6 hard-cooked eggs, sliced
2 tablespoons butter
2 tablespoons flour
1½ cups milk
½ teaspoon salt
⅛ teaspoon cayenne pepper
½ cup grated sharp Cheddar cheese
½ cup buttered soft bread crumbs.

1. Break the asparagus spears at the point where white or tough part starts and wash very well. Boil in the salted water in an asparagus cooker, with the stem bottoms in the water and tips steaming, or boil quickly, flat, in a covered skillet until barely tender.

2. Drain asparagus and arrange in a greased shallow baking dish. Top with the egg slices.

3. Preheat the oven to 350 degrees.

4. Melt the butter, blend in the flour, gradually stir in the milk and bring to a boil, stirring. Cook two minutes. Add the salt, cayenne and cheese and stir just to melt cheese. Pour over eggs and asparagus.

5. Sprinkle with the bread crumbs. Bake twenty minutes.

Yield: Six servings.

Sister Josephine's Shaker Baked Beans
Massachusetts

4 cups dried pea beans or navy beans
1 onion
½ cup unsulphured molasses
½ cup butter
1 teaspoon salt
2 teaspoons dry mustard
½ cup catchup.

1. Day before, pick over and wash beans. Cover beans with water and soak overnight. Next day, drain beans and add two and one-half cups hot water. Cook until tender, about forty-five minutes.

2. Preheat the oven to 325 degrees.

3. Place the onion in bottom of a well-buttered bean pot. Drain beans and save the liquid. Pour beans into bean pot.

4. Add the remaining ingredients to the reserved bean liquid and pour over beans to cover. Cover pot and cook two and one-half hours, adding more liquid whenever necessary. Remove cover and bake one-half hour longer to brown well.

Yield: Ten to one dozen servings.

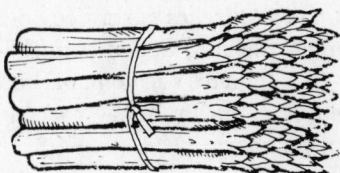

Home-Baked Beans *Maine*

> 2 pounds dried pea beans or navy beans
> Water
> ¾ pound salt pork
> 1 onion
> ⅔ cup unsulphured molasses
> 1 teaspoon dry mustard
> 1½ teaspoons salt
> Boiling water.

1. Day before, pick over the beans and wash well. Place in a bowl and cover with cold water so that water extends two inches above the beans. Soak overnight. Next morning, put beans and soaking water in a heavy pot.
2. Make one-half-inch deep cuts through the rind of the salt pork at one-half-inch intervals. Add to beans. Bring to a boil and simmer them until the skin cracks when a bean is held in the hand and blown on, about one hour.
3. Preheat the oven to 250 degrees.
4. Place the onion in the bottom of a bean pot or heavy three-quart casserole. Add the beans. Cube the salt pork and add.
5. Stir in the remaining ingredients, including enough boiling water to cover beans. Bake, uncovered, six to eight hours, stirring occasionally and adding more boiling water whenever necessary so that the beans are always just submerged.

Yield: Ten to one dozen servings.

Note: Beans and ham, most likely served with steamed brown bread (page 98) in Maine and Massachusetts and with johnnycakes (page 96) in Rhode Island, are a New England tradition on Saturday night. And there is never any problem with leftovers. Warmed-over beans are served for Sunday morning breakfast, and on Monday lunch-toting workers and children expect cold bean sandwiches garnished with crisp marinated onion rings for added texture and flavor.

To prepare Vermont baked beans, substitute maple syrup or honey for the molasses in the recipe above.

Baked Beans I *Massachusetts*

> 1 pound dried pea beans or navy beans
> 1 bay leaf
> 1 celery rib, halved
> 3 sprigs parsley
> 1 sprig fresh thyme or one-half teaspoon dried thyme
> ½ pound salt pork
> ⅔ cup unsulphured molasses
> ¼ cup brown sugar
> 2 teaspoons dry mustard
> 2 teaspoons salt
> ¼ teaspoon freshly ground black pepper
> 1 medium-size onion, coarsely chopped
> 1 cup sherry.

1. Soak the beans overnight in cold water to cover.
2. Next day, drain beans; then cover with fresh water. Tie the bay leaf, celery, parsley and thyme in a bundle. Add to the kettle. Bring to a boil and simmer slowly until bean skins blow off when blown upon lightly, thirty to sixty minutes.
3. Drain beans, reserving two quarts of the cooking liquid. Slice the salt pork into one-quarter-inch slices. Arrange the beans and half the sliced pork in alternate layers in a two-quart bean pot or casserole. Score the remaining pork and place in the center of the top layer of beans.
4. Preheat the oven to 300 degrees.
5. Combine the molasses, brown sugar, mustard, salt, pepper, onion and reserved cooking liquid. Pour over the beans. Bake, covered, six to eight hours. One hour before beans are to be done, pour the sherry over them. Replace the cover and bake one hour longer.

Yield: Six to eight servings.

Baked Beans II *Massachusetts*

> ½ pound salt pork, cut into squares
> 1 pound dried white Michigan or pea beans
> ½ cup brown sugar
> ½ cup unsulphured molasses

1 teaspoon dry mustard
1 teaspoon salt
1 onion, studded with two whole cloves.

1. Day before, place the salt pork and beans in a large mixing bowl and add water to cover to the depth of one inch. Let stand overnight.

2. Next day, drain beans and pork and pour into a three-quart saucepan. Add the remaining ingredients and bring to a boil. Simmer, partially covered, one hour.

3. Preheat the oven to 350 degrees.

4. Discard the onion and pour the beans into an earthenware crock or bean pot. Cover and bake two and one-half hours. Look at the beans occasionally and, if they are cooking too fast, reduce the oven heat. They should bubble nicely.

Yield: Six servings.

Pease Porridge Hot   *New Hampshire*

1 pound green split peas
1 teaspoon salt
1 onion, studded with two whole cloves
½ teaspoon marjoram
½ teaspoon tarragon
¼ teaspoon freshly ground black pepper
3 tablespoons butter.

1. Place the peas in a kettle and cover with water. Add the salt and onion, bring to a boil and simmer over low heat one hour, adding water as necessary.

2. Remove the cloves from the onion. Add the marjoram, tarragon and pepper and cook very slowly one hour longer, stirring occasionally to prevent sticking. The mixture should be very thick.

3. Put through a sieve, check the seasoning and dot with the butter.

Yield: Eight servings.

Samp 'n' Beans   *New York*

2 pounds dried pea beans or navy beans
1 pound salt pork, streaked lean and fat
1 onion, finely chopped
2 cans coarse pearl (or big) hominy
Salt and freshly ground black pepper to taste.

1. Cover the beans with cold water and soak overnight.

2. Next day, drain beans and place in a big kettle. Add fresh water to cover. Slice the salt pork almost all the way through so that the slices stay hinged together and add to beans.

3. Bring to a boil and simmer, covered, until the beans are tender, about forty minutes. Add the onion and hominy and simmer thirty to forty-five minutes longer. Season with salt and pepper.

Yield: About sixteen servings.

White Bean Salad   *New Jersey*

1 pound dried Great Northern beans
1 onion
2 teaspoons salt
4 ounces salt pork, sliced
⅓ cup wine vinegar
¾ cup olive oil
½ teaspoon freshly ground black pepper
1 clove garlic, crushed
1 tablespoon chopped chives
1 green pepper, cored, seeded and diced
1 small red onion, sliced and separated into rings
¼ cup finely chopped parsley
4 to six slices salami, diced
Boston lettuce cups.

1. Two days before, wash and pick over the beans. Cover with water and soak overnight. Next day, transfer to a kettle and add water, if necessary, just barely to cover the beans.

2. Bury the whole onion in the beans and add one teaspoon of the salt. Place the slices of salt

pork on the top. Bring to a boil and simmer, uncovered, until just tender, about forty-five to sixty minutes. Do not overcook or beans lose their identity.

3. Meanwhile, mix together the vinegar, oil, black pepper, garlic, chives and remaining salt.

4. Drain the beans of excess liquid. Remove and discard the salt pork and onion. Pour the oil dressing over the hot beans, cool and chill overnight.

5. Next day, add the green pepper, red onion, parsley and salami. Check the seasoning. Serve in lettuce cups.

Yield: About ten servings.

Bean Porridge   *Maine*

½ cup dried kidney beans
1 quart meat broth (from cooking corned beef is traditional)
1 tablespoon yellow corn meal
1 tablespoon flour
  Salt to taste
2 cups milk.

1. Day before, wash beans, cover with water and let soak overnight. Next morning, place beans and soaking water in saucepan and cook thirty minutes, or until beans start to become tender.

2. Drain off water. Add the broth to beans and cook until they are very tender. Mash slightly to thicken mixture.

3. Mix the corn meal and flour together and then make a paste with a little cold water. Stir into the bean mixture and boil until mixture thickens. Season with salt.

4. Add the milk and reheat.
Yield: Six servings.

Beets in Orange Sauce   *New York*

2 bunches beets
  Boiling water

1 tablespoon cider vinegar
¾ cup orange juice
3 tablespoons lemon juice
2 teaspoons grated orange rind
⅛ teaspoon ground allspice
1½ tablespoons cornstarch
1 tablespoon honey
2 tablespoons butter.

1. Scrub the beets and cut off the tops, leaving one inch attached. Place in a saucepan and add boiling water to cover. Add the vinegar and cook until tender, about twenty minutes.

2. Drain beets, reserving some liquid. Skin the beets, then slice or dice them and keep warm.

3. Strain enough reserved beet liquid to yield one-quarter cup. Combine with the orange juice, lemon juice, orange rind and allspice. Add the cornstarch slowly.

4. Bring to a boil, stirring, and cook until sauce thickens. Stir in the honey and butter and pour over the beets.

Yield: Four to six servings.

Sicilian Broccoli   *New York*

1 large bunch broccoli
  Salted water
2 tablespoons butter
1 tablespoon finely chopped shallots or scallions, including green part
1 clove garlic, finely minced
1½ tablespoons flour
1 cup fresh or canned chicken broth
4 anchovies, finely chopped
½ cup sliced ripe olives, preferably imported
  Freshly ground black pepper to taste
2 cups shredded mozzarella cheese or sharp Cheddar cheese.

1. Cook the broccoli in salted water until tender.

2. As the vegetable cooks, melt the butter in a saucepan and add the shallots and garlic. Cook, stirring, about three minutes. Do not brown.

3. Sprinkle with flour and add the broth, stirring vigorously with a wire whisk. When the mixture is thickened, simmer five minutes.

4. Add the anchovies, olives, pepper and cheese and stir until cheese melts.

5. Drain the broccoli. Pour the sauce over.

Yield: Four to six servings.

Broccoli and Onion Casserole   *Delaware*

    1 large bunch broccoli
      Salt
   18 small white onions
    3 tablespoons butter
    3 tablespoons flour
1½ cups milk
   ½ cup heavy cream
1½ cups grated sharp Cheddar cheese
      Freshly ground black pepper.

1. Preheat the oven to 350 degrees.

2. Trim off hard part of broccoli base and stand the broccoli, stem side down, in a saucepan large enough to hold broccoli while covered. Add water to the depth of one inch and sprinkle the broccoli with a little salt. Cover and cook until vegetable is crisp-tender.

3. Meanwhile, peel the onions and put them in a saucepan with salted water barely to cover. Cook, partly covered, until the onions are nearly tender. Drain.

4. While the vegetables are cooking, melt the butter in a saucepan and, with a wire whisk, stir in the flour. When blended and smooth, add the milk, stirring rapidly with the whisk. When the sauce is thickened and smooth, stir in the cream and simmer five minutes. Remove from the heat and stir in one cup of the cheese. Season to taste with salt and pepper.

5. Drain the broccoli and cut it into bite-size pieces. Arrange layers of broccoli and onions in a buttered casserole and pour the cheese sauce over all. Sprinkle with remaining cheese and bake one hour.

Yield: Four to six servings.

Golden Cabbage   *Connecticut*

    2 pounds white or green cabbage
    2 quarts water
    1 tablespoon sugar
1½ tablespoons plus one teaspoon salt
    2 cups milk
   ¼ cup cornstarch
   ¼ cup butter
   ¼ pound Swiss cheese, grated.

1. Remove and discard the core from the cabbage. Shred or chop cabbage finely and combine it with the water, sugar and one and one-half tablespoons of the salt. Bring to a boil, cover and cook over low heat one hour. Remove cabbage and drain thoroughly in a colander.

2. Preheat the oven to 400 degrees.

3. Combine the milk, cornstarch, butter and remaining salt. Bring to a boil over moderate heat, stirring. Combine with drained cabbage. Stir in all but four tablespoons grated cheese and blend well. Pour cabbage mixture into a buttered 7½-by 12-inch baking dish. Sprinkle with the remaining cheese and bake just until thoroughly heated. Run the dish briefly under the broiler and serve hot.

Yield: Six servings.

Pennsylvania Dutch Cabbage

    1 large head cabbage, coarsely shredded
   ½ cup cider vinegar
    2 tablespoons sugar
    3 tablespoons flour.

1. Place the cabbage in a large kettle. Combine the vinegar, sugar and one quart water and pour over the cabbage. Bring to a boil and boil vigorously, uncovered, twenty-five to thirty minutes.

2. Mix the flour with a little cold water and stir into the hot cabbage. Cook, stirring, until mixture thickens.

Yield: Eight servings.

Carrot Tzimmes
New York

10 to twelve medium-size carrots, diced
1 tablespoon chicken fat or kosher shortening
¼ teaspoon salt
1 teaspoon sugar
½ cup raisins
⅛ teaspoon ginger
3 tablespoons water.

1. Cook the carrots in the fat in a skillet for one minute, stirring constantly.
2. Add the remaining ingredients, bring to a boil and simmer, covered, until tender, about fifteen minutes. Evaporate any liquid remaining by boiling.
Yield: Six servings.

Candied Carrots for Passover
New York

3 tablespoons kosher shortening
4 cups sliced carrots
3 tablespoons orange juice
1½ teaspoons salt
¼ teaspoon cinnamon
4 tablespoons honey.

Combine all the ingredients in a saucepan, cover and cook, stirring occasionally, over low heat twenty-five minutes.
Yield: Six servings.

Corn Pudding
New Jersey

2 cups cooked whole kernel corn (one way to use leftover corn on the cob)
¼ cup chopped scallions, including green part
3 eggs, lightly beaten
2 tablespoons melted butter
2 cups milk, scalded
1½ teaspoons salt
¼ teaspoon freshly ground black pepper
½ cup finely chopped cooked ham (optional).

1. Preheat the oven to 325 degrees.
2. Combine all the ingredients and turn into a greased two-quart baking dish or casserole. Set in a pan with hot water extending halfway up the dish.
3. Bake one hour, replenishing the water if necessary.
Yield: Six servings.

Corn Pudding with Bacon
Rhode Island

6 slices bacon
2 cups freshly cut corn kernels
½ cup soft bread crumbs
½ green pepper, diced
1 onion, finely chopped
2 eggs, lightly beaten
2 cups milk
1 teaspoon salt
¼ teaspoon freshly ground black pepper
½ cup buttered soft bread crumbs.

1. Preheat the oven to 350 degrees.
2. Cook the bacon until crisp. Remove from skillet, crumble and combine with the corn and soft bread crumbs.
3. In the bacon drippings remaining in skillet, sauté the green pepper and onion until tender. Add to corn mixture.
4. Mix together the eggs, milk, salt and black pepper and pour over vegetable mixture. Turn into a buttered casserole, top with the buttered crumbs and bake about forty-five minutes, or until set.
Yield: Six servings.

Dandelion Stems
Vermont

12 to eighteen long dandelion stems with buds
Boiling salted water
3 hard-cooked eggs, halved
3 tablespoons olive oil
3 tablespoons lemon juice
½ clove garlic, finely chopped

Salt and freshly ground black pepper to taste.

1. Remove the dandelion buds and discard. Tie the stems in a bundle and cook in boiling salted water to cover in an uncovered skillet until tender, about ten minutes. Drain.

2. For each serving, wind two or three dandelion stems in a basket shape and place in small ramekin. Top with hard-cooked egg half.

3. Combine the remaining ingredients and drizzle over eggs and stems. Serve cold or warm. To warm, heat in 300-degree oven five minutes.

Yield: Six servings.

Sautéed Dandelion Flowers   *Vermont*

2 cups clean, freshly picked unsprayed
   dandelion flowers (see step 1)
½ cup butter
2 eggs, lightly beaten
   Flour
   Salt and freshly ground black pepper to
   taste.

1. Do not wash the flowers or they will close, so it is important that they are clean when picked.

2. Heat the butter in a skillet. Dip each blossom into eggs, then into flour, and sauté briefly in the butter.

3. Season with salt and pepper and serve as a vegetable or special side dish.

Yield: Six servings.

Veronica's Creamed Horseradish
New York

3 roots of fresh horseradish
3 cups milk
¼ cup butter
¼ cup flour
1 tablespoon sugar
1½ teaspoons salt.

1. Peel the roots and grate the horseradish on a very fine grater. There should be about two cups. Alternately, the horseradish can be grated in an electric blender in small quantities, using one cup of the milk to give the necessary liquid.

2. Melt the butter in a heavy skillet. Stir in the flour and cook, stirring, until lightly browned. Add the horseradish and cook three minutes longer, stirring constantly.

3. Stir in the sugar, salt and (remaining) milk and bring to a boil, stirring. Cover and simmer very slowly, stirring occasionally, or cook in a double boiler over boiling water, forty-five to sixty minutes, or until the horseradish is tender.

Yield: About three cups.

Note: During long cooking, the horseradish loses much of its pungency.

Serve with roast beef, ham or corned beef.

Braised Lettuce with Rosemary
New Jersey

¼ pound mushrooms, sliced
6 tablespoons butter
2 tablespoons flour
⅔ cup chicken broth
⅔ cup light cream
   Salt and freshly ground black pepper to
   taste
¼ teaspoon nutmeg
1 teaspoon fresh rosemary
1 tablespoon chopped parsley
2 tablespoons cognac
2 large or three small heads Boston lettuce
2 tablespoons chopped chives.

1. Sauté mushrooms briefly in four tablespoons butter. Sprinkle with flour. Gradually stir in the broth and cream and bring to a boil, stirring.

2. Season with salt, pepper, the nutmeg, rosemary, parsley and cognac. Hold over hot water.

3. Shred the lettuce into very wide ribbons and sauté very briefly in remaining butter. Do not overcook.

4. Toss lettuce with sauce, sprinkle with the chives and serve immediately.

Yield: Six servings.

Note: Braised lettuce goes well with poached or stuffed chicken breasts.

Wilted Lettuce   *Pennsylvania*

6 slices bacon, cubed
¼ cup cider vinegar
1 teaspoon brown sugar
½ teaspoon salt
⅛ teaspoon freshly ground black pepper
4 cups torn-up Boston lettuce.

1. Cook the bacon until crisp, remove bits and reserve. Remove and discard all but three tablespoons fat from the pan.

2. Add the vinegar, brown sugar, salt and pepper to pan. Bring to a boil and pour over lettuce. Add reserved bacon bits and toss.

Yield: Four servings.

Deep-Fried Mushrooms   *Pennsylvania*

32 medium-size white mushrooms
   Flour
   Salt and freshly ground black pepper to taste
2 eggs
1 teaspoon water
1 teaspoon peanut oil or vegetable oil
1½ cups soft bread crumbs
   Oil for deep-frying
   Tartar sauce (page 157).

1. Trim off the tips of the mushroom stems, but leave the stems on. Rinse the mushrooms under cold running water and drain. Do not dry.

2. Dredge the mushrooms in flour seasoned with salt and pepper.

3. Beat the eggs with the water and peanut or vegetable oil and place in a pie dish.

4. Toss or turn the mushrooms in the egg mix-ture until well coated. Coat the mushrooms on all sides with the bread crumbs. Let stand until ready to cook.

5. Heat oil in a large skillet and, when hot (375 degrees), add the mushrooms. Cook until golden brown all over. Drain on paper towels and serve hot with tartar sauce.

Yield: Four servings.

Mushrooms with Cream   *Pennsylvania*

¼ cup butter
½ pound medium-size mushrooms, sliced or quartered
   Salt and freshly ground black pepper to taste
1 teaspoon chopped fresh dill or one-half teaspoon dried dill
½ cup heavy cream.

1. Heat the butter in a skillet with a cover and, when butter is melted, add the mushrooms. Cover and cook over medium heat, stirring or shaking the pan, about one minute.

2. Add salt, pepper and the dill. Cover and cook five minutes. Add the cream and simmer, uncovered, until the sauce is thickened and reduced somewhat. Taste and correct the seasonings with more salt, pepper or dill if desired.

Yield: Four servings.

Stuffed Mushrooms   *Pennsylvania*

24 medium-size to large mushrooms
2 cloves garlic, finely chopped
8 tablespoons butter
1 cup soft bread crumbs
½ cup freshly grated Parmesan cheese
½ teaspoon salt
¼ teaspoon freshly ground black pepper
2 tablespoons chopped parsley.

1. Preheat the oven to 350 degrees.

2. Remove the stems from the mushrooms, re-

serving mushroom caps, and chop stems finely. Sauté with the garlic in four tablespoons of the butter.

3. Add the bread crumbs, cheese, salt, pepper and parsley.

4. Sauté the mushroom caps briefly in three tablespoons of the remaining butter.

5. Fill the caps with the stuffing and place in a buttered shallow casserole. Melt the remaining butter and drizzle over the mushrooms. Bake until very hot, about fifteen minutes.

Yield: Six to eight servings.

Stuffed Mushrooms with Anchovies
Pennsylvania

24 medium-size to large mushroom caps, or forty tiny caps
 4 tablespoons olive oil
 1 two-and-one-half-ounce can anchovy fillets
 1 clove garlic, finely chopped
 1 teaspoon lemon juice
 ¾ cup soft bread crumbs
 ¼ cup chopped parsley
   Freshly ground black pepper to taste.

1. Preheat the oven to 350 degrees.

2. Sauté the mushroom caps in three tablespoons of the oil two to three minutes.

3. Chop the anchovies with the garlic. Add the lemon juice, bread crumbs and parsley and mix. Season with pepper.

4. Fill the caps with the mixture, drizzle remaining oil over all and bake until hot, about fifteen minutes.

Yield: Six to eight servings.

Mushrooms with Fennel
Pennsylvania

 5 tablespoons butter
 1 small onion, finely chopped
 ½ cup fennel root, diced
 2 tablespoons chopped parsley
1½ pounds mushrooms, sliced

 2 tablespoons flour
 1 cup milk
 2 tablespoons chopped fennel leaves
   Salt and freshly ground black pepper to taste
 1 egg yolk
 2 tablespoons sour cream.

1. Melt four tablespoons of the butter. Sauté the onion and fennel root in the butter until wilted and tender but not browned. Add the parsley and mushrooms. Cook until mushrooms are tender and most of the liquid has evaporated, about five minutes.

2. Melt the remaining butter in a small pan and blend in the flour. Gradually stir in the milk, bring to a boil and simmer, stirring constantly, one minute. Add the fennel leaves and pour over the mushroom mixture. Stir.

3. Bring to a boil and season with salt and pepper. Blend together the egg yolk and sour cream and stir into the mushroom mixture. Reheat, but do not allow to boil.

Yield: Six servings.

Fried Onions and Apples
New Jersey

⅓ cup diced salt pork
 4 tart apples
 2 large onions, thinly sliced and separated into rings
¼ cup water, approximately.

1. Cook the salt pork in a heavy skillet until crisp. Remove bits and reserve.

2. Core the apples, leave skin on and slice into one-half-inch rings. Place in the fat remaining in the skillet. Scatter the onion rings over the apples. Cook five minutes. Add one-quarter cup water, cover and cook until apples and onions are tender, adding more water during cooking if necessary. Sprinkle with reserved pork bits.

Yield: Six servings.

Onion Sour Cream Pie   *New Jersey*

5 slices lean bacon
3 cups thin onion rings
1 cup sour cream
⅓ cup dry sherry
3 eggs, lightly beaten
½ teaspoon salt
¼ teaspoon freshly ground black pepper
⅛ teaspoon nutmeg
1 tablespoon freshly snipped dill weed
1 unbaked eight-inch to nine-inch pie shell.

1. Cook the bacon until crisp. Remove bacon, drain, crumble and reserve. Pour off all but four tablespoons of the bacon drippings.
2. Preheat the oven to 450 degrees.
3. Sauté the onions until golden in the bacon drippings in the skillet. Cool.
4. Combine the sour cream, sherry, eggs, salt, pepper, nutmeg and dill weed. Stir in onions and reserved bacon.
5. Bake the pie shell ten minutes, or until set. Reduce the oven heat to 350 degrees. Pour the sour cream mixture into the pie shell and bake twenty-five to thirty minutes, or until set.
Yield: Eight servings.

Leeks and Rice   *Connecticut*

2 or three leeks
Boiling water to cover
¼ cup butter
1 carrot, thinly sliced
1 cup uncooked rice
2 cups fresh or canned chicken broth, approximately
Salt and freshly ground black pepper to taste.

1. Trim the leeks and split them in half lengthwise. Rinse thoroughly under cold running water to remove all sand and dirt. Cut the leeks into one-inch lengths. Place in a saucepan and add boiling water to cover. Let stand five minutes.

2. Heat the butter in a saucepan and add the carrot. Cover and cook slowly ten minutes. Add the leeks, cover and cook five minutes. Add the rice and one and one-half cups of the chicken broth. Add salt and pepper. Simmer, covered, thirty minutes, or until rice is tender, adding more broth during cooking if necessary.
Yield: Four to six servings.

Roasted Italian Peppers   *Connecticut*

4 large green peppers, left whole
Salt and freshly ground black pepper to taste
1 clove garlic, finely minced
2 tablespoons finely chopped parsley
1½ tablespoons wine vinegar
4½ tablespoons olive oil
Lemon wedges.

1. Place the peppers on a hot griddle or over hot charcoal but not too close. Cook, turning occasionally, until skin is roasted and almost black all over. Set aside.
2. When peppers are cool enough to handle, peel away the charred skin. Remove the core and seeds from each pepper. Cut the peppers into strips and arrange symmetrically on a serving dish. Sprinkle with salt, pepper, the garlic, parsley, vinegar and oil. Chill. Serve garnished with lemon wedges.
Yield: Four to six servings.

Cabbage-Filled Peppers   *New York*

6 red or green sweet peppers
½ head cabbage, finely shredded
½ teaspoon salt
1 tablespoon mustard seeds
2 cups cider vinegar, approximately.

1. Wash the peppers and remove stems. Cut slice off tops and reserve. Remove cores and seeds without breaking shells.

2. Mix the cabbage with the salt and mustard seeds and press down into the pepper shells. Pack firmly. Fasten tops back on with toothpicks.

3. Arrange peppers upright in a stone jar and cover with the vinegar. Store in a cold place or in the refrigerator. Or the peppers can be packed into hot sterilized jars. Add hot vinegar, seal and process in a water bath thirty minutes. Cool, test, vacuum seal and store in a cool, dry, dark place.

Yield: Six peppers.

Potatoes with Mustard Sauce   *Maine*

3 large waxy potatoes
  Boiling salted water
6 tablespoons butter
3 tablespoons chopped onion
3 tablespoons flour
2 cups chicken broth
1 cup heavy cream
3 to four tablespoons Düsseldorf mustard
  Salt and freshly ground black pepper to taste
¼ cup soft bread crumbs
¼ cup freshly grated Parmesan cheese.

1. Scrub the potatoes and cover with boiling salted water. Simmer until barely tender, about thirty minutes.

2. Meanwhile, melt three tablespoons of the butter in a saucepan. Add the onion and sauté until tender but not browned. Sprinkle with the flour and gradually stir in the broth and cream. Bring to a boil, stirring, and simmer one minute. Stir in the mustard and hold over hot water until potatoes are done.

3. Preheat the oven to 375 degrees.

4. Peel potatoes and slice into a shallow casserole, seasoning each layer with salt and pepper.

5. Pour sauce over potatoes, sprinkle with the bread crumbs and cheese and dot with remaining butter. Bake, uncovered, until bubbly hot and lightly browned.

Yield: Six servings.

Note: Potatoes in mustard sauce go particularly well with corned beef, boiled beef or roast beef.

Potato Kugel for Passover   *New York*

6 medium-size potatoes, peeled
3 eggs
½ cup matzoh meal
½ teaspoon potato starch
1½ teaspoons salt
  Freshly ground black pepper to taste
1 onion, grated (optional).

1. Preheat the oven to 350 degrees.

2. Grate the potatoes into cold water; then drain. There should be three cups.

3. Beat the eggs until they are thick. Stir in the potatoes and remaining ingredients.

4. Turn the mixture into a one-and-one-half-quart casserole and bake, uncovered, about one hour.

Yield: Six to eight servings.

Mashed Potato Casserole   *New Jersey*

2 cups mashed potatoes
1 cup sour cream
1 cup large-curd cottage cheese
2 eggs, lightly beaten
2 tablespoons melted butter
¾ teaspoon salt
⅛ teaspoon freshly ground black pepper
1 tablespoon finely chopped green pepper
¼ cup finely chopped scallions, including
  green part.

1. Preheat the oven to 350 degrees.

2. Combine all the ingredients and place in a greased one-and-one-half-quart baking dish. Bake one hour.

Yield: Six servings.

Cheese Scalloped Rutabagas or Yellow Turnips   *Maine*

3 cups thinly sliced rutabagas or yellow turnips (about one and one-half pounds)
1 cup boiling water
2 tablespoons butter
½ cup chopped onion
⅓ cup chopped celery
⅔ cup chopped green pepper
1 teaspoon salt
¼ teaspoon freshly ground black pepper
¼ teaspoon thyme
2 teaspoons cornstarch
3 tablespoons water
½ cup grated Cheddar cheese
¼ cup buttered soft bread crumbs
2 tablespoons freshly grated Parmesan cheese.

1. Place the rutabaga or turnip slices in a saucepan and add the boiling water. Bring to a boil and simmer about twenty minutes, or until the vegetable is barely tender.

2. Meanwhile, melt the butter in a heavy skillet and sauté the onion in it until tender but not browned. Add the celery and green pepper and cook three minutes longer.

3. Season with the salt, pepper and thyme. Add the undrained cooked rutabagas to the seasoned vegetables.

4. Mix the cornstarch with the water. Stir the cornstarch mixture and the Cheddar cheese into the vegetables. Heat, stirring, until vegetable mixture thickens. Cook two minutes. Pour into a heatproof serving casserole or dish. Sprinkle with the bread crumbs and Parmesan cheese and glaze under a preheated broiler.
Yield: Four servings.

Glazed Yellow Turnip   *Vermont*

2 medium-size yellow turnips, peeled and sliced one-quarter-inch thick
Boiling salted water
1 cup brown sugar

½ cup orange juice
1 teaspoon grated orange rind
2 tablespoons butter.

1. Preheat the oven to 350 degrees.

2. Barely cover the yellow turnips with boiling salted water and boil five minutes. Drain turnips and place in a shallow baking dish.

3. Combine the brown sugar, orange juice, orange rind and butter in a pan and heat to melt the butter and dissolve the sugar. Pour over the vegetable and bake, basting frequently, forty-five to sixty minutes, until the turnip slices are tender.
Yield: Six servings.

George's Spanakopita (Spinach-Onion Pie)   *New York*

2 ten-ounce bags spinach
Salt
3 large bunches scallions, chopped, including green part
½ pound cottage cheese
½ pound feta cheese, crumbled
6 eggs, lightly beaten
White pepper to taste
1½ cups water
1½ cups flour, approximately
2 tablespoons oil
¼ cup butter.

1. Preheat the oven to 350 degrees.

2. Chop the spinach finely. Sprinkle generously with salt, add the scallions and squeeze to wilt the greens. Discard extra moisture.

3. Add the cottage cheese, feta cheese and three of the eggs to the spinach and scallions. Season with pepper.

4. Make a thin batter with the water, flour and remaining eggs (batter should be just slightly thinner than a crepe batter).

5. Put the oil in a 12-by-18-by-3-inch baking dish or roasting pan and swirl to coat the dish.

6. Pour half the batter into the dish. Top with spinach mixture. Dot with the butter. Pour re-

maining batter over all and bake about one hour, or until set and browned on top.

Yield: Ten servings.

Spinach Custard
New York

1 pound spinach, well washed
1 tablespoon bacon drippings
½ teaspoon salt
⅛ teaspoon freshly ground black pepper
⅛ teaspoon nutmeg
1 cup milk, scalded
2 eggs, lightly beaten
2 hard-cooked eggs, chopped.

1. Preheat the oven to 350 degrees.
2. Place the spinach in a large kettle with just the water clinging to the leaves. Cover and cook until spinach wilts. Drain well and chop.
3. Add the bacon drippings, salt, pepper and nutmeg to spinach. Combine the spinach mixture with the milk. Stir in the beaten eggs and hard-cooked eggs and turn into a greased shallow baking dish. Set the dish in a pan of hot water and bake thirty-five minutes, or until custard is set.

Yield: Four servings.

Cucumber in Sour Cream
New York

1 large cucumber
1 cup sour cream
1 tablespoon chopped onion
3 tablespoons cider vinegar
¼ teaspoon salt
⅛ teaspoon white pepper

1. Peel the cucumber. Run tines of fork lengthwise over cucumber and cut crosswise into thin slices.
2. Combine the remaining ingredients and pour over sliced cucumber. Marinate thirty minutes at room temperature.

Yield: Four servings.

Sandra's String Beans with Mint
Connecticut

2 pounds tiny string beans, washed, trimmed, left whole
Boiling salted water
3 sprigs mint
½ cup olive oil
¼ clove garlic
2 teaspoons wine vinegar
Salt and freshly ground black pepper to taste.

1. Cook the beans in boiling salted water to cover until crisp-tender, about six minutes. Drain beans and rinse with cold water briefly to stop cooking but not to cool beans down too much.
2. Place the remaining ingredients in an electric blender and blend until smooth. Pour over hot rinsed beans.

Yield: Eight servings.

Note: These can be eaten cold, too.

String Beans with Herb Sauce
Connecticut

3 tablespoons olive oil
1 tablespoon butter
1 onion, chopped
1 clove garlic, finely chopped
2 tomatoes, peeled, seeded and chopped
1 tablespoon chopped celery
1 tablespoon chopped parsley
1 teaspoon herbed vinegar
¼ teaspoon rosemary
¼ teaspoon sugar
Salt and freshly ground black pepper to taste
2 pounds string beans, cooked whole and drained.

1. Heat the oil and butter in a small skillet and sauté the onion and garlic in it until tender. Add the remaining ingredients except the beans. Bring to a boil and simmer ten minutes.

2. Pour over hot beans.
Yield: Eight servings.

Scalloped Sweets and Cranberries
New Jersey

6 sweet potatoes, cooked, peeled and sliced
   lengthwise
1½ cups homemade whole cranberry sauce
   (page 152)
¾ cup water
½ cup brown sugar
¾ teaspoon grated orange rind
¾ teaspoon cinnamon
1½ tablespoons butter.

1. Preheat the oven to 325 degrees.
2. Place the sweet potato slices in a greased two-quart casserole.
3. Combine the cranberry sauce, water, brown sugar, orange rind and cinnamon in a saucepan. Bring to a boil and simmer five minutes.
4. Add the butter and pour over sweet potatoes. Bake twenty minutes.
Yield: Six servings.

Tomato Fritters
New Jersey

½ cup flour
½ teaspoon baking powder
¼ teaspoon salt
⅓ cup milk
1 egg, well beaten
6 firm tomatoes
1 teaspoon basil
   Salt and freshly ground black pepper to
   taste.

1. Combine the flour, baking powder and salt in a bowl. Mix the milk and egg together and stir into the dry ingredients to make a smooth batter.
2. Cut the tomatoes into one-half-inch slices. Sprinkle with the basil, salt and pepper and let drain ten minutes.

3. Dip the tomato slices into the batter and fry on a well-greased griddle until brown on one side. Turn and brown the underside.
Yield: Eight servings.
Note: Tomato fritters are delicious with ham or bacon.

Shaker Tomato Custard
New Hampshire

8 to ten ripe tomatoes, chopped
   Salt and freshly ground black pepper to
   taste
1 teaspoon basil
4 eggs, lightly beaten
1 cup milk
⅓ cup sugar
⅛ teaspoon nutmeg.

1. Place the tomatoes, salt, pepper and basil in a saucepan and simmer gently, uncovered, thirty minutes.
2. Pass through a sieve. Cool.
3. Preheat the oven to 350 degrees.
4. Combine the remaining ingredients. Stir in tomato mixture. Pour into ten to twelve greased custard cups. Set cups in a shallow pan with hot water coming halfway up the cups. Bake thirty minutes, or until custards are set.
Yield: Ten to one dozen servings.

Fresh Tomato Risotto
Connecticut

1 cup peeled, chopped tomatoes
¾ cup uncooked rice
½ cup finely chopped onions
1 clove garlic, finely minced
½ teaspoon oregano
½ teaspoon salt
1¾ cups concentrated chicken broth.

1. Preheat the oven to 375 degrees.
2. Combine the tomatoes, rice, onions, garlic, oregano and salt in a one-and-one-half-quart casserole.

3. Heat the broth to boiling and pour over tomato mixture. Cover and bake, stirring occasionally, about thirty-five minutes, or until rice is cooked.

Yield: Four servings.

Baked Zucchini and Eggplant   *New York*

6 medium-size zucchini, thinly sliced
1 medium-size eggplant, thinly sliced
½ cup peanut oil
  Salt and freshly ground black pepper to taste
3 shallots, finely chopped
¼ teaspoon thyme
1 bay leaf
6 tomatoes, cored, peeled and stewed until thickened
3 tablespoons freshly grated Parmesan cheese.

1. Preheat the oven to 350 degrees.
2. Cook the zucchini and eggplant in half the oil until wilted and browned. Sprinkle with salt and pepper. Pour into a colander to drain.
3. Cook the shallots in the remaining oil and add the drained zucchini and eggplant.
4. Add the thyme and bay leaf. Turn into a baking dish and bake twenty minutes. Remove from the oven. Increase the oven heat to 400 degrees.
5. Put into another baking dish half the tomatoes, then the zucchini and eggplant mixture. Add the remaining tomatoes and sprinkle with the cheese. Bake ten minutes, or until cheese browns.

Yield: Four to six servings.

Cold Curried Vegetables   *New York*

¼ cup chicken broth
1 tablespoon curry powder, or to taste
½ cup chopped scallions, including green part
⅓ cup mayonnaise

1¼ cups sour cream
2 teaspoons lemon juice
1 cup cooked peas
⅓ cup chopped celery
½ cup diced cooked carrot
½ cup cooked corn kernels
¼ cup diced green pepper
  Salt and freshly ground black pepper to taste
1 teaspoon chopped fresh mint
  Lettuce leaves (optional)
  Mint sprigs.

1. Combine the broth and curry powder. Bring to a boil, stirring, and simmer gently until reduced by at least half.
2. Combine curry mixture with the scallions, mayonnaise, sour cream and lemon juice. Mix well.
3. Add the vegetables, salt, pepper and chopped mint. Chill.
4. Serve on lettuce leaves if desired. Garnish with mint sprigs.

Yield: Four servings.

Libby's Summer Vegetable Casserole
New York

3 onions, sliced
2 tablespoons oil
2 medium-size potatoes, thinly sliced
2 medium-size zucchini, thickly sliced
1 small eggplant, thinly sliced
  Salt and freshly ground black pepper to taste
1 green pepper, cored, seeded and sliced
2 tablespoons melted butter
½ teaspoon basil
2 cloves garlic, finely minced
3 large tomatoes, peeled and sliced.

1. In a heavy casserole, sauté two of the onions in the oil until tender. Add the potatoes and cook until lightly browned.
2. Add the zucchini and eggplant in two lay-

ers. Season with salt and black pepper. Make a layer of remaining onion slices and the green pepper and season with salt and pepper.

3. Drizzle the butter over all and sprinkle with the basil and garlic. Top with the tomatoes and season again. Cover, bring to a boil and simmer gently about twenty-five minutes, or until the vegetables are tender. Serve hot or cold, spooning down to the bottom to catch all layers.

Yield: Six servings.

Yette's Garden Platter   *New Jersey*

3 medium-size potatoes, sliced one-quarter-inch thick
3 medium-size zucchini, sliced one-half-inch thick
4 tomatoes, peeled, seeded and chopped
¼ cup chopped parsley
1 clove garlic, finely chopped
¾ cup olive oil
2 medium-size onions, finely chopped
Salt and freshly ground black pepper to taste.

1. Preheat the oven to 350 degrees.
2. Place the potatoes and zucchini in a shallow baking dish.
3. Combine the remaining ingredients and add to the dish. Toss to mix. Bake, uncovered, one and one-half hours.

Yield: Six servings.

Note: Peeled sliced eggplant can be added if desired.

Baked Zucchini   *Connecticut*

2 tablespoons vegetable oil or olive oil
3 large or six small zucchini, peeled and diced
1 teaspoon salt
½ teaspoon freshly ground black pepper
4 eggs, well beaten
1½ cups milk

1 tablespoon flour
¼ teaspoon cayenne pepper
½ cup grated Gruyère or Swiss cheese.

1. Pour the oil into a heavy saucepan and add the zucchini. Sprinkle with the salt and pepper. Cover and cook over very low heat, stirring occasionally, until zucchini is soft and mushy.
2. Preheat the oven to 400 degrees.
3. In a mixing bowl, combine the eggs, milk, flour and cayenne.
4. Drain the zucchini and add to egg mixture. Beat well with a rotary beater or wire whisk.
5. Pour the mixture into a buttered two-quart baking dish and sprinkle with the cheese. Bake at least twenty minutes, or until top is brown and the casserole is slightly puffed.

Yield: Six servings.

Squash and Cheese Casserole   *Vermont*

2 pounds yellow squash
Boiling water
1 cup chopped onions
3 sprigs parsley
½ teaspoon thyme
Salt and freshly ground black pepper to taste
2 tablespoons butter
2 tablespoons flour
1 cup milk
¾ cup grated Gruyère or Swiss cheese
¼ teaspoon nutmeg
2 egg yolks, lightly beaten
¼ teaspoon cayenne pepper
¼ cup buttered soft bread crumbs.

1. Preheat the oven to 325 degrees.
2. Trim ends of the squash. Cut squash into rounds and place in a suacepan. Add boiling water to cover. Add the onions, parsley, thyme, salt and black pepper. Cook briefly until squash is crisp-tender. Discard parsley and drain squash mixture.
3. Heat the butter in a saucepan and add the

flour. Stir until blended and add the milk, stirring rapidly with a wire whisk. When sauce is blended and smooth, remove from heat. Add half the cheese, the nutmeg, egg yolks and cayenne, beating rapidly.

4. Add squash mixture and pour into a buttered baking dish. Sprinkle with remaining cheese and bread crumbs. Bake twenty-five to thirty minutes, or until bubbling and golden brown.

Yield: Six servings.

Spiced Butternut Squash *New Hampshire*

2 butternut squash
8 tablespoons butter
¼ teaspoon ground allspice
½ cup light brown sugar
1 teaspoon cinnamon
¼ teaspoon nutmeg
1 tablespoon maple syrup.

1. Preheat the oven to 350 degrees.
2. Split the butternut squash in half and scoop out seeds and membranes. Dot interior and the cut surface with the butter. Place squash halves in a roasting pan or baking dish.
3. Blend the allspice, sugar, cinnamon and nutmeg and sprinkle squash cavities with mixture. Pour equal quantities of the syrup into each cavity. Bake until squash is thoroughly tender, fifty minutes to one hour.

Yield: Four servings.

Clam Salad *New York*

2 envelopes unflavored gelatin
¼ cup cold water
1 cup boiling water
Grated rind and juice of one lemon
1 seven-ounce can chopped clams, drained and liquor reserved
¼ teaspoon freshly ground black pepper
1½ cups clam broth or water
1 teaspoon Dijon or Düsseldorf mustard

2 scallions, finely chopped, including green part
6 large stuffed olives, sliced
1 cup cottage cheese, well beaten
¼ cup catchup
½ cup chopped parsley
1 hard-cooked egg, sliced
Salad greens.

1. Soften the gelatin in the cold water. Add the boiling water and stir to dissolve gelatin. Add the lemon rind, lemon juice, reserved clam liquor, pepper and clam broth or water. Stir well.
2. Halve the gelatin mixture between two bowls. Stir the clams, mustard and scallions into one bowl of gelatin mixture.
3. Pour the clam mixture into a one-and-one-half-quart mold or oblong baking dish that has been rinsed with cold water.
4. Chill until the layer just starts to set; then poke the olive slices down around the sides of the mold or dish. Chill until almost firm.
5. Reserve one-quarter cup of the gelatin mixture in the second bowl. To the remaining, add the cottage cheese, catchup and six tablespoons of the parsley. Spoon the cottage cheese mixture over the setting clam mixture. Chill until firm.
6. Sprinkle the remaining parsley over the top of firm mixture; then arrange the egg slices in an attractive pattern over all. Spoon reserved gelatin mixture over to coat the egg slices. Chill until firm.
7. Unmold or cut into squares. Serve on salad greens.

Yield: Six to eight servings.

Greek Salad *New York*

Salad:
2 red onions, thinly sliced
3 tablespoons cider or wine vinegar
Salt
1 head escarole, chopped
3 tomatoes, peeled and chopped
1 cucumber

1 green pepper, cored, seeded and diced
1 bunch radishes, sliced
1 cup Greek olives
½ pound feta cheese, cut into slivers.
Dressing:
¼ cup wine vinegar
1 teaspoon dry mustard
1 teaspoon sugar
1 cup olive oil
   Salt and freshly ground black pepper to
   taste.

1. To prepare salad, place the onions and vinegar in a bowl. Sprinkle generously with salt. Squeeze vigorously with the hand. Let mixture set twenty to thirty minutes.

2. Place the escarole, onion mixture and tomatoes in a salad bowl.

3. Cut the top off the cucumber. Salt and rub cut surfaces together several minutes. This removes the bitterness.

4. Peel cucumber and score the outside before chopping. Add to the salad bowl. Add the green pepper, radishes, olives and feta cheese.

5. To prepare dressing, shake together in a jar the vinegar, mustard and sugar. Add the oil, salt and pepper. Shake again. Toss the salad with the dressing just before serving.

Yield: Ten servings.

Canlis Salad   *Connecticut*

2 heads romaine lettuce
1 egg
1 pound bacon slices
2 teaspoons vegetable oil
1 cup one-half-inch bread cubes
   Salt to taste
1 clove garlic, peeled
⅓ cup olive oil
2 tomatoes, peeled, cored and cut into eighths
¼ cup chopped scallion, including green part
½ cup freshly grated Romano cheese or
   Parmesan cheese
   Juice of two lemons

¼ teaspoon chopped fresh mint
¼ teaspoon dried oregano
   Freshly ground black pepper to taste.

1. Trim and rinse the lettuce and cut or tear it into bite-size pieces. Pat dry, place in plastic bag and chill.

2. Place the egg in a saucepan, cover with water, bring to a simmer and simmer one minute. Drain. Set aside.

3. Cook the bacon until it is crisp. Drain on paper towels. Let bacon cool; then break or cut into small pieces.

4. Heat the vegetable oil in a skillet and add the bread cubes. Cook, shaking the skillet and stirring, until cubes are golden brown and crisp. Drain on paper towels.

5. Sprinkle the bottom of a salad bowl with salt and rub with the garlic. Remove the garlic and stir in one tablespoon of the olive oil. Add the tomato wedges and the lettuce.

6. Sprinkle with the scallion, cheese and bacon bits.

7. In a small mixing bowl, combine the remaining olive oil, the lemon juice, mint, oregano and lightly cooked egg. Stir thoroughly and pour the dressing over the salad. Add salt and pepper and toss. Add the bread cubes, toss once more and serve immediately.

Yield: Four to six servings.

Salade de Champignons   *New York*

1½ tablespoons lemon juice
3 tablespoons Dijon mustard
¼ teaspoon salt
⅛ teaspoon freshly ground black pepper
¼ cup olive oil
½ pound mushrooms, sliced.

1. Place the lemon juice, mustard, salt and pepper in a bowl. With a wire whisk, gradually whisk in the oil. Mixture will become the consistency of mayonnaise.

2. Add the mushrooms, toss and chill.
Yield: Three servings.

Brandywine River Salad   *Pennsylvania*

1 pound button mushrooms
    Boiling water
3 large cloves garlic, crushed
1 bay leaf
½ teaspoon thyme
½ teaspoon rosemary, crushed with mortar
    and pestle
¼ teaspoon basil
¼ teaspoon salt
¼ teaspoon freshly ground black pepper
2 tablespoons lemon juice
½ cup olive oil
¾ cup malt vinegar or wine vinegar
2 quarts spinach leaves, washed.

1. Trim the mushroom stems, rinse mushrooms and place in a saucepan. Cover with boiling water. Cover and boil five minutes. Drain.
2. Meanwhile, combine the remaining ingredients except the spinach. Shake or beat well. Pour over the hot drained mushrooms and chill.
3. Place spinach leaves in a salad bowl and add the mushrooms and enough of the marinade to dress the greens. Toss.
Yield: Eight servings.

Maine Sardine Salad

1 clove garlic, crushed or quartered
¾ cup oil
1½ cups small bread cubes
1 egg
1 small onion, sliced and separated into
    rings
8 cups bite-size pieces romaine lettuce
½ teaspoon salt
¼ teaspoon freshly ground black pepper
2 tablespoons lemon juice
⅓ cup freshly grated Parmesan cheese

3 three-and-three-quarter-ounce to
    four-ounce cans sardines
6 cherry tomatoes, peeled.

1. Let the garlic stand in the oil one hour or longer. Remove garlic and discard.
2. Heat one-half cup of the oil in a skillet, add the bread cubes and cook until golden and crisp. Drain on paper towels. Set aside.
3. Place the egg in a saucepan, cover with water, bring to a simmer and simmer one minute. Drain. Set aside.
4. Place the onion, romaine, salt and pepper in a salad bowl. Pour remaining oil over all and toss lightly. Break the egg into the salad.
5. Add the lemon juice and toss thoroughly. Add the cheese, bread cubes and sardines. Toss. Garnish with the tomatoes.
Yield: Six servings.

Picnic Potato Salad   *Vermont*

⅓ cup homemade French dressing (page 622)
4 cups hot diced, cooked potatoes
4 hard-cooked eggs
1 cup sour cream
¼ cup sliced scallions, including green part
2 tablespoons snipped parsley
2 tablespoons chopped dill pickle
2 tablespoons diced pimento
2 tablespoons cider vinegar
1 tablespoon prepared mustard, preferably
    Dijon or Düsseldorf
1 teaspoon salt
⅛ teaspoon freshly ground black pepper
1 cup chopped celery
    Parsley sprigs.

1. Pour the dressing over the potatoes and toss to coat. Refrigerate until potatoes are thoroughly chilled.
2. Chop three of the hard-cooked eggs.
3. Combine the sour cream, scallions, snipped parsley, pickle, pimento, vinegar, mustard, salt

and pepper. Add to potatoes along with the celery and chopped eggs. Toss gently and chill.

4. Cut remaining egg in wedges. Garnish potato salad with egg wedges and the parsley sprigs.

Yield: Six servings.

Potato Salad I   *New Jersey*

    6 medium-size baking potatoes
    1 cup chopped celery
    1 cup thinly sliced red onion rings
      Salt and freshly ground black pepper to taste
 1½ teaspoons celery seeds
    ½ cup wine vinegar
    ½ cup peanut oil
    2 tablespoons olive oil
    ⅛ teaspoon cayenne pepper
 1½ cups chopped parsley
      Lettuce leaves.

1. Cook the potatoes in jackets until tender. Peel and slice thinly while still hot.

2. Combine the potato slices, celery, onion rings, salt, black pepper, celery seeds, vinegar, peanut oil, olive oil, cayenne and one cup of the parsley. Mix well.

3. Cover with the remaining parsley. Serve at room temperature, on lettuce leaves.

Yield: Six servings.

Potato Salad II   *Massachusetts*

    1 pound waxy potatoes
    2 tender ribs celery, approximately
    ¾ cup heavy cream
    ¼ cup sour cream
    2 tablespoons cider vinegar
      Juice of half a lemon
      Salt and freshly ground black pepper to taste
    ¼ cup cooked ham.

1. Cook the potatoes in jackets, taking care not to overcook. Let cool; then chill.

2. Peel potatoes. Cut them first into thin slices; then cut each slice into thin matchlike strips. Place strips in a mixing bowl.

3. Cut the celery ribs into two-inch lengths. Cut each length of celery into very thin strips. There should be about half as much celery as potatoes. Add celery to potatoes.

4. Whip the heavy cream until it is the consistency of thin mayonnaise. Do not whip until stiff. Stir in the sour cream, vinegar, lemon juice, salt and pepper. Pour over potatoes and celery. Mix gently without breaking potatoes.

5. Cut the ham into very thin strips and scatter over the salad. Serve as soon as possible.

Yield: Four servings.

Hot Apple and Potato Salad
Massachusetts

    ½ cup golden raisins
    1 cup boiling water
    3 cups sliced cooked potatoes
    1 cup diced celery
    2 tablespoons chopped parsley
    2 teaspoons salt
    ¼ teaspoon freshly ground black pepper
    4 slices bacon
    2 tablespoons cider vinegar
    2 tablespoons tarragon vinegar
    ¼ cup sugar
    1 teaspoon grated lemon rind
    3 unpeeled Red Delicious apples, cored and diced.

1. Place the raisins in a bowl, pour the boiling water over raisins and let stand three minutes. Drain.

2. Combine the potatoes, celery, parsley, salt and pepper in a skillet.

3. In another skillet, cook the bacon until crisp. Add the cider vinegar, tarragon vinegar, sugar and lemon rind and bring to a boil.

4. Pour over the potato mixture. Heat gently.

Add the apples and raisins and heat mixture to serving temperature.

Yield: Eight servings.

Crisp Rutabaga Salad   *Maine*

½ cup grated raw rutabaga
½ cup thinly sliced celery
2 scallions, including green part, chopped
2 radishes, sliced paper-thin
3 cups shredded romaine lettuce
3 tablespoons olive oil
1 tablespoon wine vinegar
½ teaspoon salt
¼ teaspoon freshly ground black pepper
⅛ teaspoon dry mustard
¼ teaspoon sugar
¼ teaspoon basil.

1. Combine the rutabaga, celery, scallions, radishes and romaine in a bowl and chill well.
2. Combine the remaining ingredients in a jar and shake. Chill. Toss the salad with the dressing just before serving.

Yield: Four servings.

Spinach Salad   *New York*

1 pound spinach
  Salt
1 clove garlic
¼ teaspoon dry mustard
  Tabasco sauce
3 tablespoons wine vinegar
7 tablespoons olive oil
  Freshly ground black pepper to taste
2 hard-cooked eggs, finely chopped.

1. Wash the spinach well, dry it and cut into bite-size pieces. Discard any tough stems.
2. Sprinkle the bottom of a salad bowl with salt, rub with the garlic and add the mustard. Add a few drops Tabasco, the vinegar, oil and pepper. Stir with a fork until the mixture is well blended. Add the spinach and toss until leaves are coated with dressing. Lift onto individual salad plates and sprinkle with the eggs.

Yield: Four to six servings.

Marinated Bean Salad   *Connecticut*

2 cups cooked baby lima beans
2 cups cooked green beans
1 one-pound-fourteen-ounce can kidney beans, drained
1 cup button mushrooms or sliced large mushrooms
¼ cup diced pimento
½ cup finely chopped onion
2 tablespoons chopped parsley
½ cup wine vinegar
¼ cup olive oil
⅓ cup water
1 teaspoon sugar
1 clove garlic, crushed
¼ teaspoon oregano
¼ teaspoon celery salt
½ teaspoon salt
¼ teaspoon freshly ground black pepper.

1. Day before, place the lima beans, green beans, kidney beans, mushrooms, pimento, onion and parsley in a bowl.
2. Place the remaining ingredients in a jar and shake well. Pour over the beans and toss. Cover and chill well overnight.

Yield: One dozen servings.

Tossed Salad with Honey Dressing
Connecticut

Salad:
1 medium-size head leaf lettuce or romaine lettuce, washed, drained and crisped
¼ head red cabbage, finely shredded
1 cucumber, peeled and thinly sliced
1 bunch scallions, including some green part, chopped

¼ cup finely diced celery
⅓ cup finely diced carrot
½ clove garlic, finely chopped
1 teaspoon oregano
1 tablespoon finely grated onion
 Salt and freshly ground black pepper to taste.
Honey dressing:
½ cup oil
¼ cup cider vinegar
¼ cup honey.

1. To prepare salad, break the lettuce into a salad bowl. Add the cabbage, cucumber, scallions, celery and carrot. Toss.

2. Sprinkle with the garlic, oregano, grated onion, salt and pepper.

3. To prepare honey dressing, combine the oil, vinegar and honey. Mix well. Pour over salad and toss.

Yield: Eight servings.

Dandelion Greens and Bacon Dressing
Pennsylvania

4 slices bacon, diced
½ cup sugar
½ teaspoon salt
1 tablespoon cornstarch
1 egg, lightly beaten
¼ cup cider vinegar
1 cup light cream
4 cups dandelion greens
1 hard-cooked egg, chopped.

1. Cook the bacon until crisp. Reserve drippings and bacon.

2. Combine the sugar, salt and cornstarch. Mix well. Gradually stir in the egg, vinegar and cream.

3. Pour into the bacon mixture and cook, stirring, until mixture thickens. Pour over the greens and garnish with the egg.

Yield: Six servings.

Asparagus Salad
New Jersey

1 hard-cooked egg
1½ tablespoons olive oil
1 tablespoon cider vinegar
1 teaspoon salt
½ teaspoon freshly ground black pepper
1 tablespoon finely grated onion
1 tablespoon chopped parsley
2 tablespoons heavy cream, whipped
16 spears asparagus, cooked, drained and chilled.

1. Rub the yolk of the egg through a sieve. Chop the egg white. Gradually beat the oil, vinegar, salt, pepper, onion, parsley and egg white into the yolk.

2. Fold into the cream and spoon over the asparagus.

Yield: Four servings.

Cole Slaw with Cooked Dressing
Maine

Cooked dressing:
1 egg, lightly beaten
¾ cup milk
2 tablespoons flour
1½ tablespoons sugar
1 teaspoon salt
1 teaspoon dry mustard
⅛ teaspoon cayenne pepper
2 tablespoons bacon drippings or butter
¼ cup cider vinegar.
Slaw:
4 cups shredded cabbage
½ green pepper, seeded and diced
½ red sweet pepper, diced
1 teaspoon salt.

1. To prepare cooked dressing, combine the egg and milk. In the top of a double boiler, mix together the flour, sugar, salt, mustard and cayenne. Stir in the milk mixture.

2. Cook over hot water, stirring until mixture

thickens. Do not boil. Stir in the bacon drippings or butter and vinegar. Cool.

3. Combine the slaw ingredients in a bowl and toss well.

4. Stir in enough of the cooled dressing to moisten well.

Yield: Eight servings.

Poppy Seed Dressing
Connecticut

½ cup sugar
1 teaspoon dry mustard
1 teaspoon paprika
¼ teaspoon salt
5 tablespoons tarragon vinegar
⅓ cup honey
1 tablespoon lemon juice
2 tablespoons onion juice or finely grated onion
1 cup vegetable oil (not olive oil)
1 tablespoon poppy seeds.

1. Mix together the sugar, mustard, paprika, salt and vinegar until sugar dissolves completely.

2. Add the honey, lemon juice and onion juice or onion. Gradually beat in the oil. Chill.

3. Add the poppy seeds just before serving.
Yield: About one and one-half cups.
Note: Mrs. Linz uses the poppy seed dressing for orange, graepfruit and endive salad.

Mayonnaise
Connecticut

½ teaspoon dry mustard
1 teaspoon cold water
2 egg yolks
Salt to taste
Pinch of cayenne pepper
3 tablespoons wine vinegar or lemon juice
1¼ cups peanut oil or vegetable oil.

1. Place the mustard in a mixing bowl. Add the water to make a paste. Let stand ten minutes.

2. Add the egg yolks, salt, cayenne and half the vinegar or lemon juice. Start beating with a wire whisk, rotary beater or electric mixer, gradually adding the oil. Continue beating, adding the oil and remaining vinegar alternately until all the ingredients are used. Taste for seasoning and add more salt, cayenne or vinegar if desired.

Yield: About one and one-half cups.

Breads

Rhode Island johnnycakes or Massachusetts johnnycakes were originally called journey cakes because the circuit riders carried the bread with them on their travels to preach the gospel. Massachusetts johnnycakes usually have wheat flour and corn meal in them.

Johnnycakes *Rhode Island*

1 cup waterground white corn meal
1 teaspoon salt
1 cup boiling water
1 teaspoon sugar (optional)
½ cup milk, approximately
   Butter and maple syrup.

1. Place the corn meal and salt in a bowl. Gradually stir in the boiling water. Add the sugar if desired and enough milk to make a batter that is a little thicker than a regular pancake batter.
2. Spoon onto a greased griddle and cook eight to ten minutes on one side before turning to cook and brown the other side. Split cakes and serve with butter and syrup.
Yield: Fourteen.

Philipsburg Waterground Corn Bread *New York*

1½ cups flour
 1 teaspoon baking soda
 4 teaspoons baking powder
 3 tablespoons sugar
1½ teaspoons salt
1½ cups waterground yellow corn meal
 3 teaspoons caraway seeds
 ½ teaspoon nutmeg
 3 eggs, lightly beaten
1½ cups buttermilk
 5 tablespoons melted shortening or bacon
  drippings

1. Preheat the oven to 425 degrees.
2. Sift together the flour, baking soda, baking powder, sugar and salt. Add the corn meal, caraway seeds and nutmeg.
3. Stir in the eggs, buttermilk and shortening or bacon drippings. Turn into a greased nine-inch square baking tin and bake twenty-five to thirty minutes.
Yield: Six to eight servings.

Spider Corncake *Connecticut*

1⅓ cups yellow corn meal
 ⅓ cup flour
 1 teaspoon baking soda

1 cup buttermilk
2 cups regular milk
2 teaspoons sugar
½ teaspoon salt
2 tablespoons bacon drippings or butter.

1. Preheat the oven to 350 degrees.
2. Combine the corn meal, flour and baking soda in a mixing bowl. Add the buttermilk, one cup of the regular milk, sugar and salt. Stir to blend well.
3. Meanwhile, put the bacon drippings or butter in a nine-inch cast-iron skillet or other baking dish and place it in the oven.
4. When skillet is thoroughly hot, withdraw it and pour in the batter. Carefully pour the remaining milk over the top. Bake fifty minutes.

Yield: Six servings.

Potato Biscuits   *Maine*

⅓ cup shortening, melted
1 cup mashed potatoes
1½ cups flour
½ teaspoon salt
4 teaspoons baking powder
2 tablespoons sugar
½ cup milk.

1. Preheat the oven to 400 degrees.
2. Stir the shortening into the potatoes. Sift together the flour, salt, baking powder and sugar and add to the potato mixture. Mix well.
3. Add the milk all at once and mix just enough to moisten.
4. Turn out onto a lightly floured board and knead twenty times.
5. Flatten dough into one-inch-thick rectangle. Cut into rounds. Bake on a greased baking sheet about twenty minutes, or until done.

Yield: Ten to twelve.

Clam Biscuits   *Massachusetts*

2 cups flour
½ teaspoon baking soda
1 teaspoon cream of tartar
½ teaspoon salt
¼ cup lard
1 cup milk, approximately
1 cup clams, drained and chopped
2 tablespoons butter
Salt and freshly ground black pepper to taste.

1. Preheat the oven to 425 degrees.
2. Sift the flour, baking soda, cream of tartar and salt into a bowl. With the finger tips or a pastry blender, work in the lard.
3. Add enough milk to make a soft dough. Turn out onto a floured board and knead thirty seconds. Flatten with the hands to one-half-inch thickness and cut into two-inch rounds.
4. Place two teaspoons of the clams on half of biscuits. Top with dot of the butter, salt and pepper. Moisten edges of biscuits and top with second biscuit. Press to seal. Place on a greased baking sheet and bake fifteen to twenty minutes, or until done and golden.

Yield: Eight.

Quahog Popovers   *Massachusetts*

6 medium-size quahogs
¼ cup water
1 cup flour
⅛ teaspoon freshly ground black pepper
2 eggs
1 tablespoon oil
½ cup milk.

1. Preheat the oven to 425 degrees.
2. Place the quahogs and water in a pan and steam until quahogs open, about five minutes. Remove meat and chop. Reserve quahog liquid.
3. Place the flour and pepper in a bowl. Add

the eggs, oil, milk and one-half cup of the reserved quahog liquid. Beat until smooth.

4. Grease six deep muffin tins very well and
heat in oven three minutes.

5. Stir chopped quahogs into batter and pour
into muffin tins. Bake thirty-five to forty minutes.
Yield: Six.

Cranberry Corn Meal Muffins
Massachusetts

1½ cups flour
1½ cups yellow corn meal
3 tablespoons sugar
2 tablespoons baking powder
1 teaspoon salt
3 eggs, lightly beaten
1½ cups milk
⅓ cup oil
½ cup finely chopped cooked smoked ham
1 tablespoon chopped chives
1½ cups cranberries, rinsed and drained.

1. Preheat the oven to 425 degrees.
2. Combine the flour, corn meal, sugar, baking
powder and salt in a bowl.
3. Beat the eggs into the milk and oil and add
to dry ingredients. Stir to moisten. Add the ham,
chives and cranberries and mix.
4. Spoon into well-greased muffin tins. Bake
fifteen to twenty minutes, or until done. Serve
warm.
Yield: Two dozen.

Blueberry Muffins
Maine

3 cups flour
1 cup sugar
4 teaspoons baking powder
1 teaspoon salt
2 eggs, lightly beaten
½ cup oil
1 cup milk
1½ cups blueberries.

1. Preheat the oven to 400 degrees.
2. Mix together the flour, sugar, baking powder and salt in a bowl. Combine the eggs, oil and
milk and stir into the dry ingredients until just
moistened.
3. Stir the berries into the batter and spoon
into medium-size muffin tins lined with cupcake
liners until about half full. Bake twenty minutes.
Yield: Two dozen.

Brown Bread I
Massachusetts

¾ cup graham flour
¾ cup yellow corn meal
¾ cup flour
¾ cup dry bread crumbs
¾ cup molasses
2 cups sour milk or buttermilk
2 teaspoons baking soda
1 teaspoon salt
¾ cup ground raisins (optional).

1. Grease two coffee tins, each with a one-
quart capacity. Or use other one-quart utensils
suitable for steaming.
2. Combine all the ingredients in a mixing
bowl and pour the batter into the prepared tins.
The tins should be about two-thirds full. Cover
with aluminum foil.
3. Steam in a closed steamer two hours.
Yield: Two loaves.

Brown Bread II
Maine

1 cup yellow corn meal
1 cup rye flour
1 cup graham flour
2 teaspoons baking soda
1 teaspoon salt
2 cups buttermilk
¾ cup unsulphured molasses
1 cup raisins.

1. Combine the corn meal, rye flour, graham flour, baking soda and salt in a mixing bowl.

2. Mix together the buttermilk, molasses and raisins. Add to dry ingredients. Mix well. Fill well-greased pudding molds or cans two-thirds full with the batter. It will fill about three No. 2 cans or two No. 2½ cans.

3. Cover with greased mold covers or can lids and cover over with aluminum foil.

4. Place the molds or cans on a rack in a large kettle, with water extending at least halfway up the sides of the molds or cans. Cover and cook three hours, replenishing water as necessary.

Yield: Two or three loaves.

Blueberry Nut Bread   *Connecticut*

  2 cups flour
  ¼ teaspoon salt
  3 teaspoons baking powder
  1 cup sugar
  1 cup blueberries, preferably wild
  ½ cup chopped nuts
  2 eggs, well beaten
  1 cup milk
  3 tablespoons oil.

1. Sift together the flour, salt, baking powder and sugar. Add the berries and nuts.

2. Combine the eggs, milk and oil and stir in just to moisten. Pour into a wax paper-lined 9-by-5-by3-inch loaf pan. Let stand twenty minutes.

3. Preheat the oven to 350 degrees.

4. Bake loaf one hour, or until done.

Yield: One loaf.

Oatmeal Bran Bread   *Pennsylvania*

  2 cups flour
  ⅓ cup sugar
  1 tablespoon salt
  1 teaspoon baking soda
  1½ cups rolled oats
  1 cup whole bran cereal

  ½ cup raisins
  2 eggs, lightly beaten
  1⅓ cups buttermilk
  ½ cup light molasses.

1. Preheat the oven to 350 degrees.

2. Sift together the flour, sugar, salt and baking soda. Stir in the oats, bran and raisins.

3. Combine the eggs, buttermilk and molasses. Add to dry ingredients and stir until just moistened. Pour into a greased 9-by-5-by3-inch loaf pan. Bake one hour, or until done.

Yield: One loaf.

Banana Bread   *New York*

  ½ cup shortening
  1 cup sugar
  2 eggs, lightly beaten
  1 cup mashed sieved ripe bananas
  1 teaspoon lemon juice
  2 cups flour
  3 teaspoons baking powder
  ½ teaspoon salt
  1 cup chopped walnuts.

1. Preheat the oven to 375 degrees.

2. Cream the shortening and sugar together until light and fluffy. Beat in the eggs. Mix the bananas with the lemon juice and mix into batter.

3. Sift together the flour, baking powder and salt. Stir into batter. Fold in the nuts.

4. Turn into a greased loaf pan and bake one and one-quarter hours, or until done.

Yield: One loaf.

Rebecca's Challah   *New York*

  2 packages active dry yeast
  8 teaspoons plus one-half cup sugar
7¾ cups flour, approximately
2¼ cups warm water
  ½ cup plus one tablespoon oil
  2 tablespoons coarse salt

3 eggs
Poppy seeds (optional).

1. Place the yeast, two teaspoons of the sugar and two tablespoons of the flour in a tall tumbler. Add three-quarters cup of the water and mix well. Set in a warm place, uncovered.

2. In a big bowl, place four cups of the flour. Add one and one-half cups of the water, one-half cup of the oil, one-half cup of the sugar, the salt and two of the eggs and mix well.

3. When the yeast mixture reaches the top of the glass, add to the batter in the bowl. Mix well and gradually add three more cups of the flour. Knead the mixture right in the bowl until very smooth and elastic. Cover and set in a warm place about five hours, or until doubled in bulk.

4. Knock dough down and add about two-thirds cup more of the flour, kneading well to give a soft but not sticky dough. Oil the top of the dough with remaining oil. Cover and let rise again until doubled in bulk, about two and one-half hours.

5. Knead again. Divide dough in two. Shape into two loaves to fit greased 9-by-5-by-3-inch loaf pans and place in pans, or braid and set on greased baking sheet. Cover and let rise until doubled in bulk, about one hour.

6. Preheat the oven to 350 degrees.

7. Combine the remaining egg and remaining sugar and brush over top of the loaves. Sprinkle with poppy seeds if desired. Bake about forty-five minutes, or until done.

Yield: Two loaves.

Parker House Rolls   *Massachusetts*

1 cup milk, scalded
¼ cup sugar
¼ cup plus three tablespoons butter
¼ cup shortening
1 teaspoon salt
½ package active dry yeast
¼ cup warm water
2 eggs, lightly beaten

4 to five cups flour
2 tablespoons melted butter.

1. Combine the milk with the sugar, one-quarter cup of the butter, the shortening and salt. Stir to melt the shortening and dissolve the sugar. Cool to lukewarm.

2. Soften the yeast in the water. Stir until dissolved.

3. Add the eggs to the lukewarm milk mixture. Stir in the softened yeast. Add three cups of the flour and beat until smooth. Add enough remaining flour to make a soft ball of dough.

4. Knead the dough on a lightly floured board or in the bowl until dough is smooth and elastic, about eight minutes. Place the dough in a clean bowl, grease the top surface, cover with a damp towel and let dough rise in a warm place until doubled in bulk, about one hour.

5. Knock down the dough. Let rest, covered, about ten minutes. Knead three minutes on a lightly floured board.

6. Soften the remaining butter. Divide the dough in half. Roll out each half to one-quarter-inch thickness and spread each with one and one-half tablespoons softened butter. With a biscuit cutter, cut into two-inch rounds.

7. With the back of a knife, make a light cut, slightly off center, in each round and fold the smaller half over the larger, pressing edges together to secure. Place rolls close together on a greased baking sheet. Cover with a damp cloth and let rise in a warm place until doubled in bulk, about fifteen to twenty minutes.

8. Preheat the oven to 425 degrees.

9. Bake the rolls about fifteen minutes, or until golden brown. Brush with the melted butter and serve hot or, if desired, let rolls cool on a rack.

Yield: Three dozen.

Flaky Rolls   *Pennsylvania*

2½ teaspoons active dry yeast granules or one three-quarter-ounce cake compressed yeast

¼ cup warm water for dry yeast or one
  tablespoon warm water for compressed
  yeast
2½ cups flour
1 teaspoon salt
¾ cup scalded milk, cooled to lukewarm, for
  dry yeast or one cup scalded milk, cooled
  to lukewarm, for compressed yeast
1 cup plus one tablespoon butter
1 egg yolk
2 tablespoons heavy cream.

1. Dissolve or soften yeast in warm water.

2. Put the flour and salt in a bowl and make a well in the center. Into this pour the cooled milk, the dissolved or softened yeast and one tablespoon of the butter.

3. Blend well and knead until dough is smooth and elastic.

4. Refrigerate dough on bottom shelf of the refrigerator fifteen minutes. Roll out on a board to a 12-by-18-inch rectangle.

5. Soften the remaining butter. Score the dough rectangle into thirds and spread half the softened butter over the center third. Fold one end of the dough over the butter. On this spread the remaining butter. Fold the other end over this and press the edges to seal.

6. With a rolling pin, roll out the dough to a 12-by-18-inch rectangle. Fold in thirds as before. Wrap dough in wax paper and chill one hour.

7. Roll dough into 12-by-18-inch rectangle, fold in thirds, wrap in wax paper and refrigerate two hours.

8. Roll out dough to one-eighth-inch thickness in a 12-by-18-inch rectangle. Cut into six-inch squares and then cut each square into four triangles. Starting with the wide end, roll the triangles; then bend into crescents. Place on a buttered baking sheet.

9. Cover with wax paper and refrigerate thirty minutes or longer.

10. Preheat the oven to 475 degrees.

11. Blend the egg yolk with the cream and brush over the crescents. Bake five minutes and reduce oven heat to 400 degrees. Bake until crescents are golden, about ten minutes longer.

Yield: Two dozen.

Pumpkin Rolls   *New Hampshire*

1 cup canned or homemade pumpkin puree
½ cup sugar
1½ teaspoons salt
1 cup milk, scalded
1 package active dry yeast
¼ cup warm water
½ cup melted shortening
2 teaspoons grated lemon rind
5 cups flour
  Melted butter.

1. Day before, combine the pumpkin, sugar, salt and milk in a large bowl and beat until smooth and lukewarm.

2. Dissolve the yeast in the water and add to the lukewarm mixture. Add the shortening and lemon rind and mix well.

3. Add about half the flour and beat until batter is smooth. Add remaining flour to make a soft dough. Mix well with the hands or a wooden spoon. Cover and let rise in a warm place until doubled in bulk. Cover dough with wax paper and a towel and chill overnight in the refrigerator.

4. Next day, shape the dough by dividing into thirty-two equal portions. For cloverleaf rolls, make three balls out of each portion and drop into greased medium-size muffin tins. The dough may be made into other shapes if desired.

5. Brush the top of the rolls lightly with melted butter. Cover and let rise in a warm place until doubled in bulk, about one and one-quarter hours.

6. Preheat the oven to 375 degrees.

7. Bake rolls twenty-five to thirty minutes, or until done. Brush with melted butter and cool on a rack.

Yield: Thirty-two.

Anadama Bread
Connecticut

½ cup yellow corn meal, preferably
   waterground
2 cups boiling water
2 tablespoons shortening
½ cup dark molasses
1 tablespoon salt
2 packages active dry yeast
½ cup warm water
7 to eight cups sifted flour
   Melted butter.

1. Add the corn meal to the boiling water, stirring constantly. Add the shortening, molasses and salt and let cool to lukewarm.

2. Soften the yeast in the warm water and stir into the corn meal mixture. Add the flour gradually, stirring in just enough to make a stiff dough. Knead well and place in a bowl rubbed with shortening. Cover with a cloth and let stand in a warm place until doubled in bulk.

3. Slash through dough with a knife or punch dough with the fingers. Cover and let rise in a warm place forty-five minutes longer. Pull out onto a lightly floured board and knead well, adding more flour if necessary.

4. Shape the dough into two loaves and place in two 9-by-5-by-3-inch loaf pans rubbed with shortening. Cover and let stand in a warm place until nearly doubled in bulk.

5. Preheat the oven to 400 degrees.

6. Bake the two loaves fifteen minutes and reduce the oven heat to 350 degrees. Bake about forty-five minutes longer. Brush the tops of the loaves with the melted butter and remove the bread from the oven to a rack.

Yield: Two loaves.

Sour Dough White Bread
New York

Starter:
1 package active dry yeast
2 cups warm water
2 cups flour

Bread:
1 cup warm water
1 package active dry yeast
1½ cups sour dough starter
2 eggs, lightly beaten
1½ teaspoons salt
2 tablespoons sugar
6 cups flour, approximately
3 tablespoons melted butter.

1. Mix the starter ingredients together in a large bowl, cover with cheesecloth and allow to stand in a warm place about two days. Stir once or twice as mixture bubbles.

2. To prepare bread, place the water in a bowl and dissolve the yeast in it. Add one and one-half cups sour dough starter, the eggs, salt, sugar and four cups of the flour. Beat well. (Remaining starter should be kept in the refrigerator and replenished by adding equal quantities of flour and warm water and letting stand in a warm place overnight.)

3. Cover the bread dough with a damp cloth and let rise in a warm place until doubled in bulk, about one and one-half hours.

4. Place the remaining two cups flour on a board and pour out the dough onto the flour. Knead enough of the extra flour into the dough to make a soft but not sticky dough. Knead until smooth and satiny.

5. Shape into two loaves. Place in two 9-by-5-by-3-inch loaf pans that have been greased and dusted with corn meal. Brush with the melted butter, cover with a towel and let rise until doubled in bulk, about one and one-half hours.

6. Preheat the oven to 400 degrees.

7. Bake loaves about forty-five minutes, or until bread sounds hollow when tapped on the bottom. Cool on a rack. A damp cloth placed on the hot loaves will soften the crusts if the cooled loaves are to be used for sandwiches.

Yield: Two loaves.

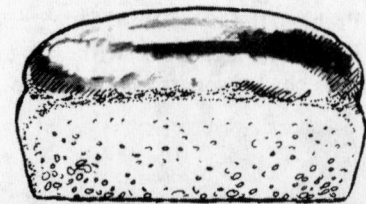

Rye Bread   *Pennsylvania*

3 packages active dry yeast
1½ cups warm water
¼ cup molasses
⅓ cup sugar
4 teaspoons salt
3 tablespoons caraway seeds
2¾ cups rye flour
2 tablespoons shortening
3½ cups to four cups flour
1 egg white
2 tablespoons water.

1. Dissolve the yeast in the warm water. Stir in the molasses, sugar, salt and caraway seeds.
2. Stir in the rye flour until smooth.
3. Work in the shortening. With the hands, work in enough of the regular flour to make a dough that can be handled. Turn onto a floured board and knead until smooth, about ten minutes.
4. Place in a clean greased bowl, cover and let rise in a warm place until doubled in bulk.
5. Shape into two round, slightly flattened loaves. Place far apart on a greased large baking sheet. Cover with damp cloth and let rise in a warm place until doubled in bulk.
6. Preheat the oven to 375 degrees.
7. Mix the egg white with the water and use to brush the loaves. Bake thirty to forty minutes, or until done.
Yield: Two loaves.

Pumpkin Bread   *New Hampshire*

1 cup warm water
¾ cup sugar
1 package active dry yeast
3 tablespoons oil
2 teaspoons salt
1 cup pumpkin puree
½ cup non-fat dry milk solids
5 cups flour, approximately.

1. Place the water, sugar and yeast in mixing bowl. Let stand five minutes.
2. Add the oil, salt, pumpkin and milk solids and beat well.
3. Gradually beat in enough flour to give a manageable dough. Knead on a lightly floured board until smooth. Place in clean greased bowl, cover and let rise until doubled in bulk.
4. Knead briefly, cover and let rise again until doubled in bulk.
5. Punch dough down and shape into two rolls to fit two greased 8½-by-4½-by-2½-inch loaf pans. Put dough into pans, cover and let rise until doubled in bulk.
6. Preheat the oven to 400 degrees.
7. Bake twenty-five to thirty minutes.
Yield: Two loaves.

Potato Bread   *Maine*

1 package active dry yeast
½ cup lukewarm water
1 cup milk, scalded
⅔ cup sugar
1 teaspoon salt
2 eggs, lightly beaten
½ cup mashed potatoes
6 cups flour, approximately.

1. Dissolve the yeast in the water. Combine the milk, sugar and salt and let stand until lukewarm.
2. Beat the eggs into the mashed potatoes and gradually beat in the cooled milk mixture. Add the dissolved yeast.
3. Stir in enough flour to make a manageable dough. Turn onto a lightly floured board and knead until smooth, about ten minutes. Place in a clean greased bowl, cover and let rise until doubled in bulk, about one hour.
4. Knock dough down and shape into two loaves. Place in two greased 9-by-5-by-3-inch loaf pans. Cover with a damp cloth and let rise in a warm place until doubled in bulk.
5. Preheat the oven to 375 degrees.

6. Bake forty minutes, or until done.
Yield: Two loaves.

Apple Bread   *Massachusetts*

1 package active dry yeast
¼ cup lukewarm water
2 cups lukewarm applesauce
2 tablespoons butter
1 teaspoon salt
¼ cup sugar
6 cups to six and one-half cups flour
  Melted butter.

1. Soften the yeast in the water.
2. Combine the applesauce, two tablespoons butter, salt and sugar. Stir to dissolve sugar. Add the softened yeast and half the flour. Mix well.
3. Continue adding flour until a soft manageable dough is formed.
4. Knead on a lightly floured board until smooth.
5. Place in a clean greased bowl, cover and let rise until doubled in bulk, about one hour.
6. Knock dough down and divide into two. Let rest, covered, ten minutes. Shape into two oblong loaves and place on a greased baking sheet. Cover and let rise until doubled in bulk, about forty-five minutes.
7. Preheat the oven to 400 degrees.
8. Bake thirty to thirty-five minutes, or until done. Brush with melted butter.
Yield: Two loaves.

Rich Tea Loaf   *Connecticut*

1 package active dry yeast
¼ cup lukewarm water
⅓ cup milk, scalded
¼ cup sugar
¼ cup butter
1 egg, lightly beaten
2 egg yolks
½ teaspoon salt

1½ teaspoons grated lemon peel
¼ teaspoon lemon extract
3 cups flour, approximately.

1. Dissolve the yeast in the water.
2. Place the milk in a large bowl and add the sugar and butter. Stir to melt butter and dissolve sugar and let cool to lukewarm.
3. Beat the egg and egg yolks together and add to the yeast. Stir into the milk mixture. Add the salt, lemon peel and lemon extract.
4. Gradually stir in the flour to make a soft dough. Beat in the bowl with dough hook of electric mixer or with a wooden spoon until smooth.
5. Place the dough in a clean greased bowl, cover and let rise in a warm place until doubled in bulk, about one and one-quarter hours.
6. Knock dough down and knead lightly on a floured board. Roll into a 10-by-14-inch rectangle and roll up from the short end. Tuck the ends under and place in a greased 9-by-5-by-3-inch loaf pan.
7. Cover and let rise until doubled in bulk, about one hour.
8. Preheat the oven to 375 degrees.
9. Bake ten minutes, reduce the oven heat to 350 degrees and bake thirty minutes longer, or until done. Cool on a rack.
Yield: One loaf.

Jennie's Coffeecake Ring   *Vermont*

Coffeecake ring:
2 packages active dry yeast
⅓ cup lukewarm water
1 cup milk, scalded
¼ cup butter
½ cup granulated sugar
1 teaspoon salt
2 eggs, lightly beaten
1 teaspoon grated lemon rind
5 cups flour, approximately.
Filling:
¼ cup melted butter
⅓ cup light brown sugar

½ cup granulated sugar
½ cup raisins
1 teaspoon cinnamon.
Frosting:
2 cups confectioners' sugar
¼ cup chopped walnuts or pecans.

1. To prepare coffeecake ring, dissolve the yeast in the water.

2. Combine the milk, butter, granulated sugar and salt in a bowl and cool to lukewarm.

3. Add the dissolved yeast, the eggs, lemon rind and enough flour to make a stiff batter. Beat well. Add more flour to make a soft dough. Turn out onto a lightly floured board and let rest, covered with a towel, ten minutes. Knead gently until smooth and satiny, about ten minutes.

4. Place in a clean greased bowl, cover and let rise in a warm place until doubled in bulk, about one hour.

5. Punch dough down and roll out into a large rectangle about one-quarter-inch thick.

6. For filling, brush the dough rectangle with the butter and sprinkle with the brown sugar, granulated sugar, raisins and cinnamon. Roll up from the long side like a jellyroll.

7. Arrange roll in a ring shape on a lightly greased baking sheet, pinching dough ends together. With scissors, cut slashes at an angle, about two inches apart, three-quarters of the way through the dough from the outer edge. Turn the sections over on their side so that they are flat on the tin or slightly twisted.

8. Cover with a towel and let rise about twenty-five minutes, until almost doubled in bulk.

9. Preheat the oven to 375 degrees.

10. Bake twenty-five minutes, or until well browned and done. Cool on a rack.

11. To prepare frosting, combine the confectioners' sugar with enough water to give a smooth coating consistency. Spoon over the hot coffeecake. Sprinkle with the nuts.

Yield: One dozen servings.

Passover Crispy Sticks   *New York*

1 egg
½ cup water
1 teaspoon salt
1 cup sifted matzoh meal
1 cup oil
1 teaspoon coarse salt.

1. Using a rotary beater, beat together the egg, water and salt. Gradually stir in the matzoh meal. Cover and chill at least one hour.

2. With lightly greased hands, take a piece of dough the size of a green pea and roll out into a pencil shape between the palm of the hand and a clean flat surface. Place on a flat plate. Repeat until all dough is used.

3. Heat the oil in a heavy skillet and add the dough strands, a few at a time, and fry until golden. Drain sticks and shake in a paper bag containing the coarse salt.

Yield: Three dozen.

Note: Serve in soup or as a snack.

Pies, Cakes, Desserts and Cookies

Squash-Apple Pie
Massachusetts

1 cup cooked, mashed and sieved squash
1 cup thick tart applesauce
½ teaspoon salt
1 cup light brown sugar
1 teaspoon cinnamon
1 teaspoon ginger
½ teaspoon mace
⅛ teaspoon ground cloves
4 eggs, lightly beaten
1½ cups heavy cream
1 unbaked ten-inch pie shell with stand-up edge.

1. Preheat the oven to 425 degrees.
2. Place the squash and applesauce in a bowl. Stir in the salt, brown sugar, cinnamon, ginger, mace and cloves.
3. Combine the eggs and cream and add to the squash mixture. Pour into the pie shell. Bake twenty minutes. Reduce oven heat to 350 degrees and bake twenty to twenty-five minutes longer (a knife inserted into filling should come out clean). Cool and chill.

Yield: Eight servings.

Note: This pie can be made with egg yolks and beaten egg whites folded in or used for a meringue topping.

Apple Pie with Sour Cream
Massachusetts

⅓ cup plus two tablespoons flour
⅓ cup plus three-quarters cup sugar
1¼ teaspoons cinnamon
⅛ teaspoon salt
1 egg
½ teaspoon vanilla
1 cup sour cream
6 medium-size apples, peeled, cored and sliced
1 unbaked nine-inch pie shell, chilled
¼ cup butter.

1. Preheat the oven to 400 degrees.
2. Sift together two tablespoons of the flour, three-quarters cup of the sugar, three-quarters teaspoon of the cinnamon and the salt. Stir in the egg, vanilla and sour cream. Fold in the apples and spoon into the pie shell. Bake fifteen minutes.
3. Reduce the oven temperature to 350 degrees and bake thirty minutes longer. Meanwhile, combine the remaining flour, sugar and cinnamon. With a pastry blender or the finger tips, blend in the butter until the mixture is crumbly.
4. Increase the oven temperature to 400 degrees. Sprinkle crumb mixture over the pie. Bake ten minutes longer.

Yield: Six servings.

Tewksbury Apple Pie *New York*

3 pounds tart green apples
Juice of half a lemon
¼ cup cognac or bourbon
½ cup sweet butter
¾ cup light brown sugar
¼ cup granulated sugar
¾ cup flour.

1. Preheat the oven to 350 degrees.
2. Take two of the apples and reserve for another use. Peel the remaining apples and core them. Cut into thick slices and immediately arrange them in a buttered baking dish. Sprinkle with the lemon juice. Pour the cognac or bourbon over the apples.
3. With the fingers, cream together the remaining ingredients. Spread this mixture over the apples and bake one hour. Serve hot.
Yield: Six servings.

Winy Apple-Raisin Pie *New York*

Pastry for a two-crust ten-inch pie
1 tablespoon butter
¼ cup dry vermouth
1 cup golden raisins
6 cups peeled, sliced tart apples
1 tablespoon lemon juice
¾ cup light brown sugar
½ cup granulated sugar
1 teaspoon cinnamon
¼ teaspoon allspice
¼ teaspoon nutmeg
Sweetened whipped cream (optional).

1. Preheat the oven to 375 degrees.
2. Roll out half the pastry and use it to line a ten-inch pie dish. Reserve remaining pastry for the top.
3. Heat the butter and vermouth in a saucepan and add the raisins. Simmer until raisins are soft. Drain and set aside.
4. Combine the apples, lemon juice, brown

sugar, granulated sugar, cinnamon, allspice and nutmeg. Add raisins and toss lightly. Pour mixture into the pie dish. Roll out remaining pastry and make a latticework top for pie. Bake about forty minutes, or until crust is golden brown. If desired, serve with sweetened whipped cream on the side.
Yield: Six to ten servings.

Dutch Apple Sack Pie *Maine*

5 to six apples, peeled and sliced
½ cup light brown sugar
⅓ cup granulated sugar
⅛ teaspoon salt
⅛ teaspoon allspice
2 tablespoons flour
1½ tablespoons butter, cut up very finely
1 unbaked nine-inch pie shell
3 tablespoons heavy cream
1 tablespoon milk
½ teaspoon cinnamon.

1. Preheat the oven to 425 degrees.
2. Mix together the apples, brown sugar, granulated sugar, salt, allspice, flour and butter. Turn into the pie shell.
3. Mix the cream and milk together and pour over the pie filling. Sprinkle with the cinnamon.
4. Slide the pie into a heavy, unglazed brown paper sack and fold over the open end. Place on shelf in middle of oven and bake about thirty minutes, or until apples are almost tender.
5. Remove pie carefully from the sack and allow to brown lightly, about fifteen minutes.
6. Cool the pie to lukewarm on a rack before serving.
Yield: Six servings.

Blueberry Pie *Maine*

Pastry:
2 cups flour
½ teaspoon salt

⅔ cup shortening
Ice water.
Filling:
 4 cups wild blueberries
¾ cup to one cup sugar, depending on tartness of berries
¼ scant cup flour
¼ teaspoon salt
¼ teaspoon lemon juice
2 tablespoons butter, cut into three pats.

1. Preheat the oven to 400 degrees.
2. To prepare pastry, combine the flour and salt in a bowl. With a pastry blender or the finger tips, blend the shortening in until the mixture resembles coarse oatmeal. With a fork, mix to a dough with ice water. Chill twenty minutes if desired.
3. Roll out two-thirds of the pastry and use to line a nine-inch pie plate.
4. To prepare filling, combine the blueberries, sugar, flour, salt and lemon juice. Pour into the pie plate. Dot with the butter. Cover with remaining pastry, rolled out.
5. Slit the crust in several places. Bake pie about fifty minutes, or until crust is well browned.
Yield: Six servings.

Deep-Dish Blueberry Pie   *New Jersey*

 4 cups blueberries, picked over, rinsed and drained
¾ cup sugar
1½ teaspoons tapioca
⅛ teaspoon salt
 Grated rind of half a lemon
1 tablespoon lemon juice
1 tablespoon butter
 Pastry for one-crust pie
 Whipped cream.

1. Preheat the oven to 400 degrees.
2. Combine the blueberries, sugar, tapioca, salt, lemon rind and lemon juice. Turn mixture

into a 10-by-6-by-2-inch baking dish. Dot with the butter.
3. Roll the pastry into a rectangle one-eighth-inch thick and about one and one-half inches larger than the baking dish. Arrange pastry lightly over berries and trim edges, leaving one-half inch overhanging. Moisten rim of dish, turn overhanging edge of pastry under and press it onto rim. Flute or crimp edge with tines of a fork. Cut slits in pastry for steam to escape. Bake pie thirty to forty-five minutes, or until crust is browned. Serve with whipped cream.
Yield: Six to eight servings.

Blueberry Velvet Custard Pie   *New Jersey*

 4 eggs
⅔ cup granulated sugar
½ teaspoon salt
½ teaspoon nutmeg
2⅔ cups milk
1 teaspoon vanilla
1 unbaked nine-inch pie shell
1 cup blueberries, picked over, rinsed and drained
2 tablespoons orange juice
3 tablespoons confectioners' sugar.

1. Preheat the oven to 425 degrees.
2. Beat the eggs with rotary beater until thoroughly blended. Add the granulated sugar, salt, nutmeg, milk and vanilla and stir until smooth.
3. Pour mixture into the pie shell. Bake fifteen minutes; then reduce oven temperature to 350 degrees and bake thirty minutes longer, or until a knife inserted in filling about one inch from pastry edge comes out clean. Cool.
4. Blend the blueberries, orange juice and confectioners' sugar and spoon over custard before serving pie.
Yield: Six to eight servings.

Cape Cod Cranberry Pie   *Massachusetts*

2 cups cranberries
1½ cups sugar
½ cup chopped nuts
2 eggs, well beaten
1 cup flour
½ cup melted butter
¼ cup melted shortening.

1. Preheat the oven to 325 degrees.
2. Spread the cranberries in the bottom of a well-greased ten-inch pie plate.
3. Sprinkle with one-half cup of the sugar and the nuts.
4. Add the remaining sugar to the eggs, beating well. Beat in the flour, butter and shortening. Pour over the cranberries.
5. Bake about one hour, or until crust is golden brown.
Yield: Six to eight servings.

Cranberry-Pumpkin Chiffon Pie
Massachusetts

1 tablespoon unflavored gelatin
¼ cup cold water
1 cup cranberries
1 cup plus two tablespoons sugar
¼ cup chopped citron
¼ cup chopped nuts
½ cup chopped raisins
1 baked nine-inch pie shell
2 eggs, separated
¼ teaspoon salt
½ teaspoon ginger
½ teaspoon nutmeg
½ teaspoon cinnamon
¾ cup mashed pumpkin
⅓ cup milk
½ cup heavy cream, whipped.

1. Soften one teaspoon of the gelatin in two tablespoons of the water and place over hot water to melt gelatin.

2. Put the cranberries through a food chopper, using medium blade. Add six tablespoons of the sugar, the citron, nuts and raisins. Add the melted gelatin and let mixture stand until thickened.
3. Spread over the bottom of the baked pie shell and chill until firm.
4. In the top part of a double boiler, beat the egg yolks with one-half cup of the sugar, the salt and spices. Stir in the pumpkin and milk. Cook over hot water, stirring constantly, until thick, ten to fifteen minutes. Remove from the heat.
5. Soften the remaining gelatin in the remaining cold water and add to the pumpkin mixture. Chill over ice water, stirring frequently, until thick.
6. Beat the egg whites until they stand in soft peaks; then gradually beat in the remaining sugar. Fold into the pumpkin mixture. Pour over the cranberry layer in the pie shell. Chill until firm. Top with whipped cream.
Yield: Six servings.

Pumpkin Pie with Cottage Cheese
Delaware

2 cups pumpkin puree
1 cup cottage cheese, sieved
½ teaspoon ginger
½ teaspoon cinnamon
1 teaspoon salt
¼ cup sour cream
2 eggs, lightly beaten
½ cup milk
¼ cup dry sherry
1 unbaked nine-inch pie shell
Whipped cream.

1. Preheat the oven to 450 degrees.
2. Mix the pumpkin with the cottage cheese, ginger, cinnamon, salt and sour cream.
3. Beat the eggs with the milk and sherry and gradually stir into the pumpkin mixture. Pour into the pie shell.
4. Bake ten minutes. Reduce the oven temper-

ature to 350 degrees and bake thirty minutes longer, or until set. Cool and chill. Serve cold, garnished with whipped cream.

Yield: Six to eight servings.

Pioneer Lemon Pie   *Massachusetts*

3 slices stale firm white bread
3 tablespoons butter
1 cup sugar
1 cup boiling water
2 eggs, separated
2 teaspoons grated lemon rind
⅓ cup lemon juice
  Pastry for a two-crust nine-inch pie.

1. Spread the bread with the butter and place in a bowl. Add the sugar and boiling water and let stand until cool.
2. Preheat the oven to 425 degrees.
3. Beat the bread mixture until smooth. Stir in the egg yolks, lemon rind and lemon juice.
4. Roll out half the pastry and use to line a nine-inch pie plate.
5. Beat the egg whites until stiff but not dry and fold into the bread mixture. Pour into the pie plate. Cover with remaining pastry, rolled out. Seal the edges.
6. Bake pie thirty-five minutes, or until golden and done. Let cool to room temperature.

Yield: Six servings.

Orange Chiffon Pie   *New Jersey*

Crumb crust:
1⅓ cups vanilla wafer crumbs (about thirty-five wafers)
¼ cup butter, melted.
Filling:
2 envelopes unflavored gelatin
½ cup plus two tablespoons sugar
1 cup water
2 cups plain yogurt

1 six-ounce can frozen orange juice concentrate, thawed
1 tablespoon grated orange rind
2 egg whites
  Toasted coconut.

1. To prepare crust, combine the crumbs and butter. Press firmly and evenly against bottom and sides of a nine-inch pie plate, building up a rim.
2. To prepare filling, combine the gelatin and one-half cup of the sugar in a saucepan. Stir in the water and heat gently until gelatin has dissolved.
3. Combine the yogurt, orange juice concentrate and orange rind in a bowl and stir into the gelatin mixture. Chill until partially set.
4. Beat the egg whites until foamy, gradually add the remaining sugar and beat until stiff. Fold into the setting mixture. Chill until mixture mounds; then turn into pie shell.
5. Chill until firm. Garnish with toasted coconut.

Yield: Six servings.

Honey Raisin Pie   *Pennsylvania*

Crust:
1 cup flour
¼ teaspoon salt
3 tablespoons butter
2 tablespoons lard or shortening
3 tablespoons cold water, approximately
Filling:
3 eggs, lightly beaten
¾ cup honey
1 cup sour cream
1 tablespoon lemon juice
1 cup cooked, pitted, chopped prunes
1 cup raisins
½ cup chopped walnuts.

1. Preheat the oven to 350 degrees.
2. To prepare crust, sift the flour and salt into a bowl. With a pastry blender or the finger tips, blend in the butter and lard or shortening.

3. Using a fork, mix to a dough with the water.

4. Roll out the dough on a lightly floured board and use to line a nine-inch pie plate. Decorate the edge.

5. To prepare filling, blend the eggs with the honey, sour cream and lemon juice. Fold in the prunes and raisins. Pour into the pie shell and sprinkle the walnuts over the top.

6. Bake fifty to sixty minutes, or until a knife inserted in the middle comes out clean.

Yield: Six servings.

Sour Cream, Raisin and Walnut Pie
Vermont

2 eggs, lightly beaten
1 cup instant superfine sugar
1 cup sour cream
1 cup chopped raisins
¼ cup coarsely chopped walnuts
½ teaspoon vanilla
⅛ teaspoon salt
2 teaspoons lemon juice
  Pastry for a two-crust nine-inch pie.

1. Preheat the oven to 450 degrees.

2. Combine the eggs and sugar and beat with a wire whisk until light and fluffy. Add the sour cream, raisins, walnuts, vanilla, salt and lemon juice. Blend well.

3. Line bottom of a nine-inch pie dish with the rolled-out pastry and pour in filling. Top with remaining pastry, rolled out, and seal. Slit top to permit steam to escape. Bake fifteen minutes and reduce oven heat to 350 degrees. Bake one-half hour longer.

Yield: Six to eight servings.

Yankee Pine Nut Pie
Massachusetts

½ cup sugar
  Salt to taste
1 tablespoon flour
1 cup dark corn syrup

2 eggs, lightly beaten
1 teaspoon vanilla
2 tablespoons melted butter
1 cup pignoli (pine nuts, see note)
1 unbaked nine-inch pie shell.

1. Preheat the oven to 300 degrees.

2. Sift the sugar, salt and flour into a mixing bowl. Stir in the syrup and eggs. Add the vanilla, butter and pignoli.

3. Pour mixture into the pie shell and bake one hour. Let cool.

Yield: Eight servings.

Note: Pignoli are available in Italian groceries and many supermarkets.

Pecan-Maple Pie
New York

4 eggs
⅔ cup sugar
½ teaspoon salt
⅓ cup melted butter
1 cup maple syrup
1 cup pecan halves
1 unbaked nine-inch pie shell, chilled.

1. Preheat the oven to 375 degrees.

2. With a rotary beater, beat together the eggs, sugar, salt, butter and syrup. Mix in the pecans and pour into the pie shell.

3. Bake fifteen minutes. Reduce the oven heat to 350 degrees and bake twenty-five minutes longer, or until filling is set and pastry is browned. Serve cold or slightly warm.

Yield: Six servings.

Rutabaga Pie
Maine

1½ cups cooked, mashed and sieved rutabaga
    or yellow turnip
1 cup light brown sugar
2 tablespoons unsulphured molasses
2 eggs, lightly beaten
1¼ cups light cream

½ teaspoon ginger
1 teaspoon cinnamon
½ teaspoon nutmeg
¼ teaspoon cloves
½ teaspoon salt
1 teaspoon vanilla
1 unbaked deep nine-inch pie shell
½ cup heavy cream, whipped
  Sliced filberts.

1. Preheat the oven to 450 degrees.
2. Beat together the rutabaga, brown sugar, molasses, eggs, light cream, ginger, cinnamon, nutmeg, cloves, salt and vanilla. Pour into the pie shell and bake fifteen minutes. Reduce the oven heat to 350 degrees and bake about forty minutes longer, or until set. Do not overbake.
3. Cool. Serve topped with the whipped cream and sliced filberts.
  Yield: Six servings.

Chocolate Pie   *Pennsylvania*

1 unbaked ten-inch pie shell
5 egg yolks, lightly beaten
2½ ounces unsweetened chocolate, grated
1¼ cups milk
1 cup plus five tablespoons sugar
1 cup evaporated milk
1 teaspoon vanilla
3 egg whites
¼ teaspoon cream of tartar.

1. Preheat the oven to 425 degrees.
2. Line the pie shell with aluminum foil and pour in dry rice or beans. Bake five to ten minutes, or until just set. Remove from oven and remove foil and rice or beans. Cool the pie shell.
3. Brush pie shell with a very small amount of the egg yolks and bake one to two minutes to set.
4. Reduce the oven heat to 325 degrees.
5. Combine the chocolate and regular milk in a saucepan and heat slowly, stirring, until chocolate melts.
6. Put one cup minus one tablespoon of the

sugar in a bowl and add remaining egg yolks. Beat the yolks and sugar together until well blended. Pour hot chocolate mixture into yolk mixture gradually, beating vigorously. Stir in the evaporated milk and vanilla and strain into the pie shell.
7. Bake about thirty-five minutes, or until set. Increase the oven heat to 400 degrees.
8. Beat the egg whites and cream of tartar together until foamy. Add remaining six tablespoons sugar gradually, beating until stiff and shiny. Spread meringue over warm pie and bake until lightly browned, about ten minutes.
  Yield: Six to eight servings.
  Note: The pie is best if made early in the day as the filling sets and becomes smooth and creamy.

Cognac Pie   *New York*

5 egg yolks
¾ cup sugar
1 envelope unflavored gelatin
¼ cup water
½ cup cognac
1½ cups heavy cream
1 ten-inch or deep nine-inch graham cracker crust, baked and cooled
2 tablespoons shaved chocolate.

1. Beat the egg yolks until thick and lemon-colored. Gradually beat in the sugar.
2. Soften the gelatin in the water and one-quarter cup of the cognac. Heat over boiling water until gelatin dissolves.
3. Pour the gelatin mixture into the yolks, stirring briskly. Stir in the remaining cognac.
4. Whip one cup of the cream and fold it into the custard. Pour the filling into the pie shell and chill.
5. When the pie filling is set, whip the remaining cream. Decorate the pie with the cream and the chocolate.
  Yield: Eight servings.

Sour Cream Pie   *Delaware*

1¼ cups graham cracker crumbs
⅓ cup melted butter
½ cup plus one teaspoon sugar
¼ pound cream cheese
2 cups sour cream
1 cup blueberries.

1. Preheat the oven to 350 degrees.
2. Combine the cracker crumbs, butter and one-quarter cup of the sugar. Line a nine-inch pie plate with the mixture and press down firmly. Bake eight to ten minutes, or until lightly browned.
3. Mix together the cream cheese, sour cream and one-quarter cup of the remaining sugar. Pour into pie shell. Top with blueberries and sprinkle with remaining sugar. Bake five minutes. Cool and chill.
Yield: Six servings.

Sour Cream Peach Pie   *New Jersey*

5 cups peeled, sliced, ripe peaches
½ cup light brown sugar
1 tablespoon cornstarch
½ teaspoon cinnamon
¼ teaspoon nutmeg
⅛ teaspoon salt
Pastry for a two-crust nine-inch or ten-inch pie
1½ cups sour cream.

1. Preheat the oven to 400 degrees.
2. Combine the peaches, brown sugar, cornstarch, cinnamon, nutmeg and salt. Line a nine-inch or ten-inch pie plate with rolled-out pastry.
3. Turn the fruit into the pie plate. Pour the sour cream over all. Top with remaining pastry, rolled out. Seal and decorate edges and make a steam hole. Bake twenty-five to thirty-five minutes, or until pastry is golden.
Yield: Six servings.

Shoofly Pie   *Pennsylvania*

1½ cups sifted flour
1 cup light or dark brown sugar
½ cup butter
¼ teaspoon salt
½ teaspoon baking soda
⅔ cup hot water
⅔ cup dark molasses
1 unbaked nine-inch pie shell.

1. Preheat the oven to 350 degrees.
2. Combine the flour, brown sugar, butter and salt and rub the mixture between the hands to form crumbs.
3. Dissolve the baking soda in the water and combine with the molasses. Pour into the pie shell. Sprinkle with the crumbs. Bake thirty to forty minutes, or until filling is set.
Yield: Six servings.

Mince Pies   *New York*

Mincemeat:
1 pound beef suet, ground
1½ pounds golden raisins, ground
½ pound prunes, pitted and ground
½ pound dates, ground
½ pound mixed candied fruit peels, ground
¼ pound citron peel, ground
3 tart green apples, peeled, cored and grated or finely chopped
1½ pounds currants
1 pound dark brown sugar
6 ounces chopped blanched almonds
Grated rind and juice of two lemons
1 teaspoon nutmeg
1 teaspoon cinnamon
½ teaspoon ground ginger
½ teaspoon allspice
1 teaspoon salt
½ cup dark rum or cognac.

Pastry:

    Short crust pastry for two-crust pie
1 egg, lightly beaten.

1. Combine all the mincemeat ingredients very well, using the hands. Turn into clean jars and store, covered, in a cool, dark, dry place. The mincemeat will keep for months.

2. Preheat the oven to 425 degrees.

3. Roll out half the pastry to one-eighth-inch thickness and cut into two-inch rounds. Fit into small muffin tins. Fill with mincemeat. Roll out remaining pastry and cut tops to fit the pies.

4. Moisten the edges and pinch to seal. Make a steam hole in each pie, brush with egg and bake about twenty-five minutes, or until golden brown. The pies are best eaten warm.

Yield: About six pounds mincemeat; pastry makes one dozen little pies.

Sour Cream Pastry Turnovers   *New York*

Pastry:
 2 cups flour
½ teaspoon salt
¾ cup butter
¼ cup sugar
½ cup sour cream.
Filling:
 2 tablespoons flour
½ cup sugar
¼ teaspoon cinnamon
 4 tart green apples, peeled, cored and thinly sliced
¼ cup butter.

1. To prepare pastry, sift the flour and salt into a bowl. With a pastry blender or two knives, cut in the butter until mixture resembles coarse oatmeal. Mix in the sugar and sour cream.

2. Roll out the dough on a lightly floured pastry cloth or board into an approximate 18-by-9-inch rectangle. Fold lengthwise into three. Wrap in aluminum foil and chill two hours.

3. Preheat the oven to 375 degrees.

4. To prepare filling, combine the flour, sugar and cinnamon and toss with the apples.

5. Roll out the chilled pastry to one-eighth-inch thickness on a lightly floured pastry cloth or board. Cut into four-and-one-half-inch rounds.

6. Place a tablespoon or two of apple mixture in the middle of each round. Dot with the butter. Moisten the edges of each round, fold over and pinch with a fork to seal.

7. Place on an ungreased baking sheet and bake twenty minutes, or until golden and done.

Yield: One dozen to fourteen.

Galakto Boureka   *New York*

Filling:
 1 cup sugar
 4 cups milk, boiling
½ cup farina
¼ cup butter
    Grated rind of half a large orange
 2 eggs, lightly beaten.
Syrup:
 2 cups sugar
 2 cups water
 1 stick cinnamon.
Pastry:
 1 pound phyllo pastry (see note)
½ cup melted butter, approximately.

1. To prepare filling, add the sugar to the boiling milk and bring to a boil, stirring. Gradually stir in the farina and cook until thickened. Stir in the butter and orange rind.

2. Add a little of the hot mixture to the eggs. Return all to the pan and cook one minute longer. Allow to cool to room temperature.

3. Preheat the oven to 350 degrees.

4. To prepare syrup, combine the sugar, water and cinnamon stick and bring to a boil. Boil five minutes. Set aside to cool.

5. Remove one leaf of the phyllo pastry at a time, keeping remaining leaves covered. Dot edges with melted butter, fold in half, dot edges with melted butter again and fold in half again.

6. Place two tablespoons of the cooled filling mixture at one end of the pastry. Dot edges of pastry with melted butter. Turn in the sides and roll up like a jellyroll. Continue shaping rolls until all filling is used.

7. Place rolls with space between in a well-oiled baking pan.

8. Bake about twenty-five minutes, or until golden brown. Spoon the cooled syrup over the hot pastries.

Yield: Three dozen to four dozen.

Note: Fresh phyllo pastry is available in New York City at Kassos Brothers, 570 Ninth Avenue (10036); Poseidon Pastry Shop, 629 Ninth Avenue (10036), and Trinacria, 415 Third Avenue (10016), and frozen in specialty food stores.

Pumpkin Cake New York

  2 cups sugar
1¼ cups oil
1½ cups canned pumpkin
  4 eggs
  3 cups flour
  2 teaspoons baking powder
  2 teaspoons baking soda
  2 teaspoons cinnamon
  1 teaspoon salt
  ½ cup dark raisins
  ½ cup golden raisins
  1 cup chopped walnuts or pecans.

1. Preheat the oven to 350 degrees.

2. Place the sugar, oil and pumpkin in a large mixer bowl and beat well with the mixer at medium speed.

3. Add the eggs, one at a time, beating well after each addition.

4. Sift together the flour, baking powder, baking soda, cinnamon and salt and fold into the batter. Stir in the raisins and nuts.

5. Pour into a greased ten-inch tube pan. Bake one and one-quarter hours, or until done. Do not open the oven door under one hour. Let cool slightly in pan before turning out onto a rack.

Yield: One dozen servings.

Honey Chocolate Cake New York

Cake:
  ½ cup shortening
  ½ cup sugar
  3 eggs
  1 teaspoon vanilla
  1 cup honey
  1 teaspoon grated orange rind
2¼ cups flour
  1 teaspoon baking soda
  1 teaspoon salt
  ⅔ cup cocoa powder
  ¾ cup sour cream
  ¼ cup orange juice.
Frosting:
1¼ cups sugar
  ¼ cup honey
  ¼ teaspoon cream of tartar
  ½ cup minus one tablespoon orange juice
  1 tablespoon lemon juice
  2 egg whites
  ¼ teaspoon salt.
Honey crumb topping:
  1 cup flour
  3 tablespoons light brown sugar
  1 tablespoon honey
  ½ cup butter
  ½ cup chopped walnuts.

1. Preheat the oven to 350 degrees.

2. To prepare cake, beat the shortening and sugar together until light and fluffy. Beat in the eggs, one at a time, very well. Stir in the vanilla, honey and orange rind.

3. Sift together the flour, baking soda, salt and cocoa powder. Stir dry ingredients into batter alternately with the sour cream and orange juice.

4. Divide the batter between two greased and floured nine-inch layer pans. Bake twenty-five to thirty minutes, or until done.

5. Let cool on a rack.

6. To prepare frosting, place all ingredients in the top of a double boiler over rapidly boiling water.

7. Beat constantly for about seven minutes, remove from the heat and continue to beat until frosting is the correct consistency for filling and frosting the layers.

8. Meanwhile, increase the oven heat to 400 degrees. Combine the ingredients for the crumb topping and spread on a baking sheet. Bake twelve to fifteen minutes, stirring every three minutes.

9. The crumb topping may be stirred into the frosting before using to fill and frost the layers or may be sprinkled over the filling and the frosted cake.

Yield: Ten servings.

French Chocolate Cake   *New York*

1 pound Maillard's Eagle sweet chocolate (see note)
1 tablespoon water
1 tablespoon flour
1 tablespoon sugar
10 tablespoons soft butter
4 eggs, separated
  Sweetened whipped cream.

1. Preheat the oven to 425 degrees.

2. Melt the chocolate gently with the water in the top of a double boiler over hot, not boiling, water. This is a critical step in the preparation and should be done very slowly.

3. Remove from the heat and stir in the flour, sugar and butter. Beat the egg yolks lightly and gradually whisk into the chocolate mixture.

4. Beat the egg whites until they hold a definite shape but are not dry and fold into the chocolate mixture. Overbeating or underbeating will ruin the cake. The beaten egg whites should be folded smoothly, quickly and easily into the chocolate mixture.

5. Pour into an eight-inch springform pan that has been lined with wax paper. Bake fifteen minutes. Turn off the oven heat. Open the oven door, leaving it ajar, and allow the cake to cool completely in the oven.

6. If the center of the cake still feels soft, refrigerate an hour or two, but cake is best served at room temperature. Decorate with whipped cream. Serve small pieces. The cake is rich.

Yield: Ten servings.

Note: Maillard's Eagle sweet chocolate is available in New York City at Bloomingdale's; Charles and Company, 340 Madison Avenue (10017) and 683 Madison Avenue (10021); Altman's, and Verde's Original Market, 534 Third Avenue (10016). The chocolate is also available at many supermarkets.

Seven-Layer Chocolate Cake for Passover
New York

½ pound Elite bittersweet chocolate (see note)
1 tablespoon margarine
½ pound orange marmalade
2 eggs
2 tablespoons brandy
1 cup semi-dry white wine
8 round matzohs
  Chopped nuts.

1. Melt the chocolate, margarine and marmalade in the top of a double boiler over hot water.

2. Add the eggs and beat with a wire whisk until the mixture is as thick as sour cream. Add the brandy and remove pan from the heat.

3. Continue beating until mixture again attains the consistency of sour cream. Pour the wine into a large shallow dish.

4. Dip the matzohs, one at a time, into the wine just to moisten but not to soak. Place moistened matzoh on a cake plate and coat with a layer of the chocolate mixture. Top with another moistened matzoh and more chocolate, continuing until all matzohs are used. Use remaining

chocolate mixture to frost sides. Decorate with nuts and let set at room temperature.

Yield: Six to eight servings.

Note: Elite bittersweet chocolate is available at Macy's and Gimbels' Passover shops.

Dark Chocolate Cake   *New York*

½ cup butter
½ cup shortening
2 cups sugar
4 eggs
2½ cups cake flour
¼ teaspoon salt
3 teaspoons baking soda
1 cup buttermilk
¾ cup cocoa powder
⅔ cup boiling water
1 teaspoon vanilla
Chocolate frosting (recipe below).

1. Preheat the oven to 350 degrees.
2. Beat the butter, shortening and sugar together very well until light and fluffy. Beat in the eggs, one at a time.
3. Sift the flour with the salt and baking soda and fold into the batter alternately with the buttermilk.
4. Stir the cocoa powder into the boiling water until smooth. Stir with the vanilla into the batter.
5. Pour into three greased and floured eight-inch layer pans and bake about thirty-five minutes, or until done. Cool. Fill and frost with chocolate frosting.

Yield: Ten to one dozen servings.

Chocolate Frosting   *New York*

6 ounces (squares) unsweetened chocolate
6 tablespoons butter
1½ pounds confectioners' sugar
⅛ teaspoon salt
¾ cup milk
1½ teaspoons vanilla.

1. Melt the chocolate and butter in the top of a double boiler over hot water. Combine the remaining ingredients in a bowl and blend.
2. Beat in the chocolate mixture and let stand, stirring occasionally, until frosting is spreading consistency.

Yield: About three and one-half cups.

Prize Angel Food Cake   *New York*

1½ cups egg whites (nine large eggs)
1 teaspoon cream of tartar
½ teaspoon salt
1 cup granulated sugar
1 teaspoon vanilla
1 cup confectioners' sugar
1 cup cake flour.

1. Preheat the oven to 375 degrees. Heat a nine-inch angel food pan in the oven five to ten minutes before using.
2. Beat the egg whites with the cream of tartar and salt until very stiff. Gradually beat in three-quarters cup of the granulated sugar until mixture is very smooth and glossy.
3. Beat in the vanilla.
4. Sift together three times the confectioners' sugar and flour. Fold with the remaining granulated sugar into the egg white mixture.
5. Turn the batter into the prepared pan. Bake thirty-five minutes. Cool in the pan turned upside down.

Yield: Ten servings.

Zuppa Inglese   *New York*

Spongecake:
6 eggs, separated
1 cup sugar
1 tablespoon lemon juice
1 tablespoon grated orange rind
1 cup cake flour
1½ teaspoons baking powder

¼ teaspoon salt.

Custard filling:

½ cup sugar

¼ cup cornstarch

⅛ teaspoon salt

2 cups milk

3 egg yolks, lightly beaten

½ cup dark rum

½ teaspoon vanilla

2 tablespoons crème de cacao

¼ cup Marsala wine

1 cup heavy cream, whipped

2 tablespoons chopped mixed candied fruits.

1. Preheat the oven to 350 degrees. Grease and flour a nine-inch springform pan.

2. To prepare spongecake, beat the egg yolks until they are very thick and pale; then gradually beat in the sugar until mixture spins a rope when dropped from the beaters.

3. Beat in the lemon juice and orange rind. Sift together twice the flour, baking powder and salt and gently fold into the yolk mixture.

4. Beat the egg whites until stiff but not dry and fold into the batter. Pour into the prepared pan and bake about forty-five minutes, or until cake tests done. Cool in pan on a rack.

5. To prepare custard filling, combine the sugar, cornstarch and salt in a saucepan. Stir in the milk. Bring to a boil, stirring, and cook one minute.

6. Pour a little of the hot mixture into the egg yolks, mix and return all to the pan. Heat one to two minutes to cook the yolks.

7. Divide the custard into three bowls. Add two tablespoons rum to the first bowl and chill. Add the vanilla to the second bowl and the crème de cacao to the third bowl and chill.

8. Combine the remaining rum with the Marsala. Split the cooled spongecake into three layers and sprinkle all layers with the rum mixture. Place the bottom layer in a shallow dish or deep plate. Spread with one of the cooled custards. Repeat with the other layers and the two other custards.

9. Frost with whipped cream and garnish with candied fruit. Serve immediately or refrigerate until serving time.

Yield: One dozen servings.

Passover Spongecake   *New York*

8 eggs, separated

1½ cups sugar

Grated rind of two lemons

Juice of half a lemon

¼ cup matzoh cake flour

¾ cup potato starch

¼ teaspoon salt.

1. Preheat the oven to 325 degrees.

2. Beat the egg whites until stiff. Beat the egg yolks with the sugar, lemon rind and lemon juice until yolks are thick and lemon-colored.

3. Sift together the matzoh cake flour, potato starch and salt. Fold the egg whites and dry ingredients alternately into the yolks. Pour the mixture into two ungreased eight-inch layer pans and bake one hour, or until done. Invert in pans, on a rack, and let cool thoroughly.

Yield: One dozen servings.

Spongecake   *New York*

9 large egg yolks

1½ cups sugar

¾ cup boiling water

1 teaspoon lemon extract

2½ cups cake flour

¾ teaspoon salt

3 teaspoons baking powder.

1. Preheat the oven to 350 degrees.

2. Beat the egg yolks until light. Gradually beat in the sugar until the mixture is light and creamy.

3. Beat in the boiling water and the lemon extract.

4. Sift the flour with the salt and baking powder and fold in. Turn into a greased 15-by-10-by-

2-inch baking or roasting pan and bake forty-five minutes, or until done. Cool in the pan, on a rack.

Yield: Ten to one dozen servings.

Bundt Cake   *Pennsylvania*

1 cup butter
1 cup granulated sugar
1 cup confectioners' sugar
4 eggs, separated
1 teaspoon vanilla
1 teaspoon almond extract
3 cups cake flour
2 teaspoons baking powder
⅛ teaspoon salt
1 cup milk.

1. Preheat the oven to 350 degrees.
2. Cream the butter and gradually beat in the granulated sugar and confectioners' sugar until mixture is light and fluffy.
3. Beat in the egg yolks, one at a time, well.
4. Beat in the vanilla and almond extract.
5. Sift together the flour, baking powder and salt and add to the batter alternately with the milk.
6. Beat the egg whites until stiff but not dry and fold into the batter. Turn into a well-greased heavy cast aluminum bundt pan and bake one and one-quarter hours. Cool in pan thirty minutes before turning onto a rack to finish cooling.

Yield: Two dozen servings.

Note: Bundt pans are sold in specialty kitchen stores and large department stores.

Maple Sugar Cake   *New York*

1 cup soft maple sugar
¼ cup shortening
2 egg yolks
1½ cups flour
1 teaspoon salt
2 teaspoons baking powder

1 cup milk
1 cup chopped nuts
Maple frosting (recipe below).

1. Preheat the oven to 350 degrees.
2. Cream together the maple sugar and shortening until light and fluffy. Beat in the egg yolks.
3. Sift together the flour, salt and baking powder. Add to the batter alternately with the milk. Fold in the nuts.
4. Spoon into two greased eight-inch layer pans and bake about twenty-five minutes, or until done. Cool on a rack before filling and frosting with maple frosting.

Yield: Six to eight servings.

Maple Frosting   *New York*

¾ cup maple syrup
¼ cup sugar
1 egg white, stiffly beaten.

1. Place the syrup and sugar in a small pan and heat until the mixture spins a thread or registers 220 degrees on a candy thermometer.
2. Immediately pour the syrup slowly into the stiffly beaten egg white, continuing to beat until mixture is cold.

Yield: About two cups.

Spice Cake   *Maine*

Cake:
1 cup raisins
2⅔ cups cake flour
1 teaspoon baking soda
1 teaspoon salt
1 teaspoon cinnamon
½ teaspoon nutmeg
½ teaspoon ground allspice
¾ cup butter
1½ cups light brown sugar
¾ cup buttermilk
3 eggs

1 cup finely chopped nuts.
Frosting:
   2 egg whites
1½ cups light brown sugar
⅛ teaspoon salt
½ cup water
   1 tablespoon light corn syrup
1¼ teaspoons vanilla
   Toasted flaked coconut (see note).

1. Preheat the oven to 350 degrees.

2. To prepare cake, rinse the raisins in hot water, drain and chop. Sift the flour with the baking soda, salt and spices.

3. Beat the butter to soften and cream it. Add the flour mixture, brown sugar and buttermilk and mix to moisten. Beat two minutes with electric mixer on medium speed. Add the eggs and beat one minute longer.

4. Stir in the raisins and nuts. Pour batter into three eight-inch layer pans lined on the bottom with paper. Bake twenty-five minutes, or until done. Cool.

5. To prepare frosting, combine the egg whites, brown sugar, salt, water and syrup in the top of a double boiler. Beat about one minute, or until mixed. Place over boiling water and beat constantly with a rotary beater or electric mixer seven minutes, or until frosting stands in stiff peaks.

6. Pour the frosting into a bowl, add the vanilla and beat until thick enough to spread. Use to fill and frost the cooled layers. Sprinkle with toasted coconut.

Yield: Ten to one dozen servings.

Note: To toast flaked coconut, spread in shallow pan and toast in 350-degree oven seven minutes.

Coconut Cake with Apricot Glaze for Passover   *New York*

¼ cup matzoh meal
½ cup potato starch
⅛ teaspoon salt

7 eggs, separated
1 cup sugar
   Juice of half a lemon
   Apricot glaze (recipe below)
   Coconut frosting (recipe below).

1. Preheat the oven to 300 degrees.

2. Sift together the matzoh meal, potato starch and salt.

3. Beat the egg yolks with the sugar and lemon juice until thick and lemon-colored. Beat the egg whites until stiff and fold them into yolk mixture. Fold in the dry ingredients and pour the batter into an ungreased nine-inch springform pan. Bake thirty minutes.

4. Increase the oven heat to 325 degrees. Bake fifteen minutes longer, or until cake tester comes out clean. Invert to cool. Cut into layers and spread with apricot glaze; then frost with coconut frosting.

Yield: Eight to ten servings.

Apricot Glaze   *New York*

Heat the contents of one twelve-ounce jar of apricot preserves over low heat. When dissolved, force the mixture through a fine sieve. Use as a glaze while hot.

Yield: About one and one-quarter cups.

Coconut Frosting   *New York*

1 tablespoon unflavored vegetable gelatin
½ cup cold water
½ cup boiling water
½ cup sugar
3 egg whites, stiffly beaten
   Juice of half a lemon
1 fresh coconut, grated.

1. Soften the gelatin in the cold water; then dissolve gelatin in the boiling water. Add the sugar and stir until dissolved. Set aside to cool.

2. When mixture begins to set, fold it into the

egg whites; then beat until mixture reaches consistency of soft marshmallow. Add the lemon juice and stir to blend. Use as a cake frosting. Coat the frosted cake with the coconut.

Yield: Enough thick frosting for filling, top and sides of nine-inch two-layer cake.

Velvet Lunch Cake   *Maine*

1 cup sugar
½ cup butter
1 egg
1 tablespoon unsulphured molasses
2 cups flour
½ teaspoon salt
1 teaspoon baking soda
½ teaspoon nutmeg
½ teaspoon ground cloves
½ teaspoon cinnamon
1 cup sour milk or buttermilk
½ cup raisins
½ cup chopped walnuts or pecans.

1. Preheat the oven to 350 degrees.
2. Cream the sugar and butter together until very light and fluffy. Beat in the egg and molasses.
3. Sift together the flour, salt, baking soda, nutmeg, cloves and cinnamon and stir into the batter alternately with the milk.
4. Stir in the raisins and nuts and spoon into two greased and lightly floured eight-inch layer pans. Bake twenty-five minutes. Cool on a rack.

Yield: One dozen servings.

Edna's Blueberry Gingerbread   *Maine*

½ cup sugar
½ cup shortening
2 eggs
1 cup unsulphured molasses
2 cups flour
½ teaspoon salt
¼ teaspoon ground cloves
¼ teaspoon nutmeg

1 teaspoon ground ginger
2 teaspoons baking soda
1 cup boiling water
1 cup blueberries, lightly floured
   Whipped cream or vanilla ice cream.

1. Preheat the oven to 350 degrees.
2. Beat the sugar and shortening together until light and fluffy. Beat in the eggs, one at a time, very well. Beat in the molasses.
3. Sift together the flour, salt, cloves, nutmeg and ginger and stir into the batter.
4. Stir the baking soda quickly into the boiling water and stir into the batter. The mixture will be thin. Pour into a well-greased 10-by-14-inch pan or 11-by-16-inch pan.
5. Sprinkle the top with the blueberries and bake thirty to thirty-five minutes, or until done. The blueberries sink to the bottom. Serve warm straight from the pan, with whipped cream or vanilla ice cream.

Yield: About twenty servings.

Note: A delicious unfruited gingerbread can be made from this recipe by omitting the blueberries and adding two teaspoons ground ginger, instead of one, to the flour mixture.

Fruitcake   *New York*

1½ cups shelled Brazil nuts, left whole
1½ cups walnut halves
1 eight-ounce package pitted dates, left whole
⅔ cup chopped candied orange peel
½ cup red maraschino cherries, drained
½ cup green maraschino cherries, drained
½ cup raisins
¾ cup flour
¾ cup sugar
½ teaspoon baking powder
½ teaspoon salt
3 eggs
1 teaspoon vanilla.

1. Preheat the oven to 300 degrees.

2. Mix together the Brazil nuts, walnut halves, dates, orange peel, red cherries, green cherries and raisins. Sift together the flour, sugar, baking powder and salt and sprinkle over fruit mixture.

3. Beat the eggs until light and fluffy, add vanilla and combine with fruit mixture. Resulting mixture will be stiff.

4. The baking utensil(s) to be used should be greased, lined with unglazed brown paper, parchment paper or wax paper and greased again. Spoon the fruitcake mixture into a prepared 9-by-5-by-3-inch loaf pan or one-and-one-half-quart mold or into two prepared one-pound coffee cans.

5. Bake loaf one and three-quarter hours and other tins two hours. Cool cake in baking utensil(s) ten minutes; then loosen and finish cooling on a rack.

Yield: About fourteen servings.

Christmas Cake   *Connecticut*

½ cup shortening
½ cup butter
1 cup granulated sugar
1 cup light brown sugar
3 eggs
1 teaspoon vanilla
1 teaspoon lemon extract
1 teaspoon almond extract
3 cups flour
1½ teaspoons baking powder
½ teaspoon salt
1 cup milk
1 cup golden raisins
½ cup green glacé cherries, chopped
¾ cup drained maraschino cherries, chopped
1 cup chopped mixed glacé fruits
½ cup chopped walnuts.

1. Preheat the oven to 250 degrees.
2. Beat the shortening, butter, granulated sugar and brown sugar together until light and fluffy. Beat in the eggs, one at a time. Beat in the vanilla, lemon and almond extracts.
3. Sift together the flour, baking powder and

salt. Reserve one-half cup of the flour mixture and stir remainder into batter alternately with the milk.

4. Mix together the raisins, glacé cherries, maraschino cherries, mixed fruits and nuts. Toss with reserved flour mixture and stir into batter.

5. Grease a nine-inch tube pan with removable bottom, line with unglazed brown paper or parchment paper and grease again. Spoon batter into pan.

6. Bake three hours, or until the cake tests done. Cool thirty minutes in the pan, remove and finish cooling on a rack.

Yield: About fourteen servings.

Boston Cream Pie   *Massachusetts*

4 eggs
⅛ teaspoon cream of tartar
1¼ cups sugar
½ cup plus three tablespoons flour
¼ teaspoon salt
2 cups milk
2 teaspoons vanilla
Sweetened whipped cream (optional).

1. Preheat the oven to 350 degrees.
2. Separate three of the eggs. Beat the yolks until they are light and lemon-colored.
3. In a separate bowl, beat the egg whites until they are foamy. Add the cream of tartar and continue beating until stiff but not dry. Beat in one-half cup of the sugar.
4. Fold the yolks into the whites; then fold in one-half cup of the flour and half the salt.
5. Butter and lightly flour the bottom of a nine-inch cake pan. Pour the batter into the pan and bake thirty-five to forty minutes. Let cool.
6. Meanwhile, heat the milk in a saucepan. Beat the remaining eggs lightly with the vanilla and remaining sugar, flour and salt. Stir into milk and cook, stirring, until thickened. Cool and chill.
7. Split the cake in half and fill with the cus-

tard. Chill. Serve with sweetened whipped cream if desired.

Yield: Six to ten servings.

Passover Apple Cake   *New York*

¾ cup matzoh cake flour
¾ cup potato flour
2⅓ cups sugar
5 eggs, separated
1 cup orange juice
2 tablespoons grated orange rind
½ teaspoon salt
4 apples, peeled, cored and sliced
2 teaspoons cinnamon.

1. Preheat the oven to 325 degrees.
2. Sift the matzoh cake flour and potato flour together into a bowl. Add one and one-half cups of the sugar. Make a well in the center and drop in the egg yolks. Add the orange juice and orange rind. Beat until smooth.
3. In a separate bowl, beat the egg whites with the salt until stiff. Gradually beat in one-half cup of the sugar and continue beating until stiff. Fold into batter and turn into a greased 13-by-9-by-2-inch baking dish.
4. Arrange the apple slices over top. Combine the remaining sugar with the cinnamon and sprinkle over apples. Bake one hour, or until done.

Yield: Eight to ten servings.

Apple Upside-Down Cake   *Connecticut*

¼ cup butter
½ cup light brown sugar
¼ teaspoon nutmeg
2 large apples, peeled, cored and thinly sliced
1 teaspoon lemon juice
1⅓ cups cake flour
¾ cup sugar
1¾ teaspoons baking powder

¼ teaspoon salt
3 tablespoons shortening, at room temperature
½ cup milk
1 teaspoon vanilla
1 egg.

1. Preheat the oven to 375 degrees.
2. Melt the butter in an eight-inch square pan. Add the brown sugar and nutmeg and blend well. Remove from heat.
3. Arrange the apple slices, slightly overlapping them, on the brown sugar mixture. Sprinkle apples with the lemon juice and set aside.
4. Sift the flour with the sugar, baking powder and salt. Stir the shortening just to soften and stir in the flour mixture, milk and vanilla. Mix until the flour is dampened.
5. Beat two minutes with electric mixer at medium speed or beat 300 strokes by hand. Add the egg and beat one minute longer with the mixer or 150 strokes by hand. Pour the batter over the apples.
6. Bake thirty-five minutes, or until done. Cool cake in the pan five minutes and then invert onto serving plate. Let stand one minute; then remove pan. Serve warm.

Yield: Six to eight servings.

Julia's Glazed Orange Cake

Massachusetts

Cake:
1 cup butter
2 cups sugar
5 eggs
½ teaspoon vanilla
2 tablespoons grated orange rind
3 cups cake flour
3 teaspoons baking powder
¼ teaspoon salt
¾ cup milk.
Glaze:
¼ cup butter

⅔ cup sugar
⅓ cup orange juice.

1. Preheat the oven to 350 degrees.
2. To prepare cake, cream the butter and sugar together until light and fluffy. Beat in the eggs, one at a time, very well. Beat in the vanilla and orange rind.
3. Sift together the flour, baking powder and salt and add to the batter alternately with the milk, ending with the flour mixture.
4. Spoon into a greased and floured ten-inch tube pan. Bake one hour, or until done. Cool in the pan on a rack two minutes.
5. Heat the glaze ingredients in a small pan until the sugar just dissolves.
6. Pour the hot glaze over the hot cake. Allow the cake to cool thoroughly in the pan before removing.
Yield: Ten to one dozen servings.

Old-Fashioned Cream Cake   *Massachusetts*

1½ cups sugar
 4 eggs
1¾ cups self-rising flour
 1 cup heavy cream
 1 teaspoon vanilla.

1. Preheat the oven to 400 degrees.
2. Beat the sugar and eggs together until very thick and pale. Fold in the flour alternately with the cream.
3. Stir in the vanilla.
4. Pour into a greased and floured nine-inch tube pan and bake fifteen minutes. Reduce the oven heat to 300 degrees and bake thirty minutes longer, or until done.
Yield: Eight to ten servings.

Apricot Lattice Cake   *New York*

6 cups flour
1 pound butter

½ teaspoon salt
1½ cups sugar
 2 teaspoons baking powder
   Grated rind and juice of half a lemon
 6 egg yolks
 2 tablespoons sour cream
 1 cup to one and one-half cups apricot
   preserves.

1. Preheat the oven to 350 degrees.
2. Place the flour in a large bowl and cut in the butter with a pastry blender or the finger tips as though starting pastry dough. Mixture should resemble coarse oatmeal.
3. Add all remaining ingredients except preserves and work with hands into a dough.
4. Cut off one-eighth of the dough and set aside. Using fingers, spread bulk of dough evenly in a lightly greased 10-by-15-inch jellyroll tin. Spread with preserves.
5. Roll out reserved dough to one-eighth-inch thickness on a lightly floured pastry cloth or board. Cut into pencil-thin strips and arrange over the cake in a crisscross lattice design. Bake twenty-five minutes, or until lightly browned.
6. Cool in the tin on a rack and cut into squares, triangles or bars. This is very rich.
Yield: About forty.

Coffeecake   *Connecticut*

½ cup soft butter
1½ cups sugar
 2 eggs
 1 cup sour cream
 2 teaspoons vanilla
 2 cups flour
 1 teaspoon baking powder
 1 teaspoon baking soda
¼ teaspoon salt
⅓ cup chopped pecans
 1 teaspoon cinnamon.

1. Preheat the oven to 325 degrees.
2. Beat the butter and one cup of the sugar

together until fluffy. Beat in the eggs, one at a time. Stir in the sour cream and the vanilla.

3. Sift together the flour, baking powder, baking soda and salt and stir into the batter until it is smooth.

4. Spoon half the batter into a greased nine-inch square baking pan. Combine the pecans, cinnamon and remaining sugar and sprinkle two-thirds of the mixture over the batter. Top with remaining batter and sprinkle with remaining nut mixture.

5. Bake fifty minutes, or until done. Serve warm.

Yield: Nine servings.

Apple Coffeecake   Connecticut

6 apples, peeled, cored and sliced (three cups)
5 tablespoons plus two cups sugar
5 teaspoons cinnamon
3 cups flour
3 teaspoons baking powder
1 teaspoon salt
1 cup oil
4 eggs
¼ cup orange juice
1 tablespoon vanilla
  Whipped cream.

1. Preheat the oven to 375 degrees.

2. Combine the apples, five tablespoons of the sugar and the cinnamon and set aside.

3. Sift the flour, baking powder, salt and remaining sugar into a bowl. Make a well in the center and pour in the oil, eggs, orange juice and vanilla. Beat with a wooden spoon until well blended.

4. Drain the reserved apple mixture of excess moisture.

5. Spoon one-third of the batter into a greased nine-inch or ten-inch angel food pan. Make a ring of half the drained apple mixture on top of batter, taking care not to have any apple touching sides of pan.

6. Spoon another third of the batter over,

make a ring of remaining apples and top with remaining batter. Bake one and one-quarter hours, or until done. Cover top with aluminum foil if top begins to overbrown.

7. Allow to cool to lukewarm in pan before turning out onto a serving plate. Serve immediately, with whipped cream.

Yield: Ten servings.

Note: This cake can also be made with peeled, pitted and sliced peaches.

Maggie Murphy's Aunt's Coffeecake
Massachusetts

½ cup butter
1¼ cups sugar
1 egg
2¼ cups flour
4 teaspoons baking powder
¼ teaspoon salt
1 cup milk
½ cup chopped dates
½ cup chopped nuts
1 teaspoon grated orange rind
2 teaspoons cinnamon.

1. Preheat the oven to 350 degrees.

2. Cream the butter and three-quarters cup of the sugar together until light and fluffy. Beat in the egg.

3. Sift the flour with the baking powder and salt. Add alternately with the milk to the batter.

4. Fold in the dates, nuts and orange rind. Spoon into a greased 9-by-9-by-2-inch pan. Mix remaining sugar with the cinnamon and sprinkle over cake. Bake forty-five minutes, or until done. Serve warm.

Yield: One dozen servings.

Sour Cream Coffeecake   *Massachusetts*

Cake:
1½ cups sour cream
1½ teaspoons baking soda

¾ cup butter
1½ cups sugar
3 eggs
3 cups flour
1½ teaspoons baking powder
1¾ teaspoons vanilla.
Topping:
¼ cup chopped pecans
½ cup sugar
1½ teaspoons cinnamon.

1. Preheat the oven to 350 degrees.
2. To prepare cake, combine the sour cream and baking soda and set aside.
3. Beat the butter with the sugar until light and fluffy. Beat in the eggs, one at a time. Sift the flour and baking powder together and add to the batter alternately with the sour cream mixture. Stir in the vanilla.
4. Pour into a greased and floured nine-inch tube pan.
5. Combine the topping ingredients and sprinkle over the top of the cake. Bake one hour and ten minutes, or until cake tests done.
Yield: Ten to one dozen servings.

Quick Coffeecake   *New York*

2 cups flour
3 teaspoons baking powder
½ teaspoon salt
¼ cup granulated sugar
⅓ cup shortening
1 egg
  Milk
2 nectarines, peeled, pitted and sliced
3 tablespoons light brown sugar.

1. Preheat the oven to 375 degrees.
2. Sift together the flour, baking powder, salt and granulated sugar. With a pastry blender or the finger tips, blend in the shortening.
3. Break the egg into measuring cup and beat lightly. Add milk to make two-thirds cup. Stir

into dry ingredients. Turn onto floured board and knead thirty seconds.
4. Press into a greased nine-inch square pan. Cover with nectarine slices and sprinkle with the brown sugar. Bake twenty-five minutes.
Yield: Nine servings.

Passover Cheesecake   *New York*

1 cup matzoh meal
1 teaspoon cinnamon
1¼ cups sugar
¼ cup butter
4 eggs, well beaten
1½ tablespoons lemon juice
⅛ teaspoon salt
1 cup milk
3 cups creamed cottage cheese
2 tablespoons potato starch
2 teaspoons grated lemon rind.

1. Preheat the oven to 350 degrees.
2. Combine the matzoh meal, cinnamon, one-quarter cup of the sugar and the butter. Press into bottom and sides of ungreased nine-inch spring-form pan.
3. Gradually beat the remaining sugar into the eggs. Beat in the lemon juice, salt, milk, cottage cheese and potato starch.
4. Stir in the lemon rind and pour into the prepared crust. Bake one hour.
5. Shut oven heat off, leave door ajar and let cake cool down to room temperature in the oven. Chill thoroughly. Remove pan sides.
Yield: Ten to one dozen servings.

Evelyn's Cheesecake   *New York*

Crust:
2 cups zwieback crumbs
½ cup sugar
1½ teaspoons cinnamon
½ cup butter, melted.

Filling:

4 eggs
1 cup sugar
1½ tablespoons lemon juice
⅛ teaspoon salt
1 cup light cream
3 cups creamed cottage cheese
¼ cup flour
2 teaspoons grated lemon rind
¼ cup chopped walnuts.

1. Preheat the oven to 350 degrees.

2. To prepare crust, combine all ingredients. Reserve three-quarters cup of the crumb mixture. With a spoon, press the remaining mixture into bottom and sides of an eight-inch springform pan.

3. To prepare filling, beat the eggs with an electric mixer on low speed until light. Add the sugar gradually; then add the lemon juice, salt, cream, cottage cheese, flour and lemon rind. Pour into prepared pan and sprinkle top with reserved crumb mixture and the walnuts.

4. Bake one hour. Turn off oven heat, leave the door ajar and let cake cool in the oven one hour. Chill on rack in the refrigerator. Remove sides of pan before serving cake.

Yield: Ten to one dozen servings.

Cheesecake with Beer　　　　*New York*

1½ cups graham cracker crumbs
¼ cup butter, melted
4 eight-ounce packages cream cheese
½ cup freshly grated Cheddar cheese
1½ cups sugar
1 teaspoon vanilla
4 eggs
2 egg yolks
¼ cup heavy cream
¼ cup beer
½ cup pineapple preserves, if desired, or three to four cups fruit glaze (see next recipe).

1. Preheat the oven to 300 degrees.

2. Mix the cracker crumbs with the butter. Press the mixture over the bottom and around the sides of a buttered nine-inch springform pan.

3. Beat the cream cheese until soft and creamy. Add the Cheddar cheese and gradually beat in the sugar.

4. Add the vanilla. Beat in the eggs and egg yolks, one at a time. Continue to beat until the mixture is smooth and satiny. Fold in the cream and beer.

5. Spoon the pineapple preserves, if used, over the bottom of the prepared pan. Pour in the cheese mixture. Bake about one and one-half hours, or until set.

6. Turn off the oven heat and allow the cheesecake to remain thirty minutes in the oven with the door ajar.

7. Cool cake on a rack. Chill thoroughly before serving. If the pineapple preserves were not used, the cake may be topped with a fruit glaze.

Yield: Eight servings.

Strawberry Glaze　　　　*New York*

2 one-pound cartons frozen whole strawberries, thawed
　Cherry juice or water
2 tablespoons cornstarch or arrowroot.

1. Drain the strawberries very well, reserving the juice. Add the cherry juice or water to it until liquid measures two cups. Set berries aside.

2. Slowly mix the cornstarch with the liquid in a small pan. Gradually bring the mixture to a boil, stirring, and cook two to three minutes, or until thick and translucent. Cool and chill. Fold in the strawberries.

Yield: Three cups.

Deluxe Cheesecake
New York

Crust:
- 1 cup flour
- ¼ teaspoon sugar
- 1 teaspoon grated lemon rind
- ½ cup butter
- 1 egg yolk, lightly beaten
- ¼ teaspoon vanilla.

Filling:
- 5 eight-ounce packages cream cheese
- ¼ teaspoon vanilla
- 1 teaspoon grated lemon rind
- 1¾ cups sugar
- 3 tablespoons flour
- ¼ teaspoon salt
- 5 eggs
- 2 egg yolks
- ¼ cup heavy cream.

1. Preheat the oven to 400 degrees.

2. To prepare crust, combine the flour, sugar and lemon rind. Cut in the butter until mixture is crumbly. Add the egg yolk and vanilla. Mix.

3. Pat one-third of the dough over bottom of a nine-inch springform pan with sides removed. Bake about six minutes, or until golden. Cool.

4. Butter the sides of the pan and attach to the bottom. Pat remaining dough around sides to a height of two inches.

5. Increase the oven heat to 475 degrees.

6. To prepare filling, beat the cream cheese until fluffy. Add the vanilla and lemon rind.

7. Combine the sugar, flour and salt. Gradually blend into the cheese mixture. Beat in the eggs and egg yolks, one at a time, and the cream. Beat until smooth and creamy.

8. Pour mixture into prepared pan. Bake eight to ten minutes, or until top edge is golden.

9. Reduce the oven heat to 200 degrees. Bake one hour longer, or until set. Turn off oven heat and allow cake to remain thirty minutes in the oven with the door ajar.

10. Cool cake on a rack. Chill before serving. Top with a fruit glaze (recipes above) if desired.

Yield: Eight servings.

Cottage Cheese Cheesecake
New York

- 16 zwieback, crushed into crumbs
- ¼ cup butter, melted
- 1¼ cups sugar
- 3 eggs, separated
- ¼ cup flour
- ⅛ teaspoon salt
- 1½ pounds small-curd cottage cheese, forced through a sieve
- 1 teaspoon grated lemon rind
- ¼ cup lemon juice
- 1 cup heavy cream, whipped.

1. Preheat the oven to 300 degrees.

2. Combine the zwieback crumbs, butter and one-quarter cup of the sugar. Press half the mixture into bottom of a buttered nine-inch springform pan.

3. Beat the egg yolks until thick. Add the flour, salt, cottage cheese, lemon rind, lemon juice and three-quarters cup of the remaining sugar. Mix well.

4. Beat the egg whites until foamy. Gradually add remaining sugar. Beat until stiff. Fold with the whipped cream into cheese mixture. Pour into prepared pan. Sprinkle with remaining crumbs. Bake one and one-half hours, or until set.

5. Turn off oven heat and allow cake to remain forty-five minutes in oven with door ajar. Cool on a rack. Chill.

Yield: Eight servings.

Passover Nut Torte
New York

- 6 eggs, separated
- 1 cup sugar
- Juice of half a lemon
- Juice and grated rind of half an orange
- ½ cup matzoh meal
- 2 tablespoons matzoh cake flour
- ½ teaspoon salt
- 1 cup walnuts, finely chopped.

1. Preheat the oven to 350 degrees.

2. Beat the egg yolks, add the sugar gradually and beat until the mixture is light in color. Add the lemon juice, orange juice and orange rind. Mix in the matzoh meal, flour, salt and walnuts.

3. Beat the egg whites until stiff but not dry. Fold into the walnut mixture. Turn into an ungreased eight-inch springform pan and bake forty-five minutes, or until the cake tests done.

Yield: Eight servings.

Fourth of July Shortcake   *New Jersey*

1¼ cups flour
¼ teaspoon salt
1 teaspoon baking powder
¾ cup 100 per cent bran
1 three-ounce package cream cheese
⅔ cup soft butter
  Sugar
1 teaspoon grated lemon rind
1 tablespoon lemon juice
1 egg, lightly beaten
¼ cup apricot preserves
1 pint strawberries
1½ cups blueberries
1 cup ricotta cheese
¼ cup milk
½ teaspoon vanilla.

1. Preheat the oven to 375 degrees. Grease an 11-by-7-by-1½-inch baking dish or a ten-inch springform pan. Line dish or pan with wax paper, allowing paper to extend one inch above top.

2. Sift together the flour, salt and baking powder. Stir in the bran.

3. Cream together the cream cheese and butter. Add one-half cup of the sugar and beat until fluffy. Beat in the lemon rind, lemon juice and egg. Stir in dry ingredients.

4. Spread dough in a very thin layer over bottom of prepared pan and up sides in a thin layer to form a shell. Press a piece of greased wax paper down into the shell. Fit close to dough at all points and let extend an inch above the pan. Fill with dried beans or rice.

5. Bake twenty minutes, or until dough is set. Remove top wax paper with beans or rice. Reduce oven heat to 350 degrees and bake fifteen minutes longer, or until done.

6. Set pan on a rack and let cool thirty minutes. Lift out shell and let cool. Spread bottom of shell with apricot preserves.

7. Slice the strawberries and sprinkle with sugar to taste. Sprinkle the blueberries with sugar to taste. Alternating the berries, arrange them in four segments on top of the preserves.

8. Beat the ricotta with the milk until smooth. Blend in two tablespoons sugar, or to taste, and the vanilla. Serve on each piece of shortcake.

Yield: Six servings.

Blueberry Shortcake   *New Jersey*

Shortcake:
2 cups flour
3 teaspoons baking powder
1 teaspoon salt
3 tablespoons sugar
½ cup shortening
⅔ cup milk
2 tablespoons butter.
Sauce:
½ cup sugar
2 teaspoons cornstarch
⅛ teaspoon salt
½ cup water
2 pints blueberries
1 tablespoon lemon juice
1 teaspoon grated lemon rind
1 cup heavy cream, whipped.

1. Preheat the oven to 450 degrees.

2. To prepare shortcake, sift the flour, baking powder, salt and sugar into a bowl. Cut in the shortening until mixture resembles oatmeal.

3. With a fork, blend in the milk until mixture is just moistened. Knead lightly twenty seconds and turn onto a lightly floured board. Pat or roll into a large round one-half-inch thick roll.

4. Place dough on a greased sheet and bake

twenty minutes, or until done. Split and spread with the butter.

5. While shortcake bakes, prepare sauce by mixing sugar, cornstarch and salt together in a small pan. Stir in the water and one pint of the blueberries. Bring to a boil and simmer until clear and thickened, about four minutes. Remove from heat and add the lemon juice and lemon rind. Cool.

6. Spoon sauce and remaining pint blueberries between and on top of shortcake layers. Decorate with the whipped cream.

Yield: Six servings.

Ginger-Apple Custard   *New York*

5 cups soft bread crumbs, made from three-day-old firm white bread with crusts removed
2 cups buttermilk
2 cups regular milk
3 pounds firm tart apples, such as greenings, peeled, cored and thickly sliced
¼ cup water
½ cup unsulphured molasses
⅓ cup sugar
4 eggs, lightly beaten
¾ teaspoon ginger
1 teaspoon cinnamon
¾ teaspoon nutmeg
⅛ teaspoon ground cloves
¼ teaspoon salt
⅛ teaspoon freshly ground black pepper.

1. Place the bread crumbs in a bowl and pour the buttermilk and regular milk over crumbs. Set aside.

2. Preheat the oven to 350 degrees.

3. Place the apples and water in a skillet. Cover and cook gently until the apples start to soften but still retain their shape. Cool slightly.

4. Beat the remaining ingredients into the soaked bread mixture. Fold in the apples. Pour into a greased three-quart casserole or baking

dish. Bake fifty to sixty minutes, or until set. Serve warm.

Yield: Ten servings.

Steamed Cranberry Pudding

Massachusetts

6 tablespoons butter
¾ cup sugar
2 eggs
2¼ cups flour
2½ teaspoons baking powder
¼ teaspoon salt
½ cup milk
2 cups cranberries
½ cup chopped pecans
Eggnog sauce (see next recipe).

1. Cream the butter and sugar together until smooth and creamy. Beat in the eggs, one at a time.

2. Sift the flour with the baking powder and salt and stir alternately with the milk into the batter. Stir in the cranberries and pecans.

3. Turn mixture into a greased six-cup mold or pudding basin. If the mold has its own cover, grease and place over pudding. If the mold has no cover, cover with aluminum foil and secure tightly.

4. Place mold on a rack in a kettle with boiling water extending halfway up the mold. Cover and steam one and one-half to two hours, or until done.

5. Let stand ten minutes. Unmold and serve with eggnog sauce.

Yield: Ten to one dozen servings.

Note: The pudding can be made several days ahead and kept refrigerated. To heat, wrap the pudding in aluminum foil and bake forty-five minutes in a 325-degree oven.

Eggnog Sauce
Massachusetts

1 cup butter
1½ cups sugar
1 cup homemade or purchased eggnog
¼ cup dark rum.

In a saucepan, combine the butter, sugar and eggnog. Heat over low heat, stirring occasionally, until mixture reaches serving temperature. Stir in the rum and serve.

Yield: Three cups.

Plum Pudding
New York

¾ pound ground beef suet
1¼ cups flour
1 teaspoon nutmeg
2 slices fresh firm white bread, crusts removed and bread made into fine crumbs
½ teaspoon salt
1 fifteen-ounce box seeded muscat raisins
1 fifteen-ounce box seedless raisins
2 eleven-ounce boxes currants
1½ pounds mixed candied fruit, finely chopped
½ pound pitted dates, chopped
6 ounces whole candied cherries, halved
4 ounces candied pineapple, chopped
Grated rind of one lemon
1⅛ cups firmly packed dark brown sugar
5 eggs, lightly beaten
1 cup cold strong black coffee
Cognac or dark rum (optional)
Hard sauce (recipe below) or foamy sauce (recipe below).

1. Place suet in a large bowl and add the flour, nutmeg, bread crumbs and salt.

2. Pull the seeded muscat raisins apart, removing any tiny stems or seeds. Add muscat raisins to flour mixture and toss to coat.

3. Pick over the seedless raisins and the currants and add. Stir in the remaining fruits and the lemon rind. Add the brown sugar, eggs and coffee and mix well.

4. Pack firmly into pudding molds or basins. Cover with aluminum foil. Steam with hot water halfway up the molds. Set in a steamer or on a rack in a pan with hot water halfway up the molds.

5. When water boils, reduce the heat and steam four hours, replenishing water as needed. Let molds cool until they can be handled. Remove foil and wash outside of molds. Cognac or rum can be poured over puddings and they can be covered with fresh foil or plastic wrap. Reheat for serving by steaming one hour longer. Serve with hard sauce or foamy sauce.

Yield: Three three-and-one-half-cup puddings, each serving eight.

Hard Sauce
New York

1 cup sweet butter
1 cup confectioners' sugar
¼ cup dark rum, cognac or dry sherry
⅛ teaspoon salt.

Cream the butter and confectioners' sugar together very well. Beat in remaining ingredients and chill thoroughly

Yield: About two cups.

Foamy Sauce
New York

½ cup butter
1 cup confectioners' sugar
1 egg, beaten
2 tablespoons hot water
1 teaspoon vanilla or two tablespoons cognac
⅛ teaspoon salt.

1. Cream the butter. Add the confectioners' sugar, egg and hot water.

2. Place bowl over hot water and beat until

sauce thickens. Stir in the vanilla or cognac and salt and serve warm.

Yield: About two cups.

Christmas Pudding   *Connecticut*

1 cup dark brown sugar
2 cups finely grated or ground beef kidney suet
1 cup soft bread crumbs
1 cup currants
1 cup raisins
1 cup mixed candied fruit peels
1 cup finely chopped, peeled tart apple
2 cups flour
½ teaspoon salt
½ teaspoon ground cloves
½ teaspoon cinnamon
½ teaspoon nutmeg
2 eggs, lightly beaten
1 cup unsulphured molasses
1 tablespoon baking soda, dissolved in one cup boiling water.

1. Mix together the brown sugar, suet, crumbs, currants, raisins, peels, apple, flour, salt and spices.

2. Beat the eggs and molasses together and add to sweet mixture. Stir in the dissolved baking soda. Spoon into greased one-pound pudding basins or coffee cans. Cover with wax paper and then a cloth or aluminum foil. Set in a steamer or on a rack in a pan with boiling water extending two-thirds the way up basins or cans.

3. Steam three hours. Cool. Store in freezer or refrigerator. Steam to reheat, about forty-five minutes. Serve with hard sauce (page 131).

Yield: Three one-pound puddings.

Chocolate Pudding   *New York*

6 tablespoons soft butter
¾ cup sugar
6 eggs, separated

5 ounces (five squares) semisweet chocolate
1 cup milk
8 small slices firm white bread, crusts removed and bread cut into small cubes (about two cups cubes)
⅓ cup ground almonds
Grated rind of half a lemon
2 tablespoons cracker crumbs
Whipped cream
Chocolate sauce (recipe below).

1. Cream the butter and sugar together and beat in the egg yolks, one at a time.

2. Melt the chocolate over low heat and beat into the creamed mixture.

3. Add the milk to the bread cubes. Soak five minutes; then squeeze dry, discarding any excess milk. Crumble the bread cubes and add with the almonds and lemon rind to the chocolate mixture. Mix well.

4. Beat the egg whites until stiff but not dry and fold into the pudding.

5. Butter a two-quart mold for steaming and sprinkle with the cracker crumbs. Pour the pudding mixture into mold and seal with a tight-fitting cover or aluminum foil and string.

6. Pour water to the depth of two to four inches in a kettle and bring to a boil. Place the sealed mold on a rack in the kettle and steam one hour.

7. To serve, unmold pudding while hot and decorate with a border of whipped cream and a little of the chocolate sauce. Serve the remaining chocolate sauce separately.

Yield: Six or more servings.

Chocolate Sauce   *New York*

2 cups plus two tablespoons water
1 cup sugar
1 teaspoon vanilla
4 ounces (four squares) semisweet chocolate
1 teaspoon cornstarch
2 tablespoons butter.

1. Combine two cups of the water and the sugar in a saucepan and bring to a boil. Stir until sugar is dissolved. Add the vanilla and chocolate and stir until chocolate is dissolved.

2. Blend the cornstarch with the remaining water. Add to the chocolate mixture and bring to a boil. Stir in the butter and serve.

Yield: About two and one-half cups.

Cazuela (A Casserole Pudding) *New York*

4 cups pureed fresh or canned sweet potatoes (see note)
4 cups canned pureed pumpkin or pureed fresh pumpkin (see note)
1 cup coconut milk (see note)
¼ cup butter
3 eggs, lightly beaten
2 cups sugar
1 teaspoon salt
¼ cup flour
½ cup water
1 small piece fresh ginger, mashed, or one-half teaspoon dried ginger
1 four-inch-long stick cinnamon
¼ teaspoon aniseed
5 whole cloves.

1. Preheat the oven to 350 degrees.

2. Combine the pureed potatoes and pureed pumpkin with the coconut milk, butter, eggs, sugar, salt and flour. Blend well.

3. Combine the remaining ingredients in a saucepan and bring to a boil. Simmer five minutes and strain into pumpkin mixture. Blend well.

4. Butter an earthenware casserole or baking dish. Line it with plantain leaves that have been rinsed and dried or with parchment paper. Butter leaves or paper generously. Pour in pumpkin mixture and fold leaves or paper over the top.

5. Bake about one and one-half hours. Let cool completely before unmolding. Remove leaves or paper and serve.

Yield: Ten servings.

Note: Fresh potatoes and pumpkin, if used, should be pared and cubed and cooked in boiling salted water until tender, about forty-five minutes, then drained and put through a food ricer.

To prepare coconut milk, place two cups diced fresh coconut meat and two cups water in an electric blender. Blend on high speed one minute. Let stand ten minutes. Strain through double thickness of cheesecloth.

Peanut-Pumpkin Pudding *New York*

⅓ cup peanut butter
1¼ cups light corn syrup
1 one-pound can pumpkin puree
½ teaspoon salt
1 teaspoon cinnamon
½ teaspoon ground ginger
¼ teaspoon nutmeg
1 cup undiluted evaporated milk
3 eggs.

1. Preheat the oven to 350 degrees.

2. Mix the peanut butter and syrup together. Add the pumpkin, salt, cinnamon, ginger and nutmeg. Mix well.

3. Add the milk and eggs and stir until well blended. Pour into a greased baking dish and bake thirty-five to forty minutes, or until set.

Yield: Four to six servings.

Note: Two cups mashed sweet potatoes may be substituted for the pumpkin puree.

Indian Pudding *Massachusetts*

4 cups milk
1 cup yellow corn meal
2 eggs, lightly beaten
⅓ cup finely minced suet
½ cup sugar
⅔ cup light molasses
¾ teaspoon salt
½ teaspoon cinnamon
¼ teaspoon ground cloves

¼ teaspoon ground ginger
⅛ teaspoon allspice
⅛ teaspoon nutmeg
  Vanilla ice cream.

1. Bring the milk to a boil and add the corn meal gradually, beating vigorously with a wire whisk. When mixture starts to thicken, set it aside to cool.

2. Preheat the oven to 325 degrees.

3. When the mixture is nearly cool, stir in the remaining ingredients except the ice cream and mix well.

4. Pour into a buttered baking dish. Bake two hours. Serve piping hot, with vanilla ice cream on top.

Yield: Ten to one dozen servings.

Charles Street Indian Pudding

Massachusetts

 4 cups milk
⅓ cup yellow corn meal
¼ cup water
½ teaspoon ground ginger
½ teaspoon cinnamon
¼ cup sugar
½ teaspoon salt
½ cup unsulphured molasses
  Butter
  Ice cream, heavy cream or hard sauce (page 131).

1. Pour three cups of the milk into a saucepan and bring just to a boil.

2. Moisten the corn meal with the water and stir mixture rapidly into the hot milk, using a wire whisk to prevent lumps. Simmer twenty minutes, stirring frequently.

3. Preheat the oven to 325 degrees.

4. Combine the ginger, cinnamon, sugar and salt and add to the mush. Stir in the molasses.

5. Butter a one-and-one-half-quart casserole and add the corn meal mixture. Gently pour the remaining cup of cold milk over the top, but do not stir milk in. Dot the casserole with butter. Bake two hours. Serve hot, with ice cream, heavy cream or hard sauce.

Yield: Six servings.

Cracker Pudding

Pennsylvania

 4 cups milk
 2 eggs, separated
½ cup plus three tablespoons sugar
 2 cups coarse cracker crumbs
 1 cup fresh or packaged shredded coconut
 1 teaspoon vanilla.

1. Preheat the oven to 350 degrees.

2. Scald the milk in the top of a double boiler. Beat the egg yolks until light and creamy and stir them into the milk. Stirring constantly, add one-half cup sugar. Cook one minute and add the cracker crumbs and coconut. Stir until crumbs are soft and the pudding thickens. Stir in the vanilla and pour pudding into a buttered two-quart baking dish.

3. Beat the egg whites, adding the remaining sugar gradually, until stiff. Spoon meringue onto the pudding and bake until meringue is golden brown.

Yield: Six to eight servings.

Apple Snow with Custard Sauce

Vermont

 2 cups applesauce
¾ cup confectioners' sugar
 1 teaspoon lemon juice
½ teaspoon grated lemon rind
½ teaspoon salt
½ teaspoon almond extract
 2 eggs, separated
 2 tablespoons granulated sugar
¾ cup milk
½ teaspoon vanilla.

1. Place the applesauce, confectioners' sugar,

lemon juice, lemon rind, salt, almond extract and egg whites in the large bowl of an electric mixer. Beat at high speed until mixture holds peaks when beaters are lifted from the bowl.

2. Spoon into dessert glasses. Chill.

3. Meanwhile, combine the egg yolks, granulated sugar, milk and vanilla in a small saucepan and heat slowly, stirring constantly until mixture coats spoon. Do not allow mixture to boil.

4. Pour custard sauce into a small bowl, cover and cool. Spoon over chilled apple snow.

Yield: Four servings.

Coffee Walnut Soufflés   *Connecticut*

2 envelopes unflavored gelatin
1 cup sugar
4 tablespoons instant coffee powder
¼ teaspoon salt
4 eggs, separated
2½ cups milk
1 teaspoon vanilla
2 cups heavy cream
½ cup finely chopped walnuts.

1. Combine the gelatin, one-half cup of the sugar, the coffee powder and salt in a two-and-one-half-quart saucepan.

2. Beat the egg yolks with the milk. Add to gelatin mixture. Stir over low heat until gelatin dissolves and mixture thickens slightly, about ten to twelve minutes.

3. Remove from heat and add the vanilla. Chill, stirring occasionally, until mixture mounds slightly when dropped from spoon.

4. Meanwhile, prepare collars on dessert glasses or demitasse cups by binding a double strip of aluminum foil firmly around top of each glass and extending one inch above top rim of glass.

5. Beat the egg whites until stiff but not dry. Add remaining sugar gradually. Beat until very stiff.

6. Fold in gelatin mixture. Whip the cream

and fold in with the walnuts. Spoon into prepared dessert glasses. Chill until firm.

7. To serve, remove collars. Garnish soufflés with additional chopped walnuts if desired.

Yield: Eight to one dozen servings.

Honey Soufflé   *New York*

4 eggs, separated
2 tablespoons flour
¼ teaspoon nutmeg
¾ cup confectioners' sugar
2 tablespoons cream sherry or sweet red or white wine
½ cup honey
½ cup unsalted, soft kosher pareve margarine, melted
1 teaspoon grated lemon rind
2 tablespoons finely ground almonds.

1. Preheat the oven to 350 degrees.

2. Beat the egg yolks until light and creamy. Sift the flour, nutmeg and confectioners' sugar together and stir into the yolks.

3. Add the wine. Mix the honey and margarine together and add slowly to the egg mixture. Add the lemon rind and beat until smooth.

4. Beat the egg whites until stiff but not dry and fold into honey mixture. Pour into an ungreased one-and-one-half-quart soufflé dish. Sprinkle with the almonds.

5. Place dish in a shallow pan of hot water and bake thirty to forty minutes.

Yield: Four servings.

Hancock Village Steamed Ginger Sponge
Massachusetts

1 cup butter
2 teaspoons granulated sugar
2 eggs, well beaten
2½ cups flour
3 teaspoons baking powder
¼ teaspoon salt

1 cup milk
½ cup Canton preserved ginger, drained and
    cut into small pieces
7 teaspoons syrup from preserved ginger
1 cup heavy cream
4 tablespoons confectioners' sugar.

1. Cream the butter and gradually add the granulated sugar. Add the eggs.

2. Sift the flour with the baking powder and salt and add alternately with the milk to the batter. Add the ginger and one teaspoon ginger syrup. Pour into a buttered one-quart mold and steam one and three-quarters hours.

3. Beat the cream until stiff, sweeten with the confectioners' sugar and flavor with the remaining ginger syrup. Unmold the ginger sponge and serve hot, with the ginger cream.

Yield: Six servings.

Orange Mousse   *New Jersey*

3 eggs, separated
¾ cup sugar
¾ cup orange juice
1 envelope unflavored gelatin
1 teaspoon grated orange rind
2 cups heavy cream, whipped.

1. Beat the egg yolks until light and lemon-colored. Gradually add the sugar and continue beating until thick and creamy.

2. Add one-half cup of the orange juice and beat well.

3. Soften the gelatin in the remaining orange juice and melt over hot water. Add the gelatin mixture and the orange rind to the egg yolk mixture and blend well.

4. Beat the egg whites stiffly. Fold the whites and the whipped cream into the orange mixture. Pour into a deep serving bowl and refrigerate at least two hours before serving.

Yield: Six servings.

Chocolate-Walnut Mousse   *Connecticut*

1 six-ounce package semisweet chocolate bits
½ cup milk
2 teaspoons unflavored gelatin
2 tablespoons cold water
2 eggs, separated
⅛ teaspoon salt
⅛ teaspoon cream of tartar
3 tablespoons sugar
¼ cup cognac
1½ cups heavy cream, whipped
½ cup chopped toasted walnuts
1 ounce (one square) semisweet chocolate,
    melted and cooled
½ teaspoon instant coffee powder
    Walnut halves.

1. Day before, combine the chocolate bits and milk in a heavy saucepan and heat over very low heat, stirring occasionally, until chocolate melts.

2. Soften the gelatin in the water.

3. Beat the egg yolks lightly and add a little of the hot chocolate mixture. Return all to the pan and cook, stirring, until mixture thickens slightly. Do not allow to boil. Stir softened gelatin into hot chocolate mixture until dissolved. Cool to room temperature.

4. Beat the egg whites with the salt and cream of tartar until stiff. Gradually beat in the sugar.

5. Stir the cognac into the cooled chocolate mixture. Fold in the egg whites, one cup of the whipped cream and the walnuts. Turn into a six-cup dish or serving bowl and chill overnight.

6. Next day, fold the melted chocolate and coffee powder into the remaining cream. Using a pastry bag fitted with a star tube, pipe rosettes around the top of the mousse. Decorate with the walnut halves.

Yield: Six to eight servings.

Cider Apples   *New York*

4 cups cider
6 whole cloves

1 two-inch piece cinnamon stick
2 slices fresh gingerroot
6 apples, peeled, cored and cut into
   three-quarter-inch slices
¼ cup grenadine syrup
   Arrowroot.

1. Combine the cider, cloves, cinnamon stick and gingerroot in a saucepan, bring to a boil and simmer fifteen minutes. (If you prefer sweet desserts, one-half cup sugar, or more to taste, can be added to the cider mixture.)

2. Add the apple slices and poach until barely tender. Remove apple slices to a serving dish and keep warm.

3. Add the grenadine to the cider syrup and boil to reduce the quantity by half. Strain the syrup, measure it and then thicken with one and one-half teaspoons arrowroot mixed with a little cold water for each cup of the syrup. Pour over the apples.

Yield: Six servings.

Maple Apples   *Vermont*

6 tart firm apples, such as Cortland or
   McIntosh
2 cups maple syrup
2 cups water
   Sweetened whipped cream (optional).

1. Remove the core from each apple, but otherwise leave them whole. Remove the peel from the upper half of each apple.

2. Combine the syrup and water, add the apples and simmer until tender, about one hour. Serve cold, with sweetened whipped cream if desired.

Yield: Six servings.

Apple Crisp   *Massachusetts*

Apple rolls:
2 cups flour
2 teaspoons baking powder
1 teaspoon salt
2 tablespoons lard
1 tablespoon butter
¾ cup milk, approximately
¼ cup melted butter
½ cup light brown sugar
2 cups peeled and diced tart apples
½ teaspoon cinnamon.

Sauce:
1 cup granulated sugar
1 tablespoon flour
½ teaspoon salt
1 cup hot water
1 teaspoon cinnamon
   Whipped cream or ice cream.

1. Preheat the oven to 350 degrees.

2. To prepare apple rolls, sift together the flour, baking powder and salt. With the finger tips, work in the lard and one tablespoon butter as though making pastry.

3. Mix to a soft dough with the milk. Knead one-half minute on a lightly floured board. Roll out to a rectangle one-quarter-inch thick.

4. Brush with the melted butter and sprinkle with the brown sugar, apples and cinnamon. Starting with the long side, roll like a jellyroll. Cut into one-inch slices and, with cut sides up, fit into a greased nine-inch square pan.

5. To prepare sauce, combine the granulated sugar, flour and salt in a small saucepan. Gradually stir in the water. Bring to a boil, stirring, and boil three minutes. Add the cinnamon and pour sauce while hot over rolls.

6. Bake forty-five to fifty-five minutes. Serve warm with whipped cream or ice cream.

Yield: Eight or nine servings.

Blueberry Roll
New Jersey

  1 cup blueberries
  2 tablespoons lemon juice
  ¼ cup plus two tablespoons sugar
  2 cups flour
2½ teaspoons baking powder
  ½ teaspoon salt
  ¼ cup butter
  2 eggs
  ½ cup milk, approximately.

   1. Place the blueberries in a bowl and sprinkle with the lemon juice and two tablespoons of the sugar.

   2. Preheat the oven to 375 degrees.

   3. Sift together the flour, baking powder, salt and remaining sugar. With a pastry blender or the finger tips, work in the butter.

   4. Beat the eggs lightly in a measuring cup and add the milk as necessary to make three-quarters cup. Stir liquid into flour mixture to make a dough.

   5. Roll out the dough on a floured board into one-half-inch-thick oblong measuring about 10 by 15 inches. Sprinkle berries over dough and press them gently into dough. Roll up dough from the long end and place on greased jellyroll pan. Bake forty-five minutes.

Yield: Eight servings.

Fresh Blueberry Buckle
Maine

  ½ cup butter, at room temperature
  1 cup sugar
  1 egg
  ½ teaspoon vanilla
1⅓ cups flour
  1 teaspoon baking powder
  ¼ teaspoon salt
  ⅓ cup milk
  2 cups blueberries, picked over, rinsed and drained
  ½ teaspoon ground cardamon or allspice
  ¼ teaspoon nutmeg
    Sweetened whipped cream.

   1. Preheat the oven to 375 degrees.

   2. Using an electric mixer, cream together half the butter and half the sugar. Beat in the egg and vanilla.

   3. Sift together one cup of the flour with the baking powder and salt. Starting and ending with the flour mixture, add alternately with the milk to the creamed mixture. Pour into a greased nine-inch square baking dish. Pour the blueberries over the batter.

   4. Combine the remaining sugar, remaining flour, the cardamon and nutmeg. Using a pastry blender, cut in the remaining butter until the texture resembles that of coarse corn meal. Sprinkle over the blueberries and bake forty to forty-five minutes. Cool slightly before serving with sweetened whipped cream.

Yield: Six to eight servings.

Down-East Blueberry Cobbler
Massachusetts

  2 tablespoons cornstarch
  ⅔ cup sugar
  ¾ cup water
  3 cups blueberries
  1 teaspoon plus three tablespoons oil
  1 teaspoon cinnamon
  1 cup flour
1½ teaspoons baking powder
  ½ teaspoon salt
  ⅓ cup milk
    Whipped cream.

   1. Mix the cornstarch and sugar together in a saucepan. Stir in the water. Bring to a boil, stirring, and cook one minute.

   2. Preheat the oven to 425 degrees.

   3. Add the blueberries to the syrup and pour into a one-and-one-half-quart baking dish or a nine-inch pie pan. Sprinkle with one teaspoon of the oil and the cinnamon.

   4. Sift together the flour, baking powder and salt. Combine the milk and remaining oil and add all at once to the flour mixture.

5. Stir with fork until mixture forms a ball. Drop spoonfuls onto fruit. Bake twenty-five to thirty minutes, or until lightly browned. Serve hot or warm, with whipped cream.

Yield: Six servings.

Cheese Blintzes   *New York*

Filling:
 8 ounces cottage cheese
 ½ teaspoon salt
 1 egg, well beaten
 ½ teaspoon vanilla
 ¼ cup raisins.
Batter:
 1 cup sifted flour
 ¼ teaspoon salt
 ¾ cup water or milk
 2 eggs, well beaten.

1. To prepare filling, cream the cottage cheese with a fork. Stir in the remaining ingredients.

2. To prepare batter, sift together the flour and salt. Stir the water or milk into the beaten eggs and add gradually to flour mixture. Beat until smooth.

3. Butter a seven-inch frying pan or griddle and heat. Drop enough batter into hot pan just to cover bottom. As soon as edges of pancake begin to curl away from side of pan, turn out onto wax paper and spread with a spoonful of the cheese filling. Fold sides over to make a neat package.

4. Make additional blintzes with remaining batter and filling.

5. Place blintzes on hot buttered frying pan and fry until browned. Turn and fry on other side. Serve at once.

Yield: Six servings.

Passover Cheese Blintzes   *New York*

Batter:
 3 eggs
 ¾ cup matzoh cake flour
 1½ cups water
 ½ teaspoon salt.

Filling:
 1 pound cottage cheese
 1 egg
 ½ teaspoon salt
 1 teaspoon sugar
   Butter.

1. Beat together the eggs, flour and water to make a thin batter. Add the salt. Pour about three tablespoons batter onto a buttered griddle or skillet, spreading as thinly as possible by tilting the pan. Fry until brown and turn out, browned side up, onto a towel.

2. To prepare filling, combine the cottage cheese, egg, salt and sugar. Spread one tablespoon of mixture on surface of each blintz. Tuck in the ends and roll up.

3. Brown the blintzes in butter and serve hot.

Yield: About ten.

Raspberry Cooler   *Connecticut*

 4 cups raspberries
 2 eight-ounce containers plain yogurt
 6 tablespoons sugar
 4 teaspoons unflavored gelatin
 ½ cup cold water.

1. Place three cups of the raspberries in an electric blender. Add the yogurt and sugar and blend until smooth.

2. Soften the gelatin in the water and then heat over hot water to dissolve. Stir into raspberry mixture.

3. Chill until mixture starts to thicken. Beat until creamy and then pile into serving dishes. Top with remaining raspberries, whole or pureed.

Yield: Six servings.

Cranberry Sherbet   *Massachusetts*

 1 envelope unflavored gelatin
 ¼ cup lemon juice
 3 cups cranberry juice cocktail

2 cups buttermilk
1½ cups sugar
1 teaspoon nutmeg.

1. Sprinkle the gelatin over the lemon juice and let stand five minutes. Heat gently, stirring until the gelatin dissolves.

2. Add the remaining ingredients, stirring until the sugar dissolves. Pour into an ice cube tray or metal pan and freeze until mushy.

3. Scoop mixture into a bowl and beat until smooth and fluffy. Return to the freezer and freeze until firm.

Yield: Five cups.

Lemon Water Ice   *Delaware*

3 cups water
2 cups sugar
2 tablespoons grated lemon rind
2 cups strained fresh lemon juice
Mint sprigs (optional).

1. Combine the water and sugar in a saucepan and bring to a boil. Simmer five minutes and cool.

2. Add the lemon rind and lemon juice.

3. Pour the mixture into a freezer tray and freeze.

4. When preparing to serve, shave the mixture by scraping the surface with a heavy spoon. Spoon into sherbet glasses and return to the freezer until ready to serve. Garnish with mint sprigs if desired.

Yield: Eight to one dozen servings.

Farmer in the Dell   *New York*

1 one-pound-six-ounce loaf extra-fresh soft white bread
1 seven-and-one-half-ounce package farmer cheese
⅓ cup granulated sugar
½ teaspoon vanilla
1 egg

½ pound butter, melted and clear yellow liquid poured off for cooking (discard milky solids)
¼ cup confectioners' sugar.

1. Remove crusts from the bread slices. With a rolling pin, roll each slice until very thin.

2. Beat together the cheese, granulated sugar, vanilla and egg and spread one tablespoon mixture on each slice of rolled bread.

3. Roll up each slice and pinch sides to hold together.

4. Heat the butter in a very heavy skillet and sauté the rolls, a few at a time, over medium heat until golden. Roll in confectioners' sugar while hot.

Yield: Twenty-six pieces; about eight servings.

Old-Fashioned Sour Cream Cookies
New Jersey

½ cup shortening
1½ cups sugar
2 eggs
2½ cups flour
½ teaspoon salt
½ teaspoon baking soda
2 teaspoons baking powder
1 cup sour cream
1 teaspoon lemon extract
Grated rind of two lemons.

1. Preheat the oven to 350 degrees.

2. Cream the shortening and sugar together until light and fluffy. Beat in the eggs, one at a time.

3. Sift together the flour, salt, baking soda and baking powder and add alternately with the sour cream to the batter. Stir in the lemon extract and lemon rind.

4. Drop by teaspoonfuls, two inches apart, onto greased baking sheets. Bake fifteen minutes, or until lightly browned at the edges. Tops will be pale.

Yield: About four dozen.

Rocks

New Hampshire

1 cup light brown sugar
¾ cup shortening
2 eggs, lightly beaten
2 cups flour
1 teaspoon allspice
¼ teaspoon salt
¾ cup chopped dates
2 cups raisins
2 cups chopped pecans or walnuts
1 teaspoon baking soda
1 tablespoon boiling water.

1. Preheat the oven to 350 degrees.
2. Cream the brown sugar and shortening together until light and fluffy. Beat in the eggs.
3. Sift the flour, allspice and salt into a bowl. Add the fruits and nuts and toss to coat. Stir into the batter.
4. Dissolve the baking soda in the boiling water and stir into the mixture. Drop by teaspoonfuls onto a lightly greased baking sheet and bake about fifteen minutes, or until lightly browned.
Yield: About four dozen.

Chocolate Surprise Cookies

Pennsylvania

½ cup butter
1 cup light brown sugar
1 egg
1 teaspoon vanilla
½ teaspoon almond extract
2 ounces (two squares) unsweetened
   chocolate, melted
2 cups flour
½ teaspoon baking soda
¼ teaspoon salt
¾ cup sour cream
½ cup fine macaroon (amaretti) crumbs
½ cup chopped glacé cherries
1 cup coarsely chopped fresh mushrooms.

1. Preheat the oven to 350 degrees.

2. Cream the butter and brown sugar together until light and fluffy.
3. Beat in the egg, vanilla and almond extract. Stir in the melted chocolate.
4. Sift together the flour, baking soda and salt and stir into the batter alternately with the sour cream. Stir in the remaining ingredients.
5. Drop by teaspoonfuls, two inches apart, onto a greased baking sheet. Bake twelve minutes, or until done.
Yield: Three dozen.

Carrot Cookies

Maine

Cookies:
1 cup shortening
¾ cup granulated sugar
1 egg
1 cup mashed cooked carrots, cooled
1 teaspoon vanilla
2 cups flour
2 teaspoons baking powder
½ teaspoon salt.
Frosting:
¼ cup orange juice
1 tablespoon grated orange rind
   Confectioners' sugar.

1. Preheat the oven to 350 degrees.
2. To prepare cookies, cream the shortening and granulated sugar together until light and fluffy. Beat in the egg.
3. Beat in the carrots and the vanilla. Sift together the flour, baking powder and salt and stir into the batter.
4. Drop by teaspoonfuls, two inches apart, onto a greased baking sheet. Bake twenty minutes, or until done. Cool on a rack.
5. To prepare frosting, combine the orange juice, orange rind and enough confectioners' sugar to make a spreading consistency. Spread over the cooled cookies.
Yield: About thirty.

Orange Oatmeal Cookies   *Rhode Island*

2 cups sifted flour
2 cups sugar
4 teaspoons baking powder
1 teaspoon salt
1 teaspoon nutmeg
1 cup soft shortening
2 eggs
2 tablespoons freshly squeezed orange juice
3 teaspoons grated orange peel
3 cups quick-cooking rolled oats.

1. Preheat the oven to 375 degrees.
2. Sift together the flour, sugar, baking powder, salt and nutmeg into a large mixing bowl.
3. Add the shortening, eggs and orange juice and beat until smooth. Stir in the orange peel and oats. Drop by teaspoonfuls onto an ungreased baking sheet. Bake twelve to fifteen minutes. Cool on a rack.
Yield: About five dozen.

Currant Cookies   *Maine*

1 cup butter
1½ cups sugar
2 eggs
2 tablespoons cognac
3½ cups flour
1½ teaspoons nutmeg
½ cup currants.

1. Beat together the butter and sugar until very light and creamy. Beat in the eggs, one at a time. Beat in the cognac.
2. Sift together the flour and nutmeg and add the currants. Toss.
3. Stir the flour mixture into the batter. Wrap in wax paper and chill several hours or overnight.
4. Preheat the oven to 350 degrees.
5. Roll out the dough to one-quarter-inch thickness and cut with a three-inch round cookie cutter. Transfer to a lightly greased baking sheet and bake fifteen to twenty minutes, or until

lightly browned at the edges. The center remains pale. Cool on a rack.
Yield: Two dozen.

Isabella's Cookies   *Massachusetts*

1 cup shortening
2 cups light brown sugar
2 eggs
3 cups flour
2½ teaspoons baking powder
½ teaspoon salt
1 teaspoon cinnamon
1 teaspoon nutmeg
½ cup cold regular-strength black coffee
2 cups raisins
1 cup chopped nuts.

1. Cream the shortening and brown sugar together until light. Beat in the eggs, one at a time.
2. Sift the flour with the baking powder, salt, cinnamon and nutmeg and add to batter alternately with the coffee. Stir in the raisins and nuts. Chill one hour or longer.
3. Preheat the oven to 375 degrees.
4. Drop batter by teaspoonfuls onto a greased baking sheet. Bake ten to twelve minutes. Remove at once from baking sheet and cool on a rack. Store tightly covered.
Yield: Six dozen.

Gingerbread Men   *Rhode Island*

¾ cup unsulphured molasses
¾ cup butter
¾ cup dark brown sugar
4½ cups flour
1 teaspoon baking powder
1 teaspoon salt
½ teaspoon baking soda
2 teaspoons ground ginger
2 teaspoons cinnamon
1 egg, lightly beaten
Royal icing (see next recipe)

Cinnamon candies
Candied cherries
Currants
Raisins.

1. Heat the molasses to the simmering point, remove from the heat and stir in the butter until it melts. Stir in the brown sugar. Cool.

2. Sift together the flour, baking powder, salt, baking soda, ginger and cinnamon. Stir along with the egg into the cooled molasses mixture. Mix well. Wrap in wax paper and chill one to two hours, or until firm enough to roll.

3. Preheat the oven to 350 degrees.

4. Roll out the dough to one-quarter-inch thickness on a lightly floured board or pastry cloth. Cut with a gingerbread man cutter.

5. Transfer to a lightly greased baking sheet and bake twelve to fifteen minutes. Cool on a rack. The gingerbread men may be decorated as desired with royal icing (recipe below), cinnamon candies, candied cherries, currants and raisins.

Yield: About eighteen.

Royal Icing　　　　　*Rhode Island*

2 to three cups confectioners' sugar
⅛ teaspoon cream of tartar
1 egg white.

Combine two cups of the confectioners' sugar with the cream of tartar and egg white and mix well. Add enough confectioners' sugar to make the icing a suitable consistency for forcing through a decorating bag or tube or for spreading with a spatula.

Yield: About three-quarters cup.

Shellbark Hickory Kisses　　*Pennsylvania*

3 egg whites
¼ teaspoon salt
¼ teaspoon cream of tartar
1 cup sifted confectioners' sugar

1½ cups whole shellbark hickory nuts or other nuts broken into pieces.

1. Preheat the oven to 375 degrees.

2. Beat the egg whites lightly until foamy and add the salt and cream of tartar. Beat, gradually adding the confectioners' sugar. Continue beating until the whites stand in peaks. Fold in the nuts.

3. Scoop up bits of meringue with a teaspoon and push off onto a buttered baking sheet. Bake seven to eight minutes.

Yield: About two dozen.

Veronica's Christmas Cookies　　*New York*

1 cup butter
1 cup shortening
1¼ cups sugar
1 egg
1 tablespoon vanilla
¼ teaspoon lemon extract
5½ cups flour
1 teaspoon salt
1 teaspoon baking powder
Chopped candied cherries or citron peel.

1. Preheat the oven to 375 degrees.

2. Cream the butter, shortening and sugar together until fluffy. Beat in the egg, vanilla and lemon extract.

3. Sift together the flour, salt and baking powder and add to the creamed mixture. Stir with a spoon or with the hand to incorporate the flour.

4. The dough can be rolled out immediately or chilled for a short period and then rolled.

5. Roll out one-sixth of the dough at a time on a lightly floured board to one-quarter-inch thickness. Cut with small, fancy cookie cutters and place on a lightly greased baking sheet. Decorate each cookie with a piece of candied cherry or citron peel.

6. Bake ten minutes, or until lightly browned. Cool on a rack. Store in an airtight tin or jar. The cookies will keep a week to ten days.

Yield: About 350 one-half-inch to one-inch cookies.

Note: If the cutting becomes too tedious, the dough can be rolled to one-quarter-inch thickness, sprinkled with sugar and cinnamon mixture (one-quarter cup sugar to one tablespoon cinnamon) and cut with a pastry wheel or knife into diamond shapes.

St. Nikoloos Cookies   *Massachusetts*

½ cup butter
½ cup lard
 1 cup sugar
 2 cups flour
 2 teaspoons cinnamon
¼ teaspoon nutmeg
¼ teaspoon ground cloves
¼ teaspoon baking soda
¼ cup buttermilk
½ cup chopped nuts.

1. Day before, beat the butter, lard and sugar together until creamy. Sift together the flour, cinnamon, nutmeg, cloves and baking soda and add with the buttermilk and nuts to the creamed mixture.

2. With the finger tips, work into a dough. With floured hands, shape the dough into two long rolls, each one inch to one and one-half inches in diameter. Wrap in wax paper and refrigerate overnight.

3. Next day, preheat the oven to 375 degrees.

4. Cut the rolls into one-eighth-inch slices and place on ungreased baking sheet. Bake until light brown, about eight minutes. Cool on a rack.

Yield: About three dozen.

Lizzies   *New York*

 1 pound raisins
½ cup whisky
¼ cup butter
¾ cup light brown sugar

 2 eggs
 2 cups flour
½ teaspoon baking soda
½ teaspoon ground cloves
½ teaspoon allspice
½ teaspoon nutmeg
½ teaspoon cinnamon
1½ tablespoons milk
¾ pound candied cherries
¾ pound candied pineapple
 3 cups pecans, chopped.

1. Soak the raisins in the whisky one hour until plump.

2. Preheat the oven to 325 degrees.

3. Cream the butter and gradually beat in the brown sugar. Add the eggs, one at a time, beating well after each addition.

4. Sift the flour with the baking soda and spices. Add to creamed mixture alternately with the milk.

5. Add the plumped raisins, candied cherries, candied pineapple and pecans. Drop by teaspoonfuls onto buttered baking sheet. Bake fifteen minutes, or until browned and done. Cool on a rack. Store in airtight container or freeze.

Yield: About four dozen.

Brownie Drops   *New Hampshire*

 2 four-ounce packages German sweet
     chocolate
 1 tablespoon butter
 2 eggs
¾ cup sugar
¼ cup flour
¼ teaspoon baking powder
⅛ teaspoon salt
¼ teaspoon cinnamon
¾ cup finely chopped pecans
½ teaspoon vanilla.

1. Preheat the oven to 350 degrees.

2. Melt the chocolate and butter together in

top of a double boiler over hot water, stirring constantly. Remove from heat and allow to cool.

3. Beat the eggs until foamy. Add the sugar, two tablespoons at a time, beating constantly until the mixture is very thick. (This takes at least five minutes with an electric mixer at high speed. It is egg, not flour, that thickens this mixture.)

4. Blend cooled chocolate mixture into egg mixture. Add the flour, baking powder, salt, cinnamon, pecans and vanilla.

5. Drop from a teaspoon onto greased baking sheets. Bake ten to twelve minutes, or until the cookies feel set when touched lightly. Cool on a rack. Store in tightly covered container.

Yield: About three dozen.

Maple Lace Wafers   *New York*

½ cup maple syrup
¼ cup butter
⅛ teaspoon baking soda
½ cup flour
¼ teaspoon baking powder
⅛ teaspoon salt.

1. Preheat the oven to 350 degrees.
2. Combine the syrup and butter in a small pan and bring to a boil. Boil hard, while stirring, thirty seconds.
3. Sift together the remaining ingredients and add all at once, stirring briskly (the batter will be lumpy).
4. Drop by half teaspoonfuls onto a greased baking sheet, about four at a time. Bake six to eight minutes, or until golden.
5. Let set on baking sheet a second or two and then, while still warm, quickly roll each wafer around the greased handle of a wooden spoon to shape a roll or a cone. Cool on a rack.

Yield: About twenty-eight.

Note: The cooled cones or rolls can be filled with whipped cream if desired.

Danish Cones with Whipped Cream   *New York*

¼ cup butter
½ cup sugar
2 eggs
¾ cup flour
1 cup heavy cream
  Strawberry jam.

1. Preheat the oven to 300 degrees.
2. Melt the butter and stir in the sugar. Beat in the eggs, one at a time, and then the flour. Drop spoonfuls of the batter about four inches apart onto a well-buttered baking sheet. Smooth the batter into ovals. Bake about six minutes.
3. Remove the cookies with a spatula and quickly roll into cone shapes while cookies are still hot and flexible. (Gloves may be handy in doing this.) Let cones cool. Rebutter the baking sheet before each addition.
4. At serving time, whip the cream and fill the cones with it. Add a little strawberry jam to the center of the cream.

Yield: About fifteen.

Filled Applesauce Squares   *Massachusetts*

½ cup butter
1 cup light brown sugar
1 egg
½ teaspoon vanilla
1⅓ cups flour
¾ teaspoon baking soda
¼ teaspoon salt
½ teaspoon cinnamon
¼ teaspoon nutmeg
⅛ teaspoon ground cloves
1⅓ cups quick-cooking rolled oats
½ cup applesauce, preferably homemade
½ cup chopped pecans
1 cup raisins.

1. Preheat the oven to 350 degrees.

2. Cream the butter and brown sugar together until light and fluffy. Beat in the egg and vanilla.

3. Sift the flour with the baking soda, salt, cinnamon, nutmeg and cloves and stir into the batter. Stir in the oats.

4. Pat two-thirds of the dough into a greased nine-inch square pan. Combine the applesauce, pecans and raisins and spread over the dough.

5. Flour a piece of wax paper generously and then, with flour-dipped finger tips, spread the remaining dough on the paper to form a nine-inch square. Invert dough square over the filling, releasing dough with the help of a spatula. (Don't be upset if there are holes in the layer; this does not spoil the end result.) Bake about thirty minutes, or until lightly browned. Cool in the pan and cut into bars or squares.

Yield: Sixteen to twenty servings.

Frazer's Cheaters (Nut Squares)
Connecticut

1 cup plus two tablespoons flour
2 tablespoons granulated sugar
1 teaspoon salt
½ cup butter
2¼ cups light brown sugar
2 eggs
1 cup coarsely chopped pecans
1 cup grated coconut.

1. Preheat the oven to 350 degrees.

2. Combine one cup flour, the granulated sugar and salt in a mixing bowl. Using a pastry blender, cut in the butter. Mix with the hands and press the dough over the bottom of an eight-inch square baking pan. Bake ten minutes.

3. Increase the oven heat to 375 degrees.

4. Blend the brown sugar, eggs, pecans, coconut and remaining flour. Spread the mixture over the bottom crust. Bake twenty minutes. Cool. Cut into squares and remove from the pan with a narrow spatula.

Yield: Sixty-four one-inch squares.

Maple Walnut Bars
New York

1 cup shortening
1 cup soft maple sugar
2 eggs
¾ cup flour
½ teaspoon baking powder
¼ teaspoon salt
1 cup chopped walnuts
Confectioners' sugar.

1. Preheat the oven to 350 degrees.

2. Cream the shortening and maple sugar together. Beat in the eggs. Sift together the flour, baking powder and salt and stir into batter.

3. Stir in the walnuts and spoon into a greased eight-inch square baking dish. Bake thirty minutes. Cool in the dish. When cold, cut into bars and coat with confectioners' sugar.

Yield: Sixteen.

Peggy's Coconut Squares
New York

1½ cups light brown sugar
½ cup butter
1 cup cake flour
2 eggs, lightly beaten
1 cup slivered blanched almonds
1 cup shredded coconut
2 tablespoons regular flour
½ teaspoon baking powder
⅛ teaspoon salt
¼ teaspoon vanilla.

1. Preheat the oven to 350 degrees.

2. Cream one-half cup brown sugar with the butter and stir in the cake flour.

3. Spread mixture in a greased nine-inch square baking pan. Bake fifteen minutes.

4. Combine the remaining ingredients and spread over the partially baked mixture. Return to the oven and bake about twenty minutes longer, or until well browned. Cool in the pan; then cut into squares.

Yield: Three dozen one-and-one-half-inch squares.

Jan Hagel   *New York*

1 cup butter
1 cup sugar
1 egg, separated
2 cups flour
½ teaspoon cinnamon
1 tablespoon water
½ cup chopped blanched almonds.

1. Preheat the oven to 350 degrees.
2. Cream together the butter and sugar until very light and fluffy. Beat in the egg yolk very well.
3. Sift together the flour and cinnamon and stir into the creamed mixture. Spread in a greased 10-by-15-inch jellyroll pan.
4. Beat the water and egg white together lightly. Brush over the top of the cake and sprinkle with the almonds. Bake twenty to twenty-five minutes, or until golden brown. Cut into squares or bars while hot.
Yield: Three dozen to four dozen.

Molasses Fruit and Nut Bars
                          New Hampshire

⅓ cup shortening
¼ cup granulated sugar
¼ teaspoon baking soda
1 teaspoon salt
1 teaspoon cinnamon
⅔ cup unsulphured molasses
1 egg
1¼ cups flour
1 cup finely cut dates
½ cup chopped walnuts
¾ cup confectioners' sugar
4 teaspoons water
1 tablespoon grated orange rind.

1. Preheat the oven to 375 degrees.
2. Cream together the shortening, granulated sugar, baking soda, salt and cinnamon. Beat in the molasses and then the egg. Stir in the flour, dates and walnuts.
3. Spread in a greased and lightly floured 9-inch square baking pan.
4. Bake twenty-five minutes. Cool. Turn out onto a cutting board.
5. Combine the confectioners' sugar, water and orange rind and spread over all. Cut into bars.
Yield: About forty-two.

Cream Cheese Brownies   *Delaware*

1 four-ounce bar German sweet chocolate
5 tablespoons butter, at room temperature
4 ounces cream cheese, at room temperature
1 cup sugar
3 eggs
½ cup plus one tablespoon flour
½ teaspoon lemon juice
1½ teaspoons vanilla
½ teaspoon baking powder
¼ teaspoon salt
½ cup chopped walnuts or pecans
½ teaspoon almond extract.

1. Preheat the oven to 350 degrees.
2. Melt the chocolate with three tablespoons of the butter over boiling water. Remove from the heat and let cool.
3. Cream together the cream cheese, one-quarter cup of the sugar and the remaining butter until light and fluffy. Beat in one of the eggs. Stir in one tablespoon of the flour, the lemon juice and one-half teaspoon of the vanilla. Set aside.
4. In another bowl, beat the remaining eggs until they are thick, gradually beat in the remaining sugar and continue beating until the mixture is thick.
5. Mix together the baking powder, salt and remaining flour and fold into the beaten egg mix-

ture. Stir in the chocolate mixture, nuts, almond extract and remaining vanilla.

6. Spread all but one cup of the chocolate batter in a greased 9-by-9-by-2-inch baking pan. Top with the reserved cream cheese mixture and then spoon remaining chocolate batter over the cheese mixture. Swirl through the batter with a spatula or knife to marble.

7. Bake twenty-five to thirty minutes. Cool. Cut into bars or squares and store in the refrigerator.

Yield: About twenty.

Passover Brownies   *New York*

2 cups sugar
5 eggs

½ cup oil
1 cup matzoh cake meal
1 tablespoon potato starch
5 tablespoons cocoa powder
⅓ cup orange juice
⅓ cup chopped nuts.

1. Preheat the oven to 350 degrees.

2. Beat the sugar and eggs together well. Beat in the oil.

3. Combine the cake meal, potato starch, cocoa powder, orange juice and nuts. Stir into the batter. Pour into a well-greased or wax-paper-lined 13-by-9-by-2-inch baking pan. Bake thirty-five to forty-five minutes, or until done. Cut into squares while warm.

Yield: About two dozen.

Miscellaneous

Pickles, Relishes and Preserves

Bread and Butter Pickles
New York

25 cucumbers, each measuring one inch to one
and one-half inches in diameter (about four
quarts), scrubbed and thinly sliced
 8 onions, thinly sliced
½ cup salt
 5 cups cider vinegar
 5 cups sugar
 2 tablespoons mustard seeds
 2 tablespoons celery seeds
 2 teaspoons turmeric
½ teaspoon ground cloves.

1. Combine the cucumbers and onions. Sprinkle with salt and let stand three hours. Drain well.

2. Add the remaining ingredients, bring to a
boil and ladle immediately into hot sterilized canning jars. Seal immediately. Store in a cool, dark,
dry place.

Yield: About six pints.

Winchester Center Bread and Butter Pickles
Connecticut

1 gallon cucumbers (about twenty-five)
8 small onions, chopped
1 green pepper, seeded and chopped
½ cup coarse salt
2 quarts ice cubes

 4 cups sugar
3½ cups cider vinegar
1½ cups water
1½ teaspoons turmeric
 1 tablespoon celery seeds
½ teaspoon ground cloves
 2 tablespoons mustard seeds.

1. Wash the cucumbers and slice thinly into a
large bowl or crock. Add the onions, green pepper and salt. Mix. Top with the ice cubes. Let
stand at room temperature eight hours. Drain.
Rinse lightly.

2. Combine the remaining ingredients in a kettle and add cucumber mixture. Heat, stirring to
dissolve sugar, until mixture comes to just below
the boiling point. Pack into hot sterilized jars.
Seal. Cool. Store in cool, dry, dark place.

Yield: About five quarts.

Ernie's Mustard Pickles
Connecticut

1½ quarts one-inch chunks halved, peeled
cucumbers
 2 large onions, chopped (about six cups)
 3 tablespoons salt
 1 quart water
1½ cups sugar
¼ cup flour
1½ teaspoons celery seeds
1½ teaspoons dry mustard

½ teaspoon turmeric
2 cups white vinegar.

1. In a crock or earthenware bowl, combine the cucumbers, onions, salt and water. Let stand at room temperature three hours.

2. In a saucepan, mix together the sugar, flour, celery seeds, mustard and turmeric. Gradually stir in the vinegar. Heat, while stirring, until mixture thickens and is smooth.

3. Drain cucumbers and onions, rinse briefly and add to boiling mustard sauce. Bring to a boil again. Pour into hot sterilized jars. Seal. Cool and store in a cool, dark, dry place.

Yield: About two quarts.

Green Tomato Mincemeat   *New York*

6 cups chopped peeled apples
6 cups chopped peeled green tomatoes
4 cups light brown sugar
1⅓ cups cider vinegar
3 cups raisins
3 teaspoons cinnamon
1 teaspoon ground cloves
¾ teaspoon ground allspice
¾ teaspoon mace
2 teaspoons salt
¾ teaspoon freshly ground black pepper
½ cup butter.

1 Mix the apples and tomatoes together and drain well. Add the remaining ingredients except the butter. Bring gradually to the boiling point and let simmer three hours, stirring often.

2. Add the butter and mix well. Spoon into hot sterilized canning jars and seal the covers. Cool and store in a cool, dark, dry place.

Yield: About five pints.

Venison Mincemeat   *New York*

5 pounds tough cuts venison, very finely cut or diced

1 tablespoon plus one-quarter teaspoon salt
¼ teaspoon freshly ground black pepper
4 pounds Northern Spy apples, peeled, cored and chopped
2 cups cider, scalded
1 cup unsulphured molasses
2 cups honey
2 cups sugar
1 teaspoon ground cloves
1 teaspoon cinnamon
1 teaspoon ground allspice
½ pound raisins
1 pint blackberry brandy.

1. Cover the venison with cold water. Add one tablespoon salt. Let stand at room temperature two hours. Drain and place in a kettle.

2. Cover with fresh water. Add remaining salt and the pepper and cook, covered, until meat is very tender.

3. Add the remaining ingredients except the brandy. Bring to a boil and simmer until apples are tender. Cool.

4. Add brandy, reheat almost to the boiling point and pack into hot sterilized jars. Seal. Cool and store in a cool, dry, dark place for at least one month before using.

Yield: About eight quarts.

Vermont Mincemeat

2 pounds cooked roast beef or venison, ground
4 pounds apples, peeled, cored and ground
1 pound beef suet, ground
2 pounds currants
2 pounds raisins, ground
6 cups light brown sugar or granulated sugar
4 cups cider, vinegar or grape juice
2 teaspoons nutmeg
1 tablespoon ground allspice
1 tablespoon cinnamon
½ teaspoon ground ginger
1 teaspoon ground cloves

1 tablespoon salt
1 pound mixed diced candied fruit peels.

1. Mix all the ingredients in a large heavy kettle. Simmer, stirring, thirty minutes, or until mixture is the correct consistency.

2. Pack into hot sterilized jars and seal the caps. Process in a water bath for three hours or in a pressure cooker for one hour at ten pounds pressure. Store in a cool, dark, dry place.

Yield: Six to eight quarts.

Piccalilli   *New York*

2 sweet red peppers, cored, seeded and chopped
2 green peppers, cored, seeded and chopped
4 cups green tomatoes, chopped
1 cup chopped celery
2 large onions, chopped
1 small head cabbage, chopped
½ cup salt
3 cups cider vinegar
1 teaspoon dry mustard
1 pound light brown sugar
1 teaspoon turmeric.

1. Day before, arrange the peppers, tomatoes, celery, onions and cabbage in alternate layers, sprinkling each layer with salt, and let stand at room temperature overnight.

2. Next day, drain well and add the remaining ingredients. Bring to a boil and cook twenty minutes, stirring frequently. Turn into hot sterilized jars. Seal. Cool and store in a cool, dark, dry place.

Yield: About five pints.

Hancock Shaker Village India Relish
Massachusetts

8 pounds very small green tomatoes
8 cups light brown sugar or maple sugar
2 cups water

3 sticks cinnamon
2 tablespoons ground ginger
3 lemons, very thinly cut
2 cups citron, shredded
3 cups raisins
Peel of one small orange, finely chopped.

1. Wash the tomatoes and cut into quarters.

2. Bring the sugar and water to a boil, stirring until the sugar dissolves, and simmer two to three minutes. Add tomatoes and remaining ingredients. Simmer, stirring, three hours, or until lemon slices and citron peel look transparent and tomatoes are very tender. Pour into hot sterilized containers and seal. Cool and store in a cool, dark, dry place. Serve with cold meat.

Yield: About eight to ten pints.

Beet Relish   *New York*

6 cups cooked chopped beets
6 cups shredded raw cabbage
¾ cup freshly grated horseradish
3 teaspoons salt
½ teaspoon freshly ground black pepper
3 cups cider vinegar
1½ cups sugar.

1. Combine the beets, cabbage, horseradish, salt and pepper. Heat the vinegar, add the sugar and stir to dissolve. Bring to a boil.

2. Add the vegetable mixture and cook twenty minutes. Pour into hot sterilized jars and seal. Cool and store in a cool, dark, dry place.

Yield: About five pints.

Uncooked Cranberry Relish
Massachusetts

4 cups cranberries
2 seedless whole oranges
Juice of one orange
2 cups sugar.

Wash the cranberries well and chop them. Chop the oranges and add to the cranberries. Add the orange juice and sugar and mix well. Refrigerate twenty-four hours before serving.

Yield: About four cups.

Onion Relish   New York

3 medium-size onions, thinly sliced
1 green pepper, cored, seeded and thinly sliced
1 tomato, peeled and thinly sliced
1 cucumber, peeled, seeded and thinly sliced
  Tabasco sauce to taste
3 teaspoons sugar
  Juice of one lemon
½ cup wine vinegar
2 tablespoons oil.

Combine all ingredients and chill until ready to serve.

Yield: Four to six servings.

Fulling Mill Farm Chili Sauce   New York

24 large ripe tomatoes, cored
 4 large onions
 4 large green peppers, cored, seeded and chopped
 1 tablespoon ground cloves
 1 teaspoon ground allspice
   Pinch cayenne pepper
 5 cups cider vinegar
 8 tablespoons sugar
 2 tablespoons salt
 1 tablespoon cinnamon.

1. Put the tomatoes through the medium-coarse blade of a grinder. Place in a kettle, bring to a boil and simmer briefly. Drain. Return the tomato pulp to the kettle.

2. Put the onions and green peppers through the grinder and add them, along with the remaining ingredients, to the tomatoes. Bring to a boil and simmer one and one-half hours.

3. Put sauce into sterilized jars and seal. Store in a cool, dark, dry place. Serve with pot roast, cold ham or loin of pork.

Yield: Two to two and one-half quarts.

Cranberry Sauce   Massachusetts

4 cups cranberries
2 cups water
1½ cups sugar.

1. Place the cranberries in a saucepan and add the water. Cover and cook until berries pop, about ten minutes.

2. Add the sugar and continue cooking fifteen minutes. Mold, if desired, and chill.

Yield: About three cups.

Apple Chutney   New York

40 good-size tart, hard cooking apples, peeled and cored
1½ pounds seeded muscat raisins
1½ pounds currants
¾ pound chopped citron peel
½ cup dried hot chili peppers, crumbled
½ cup chopped fresh gingerroot
¼ cup finely chopped garlic
 4 large onions, quartered
½ cup preserved ginger
 6 pounds sugar
 3 quarts cider vinegar
 1 tablespoon nutmeg
 1 tablespoon ground ginger
 1 tablespoon cumin seeds.

1. Put the apples, raisins, currants, citron peel, peppers, gingerroot, garlic, onions and preserved ginger through the fine blade of a meat chopper.

2. Place the sugar and vinegar in a large kettle and bring to a boil.

3. Add the nutmeg, ground ginger, cumin

seeds and the ground ingredients. Bring to a boil, stirring, and then cook, stirring frequently, until very thick, about six to eight hours. Pour into hot sterilized jars. Seal. Cool and store in cool, dark, dry place. Serve with curries, cold meats and poultry.

Yield: About twenty pints.

Bourbon "Brandied" Peaches   *New York*

9 pounds ripe peaches (about eighty good size)
9 pounds sugar
4 cups water
4 sticks cinnamon, broken
2 tablespoons whole cloves
2 fifths bourbon.

1. Scald the peaches, a few at a time, and peel.
2. Dissolve the sugar in the water. Tie the cinnamon sticks and cloves in a muslin bag and add. Bring to a boil. When syrup is clear, add the peaches, a few at a time, and simmer until barely tender. Do not overcook.
3. Drain fruit on a platter, returning excess syrup to pan, and repeat until all fruit is cooked. Boil the syrup until it is slightly thickened (222 degrees on a candy thermometer). Cool slightly.
4. Stir in the bourbon. Place the fruit as it drains in hot sterilized jars. Cover with bourbon syrup. Seal. Store in cool, dark, dry place.

Yield: Nine to one dozen quarts, depending on size of fruit.

Whole Cranberry Conserve   *Massachusetts*

4 cups cranberries
2 cups water
2 cups sugar
Juice of one lemon
Grated rind of one orange.

1. Use a darning needle and run it through each cranberry, piercing the stem end first.

2. Combine the water and sugar and simmer ten minutes to make syrup. Add cranberries, the lemon juice and orange rind and cook over high heat twenty minutes, or until syrup thickens and sheets from spoon in two streams. Pour into hot sterilized jars. Pour two thin layers of melted paraffin over. Cool, cover and store in a cool, dark, dry place.

Yield: Four to five eight-ounce jars.

Lemon-Peach-Ginger Conserve   *New York*

1 large lemon or two small lemons, finely chopped
1 small orange, finely chopped
7 cups scalded, peeled and chopped firm ripe peaches, with all bruised spots removed
5 cups sugar
½ teaspoon ground ginger or one-quarter cup chopped crystallized ginger
½ cup blanched slivered almonds.

1. Combine the lemons, orange and peaches in a stainless steel or enameled kettle and simmer gently fifteen to twenty minutes, until orange and lemon skins are tender.
2. Add the sugar and ginger and bring to a boil, stirring until the sugar is dissolved. Boil rapidly until mixture sheets off spoon or registers 220 degrees on a candy thermometer. Add almonds during last five minutes of cooking.
3. Pour into hot sterilized jelly glasses. Pour two thin layers of melted paraffin over. Cool. Cover and store in a cool, dark, dry place.

Yield: About eight and one-half pints.

Apple-Blueberry Conserve   *Maine*

4 cups chopped, cored, peeled tart apples (about four medium-size apples)
4 cups blueberries, stemmed and washed
6 cups sugar
½ cup raisins

¼ cup lemon juice
½ cup chopped pecans.

1. Combine all the ingredients except the pecans in a large saucepan. Bring to a boil slowly, stirring occasionally until the sugar is dissolved.

2. Cook rapidly until thick, about twenty minutes, stirring frequently to prevent sticking. Add the pecans during the last few minutes of cooking. Pour the boiling hot conserve into hot sterilized half-pint canning jars. Adjust the caps. Cool and store in a cool, dark, dry place.

Yield: About six half-pint jars.

New England Carrot Marmalade
New Hampshire

4 cups cooked (slightly underdone) carrots
2 lemons, seeded
2 oranges, seeded
6½ cups sugar.

1. Coarsely grind the carrots, lemons and oranges, reserving any liquid or juice that comes from them. Place carrots, lemons, oranges and any reserved liquid or juice in a large kettle and bring to a simmer.

2. Add the sugar and stir to dissolve. Cook slowly, stirring occasionally, until mixture is thick.

3. Pour into hot sterilized jelly glasses. Pour two thin layers of melted paraffin over. Cool. Cover and store in a cool, dark, dry place.

Yield: About six eight-ounce jelly glasses.

Cucumber Marmalade
New Jersey

1½ pounds cucumbers, peeled and chopped
finely or ground (two cups)
4 cups sugar
2 tablespoons grated lemon rind
⅓ cup lemon juice
Green food coloring
½ bottle liquid fruit pectin.

1. Place the cucumber pulp in a large saucepan. Stir in the sugar, lemon rind, lemon juice and a few drops of food coloring and mix well.

2. Place over high heat and bring to a full rolling boil. Boil hard one minute, stirring constantly.

3. Remove from the heat and immediately stir in the pectin. With a metal spoon, skim off foam. Stir and skim for five minutes to cool slightly and prevent floating cucumber.

4. Ladle into hot sterilized jelly glasses and cover with one-eighth inch of hot paraffin wax. Cool, cover and store in a cool, dark, dry place.

Yield: Six six-ounce jelly glasses.

Lime Marmalade
New York

12 large or 18 medium-size limes, washed
Sugar.

1. Two days before, put the limes through a food chopper. Measure the resulting pulp and add three cups water for each cup pulp. Set aside overnight in a pottery or ceramic bowl.

2. Next day, transfer the mixture to a kettle and bring to a boil. Simmer gently twenty minutes. Let stand overnight again in the bowl.

3. Next day, measure the mixture into a large kettle and add one cup sugar for each cup lime mixture. Bring to a boil, stirring until the sugar dissolves. Boil rapidly, stirring to prevent sticking, until the marmalade sheets from the spoon, a drop chilled on a plate leaves a track when pushed by the finger or the mixture registers 220 degrees on a candy thermometer.

4. Let cool in the kettle about twenty minutes and then ladle into hot sterilized jelly jars. Top with two thin layers of melted paraffin and allow to cool. Cap and store in a cool, dark, dry place.

Yield: About twenty six-ounce jelly jars.

Quince Marmalade
Massachusetts

4 to six medium-size quince
  Grated rind and juice of one orange
2 apples, peeled, cored and sliced
1 teaspoon finely chopped yellow part of
  lemon peel
  Sugar.

1. Wash the quince. Place in a pan and add water to three-quarters cover. Bring to a boil and simmer ten minutes.
2. Remove the quince from the cooking liquid. Peel and core the quince, returning the skin and cores to the cooking liquid. Chop the quince and reserve.
3. Cook the skin and cores slowly thirty minutes. Strain and reserve liquid.
4. Place the chopped quince, grated rind and juice of the orange, apples and lemon peel in a heavy pan. Add reserved liquid until pulp is covered by one-half-inch liquid. Bring to a boil and simmer gently until fruit is very tender. Mash the fruit.
5. Measure the pulp into a pan and add three-quarters cup sugar for each cup of pulp. Heat and stir until the sugar dissolves. Boil rapidly until a set is reached, about ten minutes. (To test for set, put a drop of mixture on a saucer, refrigerate and push the finger into the cooled drop. The finger should leave a clean path when the marmalade is done.)
6. Pour the marmalade into hot sterilized jelly glasses, pour a thin layer of paraffin over and cool. Cover and store in a cool, dark, dry place.
   Yield: About six six-ounce jelly glasses.

Tomato Marmalade
New York

8 pounds ripe plum tomatoes, approximately
  Boiling water
3 oranges
3 lemons
8 sticks cinnamon
1 tablespoon whole cloves
  Sugar.

1. Dip the tomatoes, a few at a time, into a kettle of boiling water. Remove skin, chop tomatoes roughly and measure four quarts. Let stand while preparing the oranges and lemons.
2. Finely chop the skin and pulp of the oranges and lemons.
3. Place in a large kettle. Add the cinnamon sticks and cloves.
4. Pour off and discard most of the tomato liquid that has accumulated in the tomatoes. Measure the tomatoes and add to the kettle. Add one cup of sugar for each cup of tomatoes.
5. Bring to a boil, stirring until the sugar is dissolved. Boil, stirring to prevent sticking, until the marmalade sheets off the spoon, registers 220 degrees on a candy thermometer or a drop chilled on a plate leaves a track when pushed by a finger.
6. Remove the cinnamon sticks and most of the cloves. Ladle the marmalade into hot sterilized jars. Top with two thin layers of melted paraffin. Allow to cool. Cover and store in a cool, dark, dry place.
   Yield: About two dozen six-ounce jars.

Beach Plum Jelly Without Pectin
New York

1. Gather as many beach plums as convenient. All jellies should be made in relatively small batches, rarely more than three to four quarts at a time.
2. Assemble enough jelly jars, glasses or canning (screw-top) jars and lids to contain the jelly when it is made. Wash in hot soapy water and rinse. Cover with hot, not boiling, water and bring to a boil. No further boiling is necessary.
3. Pick over the beach plums, rinse well and put them into a six-quart to eight-quart kettle. Add water barely to cover. Simmer just until the fruit is soft. Strain the juice through a jelly bag or cheesecloth bag all night or for several hours. Do not squeeze the bag if you want a totally clear

jelly. A faster method, however, and one that gives a greater yield, is to squeeze the bag until most of the juice is extracted and then re-strain the juice through another clean, damp jelly bag without squeezing.

4. When ready to cook, measure the juice, bring it to a boil and cook briskly ten minutes. Add one cup of sugar for each cup of juice and stir just until the sugar is dissolved.

5. Let the mixture boil furiously until it reaches the jellying point. There are two methods to determine this. One is to dip a large metal spoon into the boiling syrup. Tilt the spoon so that the syrup drips from the bottom rim. When the syrup is premature, it will run in a stream from the spoon. When the jellying point is reached, the syrup will not flow in a steady stream. Rather, two distinct drops will form and these will run together on the bottom rim.

Another method for determining the jellying point is to spoon a generous drop of the boiling mixture onto a saucer, let the mixture cool to lukewarm and then with one finger push the drop. If the jellying point has been reached, a skin will form in front of the finger and the jelly will not flow back easily and cover the finger track.

Thermometers are helpful when cooking jelly, but the jellying test with a spoon should be used in any event. The jellying point of jellies is 220 to 222 degrees F.

6. When the jelly is finished, skim off foam and pour the hot syrup into the prepared jelly jars, leaving space one-quarter inch from the top. Cover immediately with a one-eighth-inch layer of hot paraffin. Let cool; then cover with metal lids, if desired. If the screw-top jars are used, pour in the hot jelly to one-eighth inch from the top. Put lid on and screw on the metal band evenly and tightly. Invert the jar for thirty seconds; then stand it upright to cool.

The yield for this recipe will depend on the quantities of beach plums, water and sugar used.

Sauces

Pesto Alla Romano
Connecticut

2 egg yolks
1 cup olive oil
½ cup fresh basil leaves, chopped
½ cup chopped parsley
1 teaspoon salt
2 cloves garlic
¼ cup lemon juice.

1. Place the egg yolks in the container of an electric blender. Set on high speed and dribble in the oil slowly.

2. Add the remaining ingredients. Blend thirty seconds. Use as a dip for cooked shrimp.

Yield: About two and one-half cups.

Pesto Genovese for Spaghetti
Connecticut

1 cup loosely packed basil leaves
½ cup shelled walnuts or pignoli (pine nuts)
2 cloves garlic
¾ cup freshly grated Parmesan cheese
½ cup olive oil.

1. Place the basil in the container of an electric blender and add the nuts and garlic. Blend, stirring down carefully with a rubber spatula if necessary. When well blended, add the cheese.

2. Gradually add the oil while blending on low speed.

3. Pass the pesto sauce separately with spaghetti or toss with the pasta before serving.

Yield: Four servings.

Sandra's Tomato Sauce
Connecticut

½ cup olive oil
1 large onion, finely chopped

2 two-pound-three-ounce cans tomatoes in tomato puree
1 tablespoon sugar
1 teaspoon salt
3 leaves fresh basil or one-half teaspoon dried basil
1 sprig fresh oregano or one-quarter teaspoon dried oregano.

1. Heat the oil in a saucepan and sauté the onion in it until tender. Add the tomatoes and cook, uncovered, one hour or until well blended.

2. Add the remaining ingredients and cook five minutes.

Yield: About two quarts.

Marinara Sauce with Sausage

Connecticut

1 carrot, thinly sliced
1 onion, thinly sliced
¼ cup olive oil
1 clove garlic, finely minced
1 two-pound-three-ounce can tomatoes
1 six-ounce can tomato paste
2 leaves fresh basil
3 whole cloves
½ teaspoon oregano
  Salt and freshly ground black pepper to taste
6 Italian sweet or hot sausages
¾ cup dry white wine
6 tablespoons butter
6 fresh mushrooms, thinly sliced
6 dried Italian mushrooms (optional)
  Boiling water.

1. Cook the carrot and onion in the oil until lightly browned. Add the garlic, cook briefly and add the tomatoes and tomato paste. Stir and add the basil, cloves, oregano, salt and pepper.

2. Meanwhile, in another skillet, cook the sausages, turning occasionally, until brown all over. Pour off the fat from the pan. Add the wine to the skillet and partly cover. Cook until most of the wine is evaporated. Add the sausages and pan liquid to the tomato sauce. Partly cover and simmer forty-five minutes.

3. Meanwhile, heat two tablespoons of the butter and cook the fresh mushrooms in it briefly. Place the dried mushrooms in a mixing bowl and add boiling water to cover. Let stand ten minutes. Remove the dried mushrooms and slice them. Reserve the soaking liquid.

4. Remove the sausages from the sauce and put through a food mill or sieve. Return the sauce to a boil and add the sausage, fresh mushrooms, sliced dried mushrooms and the soaking liquid. Bring to a boil; then remove from the heat. Immediately stir in the remaining butter. Serve immediately, with spaghetti or polenta.

Yield: Four to six servings.

Blender Hollandaise

New York

3 egg yolks
1 teaspoon lemon juice
¼ teaspoon salt
⅛ teaspoon cayenne pepper
½ cup butter, melted.

1. Warm the blender container.

2. Place the egg yolks, lemon juice, salt and cayenne in container. Cover. Switch the blender on and off.

3. Turn blender to high speed and add the butter in a steady stream. Keep warm by standing container in hot water.

Yield: About one cup.

Tartar Sauce

Maine

1½ cups mayonnaise
2 tablespoons chopped sour pickle
1 teaspoon finely minced onion
2 tablespoons finely chopped parsley
2 tablespoons coarsely chopped capers
1 teaspoon chopped chives

1 teaspoon mustard, preferably Dijon or
  Düsseldorf
½ teaspoon finely chopped tarragon
  Lemon juice to taste
1 hard-cooked egg, sieved (optional).

Combine all ingredients and chill.
Yield: About two cups.

Sauce for Pork Chops   *Pennsylvania*

3 cloves garlic, finely minced
¼ cup finely chopped parsley
¼ cup olive oil
2 tablespoons tomato paste
¼ cup water
5 anchovy fillets, finely minced
2 teaspoons chopped capers
  Freshly ground black pepper to taste.

1. Stirring frequently, cook the garlic and
parsley five minutes in the oil over low heat. Do
not brown. Add the tomato paste and water and
simmer about ten minutes longer.
2. Remove the sauce from the heat and stir in
the anchovies, capers and pepper. Serve with
grilled pork chops.
Yield: About one cup.

Game Sauce   *Connecticut*

6 large onions, quartered
½ cup butter
2 juice oranges
1 eight-ounce jar black currant jelly
1 teaspoon salt
2 navel oranges
1 cup sugar
1 cup Duff Gordon amontillado sherry
1 jigger cassis
1 jigger cognac or armagnac
  Drippings from roasting game or stock.

1. In a heavy casserole or pan, sauté the onions

in the butter until transparent and tender.
Squeeze the juice oranges and add the juice to the
casserole. Add the jelly and salt. Cook slowly, so
that the sugar in the jelly does not burn, until the
sauce is brown, partially caramelized.
2. Meanwhile, with a vegetable peeler, peel the
navel oranges so that only the orange-colored
part is removed. Cut the strips into tiny slivers
about one and one-half inches long and one-six-
teenth inch wide.
3. Place in a small pan, cover with water, bring
to a boil and boil ten minutes. Drain and discard
water.
4. Dissolve the sugar in one-third cup water.
Boil in another small pan until syrup registers
230 degrees on a candy thermometer. Remove
from the heat and stir in the drained peel. Let
stand at least thirty minutes.
5. Remove the browned sauce from the heat
and stir in the sherry, cassis and candied orange
slivers. Just before serving, stir in the cognac and
drippings.
Yield: About two and one-half cups.

Beverages

Fisherman's Swizzle   *Maine*

12 lemons
36 oranges
 2 pounds confectioners' sugar
 2 cups cognac
 2 cups peach brandy
 3 cups Jamaica rum
 4 quarts club soda
   Ice.

1. Squeeze juice from the lemons and oranges
into a punch bowl. Add the confectioners' sugar
and stir until it dissolves.
2. Add the cognac, peach brandy and rum.

3. Just before serving, add the club soda and ice.

Yield: About two gallons.

Slemp   *New York*

1 one-inch piece cinnamon stick
  Pinch saffron
2 whole cloves
  Small piece blade mace or one-half
  teaspoon ground mace
4 cups milk
  Peel of half a lemon in strip
⅛ teaspoon salt
½ teaspoon loose tea
2 tablespoons sugar.

1. Tie the cinnamon stick, saffron, cloves and mace in a muslin bag. Bring the milk to a boil in a saucepan. Add the lemon peel, salt, tea and the spice bag. Simmer one hour.

2. Remove the spice bag and add the sugar.

Yield: Four servings.

Wassail Bowl   *Massachusetts*

1 gallon cider
½ pound dark brown sugar
1 tablespoon whole allspice
1 tablespoon whole cloves
2 sticks cinnamon
2 blades mace
¼ teaspoon salt
2 cups dark rum
2 lemons, cut into thin slices and halved
3 oranges, cut into thin slices and halved.

1. Place the cider and brown sugar in a large kettle. Tie the allspice, cloves, cinnamon and mace in a muslin bag and add with salt. Bring to a boil and simmer fifteen minutes.

2. Remove spice bag and add the rum, lemons and oranges just before serving. Serve hot.

Yield: About three dozen servings.

Hot Buttered Rum   *Connecticut*

1 teaspoon light brown sugar
¼ teaspoon minced lemon rind
3 pinches cinnamon
1 pinch nutmeg
1 jigger light rum
  Boiling water
  Sweet butter.

1. Combine the brown sugar, lemon rind, cinnamon, nutmeg and rum in a warmed ten-ounce glass.

2. Fill with boiling water and drop in a generous teaspoon of sweet butter.

Yield: One serving.

Candies

Caramel Popcorn   *New York*

3 tablespoons corn oil
½ cup yellow hull-less popcorn
½ cup butter
1 cup firmly packed light brown sugar
¼ cup light corn syrup
½ teaspoon salt
½ teaspoon vanilla
¼ teaspoon baking soda.

1. Preheat the oven to 250 degrees.

2. Pour the oil into a four-quart to five-quart heavy, deep skillet or kettle. Place over medium-high heat and add a kernel of popcorn. When the kernel pops, remove it and add the one-half cup popcorn. Place cover on kettle, leaving a small air space at the edge of the cover. Shake pot frequently until popping stops. Remove pot from heat.

3. Measure two and one-half quarts of the popcorn (the remainder can be eaten plain) and place in a large roasting pan or metal bowl. Place in oven and keep warm.

4. Melt the butter in a two-quart saucepan. Stir in the sugar, syrup and salt. Bring mixture to a boil and boil five minutes. Remove from heat and stir in the vanilla and baking soda. Pour over the warm popcorn, mixing well to coat each piece.

5. Separate pieces of popcorn and place one layer only on two large baking sheets. Bake one hour. Cool popcorn completely (it crisps on standing). Store in airtight container.

Yield: Two and one-half quarts.

Blue Ribbon Maple Syrup Fudge
New York

2 cups maple syrup
1 tablespoon light corn syrup
¾ cup light cream
1 teaspoon vanilla
¾ cup coarsely chopped walnuts or butternuts.

1. Combine the maple syrup, corn syrup and cream in a heavy saucepan.

2. Place over moderate heat and stir until mixture begins to boil. Continue boiling, without stirring, until a small amount of the mixture forms a soft ball in cold water (234 degrees on a candy thermometer).

3. Remove pan from heat and let cool, without stirring, until lukewarm (120 to 110 degrees). Beat the mixture until it thickens and loses its gloss.

4. Add the vanilla and nuts and pour into a buttered 8-by-8-by-2-inch pan. When cool, cut into squares.

Yield: About twenty-five one-and-one-half-inch squares.

Fruit Candy for Passover
New York

½ pound pitted prunes
¼ pound golden raisins
½ pound dried apricots
¼ pound candied orange peel (recipe below)
¼ pound candied grapefruit peel (recipe below)
¼ pound Elite bittersweet chocolate, melted (see note)
1 tablespoon brandy
Sugar.

1. Grind together the prunes, raisins, apricots, orange peel and grapefruit peel. Add the chocolate and brandy and work with the hands to mix.

2. Roll into logs, cut one-inch slices and roll into balls. Roll in sugar and store in a dry place. This candy lasts indefinitely and improves with age.

Yield: Two pounds.

Note: Elite chocolate is available at Macy's and Gimbels' Passover shops.

Candied Orange Peel
New York

6 oranges
Sugar
⅓ cup lemon juice.

1. Score the oranges into eight sections and remove the peel from each section. Discard the pulp.

2. Place the peel in a saucepan and cover with water. Bring to a boil and boil five minutes. Drain. Cover with fresh water and boil five minutes again.

3. Repeat the draining and boiling twice more. Cut peel into slivers one-eighth-inch to one-quarter-inch thick. Combine two cups sugar and lemon juice in a saucepan and heat to dissolve sugar.

4. Add cut peel and boil until peel is glazed and no syrup remains. Remove from heat and let cool. Line peel up neatly on wax paper. Sprinkle with sugar and let dry twenty-four hours. Store in refrigerator.

Yield: About three-quarters pound.

Candied Grapefruit Peel

New York

4 grapefruit
Sugar
⅓ cup lemon juice.

1. Using a swivel-bladed potato peeler, remove, then discard the thin yellow skin of the grapefruit.
2. Score the fruit into eight sections and remove the white peel from each section. Discard the pulp.
3. Place peel in a saucepan and cover with water. Bring to a boil and boil five minutes. Drain. Cover with fresh water and boil five minutes again.
4. Repeat the draining and boiling twice more. Cut peel into slivers one-eighth-inch to one-quarter-inch thick. Combine two cups sugar and lemon juice in a saucepan and heat to dissolve sugar.
5. Add cut peel to syrup and boil until peel is glazed and no syrup remains. Remove from heat and let cool. Line peel up neatly on wax paper. Sprinkle with sugar and let dry twenty-four hours. Store in refrigerator.

Yield: About three-quarters pound.

Homemade Lollipops or Hard Candies

New Jersey

2 cups sugar
⅔ cup light corn syrup
1 cup water
½ teaspoon oil of lemon or other concentrated flavor
Food colorings
Skewers or ice cream sticks for lollipops.

1. Place the sugar, syrup and water in a pan. Heat, stirring, until the sugar dissolves. Continue to cook, without stirring, until syrup reaches 310 degrees on a candy thermometer. Keep the pan clear of crystals by washing down the sides once or twice with a brush dipped into water.

2. Remove from the heat, add the flavoring and coloring and spoon quickly, one teaspoon at a time, onto a greased baking sheet. Immediately place a skewer or stick in position before the candy sets. Alternately, the syrup may be poured into lightly greased tiny muffin cups to give round candies.
3. Remove the lollipops or round candies as soon as they are set. Wrap in clear plastic wrap.

Yield: About two dozen.

Dressings (Stuffings)

Cranberry-Corn Bread Stuffing

Massachusetts

4 cups cranberries
1 cup water
1½ cups sugar
1 pound sausage meat, cooked and crumbled, with drippings
9 cups crumbled corn bread (page 220)
1 cup diced celery
1 small onion, chopped
½ cup diced green pepper
½ teaspoon thyme
½ teaspoon marjoram
½ teaspoon sage
1 small unpeeled red apple, cored and chopped
¼ cup lemon juice
1 cup applesauce.

1. Preheat the oven to 350 degrees.
2. In a saucepan, combine the cranberries, water and sugar. Bring to a boil and simmer ten minutes, or until berries are tender. Drain off juice.
3. Combine drained berries with the remaining ingredients. Turn into a greased casserole and bake one hour. Or use to stuff a fourteen-pound turkey.

Yield: Ten servings.

Potato Stuffing or Filling   *Pennsylvania*

2 cups mashed potatoes
2 eggs, lightly beaten
2 tablespoons butter
2 cups tiny white bread cubes
½ teaspoon marjoram
½ teaspoon thyme
    Salt and freshly ground black pepper to
    taste
1 cup milk.

1. Preheat the oven to 350 degrees.
2. Beat the potatoes with the eggs. Heat the butter in a skillet and brown the bread cubes in it. Sprinkle with the marjoram, thyme, salt and pepper and stir into potato mixture.
3. Add the milk and mix well. Turn into a greased baking dish and bake forty-five minutes. Or use to stuff a five-pound chicken.
Yield: Four servings.

Oyster Stuffing   *New York*

¼ cup butter or goose fat
1 onion, finely chopped
½ cup chopped celery
1 goose liver, chopped
6 cups stale one-quarter-inch white bread cubes
2 cups oysters with liquor
2 tablespoons chopped parsley
1 teaspoon salt
½ teaspoon freshly ground black pepper
1 egg, lightly beaten
½ teaspoon thyme
¼ teaspoon marjoram.

1. Melt the butter in a skillet and sauté the onion and celery in it until tender but not browned. Add the liver and cook quickly two to three minutes. Put the bread cubes in a bowl and add the liver mixture.
2. Strain the oyster liquor, through cheesecloth if gritty, into a saucepan. Bring to a boil and add cleaned oysters. Simmer three minutes, or until the edges just curl.
3. Skim out the oysters and quarter them if they are very large, halve them if they are average. Add to the bread mixture.
4. Add the remaining ingredients and enough oyster liquor, usually about one-third cup, to moisten the dressing.
Yield: Enough stuffing for a seven-pound to eight-pound goose or turkey.

Fruit Stuffing   *New York*

¼ cup butter
1 large onion, finely chopped
½ cup chopped celery
6 cups stale firm one-quarter-inch white bread cubes
⅓ cup currants
3 firm tart apples, peeled, cored and diced
½ tablespoon chopped fresh sage leaves or one teaspoon dried sage
2 tablespoons chopped parsley
    Grated rind of one large lemon
1 teaspoon salt
½ teaspoon freshly ground black pepper
1 tablespoon lemon juice
    Dry white wine.

1. Melt the butter in a skillet and sauté the onion and celery in it until tender but not browned. Put the bread cubes in a large bowl and add the onion mixture.
2. Add the remaining ingredients including enough wine to just moisten the stuffing.
Yield: Enough stuffing for a seven-pound goose or a six-pound duck.

Dumplings

Dumplings for Soup   *Massachusetts*

1 cup sifted flour
¼ teaspoon salt
2 teaspoons baking powder
1 tablespoon butter
6 tablespoons milk, approximately.

1. Sift together the flour, salt and baking powder into a mixing bowl. With the fingers, work in the butter.
2. Add the milk, little by little, while stirring with a fork. Add just enough milk to make a soft dough. Drop tablespoons of the batter into simmering soup, cover tightly and cook fifteen minutes.
Yield: About sixteen.

Marrow Bone Matzoh Balls   *New York*

2 large marrow bones, cut into one-and-one-half-inch pieces
1 cup matzoh meal
Salt to taste
⅛ teaspoon nutmeg
1 cup boiling water
2 eggs
Boiling salted water.

1. With a sharp-pointed knife, dig out the marrow from the bones (there should be about one-half cup) and place in a small skillet. Heat gently until the marrow is melted. Remove skillet from the heat.
2. Stir in the matzoh meal until it is completely coated with fat. Add the salt and nutmeg. Add the one cup boiling water and beat until mixture leaves the sides of the skillet.
3. Beat in the eggs, one at a time. With wet hands, form the mixture into small balls. Drop into boiling salted water and boil one-half hour.
Yield: One dozen to fifteen.

Matzoh Balls   *New York*

4 teaspoons chicken fat
2 eggs
¼ cup hot chicken soup
Salt and freshly ground black pepper to taste
⅔ cup matzoh meal
1 tablespoon finely minced parsley
8 cups rapidly boiling salted water.

1. Cream the fat with the eggs. Gradually add the hot soup, beating continuously. When thoroughly blended, add the salt, pepper, matzoh meal and parsley. Spoon into a bowl, cover and refrigerate at least four hours.
2. Shape the mixture into balls and drop into the boiling salted water. Cover, reduce the heat and simmer thirty-five minutes. Drain. Serve hot, in chicken soup.
Yield: About two dozen.

2. South

Appetizers and Soups

For a description of conch see page 186.

Conch Vinaigrette   *Florida*

4 large conchs
½ cup olive oil
2 tablespoons wine vinegar or juice of one
  lime
  Salt and freshly ground black pepper to
  taste
1 clove garlic, finely minced
2 tablespoons finely chopped parsley
1 tablespoon finely chopped chives (optional)
¼ teaspoon oregano.

1. Scrub the conchs with a brush and drop them into boiling water. Cover and simmer thirty minutes to one hour, depending on the size of each conch and until part of the body protrudes from the shell. Drain and cover immediately with cold water. Remove the meat and cut off the hard outer cover with a paring knife.

2. Cut the meat into one-half-inch slices and add the remaining ingredients. Toss well and serve at room temperature.

Yield: Six servings.

Conch Seviche   *Florida*

5 to eight conchs
1 small red onion, peeled and finely chopped
½ cup freshly squeezed lime juice or lemon
  juice
2 small tomatoes, peeled, cored and chopped
1 small hot green pepper, seeded and finely
  chopped
  Salt and freshly ground black pepper to
  taste
3 tablespoons peanut oil, approximately
1 tablespoon finely chopped cilantro (Chinese
  parsley, see note), optional.

1. If conchs in the shell are bought, rinse them thoroughly and crack the base of two shells together. If they cannot be cracked in this manner, use a large hammer to crack the shell. Using a knife and the fingers, press or pull out the flesh from the interior. Pare or scrape away the soft matter and carefully trim away the horny claw-like structure attached. Slit the outer covering of the flesh. Pull or pare away this covering.

2. Split the firm white conch flesh down the center, but do not cut in half. Using a heavy mallet, pound the flesh lightly but firmly. Slice the pounded meat into thin slivers and place in a bowl. Add the remaining ingredients. Add more peanut oil if desired. Toss and chill.

Yield: Four or more servings.

Note: Cilantro is available in Spanish and Chinese markets.

Deviled Crab Meat I   *Maryland*

    1 pound lump crab meat, picked over to
      remove bits of shell and cartilage
    ¼ cup dry sherry
      Dash of Worcestershire sauce
    2 tablespoons butter
    1½ tablespoons flour
    ½ teaspoon dry mustard
    1 cup milk
      Salt and freshly ground black pepper to
      taste
    2 egg yolks, lightly beaten
    1 hard-cooked egg, finely chopped
      Lemon juice to taste
    ½ teaspoon grated horseradish
      Cayenne pepper to taste (optional)
    ½ cup buttered soft bread crumbs
      Lemon wedges.

1. Preheat the oven to 375 degrees.
2. Put the crab meat in a mixing bowl and pour the sherry over the crab. Add the Worcestershire and set aside.
3. Melt the butter in a saucepan and stir in the flour and mustard with a wire whisk. Add the milk, stirring rapidly with the whisk. When the mixture is thickened and smooth, simmer two to three minutes.
4. Add the salt and pepper. Remove the sauce from the heat. When sauce cools slightly, stir in the egg yolks, beating rapidly with the whisk.
5. Add the crab meat, hard-cooked egg, lemon juice and horseradish. If desired, season with a bit of cayenne. Mix well, but do not break up the crab lumps.
6. Fill crab shells or individual ramekins with the mixture and sprinkle with the bread crumbs. Bake ten minutes, or until golden brown. Serve with lemon wedges.
Yield: Four servings.

Deviled Crab Meat II   *Maryland*

    4 tablespoons butter
    ½ cup finely chopped onion
    ½ cup plus four teaspoons soft bread crumbs
    1 cup heavy cream
    ½ teaspoon dry mustard
    ¼ teaspoon cayenne pepper, or to taste
      Tabasco sauce to taste
    2 egg yolks, beaten
      Salt to taste
    1 pound lump crab meat, picked over to
      remove bits of shell and cartilage
      Parsley for garnish.

1. Preheat the oven to 375 degrees.
2. Melt two tablespoons of the butter in a skillet and cook the onion in it until wilted. Add one-half cup of the bread crumbs, the cream, mustard, cayenne, Tabasco, egg yolks and salt. Gently mix with the crab meat.
3. Spoon the mixture into four individual ramekins, dot with the remaining butter and sprinkle with the remaining bread crumbs. Bake until golden brown. Serve garnished with parsley.
Yield: Four servings.

Crab Sauté   *Maryland*

    4 tablespoons butter
    1 pound lump crab meat, picked over to
      remove bits of shell and cartilage
      Salt to taste
    4 to six slices thin toast
      Chopped herbs (see note)
      Black peppermill
      Lemon wedges.

1. Melt the butter in a skillet. When butter starts to sizzle, add the crab meat. Cook, stirring as gently as possible, until crab is piping hot. The crab lumps should remain as whole and firm as possible. Season with salt.
2. Spoon the crab onto the toast and sprinkle

with chopped herbs if desired. Serve with a pep-permill and lemon wedges.

Yield: Four to six servings.

Note: Chopped fresh herbs that go well with crab include parsley, tarragon, chives and chervil. Or use a mixture of all four.

Hot Crab Meat Puffs   *Virginia*

2 egg whites, stiffly beaten
1 cup mayonnaise
1 cup flaked and picked-over crab meat
1 teaspoon lemon juice
½ teaspoon Worcestershire sauce
  Tabasco sauce to taste
  Toast rounds
  Paprika.

Fold together the egg whites, mayonnaise and crab meat. Stir in the lemon juice, Worcestershire and Tabasco. Spoon onto toast rounds, sprinkle with paprika and broil until bubbly.

Yield: Three dozen to four dozen.

Oyster Appetizer   *Maryland*

12 shucked oysters
 6 thin slices bacon, cut in half
   Finely ground black pepper
   Lemon juice
   Worcestershire sauce.

1. Place an oyster at one end of a piece of bacon. Season with pepper, lemon juice and Worcestershire. Roll bacon up to enclose oyster.

2. Place on broiler pan and repeat with re-maining ingredients. Broil in a preheated broiler, turning frequently until the bacon is crisp.

Yield: Four servings.

Oysters with Cocktail Sauce   *Louisiana*

 1 cup catchup
   Juice of one lemon
 2 tablespoons horseradish, or to taste
 2 teaspoons Worcestershire sauce
 3 dashes Tabasco sauce
½ cup finely chopped hearts of celery
24 freshly shucked oysters or oysters on the half shell.

Combine all ingredients except the oysters. Chill. Serve sauce separately with oysters.

Yield: Four servings.

Cucumber and Shad Roe   *Maryland*

3 tablespoons butter
1 pair shad roe
3 medium-size cucumbers
  Salt and freshly ground black pepper to taste
1 teaspoon onion juice or one tablespoon finely chopped chives
  Worcestershire sauce to taste
  Hollandaise sauce (see page 301).

1. Melt the butter in a skillet and gently add the shad roe. Cover and cook over low heat, turn-ing once, just until the roe are cooked through, five to twelve minutes, depending on size. Let cool slightly. Discard the connecting membrane of the roe.

2. Preheat the oven to 375 degrees.

3. Peel the cucumbers. Hollow out the whole cucumbers using an apple corer or the small scoop of a melon ball cutter.

4. Gently mash the shad roe and season with salt, pepper, onion juice or chives and Worcester-shire. Stuff the cucumbers with the roe mixture.

5. Butter three squares of aluminum foil and place one stuffed cucumber in the center of each. Wrap in foil and seal envelope fashion. Place on a baking sheet and bake twenty to forty minutes, or until cucumbers are tender. Remove foil, place

cucumbers on hot dish and serve with hollandaise sauce.

Yield: Six servings as a first course.

Note: Cucumbers may also be stuffed with a mixture of crab meat, lemon juice and tarragon to taste.

Shrimp with Lamaze Sauce   *Louisiana*

1 cup mayonnaise, preferably homemade
1 cup chili sauce
¼ cup India relish
1 to two hard-cooked eggs, chopped
½ teaspoon chopped stuffed olive
¼ green pepper, seeded and chopped
½ pimento, chopped
1 tablespoon chopped celery
1½ teaspoons prepared mustard
  Salt and freshly ground black pepper to taste
1½ teaspoons steak sauce
  Dash of paprika
36 shrimp, cooked, shelled and deveined
  Water cress for garnish.

Combine all the ingredients except the water cress and chill. Serve garnished with water cress.
Yield: Six servings.

Shrimp Cocktail with Celery-Tomato Sauce   *Mississippi*

¾ cup catchup
½ cup finely chopped heart of celery
2 tablespoons finely chopped green pepper
1 teaspoon Worcestershire sauce, or to taste
  Juice of one lemon
  Tabasco sauce to taste
1 tablespoon horseradish, preferably freshly grated
  Salt to taste (optional)
6 or more lettuce leaves
36 shrimp, cooked, shelled and deveined.

1. Combine all the ingredients except the lettuce and shrimp and chill.

2. Arrange the lettuce leaves in six ramekins, shells or cocktail dishes and cover with equal portions of shrimp.

3. Spoon equal portions of cocktail sauce over each serving.
Yield: Six servings.

Shrimp with Hot Sauce   *Alabama*

¼ pound butter
  Juice of two lemons
6 tablespoons Worcestershire sauce
  Salt and freshly ground black pepper to taste
  Tabasco sauce to taste
2 pounds shrimp, cooked, shelled, and deveined.

Combine all the ingredients except the shrimp in a chafing dish. Serve the shrimp separately on a bed of ice. Skewer the shrimp with toothpicks and let guests serve themselves by dipping shrimp into the hot sauce.
Yield: Eight or more servings.

Pickled Shrimp   *Alabama*

3 cups oil
3 teaspoons dry mustard
4 teaspoons sugar
⅔ cup cider vinegar
⅔ cup catchup
  Freshly ground black pepper to taste
4 to six cloves garlic
4 teaspoons Worcestershire sauce
3 pounds shrimp, cooked, shelled, and deveined
3 medium-size sweet onions, sliced wafer-thin
6 bay leaves.

1. This dish should be made two days in advance, and it must be made in two operations.

2. Combine the oil, mustard, sugar, vinegar, catchup, pepper, garlic and Worcestershire and blend half the mixture in an electric blender.

3. Arrange half the shrimp in a layer in a deep serving dish. Arrange over them half the onion slices and bay leaves. Pour the blended oil mixture over all.

4. Blend the remaining half of oil mixture. Repeat layers of remaining shrimp, onion slices and bay leaves and pour the oil mixture over all. Cover and refrigerate two days before using.

Yield: Eight or more servings.

Shrimp Remoulade   *Louisiana*

2 pounds shrimp
1 bay leaf
1 rib celery with leaves
2 sprigs parsley
12 peppercorns
   Salt to taste
3 tablespoons tarragon vinegar
¼ cup Creole mustard (if unavailable use Düsseldorf mustard and add Tabasco to taste)
5 anchovies, finely chopped
¾ cup oil (may be a mixture of olive oil and vegetable oil)
   Freshly ground black pepper to taste
½ teaspoon chopped fresh tarragon or one-quarter teaspoon dried tarragon
1 clove garlic, finely minced
1 tablespoon chopped parsley
1 scallion, including green part, chopped
3 tablespoons horseradish, preferably fresh
   Tabasco sauce to taste
   Chopped lettuce.

1. Day before, peel each shrimp and make a small incision along the curved back. Reserve the shrimp shells. Rinse the shrimp under cold running water to remove the sandy vein along the back.

2. Place the shrimp, shells, bay leaf, celery, parsley sprigs, peppercorns and salt in a saucepan and add water to cover. Bring to a boil and simmer about five minutes. Drain the shrimp and let cool.

3. Place the shrimp in a mixing bowl. Chill. Combine the remaining ingredients except chopped lettuce and pour over the shrimp. Let stand overnight in the refrigerator. Next day, bring to room temperature before serving. Serve on chopped lettuce.

Yield: Four to six servings.

Chilled Gulf Coast Shrimp Creole
Louisiana

2 cups mayonnaise
½ small onion, grated
1 clove garlic, finely minced
½ cup Creole mustard or Düsseldorf mustard with Tabasco added to taste
1 tablespoon grated horseradish, or to taste
½ cup finely chopped parsley
   Juice of one lemon
3 pounds shrimp, cooked, shelled and deveined.

1. Blend the mayonnaise with the onion, garlic, mustard, horseradish, parsley and lemon juice.

2. Stir in the shrimp and refrigerate at least two hours before serving.

Yield: Eight or more servings.

Shrimps Wilder   *Alabama*

2 pounds shrimp
2 cloves garlic, finely chopped
½ cup peanut oil or olive oil
¼ cup soy sauce
½ cup lime or lemon juice
3 tablespoons finely chopped parsley
2 tablespoons finely minced scallions, including green part

Salt and freshly ground black pepper to taste
Lime or lemon wedges.

1. Shell and devein the shrimp, but leave on the last tail segment. Dry and place in a shallow dish.
2. Combine the remaining ingredients and pour over shrimp. Let stand three to four hours.
3. Thread the shrimp on skewers and place them on a grill over hot coals. The coals should be approximately three inches from the shrimp. Cook quickly, about three minutes on one side, basting with the marinade. Turn and cook three to five minutes longer, basting occasionally. Serve with lime or lemon wedges.
Yield: Four to six servings.

Shrimp Paste   *Alabama*

2 pounds shrimp, cooked, shelled and deveined
6 tablespoons butter
¾ cup catchup
1 teaspoon onion juice
1½ tablespoons Worcestershire sauce
Juice of one lemon
Salt to taste
Tabasco sauce to taste
Lettuce
Mayonnaise.

1. Put shrimp through a meat grinder twice, using the finest blade.
2. Cream the butter; add shrimp and the remaining ingredients except lettuce and mayonnaise. Blend with a wooden spoon until mixture is the consistency of mayonnaise. Mold with hands into a loaf and press into a six-cup loaf pan. Refrigerate six hours. Unmold and slice in one-quarter-inch slices. Serve on lettuce with mayonnaise.
Yield: Six to eight servings.

Sea Food and Southern Cocktail Sauce
                                   Alabama

2 cups mayonnaise
1 hard-cooked egg, sieved
1 cup catchup
2 teaspoons Worcestershire sauce
Juice of one lemon
2 teaspoons anchovy paste
Tabasco sauce to taste
Salt to taste
Coarsely ground black pepper to taste
Chopped parsley
4 cups cooked, cleaned shrimp, oysters, clams, lobster pieces, crawfish.

1. Place the mayonnaise in a mixing bowl and stir in the egg. Gradually stir in the catchup; then add the Worcestershire, lemon juice, anchovy paste, Tabasco, salt and pepper.
2. Sprinkle with parsley before serving as a dip for the sea food.
Yield: About ten servings.

Chilled Red Snapper Appetizer
                                   Louisiana

2 pounds red snapper fillets
4 cups court bouillon (see below)
4 hard-cooked eggs
1 tablespoon dry mustard
⅓ cup lemon juice
¼ teaspoon salt
½ cup mayonnaise
¾ cup finely chopped scallions, including green part
⅓ cup drained capers
2 teaspoons Creole mustard, or to taste (if unavailable, use Düsseldorf mustard and add Tabasco sauce to taste)
Boston lettuce leaves.

1. Simmer the snapper in the court bouillon until fish flakes, about fifteen minutes. Cool the fish; bone and skin. Chill.

2. Mash the yolks of three of the eggs and add the dry mustard, lemon juice and salt.

3. Add the mayonnaise, scallions, capers and Creole mustard. Chop or sieve the whites of three of the eggs and stir in.

4. Arrange the chilled fish on the lettuce leaves and spoon the sauce over. Garnish with remaining egg cut into slices.

Yield: Four servings.

Court Bouillon   *Louisiana*

1 cup white wine
4 cups water
  Bones and head of snapper and/or other white fish
6 peppercorns, bruised
½ teaspoon salt
½ small onion
½ rib celery
¼ teaspoon thyme
½ bay leaf
2 sprigs parsley.

1. Place the wine, water, fish bones and head, peppercorns, salt and onion in a saucepan. Sprinkle the inside of the celery with the thyme, cover with the bay leaf and parsley sprigs and tie into a bundle. Add bundle to the pan.

2. Bring to a boil and simmer twenty-five minutes. Strain through a double thickness of cheesecloth.

Yield: About one quart.

Escabeche of Red Snapper   *Florida*

4 red snapper fillets, each about one-inch thick and each weighing about one-half pound
  Flour
  Salt and freshly ground black pepper
½ cup peanut oil
2 cloves garlic, peeled and cut in half
½ cup olive oil (see note)

2 tablespoons cider vinegar
  Juice of one sour orange or lime (see note)
  Tabasco sauce to taste.

1. Day before, dredge the fish fillets in a mixture of flour, salt and pepper. Cook the fish in hot peanut oil with the garlic six to eight minutes to a side. Transfer the fish to a flat baking dish.

2. Heat the olive oil and let it cool. Stir in the vinegar, orange or lime juice, Tabasco and salt and pepper to taste. Beat vigorously and pour the mixture over the fish. Cover and refrigerate overnight. Next day, serve cold.

Yield: Four to six servings.
Note: Some recipes call for using the oil in which the fish cooked rather than using the olive oil recommended in this recipe.

Sour Seville oranges are available in February and March.

Ham and Egg Canapés   *Virginia*

4 slices white bread
  Melted butter
1 cup ground baked Virginia or country ham
2 hard-cooked eggs
  Paprika.

1. Preheat the over to 400 degrees.

2. Using a small biscuit cutter, cut each slice of bread into four rounds. Brush generously with melted butter and place on a baking sheet. Bake, turning once, until golden brown.

3. Spoon one tablespoon of ham onto each round of toast and return to the oven just to heat through.

4. Meanwhile, split the eggs in half. Press the whites through a sieve or ricer. Press the yolks through another. Sprinkle the canapés first with white of egg, then with yolk. Dust with paprika and serve hot.

Yield: Sixteen.

Ham Biscuits *Kentucky*

1 cup flour
2 teaspoons baking powder
⅛ teaspoon salt
¼ teaspoon dry mustard
3 tablespoons shortening
1 cup ground cooked country-style ham
½ cup milk, approximately.

1. Combine the flour, baking powder, salt and mustard in a bowl. With the finger tips or a pastry blender, mix in the shortening.
2. Preheat the oven to 450 degrees.
3. Add the ham and mix to a soft dough with the milk. Knead thirty seconds on a lightly floured board. Roll out to three-eighths-inch thickness. Cut into tiny rounds and place on a lightly greased baking sheet.
4. Bake ten minutes, or until done. Serve hot with or without butter.
Yield: Eighteen to two dozen.

Eggs Sardou *Louisiana*

1 cup hot creamed spinach
2 artichoke bottoms, canned and reheated or freshly cooked
2 poached eggs
Easy hollandaise sauce (see below).

1. Spoon the spinach onto two hot plates. Top with the artichoke bottoms.
2. Place one egg on each artichoke bottom. Cover with hollandaise sauce.
Yield: Two servings.

Easy Hollandaise Sauce *Louisiana*

3 egg yolks
2 tablespoons lemon juice
¼ teaspoon salt
⅛ teaspoon cayenne pepper (optional)
½ cup butter, melted and hot.

1. Place the yolks, lemon juice, salt and cayenne if desired in an electric blender and blend on low speed.
2. Maintaining the blender at low speed, gradually pour in the butter and continue blending until sauce is thick and smooth.
Yield: About three-quarters cup.

Stuffed Cherry Tomatoes *Florida*

48 cherry tomatoes
2 tablespoons wine vinegar
6 tablespoons olive oil
Salt and freshly ground black pepper to taste
2 three and one-half-ounce cans tuna
4 tablespoons chopped capers
2 hard-cooked eggs, finely chopped
2 tablespoons chopped chives
2 teaspoons chopped onion
2 anchovies, finely chopped
2 teaspoons chopped parsley
Tabasco sauce to taste
4 drops Worcestershire sauce
2 tablespoons mayonnaise, or more to taste
1 teaspoon lemon juice.

1. With a sharp paring knife, trim off a tiny portion from the base of each tomato. This will give a slight base to help them stand upright. Cut a small slice from the top of each tomato. Run the tip of the knife around the inside of each tomato and scoop out the inside to leave the shell.
2. Place the hollowed-out tomatoes in a mixing bowl and add the vinegar, oil, salt and pepper. Refrigerate one hour or longer, tossing occasionally.
3. Combine the remaining ingredients in a mixing bowl. Mash and whip to blend well. Drain the tomatoes and fill them with the stuffing.
Yield: Four dozen.

Tomato Freeze with Avocado Topping
Florida

1 three-ounce package cream cheese
¼ cup Roquefort cheese
½ teaspoon grated onion
½ teaspoon Worcestershire sauce
3 tablespoons lemon juice
2 cups tomato juice
    Salt and freshly ground black pepper to
    taste
2 egg whites, beaten stiff but not dry
1 ripe avocado
⅛ teaspoon Tabasco sauce.

1. Cream the cream cheese and Roquefort together. Stir in the onion, Worcestershire and two tablespoons of the lemon juice. Slowly stir in the tomato juice. Season with salt and pepper.

2. Pour into a freezer tray and freeze until frozen around the edges but still mushy in the middle. Beat mixture until smooth but not completely melted. Fold in the egg whites and refreeze.

3. Peel and pit the avocado. Mash or puree the avocado and mix in the remaining lemon juice and Tabasco. Serve tomato freeze topped with avocado.

Yield: Six servings.

Cheese Balls
Mississippi

1½ cups finely grated Swiss cheese or Cheddar
    cheese
3 egg whites, beaten stiff but not dry
    Dry bread crumbs
2 egg yolks, lightly beaten
    Fat or oil for deep-frying.

1. Place the cheese in a bowl and fold in the egg whites. Shape mixture into one-inch balls and roll in bread crumbs.

2. Dip in the egg yolks and again in crumbs. Fry until golden, a few at a time, in a fry basket in fat or oil heated to 365 degrees. Drain on paper towels.

Yield: About two dozen.

Herb Dip for Raw Vegetables
Alabama

1 cup cottage cheese
½ cup sour cream
1 cup homemade mayonnaise
2 tablespoons chopped chives
1 tablespoon chopped parsley
2 cloves garlic, finely minced
2 tablespoons grated onion
½ teaspoon Worcestershire sauce
¼ teaspoon Tabasco sauce
    Salt and freshly ground black pepper to
    taste.

Place the cottage cheese in a mixing bowl and add the sour cream. Beat with a fork or wire whisk until smooth, or blend in a blender. Stir in the remaining ingredients and serve chilled as a dip for raw vegetables such as cauliflower, celery and carrots.

Yield: About three cups.

Pat's Favorite Dip
Kentucky

1 egg
3 tablespoons cider vinegar
3 tablespoons sugar
1 eight-ounce package cream cheese, softened
3 tablespoons finely chopped onions
3 tablespoons chopped pimento
3 tablespoons chopped green pepper
    Salt and freshly ground black pepper to
    taste.

1. Put the egg, vinegar and sugar in the top of a double boiler and cook over hot water, stirring until thick.

2. Stir in the remaining ingredients and cool. Chill and serve with fresh raw vegetables.

Yield: About two cups.

Benne Seed Wafers
South Carolina

⅔ cup sesame seeds
2 cups flour
　Salt to taste
　Cayenne pepper to taste
½ cup butter
¼ cup shortening
¼ cup ice water, approximately.

1. Preheat the oven to 300 degrees.
2. Place the sesame seeds on a baking sheet and bake, stirring occasionally, until lightly browned, about twenty minutes.
3. Combine the flour, salt and cayenne in a mixing bowl. Add the butter and shortening and cut in with two knives or a pastry blender until mixture has the texture of coarse corn meal. Add the water, a little at a time, using a two-pronged fork to toss the mixture. Add just enough water so that the dough will hold together. Knead in the seeds.
4. Roll the dough on a lightly floured board and cut into small round wafers with a biscuit cutter. Place on a baking sheet and bake fifteen to twenty minutes. Remove from the oven and sprinkle, while hot, with a little salt.

Yield: Two dozen to three dozen wafers, depending on size.

Cheese Straws
Alabama

1¼ pounds sharp Cheddar cheese, grated
8 tablespoons butter
1¾ cups flour
¼ teaspoon cayenne pepper
⅓ teaspoon salt.

1. Preheat the oven to 350 degrees.
2. Using an electric mixer, cream together the cheese and butter. Gradually add the flour and remaining ingredients. Work into a dough with the fingers.
3. Press the dough through a cookie press onto a baking sheet. Bake twenty to thirty minutes, or until crisp and lightly browned.

Yield: Six dozen to eight dozen, depending on size.

Deep-Fried Grits Balls
South Carolina

2 cups water
½ teaspoon salt
½ cup quick cooking grits
1 cup grated sharp Cheddar cheese or Gruyère cheese
¼ teaspoon cayenne pepper
¼ teaspoon grated nutmeg
　Freshly ground black pepper to taste
2 eggs
1½ teaspoons peanut oil
1½ cups soft bread crumbs
　Fat for deep-frying.

1. Bring the water to a boil and add salt. When water is boiling vigorously, add the grits slowly. Return to a boil and cook over direct heat, stirring occasionally, two and one-half to five minutes. Chill the grits.
2. Mash grits with a fork and stir in the cheese, cayenne, nutmeg and pepper. With hands, shape into approximately forty balls. Beat the eggs and oil together. Dip balls in mixture; then roll in the bread crumbs.
3. Fry in hot fat (375 degrees) about two minutes, or until golden brown.

Yield: Forty appetizers.

Conch Chowder
Florida

4 raw conchs
¼ pound salt pork, cut into small cubes
2 tablespoons butter
2 cups finely chopped onions
1 large green pepper, peeled, seeded and cored
1 one-pound can Italian-plum tomatoes
4 large potatoes, peeled and cut into cubes

8 cups water
Salt and freshly ground black pepper to
taste.

1. Wash and scrub the conchs. Remove the meat from the shell. Skin the flesh and remove the intestinal vein. Clean well. Grind the meat.

2. Cook the salt pork in the butter until almost crisp. Add the onions and green pepper and cook, stirring, until onions are wilted. Add the tomatoes, ground conch, potatoes and water. Season with salt and pepper. Simmer until potatoes are mushy, about one hour. This chowder is better if it is removed from the heat, cooled, then reheated.

Yield: Four servings.

One of the genuine delicacies of the Louisiana scene is the abundant crawfish or crayfish which come primarily from the Cajun country in the southern part of the state. The finest sources are said to be the Atchafalaya River basin and the region around the Belle River. The town of Breaux Bridge is said to be the crawfish capital of the world.

Because crawfish come from swamps and other shallow freshwater sources, their flavor is a trifle earthy. They have a texture that more closely resembles lobster than shrimp, although a cooked crawfish tail is about the size of a small shrimp.

An appreciation of crawfish is by no means limited to Louisiana. Each August the Swedes have a crawfish festival and the French, who call them écrevisse, *use crawfish in countless dishes.*

The commonest uses for crawfish in Louisiana are in a bisque and in étouffée. The bisque is a thickened soup garnished with stuffed crawfish heads. The étouffée is a form of stew.

Crawfish Bisque   *Louisiana*

12 to fifteen pounds live crawfish
   Boiling salted water
3 tablespoons butter

4 onions, finely chopped
5 ribs celery, finely chopped
2 green peppers, seeded and finely chopped
6 cloves garlic, finely chopped
   Salt and freshly ground black pepper to taste
3 tablespoons Worcestershire sauce
¼ cup lemon juice
3 tablespoons plus one-half cup chopped parsley
1 teaspoon thyme
1 cup finely chopped scallions, including green part
3 slices stale white bread
¾ cup flour
¾ cup oil
3 quarts hot water
1 lemon, thinly sliced
1 bay leaf
   Cooked rice.

1. Preheat the oven to 350 degrees.

2. Wash the crawfish and boil in the salted water for ten minutes. Remove meat from the tail and clean. Remove fat from heads and reserve. Clean the heads, rinse in cold water and drain.

3. Melt the butter and sauté two of the onions, three of the celery ribs, one of the green peppers and three of the garlic cloves in it until tender.

4. Grind two-thirds of the crawfish tails and add. Cook five minutes. Add salt and pepper to taste, two tablespoons of the Worcestershire, the lemon juice, three tablespoons of the parsley, the thyme, one-half cup of the scallions and one-half of the reserved crawfish fat.

5. Soak the bread briefly in water, squeeze and add. Simmer mixture ten minutes, stirring constantly. Use mixture to stuff heads. Pack tightly. Bake fifteen minutes and set aside while preparing bisque.

6. Combine the flour and oil in a saucepan and heat, stirring, until mixture forms a brown roux. Add the remaining onions, celery, green pepper and garlic and cook until tender.

7. Add the hot water all at once and blend well. Season with the remaining Worcestershire

and salt and pepper and add the lemon slices. Add remaining crawfish fat and the bay leaf and cook for one hour.

8. Remove bay leaf. Add remaining crawfish tails. Cover pot and cook ten minutes longer. Add stuffed heads, remaining scallions and remaining parsley. Cook five minutes. Serve over rice.

Yield: Eight to ten servings.

Shrimp Bisque   *Louisiana*

½ cup diced salt pork
⅓ cup finely chopped shallots
⅓ cup finely chopped celery
1 cup one-half-inch cubes potato
4 cups fish stock or bottled clam juice and water
1 bay leaf
2 sprigs parsley
½ teaspoon thyme
1½ pounds shrimp, shelled and deveined
1½ cups heavy cream
¼ cup dry white wine or one teaspoon lemon juice
  Cooked rice.

1. In a heavy kettle, render the salt pork until it gives up its fat and is crisp. Drain the bits and reserve.

2. Sauté the shallots and celery in the pork fat until tender. Add the potato cubes, fish stock or clam juice and water and the bay leaf, parsley and thyme tied in a muslin bag. Bring to a boil and simmer fifteen minutes, or until potato pieces are barely tender.

3. Add the shrimp and cook about eight minutes, or until shrimp turn pink. Remove the muslin bag. Add the cream, reserved salt pork and wine or lemon juice and reheat. Check the seasoning. Serve in deep soup plates over rice.

Yield: Four servings.

She-Crab and Lobster Soup   *Alabama*

4 cups Italian plum tomatoes
1 cup shelled green peas
  Salted water
1 cup milk
2 cups heavy cream
1 pound lump crab meat, picked over to remove bits of shell and cartilage
1 one and one-half-pound lobster, cooked
  Salt and freshly ground black pepper to taste
  Cayenne pepper to taste
¼ teaspoon ground ginger
1 tablespoon Worcestershire sauce
½ cup plus six tablespoons dry sherry
6 tablespoons whipped cream
  Paprika
  Finely chopped parsley.

1. Cook the tomatoes over moderate heat about thirty minutes, or until reduced to a paste. The tomatoes must be stirred frequently to prevent sticking and burning.

2. Cook the peas in salted water to cover until tender. Put them through a sieve or food mill and add to the tomatoes.

3. Add the milk, cream and crab meat. Remove all the meat from the lobster shell and cut lobster meat into bite-size pieces. Add to the stew. Add the salt, pepper, cayenne, ginger and Worcestershire. Cook over low heat, stirring frequently, for one hour. Add one-half of the sherry.

4. When ready to serve, add one tablespoon sherry to each of six heated soup bowls. Ladle the soup over and garnish each serving with one tablespoon whipped cream sprinkled with paprika and parsley.

Yield: Six servings.

She-Crab Soup   *Maryland*

4 tablespoons butter
¼ cup onion, finely minced
2 cups milk

½ teaspoon grated lemon rind
1 pound lump crab meat, picked over to remove bits of shell and cartilage
2 cups heavy cream
¼ cup cracker crumbs
Nutmeg to taste
Cayenne pepper to taste
Salt and freshly ground black pepper to taste
1 tablespoon dry sherry
¼ to one-half cup crab roe, if available.

1. Heat one tablespoon of the butter in the top of a double boiler. Add the onion and cook, stirring, until onion is wilted. Add the milk and lemon rind and simmer five minutes.

2. Add the crab meat to the onion and milk. Add remaining butter and the cream and simmer over boiling water fifteen minutes, stirring occasionally. Stir in the crumbs, nutmeg, cayenne, salt and pepper. Let stand until ready to serve. Before serving, stir in the sherry and roe. Heat thoroughly.

Yield: Six servings.

South River Club Crab Soup   *Maryland*

2 tablespoons butter
1½ tablespoons flour
2½ cups milk
1 teaspoon salt
¼ teaspoon freshly ground black pepper
⅛ teaspoon cayenne pepper
1 pound back fin crab meat, picked over to remove bits of shell and cartilage
1 cup heavy cream
2 hard-cooked eggs, pressed through a sieve
¼ cup dry sherry, or to taste.

1. Melt the butter in a saucepan. Blend in the flour and cook, stirring, one minute. Remove from heat and gradually stir in the milk. Add the salt, pepper and cayenne.

2. Bring to a boil, stirring constantly until sauce thickens. Cook two minutes. Add the crab

meat and cream and reheat. Add the eggs and then the sherry. Serve at once.

Yield: Six servings.

Maryland Clam Chowder

3 quarts chicken broth or broth and water mixed
1 whole chicken breast
1 teaspoon salt
2 ribs celery with leaves
1½ cups Chesapeake Bay soft-shelled clams (about 36)
1 tablespoon chopped chives
2 tablespoons minced onion
½ teaspoon celery salt
¼ teaspoon thyme leaves
¼ teaspoon white pepper
1 cup sliced carrots
1 cup diced potatoes
1 ten-ounce package frozen corn
1 ten-ounce package frozen peas
1 pimento, finely chopped
1 cup clam juice
1 teaspoon finely chopped parsley.

1. Combine the broth, chicken breast, salt and celery. Simmer one hour.

2. Discard celery. While chicken broth simmers, separate the bodies of the clams from tough outer ring; refrigerate bodies and mince the outer rings.

3. Remove chicken and chop meat finely. Add the remaining ingredients except clam juice, parsley, chicken and clam bodies, to broth. Simmer twenty minutes.

4. Add chicken, clam juice and parsley. Continue cooking five minutes. Add clam bodies just before serving.

Yield: Four quarts; about sixteen servings.

Black-Eyed Pea Soup   *Louisiana*

2 cups dried black-eyed peas
    Cold water
1 small ham hock
4 cups boiling water
1 bay leaf
2 ribs celery, coarsely chopped
1 onion, studded with two whole cloves
    Salt to taste
4 peppercorns
4 thin slices lemon
    Paprika
1 teaspoon finely chopped parsley.

1. Soak the black-eyed peas overnight in cold water to cover. Next day, drain and place in a two-quart kettle. Add the ham hock, boiling water, bay leaf, celery, onion, salt and peppercorns and bring to a boil. Cook until peas are tender, two and one-half to three hours. As the soup cooks, skim the surface as necessary.

2. Remove the ham hock and bay leaf and puree the soup either through a sieve or in an electric blender. Spoon into four hot soup plates and top each with a slice of lemon. Dot the center of each lemon slice with a little paprika and one-quarter teaspoon chopped parsley.

Yield: Four servings.

Potage d'Haricots Rouges (Louisiana Red Bean Soup)

4 cups dried Louisiana red beans or kidney
    beans
½ pound lean slab bacon, without rind, cut
    into cubes
2 large onions, finely chopped
2 cloves garlic, finely minced
1 teaspoon celery seeds
1 teaspoon sage
    Salt and freshly ground black pepper to
    taste
    Tabasco sauce to taste
    Chopped parsley

    Chopped hard-cooked egg
    Garlic croutons (optional).

1. Soak the beans overnight in water that extends one inch above their level.

2. Next day, drain the beans and put them in a heavy kettle. Add three quarts of water and bring to a boil.

3. Cook the bacon in a skillet until most of the fat is rendered. Add the onions and garlic and cook until onions are translucent. Add the celery seeds and sage. Season with salt, pepper and Tabasco and pour the mixture into the beans. Simmer the beans until they are very tender, two to two and one-half hours.

4. Let the beans cool and put them through a food mill or sieve or puree them, a little at a time, in an electric blender. If necessary, they may be thinned with a little broth or water. This soup will keep well in the refrigerator.

5. Heat the soup thoroughly and serve sprinkled with chopped parsley and hard-cooked egg and, if desired, garlic croutons.

Yield: Three and one-half quarts; about one dozen servings.

Black Bean Soup   *South Carolina*

1½ cups dried black beans
    Cold water
8 cups water
¼ pound salt pork, diced
1 onion, chopped
1 carrot, quartered
2 ribs celery, diced
2 whole cloves
⅛ teaspoon mace
1 teaspoon salt
    Pinch of cayenne pepper
2 tablespoons flour
1 tablespoon butter
¾ cup dry sherry
2 hard-cooked eggs, chopped
1 lemon, thinly sliced.

1. Day before, wash and pick over the beans. Cover with cold water and let soak overnight. Next morning, drain beans and place in a large kettle.

2. Add the eight cups water. Cook the salt pork until the fat has been rendered. Add the onion and sauté until tender.

3. Add the onion to the kettle along with the carrot, celery, cloves, mace, salt and cayenne. Bring to a boil, cover and simmer about three hours, or until beans are very tender. Stir occasionally and add more water if necessary.

4. Press mixture through a sieve or a food mill. Mix the flour with a little water. Stir in a little of the hot soup and return to the pan. Bring to a boil, stirring. Cook three minutes. Check the seasoning.

5. Add the butter and sherry. Serve in soup bowls. Garnish with the chopped egg and the lemon slices.

Yield: Six servings.

Cream of Corn Soup South Carolina

6 ears corn
3 tablespoons butter
2 hard-cooked egg yolks
1½ tablespoons flour
1 teaspoon salt
¼ teaspoon freshly ground black pepper
1 cup heavy cream
1 egg yolk.

1. Cut the kernels from the corn cobs and grind in a meat grinder. Place the cobs in a saucepan, barely cover with water and boil fifteen minutes. Remove and discard the cobs. Reserve liquid.

2. Mix together the butter, hard-cooked egg yolks and flour in a saucepan. Gradually stir in the corn cob liquid. Add the corn and bring to a boil, stirring. Cook five minutes. Press through a sieve or puree in an electric blender.

3. Season with salt and pepper. Mix the cream

with the egg yolk, add a little hot soup and return all to the pan. Cook only to just below boiling.

Yield: Six servings.

Pumpkin Soup Virginia

4 cups diced peeled pumpkin pulp (about one medium-size pumpkin)
3 carrots, diced
3 ribs celery, diced
1 small onion, finely chopped
1 bay leaf
6 cups chicken broth
1 cup heavy cream
  Salt and freshly ground black pepper to taste
½ teaspoon nutmeg
1 tablespoon sugar
  Boiling milk.

1. Place the pumpkin, carrots, celery and onion in a large kettle. Add the bay leaf and broth. Bring to a boil. Cover and simmer about one hour, or until pumpkin is tender.

2. Pass mixture through a strainer, food mill or electric blender and return to the kettle. Stir in the remaining ingredients except the milk. Adjust the consistency with the milk.

Yield: Six servings.

Tomato Soup South Carolina

4 cups finely chopped, peeled tomatoes
¾ teaspoon baking soda
2 cups light cream or milk
2 large soda crackers, made into fine crumbs
  Salt and freshly ground black pepper to taste
2 tablespoons butter
¼ cup finely grated Cheddar cheese.

1. Cook the tomatoes for about fifteen minutes, stirring to prevent sticking. Add the baking soda and stir until it stops effervescing.

2. Stir in the cream or milk and the cracker crumbs. Reheat. Season with salt and pepper. Whirl in the butter.

3. Serve in hot bowls and sprinkle one tablespoon of the cheese over each serving.

Yield: Four servings.

Cream of Spinach Soup   *South Carolina*

1½ pounds fresh spinach or one package
    frozen spinach
 2 tablespoons butter
 ½ cup finely minced onion
 2 tablespoons flour
    Salt and freshly ground black pepper to
    taste
 4 cups milk or half milk and half heavy
    cream
    Cayenne pepper to taste
    Whipped cream for garnish.

1. If fresh spinach is used, pick it over well and wash in several changes of cold water. Tear off and discard any tough stems. Cook the spinach in a covered kettle in the water that clings to the leaves. If frozen spinach is used, cook according to package directions. Drain spinach well and set aside.

2. Heat the butter in a saucepan and add the onion. Cook until onion is wilted. Sprinkle with the flour, salt and pepper. Add the milk, stirring rapidly with a wire whisk.

3. Put the spinach through a food mill or sieve or add to the sauce and blend in an electric blender. Add cayenne, bring just to a boil and serve hot or cold with a garnish of whipped cream.

Yield: Six to eight servings.

Celery Chowder   *Florida*

¼ pound salt pork, diced
3 onions, thinly sliced
4 cups milk

3 large potatoes, peeled and diced
3 cups celery, diagonally sliced into small
   pieces
2 tablespoons flour
   Salt and freshly ground black pepper to
   taste.

1. Cook the salt pork in a heavy kettle or pan until crisp and brown. Remove the pork pieces and reserve.

2. Sauté the onions in the pork fat remaining in the pan or kettle until tender but not browned.

3. Heat all but one-quarter cup of the milk to boiling and add to the pan with the potatoes and celery. Bring to a boil, cover and simmer about twenty minutes, or until potatoes are tender.

4. Blend the flour with the remaining milk, add a little of the hot soup and mix. Return to the pan and cook, stirring, until soup thickens. Season with salt and pepper and sprinkle with reserved salt pork.

Yield: About two quarts; eight to ten servings.

Field or Cow Pea Soup   *South Carolina*

2 cups dried field or cow peas
   Water
1 ham bone
8 cups water
1 onion, chopped
½ cup chopped celery
2 teaspoons salt
   Freshly ground black pepper to taste
6 slices lemon.

1. Cover the peas with water and let soak overnight.

2. Next day, drain peas and put in a kettle with the ham bone, two quarts water, onion, celery and salt and cook until peas are soft. Remove bone and puree soup in an electric blender or push through a sieve.

3. Reheat soup and add pepper. Serve in hot

soup plates and garnish each serving with a slice of lemon.

Yield: Six servings.

Okra Ham Soup   *South Carolina*

2 pounds okra, finely sliced (frozen okra can be used)
1 tablespoon bacon drippings
1 tablespoon cider vinegar
1 ham bone
6 tomatoes, peeled and chopped, or four cups canned
1 cup fresh butter or lima beans
1 small sprig thyme or one-half teaspoon dried thyme
  Salt and freshly ground black pepper to taste
  Water or chicken broth, if necessary
1½ cups corn kernels, cut from cob
3 cups hot cooked rice.

1. Cook the okra quickly in a skillet with the bacon drippings and vinegar until okra loses its slimy consistency, stirring constantly.

2. Transfer to a kettle and add the ham bone, tomatoes, beans and thyme. Season with salt and pepper. Bring to a boil and simmer until meat on bone is very tender. Remove bone. Chop ham and return to kettle. Check consistency and, if too thick, add water or chicken broth.

3. Add corn kernels to soup. Cook three minutes. Serve over the rice.

Yield: Six servings.

Chilled Peach Soup   *Georgia*

2 tablespoons butter
1 tablespoon finely chopped scallion, including green part
1 tablespoon grated carrot
1 tablespoon finely chopped celery with leaves
1 tablespoon finely chopped parsley
1 tablespoon flour

2 cups chicken broth
4 cups peeled, thinly sliced ripe peaches
⅛ teaspoon oregano
¼ teaspoon cinnamon
¼ teaspoon freshly ground black pepper
2 cups light cream
2 to four tablespoons dark rum or cognac (optional)
½ cup heavy cream, whipped
2 tablespoons toasted almond slivers.

1. Heat the butter in a heavy saucepan. Sauté the scallion, carrot, celery and parsley in it until golden. Sprinkle with the flour and cook, stirring, one minute longer.

2. Add the broth, peaches, oregano, cinnamon and pepper. Bring to a boil and simmer gently about thirty minutes.

3. Force the mixture through a food mill. Chill well.

4. Before serving, stir in the light cream and rum or cognac if desired. Pour soup into individual bowls and top with the whipped cream and almonds.

Yield: Six servings.

Strawberry Cooler   *Florida*

4 cups strawberries
1 cup orange juice
1½ tablespoons cornstarch
½ cup sugar
1 tablespoon lemon juice
1 cup buttermilk
  Sesame wafers.

1. Reserve several berries for garnish; place remainder in an electric blender with the orange juice.

2. Blend until smooth and strain into a saucepan. Mix the cornstarch with a little of the strained mixture and add to remaining mixture in the pan. Heat, stirring, until mixture comes to a boil; then cook one minute.

3. Remove from heat and add the sugar,

lemon juice and buttermilk. Chill thoroughly. Serve in chilled bowls, garnished with reserved strawberries and wafers.

Yield: Four to six servings.

Cream of Peanut Soup *Virginia*

⅓ cup butter
2 tablespoons finely chopped onion
2 tablespoons finely chopped celery
1½ tablespoons flour
1 cup peanut butter
4 cups chicken broth
1 teaspoon salt
¼ teaspoon freshly ground black pepper
1 cup heavy cream
⅓ cup finely chopped unsalted peanuts.

1. Melt the butter in a heavy saucepan and sauté the onion and celery in it until tender but not browned. Sprinkle with the flour and cook one minute longer.

2. Remove from the heat and stir in the peanut butter. Gradually stir in the broth, salt and pepper. Bring to a boil, stirring, and simmer, covered, twenty-five minutes.

3. Strain mixture and add the cream. Reheat, but do not boil. Serve garnished with the peanuts.

Yield: Six servings.

Almond Soup *Virginia*

1 large whole chicken breast
2 cups chicken broth
1 bay leaf
1 rib celery
Salt and freshly ground black pepper to taste
¼ cup blanched almonds, finely grated
1 cup heavy cream.

1. Place the chicken breast in a skillet with the broth, bay leaf, celery, salt and pepper.

2. Bring to a boil, cover and simmer fifteen minutes. Remove chicken from the bone and mash together with the almonds with a wooden spoon or in an electric blender. Mix in two tablespoons of the cream.

3. Strain the chicken broth and add gradually, while stirring, to the chicken-almond mixture. Bring to a boil and add the remaining cream. Reheat, but do not boil.

Yield: Four servings.

Fish and Shellfish

Clam-Stuffed Baked Rock Fish (Striped Bass) *Maryland*

1 eight-pound or two four-pound rock fish, heads and tails removed
Salt and freshly ground black pepper to taste
½ cup butter
1 onion, finely chopped
2 tablespoons finely chopped green pepper
1 rib celery, finely chopped
1 clove garlic, finely chopped
2 cups shucked soft-shelled clams with liquor
1 teaspoon plus one tablespoon lemon juice
¼ teaspoon oregano
2 tablespoons chopped parsley
8 slices stale white bread, finely cubed
8 slices bacon.

1. Preheat the oven to 350 degrees.
2. Season the fish inside and outside with salt and pepper.
3. Melt half the butter and sauté the onion, green pepper, celery and garlic in it until tender. Add the clams and liquor and cook until edges of clams just curl.
4. Add one teaspoon of the lemon juice, the oregano, parsley, bread and salt and pepper to taste.
5. Stuff the cavity of the fish with the stuffing. Sew or skewer to close. Make gashes on top of fish and fit the bacon in the gashes. Set fish in a greased baking dish.
6. Sprinkle with remaining lemon juice and dot with remaining butter.
7. Bake about one and one-quarter hours for an eight-pound fish and forty-five minutes for two four-pounders, or until fish flakes.
Yield: Eight servings.

Baked Catfish *Mississippi*

2 pounds skinned catfish fillets, cut into serving pieces
1 teaspoon salt
⅛ teaspoon freshly ground black pepper
½ cup chopped scallions, including green part
1 lemon, thinly sliced
½ cup catchup
2 tablespoons melted butter
2 tablespoons dry white wine.

1. Preheat the oven to 350 degrees.
2. Place the fillets in a single layer in a shallow baking dish. Season with the salt and pepper.
3. Sprinkle with the scallions and top with the lemon slices. Combine the remaining ingredients and pour over fish. Bake twenty-five minutes, or until fish flakes easily.
Yield: Four servings.

For a description of gumbo see page 205.

Catfish Gumbo   *Louisiana*

¼ cup pork fat rendered
½ cup finely chopped celery
½ cup chopped green pepper
½ cup chopped onion
1 clove garlic, finely chopped
2 cups beef broth
1 one-pound can tomatoes
½ pound fresh okra or one ten-ounce package frozen okra, sliced
2 teaspoons salt
½ teaspoon freshly ground black pepper
¼ teaspoon thyme
1 bay leaf
   Few drops of Tabasco sauce
1 pound skinned catfish fillets, cut into one-inch pieces
1½ cups hot cooked rice.

1. Heat the fat and sauté the celery, green pepper, onion and garlic in it until tender. Stir in the broth, tomatoes, okra, salt, pepper, thyme, bay leaf and Tabasco.

2. Bring to a boil and simmer thirty minutes.

3. Add the fish and simmer about ten to fifteen minutes longer, or until fish flakes easily. Remove bay leaf.

4. Place one-quarter cup of the rice in each of six hot bowls and fill with gumbo.

Yield: Six servings.

Maryland Fried Clams

4 cups shucked soft-shelled clams with liquor
2 eggs, beaten
2 tablespoons milk
2 teaspoons salt
⅛ teaspoon freshly ground black pepper
3 cups dry bread crumbs
   Fat or oil for deep-frying
   Tartar sauce (see page 187).

1. Drain the clams. Combine the eggs, milk, salt and pepper. Dip clams in egg mixture and roll in the bread crumbs.

2. Fry a few clams at a time until golden in a fry basket in fat or oil heated to 350 degrees. Drain on paper towels. Serve with tartar sauce.

Yield: Six servings.

Conchs are big sea snails, and the early settlers of the Florida Keys said that the flesh or juices of fresh conch would give those who partook of it perpetual youth. The flesh of conch may be marinated and eaten raw or it may be cooked.

Raw Conch Salad   *Florida*

4 raw conchs
   Salt and freshly ground black pepper to taste
2 to four tablespoons lime juice
½ cup tomato juice
¾ cup finely chopped heart of celery
½ cup finely chopped white onion or scallions, including green part
¼ cup finely chopped green pepper
   Tabasco sauce to taste
   Lettuce (optional).

1. Wash and scrub the conchs. Remove the meat from the shell. Skin the flesh and remove the intestinal vein. Clean well.

2. Slice the conchs and pound the meat with a mallet. Cut the meat into small cubes and combine with the remaining ingredients. Refrigerate several hours.

3. Serve chilled, with lettuce if desired.

Yield: Six to eight servings.

Crab Cakes I   *Maryland*

2 cups back fin crab meat, picked over to remove bits of shell and cartilage
¼ cup milk

2 tablespoons finely chopped parsley
Salt to taste
½ cup soft bread crumbs
2 eggs, well beaten
1 teaspoon Worcestershire sauce
4 tablespoons butter
Lemon wedges
Tartar sauce (recipe below).

Blend the crab meat with the milk, parsley, salt, bread crumbs, eggs and Worcestershire. Shape into four to six cakes and cook in the butter on all sides until golden brown. Serve with lemon wedges and tartar sauce.

Yield: Four to six servings.

Tartar Sauce   *Maryland*

1 cup mayonnaise
2 tablespoons finely chopped parsley
1 tablespoon finely chopped chives
1 tablespoon finely chopped tarragon
1 tablespoon finely chopped chervil (optional)
1 teaspoon finely chopped onion (optional)
1 tablespoon finely chopped capers
1 small sour pickle, finely chopped
Finely minced garlic (optional).

Combine all ingredients except the garlic and blend well. If desired, add a little finely minced garlic.

Yield: About one and one-quarter cups.

Crab Cakes II   *Maryland*

¼ cup chopped parsley
3 tablespoons chopped scallions including green part
1 pound crab meat, picked over to remove bits of shell and cartilage
½ teaspoon salt
⅛ teaspoon freshly ground black pepper
1 teaspoon dry mustard
1 egg

½ cup fine dry bread crumbs
8 tablespoons butter.

Combine the parsley, scallions, crab meat, salt, pepper, mustard and egg and mix well. Shape into small cakes, roll in the bread crumbs and cook in butter until golden brown on all sides.

Yield: Eight to ten cakes.

Crab Stew   *Louisiana*

2 tablespoons butter
2 tablespoons finely chopped shallots or scallions, including green part
4 white mushrooms, thinly sliced
Juice of half a lemon
2 ripe tomatoes, peeled, seeded and cubed
1 pound lump crab meat, picked over to remove bits of shell and cartilage
2 tablespoons finely chopped parsley
2 tablespoons finely chopped chives
1¼ cups heavy cream
Tabasco sauce to taste
Salt and freshly ground black pepper to taste
2 tablespoons warm cognac
Cooked rice.

1. Heat the butter in a skillet or chafing dish and add the shallots or scallions. Cook about three minutes and add the mushrooms. Sprinkle with the lemon juice and cook briefly, stirring. Add the tomatoes and simmer five minutes.

2. Add the crab meat, but treat it gently so as not to break up the lumps. Add the parsley and chives and simmer five minutes. Stir in the cream, Tabasco, salt and pepper. Add the cognac and ignite it. Serve immediately with rice.

Yield: Four to six servings.

Deep-Fried Soft-Shelled Crabs   *Maryland*

6 soft-shelled crabs
Milk

Salt and freshly ground black pepper to taste
2 eggs, lightly beaten
2 cups soft bread crumbs
Fat for deep-frying
Tartar sauce (page 187).

1. Wash the crabs well to remove all sand. Place them "face" down and, with a sharp knife, cut out the face. Remove the spongy gills under the side points and sand bags from under either side of the shell. Remove the small pointed lower portion known as the apron. Soak the crabs in milk seasoned with salt and pepper.

2. Dip each crab in the egg, then in the bread crumbs, in egg again and then again in crumbs. Heat the fat to about 375 degrees and cook the crabs, turning once, until golden brown. Drain on paper towels. Serve with tartar sauce.
Yield: Six servings.

For a description of gumbo see page 205.

Crab Gumbo
Louisiana

12 live hard-shelled crabs
Boiling water
Salt and freshly ground black pepper to taste
¼ cup butter
8 large tomatoes, cored and peeled
2 large onions, chopped
3 sprigs fresh thyme or one teaspoon dried thyme
3 sprigs fresh parsley
4 cups tender okra
2 tablespoons bacon drippings
1 bay leaf
½ pod seeded red pepper
Cayenne pepper to taste
Boiled rice.

1. Place the crabs in a kettle and add boiling water to cover. Let stand briefly; then drain. Pull away the front "apron" on the underside of the crabs. Take away and discard the "dead man's fingers," a spongy, lunglike substance inside the crabs. Crack the crab claws and cut the body of the crab into quarters. Season with salt and pepper. Wipe the kettle with a clean cloth.

2. Heat half the butter in the kettle and add the crab pieces. Cover closely and cook over low heat about five minutes. Chop the tomatoes and drain, but reserve both the pulp and juice. Add pulp to the kettle. Add the onions, thyme and parsley and stir to prevent scorching. Cook about five minutes. Brown the okra separately in bacon drippings. Add to the crab. Cook, stirring, until most of the moisture in the kettle has evaporated.

3. Add the bay leaf and reserved tomato juice. Add eight cups boiling water and the pepper pod and simmer, stirring frequently, for one hour. Season with cayenne. Serve hot with boiled rice.
Yield: Six or more servings.

One of the greatest delights of Florida's coastal regions is stone crabs or Morro crabs, with their hard shell and meat-filled claws which have a delicate flavor and admirable texture. Stone crabs are not plentiful and, when available, they are expensive. There are a few sea food shops in coastal areas, especially in the Keys, where these crabs may be bought alive.

One of these shops is Sid and Roxie's in Islamorada. The whole crabs may be purchased, but the claws alone may be ordered. The body of the stone crab has a delicious flavor, but there is not much meat to be had.

Steamed Stone Crab
Florida

24 whole stone crabs (see above)
Water
1 cup dry white wine
Salt to taste
20 peppercorns
1 large onion, coarsely chopped
3 ribs celery with leaves
½ teaspoon thyme
2 carrots, quartered

2 bay leaves
3 tablespoons cider vinegar.

1. Take special care when dealing with the crabs because they have powerful claws and their grip is dangerous.

2. In a large kettle place enough water to cover the crabs to the depth of one inch and add the wine, salt, peppercorns, onion, celery, thyme, carrots and bay leaves. Simmer fifteen minutes and add the vinegar. Immediately add the crabs, cover and bring to a boil. Simmer ten to fifteen minutes. Crack the claws and cut the bodies into quarters. To serve, see note.

Yield: Four to six servings.

Note: Stone crabs may be served hot with melted butter and lemon or lime juice or cold with mustard, mayonnaise or vinaigrette sauce.

Crab Meat Imperial   *Maryland*

1 large green pepper, diced
2 pimentos, diced
½ teaspoon salt
½ teaspoon freshly ground white pepper
1 tablespoon dry mustard
  Mayonnaise
2 eggs, lightly beaten
3 tablespoons dry sherry
2 pounds lump crab meat, picked over to remove bits of shell and cartilage
  Paprika.

1. Preheat the oven to 350 degrees.

2. Mix the diced pepper and pimentos. Add the salt, pepper, mustard, three tablespoons mayonnaise, the eggs and two tablespoons of the sherry. Mix well.

3. Carefully fold the crab meat into the pepper mixture so as not to break up the pieces of crab. Add the remaining sherry and place the mixture in a buttered casserole.

4. Coat the top of the casserole with a thin layer of mayonnaise and sprinkle with paprika. Bake fifteen minutes.

Yield: Six servings.

Steamed Hard-Shelled Crabs   *Maryland*

12 hard-shelled crabs
 1 teaspoon crushed red pepper flakes
   Salt to taste
 2 tablespoons crab boil (see note) or pickling spices
 1 cup stale beer
   Lemon wedges
   Melted butter.

1. Place the crabs on a rack in a steamer and sprinkle with the pepper flakes, salt, crab boil and beer.

2. Cover closely and bring to a boil on top of the stove. Steam the crabs twenty to thirty minutes, or until the aprons begin to lift. Serve with lemon wedges and melted butter.

Yield: Four to six servings.

Note: Crab boil is available in packages in many grocery stores.

Broiled Soft-Shelled Crabs   *Florida*

6 soft-shelled crabs
6 tablespoons melted butter
  Juice of half a lemon
  Salt and freshly ground black pepper to taste
  Few drops of Tabasco sauce
  Toast (optional).

1. Wash the crabs well to remove all sand. Place them "face" down and, with a sharp knife, cut out the face. Remove the spongy gills (sometimes called "dead man's fingers") from under the side points and sand bags from under either side of the shell. Remove the small pointed lower portion known as the apron.

2. Combine the remaining ingredients. Dip the crabs in the mixture and broil or grill the crabs

five to ten minutes. Pour over the remaining melted butter mixture. Serve on toast if desired.

Yield: Three servings.

For a description of crawfish see page 177.

Crawfish à la Nage   *Louisiana*

1 carrot, cut into rounds
1 large onion, sliced
2 shallots or scallions, including green part, coarsely chopped
2 cups water
2 cups dry white wine
  Salt to taste
12 peppercorns
2 sprigs parsley
1 bay leaf
  Pinch of thyme
48 to sixty crawfish
  Parsley for garnish.

1. Combine the carrot, onion, shallots or scallions, water, wine, salt, peppercorns, two sprigs parsley, bay leaf and thyme in a kettle and bring to a boil. Simmer fifteen minutes.

2. Wash the crawfish well and drop them into the court bouillon. Return to a boil and remove from the heat. Let the crawfish cool in the liquid. Drain and arrange in a pile with the parsley for garnish. Eat with the fingers.

Yield: Four to six servings.

Crawfish Étouffée   *Louisiana*

3 tablespoons vegetable oil or olive oil
¾ cup chopped onion
1 clove garlic, finely chopped
2 cups tomatoes, preferably Italian plum style
  Salt and freshly ground black pepper
2 tablespoons butter
1 cup chopped scallions, including green part
¼ cup crawfish stock (see note)

5 pounds crawfish tails
⅔ cup crawfish fat (see note)
  Cayenne pepper to taste
¼ teaspoon each ground rosemary, marjoram, thyme, oregano, sage and basil
  Cooked rice.

1. Heat two tablespoons of the oil and add the onion and garlic. Cook, stirring, until onion is translucent. Add the tomatoes and sprinkle with salt and pepper. Cook, stirring occasionally, approximately one hour, or until sauce is thickened. There should be about one cup of sauce.

2. Melt the butter in a large Dutch oven or kettle and add the remaining oil. Add half the scallions and cook briefly. Add sauce, crawfish stock and crawfish tails and season lightly with salt and pepper. Stir briefly and bring to a boil.

3. Add the crawfish fat and seasonings. Cook, stirring occasionally, thirty to forty minutes. Before serving, sprinkle with remaining scallions. Serve piping hot with rice.

Yield: Eight to ten servings.

Note: Crawfish stock is made by boiling shells and other discarded portions of the crawfish in water barely to cover. If the shells are not available, substitute chicken broth. When shelled crawfish are purchased, there is always a certain amount of crawfish fat clinging to the meat.

Dolphin Fillets Norsaga   *Florida*

2 dolphin fillets, each weighing approximately one-half pound
  Milk
  Oil
½ cup melted butter
  Salt and freshly ground black pepper
  Juice of half a lemon or lime
3 tablespoons finely chopped parsley or equal parts finely chopped parsley, tarragon and dill
  Lemon wedges.

1. Place the dolphin fillets in a pan and cover with milk. Let stand one hour.

2. Fifteen minutes before cooking, preheat the broiler to high.

3. Drain the dolphin fillets and wipe with paper towels. Rub the broiler rack lightly with oil. Place the fillets on the rack and brush with half the butter. Sprinkle with salt and pepper. Broil five minutes and brush again. When the fillets are browned, remove them to plates or a hot serving platter. Pour the remaining butter over them and sprinkle with the lemon or lime juice and parsley. Serve immediately with lemon wedges.

Yield: Four servings.

Out Island Grouper   *Florida*

1 two-and-one-half-pound grouper
½ cup lime juice
  Salt and freshly ground black pepper to
  taste
1 egg
⅓ cup cold water
¼ cup flour
  Oil for deep-frying
  Lemon wedges
  Tartar sauce (page 302).

1. Cut the grouper into finger-size pieces and place in a mixing bowl. Add the lime juice, salt and pepper and cover. Let stand one hour or so in the refrigerator.

2. Place the egg and water in a bowl and beat in the flour. Add salt and pepper.

3. Drain the fish and dry with paper towels. Dip a few fish pieces at a time in the batter and deep-fry in oil heated to 370 degrees. As the fish is cooked, drain on paper towels. Serve with lemon wedges and tartar sauce.

Yield: Four to six servings.

There is a giant crustacean in Florida waters that goes by the name of lobster and crawfish. Actually, it more nearly resembles the langosta or langouste of European waters. Most of the meat in a Florida lobster is in the tail and it is delicious hot or cold.

Steamed Florida Lobster

 4 Florida lobsters or crawfish
 2 cups dry white wine
   Salt to taste
20 peppercorns
 1 large onion, coarsely chopped
 3 ribs celery with leaves
 ½ teaspoon thyme
 2 carrots, quartered
 2 bay leaves
 3 tablespoons cider vinegar.

1. The lobsters should be alive when cooked. They should be cooked in a kettle large enough to hold them.

2. Add enough water to the kettle to immerse the lobsters completely. Add the wine, salt, peppercorns, onion, celery, thyme, carrots and bay leaves. Bring to a boil and simmer ten minutes. Add the vinegar. When the water is boiling violently, add the lobsters. Cover the kettle and simmer exactly fifteen minutes. Drain the lobsters; to serve, see note.

Yield: Four servings.

Note: The lobsters may be served hot with melted butter or cold with mayonnaise and lemon wedges.

How to Salt Mackerel   *Florida*

6 mackerel, each weighing one and one-half to
  two pounds
2 cups, approximately, pure salt, preferably
  coarse salt (do not use iodized salt).

1. If possible, procure a small wooden bucket

(approximately four-quart capacity) with lid. Wash the bucket inside and outside and rinse well to remove all trace of soap or detergent. Soak the bucket in pure clean water. This will act as a "seal." Test the bucket by filling it with water to ensure that it does not leak. If it leaks, seal it on the outside wherever necessary with sealing wax. A stone crock or enamel utensil may be substituted for the bucket.

2. Have the fish filleted. Add a layer of salt to the bucket. Arrange two fillets on the salt. Continue adding layers of salt and of mackerel, ending with a layer of salt. Cover and refrigerate two weeks or longer. The fish will produce its own brine.

Yield: Six salt mackerel fillets.

How to Cook Salt Mackerel   *Florida*

Remove as many pieces of salt mackerel as desired from the brine. Rinse well under cold water. Place the fish in a dish and cover with cold water. Let stand twelve hours or longer in a cool place. Change the water occasionally. When ready to cook, drain the fish and add equal parts milk and cold water to cover. Bring to a boil and simmer five to twelve minutes. Serve with melted butter and lemon wedges.

Deviled Oysters   *Mississippi*

4 cups shucked and drained oysters
8 tablespoons butter
2 cups finely chopped celery
1 cup finely chopped onions
2 teaspoons Worcestershire sauce
Salt and freshly ground black pepper to taste
12 to sixteen soda crackers, approximately.

1. Preheat the oven to 325 degrees.
2. If the oysters are large, cut them in half. Melt two tablespoons of the butter in a large

skillet and add the oysters. Cook just until the edges curl.

3. Cook the celery and onions in two tablespoons of the remaining butter, but do not brown. When the onions are wilted and transparent, add the oysters, Worcestershire, salt and pepper. Crumble the crackers and add about half of them to the oysters. Continue adding just enough crackers until all liquid is absorbed. Spoon the mixture into a two-quart baking dish. Sprinkle with the remaining crackers, dot with the remaining butter and bake twenty-five to thirty minutes.

Yield: About eight servings.

Oysters Johnny Reb   *Mississippi*

4 cups shucked and drained oysters
6 tablespoons finely chopped parsley
6 tablespoons finely chopped scallions, including green part
Salt and freshly ground black pepper to taste
Tabasco sauce to taste
2 teaspoons Worcestershire sauce
1 tablespoon lemon juice
4 tablespoons butter
1 cup cracker crumbs
1 teaspoon paprika
⅓ cup heavy cream.

1. Preheat the oven to 375 degrees.
2. Place half the oysters in a generously buttered one-quart baking dish. Sprinkle with half the parsley, half the scallions, salt, pepper, Tabasco, half the Worcestershire, half the lemon juice, half the butter and half the crumbs. Make a layer with the remaining oysters and top with the remaining parsley, scallions, salt, pepper, Tabasco, Worcestershire, lemon juice, butter and crumbs.

3. Sprinkle with paprika and, using a knife, make six or so "holes" in the top of the casserole to pour in the cream. Bake thirty minutes or until firm.

Yield: One dozen to fifteen servings.

Oysters Bienville   *Louisiana*

½ pound mushrooms, finely chopped
2 tablespoons finely chopped shallots or scallions, including green part
5 tablespoons butter
6 tablespoons flour
¼ cup dry white wine
1½ cups fish stock or clam juice
¾ cup milk
¾ cup heavy cream
2 egg yolks
Salt and freshly ground black pepper to taste
12 cooked shrimp, shelled, deveined and finely chopped
1 ounce anise liqueur such as Pernod, Ricard, anisette, etc. (optional)
48 oysters on the half shell
Rock salt
½ cup freshly grated Parmesan cheese.

1. Cook the mushrooms and shallots or scallions in butter until mushrooms give up their liquid. Sprinkle with flour.
2. Meanwhile, combine the wine and stock or clam juice and bring to a boil. Simmer five minutes and add to the mushroom mixture, stirring vigorously with a wire whisk. Add the milk, stirring. Combine the cream and egg yolks; add a little of the hot mixture; then stir this into the sauce. Bring just to a boil and add salt, pepper and shrimp. Add the anise liqueur, if desired.
3. Preheat the oven to 450 degrees.
4. Loosen the oysters on their half shells. Make a reasonably thick layer of rock salt in four pie tins. Arrange one dozen oysters on the half shell in each tin. Place in the oven and bake briefly until edges of oysters start to curl. Carefully pour off the water from each shell and replace shells on the rock salt. Spoon a generous amount of sauce over each and sprinkle lightly with Parmesan cheese. Return to the oven and bake until lightly browned. Serve immediately.
Yield: Four servings.

Hot Oysters à la Louisiane   *Louisiana*

1 cup catchup
1 cup chili sauce
3 tablespoons Worcestershire sauce
4 tablespoons butter
Grated rind of one lemon
Juice of half a lemon
1 cup minced celery
½ cup finely chopped parsley
Tabasco sauce to taste
48 oysters, shucked and drained
Buttered toast or crackers (optional).

1. Combine the catchup, chili sauce, Worcestershire, butter and lemon rind. Bring just to a boil and stir until butter is melted and blended. Remove the sauce from the heat and add the lemon juice, celery, parsley and Tabasco. The sauce may be refrigerated at this point.
2. When ready to serve, heat the sauce again to the simmering point. Add the oysters and cook just until the edges of the oysters curl. Do not overcook or the oysters will toughen. Serve with buttered toast or crackers if desired.
Yield: Four to eight servings.

Oysters Casino   *Louisiana*

48 oysters on the half shell
Rock salt
1 cup sweet butter
⅓ cup finely chopped shallots or scallions, including green part
¼ cup finely chopped chives
⅓ cup finely chopped heart of celery
½ cup finely chopped parsley
Juice of one lemon
48 small squares bacon
48 strips pimento.

1. Preheat the oven to 450 degrees.
2. Loosen the oysters in their half shells. Make a reasonably thick layer of rock salt in four pie tins. Arrange one dozen oysters on the half shell

in each tin. Place in the oven and bake briefly until edges of oysters start to curl. Carefully pour off the water from each shell and replace shells on the rock salt.

3. Cream together the butter, shallots or scallions, chives, celery, parsley and lemon juice. Spoon a little of the creamed mixture atop each oyster.

4. Place the bacon briefly under the broiler to cook partly. Top each oyster with a strip of pimento and a square of bacon. Return the oysters to the oven and bake until bacon is browned, five to eight minutes.

Yield: Four servings.

Fried Oysters   *Maryland*

12 large plump oysters
 1 egg
 2 tablespoons water
   Yellow corn meal
   Salt and freshly ground black pepper to
   taste
   Fat for deep-frying
   Lemon wedges.

1. Drain the oysters and dry on paper towels.

2. Beat the egg with water. Dip the oysters one at a time in the egg, then in corn meal seasoned with salt and pepper. Dip them in egg again, then again in corn meal. Let stand thirty minutes.

3. Preheat the fat to 375 degrees. Fry the oysters in it until corn meal is golden brown. Drain on paper towels. Serve with lemon wedges.

Yield: Two to four servings.

Oysters en Brochette   *Virginia*

48 small oysters, shucked and drained
   Salt and freshly ground black pepper
 8 slices bacon
 6 tablespoons butter
 2 tablespoons chopped fresh parsley
   Lemon juice to taste

Tabasco sauce to taste (optional)
 4 slices white or wholewheat toast.

1. Sprinkle the oysters with salt and pepper.

2. Cut each slice of bacon into six cubes. Arrange the oysters alternately with cubes of bacon on four skewers. Melt the butter. Dip the skewered food into it. Place the skewers on a grill over hot charcoal or place under the broiler. Grill or broil until bacon browns and oysters curl.

3. Add the parsley, lemon juice and Tabasco to the remaining butter. Pour the butter over the skewered food and serve immediately with or on toast.

Yield: Four servings.

Oysters Rockefeller   *Louisiana*

 1 pound spinach
 8 scallions, including green part trimmed
   and chopped
½ cup coarsely chopped heart of celery
 1 cup firmly packed, coarsely chopped
   parsley
 1 pound butter, melted
¼ cup finely chopped chives (optional)
½ teaspoon crushed anise seeds or fennel
   seeds
1½ cups soft bread crumbs
 1 tablespoon anchovy paste
 2 tablespoons Worcestershire sauce
   Salt and freshly ground black pepper to
   taste
1½ ounces anise liqueur such as Pernod,
   Ricard, anisette, etc.
48 oysters on the half shell
   Rock salt
¾ cup freshly grated Parmesan cheese.

1. Rinse the spinach in several changes of cold water. Drain. Place spinach in a large pot, cover and cook in the water that clings to the leaves. Do not add salt. Drain the spinach well, pressing to remove most of the moisture.

2. Place the spinach, scallions, celery and

parsley in an electric blender. Pour in the melted butter and blend well. It may be necessary to blend this in two batches.

3. Spoon the mixture into a mixing bowl and add the chives, anise seeds, bread crumbs, anchovy paste, Worcestershire, a little salt (the anchovy paste is salty), pepper and anise liqueur.

4. Preheat the oven to 450 degrees.

5. Loosen the oysters on their half shells. Make a reasonably thick layer of rock salt in four pie tins. Arrange 12 of the oysters on the half shell in each tin. Place in the oven and bake briefly until edges of oysters start to curl. Carefully pour off the water from each shell and replace shells on the rock salt. Spoon a generous amount of sauce over each and sprinkle lightly with the cheese. Return to the oven and bake until lightly browned. Serve immediately.

Yield: Four servings.

Creamed Oysters   *Alabama*

    4 cups shucked oysters with liquor
      Light cream, if necessary
    4 tablespoons butter
    ½ cup flour
    1 small clove garlic, finely minced
    1 teaspoon chopped fresh basil or one-half
      teaspoon dried basil
    2 teaspoons finely chopped parsley
    1 tablespoon lemon juice
      Tabasco sauce to taste
    1 tablespoon Worcestershire sauce
    1 tablespoon catchup
      Salt and freshly ground black pepper to
      taste
    ½ teaspoon paprika
    1 tablespoon dry sherry or cognac
      Toast.
      Additional chopped parsley (optional).

1. Drain the oysters and reserve the liquor.

2. Place the oysters in a skillet or saucepan and cook just until they curl. Drain oysters again and combine hot liquid with reserved liquor. If neces-

sary, add enough cream to make three cups of liquid.

3. Melt the butter over gentle heat in a heavy iron skillet. Add flour and stir constantly for about thirty minutes until flour is almost caramel-colored.

4. Add oyster liquid a little at a time while stirring rapidly with a wire whisk. Stir in the remaining ingredients. Finally, add the oysters. Serve on toast, sprinkled, if desired, with additional chopped parsley.

Yield: Six to eight servings.

Southern Scalloped Oysters   *Mississippi*

    4 tablespoons butter
  1½ cups dry bread crumbs
    2 cups shucked oysters with liquor
    1 cup heavy cream
    1 tablespoon finely chopped chives
    1 tablespoon finely chopped parsley
      Salt and freshly ground black pepper to
      taste
    1 teaspoon celery salt
    1 teaspoon paprika
    ¼ teaspoon nutmeg
    1 teaspoon Worcestershire sauce
      Tabasco sauce to taste
    ½ cup freshly grated Parmesan cheese.

1. Preheat the oven to 400 degrees.

2. Heat the butter in a small skillet and add the bread crumbs. Stir until crumbs are coated with butter. Spoon half the crumbs over the bottom of a nine-inch baking dish.

3. Drain the oysters and empty them into a mixing bowl. Add the remaining ingredients except the cheese and remaining crumbs. Spoon mixture over the crumb-lined pan.

4. Blend remaining crumbs with cheese and spread this over the oysters. Bake ten minutes, or until thoroughly hot and lightly browned.

Yield: Four to six servings.

Oyster Roast for 24   *South Carolina*

48 dozen oysters
3 pounds butter
6 tablespoons Worcestershire sauce, or to taste
Juice of four lemons
Tabasco sauce to taste.

1. Place a large cast iron slab on supports, leaving enough space beneath for a giant fire. Prepare a fire beneath the slab and keep it going two hours or longer.
2. Rinse the oysters well and add them to the slab. Dip enough burlap bags in cold water to cover the oysters. Soak them thoroughly. Cover the oysters with the burlap bags and douse with water. Roast the oysters until they are easily opened, about fifteen minutes or longer, depending on heat of the fire.
3. Meanwhile, melt the butter to bubbling and add the remaining ingredients. Equip each guest with thick gloves and oyster knives and serve the oysters with the butter sauce.
Yield: Two dozen servings.

Oyster Pie   *Virginia*

3 tablespoons butter
3 tablespoons flour
¾ cup oyster liquor
¾ cup light cream
Salt and freshly ground black pepper to taste
⅛ teaspoon mace
2 cups drained oysters
½ cup finely chopped celery
Unbaked pastry for a one-crust pie.

1. Preheat the oven to 400 degrees.
2. Melt the butter, blend in the flour and then gradually stir in the oyster liquor and cream. Bring mixture to a boil, stirring. Season with salt, pepper and mace. Simmer five minutes.
3. Stir in the oysters and celery and turn into

a one-and-one-half-quart deep baking dish. Top with the pastry. Make a steam hole and bake twenty to twenty-five minutes, or until pastry is browned and cooked.
Yield: Four servings.

Pompano Baked en Papillote   *Florida*

4 pompano fillets (see note)
¼ cup butter
5 tablespoons flour
1 cup clam juice or milk, preferably clam juice
1 egg yolk
¼ cup heavy cream
Salt and freshly ground black pepper to taste
1 tablespoon finely chopped shallots or scallions, including green part
¼ cup dry white wine
1 tablespoon cognac (optional)
1 cup crab meat, picked over to remove bits of shell and cartilage
16 to twenty-four raw or cooked shrimp, shelled and deveined.

1. Preheat the oven to 400 degrees.
2. Split the fillets lengthwise and trim away the tiny bone unit down the center of each. Cut or tear off sheets of heavy parchment paper or heavy-duty aluminum foil, each large enough to enclose one fillet envelope style. Rub the center of each sheet lightly with the butter, reserving three tablespoons for a sauce, and put one fillet on each sheet.
3. Melt the three tablespoons butter in a saucepan and blend in the flour, using a wire whisk. Add the clam juice, and milk all at once, stirring vigorously with the whisk. Continue stirring until the sauce is thickened and smooth. Continue to cook, stirring frequently, for five minutes. The sauce will be very thick.
4. Blend the egg yolk with the cream. Add a little of the hot sauce to the egg yolk mixture and stir until blended. Add the egg mixture to the hot

sauce, stirring rapidly. Heat until mixture starts to bubble, but do not boil. Season with salt and pepper.

5. Meanwhile, combine the shallots, or scallions and wine in a saucepan and cook until reduced by half. Strain the wine into the hot sauce. Blend. Stir in the cognac if desired.

6. Sprinkle each fish fillet with an equal portion of crab meat and divide the sauce among the portions. Arrange four to six shrimp over the sauce on each portion. Bring the edges of the paper or foil up and enclose the fish envelope style. Press down on edges to seal fish tightly. Bake for eighteen to twenty minutes, or until fish flakes easily when tested with a fork. Serve directly from the package.

Yield: Four servings.

Note: Small sole fillets may be substituted for the pompano.

Pompano Meunière   *Louisiana*

4 pompano fillets
  Milk
  Flour
  Salt and freshly ground black pepper to
    taste
¼ cup peanut oil, approximately
½ cup butter
¼ cup finely chopped parsley.

1. Place the fillets in a dish and add milk barely to cover. Let stand one hour.

2. Drain the fish, wipe lightly and dredge in flour seasoned with salt and pepper.

3. Cook the fish until golden brown on all sides in hot oil, turning once. Remove the fish to a warm platter.

4. Quickly wipe out the skillet and add the butter. When the butter is hot and foamy, pour it over the fish. Sprinkle with parsley.

Yield: Four servings.

Pompano Grenoble Style   *Louisiana*

Follow the above recipe for "Pompano Meunière." When the butter is added to the skillet, add two tablespoons small whole or chopped capers. Sprinkle with small bits of chopped lemon as well as parsley.

Sea Food with Eggs   *Maryland*

½ pound shrimp, cooked, shelled and
    deveined
½ pound crab meat, picked over to remove
    bits of shell and cartilage
3 tablespoons dry sherry
6 tablespoons butter
2 tablespoons flour
¾ cup heavy cream
  Salt and freshly ground black pepper to
    taste
12 eggs
6 slices white toast, crusts removed
1 tablespoon chopped chives
1 tablespoon chopped parsley
1 teaspoon chopped tarragon (optional).

1. Combine the shrimp, crab meat and sherry in a mixing bowl and set aside.

2. Heat two tablespoons of the butter in a saucepan and stir in the flour, using a wire whisk. When blended, add the cream, stirring rapidly with the whisk. When thickened and smooth, add salt and pepper. Add shrimp and crab and keep hot.

3. Heat remaining butter in a large skillet. Beat the eggs lightly and add to the skillet. Cook, stirring over low heat, until eggs are partially cooked. Do not let them scramble in the usual fashion. Add salt and pepper to taste and, while eggs are still soft, stir in the sea food mixture. Heat thoroughly and serve equal portions on the toast. Serve sprinkled with a mixture of chives and parsley and, if desired, tarragon.

Yield: Six servings.

Artichoke and Sea Food Casserole
Maryland

4 tablespoons butter
2 tablespoons chopped shallots
1 clove garlic, finely chopped
½ pound mushrooms, sliced
¼ cup flour
1 cup milk
⅔ cup dry white wine, fish stock or clam juice
1½ cups grated Swiss cheese or Gruyère cheese
Salt and freshly ground black pepper to taste
1 tablespoon freshly snipped dill weed
1 pound shrimp, cooked, shelled and deveined
1 pound lump crab meat, picked over to remove bits of shell and cartilage
1 package frozen artichoke hearts, cooked and drained
3 tablespoons buttered soft bread crumbs.

1. Preheat the oven to 375 degrees.
2. Melt the butter in a skillet and sauté the shallots and garlic in it until tender. Add the mushrooms and cook two minutes longer.
3. Sprinkle with the flour, stir and cook one minute.
4. Gradually stir in the milk and wine, stock or clam juices. Bring to a boil, stirring until thick. Remove from the heat and stir in one cup of the cheese until it melts. Season with salt and pepper and add the dill.
5. Stir in the shrimp, crab meat and artichoke hearts and pour into a buttered casserole. Sprinkle with the remaining cheese and the bread crumbs. Bake twenty-five minutes, or until bubbly, and glaze under the broiler if desired.
Yield: Six servings.

Shad Stuffed with Mousse and Roe
South Carolina

¾ pound boneless scrod or cod
3 shallots, finely chopped
4 tablespoons finely chopped parsley
1⅔ cups heavy cream
⅔ cup soft bread crumbs
Salt and freshly ground black pepper to taste
Cayenne pepper to taste
2 boneless fillets of fresh shad
1 pair shad roe
3 hard-cooked eggs
5 tablespoons butter
1½ cups thinly sliced mushrooms
1 cup dry white wine
1 tablespoon flour
1 teaspoon lemon juice
Boiled potatoes.

1. Preheat the oven to 400 degrees.
2. Cut the scrod or cod into small cubes and add to the container of an electric blender. Blend, stirring down with a rubber spatula, until well blended. Do not let the spatula touch the blender blades. It may be necessary to stop the machine at times to "stir down." When blended, add one tablespoon of the chopped shallots and one tablespoon of the parsley. Gradually add two-thirds cup of the cream. When the cream has been added, carefully scoop the mousse from the blender into a mixing bowl. Stir in the bread crumbs. Season with salt, pepper and cayenne.
3. Lay one of the shad fillets, skin side down, on a flat surface. There are two "flaps" on either side of the fillet where the bones were removed. Open these "flaps" and spread half the scrod mixture up and down the center of the fillet. Split the pair of shad roe in two and place the two parts tip to tip down the center of the mousse.
4. Quarter the eggs. Arrange six quarters along one side of the roe. Arrange the other six down the other side. Spread the remaining mousse mixture over the roe and eggs.
5. Open the "flaps" on the other shad fillet and

place this fillet, skin side up, over the stuffed fillet. This will in effect form a "box" with the mousse and roe enclosed. Tie the "box" crosswise in about four places with string.

6. Sprinkle the fish with salt and pepper and spread fish generously on top with four tablespoons of the butter. Sprinkle fish with the remaining shallots and parsley and scatter the mushrooms all around. Pour the wine around and cover with aluminum foil. Bake forty to fifty minutes, lifting the foil occasionally and basting with the wine.

7. Remove the fish to a warm platter. Remove string and keep fish warm.

8. Pour the sauce into a saucepan and reduce sauce over high heat to about two-thirds of its original volume. Add the remaining cream and cook about ten minutes. Blend together the remaining tablespoon butter and the flour and stir, bit by bit, into the sauce. When thickened, add the lemon juice.

9. Peel the skin from the top of the shad and pour a little of the sauce over and around the fish. Serve the remaining sauce separately. Serve with boiled potatoes.

Yield: About six servings.

For a description of gumbo see page 205.

Shrimp Gumbo   *Louisiana*

¼ cup flour
8 small white onions, peeled
7 tablespoons butter
2 eight-ounce bottles clam juice
1 large can Italian plum tomatoes, drained
1 bay leaf
1 teaspoon Worcestershire sauce
  Salt, if necessary
¼ teaspoon thyme
  Freshly ground black pepper to taste
  Red pepper flakes to taste
½ teaspoon sugar

2 pounds shrimp, cooked, shelled and deveined
1 package frozen okra
1 green pepper, seeded and cut into strips
2 ribs celery, trimmed and cut into one-half-inch pieces
½ teaspoon filé powder (optional)
  Chopped parsley.

1. Preheat the oven to 350 degrees.
2. Place the flour on aluminum foil and bake, stirring occasionally, until hazelnut brown, about ten minutes.
3. Combine the onions and four tablespoons of the butter in a saucepan. Toss briefly. Cover and cook until onions start to become translucent, about five minutes.
4. Sprinkle the onions with the browned flour. Stir in the clam juice with a wire whisk. Continue stirring until mixture is thickened and smooth. Add the tomatoes, bay leaf, Worcestershire, seasonings and sugar. Add the shrimp and cook ten minutes. Add the okra and cook, stirring, until pieces of okra separate.
5. Cook the green pepper and celery in the remaining butter about three minutes, stirring. The vegetables must remain crisp.
6. Add the vegetables to the onion mixture and cook ten to fifteen minutes longer, or until celery is tender but still somewhat crisp. Stir in the filé powder, sprinkle with chopped parsley and serve.

Yield: Four to six servings.

Shrimp à la Turque   *Florida*

2 pounds shrimp in the shell
1 cup oil
1½ teaspoons chili powder
1 tablespoon cider vinegar
1 teaspoon plus one tablespoon chopped fresh mint
1 teaspoon thyme
  Salt and freshly ground black pepper to taste

2 tablespoons finely minced shallots
4 lemon wedges.

1. Split the shrimp down the back with a sharp knife or with scissors. Rinse the shrimp under cold water to remove the small intestinal vein down the back. Pat dry.

2. Pour the oil into a mixing bowl. Combine the chili powder, vinegar and one teaspoon of the mint to make a paste. Add to the oil along with the thyme, salt, pepper, shallots and remaining mint. Stir well to mix and add the shrimp. Mix well and let stand four hours or overnight.

3. Preheat the broiler.

4. Pour the shrimp and the marinade into a broiler pan.

5. Broil the shrimp five or six inches from the flame. Broil six to ten minutes, depending on size, turning once. Serve, if desired, with a little of the marinade poured over. Garnish with lemon wedges.

Yield: Four servings.

Steamed Live Shrimp   *Florida*

36 live shrimp (the kind that are sold for bait)
 8 cups water
 1 cup dry white wine (optional)
 2 tablespoons salt
12 peppercorns
 1 rib celery with leaves, halved
 1 small onion, sliced
 1 carrot, quartered
 1 bay leaf
 2 sprigs parsley
¼ teaspoon thyme
 2 tablespoons cider vinegar.

1. Place the shrimp in cold running water until ready to use.

2. Place the two quarts water and the wine if desired in a large saucepan and add the salt, peppercorns, celery, onion and carrot. Tie the bay leaf, parsley and thyme in cheesecloth and add. Bring to a boil and simmer ten minutes. Add the

vinegar and shrimp. Return to a boil and remove from the heat. To serve, see note.

Yield: Three to six servings.

Note: Serve hot with melted butter or lukewarm or cold with cocktail sauce, mustard mayonnaise or with lukewarm French dressing.

Shrimp in Sour Cream   *Louisiana*

 6 tablespoons butter
 3 shallots, finely chopped
1½ pounds shrimp, shelled and deveined
½ pound mushrooms, sliced
 2 tablespoons flour
 1 teaspoon salt
¼ teaspoon freshly ground black pepper
¼ teaspoon thyme
 2 cups sour cream
 3 to four tablespoons dry sherry.

1. Melt the butter and sauté the shallots in it until tender but not browned.

2. Add the shrimp and cook over high heat, stirring occasionally, five minutes, or until shrimp just turn pink.

3. Add the mushrooms and cook three minutes longer. Sprinkle with the flour, salt and pepper and cook, stirring, two minutes.

4. Sprinkle with the thyme and gradually stir in the sour cream over low heat. Bring the mixture just to a boil, but do not allow to boil or it will curdle. Stir in the sherry.

Yield: Six servings.

Shrimp Creole   *Louisiana*

3 tablespoons butter or bacon drippings
2 cups coarsely chopped onions
2 cloves garlic, finely minced
3 ribs celery, coarsely chopped
1 green pepper, cored, seeded and chopped
3 ripe tomatoes, cored and peeled
1 bay leaf

2 sprigs fresh thyme or one-half teaspoon
  dried thyme
  Salt to taste
½ teaspoon freshly ground black pepper
¼ teaspoon cayenne pepper
2 pounds shrimp, shelled and deveined
1 teaspoon Worcestershire sauce (optional)
  Hot fluffy rice.

1. Melt the butter or bacon drippings in a large saucepan and cook the onions, garlic, celery and green pepper in it until tender and without browning. Add the tomatoes, bay leaf, thyme, salt, pepper and cayenne. Simmer ten minutes, stirring occasionally.

2. Add the shrimp and cover. Simmer ten minutes. If desired, season with Worcestershire. Serve with hot fluffy rice.

Yield: Four to six servings.

Charleston Breakfast Shrimp
South Carolina

3 tablespoons bacon drippings
1 tablespoon chopped green pepper
2 tablespoons chopped onion
1½ cups small shrimp, shelled and deveined
1 cup water
  Salt and freshly ground black pepper to
  taste
1 teaspoon Worcestershire sauce
1 tablespoon catchup
1½ tablespoons flour
  Grits.

1. Heat the bacon drippings and add the green pepper and onion. Cook until onion is wilted and add the shrimp. Cook, stirring, until shrimp turn pink. Add the water, salt and pepper and simmer three minutes.

2. Combine the Worcestershire, catchup and flour. Blend well and stir into the simmering mixture. When thickened, remove from the heat and serve. Serve with grits.

Yield: Four servings.

Broiled Red Snapper
Florida

2 red snapper fillets, each weighing about one
  pound, or four large fillet pieces, each
  weighing about one-half pound
  Melted butter
  Salt and freshly ground black pepper
  Chopped parsley
  Lemon butter
  Lemon wedges.

1. Preheat the broiler.

2. Place the fillets on a baking dish and brush generously with melted butter. Sprinkle with salt and pepper and broil about two inches from broiler heat. If fish starts to brown too quickly, reduce heat. Cook five to ten minutes, depending on size and thickness of fish. Brush the fish with additional butter during cooking. Serve fish sprinkled with parsley and lemon butter. Garnish with lemon wedges.

Yield: Two to four servings.

Red Snapper Grenobloise
Florida

1 lemon
1 one-and-one-half-pound red snapper
  Salt and freshly ground black pepper
½ cup butter
2 tablespoons capers
  Lemon slices (optional).

1. Preheat the oven to 425 degrees.

2. Peel the lemon, removing all the white pulp. Cut the lemon into thin slices and remove the seeds. Cut each slice into small cubes, discarding the membranes between sections. Reserve lemon cubes.

3. Thoroughly clean and scale the fish, but leave the head and tail intact. Rinse the fish under cold water and pat dry with paper towels. Sprinkle the fish inside and outside with salt and pepper.

4. Melt the butter in a skillet with ovenproof handle large enough to hold the fish. When skillet

is hot, put in the fish and cook only on one side for about five minutes. Tilt the pan occasionally and spoon the butter over the fish.

5. Place the fish in the oven and bake, basting occasionally, for about twenty-five minutes, or until fish flakes easily when tested with a fork.

6. Remove the fish from the oven and transfer to a serving platter. Sprinkle with the capers, reserved lemon cubes and butter from the skillet. Garnish with lemon slices if desired.

Yield: About three servings.

Note: Bluefish, porgies, striped bass and other small fish may be cooked in the same way.

Florida Keys Red Snapper   *Florida*

1 three-pound to four-pound red snapper
  Peanut oil or vegetable oil
  Salt and freshly ground black pepper
¼ cup butter
½ cup finely chopped onion
¼ cup finely chopped celery
¼ cup finely chopped green pepper
2 scallions, including green part, chopped
2 cups toasted soft bread crumbs
¼ cup finely chopped parsley
¼ cup coarsely chopped toasted almonds
6 thin tomato slices
6 thin onion slices
6 thin orange slices
6 thin lime slices
  Juice of half a lime.

1. Preheat the oven to 350 degrees.
2. Rub the fish lightly with oil and sprinkle inside and outside with salt and pepper.
3. Melt the butter and cook the chopped onion, celery, green pepper and scallions in it until onion is wilted. Stir in the bread crumbs, parsley and almonds. Season to taste with salt and pepper. Stuff the fish with the mixture and tie with string.
4. Place the fish on a length of aluminum foil and add alternating, slightly overlapping slices of tomato, onion, orange and lime. Sprinkle with

salt, pepper and lime juice. Bring up the edges of the foil and secure it envelope style. Bake thirty minutes, or until fish flakes easily when tested with a fork.

Yield: Four to six servings.

Red Snapper Creole   *Louisiana*

1 three-pound red snapper, cleaned and scaled
½ cup flour
  Salt and freshly ground black pepper to taste
6 tablespoons butter
¾ cup finely chopped onion
1 cup finely chopped celery
½ cup chopped green pepper
1 clove garlic, finely minced
3 cups fresh peeled or canned tomatoes
1 tablespoon finely chopped parsley
1 tablespoon tomato paste
  Juice of half a lemon
½ teaspoon grated lemon rind
1 bay leaf
1 teaspoon thyme
  Cayenne pepper to taste
1 teaspoon Worcestershire sauce
  Lemon slices for garnish
  Parsley for garnish.

1. Preheat the oven to 350 degrees.
2. Rub the fish inside and outside with a light coating of flour. Sprinkle inside and outside with salt and pepper. Arrange fish in a baking dish.
3. Heat the butter in a saucepan, add the onion, celery and green pepper and cook until vegetables are wilted. Stir in the garlic.
4. Press the tomatoes through a sieve or food mill and season with all the remaining ingredients except the lemon slices and parsley for garnish. Bring to a boil and add this to the onion mixture. Pour the sauce around the fish and bake, basting often with the sauce, about thirty minutes, or until fish flakes easily.

5. To serve, garnish with lemon slices and parsley.

Yield: Four to six servings.

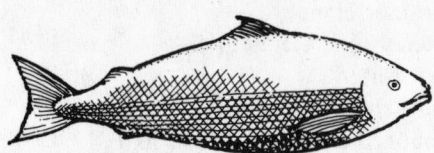

Baked Red Snapper   *Alabama*

8 tablespoons butter
2 cups finely chopped onions
2 cups finely chopped celery
1 clove garlic, finely minced
½ cup finely chopped green pepper
¼ cup finely chopped parsley
4 cups canned Italian plum tomatoes
1 bay leaf
1½ tablespoons Worcestershire sauce
1½ teaspoons chili powder
 Juice of half a lemon
 Salt and freshly ground black pepper to taste
 Cayenne pepper or Tabasco sauce to taste
1 three-pound red snapper
 Flour for dredging
3 sprigs parsley.

1. In a saucepan melt the butter and cook the onions, celery, garlic and green pepper until onions are wilted. Add the chopped parsley, tomatoes, bay leaf, Worcestershire, chili powder, lemon juice, salt, pepper and cayenne or Tabasco. Bring to a boil and simmer, stirring frequently, forty-five minutes.

2. Meanwhile, preheat the oven to 350 degrees.

3. Sprinkle the fish inside and outside with salt and pepper. Dredge fish lightly with flour. Place the parsley sprigs in the fish cavity. Place fish on a baking dish and pour the sauce over fish. Bake one hour or longer, basting frequently, or until fish flakes easily when tested with a fork.

Yield: Four to six servings.

Fish Stew   *Louisiana*

1 pound boned, skinned haddock or striped bass, cut into serving pieces
1 cup fish stock
2 tablespoons butter
½ cup finely chopped shallots
1 clove garlic, finely chopped
1 tomato, peeled and chopped
1 tablespoon finely chopped parsley
2 teaspoons salt
⅛ teaspoon freshly ground black pepper
⅛ teaspoon nutmeg
¼ teaspoon thyme
3 drops Tabasco sauce
2½ cups milk
2 tablespoons Pernod
1 teaspoon grated lemon rind.

1. Simmer the fish in the stock, covered, until fish flakes easily, about eight minutes. Reserve stock and fish separately.

2. Melt the butter in a small skillet. Add the shallots and garlic and sauté until golden.

3. Add mixture to reserved stock. Add the tomato, parsley, salt, pepper, nutmeg, thyme and Tabasco. Simmer, covered, twenty-five minutes.

4. Add the milk, Pernod and lemon rind to stock. Add fish pieces. Heat before serving, but do not boil.

Yield: Four servings.

The following dish is often used in the Pee Dee section of South Carolina for large family or community meals. The name of the stew stems from the custom of cooking it in a black pot over a pine bark fire (or because it was served on pine bark).

Pine Bark Stew   *South Carolina*

3 quarts ripe tomatoes
2 tablespoons salt
4 tablespoons sugar
1 teaspoon chili powder

1½ teaspoons freshly ground black pepper, or
   to taste
⅛ teaspoon cayenne pepper
¼ pound bacon slices
2 green peppers, cored, seeded and chopped
1½ cups chopped onions
5 pounds white fish (rock fish, bass, bream,
   mullet or grouper), cut into serving pieces
4 cups hot water
2 tablespoons Worcestershire sauce
   Hot cooked rice.

1. Peel the tomatoes and chop finely. Place in a saucepan with the salt, sugar, chili powder, pepper and cayenne. Cook, uncovered, until sauce measures three cups.

2. Cook the bacon in a skillet until crisp; remove and reserve. Sauté the green peppers and onions in the bacon drippings until lightly browned.

3. Place the fish, hot water, the sautéed vegetables, reserved bacon and the three cups sauce in a kettle. Add the Worcestershire and cook for about twenty minues, or until the fish flakes easily. Serve over rice.

Yield: Twenty-five to thirty servings.

Chesapeake Bay Fish Stew   *Maryland*

Court bouillon:
   Fish trimmings, including heads, bones,
   skin, crab claws and crab fat, from all fish
   listed below
1 onion
1 rib celery with leaves, chopped
1 bay leaf
1 carrot, cubed
1 leek, chopped
2 to three sprigs fresh thyme or one-half
   teaspoon dried thyme
2 sprigs parsley
1 four-inch strip orange peel
10 peppercorns

1 teaspoon salt
8 cups water.
Fish:
12 steamer clams
12 cherrystone clams
¼ cup water
6 hard-shelled blue crabs, claws and fat
   removed and back cut in half
½ pound sea bass fillets, cut into two-inch
   pieces
2 two-pound rock fish (striped bass), filleted
   and cut into two-inch pieces
1 small butterfish, filleted and cut into
   two-inch pieces
¼ pound Norfolk spot fillets, cut into
   two-inch pieces
¾ pound catfish, skinned, filleted and cut into
   two-inch pieces
½ pound sea trout fillets, cut into two-inch
   pieces
⅛ teaspoon whole saffron
   Salt and freshly ground black pepper to
   taste
   Buttered, baked thin French bread slices.

1. Place all ingredients for the court bouillon in a large kettle. Bring to a boil and simmer, uncovered, twenty minutes. Strain through a double layer of cheesecloth into a large heavy pot.

2. Place the clams and water in a heavy pan or casserole. Cover and heat until clams open, about eight minutes. Discard those that do not open.

3. Add the liquid from the clams to the court bouillon and, when the clams are cool enough, cut the snouts off the steamers and discard. Except for six cherrystones to be used for garnish, remove clams from shells and set aside.

4. Add the crabs to the large pot of court bouillon and simmer fifteen minutes.

5. Add the sea bass and rock and cook three minutes. Add the butterfish and spot and cook three minutes longer. Add the catfish, sea trout and saffron and cook five minutes longer, or until all fish are cooked.

6. Return the clams, those in and those out of the shells, to the pot and reheat. Serve stew imme-

diately in deep bowls either over the crisp bread slices or with the bread passed separately.

Yield: Six servings.

There is no dish in American cooking that speaks more vividly of a region than the various gumbos of the South. They may be made with shrimp or oysters or crab or ham or a combination of these things. But the essential ingredient is okra, whence the dish derives its name. The word is of African origin derived years ago from the Bantu language of Central Angola. The following recipe is an authentic creation of E. Lysle Aschaffenburg of the Pontchartrain Hotel in New Orleans. The gumbo is somewhat tedious to make, but it is well worth the effort.

Pontchartrain Creole Gumbo   *Louisiana*

- 2 pounds shrimp
- 12 live hard-shelled crabs
  Boiling water
- 3 slices bacon
- 4 large onions, finely chopped (about two quarts when chopped)
- 4 cloves garlic, finely minced
- 2 bay leaves
- 2 tablespoons finely minced green pepper
- 1 teaspoon finely chopped fresh thyme or one-half teaspoon dried thyme
- 1½ teaspoons sugar
  Salt and freshly ground black pepper to taste
- 2 pounds fresh okra or two packages frozen okra
- 2 tablespoons oil
- 1 large ham bone, split in half or quartered
- ½ pound chicken wings
- 1 pound boneless stewing veal, cut into one-inch cubes
- ⅓ cup finely chopped parsley
- 1 one-pound-three-ounce can tomatoes or four ripe tomatoes, peeled and cored
- ½ teaspoon Tabasco sauce, or to taste
- ¼ cup Worcestershire sauce
  Juice of half a lemon
- 2 cups shucked oysters with liquor
- 1 teaspoon filé powder (optional)
  Freshly cooked rice.

1. Using a pair of kitchen scissors, split the raw shrimp down the back. Pull off the shells and put them in a saucepan. Rinse the shrimp under cold running water and rinse or pull away the dark vein down the back. Set the shrimp aside. Cover the shrimp shells with water and bring to a boil. Simmer five minutes and set aside.

2. Drop the live crabs into boiling water. Cook exactly five minutes and drain. Break off the top shell, but save the juices and scrape away any "fat" inside the shell. Discard the shell.

3. With the fingers, pull away and discard the spongy "dead fingers" inside. Pull away and discard the small, tough sac between the eyes. Pull off and discard the "apron" on the underside of the crab. Save the crab claws and split the crabs in half and reserve.

4. Cut the bacon slices in half and put the bacon in a kettle. Cook the bacon, stirring, until it is rendered of its fat. Remove the cooked bacon and drain it on paper towels. Reserve the bacon.

5. Add the onions to the bacon drippings in the kettle. Cook, stirring, until the onions are golden brown. Add the garlic, bay leaves, green pepper, thyme, sugar, salt and pepper. Cook slowly, stirring, until green pepper is wilted.

6. Cut the fresh or frozen okra crosswise into one-half-inch lengths and add to the kettle. Continue cooking, stirring occasionally, about five minutes.

7. In another large skillet heat the oil, add the ham bone, chicken wings and veal. Cook over relatively high heat, shaking the skillet occasionally and turning the pieces so that they brown well on all sides. Pour off any excess fat from the skillet and add the browned meat and bones to the kettle. Add a cup or so of water to the skillet and stir with a wooden spoon to dissolve the brown particles that cling to the bottom and sides. Pour this liquid into the kettle.

8. Add to the kettle the parsley, tomatoes, Tabasco, Worcestershire and lemon juice. Add the pieces of crab, the reserved peeled shrimp, the oysters and cooked bacon. Strain the liquid from the shrimp shells into the kettle. Add enough water to cover all the ingredients. The water level should be about one inch over the ingredients. Add salt and pepper to taste and bring to a boil. Care should be taken that this gumbo does not burn. It may be wise to pour the gumbo at this point into a clean kettle. Bring the gumbo to a boil and cook two and one-half hours, skimming the surface frequently to remove scum, foam and excess fat. Stir occasionally as the gumbo cooks. When it is ready to serve, bring the gumbo to a boil and turn off the heat. Stir in the filé powder if desired. Do not boil again.

9. To serve, spoon a quarter of a cup of cooked rice into a measuring cup. Level off the top; then unmold the rice into the center of a hot soup plate. Do this for each serving. Ladle the gumbo around the rice and serve immediately. If desired, pass a bottle of Tabasco sauce with the gumbo for those who require more heat.

Yield: One dozen servings.

Jambalaya   *Mississippi*

6 tablespoons butter
1 cup finely chopped onions
2 cloves garlic, finely minced
1 green pepper, cored, seeded and chopped
1 rib celery, chopped
1 cup diced cooked ham, preferably country ham
1½ cups chicken broth
1 teaspoon chopped fresh thyme or one-half teaspoon dried thyme
¼ cup chopped parsley
¼ teaspoon nutmeg
¼ teaspoon ground cloves
   Tabasco sauce to taste
4 cups canned Italian plum tomatoes
   Salt and freshly ground black pepper to taste

1 teaspoon Worcestershire sauce
2 cups oysters with their liquor
1½ pounds shrimp, shelled and deveined
1 cup rice, cooked according to package directions.

1. Melt the butter in a large saucepan and add the onions, garlic, green pepper, celery and ham. Cook, stirring, until onions are translucent. Add the broth, thyme, parsley, nutmeg, cloves, Tabasco and tomatoes. Add salt, pepper and the Worcestershire. Simmer fifteen minutes.

2. Add the oysters, shrimp and rice and simmer ten minutes longer.

Yield: Six to eight servings.

Chartres Street Trout   *Louisiana*

6 trout, filleted
   Salt and freshly ground black pepper
½ cup butter, approximately
   Juice of one lemon
¼ cup capers
¼ cup freshly chopped parsley
   Buttered toast.

1. Preheat the oven to 350 degrees.

2. Cover a baking sheet with aluminum foil and butter it well. Arrange the fish fillets on the foil and sprinkle with salt and pepper. Dot fillets liberally with the butter and cover with another sheet of aluminum foil. Bake eight to ten minutes, or just until the fish flakes easily when tested with a fork.

3. Transfer the fish to hot dinner plates and sprinkle with lemon juice, capers and parsley. Serve with buttered toast.

Yield: Six main course servings or one dozen servings as a first course.

Trout Meunière   *Louisiana*

6 trout fillets
1 cup milk

½ cup flour
Salt and freshly ground black pepper to
  taste
⅓ cup vegetable oil or peanut oil
¼ cup butter
  Chopped parsley
  Lemon wedges.

1. Dip the fillets in the milk and let stand until ready to cook.

2. Blend the flour with salt and pepper. Drain the fillets, but do not dry. Dip them in seasoned flour.

3. Heat the oil in a large skillet and cook the fillets until golden brown, turning once. Transfer to a warm serving platter. Wipe out the skillet.

4. Add the butter to the skillet and cook until butter just begins to brown. Pour the butter over the fish, sprinkle with parsley and garnish with lemon wedges.

Yield: Three to six servings.

Trout Amandine   *Louisiana*

Follow the recipe above for "Trout Meunière," but cook one-half cup slivered blanched almonds in the butter before pouring it over the fish.

Meat, Poultry, Game and Other Main Dishes

Piccadillo *Florida*

¼ cup peanut oil
1 clove garlic, finely minced
2 large onions, chopped
1 large green pepper, cored, seeded and chopped
1 pound ground round steak
1 one-pound can tomatoes, preferably Italian plum style
¼ teaspoon oregano
Salt and freshly ground black pepper to taste
1 tablespoon capers
¼ cup chopped stuffed olives
½ cup raisins, chopped
1 tablespoon cider vinegar
Cooked rice and black beans.

1. Heat the oil in a large skillet and cook the garlic, onions and green pepper in it until onions are wilted.

2. Add the meat and cook, stirring and chopping, until meat is thoroughly crumbled and loses its red color. Add the tomatoes with their liquid and break up tomatoes with a fork.

3. Add the oregano, salt and pepper. Add the capers, olives, raisins and vinegar. Cover and simmer over low heat about one hour. Stir occasionally to prevent the piccadillo from sticking or scorching. Serve with rice and black beans.

Yield: Four to six servings.

Tamale Pie *Mississippi*

1 cup finely chopped onions
½ cup finely chopped green pepper
2 cloves garlic, finely minced
2 tablespoons olive oil or bacon drippings
2 cups shredded boiled chicken or braised beef
1 tablespoon chili powder, or more to taste
1 cup finely chopped and drained canned or fresh tomatoes
½ cup chicken broth or braised beef gravy
Salt to taste
½ teaspoon ground or crushed cumin seeds
2 cups white or yellow corn meal
5 cups boiling water
2 tablespoons butter or lard.

1. Preheat the oven to 350 degrees.

2. Cook the onions, green pepper and garlic in the oil or drippings until onions are wilted.

3. Grind the chicken or beef and add to the onion mixture. Add the chili powder, tomatoes, broth or gravy, salt and cumin seeds. Beat well with a wooden spoon.

4. Gradually add the corn meal to the boiling water, stirring vigorously with a wire whisk. When the mixture is boiling and smooth, add the butter or lard.

5. Butter a two-and-one-half-quart casserole and add about three-quarters of the mush. Using a spoon, push the mush against the bottom and

sides of the casserole to make a well in the center. Spoon in the meat mixture and add the remaining mush to cover. Bake about one hour.

Yield: Four to six servings.

Tamale Pie with Hominy Grits

Alabama

3 cloves garlic
¼ cup olive oil
¾ pound ground round steak
2 green peppers, cored, seeded and chopped
2 cups finely chopped onions, preferably the red Italian variety
2 teaspoons chili powder, or to taste
Salt to taste
1 pepperone (Italian hot sausage), cut into small pieces
4 ripe tomatoes, peeled, seeded and chopped
2 cups homemade or canned tomato sauce
3 leaves fresh basil, finely chopped, or dried basil to taste
1½ cups hominy grits
Boiling salted water.

1. Cook the garlic in the oil until garlic starts to brown. Remove the garlic and discard.

2. Add the ground meat, stirring to break up lumps, and cook until it loses its red color. Add the green peppers and onions and cook until onions are wilted, stirring frequently. Add the chili powder, salt and pepperone. Stir. Add the tomatoes, tomato sauce and basil and simmer thirty minutes.

3. Preheat the oven to 300 degrees.

4. Meanwhile, cook the hominy in boiling salted water according to package directions. When hominy is thickened and done, spread it on a two-inch-deep oval or round platter or deep pie plate and smooth out the center to make a "shell" resembling a pie shell with a thick rim. Fill the hollow with the meat mixture and bake, uncovered, about thirty minutes.

Yield: Six to eight servings.

Cuban Round Roast

Florida

3 pounds eye of beef round
¼ pound smoked ham, preferably country style
¼ pound bacon
1 cup finely chopped onions
2 tablespoons finely chopped capers
1 clove garlic, finely minced
¼ cup chopped green olives
1 tablespoon chopped green chilies (optional)
Salt and freshly ground black pepper to taste
¼ cup lard or bacon drippings
1 cup beef broth or water
½ cup homemade or canned tomato sauce
1 tablespoon cider vinegar.

1. Preheat the oven to 350 degrees.

2. Run a long, sharp, thin-bladed knife through the center of the roast. The incision should be about one and one-half to two inches deep, depending on the thickness of the roast.

3. Chop or grind the ham and bacon and mix well. Blend the ham mixture with the onions, capers, garlic, olives and chilies. Stuff the roast with the mixture. Season the roast with salt and pepper.

4. Heat the lard or bacon drippings in a Dutch oven or heavy casserole and brown the roast in it thoroughly on all sides. Do not let the fat burn.

5. Add the broth, tomato sauce and vinegar and bake, uncovered, basting occasionally, until the meat is very tender, two to two and one-half hours. Add water, if necessary, during cooking.

Yield: Eight to ten servings.

The town of Natchitoches on the western side of Louisiana is famous for its "Hot-ta-Meat Pies," which are shaped like a half-moon with delicately fluted edges and a spiced meat filling. The name of the town is pronounced, incidentally, NACK-i-tosh. The pies date from before the Civil War.

Hot-ta-Meat Pies   *Louisiana*

Filling:

 2 tablespoons flour
 1 tablespoon bacon drippings
 1½ cups finely chopped onions
 1 clove garlic, finely minced (optional)
 ½ pound ground beef
 1½ pounds ground pork
 6 scallions, including green part, trimmed
   and finely chopped
 3 tablespoons finely chopped parsley
 1 tablespoon finely chopped hot green
   pepper or a dash of cayenne pepper to
   taste
   Salt and freshly ground black pepper to
   taste

Pastry:

 ½ cup shortening
 4 cups flour
 2 teaspoons baking powder
   Salt to taste
 2 eggs
 ¼ cup milk, approximately
 4 cups oil or shortening

1. The filling should be prepared and cooled before the pastries are made.

2. Blend the flour with the bacon drippings in a skillet and cook, stirring, until flour is golden. Add the onions and garlic and cook until onions are lightly browned. Add the meat and cook, breaking up the meat with the side of a spoon and stirring, until meat loses its color. Add the remaining ingredients and remove the mixture from the heat. Cool thoroughly.

3. To prepare pastry, melt the shortening and let it cool slightly.

4. Sift together the flour, baking powder and salt into a mixing bowl. Make a well in the center and add the eggs. Stir with a wooden spoon and add the shortening. When blended, mix with the fingers, adding a little milk at a time. Continue kneading, adding just enough milk to make a stiff, manageable dough. Chill the dough if desired.

5. Divide the dough into quarters and roll it out one-eighth-inch thick or less. Using a saucer six inches in diameter, cut out circles of dough. If desired, these circles may be rolled slightly to make them larger or the pastry thinner. Spoon a little of the filling into the center of each circle. Brush the edges of each circle with cold water; then fold dough over. The water helps seal the dough. Crimp the edges with a fork. Using a sharp knife, make two small incisions in the top of each turnover to permit the escape of steam.

6. Heat the oil or shortening in a deep-fryer to 370 degrees. Drop in the turnovers, a few at a time, and, when thoroughly brown on one side, turn them to brown on the other. Drain on paper towels and serve hot.

Yield: One dozen or more pies.

One of the best dishes in Louisiana—and one that is particularly recommended for breakfast— is known as grillades. It is a braised meat dish generally made with veal, but it may be made with round steak. The usual accompaniment for breakfast grillades is grits.

Grillades   *Louisiana*

 2 pounds veal or round steak, cut into six
   thin slices, each slice measuring about four
   by six inches
 6 tablespoons bacon drippings
 ¼ cup flour
 2 cups finely chopped onions
 3 tablespoons tomato paste
 1 clove garlic, finely minced
 ½ cup finely chopped scallions, including
   green part
 ¼ teaspoon thyme
 ¼ teaspoon cayenne pepper
 1 bay leaf
   Salt and freshly ground black pepper to
   taste
 2 cups beef broth
   Worcestershire sauce to taste (optional)

Chopped parsley
Chopped scallions for garnish.

1. Pound the meat, if desired.
2. Heat two tablespoons of the bacon drippings in a skillet and brown the meat in it on both sides.
3. Heat the remaining drippings in a two-quart saucepan and add the flour. Cook over moderate heat, stirring with a wooden spoon, until flour is lightly browned. Add the onions and continue cooking and stirring until onions are golden brown. Add the tomato paste and cook, scraping the bottom of the saucepan until tomato paste browns slightly. Add the garlic, scallions, thyme, cayenne, bay leaf, salt and pepper and stir well. Pour in the broth, stirring rapidly.
4. Return the meat to the sauce and simmer one to one and one-half hours, stirring occasionally from the bottom. Add Worcestershire if desired.
5. Serve sprinkled with parsley and scallions.
Yield: Six servings.

Tripe Creole   *Louisiana*

3 pounds honeycomb tripe, cut into
  one-and-one-half-inch cubes
  Salt to taste
4 small onions, thinly sliced (about two cups)
½ pound mushrooms, sliced
2 cups peeled, chopped, ripe tomatoes or an
  equal amount canned Italian plum tomatoes
2 green peppers, cored, seeded and sliced
2 cloves garlic, minced
2 sprigs thyme, finely chopped, or one-half
  teaspoon dried thyme
1 bay leaf (see note)
2 cups chicken broth, approximately
  Freshly ground black pepper to taste
  Tabasco sauce to taste
  Boiled potatoes.

1. Preheat the oven to 375 degrees.
2. Place the tripe in a kettle and add water to cover. Bring to a boil and cook five minutes. Drain.
3. Return the tripe to the kettle and add the remaining ingredients. Bring to a boil, cover closely and bake four hours, stirring occasionally. If the tripe seems to cook too fast, reduce the oven heat and continue cooking. If it is deemed necessary, add a little more chicken broth as tripe cooks. Serve with boiled potatoes on the side.
Yield: Four to six servings.
Note: The bay leaf may be added whole, but it is better finely chopped. To chop it, break the leaf into quarters and combine it with the chopped garlic and thyme. Chop until finely minced.

Some recipes for tripe creole also call for a last-minute addition of cognac, but it is not generally considered an ingredient in the traditional sense.

Roast Marinated Pork Loin   *Virginia*

1 three- to five-pound pork loin
1½ cups dry white wine
3 cloves garlic, crushed
½ cup sliced carrot
½ cup sliced onion
1 teaspoon peppercorns
1 teaspoon thyme
1 large bay leaf
1 teaspoon juniper berries.

1. Place the pork in a dish large enough to hold it. Add the remaining ingredients and cover. Refrigerate. Let the pork stand in the refrigerator, turning occasionally in the marinade, three or four days. If this is not feasible, let pork stand overnight and the following day.
2. Preheat the oven to 325 degrees.
3. Drain the pork and reserve the marinade. Wipe the pork with paper towels and place it on a rack in a baking pan. Roast forty minutes to the pound, basting occasionally with the marinade. When cooked, the roast should be quite brown. When cooked, turn off the oven and let the pork

stay there ten minutes longer. This roast when served should be neither hot nor cold.

Yield: Four to six servings.

Pork Chops Bermudiana   *Florida*

4 pork chops, each one and one-half inches thick
  Salt and freshly ground black pepper
1 tablespoon butter
4 tablespoons uncooked rice
4 slices peeled tomato
4 slices green pepper
4 thick slices Bermuda onion
1 cup fresh or canned chicken or beef broth
1 tablespoon finely chopped parsley
1 tablespoon finely chopped chives
½ bay leaf.

1. Preheat the oven to 350 degrees.
2. Sprinkle the chops with salt and pepper. Brown the chops on both sides in butter and transfer to a baking dish. Spoon one tablespoon uncooked rice atop each chop. Top each with a slice of tomato, green pepper and onion and sprinkle with salt and pepper. Pour the broth around the chops and sprinkle with parsley and chives. Add the bay leaf half and cover. Bake one hour.

Yield: Four servings.

Boiled Spareribs   *Alabama*

2 sides baby spareribs
  Boiling water
  Salt and freshly ground black pepper to taste
1 onion, studded with two whole cloves
  Sauerkraut, cooked rice or mashed potatoes.

1. Cut the sides of spareribs in half or quarters and place in a kettle large enough to hold them.

Pour boiling water to cover over them and add salt, pepper and the onion.

2. Bring to a boil and simmer one to two hours, depending on size of spareribs, until thoroughly tender. Serve with sauerkraut, rice or mashed potatoes, or deep-fry the spareribs (recipe below). The cooking liquid may be used to cook rice.

Yield: Four to six servings.

Deep-Fried Spareribs   *Georgia*

2 sides baby spareribs, boiled (recipe above)
1 cup self-rising flour
  Freshly ground black pepper to taste
3 eggs
¼ cup milk
  Oil for deep-frying
  Cooked rice
  Tomato sauce (optional).

1. When the spareribs are cooked and cool enough to handle, cut them into individual ribs or, if they are not very meaty, cut them into two-rib sections.
2. Dredge the ribs in flour seasoned with pepper.
3. Beat the eggs and add the milk. Dip the ribs in the mixture and deep-fry in hot oil just until they are crisp and golden brown. Serve hot with rice. The ribs may also be served with a tomato sauce.

Yield: Four to six servings.

Pork-Stuffed Peppers   *Georgia*

4 pork chops or two pounds lean shoulder of pork
  Boiling water
  Salt to taste
1 cup leftover grits (page 243)
1 cup crumbled baking powder biscuits (page 261)
2 eggs, lightly beaten

Freshly ground black pepper to taste
¾ cup finely chopped onion
1 tablespoon butter
8 large green peppers, halved, membranes and seeds scooped out to give shells for stuffing.

1. Cover the meat with boiling water and add salt. Bring to a boil and simmer until meat is fork-tender. Drain, reserving a little of the cooking liquid. Shred or grind the meat.
2. Preheat the oven to 350 degrees.
3. In a mixing bowl combine the meat with the grits, biscuits, eggs and black pepper. Cook the onion in the butter until onion is translucent and add to the stuffing. Mix well. Add just enough cooking liquid to moisten.
4. Meanwhile, drop the green pepper in boiling water to cover and simmer three minutes. Drain immediately.
5. Fill the peppers with the pork mixture and place them, stuffed side up, in a buttered baking dish. Bake ten to fifteen minutes, or until thoroughly heated.
Yield: Eight servings.

Sausage with Cream Gravy and Biscuits
Tennessee

1½ pounds sausage meat
⅓ cup flour
1 cup water
2 cups evaporated milk or heavy cream
    Salt and freshly ground black pepper to taste
6 hot biscuits, split.

1. Shape the sausage meat into twelve patties and fry in a heavy skillet until brown and thoroughly cooked. Remove patties and keep warm.
2. Remove all but one-third cup fat from the skillet. Sprinkle the flour over fat in skillet and mix. Gradually add the water, stirring constantly.
3. Stir in the milk or cream. Season with salt

and pepper. Bring to a boil, stirring. Return patties to skillet and reheat.
4. Serve on top of the biscuits.
Yield: Six servings.

Cuban Sausages
Florida

3 pounds pork that is both lean and fat
2½ tablespoons salt
    Freshly ground black pepper to taste
3 cloves garlic, finely minced
1 teaspoon ground oregano
½ cup achiote coloring (see note)
2 yards pork intestines.

1. Grind the meat twice. Add the salt, pepper, garlic, oregano and achiote and mix well.
2. Use the mixture to stuff the pork intestines, using a sausage stuffer or a large funnel. These sausages may be hung for a short time in a cool, dry place. Before hanging, prick them in several places. Twist the sausage in several places to make individual sausages.
Yield: About three pounds stuffed sausages; twelve servings.
Note: Achiote coloring is available in Spanish markets.

Head Cheese (Fromage de Tête)
Louisiana

1 pig's head
    Coarse salt
1 pound salt pork
2 large carrots
2 medium-size onions, each studded with two whole cloves
1 clove garlic, peeled
4 sprigs parsley
3 ribs celery
2 bay leaves
4 sprigs thyme or one teaspoon dried thyme
    Salt to taste
20 peppercorns

1 tablespoon cider vinegar
    Freshly ground black pepper to taste, if necessary.

1. This will require a large kettle. First, however, the pig's head must be thoroughly singed, cleaned and scraped to remove all traces of hair. Remove the tongue and brains. Discard the fat part of the throat. Keep tongue and brains separate. Have the head cut into quarters.

2. Rub the head and tongue with coarse salt and place in a large bowl with the salt pork. Let stand in a cool place at least four hours. Place the head, tongue, salt pork, carrots, onions, garlic, parsley, celery, one bay leaf and half the thyme in a large kettle. Add salt, the peppercorns and water to cover.

3. Bring to a boil and simmer one and one-half hours, skimming the surface, as necessary. Remove the tongue and reserve it. Continue cooking the head and other ingredients two and one-half hours longer. Let cool to lukewarm.

4. Meanwhile, soak the brain in cold salted water. Drain and place in a saucepan. Add water to cover, one bay leaf, the remaining thyme and the vinegar. Bring to a boil and simmer two minutes. Remove from the heat and let cool.

5. Lift the pig's head from the broth and cut off all meat from the bones. Cut the brains, meat and tongue into one-half-inch squares. Reserve the pig's ears. Season meat and tongue with salt and pepper if necessary.

6. Bring the cooking liquid to a boil and cook rapidly over high heat to reduce by one-third. Strain.

7. Cut the salt pork and pig's ears into strips. Arrange layers of salt pork, pig's ears, brains, meat and tongue in a bowl and pour in enough of the strained cooking liquid to cover. Let cool slightly. Cover with aluminum foil or wax paper and add a weight to cover. Let cool twenty-four hours. Serve unmolded or directly from the bowl as an appetizer, preferably with sour pickles, the kind the French call *cornichons*.

Yield: One dozen or more servings.

Head Cheese Vinaigrette   *Louisiana*

Cut head cheese (recipe above) into cubes and arrange on lettuce leaves. Serve sprinkled with cider vinegar, oil, chopped onion, salt and freshly ground black pepper.

Chitterlings   *Mississippi*

10 pounds chitterlings (see note)
    Lemon juice
    Salt to taste
 1 tablespoon cider vinegar
    Seasoning salt to taste
 1 onion, finely chopped
 1 clove garlic, crushed
 3 bay leaves
    Vinegar
    Hot sauce.

1. Place the chitterlings in a basin and add cold water, a little lemon juice and salt. Clean chitterlings thoroughly, removing as much of the fat as possible. Change the water, adding more lemon juice and salt as necessary. Rinse chitterlings thoroughly and put them in a pot.

2. Add cold water to cover, the juice of one lemon and the remaining ingredients and bring to a boil. Cover and simmer until chitterlings are thoroughly tender, about four hours. Serve hot with vinegar and hot sauce on the side.

Yield: Eight servings.

Note: Chitterlings are the intestines of the hog and it is important to remove all excess fat and clean them thoroughly. After boiling until tender, the chitterlings may be drained, dipped in corn meal and fried, or dipped in a batter made of two cups flour, two eggs and one and one-half cups milk and deep-fried.

This recipe is as Southern as grits and red eye gravy and is always eaten on New Year's Day along with turnip greens or collards and some sort of corn bread. This is good luck for the New Year—the peas are coins, the greens are folding money, the jawl is for luck and the corn bread is to stick to your ribs.

Mrs. Jackson Porter Dick's Black-Eyed Peas and Hog Jawl (Jowl)   *Georgia*

1 one-pound package dried black-eyed peas
1 four-inch to five-inch piece of smoked hog
   jawl, sliced
   Salt
1 bird's eye pepper or other small hot red
   pepper (see note)
   Worcestershire sauce to taste.

1. Day before, rinse and pick over the peas. Cover with water and soak overnight.
2. Next day, sprinkle the jawl with 3 teaspoons salt and then fry in a skillet until browned. Transfer to a kettle. Add the soaked peas, enough water to cover by one inch, salt to taste and the pepper. Bring to a boil.
3. Cover and simmer three to four hours. Add additional water during cooking if necessary. Add Worcestershire.
Yield: Eight servings.
Note: Bird's eye peppers grow in Georgia and Bermuda.

Souse (Jellied Pork)   *Tennessee*

1 hog's head, split, eyes and brain removed
4 pig's feet
2 pig's ears
   Salt
   Freshly ground black pepper
   Sage
   Crushed hot red pepper.

1. Remove excess fat from head and clean thoroughly.
2. Singe hairs off feet and ears and scrub well under hot water.
3. Place head, feet and ears in a large kettle and cover with hot water. Bring to a boil, cover, and simmer several hours, or until meat is very tender.
4. Remove meat from the bones and season with one teaspoon each salt, pepper, sage and red pepper for each quart meat. Press into a bowl and chill. To serve, see note.
Yield: Two dozen servings.
Note: Serve cold with vinegar or cut into slices, dip in egg and bread crumbs and fry in hot lard. Hog's head cheese is prepared as above, but the meat is ground, seasoned as above plus three teaspoons allspice and two teaspoons ground cloves and mixed with two to three cups of the cooking broth before pressing into a bowl. Broth forms jelly.

Smithfield or Smithfield-Style Virginia Ham

1 ten-pound to twelve-pound country ham (see note)

1. Soak the ham in cold water to cover overnight.
2. Preheat the oven to 500 degrees.
3. Scrub the ham to remove the pepper coating and any mold that may be present. Place the ham in a covered roaster with six cups cold water. Close all vents.
4. Bake ham twenty minutes. Turn oven off. Allow ham to remain in oven without opening door three hours.
5. Turn oven heat to 500 degrees and leave fifteen minutes. Turn off the heat and allow ham to remain in the oven for at least three hours or more, or ham can be left in overnight.
6. Remove ham from roaster and cut off the rind. Ham is ready to serve or may be glazed if desired.

Yield: About two dozen servings.

Note: Country hams are dry cured, salty and usually have a pepper coating.

Boiled and Baked Country Ham

Kentucky

1 country-style ham
6 onions, sliced
2 cups cider vinegar
2 bay leaves
½ cup unsulphured molasses
¾ cup light brown sugar
2 tablespoons dry mustard
1 cup soft bread crumbs
  Whole cloves.

1. Day before, scrub the ham, removing any pepper coating and mold. Place in a large kettle, cover with water and let soak overnight.

2. Next day, drain ham. Put back in the kettle and cover with fresh water. Add the onions, vinegar, bay leaves and molasses; stir to mix. Bring to a boil and simmer gently fifteen to twenty minutes to the pound.

3. Allow ham to cool in the broth.

4. Preheat the oven to 375 degrees.

5. Remove skin from ham and score fat in diamond pattern. Combine the sugar, mustard and bread crumbs. Place cloves in centers of diamonds and pat bread crumb mixture over all. Bake twenty minutes, or until brown.

Yield: About twenty servings.

Southern Maryland Stuffed Ham

1 twelve-pound to fourteen-pound plump, thick country ham with thin layer of fat
3 pounds kale, shredded
3 pounds water cress, tough stems removed, chopped roughly
2 pounds green cabbage, shredded
1 whole stalk pascal celery, chopped
1 hot red pepper, chopped

6 tablespoons salt
2 tablespoons freshly ground black pepper
2 tablespoons red pepper flakes
2 tablespoons mustard seeds
2 tablespoons celery seeds
2 teaspoons Tabasco sauce.

1. If the ham is salty, cover with cold water and soak overnight. Place in a kettle, cover with water, bring to a boil and simmer, covered, twenty minutes. Let ham sit in the hot broth twenty minutes longer, remove the skin and cool.

2. In a large kettle, barely cover the kale, water cress, cabbage, celery and chopped pepper with boiling water and simmer one to two minutes, or until limp. Drain well.

3. Carving is easier if the ham is boned, but this is not essential.

4. Add the remaining ingredients and mix well. Starting at the butt end of the cooled ham, make several deep incisions either crosswise or lengthwise about two to three inches apart.

5. With the fingers, push the greens down into the slits to fill all the holes. Pile remaining greens over the top of the ham. If the ham has been boned, it is necessary to tie it at this point to retain the shape. Boned or unboned, tie in a muslin or fine cloth, securing with pins, to retain the stuffing in position.

6. Lower the ham back into the boiler with the broth in it and simmer, covered, fifteen minutes to the pound, or until tender. Allow to set in the "pot likker" at least two hours. Chill, still in the cloth, before removing and carving.

Yield: About two dozen servings.

Ham Steak and Red Eye Gravy

Virginia

1 center slice about three-eighths-inch thick country ham
  Black coffee (optional)
  Cooked grits
  Fried apples (page 291).

1. If the ham is salty, soak the slice in water for thirty minutes to an hour. Drain and pat dry.

2. Cook the slice in a heavy skillet slowly, until tender, about twenty minutes. Set aside on a warm platter.

3. Add one cup water to the skillet and cook, stirring to loosen all the browned particles and pieces of "red" meat. Boil two minutes. Add tablespoon or two of coffee to darken further if desired.

4. Serve ham with grits, gravy and fried apples.

Yield: Three servings.

Ham Hocks   *Georgia*

4 ham hocks
2 teaspoons salt
3 carrots, quartered
3 onions, sliced
3 potatoes, diced
¼ large head cabbage, cut into four wedges.

1. Place the hocks in a Dutch oven or casserole. Cover with water and add the salt. Bring to a boil and simmer, covered, one and one-half to two hours, or until tender.

2. Add the remaining ingredients and cook, covered, fifteen minutes longer, or until vegetables are tender.

Yield: Four servings.

Ham Croquettes with Egg Sauce
Virginia

¾ plus one-third cups butter
¾ cup flour
3½ cups milk or light cream
    Salt and freshly ground black pepper to taste
2½ cups finely ground cooked country ham
½ teaspoon Worcestershire sauce
½ teaspoon dry mustard
4 eggs, lightly beaten

    Dry bread crumbs
    Fat or oil for deep-frying
½ cup finely chopped onion
1 cup sliced mushrooms
1 green pepper, finely chopped
½ teaspoon sage
¼ teaspoon marjoram
    Light cream
6 hard-cooked eggs, chopped.

1. Melt three-quarters cup of the butter and blend in the flour. Gradually stir in the milk or cream. Season with salt and pepper and bring to a boil, stirring. Cook, stirring, three minutes.

2. Place the ham in a bowl and add Worcestershire, mustard and one and one-half cups of the sauce mixed with two of the lightly beaten eggs. Set remaining sauce over hot water.

3. Mix ham and sauce and set aside to cool. Chill. Shape the cooled mixture into croquettes, dip in remaining eggs and then in the bread crumbs. Repeat if necessary to get good coating.

4. Fry a few croquettes at a time until golden, using a fry basket, in fat or oil heated to 365 degrees. Drain on paper towels.

5. Heat remaining butter in a skillet and sauté the onion in it until tender. Add the mushrooms, green pepper, sage and marjoram and cook until vegetables are tender.

6. Add enough light cream to reserved sauce to make pouring consistency. Stir in cooked vegetables and the chopped eggs. Season to taste with salt and pepper. Serve separately with croquettes.

Yield: Six servings.

Southern Fried Chicken I   *Mississippi*

2 three-and-one-half-pound frying chickens, cut into serving pieces
    Milk to cover
½ teaspoon Tabasco sauce
1 cup flour
    Salt to taste
1 or more teaspoons freshly ground black pepper

2 pounds lard or 4 cups oil and one-half pound butter.

1. Place the chicken pieces in a large mixing bowl and add milk to cover. Add the Tabasco and refrigerate for one hour or so.

2. Combine the flour, salt and pepper in a heavy paper bag or large plastic bag. Shake to blend.

3. Use two large heavy skillets. Heat one pound of lard or half the oil and one-quarter pound of the butter in each skillet.

4. Do not drain the chicken. Take one piece at a time and shake it in the bag until well coated. Place in skillets and cook until golden brown on one side. Turn and cook until brown on the other side. When done, drain on paper towels. Serve hot or cold.

Yield: Four to six servings.

Southern Fried Chicken II   *Tennessee*

1 two-and-one-half-pound to three-pound frying chicken, cut into serving pieces
1 egg
Juice of one lemon
Milk to cover
¾ cup flour
Salt and freshly ground black pepper to taste
Shortening
Gravy
Hot biscuits.

1. Wash the chicken pieces under cold running water. Drain and dry with paper towels.

2. Beat the egg and add the lemon juice. Soak the chicken in milk to cover to which egg mixture has been added at least one-half hour or longer if possible.

3. Place the flour, salt and pepper in a medium-size brown paper bag. Add the chicken pieces, close top of bag and shake so all pieces are coated evenly and well.

4. Place melted shortening one inch deep in a

ten-inch or eleven-inch skillet. Fry the chicken in it until tender, about thirty to forty minutes. Serve with gravy and hot biscuits.

Yield: Four to six servings.

Southern Fried Chicken III   *Alabama*

1 two-and-one-half-pound to three-pound frying chicken, cut into serving pieces, or four medium-size chicken breasts, halved
Salt
1 cup flour
½ teaspoon white pepper
Shortening, lard or oil
Chicken cream gravy (page 219)
Hot biscuits.

1. Wash the chicken pieces under cold running water. Drain, but do not dry. Sprinkle liberally on both sides with salt.

2. Place the flour, pepper and one teaspoon salt in a medium-size brown paper bag. Add chicken, close top of bag and shake so all pieces are coated evenly and well. Remove chicken pieces and shake to remove excess flour.

3. Place melted shortening or lard or oil one-quarter-inch deep in a ten-inch skillet. Place over highest heat for a few minutes until fat is crackling hot. Carefully place chicken pieces in skillet side by side, fleshy side down. Cook rapidly a few minutes, making sure pieces have a firm but very light brown crust on the bottom. Turn each piece as it reaches this stage until all are turned. Continue cooking one minute over high heat. Reduce the heat to quite low and cover skillet. Cook forty minutes.

4. Remove cover and turn heat up once more to highest level. Turn each piece as the bottom becomes golden, but not too brown, and quite crisp. (The top surface of the chicken pieces will have a rather soft, dispirited look when the cover is removed, but a couple minutes turned over will change this to the desired golden crispness.)

5. Remove pieces to drain on paper towels. Serve with chicken cream gravy and hot biscuits.

Yield: Four to six servings.

Chicken Cream Gravy   *Alabama*

Cooking fat from chicken
3 tablespoons flour
Freshly ground black pepper
2 dashes Tabasco
2 cups milk

Pour through a sieve the fat left in the skillet after frying chicken. Return two or three tablespoons of the fat to the skillet, along with the brown particles remaining in the sieve. Turn the heat to high, add the flour and stir, picking up browned bits remaining in the skillet, until flour is medium brown; then turn heat off. Add a generous sprinkle of the pepper and the Tabasco. Pour in the milk all at once, turn heat to medium high and stir constantly until gravy thickens. The consistency should be similar to that of heavy cream.

Yield: Two cups

Batter-Fried Chicken   *West Virginia*

1 two-and-one-half-pound to three-pound frying chicken, cut into serving pieces
1 rib celery
1 carrot
1 bay leaf
1 small onion
  Salt and freshly ground black pepper
  Chicken broth
2 cups flour
2 teaspoons baking powder
2 eggs
1½ cups milk
2 tablespoons melted butter
  Fat or oil for deep-frying.

1. Place the chicken pieces in a skillet. Add the celery, carrot, bay leaf, onion, salt and pepper to taste and enough broth to cover barely.

2. Bring to a boil and simmer gently fifteen minutes. Drain and dry pieces of chicken and let cool.

3. Combine the flour, baking powder and one-half teaspoon salt in a bowl. Beat the eggs with the milk and stir into dry ingredients along with the butter.

4. Dip the chicken pieces in the batter and, using a fry basket, drop into the fat or oil heated to 375 degrees. Fry until golden and drain on paper towels.

Yield: Four servings.

Chicken with Corn Bread Stuffing

Arkansas

Corn bread (next recipe)
⅔ cup coarsely chopped celery
⅔ cup coarsely chopped onion
⅔ cup coarsely chopped green pepper
10 tablespoons butter
2 slices toast, coarsely chopped
⅓ cup finely chopped parsley
2 raw eggs
3 or more cups chicken broth
2 hard-cooked eggs, coarsely chopped
  Salt and freshly ground black pepper to taste
1 four-pound roasting chicken, cleaned and ready to stuff
  Chicken giblets
3 tablespoons flour.

1. Preheat the oven to 400 degrees.

2. Crumble the corn bread into a mixing bowl. Cook the celery, onion and green pepper in three tablespoons of the butter just until vegetables are crisp-tender. Add to the corn bread. Add the toast, parsley, raw eggs and enough broth to make a moist dressing. Reserve remaining broth.

3. Add the chopped eggs, salt and pepper. Melt three tablespoons of the remaining butter and add to stuffing. Stir briefly. Use just enough

filling to stuff the chicken. Spoon remaining filling into a generously buttered skillet and set aside.

4. Melt one tablespoon of the remaining butter in a skillet large enough to hold the chicken. Add the chicken and turn it around in the butter on top of the stove.

5. Place the chicken on one side and roast, uncovered, basting occasionally, about twenty minutes. Turn the chicken to the other side and continue roasting, basting, about twenty minutes longer. Turn the chicken on its back and roast, basting, twenty minutes longer.

6. Place the skillet with additional filling in the oven for the last half hour of roasting. Bake just until bubbling and golden.

7. Meanwhile, place the remaining broth in a saucepan and add the neck, gizzard and heart. Simmer about thirty minutes. Add the liver and continue cooking about ten minutes. To prepare giblet gravy, discard the neck and chop the liver, heart and gizzard. Blend the remaining butter with the flour and stir, bit by bit, into simmering broth. Serve gravy separately with chicken and stuffing.

Yield: Four to six servings.

Corn Bread   *Arkansas*

1 cup yellow corn meal
1 cup flour
1 teaspoon sugar
½ teaspoon salt
4 teaspoons baking powder
1 egg
1 cup milk
¼ cup melted lard or shortening.

1. Preheat the oven to 425 degrees.
2. Sift the corn meal, flour, sugar, salt and baking powder into a mixing bowl. Add the egg, milk and lard or shortening and stir with a wooden spoon until blended. Do not overbeat.
3. Grease an eight-inch square pan or iron skillet. Heat on top of the stove and pour in the batter. Place in the oven and bake twenty to twenty-five minutes.

Yield: Eight to ten servings.

Chicken 'n' Dumplings   *Alabama*

1 five-pound to six-pound hen or capon
2 ribs celery with leaves
1 large carrot, cut in half
1 large onion, studded with two whole cloves
12 peppercorns
Salt
2 cups self-rising flour
1½ tablespoons shortening
1 cup milk.

1. Place the hen or capon in a kettle and add the celery, carrot and onion. Add water to cover and peppercorns. Do not salt. Bring to a boil and cook until chicken is tender, four to five hours. Remove the chicken and, when it is cool enough to handle, remove the meat from the bones.
2. Strain the cooking liquid and return it to the heat. Salt lightly. Cook the broth down until it is rich-flavored.
3. Meanwhile, place the flour in a mixing bowl and cut in the shortening, using a pastry blender or two knives. Stir in the milk, adding just enough so that the dough can be handled. Roll out the dough on a lightly floured board to one-quarter-inch thickness and with a sharp knife cut into one-inch circles
4. Return the chicken to the kettle, return to a boil and drop in the dumplings a few at a time. Cook, covered, about ten minutes, stirring once, and serve immediately.

Yield: Ten to one dozen servings.

Chicken Olivette   *Arkansas*

1 five-pound fowl or two large broiler-fryers, cut into serving pieces
½ cup olive oil
6 cups water or chicken broth

Salt and freshly ground black pepper to
taste
1 onion, chopped
2 cups chopped celery
1 medium-size green pepper, diced
2 cups uncooked rice
½ cup chopped pimentos
1 cup sliced stuffed olives
1 pound shredded sharp Cheddar cheese.

1. Brown the fowl or broiler pieces in the oil
in a heavy Dutch oven or casserole. Add the
water or broth, salt and black pepper. Cover,
bring to a boil and simmer until the meat is tender, about thirty minutes for broilers and one
hour for fowl.

2. Strain the cooking broth and reserve. Take
the meat off the bones and cut into large pieces.
Discard the skin.

3. Place two or three tablespoons of the
chicken fat from the top of the reserved broth in
a skillet. Add the onion, celery and green pepper
and sauté until barely tender.

4. Measure the reserved broth and make up to
four and one-half to five cups with water and add
to the skillet with the chicken pieces and the rice.
Cover and cook until rice is tender, about twenty-
five minutes.

5. Add the remaining ingredients and stir until
the cheese melts. Check the seasoning.

Yield: Six servings.

Chicken Pudding   *Virginia*

 2 three-pound chickens
12 peppercorns
 3 celery tops
½ onion
 3 sprigs parsley
½ teaspoon thyme
   Boiling chicken broth or cold water
   Salt to taste
 5 eggs
 2 cups milk
 2 cups plus six tablespoons flour

 4 tablespoons melted butter
 4 tablespoons cold butter
   Freshly ground black pepper to taste
 2 tablespoons chopped parsley.

1. Place the chickens in a kettle and add the
peppercorns, celery, onion, parsley sprigs and
thyme. Add boiling broth or cold water to cover
and bring to a boil. Add salt. (If broth is used, use
salt sparingly because the liquid will be reduced.)
Simmer until chickens are tender, at least forty
minutes.

2. Remove the chickens from the broth and let
cool slightly. When cool enough to handle, remove the best pieces of white and dark meat and
set aside. Return the skin and bones to the kettle
and continue simmering until broth is reduced by
almost half. Strain.

3. Preheat the oven to 450 degrees.

4. Butter a ten-inch heavy iron skillet or similar utensil and add one-quarter cup of the simmering broth. Add the reserved chicken meat and
cover with aluminum foil. Place in the oven and
heat about ten minutes.

5. Meanwhile, beat the eggs lightly and add
the milk. Gradually beat in two cups of the flour,
salt to taste and the melted butter. Pour the mixture over the chicken and bake until the pudding
is set and brown, forty-five minutes to one hour.

6. While the pudding cooks, prepare a sauce.
Melt the cold butter and stir in the remaining
flour with a wire whisk. When blended, add three
cups of the strained broth, stirring vigorously
with the whisk. When thickened and smooth,
simmer ten minutes. Add pepper and chopped
parsley. Serve the pudding with the sauce.

Yield: Six to eight servings.

Mom's Arkansas Chicken Pie

1 five-pound to six-pound fowl or two
  broiler-fryers, cut into serving pieces
1 rib celery, diced
1 carrot, diced
1 onion, sliced

1 bay leaf
Salt and freshly ground black pepper to taste
6 cups water or chicken broth
½ cup chicken fat or butter
½ cup flour.
Crust:
3 cups flour
1 teaspoon salt
4 teaspoons baking powder
½ teaspoon baking soda
1½ cups soured heavy cream, made by leaving at room temperature until it thickens, by adding one and one-half tablespoons white vinegar or by adding two tablespoons buttermilk and leaving at room temperature twenty-four hours, or until it thickens
2 eggs, beaten
Light cream.

1. Place the fowl or broilers in a deep Dutch oven or heavy casserole and add the celery, carrot, onion, bay leaf, salt, pepper and water or broth. Bring to a boil, cover and simmer until tender, about one hour for fowl and thirty-five minutes for chickens.

2. Remove chicken pieces and take meat off the bones. Discard the skin. Strain the cooking liquid and measure four and one-half cups, adding milk if necessary.

3. Preheat the oven to 350 degrees.

4. Melt the chicken fat or butter and blend in the flour. Gradually stir in the broth and bring to a boil, stirring. Season with salt and pepper. Add chicken pieces and pour into a shallow baking pan about 12-by-8-by-3 inches.

5. To make crust, sift the dry ingredients together. Combine the heavy cream and eggs and stir into the dry ingredients. Spoon the mixture over the chicken in the baking dish and even out with a spatula. Brush with light cream and bake thirty-five minutes, or until done and browned.

Yield: Six to eight servings.

Stuffed Chicken Breasts   *Tennessee*

10 large whole chicken breasts, boned and halved
Salt and freshly ground black pepper
1 pound mushrooms
Juice of two lemons
8 tablespoons butter
¼ cup chopped fresh chives
Paprika
1½ cups boiling fresh or canned (twelve ounces) chicken broth
2 tablespoons arrowroot or cornstarch
½ cup water
15 canned or bottled crab apples
Parsley for garnish.

1. Preheat the oven to 450 degrees.

2. Split each half breast partly through the center to make a pocket. Sprinkle the cavity with a little salt and pepper.

3. Slice the mushrooms and immediately sprinkle with lemon juice to prevent discoloration. Add half the butter to a small skillet and cook mushrooms in it until they are wilted. Add about one tablespoon of the mushrooms to each of the chicken cavities. If there are any remaining mushrooms, reserve them.

4. Arrange the chicken breasts, skin side up, in a large buttered baking dish and sprinkle with salt, pepper and chives. Sprinkle lightly with paprika and dot with the remaining butter. Cover closely with heavy-duty aluminum foil and bake twenty-five minutes. Uncover and add the boiling broth. Continue cooking.

5. Combine the arrowroot or cornstarch with the water and stir it into the baking dish. If there are any remaining mushrooms, add them. Baste the chicken until it is nicely glazed. Place the crab apples in the center of a large platter and arrange the chicken breasts around them. Garnish the platter with parsley and serve hot.

Yield: Ten to fifteen servings.

Chicken Crab Bake   *Maryland*

¾ cup butter
1 two-and-one-half-pound broiler-fryer, cut into small serving pieces
   Salt and freshly ground black pepper to taste
½ cup finely chopped onion
1 cup uncooked rice
1½ cups chicken broth
1 cup clam juice
⅛ teaspoon saffron
2 tablespoons chopped parsley
½ cup minced clams
½ pound back fin crab meat, picked over to remove bits of shell and cartilage
1 dozen small clams in the shell
1 ten-ounce package frozen artichoke hearts, cooked
1 cup fresh peas, cooked, or frozen peas, thawed.

1. Heat one-half cup of the butter in a large ovenproof skillet or shallow casserole. Season the chicken with salt and pepper and sauté in the butter until brown on all sides. Set chicken aside.

2. Add remaining butter to skillet and sauté the onion in it until tender. Add the rice and cook five minutes longer.

3. Stir in the broth, clam juice, saffron, parsley and chicken pieces. Cover and cook about thirty minutes, or until rice and chicken are cooked. Stir occasionally.

4. Preheat the oven to 350 degrees.

5. Fold in the minced clams and crab meat. Season to taste with salt and pepper.

6. Arrange the clams in the shell, artichoke hearts and peas over the top and bake, uncovered, for ten minutes, or until clams open.
Yield: Six to eight servings.

Barbecued Chicken   *South Carolina*

1 two-and-one-half-pound to three-pound frying chicken, cut into serving pieces

2 onions, sliced
¾ cup catchup
¾ cup water
3 tablespoons cider vinegar
2 tablespoons Worcestershire sauce
1 teaspoon paprika
   Salt and freshly ground black pepper to taste
1 teaspoon chili powder.

1. Preheat the oven to 350 degrees.

2. Place the chicken pieces in a casserole. Mix together the remaining ingredients and pour over chicken.

3. Bake, uncovered, one and one-half hours.
Yield: Four servings.

Seven Hearths Chicken   *North Carolina*

3 whole chicken breasts, halved
4 chicken thighs
2 chicken legs
   Salt and freshly ground black pepper to taste
10 tablespoons butter
2 tablespoons oil
6 tablespoons flour
2 cups rich chicken broth
¼ teaspoon thyme
½ cup heavy cream
½ pound mushrooms
¼ cup Madeira wine.

1. Preheat the oven to 350 degrees.

2. Sprinkle the chicken pieces with salt and pepper. Heat two tablespoons of the butter and the oil in a large skillet and brown chicken on all sides. Transfer to a heavy two-quart casserole. Wipe out skillet and set aside for future use.

3. Heat six tablespoons of the butter in a saucepan and stir in the flour. When blended, add the broth, stirring rapidly. When mixture is thickened and smooth, add the thyme and simmer ten minutes, stirring frequently. Stir in the cream.

4. Add the remaining butter to skillet in which chicken cooked. Chop the mushrooms and add them to skillet. Cook until mushrooms give up their moisture and most of it evaporates.

5. Stir in cream sauce to dissolve brown particles that cling to bottom and sides of skillet. Add the Madeira and pour over chicken. Cover and bake thirty-five minutes, or until chicken is thoroughly tender.

Yield: Six servings.

Poulet Floride *Florida*

¼ cup catchup
¼ cup cider vinegar
2 tablespoons Worcestershire sauce
2 tablespoons butter
2 tablespoons light brown sugar
1 clove garlic, crushed
1 teaspoon salt
1 teaspoon dry mustard
1 teaspoon chili powder
¼ teaspoon cayenne pepper
  Few dashes Tabasco sauce
2 medium-size onions, sliced
1 three-pound chicken, cut into serving pieces.

1. Mix all the ingredients except the sliced onion and chicken in a large saucepan. Bring to a boil and let cool.

2. Preheat the oven to 375 degrees.

3. Add the sliced onion and chicken to the sauce.

4. Cut four pieces of heavy-duty aluminum foil 14 by 18 inches. Butter one side of each. Divide the chicken, onion and sauce evenly on the buttered foil. Fold foil in half and close by folding open edges triply. Place packages on a baking sheet and bake one hour. Serve in the foil.

Yield: Four servings.

Pressed Chicken *South Carolina*

1 envelope unflavored gelatin
2 tablespoons cold water
½ cup boiling chicken broth
2 cups cut-up or diced cooked chicken
2 cups diced celery
2 teaspoons salt
¼ teaspoon freshly ground black pepper
2 tablespoons lemon juice
1 teaspoon finely grated onion
½ cup blanched almonds, split
½ cup heavy cream, whipped
¼ cup mayonnaise
½ green pepper, finely chopped
6 hard-cooked eggs, chopped or left whole
  Salad greens.

1. Soak the gelatin in the water. Add the broth and stir to dissolve the gelatin.

2. In a bowl mix together the chicken, celery, salt, black pepper, lemon juice, onion and almonds. Fold in the cream, mayonnaise, green pepper and dissolved gelatin.

3. If the eggs are chopped, fold them into mixture. Pack mixture into a lightly oiled mold or loaf pan. If the eggs are left whole, pack half the mixture into mold or pan, arrange eggs lengthwise on top and pack in remaining mixture.

4. Chill several hours. Unmold on a bed of greens.

Yield: Four servings.

Chicken Loaf *Arkansas*

1 cup soft bread crumbs
1½ cups warm milk
2 eggs, lightly beaten
3 cups diced cooked chicken
½ cup chicken broth
1 teaspoon salt
¼ teaspoon freshly ground black pepper
½ teaspoon celery seeds
  Tabasco sauce to taste
  Mushroom sauce.

1. Preheat the oven to 325 degrees.

2. Place the bread crumbs in a bowl and pour the milk over. Let stand five minutes.

3. Stir in the eggs. Combine the chicken and broth and add to crumb mixture. Season with the salt, pepper, celery seeds and Tabasco.

4. Pack into a greased loaf pan and bake forty-five to sixty minutes, or until set. Serve with mushroom sauce.

Yield: Four to six servings.

For a description of gumbo see page 205.

Chicken Gumbo   *Louisiana*

1 five-pound stewing chicken, cut into pieces
¼ cup lard or bacon drippings
4 cups boiling chicken broth or water
  Salt to taste
4 ears corn
3 ripe tomatoes or two cups canned tomatoes
½ pound okra, trimmed and sliced lengthwise or crosswise
5 cups water
¾ cup finely chopped onion
¾ cup finely chopped celery
½ cup finely chopped green pepper
¼ cup butter or chicken fat
½ teaspoon or more red pepper flakes or Tabasco sauce to taste
½ cup uncooked rice
1 teaspoon or more Worcestershire sauce (optional)
1 to two teaspoons filé powder (optional).

1. Brown the chicken pieces in the lard or bacon drippings and transfer the pieces to a casserole. Add the broth or water and salt and simmer, partly covered, until the meat is easily removed from the bones, one and one-half hours or longer. Drain and reserve the cooking liquid. Remove the meat from the bones and shred it. Add the meat to the cooking liquid and set aside.

2. Scrape the corn from the cobs into another saucepan. Add the tomatoes, okra and water and bring to a boil.

3. Meanwhile, cook the onion, celery and green pepper in the butter or chicken fat until vegetables are wilted. Add them to the tomato mixture. Add the pepper flakes or Tabasco and rice and return to a boil. Continue cooking until rice is tender.

4. Add the reserved meat and broth and return to a boil. Taste for seasoning and add more salt and red pepper if desired. Add the Worcestershire if desired. Moisten the filé powder with water if desired and add. Do not boil gumbo. Serve immediately.

Yield: Six or more servings.

Chicken Wings, Gumbo-Style   *Louisiana*

¼ pound salt pork
3 pounds chicken wings
2 cups finely chopped onions
2 large cloves garlic, finely minced
2 cups chopped green pepper
1½ cups chopped celery
1 pound ground pork
1 pound ground round steak
5 cups fresh peeled or canned tomatoes
1½ cups fresh or canned chicken broth
  Salt and freshly ground black pepper to taste
¾ cup fresh or frozen lima beans
1 cup corn kernels, scraped from the cob
  Worcestershire sauce to taste
  Tabasco sauce to taste
  Cooked rice.

1. Cut the salt pork into small cubes or thin slices. In a large casserole, cook the salt pork, stirring occasionally, about five minutes, or until golden. Remove and reserve the salt pork, but leave the fat in the casserole.

2. Add the chicken wings and cook until golden brown on all sides. Remove and reserve the chicken wings.

3. Add the onions, garlic, green pepper and celery and cook, stirring, until onions are wilted.

4. Add the ground pork and round steak and cook, stirring to break up the meat. Cook until meat loses color. Add the chicken wings and salt pork. Add the tomatoes, broth, salt and pepper. Simmer, stirring occasionally, thirty minutes.

5. Add the lima beans and continue cooking thirty minutes. Add the remaining ingredients and cook fifteen minutes longer. Serve in soup bowls with rice on the side. Sprinkle with pork bits.

Yield: Eight or more servings.

Chicken Jambalaya   *Louisiana*

1 four-and-one-half-pound to five-pound chicken, cut into serving pieces
3 tablespoons peanut oil or vegetable oil
1 carrot, sliced
1 onion, studded with one whole clove
1 cup diced celery
2 sprigs parsley
1 bay leaf
1 clove garlic
 Salt to taste
16 peppercorns
1½ cups uncooked rice.

1. Brown the chicken pieces lightly in the oil in a Dutch oven or heavy casserole. Add the carrot, onion, celery, parsley, bay leaf, garlic, salt, peppercorns and cold water to cover. Bring to a boil and simmer until chicken is fork-tender.

2. Remove the chicken from the broth and strain the broth. When the chicken is cool enough to handle, remove the skin and bones. Leave the chicken in large pieces and return it to the broth. Add the rice, bring the dish to a boil and simmer until rice is tender, twenty minutes or longer.

Yield: Six servings.

Chicken Creole   *Louisiana*

1 three-pound chicken, cut into serving pieces
 Salt and freshly ground black pepper to taste
3 tablespoons butter
1 onion, thinly sliced
1 tablespoon flour
1 cup chopped green pepper
1 clove garlic, finely minced
1 cup chopped fresh or canned tomatoes
2 sprigs fresh thyme or one-half teaspoon dried thyme
2 sprigs parsley
1 bay leaf
1 cup boiling chicken broth
 Cooked rice.

1. Season the chicken with salt and pepper and brown on all sides in the butter. Remove the chicken and add the onion. Cook, stirring, until golden brown. Add the flour and cook, stirring, until flour is lightly browned. Add the green pepper and garlic, cook briefly and add the tomatoes, thyme, parsley and bay leaf. Bring to a boil. Return the chicken to the skillet. Cover closely and simmer twenty minutes longer.

2. Add the boiling broth, stir all around until blended, cover and continue cooking ten to fifteen minutes, or until chicken is tender. Serve with rice.

Yield: Four servings.

Chicken Spaghetti   *Mississippi*

2 three-pound chickens
2 whole ribs celery
1 carrot, cut into rounds
2 sprigs parsley
1 onion, studded with two whole cloves
 Salt to taste
12 peppercorns
8 tablespoons butter
2 green peppers, cored, seeded and chopped
1 large onion, finely chopped
2 ribs celery, finely chopped

½ pound mushrooms, sliced
5 tablespoons flour
1 cup heavy cream
2 cups tomato sauce (recipe below)
2 pounds spaghetti (see note)
2 cups freshly grated sharp Cheddar cheese
French bread
Freshly grated Parmesan cheese.

1. Place the chickens in a heavy kettle and add the whole celery ribs, carrot, parsley and onion studded with cloves. Add water to cover, salt and peppercorns. Bring the mixture to a boil and simmer until chickens are tender, about forty-five minutes to one hour. Remove the chickens from the broth and, when they are cool enough to handle, remove the meat from the bones. Discard bones and skin and reserve the meat, keeping it covered. Meanwhile, continue cooking the chicken broth until it is reduced and has more body.

2. Melt half the butter in a skillet and cook the peppers, chopped onion and chopped celery in it until vegetables are nearly tender. Add the mushrooms and cook, stirring, until mushrooms give up their juices. Continue cooking until most of the liquid is evaporated and the vegetables are tender. Reserve until ready to use.

3. Melt the remaining butter in a saucepan and add the flour, stirring it with a wire whisk. When blended, add two cups of the hot chicken broth and cook, stirring vigorously with the whisk, until the mixture is thickened and smooth. Continue cooking, stirring occasionally, five to fifteen minutes. Add the cream, blend well and return to a boil. Add the tomato sauce. Combine the sauce, chicken and mushroom mixture. The sauce should have a medium thickness. To thin it, add a little broth.

4. Cook the spaghetti according to package directions until it is nearly but not thoroughly done. (The spaghetti will cook slightly when it is reheated in the sauce.) Drain the spaghetti.

5. Use a roasting pan or other large cooking utensil and pour in a layer of sauce and a layer of spaghetti. Sprinkle with the Cheddar cheese.

Continue making layers until all the sauce, spaghetti and Cheddar cheese are used, ending with a layer of cheese. This dish may be made in advance to this point.

6. If spaghetti is allowed to stand, it will absorb much of the sauce and it may be necessary to add more chicken broth. The spaghetti should be amply steeped in sauce, but not runny.

7. When ready to serve, preheat the oven to 350 degrees.

8. Place the pan in the oven and heat spaghetti and sauce until hot and bubbling, but do not overcook. Serve on hot plates with loaves of French bread and grated Parmesan cheese.

Yield: One dozen to fifteen servings.

Note: Spaghettini may be substituted for the spaghetti.

Leftover chicken broth can be reserved for another purpose.

Tomato Sauce   *Mississippi*

3 medium-size tomatoes (about one and one-half pounds)
3 tablespoons butter
1½ cups coarsely chopped onions
½ clove garlic, finely chopped
½ teaspoon thyme
1 bay leaf
Salt and freshly ground black pepper to taste.

1. Peel the tomatoes. To facilitate peeling, pierce the stem end of the tomatoes with a two-pronged fork and dip them briefly into rapidly boiling water. Peel with a paring knife. Pare away and discard the core. Chop the tomatoes in a mixing bowl.

2. Melt the butter in a saucepan and cook the onions and garlic in it until wilted. Add the chopped tomatoes and the seasonings. Simmer fifteen minutes, stirring occasionally.

3. Pour the contents of the saucepan into a colander to drain. Reserve the tomatoes and reserve the liquid that flows from the tomatoes.

When well drained, return the liquid to the saucepan and cook over high heat until reduced by half. Add the cooked tomatoes to the reduced liquid and bring to a boil. Simmer five minutes.

Yield: About two cups.

Note: This sauce may be stored for several days in the refrigerator or may be frozen.

Cajun Jambalaya   *Louisiana*

1 three-pound frying chicken, cut into serving pieces
  Salt and freshly ground black pepper
2 tablespoons bacon drippings or shortening
2 tablespoons flour
1 pound smoked sausage or smoked country ham, diced
2 onions, chopped
1 green pepper, diced
3 cups peeled and diced tomatoes
1 clove garlic, finely chopped
2 cups shelled and deveined shrimp (about one and one-quarter pounds)
3 cups water
½ teaspoon thyme
½ teaspoon Tabasco sauce, or to taste
2 cups uncooked rice
¼ cup chopped parsley
⅓ cup finely chopped scallions, including green part.

1. Season the chicken with salt and pepper and brown on all sides in the drippings or shortening in a heavy skillet. Remove chicken.

2. Sprinkle the flour over fat remaining in the skillet and cook, stirring, until roux turns light brown. Do not allow to burn.

3. Add the sausage or ham, the chicken, onions, green pepper, tomatoes, garlic and shrimp and cook, stirring, about ten minutes.

4. Add the water, one and one-half teaspoons salt, the thyme, Tabasco, one-half teaspoon pepper and the rice. Bring to a boil and then cover and let simmer about thirty minutes, or until the

rice is tender. Stir in the parsley and scallions. Cook five minutes longer.

Yield: Eight servings.

Chicken Bog   *South Carolina*

1 five-pound to six-pound hen, cut into small serving pieces
  Chicken broth
4 cups uncooked rice
2 tablespoons salt
2 teaspoons freshly ground black pepper
½ cup butter.

1. Place the hen pieces in a deep casserole and add water to cover. Bring to a boil, cover and simmer until tender, about one hour.

2. Reserve the chicken and measure the broth in the casserole. Add enough broth to make eight cups.

3. Bring to a boil and add the rice, salt, pepper and butter. Cook, covered, very slowly until rice is tender, about forty-five to sixty minutes, stirring twice during cooking.

4. Add reserved chicken and reheat.

Yield: One dozen to fourteen servings.

Brunswick Stew   *North Carolina*

1 three-pound chicken, cut into serving pieces
8 cups fresh or canned chicken broth (or use half chicken broth and half water)
  Salt and freshly ground black pepper to taste
¼ cup diced uncooked bacon
1 cup chopped onions
2 cups peeled ripe tomatoes or one one-pound-three-ounce can tomatoes, drained
2 cups peeled, diced raw potatoes
2 cups fresh baby lima beans or one ten-ounce package frozen
2 cups corn kernels, cut from the cob (about eight ears)

1 tablespoon Worcestershire sauce, or to taste
2 tablespoons butter.

1. Place the chicken in a kettle and add the broth. Bring to a boil and add salt and pepper. Simmer until chicken is tender, about one hour, skimming surface frequently to remove fat and foam. Remove chicken from kettle, but let stock continue to boil to reduce slightly.

2. When chicken pieces are cool enough to handle, remove meat from bones. Discard bones and skin.

3. Return meat to kettle and add the bacon, onions, tomatoes, potatoes and lima beans. Simmer one hour, skimming surface as necessary to remove all fat. Stir frequently so stew does not stick.

4. Add the corn and cook ten minutes longer. When done, stew should be a thickened mass. Stir in the Worcestershire and butter. Serve piping hot.

Yield: Six to eight servings.

Deep-Fried Frogs' Legs   *Louisiana*

12 pairs large frogs' legs
   Milk to cover
   Fat for deep-frying
   Flour for dredging
   Salt and freshly ground black pepper to
   taste
   Lemon wedges
   Tartar sauce (page 302).

1. Soak the frogs' legs in the milk one hour or so.

2. Heat the fat for deep-frying (about 375 degrees).

3. Drain the frogs' legs, but do not dry. Dredge them in flour seasoned with salt and pepper and drop them, one pair at a time, into the hot fat. Cook until golden brown, turning once. Drain on paper towels and serve with lemon wedges and tartar sauce.

Yield: Four to six servings.

Braised Frogs' Legs with Sherry

Tennessee

18 pairs frogs' legs
   Salt and freshly ground black pepper
   Flour for dredging
 8 tablespoons butter
 2 tablespoons shortening
1¼ cups beef broth
 ¼ cup dry sherry
 1 tablespoon chopped fresh parsley.

1. Preheat the oven to 400 degrees.

2. Place the frogs' legs in a mixing bowl and add cold water. Drain well and sprinkle with salt and pepper.

3. Dredge the frogs' legs, one pair at a time, in flour.

4. Heat the butter and shortening in a heavy iron skillet and, when skillet is very hot, add the frogs' legs. Cook until golden brown on one side. Turn and cook until golden brown on the other. Transfer the frogs' legs to a baking dish and add the broth and sherry to the fat remaining in the skillet. Bring to a boil, stirring with a wooden spoon. Pour this over the frogs' legs and bake twenty minutes. Sprinkle with the parsley and serve.

Yield: Six servings.

Spit-Roasted Saddle of Venison

Tennessee

½ cup wine vinegar
 2 carrots, coarsely chopped
 1 onion, chopped
 3 sprigs parsley
 1 clove garlic, crushed
10 juniper berries
 1 sprig fresh rosemary
 1 teaspoon crushed sage
 1 five-pound to six-pound saddle of young
   venison
 1 bottle dry red wine

Salt and freshly ground black pepper to taste
Cranberry and horseradish sauce (page 304).

1. Day before, combine the vinegar, carrots, onion, parsley, garlic, juniper berries, rosemary and sage. Bring just to a boil and pour the mixture over the venison. Add the wine, salt and pepper and let stand overnight.

2. Next day, drain the venison and wipe it dry, reserving marinade. Sprinkle venison with salt and pepper. Place on a spit and roast, basting with the marinade, until dark brown on the surface and rare within. This will require about thirty minutes to one hour, depending on size of venison and proximity to the heat. Serve with cranberry and horseradish sauce.

Yield: Ten to one dozen servings.

Pressed Duck   *Tennessee*

6 wild ducks
¾ cup olive oil
1 large onion, coarsely chopped
3 tablespoons dry red wine, preferably a Burgundy or Bordeaux
3 tablespoons cognac
4 tablespoons sweet butter, melted
¼ teaspoon cayenne pepper
1½ teaspoons freshly grated horseradish
3 tablespoons Cointreau or other orange-flavored liqueur
12 slices bacon
Cooked wild rice.

1. With a sharp knife, carefully trim away the fleshy meat from either side of the breast of each duck. From six ducks this will yield twelve portions. Leave the skin on each portion. Place the meat in a mixing bowl and add the oil and onion. Let stand at least two hours.

2. Chop up the carcasses of the ducks with a cleaver and warm the carcasses in a skillet, stirring frequently. Place the carcasses in a duck press and press to extract as much liquid as possi-

ble from the meat and bones. This should yield a scant cup. Bring the extracted liquid to a boil.

3. To the duck juice add the wine, cognac, butter, cayenne, horseradish and Cointreau. Simmer five minutes.

4. Prepare a charcoal fire.

5. Remove the duck breasts from the oil and onion and wrap each portion in a slice of bacon. Skewer with toothpicks. Place the breasts, thus prepared, on the grill six inches away from the heat. For rare duck, cook four minutes on each side; for medium, seven minutes on each side; for well done, ten minutes on each side. Serve with wild rice and the duck sauce.

Yield: Six servings.

Wild Ducks with Madeira   *Louisiana*

4 wild ducks
Olive oil or melted butter
Salt and freshly ground black pepper
4 apples, peeled, cored and cut into eighths
4 onions, cut into eighths
1 cup chopped celery
4 slices bacon, cut in half
2 tablespoons A.1. Sauce or Piquet's Wild Game Sauce, if available
4 slices orange
4 slices lemon
2 ribs celery with leaves, quartered
½ cup Madeira wine
2 tablespoons flour
Cooked wild rice
Spiced red apples.

1. Preheat the oven to 275 degrees.

2. Clean the ducks well and rub them with the oil or butter. Sprinkle inside and outside with salt and pepper. Stuff the cavities with equal quantities of the apples, onions and chopped celery. Truss the ducks and place them side by side, breast up, in a roasting pan just large enough to hold them.

3. Arrange two pieces of the bacon on each breast and add water to the pan. There should be

only about one-half inch of water around the ducks. Stir in the A.1. or Piquet Sauce and arrange the orange and lemon slices and the celery ribs around the ducks. Bake about three hours, basting occasionally, or until birds are tender.

4. Thirty minutes before ducks are done, remove the bacon strips and add the Madeira. Baste frequently.

5. When done, remove ducks to a serving platter and strain the juices. Blend the flour with about two tablespoons of the juices to make a paste. Stir this into the sauce, using a wire whisk, until sauce boils up and is thickened. Season to taste with salt and pepper and serve wild rice and spiced red apples with the ducks.

Yield: About eight servings.

Wild Duck Country Captain   *Alabama*

½ cup flour
  Salt and freshly ground black pepper to taste
1 two-and-one-half-pound wild duck or two smaller birds, cut into serving pieces
4 tablespoons butter
⅓ cup chopped onion
⅓ cup finely chopped green pepper
1 clove garlic, finely minced
1½ teaspoons curry powder
½ teaspoon dried thyme
2 cups Italian plum tomatoes
3 teaspoons dried currants
¼ cup toasted almonds
  Buttered rice
  Chopped parsley.

1. Combine the flour, salt and pepper and coat the duck pieces with the mixture.
2. Heat the butter in a large skillet and brown the duck pieces in it. Remove duck pieces and reserve.
3. Add the onion, green pepper, garlic, curry powder and thyme to the skillet and cook, stirring, until onion is golden brown. Add the tomatoes and duck pieces. Cover and cook forty minutes, or until duck is tender. Stir in the currants and almonds and serve with buttered rice tossed with chopped parsley.

Yield: Two to four servings.

Fresh Quail with Grits and Gravy
South Carolina

6 quail, skinned and split down the back
  Salted water
  Freshly ground black pepper
  Flour
  Fat or oil for frying
2½ cups water
  Salt
  Cooked grits.

1. Wash the quail in water and clean thoroughly. Soak in salted water to cover for three hours.
2. Drain quail and pat dry. Sprinkle with pepper, coat with flour and fry in one-half-inch depth of fat or oil heated in a heavy skillet.
3. Cook about twenty to thirty minutes, turning continuously, until birds have golden crust and are cooked through. Keep warm while making gravy.
4. Pour off all but two tablespoons of the fat from the skillet. Sprinkle fat in skillet with four tablespoons flour. Cook, stirring, one minute. Gradually stir in the two and one-half cups water. Bring to a boil, stirring. Season to taste with salt and pepper and serve over grits.

Yield: Six servings.

Braised Quail   *Georgia*

18 quail
  Flour
  Salt and freshly ground black pepper
12 tablespoons butter
2 scallions, including green part, chopped
½ green pepper, seeded and chopped
2 cloves garlic, finely minced

4 cups chicken broth
¼ cup dry red wine
   White toast.

1. Preheat the oven to 350 degrees.
2. Coat the quail with a mixture of flour, salt and pepper.
3. Melt the butter in a large Dutch oven and brown four or five quail in it at a time. When all are golden brown, transfer to a roasting pan.
4. Add four tablespoons flour to the Dutch oven. Brown the flour over moderate heat, stirring constantly, but do not let the flour burn or it will have a bitter taste.
5. Add the scallions, green pepper and garlic and cook briefly, stirring. Add the broth, stirring rapidly, and the wine.
6. When the mixture is bubbling and well blended, pour it over the quail. Cover and bake twenty minutes. Reduce the oven heat to 325 degrees and cook until quail are thoroughly tender, one and one-half to two hours. Serve the quail on toast with the sauce separately.
Yield: Nine to eighteen servings.

Halidon Hill Potted Doves

South Carolina

6 doves
4 slices bacon
¼ cup finely minced onion
6 slices toasted day-old white bread
   Salt and freshly ground black pepper
1 cup hot chicken broth or water, approximately
   Flour for dredging
2½ tablespoons peanut oil, lard or butter.

1. Wipe the birds inside and outside with a damp cloth.
2. Cook the bacon in a skillet until crisp. Drain and crumble. Set aside.
3. Pour off all but one tablespoon of fat from the skillet and cook the onion in it, stirring, until onion is wilted. Crumble the toast and add it.

Add salt and pepper to taste, the bacon and three-quarters cup of the broth or water. Use the mixture to stuff the birds.
4. Sprinkle the birds with salt and pepper and dredge in flour.
5. Heat the oil, lard or butter and brown the birds in it on all sides. The birds should be quite brown. Add the remaining broth to the skillet, cover closely and cook over low heat until tender, about twenty minutes or longer.
Yield: Three to six servings.

Doves Pontchartrain

Louisiana

12 dressed doves
   Salt and freshly ground black pepper
12 slices bacon
   Boiling chicken broth or water
   Worcestershire sauce to taste
1 lemon, seeded and finely chopped
4 slices toast
   Chopped parsley.

1. If desired, remove the legs and wings from the doves. Sprinkle the doves with salt and pepper and wrap each dove in a slice of bacon. Secure bacon with toothpicks.
2. Brown the bacon-wrapped doves on all sides in a kettle or casserole. When browned, pour off most of the fat. Add the boiling broth or water to a depth of one-half inch. Add Worcestershire and the lemon. Cover and simmer gently forty-five minutes.
3. Taste the sauce for seasoning. Arrange the ducks, three to a person, on the toast and sprinkle with parsley. Strain the sauce and serve it separately.
Yield: Four servings.

Frogs' Legs Omelet

Louisiana

12 pairs frogs' legs
2 tablespoons olive oil
2 tablespoons butter

½ cup finely chopped onion
1 small clove garlic, finely minced
½ cup dry white wine
  Salt and freshly ground black pepper to
  taste
¼ cup finely chopped mushrooms
12 eggs.

1. Rinse the frogs' legs in cold water and pat dry.

2. Heat half the oil and half the butter in an enamel or stainless steel skillet and cook half the onion in it until wilted. Add the garlic and cook briefly. Add the wine and simmer until reduced by half. Add frogs' legs, salt, pepper and the mushrooms. Add water to cover barely. Cover with aluminum foil and simmer until legs are tender. Remove frogs' legs and take the meat from the bones. Set aside. Cook the liquid in the skillet until liquid has a saucelike consistency.

3. Lightly beat the eggs until blended.

4. In a large omelet pan, heat remaining oil and butter. Add remaining onion and cook until wilted. Add the meat from the frogs' legs. Pour in eggs and cook until omelet is cooked on the bottom. Flip the omelet, using a spatula if necessary. Cook until the other side is set. Pour sauce over the omelet and cut it into wedges. Serve hot.

Yield: Six servings.

Baked Christmas Mushroom Omelet
Alabama

1 pound mushrooms
4 tablespoons butter, melted
8 eggs, separated
3 tablespoons flour
2 cups hot milk
¼ cup dry sherry
  Salt and freshly ground black pepper to
  taste
¼ teaspoon cayenne pepper.

1. Preheat the oven to 350 degrees.
2. Brush the mushrooms with a little of the

butter and broil them until done. Let cool. Slice the mushrooms.

3. Beat the egg yolks until light and lemon-colored. Beat the whites until stiff.

4. Place the flour in a mixing bowl and gradually add the hot milk, stirring rapidly with a wire whisk or beater. Add two tablespoons of the melted butter, the egg yolks, sherry, salt, pepper, cayenne and mushrooms. Fold in the whites and pour the mixture into a greased six-cup baking dish. Pour remaining butter on top and bake forty-five minutes.

Yield: Four servings.

Chipped Beef Rarebit
Mississippi

3 tablespoons butter
2 small jars (two and one-half ounces each)
  chipped beef
1 teaspoon prepared mustard, preferably Dijon
  or Düsseldorf
2 teaspoons Worcestershire sauce
1 teaspoon chili powder
4 cups Italian plum tomatoes
  Freshly ground black pepper to taste
  Tabasco sauce to taste (optional)
3 cups grated sharp Cheddar cheese
3 eggs, well beaten
4 slices buttered toast.

1. Heat the butter in a large saucepan. Pull the beef apart with the fingers and add beef to the butter. Cook, stirring, until meat frizzles. Add the mustard, Worcestershire, chili powder, tomatoes, pepper and Tabasco. Do not add salt. Simmer about thirty minutes to make a sauce.

2. Remove the sauce from the heat and stir in the cheese. When the cheese melts, add the eggs. Cook, stirring, just to the boiling point when the rarebit thickens. Do not boil or the eggs may curdle. Serve hot over toast.

Yield: Four servings.

Crackus   *Mississippi*

4 tablespoons butter
4 tablespoons flour
½ cup milk
2½ cups canned tomatoes, chopped with their
   liquid
½ teaspoon dry mustard
¾ pound sharp Cheddar cheese, grated
1 small jar (two and one-half ounces) dried
   chipped beef
2 hard-cooked eggs, chopped
4 cups cooked rice.

1. Melt the butter and blend in the flour.
Gradually stir in the milk and tomatoes. Bring to
a boil, stirring.
2. Add the mustard and stir in the cheese until
it melts.
3. Fold in the beef and hard-cooked eggs and
reheat, but do not boil. Serve over rice.
Yield: Four servings.

Cheese Custard   *North Carolina*

12 saltine crackers, crumbled
1 cup grated Cheddar cheese
3 eggs, lightly beaten
2 cups milk
¼ cup butter, melted
⅛ teaspoon cayenne pepper.

1. Place the crackers in bottom of a greased
one-quart casserole. Sprinkle with the cheese.
Combine the eggs, milk, butter and cayenne and
pour over. Let stand thirty minutes.
2. Preheat the oven to 400 degrees.
3. Bake ten minutes, lower the oven heat to
275 degrees and bake about twenty minutes
longer, or until custard is set.
Yield: Four servings.

No-Fail Welsh Rabbit   *Arkansas*

2 tablespoons butter
2 tablespoons flour
1 cup stale beer
2 cups cubed sharp Cheddar cheese
2 eggs, well beaten
½ teaspoon dry mustard
1 tablespoon Worcestershire sauce, or to taste
   Salt to taste
   Cayenne pepper to taste
4 slices toast.

1. Melt the butter and add the flour. Stir in the
beer. When the mixture is thickened and smooth,
add the cheese, stirring.
2. When the cheese is melted, add the eggs and
cook just until the eggs thicken. Do not overcook
or the eggs will scramble. Add the Worcestershire, salt and cayenne. Serve with or on toast.
Yield: Four servings.

Cheese Grits Casserole   *Kentucky*

5 cups water
1 cup hominy grits
½ pound sharp Cheddar cheese, grated
½ cup butter
1 egg, separated
1 teaspoon salt.

1. Bring the water to a boil and gradually stir
jn the grits. Simmer, covered, twenty-five to
thirty minutes, stirring often.
2. Stir in the cheese and butter until melted.
Spoon a little of the hot mixture onto the egg
yolk, return to the bulk of the mixture, add the
salt and mix. Cool to room temperature.
3. Preheat the oven to 350 degrees.
4. Beat the egg white until stiff but not dry and
fold into the cooled mixture. Spoon mixture into
a greased baking dish and bake, covered, forty
minutes. Remove cover, turn oven heat to 375

degrees and bake until top of casserole is slightly browned.

Yield: Six servings.

Quick Big Hominy with Sausage

South Carolina

4 cups corn kernels
1 tablespoon baking soda
½ cup butter
2 pounds sausage meat, made into patties.

1. Cover the corn with hot water and let soak overnight.

2. Next morning, drain, cover with more hot water and add the baking soda. Soak until the husks come off and then rinse with several lots of cold water, or until all husks are removed.

3. Place corn in a kettle, cover with hot water, bring to a boil and cook until tender.

4. Drain the corn and toss with the butter. Fry the sausage patties until brown and well cooked and serve around the hot corn on a platter.

Yield: Eight servings.

Vegetables, Main Dish Accompaniments and Salads

Tomatoes and Green Beans au Gratin

Alabama

2 slices bacon, chopped, or thinly sliced salt pork, chopped
1½ cups chopped onions
3 medium-size tomatoes, peeled and chopped
   Salt and freshly ground black pepper to taste
1 pound green beans
   Salted water
½ cup heavy cream
1 cup freshly grated Parmesan cheese.

1. Preheat the oven to 350 degrees.
2. Cook the bacon or salt pork and, when the fat is rendered, add the onions. Cook until onions are wilted and add the tomatoes. Bring to a boil and simmer fifteen minutes, stirring occasionally. Add salt and pepper.
3. Remove the tip ends from the beans and break into two-inch lengths. Simmer in salted water to cover about ten minutes until crisp-tender. Drain well. Scatter the beans over a buttered flat baking dish.
4. Bring the cream to a boil and add to the tomato sauce. Pour this over the beans and sprinkle with the cheese. Bake just until thoroughly heated. Glaze lightly under a broiler flame and serve immediately.
Yield: About six servings.

Green Bean Casserole

Florida

1½ pounds green beans, picked over and cut into one-and-one-half-inch lengths (there should be about three cups)
1 tablespoon oil
3 tablespoons butter
1 clove garlic, finely minced
¾ cup chopped onion
¾ cup chopped green pepper
¼ cup chopped pimentos
2 cups homemade or canned well-seasoned tomato sauce
   Tabasco sauce to taste (optional)
1 cup grated Cheddar cheese.

1. Preheat the oven to 350 degrees.
2. Rinse and drain the beans and put them in a four-cup saucepan with cover. Add the oil. Do not add water or salt. Cover the beans and cook them over medium heat, shaking the pan occasionally so the beans do not stick. Cook five to ten minutes, depending on the age of the beans, until they are crisp-tender. Pour beans into a baking dish.
3. Meanwhile, melt the butter and cook the garlic, onion and green pepper in it until the onion is translucent. Stir occasionally.
4. Add the pimentos, tomato sauce and Tabasco if desired to the onion mixture. Simmer briefly and pour the sauce over the beans. Sprinkle with the cheese and bake twenty-five minutes,

or until casserole is thoroughly hot and cheese is melted and bubbling.

Yield: About six servings.

Green Beans, Southern Style   *Georgia*

2 pounds green beans
1 ham hock
2 teaspoons salt
1 small hot pepper (bird's eye peppers are best).

1. Wash the beans, cut off the ends and snap beans in two.
2. Place the ham hock in a large kettle, cover with water and boil fifteen minutes. Add beans, the salt and hot pepper and more water almost to cover the beans.
3. Bring to a boil, cover and boil forty minutes. Add more water if necessary. Turn off heat and let rest several hours.
4. Simmer thirty-five minutes longer before serving. Serve beans with pieces of ham from hock.

Yield: Six to eight servings.

Green Beans with Brown Butter Sauce   *Georgia*

¼ cup butter
4 tablespoons flour
2 cups chicken broth
1 bay leaf
½ cup grated sharp Cheddar cheese
1 pound green beans, cooked and drained
¼ cup chopped pecans.

1. Brown the butter lightly in a heavy saucepan, but do not allow to burn. Add the flour and gradually stir in the broth.
2. Add the bay leaf and bring to a boil, stirring. Cook one minute. Stir in the cheese until melted. Remove bay leaf.

3. Arrange the beans in a serving dish and pour sauce over. Sprinkle with the pecans.

Yield: Six servings.

Frijoles Negros (Savory Black Beans)   *Florida*

1 pound dried black beans
¼ cup olive oil
1 clove garlic, unpeeled and mashed
½ sweet green pepper, coarsely chopped
½ medium-size onion, coarsely chopped
1 cube (two inches) salt pork
   Salt to taste
   Fluffy rice.

1. Soak the beans in water to cover for twenty-four hours. Drain; place in a kettle. Add water to come one inch above the top of the beans.
2. Add the oil, garlic, green pepper, onion and salt pork. Bring to a boil and cook for one hour. Add salt and simmer for about thirty minutes longer. If desired, an extra tablespoon of oil may be added before serving. Serve hot in soup plates with fluffy rice.

Yield: About six servings.

Black Beans with Rum   *Louisiana*

2 cups dried black beans
2 medium-size onions, coarsely chopped
2 cloves garlic, finely minced
3 tablespoons bacon drippings
3 ribs celery, coarsely chopped
1 carrot, cut into fine dice
1 tablespoon salt, or more to taste
   Freshly ground black pepper to taste
1 bay leaf
1 tablespoon chopped parsley
½ teaspoon oregano
¼ cup dark rum
1 cup sour cream.

1. Soak the beans overnight in water to cover

or add enough water to cover the beans to a depth of one inch, bring to a boil and cook two minutes. Let stand one hour.

2. Cook the onions and garlic in the bacon drippings until onions are wilted. Add to the beans. Add the celery, carrot, salt, pepper, bay leaf, parsley and oregano. Cover and simmer until beans are nearly tender. Add more water if necessary as the beans cook.

3. Meanwhile, preheat the oven to 350 degrees.

4. Turn the beans into a casserole and add half the rum. Cover and bake until beans are thoroughly tender. Just before serving, stir in remaining rum. Serve beans with the sour cream.

Yield: Six servings.

One of the most famous dishes in Louisiana is red beans with rice. The beans are not kidney beans, as many suppose, but kidney beans make an acceptable substitute.

Red Beans with Rice I   *Louisiana*

  2 cups dried red beans or kidney beans
  6 cups water
  ½ cup bacon drippings
  1 onion
    Hot cooked rice.

1. Wash the beans well until water is clear. Drain. Put the beans in a large bowl and add the six cups water.

2. Heat the bacon drippings in a large kettle or Dutch oven and cook the onion in it gently, stirring occasionally, until onion is amber-colored. Add the beans with their water and bring to a boil. Partially cover and cook three to four hours, or until beans are thoroughly tender and mash easily. If necessary, add more water as the beans cook and stir beans occasionally to prevent them from sticking. When ready to thicken, mash a few beans to thicken the lot. Serve over hot cooked rice.

Yield: Six servings.

Red Beans with Rice II   *Louisiana*

  1 cup dried red beans, soaked overnight
  3 cups water
    Salt and freshly ground black pepper to taste
  3 tablespoons bacon drippings or one small ham hock
  1 small onion, studded with two whole cloves
  1 clove garlic, finely minced
  1 rib celery, chopped
  ¼ cup finely chopped parsley
  1 bay leaf, broken into pieces
  1 cup rice, cooked according to package directions.

1. Drain the beans and place in a heavy kettle with the water, salt, pepper and bacon drippings or ham hock. Bring to a boil and simmer one and one-half hours. Add the onion, garlic, celery, parsley and bay leaf. Return to a boil and cook one hour longer.

2. Serve on hot rice.

Yield: Four servings.

Fresh black-eyed peas when available are delicious and can be cooked until tender in boiling salted water to cover with bacon, salt pork or bits of ham. The dried black-eyed peas are also excellent.

Black-Eyed Peas   *Alabama*

  1 pound dried black-eyed peas
  ¼ pound salt pork
  1 onion, studded with two whole cloves
    Salt and freshly ground black pepper to taste
  2 tablespoons grated lemon rind.

1. Day before, place the peas in a bowl and add the salt pork and water to cover to a depth of one inch. Let stand overnight.

2. Next day, drain the peas and salt pork and put both in a large pot with eight cups water. Add the onion, salt and pepper and bring to a boil. Simmer two hours, or until peas are tender. If necessary, add more water as the peas cook to keep them from burning. When ready to serve, stir in the lemon rind.

Yield: About six servings.

Note: A ham bone may be cooked with the peas in place of the salt pork.

Hopping John or Black-Eyed Peas and Rice   *South Carolina*

3 cups dried black-eyed peas
½ pound salt pork
1 onion, chopped
1 bay leaf
  Salt to taste
  Pinch of crushed red pepper
1 cup uncooked rice.

1. Soak the peas overnight in water to cover. Drain.

2. Cook the salt pork in four cups water one-half hour. Add the peas, onion, bay leaf, salt and red pepper and cook one hour.

3. Add the rice and simmer very slowly until rice and peas are soft. Add more water if needed and adjust seasonings to taste.

Yield: Eight servings.

Cabbage Casserole   *North Carolina*

3 cups shredded cabbage
  Boiling water
1 cup shredded celery
¾ cup soft bread crumbs
  Salt and freshly ground black pepper to taste
1 cup milk

⅓ cup heavy cream
1 egg, lightly beaten
2 tablespoons butter
¼ cup freshly grated Parmesan or Cheddar cheese.

1. Preheat the oven to 450 degrees.

2. Place the cabbage in a saucepan and cover with boiling water. Let stand about five minutes. Drain and blend cabbage with the celery.

3. Make a layer of the vegetables in a greased one-and-one-half-quart casserole. Sprinkle with a third of the bread crumbs. Make another layer of vegetables, another of crumbs and another of vegetables. Sprinkle each layer lightly with salt and pepper.

4. Blend the milk, cream and egg; strain over the casserole. Sprinkle with remaining crumbs and dot with butter. Sprinkle with the cheese. Bake fifteen minutes.

Yield: Four servings.

Celery in Cheese Sauce   *Florida*

4 cups celery, cut into one-inch lengths
  Salt to taste
1½ cups chicken broth
2 celery rib tops with leaves
3 tablespoons butter
3 tablespoons flour
½ cup heavy cream
  Freshly ground black pepper to taste
¾ cup grated sharp Cheddar cheese
  Soft buttered or dry bread crumbs.

1. Preheat the oven to 350 degrees.

2. Place the cut-up celery in a saucepan and add water to cover and salt. Bring to a boil, simmer until crisp-tender and drain.

3. Combine the broth with the celery tops and bring to a boil. Strain and reserve the liquid.

4. Melt the butter and stir in the flour with a wire whisk. Add the strained broth, stirring rapidly with the whisk. When thickened and smooth, add the cream. Simmer five minutes and add salt

and pepper. Add the cheese and, when melted, add the celery. Pour into a one-and-one-half-quart casserole, sprinkle with bread crumbs and bake fifteen to twenty minutes.

Yield: Six to eight servings.

Celery with Egg and Lemon Sauce

Tennessee

1 cup finely chopped onion
4 tablespoons butter
1 two-pound stalk of celery
2 cups fresh or canned chicken broth
    Salt and freshly ground black pepper to taste
2 egg yolks, lightly beaten
    Juice of one lemon.

1. In a large saucepan, cook the onion in the butter until wilted.
2. Trim off the tops of the celery and discard or reserve for soups. Trim off the bottoms of the celery ribs; then cut the ribs of celery into two-inch lengths. Add to the saucepan. Add the broth, salt and pepper and bring to a boil. Simmer until the celery is tender, about half an hour.
3. Combine the egg yolks and lemon juice and stir in a little of the hot broth. Add this to the saucepan, stirring rapidly. Continue stirring and cooking until slightly thickened. Do not overcook or boil or the sauce will curdle. Cover and let stand five minutes.

Yield: Four to six servings.

Corn Oysters

Florida

8 ears corn
3 eggs, separated
    Salt and freshly ground black pepper to taste
¼ cup sifted flour.

1. Slit the kernels of the uncooked corn and scrape off the cob with the back of a knife.

2. Beat the egg whites until stiff, adding a pinch of salt.
3. Beat the egg yolks until light and lemon-colored. Add the corn, salt, pepper and flour.
4. Stir the mixture until smooth and fold in the beaten egg whites. Drop the mixture by table-spoonfuls onto a greased skillet or griddle. Cook on both sides until golden brown.

Yield: Six servings.

Francille's Stewed Corn

Arkansas

12 ears corn, approximately
¼ cup bacon drippings
2 tablespoons butter
3 cups milk, approximately
1½ teaspoons salt
2 tablespoons light brown sugar
¼ teaspoon freshly ground black pepper.

1. Cut off the corn cob tips and scrape the cobs to make one quart of kernels.
2. Heat the bacon drippings and butter in a heavy skillet. Add one cup milk, the salt, brown sugar and pepper.
3. Bring to a boil and add the corn. Turn heat down and simmer gently one and one-quarter hours, stirring frequently with a pancake turner to prevent sticking. Add remaining milk as needed to thin corn.

Yield: Six to eight servings.

Butter-Fried Corn

Florida

10 ears corn
4 tablespoons butter
    Salt and freshly ground black pepper to taste.

1. Shuck the corn and carefully remove any bits of tassel that remain.
2. Using a sharp knife or a corn scraper, cut off the kernels, not too close to the cob. Gently scrape off kernels remaining on cob.

3. Heat the butter in a saucepan and add the scraped corn. Cook, stirring, five to ten minutes and season with salt and pepper.

Yield: About four servings.

cheese and dot with remaining butter. Bake twenty to thirty minutes.

Yield: Six to eight servings.

Clara's Eggplant   *Tennessee*

2 medium-size eggplants
  Salt to taste
6 tablespoons butter
½ pound chicken livers
  Freshly ground black pepper to taste
½ pound mushrooms, sliced
2 eggs, lightly beaten
⅓ cup heavy cream
¼ teaspoon nutmeg
  Cayenne pepper to taste
½ cup soft bread crumbs
½ cup freshly grated Parmesan or Cheddar cheese.

1. Preheat the oven to 350 degrees.
2. Select firm eggplants with shiny skins. Peel the eggplants and cut them into one-inch cubes. Place the cubes in a saucepan and add cold water to cover. Add salt and bring to a boil. Simmer just until the eggplant is tender. Do not overcook. Drain the eggplant immediately.
3. Meanwhile, melt two tablespoons of the butter in a skillet and add the chicken livers. Sprinkle with salt and pepper and cook, turning the livers occasionally, until done. Remove and reserve the livers. Add two more tablespoons of the butter to the skillet and cook the mushrooms in it, stirring frequently, until they give up their juices. Cook until most of the liquid evaporates.
4. Chop the eggplant and the livers and combine them. Stir in the mushrooms.
5. Beat together the eggs, cream, nutmeg, cayenne, salt and pepper. Stir this into the eggplant mixture.
6. Pour the mixture into a buttered one-quart casserole. Sprinkle with the bread crumbs and

Eggplant Soufflé   *Florida*

1 medium-size eggplant
  Boiling salted water
2 tablespoons butter
3 tablespoons flour
1 cup milk
½ cup grated sharp Cheddar cheese
¾ cup soft bread crumbs
¼ cup finely chopped scallions, including green part
  Cayenne pepper to taste
2 tablespoons homemade or canned tomato sauce
  Salt and freshly ground black pepper to taste
3 eggs, separated.

1. Preheat the oven to 350 degrees.
2. Peel the eggplant and cut it into cubes. Add boiling salted water to cover and simmer just until tender. Drain well and mash the eggplant.
3. Melt the butter and, with a wire whisk, stir in the flour. When blended, add the milk all at once, stirring vigorously with the whisk. Remove the mixture from the heat and stir in the cheese and bread crumbs. Add the scallions, cayenne, tomato sauce, salt and pepper. Add the egg yolks and return to the heat. Bring just to a boil.
4. Beat the egg whites until stiff and fold them into the mixture. Pour the mixture into a buttered one-and-one-half-quart soufflé dish and set the dish in a pan of hot water. Place on top of the stove and bring the water in the pan just to a boil. Place in the oven and bake thirty to forty minutes.

Yield: Four servings.

Stuffed Eggplant   *Mississippi*

2 medium-size eggplants
  Salt to taste
8 tablespoons butter
1 rib celery, finely chopped
1 small onion, finely chopped
3 eggs, lightly beaten
  Freshly ground black pepper to taste
1 cup soft bread crumbs.

1. Trim off and discard the stem ends of the eggplants. Otherwise, do not peel. Place the eggplants in a large saucepan and add water to cover and salt. Bring to a boil and simmer until eggplants are tender, about thirty minutes, depending on the size of the vegetables. Drain and let cool.

2. Preheat the oven to 400 degrees.

3. Melt six tablespoons of the butter in a skillet and add the celery and onion. Cook briefly, stirring, until vegetables are tender.

4. Split the eggplants lengthwise in half and carefully scoop out the insides, leaving the casings intact. Add the eggplant pulp to the skillet and mash pulp. Cook briefly and add the eggs, salt and pepper. Cook, stirring, until mixture thickens slightly.

5. Stir in all but two tablespoons of the bread crumbs. Spoon the filling into the eggplant casings. Dot with the remaining butter and sprinkle with the remaining crumbs. Bake about fifteen minutes, or until thoroughly heated and golden brown on top.
  Yield: Six servings.

Hunt and Polo Eggplant Casserole
                              Tennessee

2 eggplants, peeled and cubed
  Boiling salted water
½ pound chicken livers
  Melted butter
2 eggs
½ cup heavy cream

6 tablespoons butter
½ pound mushrooms, thinly sliced
  Nutmeg to taste
  Salt and freshly ground black pepper to taste
½ cup soft bread crumbs
½ cup grated mild Cheddar cheese.

1. Preheat the oven to 350 degrees.

2. Drop the eggplant cubes into boiling salted water to cover. Bring to a boil and simmer just until eggplant is tender. Drain well and mash.

3. Brush the chicken livers with melted butter and place them under the broiler. Cook, turning once, until they are done. Let cool slightly and chop fine. Add them to the eggplant.

4. Beat the eggs with the cream and stir this into the eggplant mixture.

5. Heat two tablespoons of the butter and cook the mushrooms in it, stirring, until they are wilted and most of the liquid evaporates. Add the mushrooms to the eggplant. Add nutmeg, salt and pepper. The mixture will be rather liquid before baking. Turn the mixture into a one-quart casserole. Sprinkle with the bread crumbs and cheese. Melt the remaining butter and pour it over all. Bake twenty to thirty minutes.
  Yield: Six to eight servings.

Homemade Hominy   *South Carolina*

2 tablespoons lye
  Cold water
1 gallon boiling water
2 quarts corn kernels.

1. Put the lye in an iron kettle. Add two cups cold water and stir with a wooden paddle to dissolve.

2. Add the boiling water and stir. Add the corn and bring to a boil. Boil twenty-five to forty minutes, stirring all the time, and add more boiling water if corn starts to stick.

3. After twenty-five minutes, spoon some corn into a bowl of cold water and, if the part of the

kernel where it was attached to the cob (the eyes) falls off, it is ready to wash.

4. Fill kettle with cold water, stir well and pour off all the water. Repeat the washing and draining five times. The stirring is important because this is what loosens the eyes.

5. Cover corn with cold water and bring to a boil. Drain and repeat four times. Add more cold water, bring to a boil again and boil three to four hours, or until corn swells to maximum. Add water as necessary.

Yield: About two and one-half quarts big hominy.

Fried Hominy Grits　　　*Georgia*

2½ teaspoons salt
 5 cups boiling water
 1 cup hominy grits
 ¼ cup blanched sliced almonds
　 Bacon drippings or lard
　 Flour
 2 eggs
 2 tablespoons water.

1. Day before, add two teaspoons of salt to the boiling water and add the grits gradually, stirring constantly. Cook over low heat, stirring frequently, thirty to forty minutes.

2. Stir in the almonds and let mixture cool to warm.

3. Pack the warm grits into straight-sided iced tea glasses that have been rinsed out with cold water. Chill overnight.

4. Next day, loosen around the grits with a knife and allow to unmold. Cut into one-half-inch-thick circles.

5. Heat the bacon drippings or lard in a heavy iron skillet.

6. Dip the circles in flour and then in the eggs combined with the remaining salt and two tablespoons water.

7. Fry the circles in the hot fat until browned on both sides.

Yield: About twenty circles; five servings.

Sarah's Oando　　　*Tennessee*

½ cup hominy grits, cooked according to
　 package directions in a double boiler
 1 cup yellow corn meal
 2 tablespoons butter
 ½ teaspoon salt
1½ cups boiling milk
 2 eggs, well beaten.

1. Preheat the oven to 350 degrees.

2. Combine the cooked grits with the corn meal, butter and salt. Pour the milk over and stir to mix.

3. Stir a little of the hot mixture into the eggs. Return all to the bulk of the mixture. Pour into a greased casserole and bake forty to sixty minutes, or until well browned.

Yield: Six servings.

Note: This is similar to the Awendaw bread of South Carolina.

Hominy and Bean Cakes　　　*South Carolina*

　 Bacon drippings
 1 tablespoon flour
 ½ cup milk
 1 teaspoon salt
 1 cup big hominy, ground
 1 cup cooked red kidney beans, ground
　 Cayenne pepper to taste.

1. Melt one tablespoon bacon drippings and blend in the flour. Gradually stir in the milk and bring to a boil, stirring. Add the salt.

2. Add the hominy and beans to the sauce and add cayenne to taste (mixture should be hot). Form mixture into cakes.

3. Heat bacon drippings in a heavy skillet and brown the cakes in it on both sides.

Yield: Four servings.

Baked Hominy and Tomatoes   *Arkansas*

3 cups canned or homecooked hominy grits
1 tablespoon butter
2 cups canned tomatoes or tomato puree
¼ cup grated sharp Cheddar cheese
½ teaspoon salt
¼ teaspoon freshly ground black pepper.

1. Preheat the oven to 375 degrees.
2. Combine the hominy, butter, tomatoes and cheese. Add the salt and pepper and pour into an oiled baking dish or casserole.
3. Bake about forty-five minutes.
Yield: Eight servings.

Grits Soufflé   *Alabama*

4 cups cooked grits
2 cups milk
Salt to taste
8 eggs, separated.

1. The grits should be cooked according to package directions. When grits are done, let them cool to room temperature.
2. Preheat the oven to 350 degrees.
3. Bring the milk just to a boil and stir it into the grits. Add salt. Beat the egg yolks and stir them into the grits mixture.
4. Whip the egg whites until stiff and fold them into the mixture. Butter a two-quart baking dish not more than six inches high and pour the mixture into it. Set the dish in a pan of hot water and bake forty-five minutes to one hour. Serve immediately.
Yield: Eight to one dozen servings.

There are three sorts of garden greens that are frequently associated with Southern cooking. These are mustard greens, turnip greens and collard greens. Mustard greens and turnip greens are the more delicate of the three. Collard greens are frequently tough but, for those who enjoy them, they are delicious. In many Southern homes the greens are cooked for several hours before serving.

Mustard Greens, Turnip Greens and Collard Greens   *Mississippi*

3 pounds mustard greens, turnip greens or collard greens
1 onion
½ pound salt pork (see note)
Salt and freshly ground black pepper to taste.

1. Trim the greens and discard hard stems. Wash the greens in several changes of cold water. Put greens in a large pot. If the greens are young and tender, they may be cooked in the water that clings to their leaves. Or add two cups of water to the kettle. Add the remaining ingredients and bring to a boil.
2. Simmer just until greens are tender or cook them one hour or longer. Traditionally, the greens are served with corn bread.
Yield: Six to eight servings.
Note: If desired, cook the salt pork in four cups water until meat is almost tender. This will add flavor to the water. Then add the greens and cook until tender.

Southern-Style Turnip Greens   *Arkansas*

Pick turnip greens carefully. Remove all large, tough stems and brown leaves. Wash thoroughly in several changes of water. Salt may be added to first wash water if greens appear "buggy" to make them turn loose from the leaves, or the individual leaves may be held under running water.

Put the greens into a heavy pan with a tight-fitting cover. Add water to half cover the greens and a ham hock or piece of salt pork. Cover and cook slowly two to three hours. Extra bacon drippings can be added near end of cooking if desired. Check for seasoning before serving.

Mixed Greens with Corn Bread Dumplings   *Arkansas*

2 pounds turnip greens
2 pounds mustard greens
2½ quarts water
1 onion, quartered
1 pound salt pork, cubed
Salt and freshly ground black pepper
2 teaspoons sugar
1½ cups white corn meal
¼ cup flour
1 cup boiling water, approximately.

1. Tear off and discard any tough stems from the greens. If the greens are freshly picked and young, this may not be necessary. In any event, wash the greens in several changes of cold water. Drain.

2. Bring the two and one-half quarts water to a boil in a large kettle and add the onion and salt pork. Simmer thirty minutes and add the greens and salt and pepper to taste. Add one teaspoon of the sugar and simmer about two hours.

3. Meanwhile, combine the corn meal, flour, one teaspoon salt and the remaining sugar in a mixing bowl. Slowly add the boiling water, stirring. Add just enough water to make a stiff, manageable mixture.

4. Wet the palms of the hands, break off bits of corn meal dough the size of walnuts and shape into balls. Drop the balls into the boiling greens. Cover and continue cooking thirty minutes.

Yield: Four or more servings.

Note: Condiments to be served with this dish might include pepper vinegar, malt vinegar, chopped green onions, crumbled crisp bacon and chopped hot green peppers.

Assorted Greens   *Virginia*

4 pounds collard, turnip or mustard greens, or mixed
½ pound salt pork
4 cups cold water
Pinch of crushed red pepper
Salt to taste
1 onion, minced.

1. Remove large stems from greens and wash greens thoroughly.

2. Put all ingredients in a large pot and boil one to one and one-half hours, or until tender.

3. Drain greens and chop them rather fine. Serve with salt pork, sliced.

Yield: About eight servings.

Mushrooms au Gratin   *Virginia*

3 tablespoons butter
2 teaspoons fresh lemon juice
1 pound mushrooms, thinly sliced
2 tablespoons finely chopped scallions, including green part
Salt and freshly ground black pepper to taste
½ cup milk
½ cup heavy cream
¼ teaspoon nutmeg
2 tablespoons flour
⅓ cup soft bread crumbs
⅓ cup freshly grated Swiss cheese or Parmesan cheese.

1. Heat one and one-half tablespoons of the butter in a one-quart saucepan and add the lemon juice and mushrooms. Cover closely and cook, shaking the pan, until mushrooms have wilted and given up most of their juices.

2. Add the scallions, salt, pepper, milk and cream and bring to a boil. Add the nutmeg.

3. Blend the flour with the remaining butter, kneading with the fingers. Add mixture, bit by bit, to the mushroom mixture, stirring constantly. When the sauce is thickened, pour the creamed mushrooms into an ovenproof dish and sprinkle with a mixture of the bread crumbs and cheese. Brown under the broiler and serve very hot.

Yield: Four to six servings.

Fried Okra

South Carolina

1 pound tender okra
½ teaspoon salt
⅛ teaspoon freshly ground black pepper
⅓ cup yellow corn meal
¼ cup bacon drippings.

1. Wash the okra well and cut off the ends. Slice okra into one-quarter-inch rounds. Combine the salt, pepper and corn meal. Toss the okra in the corn meal mixture.

2. Heat the bacon drippings in a large skillet. Add okra slices and sauté until they are tender and golden.

Yield: Four servings.

Limping Susan

South Carolina

4 thick slices bacon, diced
¾ cup washed, sliced okra
1 cup uncooked rice
2 cups chicken broth
  Salt and freshly ground black pepper to taste.

1. Cook the bacon in a skillet until the fat is rendered. Add the okra to the skillet. Sauté until barely tender.

2. Add the rice, broth, salt and pepper. Bring to a boil, cover and simmer until the rice is tender, about twenty-five minutes.

Yield: Six servings.

Heart of Palm (Swamp Cabbage)

Florida

1 three-foot-long heart of palm or swamp cabbage, weighing about two to three pounds
  Salt to taste
¼ teaspoon thyme.

1. Trim the palm under cold water or palm will discolor. Remove the outer leaves. Cut off the base, which is occasionally bitter. Remove the fibrous upper portion.

2. Soak the trimmed heart of palm in cold water for one hour. Place in a kettle and add water to cover to the depth of one inch. Add salt and the thyme. Bring to a boil and simmer, covered, forty-five minutes, or until tender.

Yield: Four to six servings.

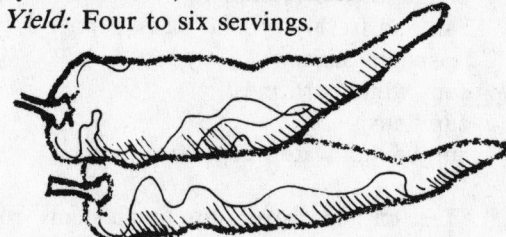

Heart of Palm au Gratin (Swamp Cabbage au Gratin)

Florida

2 cups cooked (recipe above) or canned heart of palm, cut into one-half-inch rounds
1½ tablespoons butter
1½ tablespoons flour
¾ cup milk
¼ cup light cream
¾ cup grated sharp Cheddar cheese
  Salt to taste
  Cayenne pepper to taste
½ cup toasted soft bread crumbs.

1. Preheat the oven to 400 degrees.

2. Prepare the heart of palm and place it in a buttered baking dish.

3. Melt the butter in a saucepan and stir in the flour with a wire whisk. When blended, add the milk and cream, stirring vigorously with the whisk. Bring to a boil, stirring, and, when the mixture is thickened and smooth, simmer about five minutes. Remove from the heat and add the cheese, salt and cayenne. Pour the sauce over the heart of palm and sprinkle with the bread crumbs.

4. Bake until sauce is bubbling and palm is thoroughly hot.

Yield: Four to six servings.

Fried Plantains *Florida*

3 firm plantains (see note)
1 cup peanut oil
  Salt.

1. Peel the plantains and cut them into one-quarter-inch rounds or smaller.
2. Heat the oil until it is very hot and fry the plantain rounds, a few at a time, like deep-fried potatoes. When crisp and brown, drain on paper towels. While hot, sprinkle with salt.

Yield: Six or seven servings.

Note: Plantains are available in Spanish markets.

French Potato Salad *Louisiana*

8 medium-size potatoes
  Boiling salted water
1 teaspoon salt
½ teaspoon freshly ground black pepper
¼ cup wine vinegar
1 tablespoon Pernod, Ricard or other anise-flavored liqueur
2 tablespoons beef broth
¼ cup dry white wine
½ tablespoon chopped tarragon
3 tablespoons chopped parsley
½ cup oil.

1. Cook the potatoes in boiling salted water until tender but still firm.
2. Peel the potatoes while still warm and cut into slices one-quarter-inch thick. Place in a salad bowl.
3. In another bowl, combine the salt, pepper, vinegar, Pernod, broth and wine. Mix until the salt dissolves.
4. Add the tarragon, parsley and oil and mix well. Pour over the potatoes and toss gently but thoroughly until all the liquid is absorbed.

Yield: Four to six servings.

Hot Potato Salad *Kentucky*

6 medium-size potatoes
6 hard-cooked eggs, sliced
1 bunch scallions, including green part, finely chopped
1½ teaspoons celery seeds
  Salt and freshly ground black pepper to taste
1 cup mayonnaise
6 slices bacon
¼ cup cider vinegar
¼ cup hot water
3 tablespoons sugar
1 dill pickle, diced.

1. Scrub and boil or bake the potatoes until tender. Peel and dice while hot. Add the egg slices, scallions, celery seeds, salt, pepper and mayonnaise.
2. Meanwhile, cook the bacon in a skillet until crisp. Remove and crumble into potato mixture.
3. Add the vinegar, hot water and sugar to bacon drippings in skillet. Bring to a boil and continue boiling, stirring, two minutes. Add the pickle and pour over potatoes. Toss and serve.

Yield: Six servings.

Note: This salad may be chilled and served cold if desired.

Orange-Glazed Sweet Potatoes
Kentucky

6 medium-size yams or sweet potatoes, scrubbed and boiled or baked until barely tender and peeled
1 cup orange juice
2 teaspoons grated orange rind
1 tablespoon cornstarch
3 tablespoons melted butter
⅓ cup light brown sugar
⅓ cup granulated sugar
⅛ teaspoon salt.

1. Preheat the oven to 350 degrees.

2. Place the yams or sweet potatoes in a greased shallow baking dish. Combine the remaining ingredients in a small pan and bring to a boil, stirring. Pour over the potatoes and bake thirty minutes, basting occasionally.

Yield: Six servings.

Baked Bourbon Spiced Sweet Potatoes

Tennessee

4 sweet potatoes
⅓ cup sugar
½ cup butter
2 eggs, lightly beaten
½ cup heavy cream
¼ teaspoon salt
¼ teaspoon nutmeg
½ teaspoon cinnamon
⅓ cup raisins
¼ cup bourbon.

1. Preheat the oven to 375 degrees.
2. Scrub the potatoes and bake until tender, about forty minutes. Peel and mash into a bowl.
3. Add the remaining ingredients and mix well. Turn into a greased casserole and bake until heated through, about ten minutes.

Yield: Four servings.

Green Rice Ring

Tennessee

1¾ cups uncooked long grain rice
4 quarts water
  Salt
1 pound spinach
3 scallions, including some green part, chopped
  Freshly ground black pepper to taste
4 tablespoons melted butter
2 tablespoons butter
  Buttered small carrots.

1. Preheat the oven to 300 degrees.
2. Rinse the rice under cold running water.

Bring the four quarts water to a boil and add one and one-half teaspoons salt. When water is boiling vigorously, add the rice gradually. Let boil, stirring occasionally, about twenty minutes, or until rice is tender but firm. Drain the rice in a colander and rinse under cold running water.

3. Pick over the spinach to remove any tough stems. Place the spinach and scallions in the container of an electric blender. Blend, stirring down with a rubber spatula, to make a thick puree. Blend the spinach mixture with the rice and add salt and pepper to taste and the melted butter.

4. Butter a ring mold with the two tablespoons of the butter and add the rice. Press the rice firmly in the mold and cover with aluminum foil. Sit the mold in a pan and pour boiling water around mold. Bake twenty to thirty minutes, or until piping hot. Unmold on a round platter and fill the center with buttered carrots.

Yield: Six to eight servings.

Steamboat Rice

Louisiana

2 tablespoons oil
2 cups finely chopped onions
1 clove garlic, finely minced
1 green pepper, cored, seeded and chopped
3 cups cubed cooked ham
¼ cup finely chopped parsley
¼ cup finely chopped celery
½ cup chopped scallions, including green part
¼ teaspoon thyme
1 bay leaf
  Freshly ground black pepper to taste
2 cups homemade or canned tomato sauce
2 cups fresh or canned chicken broth
2 cups uncooked rice.

1. Heat the oil and cook the onions and the garlic in it until onions are wilted. Add the green pepper and ham and cook, stirring, three minutes longer. Add the parsley, celery, scallions, thyme, bay leaf, pepper and tomato sauce. Stir, cover and simmer ten minutes.

2. Remove the cover and add the broth. Bring

to a boil; then stir in the rice. Cover and simmer twenty to thirty minutes, or until rice is tender. Remove cover and simmer ten minutes longer. Serve piping hot.

Yield: Six servings.

Dilled Rice for Shrimp   *Louisiana*

4 tablespoons butter
2 tablespoons chopped onion
1½ cups uncooked rice
1 cup fish stock or clam juice
2½ cups water
⅓ cup finely snipped fresh dill weed.

1. Melt the butter in a heavy casserole or skillet and sauté the onion in it until tender but not browned.

2. Add the rice and cook, stirring, three minutes until the rice takes on a transparent appearance and is golden. Stir in the fish stock or clam juice and the water.

3. Bring mixture to a boil, cover and simmer slowly about twenty minutes, or until the liquid has all been absorbed. Add the dill and toss.

Yield: Six servings.

One of the most interesting dishes in Louisiana cuisine bears the abrupt name of Dirty Rice. This is really a jambalaya made with chicken gizzards and livers and, when well made, it is delicious.

Dirty Rice   *Louisiana*

2 cups uncooked rice
6 cups chicken broth or water
1 bay leaf
1 cup finely chopped onions
2 tablespoons bacon drippings
¼ pound chicken livers
¼ pound chicken gizzards
1 clove garlic, finely minced
¾ cup finely chopped scallions, including green part
½ cup finely chopped parsley
Salt and freshly ground black pepper to taste
Butter.

1. Preheat the oven to 350 degrees.

2. Place the rice in a one-and-one-half-quart saucepan and add four cups broth and the bay leaf. Cover, bring to a boil and simmer exactly fifteen minutes.

3. Cook the onions in the bacon drippings until almost brown. Chop the livers and gizzards fine and add them. Cook, stirring, until brown. Add the garlic, scallions and parsley. Season with salt and pepper and add the remaining broth. Combine the partially cooked rice and the chicken giblet mixture and pour all into a baking pan. Dot with butter and bake fifteen minutes.

Yield: About six servings.

Zucchini Cheese Custard   *Florida*

4 small zucchini
2 medium-size onions
¼ cup melted butter
3 eggs, lightly beaten
⅔ cup light cream
Pinch of nutmeg
1½ cups grated sharp Cheddar cheese
Salt and freshly ground black pepper to taste.

1. Preheat the oven to 350 degrees.

2. Cut the zucchini into two-inch rounds.

3. Peel the onions and cut them into thin rings. Cook the zucchini and onions in the butter until light golden. Do not brown and do not let the zucchini become soft.

4. Spoon the zucchini and onions into a shallow casserole. Combine the eggs, cream and nutmeg and half the cheese. Pour the mixture over the vegetables. Sprinkle with salt, pepper and the

remaining cheese. Place the casserole in a baking dish, pour boiling water around casserole and bake thirty-five to forty minutes, or until custard is set.

Yield: Four servings.

Cheese-Stuffed Squash — *Tennessee*

3 medium-size yellow squash
  Boiling salted water
2 tablespoons butter
2 tablespoons finely chopped onion
6 mushrooms, finely chopped
½ teaspoon finely minced garlic
¼ cup grated Swiss cheese or Parmesan cheese
⅓ cup soft bread crumbs
1 tablespoon finely chopped parsley.

1. Preheat the oven to 350 degrees.
2. Split each squash in half lengthwise. With a sharp paring knife, cut away the pulp of each, leaving a rim about one-quarter-inch thick. Reserve the pulp.
3. Drop the shells into boiling salted water and cook three minutes, no longer. Drain.
4. Melt the butter in a skillet, add the onion, mushrooms and garlic and cook until onion is wilted. Add the squash pulp and cook briefly, stirring. Add the cheese, bread crumbs and parsley. Stuff the squash shells with the mixture. Place in a baking dish and bake thirty minutes.

Yield: Six servings.

Pecan Squash Casserole — *Tennessee*

3 tablespoons butter
½ small onion, finely chopped
1 cup hot milk
1 cup dry bread crumbs
  Salt and freshly ground black pepper to taste
¼ teaspoon nutmeg
2 eggs, lightly beaten

2 cups mashed or sieved cooked squash
½ cup finely chopped pecans.

1. Preheat the oven to 325 degrees.
2. Heat the butter in a small skillet and sauté the onion in it until tender. Add the milk and then pour over the bread crumbs.
3. Mix well. Season with salt, pepper and the nutmeg. Fold in the eggs, squash and pecans. Pour into a greased soufflé dish or baking dish and bake about thirty-five minutes, or until set.

Yield: Four servings.

Spinach and Artichokes, Asphodel Style — *Louisiana*

2 pounds spinach
1 package frozen artichoke hearts
4 slices bacon
½ cup finely chopped onion
1 tablespoon flour
1 clove garlic, finely minced
3 scallions, including green part, trimmed and chopped
½ cup heavy cream
  Salt and freshly ground black pepper to taste
  Cayenne pepper to taste
1 teaspoon or more Pernod, Ricard or other anise-flavored liqueur
¼ cup toasted soft bread crumbs
  Butter.

1. Trim off any tough stems on the spinach and wash the leaves in several changes of cold water. Shake to remove excess moisture. Put the spinach in a kettle. No additional water is needed. The spinach will cook in the water that clings to the leaves.
2. Cover the kettle and bring to a boil. Stir the spinach leaves around when they wilt and continue cooking briefly until just tender. Set aside.
3. Cook the artichoke hearts according to package directions and set aside.

4. Cook the bacon in a large saucepan until crisp. Remove the bacon, crumble it and reserve.

5. Preheat the oven to 400 degrees.

6. Pour off all but one tablespoon of the fat from the saucepan in which bacon cooked. Add the onion and flour and cook, stirring, but do not brown. Add the garlic and scallions and stir in the cream. Cook until the mixture is thickened and smooth.

7. Drain the spinach well in a colander. Drain the artichokes. Add both vegetables and the reserved bacon to the sauce and season with salt, pepper and cayenne. Add the Pernod and pour mixture into a buttered baking dish.

8. Sprinkle with the bread crumbs, dot with butter and bake until dish is thoroughly hot and nicely browned.

Yield: Six to eight servings.

Broiled Tomatoes   *Louisiana*

6 large firm ripe tomatoes
1 clove garlic
Salt
6 teaspoons olive oil
1 teaspoon chopped fresh or dried rosemary
Freshly chopped basil (optional).

1. Core the tomatoes, but do not peel. Cut the tomatoes in half.

2. Slice the garlic into wafer-thin slivers and insert the slivers into the tomato halves. Sprinkle with salt, the oil and rosemary. Rub the bottom of a baking dish with a little oil and arrange the tomatoes in the dish.

3. Place the tomatoes about three inches from a broiler flame and broil until hot and bubbling and edges of tomatoes start to burn. Sprinkle with basil if desired and serve.

Yield: Six servings.

Note: These tomatoes are also good served cold.

Fried Green Tomato Slices   *West Virginia*

4 green tomatoes, thickly sliced
½ cup white or yellow corn meal
¼ teaspoon salt
Freshly ground black pepper to taste
⅓ cup bacon drippings or pork fat.

1. Dip the tomato slices in the corn meal mixed with the salt and pepper.

2. Heat the bacon drippings or pork fat in a heavy skillet and sauté the slices in it quickly until browned on both sides.

Yield: Six servings.

Tomato Pudding   *Arkansas*

6 tablespoons butter
1 cup chopped onions
4 cups chopped peeled and cored tomatoes
Salt and freshly ground black pepper to taste
¼ cup light brown sugar
2 tablespoons chopped fresh basil
2 tablespoons chopped fresh parsley
1½ cups small white bread cubes or one cup soft bread crumbs.

1. Melt two tablespoons of the butter in a large saucepan and cook the onions in it until wilted. Add the tomatoes and stew them, stirring frequently, until they are reduced by half.

2. Preheat the oven to 375 degrees.

3. Add the salt, pepper, brown sugar, basil and parsley to the stewed tomatoes.

4. Pour the bread cubes or crumbs into a one-quart baking dish. Melt the remaining butter and pour over the bread cubes or crumbs. Spoon the tomato mixture over all and cover closely with aluminum foil or a lid. Bake thirty minutes.

Yield: Four to six servings.

Bibb Lettuce Salad
Kentucky

2 or three heads Bibb lettuce
1 teaspoon Dijon or Düsseldorf mustard
  Salt and freshly ground black pepper to
  taste
1 tablespoon wine vinegar or lemon juice
3 tablespoons or more peanut oil or olive oil
½ clove garlic, finely minced.

1. Pull off the leaves of the lettuce and rinse well under cold running water. Cut or tear the leaves into bite-size pieces. Shake to dry.
2. Put the mustard into a salad bowl and add the salt, pepper, vinegar, oil and garlic, stirring with a wire whisk. Add the lettuce and toss.
Yield: Four servings.

Cauliflower Slaw
Kentucky

1 large head cauliflower, broken into flowerets
¼ cup minced scallions, including green part
½ cup finely chopped celery leaves
1 cup sour cream
½ cup homemade French dressing (page 622)
2 teaspoons caraway seeds
  Salt and freshly ground black pepper to
  taste.

Slice the flowerets thinly and toss with the other ingredients just before serving.
Yield: Six servings.

Cole Slaw
Alabama

1 small head green cabbage
½ to one cup mayonnaise
2 tablespoons wine vinegar or lemon juice
1 tablespoon grated onion
½ teaspoon caraway seeds or celery seeds
½ cup finely slivered green or red sweet
  peppers

  Salt and freshly ground black pepper to
  taste
  Cayenne pepper to taste (optional).

1. Tear off the tough outer leaves of the cabbage and pare away the core. With a sharp knife on a flat surface, shred the cabbage. There should be about four cups. Place cabbage in a mixing bowl.
2. Add the remaining ingredients and toss well. Serve well chilled.
Yield: About six servings.

Cole Slaw with Capers
South Carolina

1 small head green cabbage
½ small onion
  Salt and freshly ground black pepper to
  taste
2 tablespoons wine vinegar
3 tablespoons olive oil
½ teaspoon Tabasco sauce, or to taste
1 teaspoon chopped fresh basil, thyme,
  tarragon, marjoram or other fresh herb
2 tablespoons capers
1½ cups mayonnaise, approximately.

1. Peel off the tough outer leaves of the cabbage and pare away the core. Slice the cabbage in half and shred it finely with a sharp knife. There should be about four cups.
2. Place the shredded cabbage in a large mixing bowl. Grate enough onion to make one or two teaspoonfuls and add to the cabbage. Add the remaining ingredients, using just enough mayonnaise to bind well. Toss and chill.
Yield: Four to six servings.

Stella's Pensacola Gazpachy Salad
Florida

6 large tomatoes, peeled
4 large green peppers, cored and seeded
2 cucumbers, peeled

2 ship biscuits (hard tack) or six to eight
    hard pilot crackers, soaked in cold water
2 cups homemade mayonnaise
¼ teaspoon dry mustard
1 small onion
    Salt and freshly ground black pepper to
    taste
    Cayenne pepper to taste.

1. Slice the tomatoes, green peppers and cucumbers as thinly as possible. Place the vegetables and biscuits or crackers in alternate layers in a large salad bowl, spreading each layer with the mayonnaise to which the mustard has been added.

2. Cut the onion in four wedges. Spear each wedge with a toothpick. Push wedges down into salad mixture. Cover and place in refrigerator six hours before serving. Remove onion before serving and stir mixture well with a wooden spoon. Add salt, pepper and cayenne. Do not serve on lettuce.

Yield: Six or more servings.

Shreveport Poppy Seed Dressing
Louisiana

½ cup tarragon vinegar
¼ cup sugar
1 tablespoon paprika
1 tablespoon dry mustard
½ teaspoon ground ginger
1½ teaspoons salt
    Cayenne pepper to taste
2 tablespoons onion juice (made by scraping
    the cut surface of half an onion with a
    knife)
1 egg yolk
1 tablespoon chopped chutney
¾ cup honey
2 cups peanut or vegetable oil
2 tablespoons poppy seeds.

1. Combine the vinegar and sugar and bring to a boil. Remove from the heat and add the pa-

prika, mustard, ginger, salt, cayenne and onion juice.

2. When cool, beat in the remaining ingredients. Chill and serve with fruit salads. In Shreveport, this dressing is frequently served with sea food cocktails.

Yield: About one quart.

Boiled Salad Dressing
Virginia

1 teaspoon dry mustard
3 tablespoons sugar
½ teaspoon salt
2 tablespoons flour
3 egg yolks
½ cup cold milk
¾ cup white vinegar.

1. Combine the mustard, sugar, salt and flour in the top of a double boiler.

2. Beat the egg yolks slightly with a wire whisk and beat them into the flour mixture. Stir in the milk and vinegar and cook over boiling water until the mixture is thickened and smooth.

Yield: One and one-half cups.

Cole Slaw Dressing
Virginia

½ cup cider vinegar
1½ teaspoons dry mustard
4 eggs
2 cups light cream
    Salt to taste
¼ to one-half cup sugar
2 tablespoons butter.

1. Combine the vinegar and mustard in the top of a double boiler and let stand ten minutes.

2. Beat the eggs lightly and add them to the vinegar. Add the cream, salt and sugar and cook, stirring with a wooden spoon, until the mixture coats the spoon. Remove the sauce from the heat and swirl in the butter.

Yield: About three cups.

Cooked Bacon Dressing

Virginia

4 slices bacon
3 eggs
1 tablespoon dry mustard
2½ tablespoons flour
⅓ cup sugar
1 teaspoon salt
½ teaspoon celery seeds, crushed
½ cup cider vinegar
1 cup water
¼ teaspoon freshly ground black pepper
1 cup mayonnaise, preferably homemade.

1. Cook the bacon until crisp. Remove and crumble strips. Reserve.

2. Combine bacon drippings with eggs, mustard, flour, sugar, salt, celery seeds, vinegar, water and pepper in a deep saucepan. Beat with a rotary beater.

3. Heat, stirring constantly, until mixture thickens. Remove. Cool slightly and stir in the mayonnaise and reserved bacon bits. Cool and chill.

Yield: About two and one-half cups.

Note: This is excellent on potato salad, chicken salad or spinach salad.

Breads

Hot Water Corn Bread (Hoe Cake)

Mississippi

1 cup white corn meal
4 teaspoons sifted flour
½ teaspoon salt
1 teaspoon sugar
2 teaspoons baking powder
6 tablespoons melted shortening
1¼ cups boiling water, approximately
    Shortening for shallow-fat frying.

1. Put the corn meal in a mixing bowl and add the flour, salt, sugar and baking powder. Mix well and stir in the melted shortening.
2. Pour in the boiling water, adding just enough to make a moist but manageable mixture. Wet the hands and shape the dough into patties about one-half-inch thick and four inches in diameter. Heat shortening in a skillet to a depth of about one-quarter inch. Add the patties and cook over moderately high heat on one side. Turn and cook until golden brown on the other.
Yield: Four patties.

Vivian's Corn Bread

Florida

2 cups yellow corn meal
1 cup flour
1 tablespoon baking powder
2 eggs, lightly beaten
1 teaspoon salt
1 teaspoon sugar (optional)
1 cup milk
3 tablespoons shortening or bacon drippings, melted.

1. Preheat the oven to 400 degrees.
2. Sift together the corn meal, flour and baking powder into a mixing bowl. Stir in the eggs, salt, sugar if desired, milk and shortening or bacon drippings. Pour into greased nine-inch square pan.
3. Bake twenty to twenty-five minutes, or until bread is firm in the center.
Yield: Six servings.

Corn Bread

South Carolina

½ cup lard
½ cup butter
¼ cup sugar
2 eggs
1¾ cups white corn meal
1¼ cups flour
6 teaspoons baking powder
1 teaspoon salt
1¼ cups milk.

1. Preheat the oven to 450 degrees.
2. Cream the lard, butter and sugar together. Beat in the eggs, one at a time.

3. Sift together the corn meal, flour, baking powder and salt and add alternately with the milk to the butter mixture. Turn into a greased 14-by-10-inch baking pan and bake about twenty-five minutes.

Yield: About thirty-five pieces, each two inches square.

Crackling Corn Bread   *Mississippi*

¼ pound cracklings, about one cup (see note)
⅓ cup sifted flour
1½ cups sifted white corn meal
1 teaspoon baking soda
½ teaspoon salt
2 eggs
1 cup buttermilk
2 cups regular milk
3 tablespoons bacon drippings, lard or butter.

1. Preheat the oven to 350 degrees.
2. Place the cracklings in an ovenproof skillet and bake about fifteen minutes. Drain and reserve the cracklings.
3. Sift the flour, corn meal, baking soda and salt into a mixing bowl. Beat the eggs until they are foamy and stir in the buttermilk and half the regular milk. Stir this into the corn meal mixture. Stir in the drained cracklings.
4. Place the bacon drippings, lard or butter in a nine-inch heavy iron skillet and heat it on top of the stove. The bacon drippings should be quite hot but not brown. Pour the corn bread mixture into the skillet. Very carefully pour the remaining cup of regular milk over the top of the corn meal mixture. Do not stir. Bake fifty minutes.

Yield: Eight servings.

Note: Cracklings are rendered pork skins and are much richer than the fried pork skins sold commercially, at least outside the South.

Spoon Bread   *Mississippi*

3 cups milk
1½ cups white corn meal
¼ cup butter
1 teaspoon salt
2 teaspoons baking powder
4 eggs, separated.

1. Preheat the oven to 350 degrees.
2. Heat two cups of the milk. Gradually stir into the corn meal set in the top of a double boiler. Add the butter.
3. Bring the mixture to a boil, stirring, and cook ten minutes. Add the salt and cool to lukewarm.
4. Dissolve the baking powder in the remaining milk and beat with the egg yolks into the corn meal mixture. Beat the egg whites until stiff and fold in. Pour into a buttered casserole. Bake about forty minutes, or until well puffed and brown. Serve from the casserole.

Yield: Six servings.

Batter Bread   *Maryland*

2 cups milk
2 tablespoons butter
2 eggs, lightly beaten
1 tablespoon sugar
1 teaspoon salt
1 tablespoon flour
⅓ cup yellow corn meal
1 cup cold cooked rice.

1. Preheat the oven to 375 degrees.
2. Heat the milk and butter together. Mix the eggs with the remaining ingredients and then gradually stir the milk mixture into it.
3 Return to the pan and stir and cook over low heat or in the top of a double boiler until mixture thickens. Pour into a buttered baking dish and bake forty mintues, or until well browned.

Yield: Four to six servings.

Deep-Fried Hot Water Corn Bread

Alabama

1 cup white corn meal
1 tablespoon plus one teaspoon flour
2 teaspoons baking powder
½ teaspoon salt
1 tablespoon sugar
1¼ cups boiling water
    Fat or oil for deep-frying.

1. Place the corn meal, flour, baking powder, salt and sugar in a bowl. Stir in the water.
2. Heat the fat or oil to 375 degrees. Drop the dough by tablespoons into the hot fat and cook until golden.
Yield: Four servings.

Southern Buttermilk Corn Bread

Tennessee

1½ tablespoons butter
⅓ cup flour
1½ cups white corn meal
1 teaspoon baking soda
½ teaspoon salt
2 eggs, beaten
1 cup buttermilk
2 cups regular milk.

1. Preheat the oven to 350 degrees.
2. Heat the butter in an ovenproof nine-inch to ten-inch skillet. A cast iron one is best. Sift together the flour, corn meal, baking soda and salt.
3. Beat in the eggs, buttermilk and one cup of the regular milk. Pour into the hot skillet. Pour remaining cup of regular milk over the top. Do not stir. Bake fifty minutes, or until done.
Yield: Four servings.
Note: Serve, buttered, with creamed chicken.

Fried Corn Meal Mush

South Carolina

½ cup white corn meal
2½ cups boiling water
¾ teaspoon salt
    Bacon drippings.

1. Sprinkle the corn meal over the boiling water, stirring briskly. Add the salt and cook thirty minutes over low heat.
2. Pour into a greased loaf pan or bowl and cool until firm. Remove from pan or bowl and cut into slices three-quarters-inch thick.
3. Melt the bacon drippings in a heavy skillet and cook the slices until brown on both sides.
Yield: Four servings.

Corn Meal Sticks

Alabama

2 cups water
1¼ teaspoons salt
1½ cups white corn meal
1 cup grated Edam cheese
    Lard for deep-frying.

1. Combine the water and salt in a saucepan. Heat to the boiling point and gradually stir in the corn meal. When thoroughly blended, cook for five minutes, stirring almost constantly. When ready, the mixture should separate from the bottom and sides of the pan.
2. Remove mixture from the heat and stir in the cheese.
3. When cool enough to handle, shape mixture, one heaping teaspoonful at a time, into balls. Using the palms of the hands, roll each ball into a small cigar shape about one-half-inch thick.
4. Drop sticks, a few at a time, into lard heated to 375 degrees. Cook until golden brown and drain on paper towels.
Yield: About fifty; ten servings.

Crackling Bread Cakes

Georgia

1 cup white corn meal
¼ teaspoon baking soda
1 teaspoon single acting (tartrate) baking
  powder
  Buttermilk
½ cup cracklings (crisp pork rind pieces).

1. Preheat the oven to 400 degrees.
2. Place the corn meal, baking soda and baking powder in a bowl. Add enough buttermilk to make a soft batter. Let rest five minutes. Stir in the cracklings and more buttermilk if needed to make a pancake consistency.
3. Drop by tablespoonfuls onto a hot greased griddle and cook until brown. Turn and brown the other side. Place on a baking pan and bake about ten minutes to complete cooking.

Yield: Four servings.

Lacy Hoe Cakes

Georgia

1 tablespoon bacon drippings
1 teaspoon salt
1 cup waterground white corn meal
1 cup boiling water, approximately.

1. Add the bacon drippings and salt to the corn meal. Cut in the drippings with a knife. Add boiling water until the batter is fairly runny. Let rest one hour. The corn meal swells.
2. Add more water if necessary to give a batter that flows easily. Spoon by the tablespoonful onto a moderately hot (375 degrees) greased griddle. Cook until brown, turn and cook underside. Hoe cakes must cook thoroughly or they will stick to the griddle. They should be paper-thin and lacy-looking.

Yield: Four servings.

Hush Puppies

Kentucky

2 cups white corn meal
2¼ teaspoons baking powder
1 teaspoon salt
½ cup finely minced onion
1½ cups milk
½ cup warm water
  Fat for deep-frying.

1. Sift the corn meal, baking powder and salt into a mixing bowl. Stir in the onion, milk and warm water. Mix well to make a manageable mass. Using the palms, shape the mixture into rounds the size of large walnuts.
2. Heat the fat to about 370 degrees and deep-fry the hush puppies until golden brown and crisp on the outside. These are traditional accompaniments for fried fish.

Yield: About two dozen.

River Road Hush Puppies

Louisiana

1 cup white corn meal
1 cup flour
1 teaspoon salt
½ teaspoon sugar
1 teaspoon baking powder
¾ cup milk
1 egg
  Cayenne pepper or chopped hot green
  peppers to taste
¼ cup chopped scallion tops
1 tablespoon finely minced or grated onion
  Lard or other fat for deep-frying.

1. Sift the corn meal, flour, salt, sugar and baking powder into a mixing bowl. Make a well in the center and stir in the milk beaten with the egg. When blended, add the cayenne, or hot green peppers, scallion tops and minced onion.
2. Heat the fat for deep-frying (about 375 degrees). Drop the corn meal batter by the spoonful into the fat and cook until golden brown.

Yield: About two dozen.

Lacy Corn Bread

North Carolina

1 cup yellow corn meal
½ cup flour
½ teaspoon baking soda
½ teaspoon salt
1½ cups water
   Peanut oil.

1. Combine the corn meal, flour, baking soda and salt in a bowl. Add the water and mix to a thin batter.
2. Heat oil to the depth of one-eighth inch in a ten-inch skillet until almost smoking. Pour in a very thin layer of the batter and cook over high heat.
3. Cook until the underside is well browned and the top is lacy over most of its area. Turn and cook a few moments longer. Drain on paper towels and keep warm. Repeat until all the batter is used, being careful to stir batter well before pouring. Thin the batter with water if batter gets too thick and add more oil to the skillet as necessary. The rounds of lacy corn bread can be broken up for serving.
Yield: Eight servings.

Molasses Corn Bread

Georgia

¾ cup white corn meal
1 cup flour
1 teaspoon salt
¾ teaspoon baking soda
½ cup light molasses
¾ cup buttermilk
1 egg, well beaten
2 tablespoons shortening, melted.

1. Preheat the oven to 425 degrees.
2. Grease an eight-inch cast iron skillet or an eight-inch square pan. Sift the corn meal, flour, salt and baking soda together into a bowl.
3. Add the remaining ingredients and stir until just blended. Pour into the prepared pan and bake twenty minutes, or until done.
Yield: Six servings.

Bacon and Cheese Spoon Bread

Georgia

½ pound bacon
1 clove garlic, finely chopped
¾ cup yellow corn meal
½ cup white hominy grits
2½ cups water
2 cups shredded sharp Cheddar cheese
¼ pound butter
½ teaspoon salt
1 cup milk
4 eggs, separated
1 four-ounce jar or can pimentos, drained and diced.

1. Preheat the oven to 325 degrees.
2. Cook the bacon in a skillet until crisp. Remove, crumble and reserve. Discard all but one tablespoon of the bacon drippings, sauté the garlic in it until tender and reserve.
3. Mix together the corn meal, hominy and water in a saucepan. Bring to a boil, stirring, and cook one minute. Remove from the heat.
4. Stir in the cheese and butter until melted. Add the salt, milk, egg yolks, reserved bacon and garlic and the pimentos.
5. Beat the egg whites until stiff but not dry and fold into the corn meal mixture. Turn into a greased three-quart casserole or soufflé dish and bake about one hour and fifteen minutes, or until set in the middle.
Yield: Six servings.

Grand Hot Cakes

Mississippi

½ cup white corn meal
1 tablespoon sugar
½ teaspoon salt
1 cup boiling water

2 eggs, separated
¾ cup milk
1 cup flour
3 teaspoons baking powder
¼ cup oil.

1. Place the corn meal, sugar and salt in a saucepan. Stir in the water and cook, stirring, two minutes. Cool.

2. Stir the egg yolks and milk into the cooled corn meal.

3. Sift the flour with the baking powder and stir into the corn meal mixture. Beat the egg whites until stiff and fold with the oil into the mixture.

4. Spoon by tablespoons onto a moderately hot lightly greased griddle and cook until browned. Turn and brown other side.

Yield: Four servings.

Waffles   *Tennessee*

1½ cups flour
3 teaspoons baking powder
½ teaspoon salt
1 tablespoon sugar
1 cup milk
2 eggs, separated
3 tablespoons melted butter, syrup,
    marmalade, jam or honey.

1. Sift the flour with the baking powder, salt and sugar into a mixing bowl. Make a well in the center and add the milk, egg yolks and melted butter. Combine rapidly with a fork or wire whisk. The mixture should remain a little lumpy.

2. Beat the egg whites until stiff and fold them into the batter. Cook the batter in waffle irons and serve with melted butter, syrup, marmalade, jelly, jam or honey.

Yield: Six to eight.

Sweet Potato Spoon Bread   *Georgia*

2 medium-size sweet potatoes
  Salt to taste
8 tablespoons butter
1 tablespoon sugar
½ teaspoon nutmeg
1 teaspoon allspice
¼ cup flour
2 eggs, separated.

1. Place the potatoes in a large saucepan and add water to cover and salt. Bring to a boil and simmer until potatoes are tender, at least thirty minutes. Drain and peel. Put the potatoes through a ricer into a hot mixing bowl. Beat in the butter, sugar, nutmeg, allspice and flour.

2. Preheat the oven to 400 degrees.

3. Beat the egg yolks lightly and beat them into the potatoes. Beat the egg whites until stiff and fold them into the mixture. Pour the mixture into a buttered one-and-one-half-quart casserole and bake until puffed and brown, about thirty minutes.

Yield: Four to six servings.

Southern-Style Biscuits   *South Carolina*

2 cups flour
3 teaspoons baking powder
½ teaspoon salt
3 tablespoons melted shortening
⅔ cup buttermilk, approximately.

1. Preheat the oven to 475 degrees.

2. Sift the flour, baking powder and salt into a bowl.

3. Stir in the shortening and buttermilk to make a soft dough. Work on a floured board lightly until dough can be rolled. Roll out to one-half-inch thickness and cut into rounds.

4. Place rounds on a lightly greased baking sheet and bake ten to twelve minutes.

Yield: About two dozen.

Cheese Biscuits
Mississippi

1½ cups flour
2 teaspoons baking powder
¼ teaspoon salt
6 tablespoons grated sharp Cheddar cheese
1 tablespoon melted butter
  Milk.

1. Preheat the oven to 450 degrees.
2. Combine the flour, baking powder and salt. Stir in the cheese. Toss lightly with the butter and approximately two-thirds cup of milk, adding enough milk to make a soft dough that can be dropped from a teaspoon. Toss dough on floured board, pat to one-half-inch thickness and cut with a small biscuit cutter or drop the dough by spoonfuls onto a baking sheet. Brush with milk. Bake ten minutes.
Yield: Three dozen.

Biscuits
Mississippi

2 cups flour
1 teaspoon sugar
½ teaspoon salt
2 teaspoons baking powder
½ cup shortening, melted
1 cup milk, approximately.

1. Preheat the oven to 425 degrees.
2. Place the flour, sugar, salt and baking powder in a mixing bowl and mix well. Pour in the melted shortening, stirring with a wooden spoon. When blended, add the milk gradually, stirring constantly. Add enough milk to form a soft, manageable dough.
3. Knead the dough about ten strokes. Roll it out on a lightly floured board to approximately one-third-inch thickness. Cut into rounds with a biscuit cutter. Arrange the biscuits about one inch apart on a lightly greased baking sheet and bake twelve to fifteen minutes.
Yield: About one dozen to two dozen.

Beaten Biscuits
Virginia

3 cups flour
½ teaspoon sugar
½ teaspoon salt
3 tablespoons cold butter
3 tablespoons cold lard
½ cup cold milk
½ cup cold water, approximately.

1. Sift the flour, sugar and salt into a mixing bowl.
2. Add the butter and lard and, with two knives or a pastry blender, cut into the flour until mixture resembles coarse corn meal. Add the milk and enough water to make a stiff dough. Toss mixture with a fork. Knead dough for fifteen minutes; then beat with a mallet for twenty minutes, or until well blistered. Or put dough through the coarse blade of a meat grinder, folding dough over frequently. Or put dough over and over through the rollers of a beaten biscuit machine. When ready, the dough should be smooth and glossy.
3. Preheat the oven to 325 degrees.
4. Roll dough one-half-inch thick and cut into rounds with a small floured biscuit cutter. Prick rounds with a fork and bake thirty minutes on baking sheets.
Yield: Three dozen or more.

Sweet Potato Biscuits
Alabama

2 cups flour
5 teaspoons baking powder
1 teaspoon salt
¼ cup sugar
2 cups mashed cooked sweet potatoes
½ cup shortening
¾ cup milk, approximately.

1. Preheat the oven to 425 degrees.
2. Sift together the flour, baking powder, salt and sugar. Mix in the potatoes and shortening.

Add enough milk to make a soft dough for rolling.

3. Knead on a lightly floured board until smooth. Roll out to one-half-inch thickness and cut into rounds with a biscuit cutter. Place rounds on lightly greased baking sheets and bake ten to fifteen minutes. Eat hot.

Yield: About thirty.

Corn Meal Muffins   *Arkansas*

1½ cups sifted self-rising white corn meal
½ cup sifted self-rising flour
1 cup milk
3 tablespoons oil
1 egg.

1. Preheat the oven to 425 degrees.
2. Mix the corn meal and flour in a bowl. Measure the milk into a two-cup measure and add the oil and unbeaten egg. Mix well.
3. Make a hole in the center of corn meal mixture and pour in milk mixture. Stir until ingredients are just moistened. Fill hot greased muffin pans two-thirds full. Bake eighteen to twenty minutes.

Yield: One dozen medium-size.

Note: In place of self-rising corn meal and flour, use one and one-half cups regular white corn meal, one-half cup flour, three teaspoons baking powder and one-half teaspoon salt.

To avoid heating oven in hot weather, bake the batter as you would pancakes on a hot greased griddle.

Banana Bread   *Mississippi*

½ cup butter
1 cup sugar
2 eggs
2 cups flour
1 teaspoon baking powder
1 teaspoon baking soda
¼ teaspoon salt

½ cup chopped pecans
3 very ripe bananas, mashed.

1. Preheat the oven to 350 degrees.
2. Cream the butter with the sugar until light and fluffy. Beat in the eggs, one at a time.
3. Sift together the flour, baking powder, baking soda and salt. Toss the pecans with one tablespoon of the flour mixture.
4. Fold the bananas into the butter mixture. Stir in the flour. Fold in the pecans. Turn into a greased 8½-by 4½-by 2½-inch loaf pan and bake forty-five minutes to one hour, or until bread tests done.

Yield: One loaf.

Fried Cream or Custard   *Alabama*

1 tablespoon plus one teaspoon flour
3 tablespoons cold milk
½ cup sugar
2 tablespoons cornstarch
2 cups hot milk
1 stick cinnamon
3 eggs, lightly beaten
¼ teaspoon salt
2 egg whites, lightly beaten
Cracker crumbs
Fat or oil for deep-frying.

1. Day before, mix the flour with the cold milk in a saucepan. Mix together the sugar and cornstarch and stir into the flour mixture. Gradually stir in the hot milk. Add the cinnamon stick and heat, stirring, until mixture boils.
2. Cook, stirring, three minutes. Remove cinnamon stick. Add one-half cup of the hot sauce to the eggs. Mix and return to the bulk of the sauce. Cook until eggs cook and mixture thickens a little bit further. Pour into a greased shallow pan so that there is about one-half inch of mixture.
3. Chill overnight. Next day, cut into two-inch squares or strips. Dip in the egg white and then in the crumbs and fry, a few pieces at a time, in

a fry basket in fat, or oil heated to 375 degrees. Drain on paper towels and keep warm in the oven while preparing remainder.

Yield: Six servings.

Note: Serve with broiled or roasted chicken.

Light Rolls   *South Carolina*

1 cup shortening
½ cup sugar
1 tablespoon salt
1½ cups boiling water
2 eggs, beaten
2 packages active dry yeast
½ cup lukewarm water
5 cups flour, approximately
  Butter.

1. Combine the shortening, sugar, salt and boiling water in a bowl and stir to dissolve the sugar. Let stand until at room temperature.

2. Beat in the eggs.

3. Soften the yeast in the lukewarm water and add to the bowl.

4. Stir in enough flour to make a soft but not sticky dough. Knead until smooth on a lightly floured board. Place in a clean greased bowl, cover and let rise in a warm place until doubled in bulk.

5. Roll out on a floured board to one-quarter-inch thickness. Cut into two-and-one-half-inch rounds. Place a small piece of butter in the center of each, fold one half over the other and pinch to seal.

6. Place on a greased baking sheet, cover and let rise until doubled in bulk, about forty-five minutes.

7. Preheat the oven to 350 degrees.

8. Bake fifteen to twenty minutes, or until browned and done.

Yield: Three dozen.

Sally Lunn   *Virginia*

1 package active dry yeast
¼ cup warm water
1 cup milk, scalded
½ cup butter
¼ cup sugar
3 eggs, beaten
4 cups flour, approximately
1 teaspoon salt.

1. Soften the yeast in the water and stir to dissolve.

2. Combine the milk, butter and sugar. Stir to melt the butter and dissolve the sugar. Cool to lukewarm.

3. In a large bowl, combine the softened yeast, milk mixture and the eggs. Add three cups of the flour and the salt and beat with a wooden spoon until smooth. Add enough extra flour to make a soft batter. Beat well until smooth and elastic.

4. Place in a clean bowl, cover with a damp cloth and let rise in a warm place until doubled in bulk, about one hour. Knock down and beat well until smooth.

5. Transfer the dough to a greased two-quart Turk's head mold, kugelhof pan or nine-inch angel food pan. Cover with a damp cloth, place in a warm place and let rise until doubled in bulk, about forty-five minutes.

6. Preheat the oven to 325 degrees.

7. Bake the Sally Lunn about forty-five minutes, or until golden brown and done. Serve hot or warm if possible.

Yield: About ten servings.

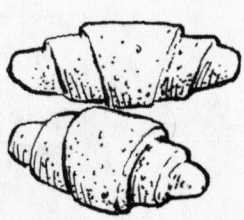

Pies, Cakes, Desserts and Cookies

Molasses-Nut Pie
Alabama

1 cup dark molasses
3 tablespoons lemon juice
½ teaspoon grated lemon rind
2 eggs, separated
¼ cup sugar
1 tablespoon flour
¼ teaspoon nutmeg
¼ teaspoon cinnamon
1 tablespoon melted butter
⅛ teaspoon salt
½ cup pecans
1 unbaked eight-inch or nine-inch pie shell.

1. Preheat the oven to 350 degrees.
2. Mix the molasses with the lemon juice and rind. Beat the egg yolks with the sugar. Gradually beat in the flour, nutmeg, cinnamon, butter and salt.
3. While beating, add the molasses slowly. Beat the egg whites until stiff but not dry and fold molasses mixture into them. Place the pecans in the bottom of the pie shell and pour the molasses mixture over.
4. Bake ten minutes, reduce oven heat to 325 degrees and bake about twenty-five minutes longer, or until set.
Yield: Six servings.

Guava Pecan Pie
Florida

1 cup guava syrup or three-quarters cup guava jelly, heated and diluted with water
¾ cup sugar
2 tablespoons flour
2 egg yolks
¼ cup evaporated milk
Pinch of salt
2 tablespoons melted butter
1 cup pecan halves
1 unbaked nine-inch pie shell.

1. Preheat the oven to 425 degrees.
2. Place the guava syrup in a bowl. Combine the sugar and flour and beat with the egg yolks. Stir in the evaporated milk and salt. Stir the mixture into the guava syrup and add the butter. Stir in the pecan halves and pour the filling into the pie shell. Bake ten minutes, reduce oven heat to 325 degrees and bake thirty-five minutes longer, or until set.
Yield: Six servings.

Black Walnut Pie
North Carolina

3 eggs, lightly beaten
1 cup dark corn syrup
1 cup firmly packed light brown sugar
3 tablespoons butter, melted
1 teaspoon vanilla

⅛ teaspoon salt
1 unbaked nine-inch pie shell, chilled
¾ cup black walnuts
    Confectioners' sugar (optional).

1. Preheat the oven to 350 degrees.
2. Combine the eggs, syrup, brown sugar, butter, vanilla and salt.
3. Turn the mixture into the pie shell and sprinkle the black walnuts over the top.
4. Bake until firm, about one hour. If desired, serve sprinkled with confectioners' sugar.
Yield: Eight servings.
Note: One cup peanuts or pecans may be substituted for the black walnuts.

Peanut Pie   *Georgia*

2 eggs
1 cup dark corn syrup
1 cup sugar
1 teaspoon vanilla
1 cup salted peanuts
1 unbaked nine-inch pie shell
2 tablespoons butter.

1. Preheat the oven to 350 degrees.
2. Combine the eggs, syrup, sugar and vanilla. Stir in the peanuts. Pour the mixture into the pie shell. Dot with the butter.
3. Bake forty-five to fifty minutes, or until the filling is set.
Yield: Six to eight servings.

Walnut Pie   *Georgia*

½ cup butter, at room temperature
1 cup firmly packed dark brown sugar
1 cup dark corn syrup
4 eggs, lightly beaten
    Pinch of salt
1 teaspoon vanilla
1 unbaked eight-inch or nine-inch pie shell
1 cup walnut meats.

1. Preheat the oven to 375 degrees.
2. Cream together the butter and brown sugar in a mixing bowl. Blend in the syrup. Beat in the eggs.
3. Add the salt and vanilla to the mixture and pour into the pie shell. Arrange the walnuts symmetrically over the top and bake forty minutes, or until set.
Yield: Six to eight servings.

Pecan Pie   *Louisiana*

½ cup sugar
2 tablespoons butter
2 eggs, lightly beaten
2 tablespoons flour
¼ teaspoon salt
1 teaspoon almond extract
1 teaspoon vanilla
1 cup light corn syrup
1½ cups chopped pecans
1 unbaked eight-inch pie shell.

1. Preheat the oven to 350 degrees.
2. Cream together the sugar, butter, eggs, flour, salt, almond extract, vanilla and syrup. Beat well and stir in pecans.
3. Pour mixture into pie shell. Bake thirty to forty-five minutes, or until filling is set.
Yield: Six servings.

Chess Pie I   *Kentucky*

1 cup light brown sugar
½ cup granulated sugar
1 teaspoon flour
2 eggs
1 teaspoon vanilla
2 tablespoons light cream
½ cup melted butter
1 unbaked nine-inch pie shell
    Sweetened whipped cream (optional).

1. Preheat the oven to 325 degrees.

2. Combine the brown sugar, granulated sugar and flour. Add the eggs and mix well. Add the vanilla and cream and blend. Stir in the butter and pour the mixture into the pie shell.

3. Bake thirty to thirty-five minutes, or until the filling is slightly firm. If desired, serve with whipped cream sweetened to taste.

Yield: Six to eight servings.

Chess Pie II   *Kentucky*

½ cup butter, at room temperature
1¼ cups sugar
1 tablespoon yellow corn meal
3 eggs
  Grated rind of one lemon
  Juice of one lemon
1 teaspoon vanilla
¼ teaspoon salt
1 unbaked nine-inch pie shell.

1. Preheat the oven to 325 degrees.

2. Cream together the butter and sugar in a mixing bowl, using a wooden spoon. Beat in the corn meal.

3. Add the eggs, one at a time, beating well after each addition. Beat in the lemon rind, lemon juice, vanilla and salt. Pour the mixture into the pie shell. Bake forty-five minutes, or until a knife inserted in the center comes out clean.

Yield: Six to eight servings.

Chess Tarts   *North Carolina*

⅓ cup butter
1 cup sugar
3 eggs, separated
1 tablespoon yellow corn meal
¼ cup heavy cream
1 teaspoon grated lemon rind
1 teaspoon lemon juice
⅛ teaspoon salt
8 individual two-inch tartlet pans lined with pastry.

1. Preheat the oven to 400 degrees.

2. Cream the butter and sugar together. Beat in the egg yolks. Combine the corn meal and cream and add to the batter. Stir in the lemon rind, lemon juice and salt.

3. Beat the egg whites until stiff but not dry and fold in.

4. Bake the unfilled shells about five minutes until set. Fill with the mixture and bake five minutes. Reduce oven heat to 350 degrees and bake about twenty minutes longer, or until browned and set.

Yield: Eight tarts.

Sweet Potato Pie   *Arkansas*

1½ cups mashed cooked sweet potatoes
½ cup sugar
½ teaspoon salt
½ teaspoon nutmeg
1 teaspoon cinnamon
¼ teaspoon ground cloves
2 eggs, well beaten
½ teaspoon vanilla
¼ cup butter
1 cup hot milk
1 unbaked nine-inch pie shell.

1. Preheat the oven to 450 degrees.

2. Combine the sweet potatoes, sugar, salt, nutmeg, cinnamon, cloves, eggs and vanilla. Melt the butter in the milk and stir into the potato mixture.

3. Beat with a rotary beater until smooth. Turn into the pie shell. Bake ten minutes, reduce oven heat to 350 degrees and bake forty-five minutes longer, or until a knife inserted in center comes out clean. Cool. Chill.

Yield: Six servings.

Sliced Yam Pie   *Kentucky*

Pastry for a nine-inch two-crust pie
5 to six cups very thinly sliced raw yams

1 cup light brown sugar
½ teaspoon salt
Cinnamon to taste
½ cup butter
2 tablespoons water or light cream.

1. Preheat the oven to 350 degrees. Line a nine-inch pie pan with the pastry.

2. Using about one-third of the ingredients at a time, arrange the yams, brown sugar, salt, cinnamon and bits of butter in layers in the pie pan. Pour the water or cream over all.

3. Cover with top crust, seal and cut slits. Bake until potatoes are soft, about one hour. Serve warm or at room temperature.

Yield: Six to eight servings.

Jeff Davis Pie   *South Carolina*

½ cup butter
1 cup sugar
1 tablespoon flour
3 eggs
1 cup heavy cream
¼ teaspoon salt
½ teaspoon vanilla
1 unbaked nine-inch pie shell.

1. Preheat the oven to 425 degrees.

2. Cream the butter and sugar together until light and fluffy. Beat in the flour, eggs, cream, salt and vanilla.

3. Pour into the pie shell and bake ten minutes. Lower the oven heat to 350 degrees and bake about thirty minutes longer, or until set.

Yield: Six servings.

Sour Cream Pie   *North Carolina*

1 cup sour cream
¾ cup sugar
2 eggs, lightly beaten
¼ teaspoon ground cloves
1 teaspoon cinnamon

½ teaspoon nutmeg
½ cup pecans
1 unbaked eight-inch or nine-inch pie shell, chilled.

1. Preheat the oven to 425 degrees.

2. Combine the sour cream, sugar and eggs. Stir in the cloves, cinnamon, nutmeg and pecans. Pour into the pie shell. Bake fifteen minutes, reduce oven heat to 325 degrees and bake fifteen to twenty minutes longer, or until set and browned.

Yield: Six servings.

Black Bottom Pie   *Kentucky*

14 gingersnaps
5 tablespoons melted butter
1 tablespoon unflavored gelatin
¼ cup cold water
1 cup sugar
½ teaspoon salt
¼ cup cornstarch
2 cups milk
4 eggs, separated
6 ounces semisweet chocolate bits
1 teaspoon vanilla
1 tablespoon dark rum
¼ teaspoon cream of tartar
Whipped cream
Shaved chocolate.

1. Preheat the oven to 350 degrees.

2. Crush and roll the ginersnaps fine with a rolling pin. Mix with the butter and pat the mixture along the bottom and side of a nine-inch pie pan. Bake seven minutes. Cool thoroughly.

3. Soften the gelatin in the cold water.

4. Combine one-half cup of the sugar with the salt and cornstarch and gradually stir in the milk, using a wire whisk. Bring to a boil and cook, stirring, until thickened.

5. Beat the egg yolks in a mixing bowl and gradually stir in the hot mixture. Return the custard to the heat and cook, stirring, two minutes.

6. Remove the saucepan from the heat and

measure out one and one-half cups custard. Add the chocolate bits and vanilla and pour into pie shell. Chill.

7. Add the gelatin to the remaining custard mixture, stirring until gelatin dissolves. Cool to lukewarm and add the rum.

8. Beat the egg whites with the cream of tartar until stiff. Gradually beat in the remaining sugar. Fold the whites into the rum-flavored custard, pour over the chocolate mixture and chill. Serve pie topped with whipped cream and garnished with shaved chocolate.

Yield: Six or more servings.

Chocolate-Butterscotch Pie   *Kentucky*

3 cups light brown sugar
½ cup butter
3 eggs
1 teaspoon vanilla
½ cup light cream
1 ounce (one square) unsweetened chocolate, melted
1 unbaked nine-inch pie shell with stand-up edge, chilled
1 cup sweetened heavy cream, whipped
Chocolate shavings.

1. Preheat the oven to 350 degrees.

2. Beat the brown sugar and butter together until creamy. Beat in the eggs, one at a time. Add the vanilla.

3. Beat in the light cream, add the melted chocolate and beat to mix completely. Pour into the pie shell and bake thirty minutes. Reduce the oven heat to 300 degrees and continue to bake about fifty minutes longer, or until set. Cool before decorating with the whipped cream and chocolate shavings. The pie puffs up during cooking, then falls as it cools.

Yield: Eight servings.

Rum Pie   *Louisiana*

5 egg yolks
¾ cup granulated sugar
1 envelope unflavored gelatin
¼ cup water
¾ cup dark rum
2 cups heavy cream
1 baked nine-inch graham cracker pie shell, cooled
3 tablespoons raw sugar (see note).

1. Beat the egg yolks until they are thick and lemon-colored. Gradually beat in the granulated sugar.

2. Soften the gelatin in the water and add one-quarter cup of the rum. Heat over boiling water until gelatin dissolves. Pour the gelatin mixture into the yolks, stirring briskly. Stir in the remaining rum.

3. Whip the cream and fold it into the custard. Pour the filling into the pie shell and chill.

4. When filling is set, sprinkle the pie with the raw sugar and serve.

Yield: Six servings.

Note: Raw sugar is available in health food stores and some supermarkets.

Chocolate Rum Pie   *Florida*

3 ounces (three squares) unsweetened chocolate
¾ cup sugar
3 tablespoons flour
½ teaspoon salt
1½ cups milk
3 tablespoons cornstarch
1 cup light cream
2 egg yolks
1 teaspoon vanilla
½ cup butter
¼ cup rum
1 baked nine-inch pie shell
Whipped cream, flavored to taste with sugar and rum.

1. Melt the chocolate over low heat.

2. Combine the sugar, flour and salt in a mixing bowl. Blend one-half cup of the milk with the cornstarch. Stir the cornstarch mixture into the flour mixture. Add the melted chocolate, the remaining milk and the cream. Add the egg yolks, vanilla and butter, beating constantly.

3. Cook the filling over boiling water until thick. Let cool.

4. Stir in the rum and pour the filling into the pie shell. Top with whipped cream and serve.

Yield: Six or more servings.

Bourbon Pie   *Kentucky*

5 egg yolks
¾ cup sugar
1 envelope unflavored gelatin
¼ cup water
⅓ cup bourbon
2 cups heavy cream, whipped
1 baked nine-inch pie shell, cooled
½ ounce (one-half square) unsweetened
   chocolate, shaved

1. Beat the egg yolks and gradually add the sugar. Beat constantly until the mixture turns a light yellow.

2. Soften the gelatin in the water and heat over boiling water until gelatin dissolves. Add to the egg yolk mixture. Mix well and add the bourbon.

3. Fold in the whipped cream and pour into the pie shell. Sprinkle with the chocolate shavings. Chill for at least six hours before serving.

Yield: Six to eight servings.

Note: One-third cup dark rum may be substituted for the bourbon.

Lime Meringue Pie   *Florida*

4 tablespoons flour
5 tablespoons cornstarch
1½ cups plus five tablespoons sugar
½ teaspoon salt

2 cups boiling water
3 eggs, separated
   Grated rind of two limes
½ cup freshly squeezed lime juice
2 drops green food coloring (optional)
1 baked nine-inch pie shell
   Pinch of cream of tartar.

1. Combine the flour, cornstarch, one and one-half cups of the sugar and the salt in a heavy saucepan and mix thoroughly with a wire whisk. When well blended, add the boiling water gradually, stirring with the whisk. Bring gradually to a boil, stirring constantly. When mixture is thickened, remove from the heat.

2. Beat the egg yolks until they are light and lemon-colored. Spoon a little of the hot mixture into the yolks; then stir the yolk mixture into the sauce. Cook, stirring, two minutes over low heat.

3. Stir in the lime rind, lime juice and food coloring if desired. When all is well blended, pour the filling into the pie shell. Let the filling cool in the shell.

4. Preheat the oven to 425 degrees.

5. Beat the egg whites until they are frothy. Add the cream of tartar. Continue beating until whites stand in peaks, and gradually add the remaining sugar. When whites are thoroughly stiff, spread them roughly on top of the pie filling, leaving peaks. Make certain that the meringue touches the pie shell all around to prevent shrinking of meringue as pie bakes.

6. Bake pie until meringue is browned on top.

Yield: Six to eight servings.

Kentucky Lemon Pie

6 eggs
1½ cups light corn syrup
¾ cup sugar
1 teaspoon cornstarch
½ cup lemon juice
   Grated rind of one lemon
1 tablespoon melted butter

1 unbaked ten-inch pie shell with stand-up edge, chilled
Meringue (recipe below).

1. Preheat the oven to 375 degrees.
2. Beat the eggs with a rotary beater until well mixed. Add the syrup and continue beating.
3. Combine the sugar and cornstarch and add to the egg mixture, beating.
4. Add the lemon juice, lemon rind and butter. Beat until thoroughly mixed.
5. Pour carefully into the pie shell. Bake fifteen minutes. Reduce the oven heat to 300 degrees and cook forty-five minutes longer, or until set. Cool and chill.
6. When ready to top the pie with the meringue, preheat the oven to 350 degrees. Spread the meringue over filling so that the meringue touches the pastry edge all around. Leave the surface rough. Bake ten minutes, or until the meringue is lightly browned. Cool and chill again before serving.

Yield: Eight to ten servings.

Meringue *Kentucky*

3 egg whites, at room temperature
¼ teaspoon cream of tartar
3 tablespoons confectioners' sugar.

1. Beat the egg whites until frothy. Add the cream of tartar and continue beating until stiff.
2. Add the sugar, one tablespoon at a time, beating very well after each addition.

Yield: Enough for one nine-inch or ten-inch pie.

Orange Liqueur Chiffon Tart *Kentucky*

1 envelope unflavored gelatin
¼ cup cold water
4 eggs, separated
¾ cup sugar
⅓ cup orange juice

¼ teaspoon salt
2 tablespoons Cointreau or Grand Marnier
1 tablespoon grated orange peel
1 baked nine-inch pie shell
1 cup heavy cream, whipped
2 tablespoons sliced toasted almonds.

1. Soften the gelatin in the water. Beat the egg yolks until thick. Beat in one-half cup of the sugar. Beat in the orange juice and salt and heat in the top of a double boiler until mixture thickens. Do not allow to boil.
2. Stir in softened gelatin until it dissolves. Add the liqueur and orange peel. Cool until mixture starts to thicken. Beat the egg whites until frothy, add the remaining sugar and continue beating until stiff and glossy. Fold into cooked mixture.
3. Pour filling into the pie shell and chill. Decorate with the whipped cream and sprinkle with the almonds just before serving.

Yield: Six servings.

Lemon Chiffon Pie *South Carolina*

¾ cup sugar
2 tablespoons milk
5 egg yolks
1 tablespoon grated lemon rind
3 tablespoons lemon juice
3 egg whites, stiffly beaten
1 baked nine-inch pie shell.

1. Preheat the oven to 400 degrees.
2. Combine one-half cup of the sugar, the milk and egg yolks in the top of a double boiler. Cook over hot water, stirring, until thickened. Stir in the lemon rind and lemon juice and remove from heat. Pour the mixture into a mixing bowl and let cool.
3. Fold the egg whites and remaining sugar into the mixture and pour into the pie shell. Bake eight to ten minutes.

Yield: Eight servings.

Spiced Carrot Pie — *Arkansas*

1 cup sugar
½ teaspoon salt
1 teaspoon ground ginger
1 teaspoon cinnamon
½ teaspoon nutmeg
⅛ teaspoon ground cloves
1½ cups mashed cooked carrots
3 eggs, lightly beaten
1½ cups milk or light cream
1 unbaked nine-inch pie shell.

1. Preheat the oven to 400 degrees.
2. Combine the sugar, salt and spices. Stir in the carrots and eggs. Add the milk or cream and mix well. Pour the mixture into the pie shell.
3. Bake one hour, or until filling is nearly set. The filling will continue to cook slightly after pie is removed from the oven.
Yield: Six to eight servings.

Apple Stack Pie — *Tennessee*

Pastry made according to a standard recipe
   using three cups flour
4 cups thick applesauce
Sugar to taste
Cinnamon, chopped preserved ginger,
   ground ginger or nutmeg
2 cups heavy cream, whipped.

1. Preheat the oven to 425 degrees.
2. Roll the pastry to one-eighth-inch thickness and cut around a nine-inch pan into circles. There should be about six circles. Bake until golden brown, about twelve minutes.
3. Sweeten the applesauce with sugar and flavor with spice to taste.
4. Just before serving, spread each pastry circle with applesauce and whipped cream, stacking circles like a layer cake.
Yield: Eight servings.

Fried Fresh Peach Turnovers — *Georgia*

2 cups flour
½ teaspoon salt
4 tablespoons granulated sugar
1 teaspoon baking powder
½ cup milk
1 egg, lightly beaten
3 tablespoons melted butter
1½ cups peeled and finely chopped peaches
½ teaspoon cinnamon
   Fat or oil for deep-frying
   Confectioners' sugar
   Whipped cream.

1. Sift the flour, salt, one tablespoon of the granulated sugar and the baking powder into a bowl. Combine the milk, egg and butter and stir into the flour mixture to make a soft but not sticky dough.
2. Roll out the dough on a lightly floured board or pastry cloth to one-eighth-inch thickness. Cut into two-and-one-half-inch rounds.
3. Mix together the peaches, cinnamon and remaining sugar and place a tablespoon of this filling in the middle of each round.
4. Moisten around the edge of the round, fold over to make a turnover and press the edge together with the tines of a fork to seal.
5. Deep-fry, two or three at a time, in the fat or oil heated to 375 degrees until golden brown and done, about three minutes. Turn once.
6. Drain on paper towels, sprinkle with confectioners' sugar and serve hot with whipped cream.
Yield: Fourteen to sixteen.

Fried Fruit Turnovers — *Georgia*

1 pound dried peaches, apricots or apples,
   cooked
1 cup sugar, approximately
   Cinnamon or nutmeg to taste
4 cups sifted flour
1 teaspoon salt

¾ cup shortening or lard
½ cup ice water, approximately
   Fat for frying.

1. Drain the selected fruit, mash and sweeten with sugar to taste. Add desired spice. Cool.

2. Sift together the flour and salt. Chop in the shortening or lard until the lumps are the size of very small peas. Add the ice water while tossing the mixture from the bottom of the bowl, using only enough water to form a fairly stiff dough. Press into a ball.

3. Roll out one-third of the dough at a time into a sheet not more than one-eighth-inch thick and about seven inches long. Using a six-inch plate as a guide, cut the dough into circles.

4. Put a one-half-inch layer of prepared fruit on half of each circle, leaving the rim uncovered. Moisten the uncovered rim and fold the other half of the circle over the fruit. Seal and cut away any excess pastry. Crimp the rim.

5. Heat fat to the depth of about one-half inch in a heavy skillet and brown the turnovers on each side. Serve warm or cold.

Yield: Sixteen.

Fresh Peach Pie   *Georgia*

   Pastry for a two-crust pie
3 cups peeled, sliced fresh peaches tossed with juice of half a lemon to prevent discoloration
¼ cup flour
⅓ cup light brown sugar
⅛ teaspoon ground ginger
1 tablespoon butter.

1. Preheat the oven to 400 degrees.
2. Line an eight-inch pie plate with the pastry.
3. Combine the peaches, flour, brown sugar and ginger and turn the mixture into pie plate. Dot with the butter. Cover with the top crust and slash the top. Flute the edges. Bake thirty to forty minutes, or until browned.

Yield: Six servings.

Peach Roll-Ups   *Georgia*

2 cups flour
4 teaspoons baking powder
½ teaspoon salt
4 tablespoons granulated sugar
⅓ cup shortening
¾ cup milk, approximately
¼ cup soft butter
½ teaspoon cinnamon
2 cups peeled, diced fresh peaches
½ cup light brown sugar
1 tablespoon lemon juice
½ cup water
   Whipped cream.

1. Preheat the oven to 400 degrees.
2. Combine the flour, baking powder, salt and one tablespoon of the granulated sugar in a bowl. Cut in the shortening until mixture resembles coarse oatmeal.
3. Gradually add enough milk to make a soft dough. Pat the dough or roll into a rectangle about one-half-inch thick.
4. Brush with the butter and sprinkle with the remaining sugar mixed with the cinnamon.
5. Spread with the peaches and roll like a jellyroll. Cut into one-and-one-half-inch slices and place, cut side up, in a greased 9-by-13-inch baking pan.
6. Combine the brown sugar, lemon juice and water and pour over slices. Bake thirty to forty minutes, or until done. Serve warm with whipped cream.

Yield: Six to eight servings.

Note: The cooked slices can be frozen and stored for up to two months. To serve, bake, uncovered, in a 350-degree oven for about twenty minutes.

Peach Cobbler   *Arkansas*

4 cups sliced fresh peaches, peeled or not as desired
1 cup sugar

3 tablespoons plus three-quarters cup flour
2 tablespoons melted butter
¼ cup shortening
¼ teaspoon salt
2 tablespoons water.

1. Preheat the oven to 400 degrees.
2. Place the peaches in the bottom of a flame-proof eight-inch square baking dish. Heat until peaches start to simmer.
3. Mix together the sugar and three tablespoons of the flour and sprinkle over the peaches. Add the butter.
4. Place the remaining flour in a bowl, add the shortening and salt and with the finger tips work in the shortening until mixture resembles coarse oatmeal. Mix to a dough with the water.
5. Roll out the pastry on a lightly floured board or pastry cloth to fit the baking dish and place over the peaches. Prick with a fork and bake thirty-five to forty minutes.
Yield: Eight servings.

Rum and Rhubarb Chess Pie   *Maryland*

2 tablespoons butter
1 cup sugar
¼ cup flour
2 eggs, separated
1 cup rhubarb, but into one-half-inch lengths
¾ cup plus two tablespoons milk
2 tablespoons dark rum
½ teaspoon salt
¼ teaspoon nutmeg
1 partially cooked nine-inch pie shell,
   prepared according to the next recipe.

1. Preheat the oven to 350 degrees.
2. In a mixing bowl and using an electric beater, cream together the butter and sugar. Beat in the flour and then the egg yolks. Stir in the rhubarb, milk, rum, salt and nutmeg.
3. In a separate bowl, beat the egg whites until stiff and fold them into the rhubarb mixture. Pour

this into the pie shell and bake forty-five minutes. Let cool before serving.
Yield: Six to eight servings.

Pastry for a Nine-Inch Pie   *Maryland*

1¼ cups sifted flour
½ teaspoon salt
¼ cup shortening
¼ cup butter
3 tablespoons water, approximately.

1. Preheat the oven to 350 degrees.
2. In a mixing bowl, combine the flour and salt. Using a pastry blender or two knives, cut in the shortening and butter until the mixture resembles coarse corn meal.
3. Sprinkle the water over the mixture a little at a time while tossing lightly with a two-pronged fork. Add just enough water to moisten the flour so that the pastry will hold together. Gather the dough into a ball and roll it out in a circle on a lightly floured board. The pastry should be about one-eighth-inch thick and one and one-half inches larger in diameter than the pie plate. Line the pie plate with pastry. Flute the edge of the pastry and bake five minutes.
Yield: One partially cooked nine-inch pie shell.

Orange Cake   *Florida*

Cake:
1 cup butter
1½ cups sugar
4 eggs
2¼ cups cake flour
2 teaspoons baking powder
½ teaspoon salt
1 tablespoon grated orange rind
¼ cup orange juice.
Filling:
3 tablespoons flour
2 tablespoons cornstarch

½ cup sugar
1 cup orange juice
1 teaspoon grated orange rind
1 teaspoon unflavored gelatin
1 tablespoon water
2 egg yolks, lightly beaten
¼ cup butter
½ cup heavy cream, whipped (optional).
Frosting:
  2 egg whites
1¾ cups sugar
  1 tablespoon light corn syrup
  5 tablespoons orange juice.

1. To prepare cake, grease and flour an eight-inch springform pan or two nine-inch layer pans. Preheat the oven to 325 degrees for the eight-inch pan or to 375 degrees for the layer pans.

2. Beat the butter with the sugar until very light in color and fluffy in texture. Beat in the eggs, one at a time.

3. Combine the flour, baking powder and salt and sift together. Add half the flour mixture, the orange rind and orange juice to the batter and fold in gently. Fold in the remaining flour mixture and pour into the prepared pan or pans.

4. Bake the eight-inch layer about one and one-quarter hours, or until a cake tester inserted in the center comes out clean. Bake the nine-inch layers about thirty minutes, or until they test done.

5. Cool the cake in the pan or pans ten minutes; then remove to a rack and cool before filling and frosting. The deep cake can be sliced into two, three or four layers, Each of the two layers may be halved, if desired, for a four-layer effect.

6. To prepare filling, combine the flour, cornstarch and sugar in a small pan. Add the orange juice and orange rind and mix well.

7. Soak the gelatin in the water.

8. Bring the orange mixture to a boil, stirring constantly. Cook two minutes. Spoon a little of the hot mixture onto the egg yolks and mix. Add the rest of the orange mixture. Cook half a minute longer.

9. Add the soaked gelatin and the butter. Stir to dissolve. Cool and chill, stirring occasionally.

10. Fold in the whipped cream, if desired, just before using to fill the cake layers.

11. To prepare frosting, place all ingredients in the top of a double boiler over rapidly boiling water. Cook seven minutes, beating rapidly all the time. Frosting will be thick and fluffy. Remove from the boiling water and continue to beat until thick enough to hold its shape. Use to frost the cake.

Yield: Ten servings.

Cake à l'Orange   *Florida*

1 cup butter, at room temperature
1½ cups sugar
3 eggs, separated
2 cups flour
1 teaspoon baking powder
1 teaspoon baking soda
1 cup sour cream
  Grated rind of one orange
½ cup chopped walnuts or pecans
¼ cup orange juice
⅓ cup Grand Marnier or other
  orange-flavored liqueur
2 tablespoons slivered blanched almonds.

1. Preheat the oven to 350 degrees.

2. Cream together the butter and one cup sugar until light and fluffy. Beat in the egg yolks.

3. Sift together the flour, baking powder and baking soda and add, alternately with the sour cream, stirring until smooth. Stir in the orange rind and nuts.

4. Beat the egg whites until stiff but not dry and fold them into the batter. Grease a nine-inch tube cake pan and pour in the batter. Bake fifty minutes, or until cake is done when tested with a cake tester.

5. Combine the orange juice, Grand Marnier and remaining sugar and spoon the mixture over the hot cake. Decorate the top with the almonds.

Let the cake cool before removing it from the pan.

Yield: Ten servings.

Butter Cake

North Carolina

1 cup chopped nuts or nuts mixed with raisins
4 eggs
2 cups sugar
1 teaspoon vanilla
2 cups flour
1 teaspoon baking powder
¼ teaspoon salt
1 cup milk
½ cup butter.

1. Preheat the oven to 350 degrees.
2. Grease a nine-inch pan generously. Line the bottom of the pan with wax paper and grease the paper.
3. Sprinkle the nuts over the bottom of the pan.
4. Beat the eggs until they are lemon-colored and very thick. Gradually beat in the sugar and continue beating until mixture is very thick. Beat in the vanilla.
5. Mix the flour with the baking powder and salt and blend in with the mixer on lowest speed or with a wooden spoon.
6. Heat the milk and butter together in a pan until the butter is melted and the mixture boiling. Pour all at once into the batter and mix just sufficiently to blend all ingredients together. Immediately pour into the prepared pan and bake about fifty minutes, or until done.
7. Cool in the pan ten to fifteen minutes before turning upside down onto a serving plate. The cake will shrink during the cooling.

Yield: Ten to one dozen servings.

Poundcake I

South Carolina

1 cup butter
2 cups sugar
4 eggs
1 teaspoon vanilla
½ teaspoon almond extract
2 cups flour, sifted four times
⅓ cup (one small can) evaporated milk.

1. Preheat the oven to 350 degrees.
2. Cream the butter and sugar together until very light and fluffy and there is no graininess left from the sugar.
3. Beat in the eggs, one at a time, very well.
4. Beat in the vanilla and almond extract. Fold in the flour alternately with the milk.
5. Pour into an eight-inch tube pan or 9-by-5-by-3-inch loaf pan that has been greased and lined with wax paper.
6. Bake about fifty-five minutes, or until done. Cool slightly in the pan before turning cake out onto a rack. The cake is very tender when hot. The flavor and texture improve on storage.

Yield: Ten to one dozen servings.

Poundcake II

South Carolina

1 cup butter
¼ cup shortening
2½ cups sugar
5 eggs
3 cups flour
½ teaspoon baking powder
⅛ teaspoon salt
1 teaspoon vanilla
½ teaspoon lemon extract
1 cup milk.

1. Cream the butter and shortening together until creamy. Gradually beat in the sugar until mixture is light and fluffy.
2. Beat in the eggs, one at a time.
3. Sift together the flour, baking powder and salt. Add the vanilla and lemon extract to the

milk. Fold dry ingredients into batter alternately with the milk.

4. Spoon batter into a lightly greased nine-inch tube pan. Place in the middle of the oven and set the oven for 325 degrees (the oven is not preheated). Bake one hour and twenty minutes, or until done.

Yield: One dozen servings.

Pecan-Cherry Cake   *Georgia*

2 cups candied cherries, halved
2 cups golden raisins
2 cups bourbon
1½ cups butter
2 cups granulated sugar
1 cup light brown sugar
6 eggs, separated
5 cups flour
1 teaspoon nutmeg
1 teaspoon cinnamon
1 teaspoon baking powder
2½ cups (about one pound) shelled pecans, chopped.

1. Day before, place the cherries and raisins in a bowl and cover with one and one-half cups of the bourbon. Let stand overnight.
2. Next day, preheat the oven to 275 degrees. Line a greased ten-inch tube pan with parchment paper, wax paper or unglazed brown paper and grease again.
3. Cream the butter together with the sugars until very light and fluffy. Beat in the egg yolks, one at a time.
4. Fold in the soaked fruit and the extra bourbon that may be in the bottom of the bowl. Sift together the flour with the nutmeg, cinnamon and baking powder. Take out one-half cup of the mixture and sprinkle over the pecans. Toss to coat.
5. Beat the egg whites until stiff but not dry. Fold the flour mixture and the egg whites into the batter. Fold in the pecans. Spoon the batter into

the prepared pan and bake three and one-half to four hours, or until cake tests done.

6. Cool in the pan, then remove from the pan and wrap in cheesecloth soaked in the remaining bourbon. Wrap in wax paper and aluminum foil or place in a tin with a tightly fitting lid. Do not attempt to cut for at least forty-eight hours.

Yield: Two dozen servings.

Jam Cake   *South Carolina*

¾ cup butter
1 cup sugar
3 eggs
1 cup black raspberry or blackberry preserves
2½ cups flour
1 teaspoon nutmeg
1 teaspoon allspice
1 teaspoon cinnamon
1 teaspoon baking soda
¾ cup buttermilk
2 tablespoons bourbon.

1. Preheat the oven to 350 degrees.
2. Beat the butter and sugar together until light and fluffy. Beat in the eggs, one at a time.
3. Fold in the preserves. Sift together the flour, nutmeg, allspice, cinnamon and baking soda. Add to batter alternately with the buttermilk, folding in. Fold in the bourbon.
4. Spoon into a greased nine-inch tube pan. Bake fifty minutes.

Yield: Ten to one dozen servings.

Lemon Cake   *Alabama*

1 cup butter
½ cup shortening
2 cups granulated sugar
3 eggs
3 cups flour
½ teaspoon baking soda
½ teaspoon salt

1 cup buttermilk
2 tablespoons grated lemon rind
½ cup, approximately, plus one tablespoon
  lemon juice
3 cups confectioners' sugar.

1. Preheat the oven to 325 degrees.
2. Beat one-half cup of the butter, the shortening and granulated sugar together until light and fluffy. Beat in the eggs, one at a time.
3. Sift together the flour, baking soda and salt and stir in alternately with the buttermilk. Stir in one tablespoon of the lemon rind and one tablespoon of the lemon juice.
4. Pour into a greased nine-inch tube pan and bake one and one-quarter hours, or until cake tests done. Cool on a rack.
5. Mix together the remaining butter and the confectioners' sugar until creamy. Add the remaining lemon rind and stir in enough remaining lemon juice to give a pouring consistency. Pour over the cooling cake.
Yield: Ten servings.

Angel Food Cake   *Tennessee*

1⅓ cups sugar, sifted twice
1 cup sifted cake flour
½ teaspoon salt
1½ cups egg whites (about twelve whites)
1¼ teaspoons cream of tartar
1 teaspoon vanilla
½ teaspoon almond extract.

1. Preheat the oven to 350 degrees.
2. Add one-third cup of the sifted sugar to the cake flour. Add the salt and sift the mixture together three times.
3. Beat the egg whites, preferably with a wire whisk, until they are foamy and add the cream of tartar. Continue beating until whites are stiff but not dry. Gradually beat in the remaining sugar, one tablespoon at a time. Fold in the vanilla and almond extract. Sift approximately one-quarter cup of the sugar and flour mixture over the batter.

Fold in with a rubber spatula. Continue adding the sugar and flour mixture, folding in after each addition.
4. Pour the batter into an ungreased nine-inch tube pan. Bake about forty-five minutes, or until the top springs back when lightly touched. Immediately turn the pan upside down, suspending tube part over the neck of a funnel or bottle. Let cake stand in the pan until cold, about one and one-half hours.
Yield: One angel food cake; about ten servings.

Sugar Plum Cake   *Tennessee*

Cake:
¾ cup shortening
1¾ cups granulated sugar
4 eggs
4 cups flour
¾ pound candied orange slices, cut finely
  with scissors
1½ cups coarsely chopped pecans
1 eight-ounce package dates, cut small
1 three-and-one-half-ounce can flaked
  coconut
⅛ teaspoon salt
1 teaspoon baking soda
⅔ cup buttermilk
1 tablespoon lemon juice
1 teaspoon orange extract.
Glaze:
2 cups confectioners' sugar
1 cup orange juice
2 teaspoons grated orange rind.

1. Preheat the oven to 300 degrees if metal pans are used or to 275 degrees if glass pans are used.
2. Cream the shortening and granulated sugar together very well until light and fluffy. Beat in the eggs, one at a time.
3. Sift half the flour over the orange slice bits, pecans, dates and coconut and mix well.
4. Sift the remaining flour with the salt and baking soda and add alternately with the butter-

milk to the creamed shortening mixture. Stir in the lemon juice and orange extract.

5. With the hands, mix in the dredged fruits. Fill two greased and floured 9-by-5-by-3-inch loaf pans with the mixture and bake about one hour and forty minutes, but start testing for doneness after one hour and fifteen minutes.

6. Let the cakes rest five minutes; then prick all over, while still in the pans, with a skewer or ice pick. Combine the glaze ingredients and spoon over the surface of the cakes while they are still hot.

Yield: Twenty servings.

White Fruitcake   *Georgia*

1½ cups butter
 2 cups sugar
 6 eggs
 1 teaspoon nutmeg
 1 teaspoon vanilla
 ½ cup bourbon
 2 teaspoons baking powder
 4 cups sifted flour
 1 pound candied cherries
 1 pound candied pineapple, cut into large pieces
 1 pound shelled pecans.

1. Preheat the oven to 275 degrees.
2. Cream together the butter and sugar. Add the eggs, one at a time, beating well after each addition. Add the nutmeg, vanilla and bourbon. Sift together the baking powder and three cups of the flour and fold into the batter.
3. Dredge the fruit with the remaining flour and place fruit in the oven about five minutes. Add the flour-coated fruit to the batter. Pour into a tube pan and bake three hours.

Yield: Eight or more servings.

Applesauce Fruitcake   *Tennessee*

 ½ cup butter
 1 cup sugar
 2 eggs
 2 cups flour
 2 teaspoons baking soda
 ½ teaspoon nutmeg
 ½ teaspoon ground cloves
 ½ teaspoon allspice
 ¼ cup port wine or whisky
1½ cups applesauce
 1 pound raisins
 1 cup diced citron
 1 cup diced mixed candied peels
 1 cup drained maraschino cherries
 2 cups chopped dates.

1. Preheat the oven to 325 degrees.
2. Cream the butter and sugar together well. Beat in the eggs, one at a time. Sift together the flour, baking soda and spices and reserve three tablespoons.
3. Stir in the bulk of the flour mixture alternately with the port or whisky. Stir in the applesauce. Toss the remaining ingredients with the reserved flour mixture and stir in.
4. Spoon the batter into a greased and floured two-and-one-half-quart to three-quart cake tin or springform pan with removable ring. Bake for one and one-half hours, or until the cake tests done.

Yield: One dozen to eighteen servings.

Note: The cake improves on wrapping and storing in a cool place.

Past Perfect Fruitcake   *Mississippi*

 4 cups shelled pecans
 2 cups unchopped crystallized cherries
 5 slices crystallized pineapple, each slice cut into eighths
 1 cup flour
1½ teaspoons baking powder
 ¼ teaspoon salt

4 eggs
1 cup sugar
1 teaspoon vanilla.

1. Preheat the oven to 250 degrees.
2. Grease the bottom and sides of a two-quart cake tin and line the bottom of it with brown paper or parchment paper.
3. Combine the pecans, cherries and pineapple in a mixing bowl. Combine the flour, baking powder and salt in a sifter and sift the dry ingredients over the fruits.
4. Combine the eggs, sugar and vanilla in another mixing bowl and beat until blended. Pour this over the fruit and stir with a slotted spoon. Pour the batter into the prepared pan and bake one and one-half hours. At the end of that time, set the cake pan into a pan of boiling water and continue baking fifteen minutes longer.

Yield: One dozen or more servings.

Lane Cake Layers   *Alabama*

1 cup butter
2 cups sugar
1 teaspoon vanilla
3¼ cups flour
3½ teaspoons baking powder
¼ teaspoon salt
1 cup milk
8 egg whites, beaten until stiff but not dry.

1. Preheat the oven to 375 degrees.
2. Grease and flour three nine-inch layer pans.
3. Beat the butter and sugar together until very light and creamy. Beat in the vanilla. Sift together the flour, baking powder and salt twice.
4. Stir the flour mixture alternately with the milk into the batter. Stir in one-quarter of the egg whites. Fold in remaining egg whites until just mixed. Spoon into the prepared pans and bake twenty to twenty-five minutes. Cool in the pans for ten minutes; then turn out onto racks for further cooling.

Yield: Three layers; about ten filled and topped servings.

Note: The batter may be baked in a greased and floured ten-inch tube pan or a 13-by-9½-by-2-inch metal pan, in an oven preheated to 350 degrees, for one to one and one-quarter hours.

The cake mellows on storage in a closed container for several days.

Wrapped in plastic wrap or aluminum foil, both layers and large cakes freeze well and are always on hand to be finished with filling and frosting.

For a firmer, closer, slightly more tender texture, three and one-quarter cups cake flour and one and three-quarters cups superfine sugar may be substituted for the flour and sugar in the above recipe. The instructions remain the same.

Lane Cake Filling   *Alabama*

8 egg yolks
1¼ cups sugar
  Grated rind of one orange
⅓ cup bourbon
½ teaspoon mace
1¼ cups pecans, chopped
¼ teaspoon salt
1 cup shredded coconut, preferably fresh
1 cup raisins
1 cup glacé cherries, quartered.

1. Mix together the egg yolks, sugar and orange rind in a heavy pan or in the top of a double boiler.
2. Stirring constantly, cook the mixture over medium heat until the sugar dissolves and the mixture thickens to coat the back of the spoon. Do not allow the mixture to boil or the egg yolks will be scrambled.
3. Remove from the heat and stir in the remaining ingredients. Cool before using to fill and top a three-layer cake.

Yield: About one quart.

Lady Baltimore Cake   *South Carolina*

Cake:
    1 recipe (three layers) lane cake (page 279).
Syrup:
    1 cup sugar
    ½ cup water
    ½ teaspoon almond extract
    1 teaspoon vanilla.
White frosting:
    3 cups sugar
    1 cup water
    ¼ teaspoon cream of tartar
    3 egg whites
    ⅛ teaspoon salt
    1 teaspoon vanilla
    2 cups pecans, coarsely chopped
1½ cups figs, coarsely chopped
    ½ cup raisins
    ⅓ cup cognac (optional).

1. While the cake layers are baking, prepare the syrup by combining the sugar and water in a small pan. Heat, stirring, until the sugar dissolves. Cook six minutes longer without stirring. Stir in the almond extract and vanilla and pour over the cake layers while they are still hot from the oven.

2. To make the frosting, combine the sugar, water and cream of tartar in a saucepan. Heat, stirring, until the sugar dissolves. Continue to heat without stirring until the syrup registers 238 degrees on a candy thermometer or spins a thread.

3. Beat the egg whites and the salt until stiff. Pour the syrup in a steady stream into the beaten egg whites, beating constantly until the frosting stands in peaks. Stir in the vanilla. There will be about two and one-quarter cups frosting. Divide the frosting into two parts.

4. Add the pecans, figs and raisins, soaked overnight in the cognac if desired, to one-half of the frosting and use to fill between the three soaked layers. Use remaining frosting to frost the top and sides of the cake.

Yield: About one dozen servings.

Mrs. D's Moravian Sugar Cake

North Carolina

    1 cup mashed potatoes
    1 cup potato water
    1 cup milk, scalded
    2 cups granulated sugar
    1 package active dry yeast
    ⅓ cup lukewarm water
    9 cups flour, approximately
    2 eggs, well beaten
    ¾ cup melted shortening
    1 tablespoon salt
    ¾ cup butter
    1 cup light brown sugar
    2 teaspoons cinnamon.

1. Mix together the potatoes, potato water, milk and one cup of the granulated sugar. Cool to lukewarm.

2. Dissolve the yeast in the lukewarm water and add one teaspoon of the remaining sugar.

3. Add yeast mixture and two cups of the flour to cooled potato mixture. Stand in a warm place, covered, for about one hour, or until mixture bubbles.

4. Stir in the eggs, shortening, salt, remaining sugar and enough remaining flour to make a soft dough. Knead lightly on a board. Place in a clean greased bowl and let rise until doubled in bulk, about one and one-half hours.

5. Punch dough down and then spread into a one-half-inch layer in three greased jellyroll pans or other shallow baking pans. Cover and let rise until doubled in bulk, about twenty minutes.

6. Preheat the oven to 375 degrees.

7. Make depressions in the dough and place a knob of butter and a tablespoon or two of the brown sugar mixed with the cinnamon in each hole. Bake about twenty minutes, or until brown and done.

Yield: About four dozen servings.

Note: After kneading, the dough can be left in a clean bowl in a cool place overnight, if desired.

Sweet Potato Pone
Georgia

2 cups grated raw sweet potatoes
1 egg, beaten
½ cup unsulphured molasses
3 tablespoons sugar
3 tablespoons melted butter
  Grated rind of one orange
2 cups milk
½ teaspoon grated fresh or ground ginger
½ teaspoon cinnamon
½ teaspoon nutmeg
½ teaspoon salt
  Heavy cream or ice cream.

1. Preheat the oven to 275 degrees.
2. Combine all the ingredients and pour into a one-and-one-half-quart baking dish. Bake three hours. Serve warm with heavy cream or ice cream.
Yield: Six servings.

Mrs. Mescal Johnston's Rice Custard with Lemon Sauce
Arkansas

Custard:
  2 cups milk
  1 cup cooked rice
  1 tablespoon butter
  ⅓ cup sugar
  ¼ teaspoon salt
  ⅓ cup raisins or nuts
  2 eggs, beaten.
Sauce:
  ½ cup sugar
  1 tablespoon cornstarch
  ⅛ teaspoon salt
  ⅛ teaspoon nutmeg
  1 cup boiling water
  2 tablespoons butter
  1½ tablespoons lemon juice.

1. Preheat the oven to 350 degrees.
2. To make custard, heat the milk and add the rice and butter. Stir the sugar, salt and raisins or nuts into the eggs and then slowly stir into hot milk mixture.
3. Pour into a greased baking dish, set in a pan of hot water and bake one hour, or until set. Or pour into four greased custard cups, set in a pan of hot water and bake twelve to fifteen minutes, or until set.
4. For sauce, combine the sugar, cornstarch, salt and nutmeg in a saucepan and gradually stir in the boiling water. Cook, stirring, until thick and clear. Add the butter and lemon juice. Serve with rice custard.
Yield: Four servings.

Banana Pudding
Arkansas

4 cups milk
1 cup sugar
⅛ teaspoon salt
4 eggs, separated
1 teaspoon vanilla
  Vanilla wafer cookies
3 to four ripe bananas.

1. Heat the milk, one-half cup of the sugar and the salt in the top of a double boiler. Beat the egg yolks slightly, mix in a little hot milk and return all to the double boiler.
2. Heat, stirring, until custard coats the back of the spoon. Remove from the heat and place in a pan of cold water and stir the custard as it cools. Stir in the vanilla.
3. Preheat the oven to 350 degrees.
4. In the bottom of a greased two-quart baking dish, put a layer of vanilla wafers. Slice over them a layer of bananas and add some of the custard.
5. Repeat until dish is three-quarters full. Beat the egg whites until stiff and gradually beat in the remaining sugar.
6. Spread the meringue on top of the pudding and bake twelve minutes, or until meringue is lightly browned. Cool and chill.
Yield: Six servings.

Bourbon Date Pudding
Kentucky

2 eggs
1 cup sugar
5 tablespoons light cream
3 tablespoons flour
1½ teaspoons baking powder
1 cup broken walnuts or pecans
1 cup chopped dates
1 or two tablespoons bourbon (see note)
Sweetened whipped cream.

1. Combine the eggs and sugar and beat well until light and creamy. Add the cream, flour, baking powder, nuts and dates and spoon into the top of a large double boiler.
2. Cover and cook over boiling water, taking care that all the water does not evaporate from the bottom. Cook about two hours, stirring occasionally. When cooked, add the bourbon. Chill and serve cold with sweetened whipped cream, flavored with bourbon if desired.
Yield: Eight or more servings.
Note: Cognac may be substituted for the bourbon.

Flan
Florida

4 cups heavy cream
12 egg yolks
1 cup plus five tablespoons sugar
Grated rind of half a lime
Juice of one lime
3 tablespoons water.

1. Preheat the oven to 350 degrees.
2. Bring the cream just to a boil.
3. Combine the egg yolks and five tablespoons of the sugar and stir until blended. Gradually add the hot cream to the yolk mixture, stirring constantly. Add the lime rind and lime juice and set aside.
4. Combine the remaining sugar and the water in a saucepan and bring to a boil, stirring. Continue cooking until sugar turns the color of deep amber. Do not burn the sugar, however. Pour caramel around bottom and sides of a warm two-quart baking dish to coat it. Pour in the cream mixture and set the dish in a larger pan. Pour hot water around dish. Bake forty-five minutes to one hour, or until a knife inserted in center comes out clean. Cool, chill and unmold.
Yield: Six to eight servings.

Chocolate Pecan Pudding
Virginia

1 envelope unflavored gelatin
2 tablespoons cold water
¼ cup boiling water
2 ounces (two squares) semisweet chocolate
1 tablespoon black coffee
4 egg whites
⅛ teaspoon salt
½ cup sugar
1 teaspoon vanilla
½ cup chopped fresh or toasted pecans
Sweetened whipped cream.

1. Soften the gelatin in the cold water. Add the boiling water, stirring until mixture dissolves. Keep warm.
2. Combine the chocolate and coffee and melt over very low heat or in a double boiler, stirring.
3. Whip the egg whites until frothy and add the salt. Beat until stiff but not dry. Gradually beat in the sugar, vanilla and melted chocolate.
4. Stir in the gelatin and pecans and turn into a 9-by-5-inch loaf pan. Chill until firm and serve cut into slices and topped with sweetened whipped cream.
Yield: Six to eight servings.

Lemon Fluff
Georgia

7 egg yolks
1¼ cups sugar
Juice of three lemons
Grated rind of two lemons
1 tablespoon unflavored gelatin

¼ cup cold water
7 egg whites
  Ladyfingers
  Sweetened whipped cream.

1. Beat the egg yolks with one cup of the sugar until they are light. Add the lemon juice and lemon rind and cook over boiling water, stirring, until thickened.

2. Soak the gelatin in the water; then add to the hot mixture, stirring to dissolve.

3. Beat the egg whites until frothy and begin adding the remaining sugar. Beat until stiff and fold the whites into the yolk mixture. Line a two-quart springform pan with ladyfingers and spoon the lemon fluff into it. Chill until set. Unmold and serve with sweetened whipped cream.

Yield: About eight servings.

Snow on the Mountain   *Louisiana*

Base:
 5 egg whites
 6 tablespoons sugar
¼ teaspoon salt
 1 envelope unflavored gelatin
¼ cup cold water
 1 cup heavy cream
 1 teaspoon vanilla
 1 cup grated coconut.
Sauce:
 5 egg yolks
 1 cup sugar
 2 tablespoons sweet sherry
 2 tablespoons light rum, or to taste.

1. To make base, beat the egg whites until stiff. Gradually beat in the sugar and salt.

2. Soak the gelatin in the water and heat over hot water to dissolve. Fold the gelatin into the beaten egg whites.

3. Whip the cream until stiff and add the vanilla. Fold the cream into the egg white mixture. Spoon the mixture into lightly oiled custard cups and chill. When ready to serve, unmold onto individual plates or arrange the "balls" in a crystal serving bowl. Sprinkle with the coconut and serve with sauce.

4. To make sauce, beat the egg yolks until they are slightly thickened and pale yellow. Beat in the sugar. Add the sherry and cook over low heat until thickened and smooth. Do not let the mixture boil. Stir in the rum and reheat without boiling.

Yield: About six servings.

Bridal Pudding   *Louisiana*

 2 envelopes unflavored gelatin
½ cup cold water
⅓ cup boiling water
 6 egg whites
¼ teaspoon salt
¾ cup sugar
 2 cups heavy cream
 1 teaspoon vanilla
 1 cup flaked coconut
  Crushed sweetened strawberries
  Rum sauce (page 306)
  Whole strawberries (optional).

1. Soften the gelatin in the cold water.

2. Pour the boiling water into the gelatin and stir to dissolve.

3. Beat the egg whites until stiff. Add the salt and gradually beat in the sugar.

4. Fold the gelatin into the egg whites.

5. Beat the cream until stiff and add the vanilla. Fold the cream into the egg whites.

6. Rub the bottom and sides of an eight-inch or nine-inch springform pan with butter. Sprinkle the bottom with half the coconut and pour in the cream mixture. Sprinkle with remaining coconut and chill four hours or overnight.

7. Unmold pudding and serve with crushed sweetened strawberries and rum sauce. If desired, the dessert may be garnished with whole strawberries.

Yield: Six to eight servings.

"Lemmon Syllabub" *Maryland*

Thinly cut peel (lemon-colored part only)
of one lemon
1 cup cream sherry
1 cup Madeira wine
4 cups heavy cream
⅓ cup lemon juice
1 cup sugar
Nutmeg.

1. Soak the lemon peel in the sherry and Madeira for at least one hour.
2. Whip the cream until it just begins to hold its shape. Remove the peel and gradually beat into the cream the wine, lemon juice and sugar until thick. Pour into parfait or wine glasses and sprinkle with nutmeg. Serve immediately.

Yield: Eight servings.

Peppermint Stick Bavarian Cream
Louisiana

1 envelope plus one and one-half teaspoons
unflavored gelatin
⅓ cup cold water
6 egg yolks
¾ cup sugar
¼ teaspoon salt
1½ cups milk
¾ cup finely crushed peppermint sticks or
candies (about six medium-size candy
canes; crushing can be done easily in an
electric blender)
¼ teaspoon peppermint essence, or to taste
Red food coloring
1½ cups heavy cream, whipped
Peppermint candies for garnish (optional)
Chocolate sauce (recipe below).

1. Soak the gelatin in the water.
2. Beat the egg yolks, sugar and salt in a saucepan until well blended. In another saucepan heat the milk and crushed peppermint candies until almost boiling, stirring to dissolve the candy.

3. Gradually beat the hot milk into the egg yolk mixture. Heat over hot water or over low direct heat, stirring continuously until the mixture thickens. Do not allow to boil.
4. Stir in the softened gelatin and stir to dissolve. Set the mixture aside to cool. Stir in the peppermint essence and the red food coloring, remembering that the cream will tone down the shade.
5. Fold in the cream gently but thoroughly and pour into a six-cup mold. Chill four hours or overnight. Unmold and decorate with the candies and serve with chocolate sauce.

Yield: Ten servings.

Chocolate Sauce *Louisiana*

4 ounces (four squares) unsweetened
chocolate
2 tablespoons butter
2 tablespoons light corn syrup
½ cup sugar
⅛ teaspoon salt
½ cup milk
¼ cup heavy cream.

1. Melt the chocolate with the butter in the top of a double boiler over hot but not boiling water. Add the syrup, sugar and salt and blend.
2. Add the milk and cream and cook, stirring, about ten minutes.

Yield: About one and one-half cups.

Fruited Eggnog Pudding *Kentucky*

1 cup chopped mixed candied fruits
¼ cup roughly chopped pecans or walnuts
2 tablespoons golden raisins
¼ cup cognac
12 egg yolks
¾ cup sugar
½ cup dark rum
3 envelopes unflavored gelatin
½ cup cold water

1 cup bourbon
2 cups heavy cream, whipped
2 tablespoons vanilla
  Whipped cream for garnish
  Pieces of candied cherries.

1. Soak the mixed fruits, nuts and raisins in the cognac.

2. Beat the egg yolks until very thick, lemon-colored and smooth. Gradually beat in the sugar.

3. Add the rum and beat in well. Chill the mixture until it is at refrigerator temperature, about forty minutes.

4. Soak the gelatin in the water. Heat to dissolve the gelatin. Add the bourbon and stir into the chilled egg mixture quickly and thoroughly.

5. Fold in the whipped cream and vanilla and continue stirring until the mixture begins to thicken. Fold in the soaked fruit and nut mixture and pour into a nine-cup mold which has been rinsed with cold water or lightly oiled.

6. Chill at least five hours or overnight. Unmold and decorate with whipped cream and candied cherries.

Yield: About one dozen servings.

Note: If a nine-cup mold is not available, divide the mixture between a six-cup mold and a three-cup mold. When ready to serve, unmold and place one atop the other.

Trifle   *Virginia*

  8 egg yolks, lightly beaten
½ cup sugar
  4 cups milk, scalded
  1 teaspoon vanilla
24 ladyfingers, or a comparable quantity of spongecake, torn into bite-size pieces
½ cup medium-dry sherry
  1 cup strawberry or raspberry preserves
⅓ cup slivered blanched almonds or crumbled macaroons (optional)
½ cup heavy cream, whipped
  Glacé cherries

Angelica or one tablespoon slivered blanched almonds.

1. Combine the egg yolks, sugar and milk in a heavy saucepan, beating with a wire whisk to mix well. Heat over medium heat until mixture thickens and coats the back of a spoon. Do not allow custard to boil.

2. Remove from the heat and pour into a cold bowl. Stir in the vanilla and cool to lukewarm.

3. Sprinkle the ladyfingers or spongecake with the sherry and let stand five to ten minutes.

4. Place a layer of the soaked ladyfingers in a two-quart serving bowl, preferably glass.

5. Spread with one-third of the preserves and one-third of the almonds or macaroons. Repeat the layers until all ladyfingers are used.

6. Pour the cooled custard over the ladyfinger arrangement and chill several hours.

7. Decorate with the whipped cream, piped through a rosette tube, and garnish with the cherries and angelica or almond pieces.

Yield: About ten servings.

Trifle Royal   *Virginia*

  1 homemade jellyroll, made from four eggs and a standard recipe
  1 cup strawberry or raspberry preserves
½ cup medium-dry sherry
  8 egg yolks, lightly beaten
½ cup sugar
  4 cups milk, scalded
1½ teaspoons vanilla
  1 teaspoon unflavored gelatin
  2 tablespoons water
  Whipped cream for garnish.

1. Spread the cooled jellyroll with the preserves. Roll and cut into three-quarter-inch slices. Arrange as many slices as necessary to cover the bottom and sides of a two-quart round glass bowl, dish or casserole. Sprinkle with the sherry.

2. Combine the egg yolks, sugar and milk in a heavy pan. Heat, stirring, over medium heat until

the mixture thickens and just coats the back of the spoon. Remove from the heat and pour into a cool bowl to stop the cooking.

3. Stir in the vanilla. Dissolve the gelatin in the water. Add to mixture. Cool to lukewarm or room temperature.

4. Pour one-third of the custard into the lined bowl. Add some of the remaining slices of jellyroll, pushing them down into the custard. Repeat with the remaining custard and jellyroll slices, ending with slices.

5. Chill well, at least several hours. Unmold onto a plate and decorate with whipped cream as desired.

Yield: About ten servings.

Note: If the trifle royal is not to be unmolded, the gelatin may be omitted.

Trifle Pudding   *Virginia*

½ cup blanched almonds
¼ pound candied cherries
¼ pound ladyfingers
¼ cup tart currant or beach plum jelly
½ pound almond macaroons
¼ cup dry sherry
1½ teaspoons cornstarch
1½ cups milk
2 large eggs
4 tablespoons sugar
2 cups heavy cream.

1. Preheat the oven to 350 degrees.

2. Place the almonds on a baking sheet and bake until they are toasted, stirring occasionally. Do not let them burn. Turn off oven and let almonds cool.

3. Chop the almonds and chop the candied cherries.

4. Split each ladyfinger in half and smear the split side of each half with jelly. Arrange layers of jelly-smeared ladyfingers and the macaroons over bottom and side of a round glass mixing bowl. Sprinkle with the sherry.

5. Place the cornstarch in a saucepan and

gradually add the milk, stirring with a wire whisk. Beat the eggs and add them along with half the sugar. Bring gently to a boil, stirring constantly, to make a custard. Do not cook over high heat or too long or the custard will curdle. Let cool and fold in chopped cherries.

6. Whip the cream and, before it is stiff, beat in the remaining sugar. Fold the whipped cream into the custard and pour the mixture into the prepared bowl. Chill. When ready to serve, sprinkle with chopped almonds.

Yield: Six servings.

Minetry McCoy's Miracle   *Tennessee*

1 pound sweet butter
2 cups sugar
12 eggs, separated
48 amaretti (Italian macaroons)
1 cup bourbon
4 ounces (four squares) unsweetened chocolate, melted
1 teaspoon vanilla
1 cup chopped pecans
24 double ladyfingers, approximately
1½ cups heavy cream, whipped.

1. Day before, cream the butter and sugar together until light and fluffy. Beat the egg yolks until light and beat into creamed mixture.

2. Soak the amaretti in the bourbon.

3. Beat the chocolate into the butter mixture. Add the vanilla and pecans. Beat the egg whites until stiff but not dry and fold into the chocolate mixture.

4. Line a ten-inch springform pan around the side and on the bottom with split ladyfingers. Alternate layers of soaked macaroons and chocolate mixture in the lined pan. Chill overnight.

5. Next day, remove the sides of the pan and decorate the top of the dessert with whipped cream.

Yield: Sixteen to twenty servings.

Stuffed Frozen Oranges   *Florida*

12 oranges
½ cup water
1 tablespoon lemon juice
   Grated rind of one orange
½ cup sugar, approximately
12 tablespoons heavy cream
6 tablespoons gin
6 sprigs fresh mint for garnish.

1. Cut a one-half-inch slice from the tops of six oranges and carefully scoop out the flesh. This is to provide a hollow shell to be filled later. Place the shells in the freezer.

2. Squeeze the scooped-out flesh to extract the juice. Cut the remaining oranges in half and squeeze to extract the juice. Combine all the juice and add the water, lemon juice and orange rind. Add the sugar according to taste. Stir to dissolve sugar. Pour the mixture into a container for freezing and freeze.

3. Remove the frozen juice for a short time before using. Spoon one tablespoon of the cream into the bottom of each shell; then add a small scoop of the frozen juice. Add another tablespoon cream and another scoop of the frozen juice. Return to the freezer until ready to serve. When ready to serve, add one tablespoon of the gin to each serving and garnish each with a sprig of mint.

Yield: Six servings.

Oranges en Surprise   *Florida*

6 large navel oranges
1 envelope unflavored gelatin
1½ cups orange juice
   Sugar to taste
   Grand Marnier or other orange liqueur to taste.

1. With a sharp paring knife, remove the peel, spiral fashion, from the oranges. Carefully sec-

tion each orange into a bowl, but leave the pulpy formation or "skeleton" of the orange intact.

2. Soak the gelatin in three-quarters cup orange juice; then heat, stirring to dissolve.

3. Dip the orange sections in gelatin; then replace them neatly in the "skeleton," using a small custard cup as a temporary base. Chill and remove to dessert places.

4. Sweeten the remaining orange juice with sugar and liqueur. Serve as a sauce with the oranges.

Yield: Six servings.

Bananas à la Turtle Cay   *Florida*

6 sugar bananas (tiny bananas in islands off
   Florida)
½ cup butter
½ cup sugar
¼ cup light rum
¼ cup dark rum
   Lime wedges.

1. Peel the bananas and cut them lengthwise.

2. Melt the butter in a heavy skillet and add the bananas, turning once. As bananas begin to color, sprinkle with the sugar and continue cooking until sugar is caramelized. Stir and turn gently so as not to break the bananas.

3. Combine the rums and heat gently. Pour over the bananas and ignite. Serve with lime wedges.

Yield: Six servings.

Bananas Flambées   *Florida*

6 ripe bananas, sliced on the bias
   Juice of half a lemon
1 cup light brown sugar
½ cup butter
½ teaspoon cinnamon
¼ cup cognac
   Vanilla ice cream.

1. Brush the banana slices with lemon juice. Melt the brown sugar and butter in a flat chafing dish. Add bananas and cook until just tender.

2. Sprinkle bananas with the cinnamon. Warm the cognac and add. Ignite and pour flaming over a ball of ice cream.

Yield: Six servings.

Cooked Custard Ice Cream   *Arkansas*

2 cups sugar
⅛ teaspoon salt
¼ cup cornstarch or one-half cup flour
4 cups regular milk, scalded
4 eggs, separated
1 teaspoon vanilla
2 large cans (thirteen ounces) evaporated milk or two and two-thirds cups heavy cream
2 cups cold regular milk, approximately.

1. Combine the sugar, salt and cornstarch or flour. Add the scalded milk. Stir until sugar dissolves.

2. Beat the egg yolks in a bowl. Pour a cup of the hot milk mixture into yolks gradually while beating; then return to bulk of milk mixture.

3. Bring to a boil, stirring, and remove from the heat. Add the vanilla and evaporated milk or cream and cool. Beat the egg whites until stiff and fold into custard. Pour into a gallon ice cream freezer can and add the cold milk to fill the can to two-thirds capacity. Freeze in crank-type or electric ice cream maker and serve, or store in home freezer for later use.

Yield: One gallon; about sixteen to twenty servings.

Ginger-Melon Ice   *Georgia*

6 cups water
3 cups sugar
1 tablespoon grated lemon rind
1¼ cups lemon juice

1½ cups finely chopped preserved ginger
3 tablespoons ginger syrup
3 cups coarsely grated peeled honeydew melon, apple or shredded pineapple.

1. Heat the water and sugar, stirring until the sugar dissolves. Bring to a boil and boil two minutes. Let cool to room temperature. Chill.

2. Add the remaining ingredients and pour into a large roasting pan. Freeze until mixture is solid around the sides but slushy in the middle. Break up and stir well. Freeze until slushy and serve. If the mixture becomes solid, remove it from the freezer about fifteen to twenty minutes before you wish to serve it.

Yield: Eight to ten servings.

Note: Frozen lemonade concentrate may be substituted for the water, sugar and lemon juice. Reconstitute three six-ounce cans with nine cups water.

Butter Fingers   *Mississippi*

½ pound butter
5 tablespoons confectioners' sugar
3 cups flour
2 teaspoons vanilla
2 cups chopped pecans
¼ teaspoon salt.

1. Preheat the oven to 350 degrees.

2. Cream the butter and sugar together until creamy.

3. Work in the flour, vanilla, pecans and salt with a wooden spoon or the fingers to make a dough.

4. Divide the mixture into about thirty-six pieces and shape each into a small cigar shape. Place on an ungreased baking sheet and bake fifteen minutes, or until lightly browned.

Yield: About three dozen.

Note: These cookies are best after they have been stored for several days in an airtight tin because the flavor mellows and the texture changes.

Sugar Cookies
Arkansas

1 cup shortening
4 cups flour
½ cup milk
2 eggs
1½ cups sugar
2 teaspoons baking soda
½ teaspoon salt
½ teaspoon almond extract.

1. Preheat the oven to 350 degrees.
2. Cut the shortening into the flour with the finger tips or a pastry blender until the mixture is the consistency of corn meal.
3. Combine the remaining ingredients and mix with flour mixture. Gather into a dough and roll to one-eighth-inch thickness.
4. Cut into various shapes and bake on ungreased baking sheets eight to ten minutes, or until lightly browned at the edges.
Yield: Seven dozen two-and-one-half-inch cookies.

Moravian Ginger Cookies
North Carolina

⅓ cup dark brown sugar
¼ cup shortening
½ cup unsulphured molasses
2¼ cups flour
¼ teaspoon baking soda
½ teaspoon ground ginger
½ teaspoon cinnamon
¼ teaspoon nutmeg
¼ teaspoon ground allspice.

1. Heat the brown sugar, shortening and molasses in a small saucepan until shortening melts. Cool.
2. Sift together the remaining ingredients and stir into the cooled mixture. Wrap in wax paper and chill several hours or overnight.
3. Preheat the oven to 375 degrees.
4. Roll out one-quarter of the dough at a time, preferably on a lightly floured pastry cloth, until dough is paper-thin. Use as little extra flour as possible.
5. Cut out with fancy cutters and transfer to a lightly greased baking sheet. Bake four minutes. Cool on a rack.
Yield: Five dozen to six dozen.

Snickerdoodles
Tennessee

2¾ cups sifted flour
2 teaspoons cream of tartar
1 teaspoon baking soda
½ teaspoon salt
1 cup shortening, at room temperature
1½ cups plus one tablespoon sugar
½ teaspoon almond extract
2 eggs
1 tablespoon cinnamon.

1. Preheat the oven to 400 degrees.
2. Sift together the flour, cream of tartar, baking soda and salt.
3. Cream the shortening with one and one-half cups of the sugar and beat in the almond extract and eggs. Combine the two mixtures and chill.
4. Roll the dough into small balls about one-half inch in diameter and roll in a mixture of the remaining sugar and the cinnamon. Place the balls about two inches apart on an ungreased baking sheet and bake eight to ten minutes.
Yield: About five dozen.

Hermits
West Virginia

4 tablespoons butter, at room temperature
½ cup packed light brown sugar
1 egg
1 cup sifted cake flour
½ teaspoon baking powder
¼ teaspoon allspice
¼ teaspoon ground ginger
¼ teaspoon nutmeg
1 cup currants or chopped raisins
¼ cup chopped walnuts or almonds.

1. Preheat the oven to 350 degrees.
2. Cream the butter in an electric mixer and beat in the brown sugar and egg.
3. Sift together the flour, baking powder, allspice, ginger and nutmeg and add. Fold in the currants and nuts and blend well. Drop by spoonfuls onto a lightly greased baking sheet and bake about ten minutes.

Yield: About two dozen.

Our Aunt Harriet's Favorite Brownies

Virginia

2 ounces (two squares) unsweetened chocolate
½ cup butter
1 teaspoon vanilla
3 eggs
1¼ cups sugar
½ cup flour
½ cup chopped walnuts.

1. Preheat the oven to 350 degrees.
2. Melt the chocolate and butter in the top of a double boiler. Stir in the vanilla.
3. Beat the eggs lightly and gradually beat in the sugar. Stir in the chocolate-butter mixture and then the flour and walnuts.
4. Pour into a greased nine-inch square pan and bake twenty-five minutes, or until a crust just forms on the top and the mixture has started to leave the sides of the dish. Let cool in pan and cut into squares.

Yield: About five dozen.

Note: This is a "cakey" style of brownie.

Miscellaneous

Pickles, Relishes and Preserves

Fried Apples   *Virginia*

6 Red Delicious or Rome apples
¼ cup water
⅓ cup butter
⅓ cup light brown sugar
2 tablespoons lemon juice.

1. Peel, core and slice the apples into thick slices. Place in a skillet with the water and butter. Cook over moderate heat, stirring to prevent sticking, until barely tender.
2. Sprinkle with the brown sugar and lemon juice. Toss, cover and let stand ten minutes before serving.
   Yield: Six servings.
   Note: Fried apples are served with fried ham slices or homemade sausage for breakfast.

Blackberry and Apple Jelly   *Arkansas*

8 cups unpeeled green apples
8 cups blackberries
4½ cups water
   Sugar.

1. Remove stem and blossom ends from the apples, wash the fruit and slice or chop it. Pick over the blackberries and wash and crush them.
2. Place the apples and water in a heavy kettle. Cook very gently for about fifteen minutes, or until almost tender, stirring occasionally.
3. Add the crushed blackberries and cook gently for another ten minutes, stirring frequently.
4. Drain the mixture through a jelly bag, damp cotton flannel or four layers of cheesecloth. Do not squeeze if a clear jelly is desired.
5. Measure the juice and add three-quarters cup sugar for each cup of juice. Stir to dissolve the sugar.
6. Bring mixture to a boil rapidly and cook rapidly, without stirring, for five to ten minutes, or until two drops run together and flake or sheet from the side of a large metal spoon.
7. Pour immediately into hot sterilized jelly glasses. Cover with a thin layer of melted paraffin and cool undisturbed. Cover and store in a cool, dark, dry place.
   Yield: About eight six-ounce glasses.

Fig Preserves   *Arkansas*

1 cup baking soda
6 quarts firm, sound ripe figs
6 quarts boiling water
4 quarts water
5 pounds (eleven and one-quarter cups) sugar.

1. Day before, sprinkle the baking soda over the figs and cover with the boiling water. Let stand fifteen minutes. Drain. Rinse figs in clear cold water and then set to drain while preparing syrup.

2. Mix the four quarts water and the sugar in a saucepan and heat, stirring, until sugar dissolves. Boil without stirring ten minutes and skim.

3. Add the well-drained figs gradually so as not to cool the syrup. Cook rapidly until figs are clear and tender, about two hours. When figs are transparent, lift out carefully and place in shallow pans.

4. Syrup should be as thick as honey. If it isn't, boil some more. Pour over figs, making sure to cover them completely. Leave overnight. Next morning, place cold figs in sterilized jars with stems up.

5. Fill each jar with syrup. Secure caps and process twenty-five minutes in a water bath at simmering temperature. Cool and store in a cool, dark, dry place.

Yield: About one dozen pints.

Quick Apple Preserves   *Virginia*

4 cups peeled and quartered tart apples that
  retain their shape
4 cups sugar
½ teaspoon whole cloves
½ teaspoon whole allspice
1 teaspoon nutmeg
4 sticks cinnamon.

1. Place the apples in a heavy pan and add water barely to cover. Add the sugar. Tie the spices in a cheesecloth bag and add. Cook slowly, stirring occasionally, until apples are tender but still retain their shape and syrup starts to jell. Remove spice bag.

2. Ladle mixture into hot sterilized jars and adjust caps. Store in the refrigerator.

Yield: About one quart.

Note: Serve with roast pork, ham and poultry.

Cantaloupe and Orange Jam   *Arkansas*

4 cups diced peeled cantaloupe
3 oranges, peeled and diced
¼ cup lemon juice
1 teaspoon grated orange rind
1 teaspoon grated lemon rind
4 cups sugar
½ teaspoon salt.

1. Combine the cantaloupe, oranges and lemon juice in a heavy kettle. Bring to a boil and simmer fifteen minutes.

2. Add the orange and lemon rinds, the sugar and salt. Boil rapidly about forty-five minutes, or until thick and clear, stirring occasionally. Skim as necessary.

3. Pour into sterilized jelly glasses and cover with a thin layer of melted paraffin. Cool, cover and store in a cool, dark, dry place.

Yield: About six six-ounce glasses.

Peach Conserve   *Georgia*

4 cups ripe peaches
1½ cups sugar.

1. Day before, dip the peaches into boiling water very briefly and peel. Remove the pits and chop the fruit into one-half-inch cubes or slices.

2. Place the peaches in a large bowl and sprinkle with the sugar. Allow to stand overnight.

3. Next day, pour the fruit and juice into a heavy pan and heat very slowly over low heat for about one hour, or until sugar is dissolved and the fruit is tender. Stir gently to prevent sticking.

4. Pour into hot sterilized jars. Seal, cool and store in a cool, dark, dry place.

Yield: About two pints.

Peach Almond Jam   *Georgia*

4 cups finely chopped unpeeled peaches
  (about three pounds)

½ cup chopped blanched almonds
¼ cup lemon juice
7 cups sugar (about three pounds)
½ bottle liquid fruit pectin
¼ teaspoon almond extract.

1. The unpeeled peaches may be ground, finely chopped or blended quickly in an electric blender. Measure four cups into a heavy kettle.

2. Stir in the almonds, lemon juice and sugar. Put over high heat and stir until the mixture comes to a full rolling boil. Boil hard for one minute, stirring constantly. Remove from the heat.

3. Immediately stir in the pectin and almond extract. Skim off the foam; stir and skim for five minutes to prevent floating fruit. Ladle into hot sterilized jars and cover with a thin layer of melted paraffin wax. Store in a cool, dry, dark place for at least two weeks before using.

Yield: Five to six pints.

Peach Melon Conserve   *Georgia*

6 cups diced peeled peaches
2 cups diced cantaloupe
6 cups sugar
¼ cup lemon juice
2 tablespoons syrup from preserved ginger
¼ cup chopped preserved ginger
½ cup chopped pecans.

1. Place the peaches and cantaloupe in a kettle and simmer gently thirty minutes, stirring to prevent sticking.

2. Add the sugar, lemon juice and syrup and boil rapidly until mixture is thick. Stir to prevent sticking.

3. Stir in the ginger and pecans and pour into hot sterilized jars. Pour two thin layers of paraffin wax over. Cool, cover and store in a cool, dry, dark place.

Yield: About ten jelly jars.

Surinam Preserves   *Florida*

2 quarts Surinam cherries
2 pounds sugar
  Juice of two lemons
½ teaspoon ground cardamom.

1. Rinse the cherries and remove stems. Pit the cherries.

2. Combine the cherries, sugar and lemon juice in a stainless steel or enamel saucepan. Bring to a boil and cook over moderately high heat exactly fifteen minutes, skimming the surface if foam forms. Stir in the cardamom and spoon the mixture into hot sterilized jars. Seal immediately. Cool and store in the refrigerator.

Yield: Three to four cups.

The mayhaw is a hawthorn that is abundant in parts of Louisiana. The fruit is used to make an excellent jelly.

Mayhaw Jelly   *Louisiana*

1 pound ripe mayhaws (part of the fruit
  should be underripe)
4 cups water, approximately
  Sugar.

1. Wash the mayhaws and put them in a preserving kettle. Add water to cover, approximately four cups. Bring to a boil and simmer the fruit until tender.

2. Strain the juice through a jelly bag. There should be about five cups. For each five cups of juice, add three cups of sugar and bring to a boil. Boil rapidly to the jelly stage.

3. To test for the jellying point, dip a spoon into the boiling liquid. When the syrup nears the jellying stage, it will drop from the side of the spoon in two drops. When the drops run together and slide off the spoon in a "sheet," the jelly is ready and should be taken off the heat at once.

Pour into sterilized glasses and seal at once. Cool and store in refrigerator.

Yield: About two pints.

Damson Jam   *Virginia*

4 pounds damson plums, pitted, and pits tied in a muslin bag
5 pounds sugar
2 cups water.

1. In a heavy preserving kettle, layer the damsons and the sugar. Add water and heat over high heat until the sugar starts to melt. Reduce heat to low and, when sugar takes on a color, stir the mixture well.

2. Add the bag of pits and continue to cook slowly, stirring occasionally to prevent scorching, until jam is thick and rich. Skim as necessary.

3. Remove bag of pits. Ladle jam into hot sterilized canning jars and adjust caps, or ladle into jelly glasses and cover with two thin (one-eighth-inch) layers of paraffin wax. Cool and store in a dark, dry, cool place.

Yield: About six pints.

A limited crop of Seville oranges is grown in Florida, and some are shipped to gourmet shops in metropolitan areas during late January or early February.

Seville (Bitter) Orange Marmalade
                                                Florida

12 medium-size Seville (bitter) oranges
 4 lemons
 3 quarts water
   Sugar.

1. Slice the oranges and lemons very thinly and place in a large bowl. Remove seeds, place in a muslin bag and add to the sliced fruit. Add the water, cover and let stand twenty-four to forty-eight hours.

2. Bring to a boil and simmer gently until the peel is soft, one hour or more. Discard the bag of seeds. Measure fruit and for every cup of fruit add one cup of sugar.

3. Bring to a boil again, stirring until the sugar dissolves. Boil rapidly until two drops form on the edge of the spoon and drop off simultaneously (or for a stiffer marmalade until the drops run together as they fall off). Skim foam from the surface. Pour marmalade into hot sterilized jars and seal. Cool and store in a cool, dark, dry place.

Yield: About nine pints.

Pepper Jelly   *Tennessee*

6 medium-size green peppers, cored, seeded and ground
5 long yellow sweet peppers if available, ground
8 hot green peppers, seeds left in and ground
1 onion, ground
9 cups sugar
1½ cups white vinegar
½ cup lemon juice
1 bottle liquid fruit pectin
  Green food coloring (optional).

1. Place the peppers, onion, sugar, vinegar and lemon juice in a kettle. Bring to a boil slowly, stirring to dissolve the sugar.

2. Boil five minutes. Stir in the pectin and food coloring if desired. Let stand five minutes, skim, stir and pour into hot sterilized jars. Top with two thin layers of paraffin wax. Cool, cover and store in a cool, dark, dry place.

Yield: About one dozen six-ounce jars.

Note: Serve with meats.

Bourbon Jelly   *Kentucky*

1 tablespoon unflavored gelatin
1⅓ cups water
⅓ cup sugar
⅓ cup orange juice
⅔ cup bourbon.

1. Soften the gelatin in one-third cup of the water. Heat remaining water to boiling. Add softened gelatin and the sugar. Stir to dissolve.
2. Stir in the orange juice and bourbon and pour into two jelly glasses. Seal. Cool and chill.
Yield: Two jelly glasses.
Note: Serve with poultry, ham or vegetables.

Cucumbers in Butter and Dill   *Virginia*

3 pounds cucumbers
6 tablespoons wine vinegar
2 teaspoons sugar
2 teaspoons salt
6 tablespoons butter
1½ teaspoons freshly snipped dillweed

1. Using a swivel-bladed paring knife, peel the cucumbers. Slice the cucumbers lengthwise and remove seeds with a melon ball cutter or a spoon. Slice each half lengthwise again. Cut each length of cucumber into one-and-one-half-inch pieces.
2. Place the cucumber pieces in a mixing bowl and add the vinegar, sugar and salt. Let stand one hour or so, turning occasionally in the marinade.
3. Meanwhile, preheat the oven to 375 degrees. Butter a baking dish and sprinkle with the dill. Drain the cucumbers and add them to the dish. Bake, uncovered, stirring occasionally, forty-five minutes. Chill and serve cold.
Yield: Four to six servings.

Pickled Garden Carrots   *Virginia*

1 pound freshly picked small carrots
2 cups water

½ cup wine vinegar
1 teaspoon salt
1 teaspoon sugar
1 teaspoon mustard seeds
1 teaspoon peppercorns
1 bay leaf.

1. Trim off the carrots at both ends. Wash the carrots well.
2. Combine the carrots with the remaining ingredients and cook until carrots are tender but still crisp. Cooking time will depend on the size of the carrots. Cool the carrots in the liquid; then drain and chill.
Yield: Four to six servings.

Quick Cucumber Pickles   *Arkansas*

4 quarts thinly sliced cucumbers
1½ cups thinly sliced onions
⅓ cup salt
2 cloves garlic
2 quarts crushed ice or ice cubes
4 cups sugar
1½ teaspoons ground turmeric
1½ teaspoons celery seeds
2 tablespoons mustard seeds
3 cups white vinegar.

1. Combine the cucumbers, onions, salt and garlic in a large crock or bowl. Cover the top with the ice and let stand for three hours. The ice removes the bitterness from the cucumbers.
2. Drain the mixture thoroughly in a colander and discard the liquid. If desired, discard the garlic cloves as well.
3. In a large pot, combine the sugar, turmeric, celery seeds, mustard seeds and vinegar. Bring the mixture to a boil and stir until all the sugar is dissolved.
4. Add the drained vegetables and bring to a boil. Cook for five minutes.
5. Pack the hot pickles into hot sterilized jars to within one-half inch of the jar tops. Adjust

caps and rings and make sure each cap is firmly sealed.

6. Process the jars in a boiling water bath for five minutes. The boiling water should extend at least one inch above the jars. Remove the jars, adjust seals if necessary, and allow the jars to cool. Store in a cool, dark, dry place.

Yield: Six pints.

Pickled Green Beans   *Tennessee*

2 cups cooked whole green beans (drained canned beans or cooked fresh or frozen beans may be used)
1 medium-size onion, thinly sliced
1 clove garlic, crushed
⅓ cup sugar
¾ cup cider vinegar
¾ cup water
3 tablespoons oil
½ teaspoon salt
1 teaspoon pickling spice, tied in a muslin bag.
Dressing:
½ cup sour cream
¼ cup mayonnaise
1 teaspoon lemon juice
¼ teaspoon dry mustard
1 tablespoon horseradish
½ teaspoon onion juice
2 teaspoons chopped chives.

1. Alternate the beans and the onion slices in a jar and slip in the garlic clove.

2. Combine the sugar, vinegar, water, oil, salt and spice bag in a small pan. Bring to a boil and allow to stand until mixture is at room temperature.

3. Remove the spice bag and pour mixture over beans and onion slices. Refrigerate twelve hours or longer.

4. To serve, drain the beans and remove garlic clove. Combine the dressing ingredients and toss beans with the dressing.

Yield: Four to six servings.

Whole Artichoke Pickles   *Kentucky*

4 quarts small Jerusalem artichokes, washed and scraped
  Salt
2 tablespoons alum (see note)
8 cups cider vinegar
2 tablespoons mustard seeds
2 tablespoons whole cloves
2 tablespoons celery seeds
2 cups sugar
1 tablespoon turmeric.

1. Day before, cover the artichokes with salted water, using one tablespoon salt to every quart water. Let stand overnight.

2. Next day, drain. Cover artichokes with water which has alum in it and let soak twenty-four hours. Drain artichokes and wash well.

3. Combine the vinegar, one cup water, the mustard seeds, cloves, celery seeds, sugar and turmeric in a saucepan. Bring to a boil and simmer twenty minutes. Pack the artichokes in hot sterilized jars and pour syrup over. Seal. Process in a water bath twenty minutes. Adjust caps. Cool and store in a cool, dark, dry place.

Yield: About four quarts.

Note: Alum is available in drugstores.

Crisp Watermelon Pickles   *Mississippi*

  Rind of one large watermelon
¼ cup slaked lime (see note)
10 cups sugar
8 cups cider vinegar
2 tablespoons whole allspice
2 tablespoons whole cloves
4 sticks cinnamon.

1. Neatly peel away all green, red and pink portions from the rind. Cut the rind into neat cubes or slices and measure enough rind to make approximately one gallon.

2. Drop the rind into a large kettle of boiling water and simmer five minutes. Drain and cool.

3. Dissolve the slaked lime in two quarts cold water and pour the solution over the rind. Let stand about three and one-half hours. Drain; rinse thoroughly.

4. Cover the rind with clear, cold water, bring to a boil and cook until rind is tender. Drain again.

5. Combine four cups sugar, two cups vinegar and eight cups water. Tie the allspice, cloves and cinnamon in a cheesecloth bag and add it. Bring to a boil and simmer five minutes. Add the rind and return to a boil. Simmer thirty minutes. Remove from the heat and let stand twelve to twenty-four hours.

6. Add the remaining vinegar and sugar and bring to a boil. Simmer until the rind is translucent. If the syrup becomes too thick as it cooks, add a little water occasionally. When rind is cooked, discard the spice bag and pack the rind and syrup into sterilized jars. Seal. Cool and store in a cool, dark, dry place.

Yield: About four quarts.

Note: Slaked lime is available at many drugstores.

Easy Pickled Watermelon Rind

Georgia

4 quarts cubed watermelon rind (red flesh and green skin pared away)
4 teaspoons salt
6 cups sugar
4 cups white vinegar or cider vinegar
1 cup water (optional)
2 teaspoons whole cloves
4 tablespoons broken cinnamon pieces.

1. Two days before, place the rind in a kettle and add water to cover. Sprinkle with the salt and simmer until rind is tender enough to be pierced with a fork. This should take five to ten minutes, depending on the size of the cubes.

2. Drain the cubes and place in a towel. Squeeze to remove most of the moisture. Place the squeezed rind in a stone crock.

3. Combine the sugar and vinegar in a saucepan. If the vinegar seems particularly acid, dilute with the one cup water. Otherwise, do not use the water. Bring to a boil and cook, stirring, until sugar dissolves. Pour the syrup over the rind. Cover and let stand overnight.

4. Next day, drain the rind and return the syrup to a boil. Pour the syrup over the rind again.

5. Combine the cloves and cinnamon in a cheesecloth bag. Drain the rind once more and bring the syrup to a boil. Pour the syrup over the rind and add the spice bag. Let stand overnight.

6. Next day, discard the spice bag. Bring the rind to a boil in the syrup. Pour into hot sterilized jars and seal. Cool and store in a cool, dark, dry place.

Yield: About four quarts.

Stuffed Oranges and Lemons   *Georgia*

Fruit:
10 medium-size lemons
10 medium-size oranges
   Boiling water.
Syrup:
 6 cups cider vinegar
 9 cups sugar
1½ cups water
 3 cups mixed lemon juice and orange juice
 3 cups grenadine syrup
 3 sticks cinnamon
   Red food coloring.
Filling:
 2 cups pitted dates
 2 cups cranberries
 2 cups raisins
 2 cups dried figs
 1 cup drained watermelon rind pickle, finely chopped
 2 cups nuts, chopped
½ cup drained maraschino cherries, chopped.

1. Test that the fruit fits quart jars. Cut a small slice from end of each piece of fruit and scoop out

all pulp. Strain and reserve juice. Discard pulp. Cover fruit shells with boiling water. Simmer twenty minutes. Drain; repeat twice with more water, simmering fifteen and ten minutes.

2. To prepare syrup, combine in a saucepan the vinegar, sugar, water, juices, grenadine, cinnamon sticks and enough food coloring to make the syrup rosy. Heat, stirring to dissolve sugar. Simmer thirty minutes. Add fruit shells. Simmer until shells are tender but not mushy. Remove shells and drain. Reserve syrup.

3. To prepare filling, use the fine blade of a food chopper to grind the dates, cranberries, raisins and figs together. Stir in the watermelon rind pickle, nuts and maraschino cherries.

4. Spoon the fruit and nut mixture into the hot, drained fruit shells. Push down to pack as tightly as possible. Drop three oranges or four lemons, cut ends up, into clean, sterilized quart canning jars.

5. Bring the reserved syrup to a boil and fill jars, leaving one-half-inch head space. Adjust caps. Place on a rack in a water bath so that the jars are covered by at least one to two inches of boiling water. Bring to a boil again. Boil fifteen minutes.

6. With tongs or special holder, remove jars and cool. Tighten caps as needed. Next day, test caps for seal. Store in dark, dry, cool place. To use, remove fruit and cut into one-half-inch slices. Spoon a little syrup over slices to moisten and flavor.

Yield: About eight quart jars, depending on size of fruit.

Pear Relish   *Georgia*

10 pounds Keiffer pears, peeled, cored and
    ground coarsely
 3 green peppers, seeded and ground
 3 red sweet peppers, seeded and ground
 6 onions, ground
 4 cups cider vinegar
 4 cups sugar
 1 teaspoon celery seeds

1 tablespoon mixed pickling spices
1 tablespoon mustard seeds.

1. Place the pears, peppers, onions, vinegar and sugar in a large kettle. Tie the celery seeds, pickling spices and mustard seeds in a muslin bag and add to the kettle.

2. Bring to a boil, stirring occasionally, and simmer about forty minutes. Discard the spice bag. Pour relish into hot sterilized jars and seal immediately. Cool and store in a cool, dark, dry place.

Yield: About eight pints.

Lime Chutney   *Florida*

2 large or three small limes
6 tart apples, peeled, cored and cut into fine
   dice
¼ pound finely chopped suet
¼ cup finely chopped candied ginger or equal
   parts ginger and candied lime peel, if
   available
2 cups currants, chopped
2 cups sugar.

1. Squeeze the limes and reserve the juice. Using a spoon, separate the white pulp from the skin. Discard the white pulp. Place the skins in a saucepan and add water barely to cover. Simmer until skins are almost mushy. Drain and mash the skins.

2. Combine the reserved lime juice, mashed lime skins and the remaining ingredients. Stir; then pack in hot sterilized jars. Seal tightly, store in refrigerator but open occasionally to stir. Let stand at least ten days in refrigerator before using.

Yield: About one quart.

Peach Chutney   *Georgia*

4 cups peeled, pitted and finely chopped
   peaches (about three pounds)

¾ cup cider vinegar
¼ cup lemon juice
1 cup raisins
⅓ cup chopped onion
¼ cup slivered, drained preserved ginger
1 tablespoon salt
1 teaspoon ground allspice
½ teaspoon cinnamon
½ teaspoon ground cloves
½ teaspoon ground ginger
7½ cups sugar (about three and one-quarter pounds)
1 bottle liquid fruit pectin.

1. Put the peaches in a large kettle and add the vinegar, lemon juice, raisins, onion, preserved ginger, salt and spices.

2. Add the sugar and mix thoroughly. Place over high heat and bring to a rolling boil, stirring occasionally. Boil hard one minute, stirring constantly.

3. Remove from the heat and stir in the pectin immediately. Skim off the foam with a metal spoon and stir and skim for five minutes to cool slightly and prevent floating fruit. Ladle into hot sterilized glasses and cover with a one-eighth-inch layer of melted paraffin wax. Store in a cool, dry, dark place.

Yield: About one dozen eight-ounce jars.

Mango Chutney   *Florida*

1½ cups light brown sugar
2 cups malt vinegar or cider vinegar
1 pound firm, slightly underripe mangoes, peeled and sliced
½ pound currants
½ pound raisins
½ pound blanched almonds
⅓ cup sliced green ginger (see note) or one-half cup chopped preserved ginger
1 tablespoon salt
½ tablespoon white mustard seeds, tied in a cheesecloth bag
½ cup chopped onion

½ cup chopped green pepper
1 teaspoon chopped hot chili pepper or red pepper flakes.

1. Combine the sugar and vinegar and bring to a boil.

2. Stir in the remaining ingredients and simmer thirty minutes, or until syrup is thick and fruit is clear. Discard the spice bag. Ladle the chutney into hot sterilized jars and seal. Cool and store in a cool, dark, dry place.

Yield: Three to four pints.

Note: Green ginger is available in Chinese markets.

Green Tomato Relish   *Louisiana*

12 green tomatoes, cored
⅓ cup coarse salt
24 green peppers
6 red sweet peppers (or use this additional amount of green peppers)
12 large sweet onions
1 gallon boiling water
4 cups white vinegar
3 cups sugar
1 tablespoon whole cloves
2 tablespoons stick cinnamon pieces
1 teaspoon celery seeds.

1. Chop the tomatoes and sprinkle with the salt. Let stand one hour. Drain.

2. Core and seed green and red peppers and trim away the white veins. Cut peppers into large cubes. Put peppers and the onions through a food chopper. Add half the water and drain immediately in a colander.

3. Add the remaining water and let stand ten minutes. Drain.

4. Add the vinegar and sugar. Tie the cloves, stick cinnamon and celery seeds in a cheesecloth bag and add it. Bring the mixture to a boil and simmer, uncovered, exactly thirty minutes. Discard the spice bag.

5. Pour the relish into hot sterilized jars and seal. Cool and store in a cool, dark, dry place.

Yield: About six quarts.

Ripe Tomato Pickle   *Georgia*

8 cups ripe tomatoes, cored and chopped
8 cups chopped green cabbage
4 cups sliced white onions
6 large green peppers, cored, seeded and chopped
4 cups cider vinegar
2 pounds light brown sugar
½ teaspoon mace
½ teaspoon ground cloves
½ teaspoon ground allspice
1 teaspoon ground ginger
1 tablespoon celery seeds
1 teaspoon turmeric
1 cup salt.

1. Day before, combine all the ingredients in a large mixing bowl and let stand, stirring occasionally, about one hour.

2. Pour the ingredients into a large cloth bag and let drip overnight. Next day, pour the contents of the bag into a large kettle. Bring to a boil and cook, stirring frequently, one hour. Pour into hot sterilized jars and seal. Cool and store in a cool, dark, dry place.

Yield: About three quarts.

Artichoke Relish   *North Carolina*

4 quarts Jerusalem artichokes, scraped and coarsely ground
6 onions, coarsely ground
4 green or red sweet peppers, coarsely ground
2 tablespoons coarse salt
1 tablespoon celery seeds
2 tablespoons mustard seeds
1 tablespoon turmeric
½ teaspoon cayenne pepper

6 cups cider vinegar
3 cups sugar.

Combine all the ingredients in a large kettle. Bring to a boil and simmer thirty minutes, stirring occasionally. Pour into hot sterilized jars and seal. Cool and store in a cool, dark, dry place.

Yield: About fourteen pints.

Green Relish   *Tennessee*

4 cups coarsely ground onions, drained
4 cups coarsely ground cucumbers, drained
8 cups coarsely ground seeded green peppers
3 hot green peppers, unseeded and ground
2 tablespoons coarse salt
1 tablespoon celery seeds
1 tablespoon mustard seeds
2 cups sugar
2 cups cider vinegar.

Put all the ingredients in a large kettle. Bring to a boil and simmer about thirty minutes. Ladle into hot sterilized jars and seal. Cool and store in cool, dark, dry place.

Yield: About ten pints.

Sauces

Chili Sauce   *Arkansas*

8 pounds ripe tomatoes
3 red sweet peppers, seeded
3 green peppers, seeded
1 small stalk celery
6 onions, chopped
3 cloves garlic, minced
1½ teaspoons whole allspice
1½ teaspoons mustard seeds
1½ teaspoons whole cloves
1½ cups light brown sugar
2 tablespoons salt

1 teaspoon freshly ground black pepper
1 teaspoon dry mustard
2 dried hot red peppers, crushed
2 cups cider vinegar.

1. Scald, peel, core and chop the tomatoes. Chop the peppers, celery and onions. Add with the garlic to the tomatoes, bring to a boil and simmer for forty-five minutes.

2. Tie the allspice, mustard seeds and cloves in a muslin bag. Add with the sugar, salt, black pepper, mustard and hot peppers. Boil, uncovered, until thick.

3. Add the vinegar and boil the sauce to correct the consistency. Discard the spice bag. Pour the sauce into hot sterilized jars and seal. Cool and store in a cool, dark, dry place.

Yield: Eight pints.

Southern Tomato Sauce   *Kentucky*

10 medium-size tomatoes (about two and
    one-half pounds)
¼ pound salt pork, diced
¼ cup olive oil
2 cloves garlic, finely chopped
1 large onion, finely chopped
1 six-ounce can tomato paste, preferably
    the imported Italian kind
1 bay leaf
1 teaspoon basil
    Salt and freshly ground black pepper to
    taste
2 tablespoons butter, cut into small pieces.

1. Drop the tomatoes two or three at a time into rapidly boiling water and boil for about 10 seconds. Remove and peel with a paring knife. Cut out the stem and discard. Cut the tomatoes in half crosswise and squeeze each half to extract the seeds. Then coarsely chop them in a mixing bowl.

2. In a saucepan gently sauté the salt pork in the oil until brown. Add the garlic and onion and cook until just wilted.

3. Add the prepared tomatoes, tomato paste, bay leaf, basil, and salt and pepper to taste. Bring to a boil and let simmer over very low heat for one hour.

4. When done, swirl in the butter bits and serve.

Yield: About one quart.
Note: This sauce may be frozen.

Hollandaise Sauce   *Louisiana*

½ cup butter, at room temperature
2 egg yolks
2 tablespoons lemon juice
¼ teaspoon salt
    Pinch of cayenne pepper.

1. Divide the butter into three parts. In the top of a double boiler, combine one part of the butter with the egg yolks.

2. Place over hot, nearly boiling water and beat constantly with a wire whisk until the butter is melted.

3. Add the second part of the butter and then the third, stirring constantly.

4. When the sauce thickens, add the lemon juice, salt and cayenne.

Yield: Four servings.

This is one of the most unusual of Florida's specialties. Called Old Sour, it is really a sauce made with lime juice and salt that is aged before using. The sauce is designed for use with fish and sea foods and in salad dressings.

Key West Old Lime Sour   *Florida*

2 cups fresh lime juice, preferably made with
    thin-skinned key limes
1½ teaspoons salt.

1. Strain the lime juice and, using a funnel, pour it into a bottle. Add the salt and shake the bottle.

2. Do not stopper the bottle, but cover the mouth with cheesecloth. Tie with a string and let the lime juice stand at room temperature for about two weeks to age. Seal the bottle and keep it in a cool place. Serve a dash of the sauce on broiled fish, cold fish, in mayonnaise or in French dressings.

Yield: About two cups.

Tartar Sauce   *Louisiana*

1 cup mayonnaise
1 clove garlic, finely minced
¼ cup finely chopped onion
2 tablespoons chopped sour pickle
1 tablespoon chopped capers
¼ cup finely chopped parsley
1 teaspoon Creole mustard or imported mustard such as Dijon or Düsseldorf.

Combine all ingredients and serve.
Yield: About one and one-quarter cups.

Lime and Herb Sauce Vinaigrette

Florida

½ cup peanut oil or vegetable oil
¼ cup olive oil
3 to four tablespoons lime juice
Salt and freshly ground black pepper to taste
2 tablespoons finely chopped chives
1 teaspoon finely chopped fresh tarragon or one-half teaspoon dried tarragon
½ teaspoon finely minced garlic
2 tablespoons finely chopped parsley
1 teaspoon Creole mustard or imported mustard such as Dijon or Düsseldorf.

Combine all ingredients in a mixing bowl and beat or shake well. Serve as a salad dressing or with sea food.
Yield: About one and one-quarter cups.

Louisiana Sauce Remoulade

¼ cup cold water
3 tablespoons dry mustard
3 cups corn oil
1 cup olive oil
2 five-ounce jars horseradish or about one cup fresh horseradish
3 tablespoons paprika
1 teaspoon celery seeds
1½ cups finely minced heart of celery
1 one-pound jar Creole mustard
1 tablespoon lemon juice
Grated rind of one lemon
12 whole cloves
6 bay leaves.

1. Pour the water into the container of an electric blender. Add the dry mustard. Stir to blend and let stand ten minutes.
2. Add all remaining ingredients except the cloves and bay leaves and blend. Add the cloves and bay leaves and store sauce in glass jars. This sauce may be kept for several weeks in the refrigerator. When the sauce is used, add more horseradish to taste if desired. Serve over chilled shrimp.

Yield: About two quarts.

Mustard Mayonnaise   *Louisiana*

2 egg yolks
1 tablespoon wine vinegar
Pinch of cayenne pepper
Salt and freshly ground white or black pepper to taste
¾ cup peanut oil
¼ cup olive oil
2 to four tablespoons mustard, preferably Creole type, or Dijon or Düsseldorf style
Lime or lemon juice (optional).

1. Place the egg yolks in a mixing bowl and add the vinegar, cayenne, salt and pepper.
2. Begin beating with a wire whisk and, when

well blended, add the oils in a thin stream. Continue beating until mayonnaise is thickened and all the oil has been added.

3. When firm, beat in the mustard. If desired, add a little lime or lemon juice to taste. Serve with cold boiled shrimp.

Yield: About one and one-quarter cups.

Aguacate (Avocado Sauce)   *Florida*

1 ripe avocado
1 clove garlic, finely minced
1 tablespoon wine vinegar
  Juice of one lime or lemon
4 tablespoons olive oil
  Salt and freshly ground black pepper to taste
1 green chile, fresh or canned, chopped (optional), or Tabasco sauce to taste
  Fresh coriander leaves, chopped (optional).

1. Peel the avocado and mash the pulp.
2. Immediately blend pulp with remaining ingredients. Serve as a sauce with fish or other sea food.

Yield: One to one and one-half cups.

Sauce for Poached Fish   *Louisiana*

2 tablespoons butter
2 tablespoons flour
1 cup boiling water
2 tablespoons catchup
1 tablespoon Worcestershire sauce
  Juice of one lemon
1 hard-cooked egg, finely chopped
  Salt to taste
  Cayenne pepper to taste.

1. Melt the butter and stir in the flour. Add the water, stirring until blended and smooth.
2. Stir in the remaining ingredients and serve hot with fish.

Yield: About one and one-half cups.

Lobster or Shrimp Cocktail Dressing
Mississippi

1 cup mayonnaise
3 tablespoons catchup
1 tablespoon tarragon vinegar
1 teaspoon Worcestershire sauce
  Lemon juice to taste
  Onion juice scraped from one cut onion.

Combine all ingredients and chill. Serve with cold lobster or shrimp.

Yield: About one and one-quarter cups.

Hot Barbecue Sauce   *Alabama*

2 teaspoons Tabasco sauce
2½ cups bottled chili sauce
1 teaspoon finely minced hot green peppers or canned chile peppers
¾ cup oil
½ cup lemon juice
2 tablespoons tarragon vinegar
2 cups chopped onions
2 cloves garlic, finely minced
1 tablespoon light brown sugar
1 bay leaf, crumbled
1 teaspoon dry mustard
1 teaspoon salt
½ cup water.

Combine all ingredients and simmer twenty minutes. Serve with charcoal-grilled hamburgers, spareribs or chicken.

Yield: Six cups.

Barbecue Sauce   *Mississippi*

1 cup catchup
  Juice of two lemons
1 tablespoon Worcestershire sauce
2 tablespoons cider vinegar
2 tablespoons butter

Salt and freshly ground black pepper to taste
1 teaspoon sugar.

Combine all ingredients, bring to a boil and use to brush poultry, meat or fish as it is barbecued.
Yield: About one and one-half cups.

Pendennis Club Barbecue Sauce
Kentucky

1 bottle chili sauce
1 medium-size bottle catchup
1 bottle Worcestershire sauce
1 bottle A.1. Sauce
1 small bottle Major Grey's chutney
1 cup bourbon
  Dry red wine or cider vinegar.

Combine all the ingredients, using enough wine or vinegar to give a pouring consistency. Serve on barbecued spareribs, chicken or hamburgers.
Yield: About seven cups.

Tomato Gravy
Alabama

2 tablespoons bacon drippings
3 tomatoes, peeled and chopped
2 tablespoons flour
½ teaspoon sugar
½ teaspoon salt
¼ teaspoon freshly ground black pepper
⅛ teaspoon baking soda
2 cups milk.

1. Heat the bacon drippings in a skillet and cook the tomatoes in it until tender. Sprinkle with the flour, sugar, salt and pepper and stir to mix well. Cook two minutes.
2. Add the baking soda to the milk and stir in the tomato mixture. Bring to a boil, stirring. Spoon over hot biscuits or grits.
Yield: Three cups.

Mississippi Steak Sauce

½ teaspoon dry mustard
¼ cup wine vinegar
¼ cup catchup
1 teaspoon Worcestershire sauce
¼ teaspoon curry powder
  Salt and freshly ground black pepper to taste
1 cup butter, at room temperature.

1. Combine the mustard with the vinegar and let stand ten minutes. Blend with the catchup, Worcestershire, curry powder, salt and pepper.
2. Place the butter in a skillet and place the skillet over very low heat. Stir continuously with a wire whisk and, when the butter is creamy but not melted, gradually stir in the catchup mixture. When all ingredients are blended, remove the sauce from the heat. Serve with charcoal-grilled steak.
Yield: About one and one-half cups.

Cranberry and Horseradish Sauce
Tennessee

4 cups cranberries
2 cups water
1½ cups sugar
  Horseradish to taste.

1. Place the berries in a saucepan and add the water. Cover and cook until berries pop.
2. Add the sugar and continue cooking fifteen minutes. Let cool and add the horseradish. Mold, if desired, and chill. Serve with game, poultry or meat.
Yield: About three cups.

Port Wine and Horseradish Sauce
Mississippi

½ cup port wine
⅛ teaspoon nutmeg or mace

⅛ teaspoon cinnamon
Salt and freshly ground black pepper to
taste
1 cup red currant jelly (eight ounces)
2 tablespoons freshly grated horseradish.

1. Pour the wine into a saucepan and add the nutmeg or mace, cinnamon, salt and pepper. Bring to a boil and reduce by one-third.

2. Heat the jelly over hot water, stirring, until jelly dissolves. Add the wine mixture and horseradish. Serve with game or poultry.

Yield: One and one-half cups.

One of the most famous sauces in Louisiana is a honey and curry sauce used on first courses at the Shreveport Club in Shreveport. The sauce is used on fresh fruit and on sea food.

Shreveport Club Honey and Curry Sauce

Louisiana

1 cup mayonnaise
2 tablespoons catchup
1 tablespoon dry mustard
2 tablespoons honey
1 tablespoon curry powder
Tabasco sauce to taste
1 teaspoon lemon juice
Salt to taste
Worcestershire sauce to taste
1 teaspoon onion juice, squeezed from grated onion
1 tablespoon preserved ginger or freshly grated ginger to taste.

1. Spoon the mayonnaise into a mixing bowl. Blend the catchup and mustard together and add to mayonnaise.

2. Stir in the remaining ingredients and chill.

Yield: About one and one-half cups.

Old-Fashioned Lemon Butter

Virginia

3 lemons
3 cups sugar
3 eggs
4 tablespoons butter.

1. Grate the rind of the lemons. Squeeze the lemons to extract the juice. Combine the grated rind and the juice.

2. Place the sugar in a mixing bowl and add the eggs, one at a time, beating well after each addition. Blend with the lemon rind and juice.

3. Add the butter bit by bit and cook the mixture in the top of a double boiler, stirring constantly, until mixture thickens. Do not boil.

4. Pour into hot sterilized jars and seal. Cool and store in a cool, dark, dry place. Serve with toast or as a filling for sponge layers.

Yield: About three cups.

Papaya Sauce

Florida

2 large ripe but fairly firm papayas
3 cups sugar
1 teaspoon grated fresh ginger or ground ginger
1 lemon, thinly sliced
6 whole cloves.

1. Peel the papayas and cut them into cubes.

2. Cover the papaya cubes with water and add the remaining ingredients. Bring to a boil and simmer until papaya is thoroughly tender.

Yield: Two to three cups.

Note: Use as you would applesauce.

Rum and Cherry Sauce

Louisiana

1 cup dark or bing cherry preserves
½ cup broken pecans, walnuts or other nuts
½ cup dark rum, or more to taste.

Combine all the ingredients and let stand until

ready to use. This sauce should be made only with dark rum and not with the light. The sauce will keep indefinitely in the refrigerator and for several weeks in a cool place if tightly sealed.

Yield: About two cups.

Custard Sauce Flavored with Pernod

Louisiana

4 egg yolks
3 tablespoons sugar
1 teaspoon cornstarch
⅛ teaspoon salt
1¾ cups milk, scalded
1 tablespoon Pernod.

1. Beat the egg yolks with the sugar until thick and pale. Beat in the cornstarch and salt. Gradually beat in the milk.
2. Pour the mixture into a heavy pan and cook over low heat, stirring constantly, until the mixture thickens and lightly coats the back of the spoon.
3. Remove from the heat and set in a pan of ice water to prevent further cooking. Cool. Stir in the Pernod. Chill.

Yield: About two cups.

Rum Sauce

Louisiana

6 egg yolks
1 cup sugar
¾ cup dark rum.

1. Beat the egg yolks until lemon-colored and slightly thickened. Gradually beat in the sugar.
2. Stir in half the rum and cook over boiling water, stirring constantly, until sauce coats a wooden spoon. Do not allow to boil. Stir in the remaining rum.

Yield: About one and one-half cups.

Note: Cognac or kirsch may be substituted for the rum.

Beverages

Eggnog

Mississippi

6 eggs, separated
12 tablespoons sugar
½ cup bourbon, or more to taste
1 cup heavy cream
Nutmeg.

1. Place the egg yolks in a mixing bowl and add six tablespoons of the sugar. Beat thoroughly until light and lemon-colored.
2. Beat the egg whites until stiff and gradually add the remaining sugar. Fold the whites into the yolks and add the bourbon gradually, beating thoroughly.
3. Whip the cream and fold it into the egg mixture. Serve immediately in chilled silver mugs or glasses and sprinkle each serving with a little nutmeg.

Yield: Six servings.

John's Eggnog

North Carolina

¾ cup sugar
12 eggs, separated
1 pint bourbon
2 cups heavy cream, whipped.

1. Slowly add the sugar to the egg yolks and beat until very stiff and white.
2. Beat the egg whites until stiff. Stir the bourbon into yolk mixture. Mix in whites and the cream with a wire whisk. Chill until served. This is better on the second day.

Yield: One dozen servings.

One of the gentlest and most delicious restoratives for the morning-after is a well-chilled milk punch delicately seasoned with nutmeg. The milk punch served in certain Louisiana homes prior to Sunday brunch also contains cream.

Milk Punch
Louisiana

3 cups milk
1 cup light cream
3 tablespoons sugar, or to taste
1 cup bourbon or rye whisky
  Nutmeg.

1. Combine the milk, cream and sugar and stir until sugar dissolves.
2. Add the bourbon or whisky and serve with an ice cube in chilled glasses. Sprinkle with nutmeg before serving.
Yield: Four to six servings.

Café Brûlot
Louisiana

13 lumps sugar
 5 whole cloves
2½ sticks cinnamon
 1 lemon
 1 orange
 1 cup warm cognac
 4 to six cups piping-hot strong black coffee.

1. Place the lump sugar in a silver bowl or other suitable container. Add the cloves and cinnamon.
2. Cut the skin from the lemon and the orange, spiral fashion. Add the skins to the bowl and reserve the fruit for another use.
3. Add the cognac and ignite it. Ladle the mixture over and over while flame burns, and pour in coffee. Serve immediately in demitasse cups.
Yield: Ten servings.

Edenton Punch
North Carolina

2 fifths cognac
1 bottle Sauterne wine
2 quarts ice cold sparkling water
5 fifths ice cold dry or brut champagne.

1. Place a large block of ice in a punch bowl. Pour the cognac and Sauterne over ice.
2. When mixture is thoroughly cold, add the sparkling water and champagne. Serve immediately.
Yield: Fifty servings.
Note: This is served at hunt breakfasts.

Blackberry Syrup
South Carolina

6 to ten quarts blackberries
3 cups cider vinegar
  Sugar.

1. Place sound ripe fruit in a stone crock and pour the vinegar over the top. Cover top of crock with muslin. Let stand in a cool place for three to four days, stirring twice a day.
2. Strain the mixture through a jelly bag without crushing the fruit. Measure the juice into a pan and add one pound of sugar for every pint of juice.
3. Heat, stirring, until sugar dissolves, bring to a boil and boil gently for five minutes. Bottle and seal and dilute to taste for making a blackberry drink. Store in the refrigerator or in a cool, dark, dry place.
Yield: About three quarts.

Elderberry Blossom Wine
Kentucky

3 quarts elderberry blossoms without stems
4 gallons boiling water
9 pounds sugar
½ package active dry yeast
¼ cup lukewarm water
3 pounds raisins.

1. Place the blossoms in a five-gallon crock and add the boiling water. Add the sugar and stir until it is dissolved. Let cool.

2. Dissolve the yeast in the lukewarm water and add to the crock. Let stand ten days, stirring several times each day.

3. Strain the mixture into a large glass jug and add the raisins. Let stand three months; then strain into bottles or fruit jars. Seal well.

Yield: About three and one-half gallons.

Scuppernong Nectar   *South Carolina*

12 pounds scuppernong grapes
1 cup white vinegar
1 cup water
  Sugar.

1. Day before, crush the grapes and put in large crock or earthenware bowl. Add the vinegar and water, stir and let stand overnight.

2. Next day, drain juice through a cheesecloth bag. Measure juice into a kettle and for each two cups juice add one cup sugar.

3. Bring to a boil and boil five minutes. Bottle in hot sterilized bottles. Seal and store in a cool, dark, dry place.

Yield: About two quarts.

Mint Julep   *Kentucky*

1 teaspoon sugar
1 tablespoon water
4 or five mint leaves
  Crushed ice
2 ounces bourbon
  Mint sprig.

1. In a bowl, dissolve the sugar in the water. Add the mint leaves and bruise with muddler or wooden spoon until syrup is green-colored.

2. Fill a julep cup or old-fashioned glass with crushed ice.

3. Pour in the mint syrup and the bourbon. Set the cup in the refrigerator from thirty to sixty minutes to frost. Garnish with mint sprig. Serve with a half-sized straw.

Yield: One serving.

Tarpon Isle Rum Cocktail   *Florida*

  Juice of one sour orange
1 jigger dark rum
2 teaspoons unrefined sugar (sometimes called raw sugar or crude sugar)
  Shaved ice
1 slice sour orange.

Combine all ingredients except sour orange slice in a cocktail shaker and shake well. Strain and garnish with the sour orange slice.

Yield: One serving.

Salty Dog Cocktail   *Florida*

3 large grapefruit
3 teaspoons salt, or to taste
9 ounces vodka or gin
  Ice cubes.

1. Peel the grapefruit before squeezing because the peel gives a bitter, oily flavor to the juice. Squeeze or press the grapefruit. Divide the juice equally among six all-purpose wine glasses, small tumblers or on-the-rocks glasses. Add one-half teaspoon salt or salt to taste to each glass. Stir until salt is dissolved.

2. Add one and one-half ounces of vodka or gin to each glass. Add two or three ice cubes. Stir and serve.

Yield: Six servings.

Sazerac Cocktail   *Louisiana*

4 dashes absinthe (or use Pernod, Ricard or other anise-flavored liqueur)
4 dashes Angostura or Peychaud bitters

4 teaspoons sugar (optional)
8 ounces bourbon
   Ice cubes
   Lemon peel.

1. Thoroughly chill four old-fashioned glasses.

2. Put a dash of absinthe in each glass and swirl the glass around to coat the inside.

3. Add the bitters to a mixing glass. Add the sugar if desired. Add the bourbon and several large ice cubes. Stir until thoroughly chilled; then strain into the old-fashioned glasses. Twist lemon peel over each glass and serve.

Yield: Four servings.

Candies

Pralines   *Louisiana*

2 cups light brown sugar
1 cup granulated sugar
1 cup water
1 cup heavy cream
1 teaspoon vanilla
2 tablespoons butter
3 cups pecans.

1. Combine the sugars, water and cream in a heavy saucepan. Bring to a boil, stirring until sugars dissolve. Cook to the soft ball stage, or until mixture registers 238 degrees on a candy thermometer.

2. Remove from the heat and add the vanilla and butter. Beat until creamy. Add the pecans and spoon mixture onto a buttered marble slab or wax paper.

Yield: Three dozen.

Fudge   *Mississippi*

2 cups sugar
¾ cup heavy cream
2 tablespoons light corn syrup
⅛ teaspoon cream of tartar
⅛ teaspoon salt
2 tablespoons butter
1 teaspoon vanilla.

1. Place the sugar, cream, syrup, cream of tartar and salt in a heavy pan. Heat, stirring, until the sugar dissolves. Brush down the sides of the pan with hot water to remove splashes and crystals.

2. Heat mixture to boiling and boil without stirring to 234 degrees on a candy thermometer, or until the mixture forms a soft ball when dropped into cold water.

3. Add the butter, but do not stir. Cool to lukewarm, about 110 degrees.

4. Add the vanilla and beat the fudge with a wooden spoon until fudge loses its gloss and is thick and creamy. Pour into a buttered dish (8-by-8-by-2 inches). Mark into squares and cool.

Yield: One pound, about two dozen pieces.

Chocolate fudge: Add two to four ounces (two to four squares) unsweetened chocolate to the sugar mixture at the beginning of the recipe.

Nut fudge: Add one cup chopped walnuts, pecans, almonds or Brazil nuts just before pouring the fudge into the dish.

Penuche fudge: Substitute light brown sugar for the granulated sugar.

Ginger fudge: Add three-quarters cup finely chopped crystallized gingerroot just before pouring the fudge into the dish.

Chocolate Candy   *Mississippi*

3 tablespoons butter
1 teaspoon vanilla
¼ teaspoon salt
3 cups sugar
3 tablespoons cocoa powder

1½ cups milk
1 cup pecans or other nuts.

1. Rub a large platter with lumps of the butter and sprinkle with the vanilla and salt.

2. Combine the sugar and cocoa powder in a mixing bowl and gradually stir in the milk. Scrape the mixture into an aluminum saucepan and bring to a boil. Cook without stirring to form a medium ball when tested in cold water, or until mixture registers 240 degrees on a candy thermometer.

3. Pour the chocolate mixture onto the platter and, when mixture is cool but not firm, beat well until candy begins to harden. Beat in the nuts and drop the mixture, one teaspoonful at a time, onto a lightly buttered surface.

Yield: About one and one-half pounds.

Caramels   *Mississippi*

1¾ cups light corn syrup
2 cups sugar
1 cup butter
2 cups heavy cream
1 teaspoon vanilla
1 cup chopped nuts.

1. Combine the syrup, sugar, butter and one cup of the cream in a saucepan. Bring to a boil and stir in the remaining cream.

2. Cook until mixture forms a firm ball in cold water or registers 242 to 248 degrees on a candy thermometer. Add the vanilla and nuts and turn the mixture into a well-buttered pan. When mixture is nearly cold, cut with scissors into squares.

Yield: About two pounds.

Candied Orange Pecans   *Georgia*

3 cups sugar
1 cup orange juice
1½ tablespoons butter

1 teaspoon grated orange rind
3 cups pecans.

1. Combine the sugar and orange juice in a saucepan. Use a candy thermometer and cook the mixture to the soft ball stage, 236 degrees. Grease a flat surface with oil or butter.

2. Remove the saucepan from the heat and immediately add the butter and orange rind. Beat with a wooden spoon until the mixture is just ready to set. Quickly add the pecans and continue to beat the mixture until it becomes sugary.

3. Turn the candy onto the greased surface to cool. Quickly separate the nuts with two forks.

Yield: About three cups.

Sugar-Glazed Nuts   *Georgia*

1 cup mixed nuts, such as pecans, walnuts, almonds or filberts
1 cup sugar
⅓ cup light corn syrup
½ cup water.

1. This recipe is a little tricky because there are several variables to be taken into account. It is best prepared on a day with low humidity. In any case, the recipe must be carefully followed where temperatures and sugar crystals are concerned. To begin, fill a skillet with water and bring to a boil. Let the water simmer while proceeding with the recipe.

2. If the nuts are not of freshest quality, place them in a moderately hot oven briefly until they become crisp.

3. Combine the sugar, syrup and one-half cup water in a small saucepan and cook, stirring with a wooden spoon, until the sugar is dissolved. Stop stirring, but continue to cook until 300 degrees is reached on a candy thermometer. As sugar crystals form on the side of the pan, wipe them away with a wet cloth. Cook the syrup until it is a delicate straw color. Do not let syrup become too brown.

4. When the syrup is ready, immediately set

the saucepan in the simmering water in the skillet. This is to prevent the syrup from hardening.

5. Drop a few nuts into the syrup and dip them out, one by one. Place them on a greased flat surface to harden. The best way to retrieve the nuts from the syrup is with two forks. Use one to lift one nut at a time, the other to push the glazed nut onto the greased surface. Continue, a few nuts at a time, until all are glazed. One authority on candy-making has written, "A superfluous amount of glaze around the base of the nut indicates the work of an amateur."

Yield: One and one-half cups.

Note: Stir the syrup as little as possible while dipping nuts, to prevent crystallization. If the syrup becomes too thick, it may be reheated, but do not let it brown. If the syrup becomes too solid, add a little water and cook again to original temperature.

Crystallized Grapes   *Georgia*

1 pound Thompson seedless grapes
½ cup water
  Sugar.

1. Cut the grapes into small clusters.
2. Combine the water and one cup sugar and boil five minutes. Remove from the heat. Immediately dip the clusters, one at a time, into the syrup. Sprinkle each cluster generously with sugar and let stand until set.

Yield: One pound.

3. Midwest

Appetizers and Soups

Smoked Fish Appetizer — *Michigan*

¾ pound smoked whitefish or sablefish
1 eight-ounce package cream cheese, softened
2 tablespoons light cream
2 tablespoons lemon juice
1 tablespoon drained and chopped capers
Freshly ground black pepper to taste
Pumpernickel bread squares or rounds
Thin lemon slices
Fresh dill weed.

1. Remove skin and bones from the fish and flake. Combine fish with the cream cheese, cream, lemon juice, capers and pepper. Chill.
2. Serve on pumpernickel bread, garnished with tiny piece of lemon and bit of dill weed.
Yield: Two cups.

Pickled Perch Appetizer — *Michigan*

10 one-half-pound perch, filleted
1 teaspoon salt
1 cup water
1 cup white vinegar
1 large onion, sliced
½ cup sugar
1½ tablespoons mixed pickling spices
Salad greens
Sour cream
Düsseldorf mustard to taste.

1. Day before, cut the fish fillets into two or three pieces and steam over boiling water on a rack or in a colander about seven minutes.
2. Meanwhile, combine the salt, water, vinegar, onion, sugar and spices in a saucepan and bring to a boil. Place steamed fish in a ceramic bowl or glass jar and pour hot pickling mixture over. Cool. Chill overnight.
3. Next day, drain fish. Serve on salad greens with sour cream flavored with mustard.
Yield: Ten servings.

Pickled Lake Herring — *Michigan*

2 pounds lake herring fillets
2 teaspoons salt
2 thin slices lemon
2 thin slices onion, separated into rings
½ cup cider vinegar
½ cup water
1 tablespoon mixed pickling spices
1 teaspoon sugar
1 small bay leaf
⅓ cup sour cream
1 tablespoon lemon juice
1 teaspoon grated horseradish
1 tablespoon finely chopped parsley.

1. Preheat the oven to 350 degrees.
2. Skin the fillets if necessary. Cut into serving

pieces and place in a shallow baking dish or casserole.

3. Sprinkle with the salt. Arrange the lemon slices and onion rings over fish. Combine the vinegar, water, spices, sugar and bay leaf and pour over fish. Cover with lid or aluminum foil and bake about twenty minutes, or until fish flakes easily. Allow fish to cool in the pickling liquid. Chill.

4. Mix the sour cream with the lemon juice, horseradish and parsley. Drain the fish and serve as an appetizer topped with the sour cream mixture.

Yield: Six servings.

Cheese-Olive Appetizers   *Michigan*

1½ cups flour
½ cup shortening
½ cup grated sharp Cheddar cheese
18 stuffed green olives.

1. Preheat the oven to 400 degrees.
2. Place the flour in a bowl and work in the shortening with a pastry blender or the finger tips until mixture resembles coarse oatmeal. Mix to a dough with water as though making pastry.
3. Roll out the dough on a lightly floured board or pastry cloth until one-eighth-inch thick. Sprinkle with the cheese. Fold in half.
4. Roll out again and cut into two-inch circles. Wrap each olive in a round of pastry and place on an ungreased baking sheet. Bake ten minutes, or until done. Serve hot.

Yield: Eighteen.

Onion Cheese Tart   *Wisconsin*

6 onions, thinly sliced
2 tablespoons olive oil
2 tablespoons butter
   Salt and freshly ground black pepper to taste
   Rich pie pastry (recipe below)

3 egg whites
⅓ cup freshly grated Parmesan cheese
2 ounces, approximately, sharp Cheddar cheese, cut into matchstick-size strips.

1. Preheat the oven to 425 degrees.
2. Sauté the onions very slowly in the oil and butter until golden and tender but not browned. Season with salt and pepper.
3. Roll out the pastry and fit over the bottom and halfway up the sides of an eight-inch or nine-inch layer pan. Bake five to eight minutes, or until just set. Spoon onions into pastry shell.
4. Reduce the oven heat to 375 degrees. Beat the egg whites until very stiff. Fold in two tablespoons of the grated cheese.
5. Spread the mixture over the onions and arrange the cheese strips lattice-fashion over the top. Sprinkle with remaining grated cheese. Bake about thirty-five minutes, or until golden and set.

Yield: Six servings.

Rich Pie Pastry   *Wisconsin*

1 cup flour
⅛ teaspoon salt
⅓ cup butter
1 egg yolk.

1. Place the flour and salt in a bowl. With two knives of the finger tips, work the butter into the flour until the mixture resembles coarse oatmeal.
2. Add the egg yolk and enough water to make a dough.

Yield: Pastry for one eight-inch or nine-inch shell.

Cheese Wafers   *Minnesota*

1 pound sharp Cheddar cheese, grated
¼ pound butter
1 teaspoon salt
2 teaspoons Worcestershire sauce

½ teaspoon cayenne pepper
1 cup flour.

1. Combine all the ingredients in a mixing bowl and knead well. Shape into a roll about two inches in diameter and wrap in wax paper. Refrigerate for several hours or freeze.
2. Preheat the oven to 450 degrees.
3. Slice the roll into thin rounds and place on a greased baking sheet. Bake seven minutes and serve hot.
Yield: About four dozen.

Cottage Cheese Spread   *Ohio*

1 pound large curd cottage cheese
Light cream
Salt and freshly ground black pepper to taste
2 tablespoons caraway seeds
2 tablespoons finely chopped chives
1 teaspoon Worcestershire sauce
Thinly sliced rye bread cut into rounds
Stuffed olive slices or parsley sprigs.

1. Day before, moisten cottage cheese with enough cream to make of spreading consistency. Stir in salt, pepper, the caraway seeds, chives and Worcestershire. Pack into a jar and chill overnight.
2. Next day, serve on rye rounds garnished with an olive slice or a parsley sprig.
Yield: About two cups.

Holiday Folk Fair Danish Liver Paste
Wisconsin

1 pound pork liver
¾ pound pork fat
½ pound boneless pork
1 onion
3 tablespoons butter
3 tablespoons flour
3 cups milk
1½ teaspoons salt

½ teaspoon freshly ground black pepper
4 eggs.

1. Preheat the oven to 350 degrees.
2. Grind together twice the liver, pork fat, boneless pork and onion.
3. Melt the butter, blend in the flour and gradually stir in the milk. Bring to a boil, stirring. Season with the salt and pepper and cook five minutes. Remove mixture from the heat and let cool until lukewarm.
4. Mix the cooled sauce with the ground meat mixture. Beat in the eggs. Check the seasoning. Pour into two loaf pans.
5. Set the loaf pans in a shallow pan of boiling water and bake two hours, or until set. Allow to cool in the pans before turning out.
Yield: Two loaves; one dozen to sixteen servings.
Note: The liver paste can be served as part of a smorgasbord or can be sliced, used on buttered pumpernickel and garnished with slivered beets and cucumber slices as an open-faced sandwich.

Danish Liver Pâté   *Minnesota*

1 pound pork liver
¾ pound pork fat
1 onion, quartered
4 flat anchovies
2 tablespoons butter
2 tablespoons flour
2 cups milk
2 large eggs
1 teaspoon salt, or to taste
¾ teaspoon freshly ground black pepper
½ teaspoon allspice
¼ teaspoon ground cloves

1. Preheat the oven to 350 degrees.
2. Grind the liver, pork fat, onion and anchovies together three times.

3. Melt the butter in a saucepan and, using a wire whisk, stir in the flour. Add the milk, stirring rapidly with the whisk. Cook, stirring, until sauce is thickened and smooth. Cool slightly and add the sauce to the liver mixture. Beat with a wooden spoon and add the eggs, one at a time, beating well after each addition. Beat in the remaining ingredients and pour the mixture into a loaf pan. Set the loaf pan in a shallow pan of water and bring the water to a boil on top of the stove. Place in the oven and bake one and one-quarter hours. Cool. Serve sliced.

Yield: Eight or more servings.

Oven-Barbecued Chicken Wings

Missouri

3 pounds chicken wings
  Salt and freshly ground black pepper to taste
2 tablespoons oil
1 cup honey
½ cup soy sauce
½ clove garlic, chopped
2 tablespoons catchup.

1. Cut off small wing tips of each chicken wing and discard. Cut remaining wing into two parts. Sprinkle with salt, pepper and the oil and set aside.
2. Preheat the oven to 375 degrees.
3. Combine the remaining ingredients and pour over chicken pieces. Make one layer of coated chicken pieces in a baking dish. Bake one hour, or until chicken pieces are thoroughly cooked and the sauce is caramelized. If chicken starts to burn, reduce oven heat.

Yield: Six or more servings.

Sauerkraut Balls

Missouri

¼ pound lean ham
¼ pound lean raw pork
¼ pound corned beef

1 cup chopped onions
3 tablespoons bacon drippings or shortening
1 cup milk
  Flour
1 teaspoon dry mustard
½ teaspoon salt
  Freshly ground black pepper to taste
1 tablespoon finely chopped parsley
1 pound sauerkraut
2 eggs, lightly beaten
  Soft bread crumbs
  Fat for deep frying.

1. Put the ham, pork, corned beef and onions through the fine blade of a meat grinder.
2. Heat the bacon drippings or shortening and cook the meat mixture in it until lightly browned.
3. Put the milk into the container of an electric blender and add one cup flour, the mustard, salt, pepper and parsley. Add mixture to the meat and cook, stirring and blending, until thick.
4. Meanwhile, bring the sauerkraut to a boil in its natural liquid and simmer about fifteen minutes. Drain well and add to the meat mixture. Put the entire mixture through the food chopper and beat with a wooden spoon.
5. Return the mixture to the skillet and continue cooking and stirring about five minutes. Cool thoroughly.
6. Shape the mixture into balls the size of a walnut. There should be forty to fifty balls. Roll each ball in flour, dip in the beaten egg, then roll in bread crumbs. Deep-fry the balls, a few at a time, in fat heated to about 370 degrees. Serve skewered on toothpicks.

Yield: Forty to fifty.

Chili Soup

Ohio

1 pound ground beef chuck
1 large onion, finely chopped
2 two-pound three-ounce cans Italian plum tomatoes
3 teaspoons salt
½ teaspoon freshly ground black pepper

1 tablespoon chili powder, or to taste (the
dish is not made too hot in most
Midwestern homes)
½ teaspoon thyme
1 bay leaf
1 twenty-ounce can red kidney beans, drained
Cayenne pepper to taste
Beef broth or water if necessary.

1. Brown the beef in a skillet, stirring frequently. Add the onion and cook five minutes longer. Add the tomatoes, salt, pepper, chili, thyme and bay leaf.

2. Bring to a boil, cover and simmer about one hour. Add the beans and simmer fifteen minutes longer. Season with cayenne and add beef broth or water if soup is too thick.

Yield: Six servings.

Note: Many Midwestern homemakers add spaghetti as well as beans to their chili soup.

Holiday Folk Fair Ukrainian Borscht
Wisconsin

1½ pounds beef soup meat with bones
1 pound fresh pork butt or shank
½ pound smoked ham butt
12 cups plus three tablespoons cold water
Salt
1 medium-size onion, chopped
2 medium-size beets, peeled and cut into thin
strips or coarsely shredded on a grater
1 carrot, cut into thin strips
1 potato, diced
½ cup thinly sliced celery
½ cup diced string beans or cooked white
beans
2 to three cups shredded cabbage
¾ cup tomatoes put through a food mill or
tomato juice
½ clove garlic
1 tablespoon flour
Lemon juice
Freshly ground black pepper to taste

3 tablespoons freshly snipped dill weed
½ cup sour cream.

1. Cover the beef, pork and ham with twelve cups of the water, add one teaspoon salt and slowly bring to a boil. Skim off the scum, cover and simmer for one and one-half hours, or until the meat is tender.

2. Add the onions and beets and cook ten to fifteen minutes, or until the beets are almost done. Add the carrot, potato, celery and string beans, if used, and cook ten minutes. If white beans are used, they should be added later.

3. Add the cabbage and cook until it is tender, about five minutes. Do not overcook.

4. Stir in the tomatoes or tomato juice, garlic and white beans, if used. Blend the flour with the three tablespoons water, add a little hot soup and return all to the kettle. Add lemon juice to taste so that the soup is tart but not sour. Season to taste with salt and pepper and bring to a boil. The meat can be cut from the bones and diced, if desired.

5. Add the snipped dill. As each portion is served, stir one tablespoon sour cream into each bowlful.

Yield: Eight servings.

Vegetable Beef Soup
Illinois

3 pounds beef shin, plate or brisket
3 quarts water
1 tablespoon salt
½ teaspoon freshly ground black pepper
2 carrots, quartered
3 onions, chopped
½ head cabbage, coarsely shredded
4 ribs celery, chopped
3 tablespoons tomato paste
1 cup diced potatoes
1½ cups fresh peas
2 tablespoons uncooked rice, soaked for one
hour in cold water and drained.

1. Place the beef in a heavy kettle and add the

water, salt and pepper. Bring to a boil and simmer, covered, one and one-half hours.

2. Add the carrots, onions, cabbage and celery and cook one-half hour. Add the tomato paste, potatoes, peas and rice. Cook until rice and vegetables are tender. Shred meat and serve in soup or serve separately.

Yield: Eight servings.

Oxtail Soup   *Illinois*

3 to four pounds oxtails, cut into pieces
2 tablespoons oil or lard
6 cups beef broth
1 teaspoon salt
½ teaspoon freshly ground black pepper
1 onion, sliced
1 rib celery, diced
½ teaspoon thyme
¼ teaspoon marjoram
1 bay leaf
3 potatoes, diced
2 carrots, sliced
1 white turnip, peeled and diced
1 one-pound can tomatoes.

1. Brown the oxtail joints in the oil or lard. Transfer to a kettle and discard drippings. Add the broth, salt, pepper, onion, celery, thyme, marjoram and bay leaf and bring to a boil.

2. Cover and simmer two and one-half hours. Add the potatoes, carrots, turnip and tomatoes. Cover and simmer twenty minutes, or until vegetables are tender.

Yield: Six servings.

Vegetable Soup with Dumplings

Iowa

1½ pounds beef soup bones
1½ pounds beef shin
4 quarts water
3 onions, sliced
1½ teaspoons salt

½ teaspoon freshly ground black pepper
2 cups diced celery
2 cups diced carrots
2 cups shredded cabbage
1 one-pound can tomatoes
½ teaspoon thyme
2 cups flour
4 teaspoons baking powder
1 egg
Milk.

1. Place the soup bones, beef, water, onions, one teaspoon of the salt and the pepper in a kettle. Bring to a boil and simmer three hours. Remove soup bones and discard. Take meat from shin, discarding shin bones. Dice meat and reserve.

2. Strain the broth back into the kettle. Add the celery, carrots, cabbage, tomatoes and thyme and simmer until the vegetables are tender, about twenty minutes.

3. Return the meat to the kettle. Check seasoning.

4. Sift together the flour, one-half teaspoon of the salt and the baking powder. Break the egg into a standard measuring cup and fill the cup with milk. Stir into the dry ingredients. Drop by tablespoonfuls on top of simmering soup.

5. Cover and cook twenty minutes.

Yield: Eight servings.

Vegetable Soup   *Ohio*

1 pound cubed beef chuck
1 tablespoon oil
2 cups beef broth
1 two-pound three-ounce can Italian plum tomatoes
⅓ cup diced carrots
⅓ cup diced onion
⅓ cup diced white turnip
1½ teaspoons salt
⅓ teaspoon freshly ground black pepper
3 whole cloves
2 tablespoons butter

2 tablespoons flour
2 tablespoons chopped parsley.

1. Brown the beef in the oil quickly in a skillet. Add the broth and scrape all cooked-on beef bits off pan. Transfer to a heavy saucepan.

2. Bring to a boil and simmer, covered, one and one-half hours.

3. Add the tomatoes, carrots, onion, turnip, salt, pepper and cloves. Simmer one-half hour.

4. Melt the butter and blend in the flour. Cook until lightly browned. Add a little hot soup. Return to the pan and heat, stirring, until mixture thickens. Add the parsley.

Yield: Four servings.

Cold Vegetable Soup   *Michigan*

    1 two-pound three-ounce can Italian plum
      tomatoes
    4 ribs celery with leaves, diced
    ½ green pepper, diced
    ½ large red onion, chopped
    2 small cucumbers, peeled, seeded and diced
    ¼ cup lemon juice
      Salt to taste
    1 tablespoon olive oil
    2 tablespoons cider vinegar
 1½ tablespoons honey
      Cayenne pepper to taste
      Red food coloring.

1. Day before, in an electric blender, blend the tomatoes until smooth and strain into a bowl.

2. In batches blend the celery, green pepper, onion and cucumbers in an electric blender until smooth and add to the tomatoes.

3. Stir in the lemon juice, salt, oil, vinegar, honey and cayenne. Add a drop or two of food coloring. Chill soup overnight. Next day, serve in chilled glasses or soup cups.

Yield: Six servings.

Festsuppe (Danish Banquet Soup)

Minnesota

    1 four-pound chicken
    1 pound lean beef stewing meat
    1 cracked veal knuckle or large veal bone
    2 beef knuckles
    4 carrots
    1 large onion
    6 sprigs parsley
    3 leeks (if available), split, rinsed well and
      tied
    2 ribs celery
      Salt to taste
   15 peppercorns
    ½ cup butter
    1 cup plus three tablespoons flour
    1 cup boiling water
    6 eggs
      Boiling salted water
    1 pound round steak, ground four times
      Freshly ground black pepper to taste
    4 cups hot cooked rice
      Chopped parsley.

1. Place the chicken, stewing meat, veal knuckle and beef knuckles in a large kettle. Add the carrots, onion, parsley sprigs, leeks, celery and water to cover. Water level should be about two inches above meats. Add the salt and peppercorns. Bring to a boil and skim the surface. Continue cooking, skimming surface as necessary, until meat is fork-tender and chicken is almost falling off the bones.

2. Remove and reserve the meat and chicken. Chop the carrots and reserve them.

3. Strain the broth and return to a boil. Continue cooking until ready to serve. Total cooking time for this soup is from six to twelve hours.

4. To prepare dumplings, melt the butter in a saucepan. Add one cup of the flour and stir to blend. Gradually add the boiling water while stirring with a wooden spoon. Stir briskly until mixture leaves the sides of the pan. Take off heat and add five of the eggs, one at a time. Beat well after each addition. Bring a kettle of salted water to a

boil and add the dumplings, which should be no larger than almonds, to the water. Cook two minutes, turn with a slotted spoon and continue cooking one minute longer. When drained, the dumplings are ready to be served in the soup.

5. To prepare meat balls, combine the ground meat, the remaining three tablespoons flour, the remaining egg and the pepper in a mixing bowl. Mix well and shape into small balls. Drop into boiling salted water and simmer three to four minutes, turning with a slotted spoon. Simmer only three to four minutes.

6. Serve the soup garnished with chopped carrots, dumplings, meat balls and rice. Sprinkle with chopped parsley. The reserved meat and chicken may be sliced and eaten with the soup or at another meal.

Yield: Eight to one dozen servings.

Chicken Soup with Noodles   *Indiana*

1 four-pound to five-pound stewing chicken
  Salt and freshly ground black pepper
1 teaspoon curry powder
2 ribs celery, diced
1 bay leaf
1 cup peas
2 cups diced potatoes
¼ finely chopped onion
3 cups finely cut homemade noodles
1 tomato, peeled and chopped.

1. Place the chicken in a heavy casserole with two tablespoons salt, one teaspoon pepper, the curry powder, water to cover, the celery and bay leaf. Bring to a boil and simmer, covered, until chicken is tender, about one and one-half hours.

2. Skin and bone the chicken. Coarsely chop the meat and add with the remaining ingredients to the chicken broth. Season to taste. Simmer fifteen minutes, or until vegetables are tender. Add water during cooking if necessary.

Yield: Six servings.

Turkey Soup   *Iowa*

1 turkey carcass, broken up
  Leftover turkey gravy
  Turkey giblets, if available
8 cups water
2 teaspoons salt
2 sprigs parsley
2 ribs celery with leaves, diced
2 onions, sliced
1 bay leaf
½ teaspoon thyme
2 tablespoons uncooked rice
1 carrot, thinly sliced
1 cup diced cooked turkey meat
  Tabasco sauce to taste
2 tablespoons chopped parsley.

1. Place the carcass, gravy, giblets, water, salt, parsley sprigs, celery, onions, bay leaf and thyme in a large kettle. Bring to a boil and simmer three hours.

2. Strain soup and skim off the fat. Add the rice and carrot and cook fifteen minutes, or until rice is tender.

3. Add the turkey meat, Tabasco and chopped parsley.

Yield: About one and one-half quarts; six servings.

Liver Dumplings in Broth (Leberkloesse)
          Missouri

¾ pound pork or calf's liver
¼ pound lean pork
1 cup soft bread crumbs
  Milk
2 eggs, separated
¼ cup soft butter
2 teaspoons grated onion
2 tablespoons finely chopped parsley
1 tablespoon chopped fresh basil or one-half teaspoon dried basil
  Salt and freshly ground black pepper to taste

2 tablespoons flour
8 cups simmering chicken broth.

1. Remove all tough fibers from the liver. Grind the liver and pork together twice.

2. Soak the bread crumbs in a little milk; then squeeze to remove most of the liquid. Add the crumbs to the liver mixture.

3. Combine the egg yolks, butter, onion, parsley, basil, salt, pepper and flour in a mixing bowl. Beat well to blend. Stir this into the liver mixture.

4. Beat the egg whites until stiff and fold them into the liver mixture. Shape this into balls the size of walnuts and drop them into the broth. Cook five to six minutes and serve dumplings with broth.

Yield: Six to eight servings.

Barley Soup   *Wisconsin*

¼ pound coarse pearl barley
1 onion, finely chopped
¼ cup finely chopped carrot
½ cup finely chopped celery
3 tablespoons butter
8 cups chicken broth
  Salt and freshly ground black pepper to taste
1 cup heavy cream
  Croutons.

1. Rinse the barley in warm water and place in a kettle.

2. Sauté the onion, carrot and celery in the butter in a heavy skillet until tender. Add the broth, bring to a boil and pour over the barley. Add salt and pepper.

3. Bring to a boil, cover and simmer until barley is very tender, about one hour. Pass through a food mill or an electric blender.

4. Add the cream and reheat. Check the seasoning. Serve soup garnished with croutons.

Yield: Six servings.

Lentil Soup   *Missouri*

2 cups dried lentils
½ pound salt pork or ham bone
1 cup chopped celery
1 cup chopped onions
2 sprigs fresh thyme or one-half teaspoon dried thyme
1 bay leaf
2 tablespoons butter
2 tablespoons flour
  Juice of one lemon
1 tablespoon salt
¼ teaspoon freshly ground black pepper
½ cup chopped parsley
  Lemon slices.

1. Cover the lentils with water and soak overnight.

2. Next day, drain lentils and pour into a large kettle. Add two quarts water and the salt pork or ham bone. Cover and simmer three hours. Add the celery, onions, thyme and bay leaf. Cover and simmer thirty minutes longer. Remove bay leaf and salt pork. Put soup through a sieve or puree in an electric blender.

3. Melt the butter in a saucepan and blend in the flour. Add a little of the soup and mix well. Stir mixture back into rest of soup. Simmer ten minutes. Add the lemon juice, salt and pepper. Sprinkle with the parsley and top each serving with lemon slices.

Yield: Eight to ten servings.

Spring Beet Borscht   *Wisconsin*

8 small beets with tops
1 medium-size onion, finely chopped
1 carrot, cut into thin strips
1 tomato, peeled and diced
½ cup diced string beans
1 small rib celery, diced
2 cups shredded cabbage
6 cups beef broth
5 cups water

½ cup tomato juice
Sour salt or lemon juice
1 tablespoon flour
½ cup sour cream
1 tablespoon chopped dill weed
Salt and freshly ground black pepper to taste.

1. Wash the beets well. Cut off the tops and wash thoroughly. Chop tops. Cut the unpeeled beets into thin strips.

2. Place beets and tops in a large kettle along with the onion, carrot, tomato, beans, celery, cabbage, broth and water. Bring to a boil and simmer, covered, until the vegetables are tender.

3. Add the tomato juice and enough sour salt or lemon juice to give desired tartness. Blend the flour with the sour cream and stir a little of the soup into the mixture. Return all to the kettle and heat, but do not boil.

4. Add the dill and season with salt and pepper.

Yield: Six to eight servings.

Chilled Borscht   *Wisconsin*

3 tablespoons butter
4 medium-size beets, peeled and roughly grated
1 carrot, thinly sliced
1 onion, sliced
2 ribs celery with leaves, diced
1 small white turnip, peeled and diced
Salt and freshly ground black pepper to taste
½ pound beef shin, ground or finely diced
6 cups beef broth
2 egg whites, lightly beaten (optional)
2 crumbled eggshells (optional)
1 tablespoon lemon juice, or to taste
Sour cream.

1. Melt the butter in a large kettle and add the beets, carrot, onion, celery and turnip. Sauté five minutes.

2. Season with salt and pepper and add the beef and broth. Bring to a boil and simmer, covered, forty-five minutes. Strain soup and discard the vegetables and bits of meat.

3. To clarify the borscht, if desired, let the broth cool. Add the egg whites and eggshells and bring to a boil slowly, stirring occasionally. Strain through damp flannel.

4. Whether the soup is clarified or not, cool and add the lemon juice. Chill soup and serve topped with sour cream.

Yield: Six servings.

Salsify or Vegetable Oyster Soup

Iowa

5 medium-size salsify roots (see note)
Boiling salted water
4 cups milk
2 tablespoons butter
Salt and freshly ground black pepper to taste.

1. Peel the roots and slice finely or run through a food grinder. Cover with boiling salted water and simmer until tender.

2. Mash the salsify in the liquid. Add the remaining ingredients, bring to a boil and serve.

Yield: Four servings.

Note: Salsify roots have a mild, sweet flavor that's similar to oysters and it is sometimes called oyster plant.

Corn Soup   *Ohio*

½ small onion, finely chopped
2 tablespoons butter
2 tablespoons flour
2 cups corn kernels, cut from cobs
2 cups boiling water
2 cups milk
1 teaspoon salt
¼ teaspoon freshly ground black pepper.

1. Sauté the onion in the butter until tender but not browned. Sprinkle with the flour, stir and set aside.

2. Place the corn in a saucepan and cover with the water. Simmer five minutes; drain.

3. Add the milk to corn and bring to a boil. With a wire whisk, beat in the onion mixture. Add the salt and pepper and cook to thicken.

Yield: Four servings.

Corn Chowder Kansas

½ pound salt pork, diced
¼ cup chopped onion
½ cup chopped celery
¼ cup chopped green pepper
1 cup diced potatoes
2 cups water
2 teaspoons turmeric
½ bay leaf
  Salt and freshly ground black pepper to taste
3 tablespoons flour
2 cups milk
2 cups freshly cut corn kernels (about four large ears)
2 tablespoons chopped parsley.

1. In a heavy pan or kettle, cook the salt pork until crisp and golden. Add the onion and celery and cook until tender but not browned. Add the green pepper, potatoes, water, turmeric, bay leaf, salt and pepper. Bring to a boil and simmer about twenty minutes, or until the potatoes are barely tender.

2. Mix the flour with one-half cup of the milk. Heat remaining milk and add to the blended flour. Stir into hot soup and heat, stirring until the mixture thickens.

3. Add the corn and parsley and cook until corn is barely tender, about four minutes. Check the seasoning.

Yield: About seven cups; eight servings.

Potato Soup with Rivals Indiana

5 medium-size potatoes, diced
3 teaspoons salt
½ teaspoon freshly ground black pepper
2 tablespoons butter
¾ cup flour
1 egg
2 cups milk
2 cups light cream
3 tablespoons chopped onion
1 tablespoon chopped parsley.

1. Place the potatoes in a saucepan with the salt, pepper and butter. Add water barely to cover and cook until potatoes are tender.

2. Meanwhile, for the rivals, place the flour in a bowl and add the egg. Mix lightly with the fingers until mixture is crumbly or the pieces are the size of peas.

3. Add the milk and cream to the cooked potato mixture and, when mixture comes to a boil, add the rivals (flour and egg mixture) and simmer, covered, until done, about five minutes. If soup becomes too thick, thin with more milk.

4. Serve topped with the onion mixed with parsley.

Yield: Six servings.

Turnip and Potato Soup Minnesota

1 small yellow turnip, peeled and diced
1½ cups water
1 teaspoon salt
3 potatoes, diced
2 cups milk, scalded
¾ teaspoon sugar
2 tablespoons butter
¼ teaspoon freshly ground black pepper
⅛ teaspoon nutmeg
2 tablespoons chopped parsley.

1. Place the turnip in a saucepan and add the water and salt. Bring to a boil and simmer fifteen minutes, or until turnip is tender.

2. Add the potatoes and cook ten minutes longer, or until tender.

3. Do not drain. Mash turnip and potato in cooking liquid. Add the milk, sugar, butter, pepper and nutmeg and bring to a boil. Serve with a sprinkling of parsley.

Yield: Four servings.

Grandmother's Tomato Soup   *Oklahoma*

20 pounds tomatoes
 4 large onions, chopped
 8 cups water
 4 teaspoons cornstarch
 1 teaspoon ground allspice
 1 teaspoon cinnamon
 1 teaspoon ground cloves
 ½ cup sugar
 ½ cup coarse salt
 ⅓ cup cold water
 ½ pound butter.

1. Chop the tomatoes roughly and put in a large kettle with the onions and eight cups water. Bring to a boil and simmer until tender.

2. Strain. Mix the cornstarch with the allspice, cinnamon, cloves, sugar and salt. Mix with the cold water. Add a little hot strained tomato broth. Whirl in the butter.

3. Pour into hot sterilized jars and seal, or serve.

Yield: About one dozen quarts.

Cream of Tomato Soup   *Iowa*

 2 cups stewed tomatoes
 ¼ cup finely chopped onion
 ½ cup finely chopped celery
 2 teaspoons sugar
 4 tablespoons butter
 4 tablespoons flour
 4 cups milk, scalded
 1 teaspoon salt
 ¼ teaspoon freshly ground black pepper.

1. Place the tomatoes, onion, celery and sugar in a saucepan and simmer fifteen minutes.

2. Melt the butter, blend in the flour and gradually stir in the milk. Season with the salt and pepper. Strain the tomato mixture into the sauce and hold over hot water for at least fifteen minutes. Do not allow to boil.

Yield: Four servings.

Five Bean Soup for a Crowd   *Michigan*

 1 cup dried pea beans or navy beans
 ⅔ cup dried pinto beans
 ⅔ cup dried kidney beans
 ⅔ cup dried lima beans
 ⅔ cup dried white haricot beans
 3 smoked ham hocks
 1 pound soup bones
 5 onions, chopped
 5 carrots, quartered
 5 ribs celery, diced
 1 small can tomatoes
   Salt and freshly ground black pepper to taste
 ½ head cabbage, shredded
 ½ pound hot sausage (Italian, Spanish chorizo or Portuguese), sliced on the bias.

1. Soak the beans overnight in water to cover. Next day, drain. Place beans in a large kettle. Add ham hocks and soup bones. Add water to cover.

2. Simmer for one hour or longer, or until the beans are tender. Add more water as necessary. Add the onions, carrots, celery and tomatoes and cook until vegetables are tender. Season with salt and pepper. Remove the hocks and bones. Add the cabbage and cook fifteen minutes.

3. Fry the sausage slices in a skillet and use to garnish individual portions of the soup.

Yield: Ten to one dozen servings.

Lima Bean with Dumplings Soup
Michigan

½ cup diced salt pork
1 cup chopped onions
1 twenty-ounce can tomatoes
2 cups diced potatoes
6 cups chicken broth
4 cups fresh lima beans
  Salt and freshly ground black pepper
1 cup flour
1 teaspoon baking powder
1 tablespoon shortening
1 cup freshly cut corn kernels.

1. Cook the salt pork to render the fat. Add the onions and sauté until tender. Add the tomatoes and potatoes, bring to a boil and simmer ten minutes. Add the broth and bring to a boil.

2. Add the limas, season to taste with salt and pepper and simmer ten minutes.

3. Sift together the flour, baking powder and one teaspoon salt. Blend in the shortening and stir in enough water to give a soft dough.

4. Spoon dough by tablespoonfuls on top of boiling soup. Cover and cook twenty minutes. Add the corn and cook five minutes longer.
  Yield: Eight servings.

Beer Soup
Wisconsin

3 tablespoons butter
2 tablespoons finely chopped onion
4 cups finely shredded green cabbage (about half a large head)
1 tablespoon flour
2 cups chicken broth
2 cups strong ale
  Salt and freshly ground black pepper to taste
1 cup hot milk
  Chunks of dark rye bread.

1. Melt the butter in a large heavy saucepan and add the onion and cabbage. Sauté, stirring occasionally, until the onion and cabbage become translucent-looking.

2. Sprinkle with the flour, stir and cook one minute. Stir in the broth, ale, salt and pepper. Bring to a boil. Cover and simmer one hour.

3. Puree the mixture in an electric blender or rub through a sieve. Return to the pan. Add the hot milk and heat. Serve with the bread.
  Yield: Four servings.

Buffalo Fish Chowder
Michigan

¼ cup diced bacon or salt pork
½ cup finely chopped onion
½ cup chopped green pepper
1 cup chopped celery
2 cups boiling fish stock or water
1 cup diced potatoes
1 teaspoon salt
⅛ teaspoon freshly ground black pepper
¼ teaspoon thyme
1 pound buffalo fish fillets, skinned and cut into one-half-inch pieces
2 cups tomato juice.

1. Cook the bacon or salt pork until tender and browned. Add the onion, green pepper and celery and cook until tender.

2. Add the stock or water, potatoes, salt, pepper, thyme and fish and cook ten minutes, or until potatoes are tender. Add the tomato juice. Reheat.
  Yield: Six servings.

Cherry Soup
Minnesota

4 cups ripe red or black cherries
½ lemon, seeded and thinly sliced
1 two-inch piece cinnamon stick
¼ cup sugar
  Juice of one lemon
2 tablespoons cornstarch
  Shaved ice.

1. Place the cherries in a kettle with one cup water and the lemon slices. Break the cinnamon stick in half and add. Bring to a boil and simmer fifteen minutes.

2. Strain the soup, pressing it lightly in a food mill or sieve. Discard the remnants of lemon, the cherry pits and cinnamon. Pour the liquid into a one-quart measure. Add enough water to make one quart. Return the liquid to the kettle and add the sugar. Bring to a boil and stir until the sugar dissolves. Add the lemon juice.

3. Blend the cornstarch with one-quarter cup cold water and stir into the simmering soup. When thickened, remove the soup from the heat and chill. Serve in cold soup plates with a little shaved ice in each serving.

Yield: Six servings.

Duchess Soup   *Iowa*

1 small onion, finely chopped
2 tablespoons butter
2 tablespoons flour
4 cups milk, scalded
2 tablespoons grated Cheddar cheese
1 teaspoon salt
⅛ teaspoon white pepper
3 egg yolks.

1. Sauté the onion in the butter until golden brown. Sprinkle with the flour and cook until frothy. Blend in the milk and cook slowly ten minutes.

2. Strain and return to the heat. Add the cheese, salt and pepper.

3. Beat the egg yolks until light, dilute with one-half cup of the soup and put in the bottom of a tureen. Pour the remainder of the hot soup over, stirring briskly.

Yield: Four servings.

Sour Cream Soup with Egg Drops
Wisconsin

Soup:
1 four-pound to five-pound chicken, cut up
2 ribs celery
1 leek, sliced
3 sprigs parsley
Salt and freshly ground black pepper to taste
1 three-inch strip orange peel
1 three-inch strip lemon peel
1 small piece fresh or dried gingerroot
⅛ teaspoon allspice
1 stick cinnamon
4 cups water
1 cup sour cream
2 tablespoons cider vinegar
2 tablespoons flour
¼ teaspoon saffron.
Egg drops:
3 hard-cooked egg yolks
1 egg
1 tablespoon flour
Salt and freshly ground black pepper to taste
1 teaspoon chopped parsley
Milk
Boiling water.

1. To prepare soup, place the chicken pieces in a heavy casserole or Dutch oven. Add the celery, leek, parsley, salt, pepper, orange peel, lemon peel, gingerroot, allspice, cinnamon and water.

2. Bring to a boil, cover and simmer one hour, or until chicken is tender. Strain broth. Chicken can be used for salad, casseroles, etc.

3. Combine the sour cream, vinegar and flour and gradually stir in the hot strained broth. Heat, but do not allow to boil. Stir in the saffron.

4. Meanwhile, to prepare egg drops, mash the egg yolks and mix with the egg, flour, salt, pepper, parsley and enough milk to shape easily. Form into tiny one-inch balls and drop into a kettle of boiling water. Cook two minutes.

5. Add to sour cream soup.
Yield: Eight servings.

Cold Buttermilk Soup   *Minnesota*

2 eggs
¼ cup sugar

1 teaspoon vanilla
¼ cup lemon juice
4 cups buttermilk.

1. Beat the eggs, sugar, vanilla and lemon juice together in a bowl.
2. Beat the buttermilk and fold slowly into the egg mixture.
Yield: Four servings.

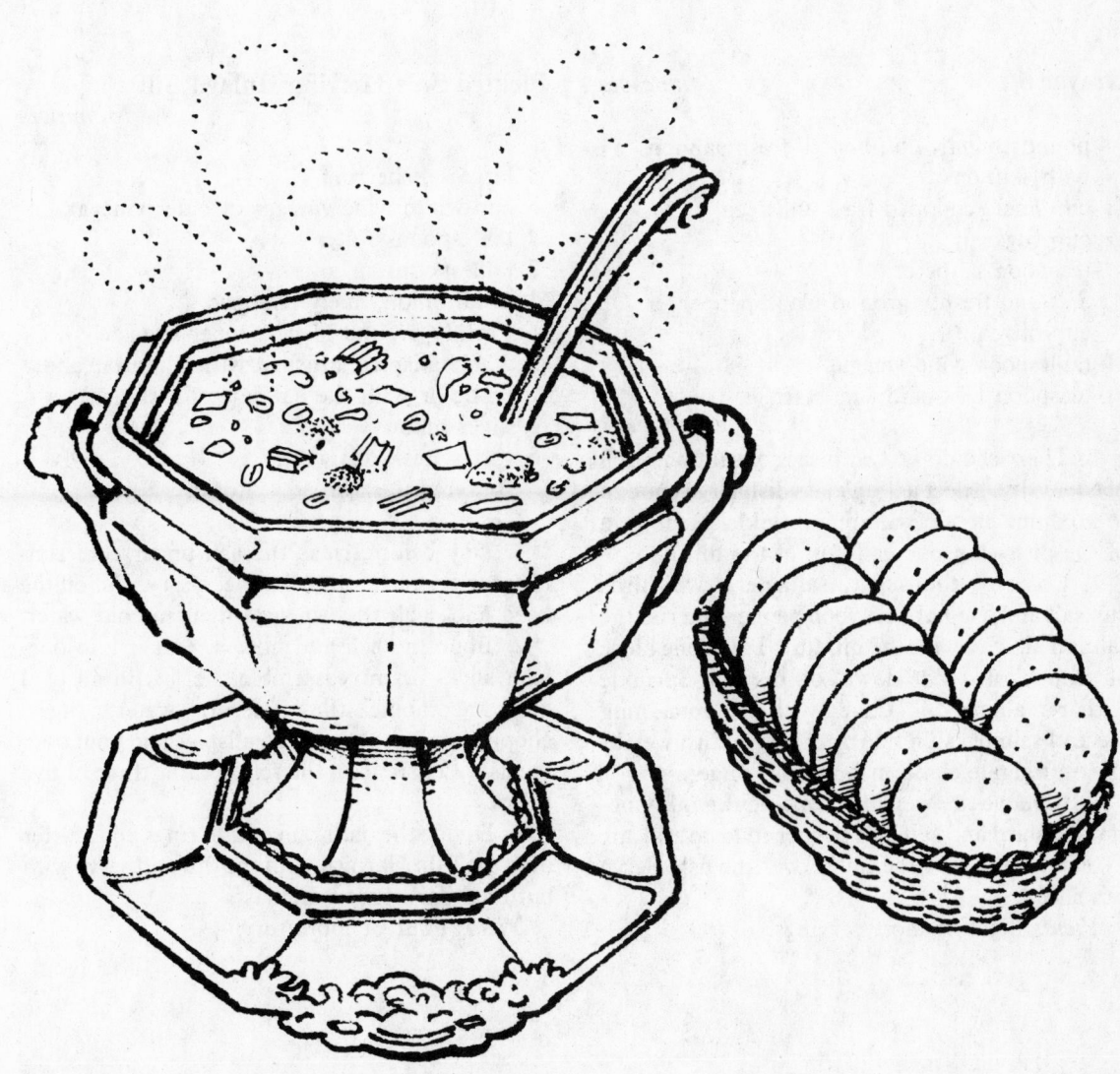

Fish and Shellfish

Gravad Lax
Minnesota

4 pounds middle-cut, boned, fresh salmon
  with skin on
1 cup finely chopped fresh dillweed
½ cup sugar
½ teaspoon saltpeter
  Salt and freshly ground black pepper
¼ cup olive oil
1 tablespoon wine vinegar
1 teaspoon Düsseldorf mustard.

1. There should be two pieces of salmon, each of equal size. Select a deep glass dish large enough to hold one piece of salmon. Sprinkle the bottom of the dish with one-half cup of the dill.

2. Combine the sugar, saltpeter, two-thirds cup salt and one-half teaspoon pepper and rub the salmon all over with the mixture. Place one piece of salmon, skin side down, on the dill. Sprinkle with remaining dill. Cover with the remaining piece of salmon, skin side up. Cover with a weight and refrigerate eighteen hours or longer.

3. Remove the weight. Combine the oil, vinegar, mustard and salt and pepper to taste and stir to blend well. Pour the sauce over the fish. Serve fish sliced.

Yield: Eight or more servings.

Pickled Salt Herring (Inlagd Sill)
Minnesota

1 large salt herring
½ cup white wine vinegar or cider vinegar
2 tablespoons water
3 tablespoons sugar
1 small onion, finely chopped
  Freshly ground black pepper to taste
3 whole allspice, crushed with a mortar and
  pestle or with the flat side of a skillet
2 slices onion
6 sprigs fresh dill weed
  Buttered dark bread or toast.

1. Day before, rinse the fish under cold running water. Clean the fish if necessary. Cut off the head and soak the fish overnight in cold water.

2. Bone the fish and fillet it. Cut it into one-inch slices; then reassemble the fish in an oval plate. Combine the vinegar, water, sugar, chopped onion, pepper and allspice and pour over the fish. Let stand in the refrigerator three or five hours.

3. Divide the onion slices into rings and scatter over the fish. Garnish with the dill and serve with buttered dark bread or toast.

Yield: Four or more servings.

Creamed Shad Roe with Sherry

Minnesota

3 large pair fresh shad roe
  Boiling salted water
7 tablespoons butter
½ cup flour
3 cups milk
2 teaspoons salt
  Freshly ground black pepper to taste
1 cup heavy cream
¼ cup dry sherry
  Buttered toasted soft bread crumbs or
  buttered toast.

1. Poach the shad roe in boiling salted water to cover ten minutes, or until firm. Drain the roe and remove the outside fiber or "skin." Break up the roe with a fork.

2. Melt the butter and stir in the flour, using a wire whisk. Cook over low heat about five minutes, stirring, but do not brown. Add the milk, stirring vigorously with the whisk, until the sauce boils and is thickened and smooth. Add the salt, pepper and cream. Cover and simmer fifteen minutes. Add the roe and heat thoroughly. Add the sherry. Serve in individual ramekins or patty shells topped with buttered toasted bread crumbs or serve on buttered toast.

Yield: Four to six servings.

Baked Trout Oklahoma

4 one-pound trout
  Salt and freshly ground black pepper
1 clove garlic, very finely chopped
8 thin slices lemon
4 tablespoons dry white wine
4 tablespoons orange juice
¼ cup butter.

1. Preheat the oven to 350 degrees.

2. Leave fish whole; clean, wash and pat dry. Place each fish on a piece of aluminum foil big enough to enclose it in a package.

3. Sprinkle inside the cavity of each fish with salt, pepper and garlic. Season outside of fish and place two lemon slices on each. Sprinkle each with one tablespoon wine and one tablespoon orange juice. Dot each with one tablespoon butter.

4. Fold up foil and seal with drugstore wrap, leaving a small space on top. Bake about twenty-five minutes, or until fish flakes easily.

Yield: Four servings.

Note: The foil-wrapped packages can also be cooked on top of a campfire. The recipe can also be used with Oklahoma bass or crappie.

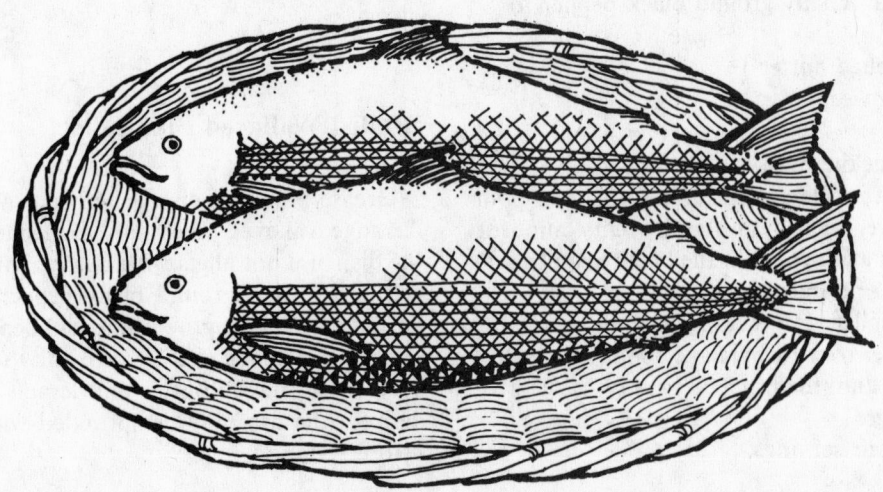

Planked Lake Trout   *Wisconsin*

3 two-pound lake trout, cleaned, heads
   removed but fish left whole
   Salt and freshly ground black pepper
6 tablespoons lemon juice
3 tablespoons melted butter
4 cups hot seasoned mashed potatoes
1 egg yolk, lightly beaten
2 tablespoons finely grated Parmesan cheese.

1. Preheat the oven to 350 degrees.
2. Season the fish inside and outside with salt
and pepper. Sprinkle with lemon juice and place
on a seasoned plank.
3. Brush with the butter and bake about forty
minutes, or until the fish flakes easily. Meanwhile,
beat the potatoes with the egg yolk. Put the mixture into a large piping bag fitted with a star tube.
4. Pipe the potato mixture around the fish in
swirls. Sprinkle with the cheese and brown briefly
under a preheated broiler.
Yield: Six servings.

Baked Pike   *Michigan*

1½ pounds pike fillets
1 cup milk
½ cup dry bread crumbs
   Salt and freshly ground black pepper to
   taste
½ cup melted butter
   Lemon wedges.

1. Preheat the oven to 350 degrees.
2. Place the fillets in a shallow dish and pour
the milk over them. Let stand twenty minutes.
Drain fillets and dredge in the bread crumbs seasoned with salt and pepper.
3. Place fillets in a baking dish and pour the
melted butter over them. Bake about twenty-five
minutes, or until the fish flakes easily. Serve with
lemon wedges.
Yield: Four servings.

Baked Minnesota Pike

1 four-pound Northern pike
6 tablespoons butter
½ cup finely chopped onion
½ cup finely chopped celery
3 tablespoons finely chopped green pepper
2 tablespoons finely chopped parsley
2 cups soft bread crumbs
3 eggs, lightly beaten
½ cup finely chopped cooked shrimp or crab
   meat
   Salt and freshly ground black pepper.

1. Preheat the oven to 350 degrees.
2. Clean the fish, but leave it whole.
3. Melt four tablespoons of the butter in a skillet and add the onion, celery and green pepper.
Cook, stirring, until onion is wilted. Combine
with the parsley, bread crumbs, eggs and shrimp
or crab meat. Mix well and add salt and pepper
to taste.
4. Sprinkle the inside of the fish with salt and
pepper and stuff the cavity with the bread crumb
mixture. Sew up the opening and place the fish in
a greased baking dish. Dot the fish with the remaining butter and sprinkle with salt and pepper.
Bake, basting occasionally, about forty minutes,
or until fish flakes easily.
Yield: Six to eight servings.

Broiled Walleyed Pike Fillets   *Minnesota*

Grease a baking dish generously with butter.
Arrange walleyed pike fillets, skin side down, on
the dish and dot fillets with butter. Sprinkle with
salt and freshly ground black pepper and broil
until done. The length of time will depend on the
size of the fillets and their proximity to the heat.
Serve with melted butter and lemon wedges. If
desired, the fish may be sprinkled with paprika
before serving.

Baked Walleyed Pike   *Minnesota*

1 three-pound to four-pound walleyed pike or two saugers
Salt and freshly ground black pepper to taste
1 cup water
2 slices lean bacon
2 scallions, including green part finely chopped
½ cup butter
¼ cup lemon juice.

1. Preheat the oven to 325 degrees.
2. Clean fish, scale and remove the head. Split fish and lay, skin side down, on a rack in a baking pan. Season with salt and pepper. Add the water to the pan.
3. Cover the pan and bake about forty minutes, or until fish flakes easily. Drain off liquid.
4. Meanwhile, cook the bacon until crisp; remove, crumble and reserve. Add the scallions to the bacon drippings and cook until tender; drain and reserve. Combine the butter and lemon juice, season with salt and pepper and brush over the fish. Broil fish under preheated broiler, basting with the butter mixture, until fish is golden. Sprinkle with the crumbled bacon and the scallions.
Yield: Six servings.

Baked Pickerel   *Michigan*

2 pounds pickerel fillets
Salt and freshly ground black pepper to taste
¼ cup butter
¼ cup finely chopped onion
½ pound mushrooms, sliced
2 tablespoons chopped parsley
2 large tomatoes, peeled, seeded and chopped
1½ cups buttered soft bread crumbs
3 tablespoons grated sharp Cheddar cheese.

1. Preheat the oven to 350 degrees.
2. Place the fillets in a well-greased shallow baking dish and season with salt and pepper.
3. Melt the butter in a skillet and sauté the onion in it until tender. Add the mushrooms and cook until moisture evaporates.
4. Add the parsley and tomatoes. Season with salt and pepper. Pour over the fish. Top with the bread crumbs mixed with the cheese. Bake thirty minutes, or until fish flakes easily.
Yield: Six servings

Baked Ciscoes   *Minnesota*

10 ciscoes, filleted (see note)
1½ tablespoons lemon juice
2 cups heavy cream
1 cup light cream
1 teaspoon flour
1 tablespoon butter
Salt and freshly ground black pepper to taste
Buttered toast.

1. Preheat the oven to 325 degrees.
2. Quarter the fillets or cut them into small pieces. Place the fish in a buttered flat baking dish. Sprinkle with the lemon juice.
3. Combine the heavy cream and light cream and bring to a boil. Blend the flour and butter with the fingers and add, bit by bit, to the cream, stirring. Pour sauce over fish and sprinkle with salt and pepper. Bake one hour. Serve on buttered toast.
Yield: Six or more servings, depending on size of fish.
Note: A cisco is a fresh-water fish found in the Great Lakes region.

Whitefish with Capers   *Michigan*

1 two-pound to two-and-one-half-pound slice whitefish, about one-inch thick

Salt and freshly ground black pepper to
taste
¼ cup finely grated onion
2 tablespoons vinegar from capers
2 cups sour cream, at room temperature
Paprika
½ cup capers.

1. Preheat the oven to 350 degrees.
2. Place the fish in a shallow baking dish and
season with salt and pepper. Sprinkle the onion
and vinegar over fish.
3. Spoon the sour cream over fish, sprinkle
with paprika and bake about thirty minutes, or
until fish flakes easily. Sprinkle with the capers
and reheat briefly.
Yield: Six servings.

Stuffed Whitefish   *Wisconsin*

2 pounds whitefish fillets
   Salt and freshly ground black pepper to
   taste
2 cups soft bread crumbs
⅓ cup melted butter
2 tablespoons chopped parsley
½ teaspoon thyme
½ teaspoon grated lemon rind
1 tablespoon finely grated onion
¼ cup finely chopped celery
⅓ cup finely chopped mushrooms
   Lemon wedges.

1. Preheat the oven to 350 degrees.
2. Place half the fillets in a single layer in a
shallow baking dish. Season with salt and pepper.
3. Mix together the bread crumbs, butter,
parsley, thyme, lemon rind, onion, celery and
mushrooms. Season with salt and pepper. Spread
over the fillets in the dish.
4. Top with remaining fillets and bake about
twenty-five minutes, or until fish flakes easily.
Serve with lemon wedges.
Yield: Four to six servings.

Sole with White Wine   *Missouri*

1½ pounds fresh or frozen fillet of sole,
   thawed if frozen
2 tablespoons cider vinegar
5 tablespoons olive oil
1 teaspoon paprika
1 clove garlic, finely chopped
1 teaspoon sugar
½ cup dry white wine
½ teaspoon oregano
   Salt and freshly ground black pepper to
   taste
   Flour
3 tablespoons butter
   Parsley
   Lemon slices.

1. Place the fish in a flat baking dish.
2. Combine the vinegar, two tablespoons of
the oil, the paprika, garlic, sugar, wine, oregano,
salt and pepper. Pour the mixture over and
around the fish. Let stand in the refrigerator,
turning once or twice, at least one hour. Remove
the fish and drain the marinade, reserving it.
3. Dredge the fish lightly in flour. Heat the
remaining oil and the butter in a large skillet.
Brown the fish on all sides in the skillet and transfer to a warm platter. Pour out the cooking fat
and add the reserved marinade to the skillet. Simmer until sauce is slightly thickened. Pour the
sauce over the fish and garnish with parsley and
lemon slices.
Yield: Four servings.

Shrimp à la Mann   *Illinois*

1 pound jumbo shrimp, peeled and deveined
2 tablespoons butter, at room temperature
1 tablespoon finely minced parsley
1 clove garlic, finely minced
2 tablespoons dry sherry
¼ teaspoon Worcestershire sauce
1 tablespoon soft bread crumbs

6 slices bacon, approximately, each cut in half
1 cup uncooked wild rice
3 cups fresh or canned clear chicken broth

1. Make a deep cut along the back of each shrimp, but do not cut the shrimp in two. The cut is to receive a filling.
2. Cream together the butter, parsley, garlic, sherry, Worcestershire and bread crumbs. Use the mixture to fill the cut portion of each shrimp. Wrap each shrimp in half a slice of bacon and skewer. Chill until ready to cook.
3. Cook the wild rice in the chicken broth until tender.
4. Preheat the oven to 450 degrees.
5. Broil the shrimp under a medium flame until bacon is crisp, turning once.
6. Spoon the rice into an ovenproof serving dish and arrange the broiled shrimp on top. Place the dish in the oven about two minutes, no longer, and serve immediately.
Yield: Four servings.

Lutefisk is codfish that has been dried and cured with lye and is available in Scandinavian stores especially at holiday time.

Lutefisk   *Minnesota*

2 pounds lutefisk, thawed if frozen
  Salt
4½ tablespoons butter
4½ tablespoons flour
3 cups light cream
  Freshly ground black pepper
¼ teaspoon allspice
2 teaspoons Düsseldorf mustard
  Boiled potatoes
  Cooked peas.

1. Preheat the oven to 350 degrees.
2. Place the fish in a buttered baking dish and sprinkle with salt. Cover with lid or aluminum foil and bake about thirty minutes, or until fish flakes easily.
3. Meanwhile, melt the butter in a saucepan and blend in the flour. Gradually stir in the cream. Bring to a boil, stirring until mixture thickens. Season to taste with salt and pepper. Add the allspice and mustard and set sauce over hot water until fish is ready to serve.
4. Drain fish of liquid. Serve fish with the sauce, potatoes and peas.
Yield: Six servings.

Lutefisk Pudding   *Minnesota*

1¾ cups water
   Salt
¾ cup uncooked rice
2 cups cooked lutefisk (recipe above), flaked
2 eggs, lightly beaten
2 cups light cream
3 tablespoons melted butter
  Freshly ground black pepper.

1. Preheat the oven to 325 degrees.
2. Heat the water and one-half teaspoon salt to boiling and add the rice. Cover and simmer twenty minutes, or until rice is done and water absorbed.
3. Mix together the lutefisk and rice. Mix together the eggs, cream and butter and stir into lutefisk mixture. Season to taste with salt and pepper. Turn into a buttered baking dish and bake forty minutes, or until set.
Yield: Six servings.

Fish Boil   *Wisconsin*

2 pounds haddock, or other round whitefish, fillets
12 new potatoes, scrubbed
8 medium-size onions, peeled
  Boiling salted water
1½ cups melted butter
2 lemons, cut into wedges or slices.

1. Cut the fish into serving pieces and tie in a double muslin bag, leaving a long string. Tie the potatoes in a double muslin bag and the onions in another, leaving a long string on both.

2. Lower the potatoes and onions into a kettle of boiling salted water and tie strings to handle. Boil twenty minutes.

3. Add the fish bag, tying string to handle, and cook slowly another ten to fifteen minutes, or until fish and vegetables are cooked.

4. Serve contents of the bags with the melted butter poured over and with lemon wedges or slices.

Yield: Four servings.

Fish Balls   *Minnesota*

2 pounds haddock, codfish or other firm-fleshed whitefish
1 tablespoon melted butter
  Salt and freshly ground black pepper to taste
⅛ teaspoon cayenne pepper
¼ teaspoon nutmeg
2 eggs
¼ cup milk
1 tablespoon finely chopped scallion, including green part
2 tablespoons water
½ cup soft bread crumbs
3 tablespoons butter
3 tablespoons oil
  Buttered boiled potatoes with dill and sour cream (optional).

1. Grind the fish three times, using the fine blade of a food grinder. Spoon the fish into a mixing bowl and add the melted butter, salt, pepper, cayenne and nutmeg. Beat one egg and add. Beat mixture thoroughly with a wooden spoon.

2. Gradually add the milk, beating well with the spoon. Add the scallion. Shape mixture into one-and-one-half-inch balls.

3. As the balls are shaped, dip them into the remaining egg, lightly beaten with the water. Dip

balls in the bread crumbs and refrigerate two hours or longer. Cook fish balls in a skillet containing the butter and oil until golden brown all over. Serve with buttered boiled potatoes with dill and, if desired, sour cream.

Yield: About two dozen.

Fish Soufflé   *Minnesota*

4 tablespoons butter
5 tablespoons flour
1½ cups milk
4 eggs, separated
1 cup raw haddock or other whitefish, finely ground
  Salt and freshly ground black pepper to taste
¼ teaspoon nutmeg.

1. Preheat the oven to 350 degrees.

2. Melt the butter in a saucepan and stir in the flour, using a wire whisk. Add the milk, stirring. Continue stirring until mixture is thickened and smooth.

3. Remove the sauce from the heat and beat in the egg yolks, one at a time, stirring rapidly. Stir in the fish and season with salt, pepper and nutmeg.

4. Beat the egg whites until stiff. Stir in half the whites, using the whisk. Fold in the remaining whites, using a rubber spatula. Do not overmix. Pour into a soufflé dish and bake thirty-five to forty-five minutes, or until soufflé is puffed and browned. Serve with lobster sauce, mushroom sauce or hollandaise sauce (page 174).

Yield: Four to six servings.

Salmon Cakes   *Indiana*

½ cup heavy cream
3 cups cracker crumbs, approximately
3 eggs, lightly beaten
1 one-pound can salmon, drained, boned, skinned and flaked

Salt and freshly ground black pepper to taste
1 tablespoon chopped parsley
¼ cup butter.

1. Add the cream to three cups cracker crumbs and let stand fifteen minutes.
2. Add the eggs, salmon, salt, pepper and parsley. Mix well.

3. Shape mixture into patties about one-half-inch thick. Add extra cracker crumbs if mixture is too wet to shape.
4. Melt the butter in a skillet and sauté the cakes in it until lightly browned on one side; turn and brown other side.

Yield: Four servings.

Note: You can add an extra cup of cracker crumbs, form the mixture into balls and then fry them in deep-fat heated to 365 degrees until golden for an appetizer.

Meat, Poultry, Game and Other Main Dishes

Steak and Lobster on a Skewer

Missouri

1 clove garlic, crushed
½ cup oil
3 tablespoons lemon juice
1 teaspoon salt
¼ teaspoon freshly ground black pepper
   Tabasco sauce to taste
¼ teaspoon dry mustard
¼ teaspoon sugar
½ teaspoon chopped fresh thyme or
   one-quarter teaspoon dried thyme
2 pounds boneless sirloin, cut into
   one-and-one-half-inch cubes
6 large lobster tails, shells removed, quartered
1 cup hot melted butter
12 lemon wedges.

1. Combine the garlic, oil, lemon juice, salt, pepper, Tabasco, mustard, sugar and thyme. Divide the mixture between two bowls.

2. Place the sirloin in one bowl and the lobster in the other. Toss to coat and marinate in the refrigerator at least one hour.

3. Alternate the lobster and sirloin on skewers and broil under a preheated broiler or over a charcoal fire until the lobster is cooked, turning frequently and brushing with melted butter as needed, about fifteen minutes.

4. Pour remaining hot melted butter over when ready to serve. Serve with lemon wedges.

Yield: Six servings.

Note: There are dozens of variations on this dish, which is basically a shashlik. The meat may very well be cubed filet mignon rather than the sirloin, and rock lobster tails may be used in lieu of Maine lobster tails. Rock lobster tails, in fact, are used principally for making the dish.

The seasonings, too, may be varied. Oregano, for example, may be substituted for the thyme.

Chicken Fried Round Steak with Cream Gravy

Iowa

2 pounds round steak, cut one-half-inch
   thick and pounded thin
2 eggs, lightly beaten
2 tablespoons milk
1 cup flour or cracker crumbs
1½ teaspoons salt
¼ teaspoon freshly ground black pepper
3 tablespoons oil or rendered beef fat
1 cup heavy cream.

1. Cut the pounded steak into serving pieces. Dip in the eggs mixed with the milk and then in the flour or cracker crumbs mixed with the salt and pepper.

2. Heat the oil or fat in a heavy skillet (400 degrees on an electric skillet) and brown the steaks in it very quickly on both sides. Remove to a warm platter.

3. Stir in the cream and cook, stirring to loosen all browned-on bits. Serve gravy over mashed potatoes or bread. If steak is not tender enough after just frying, it can be returned to cream gravy, covered and cooked further.

Yield: Six servings.

Round Steak with Green Peppers

Ohio

1½ pounds round steak, cut one-half-inch thick and into one-quarter-inch strips
¼ cup flour
½ teaspoon salt
¼ teaspoon freshly ground black pepper
¼ cup oil or shortening
1 cup canned tomatoes
½ cup chopped onion
1 clove garlic, finely chopped
1¾ cups beef broth
1½ teaspoons Worcestershire sauce
2 large green peppers, cored and cut into strips
Cooked noodles.

1. Coat the meat with the flour mixed with the salt and pepper. Heat the oil in a large skillet and brown the meat in it on all sides.

2. Drain the tomatoes, reserving both tomatoes and liquid. Add liquid, the onion, garlic and broth to meat. Cover and simmer until meat is tender, about one hour.

3. Stir in the Worcestershire and pepper strips and cook five minutes. Add reserved tomatoes. Serve over noodles.

Yield: Six servings.

German Rolled Steak

Kansas

1½ pounds round steak
1 tablespoon Düsseldorf mustard
2 dill pickles, sliced lengthwise into three sticks each
¾ pound bacon, diced

1 onion, finely chopped
1 tablespoon light brown sugar
Salt and freshly ground black pepper to taste
⅓ cup flour
1¼ cups beef broth.

1. Preheat the oven to 325 degrees.

2. Pound the round steak until it is one-eighth-inch thick. Cut into six rectangles about five by three inches.

3. Spread meat with the mustard. Place a slice of the pickle on each piece of meat.

4. Cook the bacon until crisp, remove and sprinkle over meat. In two tablespoons of the bacon drippings (reserve remaining drippings), sauté the onion until tender. Divide onions among pieces of meat. Sprinkle with brown sugar and season with salt and pepper.

5. Roll each piece of steak as for jellyroll and secure with string. Dredge the rolls in the flour and brown quickly in a skillet in the reserved bacon drippings. Transfer rolls to a casserole.

6. Measure two tablespoons flour from dredging flour left and sprinkle over drippings in skillet. Cook, stirring. Add the broth and bring to a boil.

7. Pour over beef rolls, cover and bake about one hour, or until meat is very tender.

Yield: Six servings.

Flamed Filet

Missouri

4 small filet mignons, each about one-inch thick
4 tablespoons butter
¼ pound mushrooms, thinly sliced
½ cup chopped scallions, including green part
Freshly ground black pepper
1 tablespoon Worcestershire sauce or soy sauce
3 tablespoons cognac
4 toast points.

1. Trim off any bits of fat from the steak.

2. Heat the butter in a skillet and brown the meat on one side. Turn the meat and scatter the mushrooms and scallions over it. Sprinkle with pepper. Cook to the desired degree of doneness, five minutes or longer.

3. Combine the Worcestershire or soy sauce and cognac and pour over the meat. Ignite the cognac. Stir all ingredients around in the sauce and serve the meat on toast points with the sauce poured over.

Yield: Four servings.

Roast Fillet of Beef　　　　　*Illinois*

1 four-pound beef fillet, well larded with fat
Salt and freshly ground black pepper to taste
1 carrot, diced
1 onion, chopped
1 rib celery, chopped
1 clove garlic, crushed
3 tablespoons flour
1½ cups beef broth
1 pound mushrooms, sliced
½ cup butter
1 teaspoon lemon juice
¼ cup Madeira wine
1 tablespoon chopped parsley.

1. Preheat the oven to 425 degrees.

2. Season the fillet with salt and pepper and place on a rack in a shallow roasting pan. Scatter the carrot, onion, celery and garlic around the meat.

3. Roast about thirty minutes or until a meat thermometer placed in the thickest part of the fillet registers 140 degrees for rare, 160 degrees for medium or 170 degrees for well done, as desired.

4. Place fillet on a warm platter. Pour off all but three tablespoons of the drippings from the roasting pan. Sprinkle with the flour and cook, stirring, until it just starts to color.

5. Add the broth and bring to a boil, stirring. Simmer ten minutes. Sauté the mushrooms

briefly in the butter. Strain the sauce and add to the mushrooms.

6. Add the lemon juice, Madeira, parsley, salt and pepper. Reheat, but do not boil. Serve sauce separately.

Yield: Eight servings.

Barbecued Beef Roast　　　　*Illinois*

¼ cup cider vinegar
3 teaspoons Worcestershire sauce
1 cup catchup
¾ cup water
¼ cup chopped onion
1 teaspoon light brown sugar
¼ teaspoon dry mustard
3 tablespoons liquid smoke (see note)
1 four-pound eye round or sirloin tip beef roast.

1. In a saucepan, combine the vinegar, Worcestershire, catchup, water, onion, brown sugar and mustard. Bring to a boil and simmer ten minutes.

2. Add the liquid smoke. Place the roast in the marinade and let stand two to four hours at room temperature.

3. Drain meat, reserving marinade, and insert barbecue spit through the roast. Roast over charcoal fire, basting frequently with marinade, about two hours, or until meat is done to desired degree of doneness.

Yield: Ten servings.

Note: Liquid smoke is available at specialty stores.

Beef 'n' Beans　　　　　*Michigan*

1 three-pound to four-pound piece brisket of beef
3 tablespoons oil
8 small white onions
1 carrot, quartered

1 onion, sliced
2 ribs celery, quartered
1 leek, chopped
1 clove garlic, chopped
1 bay leaf
8 peppercorns
 Salt to taste
2 sprigs parsley
2 cups dried navy beans or pea beans
¼ pound salt pork
 Freshly ground black pepper to taste
1 pound smoked deer sausage, pork sausage
 or knockwurst, sliced
2 tablespoons unsulphured molasses
1 teaspoon dry mustard.

1. Day before, brown the beef on all sides in the oil in a heavy casserole or Dutch oven. Remove meat. Brown the whole onions in casserole; remove and reserve.

2. Add the carrot, sliced onion, celery, leek and garlic to the casserole and cook, stirring, three minutes. Return the meat to the casserole and add the bay leaf, peppercorns and salt. Add water to three-quarters cover the meat and the parsley sprigs.

3. Bring to a boil, cover and simmer gently about one and one-half hours, or until the meat is barely tender. Let set in broth overnight.

4. Wash and pick over the beans, cover with water and let soak overnight. Next morning, drain beans and place in kettle with the salt pork and two quarts water. Bring to a boil and cook, covered, for about one hour, or until beans are tender. Season with pepper.

5. Preheat the oven to 325 degrees.

6. Remove brisket from broth and slice meat. Strain the broth. Drain the beans, reserving salt pork and cooking liquid. In a heavy casserole, layer half the drained beans, then slices of beef and slices of sausage or wurst. Top with remaining beans and salt pork and bury the reserved white onions in the beans.

7. Add the molasses and mustard to the meat broth and pour over beans so that liquid is just visible. Use bean-cooking liquid as required to maintain level of liquid while casserole bakes. Bake, uncovered, at least two hours.

Yield: Six to eight servings.

Note: This dish can be made with leftover boiled beef.

Sauerbraten   *Missouri*

1 six-pound pot roast of beef
½ bottle dry red wine
1 cup red wine vinegar
12 peppercorns
1 teaspoon salt
2 bay leaves, broken
1 teaspoon leaf sage
1 teaspoon crushed rosemary
2 cloves garlic, crushed
1 onion, sliced
3 ribs celery, chopped
2 carrots, chopped
3 sprigs parsley
¼ cup peanut oil or vegetable oil
2 cups beef broth
3 tablespoons cornstarch
 Salt and freshly ground black pepper to taste.

1. Wipe the meat with a damp cloth and place meat in an enamel or stainless steel pot.

2. Combine the wine, vinegar, peppercorns, salt, bay leaves, sage, rosemary, garlic, onion, celery, carrots and parsley. Pour the mixture over the meat. Cover and let stand eighteen to twenty-four hours.

3. Remove the meat from the marinade and wipe meat with paper towels. Strain the marinade, partly cover and bring to a gentle boil on top of the stove. The marinade should barely boil.

4. Heat the oil in a Dutch oven and brown the meat in it slowly but well on all sides. Pour off excess fat. Add one cup of the broth and cover. Let cook on top of the stove three and one-half hours. As the meat cooks, baste it with the remaining broth and the simmering marinade.

5. When the meat is thoroughly tender, re-

move it to a hot platter. Strain the gravy, pressing as much of the solids through as possible. Skim it to remove fat. Bring to a boil. Blend the cornstarch with a little water and stir into the gravy. Add salt and pepper and serve gravy with the meat.

Yield: Eight to ten servings.

Boiled Beef with Stappa (Mashed Rutabagas) *Minnesota*

1 large beef shin
3 carrots, quartered
2 ribs celery with leaves
  Salt to taste
20 peppercorns
2 rutabagas, peeled and thickly sliced
3 large potatoes, scrubbed
  Freshly ground black pepper to taste
¼ teaspoon ground ginger, or to taste
4 tablespoons butter.

1. Place the beef shin in a kettle and add water to cover. Add the carrots, celery, salt and peppercorns. Bring to a boil, skim the surface to remove foam and scum and partly cover. Simmer about two hours.

2. Add the rutabagas and potatoes and cook until tender, thirty minutes or longer. When the rutabagas and potatoes are tender, remove them. Peel the potatoes and put both vegetables through a food ricer. Season with salt, pepper and ginger and stir in the butter. Serve with beef shin, sliced.

Yield: Six to eight servings.

How to Corn Beef *Illinois*

1 three-pound to five-pound piece beef brisket, flanken or plate
  Salt
1 tablespoon pickling spices
1 teaspoon saltpeter
1 clove garlic, crushed

1 tablespoon sugar
1 tablespoon peppercorns
1 onion, sliced.

1. Prick the meat all over with a two-pronged fork or ice pick. Refrigerate until ready to use.

2. Place enough water to cover the meat in an earthenware or glass crock and add about one-half cup salt. Stir to dissolve. Continue adding and stirring salt, a little at a time, until an egg will float in the liquid. Do not add the meat, but add the pickling spices, saltpeter, garlic, sugar and peppercorns. Bring the brine to a boil. Let brine cool thoroughly.

3. Add the meat and onion and cover with heavy-duty aluminum foil. Let stand at least forty-eight hours.

Yield: One piece corned beef.

Corned Beef in a Pot *Illinois*

1 three-pound to five-pound piece corned beef
1 leek, trimmed and well washed
2 sprigs parsley
  Pinch of thyme
1 bay leaf
½ pound salt pork
8 small potatoes, peeled
8 small white turnips, peeled
8 small carrots
1 cabbage, cut into eighths
  Boiling salted water
  Hot mustard, grated horseradish, sour pickles or mustard pickles.

1. Rinse the corned beef under cold running water to remove surface salt. Place corned beef in a kettle and add water to cover.

2. Split the leek down to but not through the root end. Place the parsley, thyme and bay leaf in the middle and tie the leek together with a string. Add to the corned beef and bring to a boil. Simmer three to four hours. Cooking time will depend on the weight of the corned beef. The meat

is done when it can be easily pierced through the center with a two-pronged fork.

3. Meanwhile, when the beef has cooked about two hours, add the salt pork and continue cooking.

4. About thirty minutes before the meat is done, add the potatoes, turnips and carrots. Cook until vegetables are tender.

5. Meanwhile, cook the cabbage separately until tender in boiling salted water.

6. Drain the meat and slice it. Serve the meat surrounded by the vegetables on a hot platter. Serve hot mustard, grated horseradish, sour pickles or mustard pickles separately.

Yield: Six to ten servings.

Charlie's Café Peppered Tenderloin Casserole   *Minnesota*

¼ cup butter
2 tablespoons olive oil
2 pounds beef tenderloin or boneless sirloin, cut into one-quarter-inch strips
1 teaspoon salt
½ teaspoon freshly ground black pepper
⅛ teaspoon ground sage
⅛ teaspoon ground cumin
1 pound mushrooms, quartered
2 cloves garlic, finely chopped
1 onion, chopped
2 green peppers, diced
2 tomatoes, peeled and cut into eight wedges each
½ cup soy sauce
2 tablespoons cider vinegar
2 tablespoons tomato paste.

1. Preheat the oven to 325 degrees.

2. Heat two tablespoons of the butter and one tablespoon of the oil in a heavy skillet and quickly brown the beef in it on all sides.

3. Transfer to a four-quart casserole. Sprinkle with the salt, pepper, sage and cumin. Toss lightly to mix.

4. Sauté the mushrooms in the remaining but-

ter and oil in the skillet used to brown the beef. Add to meat.

5. Add the garlic, onion and peppers to skillet and sauté two minutes. Add with the tomatoes to casserole.

6. Combine the soy sauce, vinegar and tomato paste and add to skillet. Cook, stirring to loosen all browned-on particles. Bring to a boil and pour over meat and vegetables. Toss lightly.

7. Cover and bake thirty minutes, or until meat is tender and mixture bubbling hot.

Yield: Six servings.

Meat and Cheese Loaf   *Kansas*

2 pounds ground beef chuck
1½ cups grated Swiss cheese
2 eggs, lightly beaten
½ cup chopped onion
½ cup chopped green pepper
1½ teaspoons salt
½ teaspoon freshly ground black pepper
1 teaspoon celery salt
2 cups milk
1 cup dry bread crumbs
4 slices lean bacon.

1. Preheat the oven to 350 degrees.

2. Mix all the ingredients except the bacon together. Pack into a large loaf pan. Top with the bacon and bake one and one-half hours.

Yield: Eight servings.

Anne's Hamburgers   *Missouri*

½ pound ground chuck
½ pound ground neck meat
1 egg
2 tablespoons heavy cream
1 tablespoon soft bread crumbs
  Salt and freshly ground black pepper to taste
2 tablespoons butter or other fat.

1. Combine the meats in a mixing bowl. Beat the egg with the cream and add. Add the bread crumbs, salt and pepper and mix with the fingers.

2. Shape mixture into four patties and cook on all sides in the butter or other fat until done.

Yield: Four servings.

Camping Hamburger   *Iowa*

1 pound ground beef chuck
1 onion, chopped
1 cup broken-up spaghetti
2½ cups tomato juice
½ cup catchup
1 teaspoon salt
¼ teaspoon freshly ground black pepper
½ teaspoon oregano
½ teaspoon basil.

Brown the meat and onion in a heavy kettle. Add the remaining ingredients, stir and cook very slowly about forty-five minutes.

Yield: Four servings.

Meat and Potato Burgers   *Iowa*

1 pound ground beef round
¾ cup cold cooked mashed potato
1 egg, lightly beaten
2 tablespoons finely chopped onion
¼ cup water
½ cup chopped drained pickled beets
1 tablespoon chopped drained capers
1 teaspoon salt
¼ teaspoon freshly ground black pepper
1 tablespoon freshly snipped dill weed
3 tablespoons butter.

1. With the hands, mix all the ingredients except the butter together in a bowl. Shape into patties.

2. Heat the butter in a heavy skillet and brown the patties in it on both sides. Burgers should be served rare or medium rare.

Yield: Four servings.

Meat Balls I   *Iowa*

3 pounds well-trimmed beef round
½ pound beef suet
1 tablespoon salt
1 teaspoon mace or nutmeg
4 cups heavy cream
½ cup butter
4 tablespoons flour
3 cups beef broth.

1. Grind the beef with the suet through the finest blade of the meat chopper three times.

2. Beat the meat mixture well. Beat in the salt and mace or nutmeg.

3. Using the hands, gradually work in the cream. Shape mixture into balls the size of walnuts.

4. Fry the balls, a few at a time, in the butter. Drain on paper towels.

5. Remove all but three tablespoons drippings. Sprinkle with the flour and cook until lightly browned. Stir in the broth and cook, stirring to loosen all cooked-on bits, until gravy thickens. Pour over meat balls.

Yield: About four dozen; eight servings.

Meat Balls II   *Minnesota*

¾ pound beef or veal, ground twice
¼ pound pork, ground twice
¼ cup finely chopped onion
6 tablespoons butter
⅓ cup soft bread crumbs
½ cup water
½ cup heavy cream
Salt and freshly ground black pepper to taste
¼ teaspoon nutmeg
2 tablespoons oil.

1. Place the ground meats in a mixing bowl.

2. Cook the onion in two tablespoons of the butter until wilted. Cool slightly and add to the meats.

3. Soak the bread crumbs in the water and cream; then squeeze to remove most of the liquid. Add the crumbs to the meats. Season with salt, pepper and nutmeg and shape mixture into small balls.

4. Melt the remaining butter in a skillet and add the oil. Cook the meat balls in the skillet until golden brown on all sides and thoroughly cooked. Serve hot or cold.

Yield: About two dozen; four servings.

Meat Balls III   *Iowa*

1 pound ground chuck
  Salt and freshly ground black pepper
¼ teaspoon allspice
⅛ teaspoon ginger
⅛ teaspoon dry mustard
¼ cup quick-cooking (dry) oatmeal
⅓ cup milk
¼ cup bacon drippings
2 tablespoons flour
1 cup heavy cream
¼ pound mushrooms, finely chopped.

1. Preheat the oven to 325 degrees.

2. Mix together the meat, one-half teaspoon salt, one-eighth teaspoon pepper, the allspice, ginger, mustard, oatmeal and milk. Shape into one-inch balls.

3. Heat the bacon drippings in a heavy skillet and brown the balls, a few at a time, in it. Place meat balls in a casserole.

4. Pour off all but two tablespoons fat from the skillet. Sprinkle with the flour and cook three minutes. Add the cream and bring to a boil. Cook, stirring, five minutes. Add the mushrooms. Season to taste with salt and pepper.

5. Pour mushroom mixture over meat balls in casserole and bake one hour.

Yield: About thirty; four to five servings.

Barbecued Meat Balls   *Iowa*

1½ pounds ground beef chuck
  3 teaspoons finely chopped onion
  1 cup milk
  ¾ cup quick-cooking (dry) oatmeal
  1 teaspoon salt
  ¼ teaspoon freshly ground black pepper
  2 tablespoons shortening.
Sauce:
  1 cup catchup
  1 small onion, finely chopped
  2 tablespoons Worcestershire sauce
  1 teaspoon light brown sugar
  2 tablespoons cider vinegar.

1. Mix together the meat, onion, milk, oatmeal, salt and pepper. Form into one-inch balls and brown in the shortening ten minutes, turning often.

2. Drain off excess fat.

3. Meanwhile, combine all the sauce ingredients in a saucepan, bring to a boil, simmer five minutes and pour over meat balls. Simmer twenty minutes.

Yield: About three dozen; six servings.

One Dish Supper   *Michigan*

2 large green peppers, halved and seeded
  Boiling salted water
8 small onions
4 ribs celery, cut into one-half-inch pieces
1 slice lemon
1 pound ground beef
  Salt and freshly ground black pepper to taste
1 tablespoon freshly snipped dill weed
2 tablespoons soft bread crumbs
1 cup tomato sauce, preferably homemade
2 tablespoons buttered soft bread crumbs.

1. Preheat the oven to 350 degrees.

2. Plunge the pepper halves into a pan of boiling salted water and simmer five minutes. Drain.

3. Place the onions, celery and lemon slice in

a small pan and add a small amount of boiling salted water. Cover and cook until onions are barely tender. Drain, reserving onions and celery.

4. In a bowl, mix the beef, salt, pepper, dill, bread crumbs and two tablespoons of the tomato sauce. Place pepper halves in a greased baking dish and fill with meat mixture. Place onions and celery around and spoon remaining tomato sauce over all. Sprinkle with buttered crumbs. Bake forty minutes.

Yield: Four servings.

Meat Loaf with Parsley   *Indiana*

2 slices white bread
1 cup coarsely chopped onions
2 cups loosely packed parsley, stems removed
1 small clove garlic, finely chopped
3 ribs celery, chopped
½ cup water
2 pounds ground beef round
1 egg, lightly beaten
1 teaspoon salt
1 teaspoon freshly ground black pepper
6 to eight slices bacon.

1. Preheat the oven to 325 degrees.
2. Blend the bread in an electric blender or grate to make fine crumbs.
3. Place the onions, parsley, garlic, celery and water in the container of an electric blender and blend on high speed until ingredients are chopped and blended.
4. Place meat in a mixing bowl and add parsley mixture, the egg, bread crumbs, the salt and pepper. Blend with fingers. Shape into a round or oval loaf on a baking dish. Cover loaf with bacon and bake two hours.

Yield: Six to eight servings.

Wild Rice and Beef Casserole   *Minnesota*

4 cups boiling water
1⅓ cups wild rice

3 cups chicken broth
1½ teaspoons salt
1 bay leaf, crumbled
1 tablespoon soy sauce
½ teaspoon curry powder
½ cup butter
⅓ cup finely chopped onion
1 pound mushrooms, sliced
1 pound ground beef
½ pound grated sharp Cheddar cheese.

1. Preheat the oven to 350 degrees.
2. Pour the boiling water over the rice and let stand fifteen minutes. Drain. Add the broth, salt, bay leaf, soy sauce and curry powder to rice.
3. Melt the butter in a heavy skillet and sauté the onion in it until tender. Add the mushrooms and sauté three minutes. Add the beef and cook, stirring, until it loses its pink color.
4. Combine rice mixture with meat mixture in a 14-by-9-inch casserole. Top with the cheese and bake one hour.

Yield: Six servings.

Hazel's Tallerine   *Indiana*

2 tablespoons bacon drippings
2 pounds ground beef chuck
1 large onion, chopped
8 ounces noodles, cooked al dente, drained
1 green pepper, diced
¼ pound mushrooms, sliced
1 cup stuffed olives, chopped
2 cups tomato juice
1 cup freshly cut corn kernels or canned, drained corn kernels
  Cayenne pepper to taste
1 cup grated sharp Cheddar cheese.

1. Preheat the oven to 375 degrees.
2. Heat the bacon drippings in a skillet. Add the beef and onion and cook until beef is lightly browned.
3. Mix meat and onion with all remaining ingredients except the cheese and pour into a

greased casserole. Top with cheese and bake thirty minutes, or until bubbly hot and lightly browned.

Yield: Six to eight servings.

Savory Veal Cutlet   *Kansas*

3 medium-size onions, sliced
2 tablespoons butter
1 veal cutlet, one and one-half inches thick
¼ cup flour
1 teaspoon salt
1 teaspoon paprika
¾ cup sour cream.

1. Sauté the onions in the butter until golden. Coat the veal cutlet with the flour, add to the pan and sauté on both sides.

2. Season the meat with the salt and paprika. Stir in the sour cream, cover and cook over very low heat until veal is tender. Do not allow mixture to boil.

Yield: Four servings.

Scaloppine of Veal   *Michigan*

1 pound veal from the top of the leg, thinly cut
3 tablespoons flour
Salt and freshly ground black pepper to taste
1 tablespoon butter
3 tablespoons olive oil
1 clove garlic, finely chopped
½ small onion, finely chopped
⅔ cup chicken broth
⅓ cup dry white wine
⅔ cup tomato juice
½ teaspoon rosemary
1 tablespoon chopped parsley.

1. Cut the veal into serving pieces and pound well between pieces of wax paper with a mallet or rolling pin.

2. Dredge the veal pieces in the flour seasoned with salt and pepper. Heat the butter and oil in a skillet and brown the veal in it on all sides. Remove veal and drain on paper towels.

3. Add the garlic and onion to the skillet and sauté until tender. Add the broth, wine and tomato juice and cook ten minutes.

4. Add the herbs and return the meat to the skillet. Simmer gently five minutes, or until veal is tender.

Yield: Two or three servings.

Veal and Eggplant Casserole   *Ohio*

½ cup oil
4 onions, finely chopped
2 pounds ground veal
Salt and freshly ground black pepper
3 tablespoons chopped parsley
½ teaspoon thyme
2 tomatoes, peeled and chopped
¼ cup dry red wine
3 medium-size eggplants, sliced
2 eggs, separated
6 tablespoons soft bread crumbs
1 cup milk
⅓ cup grated feta cheese or Swiss cheese
2 tablespoons butter.

1. Preheat the oven to 350 degrees.

2. Heat half the oil in a large skillet and sauté the onions in it until tender but not browned. Add the veal and salt and pepper to taste and cook until meat loses all pinkness.

3. Add the parsley, thyme, tomatoes and wine and simmer, uncovered, until most of the liquid has been absorbed. Cool slightly.

4. Meanwhile, sprinkle the eggplant slices with salt and let stand twenty-five minutes. Rinse, drain and pat dry. Heat remaining oil in another skillet and brown the eggplant slices in it quickly on both sides.

5. Beat the egg whites until stiff but not dry and fold into the meat mixture with half the bread crumbs.

6. Sprinkle remaining bread crumbs over the bottom of a greased casserole. Alternate layers of eggplant and meat mixture in the casserole, finishing with eggplant.

7. Beat the egg yolks lightly and combine with the milk and cheese. Pour over the casserole. Dot top with the butter. Bake one hour. Serve warm.

Yield: Eight servings.

Fried Ravioli   *Missouri*

3 cups flour
¼ teaspoon salt
4 eggs
6 tablespoons water, approximately
  Ravioli filling (recipes below)
  Fat or oil for deep-frying
  Homemade tomato sauce.

1. Place the flour and salt on a board and make a well in the center. Break the eggs into the well and add the water.

2. Gradually mix to a dough, using the fingers. A minimum of water will give a harder-to-roll but crisp end product and adding one or two extra tablespoons of water will give an easy-to-roll dough which is softer.

3. Knead the dough on a lightly floured board until smooth. Cover with a cloth and let stand twenty to thirty minutes.

4. Divide the dough into three portions and roll out one part on a lightly floured board until very thin. Fit into ravioli pans, fill the depressions with either the veal filling or the spinach and ricotta filling and top with some of the remaining dough. Roll over the top of the pan to cut ravioli into squares.

5. Repeat with the remaining dough until all is used.

6. The ravioli may be fried immediately or held refrigerated or frozen until just before serving.

7. Heat a pan of deep fat or oil to 360 degrees. Place a few ravioli at a time into a deep-frying basket and lower gently into the fat. Cook until golden, turning if necessary, about two to three minutes. Drain on paper towels and keep warm while remaining ravioli are fried. Serve with tomato sauce.

Yield: About seventy-five to 100, depending on size; about ten servings.

Veal Filling for Ravioli   *Missouri*

¼ cup butter
½ cup finely chopped onion
½ pound ground veal
¼ teaspoon salt
⅛ teaspoon freshly ground black pepper
½ teaspoon basil
⅛ teaspoon grated nutmeg
¼ cup freshly grated Parmesan cheese
¼ cup soft bread crumbs
1 egg.

Melt the butter in a small skillet and sauté the onion in it. Add the veal and cook, stirring, until lightly browned. Add the remaining ingredients and stir to mix.

Yield: About one and one-quarter cups, enough to fill about seventy-five ravioli.

Spinach and Ricotta Filling for Ravioli
Missouri

½ cup cooked spinach, chopped
½ cup ricotta cheese
½ cup freshly grated Parmesan cheese
2 eggs, lightly beaten
  Salt and freshly ground black pepper to taste
¼ teaspoon nutmeg.

Mix all ingredients together.

Yield: About one and three-quarters cups, enough to fill about 100 ravioli.

Jellied Veal Loaf (Sylta)   *Minnesota*

2 veal shanks, cracked
1 pound veal neck, cubed
2 bay leaves
⅛ teaspoon allspice
4 whole cloves
  Salt and freshly ground black pepper to
  taste
1 teaspoon unflavored gelatin
1 tablespoon cider vinegar.

1. Place the veal shanks, veal neck, bay leaves, allspice, cloves, salt, pepper and enough water to cover in a heavy kettle.
2. Bring to a boil, cover and simmer slowly one and one-half to two hours, or until the meat is very tender. Remove meat from bones. Grind or finely chop meat. Strain the broth into a saucepan.
3. Reduce the amount of broth to three cups by boiling uncovered. Soften the gelatin in two tablespoons water. Add to concentrated broth along with vinegar. Add meat and pour into an oiled loaf pan. Chill until firm. Unmold and serve sliced.
    Yield: Six to eight servings.

Armenian Squash Dolma   *Wisconsin*

10 small summer squash
   Salt
 1 pound ground lamb
½ cup chopped onion
½ cup cooked rice
 1 cup canned tomatoes
 2 tablespoons chopped parsley
   Freshly ground black pepper
 2 tablespoons hot water.

1. Preheat the oven to 350 degrees.
2. Cut off the end of each squash and scoop out the seeds. Sprinkle inside lightly with salt.
3. Combine the lamb, onion, rice, tomatoes and parsley. Season to taste with salt and pepper

and use to stuff the squash. Place in a greased shallow baking dish. Add the hot water to the baking dish and bake one hour, or until done.
    Yield: Five servings.

Lamb and Eggplant, Syrian Style   *Wisconsin*

2 medium-size eggplants, sliced
  Salt
2 tablespoons butter
3 pounds boneless leg of lamb, finely diced
3 onions, chopped
½ clove garlic, finely chopped
2 ribs celery, diced
  Freshly ground black pepper
1 one-pound can tomatoes.

1. Preheat the oven to 350 degrees.
2. Sprinkle the eggplant with salt and set aside fifteen to twenty minutes.
3. Rinse, drain and pat dry eggplant slices and place on broiler pan. Broil until lightly browned, turn and broil other side.
4. Melt the butter in a skillet and brown the lamb in it on all sides. Add the onions, garlic and celery and cook fifteen minutes longer.
5. Season to taste with salt and pepper and add the tomatoes.
6. Cook slowly five minutes. Place half of the eggplant slices in a single layer in the bottom of a greased baking dish. Top with spoonfuls of the meat-tomato mixture.
7. Cover with remaining eggplant slices. Pour remaining meat-tomato mixture over slices and bake thirty minutes, or until done.
    Yield: Eight servings.

Dilled Lamb Stew   *Minnesota*

2 pounds boneless neck or shoulder of lamb,
  cut into large chunks
1 teaspoon salt
¼ teaspoon freshly ground black pepper

2 tablespoons freshly snipped dill weed
2 cups chicken broth or water
2 cups sliced carrots
2 cups diced peeled tomatoes
3 tablespoons flour
1 cup sour cream.

1. Trim the extra fat from the lamb and render in a large skillet. Brown the lamb in the rendered fat until browned on all sides.

2. Transfer meat to a casserole and sprinkle with the salt, pepper and dill. Add the broth or water, bring to a boil, cover and simmer until meat is tender, about one hour.

3. Add the carrots and tomatoes and cook fifteen minutes longer. Mix the flour to a paste with a little water, add a little of the hot broth and return to casserole. Heat, stirring, until thick. Stir in the sour cream. Heat, but do not boil.

Yield: Six servings.

Leg of Lamb in Sour Cream Sauce
Wisconsin

1 five-pound to six-pound leg of lamb,
    oven-ready with all surface fat removed.
1 clove garlic, cut into slivers
    Salt and freshly ground black pepper
    White vinegar
    Flour
    Chicken broth
1 onion, chopped
2 tablespoons tomato paste
¼ pound mushrooms, finely chopped
2 cups sour cream.

1. Day before, make several small incisions in the lamb flesh and insert the garlic slivers. Sprinkle generously with salt and pepper and rub into the meat.

2. Soak a triple thickness of cheesecloth with vinegar and wrap around the meat. Cover with wax paper and refrigerate overnight.

3. Next day, preheat the oven to 450 degrees.

4. Remove the cheesecloth, wipe the meat with a damp cloth and place meat on a rack in a roasting pan. Sprinkle with two tablespoons flour.

5. Bring one cup broth to a boil, combine with onion and tomato paste and pour into the pan under the roast.

6. Roast, uncovered, forty minutes, checking two or three times to see that liquid in the bottom is not burning or drying up; add more broth if necessary.

7. Reduce the oven heat to 300 degrees.

8. Remove roast from pan and keep warm. Strain the pan juices and measure into a saucepan. For each cup pan juices, add two tablespoons flour mixed with a small quantity of water.

9. Add the mushrooms and bring to a boil, stirring. Gradually stir the hot sauce into the sour cream. Return the roast without the rack to the roasting pan. Pour the sauce over the roast.

10. Cover the pan, with aluminum foil if necessary, and roast one hour longer, or until the lamb is the desired degree of doneness, basting with the sauce three times. In one hour the lamb is a delightful pink in the middle. Serve extra sauce separately. It may show slight signs of curdling because of the sour cream but tastes delicious.

Yield: Six servings.

Lamb Loaf
Minnesota

2 pounds ground lamb
1 cup soft bread crumbs
2 tablespoons chopped celery
2 tablespoons finely chopped onion
2 tablespoons freshly snipped dill weed
1½ teaspoons salt
¼ teaspoon freshly ground black pepper
2 eggs.

1. Preheat the oven to 350 degrees.

2. Mix all the ingredients together and pack into a greased loaf pan.

3. Bake one hour, or until done.

Yield: Four servings.

Paula's Bosnian Casserole　　　*Wisconsin*

¼ pound lean bacon, diced
½ pound cubed boneless beef chuck
½ pound cubed boneless lean pork shoulder
½ pound cubed lamb shoulder
½ pound cubed boneless veal shoulder
1 large onion, sliced
1 large clove garlic, finely chopped
1 carrot, sliced
1 parsnip, sliced
1 white turnip, peeled and sliced
2 tomatoes, peeled and sliced
2 ribs celery with leaves, sliced
10 tiny potatoes, peeled and left whole, or six
 medium-size potatoes, peeled and halved
3 tablespoons chopped parsley
 Salt and freshly ground black pepper to
 taste
2 tablespoons cider vinegar
2 cups dry white wine
 Chicken broth.

1. Preheat the oven to 300 degrees.
2. Cook the bacon in a heavy skillet; remove bacon and reserve. Brown the meats, a few pieces at a time, in the bacon drippings.
3. In a heavy casserole, layer the browned meats and bacon bits alternately with the vegetables, sprinkling each layer with parsley, salt and pepper.
4. Pour in the vinegar and wine and enough broth to three-quarters cover the meat and vegetables. Bring to a boil on top of the stove, cover very tightly and bake three to four hours.
5. The gravy may be thickened with flour if desired or dumplings can be cooked in the liquid for the last twenty-five minutes.
Yield: Eight servings.

Pork Chops with Capers　　　*Wisconsin*

6 shoulder pork chops
 Freshly ground black pepper to taste
1 onion, finely chopped

2 cloves garlic, finely chopped
2 tablespoons tomato paste
1 one-and-three-quarters-ounce can anchovy
 fillets, finely chopped
1 tablespoon capers, drained
¾ cup chicken broth
1 tablespoon chopped parsley.

1. Brown the pork chops on both sides in a large heavy skillet. Season with pepper. Remove and keep warm.
2. Add the onion and garlic to the skillet and cook until tender. Stir in the tomato paste, anchovies, capers and broth. Bring to a boil, stirring to loosen browned-on particles.
3. Return the chops to the skillet and simmer, covered, thirty minutes, or until tender. Spoon sauce over occasionally. Check seasoning and sprinkle with the parsley before serving.
Yield: Six servings.

Apricot-Stuffed Pork Chops　　　*Iowa*

1 cup diced dried apricots
½ cup boiling water
1 tablespoon sugar
4 rib pork chops, cut one-inch thick
¼ cup flour
 Salt and freshly ground black pepper to
 taste
2 tablespoons shortening
3 cups toasted one-quarter-inch white bread
 cubes
1 cup peeled, cored and diced tart apple
½ cup chopped celery
¼ cup finely chopped onion
½ teaspoon thyme
¼ teaspoon marjoram.

1. Preheat the oven to 325 degrees.
2. Combine the apricots, water and sugar. Set aside.
3. Trim the chops and coat with the flour seasoned with salt and pepper. Heat the shortening

in a skillet and brown the chops in it on both sides.

4. Combine the apricot mixture, bread cubes, apple, celery, onion, thyme and marjoram. Mix lightly and season with salt and pepper.

5. Place the fruit stuffing in the bottom of a casserole and arrange the browned chops on top. Cover and bake one and one-half hours, or until chops are well done.

Yield: Four servings.

Baked Pork Chops with Rice   *Iowa*

 6 pork shoulder chops (one and one-half pounds)
 2 tablespoons oil
1½ teaspoons salt
 ¼ teaspoon freshly ground black pepper
 1 cup uncooked rice
 ½ cup chopped onion
 1 cup peeled, chopped tomatoes
 ½ teaspoon sage
 ¼ teaspoon thyme
 ¼ teaspoon marjoram
 2 tablespoons chopped parsley
 2 cups chicken broth.

1. Preheat the oven to 350 degrees.
2. Brown the chops on both sides in the oil. Season with the salt and pepper and set aside. Remove all but two tablespoons drippings.
3. Add the rice and onion and cook slowly until onion is tender and rice golden. Add the tomatoes, sage, thyme, marjoram, parsley and broth. Pour into a three-quart casserole and top with chops.
4. Cover and bake one hour.
Yield: Six servings.

Pork Chops and Potato Casserole   *Iowa*

6 thick rib pork chops
2 tablespoons oil

3 tablespoons flour
1½ cups chicken broth or water
   Salt and freshly ground black pepper to taste
6 potatoes, peeled and sliced.

1. Preheat the oven to 350 degrees.
2. Brown the chops in the oil in a heavy skillet, turning once. Remove chops and keep warm.
3. Pour off all but three tablespoons drippings from the skillet. Sprinkle with the flour and cook, stirring, until lightly browned. Stir in the broth or water. Bring to a boil, stirring until gravy thickens. Season with salt and pepper.
4. Place the potatoes in the bottom of a casserole, pour the gravy over and top with the chops. Season chops. Cover and bake one and one-half hours. Remove cover and bake thirty minutes longer.
Yield: Six servings.

Kraut, Pork and Apple   *Iowa*

¼ cup butter
¼ cup currant jelly
3 medium-size unpeeled Rome apples, cored and cut into one-half-inch rings
4 double loin pork chops
  Salt and freshly ground black pepper to taste
1 twenty-ounce can sauerkraut
1 cup finely chopped onions.

1. Melt the butter in a skillet. Add the currant jelly and apple rings and cook until rings are browned, turning once.
2. Remove rings and reserve. Brown the chops on both sides in the skillet. Season with salt and pepper. Combine the kraut and onions and place on top of chops.
3. Cover and cook thirty minutes over low heat.
4. Uncover skillet and arrange apple rings

over kraut. Cover and cook thirty minutes longer, or until pork is well done.

Yield: Four servings.

Braised Stuffed Pork Chops   *Iowa*

    4 double thick loin pork chops
    ¼ cup raisins, chopped
    1¾ cups bread crumbs made from day-old
        white bread
    ¼ cup finely chopped onion
    2 tablespoons melted butter
    ¾ cup finely diced, peeled tart apple
    ½ teaspoon salt
    ⅛ teaspoon freshly ground black pepper
    ¼ teaspoon sage
    1 teaspoon sugar
      Flour
    2 tablespoons oil
    ¼ cup chicken broth.

1. Cut a pocket in each of the chops.
2. Combine the raisins, bread crumbs, onion, butter, apple, salt, pepper, sage and sugar. Mix well and use to stuff chops. Close opening with toothpicks.
3. Dredge the chops in flour. Brown in the oil heated in a heavy skillet. Pour off the drippings. Add the broth. Cover and cook slowly forty minutes, or until chops are well done. Remove toothpicks before serving.

Yield: Four servings.

Pork Steaks and Apple Kraut   *Iowa*

    4 pork steaks (one-half-inch slices cut from
        fresh ham)
    2 tablespoons lard
    1 teaspoon salt
    ¼ teaspoon freshly ground black pepper
    1 tablespoon horseradish
    1 tablespoon Düsseldorf mustard
    1 twenty-nine-ounce can sauerkraut, drained
    2 tart apples, cored, peeled and diced

    ½ cup chopped onion
    1 teaspoon caraway seeds.

1. Preheat the oven to 350 degrees.
2. Brown the steaks in the lard on both sides.
3. Pour off the drippings and season the steaks with the salt and pepper. Combine the horseradish and mustard and spread over steaks.
4. Combine the remaining ingredients and place in a two-quart shallow baking dish or casserole. Top with the steaks. Cover tightly and bake thirty minutes, or until pork is well cooked.

Yield: Four servings.

Sauerkraut with Spareribs   *Missouri*

    8 slices bacon, approximately
    2 pounds sauerkraut
    3 cups finely chopped onions
    1 clove garlic, finely minced
   12 peppercorns
    4 whole cloves
    2 sprigs parsley
    2 large carrots, quartered
    2 cups dry white wine
    2 cups chicken broth
    3 tablespoons lemon juice
    4 pounds spareribs, approximately
      Salt and freshly ground black pepper to
      taste.

1. Preheat the oven to 250 degrees.
2. Line a heavy three-quart kettle with the bacon.
3. Rinse the sauerkraut and squeeze out most of the liquid. Pull the sauerkraut apart to remove lumps and sprinkle half of it over the bacon. Add the onions and garlic.
4. Tie the peppercorns, cloves and parsley in a cheesecloth bag and add it. Add the remaining sauerkraut and the carrots. Pour the wine, broth and lemon juice over all. Cover closely and bring to a boil. Place in the oven and bake three to four hours.
5. When the sauerkraut has cooked one hour,

place the spareribs on a rack in a roasting pan and sprinkle with salt and pepper. Bake one and one-half hours.

6. Add the spareribs to the sauerkraut and continue cooking until sauerkraut is done. Uncover the kettle for the last forty-five minutes of baking.

Yield: Four to six servings.

Barbecued Spareribs   *Missouri*

 1 medium-size onion, finely chopped
 2 tablespoons butter
 2 tablespoons vinegar
 2 tablespoons dark brown sugar
¼ cup lemon juice
 1 cup catchup
 3 tablespoons Worcestershire sauce
½ tablespoon prepared mustard
½ cup water
½ cup chopped parsley
 2 racks spareribs, the smaller the better
   Salt and freshly ground black pepper to taste.

1. Cook the onion in the butter until wilted. Add the vinegar, brown sugar, lemon juice, catchup, Worcestershire, mustard, water and parsley. Simmer one-half hour.

2. Preheat the oven to 450 degrees.

3. Sprinkle the spareribs with salt and pepper, place on a rack in a roasting pan and bake thirty minutes. Remove spareribs. Pour off fat from pan. Return spareribs without rack to pan and brush with sauce. Reduce oven heat to 300 degrees and continue baking forty-five minutes. Turn spareribs as they cook and brush frequently with sauce.

Yield: Eight to one dozen servings.

Grilled Pig with a Blanket   *Missouri*

 1 length of pork tenderloin, about eleven inches long (see step 1)

 1 thin sheet flank or round steak, about 7 by 11 inches
   Olive oil
   Salt and freshly ground black pepper
   Juice of one lemon
¼ pound butter, melted
¼ cup finely chopped parsley
   Mushrooms au beurre (page 380).

1. If pork tenderloin is not available, trim out the eyes of six small pork chops. If the tenderloin is used, wrap it carefully in the steak. Skewer with six skewers equally spaced. Slice between the skewers to provide six servings. Or, if the chops are used, roll each piece of meat with a length of steak trimmed to fit.

2. Place the meat on a grill over hot coals. When seared on one side, turn and brush the top of each serving with oil. Sprinkle the seared side with salt and pepper.

3. When the meat is cooked through, transfer to a hot serving platter. Squeeze half the lemon juice over meat. Squeeze the remaining juice into the butter and stir in the parsley.

4. Spoon the hot butter sauce over the meat and serve immediately. Garnish with mushrooms au beurre.

Yield: Six servings.

Head Cheese   *Iowa*

 1 hog's head
 1 hog's tongue
   Lightly salted water
 1 teaspoon sage
1½ teaspoons chili powder
   Salt and freshly ground black pepper to taste.

1. Clean and scrape the hog's head, wash thoroughly and saw into pieces. Wash and trim the tongue. Place 'head pieces and tongue in heavy kettle and add lightly salted water to cover.

2. Simmer until meat is very tender, about two

hours. Remove meat from bones and grind in food chopper.

3. Season meat with the sage, chili powder, salt and pepper. Mix well. Pack tightly into a loaf pan or bowl. Cover and weight down. Refrigerate three days. Slice and serve.

Yield: One dozen servings.

Bologna Gravy   *Iowa*

2 tablespoons butter
2 tablespoons flour
2 cups milk
½ teaspoon salt
  Tabasco sauce to taste
½ teaspoon Worcestershire sauce
2 cups ground bologna
  Corn bread squares (page 355).

1. Melt the butter and blend in the flour. Gradually stir in the milk. Bring to a boil, stirring, and cook, stirring, until thickened.

2. Season with the salt, Tabasco and Worcestershire. Stir in the bologna and set over hot water until ready to serve. Check seasoning.

3. Serve over corn bread squares.

Yield: Four servings.

Pioneer Sausage   *Michigan*

10 pounds ground pork
 3 ounces salt (about one-quarter cup)
½ ounce dry powdered sage (about one-half cup), or to taste
 1 ounce black pepper (about two tablespoons), or to taste
¼ cup flour
¼ cup sugar.

1. Day before, mix ingredients together in a large container and let stand in the refrigerator or a cool place overnight.

2. Next day, shape into patties and pan-fry or broil.

Yield: About sixty patties; thirty servings.

Ham Loaf   *Iowa*

1 pound smoked ham, ground
1 pound ground lean pork
2 eggs, lightly beaten
½ cup milk
½ cup cracker crumbs
1 teaspoon salt
⅛ teaspoon freshly ground black pepper
1 cup light brown sugar
2 teaspoons dry mustard
⅓ cup cider vinegar
⅓ cup water.

1. Preheat the oven to 350 degrees.

2. Combine the ham, pork, eggs, milk, cracker crumbs, salt and pepper and pack into a loaf pan.

3. Bake forty-five minutes.

4. Meanwhile, combine remaining ingredients in a saucepan, bring to a boil and boil five minutes.

5. Bake ham loaf forty-five minutes longer, basting frequently with the sauce.

Yield: Eight servings.

Sunday Brunch Omelet   *Illinois*

3 medium-size potatoes, diced
  Boiling salted water
¼ cup butter
⅓ cup finely chopped onion
1 cup diced cooked ham
6 eggs, lightly beaten
1 teaspoon salt
¼ teaspoon freshly ground black pepper
2 tablespoons milk
1 tablespoon chopped parsley
½ cup finely chopped mushrooms
½ cup grated Swiss cheese.

1. Place the potatoes in a saucepan, cover with the salted water and cook ten minutes, or until barely done. Drain well.

2. Melt the butter in a large skillet with flame-proof handle. Sauté the onion in skillet until tender. Add the potatoes and ham and cook three minutes.

3. Combine the eggs, salt, pepper, milk and parsley and pour over potato mixture. Cook over high heat, stirring with a fork until all mixture starts to coagulate. Cook until underside is browned. Sprinkle with the mushrooms and cheese and place under a preheated broiler to melt the cheese.

Yield: Four servings.

Sour Cream Omelet   *Wisconsin*

6 eggs, separated
¾ cup sour cream, at room temperature
1 teaspoon salt
¼ teaspoon freshly ground black pepper
⅛ teaspoon nutmeg
1 tablespoon butter.

1. Preheat the oven to 375 degrees.

2. Beat the egg yolks and stir in the sour cream, salt, pepper and nutmeg. Beat the egg whites until stiff but not dry. Fold into batter.

3. Heat the butter in a seasoned omelet pan. Pour in the mixture and cook quickly, stirring with a fork until all the mixture starts to coagulate. Cook until lightly browned on underside.

4. Bake eight minutes, or until top is cooked. Fold in half and slide onto serving platter.

Yield: Two servings.

Liver Pancakes   *Iowa*

½ pig's liver, finely ground
6 eggs, lightly beaten
¾ cup flour
⅓ cup lard, melted and cooled
1 teaspoon ginger

1 teaspoon cinnamon
1 teaspoon salt
Milk.

Mix all ingredients together well, adding enough milk to give mixture a thin pancake consistency. Spoon onto hot greased griddle and fry like pancakes.

Yield: Six servings.

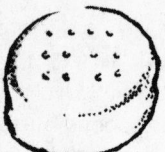

Blood Sausage (Blod Polse)   *Iowa*

½ cup pearl barley
Boiling salted water
8 cups pig's blood
½ pound fresh side pork, diced
½ teaspoon ground ginger
¼ teaspoon ground cloves
1 teaspoon ground allspice
1 tablespoon salt
¼ teaspoon freshly ground black pepper
Flour
2 teaspoons baking powder
Butter
Syrup.

1. Cover the barley with the water and simmer until tender, about fifteen minutes. Drain and cool.

2. Combine the cooled barley with the blood, pork, ginger, cloves, allspice, salt and pepper. Stir in enough flour to make mixture a little thicker than pancake batter. Stir in the baking powder.

3. Fill strong linen sacks three-quarters full with the mixture. Tie and place in boiling salted water. Cook until sacks are entirely full, one and one-half to two hours.

4. Serve sausage hot with butter and syrup.

Yield: Six servings.

Old-Fashioned Brunswick Stew, Michigan Style

1 five-pound to six-pound hen
1 rib celery
1 onion, quartered
1 carrot, cut up
1 bay leaf
1 sprig parsley
  Salt and freshly ground black pepper to taste
3 onions, chopped
10 tablespoons butter
4 cups fresh lima beans, shelled
4 to six medium-size potatoes, peeled and cut into one-half-inch cubes
6 ears corn, kernels removed
6 tomatoes, peeled and chopped.

1. Place the hen in a large deep casserole or kettle and barely cover with cold water. Add the celery, quartered onion, carrot, bay leaf, parsley, salt and pepper.

2. Bring to a boil, cover and simmer gently until the hen is tender, about one and one-quarter hours. Remove hen and take chicken meat off bones. Reserve chicken meat. Strain and reserve broth.

3. Sauté the chopped onions in the butter in a heavy casserole or Dutch oven.

4. Add the beans and potatoes and enough of the reserved broth to barely cover. Bring to a boil and simmer until barely tender.

5. Add the corn kernels, tomatoes and reserved chicken meat and simmer until all is tender. Add more broth during cooking as necessary.

Yield: Fifteen to twenty servings.

Roast Young Capon with Wild Rice and Almond Stuffing   *Minnesota*

1 five-pound to six-pound capon
8 tablespoons butter
  Salt and freshly ground black pepper to taste
1 small clove garlic, finely minced
1 large onion, finely chopped
½ cup finely diced green pepper
½ cup finely diced celery with leaves
½ cup sliced mushrooms
2 cups cooked wild rice
½ cup chopped toasted almonds
¼ teaspoon ground sage
¼ teaspoon thyme.

1. Preheat the oven to 450 degrees.

2. Rub the capon inside and outside with two tablespoons of the butter. Sprinkle inside with salt and pepper.

3. Heat four tablespoons of the butter in a skillet and cook the garlic, onion, green pepper and celery in it, stirring, until onion is translucent.

4. In a separate skillet, cook the mushrooms in remaining butter until mushrooms are wilted.

5. Combine the wild rice, onion mixture, mushrooms, almonds, sage and thyme. Add salt and pepper. Stuff the capon with the mixture. Truss capon.

6. Place the capon, breast side up, on a rack in a roasting pan and place in the oven. Immediately reduce the oven heat to 350 degrees. Bake capon, basting frequently with pan juices, twenty to twenty-five minutes to the pound.

Yield: Six servings.

Chicken with Wild Rice Casserole
Minnesota

1 cup uncooked wild rice
3 tablespoons finely chopped shallots or one-half cup chopped onion
4 tablespoons butter
4 tablespoons flour
1½ cups chicken broth
1½ cups light cream
¼ teaspoon nutmeg
  Salt and freshly ground black pepper to taste

¼ pound mushrooms, thinly sliced
3 cups diced cooked chicken
2 tablespoons finely chopped parsley
2 tablespoons freshly grated Parmesan
   cheese.

1. Preheat the oven to 350 degrees.
2. Cook the rice until tender according to any standard recipe. Set aside.
3. Cook the shallots or onion in two tablespoons of the butter, but do not brown. Sprinkle with the flour and stir until blended. Add the broth and cream, stirring rapidly with a wire whisk. When blended and smooth, simmer, stirring, about five minutes. Season with the nutmeg, salt and pepper.
4. Sauté the mushrooms in the remaining butter and add to sauce. Add the rice, chicken and parsley. Spoon mixture into a two-quart casserole and sprinkle with the cheese. Bake twenty-five to thirty minutes.
Yield: Eight servings.

Chicken with Caraway Seeds   *Iowa*

2 tablespoons flour
2 tablespoons potato flour (if not available, use all regular flour)
   Salt and freshly ground black pepper to taste
1 four-pound chicken, cut into serving pieces
⅓ cup shortening
2 tablespoons caraway seeds, lightly crushed
½ cup chicken broth
2 cups sour cream, at room temperature.

1. Preheat the oven to 300 degrees.
2. Combine the flour and potato flour, season with salt and pepper and coat chicken pieces with the mixture.
3. Heat the shortening in a heavy skillet and brown the chicken pieces in it on all sides. Transfer chicken to a casserole.
4. Add the caraway seeds, broth and one cup of the sour cream. Cover the casserole and bake

one and one-half hours. Just before serving, stir in the remaining sour cream.
Yield: Four to six servings.

Iowa Fried Chicken

1 three-pound chicken, cut into serving pieces
3 cups milk
⅓ cup flour
   Salt and freshly ground black pepper to taste
½ teaspoon sweet paprika
¼ cup shortening.

1. Dip the chicken pieces in one cup of the milk. Place the flour, salt, pepper and paprika in a sack. Shake two chicken pieces at a time in the sack until well coated. Reserve remaining flour.
2. Melt the shortening in a heavy skillet. If electric skillet is used, set at 300 degrees. Over burner, use medium heat. Fry the chicken on one side fifteen minutes, or until well browned. Turn with tongs and brown the other side.
3. Season with salt and pepper and cover. Lower heat in electric skillet to 275 degrees or to medium-low on burner and cook twenty minutes. Transfer chicken to a warm platter.
4. Remove and discard all but three tablespoons of the drippings. Measure three tablespoons reserved flour and add. Stir and cook until browned lightly. Lower heat to 225 degrees and stir in the remaining milk. Cook, stirring, until gravy thickens. Serve separately.
Yield: Four servings.

Barbecued Chicken   *Ohio*

2 two-pound chickens, split for broiling
1 teaspoon salt
¼ teaspoon freshly ground black pepper
   Cayenne pepper to taste
½ teaspoon sweet paprika
½ teaspoon oregano
2 tablespoons cider vinegar
6 tablespoons olive oil

¾ cup butter, melted, yellow liquid poured off
and milky sediment discarded (clarified)
1 tablespoon Worcestershire sauce
2 tablespoons lemon juice.

1. Day before, rub the chicken halves with
salt, pepper, cayenne and paprika. Combine the
oregano, vinegar and oil and brush all over the
chicken. Put chicken in a bowl or dish. Pour
remaining oil mixture over chicken, cover and
refrigerate overnight. Turn three times.

2. Next day, prepare a charcoal fire, starting at
least forty-five minutes before you intend to cook.
Let the fire burn until it dies down to a moderate
heat. Remove chicken from marinade, reserving
marinade. Place chicken halves, bony side down,
on a grill over fire and grill until lightly browned.

3. Turn and lightly brown the skin side. Then
raise the grill away from the flame so chicken will
cook slowly.

4. Combine the clarified butter, Worcestershire and lemon juice and add to remaining marinade. Brush the marinade on the chicken as it
cooks or mop chicken with marinade with a wad
of cheesecloth on the end of a stick. Cook chicken
slowly, brushing or mopping with the sauce and
turning often, until done, about one hour.
Yield: Four servings.

Stuffed Chicken Legs   *Kansas*

⅓ cup butter
½ onion, finely chopped
½ cup finely diced celery
2 cups soft bread crumbs
  Salt and freshly ground black pepper to
  taste
¼ teaspoon thyme
⅛ teaspoon marjoram
2 teaspoons grated lemon rind
2 tablespoons chopped parsley
1 egg, lightly beaten
12 chicken legs, boned.

1. Preheat the oven to 350 degrees.

2. Melt one-quarter cup of the butter in a skillet and sauté the onion in it until tender. Add the
celery and cook one minute. Stir in the bread
crumbs, salt, pepper, thyme, marjoram, lemon
rind and parsley. Add the egg and mix well.

3. Stuff the legs loosely, drawing the skin over
to enclose the stuffing. Sew or secure with toothpicks. Place in a greased shallow baking dish.
Melt remaining butter and pour over chicken.
Bake fifty minutes, basting four times with pan
drippings.
Yield: Six servings.

Iowa Scalloped Chicken

1 five-pound to six-pound chicken, cut into
  serving pieces
1 bay leaf
2 ribs celery with leaves
2 sprigs parsley
1 onion, sliced
2 carrots, quartered
10 peppercorns, lightly crushed
  Salt to taste
6 tablespoons flour
⅓ cup light cream or milk
  Freshly ground black pepper to taste
1½ quarts stale bread cubes, crusts removed
½ cup butter, melted
1 cup diced celery
2 tablespoons grated onion
½ green pepper, finely diced
1 teaspoon powdered sage.

1. Place the chicken in a heavy casserole or
Dutch oven. Add water barely to cover. Add bay
leaf, celery ribs, parsley, sliced onion, carrots,
peppercorns and salt.

2. Bring to a boil, cover and simmer until tender, about one hour. Let chicken cool in the
broth, overnight if possible, because it is easier to
remove the chicken fat for use in the sauce.

3. Remove skin and bones from chicken and
cut meat into large cubes; reserve. Remove fat
and reserve. Boil the broth in the casserole until

it is reduced to five cups and has good flavor. Strain the broth; reserve.

4. Preheat the oven to 350 degrees.

5. Melt six tablespoons reserved chicken fat, blend in the flour and gradually stir in the cream and one quart of the broth. Bring to a boil, stirring. Season with salt and pepper and cook over boiling water two to three minutes or longer.

6. Combine the bread cubes with the butter, diced celery, grated onion, green pepper, sage and remaining strained broth. Season with salt and pepper.

7. Place reserved chicken in the bottom of a greased three-quart casserole or baking dish. Top with the bread mixture and pour the sauce over all, using a fork to help sauce to be distributed evenly. Bake forty-five minutes, or until browned on top and hot.

Yield: Six to eight servings.

Iowa Chicken and Corn Pudding

1 three-pound chicken, cut into small serving pieces
  Salt and freshly ground black pepper
1 bay leaf
1 three-inch piece celery and sprig of parsley, tied together
2 cups water
2 cups milk, scalded
3 eggs, lightly beaten
4 cups corn kernels, cut from the cob, or three cups drained canned corn
⅛ teaspoon cayenne pepper
¼ cup buttered soft bread crumbs
2 tablespoons flour
  Cold water.

1. Preheat the oven to 350 degrees.

2. Place the chicken, salt and pepper to taste, bay leaf, celery and parsley and two cups water in a heavy pan. Bring to a boil, cover and simmer until chicken is barely tender, about thirty-five minutes.

3. Remove the chicken to a buttered baking dish and season with salt and pepper to taste. Strain broth and reduce by boiling to give two cups; reserve.

4. Beat the milk into the eggs. Add the corn, one teaspoon salt, one-quarter teaspoon black pepper and the cayenne and pour over the chicken. Top with the bread crumbs and bake twenty to twenty-five minutes, or until set.

5. Mix the flour with a little cold water and gradually stir in the reduced broth. Heat, stirring, until the mixture thickens. Season to taste. Serve separately with the chicken and corn pudding.

Yield: Four servings.

Chicken Loaf   *Iowa*

3 cups cooked chicken, finely diced or ground
1 cup soft bread crumbs
3 eggs, lightly beaten
1 cup heavy cream
  Salt and freshly ground black pepper to taste
2 tablespoons melted butter
1 tablespoon chopped parsley
4 slices lean bacon.

1. Preheat the oven to 350 degrees.

2. Place the chicken and bread crumbs in a bowl. Combine the eggs and cream and pour over chicken and crumbs. Mix well. Season with salt and pepper.

3. Stir in the butter and parsley. Pack into a greased loaf pan. Top with the bacon and bake one hour, or until set.

Yield: Four servings.

Chicken à la King   *Indiana*

4 tablespoons butter
1 cup thinly sliced mushrooms
¼ cup chopped green pepper
¼ cup flour
1½ cups rich chicken broth
1 cup heavy cream

Salt and freshly ground black pepper to taste
3 cups cooked, boneless, skinless chicken, cut into large cubes
1 tablespoon finely chopped parsley
2 tablespoons diced pimentos
1 cup fresh or frozen green peas, cooked
2 egg yolks
3 tablespoons medium-dry sherry.

1. Melt the butter in a saucepan and cook the mushrooms in it, stirring occasionally, until they give up most of their liquid. Continue cooking until most of the moisture evaporates. Add the green pepper. Sprinkle with the flour and blend, using a wire whisk.

2. Add the broth, stirring rapidly with whisk. Bring to a boil and, when thickened and smooth, stir in the cream. Season with salt and pepper. Cook, stirring, about ten minutes.

3. Add the chicken, parsley, pimentos and peas. Bring mixture to a boil; then lower heat. Blend the egg yolks with the sherry and stir into sauce. Do not boil or sauce might curdle. Serve piping hot on toast triangles.

Yield: Six to eight servings.

Chicken Corn Bread   Ohio

1 recipe chicken à la king (page 360), omitting the egg yolks and sherry
1 pound link pork sausages
¼ cup yellow corn meal
¾ cup flour
1 teaspoon baking powder
¼ teaspoon salt
1 tablespoon sugar
1 egg, beaten
½ cup milk
3 tablespoons melted butter.

1. Preheat the oven to 425 degrees.
2. Use the chicken mixture to half fill a casserole.

3. Cook the sausages in a skillet until they are almost done.

4. Sift together the corn meal, flour, baking powder, salt and sugar. Combine the egg, milk and butter and stir into the dry ingredients. Stir only to mix. Spoon over chicken.

5. Top with sausage. Bake twenty-five minutes.

Yield: Six servings.

Hot Chicken Salad   Oklahoma

2 cups diced cooked chicken
½ teaspoon salt
⅛ teaspoon freshly ground black pepper
1 tablespoon grated onion
2 cups diced celery
1 cup mayonnaise
2 tablespoons lemon juice
½ cup slivered almonds
½ cup grated sharp Cheddar cheese
½ cup buttered croutons.

1. Preheat the oven to 450 degrees.
2. Mix together all the ingredients except the cheese and croutons and turn into a greased baking dish.
3. Combine the cheese and croutons and sprinkle over top. Bake fifteen minutes.

Yield: Four servings.

Pressed Chicken   Iowa

1 four-pound to five-pound chicken, cut into serving pieces
1 bay leaf
2 ribs celery, quartered
2 sprigs parsley
1 small onion, sliced
Salt and freshly ground black pepper to taste
1 envelope unflavored gelatin
Cayenne pepper to taste
1 tablespoon finely grated onion

Mayonnaise
10 hard-cooked eggs, yolks and whites
separated
1 tablespoon chopped parsley
⅓ cup very finely chopped celery
Salad greens.

1. Place the chicken pieces in a heavy casserole or Dutch oven. Add the bay leaf, celery ribs, parsley sprigs, sliced onion and enough water barely to cover the chicken. Season with salt and pepper.

2. Bring to a boil, cover and simmer slowly until chicken is tender, about one hour. Remove chicken. Discard skin and bones and grind chicken meat. There should be about three to four cups. Season lightly and reserve.

3. Strain the cooking broth into a saucepan and boil to reduce to two cups.

4. Soften the gelatin in one-half cup cold water. Add to the two cups hot concentrated broth. Season with cayenne. Allow to cool slightly.

5. Mix the grated onion and one tablespoon mayonnaise, stir in a little cooled gelatin mixture and return to bulk of mixture. Cool.

6. Lightly oil a loaf pan and line lengthwise with a double strip of wax paper with the ends extending above each end of pan. Arrange chicken in pan. Pour three-quarters cup of the cooled gelatin-broth mixture over chicken.

7. Mash the hard-cooked egg yolks, mix with the chopped parsley and add in a layer to the loaf pan. Add one-half cup gelatin-broth mixture.

8. Mash the hard-cooked egg whites, mix with the chopped celery and add in a top layer to the loaf pan. Pour remaining gelatin-broth mixture over all. Press down with hands. Chill until firm.

9. Unmold on salad greens and serve, sliced, with mayonnaise.

Yield: Six servings.

Tongue and Chicken Mold   *Iowa*

2 eggs, lightly beaten
½ cup cider vinegar

2 teaspoons sugar
¼ teaspon dry mustard
Salt and freshly ground black pepper to taste
1 tablespoon butter
2 cups diced cooked chicken
1½ cups chopped celery
3 tablespoons chopped parsley
1 teaspoon finely grated onion
2 tablespoons mayonnaise
1 envelope unflavored gelatin
2 tablespoons cold water
1 cup boiling chicken broth
½ cup beef broth
1 tablespoon lemon juice
¼ teaspoon Worcestershire sauce
12 one-eighth-inch-thick slices cooked beef tongue
Salad greens.

1. Combine the eggs, vinegar, sugar, mustard, salt and pepper in the top of a double boiler. Cook over hot water, stirring, until mixture thickens. Do not allow to boil.

2. Whirl in the butter and cool.

3. Mix together the chicken, celery, parsley, onion, mayonnaise and cooled salad dressing. Season with salt and pepper.

4. Soften the gelatin in the cold water. Add the boiling broth and stir to dissolve gelatin. Add the beef broth, lemon juice and Worcestershire and cool mixture until it starts to thicken.

5. Dip the tongue slices in the gelatin mixture and line the bottom and sides of a lightly oiled loaf pan. Add remaining gelatin mixture to the chicken salad and spoon into the pan. Chill well.

6. Unmold on a bed of salad greens.

Yield: Six servings.

Barbecued Venison   *Oklahoma*

6 venison steaks or one-half-inch-thick slices from roast
1 tablespoon salt
½ teaspoon rosemary

½ teaspoon oregano
1 tablespoon whole pickling spices
¼ cup dry red wine
1 clove garlic, finely chopped
½ cup chopped onion
2 tablespoons butter
2 tablespoons cider vinegar
⅛ teaspoon freshly ground black pepper
½ teaspoon dry mustard
1 eight-ounce can tomato sauce
2 tablespoons lemon juice
2 tablespoons light brown sugar
2 tablespoons Worcestershire sauce.

1. Place the steaks or slices in a large porcelainized iron casserole. Add the salt, rosemary, oregano, pickling spices, wine, garlic and enough water barely to cover.

2. Bring to a boil, cover and simmer until the meat is tender, about one hour, depending on the cut and tenderness of venison. Allow meat to cool in liquid.

3. Sauté the onion in the butter in a saucepan. Add the vinegar, pepper, mustard, tomato sauce, one-half cup water, the lemon juice, brown sugar and Worcestershire. Bring to a boil and simmer five minutes.

4. Grill the venison meat six inches from a moderately hot charcoal fire, basting frequently with the hot barbecue sauce and turning often until well glazed. Serve extra sauce separately.

Yield: Six servings.

Roast Saddle or Leg of Venison

Indiana

20 thin shoestring strips of salt pork
 1 six-pound to seven-pound saddle or leg of venison
 1 clove garlic
   Salt and freshly ground black pepper
 6 tablespoons butter
 6 slices bacon.

1. Preheat the oven to 550 degrees.

2. Use a larding needle to insert salt pork into venison. Or pierce meat in various places with an ice pick and insert salt pork. Rub meat with garlic and sprinkle with salt and pepper. Rub meat with butter and place, fat side up, on a rack in an open roasting pan. Arrange bacon over roast.

3. Place the roast in the oven and reduce oven heat to 350 degrees. Cook meat twenty minutes to the pound, basting frequently with pan juices. Serve with herbed game sauce (recipe below).

Yield: Eight servings.

Herbed Game Sauce

Indiana

½ cup butter
⅓ cup currant jelly
1 teaspoon Worcestershire sauce, or more to taste
  Salt to taste
½ teaspoon each chopped rosemary, savory and thyme.

1. In a small saucepan, heat the butter and stir in the jelly. Cook over low heat, stirring, just until jelly melts. Add the remaining ingredients.

2. Bring just to the boiling point, but do not boil. Remove the sauce from the heat and let stand thirty minutes.

Yield: About one cup.

Note: When game is to be charcoal grilled, baste lightly with this sauce just before removing the meat from the grill. Serve remaining sauce separately. The sauce should be hot, but it should never be allowed to boil. Serve with deer, duck, goose and other wild game. Do not serve with pheasant, quail or grouse.

Venison Braten

Minnesota

2 cups dry red wine
1 cup red wine vinegar
1 tablespoon peppercorns
1 teaspoon salt
1 large bay leaf

4 whole allspice
4 whole cloves
1 clove garlic, peeled
1 onion, thinly sliced
3 ribs celery, coarsely chopped
2 carrots, coarsely chopped
4 sprigs parsley
1 four-pound to six-pound
   venison roast
¼ cup diced salt pork
2 cups fresh or canned beef broth
3 tablespoons cornstarch
   Buttered noodles.

1. Combine the wine, vinegar, peppercorns, salt, bay leaf, allspice, cloves, garlic, onion, celery, carrots and parsley in a large mixing bowl. Add the venison and cover. Let stand in a cold place or refrigerate for three days, turning the meat in the marinade twice a day.

2. Remove the meat. Strain the marinating liquid and reserve both the liquid and the vegetables. Pat the meat dry with paper towels. Bring the liquid to a boil and simmer over very low heat while the venison cooks. The liquid will be used for basting.

3. Heat the salt pork in a large heavy casserole and, when salt pork is rendered of fat, remove the cubes of pork. Add the venison and brown it thoroughly on all sides. Pour off excess fat from the casserole. Add the reserved vegetables and one cup of the broth. Cover tightly and cook over low heat three and one-half to four hours, or until meat is tender. As the meat cooks, it must be basted frequently with the simmering marinade and the remaining broth. Before the meat is done, all this liquid should be added.

4. Remove the meat to a hot platter and keep warm. Strain the cooking liquid and press as much of the reserved vegetables through the sieve as possible. Skim off the fat. Blend the cornstarch with a little cold water and stir into the sauce. Slice venison and serve the sauce separately. Serve with buttered noodles.

Yield: Eight to ten servings.

Wild Burgers   *Oklahoma*

2 pounds ground venison, elk
   or antelope
1 large onion, chopped
2 teaspoons dry mustard
1 clove garlic, finely chopped
1 tablespoon Worcestershire sauce
   Salt and freshly ground black pepper to
   taste
¼ cup oil or shortening.

1. Combine the meat. onion, mustard, garlic, Worcestershire, salt and pepper. Shape into patties.

2. Heat the oil or shortening in a skillet and fry the patties in it slowly until cooked through and browned.

Yield: Eight servings.

Wichita Duck   *Kansas*

1 five-and-one-half-pound duck
½ seedless orange, peeled
   Salt
   Duck giblets
½ cup orange juice
1 cup dry white wine
   Peel of one orange
¼ cup bitter orange marmalade
   Madeira wine to taste (optional)
1 tablespoon cornstarch
1 tablespoon butter.

1. Preheat the oven to 400 degrees.

2. Wipe the duck inside and outside and place the orange half in the cavity. Truss or skewer the duck. Rub the breast with salt. Roast the duck fifteen minutes to the pound, basting with pan drippings. The duck is done when drippings from the cavity run clear when the duck is lifted.

3. While the duck cooks, place the giblets in a saucepan and add water to cover. Add a little salt and simmer until giblets are thoroughly tender.

Let cool slightly; then chop. Reserve one-half cup of the liquid in which giblets cooked.

4. When the duck is done, remove it from the pan and pour off the fat. Add the reserved giblet liquid to the pan and scrape to dissolve brown particles that cling to the bottom and sides. Add the orange juice and white wine.

5. Cut the orange peel into very thin strips and cook briefly in water. Drain. Add the peel to the sauce. Add the marmalade and the chopped giblets. Stir. Add the Madeira.

6. Using the fingers, blend the cornstarch and butter. Stir bit by bit into the simmering sauce and thicken slightly. Serve with carved duck.

Yield: Four servings.

Cold Pickled Duck   *Minnesota*

 1 four-pound to five-pound duck
½ lemon
½ cup sugar
 1 cup coarse salt
1½ teaspoons saltpeter
 1 tablespoon juniper berries, crushed (optional)
½ leek, sliced
 1 bay leaf
 2 sprigs parsley
 2 ribs celery, diced.

1. Wash and dry the duck. Rub inside and outside with the lemon half. Combine one-quarter cup sugar, one-half cup salt and one teaspoon saltpeter and rub into the inside and outside of the duck.

2. Refrigerate the duck for twenty-four hours.

3. Prepare a brine in a large kettle by combining remaining sugar, salt and saltpeter with eight cups water and the crushed juniper berries if desired. Heat, stirring, until boiling. Cool.

4. Place duck in the brine so that duck is completely submerged. Refrigerate two to three days.

5. Remove duck from brine and place in a heavy casserole with the leek, bay leaf, parsley, celery and enough water to cover. Bring to a boil,

cover and simmer gently about one hour, or until duck is tender. Allow duck to cool in the liquid.

6. Serve duck cold, thinly sliced, as an appetizer or luncheon entree.

Yield: One dozen appetizer servings or four entree servings.

Grilled Duck Breasts   *Indiana*

 3 wild ducks
10 tablespoons butter
   Salt and freshly ground black pepper to taste
¼ cup medium-dry sherry or dry white wine
¼ cup strong-flavored chicken broth
¼ pound mushrooms, sliced
   Wild or brown rice.

1. Prepare a charcoal fire for broiling.

2. Carefully remove the breasts from the ducks. This will yield six whole pieces plus six thin strips called fillets.

3. Melt eight tablespoons of the butter in a skillet. Sprinkle breasts with salt and pepper. Dip the breast meat in the melted butter and place the pieces, including the fillets, on the grill. Cook the breast meat about two and one-half minutes to each side. The fillets will cook more quickly. Slice the breast meat into bite-size pieces.

4. Add the sherry or white wine and broth to the melted butter. Add the duck pieces and simmer about one minute.

5. Meanwhile, cook the mushrooms in the remaining butter and add to the saucepan. Serve with wild or brown rice.

Yield: Six servings.

Baked Wild Duck Breasts en Casserole
                           Minnesota

3 wild ducks
  Flour
  Salt to taste
¼ cup butter

Grated rind of one orange
1½ cups heavy cream, approximately
½ cup dry sherry
Freshly ground black pepper to taste.

1. Preheat the oven to 350 degrees.
2. Carefully remove the breasts from the ducks and dredge breasts in flour seasoned with salt.
3. Brown breasts in the butter in a heavy skillet. Arrange the breasts in a casserole.
4. Sprinkle the orange rind on top of the breasts. Pour the cream and sherry over the ducks and sprinkle with salt and pepper. Bake two hours, adding more cream during baking if necessary.
Yield: Three to six servings.

Smothered Quail   *Minnesota*

6 quail, cleaned
   Salt and freshly ground black pepper to taste
   Flour
¼ cup bacon drippings
2 tablespoons butter
3 tablespoons water
12 slices crisp bacon.

1. Sprinkle the quail inside and outside with salt and pepper. Dredge lightly on the outside with flour.
2. Heat the bacon drippings and butter in a heavy iron skillet and place the quail, breast side down, in the skillet. Cook until browned. Turn breast side up. When quail are brown on the bottom, add the water.
3. Put on a cover that will fit inside the skillet. The quail must be covered closely. Add a weight such as a flat iron to the cover and cook quail over moderate heat about thirty minutes, or until tender. Serve topped with bacon.
Yield: Six servings.

Braised Quail with Sherry   *Indiana*

6 quail, halved or quartered
   Salt and freshly ground black pepper
   Flour
7 tablespoons butter
12 small white onions
½ teaspoon sugar
½ cup finely chopped celery
1 tablespoon cornstarch
1 cup fresh or canned chicken broth
½ bay leaf
2 tablespoons sherry
2 tablespoons finely chopped parsley.

1. Preheat the oven to 325 degrees.
2. Sprinkle the quail with salt and pepper and dredge them lightly in flour.
3. Heat two tablespoons of the butter in a small skillet and add the onions. Sprinkle with the sugar and brown all over. Cover and cook fifteen minutes.
4. Heat the remaining butter in a large heavy skillet and brown the quail pieces in it on all sides. Remove quail pieces to a casserole and keep warm. Add the celery to the skillet and cook briefly, stirring. Add celery to the casserole.
5. Blend the cornstarch with the broth and pour this over quail. Add the bay leaf, cover and bake thirty minutes.
6. Add onions and the sherry to casserole. Bake, covered, fifteen minutes longer, or until quail are thoroughly tender. Serve sprinkled with the parsley.
Yield: Six servings.

Doves Wyatt Earp   *Minnesota*

10 doves, well cleaned
    Salt and freshly ground black pepper to taste
2 tablespoons butter
2 tablespoons beef suet
1 medium-size head cabbage, trimmed and cut into eighths

6 large carrots
1 teaspoon sage leaves
1 cup cooked lima beans
1 large onion, diced
  Buttered boiled potatoes
1 cup cooked macaroni.

1. Split the doves in half; then separate the legs, back sections and breasts. Sprinkle with salt and pepper.

2. Melt the butter and suet in a skillet and brown the dove pieces in it on all sides.

3. Place the cabbage, carrots, sage, lima beans and onion in a large kettle. Add the browned dove pieces and enough water to cover all by a depth of two inches. Add the drippings from the skillet in which the birds were browned. Add salt and pepper and bring to a boil.

4. Simmer slowly about one and one-half hours, or until vegetables and meat are tender. Serve the dove pieces with boiled potatoes. Serve the kettle vegetables separately. Add the cooked macaroni to the soup liquid and serve separately.

Yield: Six or more servings.

Fried Squirrel   *Indiana*

1 squirrel, cleaned and cut into serving pieces
  Milk
  Tabasco sauce to taste
  Flour
  Salt and freshly ground black pepper
¼ pound butter
½ pound lard or other shortening.

1. Place the squirrel pieces in a mixing bowl and add milk to cover and Tabasco. Let stand an hour or so in the refrigerator.

2. Drain the squirrel pieces and dredge lightly in flour seasoned with salt and pepper.

3. In a skillet, heat the butter and lard or other shortening and, when butter is just melted, add squirrel pieces. Cook until golden brown on both sides. If desired, skillet may be partially covered

while squirrel cooks. When squirrel is done, drain on paper towels.

Yield: Four servings.

Rabbit à la Crème   *Minnesota*

1 large rabbit, skinned, cleaned and cut into serving pieces
  Cider vinegar
1 onion, sliced
1 carrot, sliced
2 sprigs parsley
1 bay leaf
2 sprigs fresh thyme or one-half teaspoon dried thyme
12 peppercorns
  Salt
¾ cup flour
  Freshly ground black pepper to taste
¼ cup butter, lard or oil
½ cup chicken broth
¾ cup heavy cream or sour cream
  Buttered noodles.

1. Place the rabbit in a large mixing bowl and add equal parts water and vinegar to cover. Add the onion, carrot, parsley, bay leaf, thyme, peppercorns and one teaspoon salt. Cover and let stand in the refrigerator two days.

2. Drain the rabbit. Strain and reserve the liquid.

3. Dredge the rabbit pieces in the flour seasoned with salt and pepper. Brown rabbit well in the butter, lard or oil, but do not burn.

4. Add enough of the reserved liquid to cover the bottom of the skillet to the depth of one-quarter inch. Cover and simmer over low heat until rabbit is done, one hour or longer.

5. Transfer the rabbit to a warm platter and add the broth to the skillet. Cook, stirring, until well blended. Turn off the heat. Stir in the cream. Heat thoroughly and season to taste with salt and pepper. If the sour cream is used, do not let it boil

or it will curdle. Pour the sauce over the rabbit and serve with buttered noodles.

Yield: Four to six servings.

Pan-Fried Frogs' Legs   *Oklahoma*

12 pairs frogs' legs
 3 tablespoons cider vinegar
 3 tablespoons salt
½ cup heavy cream or evaporated milk
 1 cup flour
¼ teaspoon freshly ground black pepper

½ clove garlic, finely chopped
½ cup butter.

1. Clean and skin the legs and place in a shallow dish. Combine the vinegar and salt, pour over legs and add enough water just to cover the legs.

2. Soak at least two hours. Drain and pat dry. Dip in the cream or milk. Coat with the flour mixed with the pepper and garlic.

3. Heat the butter in a large skillet and fry the legs in it quickly, turning once, until tender, about ten minutes. Do not overcook.

Yield: Four servings.

Vegetables, Main Dish Accompaniments and Salads

Asparagus Pudding   *Ohio*

4 eggs, lightly beaten
2 tablespoons flour
2 tablespoons melted butter
1 cup milk
2 tablespoons ground cooked smoked ham
1 cup asparagus tips, diced
  Salt and freshly ground black pepper to
  taste.

1. Beat the eggs with the flour, melted butter
and milk until smooth. Beat in the ham.
2. Stir in the asparagus tips and season with
salt and pepper. Pour into a greased mold or
basin. Cover with wax paper and then aluminum
foil. Set on a rack in a pan of boiling water and
steam one and one-half to two hours, or until set.
Turn out and serve with butter sauce (recipe below).
Yield: Four servings.

Butter Sauce   *Ohio*

1 tablespoon flour
3 tablespoons water
½ cup butter
½ teaspoon lemon juice
  Salt to taste
⅛ teaspoon nutmeg.

Mix the flour to a paste with the water. Place
in a saucepan and add the remaining ingredients.
Heat, stirring, until mixture thickens, but do not
allow to boil.
Yield: About one-half cup.

Snibbled Beans   *Ohio*

2 pounds string beans, trimmed and cut into
    very thin lengthwise strips (French style),
    or two packages frozen French-style beans
    Salt to taste
1 large white onion
6 slices bacon
2 eggs
½ cup cider vinegar
½ cup sugar
    Freshly ground black pepper to taste.

1. If fresh beans are used, place them in a kettle and add water to cover and salt. Bring to a boil
and cook until beans are crisp-tender. If frozen
beans are used, cook them according to package
directions. Drain the beans.
2. Cut the onion into wafer-thin rings and
sprinkle over the beans.
3. Cook the bacon until crisp, but do not let
bacon drippings burn. Crumble the bacon and
sprinkle it over the onion rings. Pour off half the
drippings from the skillet.
4. Blend together the eggs, vinegar and sugar.

Beat well. Pour this into the hot drippings and stir just until thoroughly hot. Pour the sauce over the beans, add salt and pepper and toss.

Yield: Six to eight servings.

Rice and Green Bean Casserole   *Ohio*

1 pound green beans, cut diagonally into one-inch pieces
  Boiling salted water
1 cup uncooked rice
2 cups boiling chicken broth
1 teaspoon salt
1 small onion, finely chopped
3 tablespoons butter
1 cup diced celery
1 sixteen-ounce can tomatoes
1¼ cups grated sharp Cheddar cheese
½ cup buttered soft bread crumbs.

1. Preheat the oven to 350 degrees.
2. Cook the beans until barely tender in a little boiling salted water. Drain. Add the rice to the broth and add one-half teaspoon of the salt. Cover and simmer twenty minutes until water has been absorbed.
3. Sauté the onion in the butter and add to the rice. Stir in the beans, celery, tomatoes, remaining salt and one cup of the cheese.
4. Turn into a greased casserole. Sprinkle with the buttered bread crumbs and remaining cheese. Bake twenty minutes.

Yield: Eight servings.

Pioneer Leatherbritches   *Ohio*

2 pounds string beans, washed, dried, ends and strings removed if tough
  Piece of salt pork or a ham hock.

1. With a strong needle and button thread, string the beans on the thread. Hang up to dry either in the sun or near the stove.

2. To cook, remove beans from thread and soak overnight in water to cover. Next day, place beans and soak water in a kettle. Add a piece of salt pork or a ham hock and simmer until tender, three to four hours.

Yield: Eight servings.

Missouri Country-Style Green Beans

3½ pounds green beans, preferably the pole variety
¼ cup bacon drippings
1 cup water, approximately
2 fresh ham hocks
4 small white onions
2 teaspoons salt.

1. Wash the beans, remove strings and break beans into large, three-inch pieces. Heat the bacon drippings in a large heavy kettle.
2. Add beans and stir to coat. When beans have turned a bright green, add one cup water. Bring to a boil and then simmer.
3. Trim skin from hocks and add hocks to beans. Lift up beans and place hocks under beans. Cover kettle and simmer four to six hours.
4. Add more water during cooking if needed to maintain about one cup. Add the onions during the last forty-five minutes of cooking. Season with salt.

Yield: One dozen servings.

Tangy Beets   *Indiana*

8 small beets, trimmed and scrubbed
  Boiling salted water
1 tablespoon cornstarch
1 tablespoon sugar
⅔ cup orange juice
2 tablespoons lemon juice
2 tablespoons butter
¼ teaspoon salt
2 teaspoons grated horseradish.

1. Place the beets in a saucepan, cover with boiling salted water and simmer until beets are tender, about twenty minutes if small. Peel beets and slice.

2. Combine the cornstarch and sugar in a small saucepan. Stir in the orange juice, lemon juice, butter and salt. Bring to a boil, stirring, and cook two minutes. Add the horseradish and pour sauce over the beets.

Yield: Six servings.

Beanhole Beans
Michigan

2 cups dried pea beans or navy beans
¼ pound salt pork
1 onion
1 teaspoon salt
2 tablespoons molasses
2 tablespoons light brown sugar
½ cup tomato sauce.

1. Day before, pick over and wash the beans. Cover with water and let soak overnight.

2. Next day, put beans and liquid in a heavy kettle with the salt pork, onion and salt. Bring to a boil and simmer until beans are barely tender, about forty-five minutes.

3. Turn into an old-fashioned Dutch oven and add the remaining ingredients. Dig a hole twice as deep as the pot. Place flat rocks in the bottom of hole and build a charcoal or wood fire on top. When beans are ready, remove coals onto more rocks, set pot down in hole, cover and push a layer of dirt on top. Set coals and hot rocks on top. Leave overnight or all day.

Yield: Eight servings.

Lima Bean and Cottage Cheese Loaf
Ohio

1 cup dried lima beans
Salt
1 cup drained canned tomatoes
1 tablespoon finely chopped onion

2 cups cottage cheese
¼ teaspoon freshly ground black pepper
1½ cups dry bread crumbs
2 tablespoons melted butter
1 egg, lightly beaten
2 cups homemade tomato sauce.

1. Day before, pick over and wash the beans. Cover with water and let soak overnight. Next day, drain beans and cover with lightly salted water. Bring to a boil and simmer until beans are tender, about forty-five minutes. Drain beans and chop coarsely.

2. Preheat the oven to 350 degrees.

3. Add the tomatoes, onion, cottage cheese, pepper, bread crumbs, butter, egg and salt to taste to beans. Mix well. Turn into a greased loaf pan or casserole and bake forty-five minutes, or until firm. Serve with the tomato sauce.

Yield: Six servings.

Mrs. Sylvester's Baked Kidney Beans
Illinois

1 pound dried kidney beans
Salt
2 large onions, chopped
2 large green peppers, cored, seeded and chopped
1 cup light brown sugar
1 cup catchup
6 slices bacon.

1. Day before, pick over and wash the beans. Cover with water and soak overnight. Next day, put in a kettle with one teaspoon salt, bring to a boil and simmer until tender, about forty-five minutes.

2. Preheat the oven to 350 degrees.

3. Drain beans and keep liquid. Place beans in a large casserole and add the onions, green peppers, brown sugar and catchup. Add reserved liquid until it is just visible. Top with the bacon and bake two hours. Add more liquid during bak-

ing as necessary. Check seasoning and add salt if necessary.

Yield: Eight servings.

Grandmother's Lima Bean Bake

Iowa

2 cups dried lima beans
1½ teaspoons salt
¼ cup unsulphured molasses
¼ cup chili sauce
1 tablespoon cider vinegar
  Cayenne pepper to taste
½ teaspoon dry mustard
1 onion, chopped
1 cup diced cooked smoked ham
6 slices bacon.

1. Day before, wash and pick over the beans. Cover with water and let soak overnight. Next day, add the salt and simmer until beans are almost tender, about forty-five minutes.
2. Preheat the oven to 325 degrees.
3. Drain beans, reserving liquid. Combine the molasses, chili sauce, vinegar, cayenne and mustard. Mix with one cup of reserved liquid.
4. Layer the beans with the onion and ham in a deep casserole. Pour the molasses mixture over all. Top with the bacon. Bake, uncovered, one and one-half hours, adding more liquid during baking if necessary.

Yield: Six servings.

Broccoli Ring

Kansas

1½ bunches broccoli, trimmed into single
     stalks and washed
     Boiling salted water
¼ cup lemon juice
1 tablespoon finely grated onion
1 teaspoon salt
¼ teaspoon freshly ground black pepper
6 eggs, lightly beaten

2¼ cups milk
½ cup soft bread crumbs.

1. Preheat the oven to 325 degrees.
2. Cook one bunch broccoli in boiling salted water until tender; drain. Mash or chop very finely. Add the lemon juice, onion, salt and pepper.
3. Mix the eggs and milk together, pour over mashed broccoli and stir in the bread crumbs. Pour into a well-greased ring mold, set in a pan of hot water and bake one hour, or until set. Cook remaining broccoli.
4. Allow ring to stand five minutes before unmolding. Fill center with remaining cooked broccoli.

Yield: Ten servings.

Broccoli with Ham and Cheese

Illinois

1 large bunch broccoli
  Boiling salted water
½ cup olive oil
2 cloves garlic, finely chopped
3 tablespoons lemon juice
½ teaspoon oregano
⅓ cup finely diced or ground ham
  Salt and freshly ground black pepper to
  taste
⅓ cup freshly grated Parmesan cheese.

1. Trim the broccoli and separate into stalks. Wash and drain. Cook by placing stalks in boiling salted water so that the flower part is upright and will steam. Cover and cook ten to fifteen minutes, or until crisp-tender. Drain broccoli and place in a heatproof casserole or serving dish.
2. Heat the oil and sauté the garlic in it a minute or two without browning. Stir in the lemon juice, oregano, ham, salt and pepper.
3. Pour ham mixture over the broccoli, sprinkle with the cheese and brown briefly under a preheated broiler.

Yield: Six servings.

Cream Cabbage
Michigan

1 small head cabbage, shredded
Boiling salted water
2 egg yolks
½ cup sugar
½ cup cider vinegar
3 tablespoons butter
1 cup heavy cream
Salt and freshly ground black pepper to taste.

1. Barely cover the shredded cabbage with boiling salted water, cover and cook until barely tender, about eight minutes. Drain well.

2. Combine the egg yolks, sugar, vinegar and butter in a saucepan and heat, stirring, until mixture thickens. Gradually stir in the cream and heat. Season with salt and pepper. Pour sauce over hot drained cabbage.

Yield: Four to six servings.

Kale
Indiana

5 pounds kale
Boiling water
2 teaspoons salt
¼ cup butter.

1. Remove the coarse stems and the center ribs from the kale leaves. Wash very thoroughly until no sand remains.

2. Cover leaves with boiling water. Bring to a boil. Drain.

3. Cover with boiling water again and add the salt. Cover and cook until tender, about twenty-five minutes. Drain and chop.

4. Toss with the butter.

Yield: Six servings.

Wilted Lettuce
Ohio

6 slices bacon
½ clove garlic, finely chopped
¼ cup cider vinegar
2 tablespoons water
1 teaspoon sugar
1 teaspoon salt
¼ teaspoon freshly ground black pepper
8 cups lettuce leaves (Bibb, Boston or leaf lettuce), washed, drained and dried
6 scallions, including green part, chopped.

1. Cook the bacon until crisp. Drain bacon, crumble into bits and reserve in a warm place.

2. To the bacon drippings add the garlic, vinegar, water, sugar, salt and pepper. Stir and heat to boiling.

3. Place the lettuce in a large bowl and sprinkle with the scallions. Pour the hot sauce over all and toss to mix. Sprinkle with the reserved bacon bits.

Yield: Six servings.

Cabbage Casserole
Wisconsin

1 firm head cabbage, quartered
1 cup boiling salted water
½ pound sausage meat
2 tablespoons finely chopped onion
1 cup ground cooked smoked ham
1 cup soft bread crumbs
2 eggs, lightly beaten
¼ cup milk
Salt and freshly ground black pepper to taste
1 teaspoon caraway seeds.

1. Preheat the oven to 350 degrees.

2. Place the cabbage and water in a saucepan. Cover and cook until barely tender, about fifteen minutes. Drain cabbage and shred finely.

3. Meanwhile, cook the sausage meat in a skillet, stirring often, until all pinkness disappears. Remove all but one tablespoon of the fat as it forms. Add the onion and cook five minutes longer.

4. Add the ham, bread crumbs, eggs and milk to skillet. Season with salt and pepper. Stir in the

caraway seeds and cabbage. Turn into a greased casserole. Bake thirty minutes.

Yield: Six servings.

Red Cabbage and Apple   *Minnesota*

1½ tablespoons butter
 1 small head red cabbage, quartered and thinly shredded
 2 tart apples, peeled, cored and grated
 ¼ cup cider vinegar
 ½ cup red currant jelly
 ¼ cup water
 ¼ teaspoon salt
 1 teaspoon sugar.

1. Melt the butter in a heavy kettle and add the cabbage, apples, vinegar, jelly, water and salt.

2. Cover and simmer until cabbage is tender, about one hour. Stir occasionally. Stir in the sugar.

Yield: Six to eight servings.

Carrots with Celery   *Minnesota*

 6 medium-size carrots, diced
 ¾ cup boiling salted water
 1 cup diced celery
 1 small onion, finely chopped
 2 tablespoons butter
   Salt and freshly ground black pepper to taste
 1 teaspoon caraway seeds
 1 tablespoon flour
 1 tablespoon light brown sugar.

1. Place the carrots in a saucepan and add the water. Cover and simmer until carrots are barely tender, about ten minutes.

2. Meanwhile, briefly sauté the celery and onion in the butter. Add to cooked carrots. Season with salt and pepper.

3. Stir in the remaining ingredients and cook,

stirring, until mixture thickens slightly. Evaporate any excess sauce by quick boiling.

Yield: Four servings.

Crystal Carrots   *Indiana*

 1 tablespoon oil
 1 teaspoon plus two tablespoons butter
12 medium-size carrots, cut on the bias into one-half-inch-thick slices
 ⅓ cup boiling water
 ½ teaspoon salt
 2 tablespoons light brown sugar
 1 teaspoon grated lemon rind
 1 tablespoon lemon juice
 2 tablespoons chopped parsley.

1. Heat the oil and one teaspoon butter in a skillet. Add the carrots and sauté, while stirring, until carrots are shiny, about two minutes.

2. Add the water and salt, cover and simmer ten minutes or until carrots are barely tender.

3. Add the brown sugar, lemon rind, lemon juice and remaining butter. Simmer, uncovered, until sugar is melted, extra liquid evaporates and carrots are glazed. Sprinkle with the parsley.

Yield: Six servings.

Corn Pudding   *Oklahoma*

 ¼ cup butter
 ¾ cup finely chopped onion
 1 cup freshly cut corn kernels or canned whole kernel corn
 1 tablespoon sugar
   Salt and freshly ground black pepper to taste
 ½ cup grated sharp Cheddar cheese
 3 egg yolks, well beaten
 3 egg whites, stiffly beaten.

1. Preheat the oven to 350 degrees.

2. Melt the butter and cook the onion in it

until wilted. Do not brown. Add the corn, sugar, salt and pepper and cook briefly. Let cool.

3. Stir in the cheese and egg yolks. Fold in the egg whites. Pour into an oiled one-quart casserole and bake one hour. Serve immediately.

Yield: Four servings.

Corn Fritters   *Ohio*

2 eggs, lightly beaten
⅔ cup milk
½ teaspoon salt
1 tablespoon melted butter
1 cup flour
1 teaspoon baking powder
1 cup freshly cut corn kernels
   Fat or oil for deep-frying.

1. Beat the eggs with the milk, salt and butter. Sift the flour with the baking powder and beat in until smooth.

2. Stir in the corn. Drop mixture by table-spoonfuls into fat or oil for deep-frying heated to 380 degrees. Fry until golden. Drain on paper towels.

Yield: Four servings.

Corn with Chipped Beef   *Iowa*

4 tablespoons butter
1 cup (five ounces) dried beef, shredded
1½ tablespoons flour
1 twelve-ounce can whole kernel corn
   Light cream
   Salt to taste
⅛ teaspoon freshly ground black pepper
2 eggs, lightly beaten
½ cup dry bread crumbs.

1. Preheat the oven to 350 degrees.

2. Melt two tablespoons of the butter in a saucepan and frizzle the beef in it. Blend in the flour. Drain the corn and measure the corn liquid

in a one-cup measure and make up with cream. Stir into beef mixture.

3. Bring to a boil, stirring. Season with salt and pepper.

4. Remove from heat and add the eggs and corn. Turn into a greased casserole. Melt the remaining butter, combine with the bread crumbs and sprinkle over top. Set casserole in a pan of hot water and bake forty-five minutes, or until set.

Yield: Four servings.

Scalloped Corn   *Iowa*

2 cups freshly cut corn kernels
1 tablespoon butter
1 onion, finely chopped
8 soda crackers, crushed
   Salt and freshly ground black pepper to taste
1 cup milk
2 eggs, lightly beaten
1 green pepper, cored, seeded and diced
1 cup oysters with liquor (optional).

1. Preheat the oven to 350 degrees.

2. Mix all ingredients together and turn into a greased casserole. Bake forty-five to fifty minutes, or until set.

Yield: Six servings.

Corn Casserole   *Iowa*

¼ cup butter
¼ cup flour
2 teaspoons salt
4 teaspoons sugar
1⅔ cups milk
3 cups freshly cut corn kernels, chopped
3 eggs, lightly beaten
2 tablespoons freshly grated Parmesan cheese.

1. Preheat the oven to 350 degrees.

2. Melt the butter and blend in the flour, salt

and sugar. Gradually stir in the milk and bring to a boil, stirring, until mixture is thickened.

3. Stir in the corn and eggs and pour into a well-greased casserole. Sprinkle with the cheese, set casserole in a pan of hot water and bake forty minutes, or until set.

Yield: Six servings.

Eggplant Casserole   *Wisconsin*

1 medium-size eggplant
  Salt
¼ cup oil
4 tomatoes, peeled and sliced
2 green peppers, cored, seeded, and sliced
2 onions, finely chopped
1 clove garlic, finely chopped
2 teaspoons sugar
  Freshly ground black pepper to taste
¼ teaspoon thyme
½ pound grated sharp Cheddar cheese.

1. Slice the eggplant and sprinkle with salt. Let stand twenty minutes. Rinse, drain and pat dry. Heat the oil in a skillet and sauté the eggplant slices in it until browned on both sides.

2. Preheat the oven to 400 degrees.

3. In a greased casserole, alternate a layer of eggplant slices with a layer of tomatoes, green peppers, onions and garlic. Season each tomato layer with sugar, salt to taste, pepper and thyme.

4. Top with the cheese. Cover and bake ten minutes. Reduce the oven heat to 350 degrees. Remove cover and bake casserole thirty minutes longer, or until eggplant is tender.

Yield: Six servings.

Slippery Jims   *Iowa*

8 large ripe cucumbers
  Salt
4 cups white vinegar
2 cups sugar

2 tablespoons mustard seeds
1 tablespoon celery seeds.

1. Peel cucumbers, cut in half and scoop out seeds. Cut into long strips, sprinkle with salt and let stand twenty-four hours.

2. Rinse cucumber sticks and place in a skillet.

3. Combine the remaining ingredients and pour over cucumbers. Bring to a boil and simmer until cucumbers are translucent. Cool and chill.

Yield: One dozen servings.

Homemade Noodles   *Iowa*

1½ cups flour
½ teaspoon salt
1 teaspoon baking powder
3 eggs
3 tablespoons heavy cream
  Boiling chicken broth.

1. Sift the dry ingredients into a bowl. Make a well in the center and add the eggs and cream. Stir with a fork to make a dough.

2. Cover and let set ten minutes. Knead until smooth.

3. Roll out on a lightly floured table until dough is very thin. Cover with a cloth and let stand one-half hour.

4. Roll dough up from long side and cut into one-half-inch pieces. Unroll noodles and allow to dry at least two hours before boiling for about eight minutes in a kettle of boiling broth.

Yield: About one-half pound noodles; eight servings in broth.

Macaroni Deluxe   *Indiana*

1 cup uncooked elbow macaroni
  Boiling salted water
⅓ cup diced celery
½ cup heavy cream
½ cup grated sharp Cheddar cheese
1 one-pound-one-ounce can cream-style corn

½ teaspoon salt
⅛ teaspoon freshly ground black pepper
½ cup buttered soft bread crumbs.

1. Preheat the oven to 375 degrees.
2. Cook the macaroni in boiling salted water until barely tender, about eight minutes. Drain macaroni and toss with the celery.
3. Combine the remaining ingredients except the bread crumbs and stir into the macaroni and celery. Turn into a one-and-one-half-quart casserole, sprinkle with the bread crumbs and bake fifteen minutes, or until lightly browned and hot.
Yield: Four servings.

Macaroni with Mushrooms   *Michigan*

½ pound uncooked elbow macaroni
    Boiling salted water
5 tablespoons butter
1 small onion, chopped
1 pound mushrooms, sliced
1½ teaspoons flour
1 cup chicken broth
2 cups peeled, chopped and drained fresh tomatoes or strained canned tomatoes, chopped
    Salt to taste
    Cayenne pepper to taste
2 tablespoons chopped parsley
⅓ cup grated sharp Cheddar cheese.

1. Preheat the oven to 375 degrees.
2. Cook the macaroni in boiling salted water until barely tender, about eight minutes. Drain.
3. Melt the butter and sauté the onion in it until tender. Add the mushrooms and cook five minutes. Sprinkle with the flour. Stir.
4. Stir in the broth and tomatoes. Season with salt and cayenne. Add macaroni and the parsley and turn into a greased casserole.
5. Sprinkle with the cheese and bake twenty minutes, or until cheese melts.
Yield: Eight servings.

Cheese and Rice Soufflé   *Illinois*

3 tablespoons butter
3 tablespoons flour
1 cup milk
1 cup grated sharp Cheddar cheese
3 eggs, separated
½ teaspoon onion juice
    Salt and freshly ground black pepper to taste
1 cup cooked rice
    Chicken à la king (page 360) or mushroom sauce.

1. Preheat the oven to 375 degrees.
2. Melt the butter in a saucepan. Blend in the flour and gradually stir in the milk. Bring to a boil, stirring until mixture thickens. Remove from heat and stir in the cheese.
3. Beat the egg yolks and add with the onion juice, salt, pepper and rice.
4. Beat the egg whites until stiff but not dry and fold in. Turn into a greased ring mold or soufflé dish. Place in a pan of hot water. Bake forty minutes, or until well risen and brown.
5. If in a ring mold, let set five minutes and then unmold. Or serve directly from soufflé dish. Serve with chicken à la king or mushroom sauce.
Yield: Four servings.

Scallion Rice   *Illinois*

3 cups cooked rice
½ cup finely chopped scallions, including green part
1½ cups large curd cottage cheese
1 clove garlic, finely minced
1 cup sour cream
¼ cup milk
    Tabasco sauce or cayenne pepper to taste
½ teaspoon salt, or more to taste
½ cup freshly grated Parmesan cheese.

1. Preheat the oven to 350 degrees.

2. Combine the rice and scallions in a mixing bowl.

3. Blend the cottage cheese, garlic, sour cream, milk, Tabasco or cayenne and salt. Stir this into the rice mixture and turn into greased one-and-one-half-quart casserole. Sprinkle with the cheese. Bake twenty-five minutes.

Yield: Six servings.

Rice and Parsley Casserole   *Illinois*

½ cup finely chopped onion
1 clove garlic, finely minced
3 tablespoons butter
2 cups cooked rice
1 teaspoon salt
½ cup finely chopped parsley
1 cup milk
2 eggs, lightly beaten.

1. Preheat the oven to 325 degrees.
2. Cook the onion and garlic in one tablespoon of the butter until onion is wilted. Remove the skillet from the heat and add the rice.
3. Combine the salt, parsley, milk and eggs and mix thoroughly. Stir into the rice mixture.
4. Melt the remaining butter in a one-quart ovenproof casserole. Add the rice mixture and bake forty minutes.

Yield: Four to six servings.

Wild Rice and Olive Casserole   *Minnesota*

1 cup uncooked wild rice
  Boiling water
1 onion, finely chopped
6 tablespoons butter
1 cup chopped ripe olives
1 cup sliced mushrooms
1 cup grated sharp Cheddar cheese
1½ cups boiling chicken broth, approximately
1 cup drained canned tomatoes

Salt and freshly ground black pepper to taste.

1. Wash the rice in a colander. Cover rice with boiling water and let soak several hours. Drain.
2. Preheat the oven to 350 degrees.
3. Sauté the onion in four tablespoons of the butter. Place the rice, olives, mushrooms and sautéed onion in a casserole. Stir in the cheese, one and one-half cups broth and the tomatoes. Season with salt and pepper. Bake one hour, adding more broth during baking if mixture becomes too dry. Add remaining butter and toss to mix.

Yield: Six servings.

Baked Wild Rice with Carrots   *Minnesota*

1½ cups wild rice, rinsed well in cold water
2½ cups water
2 teaspoons salt
4 slices bacon, cut into tiny cubes
1 onion, finely chopped
1 cup sliced mushrooms
1 cup finely grated carrots
½ cup light cream
1 egg.

1. Combine the rice, water and salt in a large saucepan. Bring to a boil and cook vigorously ten minutes. Remove the saucepan from the heat and cover. Let stand twenty minutes, or until water has been absorbed.
2. Cook the bacon. With a slotted spoon, remove the cubes to drain on paper towels. Reserve the drippings.
3. Preheat the oven to 325 degrees.
4. Cook the onion and mushrooms in the bacon drippings until onion is wilted. Add the reserved bacon cubes, wild rice and carrots. Stir to blend.
5. Beat the cream and egg together and stir into the wild rice mixture. Cover and bake in a buttered one-and-one-half-quart casserole for one-half hour. Stir with a fork and bake fifteen minutes longer.

6. Remove the cover and stir once more. Bake fifteen minutes longer.

Yield: Six servings.

Wild Rice with Chicken Livers
Minnesota

6 ounces wild rice
2 cups chicken broth
½ cup butter
3 onions, finely chopped
1 clove garlic, finely chopped
¼ pound mushrooms, sliced
12 chicken livers (approximately three-quarters pound)
3 tablespoons cognac
Salt and freshly ground black pepper to taste
¾ teaspoon thyme
¼ teaspoon nutmeg.

1. Prepare the wild rice according to package directions, using the broth for final cooking.

2. Heat the butter in a heavy skillet and sauté the onions and garlic in it until tender but not browned. Add the mushrooms and cook three minutes.

3. Increase the heat, add the livers and brown quickly on all sides. Add the cognac and stir to loosen cooked-on particles. Add the cooked rice and toss to mix.

4. Reheat the mixture and season with salt, pepper, the thyme and nutmeg.

Yield: Six to eight servings.

Note: The wild rice and chicken liver mixture may be served as a separate vegetable, as a base for squab, poultry or game or as a stuffing.

Wild Rice Casserole
Minnesota

1½ cups uncooked wild rice
Boiling water
Salt to taste
4 slices bacon, cut into cubes

¼ pound mushrooms, sliced
¾ cup chopped onion
¼ cup chopped green pepper
½ cup chopped heart of celery
½ cup chicken broth
Chopped scallions (optional).

1. Place the wild rice in a colander and rinse well under cold water. Scoop rice into a large saucepan and add boiling water to cover. Let stand twenty minutes and drain. Add more boiling water and let stand twenty minutes longer. Drain. Continue adding water and draining until rice is almost tender, three times or more. When the last boiling water is to be used, add salt. Drain rice and turn into a baking dish.

2. Preheat the oven to 350 degrees.

3. Cook the bacon until it is golden brown. Pour off all but two tablespoons bacon drippings and add the mushrooms, onion, green pepper and celery. Cook until vegetables are wilted. Spoon all of this onto the rice. Add the broth and cover. Bake thirty minutes, stirring once or twice. Serve sprinkled with chopped scallions if desired.

Yield: Four servings.

Wild Rice I
Minnesota

Wash one cup of wild rice in cold water. Cover the rice with boiling water and simmer five minutes. Drain well and rinse once more, this time in hot water. Return the rice to a saucepan and add four cups of boiling water and salt to taste. Bring to a boil and simmer twenty to thirty minutes, or until rice is tender. Stir the rice occasionally with a fork as rice cooks. Drain and season to taste with salt, freshly ground black pepper and a generous amount of melted butter. Keep the rice warm in the oven or in a double boiler.

Yield: About four cups; eight servings.

Wild Rice II
Minnesota

Wash one cup of wild rice in cold water. Add four cups of boiling water and cover. Let stand twenty minutes. Drain and repeat this three times or more, using fresh boiling water each time. When the last boiling water is to be used, add salt to taste. Drain rice and season with salt, freshly ground black pepper and a generous amount of melted butter. Keep the rice warm in the oven or in a double boiler.

Yield: About four cups; eight servings.

Mushrooms au Beurre
Missouri

¼ cup butter
2 teaspoons olive oil
1 clove garlic, sliced
6 large mushrooms
  Salt to taste.

1. Heat the butter and oil in a skillet. Add the garlic and cook over medium heat, stirring briefly. Remove the garlic and discard.
2. Place the mushrooms, cap side down, in the skillet. Cook, turning, until tender. Sprinkle with salt.

Yield: Six mushrooms for garnish.

Onion Sour Cream Pie
Wisconsin

½ pound lean bacon
3 cups thin onion rings
1 cup sour cream
⅓ cup dry sherry
3 eggs, lightly beaten
½ teaspoon salt
¼ teaspoon freshly ground black pepper
⅛ teaspoon nutmeg
2 tablespoons chopped parsley
1 unbaked eight-inch to nine-inch pie shell.

1. Cook the bacon until crisp. Remove bacon, drain on paper towels, crumble and reserve. Pour off all but four tablespoons of the bacon drippings.
2. Preheat the oven to 450 degrees.
3. Sauté the onion rings in the bacon drippings until golden. Remove and cool.
4. Combine the sour cream, sherry, eggs, salt, pepper, nutmeg and parsley. Stir in reserved onions and bacon.
5. Bake the pie shell ten minutes, or until set.
6. Reduce the oven heat to 350 degrees. Pour sour cream mixture into pie shell and bake twenty-five to thirty minutes, or until set.

Yield: Eight servings.

Onions Delicious
Indiana

18 small white onions
  Boiling salted water
½ cup sugar
½ cup butter
½ cup heavy cream
  Salt and freshly ground black pepper to taste.

1. Place onions in a saucepan. Cover with boiling salted water and cook, covered, until tender, about twenty minutes. Drain.
2. Place the sugar and butter in a skillet and heat to melt. Add the onions and cook until lightly glazed. Just before serving, add the cream, reheat and season with salt and pepper.

Yield: Four servings.

Fried Pumpkin Blossoms
Ohio

24 pumpkin blossoms
2 eggs, lightly beaten
⅛ teaspoon freshly ground black pepper
½ teaspoon salt
⅓ cup milk
⅔ cup yellow corn meal
  Fat or oil for deep-frying.

1. Remove and discard centers of the blos-

soms. Wash blossoms well. Beat together the eggs, pepper, salt and milk to make a dip.

2. Dip blossoms in the mixture and then coat with the corn meal. Fry briefly until golden in the fat or oil heated to 350 degrees. Serve immediately.

Yield: Four servings.

Squash Bake   *Kansas*

6 medium-size zucchini or summer squash
2 to three tablespoons water
  Salt and freshly ground black pepper to taste
4 tablespoons butter
2 tablespoons chopped onion
2 tablespoons sugar
1 cup soft bread crumbs
2 eggs, lightly beaten
½ teaspoon oregano
⅔ cup grated mild Cheddar cheese.

1. Preheat the oven to 350 degrees.
2. Wash the squash and slice into a saucepan. Add the water, salt and pepper. Cover and cook slowly until tender, about ten minutes. Drain squash and mash well.
3. Melt two tablespoons of the butter in a small skillet and sauté the onion in it until tender. Mix onion with two and one-half cups of the mashed squash, the sugar, bread crumbs, eggs and oregano. Season with salt and pepper.
4. Turn mixture into a small casserole, sprinkle with the cheese and dot with remaining butter. Bake, uncovered, about thirty minutes.

Yield: Four servings.

Turnip-Potato Puree   *Wisconsin*

4 cups diced yellow turnips or rutabagas
4 cups diced potatoes
2 cups boiling chicken broth
1 tablespoon light brown sugar
¼ teaspoon freshly ground black pepper

2 tablespoons finely grated onion
½ cup finely grated sharp Cheddar cheese
3 tablespoons butter.

1. Place the turnips and potatoes in a saucepan. Add the broth and sugar. Cover and simmer until vegetables are tender, about fifteen minutes. Drain well; mash.
2. Add the remaining ingredients and beat well to melt the cheese.

Yield: Six servings.

Pioneer Potatoes   *Ohio*

3 baking potatoes, scrubbed and sliced
½ cup bacon drippings
½ cup chopped onion
  Salt and freshly ground black pepper to taste.

Place the potatoes, bacon drippings and onion in a heavy skillet and cook slowly, turning frequently with a spatula, until tender, about thirty minutes. Season with salt and pepper.

Yield: Four servings.

Potato Casserole   *Wisconsin*

8 large potatoes, scrubbed
  Boiling salted water
1 eight-ounce package cream cheese, softened
1 cup sour cream, at room temperature
2 tablespoons chopped chives
  Salt and freshly ground black pepper to taste
2 tablespoons butter.

1. Place the potatoes in a saucepan and cover with boiling salted water. Cover and cook until tender, about twenty-five minutes. Drain, peel and put through a potato ricer.
2. Preheat the oven to 350 degrees.
3. Beat the cream cheese and sour cream into the potatoes, Stir in the chives and season with salt and pepper. Turn into a greased casserole.

Decorate top with a knife, dot with the butter and bake until browned on top.

Yield: Eight to ten servings.

Skillet Potatoes   *Wisconsin*

4 large, firm potatoes, cooked, chilled and peeled
4 tablespoons butter
Salt to taste
2 tablespoons grated Swiss cheese.

1. Shred the potatoes on a coarse grater.
2. Melt two tablespoons of the butter in a heavy skillet, add the potatoes and cook over high heat until browned. Melt the remaining butter, pour over the potatoes and turn them with a spatula. Season with salt.
3. Cook over high heat until browned. Sprinkle with the cheese and either place under a preheated broiler or turn again in the skillet.

Yield: Four servings.

Holiday Folk Fair Potato Pancakes
Wisconsin

2½ medium-size potatoes, peeled, grated and drained of all liquid
1 teaspoon salt
2 eggs, lightly beaten
1½ tablespoons flour
⅓ cup shortening
Applesauce.

1. Toss the potatoes with the salt, eggs and flour. Heat the shortening in a heavy skillet and drop spoonfuls of the potato mixture in. Fry until golden, turn and fry other side.
2. Serve immediately, with applesauce.

Yield: Two servings.

Potato Puffs   *Missouri*

3 cups hot cooked riced potatoes
2 tablespoons butter
½ teaspoon salt
⅛ teaspoon freshly ground black pepper
½ cup heavy cream, whipped
⅓ cup grated sharp Cheddar cheese.

1. Preheat the oven to 350 degrees.
2. Beat the potatoes with the butter, salt and pepper. Three-quarters fill greased custard cups with the potatoes.
3. Combine the cream and cheese and spread over top of potatoes. Bake until brown, about fifteen minutes.

Yield: Six servings.

Hash Brown Potatoes   *Ohio*

1 onion, finely chopped
3 tablespoons shortening
¼ cup butter or bacon drippings
6 potatoes, peeled and sliced
Salt and freshly ground black pepper to taste.

Sauté the onion in the shortening and butter or bacon drippings until tender. Add the potato slices. Cover and cook over medium flame, stirring now and then, until cooked and browned. Season with salt and pepper.

Yield: Four servings.

Aunt Willie's Stuffed Tomatoes
Oklahoma

12 medium-size firm ripe tomatoes
2 cup fine dry bread crumbs
1 tablespoon grated onion
1 teaspoon salt
⅛ teaspoon freshly ground black pepper
¼ teaspoon basil
¼ cup butter.

1. Preheat the oven to 350 degrees.

2. Remove and reserve a slice from the stem end of each tomato. Scoop out and reserve the juicy pulp inside each tomato. Turn shells upside down on a rack to drain.

3. Mix pulp with the bread crumbs, onion, salt, pepper and basil. Stuff tomato shells with mixture. Dot with the butter and replace caps.

4. Bake twenty minutes, or until tomatoes are tender but not broken.

Yield: One dozen servings.

Peggy's Stewed Vegetables   *Oklahoma*

4 cups thinly sliced zucchini
1 onion, finely chopped
1 tablespoon water
2 tomatoes, peeled and chopped
1 sprig basil, chopped
2 tablespoons butter
    Salt and freshly ground black pepper to taste.

Place the zucchini, onion and water in a skillet and cook five minutes. Add the tomatoes and basil, cover and cook fifteen minutes, or until zucchini is tender. Add the butter, salt and pepper.

Yield: Six servings.

Tomato Pudding   *Ohio*

1 ten-ounce can tomato puree
1 tablespoon finely grated onion
½ cup boiling water
1 cup light brown sugar
¼ teaspoon salt
⅛ teaspoon freshly ground black pepper
¼ teaspoon thyme
 2 cups one-half-inch soft bread cubes
½ cup melted butter.

1. Preheat the oven to 375 degrees.

2. Combine the tomato puree, onion, water,

brown sugar, salt, pepper and thyme in a saucepan. Bring to a boil and simmer five minutes.

3. Toss the bread cubes with the butter and place in a buttered casserole. Pour the puree mixture over bread cubes and bake thirty minutes.

Yield: Four servings.

Scalloped Turnip and Apple   *Michigan*

1 large yellow turnip or rutabaga, peeled and diced
    Boiling salted water
3 tablespoons butter
1½ cups peeled, cored and sliced tart apples
⅓ cup plus three tablespoons light brown sugar
⅛ teaspoon cinnamon
⅓ cup flour.

1. Preheat the oven to 350 degrees.

2. Cover the turnip with a small quantity of boiling salted water. Cover and cook until tender, about ten minutes.

3. Drain and mash the turnip. Beat in one tablespoon of the butter.

4. Toss the apples with three tablespoons of the brown sugar and the cinnamon. Arrange alternate layers of turnip and apples in a two-quart casserole, beginning and ending with turnip.

5. Mix together until crumbly the flour, remaining butter and remaining brown sugar. Sprinkle over top of the casserole. Bake one hour.

Yield: Six servings.

Mixed Vegetables   *Iowa*

3 tablespoons butter
3 tablespoons flour
2 cups light cream
    Salt and freshly ground black pepper to taste
⅛ teaspoon nutmeg
2 medium-size potatoes, peeled, cooked and diced

1 cup cooked carrot slices
1 cup cooked cut wax beans
½ cup cooked peas
1 tablespoon finely chopped parsley.

1. Melt the butter and blend in the flour. Gradually stir in the cream and bring to a boil, stirring. Season with salt, pepper and nutmeg. Cover and set over hot water ten minutes.

2. Add the vegetables and parsley to the sauce.

Yield: Six servings.

Vegetable Bake   *Kansas*

1 medium-size head cauliflower, broken into flowerets
2 cups diced celery
1½ teaspoons salt
1 cup boiling water
¼ cup butter
¼ cup flour
⅛ teaspoon freshly ground black pepper
1¼ cups milk
2 tablespoons chopped pimentos
¼ cup finely chopped onion
1 tablespoon chopped green pepper
½ cup grated sharp Cheddar cheese.

1. Preheat the oven to 375 degrees.

2. Place the cauliflower and celery in a saucepan. Add the salt and water. Cover and cook twelve minutes. Drain vegetables and reserve three-quarters cup liquid.

3. Place the cooked vegetables in a greased one-and-one-half-quart casserole.

4. Melt the butter and blend in the flour and pepper. Gradually stir in the reserved vegetable liquid and the milk. Bring to a boil, stirring until mixture thickens. Add the pimentoes, onion and green pepper.

5. Pour sauce over vegetables, sprinkle with the cheese and bake twenty-five minutes.

Yield: Eight servings.

Cole Slaw   *Iowa*

2 cups cider vinegar
1½ cups sugar
1 teaspoon celery seeds
1 teaspoon dry mustard
1 medium-size head cabbage, shredded
1 green pepper, cored, seeded and shredded
1 onion, finely chopped
Lightly salted ice water.

1. Combine the vinegar, sugar, celery seeds and mustard in a saucepan. Bring to a boil, stirring until sugar is dissolved. Boil twenty minutes. Cool.

2. Combine the cabbage, green pepper and onion. Cover with the ice water and let stand one hour. Drain vegetables through a double thickness of muslin, pressing to remove all moisture.

3. Combine drained vegetables with cooled vinegar mixture and refrigerate twelve hours before serving.

Yield: One dozen servings.

Cabbage Salad   *Wisconsin*

1 medium-size head cabbage, shredded
2 large white onions, cut into rings
⅔ cup plus one tablespoon sugar
1 cup cider vinegar
1¼ teaspoons salt
1 teaspoon prepared mustard
1 teaspoon celery seeds
1 cup oil.

1. Alternate layers of shredded cabbage and onion rings in a glass or ceramic bowl. Sprinkle with two-thirds cup of the sugar.

2. In a saucepan, combine the vinegar, remaining sugar, salt, mustard and celery seeds. Bring to a boil, add oil and bring to a boil again.

3. Pour hot vinegar-oil mixture over cabbage and onions. Cover, cool and chill at least four hours before serving.

Yield: One dozen servings.

Whipped Cream Cole Slaw   *Iowa*

½ head red or green cabbage, grated with
   medium grater
1 small onion, grated
1 green pepper, cored, seeded and diced
3 tablespoons cider vinegar
2 tablespoons sugar
½ teaspoon salt
1 cup heavy cream, whipped.

1. Combine the cabbage, onion and green pepper in a bowl.
2. Add the vinegar, sugar and salt to the cream
and gently combine with the vegetables.
Yield: Six servings.

Greta's Cabbage Salad   *Iowa*

1 cup sugar
1 teaspoon mustard seeds
1 tablespoon salt
1 clove garlic, finely chopped
2 cups cider vinegar
2 medium-size heads cabbage, shredded or
   finely grated
1 green pepper, cored, seeded and shredded
1 small can pimentos, chopped
4 medium-size onions, finely chopped
4 carrots, grated
4 tomatoes, peeled, seeded and chopped.

1. Heat together the sugar, mustard seeds,
salt, garlic and vinegar. Cool.
2. Combine the cabbage, green pepper, pimentos, onions and carrots. Pour over cooled dressing. Toss.
3. Add tomatoes just before serving.
Yield: Eighteen servings.

Cucumber Salad   *Minnesota*

2 medium-size cucumbers, peeled and thinly
   sliced

Salt
1 cup white vinegar
½ cup sugar
⅛ teaspoon freshly ground black pepper
1 tablespoon chopped parsley.

1. Sprinkle the cucumbers lightly with salt.
Let stand ten minutes. Rinse, drain and place in
serving dish.
2. Meanwhile, combine the vinegar, sugar and
pepper and let stand five minutes. Pour over
cucumbers and sprinkle with the parsley. Chill
two hours.
Yield: Six servings.

Cucumbers in Sour Cream   *Iowa*

2 large cucumbers, peeled and thinly sliced
1 large onion, thinly sliced and separated into
   rings
¾ cup sour cream
3 tablespoons cider vinegar
2 tablespoons sugar
½ teaspoon salt
⅛ teaspoon freshly ground black pepper.

Combine the cucumber slices and onion rings.
Mix together the remaining ingredients and pour
over vegetables. Chill.
Yield: Six servings.

Twenty-Four-Hour Bean Salad
                                Michigan

1 fifteen-ounce can cut wax beans
1 sixteen-ounce can French-style green beans
1 seventeen-ounce can kidney beans
1 cup thinly sliced onions
½ cup cider vinegar
½ cup oil
½ teaspoon salt
¾ cup sugar
¼ teaspoon freshly ground black pepper.

Drain the beans and discard liquid. Combine beans in a bowl. In a jar, combine the remaining ingredients and shake well. Pour over beans and toss. Chill twenty-four hours. Drain before serving.

Yield: One dozen servings.

Sour Cream Potato Salad   *Wisconsin*

3 to four medium-size potatoes
¼ cup finely chopped red onions or scallions, including green part
1 tablespoon finely chopped green pepper
2 hard-cooked eggs, finely chopped
¼ cup mayonnaise
¼ cup sour cream
¼ teaspoon cayenne pepper or Tabasco sauce to taste
2 tablespoons white vinegar
¼ teaspoon sugar
Salt and freshly ground black pepper to taste
¾ teaspoon caraway seeds.

1. Cook the potatoes in their jackets and peel while hot. When cool enough to handle, cut into cubes.

2. Place in a mixing bowl and add the remaining ingredients. Stir gently with a rubber spatula until blended. Serve at room temperature.

Yield: Four to six servings.

Spinach Salad   *Illinois*

3 cups washed fresh spinach leaves, torn apart
1 cup slivered cooked smoked ham
3 hard-cooked eggs, chopped
2 tablespoons wine vinegar
4 tablespoons olive oil
1 teaspoon salt
¼ teaspoon freshly ground black pepper
¼ teaspoon sugar
¼ teaspoon dry mustard.

In a salad bowl, toss together the spinach, ham and chopped eggs. Put the vinegar in a jar and add the oil, salt, pepper, sugar and mustard. Shake vigorously, pour over spinach mixture and toss.

Yield: Six servings.

Peggy's Fruited Chicken Salad
Oklahoma

2 cups diced cooked chicken
¾ cup diced celery
½ cup coarsely broken nuts
1 cup halved orange segments
¾ cup seedless grapes
Homemade salad dressing or mayonnaise
Water cress.

Combine the chicken, celery, nuts, orange segments and grapes. Mix with just enough dressing or mayonnaise to moisten. Serve on a bed of water cress.

Yield: Four servings.

Hot Slaw   *Iowa*

2 egg yolks
¼ cup water
1 tablespoon butter
½ cup cider vinegar
½ teaspoon salt
1 tablespoon sugar
½ head cabbage, grated medium fine.

Combine all the ingredients except the cabbage in the top of a double broiler and cook, stirring, until thick. Add cabbage and mix. Put on direct low heat, cover and heat, stirring occasionally, until cabbage is just steamy and warm. Do not "cook" it so that cabbage gets soft.

Yield: Six servings.

Sauerkraut Salad
Wisconsin

1 twenty-nine-ounce can sauerkraut, drained
1 small onion, finely chopped
1 cup diced celery
1 green pepper, cored, seeded and diced
⅔ cup sugar.

Combine all ingredients and refrigerate overnight.
Yield: About three cups; six servings.

Corned Beef and Slaw Salad
Kansas

Slaw layer:
1 envelope unflavored gelatin
2 tablespoons sugar
½ teaspoon salt
1¼ cups water
2 tablespoons lemon juice
¼ cup cider vinegar
2 tablespoons chopped green pepper
2 cups finely shredded cabbage.
Corned beef layer:
1 envelope unflavored gelatin
½ cup water
2 tablespoons lemon juice
¼ teaspoon salt
¾ cup mayonnaise
¼ cup finely chopped onion
½ cup chopped sweet pickle
½ cup chopped celery
1 cup finely cut homemade corned beef.

1. To prepare slaw layer of salad, mix the gelatin, sugar, salt and one-half cup of the water in a saucepan. Stir over low heat until gelatin dissolves. Remove from heat.
2. Stir in the remaining water, lemon juice and vinegar. Cool and chill until the consistency of unbeaten egg white. Fold in the green pepper and cabbage. Turn into an oiled eight-inch square pan. Chill until almost firm.
3. To prepare corned beef layer of salad, soften the gelatin in the water. Place over low heat and stir to dissolve gelatin. Remove from heat. Stir in the lemon juice and salt. Cool.
4. Gradually add the mayonnaise and fold in the onion, pickle, celery and corned beef.
5. Pour or spoon the corned beef mixture on the top of cabbage layer. Chill until firm. Unmold and cut into squares.
Yield: Four to six servings.

Molded Cranberry Salad
Kansas

2 cups cranberries, washed and ground
1½ cups cold water
2 cups sugar
2 envelopes unflavored gelatin
2 cups finely diced celery
1 cup crushed pineapple with juice
¼ cup lemon juice
⅓ cup chopped nuts.

1. In a saucepan, combine the cranberries and one cup of the water. Bring to a boil and cook eight minutes. Stir in the sugar.
2. Bring to a boil again and cook three minutes.
3. Soak the gelatin in the remaining water and add to hot cranberries. Stir to dissolve gelatin.
4. Stir in the remaining ingredients and pour into a mold. Chill well before unmolding.
Yield: Eight servings.

Peggy's Tomato Dressing
Oklahoma

1 tablespoon sugar
¼ teaspoon paprika
¾ cup oil
1 eight-ounce can tomato sauce
½ cup cider vinegar
2 teaspoons A.1. Sauce
Salt and freshly ground black pepper to taste.

Mix the sugar and paprika. Beat in the oil,

tomato sauce, vinegar and meat sauce. Season with salt and pepper. Use for tossed salads.

Yield: About two and one-quarter cups.

Russian Salad Dressing   *Michigan*

    1 cup oil
    ½ cup tomato juice
    ¼ cup cider vinegar
    1 medium-size onion, finely chopped
    ½ cup light corn syrup
    ¼ cup lemon juice
    2 teaspoons salt
    2 teaspoons paprika
    2 teaspoons Worcestershire sauce
    2 teaspoons dry mustard
    1 egg, lightly beaten.

1. Combine the oil, tomato juice, vinegar and onion and let stand thirty minutes.

2. Add the remaining ingredients and beat five minutes.

Yield: About two cups.

Celery Seed Dressing   *Missouri*

    ½ teaspoon salt
    1 teaspoon sugar
    1 teaspoon dry mustard
    1 teaspoon celery seeds
    2 tablespoons cider vinegar
    7 tablespoons olive oil.

1. Place the salt, sugar, mustard and celery seeds in a mixing bowl and stir in the vinegar to make a paste.

2. Stir in the oil until well blended. Serve over salad greens.

Yield: About two-thirds cup.

Sour Cream Dressing   *Wisconsin*

    1 cup sour cream
    1 cup mayonnaise
    1 clove garlic, finely chopped
    ¼ cup finely chopped parsley
    1 tablespoon lemon juice
    1 tablespoon tarragon vinegar
    1 teaspoon salt
    ¼ teaspoon freshly ground black pepper.

Combine all ingredients thoroughly. Chill until ready to use. This dressing is good with tossed salads or vegetable salads.

Yield: About two cups.

Note: Blue cheese can be added for flavor variation.

Minute Egg Dressing   *Ohio*

    1 tablespoon butter
    1½ slices white bread, crusts removed and
       slices diced
    1 egg
    1 clove garlic, finely chopped
    ½ cup oil
    ¾ cup freshly grated Parmesan cheese
    ¼ teaspoon cayenne pepper
    ¼ teaspoon salt
    1 tablespoon cider vinegar.

1. Heat the butter in a small skillet and sauté the bread cubes in it until golden and crisp, turning frequently.

2. Put the egg in a bowl and beat with a rotary beater. Add the garlic and gradually pour in the oil while beating vigorously. Mixture will thicken as you beat. Beat in the cheese, cayenne and salt.

3. Beat in the vinegar. Just before using to toss a salad, add the bread cubes.

Yield: About one and one-half cups.

Anchovy Salad Dressing

Illinois

½ cup heavy cream
1 cup mayonnaise
3 tablespoons cider vinegar
1 tablespoon anchovy paste
1 tablespoon finely grated onion
⅛ teaspoon sugar
1 tablespoon chopped parsley

Mix all ingredients together well.
Yield: About one and one-half cups.

Fruit Salad Dressing

Kansas

¼ cup lemon juice
2 tablespoons sugar
1 egg, lightly beaten
1 cup heavy cream, whipped.

1. Combine the lemon juice, sugar and egg in the top of a double boiler. Heat, stirring, until mixture thickens. Cool.
2. Fold the cream into cooled mixture.
Yield: About two and one-quarter cups.

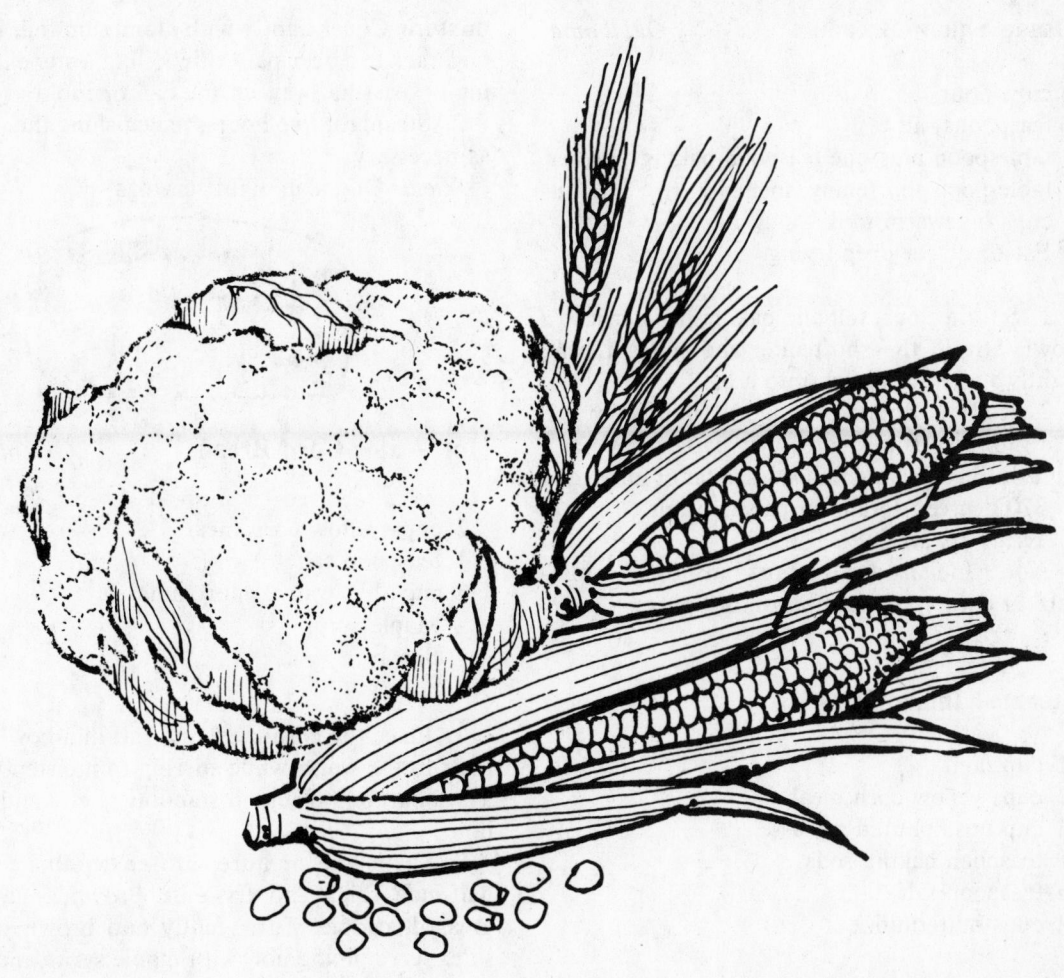

Breads

Osage Squaw Bread   *Oklahoma*

4 cups flour
2 teaspoons salt
1 tablespoon plus one teaspoon baking powder
1 tablespoon shortening, melted
2 cups lukewarm milk
   Fat or oil for deep-frying.

1. Sift the flour, salt and baking powder into a bowl. Stir in the shortening and milk. Knead lightly to gather dough into a ball.

2. Roll out dough on a lightly floured board. Cut into two-inch squares. Fry two or three at a time until golden on both sides in fat or oil heated to 370 degrees. Drain on paper towels.

Yield: Six servings.

Note: Indians dip the bread in "sop," a mixture of corn syrup and bacon drippings.

Steamed Indian Bread   *Oklahoma*

1 cup flour
2 cups yellow corn meal
¾ cup unsulphured molasses
½ teaspoon baking soda
½ teaspoon salt
2 cups buttermilk.

1. Mix all the ingredients together well. Three-quarters fill a well-greased can or mold with the mixture. Cover tightly with aluminum foil. Place on a rack in a deep pan with boiling water extending at least halfway up the can or mold.

2. Steam for two hours, replenishing the water as necessary.

Yield: One loaf; eight servings.

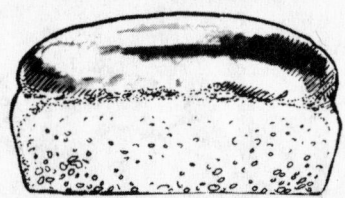

Hot Water Corn Bread   *Oklahoma*

2 cups yellow corn meal
1 teaspoon salt
1½ cups hot water, approximately
   Maple syrup
   Bacon.

1. Place the corn meal and salt in a bowl and pour in the water while stirring to moisten well. The mixture stiffens on standing. Let stand one hour.

2. Shape the mixture into cakes about one-half-inch thick and fry until brown on a hot greased griddle. Turn gently and brown other side. Serve piping hot, with maple syrup and bacon.

Yield: Six servings.

American Indian Corn Puffs   *Oklahoma*

2 eggs, lightly beaten
1 cup freshly scraped corn kernels (two to three ears corn)
⅓ cup flour
1 teaspoon baking powder
½ teaspoon salt
¼ teaspoon paprika
  Freshly ground black pepper to taste
  Fat for deep-frying.

1. Combine the eggs and corn in a mixing bowl.
2. Sift together the flour, baking powder, salt, paprika and pepper. Fold this into the corn mixture. Drop by small spoonfuls into deep fat heated to 365 degrees. Cook until golden brown all over. Drain on paper towels and serve hot. The puffs may be reheated in the oven.

Yield: About four dozen.

Harvest Corn Bread   *Oklahoma*

1 cup flour
2 teaspoons baking powder
½ teaspoon salt
1 cup white or yellow corn meal
2 tablespoons sugar
1 egg
1 cup milk
⅓ cup melted butter
¼ cup chopped green pepper
9 cherry tomatoes, quartered
3 thin green pepper rings
½ cup grated sharp Cheddar cheese.

1. Preheat the oven to 425 degrees.
2. Sift together the flour, baking powder, salt, corn meal and sugar. Add the egg, milk and butter and beat until smooth.
3. Fold in the chopped green pepper and tomatoes. Pour into a buttered eight-inch square baking pan. Arrange the pepper rings over the surface and bake eighteen minutes. Sprinkle with the cheese and bake five to eight minutes longer.

Yield: Nine servings.

Water Cress Biscuits   *Missouri*

2 cups sifted flour
3 teaspoons baking powder
  Salt to taste
⅛ teaspoon cayenne pepper
⅔ cup finely chopped water cress leaves and stems
2 tablespoons finely chopped chives
⅓ cup melted butter
¾ cup milk, approximately.

1. Preheat the oven to 450 degrees.
2. Sift the flour, baking powder, salt and cayenne into a mixing bowl.
3. Place the water cress in a piece of clean cheesecloth or kitchen toweling and squeeze to remove part of the moisture. Add the water cress and chives to the flour and toss. Gradually add the butter, tossing with a two-pronged fork or a pastry blender. Gradually add the milk, tossing with the fork. Use just enough milk to make a soft, manageable dough.
4. Roll the dough out to one-half-inch thickness on a lightly floured board. Cut the dough into rounds with a one-and-one-half-inch biscuit cutter and place on an ungreased baking sheet. Bake twelve minutes, or until browned on top.

Yield: One dozen to fourteen.

Popovers   *Illinois*

1 cup flour
¼ teaspoon salt
2 large eggs
1 cup milk
2 tablespoons melted butter or oil.

1. Preheat the oven to 425 degrees.

2. Sift together the flour and salt. Beat in the eggs, milk and butter or oil.

3. Heat greased muffin tins in the oven three minutes. Pour in the batter to three-quarters fill tins. Bake thirty-five minutes, or until well puffed and golden. Prick the top of each popover while still in the oven and bake five minutes longer.

Yield: Six.

Pumpkin Bread   *Illinois*

1⅓ cups sugar
⅓ cup shortening
2 eggs
1 cup pumpkin puree
1⅔ cups flour
¼ teaspoon baking powder
¼ teaspoon ground cloves
1 teaspoon baking soda
½ teaspoon cinnamon
¾ teaspoon salt
⅓ cup water
½ cup chopped nuts.

1. Preheat the oven to 350 degrees.
2. Beat the sugar and shortening together until light and fluffy. Beat in the eggs, one at a time. Stir in the pumpkin.
3. Sift together the flour, baking powder, cloves, baking soda, cinnamon and salt and add alternately with the water to the batter.
4. Stir in the nuts, spoon batter into a well-greased and floured 9-by-5-by-3-inch loaf pan and bake thirty minutes, or until done.

Yield: One loaf.

Fruit Bread   *Kansas*

1¾ cups plus one tablespoon flour
2 teaspoons baking powder
¼ teaspoon baking soda
¼ teaspoon salt
⅔ cup sugar
⅓ cup shortening, melted

2 eggs
1 cup chopped dates
2 tablespoons chopped maraschino cherries
1 cup mashed ripe bananas
½ cup chopped walnuts.

1. Preheat the oven to 350 degrees.
2. Mix together one and three-quarters cup of the flour, the baking powder, baking soda, salt and sugar.
3. Beat in the shortening and eggs (mixture will be stiff). Toss the dates and cherries in the remaining flour and stir in with the bananas and walnuts.
4. Spoon into a greased and floured 8½-by-4½-by-2½-inch loaf pan. Bake one hour, or until done.

Yield: One loaf.

Float Away Oatmeal Muffins   *Oklahoma*

1 cup quick-cooking (dry) oatmeal
1 cup buttermilk
1 cup flour
1 teaspoon salt
1½ teaspoons baking powder
½ teaspoon baking soda
1 egg
½ cup dark brown sugar
¼ cup melted shortening.

1. Preheat the oven to 400 degrees.
2. Place the oatmeal in a bowl and pour the buttermilk over oatmeal. Let stand while sifting together the flour, salt, baking powder and baking soda.
3. Beat the egg into the oatmeal mixture. Beat in the brown sugar. Stir in the sifted dry ingredients and then the shortening.
4. Pour into greased muffin tins and bake about eighteen minutes. Serve warm.

Yield: Two dozen "two-bite"-size muffins.

Banana Muffins
Ohio

1¾ cups flour
2 teaspoons baking powder
¼ teaspoon baking soda
¼ teaspoon salt
⅓ cup sugar
3 tablespoons melted shortening
1 egg, lightly beaten
1 cup mashed very ripe bananas.

1. Preheat the oven to 400 degrees.
2. Sift together the flour, baking powder, baking soda, salt and sugar.
3. Combine the shortening, egg and bananas and stir into dry ingredients only until just moistened. Fill greased muffin tins two-thirds full. Bake fifteen to twenty minutes, or until done.

Yield: Eighteen to two dozen, depending on size.

Brown Sugar Muffins
Kansas

1½ cups flour
¼ cup granulated sugar
¼ teaspoon salt
½ teaspoon cinnamon
3½ teaspoons baking powder
¼ cup light brown sugar
1 egg, lightly beaten
½ cup oil
½ cup milk.

1. Preheat the oven to 400 degrees.
2. Sift together the flour, granulated sugar, salt, cinnamon and baking powder. Stir in the brown sugar.
3. Combine the egg, oil and milk and stir into dry ingredients just enough to moisten. Fill greased muffin tins two-thirds full and bake twenty to twenty-five minutes, or until done.

Yield: About eighteen.

Graham Muffins
Iowa

¼ cup butter
¼ cup sugar
1 egg
½ cup regular flour
½ teaspoon baking powder
1 cup graham or whole wheat flour
1 cup buttermilk
1 teaspoon baking soda.

1. Preheat the oven to 400 degrees.
2. Cream the butter and sugar together until light and fluffy. Beat in the egg.
3. Sift together the regular flour and baking powder. Stir in the graham flour. Combine the buttermilk and baking soda. Add graham flour mixture alternately with buttermilk to the creamed mixture.
4. Fill greased muffin tins two-thirds full. Bake twenty-five minutes, or until done.

Yield: About one dozen medium size.

Polish Paluski
Wisconsin

3 cups flour
½ teaspoon salt
1 cup butter
½ pound cottage cheese
1 pound prunes, lightly cooked, drained and pitted
Confectioners' sugar.

1. Preheat the oven to 375 degrees.
2. Sift the flour and salt into a bowl. With the finger tips or a pastry blender, work in the butter as though making pastry.
3. Stir in the cottage cheese and work into a dough.
4. Roll out half the dough on a lightly floured pastry cloth or board. Cut into three-inch squares. Place one prune in the center of each square. Roll and pinch ends to seal.
5. Place on an ungreased baking sheet and

bake twenty minutes, or until lightly browned. Dust with confectioners' sugar while hot.

Yield: About two dozen.

These fat cakes are also known as knee patches, number one fried cakes, celestine crusts or Grebel and they have been a favorite with people of Czech background in Oklahoma since before 1895.

Kuechlie (Fat Cakes)   *Oklahoma*

2 large eggs, lightly beaten
2½ tablespoons heavy cream
2½ tablespoons plus one-half cup sugar
¾ teaspoon salt
3½ to four cups flour
  Fat or oil for deep-frying
1 teaspoon cinnamon.

1. Mix the eggs, cream, two and one-half tablespoons of the sugar and the salt in a bowl. Stir in enough flour to make a rollable dough. Chill.

2. Roll out the dough as thin as possible. This is best done on a lightly floured pastry cloth. Cut dough into 2-by-4-inch pieces and fry until golden, two or three at a time, in the fat or oil heated to 370 degrees, turning once.

3. Drain on paper towels. Sprinkle with the cinnamon mixed with the remaining sugar.

Yield: About thirty.

Lefsa   *Iowa*

3 cups mashed potatoes, cooled and forced through a potato ricer
1 teaspoon salt
5 tablespoons oil
1 cup flour, approximately
  Butter
  Sugar.

1. Place the cold riced potatoes in a bowl and stir in the salt and oil. Gradually stir in enough flour to make a soft dough. The less flour used, the lighter the lefsa, and good cooks of Norwegian background from Brooklyn to Iowa are judged by their prowess at lefsa-making.

2. Form the dough into a roll about twelve inches long and wrap in wax paper. Chill well.

3. Cut roll into eighteen pieces and roll out, one piece at a time, with stocking-covered rolling pin to a thin eight-inch circle on a lightly floured pastry cloth. This is not easy for the novice, who may need to use a bit more flour.

4. With wide spatula or thin flat stick, transfer to a hot greased griddle (not easy at first either) and cook until just lightly browned and bubbly. Turn and brown the other side. Watch that circles do not burn. Spread with butter, sprinkle with sugar and roll up to eat.

Yield: Eighteen.

Note: Lefsa are often served with lutefisk (page 335) at Christmas.

Large Yeast Bread Recipe   *Iowa*

3 cups milk, scalded
½ cup lard
1 cup sugar
4 teaspoons salt
4 eggs
4 packages active dry yeast
1 cup lukewarm potato water
12 cups flour, approximately.

1. Put the milk in a large bowl. Add the lard, sugar and salt and cool to lukewarm. Beat the eggs into cooled mixture.

2. Soften the yeast in the potato water and stir into milk mixture.

3. Beat in enough flour to make a soft dough that is just stiff enough to knead. Knead on a board for twenty minutes. Place in a clean bowl, grease top, cover and let rise in a warm place until doubled in bulk, about one and one-half hours.

4. Punch dough down. Shape mixture into

four loaves, fit into greased loaf pans, cover and let rise until doubled in bulk.

5. Preheat the oven to 350 degrees.

6. Bake loaves forty-five to sixty minutes, or until loaves sound hollow when tapped on the bottom. Cool on a rack.

Yield: Four loaves.

Casserole Bread   *Minnesota*

1 package active dry yeast
¼ cup lukewarm water
1 cup cottage cheese, heated to lukewarm
2 tablespoons sugar
2 tablespoons grated onion
2 tablespoons butter
2 teaspoons dill seeds
1 teaspoon salt
¼ teaspoon baking soda
1 egg
2¼ to two and one-half cups flour.

1. Soften the yeast in the water. In a mixing bowl, combine the cottage cheese, sugar, onion butter, dill seeds, salt, baking soda and egg.

2. Stir in the softened yeast and enough flour to make a moderately stiff dough, beating well as flour is added. Cover the mixture and let rise in a warm place until doubled in bulk, about one hour.

3. Stir down and turn into a well-greased two-quart casserole. Cover and let rise until doubled in bulk, about forty minutes.

4. Preheat the oven to 350 degrees.

5. Bake forty to fifty minutes.

Yield: One loaf.

Sausage Bread   *Indiana*

6 to seven cups flour
1 package active dry yeast
1 teaspoon coarsely ground black pepper
2¼ cups warm water
2 tablespoons sugar

2 teaspoons salt
1 pound cooked Italian hot and/or sweet sausage, chopped
Sausage drippings.

1. Stir two cups of the flour with the yeast and pepper.

2. Combine the water, sugar and salt. Add to the flour mixture and beat until smooth, about two minutes.

3. Add the sausage and enough remaining flour to make a fairly stiff dough. Knead on a lightly floured board until smooth.

4. Place in a greased bowl and grease the top of the dough. Cover and let rise in a warm place until doubled in bulk, about one and one-half hours. Punch down. Cover dough and let rest ten minutes.

5. Divide the dough into six pieces. Roll each piece into a rope about one inch in diameter. Braid three together to make a loaf. Place on a greased baking sheet. Repeat with other three pieces. Brush loaves with sausage drippings.

6. Cover the loaves and let rise in a warm place until doubled in bulk, about one and one-quarter hours.

7. Preheat the oven to 375 degrees.

8. Bake the loaves about one hour, or until they are golden and sound hollow when tapped on the bottom.

Yield: Two loaves.

Adobe Bread   *Oklahoma*

1 package active dry yeast
1¼ cups warm water
2 tablespoons melted lard or shortening, cooled
1 teaspoon salt
4½ cups flour
Oil.

1. Put the yeast in a dry, warm mixing bowl. Stir in one-quarter cup of the water. When yeast is softened, add the lard or shortening and salt.

2. Add the flour alternately with the remaining water, sifting the flour in a little at a time. Beat well after each addition. It may be necessary to knead in the final cup of flour with the hands. Knead until the mixture is smooth.

3. Shape the dough into a ball and place it in a greased mixing bowl. Brush dough lightly with oil and cover with a dry cloth. Let rise one to one and one-half hours, or until doubled in bulk.

4. Punch the dough down and turn it onto a floured board. Knead dough about five minutes. Divide into two equal parts. Pat each part into a round about five inches in diameter. Place the rounds on oiled ovenproof wooden boards or baking sheets and cover with a dry cloth. Let rise in warm dry place about fifteen minutes.

5. Meanwhile, preheat the oven to 400 degrees.

6. Bake the loaves fifty minutes, or until lightly browned.

Yield: Two loaves.

Norwegian Dark Bread *Minnesota*

1 package active dry yeast
2½ cups lukewarm water
2 cups dry milk solids
2 cups rye flour, preferably stone-ground
5 cups whole wheat flour, preferably stone-ground
2 teaspoons salt
1 teaspoon sugar
¼ cup water.

1. Soften the yeast in the lukewarm water about five minutes. Stir to combine. Add the dry milk solids, rye flour, two cups of the whole wheat flour, the salt and sugar. Stir until well mixed.

2. Blend the mixture, about one cup at a time, in an electric blender for sixty seconds, or until the dough turns light in color. When all the dough has been blended, rinse out the container by blending the one-quarter cup water. Add the

liquid to the blended dough. Cover the dough and let rise forty-five minutes.

3. Stir down and let rise again thirty minutes.

4. Stir in two cups more of the whole wheat flour. Sprinkle a pastry board with the remaining whole wheat flour. With greased hands, pick up the dough and knead in the flour on the board. Put the dough into a greased bowl, grease the top well, cover and let rise one hour, or until doubled in bulk.

5. Knead the dough. Shape it into four small loaves. Place the loaves in well-greased small shallow baking dishes, grease the surfaces liberally and let dough rise again thirty minutes.

6. Preheat the oven to 325 degrees.

7. Bake loaves thirty minutes.

Yield: Four small loaves.

Sour Dough Rye *Minnesota*

Starter:
1 package active dry yeast
2 cups warm water
2 cups regular flour.
Bread:
1 cup starter
2 cups rye flour
1¼ cups warm water
1 package active dry yeast
2 teaspoons salt
1 tablespoon caraway seeds
1½ teaspoons poppy seeds
2 tablespoons butter, melted
3 tablespoons sugar
4 cups regular flour, approximately
Yellow corn meal
1 egg, lightly beaten
1 tablespoon water.

1. Three to four days ahead, combine the ingredients for the starter in a container with lid. Let stand at room temperature two days; then store in refrigerator until ready to use. After using some of the starter, replenish the "mother" with equal parts of regular flour and water; let

stand at room temperature for a few hours; then put in refrigerator. If used regularly, the starter is good indefinitely.

2. The day before making bread, combine the one cup starter, the rye flour and one cup of the warm water. Cover with a piece of plastic wrap and let stand overnight at room temperature.

3. Next morning, stir the dough down. Dissolve the yeast in the remaining warm water. Add to the dough the dissolved yeast, salt, caraway seeds, poppy seeds, butter, sugar and enough regular flour to make a workable but stiff dough.

4. Knead the dough thoroughly. Shape into a ball and place it in a greased bowl. Grease the top of the dough, cover and let rise in a warm place until doubled in bulk, about two hours.

5. Punch dough down and shape into two round loaves. Place them on greased baking sheets liberally sprinkled with corn meal. Cover and let loaves rise again, about one hour.

6. Preheat the oven to 375 degrees.

7. Mix the egg with the tablespoon water. Brush over the loaves. Bake thirty minutes, or until lightly browned.

8. Cool loaves with towel covering them to prevent the crust from becoming too hard.

Yield: Two loaves.

Note: For onion rye, add one-third cup chopped raw onion to the dough and put additional chopped onion on top of the loaves before baking.

Swedish Rye Bread   *Kansas*

4 cups lukewarm water including potato
  water if available
1 cake compressed yeast or one package
  active dry yeast
¾ cup dark sorghum or molasses
¼ cup shortening, melted and cooled
1 tablespoon caraway seeds
2 tablespoons salt
2 cups rye flour
1 cup mashed potatoes

Flour
Shortening.

1. Place three and one-half cups of the water in a large bowl. Dissolve the yeast in the remaining water. Add dissolved yeast with the sorghum or molasses, cooled shortening, caraway seeds and salt to the bowl of water.

2. Beat in the rye flour, mashed potatoes and enough regular flour to make a dough stiff enough to handle and knead.

3. Knead on a lightly floured board until smooth and elastic, about ten minutes. Place in a clean bowl, grease the top of the dough with shortening, cover and let rise in a warm place until doubled in bulk, one and one-half to two hours.

4. Punch dough down and divide into four pieces. Shape into four loaves and place in four greased 8½-by-4½-by-2½-inch loaf pans. Cover and let rise in a warm place until doubled in bulk, about one and one-half hours.

5. Preheat the oven to 375 degrees.

6. Bake loaves about forty-five minutes, or until bottom sounds hollow when tapped. Cool on a rack.

Yield: Four loaves.

Finnish Sour Rye Bread (Ruisleipa)
Minnesota

Starter:
1 cup rye flour
1 cup warm water, flat beer, buttermilk or
  potato water, approximately.
Bread:
2 cups water, flat beer, buttermilk or potato
  water, warmed
1 package active dry yeast
2 tablespoons salt
¼ cup lukewarm water
2½ cups rye flour
3½ cups unbleached bread flour, such as
  Heckers or Robin Hood brands

1 egg, lightly beaten
1 tablespoon water.

1. Four days ahead, mix together the rye flour and one cup liquid for starter, cover loosely with wax paper and set in a warm place. Stir once or twice a day. If liquid evaporates, add more. Mixture will become bubbly and emit a strong fragrance.

2. To make bread, turn the soured dough mixture into a large bowl. Add the warmed liquid and stir until mixture is smooth.

3. Dissolve the yeast and salt in the lukewarm water and stir into the dough.

4. Gradually beat in the rye flour and regular flour until the mixture is the consistency of biscuit dough.

5. Knead the dough on a lightly floured board until smooth. Divide the dough into two equal parts and shape each into a ball. Place in two greased bowls, grease top of dough, cover and let rise in a warm place until doubled in bulk, about one and one-half hours.

6. Shape each piece of dough into a round loaf which may have a hole in the center, like a huge doughnut. In Finland the bread is strung up on a line to hang out of the way in the kitchen.

7. Place loaves on a greased baking sheet, cover and let rise until doubled in bulk, about forty minutes.

8. Preheat the oven to 400 degrees.

9. If desired, loaves may be pricked all over with a fork before baking. Bake the loaves about forty-five minutes, or until lightly browned.

10. Before the last ten minutes of baking, brush the top of the bread with the egg mixed with the tablespoon water.

11. Cool loaves with a towel covering them to prevent crust from becoming too hard.

Yield: Two loaves.

Addie's Squash Rolls   *Oklahoma*

 2 cups milk, scalded
 ½ cup shortening

 2 packages active dry yeast
 ⅓ cup lukewarm water
 1 egg, lightly beaten
 ½ cup sugar
 1 cup sieved squash
 1 teaspoon salt
 8 cups flour, approximately.

1. Combine the milk and shortening and set aside until lukewarm. Dissolve the yeast in the water.

2. Add yeast mixture to cooled milk mixture. Stir in the egg, sugar, squash, salt and enough flour to make a soft dough. Beat well as flour is added

3. Place dough in a clean bowl, cover and let rise in a warm place until doubled in bulk, about one and one-quarter hours. Punch down and let rise again.

4. Divide dough into quarters. Roll out, one piece at a time, to one-half-inch thickness. Cut with a biscuit cutter and place on a greased baking sheet.

5. Cover and let rise until doubled in bulk.

6. Preheat the oven to 350 degrees.

7. Bake thirty minutes, or until done.

Yield: Four dozen.

Quick Mixer Rolls   *Iowa*

 2 cups lukewarm water
 2 teaspoons salt
 2 packages active dry yeast
 ½ cup sugar
 6 cups flour
 2 eggs
 ⅓ cup oil.

1. Place the water, salt, yeast, sugar and two cups of the flour in a large mixing bowl. Beat with an electric mixer at medium speed two minutes.

2. Add the eggs and oil and beat one minute longer.

3. With a wooden spoon, beat in remaining flour very well. Place dough in a clean bowl,

cover and let rise until doubled in bulk, about one and one-quarter hours.

4. Divide dough into thirds and roll out each, on a floured pastry cloth, into a ten-inch circle. Cut each circle into twelve to sixteen wedge-shaped pieces. Starting from the wide end, roll each wedge into a butterhorn shape. Place on greased baking sheets, cover and let rise until doubled in bulk, about thirty-five minutes.

5. Preheat the oven to 450 degrees.

6. Bake rolls ten to twelve minutes, or until done.

Yield: Three dozen to four dozen.

Refrigerator Rolls   *Kansas*

1 cup hot water
1 cup shortening
½ cup sugar
2 teaspoons salt
2 packages active dry yeast
1 cup lukewarm water
3 eggs, lightly beaten
7 cups flour.

1. Day before, put the hot water in a bowl. Add the shortening, sugar and salt. Cool to lukewarm.

2. Dissolve the yeast in the lukewarm water. Add the eggs and the dissolved yeast to the shortening mixture. Gradually beat in flour. Cover and refrigerate overnight.

3. Next day, remove dough from refrigerator and allow dough to warm up enough so that it can be handled. Shape into rolls and place on greased baking sheets. Cover and let rise until doubled in bulk, about two and one-half hours.

4. Preheat the oven to 425 degrees.

5. Bake rolls twelve to fifteen minutes, or until done.

Yield: About three dozen.

Filled Danish   *Michigan*

Dough:
1 package active dry yeast
2 tablespoons lukewarm water
2 cups flour
¾ cup lightly salted butter
2 eggs, lightly beaten, two tablespoons removed.
Filling:
½ cup sweet butter
½ cup sugar
½ teaspoon vanilla.

1. To prepare dough, dissolve the yeast in the water. Place the flour in a bowl and, with the finger tips, work in the lightly salted butter until the mixture resembles coarse corn meal.

2. Mix the eggs and dissolved yeast and add to flour mixture to make a dough. Knead the dough on a lightly floured board until smooth.

3. Divide the dough into thirds and roll two thirds into a square 14-by-14 inches. Cream together the sweet butter and sugar for the filling and add the vanilla. Spread over the square.

4. Roll remaining dough and cut into one-half-inch strips. Place in diamond pattern over filling. Press down into filling. Cover and let rise in a warm place thirty minutes.

5. Preheat the oven to 375 degrees.

6. Bake twenty minutes, or until done.

Yield: Thirty servings.

Ukrainian Twist Loaf   *Wisconsin*

1 package active dry yeast
¼ cup warm water
¼ cup butter
½ cup sugar
2 eggs
2 egg yolks
½ teaspoon salt
½ teaspoon vanilla
1½ teaspoons grated lemon peel
3 cups flour, approximately

⅓ cup milk, scalded and cooled to lukewarm
½ cup chopped raisins
¼ cup chopped glacé cherries
¼ cup chopped walnuts
1 tablespoon lemon juice.

1. Dissolve the yeast in the warm water. Beat the butter and one-quarter cup of the sugar together until light and fluffy. Beat in one of the eggs and the egg yolks, salt and vanilla. Beat in the lemon peel.

2. Beat in half the flour and the dissolved yeast. Then beat in the remaining flour with the milk to make a soft dough. Beat until smooth.

3. Place in a greased bowl, cover and let rise in a warm place until doubled in bulk, about one and one-quarter hours.

4. Meanwhile, combine the raisins, cherries, walnuts, lemon juice and remaining sugar.

5. Divide the dough into three portions. Roll out each portion into a strip 9 by 3 inches. Divide the fruit mixture evenly among the three strips, placing fruit mixture along the length in the middle. Overlap edges lengthwise and seal. Pinch ends and edges.

6. Braid the three fingers and fit into a greased 9-by-5-by-3-inch loaf pan. Cover and let rise in a warm place until doubled in bulk, about one and one-quarter hours.

7. Preheat the oven to 375 degrees.

8. Beat the remaining egg and brush over top of risen dough. Bake ten minutes, reduce oven heat to 350 degrees and bake thirty minutes longer, or until done. Cover top with aluminum foil if loaf overbrowns.

9. Cool on a rack. Serve sliced, spread with soft butter.

Yield: One loaf.

German Apple Coffecake   *Wisconsin*

1 package active dry yeast
¼ cup lukewarm water
¾ cup milk, scalded
½ cup butter

¾ cup granulated sugar
3½ cups flour, approximately
2 egg yolks, lightly beaten
¼ teaspoon salt
4 large apples, peeled and sliced
⅓ cup light brown sugar
1 teaspoon cinnamon.

1. Dissolve the yeast in the water.

2. Place the milk in a large bowl. Add one-quarter cup of the butter. Add the granulated sugar. Stir to melt butter and dissolve sugar. Cool to lukewarm.

3. Stir in the dissolved yeast. Beat in half the flour. Stir in the egg yolks and salt and then enough additional flour to make a soft but not sticky dough. Knead on a lightly floured board until smooth, about eight minutes.

4. Place the kneaded dough in a clean greased bowl, cover and let rise in a warm place until doubled in bulk, about one and one-half hours.

5. Knock down the dough and fit into a greased 13-by-9-by-2-inch baking pan. Cover and let rise in a warm place until dough has doubled in bulk and three-quarters fills the pan.

6. Preheat the oven to 375 degrees.

7. Melt the remaining butter. Brush half of it over the top of the dough. Arrange the apple slices in neat rows over the surface. Brush with remaining melted butter and sprinkle with the brown sugar and cinnamon.

8. Bake eight minutes, reduce the oven heat to 325 degrees and bake twenty-five to thirty minutes longer, or until done. Serve warm.

Yield: Eight servings.

Julekage (Christmas Bread)   *Minnesota*

1 package active dry yeast
¼ cup lukewarm water
¼ cup plus one teaspoon sugar
¾ cup milk
¼ cup butter
1 teaspoon salt
1 egg, lightly beaten

¼ teaspoon ground cardamom
3½ cups flour, approximately
¼ cup raisins
¼ cup chopped candied fruits
   Thin sugar frosting (recipe below).

1. Combine the yeast, water and one teaspoon of the sugar in a warm mixing bowl. Stir to dissolve.

2. Bring the milk just to a boil and remove from the heat.

3. Combine the butter, salt and remaining sugar in another mixing bowl. Add the hot milk and stir to blend. Let the mixture cool.

4. Add the yeast mixture, the egg and cardamom. Sift in one and one-half cups of the flour. Beat well with a wooden spoon.

5. Turn the dough onto a floured board and knead in more flour gradually to make a soft dough. The dough must not be too firm. Shape the dough into a ball and place it in a greased mixing bowl. Cover and let rise until doubled in bulk.

6. Punch the dough down and knead in the raisins and candied fruits. Let dough rise again; then shape into one large or two small loaves. Place the loaf or loaves on a greased baking sheet and let rise.

7. Preheat the oven to 350 degrees.

8. Bake forty to forty-five minutes. Spread with thin sugar frosting and let cool.

Yield: One large or two small loaves.

Thin Sugar Frosting   *Minnesota*

½ cup sifted confectioners' sugar
½ teaspoon vanilla
2 tablespoons warm milk.

Combine the ingredients and use to spread over pastry.

Yield: About one-half cup.

Aunt Mary's Kolaches   *Iowa*

1 package active dry yeast
2 tablespoons warm water
1 cup milk, scalded and cooled
¼ cup sugar
½ cup melted duck fat, chicken fat or butter
2 egg yolks
4 cups flour, approximately
   Kolache filling (recipes below).

1. Dissolve the yeast in the water. To the cooled milk add the sugar, one-third cup of the fat or butter, the egg yolks, the dissolved yeast and two cups of the flour. Beat with electric mixer until mixture balls up on beaters and is smooth and shiny.

2. Beating by hand, work in remaining flour. Beat until dough is shiny and elastic, at least five minutes. Grease top of dough with one tablespoon of the remaining fat or butter. Cover and let rise in a warm place until doubled in bulk.

3. Punch dough down and let rise again. With greased hands, turn dough out onto a greased board. Divide dough into walnut-size pieces and shape into balls. Place on greased baking sheet. Flatten slightly, cover and let rise until doubled in bulk.

4. Preheat the oven to 425 degrees.

5. Make a small depression in each kolache and fill with a teaspoon of desired filling. Let rise ten minutes.

6. Bake twelve to fifteen minutes, or until golden. Brush with remaining fat or butter.

Yield: Three dozen.

Note: The dough can be quadrupled to make 100 to 125 kolaches at a time. Each recipe for filling is more than ample for one recipe of the dough.

Cottage Cheese Filling for Kolaches
                                          Iowa

1 cup cottage cheese
1 egg yolk

¼ cup sugar
¼ cup raisins
1 teaspoon vanilla
1 teaspoon instant tapioca
1 teaspoon grated lemon rind.

Mix all ingredients together.
Yield: About one and one-quarter cups.

Prune or Apricot Filling for Kolaches

Iowa

1 pound dried prunes or apricots
½ cup sugar
½ teaspoon vanilla
¼ teaspoon cinnamon.

Place fruit in a saucepan, barely cover with water and cook until tender. Pit prunes, if used. Mash the fruit well and beat with remaining ingredients.
Yield: About two cups.

Poppy Seed Filling for Kolaches

Iowa

½ pound poppy seeds, ground (see note)
½ cup pecans, ground (optional)
1 cup water
½ cup milk
¼ teaspoon salt
1 tablespoon vanilla
½ cup sugar
½ cup graham cracker crumbs or vanilla
   wafer crumbs
1 tablespoon grated lemon rind.

Place the poppy seeds and pecans if desired in a saucepan, add the water and cook twenty minutes. Add the milk, salt, vanilla, sugar, crumbs and lemon rind.
Yield: About three and one-half cups.
Note: Ground poppy seeds can be bought in stores specializing in German, Viennese and Hungarian ingredients. Otherwise, poppy seeds can be ground in a coffee grinder or electric blender.

Saffron Bread

Minnesota

2 packages active dry yeast
½ cup lukewarm water
½ cup butter, melted and cooled
1 cup light cream
½ cup sugar
2 eggs, lightly beaten
¼ teaspoon powdered saffron
4 cups flour.

1. Day before, dissolve the yeast in the water. Mix the butter and cream together and stir into yeast mixture. Stir in the sugar, one of the eggs and the saffron.
2. Gradually beat in the flour until mixture is smooth. Cover bowl and refrigerate overnight.
3. Next day, knead dough on a lightly floured board until smooth and shiny.
4. Divide dough in half and roll out each half into an eighteen-inch roll. Set rolls side by side on greased baking sheet and curl last two inches on all four ends outward into snail. Cover and let rise until doubled in bulk, about two hours.
5. Preheat the oven to 350 degrees.
6. Brush dough with remaining egg and bake twenty-five minutes, or until done. Cool on a rack.
Yield: One loaf.

Marmalade Bread and Fruit Loaves

Iowa

2 packages active dry yeast
¼ cup lukewarm water
½ cup granulated sugar
2 teaspoons salt
¼ cup shortening

1 cup milk, scalded
2 eggs, lightly beaten
5 cups flour, approximately
6 tablespoons soft butter
½ cup orange marmalade
¼ cup raisins
¼ cup chopped candied fruits
¼ cup chopped candied cherries
2 cups confectioners' sugar
   Lemon juice.
¼ cup chopped nuts.

1. Disslove the yeast in the water. Add the granulated sugar, salt and shortening to the milk. Cool to lukewarm.

2. Beat in yeast mixture and the eggs. Beat in enough flour to give a soft dough. Turn onto a lightly floured board and knead until smooth and elastic.

3. Place dough in a clean greased bowl, cover and let rise in a warm place until doubled in bulk, about one and one-half hours.

4. Punch dough down and let rest ten minutes.

5. Roll out half the dough to fit a greased nine-inch square baking dish. Place in the dish and spread with two tablespoons of the butter. Cover and let rise until doubled in bulk.

6. Preheat the oven to 375 degrees.

7. With the end of a wooden spoon handle dipped in flour, make depressions over surface of dough about one inch apart. Place one-half teaspoon of the marmalade in each. Bake twenty-five minutes, or until done.

8. Knead the raisins, candied fruits and candied cherries into the other half of the dough. Cover and let rest ten minutes. Divide dough in half and roll each half into an oval three-quarters-inch thick. Brush one half of each oval with one tablespoon butter each. Fold each oval over like large Parker House roll. Place on a greased baking sheet, brush lightly with remaining butter, cover and let rise until doubled in bulk, about one hour.

9. Preheat oven to 350 degrees.

10. Bake loaves twenty-five to thirty minutes. Cool on a rack. Frost with confectioners' sugar moistened with lemon juice. Sprinkle with chopped nuts.

Yield: One marmalade bread and two fruit loaves.

Swedish Limpa   *Minnesota*

1 package active dry yeast
¼ cup lukewarm water
¼ cup butter, melted and cooled
2 cups lukewarm milk
¼ cup dark corn syrup
1 teaspoon salt
1 cup lingonberry preserves (see note)
5 cups light rye flour
5 cups regular flour, approximately.

1. Dissolve the yeast in the water. Stir in the butter, milk, syrup, salt and preserves. Stir in the rye flour and enough regular flour to give a soft dough.

2. Cover and let rise in a warm place until doubled in bulk, about one and one-half hours.

3. Turn onto a lightly floured board and knead until smooth. Shape into two loaves and place in greased 9-by-5-by-3-inch loaf pans.

4. Let rise, covered, until doubled in bulk.

5. Preheat the oven to 350 degrees.

6. Bake loaves about forty-five minutes, or until done.

Yield: Two loaves.

Note: Lingonberry preserves are available in Scandinavian stores.

Almond Strips   *Iowa*

Dough:
½ cup milk, scalded
½ cup butter
1 package active dry yeast
¼ cup warm water
3 tablespoons granulated sugar
1 teaspoon vanilla
2 egg yolks, lightly beaten

2½ cups flour
½ teaspoon salt.
Almond filling:
  1 pound marzipan (see note)
½ cup soft butter
⅓ cup light corn syrup.
Glaze (optional):
  2 cups confectioners' sugar
    Lemon juice.

1. Day before, to prepare dough, place the milk in a bowl and add the butter. Stir to melt the butter. Set mixture aside until lukewarm.

2. Dissolve the yeast in the water. Stir in the granulated sugar and add to the cooled milk mixture. Stir in the vanilla and egg yolks.

3. Beat in the flour and salt until mixture is smooth.

4. Place in a clean bowl, cover with clear plastic wrap and refrigerate overnight.

5. Next day, prepare filling. Place the marzipan, butter and syrup in a bowl and work with the hands until mixture is soft and pliable.

6. Preheat the oven to 375 degrees.

7. Divide the dough into quarters.

8. FOR AN OPEN-FACED STRIP, roll out one-quarter of the dough on a lightly floured board or cloth to a rectangle about 6 by 8 inches.

9. Cut a four-inch piece off one end for the lattice top. Place remaining strip on a lightly greased baking sheet. Spread one-quarter of the almond mixture in a four-inch strip over the length of the dough. Push up the sides and ends to form a slightly raised edge.

10. Cut the reserved rolled dough into very thin strips and make a lattice over the filling. Repeat with remaining three-quarters dough and filling.

OR 11. FOR A CLOSED STRIP, roll out one-quarter of the dough into a very thin rectangle about 8 by 12 inches. Cut in half lengthwise. Spread one-quarter of almond mixture over the middle of one strip.

12. Moisten the edges and top with second strip. Pinch edges and ends together very well.

13. Place on a lightly greased baking sheet.

With scissors, cut decorative holes at intervals over dough. Repeat with remaining three-quarters dough and filling.

14. Preheat the oven to 375 degrees.

15. Allow open-faced or closed strips to rise in a warm place about ten minutes.

16. Bake twenty-five minutes, or until well browned. Cool on a rack.

17. If desired, frost with confectioners' sugar moistened with lemon juice. Cut into one-inch strips.

Yield: About four dozen strips.

Note: Odense brand marzipan, imported from Denmark, is available in most specialty stores and many supermarkets.

Valborg's Coffeecake   *Iowa*

  1 cup milk, scalded
½ cup shortening
    Sugar
  2 packages active dry yeast
¼ cup lukewarm water
  2 eggs, lightly beaten
4½ cups flour, approximately
    Melted butter
  1 teaspoon ground cardamom
⅔ cup raisins
⅓ cup candied orange peel, finely chopped
⅓ cup candied citron peel, finely chopped.

1. Place the milk in a bowl. Add the shortening and one-half cup sugar. Stir to dissolve sugar and melt shortening. Let mixture stand until lukewarm.

2. Dissolve the yeast in the water and add to cooled milk mixture. Stir in the eggs and enough flour to make a soft dough.

3. Knead the dough in the bowl or on a lightly floured board until smooth and elastic.

4. Place dough in a clean greased bowl, cover and let rise in a warm place until doubled in bulk, about one hour.

5. Punch dough down and roll out half the dough into a rectangle about 9 by 14 inches.

Brush with one-quarter cup melted butter. Combine one cup sugar with the cardamom and sprinkle half over the dough.

6. Sprinkle with half the fruits and roll up from long end. Place on a greased baking sheet and shape into a ring or a horseshoe. Brush with melted butter, sprinkle with sugar, cover and let rise until doubled in bulk, about twenty-five minutes.

7. Using remaining half of dough and other ingredients, prepare another coffeecake in the same way.

8. Preheat the oven to 350 degrees.

9. If desired, top layer of dough can be snipped with scissors. Bake coffeecakes thirty-five minutes, or until well browned and done.

Yield: Two coffeecakes.

Note: If desired, coffeecakes may be iced with confectioners' sugar moistened with water or fruit juice.

Cinnamon Rolls, Plain and Fancy
Illinois

2 packages active dry yeast
¼ cup lukewarm water
2 cups milk, scalded and cooled to lukewarm
2 eggs, lightly beaten
¾ cup granulated sugar
6 cups flour, approximately
3 teaspoons salt
¼ cup melted shortening, cooled
½ cup butter, melted
1 cup light brown sugar
2 teaspoons cinnamon
  Raisins (optional)
1 cup sour cream
1 teaspoon vanilla.

1. Dissolve the yeast in the water. Gradually beat the milk into the eggs. Beat in one-quarter cup of the granulated sugar and the dissolved yeast. Stir in half the flour and the salt.

2. Stir in the shortening and enough additional flour to make a soft dough.

3. Turn out the dough onto a lightly floured board, cover and let stand ten minutes. Knead the dough ten minutes.

4. Place in a clean greased bowl, cover and let rise until doubled in bulk, about one hour. Punch dough down, cover and let rise in a warm place forty-five minutes.

5. Divide the dough in half. Roll out one half on a lightly floured board to a rectangle about 12 by 18 inches. Brush with half the butter.

6. Combine the remaining granulated sugar, one-half cup of the brown sugar and one and one-half teaspoons of the cinnamon and sprinkle half over the dough. Sprinkle with raisins if desired.

7. Roll dough up from the long side like a jellyroll. Cut into eighteen one-inch slices and place, cut side up, in two greased nine-inch square or round baking pans. Repeat with the other half of the dough, butter and cinnamon-sugar mixture and raisins.

8. Cover rolls and let rise until doubled in bulk, about forty minutes.

9. Preheat the oven to 375 degrees.

10. Bake two pans plain rolls about twenty to twenty-five minutes, or until done. Turn onto a rack to cool.

11. Bake the other two pans of rolls ten to fifteen minutes or until rolls just start to brown. Combine the sour cream with remaining brown sugar and cinnamon and the vanilla. Spoon evenly over rolls. Return to oven and bake ten to fifteen minutes, or until frosting boils into thick sticky frosting. Serve warm.

Yield: Eighteen plain and eighteen fancy cinnamon rolls.

Christmas Crullers (Swedish Klenater)
Minnesota

6 egg yolks
6 tablespoons confectioners' sugar
¼ cup butter
1 tablespoon cognac or dark rum
1 tablespoon grated lemon rind

2 cups flour
Oil for deep-frying.

1. Place the egg yolks in a mixing bowl and stir in the sugar and butter. Stir in the cognac or rum and lemon rind and fold in the flour to make a dough. Cover and chill several hours.

2. Shape the dough into a ball on a floured board. Roll dough out to about one-quarter-inch thickness. Use a pastry wheel to cut the dough into strips about three-quarters-inch wide and three inches long. Make a slash lengthwise in the center of each strip and twist one end through the slash.

3. Heat the oil to 375 degrees and cook the crullers in it until golden brown. Drain on paper towels.

Yield: About seventy-five.

Sour Cream Doughnuts   *Iowa*

1 egg
  Sugar
½ cup sour cream
½ cup buttermilk
5 tablespoons regular milk
1 teaspoon salt
1 teaspoon baking soda
½ teaspoon nutmeg
4 cups flour, approximately
  Fat or oil for deep-frying.

1. Beat the egg and gradually beat in one cup sugar. Stir in the sour cream, buttermilk and regular milk. Sift the salt, baking soda and nutmeg with two cups of the flour and stir into sour cream mixture.

2. Add enough additional flour to make a soft dough that can just be handled. Roll out on a floured board and cut with doughnut cutter. Fry, a few at a time, in the fat or oil heated to 370 degrees, turning often.

3. Drain on paper towels. Roll doughnuts in sugar.

Yield: About three dozen.

Pancakes with Bread   *Illinois*

3 cups buttermilk
3 slices stale white bread
2 eggs, lightly beaten
2 tablespoons melted butter
1 cup flour
1 teaspoon salt
1 teaspoon baking soda
1 teaspoon baking powder.

1. Pour the buttermilk over the bread and let stand several hours. Beat well. Add the eggs and butter.

2. Sift together the flour, salt, baking soda and baking powder and stir into the batter. Test two to three tablespoons on a hot greased griddle. Batter should be consistency of thick cream. If mixture is too thin, add a tablespoon or two of bread moistened in buttermilk, and if too thick, add a little buttermilk. The pancakes are moist inside.

Yield: About one dozen.

Buckwheat Griddlecakes   *Ohio*

½ package (one and one-half teaspoons)
  active dry yeast
1½ cups plus one tablespoon lukewarm water
2½ cups buckwheat flour
¼ teaspoon salt
1 cup milk, scalded and cooled to lukewarm
½ teaspoon baking soda.

1. Night before, dissolve the yeast in one and one-half cups of the water. Combine the flour, salt, dissolved yeast and the milk in a glass or ceramic bowl. Beat well. Cover and set in a warm place.

2. Next morning, dissolve the baking soda in the remaining water and add to the batter. Make a test cake on a greased griddle heated to 400 degrees. If batter is too thin, stir in a small quan-

tity of buckwheat flour, and if too thick, thin with warm water or milk.

Yield: Two dozen to three dozen.

Buttermilk Pancakes   *Oklahoma*

3 eggs, separated
½ cup flour
2½ teaspoons baking powder
¼ teaspoon salt
½ cup buttermilk.

1. Beat the egg yolks until light.
2. Sift together the flour, baking powder and salt and add to the yolks alternately with the buttermilk.
3. Beat the egg whites until stiff but not dry and fold into mixture. Bake on a greased griddle heated to 380 degrees.

Yield: About one dozen small pancakes.

Apple Toast   *Indiana*

6 tart apples, cored, peeled and sliced
6 tablespoons butter
⅓ cup confectioners' sugar
2 tablespoons water
3 slices bread
2 tablespoons granulated sugar
¼ teaspoon cinnamon.

1. Place the apple slices in a saucepan with two tablespoons of the butter, the confectioners' sugar and water. Cook quickly, tossing lightly, over medium-high heat until barely tender.

2. Melt remaining butter in a skillet and fry the bread slices in it until golden on both sides. Place a slice of bread on a plate, top with apple mixture and sprinkle with the granulated sugar mixed with the cinnamon.

Yield: Three servings.

Aebleskiver (Danish Doughnuts)   *Iowa*

2 cups buttermilk
2 eggs, separated
2 cups flour
½ teaspoon salt
  Sugar
1 teaspoon baking soda
  Shortening
  Jelly or applesauce.

1. Beat together the buttermilk and egg yolks.
2. Sift together the flour, salt, one teaspoon sugar and baking soda and stir into the buttermilk mixture. Beat the egg whites until stiff but not dry and fold into batter.
3. Heat an aebleskiver pan (cast-iron pan with hemispherical holes; see note). Brush with shortening.
4. Two-thirds fill each hole in pan with batter and cook slowly until bottom is lightly brown. With an ice pick, turn the balls and brown the top side. Serve immediately with sugar and jelly or applesauce.

Yield: About two dozen.

Note: Aebleskiver pans are available by mail from Maid of Scandinavia, 3245 Raleigh Avenue, Minneapolis, Minnesota 55416; at Nyborg & Nelson, 937 Second Avenue, New York, New York, 10022; and at most Scandinavian stores.

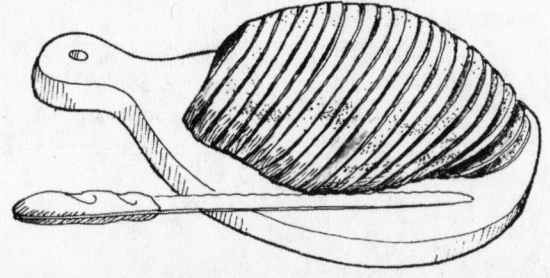

Pies, Cakes, Desserts and Cookies

Regular Pie Crust Kansas

2¼ cups flour
¼ teaspoon salt
¾ cup shortening
2 tablespoons heavy cream.

1. Place the flour and salt in a bowl. With a pastry blender or the finger tips, blend the shortening into the flour until mixture resembles coarse oatmeal.
2. With a fork, stir in the cream and enough water to make a dough. Wrap in wax paper and chill twenty minutes before rolling.
Yield: Enough for a two-crust nine-inch pie.

No-Fail Pie Crust Ohio

3 cups flour
1 teaspoon salt
1 teaspoon baking powder
1 cup plus two tablespoons shortening
1 egg
⅓ cup water
1 tablespoon vinegar.

1. Sift the flour, salt and baking powder into a bowl. With a pastry blender or the finger tips, blend the shortening into the flour until mixture resembles coarse oatmeal.
2. Beat the egg, water and vinegar together

and stir into the flour mixture. The dough may be used immediately or held refrigerated two days.
Yield: Enough for three pie shells or one large (ten-inch) two-crust pie.

Hot Water Pie Crust Iowa

½ cup water
1 cup shortening
3 cups flour
1 teaspoon salt
1 teaspoon baking powder
½ teaspoon sugar.

1. Place the water and shortening in a small saucepan and heat until shortening melts.
2. Sift together the remaining ingredients. Using a two-pronged fork, stir shortening mixture into the dry ingredients. Shape into a ball.
3. Wrap in wax paper and refrigerate overnight.
Yield: Enough for one two-crust pie or three pie shells.

Lemon-Nutmeg Custard Pie Illinois

6 eggs
1½ cups sugar
¼ teaspoon salt
2 teaspoons grated lemon rind

⅔ cup freshly squeezed lemon juice
1½ cups water
1 unbaked nine-inch pie shell
  Nutmeg.

1. Preheat the oven to 425 degrees.
2. Combine the eggs, sugar, salt, lemon rind, lemon juice and water in a large mixer bowl. Beat five minutes with electric mixer at low speed. Pour into the pie shell and bake twenty-five minutes.
3. Reduce the oven heat to 250 degrees and bake ten minutes longer. Sprinkle with nutmeg. Cool on a rack.
Yield: Six to eight servings.

'89er Lemon Pie   *Oklahoma*

1½ cups sugar
3 tablespoons cornstarch
1½ cups hot water
½ cup cider vinegar
1 tablespoon butter
2 eggs, separated
1 baked eight-inch to nine-inch pie shell
¼ teaspoon cream of tartar.

1. Mix one and one-quarter cups of the sugar with the cornstarch in a saucepan. Stir in the water, vinegar and butter.
2. Bring to a boil, stirring constantly until mixture is thick and clear. Remove from the heat.
3. Stir a small amount of the mixture into the egg yolks, return to bulk of the mixture in the pan and cook, stirring, two minutes longer.
4. Pour into the pie shell. Cool and chill.
5. Preheat the oven to 325 degrees.
6. Beat the egg whites until frothy. Add the cream of tartar and continue to beat, adding the remaining sugar very gradually until mixture is very stiff. Spread the meringue over the cooled pie, sealing meringue all the way to the edge of the pastry. Bake ten to twelve minutes, or until meringue is lightly browned.

Yield: Six servings.
Note: This is the mock "lemon pie" that the pioneers made because they could not get lemons.

Vinegar Pie   *Ohio*

2 tablespoons butter
½ cup sugar
3 tablespoons flour
2 teaspoons cinnamon
½ teaspoon ground cloves
½ teaspoon ground allspice
1 egg, lightly beaten
2 tablespoons cider vinegar
1 cup water
1 eight-inch to nine-inch pie shell that has been baked for two or three minutes at 450 degrees.

1. Preheat the oven to 350 degrees.
2. Cream the butter and sugar together. Sift the flour with the cinnamon, cloves and allspice and add to butter mixture. Stir in the egg, vinegar and water. Transfer to top of a double boiler.
3. Cook over boiling water until thick. Pour into the pie shell and bake thirty minutes.
Yield: Six servings.

Amber Pie   *Illinois*

3 eggs, separated
1 cup plus six tablespoons sugar
½ cup buttermilk
¼ teaspoon ground allspice
1 tablespoon flour
1½ teaspoons cider vinegar
½ cup chopped nuts
½ cup raisins
1 unbaked nine-inch pie shell
2 tablespoons butter
1 teaspoon vanilla.

1. Preheat the oven to 400 degrees.
2. Mix together the egg yolks, one cup of the

sugar, the buttermilk, allspice, flour, vinegar, nuts and raisins. Pour into the pie shell.

3. Dot with the butter and bake about forty-five minutes, or until golden brown and firm. Cool slightly.

4. Reduce the oven heat to 350 degrees.

5. Beat the egg whites until frothy and gradually beat in the remaining sugar until mixture is stiff. Add the vanilla.

6. Spread meringue over pie and bake ten to fifteen minutes, or until meringue is lightly browned.

Yield: Six servings.

Osgood Pie   *Illinois*

1 cup raisins
2 cups sugar
4 eggs, separated
2 tablespoons butter
3 tablespoons cider vinegar
1 teaspoon cinnamon
1 teaspoon ground cloves
1 unbaked nine-inch to ten-inch pie shell.

1. Preheat the oven to 400 degrees.

2. Cover the raisins with water and let soak five minutes. Drain raisins and pat dry.

3. In a bowl, mix the sugar and egg yolks well. Add the butter, vinegar, cinnamon, cloves and raisins. Stir to mix.

4. Beat the egg whites until stiff but not dry and fold into the raisin mixture. Pour into the pie shell and bake about ten minutes.

5. Reduce the oven heat to 325 degrees. Bake the pie until a knife inserted in center of filling tests clean, about forty minutes longer.

Yield: Six servings.

Retha's Rum Cream Pie   *Oklahoma*

½ envelope unflavored gelatin
¼ cup water
½ cup sugar

⅛ teaspoon salt
3 egg yolks
¼ cup dark rum
1 cup heavy cream, whipped
1 eight-inch to nine-inch graham cracker crust
  Whipped cream and /or chocolate curls for garnish (optional).

1. Sprinkle the gelatin over the water to soften. Add the sugar, salt and egg yolks and stir over medium heat until the gelatin dissolves and the yolks thicken. Do not boil.

2. Stir in the rum and cool until the mixture starts to thicken. Fold in the whipped cream and pour into the prepared crust. Chill several hours before serving. Pie may be garnished with whipped cream and/or chocolate curls.

Yield: Six servings.

Grandmother's Angel Food Pie

Oklahoma

1 cup sugar
2½ tablespoons cornstarch
1 cup water
⅛ teaspoon salt
1 cup shredded pineapple
2 tablespoons butter
2 egg whites, beaten until stiff but not dry
1 baked nine-inch pie shell
  Whipped cream and nuts for garnish.

1. Combine the sugar and cornstarch in a small saucepan and gradually stir in the water. Add the salt, pineapple and butter.

2. Bring to a boil, stirring, and cook until mixture is thick. Cool to lukewarm. Fold in the egg whites and pour mixture into the pie shell. Cool and chill. Garnish with whipped cream and nuts.

Yield: Six servings.

St. Genevieve Angel Pie   *Missouri*

6 eggs, separated
1⅓ cups sugar
⅓ cup plus one tablespoon fresh lemon juice
1 baked nine-inch pie shell.

1. Preheat the oven to 300 degrees.
2. Beat the egg yolks until they are light and lemon-colored while gradually beating in one cup of the sugar. Beat in one-third cup of the lemon juice. Spoon the mixture into the top of a double boiler and cook over boiling water, stirring, until the mixture thickens. Cool almost to room temperature.
3. Beat three of the egg whites until stiff and fold them into the yolk mixture. Spoon the mixture into pie shell.
4. Beat the remaining whites until frothy and add the remaining lemon juice. Continue beating until whites are stiff and gradually beat in remaining sugar. Spread the meringue over the filled pie shell and bake briefly until lightly browned. Cool and serve.
Yield: Six servings.

This pie dates from 1885.

Poorman's Pie   *Oklahoma*

Pastry for single 8-inch pie shell (made with one cup flour)
2 baking powder biscuits
¾ cup sugar
½ teaspoon cinnamon
1 cup light cream, approximately
⅓ cup chopped nuts (optional).

1. Preheat the oven to 350 degrees.
2. Line an eight-inch pie plate with pastry. Break or crumble the biscuits into pie shell.
3. Sprinkle with the sugar and cinnamon. Fill pie shell with the cream. Sprinkle with the nuts, if desired. Bake until a knife inserted in center of filling comes out clean, about forty-five minutes. Serve warm.
Yield: Six servings.

Graham Cracker Pie   *Ohio*

11 graham crackers, rolled or blended into crumbs
1 cup chopped nuts
1 cup sugar
1 teaspoon baking powder
3 eggs, well beaten
¼ cup raisins
¼ cup flaked coconut
Whipped cream.

1. Preheat the oven to 300 degrees.
2. Combine the cracker crumbs, nuts, sugar and baking powder in a bowl. Stir in the eggs, raisins and coconut.
3. Pour into a greased pie plate and bake twenty minutes. Cool and serve with whipped cream.
Yield: Six servings.

French Silk Chocolate Pie   *Oklahoma*

1 cup butter
1½ cups sugar
4 ounces (4 squares) unsweetened chocolate, melted and cooled
2 teaspoons vanilla
4 eggs
1 baked nine-inch pie shell, cooled
Whipped cream.

1. Beat the butter with the sugar until very well blended. Mixture should be smooth, fluffy and pale yellow.
2. Blend in the chocolate and vanilla.
3. Using an electric mixer at medium speed, beat in the eggs, one at a time, taking five minutes to incorporate each.
4. Turn the mixture into the pie shell and chill

several hours. Decorate with whipped cream before serving.

Yield: Eight servings.

Strawberry Pie　　　　*Illinois*

Filling:
⅓ cup sugar
6 tablespoons flour
6 egg yolks, lightly beaten
2 cups milk, scalded
1 teaspoon vanilla
1 baked nine-inch pie shell
½ cup slivered blanched almonds, toasted.
Topping and glaze:
2½ cups fresh strawberries
½ cup water
¼ cup sugar
2 teaspoons cornstarch
Few drops red food coloring
Whipped cream.

1. To prepare filling, mix the sugar and flour together in a saucepan. Stir in the egg yolks and then the milk, beating vigorously.

2. Cook, stirring constantly, until mixture thickens. Cook two to three minutes longer. Cool and stir in the vanilla.

3. Sprinkle the bottom of the pie shell with the almonds and pour in the cooled pastry cream. Chill.

4. Meanwhile, crush one-half cup of the berries in a saucepan and add the water, sugar and cornstarch. Bring to a boil, stirring, and cook two minutes. Tint with food coloring and cool slightly.

5. Slice remaining berries if large, or leave whole if small, and pile on top of chilled cream filling. Spoon the cooled glaze over all. Chill. Decorate with whipped cream before serving.

Yield: Six servings.

Old-Fashioned Raisin Pie　　　*Illinois*

Pastry for a two-crust nine-inch pie
2 cups raisins
1 cup boiling water
2 eggs
2 tablespoons flour
1 cup sugar
2 tablespoons butter
Grated rind of one lemon
2 tablespoons lemon juice.

1. Line a nine-inch pie plate with two-thirds of the pastry.

2. Place the raisins in a small saucepan, cover with the boiling water, bring to a simmer and cook slowly eight minutes. Cool to room temperature.

3. Preheat the oven to 425 degrees.

4. Beat the eggs. Combine the flour and sugar and gradually beat into the eggs. Cut the butter into little pieces and add.

5. Combine egg mixture with raisins and their liquid, the lemon rind and lemon juice. Turn mixture into pastry-lined pie plate. Roll out the remaining pastry and cut into one-half-inch strips. Arrange in lattice pattern over pie. Bake ten minutes.

6. Reduce the oven heat to 350 degrees. Bake pie twenty minutes longer, or until pastry is done.

Yield: Six servings.

St. Louis Pumpkin Pie　　　*Missouri*

2 cups canned pumpkin
1 cup milk
1 cup light cream
½ cup dark brown sugar
½ cup granulated sugar
1½ teaspoons cinnamon
¼ teaspoon salt
½ teaspoon nutmeg
1 tablespoon flour
2 eggs, lightly beaten

1 unbaked nine-inch pie shell
¾ cup toasted pecans.

1. Preheat the oven to 450 degrees.
2. Combine the pumpkin, milk, cream, sugars, cinnamon, salt, nutmeg, flour and eggs and beat well. Pour the mixture into the pie shell and sprinkle with pecans. Bake ten minutes.
3. Reduce the oven heat to 325 degrees and bake fifty minutes longer, or until set.
Yield: Six to eight servings.
Note: Fresh honey and whipped cream may be spooned onto each slice before serving.

Frozen Pumpkin Pie *Illinois*

2 cups heavy cream
2 tablespoons confectioners' sugar
1½ cups canned pumpkin
1¼ cups light brown sugar
¼ teaspoon ginger
1½ teaspoons cinnamon
¼ teaspoon nutmeg
½ teaspoon salt
1 pint vanilla ice cream, softened.

1. Chill a nine-inch pie plate in the freezer. Whip one and one-half cups of the heavy cream with the confectioners' sugar.
2. Using a spoon or spatula, make a "crust" on the bottom and up the sides of the pie plate with the whipped cream. Freeze until firm.
3. Mix the pumpkin with the brown sugar, ginger, cinnamon, nutmeg and salt. Stir in the ice cream and either mix thoroughly to incorporate or mix slightly to give a marbleized effect.
4. Whip the remaining heavy cream for garnish.
5. Spoon pumpkin mixture into the cream "crust," garnish with whipped cream and freeze until firm. Remove from the freezer fifteen minutes before serving.
Yield: Six servings.

Annie's Pumpkin Chiffon Pie *Kansas*

3 eggs, separated
1 cup sugar
1¼ cups canned pumpkin
½ cup milk
½ teaspoon salt
½ teaspoon cinnamon
½ teaspoon nutmeg
½ teaspoon ginger
1 envelope unflavored gelatin
¼ cup cold water
1 baked nine-inch pie shell
Whipped cream (optional).

1. In a saucepan or the top of a double boiler, beat the egg yolks with one-half cup of the sugar. Add the pumpkin, milk, salt, cinnamon, nutmeg and ginger.
2. Cook, stirring, over direct heat or over boiling water until the mixture thickens. Do not allow to boil.
3. Sprinkle the gelatin over the water. Stir into the hot mixture, cool and chill until mixture starts to thicken.
4. Whip the egg whites until frothy. Gradually beat in the remaining sugar and fold into the setting pumpkin mixture.
5. Turn into the pie shell and chill well. Decorate with whipped cream if desired.
Yield: Six servings.

Grandmother's Squash Pie *Oklahoma*

1½ cups sieved cooked squash
1 cup dark brown sugar
1 teaspoon cinnamon
1 teaspoon ground ginger
1 teaspoon ground cloves
¼ teaspoon nutmeg
1 teaspoon salt
3 eggs, well beaten
1 cup milk
1 unbaked nine-inch pie shell.

1. Preheat the oven to 350 degrees.
2. Place the squash in a bowl and add brown sugar, cinnamon, ginger, cloves, nutmeg and salt. Mix well. Combine the eggs and milk and gradually stir into the squash mixture.
3. Pour into the pie shell and bake fifty-five minutes, or until knife inserted in center of filling tests clean. Cool and chill.
Yield: Six servings.

Cherokee Hickory Nut Pie   *Oklahoma*

½ cup soft butter
3 eggs, lightly beaten
¼ teaspoon salt
1½ cups chopped hickory nuts or black walnuts
1 cup sugar
¾ cup dark corn syrup
1 teaspoon vanilla
1 unbaked nine-inch pie shell.

1. Preheat the oven to 450 degrees.
2. Combine the butter, eggs, salt, nuts, sugar, syrup and vanilla. Beat with a spoon to blend. Pour the mixture into the pie shell and bake fifteen minutes.
3. Reduce the oven heat to 350 degrees. Bake thirty to forty minutes longer, or until set.
Yield: Six servings.

Glazed Apple Cheese Pie   *Iowa*

1 three-ounce package cream cheese
1 tablespoon milk or sour cream
1 baked nine-inch pie shell
6 large apples that hold their shape as they cook, such as Rome or Delicious
1½ cups plus two tablespoons water
1 cup sugar
1 stick cinnamon
2 tablespoons lemon juice
1 teaspoon grated lemon rind

2 tablespoons cornstarch
Red food coloring.

1. Soften the cream cheese with the milk or sour cream and spread over the bottom of the pie shell.
2. Peel the apples and cut into eighths. Place one and one-half cups of the water and the sugar in a saucepan and bring to a boil. Drop in the apple pieces and cinnamon stick and simmer until apples are barely tender but not broken.
3. With a slotted spoon, remove apple pieces. Drain and let cool. Discard cinnamon stick. Measure one and one-quarter cups of the apple syrup.
4. Add the lemon juice and lemon rind to apple syrup. Mix together the cornstarch and remaining water. Stir into apple syrup mixture. Bring to a boil, stirring, and cook two minutes over very low heat, stirring constantly. Color faintly pink with food coloring.
5. Fill the pie shell with the apple pieces, arranging the top layer in an attractive pattern. Spoon glaze over the apples. Serve at room temperature.
Yield: Six servings.

Greta's Apple Pie   *Iowa*

Pastry:
3 cups flour
1¼ cups lard or shortening
1 teaspoon salt
1 egg, beaten
5 tablespoons water
1 tablespoon cider vinegar.
Filling:
5 to six cups peeled, cored and finely sliced or diced apples
Sugar
2 tablespoons flour
¼ teaspoon salt
¾ teaspoon cinnamon
½ teaspoon nutmeg
3 tablespoons butter.

1. To prepare pastry, place flour, lard or shortening and salt in a bowl and, with the finger tips or a pastry blender, work the fat into the flour. Mixture should resemble coarse oatmeal.

2. Mix the egg, water and vinegar together and, using a fork, stir into the fat-flour mixture. Wrap in wax paper and chill in the refrigerator. This quantity of pastry will make a two-crust nine-inch to ten-inch pie and a pie shell, or four eight-inch to nine-inch pie shells. The pastry will keep in the refrigerator several days.

3. Preheat the oven to 425 degrees.

4. Roll out one-third of the pastry on a lightly floured board or pastry cloth to fit a nine-inch to ten-inch pie plate. Put pastry in pie plate.

5. To prepare filling, combine the apples with one and one-half cups sugar, the flour, salt, cinnamon and nutmeg. Dot bottom crust with half the butter. Place filling in the crust.

6. Roll out another third of the pastry and top the pie. Seal and decorate the edges and make a steam hole. Dot the crust with the remaining butter and sprinkle with sugar. Bake forty to forty-five minutes, or until crust is golden brown and done.

Yield: Six servings.

Cider Apple Pie   *Oklahoma*

½ pound dried apples
3 cups cider
½ cup sugar
½ teaspoon cinnamon
¼ teaspoon nutmeg
  Pastry for a two-crust nine-inch pie
2 tablespoons butter.

1. Place the apples and cider in a saucepan. Bring to a boil and simmer until apples are tender and plump.

2. Combine the sugar, cinnamon and nutmeg, add to apples and cook ten minutes longer. The apples should have absorbed most of the juice. Cool slightly.

3. Preheat the oven to 425 degrees.

4. Line a nine-inch pie plate with half the pastry. Pour in the apple filling. Roll remaining pastry into a rectangle and cut into one-half-inch strips. Dot apple mixture with butter and make a lattice of pastry. Bake twenty-five to thirty minutes, or until pastry is cooked.

Yield: Six servings.

Pie Plant or Rhubarb Cream Pie   *Illinois*

3 eggs, separated
2 cups heavy cream
½ teaspoon salt
1¼ cups plus six tablespoons sugar
2 tablespoons flour
2 cups diced rhubarb
1 unbaked nine-inch to ten-inch pie shell, chilled.

1. Preheat the oven to 400 degrees.

2. Beat the egg yolks with the cream. Combine the salt, one and one-quarter cups of the sugar and the flour and add to the cream mixture.

3. Place the rhubarb in the pie shell and pour cream mixture over rhubarb. Bake ten minutes.

4. Reduce the oven heat to 350 degrees and bake thirty-five minutes longer, or until set. Cool slightly.

5. Beat the egg whites until frothy and gradually beat in the remaining sugar until mixture is stiff and glossy. Top the pie with the meringue and bake ten minutes, or until meringue is lightly browned.

Yield: Six servings.

Rhubarb and Strawberry Custard Pie   *Ohio*

  Pastry for a two-crust nine-inch pie
2 cups one-inch-long pieces washed rhubarb
2 cups strawberries, hulled and quartered if large
1¼ cups sugar

3 tablespoons flour
½ teaspoon nutmeg
1 tablespoon butter
2 eggs, lightly beaten.

1. Line a nine-inch pie plate with two-thirds of the pastry.
2. Preheat the oven to 400 degrees.
3. Combine the rhubarb and strawberries and place in the pastry-lined pie plate.
4. Combine the sugar, flour and nutmeg in a bowl. Cut the butter into little pieces and add along with the eggs. Mix well.
5. Pour sugar and mixture over the fruit in the pie plate. Roll out the remaining pastry and cut into one-half-inch strips. Arrange over the pie in a lattice design.
6. Place pie in the oven. Immediately reduce the oven heat to 350 degrees. Bake about thirty-five minutes, or until the pastry is done and rhubarb is tender.
Yield: Six servings.

Mulberry Pie   *Iowa*

2 cups mulberries
2 cups diced rhubarb
¾ cup plus one tablespoon sugar
¼ cup flour
    Pastry for a two-crust nine-inch pie
3 tablespoons light cream.

1. Preheat the oven to 400 degrees.
2. Combine the mulberries, rhubarb, three-quarters cup of the sugar and the flour.
3. Line a nine-inch pie plate with half the pastry. Fill with the fruit mixture. Roll out the remaining pastry for a top crust and use to cover pie. Seal and decorate the edge. Brush crust with the cream and sprinkle with remaining sugar. Make a steam hole.
4. Bake forty-five minutes, or until pastry is golden and done.
Yield: Six servings.

Danish Raspberry Pie   *Kansas*

1 sixteen-ounce to seventeen-ounce can black raspberries in heavy syrup
2 tablespoons sugar
1 envelope unflavored gelatin
3 tablespoons cold water
2 egg whites
⅛ teaspoon salt
1 baked eight-inch to nine-inch pie shell
    Whipped cream.

1. Drain the raspberries. Measure the juice and if necessary add water to make one cup. Add the sugar to the juice and heat.
2. Soften the gelatin in the cold water, add to hot syrup and stir to dissolve. Cool and chill until mixture starts to thicken.
3. Beat mixture until light and fluffy. Beat the egg whites until stiff but not dry and fold in. Carefully fold in raspberries and pour the mixture into pie shell. Chill. Decorate with whipped cream just before serving.
Yield: Six servings.

Crumb-Topped Cherry Pie   *Michigan*

2 one-pound cans tart red cherries
¾ cup sugar
3½ tablespoons cornstarch
¼ teaspoon salt
½ teaspoon grated lemon rind
2 tablespoons lemon juice
    Red food coloring
1 unbaked nine-inch pie shell.
Topping:
½ cup flour
½ cup sugar
½ teaspoon cinnamon
¼ teaspoon mace
⅓ cup butter.

1. Preheat the oven to 400 degrees.
2. Drain the cherries and reserve one and one-quarter cups liquid. Combine the sugar, corn-

starch and salt. Add the reserved cherry liquid and cook until thick, stirring constantly.

3. Add cherries, the lemon rind, lemon juice and a drop or two of food coloring.

4. Pour cherry mixture into the pie shell.

5. To prepare topping, combine the flour, sugar, cinnamon and mace in a bowl and cut in the butter until the mixture is crumbly. Sprinkle over the cherries.

6. Bake about thirty minutes, or until the crust is lightly browned. Serve warm.

Yield: Six servings.

Green Tomato Pie   *Oklahoma*

8 medium-size green tomatoes
2 tablespoons lemon juice
2 teaspoons grated lemon rind
½ teaspoon salt
½ teaspoon cinnamon
¾ cup sugar
2 tablespoons cornstarch
1 tablespoon butter
   Pastry for a two-crust nine-inch pie.

1. Wash and peel the tomatoes and slice fairly thickly.

2. Place in a pan with the lemon juice, lemon rind, salt and cinnamon. Bring to a simmer and simmer about ten minutes, or until tomatoes are barely tender.

3. Mix together the sugar and cornstarch and stir into the tomato mixture. Cook, stirring gently, until clear. Add the butter and allow to cool.

4. Preheat the oven to 425 degrees.

5. Line a nine-inch pie plate with half the pastry. Pour in the cooled filling and top with remaining pastry. Seal and decorate the edge and make a steam hole.

6. Bake forty to fifty minutes, or until pastry is cooked.

Yield: Six servings.

Poundcake   *Iowa*

1 cup butter
2 cups sugar
5 eggs
2 cups flour
¼ teaspoon lemon extract.

1. Cream the butter and sugar together until very light and fluffy. It is important to the success of this cake to do sufficient beating at this stage so that the grainy feel of the sugar completely disappears.

2. Beat in the eggs, one at a time, very well. At any hint of curdling, add one tablespoon of the measured flour.

3. Stir in the extract and fold in the flour. Grease and flour a heavy bundt pan and spoon in the batter. Set in a cold oven and light oven immediately, setting for a temperature of 350 degrees. Bake one hour, or until done.

Yield: Ten servings.

Golden Cake   *Oklahoma*

Cake:
4 eggs, separated
1 cup sugar
3 tablespoons water
1 teaspoon vanilla
1 cup cake flour
1½ tablespoons cornstarch
¼ teaspoon salt
1 teaspoon baking powder.
Frosting:
1 envelope unflavored gelatin
1 cup cold milk
2 egg yolks, beaten
1 teaspoon vanilla
1 cup sugar
1 cup heavy cream, whipped
½ cup buttered and lightly salted pecans.

1. Preheat the oven to 325 degrees.

2. To prepare cake, beat the egg yolks with the

sugar and water until very stiff and pale. Beat in the vanilla.

3. Sift together the flour, cornstarch, salt and baking powder and fold into the batter.

4. Beat the egg whites until stiff but not dry and fold in. Pour the batter into a lightly greased and floured nine-inch angel food pan. Bake forty minutes, or until done. Turn cake upside down in pan to cool.

5. To make frosting, sprinkle the gelatin over the milk to soften. Gradually bring to a boil and pour over the egg yolks, stirring vigorously. Stir in the vanilla and sugar until dissolved.

6. Let mixture cool and, when stiff, fold in the whipped cream.

7. Remove cake from the pan after loosening with a spatula. Pour frosting over. Sprinkle with the pecans. If desired, cake may be sliced across the middle and filled with some of the frosting and pecans.

Yield: Eight to ten servings.

Slovak Prune and Apricot Upside-Down Cake   *Wisconsin*

½ pound prunes
½ pound dried apricots
¼ cup soft butter
½ cup light brown sugar
½ teaspoon grated lemon rind
5 tablespoons shortening
⅔ cup granulated sugar
1 egg
2¼ cups flour
4 teaspoons baking powder
½ teaspoon salt
1 cup milk
Whipped cream.

1. Preheat the oven to 350 degrees.

2. Cover the prunes and apricots with water and simmer gently until tender, about twenty minutes. Cool. Drain, halve and pit the prunes. Drain the apricots.

3. Cream the butter and brown sugar together until smooth. Stir in the lemon rind and spread mixture in the bottom of a greased eight-inch square pan.

4. Arrange the apricots and prune halves slightly overlapping in neat rows on top of the butter-sugar mixture.

5. Cream the shortening and granulated sugar together. Beat in the egg. Sift the flour with the baking powder and salt and add alternately with the milk to the creamed mixture.

6. Spoon the batter carefully over the fruit and bake fifty minutes, or until done. Turn upside down onto a warm plate and serve warm with whipped cream.

Yield: Eight servings.

Banana Fruitcake   *Ohio*

3½ cups sifted flour
4 teaspoons baking powder
1 teaspoon salt
½ teaspoon baking soda
2 teaspoons cinnamon
2 teaspoons ginger
½ teaspoon freshly ground nutmeg
½ teaspoon ground allspice
1⅓ cups shortening
1⅓ cups sugar
4 eggs
2 cups mashed banana pulp (four to six ripe bananas)
1 cup raisins
1½ cups chopped almonds
4 cups diced glazed fruit.

1. Preheat the oven to 300 degrees.

2. Sift together the flour, baking powder and salt into a mixing bowl.

3. Blend the baking soda and spices with the shortening. Add the sugar gradually while beating. Beat in the eggs, one at a time. Add flour mixture alternately with the banana pulp.

4. Combine the raisins, almonds and glazed fruits and stir into batter.

5. Grease a 10-by-4-inch tube pan and line it

with brown paper. Pour in batter and place the pan on the center shelf of the oven. Place a pan of hot water on the shelf below it. Bake cake three and one-half to four hours.

Yield: One cake; one dozen servings.

bon-soaked cheesecloth and store in an airtight tin for at least a week before cutting.

Yield: About two dozen servings.

Dymple's Fruitcake   *Indiana*

½ pound butter
1 cup sugar
6 eggs
2 cups flour
¼ teaspoon cinnamon
¼ teaspoon ground cloves
¼ teaspoon nutmeg
2½ teaspoons baking powder
1 pound prunes, pitted and chopped
1 pound raisins
1 pound finely chopped citron
1 pound chopped nuts
¼ pound candied cherries
½ cup orange juice
Bourbon.

1. Preheat the oven to 275 degrees.
2. Line a nine-inch to ten-inch tube pan or two 9-by-5-by-3-inch loaf pans with brown paper or parchment.
3. Cream the butter and sugar together until very light and fluffy.
4. Beat in the eggs, one at a time.
5. Sift together the flour, cinnamon, cloves, nutmeg and baking powder. Combine the prunes, raisins, citron, nuts and cherries and dredge with one-third cup of the flour mixture.
6. Fold the remaining flour mixture into the butter and egg batter alternately with the orange juice. Fold in the fruits, nuts and flour.
7. Pack into the prepared pan or pans. Bake loaves about two and one-quarter hours and the tube pan three and one-quarter hours, or until a cake tester inserted in the center comes out clean.
8. Cool in the pan or pans. Wrap cake in bour-

Lizzies   *Kansas*

1 fifteen-ounce box raisins
½ cup bourbon, dark rum or cognac
¼ cup butter
¾ cup light brown sugar
2 eggs
2 cups flour
½ teaspoon ground cloves
½ teaspoon nutmeg
½ teaspoon ground allspice
½ teaspoon salt
½ teaspoon baking soda
½ pound candied pineapple, chopped
¼ pound candied orange, chopped
¼ pound candied citron, chopped
¼ pound glacé cherries, quartered
¼ pound candied lemon, chopped
3 cups chopped pecans, walnuts or almonds.

1. Preheat the oven to 325 degrees.
2. Soak the raisins in the bourbon, rum or cognac.
3. Cream the butter and brown sugar together. Beat in the eggs.
4. Sift together the flour, cloves, nutmeg, allspice, salt and baking soda. Fold into the batter.
5. Mix the soaked raisins and liquor with the remaining ingredients and stir into the flour mixture.
6. Drop by tablespoonfuls onto greased baking sheets and bake about fifteen minutes, or until lightly browned. Cool on a rack and then store in an airtight tin.

Yield: About four dozen.

Note: These are really miniature fruitcakes and they keep for months.

Dymple's Sausage Cake   *Indiana*

1 pound lean sausage meat
1 cup raisins
1 cup chopped walnuts
1 cup gum drops, all flavors except licorice,
  cut or ground finely
2 cups sugar
2½ cups flour
1 teaspoon baking powder
1 teaspoon cinnamon
1 teaspoon baking soda
1 teaspoon ground allspice
1 cup cold strong black coffee.

1. Preheat the oven to 300 degrees.
2. Place the sausage meat, raisins, walnuts, gum drops and sugar in a large bowl. With the fingers, mix all together, breaking up the sausage meat to get it evenly distributed.
3. Sift the flour with the baking powder, cinnamon, baking soda and allspice. Again with the fingers, mix dry ingredients into the sausage mixture alternately with the coffee.
4. Spoon into an ungreased nine-inch angel food pan and bake one and one-half hours. Cool thirty minutes in the pan before turning onto a rack.
Yield: One dozen servings.

Buttermilk Glazed Pineapple Carrot Cake
Oklahoma

Cake:
2 cups flour
1 teaspoon baking soda
½ teaspoon salt
1½ cups sugar
2 teaspoons cinnamon
3 eggs
¾ cup buttermilk
½ cup oil
2 teaspoons vanilla
1 eight-and-one-half-ounce can crushed
  pineapple

2 cups finely grated carrots (there should
  not be any liquid)
1 cup coarsely chopped nuts
1 cup flaked coconut.
Buttermilk glaze:
⅔ cup sugar
¼ teaspoon baking soda
⅓ cup buttermilk
⅓ cup butter
2 tablespoons light corn syrup
½ teaspoon vanilla.

1. Preheat the oven to 350 degrees.
2. To prepare cake, sift the flour, baking soda, salt, sugar and cinnamon together into a bowl. Beat the eggs with the buttermilk, oil and vanilla and add all at once to dry ingredients. Mix until smooth.
3. Fold in the pineapple, carrots, nuts and coconut and pour into a greased and floured 9-by-13-inch baking pan. Bake forty-five minutes, or until the center of cake springs back when lightly touched.
4. Meanwhile, prepare glaze. Combine all the ingredients except the vanilla in a small saucepan, bring to a boil, stirring, over medium heat and boil gently five minutes.
5. Remove from the heat and stir in the vanilla.
6. When cake is done, remove from oven and immediately prick the cake all over with a fork. Slowly pour the buttermilk glaze over cake. Cool in the pan and cut into slices.
Yield: Four dozen pieces.

White Cake with Choice of Frostings
Illinois

⅔ cup butter
2 cups sugar
3 cups flour
3 teaspoons baking powder
½ teaspoon salt
½ cup milk
½ cup water

1 teaspoon vanilla
½ teaspoon almond extract
6 egg whites
   Chocolate frosting or $100 frosting (recipes below).

1. Preheat the oven to 350 degrees.
2. Cream the butter and sugar together until light and fluffy. This is an important step, so do not skimp on the beating.
3. Sift together the flour, baking powder and salt three times. Mix the milk and water together and add the vanilla and almond extract.
4. Fold the flour mixture alternately with the liquid into the creamed mixture until well blended.
5. Beat the egg whites until stiff but not dry and fold into the batter. Pour into three greased and floured nine-inch layer pans. Bake twenty-five minutes, or until done. Cool in the pans five minutes; then turn out onto a rack to finish cooling. Fill and frost the layers with one of the frostings.
   Yield: Ten to one dozen servings.

Chocolate Frosting   *Illinois*

3 ounces (three squares) unsweetened
   chocolate, melted
3 cups confectioners' sugar
⅛ teaspoon salt
¼ cup hot water
3 egg yolks
¼ cup soft butter
1 teaspoon vanilla.

1. Remove the chocolate from the heat and stir in the confectioners' sugar, salt and water.
2. Beat in the egg yolks, one at a time. Beat in the butter bit by bit and the vanilla. Chill until right consistency to spread. Use to fill and frost layers.
   Yield: About two cups.

$100 Frosting   *Illinois*

½ cup butter
2 cups confectioners' sugar
2 tablespoons buttermilk
3 tablespoons strong black coffee
½ teaspoon vanilla
1 egg yolk.

Cream the butter and confectioners' sugar together very well and beat in the remaining ingredients. Beat until mixture is the consistency of whipped cream. Use to fill and frost layers.
   Yield: About two cups.

Banana Chiffon Cake   *Kansas*

2¼ cups cake flour
1½ cups sugar
3 teaspoons baking powder
½ teaspoon salt
½ cup oil
5 egg yolks, unbeaten
⅓ cup cold water
1 cup mashed ripe bananas
1 teaspoon vanilla
1 cup egg whites (seven or eight)
½ teaspoon cream of tartar.

1. Preheat the oven to 325 degrees.
2. Sift together the flour, sugar, baking powder and salt. Make a well in the center and add the oil, egg yolks, water, bananas and vanilla. Beat well.
3. Beat the egg whites until frothy. Add the cream of tartar and continue beating until stiff but not dry.
4. Pour the egg yolk mixture in a steady stream into the whites while folding in gently with a rubber spatula until completely blended. Turn into an ungreased nine-inch angel food pan and bake fifty-five minutes.
5. Increase the oven temperature to 350 degrees and bake five minutes longer.

6. Invert pan and let stand until cold.
Yield: Ten servings.

Greta's Chocolate Cake   *Iowa*

Cake:
1 cup butter
2 cups granulated sugar
1 teaspoon vanilla
4 eggs, well beaten
4 ounces (four squares) unsweetened
  chocolate, melted
3 cups cake flour
3 teaspoons baking powder
1 teaspoon salt
1 cup milk.
Frosting:
4 ounces (four squares) unsweetened
  chocolate
1 cup confectioners' sugar
3 tablespoons light cream
2 egg yolks
½ teaspoon vanilla.

1. Preheat the oven to 375 degrees.
2. To prepare cake, cream the butter and granulated sugar together until very light and fluffy.
3. Beat in the vanilla. Beat in the eggs until thoroughly mixed. Blend in the melted chocolate.
4. Sift together the flour, baking powder and salt and add alternately with the milk to the creamed mixture. Mix until blended.
5. Turn into three greased nine-inch layer pans and bake twenty-five minutes, or until done. Let cool in pans fifteen to twenty minutes before turning out onto a rack. Cool.
6. To prepare frosting, melt the chocolate. Stir in one-half cup of the confectioners' sugar and the cream. Beat the egg yolks with remaining sugar and add to the chocolate mixture. Heat, stirring, over simmering water until mixture thickens. Stir in the vanilla.

7. Cool to spreading consistency and use to fill and frost the layers.
Yield: Ten to one dozen servings.

Red Velvet Cake   *Indiana*

½ cup shortening
1½ cups sugar
2 eggs
2 cups flour
1 tablespoon cocoa powder
½ teaspoon salt
1 cup buttermilk
1 two-ounce bottle red food coloring
1 teaspoon baking soda
1 tablespoon vinegar
  Red velvet cake frosting (recipe below).

1. Preheat the oven to 350 degrees.
2. Cream the shortening and sugar together until light and fluffy. Beat in the eggs.
3. Sift together the flour, cocoa powder and salt and add alternately with the buttermilk and food coloring to the creamed mixture.
4. Dissolve the baking soda in the vinegar and fold in. Turn into three greased and floured eight-inch layer pans. Bake twenty-five minutes, or until done. Cool on racks and then fill and frost with frosting.
Yield: Ten to one dozen servings.

Red Velvet Cake Frosting   *Indiana*

1 cup milk
4½ tablespoons flour
¾ cup butter
4½ tablespoons shortening
1¼ cups sugar
⅛ teaspoon salt
3 teaspoons vanilla
⅓ cup flaked coconut.

1. Gradually add the milk to the flour to make

a smooth mixture. Bring to a boil, stirring until mixture thickens. Cool.

2. Cream the butter, shortening, sugar and salt together until creamy. Beat in the vanilla. Combine the cooked milk mixture and the creamed mixture. Chill and then use to fill and frost the layers. The coconut can be stirred into the frosting before using or sprinkled over after frosting is on the cake.

Yield: About three cups.

1870 Mahogany Cake   *Oklahoma*

Cake:
1¼ cups milk
½ cup cocoa powder
½ cup butter
1½ cups sugar
3 eggs, separated
1 teaspoon vanilla
2 cups flour
1 teaspoon baking soda, dissolved in one
  tablespoon hot water
½ cup chopped nuts.
Frosting:
1 cup sugar
½ cup boiling water
⅛ teaspoon salt
2 egg whites
2 teaspoons light corn syrup
¼ teaspoon cream of tartar
1 teaspoon vanilla.

1. Preheat the oven to 350 degrees. Grease two nine-inch layer pans and line the bottoms with wax paper. Grease again.

2. To prepare cake, heat one-half cup of the milk with the cocoa powder in a small pan, stirring until mixture thickens. Cool.

3. Cream the butter and sugar together very well. Beat in the egg yolks, one at a time. Beat in the cooled cocoa mixture.

4. Stir in the vanilla, flour, remaining milk, dissolved baking soda and nuts. Beat the egg whites until stiff and fold in. Spoon into prepared

layer pans and bake about twenty-five minutes, or until done. Cool on a rack.

5. To prepare frosting, place the sugar and water in a saucepan and heat, stirring, until sugar dissolves. Boil without stirring until sugar syrup reaches the soft ball stage or 238 degrees on a candy thermometer.

6. Add the salt to the egg whites and beat into the hot sugar syrup in a steady stream. Beat in the syrup and cream of tartar. Beat in the vanilla and continue beating until mixture is spreading consistency. Use to fill and frost the layers.

Yield: Six to eight servings.

Oatmeal Cake   *Kansas*

⅔ cup shortening
2 cups sugar
2 cups milk
1½ cups cooked oatmeal
2 cups flour
4 tablespoons cocoa powder
2 teaspoons ginger
1 teaspoon cinnamon
2 cups raisins
2 cups nutmeats, chopped
¼ teaspoon salt
2 teaspoons baking soda, dissolved in one or
  two tablespoons warm water.

1. Preheat the oven to 300 degrees.

2. Combine all the ingredients together in a bowl.

3. Pour into a greased nine-inch angel food pan.

4. Bake one and one-quarter hours, or until done. Cool in the pan on a rack.

Yield: Eight to ten servings.

Applesauce Cake   *Oklahoma*

1 cup butter
2 cups sugar
2 cups thick applesauce

3 cups flour
1 teaspoon cinnamon
1 teaspoon nutmeg
1¾ teaspoons baking soda
1 cup chopped pecans
1 cup raisins
1 teaspoon vanilla
Fudge frosting (recipe below).

1. Preheat the oven to 325 degrees.
2. Cream the butter and sugar together until very light and fluffy. Fold in the applesauce.
3. Sift together the flour, cinnamon, nutmeg and baking soda. Remove one-quarter cup of the mixture and toss with the pecans and raisins.
4. Fold the bulk of the flour mixture into the batter. Fold in the vanilla and the coated fruit and pecan mixture.
5. Pour into a nine-inch tube pan that has been either greased and floured or greased and lined with wax paper. Bake one and one-half hours, or until done. Cool slightly in the pan before turning onto a rack to cool completely.
6. When cool, frost with the frosting.
Yield: Ten to one dozen servings.
Note: Do not be disturbed if the top surface of the cake is not completely flat. The frosting smooths it out. The cake will keep for weeks.

Fudge Frosting   *Oklahoma*

2 cups light brown sugar
6 tablespoons heavy cream
4 tablespoons butter
1 teaspoon vanilla
1 cup confectioners' sugar.

1. Place the brown sugar, cream and butter in a pan. Heat slowly, stirring, until mixture reaches a full, rolling boil.
2. Remove from heat and stir in the vanilla and confectioners' sugar. Beat the frosting until it reaches a thick coating consistency. Spoon over the cake. Extra frosting can be poured into a buttered pan and, when set, eaten as fudge.
Yield: About two cups.

Buckeye Maple Syrup Cake   *Ohio*

Cake:
⅓ cup shortening
½ cup granulated sugar
¾ cup maple syrup
2¼ cups cake flour
3 teaspoons baking powder
¼ teaspoon salt
½ cup milk
3 egg whites.
Frosting:
3 cups confectioners' sugar
2 tablespoons cold strong black coffee
1 tablespoon melted butter
3 drops maple flavoring
Heavy cream
⅓ cup chopped nuts.

1. Preheat the oven to 350 degrees.
2. To prepare cake, cream the shortening and granulated sugar together until light and fluffy.
3. Stir in the syrup. Sift together the flour, baking powder and salt and add alternately with the milk to the syrup mixture.
4. Beat the egg whites until stiff but not dry and fold in. Pour batter into a nine-inch square pan that has been greased, lined with wax paper and greased again. Bake forty-five minutes, or until done. Cool on a rack.
5. To prepare frosting, combine the confectioners' sugar, coffee, butter, flavoring and enough cream to make spreading consistency.
6. Frost cake and sprinkle with the nuts.
Yield: One dozen servings.

Persimmon Upside-Down Cake

Indiana

¼ cup butter
2 cups light brown sugar
1 egg
2 cups flour
⅛ teaspoon salt
2 teaspoons baking powder
1 cup persimmon pulp
½ cup chopped nuts
1 cup water.

1. Preheat the oven to 350 degrees.
2. Cream the butter and one cup of the brown sugar together until light and fluffy. Beat in the egg. Sift together the flour, salt and baking powder and add alternately with the persimmon pulp to the creamed mixture.
3. Stir in the nuts. Batter will be thick.
4. Heat remaining brown sugar with the water until it boils. Boil one minute and pour into a greased 9-by-5-by-3-inch loaf pan. Pour the batter on top and bake forty minutes, or until done.
Yield: Eight servings.

Grandmother's Sorghum Cake

Iowa

Cake:
¾ cup shortening
¾ cup granulated sugar
2 eggs
1 cup sorghum or unsulphured molasses
1 cup thick applesauce
2½ cups flour
1½ teaspoons baking soda
1 teaspoon salt
1 teaspoon cinnamon
½ teaspoon nutmeg
½ teaspoon ground cloves
½ cup chopped nuts.
Frosting:
¼ cup butter
3 cups confectioners' sugar
Milk or light cream.

1. Preheat the oven to 350 degrees.
2. To prepare cake, beat the shortening and granulated sugar together until light and fluffy. Beat in the eggs, one at a time.
3. Beat in the sorghum or molasses and applesauce.
4. Sift together the flour, baking soda, salt, cinnamon, nutmeg and cloves and stir into the batter. Stir in the nuts. Pour into three greased and floured eight-inch layer pans and bake twenty minutes, or until done. Cool on a rack.
5. To prepare frosting, beat the butter and gradually beat in the confectioners' sugar and enough milk or cream to make spreading consistency. Use to fill and frost cooled layers.
Yield: Ten servings.

Molasses Cake

Indiana

¾ cup shortening
⅔ cup sugar
3 eggs
¾ cup dark molasses
2¾ cups flour
1 teaspoon baking soda
1 teaspoon cinnamon
½ teaspoon nutmeg
½ teaspoon ground cloves
¾ teaspoon salt
1 cup milk.

1. Preheat the oven to 350 degrees.
2. Cream the shortening and sugar together until light and creamy. Beat in the eggs, one at a time. Beat in the molasses.
3. Sift together the flour, baking soda, cinnamon, nutmeg, cloves and salt and stir into the batter alternately with the milk.
4. Pour into a greased nine-inch springform pan and bake one and one-quarter hours, or until done. Let cool in the pan five minutes. Remove pan sides and cool cake on a rack.
Yield: Ten servings.

No-Crust Cheesecake
Wisconsin

    1 pound cottage cheese
    1 pound soft cream cheese
1½ cups sugar
    4 eggs
    3 tablespoons cornstarch
    3 tablespoons flour
    2 tablespoons lemon juice
    1 teaspoon vanilla
    ½ cup melted butter, cooled
    2 cups sour cream.

1. Preheat the oven to 325 degrees.
2. Sieve the cottage cheese into a mixer bowl. Add the cream cheese and beat with an electric mixer until well blended and creamy.
3. Beat in the sugar and then the eggs. Beat in the cornstarch, flour, lemon juice and vanilla. Beat well.
4. Fold in the butter and sour cream or beat in at low speed. Pour into a lightly greased nine-inch springform pan and bake one hour and fifteen minutes, or until set. Turn oven heat off and let cake cool in oven three hours. Chill well.
Yield: One dozen servings.

Serbian Torte
Wisconsin

10 eggs, separated
1¾ cups sugar
    ¼ cup zwieback crumbs or dry bread crumbs
    1 teaspoon grated lemon rind
    ¼ cup lemon juice
    ½ pound blanched almonds, very finely ground
    3 ounces (three squares) unsweetened chocolate, melted
    ½ pound soft butter
    ¼ cup sliced toasted almonds.

1. Preheat the oven to 350 degrees.
2. Beat the egg whites until stiff and gradually beat in one cup of the sugar. Fold in the crumbs, lemon rind and lemon juice.

3. Fold in the ground almonds and divide the mixture among four greased nine-inch layer pans lined on the bottom with parchment paper or unglazed brown paper. Bake fifteen to twenty minutes, or until layers are faintly browned. Cool on a rack.
4. Beat the egg yolks lightly. Place the yolks and the remaining sugar in the top of a double boiler and cook over hot water until sugar dissolves and mixture thickens. Do not allow mixture to boil; it will curdle.
5. Remove from the hot water, beat in the chocolate and gradually beat in the butter. Refrigerate until mixture is spreading consistency. Use to fill and frost the layers.
6. Garnish with the sliced almonds. Refrigerate until firm.
Yield: Ten servings.

Poppy Seed Cake
Iowa

Cake:
    ½ cup ground poppy seeds (see note)
1½ cups milk
    ⅔ cup butter
    2 cups sugar
    ¼ teaspoon lemon extract
    ½ teaspoon vanilla
    3 cups cake flour
    1 teaspoon salt
    4 teaspoons baking powder
    4 egg whites.
Frosting:
4½ tablespoons cake flour
    1 cup milk
    1 cup butter
    1 cup sugar
    1 teaspoon vanilla
    ½ cup chopped walnuts.

1. Preheat the oven to 350 degrees.
2. To prepare cake, combine the ground poppy seeds and milk and let stand thirty minutes. Cream the butter and sugar together until light and fluffy. Beat in the lemon extract and vanilla.

3. Sift together the flour, salt and baking powder and fold alternately with the milk mixture into the batter.

4. Beat the egg whites until stiff but not dry and fold into the mixture. Turn into three greased and floured eight-inch layer pans and bake about twenty minutes, or until done.

5. Cool on a rack.

6. Meanwhile, prepare frosting by blending the flour and milk together in a small saucepan. Heat, stirring, until thick. Cook two minutes until very thick. Cool.

7. Cream the butter in a bowl. Gradually beat in the sugar until mixture is very light and fluffy. Gradually add cooled flour mixture and the vanilla. Beat five minutes longer. Use to fill and frost the layers. Decorate with the walnuts.

Yield: One dozen servings.

Note: Ground poppy seeds can be bought already ground in stores specializing in German, Viennese and Hungarian ingredients or poppy seeds can be ground in an electric blender.

Baked Custard   *Illinois*

3 eggs, lightly beaten
⅓ cup sugar
⅛ teaspoon salt
1 teaspoon vanilla
3 cups milk, scalded
¼ teaspoon nutmeg.

1. Preheat the oven to 350 degrees.

2. Beat the eggs with the sugar, salt and vanilla. Stir in the milk. Pour into a baking dish or casserole that has been greased on the bottom. Sprinkle with the nutmeg. Set baking dish or casserole in a pan of hot water and bake twenty-five to thirty minutes, or until a knife inserted in custard comes out clean.

Yield: Four servings.

Swedish Porridge   *Minnesota*

1 cup uncooked rice
1 cup water
4 cups light cream
1 stick cinnamon
½ teaspoon salt
½ cup sugar
½ cup heavy cream, whipped.

1. Place the rice and water in a heavy pan. Bring to a boil, cover and simmer ten minutes.

2. Add the light cream and cinnamon stick. Bring to a boil, cover and simmer forty-five minutes, or until the rice is tender. Remove cinnamon stick.

3. Add the salt and sugar and fold in the whipped cream.

Yield: Four servings.

Homemade Ice Cream   *Iowa*

2 cups sugar
2 eggs
⅛ teaspoon salt
2 tablespoons flour
4 cups milk, scalded
2 cups heavy cream
2 teaspoons vanilla.

1. Beat the sugar well with the eggs, salt and flour. Add two cups of the milk (cool the remaining milk). Pour into a saucepan and heat, stirring, until mixture thickens. Cool.

2. Add the cream and vanilla and pour into the can of an ice cream freezer. Add enough remaining cooled milk to fill can to within one inch of the top. Freeze according to manufacturer's directions.

Yield: About one gallon.

Variations:

Chocolate: Add two tablespoons cocoa powder and an extra half cup sugar to egg mixture.

Maple nut: Add one teaspoon maple nut

flavoring and one-half cup chopped nuts when ice cream is at mushy stage.

Banana: Add two cups mashed bananas to cooled custard.

Frozen Raspberry Dessert   *Iowa*

  1 ten-ounce package frozen raspberries, thawed
  2 egg whites
1⅓ cups sugar
  1 tablespoon lemon juice
  1 cup heavy cream, whipped
25 graham crackers, made into crumbs
  ½ cup butter, melted.

  1. Combine the raspberries, egg whites, one cup of the sugar and the lemon juice in a large mixing bowl. Beat for about fifteen minutes until mixture is quadrupled in bulk and is thick.
  2. Fold in the whipped cream.
  3. Mix the crumbs with the remaining sugar and the butter and spread three-quarters of the mixture in the bottom of a 10-by-14-inch pan. Pour the fruit mixture over crumbs.
  4. Sprinkle remaining crumbs on top and freeze.
  Yield: Fifteen servings.

Lemon Ice Cream   *Iowa*

  3 tablespoons lemon juice
  2 teaspoons grated lemon rind
  1 cup sugar
  2 cups light cream
  ⅛ teaspoon salt
    Yellow food coloring.

  1. Add the lemon juice and lemon rind to the sugar and blend well.
  2. Slowly stir in the cream, salt and one or two drops food coloring. Mix well.
  3. Pour into a freezing tray and freeze until firm. Or, mixture may be stirred when it reaches

the mushy stage and then refrozen for a smoother texture.
  Yield: About three cups.

Vanilla Ice Cream   *Oklahoma*

4½ cups milk
  6 eggs, lightly beaten
4½ teaspoons vanilla
  ⅛ teaspoon salt
2¼ cups light corn syrup
  1 cup plus two tablespoons sugar
  3 cups heavy cream.

  1. Gradually stir the milk into the eggs in the top of a double boiler. Place over hot but not boiling water and heat, stirring, until mixture just coats the spoon.
  2. Stir in the vanilla, salt, syrup and sugar. Cool. Stir in the cream and freeze in an ice cream freezer according to manufacturer's directions until it is hard to turn.
  Yield: About three quarts.
  Note: To make strawberry ice cream, reduce milk to three cups and substitute evaporated milk for the cream. When custard has cooled, add one quart washed, hulled fresh strawberries mashed with one-quarter cup extra sugar. Blend thoroughly and then add the evaporated milk and freeze.

Mary Alice's Homemade Cooked Ice Cream   *Illinois*

  4 cups milk
  6 eggs, separated
  1 cup sugar
  2 tablespoons cornstarch
  ¼ cup water
  2 teaspoons vanilla
  1 cup heavy cream.

  1. Mix together the milk, egg yolks and sugar in a saucepan and heat, stirring constantly, until

mixture thickens. Mix the cornstarch with the water and add. Cook, stirring until mixture thickens further. Cook two minutes, maintaining mixture just below boiling point.

2. Let cool. Add the vanilla. Chill to refrigerator temperature.

3. Stir in the cream. Beat the egg whites until stiff but not dry and fold in. Freeze in an ice cream freezer according to manufacturer's directions.

Yield: Three quarts.

Floating Island   *Michigan*

Custard:
 2 teaspoons cornstarch
 4 tablespoons sugar
 ¼ teaspoon salt
 ⅛ teaspoon nutmeg
 3 egg yolks, beaten
 2 cups milk
 ½ teaspoon vanilla
 ⅛ teaspoon almond extract.
Meringue:
 3 egg whites
 6 tablespoons sugar.

1. To prepare custard, mix together the cornstarch, sugar, salt and nutmeg. Beat in the egg yolks and then the milk. Cook over medium heat until mixture thickens and coats the spoon. Add the flavorings.

2. Pour into a round serving dish and cool.

3. Preheat the oven to 325 degrees.

4. To prepare meringue, beat the egg whites until stiff but not dry and then gradually beat in the sugar. Pile meringue into greased pie plate. Place pie plate in a pan of hot water and bake twenty minutes. Cool. Slide meringue onto custard.

Yield: Four servings.

Buttermilk Dessert   *Wisconsin*

2¾ cups buttermilk
 ¾ cup sugar
 2 envelopes unflavored gelatin
 ½ cup water
   Grated rind of one large lemon
 ⅓ cup lemon juice
   Compote of freshly sectioned citrus fruits or stewed dried fruits.

1. Mix the buttermilk and sugar together until the sugar dissolves.

2. Soak the gelatin in the water and then heat to dissolve the gelatin.

3. Stir the lemon rind and lemon juice into the buttermilk. While beating vigorously, slowly add the dissolved gelatin. Pour into a serving dish and chill two hours or until firm. Serve with the fruits.

Yield: Six servings.

Buttermilk Sherbet   *Ohio*

 2 cups buttermilk
 ⅔ cup confectioners' sugar
 1 teaspoon vanilla
1½ cups drained crushed pineapple
 ¼ teaspoon salt.

Combine all the ingredients thoroughly. Pour into a freezing tray and freeze until mushy. Beat until smooth and freeze again until just mushy. Serve.

Yield: Four servings.

Lemon Mousse   *Michigan*

 3 eggs, separated
 1 cup plus one tablespoon sugar
   Grated rind and juice of one lemon
 1 cup heavy cream, whipped
 ½ cup vanilla cookie crumbs.

1. Combine the egg yolks, one cup of the

sugar, the lemon rind and lemon juice in the top of a double boiler. Heat over hot water, stirring until mixture thickens. Do not boil. Cool.

2. Beat the egg whites until frothy, add remaining sugar and beat until stiff. Fold into cooled custard. Fold in the cream.

3. Pour into a buttered freezer tray. Sprinkle with the cookie crumbs and freeze.

Yield: Four servings.

Wild Grape Dumplings *Oklahoma*

2 cups flour
4 teaspoons baking powder
½ teaspoon salt
1 tablespoon plus one-quarter cup sugar
⅓ cup butter
¾ cup milk
4 cups grape juice (made from wild grapes, if possible)
4 cups wild grapes, seeded (Concord grapes may be substituted).

1. Sift together the flour, baking powder, salt and one tablespoon of the sugar. With a pastry blender, work in the butter.

2. Stir in the milk to make a dough. Roll out the dough on a lightly floured board and cut into two-inch squares.

3. Heat the grape juice, grapes and remaining sugar in a heavy kettle until boiling. Drop in the dumplings. Cover closely and steam fifteen to twenty minutes, or until tender. Serve hot.

Yield: Four servings.

Rum Chocolate Dessert *Illinois*

4½ ounces (nine rectangles) Maillard's Eagle sweet chocolate (see note) or four and one-half squares semisweet chocolate
2 tablespoons very strong black coffee
¾ cup sugar
¼ teaspoon salt
4½ tablespoons flour
¾ cup butter, melted
¼ cup dark rum
6 eggs, separated
1 cup heavy cream, whipped
Candied violets (see note)
Rum sauce (optional).

1. Preheat the oven to 350 degrees.

2. Line the bottom of a greased two-and-one-half-quart or three-quart soufflé dish with wax paper or parchment paper. Or, line the bottom and one inch up the sides of a greased eight-inch springform pan with wax paper or parchment paper. Grease the paper.

3. Melt the chocolate together with the coffee in the top of a double boiler over hot but not boiling water.

4. Mix together the sugar, salt and flour and add to the chocolate along with the butter and rum. Mix well.

5. Place the egg yolks in a large bowl and beat lightly. Remove double boiler from heat and gradually add the chocolate mixture to egg yolks, stirring well to mix.

6. Beat the egg whites until stiff but not dry and carefully fold into the chocolate mixture until no white is visible. Do not overmix. Pour the batter into prepared dish or pan. Set in a shallow pan of hot water and bake one hour, or until set.

7. Allow to cool to room temperature. Chill. The dessert will shrink as it cools.

8. If dessert has been baked in a soufflé dish, unmold the dessert onto a serving platter and peel off the paper. If dessert has been baked in a springform pan, remove the sides of the pan and, with the help of a spatula, slide the dessert from the base of the pan onto a serving plate.

9. Frost or pipe with the whipped cream and decorate with the violets. Chill until served. Serve with rum sauce if desired.

Yield: Ten servings.

Note: Maillard chocolate and candied violets are available at specialty gourmet stores.

Apple Pie Pudding
Illinois

Pudding:
½ cup butter
1 cup sugar
1 egg
1 cup flour
1 teaspoon baking soda
¼ teaspoon cinnamon
¼ teaspoon nutmeg
2 cups peeled, diced apples
½ cup chopped black walnuts.
Butter sauce:
1 cup sugar
2 tablespoons cornstarch
1 cup hot water
2 tablespoons butter
1 teaspoon vanilla.

1. Preheat the oven to 350 degrees.
2. To prepare pudding, cream the butter and sugar together until light and fluffy.
3. Beat in the egg. Sift together the flour, baking soda, cinnamon and nutmeg and stir into creamed mixture. Fold in the apples and walnuts.
4. Spoon into a greased nine-inch pie plate and bake forty-five minutes.
5. To prepare sauce, combine the sugar and cornstarch and stir in the water. Heat, stirring, until mixture thickens. Stir in the butter and vanilla.
6. Serve the apple pie pudding in wedges with the sauce.
Yield: Six servings.

Rice Pudding with Lingonberries
Minnesota

1 cup uncooked regular long grain rice
1 cup water
1 cup heavy cream
1 quart milk
1 stick cinnamon
½ teaspoon salt
⅓ cup sugar, or to taste

2 eggs, beaten
⅔ cup raisins
½ cup lingonberry preserves.

1. Place the rice and water in a heavy large pan and bring to a boil. Cover and cook ten minutes. Add the cream, milk and cinnamon stick. Bring to a boil, cover and simmer one hour.
2. Preheat the oven to 400 degrees.
3. Cool rice mixture slightly. Remove the cinnamon stick. Stir in the salt, sugar, eggs and raisins. Pour into a well-buttered baking dish and bake about thirty minutes, or until set. Serve warm or chilled, topped with the preserves.
Yield: Six servings.

Orange Pudding
Illinois

12 ladyfingers
2 tablespoons dark rum or dry sherry
5 oranges, peeled and thinly sliced
1¼ cups plus five tablespoons sugar
6 eggs, separated
2 teaspoons grated orange rind
⅛ teaspoon salt
4 cups milk, scalded
2 tablespoons orange liqueur (optional).

1. Arrange the ladyfingers in a shallow baking dish. Sprinkle with the rum or sherry. Top with the orange slices and sprinkle with one-half cup of the sugar.
2. Beat the egg yolks and two of the egg whites with three-quarters cup of remaining sugar. Add the orange rind and salt. Gradually beat in the milk. Pour into a saucepan and heat, stirring, until custard thickens but do not boil. Stir in the liqueur if desired and pour over orange slices. Cool to lukewarm.
3. Preheat the oven to 350 degrees.
4. Beat the remaining egg whites until frothy. Gradually beat in the remaining sugar and continue beating until stiff.
5. Pile meringue on top of pudding and bake

ten minutes, or until meringue is lightly browned. Serve warm or chilled.

Yield: Six servings.

Ozark's Bread Pudding   *Missouri*

10 slices French bread, lightly toasted
½ cup raisins (optional)
8 eggs, lightly beaten
1½ cups sugar
3 cups milk, scalded
3 cups heavy cream, scalded
⅛ teaspoon salt
2 teaspoons vanilla
½ teaspoon cinnamon
  Whipped cream (optional).

1. Preheat the oven to 350 degrees.
2. Arrange the bread in a two-quart baking dish or casserole. Sprinkle with the raisins if desired.
3. Beat the eggs very well with the sugar. Gradually beat in the milk and cream. Stir in the salt and vanilla and pour over the bread. Sprinkle with the cinnamon and bake thirty to forty minutes, or until set. Serve hot or chilled, with whipped cream if desired.

Yield: Ten to one dozen servings.

Royal Bread Pudding   *Michigan*

2 tablespoons butter
2 cups hot milk
1 cup soft bread crumbs
2 eggs, separated
⅓ cup plus three tablespoons sugar
¼ teaspoon salt
1 tablespoon cognac or one teaspoon vanilla
  Currant jelly.

1. Preheat the oven to 350 degrees.
2. Melt the butter in the milk and stir in the bread crumbs. Beat the egg yolks. Add one-third

cup of the sugar and the salt to the egg yolks and mix well. Add to milk mixture.
3. Stir in the cognac or vanilla and pour into a greased baking dish. Place dish in a pan of hot water and bake thirty-five to forty minutes, or until set.
4. Spread with currant jelly. Beat the egg whites until stiff and gradually beat in the remaining sugar. Spread meringue on top of the pudding and bake ten minutes, or until meringue is browned.

Yield: Four to six servings.

Persimmon Pudding   *Indiana*

½ cup butter
1 cup sugar
2 eggs
2 cups sieved persimmon pulp
1 teaspoon vanilla
1 teaspoon cinnamon
1 teaspoon baking soda
2 cups buttermilk
2 cups flour.

1. Preheat the oven to 325 degrees.
2. Cream the butter and sugar together until light and fluffy.
3. Beat in the eggs. Stir the persimmon pulp, vanilla and cinnamon into mixture. Add the baking soda to the buttermilk and stir alternately with the flour into persimmon mixture. Pour into a greased baking dish and bake about forty-five minutes, or until set.

Yield: Six servings.

Pecan Pudding   *Missouri*

1 egg
¾ cup sugar
2 tablespoons flour
1 teaspoon baking powder
¹⁄₁₆ teaspoon salt
½ cup chopped pecans or black walnuts

½ cup peeled, grated apple
½ teaspoon vanilla
   Sweetened whipped cream (optional).

1. Preheat the oven to 350 degrees.
2. Beat the egg and sugar together until light and lemon-colored. Sift together the flour, baking powder and salt. Stir into the egg mixture.
3. Stir the nuts, apple and vanilla into the mixture and pour into a greased eight-inch pie plate. Bake thirty-five to forty minutes. Serve with sweetened whipped cream if desired.
Yield: Four servings.

Pioneer Popcorn Pudding   *Oklahoma*

5 quarts popped corn, crushed with a rolling pin and then run through an electric blender or coffee mill
8 cups milk, scalded
2 eggs, lightly beaten
1½ cups sugar
1½ cups raisins
1 teaspoon nutmeg
1 teaspoon cinnamon
1 teaspoon ground allspice.

1. Mix the popcorn meal with the milk and set in a warm place to soak at least two hours.
2. Preheat the oven to 300 degrees.
3. Add the eggs, sugar, raisins and spices to the meal mixture and bring to a boil on top of the stove. Pour into a greased casserole or baking dish and bake about one hour. Serve hot.
Yield: About one dozen servings.

Chocolate Puff Balls   *Ohio*

Pudding:
½ cup granulated sugar
2 tablespoons butter
1 egg
1½ ounces (one and one-half squares) unsweetened chocolate, melted

1 teaspoon vanilla
1 cup flour
2 teaspoons baking powder
⅛ teaspoon salt
½ cup milk.
Sauce:
3 tablespoons butter
2 tablespoons flour
½ cup light brown sugar
1 cup milk, approximately.

1. To prepare pudding, cream the granulated sugar and butter together. Beat in the egg and then the chocolate and vanilla. Sift the flour with the baking powder and salt and add alternately with the milk to the chocolate mixture.
2. Spoon into four greased custard cups, ramekins or individual soufflé molds. Cover with aluminum foil. Set on a rack in boiling water and steam twenty minutes, or until done.
3. To prepare sauce, melt the butter in a saucepan. Stir in the flour and brown sugar and gradually add one cup milk. Bring to a boil, stirring, and hold over hot water. Thin with more milk if necessary.
4. Unmold the chocolate puddings and coat with sauce.
Yield: Four servings.

Raisin-Suet Pudding   *Kansas*

1 cup finely chopped or grated beef suet
1 cup plus one tablespoon sugar
1 teaspoon cinnamon
½ teaspoon nutmeg
¼ teaspoon ground cloves
1 teaspoon baking powder
½ teaspoon baking soda, dissolved in small amount of hot water
2 cups flour
1 teaspoon salt
1 egg
1 cup soft bread crumbs, soaked in water
1 cup raisins

½ cup buttermilk
    Hard sauce.

1. Combine all the ingredients in a large bowl and mix well.
2. Spoon into a greased three-pound shortening can. Cover with greased aluminum foil and set in a pan of boiling water with the water extending halfway up the side of the shortening can. Boil three hours. Serve with hard sauce.
Yield: Ten servings.

Date Pudding   *Michigan*

    1 eight-ounce package dates, chopped
    1 teaspoon baking soda
    1 cup boiling water
    ¼ cup butter
    1 cup sugar
    1 egg
    1¼ cups flour
    ¼ teaspoon baking powder
    ¼ teaspoon salt
    1 cup chopped pecans
    White sugar sauce (recipe below)
    Whipped cream.

1. Preheat the oven to 300 degrees.
2. Place the dates in a bowl, sprinkle the baking soda over dates and stir in the water. Set aside.
3. Cream the butter and sugar together until light and fluffy. Beat in the egg.
4. Sift together the flour, baking powder and salt and stir with the date mixture into the creamed mixture. Stir in the pecans. Pour into a greased nine-inch square baking dish and bake one hour.
5. Serve pudding warm with white sugar sauce poured over while it is hot. Top with whipped cream.
Yield: One dozen servings.

White Sugar Sauce   *Michigan*

    1 cup sugar
    ½ cup cold water
    ¼ teaspoon salt
    1 tablespoon butter
    ½ teaspoon vanilla
    2 tablespoons bourbon.

1. Mix the sugar, water and salt together in a saucepan. Heat, stirring, until sugar dissolves. Bring to a boil and boil five minutes.
2. Remove from heat and stir in the remaining ingredients. Use hot.
Yield: About three-quarters cup.

Steamed Pudding   *Ohio*

    ½ cup butter
    1 cup light brown sugar
    1 egg
    2 cups flour
    1 teaspoon baking soda
    2 teaspoons baking powder
    1 teaspoon cinnamon
    1 teaspoon nutmeg
    ⅛ teaspoon salt
    1 cup raisins
    ½ cup chopped walnuts
    1 cup milk
    Whipped cream or custard sauce.

1. Cream the butter and brown sugar together until light and fluffy. Beat in the egg. Sift together the flour, baking soda, baking powder, cinnamon, nutmeg and salt. Add the raisins and walnuts to flour mixture.
2. Stir the flour and fruit mixture alternately with the milk into the creamed mixture.
3. Spoon into a greased pudding basin or coffee can so that mixture only fills container to three-quarters capacity. Cover tightly with aluminum foil and stand on a rack in a pan of boiling water with the water extending at least halfway up the bowl or can. Steam one and one-half

hours. Serve hot, with whipped cream or custard sauce.

Yield: Six servings.

Hungarian Linzer Cookies   *Wisconsin*

½ cup plus two tablespoons sweet butter
½ cup sugar
1 egg
1 teaspoon vanilla
1¼ cups flour
1 teaspoon baking powder
2 tablespoons milk
Raspberry or apricot preserves.

1. Day before, cream the butter and sugar together until light and creamy. Beat in the egg and the vanilla.

2. Sift together the flour and baking powder and stir into the creamed mixture alternately with the milk. Wrap the dough in wax paper and chill overnight.

3. Next day, preheat the oven to 375 degrees.

4. Roll out a small portion of the dough on a lightly floured board to one-eighth-inch thickness. Keep remaining dough refrigerated. Cut out an equal number of two-inch rounds and of two-inch cookies with hole in the middle.

5. Bake on an ungreased baking sheet about eight minutes, or until lightly browned on the edges. Let set on sheet a few minutes before transferring to a rack. Repeat procedure until all remaining dough is used.

6. To assemble, place preserves on a plain cookie and top with one with a hole.

Yield: About four dozen.

Makova Zavin (Czech Poppy Seed Roll Cookies)   *Wisconsin*

Cookie dough:
½ cup butter
⅓ cup sugar
1 egg

2 tablespoons sour cream
2 cups flour
½ teaspoon salt
1 teaspoon grated lemon rind.
Filling:
1 cup ground poppy seeds (see note)
2 tablespoons sugar
1 teaspoon ground allspice
½ cup milk
1 tablespoon honey.

1. To prepare cookie dough, beat together the butter, sugar, egg and sour cream.

2. Place the flour and salt in a pile on a board and make a well in the center. Add the butter mixture to the well and work with the finger tips to make a dough. Add the lemon rind.

3. To prepare filling, combine all ingredients in a small pan. Bring to a boil, stirring, and cook slowly five minutes, still stirring. Cool to room temperature.

4. Preheat the oven to 350 degrees.

5. Roll out the dough into a rectangle about one-third-inch thick. Spread with the cooled poppy seed filling and roll from the long side like a jellyroll.

6. Place on a greased baking sheet and bake about forty-five minutes, or until done. Cool and slice.

Yield: About two dozen slices.

Note: Ground poppy seeds can be bought already ground in stores specializing in German, Viennese and Hungarian ingredients or poppy seeds can be ground in an electric blender.

Spice Cookies   *Minnesota*

Cookies:
½ cup butter
¾ cup granulated sugar
1 egg
¾ cup unsulphured molasses
2 teaspoons grated orange rind
3½ cups flour
½ teaspoon baking soda

½ teaspoon salt
1½ teaspoons ginger
1½ teaspoons cinnamon
1 teaspoon ground cloves
¼ teaspoon ground cardamom.
Ornamental frosting:
2 egg whites, lightly beaten
2½ cups confectioners' sugar
½ teaspoon vanilla.

1. To prepare cookies, cream the butter and granulated sugar together well. Beat in the egg and then the molasses and orange rind.

2. Sift together the remaining cookie ingredients and gradually stir into the creamed mixture.

3. Mix the ingredients to form a dough. Wrap in wax paper and chill in the refrigerator at least four hours or overnight.

4. Preheat the oven to 375 degrees.

5. Roll out the dough to one-quarter-inch to one-eighth-inch thickness. Cut out shapes with floured cutters and place cookies on greased baking sheets. (If desired, the cookies may be decorated at this point with sprinkles, raisins, cinnamon candies and silver dragées. Make a small hole in one end of the cookie if it is to be hung on the Christmas tree.)

6. Bake about ten minutes. Cool on a rack.

7. To prepare frosting, combine all the ingredients. If desired, mixture may be thickened with additional confectioners' sugar or thinned with extra egg white.

8. Use mixture to frost cooled cookies. A parchment cone bag or a decorating set can be used.

Yield: About six dozen.

Serbian Walnut Strips   *Wisconsin*

Cookie dough:
1 pound walnuts, finely ground
2 egg whites
1 cup granulated sugar
1 teaspoon lemon juice.

Frosting:
¾ cup confectioners' sugar
1 egg white, beaten until stiff.

1. Preheat the oven to 150 degrees or warm.

2. To prepare cookie dough, mix all dough ingredients together and knead until dough sticks together. Pat the dough out to one-half-inch thickness on a board sprinkled with confectioners' sugar.

3. To prepare frosting, fold the confectioners' sugar into the egg white. Spread over the cookie dough.

4. Cut into three-quarter-inch strips and one-and-one-half-inch bars. Transfer to a greased and floured baking sheet and bake twenty-five minutes.

5. Allow to cool before removing from the pan.

Yield: Two dozen bars.

Austrian Butter Horns   *Wisconsin*

Cookie dough:
4 cups flour, approximately
1½ cups soft butter
1 package active dry yeast
¼ cup warm water
¼ teaspoon salt
3 egg yolks, lightly beaten
½ cup sour cream
1 teaspoon vanilla.
Filling:
1 cup granulated sugar
3 egg whites, beaten until stiff
2 cups finely chopped walnuts
1 teaspoon vanilla.
Frosting:
2 tablespoons soft butter
2 cups confectioners' sugar
½ teaspoon vanilla
Milk.

1. Preheat the oven to 350 degrees.

2. To prepare cookie dough, put the flour in a

bowl and, with the finger tips, work in the butter until mixture resembles coarse oatmeal.

3. Dissolve the yeast in the warm water and add to the flour mixture. Add the remaining dough ingredients and mix with a wooden spoon or the fingers to give a soft but not sticky dough. If necessary, add one-quarter cup extra flour.

4. Turn dough onto a board sprinkled with confectioners' sugar and knead until smooth. Divide dough into twelve equal pieces and roll each piece into an eight-inch circle on the board sprinkled with confectioners' sugar. Divide each circle into eight wedges.

5. To prepare filling, gradually beat the granulated sugar into the stiffly beaten egg whites to give a meringue. Stir in the walnuts and vanilla. Put one to two teaspoons of the filling on each cookie dough wedge. Roll up, starting at the wide edge; then shape like crescents. Place on an ungreased baking sheet. Bake fifteen minutes. Cool on a rack.

6. To prepare frosting, mix together the butter, confectioners' sugar, vanilla and enough milk to make a coating consistency. Spoon over the cooled crescents.

Yield: Eight dozen.

Jam Biscuits   *Indiana*

2 cups flour
1 tablespoon baking powder
1 teaspoon salt
¼ cup butter
½ to three-quarters cup milk
  Strawberry or raspberry preserves.

1. Preheat the oven to 450 degrees.
2. Sift together the flour, baking powder and salt. Work the butter into the flour mixture until it resembles coarse oatmeal.
3. Stir in enough milk to make a soft dough. Turn onto a lightly floured board and knead thirty seconds.
4. Roll dough out one-quarter-inch thick. Cut biscuits with a floured two-inch cutter and place

on ungreased baking sheet. With the thumb, make a depression in the middle of each biscuit and fill with preserves.

5. Bake ten to twelve minutes, or until golden. *Yield:* Two dozen.

Danish Pastry   *Michigan*

Dough:
¾ cup butter, half sweet and half lightly
  salted
2 cups flour
1 package active dry yeast
2 tablespoons lukewarm water
2 eggs, lightly beaten, two tablespoons
  removed.
Filling:
½ cup sugar
½ cup sweet butter
½ teaspoon vanilla.

1. To prepare dough, use the finger tips, two knives or a pastry blender to work the butter into the flour as though making pastry. Mixture should resemble coarse oatmeal.

2. Dissolve the yeast in the water and gradually stir in the eggs. With a fork, stir egg mixture into the flour mixture to make a dough.

3. Knead on a lightly floured board until smooth, about four minutes. Roll out three-quarters of the dough into a rectangle about 18 by 10 inches. Dough will be thin. Transfer to a baking sheet.

4. To prepare filling, beat the sugar and butter together until light and fluffy. Beat in the vanilla.

5. With a spatula, spread the filling over the rectangle of dough. Roll out remaining dough and cut into one-half-inch strips. Arrange strips in lattice fashion over the filling.

6. Cover with wax paper and set in a warm place for thirty minutes.

7. Preheat the oven to 375 degrees.

8. Bake fifteen minutes, or until golden brown. Cool on a rack and cut into squares.

Yield: About thirty.

Refrigerator Cookies
Michigan

1 cup butter
2 cups light brown sugar
2 eggs, lightly beaten
1 teaspoon vanilla
3½ cups flour
1 teaspoon baking soda
1 teaspoon salt
1 cup finely chopped nuts.

1. Beat the butter and brown sugar together until light and fluffy. Beat in the eggs, one at a time. Beat in the vanilla.
2. Sift together the flour, baking soda and salt and stir into creamed mixture. Stir in the nuts. Form into a roll two inches in diameter, wrap in wax paper and chill until firm enough to cut, about half a day.
3. Preheat the oven to 350 degrees.
4. Cut roll into one-quarter-inch slices and bake about eight minutes, or until lightly browned.
Yield: About five dozen.

Fattigman (Scandinavian Cookies)
Minnesota

2 large egg yolks
1 egg white
3 tablespoons heavy cream
⅛ teaspoon salt
3½ tablespoons sugar
½ teaspoon cardamom
1½ tablespoons dark rum
1½ cups flour
Fat for deep-frying.

1. Combine the egg yolks and egg white in a mixing bowl and beat with a rotary beater until frothy. Add the cream, salt, sugar and cardamom and beat again. Stir in the rum.
2. Fold in the flour and knead. Shape the dough into a ball and chill.
3. Roll out the dough on a lightly floured board until thin and cut with a cutter into small triangles.
4. Heat the fat and cook the triangles in it two to three minutes, or until brown. Drain on paper towels.
Yield: About forty.

Rose Water Cookies
Missouri

1 cup butter
1 cup granulated sugar
1 egg
2 tablespoons rose water (see note)
Red food coloring
2¾ cups flour
⅛ teaspoon salt
½ cup confectioners' sugar
Crystallized rose petals, purchased or home-prepared (page 463).

1. Cream the butter and granulated sugar together until light and fluffy. Beat in the egg, rose water and one drop of food coloring to tint the batter pale pink.
2. Sift the flour and salt together and stir into the batter. Divide dough in half, wrap each half in wax paper and chill several hours.
3. Preheat the oven to 375 degrees.
4. On a lightly floured pastry cloth, roll out half the dough to one-eighth-inch thickness. This is a very rich dough and speed is needed to roll dough out before it softens too much.
5. Cut the dough into heart or other shapes as desired and transfer to an ungreased baking sheet. Bake six to eight minutes, or until beginning to brown around the edges. Cool on a rack.
6. Repeat the rolling and cutting with the second half of the dough. Bake. Chill the scraps again before attempting to roll them out.
7. Mix the confectioners' sugar with one drop of food coloring and enough drops of water to make a stiff paste. Use the frosting to secure a crystallized rose petal on each cookie.
Yield: Six to seven dozen thin cookies.
Note: Rose water is available in old-fashioned

pharmacies or in stores specializing in Middle Eastern foods.

Alison's Shortbread *Illinois*

2 cups flour
1 cup cornstarch
1 cup confectioners' sugar
  Pinch of salt
1 cup butter.

1. Preheat the oven to 250 degrees.
2. Sift the dry ingredients together. Add the butter and, using the hands, mix well. Flatten to about one-inch thickness in a circle or oblong shape. Put dough on a baking sheet and mark for cutting into cookies, cutting only halfway through the dough. Bake on the top shelf of the oven thirty minutes, turning the baking sheet after twenty minutes for even cooking.
3. Cool cookies and cut into the indicated shapes. Surface will be pale.
Yield: Eighteen to two dozen cookies, depending on size.

Finnish Shortbread *Minnesota*

4 cups flour
¼ teaspoon salt
1½ cups sugar
2 cups soft butter
½ cup finely chopped almonds
2 eggs, well beaten.

1. Preheat the oven to 375 degrees.
2. Sift the flour into a mixing bowl. Add the salt, one cup of the sugar and the butter. With the fingers, work butter into mixture and knead into a dough.
3. Divide the dough in half. Roll each half until it is long and slender, one-half to one inch in diameter. Cut the rolls into two-inch lengths. Press each slice with the back of the fingers to shape into cookies.

4. Combine the remaining sugar with the almonds. Brush the tops of the cookies with the beaten eggs, then sprinkle with the sugar and almond mixture. Arrange on baking sheets and bake seven to ten minutes.
Yield: About four dozen.

Almond Butter Cookies *Illinois*

1 cup butter
1⅓ cups plus six tablespoons sugar
2 eggs, separated
¼ cup heavy cream
2 teaspoons vanilla
1 teaspoon salt
⅛ teaspoon almond extract
3 cups flour
4 teaspoons baking powder
1 cup finely chopped sliced almonds.

1. Cream the butter and one and one-third cups of the sugar until light and fluffy. Beat in the egg yolks and then the cream, vanilla, salt and almond extract.
2. Sift the flour with the baking powder and stir into mixture.
3. Quarter the dough and roll each piece into a roll one inch in diameter. Wrap in wax paper and chill several hours.
4. Preheat the oven to 400 degrees.
5. Beat the egg whites slightly. Combine the almonds and remaining sugar. Brush each roll of dough with egg white and then roll in the sugar mixture.
6. Slice thinly and place on greased baking sheets. Bake seven to ten minutes, or until lightly browned.
Yield: About 100.

Christmas Wreaths (Berlinerkranser)
Minnesota

1 cup soft butter
½ cup granulated sugar

2 egg yolks
2 hard-cooked egg yolks, sieved
3 cups flour
1 egg white, lightly beaten
  Colored sugar.

1. Beat the butter with the granulated sugar until light and fluffy. Beat in the egg yolks and the sieved yolks.

2. Add the flour and work into a dough. Wrap in wax paper and chill about one hour.

3. Preheat the oven to 350 degrees.

4. Roll out the dough on a lightly floured board or cloth until dough is one-eighth-inch thick. It is easier to do this in three batches.

5. Cut dough into one-half-inch strips and then measure off five-inch pieces. Place on ungreased baking sheet, shaping into rings by overlapping the two ends. Brush with the egg white and sprinkle with colored sugar. Bake about ten minutes, or until lightly browned. Cool on a rack.

Yield: About five dozen.

Finnish Christmas Cookies *Minnesota*

Cookie dough:
 2 cups soft butter
 4 cups flour
 1 teaspoon salt
 ½ teaspoon baking soda
 ¾ cup ice water.
Filling:
 1 pound prunes, cooked, pitted and mashed
 ½ cup sugar
 1 teaspoon lemon juice.

1. To prepare cookie dough, place one cup of the butter in a bowl. Add the flour and salt. With the fingers or a pastry blender, work the butter into the flour as though making pastry until mixture resembles coarse oatmeal.

2. Dissolve the baking soda in the water and stir into the flour mixture. Make a dough and wrap in wax paper. Chill well.

3. Meanwhile, to prepare filling, mix the prune pulp with the sugar and lemon juice.

4. Roll out the dough into a rectangle one-eighth-inch thick. Spread half of the dough with half the remaining butter. Fold over and chill fifteen minutes. Repeat with remaining butter and chill again.

5. Preheat the oven to 400 degrees.

6. Divide dough in half and roll each half to one-eighth-inch thickness. Cut into two-and-one-half-inch squares. Make one-inch diagonal cut toward center from each corner of each square.

7. Place a teaspoon of the prune mixture in the center of each square, bring alternate corners together and pinch to form a pinwheel. Place on an ungreased baking sheet and bake about fifteen minutes, or until lightly browned. Cool on a rack.

Yield: About five dozen.

Buttergebachtness *Ohio*

1 pound confectioners' sugar
1 cup butter
4 eggs
  Grated rind of one lemon
4½ cups flour
1½ teaspoons cinnamon.

1. Cream the confectioners' sugar and butter together until light and fluffy. Beat in the eggs, one at a time, very well.

2. Stir in the lemon rind. Sift the flour with the cinnamon and stir in. Form dough into a ball, wrap in wax paper and chill until mixture can be rolled.

3. Preheat the oven to 350 degrees.

4. Roll out the dough, one-quarter at a time, to one-quarter-inch thickness. Cut with plain or fancy cutters and place on ungreased baking sheets. Bake ten to fifteen minutes, or until done. Cool on a rack.

Yield: About four dozen.

Tea Biscuits

Iowa

1 cup raisins
3½ cups flour
 Sugar
1 teaspoon salt
2 teaspoons baking powder
1 teaspoon nutmeg
1 cup shortening
1 teaspoon baking soda
1 cup buttermilk
1 teaspoon vanilla.

1. Preheat the oven to 400 degrees.
2. Place the raisins in a bowl, cover with hot water and let soak ten minutes. Drain. Toss with one-half cup of the flour.
3. In a mixing bowl, combine the remaining flour, one and one-half cups sugar, the salt, baking powder and nutmeg. With the finger tips or a pastry blender, work the shortening into the dry ingredients until mixture resembles coarse oatmeal.
4. Stir the baking soda into the buttermilk and add with the vanilla to the dry mixture. Stir in the raisin-flour mixture.
5. Pat or roll dough out on a lightly floured board or cloth to one-quarter-inch thickness and cut into two-inch rounds. Place on a lightly greased baking sheet, sprinkle with sugar and bake ten to twelve minutes or until lightly browned. Cool on a rack.

Yield: Three dozen, to four dozen, depending on size.

Rose's Prune-Filled Cookies

Illinois

Cookie dough:
5 cups flour
4 teaspoons baking powder
1 teaspoon salt
½ teaspoon nutmeg
1½ cups sugar
¾ cup lard
¾ cup butter

2 eggs
1 teaspoon vanilla
1¼ cups milk, approximately.
Filling:
1 pound prunes, cooked, pitted and mashed
¼ cup sugar
1 teaspoon flour
¼ teaspoon cinnamon
¼ teaspoon ground cloves
¼ teaspoon ground allspice.

1. Preheat the oven to 400 degrees.
2. To prepare cookie dough, place the flour, baking powder, salt, nutmeg and sugar in a bowl. With the fingertips or a pastry blender, work in the lard and butter until mixture resembles coarse oatmeal.
3. Stir in the eggs, vanilla and enough milk to make a manageable dough for rolling. Roll out the dough, one-quarter at a time, to one-eighth-inch thickness. Cut into two-inch squares.
4. To prepare filling, mix the prune pulp with the sugar, flour and spices.
5. Place one teaspoon of the filling in the center of each square. Moisten the edges and either fold over to make a triangle or gather up toward the center and pinch to seal. Place on a lightly greased baking sheet and bake about fifteen minutes, or until lightly browned.

Yield: About six dozen.

Peggy's Filled Cookies

Oklahoma

Cookie dough:
1 cup light brown sugar
1 cup granulated sugar
1 cup lard
3 eggs
5 cups flour
1 teaspoon baking soda
¼ teaspoon nutmeg
½ teaspoon salt
1 tablespoon buttermilk or sour milk.
Filling:
1 pound pitted dates, ground

1 cup orange juice
½ cup granulated sugar
1 cup chopped nuts.

1. To prepare cookie dough, cream together the sugars and lard until smooth and creamy. Beat in the eggs, one at a time.

2. Sift together the flour, baking soda, nutmeg and salt. Stir with the buttermilk or sour milk into the creamed mixture. Blend well.

3. Chill the dough until it is stiff enough to be rolled, one to two hours at least.

4. Meanwhile, to prepare filling, place the dates, orange juice and granulated sugar in a small saucepan and bring to a boil, stirring. Cook slowly until the mixture is spreading consistency. Cool; then stir in the nuts.

5. Preheat the oven to 350 degrees.

6. Take one-quarter of the chilled dough at a time and roll it out to one-eighth-inch thickness on a floured board or pastry cloth.

7. Cut dough into two-inch rounds or larger if desired. Place on a baking sheet. Put a spoonful of the filling in the center of each round and top with a second round.

8. Pinch the edges together with the end of a fork, a spoon or the fingers to seal. Bake about ten minutes, or until golden. Cool on a rack.

Yield: About six dozen two-inch cookies.

Rocks   *Ohio*

1 cup light brown sugar
¾ cup shortening
2 eggs, lightly beaten
2 cups flour
1 teaspoon ground allspice
¼ teaspoon salt
¾ cup chopped dates
2 cups raisins
2 cups chopped pecans or walnuts
1 teaspoon baking soda
1 tablespoon boiling water.

1. Preheat the oven to 350 degrees.

2. Cream the brown sugar and shortening together until light and fluffy. Beat in the eggs.

3. Sift the flour, allspice and salt into a bowl. Add the fruits and nuts and toss to coat. Stir into the batter.

4. Dissolve the baking soda in the boiling water and stir into the batter. Drop by teaspoonfuls onto a lightly greased baking sheet and bake about fifteen minutes, or until lightly browned.

Yield: About four dozen.

Chocolate "Macaroons"   *Oklahoma*

½ cup shortening
4 ounces (four squares) unsweetened chocolate
2 cups granulated sugar
4 eggs
2 teaspoons vanilla
2 cups flour
2 teaspoons baking powder
½ teaspoon salt
Confectioners' sugar.

1. Melt the shortening and the chocolate together over gentle heat or in the top of a double boiler.

2. Stir in the granulated sugar. Transfer mixture to a bowl and beat with an electric or hand mixer until the sugar is no longer grainy. Beat in the eggs, one at a time. Beat in the vanilla.

3. Sift the flour with the baking powder and salt and fold into dough. Chill at least three hours.

4. Preheat the oven to 375 degrees.

5. Shape rounded teaspoonfuls of dough into balls. Roll in confectioners' sugar. Place on a lightly greased baking sheet.

6. Bake ten minutes. The cookies will be soft when taken from the oven. Cool on a rack.

Yield: About five dozen.

Pfirsiche ("Peaches")   *Wisconsin*

1 cup milk
1½ cups peanut oil
2 cups sugar
4 eggs, lightly beaten
1 teaspoon vanilla
1½ teaspoons baking powder
6½ to seven-and-one-half cups plus six
   tablespoons flour
1 twelve-ounce jar apricot preserves
1 four-ounce bar German sweet chocolate,
   melted
1 cup chopped walnuts
   Dark rum
4 egg whites, lightly beaten
   Red and yellow colored sugars
   Artificial leaves.

1. Combine the milk, oil, sugar, eggs, vanilla
and baking powder and beat to mix. Gradually
beat in six tablespoons of the flour until well
mixed. Set aside two hours.

2. Preheat the oven to 325 degrees.

3. Beat in enough of the remaining flour to
make a dough that resembles a rich, soft yeast
dough. Pinch off inch-size balls and make into
balls about the size of walnuts. Place on greased
baking sheets and bake ten to fifteen minutes.
Balls will be pale in color. Cool on a rack.

4. When the balls are cool, take the point of a
knife and, starting from the flat side of the cookie,
scrape out and reserve most of the inside cookie
crumbs, leaving just the shell.

5. Take three to four cups cookie crumbs and
mix with the preserves, chocolate, walnuts and
enough rum to moisten well. Use to fill the
scooped-out cookies.

6. Stick two filled cookies together to form a
"peach."

7. Roll in the egg whites. Dot in a couple of
spots with red sugar and immediately roll in yellow sugar to resemble peach coloring. Dry on a
rack before storing in a tin. Stick a leaf in each
"peach" before serving.
   Yield: Four dozen to six dozen "peaches."

Mary Lu's Pecan Shortbread Rolls
Michigan

1 cup butter
⅓ cup confectioners' sugar
1 teaspoon water
1 teaspoon vanilla
2 cups flour
1 cup chopped pecans
   Granulated sugar.

1. Preheat the oven to 325 degrees.

2. Cream the butter and confectioners' sugar
together until light and fluffy. Beat in the water
and vanilla.

3. Stir in the flour and pecans.

4. Drop teaspoonfuls of the soft dough into a
pile of granulated sugar on a piece of wax paper.
With the fingers, shape each sugar-coated piece
into a two-inch-long roll. Place on an ungreased
baking sheet and bake about thirty minutes, or
until just pale brown on the bottom. Cool on a
rack.
   Yield: About three dozen.

Chocolate Balls   *Illinois*

¾ cup butter
1 cup sugar
1 egg
2 ounces (two squares) unsweetened
   chocolate, melted
2 tablespoons milk
1 teaspoon vanilla
2⅓ cups flour
¼ teaspoon salt
   Chocolate sprinkles
   Slivered blanched almonds.

1. Cream together the butter and sugar until
light and fluffy. Beat in the egg.

2. Beat in the chocolate, milk and vanilla.

3. Sift the flour with the salt and stir into the
mixture. Wrap the dough in wax paper and chill

several hours, or until dough can be handled easily.

4. Preheat the oven to 375 degrees.

5. Shape the dough into one-inch balls, roll in the sprinkles, place on an ungreased baking sheet and top each ball with an almond sliver.

6. Bake ten to twelve minutes, or until done.
Yield: About six dozen.

Lemon Bonbons   *Iowa*

Cookies:
 1 cup butter
⅓ cup confectioners' sugar
 1 teaspoon vanilla
¾ cup cornstarch
 1 cup flour
 1 teaspoon grated lemon rind
½ cup finely ground pecans.
Frosting:
 1 cup confectioners' sugar
 1 tablespoon soft butter
¼ teaspoon grated lemon rind
   Lemon juice.

1. To prepare cookies, cream the butter and confectioners' sugar together until light and fluffy. Beat in the vanilla.

2. Combine the cornstarch and flour. With a wooden spoon and then with the hands, work the flour mixture and lemon rind into the creamed mixture until a dough is formed. Wrap in wax paper and chill one hour.

3. Preheat the oven to 375 degrees.

4. Form the dough into one-inch balls. Dip one end in the pecans and place, pecans up, on baking sheet. Press down slightly with bottom of a tumbler.

5. Bake about ten minutes, or until lightly browned. Cool on a rack.

6. To prepare frosting, beat the confectioners' sugar with the butter, lemon rind and enough lemon juice to give a spreading consistency. Use to frost cooled cookies.
Yield: About two dozen.

Rum Kegeln (Rum Balls)   *Wisconsin*

½ pound shelled walnuts, finely ground
 8 ounces (two bars) German sweet chocolate, finely grated (this can be done in an electric blender)
 1 cup sugar
 3 egg whites, lightly beaten
   Dark rum
 4 to six ounces chocolate sprinkles.

1. Mix together the walnuts, sweet chocolate, sugar and half the egg whites. Add enough rum to moisten the mixture so that it holds together to form a dough.

2. Shape the mixture into one-inch balls. Roll the balls in remaining egg whites and then in the chocolate sprinkles. Set aside to dry.

3. Store in a covered tin until serving time. These rum balls will keep fresh for a week or two.
Yield: About thirty.

Sugar-Coated Banana Drops   *Kansas*

1½ cups sugar
1½ cups whole bran cereal
 ½ teaspoon cinnamon
 ½ cup shortening
 ¼ cup butter
 2 eggs
1½ teaspoons vanilla
2½ cups flour
 3 teaspoons baking powder
1½ teaspoons salt
 1 cup mashed bananas (three medium-size).

1. Preheat the oven to 400 degrees.

2. Combine one-half cup of the sugar with the cereal and cinnamon and roll or blend until fine. Place on wax paper.

3. Beat the remaining sugar with the shortening and butter until light and creamy. Beat in the eggs and vanilla.

4. Sift the flour with the baking powder and

salt. Stir with the bananas into creamed mixture. Drop by teaspoonfuls into the coating mixture.

5. Shape with the fingers into balls and place on a greased baking sheet. Bake ten minutes.

Yield: Five dozen.

Persimmon Cookies   *Indiana*

½ cup butter
1 cup sugar
1 egg
1 teaspoon baking soda
1 cup persimmon pulp
2 cups flour
½ teaspoon ground cloves
½ teaspoon cinnamon
½ teaspoon nutmeg
1 cup chopped nuts
1 cup raisins.

1. Preheat the oven to 350 degrees.
2. Cream the butter with the sugar until light and fluffy. Beat in the egg. Stir the baking soda into the persimmon pulp and stir into the batter.
3. Add the flour, cloves, cinnamon and nutmeg. Stir in the nuts and raisins. Drop by teaspoonfuls onto a greased baking sheet and bake fifteen minutes, or until lightly browned.

Yield: About three dozen.

Swedish Almond Gingersnaps

Minnesota

¾ cup sweet butter
1 cup sugar
¼ cup dark corn syrup
2¾ cups sifted flour
1 teaspoon baking soda
1½ teaspoons ginger
2 teaspoons cinnamon
1 teaspoon ground cloves
½ teaspoon nutmeg
½ cup chopped blanched almonds.

1. Preheat the oven to 400 degrees.

2. Cream the butter with the sugar until light and fluffy. Add the corn syrup to the butter mixture. Sift the flour with the baking soda and spices and add to the butter mixture along with the almonds.
3. Knead the dough briefly until smooth on a lightly floured board. Shape the dough into a slightly flattened roll. Wrap in wax paper and chill for one hour.
4. With a sharp knife cut the dough into thin slices. Place on greased baking sheet and bake for eight to ten minutes.

Yield: About five dozen.

Fudge Brownies   *Ohio*

4 ounces (four squares) unsweetened chocolate
½ cup butter
4 eggs
2 cups sugar
1 cup flour
1 teaspoon vanilla
1 cup chopped walnuts or pecans.

1. Preheat the oven to 350 degrees.
2. Melt the chocolate with the butter in the top of a double boiler over simmering water. Cool.
3. Beat the eggs until they are thick and very light in color. Gradually beat in the sugar, maintaining a marshmallow consistency.
4. Fold the chocolate mixture into the eggs. Fold in the flour. Stir in the vanilla and finally the nuts.
5. Spread the batter in a greased 9-by-13-by-2-inch baking pan and bake about thirty minutes. Cool. Cut into squares.

Yield: Two dozen.

Note: This batter may be spread in a nine-inch square pan and baked in a 325-degree oven for about one hour for very sticky, fudgy brownies.

Fruit Bars   *Illinois*

1 cup dried apricots, washed, dried and put through a food chopper

1 cup currants, washed and dried
1 cup raisins, washed and dried
1 cup raspberry or strawberry preserves
2 eggs
1 teaspoon vanilla
1 teaspoon grated lemon rind
2 cups flour.

   1. Preheat the oven to 300 degrees.

2. Mix all ingredients except the flour together very well. Sprinkle the flour over mixture and mix again. Spread the mixture in a greased 10-by-15-inch jellyroll pan. Bake thirty-five minutes.

3. Cut into bars, triangles or diamonds and return to the oven for five minutes to dry out the cut surfaces. Cool on a rack.

Yield: One to two dozen bars, according to size.

Miscellaneous

Pickles, Relishes and Preserves

Easy Pickles   *Michigan*

12 medium-size cucumbers, peeled and cut
     into one-inch pieces
     Salt
½ cup flour
 2 tablespoons dry mustard
 2 teaspoons turmeric
 2 teaspoons celery seeds
1½ cups sugar
⅔ cup water
2¼ cups cider vinegar
 4 onions, sliced and separated into rings.

1. Sprinkle the cucumber pieces with salt and
let stand one hour.

2. Combine the flour, mustard, turmeric, celery seeds and sugar. Gradually stir in the water
and vinegar. Bring the mixture to a boil, stirring
until thickened.

3. Rinse off the cucumbers, drain and add with
the onion rings to the sauce. Cook five to ten
minutes. Pack into jars, cover and store in a cool,
dry, dark place several days before using. Use
within three to four weeks.

Yield: About two and one-half quarts.

Audrey's Pickle Chips   *Indiana*

 4 quarts medium-size cucumbers
 6 medium-size onions, thinly sliced
 1 green pepper, cut into strips
 1 red pepper, cut into strips
⅓ cup coarse flake pickling salt
 2 trays ice cubes
 3 cups cider vinegar
 5 cups sugar
1½ teaspoons celery seeds
 2 tablespoons mustard seeds
1½ teaspoons turmeric.

1. Scrub the cucumbers and slice one-eighth-
inch thick. Mix cucumbers, onions and pepper
strips. In an earthenware crock arrange vegetables in layers, sprinkle with salt and top with a
tray of ice cubes.

2. Repeat until all vegetables are used. Let
stand three hours. Drain well.

3. Mix the remaining ingredients together.
Add drained vegetables. Heat to boiling and pack
into hot sterilized jars. Seal. Cool and store in a
cool, dark, dry place.

Yield: About six pints.

Special Dills   *Ohio*

18 large barrel dill pickles
 4 cups sugar

3 cups white vinegar
½ cup dry mustard
1 bottle horseradish
1 clove garlic.

1. Place the dills in a crock or earthenware bowl. Dissolve the sugar in the vinegar. Mix the mustard with the horseradish and add with the garlic to vinegar mixture. Pour over dills.

2. Let pickles stand in a cool place several days before serving.

Yield: Eighteen pickles.

Peggy's Carrot Pickles   *Oklahoma*

4 cups three-quarter-inch slices carrots
  Boiling salted water
1 cup cider vinegar
¾ cup water
¾ cup sugar
10 whole cloves
2 sticks cinnamon, broken into small pieces
1½ teaspoons salt.

1. Place carrot slices in a saucepan and add a small amount of boiling salted water to come about halfway up the carrots. Cover and cook until carrots are crisp-tender, about five minutes. Drain.

2. Combine the remaining ingredients in a small saucepan and bring to a boil. Boil three minutes.

3. Pack carrots in hot sterilized jars and pour boiling syrup over. Cover. Cool and refrigerate a day or two before using. Pickles will keep a week or two. Serve with meats.

Yield: About two pints.

Bread and Butter Pickles   *Iowa*

35 small unpeeled cucumbers, washed and sliced
3 tablespoons salt
4 cups cider vinegar

4 cups sugar
¼ cup mustard seeds
1 tablespoon celery seeds
1 tablespoon curry powder
5 slices onion.

1. Day before, sprinkle the cucumbers with the salt and let stand overnight. Next day, drain and rinse.

2. Mix together the vinegar, sugar, mustard seeds, celery seeds and curry powder in a saucepan. Bring to a boil and boil five minutes.

3. Add the cucumber slices and let stand in the hot liquid fifteen minutes. Pack into hot sterilized jars, adding one slice raw onion to each jar. Seal. Store in cool, dark, dry place.

Yield: About five pints.

Best Ever Beet Pickles   *Oklahoma*

3 quarts tiny beets
  Boiling water
2 cups sugar
2 cups cider vinegar
2 cups water
1½ teaspoons salt
2 sticks cinnamon
1 tablespoon whole allspice.

1. Wash and drain the beets. Cover with boiling water and cook until tender, about twenty minutes. Drain. When beets are cool enough to handle, remove skin, stem and root ends.

2. Combine the sugar, vinegar, water, salt, cinnamon sticks and allspice in a saucepan. Bring to a boil and simmer fifteen minutes.

3. Pack the hot beets into hot sterilized canning jars and pour boiling vinegar mixture over beets. Cap the jars and process in a water bath thirty minutes. Cool and test for seal. Store in a cool, dark, dry place.

Yield: About three quarts.

Crab Apple Pickles
Indiana

1 gallon crab apples, washed
4 cups vinegar
6 cups sugar
2 cups water
1 teaspoon whole cloves
1 stick cinnamon, broken into four pieces
1 tablespoon whole allspice.

1. Thrust a large darning needle through each apple to prevent apples from bursting. Place apples in the upper half of a steamer or in a colander over rapidly boiling water and steam ten minutes. Stir a couple of times.

2. Combine the vinegar, sugar and water in a saucepan. Tie the cloves, cinnamon pieces and allspice in a muslin bag, add to vinegar mixture and bring to a boil. Cook ten minutes.

3. Add the apples and cook until tender, about five minutes; do not overcook. Place apples in hot sterilized jars and pour the boiling syrup over apples.

4. Seal jars and process in a water bath ten minutes for lengthy storage. Cool and check seal. Store in a cool, dark, dry place.

Yield: About three quarts.

Latvian Pumpkin Pickle
Wisconsin

2 cups water
1 cup sugar
½ cup cider vinegar
1 teaspoon whole cloves, tied in a muslin bag
3 to four cups peeled pumpkin cubes (¾ by ¾ by 1 inch).

1. Combine the water and sugar and stir while heating until the sugar dissolves. Boil without stirring five minutes.

2. Add the vinegar, bag of cloves and pumpkin pieces and simmer, covered, until pumpkin pieces are translucent and tender but not mushy, about one hour. Cool and chill before serving.

Yield: Three cups.

Mom Abram's Mustard Pickle
Oklahoma

Vegetables:
8 cups small pickling cucumbers
8 cups pickling (button) onions
1 large cauliflower, broken into small flowerets
4 sweet red peppers, coarsely diced
2 cups salt
2 cups water.
Sauce:
1 cup flour
6 tablespoons dry mustard
1½ cups sugar
1 tablespoon turmeric
8 cups cider vinegar.

1. Day before, to prepare vegetables, cut the cucumbers into slices or chunks and place in a large bowl. Add the onions, cauliflower and peppers.

2. Make a brine with the salt and water. Pour over the vegetables and let stand overnight.

3. In the morning, heat the vegetables and brine just to the boiling point, but do not boil. Drain.

4. Meanwhile, to prepare sauce, mix together the flour, mustard, sugar and turmeric. Add enough vinegar to make a paste and then stir into remaining vinegar. Bring to a boil, stirring, and cook, stirring, until thick and creamy.

5. Pour sauce over drained vegetables and simmer mixture until the vegetables are just tender. Pack into hot sterilized jars. Seal. Process for ten minutes in a water bath. Cool and test for seal. Store in a cool, dark, dry place.

Yield: About five quarts.

Cabbage and Pepper Relish
Ohio

2 medium-size heads cabbage
12 green and red sweet peppers, seeded
8 carrots
8 medium-size onions
½ cup salt

6 cups sugar
6 cups cider vinegar
1 teaspoon celery seeds
1 teaspoon mustard seeds.

1. Grind the cabbage, peppers, carrots and onions into a bowl and mix well. Cover with the salt and let stand two to three hours. Drain.

2. Heat together the remaining ingredients and pour over the vegetable mixture.

3. Ladle into jars and keep refrigerated. This relish will keep several weeks.

Yield: About five quarts.

Lemon Relish   *Illinois*

2 large lemons, peeled and quartered
1 two-inch piece lemon rind without white pith
6 scallions, including green part
½ green pepper, seeded
¼ cup parsley sprigs
2 cups diced celery
½ cup sugar
½ teaspoon dry mustard
⅛ teaspoon ground allspice
1 teaspoon salt
1 teaspoon celery seeds
1 small hot pepper, finely chopped, or to taste.

1. Put the lemon pulp, lemon rind, scallions, green pepper, parsley and celery through a meat chopper, using a coarse blade.

2. Stir in the remaining ingredients and chill in refrigerator overnight to blend flavors.

Yield: About two cups.

Mixed-Up Relish   *Minnesota*

4 cups chopped onions
4 cups finely chopped cabbage
4 cups chopped, peeled green tomatoes
6 hot red peppers, chopped

12 green peppers, finely chopped
½ cup salt
2 cups finely chopped celery
4 cups sugar
4 cups cider vinegar
2 cups water
1 tablespoon celery seeds
2 tablespoons mustard seeds
1½ tablespoons turmeric.

1. Day before, combine the onions, cabbage, tomatoes and peppers. Sprinkle with the salt and let stand overnight. Next day, drain.

2. Mix the remaining ingredients in a saucepan and bring to a boil. Simmer four minutes. Pour over vegetables. Cook ten minutes. Ladle into hot sterilized jars and seal. Store in a cool, dark, dry place.

Yield: About four quarts.

Corn and Pepper Relish   *Missouri*

18 ears corn
1 small head cabbage, cored
6 white onions
3 red sweet peppers, cored, seeded and membranes removed
3 green sweet peppers, cored, seeded and membranes removed
1 tablespoon hot crushed dried pepper pods
2 teaspoons celery seeds
1 tablespoon mustard seeds
8 cups cider vinegar
¼ cup salt
2 cups sugar.

1. Slice and scrape the kernels from the corn and place in a kettle.

2. Grind the cabbage, onions, red and green peppers and hot pepper. Add to the kettle. Add the remaining ingredients and bring to a boil. Simmer thirty-five minutes.

3. Spoon the relish into sterilized jars and seal.

Process fifteen minutes in a boiling water bath. Cool and test seal. Store in a cool, dark, dry place.

Yield: About ten pints.

In Illinois and other parts of the Midwest, peppers are referred to as mangoes, leading to much confusion for the outsider.

Sweet Relish   *Illinois*

4 cups red mangoes, chopped
4 cups green mangoes, chopped
4 cups yellow mangoes, chopped
½ cup salt
4 cups celery, diced
4 cups cauliflower flowerets, diced
4 cups sweet cucumber pickles, chopped
4 cups diced apples that will retain their shape
4 cups cider vinegar
4 cups sugar
1 teaspoon celery seeds.

1. Day before, place the three varieties of peppers in a large bowl. Add water to cover and sprinkle with the salt. Let stand overnight. Next day, drain.
2. Mix drained peppers with the celery, cauliflower, pickles and apples. Heat the vinegar and sugar together and add pepper mixture and celery seeds. Cook until apples are tender, about fifteen minutes. Pack into hot sterilized jars and seal. Process in a water bath thirty minutes for long-term storage in a cool, dark, dry place, or keep in the refrigerator.

Yield: About eleven pints.

Green Tomato Pickle   *Kansas*

1 gallon green tomatoes, peeled and chopped
½ head cabbage, chopped
2 cups chopped onions
6 cucumbers, chopped

24 snap beans, diced
3 green peppers, diced
4 tablespoons turmeric
½ cup mustard seeds
2 tablespoons freshly ground black pepper
2 tablespoons ground allspice
2 teaspoons ground cloves
1 tablespoon celery seeds
1 cup salt
4 pounds light brown sugar
3 quarts cider vinegar
1 cup freshly grated horseradish
1 tablespoon ground cinnamon.

Combine all ingredients in a kettle, bring to a boil and cook about thirty minutes, or until beans are cooked. Pack into hot sterilized jars and seal. Store in a cool, dark, dry place.

Yield: About eight quarts.

Tomato and Apple Relish   *Minnesota*

12 ripe tomatoes, peeled
12 tart apples, peeled, cored and quartered
9 large sweet Bermuda onions
1 red sweet pepper
2½ cups sugar
3 cups cider vinegar
⅓ cup salt
1 teaspoon cinnamon
1 teaspoon ginger
1 teaspoon dry mustard
½ teaspoon ground cloves
½ teaspoon cayenne pepper.

1. Using the coarsest blade of the meat chopper, grind the tomatoes, apples, onions and red pepper together into a big kettle.
2. Add the remaining ingredients. Bring to a boil, stirring occasionally to prevent sticking, and simmer two hours. Pack into hot sterilized jars. Cap and cool before storing in a dark, dry, cool place or in the refrigerator.

Yield: About one and one-half quarts.

Tomato Butter   *Oklahoma*

5 pounds ripe tomatoes, peeled and cut into small pieces
1 teaspoon salt
3½ cups light brown sugar
½ teaspoon ground allspice
1½ teaspoons ground cloves
1½ teaspoons cinnamon.

1. Place the tomatoes and salt in a kettle and cook about fifteen minutes, or until tomatoes are mushy. Measure tomatoes. There should be two quarts.
2. Return tomatoes to the kettle and add the remaining ingredients. Bring to a boil and simmer slowly, stirring occasionally, one hour, or until very thick. Pour into hot sterilized jars and seal. Store in a cool, dark, dry place.
Yield: About six half-pint jars.

Gooseberry Catchup   *Indiana*

2 cups cider vinegar
2 tablespoons ground cloves
2 tablespoons cinnamon
2 tablespoons ground allspice
5 quarts gooseberries
4 pounds sugar.

Place the vinegar, cloves, cinnamon and allspice in a kettle and bring to a boil. Add the berries and sugar and boil one hour, stirring occasionally. Pour into hot sterilized jars. Seal. Cool and test seal. Store in a cool, dark, dry place.
Yield: About three quarts.

Brandied Peaches   *Kansas*

Whole cloves
6 pounds peaches, peeled
6 pounds sugar
5¼ cups water
3 cups cognac.

1. Insert two cloves in each peach. Combine the sugar and water in a saucepan and bring to a boil, stirring to dissolve the sugar. Boil five minutes.
2. Place one layer of peaches at a time in the saucepan and cook slowly until peaches are tender when pierced with a straw, about five minutes.
3. Drain fruit on a platter, reserving drippings.
4. Pack the fruit in hot sterilized jars. Return syrup drippings on platter to saucepan and boil syrup ten minutes longer. Remove from heat and stir in the cognac. Pour over fruit and seal. Store in a cool, dark, dry place. Keep at least two weeks before eating.
Yield: About seven pints.

Peggy's Pumpkin Chip Preserves
                                     Oklahoma

1 pound peeled pumpkin rind, cut into small chips
1⅔ cups sugar
1 teaspoon grated lemon rind
⅓ cup lemon juice
1½ tablespoons chopped candied ginger.

1. Day before, place the pumpkin rind in a bowl. Sprinkle the sugar over pumpkin and let stand overnight.
2. Next day, add the lemon rind, lemon juice and ginger to pumpkin. Place in a saucepan and cook slowly until pumpkin rind becomes clear and tender and syrup coats the spoon. Spoon into hot sterilized jars and seal. Store in a cool, dark, dry place.
Yield: About three jelly jars.
Note: If too large a quantity of this is attempted at one time, the color darkens during the cooking and the clear golden look is lost.

Rhubarb Marmalade   *Ohio*

3 quarts rhubarb, cut into one and
   one-half-inch pieces
1 whole orange, ground
1 whole lemon, ground
6 cups sugar
1 cup raisins
½ cup chopped nuts.

1. Place the rhubarb, orange and lemon in a saucepan. Add the sugar. Let stand one-half hour.
2. Bring to a boil and simmer forty-five minutes, stirring frequently. Stir in the raisins and nuts and pour into hot sterilized jars. Pour two thin layers of melted paraffin over. Cool, cover and store in a cool, dark, dry place.
Yield: About one and one-half quarts.

Cantaloupe-Peach Preserve   *Indiana*

4 cups diced cantaloupe
4 cups peeled, pitted, diced peaches
6 cups sugar
¼ cup lemon juice
½ teaspoon ginger
2 tablespoons chopped crystallized ginger
½ cup blanched almonds, chopped
¼ teaspoon salt.

1. Place the cantaloupe and peaches in a heavy kettle. Bring to a boil and simmer very slowly forty minutes.
2. Add the sugar and lemon juice and boil rapidly until thick. Add the remaining ingredients and pour into hot sterilized jars. Pour two thin layers of melted paraffin over. Cool, cover and store in a cool, dark, dry place.
Yield: About eight jelly glasses.

Pumpkin Preserves   *Ohio*

3 quarts peeled, cubed pumpkin
3 cups sugar
1½ lemons, ground.

1. Day before, place the pumpkin in a kettle. Sprinkle with the sugar and let stand overnight.
2. Next day, add the lemon, bring to a boil and cook until the syrup is thick. Turn into hot sterilized jars. Pour two thin layers of melted paraffin over. Cool, cover and store in a cool, dark, dry place.
Yield: About six jelly glasses.

Pear and Apple Preserves   *Indiana*

2 cups diced, peeled and cored pears
2 cups diced, peeled and cored apples
3½ cups sugar
¼ cup lemon juice
1 teaspoon grated lemon rind.

1. Mix all the ingredients together in a heavy saucepan. Bring to a boil and boil until mixture is thick and clear, about twenty-five minutes.
2. Pour into hot sterilized jars and pour two thin layers of melted paraffin over. Cool, cover and store in a dark, cool, dry place.
Yield: About three jelly jars.

Apple Butter   *Ohio*

4 quarts apples, washed and cut into pieces
8 cups water
1½ quarts cider
1½ pounds sugar
1 teaspoon cinnamon
1 teaspoon ground allspice
1 teaspoon ground cloves.

1. Place the apples in a large kettle and cover with the water.
2. Bring to a boil and simmer until the apples

are quite soft. Press through a sieve or food mill to remove seeds and skin.

3. Bring the cider to a boil and add the sieved apple pulp. Add the sugar and cook slowly, uncovered, until mixture is thick and dark in color, stirring frequently to prevent sticking.

4. Add the spices and cook twenty minutes longer.

5. Spoon into hot sterilized jars and seal. Store in a cool, dark, dry place.

Yield: About three quarts.

Peggy's Wild Sandplum Jelly   *Oklahoma*

4 quarts red sandplums, stemmed and washed
Sugar.

1. Day before, cover the wild plums with cold water and heat to boiling. Drain. Cover plums with boiling water and cook slowly until they are soft.

2. Pour the plum pulp into a jelly bag and drain overnight.

3. Next day, measure the plum juice into a large kettle and place over medium heat. Measure an equal amount of sugar and heat it in the oven set at 225 degrees.

4. Boil the juice ten minutes; then add the heated sugar. Stir to dissolve sugar and then boil, without stirring, until a drop of the mixture on a cooled dish gels. Pour into clean sterilized jelly glasses. Pour two thin layers of melted paraffin over. Cool, cover and store in a cool, dark, dry place.

Yield: Ten to one dozen jelly glasses.

Tomato Marmalade   *Oklahoma*

8 pounds ripe plum tomatoes, approximately
  Boiling water
3 oranges
3 lemons
8 sticks cinnamon

1 tablespoon whole cloves
  Sugar.

1. Dip the tomatoes, a few at a time, into a kettle of boiling water. Remove, skin, chop roughly and measure four quarts. Let stand while preparing fruit.

2. Finely chop the skin and pulp of the oranges and lemons.

3. Place the chopped oranges and lemons in a large kettle with the cinnamon sticks and cloves.

4. Pour off and discard most of the tomato liquid that has accumulated in the tomatoes. Add tomatoes to kettle, adding one cup sugar for each cup tomatoes.

5. Bring to a boil, stirring until sugar has dissolved. Boil, stirring to prevent sticking, until the marmalade sheets off the spoon, registers 220 degrees on a candy thermometer or keeps the track left by a finger pushed through a drop chilled on a plate.

6. Remove the cinnamon sticks and most of the cloves. Ladle the marmalade into hot sterilized jars. Pour two thin layers of melted paraffin over. Cool. Cover and store in a dark, cool, dry place.

Yield: About eighteen six-ounce jars.

Rose Jelly   *Missouri*

 8 cups wild, unsprayed rose petals picked in
    the early morning
10 cups cold water
½ cup strained fresh strawberry juice
 7 pounds sugar
 2 cups liquid fruit pectin
24 rose leaves, washed.

1. Wash and drain the rose petals and place in a large enamel pan with the cold water. Bring the mixture to a boil and simmer gently fifteen minutes. Strain through a jelly bag or through several thicknesses of cheesecloth.

2. Add the strawberry juice to the strained

rose juice. Add water if necessary to make up two quarts and return to the pan.

3. Add the sugar and bring to a boil, stirring until the sugar dissolves. When the mixture is boiling rapidly, pour and stir in the pectin all at once. Continue stirring the boiling mixture one minute.

4. Pour into hot sterilized jelly jars, decorate the surface of each with a washed rose leaf and seal with two thin layers of melted paraffin. Let stand undisturbed until cool and then store in a cool, dark, dry place.

Yield: About two dozen six-ounce jars.

Mincemeat   *Iowa*

1 pound lean beef
1 pound currants
1 pound raisins
2 pounds tart apples, peeled, cored and quartered
½ pound suet
1 cup cider
½ teaspoon salt
½ teaspoon cinnamon
½ teaspoon ground cloves
½ teaspoon freshly ground black pepper
½ teaspoon nutmeg
¼ pound citron, finely chopped
1 teaspoon grated lemon rind
⅓ cup lemon juice
1 tablespoon grated orange rind
⅔ cup orange juice
3 cups sugar
¾ cup pickle syrup from peaches or watermelon rind.

1. Wipe the beef with a damp cloth and place meat in a kettle with water to cover. Bring to a boil, cover and cook very slowly until very tender, about three hours. Allow to cool in the liquid.

2. Cover the currants and raisins with water and let stand thirty minutes. Drain.

3. Drain meat and put through a food chopper

with the apples, currants, raisins and suet. Add the remaining ingredients and mix well.

4. Turn into a heavy kettle and bring to a boil. Simmer slowly, stirring frequently, one hour. Store in the refrigerator and use within three to four weeks.

Yield: About three quarts.

Sauces

Cocktail Sauce for Sea Foods   *Illinois*

2 egg yolks
1 teaspoon salt
½ teaspoon dry mustard
2 tablespoons cider vinegar
1 cup olive oil
2 hard-cooked eggs, finely chopped
¼ cup finely chopped celery
2 tablespoons finely chopped green pepper
2 tablespoons finely chopped sweet pickle
2 tablespoons finely chopped onion
¼ cup chili sauce.

Mix the egg yolks, salt, mustard and vinegar together in a bowl. Very slowly beat in the oil. Stir in the remaining ingredients.

Yield: About three cups.

Hornersville Barbecue Sauce   *Missouri*

1¼ cups cider vinegar
1 teaspoon freshly ground black pepper
2½ teaspoons salt
1½ teaspoons sugar
4 teaspoons chili powder
1 teaspoon dry mustard
1 teaspoon paprika
½ teaspoon ground cumin (optional).

Combine all the ingredients in a bottle and

shake well. Use the sauce to brush on meats as they are grilled over charcoal.

Yield: About one and one-half cups.

Lion's Club Barbecue Sauce   *Indiana*

4 large bottles catchup
2 eight-ounce cans tomato puree
2 tablespoons chopped onion
3 tablespoons Worcestershire sauce
1½ cups light brown sugar
2 cups cider vinegar
1 teaspoon garlic salt
1 teaspoon freshly ground black pepper
2 tablespoons chili powder.

Combine all ingredients in a kettle. Add water to adjust the consistency to a brush-on sauce. Bring to a boil and simmer thirty minutes.

Yield: About one gallon, enough to baste eighty to 100 chickens.

Honey Curry Sauce   *Illinois*

1 cup plus two tablespoons catchup
2 tablespoons honey
1 tablespoon curry powder
1 tablespoon lemon juice
1 tablespoon finely grated onion
1 tablespoon powdered ginger
1 tablespoon dry mustard
   Tabasco sauce to taste
1 teaspoon Worcestershire sauce
   Salt to taste.

Combine all the ingredients and use for basting chicken, ham, hamburgers or meat loaf. Beware —the sauce is spicy.

Yield: About one and one-half cups.

End-of-the-Garden Sauce   *Iowa*

15 large ripe tomatoes, peeled
 8 large apples, peeled, cored and quartered
 6 large sweet peppers
 5 medium-size onions
 1 teaspoon cinnamon
 ½ teaspoon ground cloves
 ½ teaspoon celery seeds
 ¼ teaspoon freshly ground black pepper
 2 cups cider vinegar
 3 cups sugar.

Grind the tomatoes, apples, peppers and onions, using the coarse blade of a food chopper. Combine with the remaining ingredients in a heavy kettle and bring to a boil, stirring. Cook, stirring constantly, until mixture is thick. Pour into hot sterilized jars and seal. Store in a cool, dark, dry place.

Yield: About eight pints.

Quick and Easy Sauce   *Iowa*

1 small onion, finely chopped
1 large apple, peeled, cored and diced
1 medium-size green pepper, cored, seeded and diced
1 cup catchup.

Combine all the ingredients in a small saucepan and bring to a simmer. Cook slowly fifteen minutes. Use for meat loaves, meat balls, chicken, etc.

Yield: About two cups.

Koprova Omacka (Dill Gravy)   *Wisconsin*

3 tablespoons butter
3 tablespoons flour
1 cup milk
1 cup pork broth or beef broth
½ cup sour cream
1 teaspoon sugar

¾ teaspoon salt
¼ teaspoon freshly ground black pepper
3 tablespoons freshly snipped dill weed.

1. Melt the butter and blend in the flour. Gradually stir in the milk and broth. Bring to a boil, stirring, and cook three minutes.

2. Mix some of the hot sauce with the sour cream and return all to the pan. Add the remaining ingredients and reheat, but do not boil.

Yield: Two cups.

Note: To make horseradish gravy, omit the dill and add two tablespoons freshly grated horseradish, or to taste, just before serving.

Mae's Tomato Gravy   *Indiana*

    5 very ripe tomatoes, peeled and chopped
    ½ cup light brown sugar
    ⅓ cup granulated sugar
    2½ tablespoons flour
    1 cup heavy cream
    2 cups water, approximately
      Salt and freshly ground black pepper to taste.

1. Place the tomatoes in a skillet and cook until tomatoes are soft and most of the moisture has evaporated. Add the sugars and cook, stirring constantly, until mixture is thick and beginning to brown.

2. Make a paste with the flour and a little of the cream. Gradually stir in the remaining cream and two cups water. Add to tomato mixture. If too thick, add more water. Season with salt and pepper. Serve on toast or crackers.

Yield: About four cups.

Czech Gravies for Dumplings   *Wisconsin*

Basic Roux
1 cup flour
3 tablespoons shortening.

Place the flour and shortening in a heavy skillet over medium heat and cook, stirring constantly, until the mixture turns golden brown. Do not allow to burn or flavor will be bitter.

Yield: About three-quarters cup.

I. Tomato Gravy   *Wisconsin*

2 cups tomatoes, canned or fresh, peeled and chopped
2 teaspoons mixed pickling spices
2 teaspoons cider vinegar
1 teaspoon salt
2 teaspoons sugar
3 tablespoons basic roux (recipe above).

Combine the tomatoes, pickling spices, vinegar, salt and sugar and cook ten minutes. Mix a little hot sauce with the roux and return to the pan. Cook until gravy is smooth and thickened. Strain to remove spices.

Yield: About two cups.

II. Dill Pickle Gravy   *Wisconsin*

½ cup beef broth
½ cup dill pickle juice
6 tablespoons basic roux (recipe above)
2 dill pickles, sliced across.

Combine the broth and pickle juice and thicken with the roux. Add the sliced pickles and cook thoroughly.

Yield: About one and one-quarter cups.

III. Onion Gravy   *Wisconsin*

Skin of three to four large red onions
1 small onion, finely chopped
3 tablespoons oil
2 cups beef broth
4 to five tablespoons basic roux (recipe above).

Sauté the onion skins and the chopped onion in the oil until red color comes from the skins and chopped onion is browned. Gradually mix the broth with the roux and add. Cook until thickened. Strain.

Yield: About two cups.

IV. Mushroom Gravy   *Wisconsin*

1 medium-size onion, finely chopped
3 tablespoons oil
¼ pound mushrooms, diced
3 tablespoons flour
2 cups beef broth or chicken broth
Salt and freshly ground black pepper to taste.

1. Sauté the onion in the oil until golden. Add the mushrooms and cook several minutes longer.
2. Stir in the flour and then the broth. Bring to a boil, stirring, and cook until smooth. Season with salt and pepper.

Yield: About two cups.

Holiday Folk Fair Horseradish and Dill Gravies for Boiled Beef   *Wisconsin*

3 tablespoons butter
3 tablespoons flour
2 cups milk
½ cup sour cream
¾ teaspoon salt
⅛ teaspoon freshly ground black pepper
1 tablespoon freshly grated horseradish, or to taste
2 tablespoons freshly snipped dill weed.

1. Melt the butter and blend in the flour. Gradually stir in the milk and bring to a boil, stirring. Cook until smooth and thickened. Stir in the sour cream, but do not heat further. Season with the salt and pepper.

2. Divide the sauce in half. Add the horseradish to one half and the dill weed to the other.
Yield: About one cup of each gravy.

Lobster Sauce   *Minnesota*

1 boiled lobster
2 tablespoons butter
2½ tablespoons flour
1¼ cups fish stock or equal parts clam juice diluted with water
1 cup heavy cream
Salt and freshly ground black pepper to taste
Cayenne pepper to taste.

1. Remove meat from the tail and claws of the lobster. Chop the meat and reserve. Put the coral and tomalley of the lobster through a fine sieve and add to the chopped lobster meat.
2. Heat the butter in a saucepan and stir in the flour. When blended, add the stock or clam juice, stirring rapidly. When blended and smooth, continue cooking, stirring frequently, about ten minutes. Stir in the cream and cook five minutes longer. Season with salt, pepper and cayenne and add the lobster meat. Heat thoroughly and serve.
Yield: About three cups.

Warm Lemon Sauce   *Ohio*

¾ cup sugar
3 tablespoons cornstarch
¼ teaspoon salt
⅛ teaspoon nutmeg
6 tablespoons freshly squeezed lemon juice
2 tablespoons butter
1½ cups boiling water
2 teaspoons grated lemon rind.

Combine thoroughly the sugar, cornstarch, salt and nutmeg in a saucepan. Blend in the lemon juice until very smooth. Add the butter and boiling water. Bring to a boil over medium heat, stirring constantly, and boil two minutes. Stir in the lemon rind. Serve warm, with pound-cake, puddings and warm desserts.

Yield: Two cups.

Orange Sauce   *Ohio*

2 egg yolks
½ cup sugar
 Grated rind and juice of one small orange
1 cup heavy cream, whipped.

1. Beat the egg yolks and sugar together in the top of a double boiler. Stir in the orange rind and orange juice and cook over simmering water until the mixture coats the back of the spoon.
2. Cool and chill. Fold in the cream. Serve over angel food cake or spongecake.

Yield: About two cups.

Chocolate Sauce   *Illinois*

¼ cup butter
½ pound unsweetened chocolate
3 cups sugar
1 thirteen-and-one-half-ounce can evaporated milk
½ cup light corn syrup.

1. Melt the butter and chocolate together slowly over hot water. Stir in the sugar, milk and syrup.
2. Cook over medium heat until mixture is thickness of white syrup. Turn into a jar. Cool and store in the refrigerator. Use over ice cream, desserts and cake. Thin with a little heavy cream if sauce is too thick.

Yield: About three cups.

Beverages

Fourth of July Lemonade   *Ohio*

2 cups sugar
2½ cups water
2 cups lemon juice
1 cup orange juice
2 teaspoons grated lemon rind
1 tablespoon grated orange rind
1 cup crushed fresh mint leaves
 Crushed ice
 Ice water or chilled soda water.

1. Place the sugar and water in a saucepan and heat, stirring, until sugar is dissolved. Boil five minutes. Add the juices and rinds and pour over the mint leaves. Cover and let stand one hour.
2. Refrigerate, covered.
3. For each serving, pour one-third cup of the syrup over crushed ice in a glass and fill up with ice water or chilled soda water.

Yield: About one dozen servings.

Buttermilk Shake   *Wisconsin*

3 cups chilled buttermilk
½ cup cold lemon juice
½ cup sugar
⅛ teaspoon grated lemon rind
2 scoops vanilla ice cream
⅛ teaspoon ginger.

Shake, or blend in an electric blender, all the ingredients together until smooth and well mixed.

Yield: About three and one-half cups.

Joe's Eggnog   *Illinois*

60 eggs, separated
4 cups cognac or bourbon

2 cups sugar, or to taste
1 cup dark rum
1 teaspoon salt
1 teaspoon vanilla
4 cups heavy cream, whipped
   Nutmeg.

1. Beat the egg yolks until light. Beating constantly, slowly add the cognac or bourbon. Dissolve the sugar in the rum and stir into egg yolk mixture. Add the salt and vanilla.

2. Stir in the whipped cream. Beat the egg whites until stiff but not dry and fold in. Sprinkle with nutmeg.

Yield: Enough for fifty punch cups.

Hot Grape Punch   *Ohio*

1 gallon grape juice
1 teaspoon whole cloves
2 sticks cinnamon, broken into quarters
1 teaspoon freshly grated nutmeg
⅔ cup sugar
¾ cup lemon juice
1 cup orange juice.

Heat the grape juice, cloves, cinnamon pieces, nutmeg and sugar together and simmer fifteen minutes. Strain mixture and add the fruit juices. Serve hot.

Yield: About one gallon.

Jefferson Davis Punch   *Oklahoma*

12 bottles red Bordeaux
1½ bottles dry sherry
½ bottle cognac
1 cup Jamaican rum
1 cup maraschino cherry liqueur
3 cups lemon juice
3¼ pounds sugar, dissolved in a minimum
   amount of water
   Ice
3 large bottles ginger ale

6 large bottles soda water
2 lemons, thinly sliced
1 orange, thinly sliced
½ cucumber, thinly sliced.

1. Day before, combine the Bordeaux, sherry, cognac, rum, cherry liqueur, lemon juice and dissolved sugar. Mix well and refrigerate overnight.

2. Next day, pour over ice in punch bowls and add the ginger ale and soda water. Mix. Garnish with the fruit and cucumber slices.

Yield: About five gallons.

Dandelion Wine   *Michigan*

4 quarts boiling water
4 quarts dandelion blossoms, washed
3 lemons
3 oranges
3½ pounds sugar
½ cake compressed yeast or one and one-half
   teaspoons active dry yeast, dissolved in
   two tablespoons lukewarm water.

1. Pour the boiling water over the washed blossoms and bring to a boil. Cool and set aside three days. Strain, discarding blossoms.

2. Cut the colored rind from the lemons and oranges and add to strained liquid. Bring to a boil and boil fifteen minutes. Add the lemon and orange pulp and the sugar and stir well. Cool.

3. Add the yeast and set the brew in a cool place for a week to ten days. Strain and bottle.

Yield: About five quarts.

Candies

Peanut Brittle   *Oklahoma*

    3 cups sugar
    1 cup light corn syrup
    ½ cup water
    2 cups raw peanuts
    4 teaspoons baking soda
    1½ tablespoons butter
    1½ teaspoons vanilla.

1. Place the sugar, syrup and water in a heavy saucepan and heat, stirring, until sugar is dissolved. Continue cooking without stirring until the mixture registers 240 degrees on a candy thermometer.

2. Add the peanuts and continue boiling, stirring, until mixture registers 300 degrees on thermometer, the hard crack stage.

3. Remove from the heat and stir in the baking soda, butter and vanilla. Pour onto a greased marble surface. Let cool. When cold, break candy into pieces.

Yield: About two pounds.

Peppermint Taffy   *Kansas*

    2 cups sugar
    ½ cup light corn syrup
    ½ cup water
    ¼ teaspoon cream of tartar
    ¾ teaspoon peppermint extract
      Red food coloring.

1. Combine the sugar, syrup, water and cream of tartar in a heavy pan. Heat, stirring, until sugar dissolves.

2. Cook without stirring to hard ball stage, 265 degrees on a candy thermometer. Remove from the heat and add the peppermint extract and food coloring. Pour onto a greased platter or piece of marble.

3. When taffy is cool enough to handle, pull it until it is snow white and porous. To pull taffy, use greased surface and greased hands. Hold candy in left hand; pull half with right hand until stretched twelve inches; then double back strand to bulk of candy in left hand. Pull another section and loop it back.

4. Twist taffy into ropes. Cut with scissors or break into pieces.

Yield: About two dozen pieces.

Butterscotch Candy   *Illinois*

    2 cups light brown sugar
    ¼ cup light corn syrup
    1 cup water
    ¼ teaspoon salt
    ⅓ cup butter
    ¼ teaspoon vanilla.

1. Place the brown sugar, syrup, water and salt in a heavy saucepan. Stir over low heat until sugar is dissolved.

2. Increase heat and cook until mixture registers 250 degrees on a candy thermometer, the firm ball stage.

3. Add the butter and cook with occasional stirring until mixture registers 300 degrees on the thermometer, the brittle stage.

4. Remove mixture from the heat, add the vanilla and pour into a buttered shallow pan so that candy is in a one-quarter-inch layer. While warm, crease into squares with the blunt side of a knife. When cold, break into pieces.

Yield: About one and one-quarter pounds.

Peanut Butter Fudge   *Iowa*

    ½ cup peanut butter
    ½ cup milk
    2½ cups sugar
    1 to two tablespoons light corn syrup
    1 tablespoon butter
    1 teaspoon vanilla.

1. Combine the peanut butter, milk, sugar and syrup and boil gently, stirring constantly, until a little of the mixture forms a soft ball when tried in cold water (236 degrees on a candy thermometer).

2. Add the butter and vanilla and cool mixture until tepid. Beat until creamy.

3. Pour into buttered pan and cut into squares.

Yield: About one and one-half pounds.

Peggy's Caramels   *Oklahoma*

3 pounds light brown sugar
1 bottle light corn syrup
8 cups heavy cream
1 tablespoon vanilla.

1. Put the brown sugar, syrup and one quart of the cream in a large, heavy kettle. Bring to a boil, stirring, and then cook, still stirring, until mixture registers 238 degrees on a candy thermometer or forms a soft ball.

2. Add two cups of remaining cream and bring mixture to 238 degrees again, stirring constantly.

3. Add remaining cream and cook, stirring, to 240 degrees on the thermometer. Remove mixture from heat and add the vanilla. Pour into well-buttered pans. Cool and cut into squares.

Yield: About seven pounds.

Grandmother's Thanksgiving Special Candy   *Oklahoma*

6 cups sugar
1 large can (thirteen and one-half ounces) and one small can (five and one-third ounces) evaporated milk
2 cups dark corn syrup
1½ cups chopped walnuts.

1. In a large, heavy kettle, combine the sugar, milk and syrup. Heat, stirring, until the sugar is dissolved and mixture comes to a boil. Continue stirring until mixture reaches 238 degrees on a candy thermometer or forms a soft ball when dropped into cold water.

2. Cool slightly and then beat until smooth and thick. Add the walnuts and pour into greased pans. Let stand twenty-four hours before cutting.

Yield: About six pounds.

Salami Sweetmeat (Uncooked)   *Wisconsin*

½ pound shelled walnuts, finely ground
2 four-ounce bars German sweet chocolate, melted
1 egg
½ cup finely chopped candied fruits
⅓ cup chopped raisins
½ cup sliced toasted almonds
¼ cup flaked coconut (optional)
  Sugar
  Dark rum.

1. Place the walnuts, chocolate, egg, candied fruits, raisins, almonds, coconut and one-half cup sugar in a bowl and mix with the fingers until mixture forms a well-mixed mass.

2. Add enough rum to flavor and make a dough that will stick together when pressed.

3. Divide the mixture in two and form on a sugared board into two sausage-shaped rolls about one to one-half inches in diameter. Roll in sugar. Wrap in wax paper and then in clear plastic wrap.

4. Let sweetmeat mellow a day or two. The sweetmeat will keep without refrigeration and even improve for two weeks or so. Cut in one-quarter-inch slices just before serving.

Yield: About three dozen slices.

Popcorn Balls   *Kansas*

1 cup dark molasses
½ cup sugar
½ cup water
2 tablespoons cider vinegar
1 tablespoon butter

¼ teaspoon baking soda
3 quarts popped corn.

1. Mix the molasses, sugar, water, vinegar and butter in a heavy saucepan. Bring to a boil, stirring just until sugar is dissolved.
2. Boil without stirring until mixture registers 290 degrees on a candy thermometer. Stir in the baking soda.
3. Pour mixture over the corn and let stand until cool. With the hands, shape into two-inch balls.
Yield: About three dozen.

Crystallized Rose Petals   *Missouri*

2 cups water
3½ cups granulated sugar
1 pound wild, unsprayed rose petals, picked early in the day
  Confectioners' sugar.

1. Place the water in a pan and add the granulated sugar. Heat the mixture, stirring constantly, until the sugar dissolves.
2. Boil without stirring until the syrup spins a thread or registers 230 degrees on a candy thermometer.
3. Place a rack in a 13-by-9-by-2-inch baking dish. Pour in the syrup to a depth of one inch. Allow to cool. Reserve remaining syrup.
4. When syrup in pan is cool, add the petals. Make sure they are submerged in the syrup. Cover pan with a wet towel and let stand six hours.
5. Add remaining syrup, cover again and let stand twenty-four hours.
6. Remove the rack from the pan and let petals drain. Allow the petals to dry thoroughly; then dust with confectioners' sugar. Store in an airtight box.
Yield: About two cups.
Note: Petals are used as a sweetmeat or as decoration on cakes, cookies and desserts.

Dressings (Stuffings)

Potato Dressing for Roast Duck
Minnesota

5 medium-size potatoes, boiled without salt
1 onion, finely chopped
3 ribs celery, finely chopped
½ cup butter
  Salt and freshly ground black pepper to taste.

Peel and mash the cooked potatoes and add the remaining ingredients. Use to fill duck cavity.
Yield: Enough for a four-pound to six-pound duck.

Wild Rice Stuffing for Wild or Domestic Fowl
Minnesota

1½ cups uncooked wild rice
1 cup finely minced onions
½ cup butter
1 tablespoon finely chopped parsley
4 cups well-seasoned chicken broth or beef broth
  Salt, if necessary
  Freshly ground black pepper to taste.

1. Place the rice in a colander and wash well under cold running water. Drain well.
2. Cook the onions in the butter, stirring, until wilted, then add the parsley and rice. Continue cooking and stirring five to ten minutes, then add the broth, salt if necessary, and pepper. Bring to a boil, cover and simmer until rice is tender, about forty minutes.
Yield: Five to six cups.

Rice Stuffing for Chicken   *Minnesota*

1 cup uncooked rice
2 cups fresh or canned chicken broth
  Salt to taste
1 bay leaf
3 tablespoons butter or chicken fat
½ cup finely chopped onion
½ cup finely chopped heart of celery
¼ cup finely chopped green pepper
1 to two cloves garlic, finely minced
1 chicken liver, coarsely chopped
3 tablespoons finely chopped parsley.

1. Combine the rice, broth, salt and bay leaf. Bring to a boil, cover and simmer exactly twenty minutes. Let cool slightly.

2. Heat the butter or fat and cook the onion, celery, green pepper and garlic in it until onion is wilted. Add the liver and cook, stirring, until it loses its red color. Stir the liver mixture and parsley into the rice.

Yield: Enough for a three-pound to four-pound chicken.

In Missouri as in much of the Midwest, South and Southwest, "dressing" is served as a side dish when roast chicken or turkey is served. This is a rice "dressing."

Rice Dressing   *Missouri*

8 cups water
1 teaspoon salt
½ pound uncooked rice
¼ cup butter
1 cup finely chopped onions
1 green pepper, cored, seeded and chopped
1 cup chopped heart of celery with leaves
½ pound ground round steak
½ pound bulk sausage meat
2 tablespoons chopped parsley
3 tablespoons rubbed sage
1 cup strong-flavored chicken broth.

1. Preheat the oven to 200 degrees.

2. Combine the water and salt, bring to a boil and gradually add the rice. Cook rapidly about twenty minutes, or until rice is thoroughly tender. Drain rice under cold running water. Let stand until ready to use.

3. Melt the butter and add the onions, green pepper and celery. Cook, stirring, until onions are wilted. Add the ground round and sausage meat and cook, breaking up the meat with a wooden spoon. Cook, stirring, until meat loses its color. Add the parsley and sage. Bring the broth to a boil and add to meat mixture.

4. Spoon the rice into a well-buttered baking dish and spoon the meat mixture over the rice. Cover with aluminum foil and bake thirty minutes. Remove foil and bake fifteen minutes longer.

Yield: About six servings.

Cranberry-Sausage Stuffing   *Indiana*

1 pound (four cups) cranberries
1 cup water
1½ cups sugar
1 pound sausage meat, cooked until browned with drippings reserved
8 to nine cups coarsely crumbled corn bread
1 cup diced celery
1 small onion, chopped
½ cup diced green pepper
½ teaspoon thyme
½ teaspoon marjoram
1 tablespoon chopped parsley
1 unpeeled small red apple, cored and chopped.

1. Place the cranberries, water and sugar in a saucepan and cook until cranberries are tender, about ten minutes. Drain off excess juice.

2. Combine the drained berries, sausage, drippings and remaining ingredients. Use to stuff turkey or capons. Or place the stuffing in a casserole

and bake one hour in a preheated 325-degree oven.

Yield: As stuffing, enough for one twelve-pound turkey or two five-pound to six-pound capons; as casserole, about three quarts.

Dressing for Fowl   *Iowa*

Gizzards, livers and hearts of two chickens
or ducks
¼ cup butter
2 onions, finely chopped
4 cups soft bread crumbs
2 cups thick applesauce, preferably
homemade
Salt and freshly ground black pepper to
taste
1 teaspoon sage.

1. Grind the gizzards, livers and hearts. Set aside.

2. Melt the butter and sauté the onions in it until tender but not browned.

3. Add the ground mixture and cook quickly over medium-high heat while stirring until mixture loses all its pink color.

4. Remove from the heat and add the remaining ingredients. Mix lightly.

Yield: Enough stuffing for two four-pound chickens or two ducks.

Fruit Dressing for Poultry   *Minnesota*

½ pound prunes
¼ cup raisins
¼ cup currants
4 large tart apples, peeled, cored and diced
½ cup water
2 tablespoons sugar
½ teaspoon salt
⅓ teaspoon cinnamon
2 tablespoons butter
3 cups stale white bread, cut into tiny cubes
¼ teaspoon thyme.

1. Pit the prunes and place in a pan with the raisins, currants and apples. Add the water, bring to a boil, cover and simmer until the fruit is tender.

2. Add the sugar, salt, cinnamon and butter. Fold in the bread cubes and thyme.

Yield: Enough stuffing for two four-pound chickens, two ducks, a goose or a small turkey.

Dumplings

Soup Dumplings (Kleppas)   *Minnesota*

1 egg
½ cup milk
1 cup flour
¼ teaspoon salt
4 cups boiling beef broth.

1. Break the egg into a mixing bowl and beat with a wire whisk. Stir in the milk and then the flour and salt. This should be a medium-thick batter. Test the batter by dropping a small spoonful of it into the boiling broth. If batter is too thin, stir in more flour. If batter is too thick, stir in more milk. Continue adding dumplings to the soup until all the batter is used.

2. When all the dumplings have been added, simmer soup fifteen minutes and serve immediately.

Yield: Four to six servings.

Dumplings for Chicken Stew   *Iowa*

1 cup flour
2 teaspoons baking powder

¾ teaspoon salt
1 egg, lightly beaten
2 tablespoons chopped parsley
¼ cup half and half or milk.

1. Sift the flour, baking powder and salt together. Add the egg, parsley and half and half or milk. Stir only enough to blend. The dough should be quite soft.

2. Drop from spoon into a rich, well-seasoned, hot stewing chicken gravy. To prevent sticking, dip spoon into hot gravy after dropping each dumpling.

3. Cover pan tightly and cook fifteen minutes. Do not remove cover while dumplings are cooking.

Yield: Six dumplings.

Note: If you do not happen to have stewing chicken in gravy, the dumplings can be cooked in chicken broth lightly thickened with flour.

Bavarian Dumplings (Semmel Knodel)
Wisconsin

1 cup warm milk
6 dry rolls, pulled apart and then cut up into very small pieces
  Salt and freshly ground black pepper to taste
2 eggs, lightly beaten
  Boiling salted water.

1. Pour the milk over the roll pieces and let stand at least one hour. Season with salt and pepper and mix in the eggs well.

2. Form the mixture into one-and-one-half-inch to two-inch balls and boil, a few at a time, in boiling salted water about twenty minutes. Serve with sauerbraten, roast pork and gravy such as the Czech gravies for dumplings (page 457).

Yield: Eight servings.

4. Mountain/ Northern Plains

Appetizers and Soups

Cheese Crisps   *Idaho*

¼ cup butter
1 cup freshly grated Parmesan cheese
1 cup flour
½ cup sour cream
1 tablespoon caraway seeds
1 egg white, lightly beaten.

1. Preheat the oven to 350 degrees.
2. Cream the butter and beat in the cheese. Gradually stir in the flour alternately with the sour cream. Add the caraway seeds and gather dough into a ball.
3. Roll out half of the dough to one-eighth-inch thickness on a lightly floured pastry cloth or board. Cut into one-and-one-half-inch rounds. Place on greased baking sheet. Brush with the egg white and bake ten to twelve minutes, or until golden and crisp. Cool on a rack.
4. Repeat with remaining dough.
Yield: About six dozen tiny crisps.

Cocktail Meat Balls   *North Dakota*

1 pound ground lean pork
1 pound ground lean beef round
2 eggs, lightly beaten
⅔ cup cracker crumbs
1 small onion, finely chopped
1 teaspoon nutmeg

1 teaspoon ground allspice
½ teaspoon freshly ground black pepper
1 teaspoon salt
¼ teaspoon sugar
¼ cup butter
1 cup beef broth
1 tablespoon flour.

1. Combine the pork, beef, eggs, cracker crumbs, onion, nutmeg, allspice, pepper, salt and sugar in a bowl. Mix well.
2. Form into one-half-inch balls. Melt the butter in a skillet and fry the balls in it, a few at a time, until browned on all sides.
3. Drain off excess fat. Return balls to skillet and add one-quarter cup of the broth. Cover skillet and steam the balls ten minutes.
4. Blend the flour with the remaining broth. Add to skillet and bring to a boil, stirring.
Yield: About four dozen.

Rullepolse (Spiced Meat Roll)
North Dakota

Meat roll:
1 beef or veal flank steak
1 cup coarse salt
1 teaspoon saltpeter (see note)
½ teaspoon ground allspice
½ teaspoon ground cloves

1 teaspoon freshly ground black pepper
1 teaspoon baking soda
2 tablespoons brown sugar
⅛ teaspoon mace
3 slices one-quarter-inch-thick fresh ham, bone removed.
Brine:
2 cups coarse salt
3 quarts hot water
1 teaspoon saltpeter
½ teaspoon baking soda
¼ cup brown sugar
Buttered rye or pumpernickel.

1. Two weeks before serving, prepare the meat roll by trimming off the fat and gristle from the flank steak.

2. Combine the remaining meat roll ingredients except the ham slices and rub half the combined mixture into the meat. Lay the ham slices on top of the flank and rub in remaining combined mixture.

3. Roll up the flank, enclosing the ham and spices. Tie firmly with string. Wrap in three layers of muslin, pulling it tightly to form a neat shape.

4. Combine the ingredients for the brine in a porcelainized steel or ceramic dish, stirring to dissolve the salt. Place the muslin-wrapped meat in the brine so that meat is completely submerged. Cover and refrigerate ten to fourteen days.

5. Remove the meat and discard the brine. Place the meat in a clean casserole and cover with cold water. Bring to a boil, cover and simmer very gently three and one-half to four hours or until meat is fork-tender.

6. Remove meat to a platter. Place a board on top and weight it down. Refrigerate overnight.

7. Remove muslin and string. Slice meat very thinly and serve on buttered rye or pumpernickel as an hors d'oeuvre or open-faced sandwich.

Yield: One dozen servings.

Note: Saltpeter is available in many pharmacies and, in New York City, also at Lekvar by the Barrel, 1577 First Avenue (10028) and 968 Second Avenue (10022) and at Paprikas Weiss, 1546 Second Avenue (10028).

Smelts in Aspic   *North Dakota*

1 pound smelts
1 teaspoon salt
1 teaspoon sugar
2 tablespoons cider vinegar
8 whole allspice
1 bay leaf
2½ cups water
1 envelope unflavored gelatin
2 tablespoons cold water.

1. Wash and bone the smelts and roll up. Place close together, rolled side up, in a large skillet. Add the salt, sugar, vinegar, allspice, bay leaf and water.

2. Bring to a boil, cover and simmer ten to fifteen minutes or until fish is cooked.

3. Transfer smelts to a shallow serving dish. Strain the stock. Soften the gelatin in the cold water and add to hot stock, stirring to dissolve gelatin. Pour over smelts and chill. Unmold to serve.

Yield: Four to six servings.

Mountain Fish Chowder   *Wyoming*

3 two-pound trout, filleted, skinned and cut into serving pieces
1 onion, finely chopped
2 cups finely chopped celery
1 two pound three-ounce can Italian plum tomatoes
2 cups fish stock or potato water
1 cup cooked peas
1 cup creamed corn
2 cups diced cooked potatoes
Salt and freshly ground black pepper to taste
½ teaspoon thyme
2 cups heavy cream.

1. Place the trout, onion, celery and enough water barely to cover in a saucepan. Bring to a boil and simmer five minutes.

2. Add the remaining ingredients except for the cream and cook twenty-five minutes. Stir in the cream, reheat, but do not boil, and serve.

Yield: Six servings.

Bean Soup   *Idaho*

2 cups dried great Northern beans (large white)
12 cups water
1 meaty ham bone
1 cup finely chopped onions
1 bay leaf
1 clove garlic, crushed
  Salt
1 cup diced carrots
2 cups diced potatoes
1 cup diced celery
1 white turnip, peeled and diced
1 leek, sliced
  Freshly ground black pepper
½ cup heavy cream.

1. Day before, wash the beans and cover with the water. Let soak overnight. Next day, transfer water and beans to a large kettle and add the ham bone, onions, bay leaf and garlic. Add two teaspoons salt. Bring to a boil and simmer one and one-half hours, or until beans are tender.

2. Add the carrots, potatoes, celery, turnip, leek and salt and pepper to taste. Cover and cook about thirty-five minutes. Remove ham bone and take off meat. Dice meat and return to kettle.

3. Stir in the cream. Reheat, but do not boil.

Yield: About ten servings.

Yellow Split Pea Soup   *Colorado*

1 cup yellow split peas
1 onion, sliced
1 rib celery, diced

4 cups ham broth
½ teaspoon celery seeds
½ teaspoon ginger
1 cup diced ham
  Salt and freshly ground black pepper to taste.

1. Cover the yellow split peas with water and let soak several hours.

2. Add the onion and celery and boil until peas are tender, about one hour. Drain vegetables and add to them the broth, celery seeds, ginger and ham. Bring to a boil. Season with salt and pepper.

Yield: Four servings.

Potato Dill Soup   *South Dakota*

½ cup finely chopped onion
2 tablespoons butter
4 medium-size potatoes, diced
2 cups water
1½ teaspoons salt
2½ cups milk
⅓ cup freshly snipped dill weed, or to taste
2 tablespoons flour
1 cup sour cream.

1. Sauté the onion in the butter, add the potatoes and cook two minutes without browning. Add the water and salt. Bring to a boil, cover and simmer until potatoes are tender, about fifteen minutes.

2. Add the milk and dill and bring to a boil again.

3. Gradually blend the flour with the sour cream. Stir a little hot soup into the mixture and return all to the pan. Heat soup to thicken, but do not allow to boil.

Yield: Four servings.

Bohemian Oukrop   *South Dakota*

6 cups water
4 cloves garlic

Salt
¼ teaspoon caraway seeds
3 potatoes, diced
¼ teaspoon marjoram
1 tablespoon lard
Freshly ground black pepper
4 slices hard rye bread, cubed
2 tablespoons goose grease or chicken fat.

1. Place the water in a kettle. Mash the garlic with one teaspoon salt and add to water. Add the caraway seeds, potatoes, marjoram and lard. Bring to a boil and simmer until potatoes are tender, about twenty minutes. Season with salt and pepper to taste.

2. Fry the bread cubes in the grease or fat until browned. Place bread cubes in a warm tureen and ladle the hot potato soup over them. Let stand until bread is soaked.

Yield: Four to six servings.

Beer Cheese Soup   *South Dakota*

8 cups beef broth
2 tablespoons diced carrot
¼ cup diced green pepper
¼ cup flour
2 cups beer
1 pound Gruyère cheese or Swiss cheese, shredded
Salt and freshly ground black pepper to taste.

1. Place the broth, carrot and green pepper in a saucepan and bring to a boil. Mix the flour with one-half cup of the beer and stir in.

2. Bring to a boil, stirring until mixture thickens. Stir in the cheese until it melts. Season with salt and pepper. Stir in the remaining beer. Reheat, but do not boil.

Yield: Six servings.

Barley Soup   *North Dakota*

7 onions
3 pounds beef shin or other soup meat, cut up
Salt
1 clove garlic, chopped
1 parsnip, peeled and diced
½ cup pearl barley
2 white turnips, peeled and diced
6 large carrots, sliced
2 potatoes, peeled and diced
Freshly ground black pepper.

1. Quarter four of the onions and place in a kettle with the meat, three quarts water, one and one-half tablespoon salt and the garlic. Bring to a boil and simmer five hours, adding water as needed to maintain level.

2. Strain broth. Remove meat from bone and gristle and return meat to strained broth. Remove surface fat.

3. Add the parsnip and barley and cook one hour, or until the barley is tender.

4. Slice the remaining onions. Add with the turnips, carrots and potatoes to the soup. Season to taste with salt and pepper. Cook twenty-five minutes longer. Check the seasoning.

Yield: About ten servings.

Fresh Vegetable Soup   *South Dakota*

½ cup sliced carrots
½ cup peas
½ cup crosscut string beans
½ cup diced celery
2 cups diced potatoes
6 cups water
Salt and freshly ground black pepper to taste
1 tablespoon butter
2 tablespoons flour.

1. Place the carrots, peas, beans, celery and

potatoes in a saucepan, add the water and season with salt and pepper.

2. Bring to a boil and simmer, covered, until vegetables are tender, about twenty-five minutes.

3. Melt the butter in a small skillet, add the flour and cook, stirring, until the mixture browns slightly. Stir in a little of the vegetable liquid. Return all to the saucepan and cook, stirring. Check the seasoning.

Yield: Four servings.

Kale Soup   *North Dakota*

1 ham bone
8 cups water
½ cup uncooked rice
⅓ cup chopped parsley
1 cup ground pressed-down kale
1 onion, sliced
2 large carrots, sliced
2 cups peeled tiny new potatoes
  Salt and freshly ground black pepper to taste
1 cup heavy cream.

1. Cover the ham bone with the water in a large kettle. Bring to a boil and simmer three hours. Remove bone and cut off any meat. Return meat to stock in kettle.

2. Add the rice, parsley, kale, onion, carrots and potatoes. Season with salt and pepper.

3. Cover and simmer thirty-five minutes. Stir in the cream.

Yield: Eight servings.

Chicken Liver Soup   *Nebraska*

2 twenty-ounce cans tomatoes
½ bay leaf
¼ cup chopped onion
½ cup chopped celery
2 cups chicken broth
  Salt and freshly ground black pepper to taste

½ pound chicken livers, chopped
3 tablespoons butter
2 tablespoons chopped parsley.

1. Place the tomatoes, bay leaf, onion, celery and broth in a saucepan. Bring to a boil, season with salt and pepper, cover and simmer twenty-five minutes.

2. Strain the broth.

3. Sauté the chicken livers in the butter over high heat until browned. Place a spoonful of chicken livers in each soup plate and spoon broth over. Sprinkle with the parsley.

Yield: Six servings.

Pear Soup   *Montana*

½ cup pearl barley
  Lightly salted water
4 cups milk
¼ teaspoon baking soda
2 unripe green pears, peeled, cored and diced
¼ teaspoon salt
3 tablespoons sugar.

1. Day before, cover the barley with the water and let soak overnight. Next day, transfer to a saucepan and cook until barley is tender, about one hour. Drain.

2. Place barley, the milk and baking soda in a pan and bring to a boil. Add the pears and cook until tender. Add the salt and sugar.

Yield: Four servings.

Fish

Trout Poached in Wine

Idaho

2 one-pound to two-pound trout
1 cup dry white wine
1 tablespoon lemon juice
  Salt and freshly ground black pepper to taste
2 sprigs parsley
2 tablespoons finely chopped shallots
2 tablespoons butter.

1. Clean, fillet and skin the trout, reserving the bones and skin.
2. Place bones, skin, the wine, lemon juice, salt, pepper and parsley in a pan and simmer gently at least twenty-five minutes. Strain and reserve the liquid.
3. Preheat the oven to 350 degrees.
4. Sprinkle half the shallots in the bottom of a buttered small shallow baking dish. Arrange the fillets on top, slightly overlapping, and season with salt and pepper. Sprinkle the remaining shallots over the fish and dot with the butter.
5. Pour the reserved wine stock over all, cover tightly and bake about fifteen minutes, or until the fish flakes easily.

Yield: Four servings.

Trout with Anchovies

Idaho

 4 one-pound trout
¾ cup milk
¾ cup flour
  Salt and freshly ground black pepper to taste
¼ cup oil
¼ cup butter
4 anchovy fillets, finely chopped
½ cup dry white wine
1 teaspoon chopped fresh thyme or one-half teaspoon dried thyme
2 tablespoons finely chopped parsley
  Juice of one lemon.

1. Soak the trout in the milk. Combine the flour, salt and pepper. Dredge the wet trout in the mixture.
2. Place the oil in a large skillet and cook the trout in it on one side until golden brown, about five minutes. Turn and cook the other side about five minutes. Transfer the trout to a hot serving platter.
3. Wipe out the skillet with paper towels. Put the butter, anchovies and wine in the skillet. Simmer five minutes and add the thyme, parsley and lemon juice. Pour the hot sauce over the fish and serve.

Yield: Four servings.

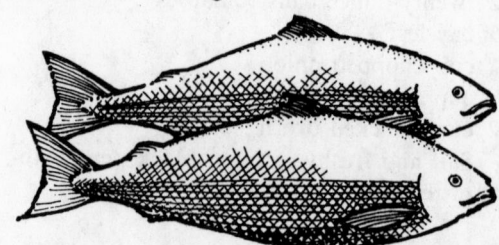

Trout Meunière
Wyoming

2 cups milk
  Salt and freshly ground black pepper to taste
2 one-pound trout, tails and fins removed
¼ cup flour
½ cup butter
2 tablespoons lemon juice
2 tablespoons chopped parsley
  Lemon wedges

1. Season the milk with salt and pepper and soak the trout in the mixture five minutes.
2. Holding each fish by the head, dredge in the flour.
3. Melt the butter in a heavy skillet and brown the fish in it on both sides. Sprinkle with the lemon juice. Lower the heat and cook slowly until fish flakes easily, about eight minutes.
4. Place fish on a warm platter. Sprinkle fish with the parsley and serve with lemon wedges.
Yield: Two servings.

Baked Trout
Wyoming

1 two-pound to three-pound trout, cleaned
1 tomato, peeled and sliced
1 small onion, thinly sliced
¼ cup butter
1 cup dry white wine
  Salt and freshly ground black pepper to taste.

1. Preheat the oven to 375 degrees.
2. Place the trout in a buttered baking dish. Top with the tomato and onion slices and dot with the butter. Pour the wine over all and season with salt and pepper.
3. Bake thirty minutes, or until fish flakes easily.
Yield: Three servings.

Baked Mackinaw
Wyoming

1 three-and-one-half-pound Mackinaw trout, cleaned, left whole
2 small onions, sliced
1 cup sour cream
⅓ cup prepared mustard
1 cup dried bread cubes
  Salt and freshly ground black pepper to taste
¼ cup melted butter.

1. Preheat the oven to 375 degrees.
2. Place the trout on a sheet of buttered aluminum foil. Mix together the onion slices, sour cream, mustard, bread cubes, salt and pepper. Stuff the fish with the mixture.
3. Brush fish with half the butter and draw up the foil to form a package. Place in a baking pan and bake thirty minutes.
4. Open up the foil and brush fish with remaining butter. Bake five minutes longer, or until fish flakes easily.
Yield: Four servings.

Jackson Lake Trout Shish Kebab
Wyoming

2 pounds trout fillets, cut into one-inch slices
  Salt and freshly ground black pepper to taste
¼ cup lemon juice
½ cup dry red wine
½ teaspoon grated lemon rind
  Bay leaf or sage leaf branches.

1. Place the fish pieces in a ceramic or glass dish. Season with salt and pepper. Pour the lemon juice and wine over fish and sprinkle with the lemon rind. Refrigerate and marinate two hours, turning occasionally.
2. Thread the fish on individual skewers. Broil over hot coals until fish flakes, about five minutes, turning to brown all sides.
3. Place skewers on a metal rack set on a metal

pan. Under the rack, stuff the bay or sage and set fire to it. Let fish smoke ten minutes.

Yield: Six servings.

Baked Stuffed Trout   *Idaho*

2 tablespoons butter
¼ cup diced salt pork
½ cup finely chopped onion
¼ cup finely chopped celery
¼ cup finely chopped green pepper
1 cup soft bread crumbs
1 teaspoon thyme
¼ cup toasted almonds, chopped
  Salt and freshly ground black pepper
2 two-pound trout, heads and tails left on, cleaned
4 slices bacon.

1. Preheat the oven to 400 degrees.
2. Place the butter and salt pork in a skillet and cook until salt pork bits are crisp. Add the onion and sauté until tender.
3. Remove skillet from the heat and add the celery, green pepper, bread crumbs, thyme, almonds and salt and pepper to taste.
4. Use the mixture to stuff the trout. Secure with string or toothpicks. Place each fish on a sheet of buttered aluminum foil.
5. Season fish with pepper and lay two slices of bacon over each. Bring up the foil and close to make two packages. Place on a baking sheet and bake twenty minutes.
6. Turn back the foil to expose top of fish. Baste with fish liquid. Bake five to ten minutes longer, or until fish flakes easily.

Yield: Four servings.

Baked Catfish or Bullhead   *Nebraska*

1 three-pound to four-pound catfish or bullhead, cleaned, head and tail removed
  Salt and freshly ground black pepper to taste

1 cup warm bacon drippings
1½ cups soft bread crumbs.

1. Preheat the oven to 475 degrees.
2. Sprinkle the fish with salt and pepper and dip in the warm bacon drippings to coat. Roll in the bread crumbs.
3. Dip fish in the drippings to coat a second time and roll again in the crumbs. Set in a baking dish and bake twenty-five minutes, or until the fish is well browned and the flesh flakes easily.

Yield: Four servings.

Mama's Herring Salad   *North Dakota*

1 large, firm salt herring, skin and bones removed
4 cups diced boiled potatoes
3 cups diced pickled beets, drained, juice reserved
1 cup diced peeled cucumber
½ cup chopped scallions, including green part
2 apples, peeled, cored and diced
1 teaspoon salt
¼ teaspoon freshly ground white pepper
3 tablespoons sugar
2 hard-cooked eggs, sliced
1 cup heavy cream, whipped.

1. Day before, wash the herring and soak overnight in water to cover.
2. Next day, drain herring and chop finely. Add the potatoes, beets, cucumber, scallions, apples, salt, pepper and sugar. Add enough beet juice to moisten, reserving remaining juice. Pack mixture into a mold or basin. Chill until firm.
3. Unmold and garnish with the egg slices. Add beet juice to the whipped cream until it is pale pink. Serve separately.

Yield: Eight servings.

Meat, Poultry, and Game

Beef Cubes with Biscuits *North Dakota*

Beef:
1½ pounds round steak, cut into cubes
¼ cup shortening
1½ cups chopped onions
2 tablespoons flour
1 cup beef broth
1 tablespoon sugar
1½ teaspoons salt
½ teaspoon freshly ground black pepper
1 cup canned tomatoes
1 six-ounce can tomato paste
½ teaspoon Worcestershire sauce
1 cup sliced mushrooms
¾ cup sour cream, at room temperature.
Sour cream puff biscuits:
1½ cups flour
2 teaspoons baking powder
¼ teaspoon salt
⅓ cup shortening
¾ cup sour cream, at room temperature
2 tablespoons heavy cream
2 tablespoons sesame seeds.

1. To prepare beef, brown the meat in the shortening in a heavy skillet. Add the onions and cook until they are tender. Sprinkle with the flour and cook two minutes longer.

2. Add the broth, sugar, salt, pepper, tomatoes, tomato paste and Worcestershire. Bring to a boil, cover and simmer one and one-half hours, or until meat is very tender. Stir in the mushrooms and sour cream and pour into a casserole.

3. Preheat the oven to 425 degrees.

4. To prepare biscuits, sift together the flour, baking powder and salt. Cut in the shortening. Stir in the sour cream to make a dough. Pat out on a floured board to one-half-inch thickness and cut six to eight small biscuits. Brush with the cream, sprinkle with the seeds and place on top of meat. Bake twenty to twenty-five minutes, or until biscuits are done.

Yield: Six servings.

Steak in a Sack *Wyoming*

1 two-pound to three-pound slice top sirloin, about two and one-half inches thick
½ cup melted butter
2 cloves garlic, crushed
Salt and freshly ground black pepper
4 slices crisp toast, made into crumbs.

1. Preheat the oven to 425 degrees.

2. Rub the meat on all sides with the melted butter, then with the garlic. Season generously with salt and pepper.

3. Flatten out a heavy paper sack, rub with remaining butter and sprinkle with the toast crumbs. Dredge the meat in the crumbs and press

to make them adhere. Wrap the meat in the paper and tie with string.

4. Place the package on a rack in a roasting pan and bake forty-five minutes for rare beef and about one hour for medium rare.

Yield: Six servings.

Grandmother's Beef-Over   *South Dakota*

1½ pounds ground beef chuck
1 onion, finely chopped
3 tablespoons flour
3 cups milk or light cream
  Salt and freshly ground black pepper to taste
  Mashed potatoes, cooked rice or toast.

1. Brown the ground chuck and onion in a skillet until beef loses its pink color and the onion is tender.

2. Sprinkle with the flour and cook until flour browns slightly.

3. Stir in the milk or cream and season with salt and pepper. Bring to a boil, stirring, and cook until thickened. Spoon over mashed potatoes, rice or toast.

Yield: Six servings.

Norwegian Meat Balls in Cream
North Dakota

1 pound ground round steak
½ pound ground pork
1 egg, lightly beaten
½ cup mashed potatoes
½ cup dry bread crumbs
½ cup milk
2 teaspoons salt
¼ teaspoon each nutmeg, ground cloves, ground allspice, ginger and freshly ground black pepper
½ teaspoon light brown sugar
  Flour
2 tablespoons peanut oil

2 tablespoons butter
1 cup heavy cream.

1. Preheat the oven to 325 degrees.

2. Combine the meats, egg, potatoes, bread crumbs, milk, salt, spices and brown sugar. Blend well and shape into twenty-four meat balls. Roll the balls in flour.

3. Heat the oil and butter, add the meat balls and brown them on all sides. Spoon the balls into a heatproof casserole and pour the cream over them. Set the casserole in a pan and pour boiling water around casserole. Cover and bake forty minutes.

Yield: Six servings.

Dakota Beef Loaf   *South Dakota*

1 pound ground beef round
1 egg, lightly beaten
½ teaspoon salt
⅛ teaspoon freshly ground black pepper
½ teaspoon paprika
1 tablespoon grated onion
¼ cup finely chopped celery leaves
1 cup tomato juice
10 small saltines, rolled into crumbs.

1. Preheat the oven to 350 degrees.

2. Mix the beef with the remaining ingredients and pack into an 8½-by-4½-by-2½-inch loaf pan. Bake twenty minutes on lowest shelf in oven.

3. Raise to high shelf and bake forty minutes longer.

Yield: Four servings.

Fleischkuechle (Meat Patties)
North Dakota

Dough:
2 cups flour
¼ cup heavy cream
1 egg, lightly beaten
¼ teaspoon baking powder

½ teaspoon salt
  Milk.
Filling:
 1 cup ground cooked beef
 1 cup ground cooked pork
 ½ cup water
 2 teaspoons grated onion
 1 teaspoon salt
 ¼ teaspoon freshly ground black pepper
  Fat or oil for deep-frying.

1. Mix all the dough ingredients together, using just enough milk to mix into a soft dough that can be rolled and will not stick. Let the dough stand, covered, two hours.

2. Meanwhile, to prepare filling, mix together the beef, pork, water, onion, salt and pepper.

3. Divide the dough into one-inch balls and roll each on a lightly floured board to one-sixteenth-inch thick circles about nine inches in diameter. Spread the meat mixture one-quarter-inch thick over one half of each circle, keeping meat mixture away from the edges.

4. Moisten the edges, fold circles in half and seal the edges together with fork tines. Fry, two at a time, until golden in the fat or oil heated to 375 degrees. Drain on paper towels.

Yield: Four servings.

Jellied Beef Mold   *South Dakota*

1½ pounds boneless beef chuck cubes
 1 cup water
 1 envelope unflavored gelatin
 ⅓ cup diced celery
 ¼ cup chopped onion
 ¼ cup diced dill pickle
1¼ cups beef broth
 ½ teaspoon salt
 ¼ teaspoon freshly ground black pepper
 ¼ teaspoon allspice
 ¼ cup stuffed olives, sliced
  Parsley sprigs
  Whole stuffed olives.

1. Place the beef and water in a saucepan and simmer, covered, until meat is very tender, about two hours. Remove meat, reserve and cool broth and put meat through a meat chopper. There should be about two cups.

2. Soften the gelatin in two tablespoons cooled broth.

3. Heat remaining broth with the celery and onion and cook ten minutes. Drain and reserve broth.

4. Add celery and onion to meat and stir in the pickle. Add three-quarters cup reserved broth to the beef broth, heat and stir in softened gelatin. Stir to dissolve gelatin. Pour a thin layer of gelatin mixture into an 8½-by-4½-by-2½-inch loaf pan. Chill.

5. Add the salt, pepper, allspice and meat mixture to remaining gelatin mixture. Arrange the stuffed olive slices in a pattern over firm gelatin mixture in pan. Spoon in the meat mixture and chill several hours.

6. Unmold and garnish with parsley and whole olives.

Yield: Eight servings.

Ky-Va (Jellied Meat Loaf)   *North Dakota*

 3 onions
 3 pounds veal shoulder with bones
 3 pounds lamb shoulder with bones
 2 bay leaves
 4 teaspoons salt
10 peppercorns
 1 teaspoon freshly ground black pepper
 1 teaspoon ginger
 1 teaspoon ground allspice
 2 envelopes unflavored gelatin
 1 cup chicken broth or water.

1. Day before, slice one of the onions and place with the veal and lamb in a large kettle. Add the bay leaves, two teaspoons of the salt, the peppercorns and water to cover the meat.

2. Bring to a boil, cover and simmer until meat is very tender, about three hours.

3. Remove the meat from the bones, discarding bones. Strain the broth in the kettle and return to the kettle. Boil rapidly until broth measures about two quarts.

4. Grind the meat and remaining onions. Add the remaining salt, the pepper, ginger and allspice. Return meat mixture to the concentrated broth in kettle. Cook gently fifteen to twenty minutes.

5. Soak the gelatin in the chicken broth or water and stir into the hot meat mixture. Stir to dissolve gelatin.

6. Turn into two oiled 9-by-5-by-3-inch loaf pans and chill overnight. Next day, unmold onto cold platter and garnish as desired.

Yield: Two loaves; about sixteen servings.

Swedish Potatis Korv (Potato Sausage)
North Dakota

2½ pounds ground pork shoulder
2½ pounds ground beef round
6 medium-size raw potatoes, ground
1 cup beef broth
2 onions, ground
1 teaspoon freshly ground black pepper
1 tablespoon salt
1 teaspoon ground allspice
1 teaspoon nutmeg
About five yards pork casing (see note).

1. Day before, mix all the ingredients except the casing in a large bowl. The easiest way is to use the hands.

2. Using a sausage stuffing attachment according to manufacturer's directions, stuff the casing with the mixture. Let the sausages set in the refrigerator overnight.

3. Next day, cover the sausages with cold water, bring to a boil and simmer gently one hour. Or the sausages can be placed in a large roasting pan and roasted in a preheated 350-degree oven for one hour. The sausage is good hot or cold. If desired, these sausages can be smoked after storing in the refrigerator overnight, then partially

dried to give a summer sausage that can be fried.

Yield: About seven pounds.

Note: Sausage casing can be purchased from most pork butchers. In New York City, these include Frank's Pork Store, 26 Carmine Street (10014); Faicco's Market, 260 Bleecker Street (10014); Esposito Meat Market, 516 Ninth Avenue (10018); and Molinari's, 776 Ninth Avenue (10019).

Cabbage Rolls
North Dakota

1 pound ground cooked smoked ham
1½ pounds ground fresh pork shoulder
1½ cups cooked rice
1 teaspoon salt
½ teaspoon freshly ground black pepper
1½ cups well-drained sauerkraut
½ teaspoon sage
¼ teaspoon nutmeg
1 medium-size head cabbage
Ham broth or chicken broth.

1. Preheat the oven to 375 degrees.

2. Combine the ham, pork, rice, salt, pepper, sauerkraut, sage and nutmeg in a bowl.

3. Steam the cabbage head until the leaves wilt. Remove leaves carefully. Place a tablespoon of the filling on each cabbage leaf and roll, tucking in the edges. Place in a shallow baking dish or roasting pan. Pour the broth over the cabbage rolls to cover and bake one and one-half hours, or until filling is well done.

Yield: Eight to ten servings.

Bohemian Spareribs
South Dakota

2 pounds spareribs
Salt and freshly ground black pepper to taste
1 twenty-ounce can sauerkraut
1 tablespoon caraway seeds
1 onion, sliced
1 twenty-ounce can tomatoes.

1. Preheat the oven to 350 degrees.

2. Cut the ribs into serving pieces and season with salt and pepper.

3. Mix the sauerkraut and caraway seeds and place in a shallow baking dish. Arrange the onion slices on top. Pour the tomatoes over onion slices and arrange the ribs on top of all.

4. Bake two hours, or until ribs are thoroughly cooked.

Yield: Four servings.

Pork Goulash South Dakota

1½ pounds boneless pork shoulder, cubed
1 tablespoon lard
1 large onion, finely chopped
¼ teaspoon caraway seeds
  Salt and freshly ground black pepper to taste
3 tablespoons grated hard rye bread
3 cups pork broth made from bones
½ cup beer.

1. Brown the pork cubes in the lard. Add the onion and caraway seeds and cook five minutes longer. Season with salt and pepper.

2. Add the bread and broth, bring to a boil and simmer until pork is tender and cooked, about two hours.

3. Stir in the beer just before serving.

Yield: Six servings.

Veal-Sour Cream Meat Loaf Utah

1½ pounds ground veal
½ pound ground pork
2 tablespoons grated onion
2 carrots, finely grated or ground
½ teaspoon rubbed leaf sage or one teaspoon chopped fresh sage
1½ teaspoons salt
¼ teaspoon freshly ground black pepper
½ teaspoon grated lemon rind
½ cup sour cream.

1. Preheat the oven to 350 degrees.

2. Mix all ingredients together and pack into a 9-by-5-by-3-inch loaf pan. Bake one and one-half hours.

Yield: Six servings.

Rocky Mountain (or Prairie) Oysters Montana

Calves' testicles (see note)
Salted water
Fine cracker crumbs
Salt and freshly ground black pepper
Bacon drippings.

1. Soak the testicles in salted water one hour. Drain. Roll in cracker crumbs seasoned with salt and pepper.

2. Heat bacon drippings in a heavy skillet and fry the testicles in it until brown and cooked through.

Note: Calves' testicles are available at roundup time from castrated calves and at some Ninth Avenue markets between 42d and 37th streets in New York City.

Lemon Shanks with Potatoes Colorado

4 pounds veal or lamb shanks, sliced through the bone
¼ cup olive oil
2 pounds small potatoes, peeled and cut in half lengthwise
1 pound small white onions
2 cups canned tomatoes
1 six-ounce can tomato paste
1 clove garlic
¾ cup dry red wine
2 tablespoons wine vinegar
2 teaspoons salt
3 small bay leaves
1 three-inch strip lemon peel
½ cup blanched almonds
¼ pound feta cheese, crumbled.

1. Brown the shanks in the oil in a heavy Dutch oven or casserole. Remove meat and reserve. Brown the potato pieces and onions in the fat remaining in the casserole.

2. Return the meat to the casserole. In an electric blender, combine the tomatoes, tomato paste, garlic, wine, vinegar and salt. Blend until smooth and pour over meat and vegetables.

3. Add the bay leaves and lemon peel. Bring to a boil, cover and simmer about one and one-half hours, or until meat is tender.

4. Add the almonds and cheese and stir to melt the cheese.

Yield: Four to six servings.

Parsleyed Lamb Riblets   *Colorado*

3 pounds lamb riblets
   Salt and freshly ground black pepper
¾ cup soft bread crumbs
¼ cup chopped parsley
3 sprigs fresh thyme, chopped, or one-half teaspoon dried thyme
1 clove garlic, finely minced.

1. Preheat the oven to 400 degrees.

2. Sprinkle the riblets on both sides with salt and pepper. Combine the remaining ingredients. Toss well.

3. Place the riblets on a rack in a roasting pan and bake one hour, turning occasionally. Sprinkle the riblets with half the bread crumb mixture and return to the oven. Reduce the oven heat to 325 degrees. Bake ten minutes and turn the riblets. Sprinkle with remaining crumb mixture and bake thirty minutes longer.

Yield: Four servings.

Chicken with Noodle Balls   *South Dakota*

Chicken:
1 four-pound to five-pound stewing chicken
2 ribs celery with leaves, sliced
4 carrots, sliced

1 onion, sliced
1 bay leaf
2 sprigs parsley
2 teaspoons salt
¼ teaspoon freshly ground black pepper
   Flour.
Noodle ball dough:
6 eggs
2 tablespoons water
⅛ teaspoon salt
4 cups flour, approximately.

1. To prepare chicken, place it in a heavy Dutch oven not much larger than the chicken and add water to come halfway up the bird.

2. Add the celery, carrots, onion, bay leaf, parsley, salt and pepper. Bring to a boil, cover and simmer two hours. Turn chicken over and cook one hour longer. Remove from heat and let chicken cool, breast side down, in broth.

3. When chicken is cool enough to handle, remove meat from bones and skin and return meat to broth. Heat to boiling and check seasoning.

4. Thicken gravy by mixing two teaspoons flour with two tablespoons cold water for every cup of broth. Add and cook, stirring, until gravy thickens.

5. To prepare noodle balls, beat the eggs, water and salt together. Beat in the flour until mixture is like heavy cake batter.

6. Drop teaspoonfuls of dough into simmering gravy and chicken. Cover and cook one-half hour, or until done.

Yield: Four to six servings.

Chicken and Dumplings   *Utah*

1 four-pound to five-pound fowl or stewing chicken
2 ribs celery with leaves, sliced
2 onions, sliced
1 carrot, quartered
   Salt and freshly ground black pepper
1¼ cups flour
1½ teaspoons baking powder

½ cup milk
2 tablespoons melted shortening.

1. Day before, place the fowl in a large Dutch oven or casserole. Barely cover with cold water and add the celery, onions, carrot and salt and pepper to taste. Bring to a simmer, cover and cook one hour, or until chicken is tender.

2. Let the chicken sit in the broth overnight in the refrigerator. Next day, remove surface fat and reserve. Remove chicken pieces from bones and set pieces aside. Strain broth and measure four cups.

3. Melt one-quarter cup reserved chicken fat in a saucepan. Stir in one-quarter cup of the flour and blend. Gradually stir in the reserved broth. Bring to a boil, stirring, and cook two minutes. Season to taste with salt and pepper.

4. Add chicken pieces to the sauce.

5. Sift together the remaining flour, one-half teaspoon salt and the baking powder. Stir in the milk and melted shortening to make a soft dough. Drop dough by spoonfuls onto simmering chicken mixture. Cover tightly and cook, without lifting cover, fifteen minutes.

Yield: Six servings.

Pecan-Stuffed Wild Duck *Nebraska*

2 wild ducks
   Salt and freshly ground black pepper
¼ cup butter
1 cup finely chopped onion
¾ cup finely chopped celery with leaves
2 tablespoons chopped parsley
½ cup raisins
1 cup roughly chopped pecans
4 cups soft bread crumbs
⅓ cup chicken broth or milk
8 slices bacon
1 cup catchup
2 tablespoons Worcestershire sauce
½ cup chili sauce
1 tablespoon light brown sugar
¼ teaspoon dry mustard.

1. Preheat the oven to 350 degrees.

2. Season the birds inside and outside with salt and pepper.

3. Melt the butter and sauté the onion in it until tender. Add the celery, parsley, raisins, pecans, bread crumbs and broth or milk. Season to taste with salt and pepper.

4. Stuff the birds with the pecan mixture. Close the cavities and truss the birds. Place the slices of bacon over the breasts and set birds on a rack in a shallow roasting pan. Roast twenty minutes to the pound.

5. Combine the catchup, Worcestershire, chili sauce, brown sugar and mustard and spoon over the ducks during the last twenty-five minutes of cooking.

Yield: Four servings.

Note: The glaze below may be substituted for the catchup mixture.

½ cup melted butter
1 cup dry red burgundy
1 cup currant jelly.

Mix ingredients in a saucepan. Boil one minute. Use to baste ducks during last thirty minutes of roasting.

Yield: Two and one-half cups.

Wild Duck I *Wyoming*

1 wild duck, cut into serving pieces
½ cup butter or bacon drippings
1 onion, sliced
   Salt and freshly ground black pepper to taste
2 cups game or beef broth
1 bay leaf
1 cup sliced mushrooms
2 tablespoons flour
⅛ teaspoon thyme.

1. Brown the duck pieces in the butter or bacon drippings in a heavy skillet; transfer to a heavy casserole. Brown the onion slices in the fat remaining in the skillet and add onion slices to

the casserole. Add salt, pepper, the broth and bay leaf. Cover and simmer one and one-half hours.

2. Sauté the mushrooms in the fat remaining in the skillet. Sprinkle with the flour and cook two minutes, stirring. Add the thyme. Add mushroom mixture to the casserole and cook thirty minutes longer, or until the duck is tender.

Yield: Two to three servings.

Wild Duck II   *Wyoming*

1 wild duck, quartered
  Salt and freshly ground black pepper
¼ cup bacon drippings
1 cup beef broth
1 cup orange juice
3 tablespoons grated orange rind
½ cup dry vermouth
⅓ cup light brown sugar
  Flour.

1. Season the duck quarters with one and one-half teaspoons salt and one-half teaspoon pepper and brown in the bacon drippings in a heavy skillet. Transfer to a casserole.

2. Add the broth, cover and simmer one hour.

3. Add the orange juice, orange rind, vermouth and brown sugar. Cover and simmer until duck is tender, about twenty minutes. Remove duck to a warm platter.

4. For each cup liquid in casserole, add one and one-half tablespoons flour mixed with three tablespoons water. Bring to a boil, stirring. Season to taste with salt and pepper. Serve separately.

Yield: Two servings.

Wild Goose with Apricot Stuffing
South Dakota

1 young wild goose (about six pounds)
  Salt and freshly ground black pepper to taste
¼ cup lemon juice

¼ cup butter
¼ cup finely chopped onion
1 goose liver, chopped
1 cup peeled, cored and diced tart green apple
1 cup diced dried apricots
3 cups soft bread crumbs
6 slices bacon
  Melted bacon drippings
1 cup dry red wine (if necessary).

1. Preheat the oven to 325 degrees.

2. Sprinkle the inside and outside of the goose with salt and pepper and sprinkle inside of the cavity with the lemon juice.

3. Melt the butter in a small skillet and sauté the onion in it until tender. Add the goose liver and cook quickly until browned.

4. Stir in the apple, apricots, bread crumbs, salt and pepper. Stuff the goose with the mixture. Close the cavity and truss the bird. Set goose, breast up, on a rack in a roasting pan.

5. Cover breast with the bacon slices. Dip a piece of cheesecloth into melted bacon drippings and place over goose. Roast two and one-half to three hours, basting frequently with pan drippings.

6. If goose is old, add one cup red wine and cover during last hour of cooking.

Yield: Six servings.

Stuffed Snow Goose   *North Dakota*

1 four-pound to six-pound snow goose
  Salt and freshly ground black pepper to taste
2 tablespoons cognac
½ pound mixed dried fruits
2 cups port wine
½ cup dry white wine
2 cups beef broth
2 tablespoons plus one-third cup butter
1 goose liver, chopped

2 tablespoons finely chopped shallots or
 scallions
¼ teaspoon thyme
⅛ teaspoon ground allspice
3 to four cups soft bread crumbs
 Flour
6 thin slices salt pork
½ cup melted butter
1 tablespoon crushed black peppercorns
¼ cup lemon juice.

1. Two days before, season the snow goose in-side and outside with salt and pepper. Sprinkle inside with the cognac and refrigerate overnight.

2. Day before, place the dried fruits in a bowl and pour the port over fruits. Let stand over-night.

3. Next day, drain the fruits, reserving the port. Place fruits, dry white wine and broth in a saucepan and simmer until fruits are tender, about twenty minutes. Chop fruits roughly.

4. Preheat the oven to 500 degrees.

5. Melt two tablespoons of the butter and quickly sauté the liver and shallots or scallions in it until browned. Add to the fruit mixture. Take one-half cup of reserved port and reduce by boil-ing to one-quarter cup. Add to fruit-liver mix-ture. Add the thyme and allspice.

6. Add enough bread crumbs to make a soft stuffing. Season with salt and pepper. Stuff the goose. Close the cavity and truss the bird.

7. Beat together one-third cup of the butter and one-quarter cup flour and rub into the skin of the goose. Cover breast with the salt pork and place goose on a rack in a roasting pan. Roast thirty minutes.

8. Reduce oven heat to 300 degrees. Combine the melted butter, peppercorns and lemon juice and pour over goose. Roast one and one-half hours longer, or until goose is tender, basting occasionally.

9. Transfer the goose to a warm platter.

10. Remove the surface fat from the drippings and strain the liquid into a saucepan. For each cup, add one and one-half tablespoons flour mixed with two tablespoons water. Bring to a boil, stirring, and cook until thickened. Season with salt and pepper. Serve separately.
Yield: Six servings.

Wild Goose with Stuffing   *Wyoming*

1 twenty-nine-ounce can sauerkraut
1 large green apple, peeled, cored and
 quartered
1 small onion
1 four-pound to five-pound wild goose
 Salt and freshly ground black pepper
⅓ cup bacon drippings.

1. Preheat the oven to 400 degrees.

2. Combine the sauerkraut, apple and onion. Season the goose inside and outside with salt and pepper. Stuff with the sauerkraut mixture. Close the cavity and truss the bird. Place on a rack in a roasting pan.

3. Rub the bacon drippings into the bird, espe-cially the breast. Roast about one hour, or until done.
Yield: Four servings.

Roast Stuffed Wild Goose   *North Dakota*

1 six-pound wild goose
 Salt and freshly ground black pepper to
 taste
½ pound chicken livers
1 goose liver and heart
⅓ cup Madeira wine
1 cup chicken broth
½ teaspoon rosemary
¼ teaspoon tarragon
½ pound sausage meat
1 pound chestnuts, scored on the flat surface
 Boiling salted water
¼ cup chopped mushrooms
1 cup soft bread crumbs
4 slices salt pork
1 cup dry white wine
1 cup orange juice

1 tablespoon grated orange rind
1 tablespoon lemon juice
½ cup water
1 cup heavy cream
2 tablespoons currant jelly.

1. Preheat the oven to 450 degrees.
2. Season the goose inside and outside with salt and pepper.
3. Place the chicken livers, goose liver and heart, Madeira, broth, rosemary and tarragon in a small saucepan and simmer until the livers are tender, about eight minutes. Drain livers and heart and chop finely; discard liquid.
4. Cook the sausage meat, draining off and discarding the fat. Place the chestnuts in a saucepan and cover with boiling salted water. Boil fifteen minutes, or until tender. Peel and mash well.
5. Combine liver mixture, sausage, chestnuts, the mushrooms and bread crumbs. Season with salt and pepper. Use to stuff the goose.
6. Sew the cavity closed and truss the bird. Place the salt pork over the breast and place bird on a rack in a roasting pan. Roast fifteen minutes. Reduce oven heat to 350 degrees. Roast about two hours longer, or until tender. Baste frequently with a mixture of the white wine, orange juice, orange rind and lemon juice.
7. Transfer the bird to a warm platter. Remove excess fat from drippings and pour in the water. Heat over low heat, scraping to loosen browned-on bits. Slowly stir in the cream and then the jelly. Serve separately.
Yield: Eight to ten servings.

Roast Wild Turkey   *North Dakota*

1 eight-pound to nine-pound wild turkey
Salt and freshly ground black pepper to taste
¼ cup lemon juice
6 slices bacon, diced
½ cup butter
1 turkey liver, ground

1 turkey heart, ground
2 onions, finely chopped
3 ribs celery, diced
2 green peppers, diced
6 cups soft bread crumbs
1¼ cups chicken broth
¼ cup chopped parsley
2 teaspoons sage
4 thin slices salt pork.

1. Preheat the oven to 375 degrees.
2. Sprinkle the turkey outside and inside with salt and pepper. Sprinkle the cavity with the lemon juice.
3. Cook the bacon until crisp. Remove bacon and reserve. Add the butter to the drippings and sauté the liver, heart and onions in them until brown. Add the celery and peppers and cook three minutes longer.
4. Soak the bread crumbs in the broth and stir in with the parsley, sage, pepper and reserved bacon. Use to stuff the bird. Close the cavity and truss the bird. Place, breast side up, on a rack in a roasting pan.
5. Place the salt pork over breast and roast twenty minutes. Reduce oven heat to 325 degrees. Cover and roast turkey about thirty minutes a pound, or until tender. Baste frequently with pan drippings.
Yield: About one dozen servings.

Grouse Breasts with Ham   *Nebraska*

4 grouse breasts, halved
2 tablespoons flour
Salt and freshly ground black pepper to taste
½ cup butter
3 tablespoons finely chopped shallots or scallions
1 cup ground or very finely chopped cooked smoked ham
¾ cup chicken broth
1½ cups heavy cream
½ teaspoon celery seeds, crushed

¼ cup dry sherry
2 tablespoons chopped parsley
4 slices toast.

1. Rub the breast pieces with the flour seasoned with salt and pepper. Heat the butter in a heavy skillet and slowly brown the breast pieces in it until tender, about thirty minutes.

2. Remove breasts to a warm dish and keep warm. Add the shallots or scallions to the skillet and cook until tender but not browned.

3. Stir in the ham, broth, cream and celery seeds. Bring to a boil and cook five minutes. Season with salt and pepper.

4. Return breasts to sauce, add the sherry and parsley and reheat, but do not cook.

5. Serve each breast on top of a toast slice and spoon sauce over.

Yield: Four servings.

Breasts of Grouse in Madeira Sauce
South Dakota

3 grouse breasts, halved and boned
⅓ cup flour
  Salt and freshly ground black pepper
¼ cup butter
¼ cup oil
1 cup cooked white rice or wild rice
2 tablespoons finely chopped shallots or scallions
½ pound mushrooms, sliced
½ cup Madeira wine
1 cup heavy cream, scalded.

1. Preheat the oven to 350 degrees.

2. Cut the breast halves lengthwise into one-half-inch-thick slices. Dredge in the flour mixed with one teaspoon salt and one-quarter teaspoon pepper.

3. Heat the butter and oil in a heavy skillet and brown the breast pieces in it well on both sides.

4. Place the white rice or wild rice in the bottom of a shallow baking dish. Arrange the breast pieces on top of the rice.

5. Add the shallots or scallions to the drippings left in the skillet and cook until tender. Add the mushrooms and cook five minutes longer. Stir in the Madeira.

6. Add the cream, bring mixture to a boil and season to taste with salt and pepper. Pour over the breasts and bake fifteen minutes.

Yield: Three servings.

Stuffed Roast Pheasant
Nebraska

2 young pheasants
  Salt and freshly ground black pepper to taste
6 chicken livers
½ pound ground lean pork
2 cups soft bread crumbs
¼ cup canned beef gravy or brown sauce
½ teaspoon sage
6 thin slices salt pork
2 cups chicken broth
1 rib celery, chopped
1 small onion, sliced
1 carrot, diced
¼ teaspoon ground allspice
  Flour.

1. Preheat the oven to 350 degrees.

2. Sprinkle the pheasants inside and outside with salt and pepper.

3. Grind the livers and pork together. Add the bread crumbs, beef gravy or brown sauce, the sage, salt and pepper.

4. Stuff the birds with the pork mixture. Truss the birds. Place the slices of salt pork over the birds, tying slices in position.

5. Place birds on a rack in a shallow roasting pan, cover and roast thirty minutes.

6. Remove cover. Add the broth, celery, onion, carrot and allspice. Bake, uncovered, about one hour longer, or until tender, basting frequently with the liquid. Remove the salt pork slices about ten minutes before the end of the cooking time and increase oven heat to 400 de-

grees to brown birds. Transfer birds to warm platter.

7. Strain liquid in pan, remove surface fat and thicken liquid with one tablespoon flour mixed with two tablespoons water for each cup. Bring to a boil, stirring, and serve separately.

Yield: Six servings.

Roast Pheasant with Sour Cream Sauce
South Dakota

2 young pheasants
   Salt and freshly ground black pepper to taste
¼ cup chopped celery with leaves
2 cloves garlic, crushed
2 slices lemon
8 slices bacon
1½ cups dry white wine
3 tablespoons currant jelly
½ cup sour cream, at room temperature.

1. Preheat the oven to 325 degrees.
2. Sprinkle the birds inside and outside with salt and pepper. Place two tablespoons of the celery, one garlic clove and one lemon slice in each cavity. Truss the birds.
3. Lay four of the bacon slices over each bird and tie in place. Place birds on a rack in a shallow roasting pan and roast one and one-half hours, or until tender, basting frequently with the wine.
4. Transfer the birds to a warm platter. Skim excess fat from pan drippings. Measure one cup drippings and bring to a boil in a small saucepan. Stir in the jelly and the sour cream. Heat, but do not boil. Serve separately.

Yield: Six servings.

Roast Young Pheasant
South Dakota

2 young pheasants
   Salt and freshly ground black pepper to taste
¼ cup butter

1 small onion, finely chopped
¼ cup finely chopped celery with leaves
1 tablespoon chopped parsley
1 teaspoon summer savory
¼ teaspoon thyme
3 cups soft bread crumbs
¼ cup chicken broth
3 tablespoons oil
16 thin slices bacon or salt pork.

1. Preheat the oven to 400 degrees.
2. Season the birds inside and outside with salt and pepper.
3. Heat the butter in a small skillet and cook the onion in it until tender. Add the celery and cook two minutes longer. Add the parsley, savory, thyme, bread crumbs and broth. Season with salt and pepper. Stuff the birds with the bread mixture (see recipe below for alternate cabbage dressing). Sew cavity closed and truss birds.
4. Massage the birds with the oil.
5. Place the bacon slices overlapping all over the birds and tie in place. Place birds, breast side up, on a rack in a shallow roasting pan and roast about thirty minutes.
6. Roast, basting frequently with pan juices, about twenty minutes longer, or until tender.

Yield: Four servings.

Cabbage Dressing for Roast Pheasant
South Dakota

¼ cup butter
½ cup chopped onion
1 cup shredded cabbage
1 egg, lightly beaten
¼ teaspoon freshly ground black pepper
½ teaspoon salt
1 cup soft bread crumbs
2 tablespoons chicken broth
¼ teaspoon caraway seeds, crushed.

1. Melt the butter and cook the onion in it until tender but not browned. Add the cabbage and cook until barely wilted, about three minutes.

2. Add the remaining ingredients and use to stuff pheasants.

Yield: Enough for two young pheasants.

Pheasant in Sour Cream   *North Dakota*

1 pheasant, cut into serving pieces
⅓ cup flour
1 teaspoon salt
1 tablespoon sweet paprika
½ teaspoon freshly ground black pepper
3 tablespoons butter
1 cup sour cream, at room temperature
1 cup light cream.

1. Preheat the oven to 275 degrees.
2. Rub the pheasant pieces in the flour mixed with the salt, paprika and pepper. Reserve one tablespoon unused flour mixture. Heat the butter in a heavy skillet and brown the pheasant pieces in it on all sides. Place in a buttered casserole.
3. Stir the reserved seasoned flour mixture into the skillet drippings. Blend in the sour cream and light cream. Pour mixture over the pheasant and bake three hours. Stir before serving.

Yield: Three servings.

Braised Pheasant   *South Dakota*

1 pheasant, cut into serving pieces
¼ cup flour
½ teaspoon salt
¼ teaspoon freshly ground black pepper
¼ cup butter
¼ pound mushrooms, sliced
½ cup strong black coffee
1 cup heavy cream.

1. Preheat the oven to 350 degrees.
2. Dredge the pheasant pieces in the flour mixed with the salt and pepper. Heat the butter in a heavy skillet.
3. Brown the pheasant in the butter and transfer to a casserole. Add the mushrooms to the skillet and cook five minutes. Stir in the coffee and cook, stirring to loosen all browned-on bits. Stir in the cream. Pour over the pheasant.
4. Cover and bake thirty minutes. Remove cover and bake thirty minutes longer, or until tender.

Yield: Three servings.

Fried Pheasant Breasts   *South Dakota*

2 pheasant breasts, boned and halved
4 pheasant thighs, boned
1½ cups buttermilk
½ cup flour
1 egg, lightly beaten
1 teaspoon Worcestershire sauce
⅛ teaspoon ground allspice
½ teaspoon salt
¼ teaspoon freshly ground black pepper
½ cup milk, approximately
Fat or oil for deep-frying.

1. Place the pheasant pieces in a shallow dish and pour the buttermilk over pieces. Cover and refrigerate two hours, turning three times.
2. Drain pheasant pieces and pat dry.
3. Combine the flour, egg, Worcestershire, allspice, salt, pepper and enough milk to make a thick coating batter.
4. Dip the pheasant pieces in the batter and fry until golden, turning once, in a hot, deep-fat frying basket in the fat or oil heated to 360 degrees. Drain on paper towels.

Yield: Two servings.

Pheasant Loaf   *North Dakota*

4 cups ground cooked pheasant
1 cup milk
1 cup chicken broth
1½ teaspoons salt
½ teaspoon freshly ground black pepper
2 tablespoons grated onion
2 eggs, lightly beaten

2 cups soft bread crumbs
¼ teaspoon marjoram.

1. Preheat the oven to 375 degrees.
2. Mix all the ingredients together lightly. Pour into a greased 9-by-5-by-3-inch loaf pan and bake one hour. Serve hot or cold.
Yield: Six servings.

Hasenpfeffer South Dakota

1 four-pound rabbit, cut into serving pieces
3 cups water
3 cups cider vinegar
½ cup light brown sugar
1 onion, sliced
2 teaspoons salt
½ teaspoon freshly ground black pepper
1 clove garlic, crushed
1 bay leaf
2 teaspoons mixed pickling spices
¼ cup flour
3 tablespoons butter.

1. Place the rabbit pieces in a ceramic or glass bowl. Mix together the water, vinegar, brown sugar, onion, salt, pepper, garlic, bay leaf and pickling spices and pour over the rabbit.
2. Cover and refrigerate two days, turning the pieces or weighting them so that they are covered by the marinade.
3. Preheat the oven to 350 degrees.
4. Drain the rabbit pieces, pat dry and rub with the flour.
5. Heat the butter in a heavy skillet and brown the rabbit pieces in it on all sides. Transfer to a casserole.
6. Pour enough of the marinade into the casserole to come about halfway up the rabbit pieces. Bring to a boil, cover and bake about one hour, or until tender.
Yield: Six servings.

Rabbit in Cream Gravy Nebraska

1 three-pound to four-pound rabbit, cut into serving pieces
5 tablespoons flour
Salt and freshly ground black pepper to taste
5 tablespoons butter
2 onions, chopped
2 celery ribs with leaves, chopped
6 whole allspice
2 bay leaves
5 whole cloves
¼ cup cider vinegar
2 cups chicken broth, approximately
½ cup heavy cream
1 tablespoon plum or apple butter.

1. Rub the rabbit pieces in three tablespoons of the flour seasoned with salt and pepper. Heat three tablespoons of the butter in a heavy skillet and brown the rabbit pieces in it.
2. Transfer rabbit pieces to heavy casserole or Dutch oven.
3. Add the onion to the skillet and cook until tender but not browned and add to the casserole. Add the celery, allspice, bay leaves, cloves, vinegar and enough broth barely to cover the rabbit.
4. Bring to a boil, cover and simmer until tender, about forty-five minutes.
5. Meanwhile, melt the remaining butter in a small saucepan, add the remaining flour and cook, stirring, until lightly browned.
6. Using a wire whisk, whisk the browned flour mixture into the casserole. Cook three minutes. Check seasoning. Stir in the cream and plum or apple butter.
Yield: Four to six servings.

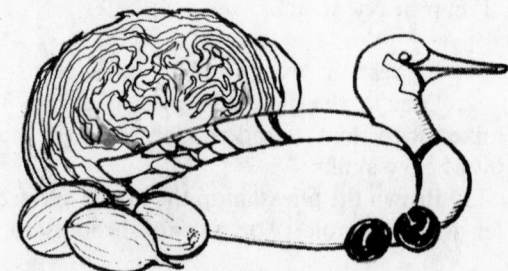

All the recipes calling for buffalo could be made using comparable cuts of beef or venison. Buffalo, bear and other exotic game meat can be bought from Maryland Gourmet Market, 414 Amsterdam Avenue, New York City 10024, and Hammacher Schlemmer, 147 57th Street, New York City 10022.

Buffalo Birds   *South Dakota*

2 pounds buffalo round steak, cut into six thin pieces suitable for rolling.
Marinade:
2 cups dry red wine
¼ cup lime juice
½ cup lemon juice
1 bay leaf
2 whole cloves
1 clove garlic, crushed
1 small onion, sliced
  Green tops from two celery ribs
6 black peppercorns, crushed
½ teaspoon tarragon
¼ teaspoon thyme
3 juniper berries, crushed.
Filling:
1 clove garlic
  Salt and freshly ground black pepper to taste
1 pound sausage meat, cooked until well browned, drained of fat
¼ cup soft bread crumbs
2 tablespoons chopped parsley
2 tablespoons grated onion
1 egg, lightly beaten
6 strips dill pickle
¼ cup flour
¼ cup sausage drippings or oil
1½ cups dry red wine
2 tablespoons tomato paste.

1. Day before, place the meat slices in a ceramic porcelainized iron or glass dish. Combine all the ingredients for the marinade and pour over meat. Refrigerate overnight.

2. Next day, drain the pieces of meat and pat dry with paper towels. Rub with the garlic clove and sprinkle with salt and pepper.

3. Mix together the sausage meat, bread crumbs, parsley, onion and egg. Spread over the pieces of meat. Place a pickle strip on each and roll like a jellyroll. Tie or secure with toothpicks.

4. Dredge the rolls in the flour and brown in the drippings or oil in a large skillet. Transfer rolls to a heavy Dutch oven or casserole. Mix together the wine and tomato paste and pour over. Bring to a boil, cover and simmer until meat is tender, about one hour.
Yield: Six servings.

Apple-Stuffed Buffalo Ribs   *South Dakota*

¼ pound salt pork, diced
1 onion, chopped
¼ cup diced celery
2 tablespoons chopped parsley
4 large tart cooking apples, peeled, cored and sliced
⅓ cup sugar
1 cup dry bread crumbs
  Salt
¼ teaspoon freshly ground black pepper
¼ teaspoon thyme
1 six-pound to eight-pound boned rib of buffalo
  Flour.

1. Preheat the oven to 400 degrees.

2. Cook the diced pork until crisp. Remove bits and reserve.

3. Sauté the onion in the drippings until tender. Add celery, parsley, apples and sugar and simmer until apples are tender.

4. Add the bread crumbs, one teaspoon salt, the pepper, thyme and reserved pork bits. Pile the stuffing over the meat, roll and tie to make a neat roast.

5. Sprinkle the roast with salt and flour. Roast thirty minutes.

6. Reduce oven heat to 350 degrees and roast

about three hours longer, or until meat is very tender.

Yield: Eight servings.

Buffalo Meat Balls in Wine Sauce
South Dakota

1¼ pounds ground buffalo meat
¼ pound ground pork
1 onion, finely chopped
1 clove garlic, finely chopped
1 egg
1 tablespoon chopped parsley
1 teaspoon lemon juice
2 teaspoons Worcestershire sauce
  Salt and freshly ground black pepper to taste
1 cup olive oil
1 cup chicken broth
2 tablespoons tomato paste
1 cup dry red wine.

1. Combine the buffalo meat, pork, onion, garlic, egg, parsley, lemon juice and Worcestershire in a bowl and mix well. Season with salt and pepper. Form into balls, one inch for cocktail size and two and one-half inches for regular balls.

2. Brown the balls, a few at a time, in the oil. Drain and place in a saucepan.

3. In another small saucepan, combine the broth, tomato paste and wine. Bring to a boil.

4. Pour the wine mixture over the balls, cover and simmer fifteen minutes.

Yield: Six servings.

Deviled Buffalo Steak
South Dakota

1 two-pound slice buffalo round steak, cut about one and one-half inches thick
  Salt and freshly ground black pepper to taste
¼ cup flour
3 tablespoons bacon drippings or oil
2 onions, sliced

1 green pepper, diced
2 cups canned tomatoes
¼ pound mushrooms, sliced
1 teaspoon sugar
1 teaspoon Worcestershire sauce
⅛ teaspoon celery seeds.

1. Preheat the oven to 350 degrees.

2. Season the steak well with salt and pepper. Dredge in the flour and brown on both sides in the bacon drippings or oil. Place in a baking dish and add the remaining ingredients. Season with salt and pepper. Cover and bake two hours, or until tender.

Yield: Six servings.

Buffalo Steaks with Wild Rice Dressing
South Dakota

1 cup uncooked wild rice
  Salt
1 pound ground buffalo meat
2 tablespoons oil
½ cup finely chopped onion
½ pound mushrooms, sliced
6 slices French bread, crusts removed, cubed
1 cup beef broth
½ teaspoon sage
¼ teaspoon freshly ground black pepper
6 buffalo T-bone or rib steaks
6 tablespoons soft butter
¼ teaspoon tarragon
1 tablespoon chopped parsley
½ teaspoon lemon juice.

1. Preheat the oven to 350 degrees.

2. Cover the wild rice with boiling water and let stand fifteen minutes. Drain. Cover with fresh water and let stand ten minutes. Drain. Add two cups water and one-half teaspoon salt. Bring to a boil, cover and simmer thirty minutes, or until tender. Drain well.

3. Brown the ground buffalo meat in the oil in a skillet, breaking up the lumps with a fork. Add

the onion and cook five minutes. Add the mushrooms and cook three minutes longer.

4. Combine the bread cubes and broth in a bowl. Stir in the meat mixture, one-half teaspoon salt, the sage, pepper and wild rice and turn into a greased two-quart casserole. Cover and bake one hour.

5. Broil or barbecue the steaks and season with salt. Combine the butter, tarragon, parsley and lemon juice. Chill. Place a pat of herbed butter on each steak and serve with the wild rice casserole.

Yield: Six servings.

Buffaloaf
South Dakota

1 cup fine dry bread crumbs
1 teaspoon salt
⅛ teaspoon freshly ground black pepper
½ teaspoon thyme
¼ teaspoon marjoram
1 tablespoon chopped parsley
¼ teaspoon nutmeg
3 eggs, lightly beaten
1 cup milk
2 pounds ground buffalo meat
1 cup shredded carrot
1 cup finely chopped onion
1 cup finely chopped celery
½ cup catchup.

1. Preheat the oven to 350 degrees.
2. Place the bread crumbs, salt, pepper, thyme, marjoram, parsley and nutmeg in a bowl. Mix the eggs and milk together and add to crumb mixture. Let stand ten minutes.
3. Add the remaining ingredients except for the catchup and spread in a 9-by-13-inch baking pan. Spread catchup over all and bake one hour. Let stand five minutes before serving.

Yield: Six to eight servings.

Buffalo and Beer Pie
South Dakota

4 pounds buffalo meat, cut into one-inch cubes
1 tablespoon salt
½ teaspoon freshly ground black pepper
2 teaspoons sage
⅓ cup plus three tablespoons flour
⅓ cup oil
3 onions, cubed
3 carrots, cubed
3 ribs celery, diced
3 potatoes, cubed
4 cups beef broth
¼ cup tomato puree
2 cups beer
1 clove garlic, crushed
1 bay leaf
3 sprigs parsley
3 whole cloves
½ teaspoon thyme
Pie crust pastry made from two cups flour.

1. Season the meat cubes with the salt, pepper and sage and dredge in one-third cup of the flour. Heat the oil in a large skillet and brown the meat in it on all sides. Transfer meat to heavy Dutch oven or casserole.
2. Sauté the onions, carrots, celery and potatoes until lightly browned in the oil remaining in the skillet. Add vegetables to meat in casserole.
3. Sprinkle the remaining flour over drippings in skillet and cook, stirring, until lightly browned. Stir in the broth, puree, beer, garlic, bay leaf, parsley, cloves and thyme. Add to casserole.
4. Bring to a boil, cover and simmer until meat is tender, about two hours.
5. Pour meat mixture into two deep pie dishes and let cool.
6. Preheat the oven to 425 degrees.
7. When meat is cool, cover dishes with rolled-out pastry. Make a steam hole in each crust and bake thirty-five to forty-five minutes, or until pastry is browned and done.

Yield: Ten to one dozen servings.

Black Bear Stroganoff　　　*Wyoming*

4 pounds black bear meat, cut into cubes
1 bottle (three and one-third cups) dry red wine
3 whole cloves
1 bay leaf
3 ribs celery, chopped
1 clove garlic, crushed
½ cup flour
½ cup bacon drippings or oil
4 onions, sliced
6 tablespoons butter
4 cups beef broth or buffalo broth
　Salt and freshly ground black pepper to taste
1 pound mushrooms, sliced
4 cups sour cream.

1. Place the bear meat in a ceramic bowl and pour the wine over the meat. Add the cloves, bay leaf, celery and garlic. Let marinate in a cool place three days.

2. Drain the meat and pat dry. Pound each cube flat. Dredge meat pieces in the flour and brown, a few at a time, in the bacon drippings or oil. Transfer meat as it is browned to a large casserole.

3. Sauté the onions in three tablespoons of the butter and add to the casserole. Add the broth, salt and pepper and simmer, covered, until meat is tender, about one hour.

4. Sauté the mushrooms in the remaining butter. Add to the meat. Warm the sour cream; mix in a little hot broth; then stir into the bulk of the meat mixture. Reheat, but do not boil.

Yield: About sixteen servings.

Bear Steak　　　*Wyoming*

2 two-and-one-half-pound bear steaks, cut two inches thick
　Marinade for game (page 499)
½ cup butter, melted
¼ cup chopped chives

2 tablespoons prepared mustard
2 tablespoons tomato paste
½ teaspoon Worcestershire sauce
1 clove garlic, finely chopped
　Salt and freshly ground black pepper to taste.

1. Marinate the steaks in the marinade twenty-four hours.

2. Drain meat and pat dry. Combine the butter, chives, mustard, tomato paste, Worcestershire and garlic. Heat to warm. Broil steaks under medium heat, basting constantly with chive mixture, until medium-rare. Season with salt and pepper.

Yield: Six servings.

Venison Roast　　　*Wyoming*

1 five-pound to six-pound venison roast
½ cup dry red wine
¼ cup olive oil
1 tablespoon salt
½ teaspoon freshly ground black pepper
¼ teaspoon ground cloves
1 clove garlic, finely chopped
1 tablespoon rosemary, roughly crushed
8 slices bacon
1 cup chopped onions
1 cup diced carrot
1 cup diced celery
1¼ cups beef broth
2 tablespoons flour.

1. Day before, place the venison in a large bowl. Combine the wine, oil, salt, pepper, cloves, garlic and rosemary and pour over venison. Let marinate overnight.

2. Next day, preheat the oven to 400 degrees.

3. Cover top of roast with the bacon. Place the onions, carrot, celery and one cup of the broth in the bottom of a roasting pan. Place the roast on top of the vegetables. Pour the marinade over and roast fifteen minutes.

4. Reduce oven heat to 350 degrees and roast one and one-half hours longer, basting frequently. Remove roast to a warm platter and surround with the vegetables. Strain the liquid into a small saucepan.

5. Mix the flour with remaining broth and stir into the strained liquid. Bring to a boil and cook two minutes. Check seasoning. Serve separately.

Yield: About eighteen servings.

Venison Ragout   *North Dakota*

    3 pounds venison sirloin, cut into
        one-half-inch cubes
    3 tablespoons flour
    1 teaspoon salt
    ¼ teaspoon freshly ground black pepper
    ¼ cup olive oil
    3 onions, quartered
    2 cups dry red wine
    1 twenty-ounce can (two and one-half cups)
        tomatoes
    2 cloves garlic, crushed
    1 tablespoon chopped fresh ginger or one
        teaspoon ground ginger.

1. Dredge the venison pieces in the flour mixed with the salt and pepper. Brown slowly in the oil in a large heavy skillet.

2. Transfer meat to a heavy casserole or Dutch oven.

3. Sauté the onions in the fat remaining in the skillet. Add the wine, tomatoes, garlic and ginger. Bring to a boil, stirring, and pour into the casserole. Cover and let simmer four hours, or until the venison is very tender.

Yield: Six servings.

Venison with Sour Cream   *Colorado*

    2 pounds boneless venison, cut into
        one-and-one-half-inch cubes
    ¼ pound salt pork, in one piece
    1 clove garlic, crushed

    1 cup finely diced celery
    1 cup finely diced carrots
    ½ cup minced onion
    1 cup dry red wine
    2 cups water
    2 sprigs fresh thyme or one-half teaspoon
        dried thyme
    1 bay leaf
   15 peppercorns
    1 teaspoon salt
    ¼ cup butter
    ¼ cup flour
    1 cup sour cream
      Buttered noodles.

1. Day before, place the venison cubes in a large mixing bowl. Add the salt pork, garlic, celery, carrots, onion, wine, water, thyme, bay leaf, peppercorns and salt. Cover and let stand overnight in a cold place or refrigerate.

2. Next day, preheat the oven to 325 degrees.

3. Drain the meat, reserving the marinade, vegetables, garlic and bay leaf. Pat the salt pork and cubes of meat dry.

4. Slice the salt pork and heat it in a large heavy skillet. When the salt pork is rendered of its fat, brown the venison cubes in it on all sides. Transfer the pieces as they are browned to a two-quart casserole or Dutch oven.

5. Add the reserved celery, carrots and onion to the skillet in which meat cooked and cook, stirring, until onion is wilted. Add to the meat. Add the reserved marinade, garlic and bay leaf to casserole and bring to a boil on top of the stove.

6. Place the casserole in the oven and bake one to two hours, or until meat is tender.

7. Transfer the venison cubes to a hot serving dish. Strain the cooking liquid into a saucepan. Blend the butter and flour with the fingers and add it, bit by bit, to the liquid, stirring.

8. When the mixture is thickened, remove the saucepan from heat. Let cool slightly and add the sour cream, stirring rapidly. Reheat, but do not boil or the cream will curdle. Serve venison and sauce with buttered noodles.

Yield: Four to six servings.

Spicy, Oven-Barbecued Venison
South Dakota

⅓ cup vinegar
½ cup catchup
¼ cup beef broth
2 tablespoons light brown sugar
1 tablespoon Worcestershire sauce
1 tablespoon lemon juice
Salt to taste
¼ teaspoon freshly ground black pepper
1 clove garlic, crushed
¼ teaspoon Tabasco sauce
1½ pounds venison, cut into one-inch cubes
¼ cup bacon drippings or oil
1 large onion, sliced
½ cup heavy cream.

1. In a saucepan, combine the vinegar, catchup, broth, brown sugar, Worcestershire, lemon juice, salt, pepper, garlic and Tabasco. Bring to a boil and simmer fifteen minutes.
2. Preheat the oven to 350 degrees.
3. Brown the venison in the bacon drippings or oil in a heavy skillet. Transfer to a heavy casserole or Dutch oven. Add the onion slices and one-half of the barbecue sauce to the casserole. Bake, uncovered, until meat is tender, about one hour, adding remainder of sauce as dish becomes dry.
4. Transfer venison to a warm serving platter. Add the cream to liquid remaining in the casserole and bring to a boil, stirring. Pour over meat.
Yield: Four servings.

Stuffed Venison Slices
Wyoming

2 pounds thinly sliced venison steak
2 cups soft bread crumbs
6 tablespoons butter
1 onion, thinly sliced
2 tablespoons chopped parsley
4 egg yolks
2 tablespoons chopped baked ham
2 tablespoons freshly grated Parmesan cheese

¼ teaspoon thyme
Salt and freshly ground black pepper to taste
Melted butter.

1. Preheat the oven to 375 degrees.
2. Pound the venison slices with a mallet or the edge of a plate.
3. Brown the bread crumbs in four tablespoons of the butter.
4. Sauté the onion in the remaining butter. Add the parsley, egg yolks, ham, cheese, thyme, salt and pepper.
5. Place one tablespoon of the stuffing on each slice of venison and roll to enclose. Secure with string or toothpicks.
6. Dip the rolls in melted butter and then in the bread crumbs to coat. Bake in a shallow dish twenty-five to thirty minutes, or until tender.
Yield: Six servings.

Venison Shish Kebabs
South Dakota

2 pounds venison, cut into one-inch cubes
½ cup homemade French dressing
2 green peppers, cut into squares
1 large onion, cut into one-inch pieces
⅓ pound mushroom caps.

1. Place the venison cubes in ceramic bowl and pour the dressing over venison. Let marinate at least two hours. Remove venison, reserving marinade.
2. Alternate the meat with green pepper squares, onion pieces and mushroom caps on skewers. Brush all with reserved marinade and broil over hot coals until done to desired degree, about fifteen minutes for rare, twenty to twenty-five minutes for well done. Turn frequently and baste with marinade as needed.
Yield: Six servings.

Broiled Venison Steaks   *North Dakota*

2 slices (about three-quarters-inch thick) cut from the leg or loin of venison
2 tablespoons oil
¼ cup soft butter
1 tablespoon chopped parsley
½ teaspoon salt
⅛ teaspoon cayenne pepper
¼ teaspoon grated onion
4 teaspoons lemon juice.

1. Brush the venison steaks with the oil and broil quickly over hot coals or in an oven broiler about three and one-half minutes. Turn and broil second side four minutes.
2. Meanwhile, beat the butter with remaining ingredients and top each steak with the butter mixture.
Yield: Four servings.

Venison or Elk Fondue   *Wyoming*

2 pounds venison or elk tenderloin, cut into three-quarter-inch cubes
Deep oil heated to 400 degrees in a fondue pot and placed over a heater.
Herb sauce:
2 egg yolks
2 tablespoons lemon juice
1 teaspoon salt
¼ teaspoon freshly ground black pepper
1½ cups oil, approximately
½ cup chopped chives
½ cup chopped parsley
1 tablespoon grated onion.
Curry sauce:
1 cup mayonnaise
½ cup sour cream
1 tablespoon red wine vinegar
1 tablespoon olive oil
3 teaspoons curry powder, or to taste
¼ teaspoon salt
1 clove garlic, crushed
1 tablespoon grated onion.

Tomato sauce:
6 tablespoons catchup
2 tablespoons prepared mustard
¼ cup oil
1 small onion, finely chopped
2 teaspoons chopped chives
2 teaspoons chopped parsley
Salt and freshly ground black pepper to taste.

1. Guests spear the meat cubes on long forks and cook cubes to the desired degree of doneness in the hot oil right at the table. They are transferred to regular forks and dipped in one or more of the sauces.
2. To prepare herb sauce, beat the egg yolks until frothy; then beat in the lemon juice, salt and pepper. Beat in the oil, one teaspoon at a time, until one-half cup has been added. Add rest of oil, beating until mixture is thick like mayonnaise. Stir in the chives, parsley and onion. Chill.
3. To prepare curry sauce, combine all the ingredients and chill.
4. To prepare tomato sauce, beat all the ingredients together.
Yield: Six servings.

Venison Meat Balls   *Colorado*

3 slices soft white bread
¼ cup water
⅓ cup butter
⅔ cup chopped onion
1½ pounds ground venison
Salt and freshly ground black pepper
1 tablespoon chopped parsley
1 tablespoon flour
¾ cup milk.

1. Soak the bread in the water five minutes; then squeeze excess water out. Melt two tablespoons of the butter in a skillet and sauté the onion in it until tender.
2. Combine the squeezed bread, onion, venison, two teaspoons salt, one-quarter teaspoon

pepper and the parsley. Form mixture into one-inch balls. Chill twenty minutes.

3. Heat remaining butter in the skillet and brown the balls in it on all sides. Cover pan and cook slowly fifteen minutes. Remove balls to a warm platter.

4. Sprinkle the flour over skillet drippings. Stir and cook one minute. Stir in the milk and bring to a boil. Season to taste with salt and pepper and return the balls to the skillet. Simmer four minutes.

Yield: Four servings.

Oven Method Jerky (Dried Venison)

Montana

3 pounds venison, fat removed, cut into
    one-quarter-inch slices
½ teaspoon liquid smoke (see note)
2 tablespoons water
    Salt and freshly ground black pepper to
    taste.

1. Day before, brush the venison slices with the liquid smoke mixed with the water. Sprinkle slices generously with salt and pepper.

2. Place venison in a large bowl, weight down and let stand in a cool place overnight. Next day, remove meat and pat dry.

3. Preheat the oven to 150 degrees.

4. Arrange the meat strips close together on the oven racks, leaving room for air to circulate around the outside edges.

5. Let dry twelve hours, catching drips on aluminum foil if necessary. Cool and store in a tight tin.

Yield: Six servings.

Note: Liquid smoke is available in specialty food stores.

Venison Hash

Montana

2 tablespoons butter
⅓ cup finely chopped onion

¼ cup grated carrot
2 tablespoons finely chopped parsley
2 cups chopped cooked venison
2 cups diced cooked potatoes
½ teaspoon salt
¼ teaspoon freshly ground black pepper
⅛ teaspoon Worcestershire sauce
½ cup light cream.

1. Melt the butter in a large heavy skillet and sauté the onion in it until tender. Add the carrot and cook two minutes.

2. Add the remaining ingredients except the cream and cook five minutes. Pour the cream over all and cook mixture until thoroughly heated.

Yield: Four servings.

Elk Carbonnades à la Flamande

Wyoming

4 pounds elk, cut one-half-inch thick and
    into pieces one inch by two inches
½ cup flour
⅓ cup oil
2 pounds onions, thickly sliced
6 cloves garlic, crushed
3 tablespoons light brown sugar
¼ cup wine vinegar
½ cup chopped parsley
2 bay leaves
2 teaspoons thyme
1 tablespoon salt
¼ teaspoon freshly ground black pepper
2½ cups beef broth
3 cups beer.
Dumplings:
2 cups self-rising cake flour
¾ cup milk
2 tablespoons melted butter.

1. Preheat the oven to 325 degrees.

2. Dredge the elk meat in the flour and brown, a few pieces at a time, in the oil in a large heavy

skillet. Transfer browned meat to a large heavy casserole.

3. Brown the onions and garlic in the oil remaining in the skillet and add onions and garlic to the casserole. Add the brown sugar, two tablespoons of the vinegar, the parsley, bay leaves, thyme, salt and pepper to casserole.

4. Pour off all extra oil from the skillet and add the broth to the skillet. Heat, stirring, to remove all the browned-on bits. Pour with the beer into casserole. Cover and bake two hours, or until meat is tender. Add remaining vinegar.

5. Combine the dumpling ingredients and drop by teaspoonfuls onto the simmering stew. Cover and cook slowly fifteen minutes, or until dumplings are done.

Yield: One dozen servings.

Elk Steak and Kidney Pie   *Wyoming*

1½ pounds elk round steak, cut into one-inch cubes
½ pound lamb kidneys, cored and sliced
½ pound mushrooms
1 cup chopped onions
2 bay leaves
1 cup dry red wine
1 cup beef broth or game broth
  Salt and freshly ground black pepper to taste
2 tablespoons chopped parsley
1½ cups flour
½ teaspoon baking powder
½ cup butter
½ cup milk, approximately.

1. Preheat the oven to 325 degrees.
2. Combine the elk meat, kidneys, mushrooms, onions, bay leaves, wine, broth, salt and pepper and place in a shallow round casserole. Sprinkle with the parsley.
3. Sift the flour and baking powder into a bowl. Cut in the butter until mixture resembles coarse oatmeal.
4. Mix to a soft springy dough with the milk.

Roll out to fit the top of the casserole and place in position. Make a steam hole. Bake one and one-half to two hours, or until meat is tender.
Yield: Six servings.

Pickled Elk's Heart   *Wyoming*

1 elk's heart, well cleaned
2 teaspoons whole cloves
1 bay leaf
4 cups cider vinegar
1 tablespoon salt
1 onion, sliced
½ teaspoon dry mustard.

1. Place the elk heart in a deep saucepan and cover with water. Bring to a boil, cover and simmer until tender, about three hours.
2. Measure two cups of the cooking liquid and add remaining ingredients to it. Bring to a boil and cool.
3. Drain the heart and place in the cooled vinegar mixture so that heart is submerged. Soak ten days to two weeks in a cool place. Slice thinly.
Yield: One dozen servings.

Marinade for Game   *Wyoming*

1 small onion, chopped
2 carrots, diced
1 small rib celery, chopped
¼ cup oil
3½ cups dry red wine
¾ cup cider vinegar
½ teaspoon black peppercorns
1 whole clove
1 bay leaf
½ teaspoon thyme
½ teaspoon marjoram
1 teaspoon salt.

1. Sauté the onion, carrots and celery in the oil until tender but not browned. Add the remaining

ingredients, bring to a boil and simmer twenty minutes. Allow to cool completely before using.

2. To use marinade, place game in a bowl, pour cooled marinade over game and let stand in the refrigerator two to five days, turning meat two or three times a day. Drain meat and pat dry before roasting or broiling.

Yield: About four cups.

Pepper Sauce for Game   *Wyoming*

  2 cups game trimmings and bones
  3 tablespoons oil
  1 carrot, diced
  ½ small onion, diced
  2 tablespoons flour
2½ cups beef broth
  2 sprigs parsley
  ½ bay leaf
  ¼ teaspoon thyme
  ½ cup marinade for game (see preceding recipe)
  Salt to taste
  ½ teaspoon black peppercorns, roughly crushed.

1. In a skillet, brown the game trimmings and bones in the oil; remove and reserve.

2. Add the carrot and onion to the skillet and sauté them until lightly browned; remove and reserve. Sprinkle the flour into oil remaining in the skillet and cook, stirring, until lightly browned.

3. Stir in the broth and bring to a boil, stirring.

4. Tie the parsley, bay leaf and thyme in a muslin bag and add with the marinade and salt to sauce. Add reserved game trimmings and bones, carrot and onion. Simmer, uncovered, two hours. Remove excess fat and muslin bag. Stir the peppercorns into sauce.

Yield: About two cups.

Note: For a variation, add two tablespoons currant jelly to finished sauce. Stir to melt jelly and then add one-half cup heavy cream. Serve at once.

Currant Sauce   *Wyoming*

1 cup currant jelly
1 tablespoon lemon juice
1 teaspoon dry mustard
¼ teaspoon ground cloves
¼ teaspoon cinnamon.

Combine all ingredients in a small saucepan and heat, stirring, until jelly is melted. Serve sauce warm with game or roast lamb.

Yield: One cup.

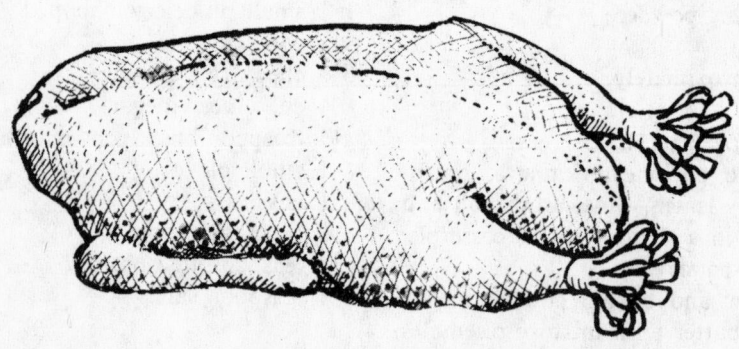

Vegetables, Main Dish Accompaniments and Salads

Corn Casserole   *Utah*

¼ cup butter
⅓ cup flour
1½ cups light cream
2 eggs, separated
1 teaspoon salt
1 teaspoon prepared mustard
Cayenne pepper to taste
2 cups corn kernels, cut from the cob
2 teaspoons Worcestershire sauce
1 tablespoon chopped parsley
1 cup buttered soft bread crumbs.

1. Preheat the oven to 350 degrees.
2. Melt the butter, stir in the flour and gradually blend in the cream. Bring to a boil, stirring.
3. Beat the egg yolks lightly and add with the salt, mustard, cayenne, corn, Worcestershire and parsley.
4. Beat the egg whites until stiff but not dry and fold into corn mixture. Turn into a greased casserole. Top with the bread crumbs and bake thirty minutes, or until lightly browned.
    Yield: Six servings.

Fried Celery   *South Dakota*

1 stalk celery
Boiling water
Salt

2 eggs, separated
½ cup light cream
1 cup flour
1 teaspoon baking powder
Fat or oil for deep-frying.

1. Break the celery into ribs and cut into three-inch to four-inch lengths. Place in a large skillet and add boiling water barely to cover. Add salt to taste. Cover and simmer only three to five minutes, or until celery is barely tender. Drain well and pat dry.
2. Combine the egg yolks and cream. Sift together the flour, one-quarter teaspoon salt and the baking powder and add egg yolk mixture to make a batter. Beat the egg whites until stiff but not dry and fold into batter.
3. Dip the celery pieces into the batter and fry, a few at a time, in the fat or oil heated to 365 degrees.
4. Drain on paper towels and serve at once.
    Yield: Eight servings.
    Note: Sticks of barely tender, cooked parsnip can be dipped into the batter and deep-fried in a similar fashion to give parsnip fritters.

Vegetable Casserole   *Nebraska*

1 eggplant, sliced
Salt
3 large onions, thinly sliced

1 clove garlic, finely chopped
½ cup butter
3 tablespoons olive oil
1 pound sharp Cheddar cheese, grated
½ pound mushrooms, sliced
3 small zucchini, sliced
  Freshly ground black pepper to taste
4 tomatoes, peeled and thickly sliced
1 teaspoon basil.

1. Preheat the oven to 350 degrees.
2. Sprinkle the eggplant slices with salt and set aside.
3. Sauté the onions and garlic in the butter and oil in a heavy skillet until tender. Drain off extra fat and transfer onions and garlic to a casserole.
4. Rinse off the eggplant slices, pat dry and brown quickly in the fat remaining in skillet. Transfer eggplant to casserole. Sprinkle with one-third of the cheese.
5. Sauté the mushrooms and zucchini in the skillet until barely tender and add to casserole. Sprinkle with one-half of the remaining cheese and add pepper.
6. Top casserole with the tomato slices, season with salt to taste, pepper and the basil and sprinkle with remaining cheese. Bake thirty-five to forty-five minutes.
Yield: Six servings.

Lima Bean Bake   *South Dakota*

2 cups cooked dried or fresh lima beans
¼ cup chopped sweet red pepper
¼ cup finely chopped onion
1 cup grated sharp Cheddar cheese
2 tablespoons catchup
3 tablespoons butter
2½ tablespoons flour
1¾ cups light cream or milk
  Salt and freshly ground black pepper to taste
⅛ teaspoon ground allspice
¼ cup buttered soft bread crumbs.

1. Preheat the oven to 350 degrees.
2. Combine the beans, red pepper, onion, cheese and catchup in a greased one-and-one-half-quart casserole.
3. Melt the butter, blend in the flour and gradually stir in the cream or milk. Bring to a boil, stirring. Season with salt, pepper and the allspice. Pour sauce into casserole. Stir to mix. Top with the bread crumbs and bake forty-five minutes.
Yield: Six servings.

Idaho Baked Beans

2 cups dried red beans (one pound)
  Salt
1 pound sausage meat
1 cup chopped onions
2 cloves garlic, finely chopped
2 cups peeled and cored tart apple slices
1 teaspoon chili powder
1 teaspoon dry mustard
¼ cup light brown sugar
  Freshly ground black pepper
1½ cups tomato or vegetable-tomato juice, approximately
2 cups sour cream.

1. Day before, pick over and wash the beans. Cover with water and let soak overnight. Next day, drain beans and place in a kettle with six cups water and two teaspoons salt.
2. Bring to a boil and simmer until tender, about one and one-half hours.
3. Meanwhile, cook the sausage meat in a skillet, breaking up meat with a spoon until all pinkness has disappeared and meat is lightly browned. Remove meat and reserve. Pour off all but three tablespoons of the fat.
4. Preheat the oven to 325 degrees.
5. Sauté the onions and garlic in the three tablespoons fat.
6. Place beans in a bean pot or casserole. Add sausage meat, onion mixture, the apple slices, chili powder, mustard, brown sugar and salt and pepper to taste and stir to mix. Add the tomato

or vegetable-tomato juice until it just covers beans.

7. Bake beans two to three hours, adding more juice as needed during cooking.

8. Serve a dollop of the sour cream on top of each serving.

Yield: One dozen servings.

Grandma's Squash Bake   *Idaho*

½ cup butter
1 large Hubbard or butternut squash or two large acorn squash
½ cup heavy cream, scalded
½ teaspoon salt
1 teaspoon freshly ground black pepper
1 teaspoon sugar
⅛ teaspoon nutmeg.

1. Preheat the oven to 375 degrees.

2. Melt three tablespoons of the butter. Cut the squash in half and remove the seeds. Cut squash in pieces if very large. Place in a roasting pan. Brush cut surfaces with the melted butter. Bake forty minutes, or until tender.

3. Scoop out the squash flesh and press through a colander. Beat pulp with the remaining ingredients and turn into a greased baking dish or casserole. Bake twenty minutes, or until top is browned.

Yield: Six servings.

Honey Fruited Beets   *Utah*

¼ cup butter, melted
¼ cup honey
¼ cup light brown sugar
1 orange, including the rind, very thinly sliced and seeded
3 cups cooked sliced or diced beets
Salt to taste.

1. Combine the butter, honey and brown sugar in a saucepan and heat.

2. Add the orange slices and beets to hot sauce. Simmer fifteen to twenty minutes. Season with salt.

Yield: Six servings.

Creamed Kohlrabi   *South Dakota*

2 bunches young kohlrabi, peeled and diced
   Boiling salted water
3 tablespoons butter
1 tablespoon finely chopped onion
2 tablespoons flour
1 cup light cream
   Salt and freshly ground black pepper to taste
⅛ teaspoon nutmeg.

1. Place the diced kohlrabi in a saucepan and add boiling salted water to cover. Cover and cook fifteen minutes, or until tender. Drain.

2. Meanwhile, melt the butter and sauté the onion in it until tender. Sprinkle with the flour. Gradually stir in the cream and bring to a boil, stirring. Season with salt, pepper and the nutmeg.

3. Stir in the kohlrabi.

Yield: Six servings.

Carrot Loaf   *Utah*

2 cups grated carrots
2 cups crumbled soda crackers
½ cup grated Cheddar cheese
1 large onion, finely grated
½ cup chopped nuts
½ teaspoon salt
⅛ teaspoon freshly ground black pepper
½ teaspoon sage
3 eggs, lightly beaten
1 cup light cream.

1. Preheat the oven to 350 degrees.

2. Combine the carrots, crackers, cheese, onion, nuts, salt, pepper and sage. Mix together the eggs and cream and stir into carrot mixture. Turn

into a greased loaf pan and bake one and one-half hours.

Yield: Four servings.

Fried Cabbage   *Idaho*

1 head cabbage, finely shredded
1 cup bacon drippings
1 cup boiling water
2 teaspoons sugar
½ hot red pepper pod
  Salt to taste
1 to two tablespoons vinegar, or to taste.

1. Place all the ingredients except the vinegar in a heavy skillet and cook, stirring occasionally, until cabbage is lightly browned and crisp-tender.

2. Just before serving, add the vinegar.

Yield: Six servings.

Baked Cabbage   *South Dakota*

1 medium-size head cabbage, shredded
  Boiling salted water
3 tablespoons butter
3 tablespoons flour
1½ cups light cream
  Salt and freshly ground black pepper to taste
1 teaspoon caraway seeds
⅛ teaspoon nutmeg
½ cup grated sharp Cheddar cheese
¾ cup buttered soft bread crumbs.

1. Preheat the oven to 350 degrees.

2. Cook the cabbage in boiling salted water barely to cover ten minutes, or until crisp-tender. Drain well and place in a large greased baking dish or oblong roasting pan.

3. Melt the butter and blend in the flour. Gradually stir in the cream and bring to a boil, stirring. Cook two minutes.

4. Add salt, pepper, the caraway seeds, nut-

meg and cheese. Stir to melt cheese. Pour sauce over the cabbage and top with the bread crumbs.

5. Bake fifteen to twenty minutes, or until lightly browned.

Yield: Eight servings.

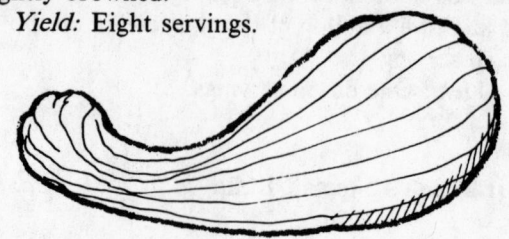

Cabbage and Potato   *South Dakota*

½ head cabbage, roughly shredded
  Salt
½ cup boiling water
5 medium-size potatoes, boiled in their jackets, peeled and riced
¼ cup butter, melted
  Freshly ground black pepper
⅓ cup heavy cream, scalded, approximately
½ pound bacon, diced and cooked until crisp
3 tablespoons flour
2 cups milk.

1. Place the cabbage, one teaspoon salt and the boiling water in a saucepan. Cover and cook ten minutes, or until cabbage is tender. Drain well.

2. Beat the hot riced potatoes with the butter, salt and pepper to taste and enough cream to give smooth consistency that still holds its shape. Stir in the cabbage.

3. Remove the bacon bits from skillet in which they cooked and reserve. Discard all but three tablespoons of the bacon drippings. Add the flour to the drippings and cook, stirring, until the mixture browns slightly.

4. Stir in the milk and bring to a boil, stirring. Season to taste with salt and pepper. Pile the cabbage-potato mixture in a serving dish. Make a depression in the middle and pour in the gravy.

5. Sprinkle the reserved bacon bits around the edge.

Yield: Six to eight servings.

Turnip, Mustard or Dandelion Greens

Utah

4 slices bacon, diced
2 tablespoons finely chopped onion
2 tablespoons flour
2 tablespoons water
¼ cup cider vinegar
2 tablespoons sugar
¼ teaspoon salt
⅛ teaspoon freshly ground black pepper
1 egg, lightly beaten
1 cup light cream or half and half
3 cups chopped cooked greens (turnip, mustard or dandelion).

1. Cook the bacon bits until crisp; remove and reserve.
2. In the bacon drippings, sauté the onion until golden. Sprinkle with the flour and cook two minutes. Stir in the water and vinegar.
3. Add the sugar, salt and pepper. Combine the egg with the cream or half and half and add. Heat, stirring, until thick. Do not boil.
4. Pour sauce over the greens, toss and sprinkle with reserved bacon bits.

Yield: Eight servings.

The pioneers used to cut the sturdy pokeweed and poke the oxen with the forked end to keep them moving, hence the name. The young leaves and shoots are cut in the spring. They must not be eaten raw, and the roots of the plant are poisonous.

Pokeweed or Pokeberry Greens

Wyoming

8 cups poke greens, washed
  Boiling salted water
  Salt and freshly ground black pepper to taste
3 tablespoons butter
1 tablespoon lemon juice.

1. Place the washed greens in a saucepan with the bottom of the pan covered with boiling salted water to a depth of one inch. Cover and boil until greens are tender like spinach.
2. Drain greens well, chop and toss with remaining ingredients.

Yield: Four servings.

Kohlrabi Cabbage

South Dakota

4 cups shredded young kohlrabi tops, ribs removed
1 small onion, thinly sliced
1 teaspoon salt
1½ tablespoons cider vinegar
½ teaspoon sugar
½ teaspoon caraway seeds
2 tablespoons bacon drippings
  Boiling water
2 tablespoons flour
¼ cup cold water.

1. Place the kohlrabi, onion, salt, vinegar, sugar, caraway seeds and bacon drippings in a heavy saucepan. Add boiling water to cover. Cover and boil fifteen minutes, or until kohlrabi is tender.
2. Combine the flour and cold water and stir into greens. This is traditionally served with pork.

Yield: Four servings.

Kale and Oatmeal

North Dakota

6 cups shredded kale leaves, ribs removed
  Boiling salted water
½ cup diced bacon
1 small onion, finely chopped
  Old-fashioned (dry) oatmeal
  Salt and freshly ground black pepper to taste.

1. Place kale leaves in a saucepan and cover

with boiling salted water. Bring to a boil and simmer five minutes.

2. Add the bacon and onion and continue cooking about one and one-half hours, or until leaves are very tender. Measure the kale and liquid and for each cup add one-quarter cup oatmeal. Cook slowly, stirring to prevent sticking, twenty-five minutes longer, or until oatmeal is cooked.

3. Season with salt and pepper.

Yield: Four servings.

Baked Mushrooms   *Wyoming*

½ pound wild or cultivated mushrooms, sliced
2 tablespoons lemon juice
1 tablespoon finely chopped onion
¼ cup butter
¼ teaspoon salt
⅛ teaspoon freshly ground black pepper
1 tablespoon flour
2 tablespoons freshly grated Parmesan cheese
1 cup heavy cream
2 egg yolks, lightly beaten
2 tablespoons fine soft bread crumbs.

1. Preheat the oven to 425 degrees.

2. Sprinkle the mushrooms with the lemon juice and place in a small saucepan with the onion and two tablespoons of the butter. Add the salt, pepper, flour and cheese and stir to mix. Cover and simmer three minutes. Turn into a shallow baking dish.

3. Mix together the cream and egg yolks and pour over mushroom mixture. Sprinkle with the bread crumbs and dot with remaining butter. Bake ten minutes, or until golden.

Yield: Four servings.

Deep-Dish Mushroom Pies   *Wyoming*

¼ cup chicken fat or butter
1 pound wild or cultivated mushrooms
1 large onion, finely chopped

¼ cup flour
¼ teaspoon salt
⅛ teaspoon freshly ground black pepper
1 cup light cream
1 cup chicken broth
2 tablespoons dry sherry
  Pie crust pastry made from one cup flour.

1. Preheat the oven to 400 degrees.

2. Melt the chicken fat or butter in a small skillet. Chop the tough stem ends of mushrooms and add with the onion to skillet. Cook until tender but not browned.

3. Add the mushrooms, sliced if large, and cook until just tender. Mushrooms should be wilted but not black.

4. Sprinkle with the flour, salt and pepper.

5. Gradually stir in the cream and broth and bring to a boil, stirring. Add the sherry and pour mixture into four greased individual ramekins.

6. While still hot, top each with rolled-out pastry, make a steam hole in each and bake fifteen minutes, or until pastry is golden and done.

Yield: Four to six servings.

Puffballs   *Wyoming*

½ pound young puffballs
2 tablespoons butter
1 teaspoon lemon juice
  Salt and freshly ground black pepper to taste.

Wash, peel and slice the puffballs. Sauté in the butter over medium heat until edges are brown. Season with the lemon juice, salt and pepper.

Yield: Three servings.

Wild Mushroom Fritters   *Wyoming*

½ pound wild boletus, shaggy manes or puffballs, cut into three-quarter-inch slices
1 tablespoon lemon juice
¼ teaspoon salt

⅛ teaspoon freshly ground black pepper
⅓ cup flour
2 eggs, lightly beaten
1 cup dry bread crumbs
  Oil for frying.

Sprinkle the mushroom slices with the lemon juice, salt and pepper. Dip each slice into the flour to coat, then dip into the eggs, and, finally, coat with the bread crumbs. Fry until golden in hot oil to cover in a large skillet. Drain.

Yield: Three servings.

Mushroom Stew   *Colorado*

½ onion, finely chopped
¼ cup butter
1 pound wild or cultivated mushrooms, sliced
½ teaspoon salt
¼ teaspoon freshly ground black pepper
½ cup milk
1 tablespoon flour
2 teaspoons freshly snipped dill weed
1 tablespoon chopped parsley
¾ cup buttermilk
  Bread dumplings (page 557).

1. Sauté the onion in the butter in a heavy skillet. Add the mushrooms, salt and pepper and sauté five minutes. Mix the milk with the flour and add with the dill and parsley. Simmer ten minutes.

2. Stir in the buttermilk and simmer five minutes longer. Serve over dumplings.

Yield: Four servings.

Stewed Tomatoes   *Nebraska*

8 ripe tomatoes, peeled and chopped
4 ribs celery, diced
1 small green pepper, diced
1 small onion, finely chopped
  Salt and freshly ground black pepper to taste

1 teaspoon basil
½ cup soft white bread cubes
3 tablespoons butter.

1. Place the tomatoes, celery, green pepper and onion in a saucepan. Bring to a boil and simmer ten minutes. Season with salt, pepper and the basil.

2. Just before serving, brown the bread cubes in the butter until golden and add to tomatoes.

Yield: Four servings.

Church Supper Scalloped Potatoes   *Idaho*

6 to eight potatoes, thinly sliced
¼ cup butter
1 small onion, finely chopped
2½ tablespoons flour
3½ cups light cream or half and half
1 teaspoon salt
½ teaspoon freshly ground black pepper.

1. Preheat the oven to 350 degrees.

2. Place the potatoes in a greased two-quart casserole.

3. Melt the butter and sauté the onion in it until tender. Stir in the flour and gradually blend in the cream or half-and-half. Bring to a boil, stirring. Season with the salt and pepper and pour over the potatoes. Bake one and one-half hours, or until potatoes are tender and top is lightly browned.

Yield: Six to eight servings.

Onion Gulch Potatoes   *Wyoming*

6 medium-size potatoes, shredded
4 medium-size onions, finely chopped or ground
¼ cup melted butter
¼ cup heavy cream
1½ teaspoons salt

¼ teaspoon freshly ground black pepper
¼ teaspoon nutmeg.

1. Preheat the oven to 250 degrees.
2. Combine all the ingredients in a buttered casserole and bake three to four hours, or until browned and cooked.
Yield: Six servings.

Cheese-Potato Bake   *Nebraska*

6 medium-size potatoes, sliced
1½ cups grated Gruyère cheese or Swiss cheese
1 teaspoon salt
¼ teaspoon freshly ground black pepper
3 tablespoons finely grated onion
1 cup heavy cream
1 teaspoon paprika.

1. Preheat the oven to 325 degrees.
2. In a greased 9-by-13-inch baking pan, place one-third of the potatoes. Sprinkle with one-third of the cheese, salt, pepper and onion.
3. Repeat with two more layers of potatoes, cheese and seasonings. Pour the cream over all. Sprinkle with the paprika and bake two hours, or until done.
Yield: Six servings.

Scalloped Carrots and Potatoes

Idaho

3 cups sliced potatoes
3 cups sliced carrots
¼ cup flour
¼ cup butter
2 teaspoons salt
¼ teaspoon freshly ground black pepper
¼ teaspoon nutmeg
2 cups light cream or milk.

1. Preheat the oven to 400 degrees.
2. Make a layer of half the potatoes in the bottom of a greased baking dish or casserole. Top with half the carrots.
3. Sprinkle with half the flour and dot with half the butter. Season with half the salt, pepper and nutmeg.
4. Make a layer of remaining carrots and another of remaining potatoes. Sprinkle with remaining flour, dot with remaining butter and season with remaining seasonings. Pour the cream or milk over all and bake about one hour, or until browned and tender.
Yield: Six to eight servings.

Creamed Potatoes   *Idaho*

¼ cup butter
¼ cup finely chopped onion
2 tablespoons flour
½ teaspoon celery seeds
½ teaspoon salt
⅛ teaspoon freshly ground black pepper
2 cups light cream
2 cups diced cooked potatoes
3 tablespoons chopped parsley.

1. Melt the butter in a heavy skillet and sauté the onion in it until tender and golden. Stir in the flour, celery seeds, salt and pepper.
2. Gradually blend in the cream and bring to a boil, stirring. Add the potatoes and heat, but do not cook. Add the parsley.
Yield: Four servings.

Mining Camp Potatoes   *Colorado*

¼ pound bacon, diced
6 potatoes, thinly sliced
¼ cup finely grated onion
1½ teaspoons salt
¼ teaspoon freshly ground black pepper.

1. Cook the bacon until crisp. Add the potatoes, onion, salt and pepper. Add water so that it

comes about three-quarters the way up through the potatoes.

2. Cover and cook about twenty minutes, or until potatoes are done. Stir gently once to prevent sticking.

Yield: Six servings.

Tomato Bulghur or Cracked Wheat
Utah

¼ cup butter
2 cups bulghur or cracked wheat
4 cups tomato juice
1 tablespoon finely chopped onion
1½ teaspoons salt
1 teaspoon oregano
1 teaspoon basil
1 teaspoon chili powder
1 large green pepper, diced
1 cup grated longhorn or Cheddar cheese.

1. Melt the butter in a skillet and add the wheat. Stir over low heat until wheat is hot and slightly browned.

2. Add the remaining ingredients except the cheese. Bring to a boil, cover and simmer twenty minutes, or until done. Stir in the cheese and serve.

Yield: Six servings.

Green Rice
Nebraska

2 cups cooked rice
2 cups grated Cheddar cheese
1 cup chopped parsley
¾ cup melted butter
1 onion, finely chopped
Salt and freshly ground black pepper to taste
2 eggs, lightly beaten
2 cups milk.

1. Preheat the oven to 350 degrees.
2. Combine the rice, cheese and parsley. Heat

the butter in a skillet and sauté the onion in it until tender. Add to the rice mixture and toss.

3. Season mixture with salt and pepper. Combine the eggs and milk and pour over rice mixture. Bake forty-five minutes, or until set.

Yield: Eight servings.

Cabbage Slaw
South Dakota

4 pounds cabbage, shredded
2 green peppers, shredded
2 carrots, shredded
1 onion, shredded or grated
1½ cups sugar
1 cup cider vinegar
1 teaspoon celery seeds
1 teaspoon salt
¼ teaspoon freshly ground black pepper
1 envelope unflavored gelatin
¼ cup cold water
1 cup oil.

1. Combine all the vegetables and chill.
2. Heat the sugar and vinegar, stirring to dissolve sugar. Let cool. Add the celery seeds, salt and pepper.

3. Soak the gelatin in the water and then heat to dissolve gelatin. Add to vinegar mixture. Cool until mixture starts to thicken. Add the oil and mix with vegetables. Chill at least twenty-four hours. The slaw will keep several days.

Yield: Two dozen servings.

Dandelion Green Salad
South Dakota

½ pound bacon, diced
4 hard cooked eggs
½ cup cider vinegar
½ cup water
1 bunch scallions, including green part, chopped
4 cooked potatoes, diced
4 cups young, tender dandelion greens, cut into strips.

1. Cook the bacon until crisp. Remove bacon, crumble and reserve. Separate the egg yolks from the whites. Mash the yolks with the vinegar and water. Add with the scallions to the bacon drippings. Cook, stirring, until scallions are tender.

2. Cut the egg whites into strips. In a bowl, combine the strips with the potatoes and dandelion greens. Pour the hot dressing over all and toss. Sprinkle with reserved bacon. Serve at once.

Yield: Four servings.

Wilted Leaf Lettuce   *South Dakota*

4 slices bacon, diced
¼ cup cider vinegar
3 tablespoons water
1 tablespoon sugar
3 scallions, including green part, finely chopped
  Salt and freshly ground black pepper to taste
8 cups shredded leaf lettuce.

1. Cook the bacon until crisp. Add the vinegar, water, sugar and scallions. Cook until scallions are barely tender. Season with salt and pepper.

2. Add the greens and toss until wilted. Serve immediately.

Yield: Six servings.

Cole Slaw with Bulghur   *North Dakota*

½ cup bulghur or cracked wheat
1 cup water
1 teaspoon salt
2 tablespoons cider vinegar
½ cup mayonnaise
1½ tablespoons finely chopped onion
2 tablespoons sugar
¼ teaspoon freshly ground black pepper
1½ cups shredded cabbage
½ cup finely chopped celery
½ cup shredded carrot.

1. Place the bulghur, water and one-quarter teaspoon of the salt in a saucepan. Bring to a boil, stir, cover and simmer slowly fifteen minutes.

2. Blend the vinegar, mayonnaise, onion, sugar, remaining salt and the pepper.

3. Add dressing to chilled bulghur and mix well. This can be chilled overnight.

4. Add the vegetables to bulghur mixture and mix well. Cover and chill.

Yield: Six servings.

Sour Cream Hot Potato Salad   *Idaho*

¼ pound bacon, cooked until crisp
1 small onion, finely chopped
¼ cup cider vinegar
¾ teaspoon salt
⅛ teaspoon freshly ground black pepper
¼ cup sour cream
3 cups hot boiled, peeled and sliced new potatoes.

1. Remove the bacon from the skillet in which it cooked; crumble and reserve. Add the onion to the bacon drippings and cook until tender. Add the vinegar, salt, pepper and sour cream. Heat, stirring, but do not boil.

2. Add the hot potatoes and reserved bacon. Serve hot.

Yield: Four servings.

Pickle and Frank Hot Potato Salad
     Idaho

¼ pound bacon
3 tablespoons finely chopped onion
1 teaspoon flour
2 tablespoons sugar
1½ teaspoons salt
1 teaspoon dry mustard
⅓ cup cider vinegar
1 teaspoon freshly grated horseradish
¼ cup water
2 egg yolks, lightly beaten

6 potatoes, boiled in their jackets
½ cup chopped celery
¼ cup chopped green pepper
6 small pickles, dill or sweet
4 frankfurters, sautéed to heat through and
　　sliced.

1. Cook the bacon until crisp; remove, crumble and reserve.

2. Sauté the onion in the bacon drippings until tender.

3. Combine the flour and sugar and add to the onion mixture. Add one-half teaspoon of the salt, the mustard, vinegar, horseradish and water. Bring to a boil, stirring, and cook until thickened.

4. Add a little of the hot mixture to the egg yolks, mix and return to the skillet. Keep warm, but do not boil.

5. Peel and cube the hot potatoes, sprinkle with remaining salt and add the celery, green pepper, pickles and frankfurter slices. Pour hot dressing over all and garnish with reserved bacon. Serve at once.

Yield: Six servings.

Fourth of July Potato Salad　　*Idaho*

2½ quarts cooked diced potatoes
 1 large cucumber, peeled, seeded and diced
 1 small green pepper, diced
 2 cups diced hearts of celery with leaves
 ½ cup finely grated onion or chopped
　　scallions
 2 cups mayonnaise
 3 tablespoons lemon juice
 2 tablespoons prepared mustard
 2 teaspoons sugar
1½ tablespoons salt, or to taste
 ½ teaspoon freshly ground black pepper
 6 hard-cooked eggs, roughly chopped.

1. Combine the potatoes, cucumber, green pepper, celery and onion or scallions in a large bowl and chill well.

2. Combine the mayonnaise, lemon juice, mustard, sugar, salt and pepper.

3. Add the eggs to the potato mixture and pour the dressing over all. Toss to mix. Refrigerate until serving time.

Yield: Two dozen servings.

Creamed Potato Salad　　*South Dakota*

5 cups diced cooked potatoes
3 hard-cooked eggs, roughly chopped
¼ cup chopped scallions
　Salt and freshly ground black pepper
2 eggs, lightly beaten
1 teaspoon dry mustard
2 tablespoons sugar
3 tablespoons butter
½ cup vinegar
1 cup heavy cream, whipped.

1. Combine the potatoes, hard-cooked eggs and scallions. Season to taste with salt and pepper.

2. Place the lightly beaten eggs, mustard, sugar, one teaspoon salt, the butter and vinegar in the top of a double boiler and heat over hot water, stirring until the mixture thickens.

3. Cool and chill dressing mixture. Fold in the whipped cream and add to potato mixture. Toss to mix.

Yield: Six servings.

Dilled Potato Salad　　*North Dakota*

6 potatoes, boiled in their jackets
3 hard-cooked eggs, sliced
1 medium-size sweet red onion, thinly sliced
2 tablespoons freshly snipped dill weed
8 radishes, sliced
1½ cups peas, cooked and chilled
1 teaspoon salt
1 teaspoon celery seeds
¼ teaspoon freshly ground black pepper
1 tablespoon prepared mustard

2 cups mayonnaise
1 tablespoon sugar.

1. Peel the potatoes and cut into one-quarter-inch dice. Add the eggs, onion, dill, radishes, peas, salt, celery seeds and pepper.

2. Combine the mustard, mayonnaise and sugar and stir into the potato mixture. Chill twenty-four hours before serving.
Yield: Eight servings.

Red Bean Salad   *Idaho*

3 cups cooked, drained and chilled red or
    kidney beans
1½ cups diced hearts of celery
1 red onion, thinly sliced
½ cup diced pickle
½ cup diced Cheddar cheese
2 tablespoons vinegar
⅓ cup oil
1 teaspoon salt
¼ teaspoon freshly ground black pepper
⅛ teaspoon dry mustard
½ teaspoon sugar.

1. Day before, combine the beans, celery, onion, pickle and cheese.

2. Place the remaining ingredients in a jar and shake to mix. Pour over the bean mixture and chill overnight.
Yield: Eight servings.

Boiled Dressing   *South Dakota*

3 egg yolks, beaten
¼ teaspoon salt
½ cup cider vinegar
1 tablespoon butter
¼ cup sugar
1 tablespoon dry mustard.

Place the egg yolks in the top of a double boiler and add the remaining ingredients. Heat over hot

water, stirring constantly, until mixture thickens. Cool and chill.
Yield: About three-quarters cup.

Sour Cream Dressing   *South Dakota*

4 cups homemade mayonnaise, made with
    lemon juice
1 three-ounce package cream cheese, softened
1 small clove garlic, finely chopped
2 teaspoons chopped parsley
2 cups buttermilk
Salt and freshly ground black pepper to
taste.

Place the mayonnaise in a bowl and beat in the remaining ingredients. Use on salads and baked potatoes and as a dip for raw vegetables.
Yield: About one and one-half quarts.

Cream Dressing   *Idaho*

½ cup heavy cream, whipped
1 hard-cooked egg yolk, mashed
¼ teaspoon salt
⅛ teaspoon freshly ground black pepper
¼ teaspoon dry mustard
½ teaspoon sugar.

Place the whipped cream in a bowl and beat in the remaining ingredients. Use on salads or fish.
Yield: About one cup.

Breads

In the case of quick breads raised by baking soda or baking powder, the same rules should be applied as given for cake baking at high altitudes (page 524).

In breads raised by yeast, the amount of yeast called for should be halved for elevations above 5,500 feet. It may be necessary to add more liquid or less flour and to bake the breads longer.

Grandmother Rezac's Rye Bread
South Dakota

4 cups warm water
1 package active dry yeast
1 tablespoon salt
1 tablespoon caraway seeds
1 tablespoon unsulphured molasses
1 tablespoon bacon drippings
2 cups rye flour
8 cups regular flour, approximately
   Melted lard.

1. Place one-half cup of the water in a large bowl and dissolve the yeast in the water. Add the remaining water, the salt, caraway seeds, molasses, bacon drippings, rye flour and enough regular flour to make a dough.
2. Turn out onto a floured board and knead until smooth and satiny, at least twenty minutes.
3. Place dough in a clean greased bowl, cover and let rise in a warm place until doubled in bulk, about two hours.
4. Shape into four loaves and place on greased baking sheets. Cover and let rise until doubled in bulk, about one hour.
5. Preheat the oven to 425 degrees.
6. Brush the loaves with melted lard and bake twenty minutes. Lower the oven heat to 350 degrees and continue baking about thirty minutes longer, or until bread sounds hollow when tapped on the bottom.
7. Brush hot loaves with melted lard and cool on a rack.
Yield: Four loaves.

Jamestown Buffalo Bread
North Dakota

2 cups milk, scalded
⅓ cup peanut butter
1 tablespoon shortening
½ cup light brown sugar
1 teaspoon salt
3 tablespoons unsulphured molasses
2 to two and one-half cups whole wheat flour, sifted before measuring and chaff discarded
1 package active dry yeast
½ cup lukewarm water
1 teaspoon sugar
3 cups regular flour
1 cup peanuts, unroasted, roughly chopped, with or without the skins.

1. Place the milk in a large bowl and add the peanut butter, shortening, brown sugar, salt, molasses and two cups of the whole wheat flour. Stir and set aside to cool to lukewarm.

2. Dissolve the yeast in the water, add the sugar and set in a warm place ten minutes.

3. Add the yeast mixture and the regular flour to the cooled whole wheat mixture to make a soft dough. If too soft, add more whole wheat flour.

4. Turn out onto a lightly floured board and knead well. Knead in the peanuts. Place in a clean bowl, cover and let rise in a warm place until doubled in bulk, about two hours.

5. Punch dough down and shape into two round loaves. Set in two greased nine-inch layer pans, cover with greased wax paper and a towel and let rise until doubled in bulk, about one hour.

6. Preheat the oven to 350 degrees.

7. Bake loaves forty-five minutes, or until done. Cool on a rack.

Yield: Two loaves.

board and knead until smooth and satiny, about fifteen minutes.

4. Place in a clean greased bowl, cover and let rise in a warm place until doubled in bulk, about one and one-half hours.

5. Punch down the dough and shape.

For Parker House rolls, roll dough to one-half-inch thickness. Cut with biscuit cutter, dip in melted butter, fold in half and pinch. Place on a greased baking sheet.

For hamburger buns, pull off pieces the size of eggs and shape each with the hands into a round. Place on greased baking sheet.

For cloverleaf rolls, form dough into one-inch balls and place three in greased muffin tins.

6. Cover rolls and let rise in a warm place until doubled in bulk, about forty-five minutes.

7. Preheat the oven to 400 degrees.

8. Bake about twenty minutes, or until done. Cool on a rack.

Yield: About thirty Parker House rolls or cloverleaf rolls or two dozen hamburger rolls.

Whole Wheat Rolls   *Utah*

  2 packages active dry yeast
½ cup lukewarm water
⅓ cup melted butter
  1 cup milk, scalded and cooled to lukewarm
⅓ cup light brown sugar or one-half cup honey
  2 eggs, lightly beaten
  2 teaspoons salt
4½ to five cups whole wheat flour, sifted before measuring and chaff discarded
  1 tablespoon grated orange rind (optional).

1. Dissolve the yeast in the water and let stand five minutes.

2. Combine the butter, milk, brown sugar or honey, eggs and salt and stir into the yeast mixture.

3. Stir in enough flour to make a soft dough that leaves the sides of the bowl. Add rind if desired. Turn dough out onto a lightly floured

Ranch Bread   *North Dakota*

  1 cup water
⅓ cup plus one teaspoon sugar
  1 cup cooked ground beef
  1 cup raisins
1½ cups potato water
  3 tablespoons melted lard
  1 tablespoon unsulphured molasses
  2 packages active dry yeast
½ cup lukewarm water
  1 cup 100% bran cereal
  2 cups whole wheat flour
  4 cups regular flour, approximately
  3 teaspoons salt
½ cup coarsely cut walnuts.

1. Place the one cup water, one-third cup of the sugar, the cooked beef and raisins in a small saucepan and bring to a boil.

2. Remove from the heat, add the potato water, lard and molasses and cool to lukewarm.

3. Dissolve the yeast in the lukewarm water, add remaining sugar and set aside ten minutes. Add to cooled beef mixture.

4. Stir in the bran, whole wheat flour and two cups of the white flour. Let rise ten minutes.

5. Add the salt, walnuts and enough remaining regular flour to make a soft dough. Knead on a lightly floured board until smooth and satiny. Place in a clean greased bowl, cover and let rise in a warm place until doubled in bulk, about one and one-half hours. Punch dough down and let rise again about thirty minutes.

6. Divide dough into three loaves and place in three greased 9-by-5-by-3-inch loaf pans. Cover and let rise until doubled in bulk, about forty-five minutes.

7. Preheat the oven to 350 degrees.

8. Bake the loaves about forty minutes, or until done.

Yield: Three loaves.

Dakota Rolls   *North Dakota*

Rolls:
 1 package active dry yeast
 ¼ cup lukewarm water
 1 cup milk, scalded
 3 tablespoons shortening
 3 tablespoons granulated sugar
 1 teaspoon salt
 1 egg, well beaten
 3½ cups flour, approximately
 3 tablespoons melted butter
 ¼ cup light brown sugar.
Caramel topping:
 1 cup light brown sugar
 2 tablespoons light corn syrup
 1 tablespoon butter.

1. To prepare rolls, dissolve the yeast in the water.

2. Combine the milk, shortening, granulated sugar and salt and let cool to lukewarm. Add yeast mixture, the egg and enough flour to make a soft dough. Beat vigorously.

3. Cover bowl and let dough rise in a warm place until doubled in bulk, about two hours.

4. Turn out onto a cloth-covered board or lightly floured board and roll into a rectangle 8 by 16 inches and about one-quarter-inch thick.

5. Brush with the melted butter and sprinkle with the brown sugar. Starting from the long side, roll up like a jellyroll. Cut into one-inch slices.

6. To prepare topping, combine the brown sugar, syrup and butter in a saucepan and heat to melt. Pour into twenty-four greased muffin tins or two greased nine-inch square pans.

7. Put the roll slices, cut side down, in the muffin tins or in the square pans. Cover and let rise until doubled in bulk, about forty-five minutes.

8. Preheat the oven to 375 degrees.

9. Bake twenty-five minutes for the muffin tins and thirty-five to forty minutes for the square pans. Tip rolls upside down onto serving platter to cool.

Yield: Two dozen.

Easy 100 Per Cent Whole Wheat Bread
Utah

 4 cups warm (110 to 112 degrees) water
 2 packages active dry yeast
 1 tablespoon salt
 ¼ cup oil
 ⅔ cup honey
 8 cups whole wheat flour, approximately.

1. Place the water in a large mixing bowl. Stir in the yeast, salt, oil and honey until well blended.

2. Add the flour gradually, beating well, until a dough slightly more moist than regular bread dough is obtained. Let rest ten minutes.

3. Turn out onto a floured board and knead dough until smooth and satiny, about fifteen minutes. Place in a clean greased bowl, cover and let rise in a warm place until doubled in bulk, about one and one-half to two hours.

4. Punch dough down and shape into four loaves. Place in four greased loaf pans. Cover and

let rise until doubled in bulk, about forty-five minutes.

5. Preheat the oven to 450 degrees.

6. Put loaves in oven and reduce oven heat to 350 degrees. Bake forty-five to sixty minutes, or until done.

Yield: Four loaves.

Kause seed is one of the first plants to mature in the spring. The seeds are pungent and resemble dill seed.

Kause Seed Bread   *Idaho*

1 cup small curd cottage cheese
2 tablespoons sugar
2 tablespoons kause seed
1 teaspoon salt
1½ tablespoons finely chopped onion
¼ cup butter
2¼ cups flour
¼ teaspoon baking soda
1 egg
1 package active dry yeast
¼ cup lukewarm water
2 tablespoons melted butter
1 tablespoon coarse salt

1. Place the cottage cheese, sugar, kause seed, one teaspoon salt, onion and one-quarter cup butter in a saucepan and heat to lukewarm. Sift the flour with the baking soda. Stir with the egg into the cottage cheese mixture.

2. Soften the yeast in the water and add. Beat well.

3. Place in a clean bowl and let rise until doubled in bulk, about one hour. Punch dough down and put in a well-greased 9-by-13-inch baking pan.

4. Cover and let rise in a warm place until doubled in bulk, about forty-five minutes.

5. Preheat the oven to 375 degrees.

6. Bake loaf about thirty minutes, or until done. Brush with the melted butter and sprinkle with the coarse salt.

Yield: One dozen servings.

Mylah's Flat Bread   *Idaho*

1 cup whole wheat flour
1 cup yellow corn meal
3 cups regular flour
⅓ cup shortening
1 teaspoon salt
1 teaspoon sugar
2 cups water, approximately.

1. Preheat the oven to 375 degrees.

2. Place the whole wheat flour, corn meal and regular flour in a bowl. With two knives, a pastry blender or the finger tips, work in the shortening.

3. Add the salt and sugar and enough water to make a dough that can be formed into balls. Make balls the size of large duck eggs. Pat down and then roll on a lightly floured board until very thin. A pastry cloth helps. Turn dough frequently to prevent sticking.

4. Place dough on a lightly greased baking sheet. Bake five to seven minutes on the shelf in the middle of the oven; then transfer to shelf in upper half of the oven for five to seven minutes longer, or until done.

Yield: Four loaves.

Ethel's Flat Bread   *North Dakota*

2 cups buttermilk
¼ cup sugar
½ cup melted butter
1 teaspoon salt
¾ teaspoon baking soda
5 cups flour, approximately.

1. Preheat the oven to 425 degrees.

2. Combine the buttermilk, sugar, butter, salt and baking soda in a bowl and stir in enough flour to make a dough that can be rolled.

3. Divide the dough into eighteen to twenty-four pieces and roll out each until very thin on a floured board. (There is a special ridged rolling pin available from stores specializing in Scandinavian specialties that makes this easier.) Place on baking sheet and bake about fifteen minutes, or until lightly browned.

Yield: Eighteen to two dozen servings.

Salt-Rising Bread   *Idaho*

    2 medium-size potatoes, peeled and sliced
 3½ tablespoons white or yellow corn meal
 2½ tablespoons plus one-half cup sugar
    ½ teaspoon baking soda
    1 teaspoon baking powder
    ½ teaspoon plus one tablespoon salt
      Boiling water
    7 to eight cups flour
    2 cups lukewarm milk
    ½ cup melted butter.

1. Day before, place the potatoes, corn meal, two tablespoons of the sugar, the baking soda, baking powder and one-half teaspoon of the salt in a plastic or ceramic container.

2. Add boiling water to cover and stir. Set in a warm place overnight. The mixture will foam up. Do not continue if mixture is not working.

3. Next morning, pour off and reserve the liquid and discard the solid. Add one cup of the flour to liquid and beat to make a batter. Set in a warm place until batter rises.

4. Add the milk, butter, remaining salt, remaining sugar and enough remaining flour to make a soft dough. Knead fifteen minutes. Shape into two loaves.

5. Place in two greased 9-by-5-by-3-inch loaf pans. Let rise until doubled in bulk.

6. Preheat the oven to 350 degrees.

7. Bake loaves forty-five minutes, or until done. Cool on a rack.

Yield: Two loaves.

Orange Rye Bread   *Nebraska*

 1½ cups milk, scalded
    ⅓ cup lard
    1 cup cold water
    2 teaspoons salt
 2½ cups rye flour
    1 package active dry yeast
    ¼ cup lukewarm water
    1 cup sorghum or unsulphured molasses
    1 teaspoon caraway seeds
    3 oranges
    5 cups regular flour, approximately.

1. Pour the milk over the lard and stir until melted. Add the water and salt and let mixture stand until lukewarm.

2. Beat in the rye flour well. Soften the yeast in the lukewarm water. Beat the sorghum or molasses, caraway seeds and softened yeast into the rye flour mixture. Mix well. Cover and let rise in a warm place until doubled in bulk, about two hours.

3. Meanwhile, using a swivel-bladed potato peeler, peel the orange-colored part of the skin of the oranges into a small saucepan.

4. Barely cover with water and cook peel until soft, about ten minutes. Grind mixture.

5. To the rye flour mixture, add orange peel and liquid and enough regular flour to make a soft dough. Turn out onto a lightly floured board and knead until smooth and satiny.

6. Place in a clean greased bowl, cover and let rise until doubled in bulk, about two hours.

7. Form dough into three loaves and put in three greased 9-by-5-by-3-inch loaf pans. Cover and let rise until doubled in bulk, about thirty-five minutes.

8. Preheat the oven to 350 degrees.

9. Bake loaves one hour, or until they test done. Wrap in cloth while hot to prevent crust from hardening.

Yield: Three loaves.

Kuchen I

¾ cup lukewarm milk
¾ cup sugar
1 teaspoon salt
3 eggs
¼ cup soft shortening
1 package active dry yeast
½ cup warm water
3 to three and one-half cups plus two
   tablespoons flour
1 one-pound-fourteen-ounce can peeled
   apricots
1 one-pound-fourteen-ounce can freestone
   peaches, halves or slices
1 one-pound-nine-ounce jar cooked prunes
2 cups heavy cream, scalded
¾ cup ricotta or pot cheese
1 teaspoon cinnamon.

1. Combine the milk, one-quarter cup of the sugar, the salt, one of the eggs and the shortening in a bowl. Dissolve the yeast in the water and add to bowl. Beat in two and one-half cups of the flour. Beat until smooth.

2. Gradually add the remaining flour except the two tablespoons until dough is soft and still slightly sticky. Knead on a lightly floured board until dough is nonsticky and pliable, about three minutes.

3. Place dough in a greased bowl, grease the top of dough, cover with a cloth and let rise until doubled in bulk, about one and one-quarter hours.

4. Meanwhile, drain the fruit in separate strainers. Pit and halve the apricots; pit the prunes.

5. Beat the remaining eggs lightly. Combine the remaining sugar with the remaining flour. Gradually beat the flour-sugar mixture into the eggs. Using a wire whisk, whisk this mixture into the hot cream in a saucepan and continue heating, while stirring, until the mixture thickens. Set custard aside to cool.

6. When dough has doubled in bulk, divide into four equal portions. Roll each piece into an eight-inch to nine-inch round and fit into four lightly greased eight-inch or nine-inch layer pans or pie plates.

7. Cover and let rise until doubled in bulk, about thirty minutes.

8. Preheat the oven to 400 degrees.

9. Top each of the yeast rounds with one of the fruits or the cheese. Divide and spoon the cooled custard topping over all four. Sprinkle with cinnamon. Bake twenty to twenty-five minutes. Serve warm.

Yield: Four cakes, each serving two.

Kuchen II

1½ cups lukewarm milk
½ cup sugar
2 teaspoons salt
2 packages active dry yeast
½ cup warm water
2 eggs, lightly beaten
½ cup soft shortening
6 to seven cups flour
4 cups cooked, drained apple slices, cooked
   pitted prunes or cooked apricots.
Topping:
4 tablespoons flour
1 cup sugar
4 eggs, beaten
4 cups heavy cream, scalded
4 teaspoons cinnamon.

1. Combine the milk, sugar and salt in a large bowl. Soften the yeast in the water and add along with the eggs and shortening.

2. Stir in enough flour to make a soft dough. Knead on a lightly floured board until smooth and satiny. Place in a clean greased bowl and let rise in a warm place until doubled in bulk about two hours.

3. Punch dough down and let rise a second time.

4. Divide dough into eight balls. On a lightly floured board, roll each to fit a nine-inch layer pan or pie plate. Put each into a greased nine-inch

layer pan or greased nine-inch pie plate. Cover and let rise until doubled in bulk, about twenty-five minutes.

5. Preheat the oven to 400 degrees.

6. While dough is rising, prepare the topping. Combine the flour and sugar; beat in the eggs and then the cream. Return to the saucepan in which cream was scalded and heat, stirring, until thick. Cool.

7. Top dough rounds with the cooked fruit.

8. Spoon the topping over the fruit and sprinkle with the cinnamon. Bake twenty to twenty-five minutes, or until done.

Yield: Eight cakes, each serving two.

Whole Wheat Cinnamon Rolls   *Utah*

  2 packages active dry yeast
  ½ cup warm water
  1 cup granulated sugar
  2 eggs, well beaten
  ⅓ cup butter, melted
1½ cups milk, scalded and cooled to
    lukewarm
  2 teaspoons salt
  1 teaspoon cardamom
4½ cups unsifted but stirred whole wheat
    flour, approximately
  3 tablespoons soft butter
  2 teaspoons cinnamon
    Fat or oil for deep-frying (optional)
  1 cup confectioners' sugar
    Lemon juice.

1. Dissolve the yeast in the water. Stir in two tablespoons of the granulated sugar and set aside in a warm place ten minutes.

2. Add six tablespoons of the remaining granulated sugar, the eggs, melted butter, milk, salt and cardamom.

3. Stir in enough flour to make a soft dough that leaves the sides of the bowl. Knead the dough on a lightly floured board ten minutes. Place in a clean bowl, cover and let rise in a warm

place until doubled in bulk, about one and one-half hours.

4. Punch dough down and let rise again until doubled in bulk, about one hour.

5. Roll out the dough into a rectangle one-quarter-inch thick and about 9 by 18 inches. Spread with the soft butter. Combine the remaining granulated sugar with the cinnamon and sprinkle over dough. Roll up, starting from the long end.

6. Cut into one-inch slices, set on a greased baking sheet, cover and let rise until doubled in bulk, about forty-five minutes.

7. The cinnamon rolls can be either baked in a preheated 375-degree oven twenty-five to thirty minutes or fried until golden in deep fat or oil heated to 400 degrees and drained.

8. Mix the confectioners' sugar with lemon juice to give pouring consistency. Use to glaze baked or fried rolls while hot.

Yield: About eighteen.

Coffeecake   *Nebraska*

2 packages active dry yeast
1 teaspoon plus one-third cup granulated
  sugar
1 teaspoon plus five cups flour, approximately
½ cup warm water
1 teaspoon salt
⅓ cup shortening
2 eggs, lightly beaten
¾ cup milk
2 tablespoons orange juice
1 tablespoon grated orange rind.
Topping:
2 cups sour cream
3 cups light brown sugar
2 teaspoons cinnamon
⅔ cup fine dry bread crumbs.

1. Add the yeast, one teaspoon of the granulated sugar and one teaspoon of the flour to the water and mix well. Set aside in a warm place ten minutes.

2. Mix remaining granulated sugar, the salt and shortening together well. Stir in the eggs, two cups of the remaining flour, the milk, orange juice and orange rind.

3. Add yeast mixture and mix well.

4. Stir in enough remaining flour to make a soft dough. Turn out onto a lightly floured board and knead until smooth.

5. Place in a clean greased bowl, cover and let rise in a warm place until doubled in bulk, about one hour.

6. Punch dough down and let rise again.

7. Preheat the oven to 375 degrees.

8. Divide dough in two, cover and let rest five minutes.

9. Roll out each half to fit a 10-by-15-inch jellyroll pan. Place in two greased jellyroll pans. Cover and let rise ten to fifteen minutes. Check that dough is touching edges of pans at all points.

10. To make topping, spread one cup of the sour cream over each cake. Combine the brown sugar and cinnamon and sprinkle over. Sprinkle one-third cup of the bread crumbs over each cake. Bake twenty-five minutes, or until done. Serve hot.

Yield: Two dozen to three dozen servings.

Yeast Fruit Dumplings   *South Dakota*

 1 package active dry yeast
 ⅓ cup lukewarm water
 2 teaspoons plus three tablespoons sugar
 ½ cup milk, scalded and cooled to lukewarm
 2 tablespoons plus one-quarter cup melted butter
 1 teaspoon salt
 1 egg, lightly beaten
 2 cups flour, approximately
16 cooked, drained and pitted Italian plums
 ½ teaspoon cinnamon.

1. Soften the yeast in the water. Add two teaspoons of the sugar and set aside in a warm place ten to fifteen minutes.

2. Combine the milk with two tablespoons of the butter, the salt and egg. Add yeast mixture and the flour to make a dough.

3. Knead on a lightly floured board until smooth. Place in a clean greased bowl, cover and let rise until doubled in bulk, about one hour.

4. Divide dough into eight balls and roll out each into a rectangle. Place two plums in each rectangle. Gather dough around and pinch to seal. Set on a baking sheet and let rise until doubled in bulk, about thirty minutes.

5. Cook in a steamer over boiling water. Or drop into a large kettle of boiling water, cover and boil ten to fifteen minutes.

6. Remove dumplings to a warm platter and immediately cut them in half. Pour remaining melted butter over. Combine remaining sugar with the cinnamon and sprinkle over.

Yield: Eight servings.

Czech Christmas Bread   *South Dakota*

 2 packages active dry yeast
 ½ cup lukewarm water
 ½ cup sugar
 ½ cup shortening
 2 teaspoons salt
1½ cups milk, scalded
 2 large eggs, lightly beaten
 7 cups flour, approximately
 2 cups raisins
 1 cup blanched almonds, slivered
 ⅓ cup melted butter.

1. Soften the yeast in the water.

2. Put the sugar, shortening and salt in a bowl and pour the milk over. Stir to blend and let cool to lukewarm. Add the eggs, softened yeast and three and one-third cups of the flour. Beat very well.

3. Add enough remaining flour to make a soft dough. Turn out onto a floured board and knead dough until smooth and satiny. Place in a clean greased bowl, cover and let rise in a warm place until doubled in bulk, about two hours.

4. Meanwhile, rinse the raisins and pat dry.

5. Roll out the dough on a lightly floured board to an oblong about one-half-inch thick. Sprinkle with raisins and the almonds. Gather into a ball and knead gently to distribute fruit.

6. Let rest, covered, on board fifteen minutes.

7. Divide dough in half and then cut each half into three equal pieces. Roll the six pieces into fourteen-inch ropes. Braid three of the ropes together loosely, tucking under the ends. Set on a lightly greased baking sheet. Repeat with remaining ropes.

8. Brush with the melted butter, cover and let rise until doubled in bulk, about fifty minutes.

9. Preheat the oven to 375 degrees.

10. Bake loaves about twenty-five minutes, or until done.

Yield: Two loaves.

Julekage (Christmas Bread)   *North Dakota*

2 packages active dry yeast
⅓ cup lukewarm water
3 cups milk, scalded
¾ cup plus two tablespoons sugar
½ cup butter
8 cups flour, approximately
2 teaspoons salt
2 eggs, lightly beaten
½ cup currants
½ cup chopped citron
¾ cup raisins
½ cup candied cherries
½ teaspoon cardamom (optional)
1 egg white, lightly beaten
2 tablespoons melted butter
½ teaspoon cinnamon.

1. Dissolve the yeast in the water.

2. Pour the milk over three-quarters cup of the sugar and the butter and stir to melt butter. Let cool to lukewarm.

3. Add softened yeast, four cups of the flour and the salt. Beat well ten minutes. Add the eggs, one at a time, beating well.

4. Stir in the currants, citron, raisins, cherries, cardamom if desired and enough remaining flour to make a soft dough.

5. Turn out onto a lightly floured board and knead dough until smooth and satiny. Place in a clean greased bowl, cover and let rise in a warm place until doubled in bulk. Punch down and knead again.

6. Return to the bowl and let rise again.

7. Divide the dough into three pieces and shape into loaves. Place in three greased loaf pans, brush tops with the egg white, cover and let rise until doubled in bulk, about forty-five minutes.

8. Preheat the oven to 350 degrees.

9. Bake loaves about fifty minutes, or until done. Brush with the melted butter. Combine the remaining sugar with the cinnamon and sprinkle over.

Yield: Three loaves.

Sour Cream Doughnuts   *Montana*

3 eggs
1 cup granulated sugar
1 cup sour cream
4 cups flour
½ teaspoon salt
½ teaspoon baking soda
1½ teaspoons baking powder
½ teaspoon nutmeg
½ teaspoon cinnamon
Fat or oil for deep-frying
Confectioners' sugar.

1. Beat the eggs until thick. Gradually beat in the granulated sugar. Stir in the sour cream. Sift together the flour, salt, baking soda, baking powder, nutmeg and cinnamon and stir in to make a soft dough.

2. Roll out the dough to one-half-inch thickness on a lightly floured pastry cloth or board and cut with a doughnut cutter.

3. Fry until golden, a few at a time, in the fat or oil heated to 375 degrees, turning once. Drain

doughnuts on paper towels. While doughnuts are hot, coat with confectioners' sugar.

Yield: About three dozen.

Potato Doughnuts   *North Dakota*

1 cup hot mashed potatoes
1½ cups sugar
1 cup buttermilk
½ teaspoon salt
3 eggs, lightly beaten
1 teaspoon nutmeg
4½ to five cups flour
2 teaspoons baking soda
  Fat or oil for deep-frying.

1. Beat together the potatoes and sugar very well. Beat in the buttermilk, salt and eggs.

2. Sift the nutmeg, flour and baking soda together and stir into the potato mixture to give a soft dough.

3. Roll out on a floured board and cut with a doughnut cutter. Fry until golden, a few at a time, in the fat or oil heated to 360 degrees, turning once. Drain on paper towels. Serve hot.

Yield: About fifty-four.

Banana Bread   *South Dakota*

¾ cup butter
1½ cups sugar
2 eggs
1½ cups mashed ripe bananas
1 teaspoon vanilla
2 cups flour
1 teaspoon baking soda
1 teaspoon salt
½ cup buttermilk
½ cup chopped nuts.

1. Preheat the oven to 350 degrees.

2. Cream the butter and sugar together until very light and fluffy. Beat in the eggs, one at a time.

3. Beat in the bananas and vanilla.

4. Sift together the flour, baking soda and salt and add alternately with the buttermilk to the batter. Fold in the nuts. Turn the mixture into two well-greased 8½-by-4½-by-2½-inch loaf pans and bake one and one-half hours. Cool on a rack.

Yield: Two loaves.

Oat Scones   *North Dakota*

1 cup flour
1 cup rolled oats
½ teaspoon salt
1 teaspoon baking soda
1 tablespoon sugar
  Butter
¾ cup buttermilk, approximately
  Jelly.

1. Preheat the oven to 400 degrees.

2. Mix the dry ingredients together in a bowl. With the fingertips, rub in one tablespoon butter.

3. With a fork, mix in the buttermilk to make a fairly soft but manageable dough. Form into a round about one-half-inch thick on a greased baking sheet. Score into six triangles.

4. Bake fifteen minutes, or until browned and done. Serve warm, with butter and jelly.

Yield: Six servings.

Note: The scones can be cooked on a hot greased griddle on top of the stove, turning once.

Whole Wheat Biscuits   *Utah*

2 cups whole wheat flour, sifted before measuring and chaff discarded
3 teaspoons baking powder
1 teaspoon salt
⅓ cup oil
⅔ cup milk.

1. Preheat the oven to 475 degrees.

2. Sift together the flour, baking powder and salt.

3. Pour the oil and milk into a measuring cup, but do not stir. Pour liquid into flour mixture all at once and stir with a fork until mixture forms a ball of dough. Pat out the dough to one-half-inch thickness on a lightly floured board.

4. Cut dough with a biscuit cutter and place on a greased baking sheet. Bake ten to twelve minutes. Cool on a rack.

Yield: About one dozen.

Note: To make delicious luncheon biscuits, substitute tomato juice for the milk in the above recipe and add one-half teaspoon basil and one-half cup grated sharp Cheddar cheese to the flour mixture.

Sour Dough Pancakes   *Wyoming*

Starter:
½ cake or one-half package active dry yeast
 2 tablespoons sugar
½ cup flour
   Lukewarm water.
Pancake batter:
 2 cups flour (you may use part whole wheat, corn meal, 100% bran cereal and regular flour)
   Cold water
 1 egg

 2 tablespoons unsulphured molasses
½ teaspoon salt
½ teaspoon baking soda
   Lukewarm water.

1. For the starter, combine the yeast, sugar, flour and enough lukewarm water to make a thin batter. Cover loosely and let stand at room temperature four to five days, or until mixture smells like vinegar.

2. The starter should be kept lightly covered in a large china, pottery or stone jug or bowl in the refrigerator.

3. The night before serving pancakes, begin to prepare pancake batter. Add the flour mixture to the starter. Add enough cold water to make a batter the consistency of heavy cream for thick pancakes or of light cream for thin pancakes. Leave at room temperature.

4. In the morning, return about one cup of the starter batter to the starter's original bowl or jug.

5. Beat together the egg, molasses and salt and pour into the remaining batter. Mix well, but do not beat.

6. Heat the griddle and dissolve the baking soda in a small quantity of lukewarm water. When the griddle is hot, fold the dissolved baking soda into the batter. Batter will puff up and be the consistency of whipped cream. Cook immediately on a very hot griddle.

Yield: About eight large pancakes.

Pies, Cakes, Desserts and Cookies

Recipes in this book are designed for preparation at elevations below 2,000 feet. In areas above 2,000 feet, it is recommended that for each teaspoon of baking powder, baking soda or cream of tartar listed, the amount should be reduced by one-quarter teaspoon for each 1,000-foot rise in elevation.

Also, the amount of sugar called for should be reduced by one-half tablespoon for each cup listed for each 1,000-foot rise in elevation.

There is greater and faster evaporation at higher elevations and so, for each cup of liquid called for, add one or two extra tablespoons liquid for each 1,000-foot rise in elevation.

Baking temperatures at high altitudes should be raised about 25 degrees, and there may be need for longer cooking time.

Dona's Favorite Pie Crust   *South Dakota*

3 cups flour
1 cup plus one tablespoon lard
1 teaspoon salt
5 tablespoons water
1 tablespoon cider vinegar
1 egg white, lightly beaten.

1. Place the flour, lard and salt in a bowl. With two knives, a pastry blender or the finger tips, blend the fat into the flour until the mixture resembles coarse oatmeal.

2. Mix together the remaining ingredients and add. Stir to mix and form into a dough.

Yield: Enough for a two-crust nine-inch pie and one nine-inch pie shell or for three nine-inch pie shells.

Lard Pie Crust   *South Dakota*

2 cups flour
½ teaspoon salt
½ cup lard
2 tablespoons butter
6 tablespoons milk.

1. Place the flour, salt, lard and butter in a bowl. With the finger tips or a pastry blender, work the fat into the flour until the mixture resembles coarse oatmeal.

2. Add the milk and pat dough together rather than mix it. Roll out the dough on a lightly floured pastry cloth or board.

Yield: Enough for a two-crust nine-inch pie.

Lou's Pie Crust   *Wyoming*

3 cups flour
½ teaspoon salt
2 teaspoons sugar
⅛ teaspoon baking soda
1 cup lard

1 egg
2 tablespoons lemon juice
2 tablespoons cold water.

1. Sift the flour, salt, sugar and baking soda into a bowl. Add the lard and cut in with two knives or a pastry blender until mixture forms into pieces the size of peas.

2. In a small bowl, combine the egg, lemon juice and water. Using a fork, add the egg mixture to flour mixture while stirring to give a dough.

3. Work the dough as little as possible and roll out on a floured pastry cloth or board.

Yield: Enough for a two-crust nine-inch pie and one nine-inch pie shell or for three nine-inch pie shells.

Peggy's Green Tomato Pie   *Idaho*

6 to eight medium-size green tomatoes, peeled and sliced
2 tablespoons lemon juice
2 teaspoons grated lemon rind
½ teaspoon salt
½ teaspoon cinnamon
2½ tablespoons cornstarch
¾ cup sugar
1 tablespoon butter
Pastry for a two-crust nine-inch pie.

1. Place the tomato slices in a skillet. Add the lemon juice, lemon rind, salt and cinnamon. Bring to a simmer and cook, uncovered, about fifteen minutes, or until tomatoes are barely tender. Stir frequently.

2. Combine the cornstarch and sugar and stir into the hot mixture. Cook, stirring, until it thickens. Add the butter. Cool mixture to room temperature.

3. Preheat the oven to 425 degrees.

4. Line a nine-inch pie plate with the pastry and turn the cooled tomato mixture into it. Top with remaining pastry. Seal and decorate edges and make a steam hole. Bake about thirty-five minutes, or until pastry is cooked. Serve warm or cool.

Yield: Six servings.

Cherry-Apple Pie   *Utah*

Pastry for a two-crust nine-inch pie
1 egg white, lightly beaten
4 large apples, peeled and sliced
2½ cups pitted sour cherries, fresh or drained canned
1 cup sugar
3 tablespoons flour
1½ teaspoons cinnamon
½ teaspoon nutmeg
3 tablespoons butter.

1. Preheat the oven to 425 degrees.

2. Line a nine-inch pie plate with pastry. Brush with the egg white. Mix the apples and cherries in a bowl. Combine the sugar, flour, cinnamon and nutmeg and fold into the fruit. Turn into pastry-lined pie plate.

3. Dot with the butter and top with remaining pastry. Seal and decorate edges and make a steam hole. Bake thirty to forty minutes, or until pastry is done. Cool to room temperature.

Yield: Six servings.

Apple Strudel   *North Dakota*

Strudel:
2 cups flour
3 teaspoons baking powder
⅔ cup plus two tablespoons granulated sugar
½ teaspoon salt
¼ cup shortening
⅔ cup milk
¼ cup melted butter
3 cups chopped peeled apples
1 teaspoon cinnamon.
Frosting:
2 cups confectioners' sugar
1 teaspoon cinnamon

1 tablespoon butter
3 tablespoons heavy cream
¼ cup chopped nuts.

1. Preheat the oven to 325 degrees.

2. To prepare strudel, sift together the flour, baking powder, two tablespoons granulated sugar and the salt. With the fingertips or a pastry blender, blend in the shortening. Stir in the milk to make a soft dough.

3. Turn dough out onto a lightly floured board and knead twenty-five to thirty times. Roll out to one-quarter-inch thickness. Brush with the melted butter.

4. Cover with the apples and sprinkle with the remaining granulated sugar and the cinnamon. Starting at the long end, roll like a jellyroll.

5. Transfer to a greased baking sheet. Curve strudel into a crescent.

6. Bake about thirty minutes, or until done.

7. To prepare frosting, combine the confectioners' sugar with the cinnamon, butter and cream.

8. Frost the strudel while warm. Sprinkle with the nuts.

Yield: Six to eight servings.

Pecan Tarts *North Dakota*

1 three-ounce package cream cheese
¼ cup plus one tablespoon butter
1 cup flour
⅛ teaspoon salt
1 egg, lightly beaten
1 teaspoon vanilla
¾ cup light brown sugar
1 cup chopped pecans.

1. Place the cream cheese, one-quarter cup of the butter and the flour in a bowl. With the finger tips or a pastry blender, work as though making pastry. Gather dough into a ball, wrap in wax paper and chill at least one hour.

2. Preheat the oven to 325 degrees.

3. Combine the remaining ingredients.

4. Roll out the chilled dough on a lightly floured pastry cloth or board and cut into rounds to fit two-inch muffin tins. Line the tins with the pastry.

5. Three-quarters fill the lined tins with the pecan mixture. Bake twenty-five minutes, or until done. Cool on a rack.

Yield: One dozen to eighteen, depending on size.

Peg's Lemon Pie-Cake *Colorado*

1½ teaspoons grated lemon rind
¼ cup lemon juice
2 tablespoons butter, melted and cooled
2 tablespoons flour
1 cup sugar
2 eggs, separated
1 cup milk
1 unbaked nine-inch pie shell, chilled.

1. Preheat the oven to 375 degrees.

2. Combine the lemon rind, lemon juice and butter in a small bowl. Mix the flour with the sugar and beat into the lemon mixture.

3. Beat the egg yolks lightly and combine with the milk. Using a wire whisk, whisk the lemon mixture. Beat the egg whites until stiff but not dry and fold into the mixture.

4. Pour the mixture into pie shell and bake ten minutes. Reduce the oven heat to 350 degrees and bake twenty-five minutes longer, or until filling is lightly browned and set.

Yield: Six servings.

Raisin Sour Cream Pie *Idaho*

1 cup sugar
2 tablespoons cornstarch
¼ teaspoon salt
1 teaspoon cinnamon
½ teaspoon nutmeg
¼ teaspoon ground cloves
3 eggs, separated

1 cup sour cream
1 cup raisins
1 baked nine-inch pie shell, cooled.

1. Combine three-quarters cup of the sugar and the cornstarch in a small saucepan. Add the salt, cinnamon, nutmeg and cloves.

2. Stir in the egg yolks, sour cream and raisins. Heat gently, stirring constantly, until mixture thickens. Do not allow to boil. Cool mixture.

3. Preheat the oven to 350 degrees.

4. Pour cooled filling into pie shell. Beat the egg whites until they just hold their shape. Gradually beat in the remaining sugar and continue beating until mixture is glossy and stiff.

5. Spread meringue over the pie and bake ten minutes, or until meringue is lightly browned. Cool.

Yield: Eight servings.

Juneberry Pie   *North Dakota*

Pastry for a two-crust nine-inch pie
2 cups Juneberries or chokecherries (see note)
¾ cup sugar
2 tablespoons flour
½ teaspoon salt
2 tablespoons lemon juice.

1. Preheat the oven to 425 degrees.

2. Roll out just over half the pastry on a lightly floured board. Line a nine-inch pie plate with the pastry.

3. Combine the remaining ingredients and toss to mix. Turn into the pastry-lined pie plate. Roll out remaining pastry and cover pie. Seal and decorate edges and make a steam hole. Bake pie about fifty minutes.

Yield: Six servings.

Note: Juneberries or chokecherries grow wild in many Western states and are ripe for picking in June.

Blitz Torte   *North Dakota*

Torte layers:
½ cup butter
½ cup confectioners' sugar
4 eggs, separated
1½ teaspoons vanilla
1 cup flour
1 teaspoon baking powder
3 tablespoons milk
¼ teaspoon cream of tartar
1 cup granulated sugar
1 teaspoon cider vinegar
1 three-ounce package blanched slivered almonds.
Sour cream filling:
1 cup granulated sugar
3 tablespoons flour
4 egg yolks
1 cup sour cream
Salt to taste.

1. Preheat the oven to 325 degrees.

2. To prepare torte layers, cream together the butter and confectioners' sugar. Beat in the egg yolks and one-half teaspoon of the vanilla. Sift together the flour and baking powder and fold alternately with the milk into the mixture.

3. Pour the batter into two greased nine-inch layer cake pans.

4. Make a meringue by beating the egg whites with the cream of tartar until stiff. Gradually add the granulated sugar, vinegar and remaining vanilla. Spread over the batter in the pans. Sprinkle one layer with the almonds. Bake the layers twenty-five to thirty-five minutes. Let cool and remove the layers from the pans.

5. To prepare filling, combine the filling ingredients and cook, but do not boil, in a double boiler until thick, stirring constantly. It takes twenty to thirty minutes to cook the flour completely without boiling the mixture.

6. Cool; then chill the filling. Spread on the plain torte layer and top with the almond-topped layer.

Yield: Ten to one dozen servings.

Raw Apple Cake   *South Dakota*

1 cup sugar
½ cup butter
1 egg
1½ cups flour
½ teaspoon cinnamon
¼ teaspoon ground cloves
¼ teaspoon nutmeg
1 teaspoon baking soda
½ cup cold black coffee
½ cup chopped raisins
½ cup grated or very finely chopped peeled and cored apple
½ cup chopped nuts.

1. Preheat the oven to 375 degrees.
2. Cream the sugar and butter together very well. Beat in the egg. Sift together the flour, spices and baking soda. Combine the coffee, raisins, apple and nuts. Stir dry ingredients alternately with apple mixture into the batter.
3. Place in a greased 8½-by-4½-by-2½-inch loaf pan and bake forty-five minutes, or until done.
   Yield: One loaf; eight servings.

Apple Cake   *North Dakota*

Cake:
½ cup butter
2 cups sugar
2 eggs
6 medium-size apples, peeled, cored and put through the fine setting of a food chopper
2 cups flour
2 teaspoons baking soda
½ teaspoon salt
1 teaspoon cinnamon
1 teaspoon nutmeg
½ cup chopped nuts.
Sauce:
½ cup butter
1 cup sugar
1 cup heavy cream

⅛ teaspoon salt
Sweetened whipped cream.

1. Preheat the oven to 350 degrees.
2. To prepare cake, cream the butter and sugar together until very light and fluffy.
3. Beat in the eggs, one at a time, very well. Stir in the apples.
4. Sift together the flour, baking soda, salt, cinnamon and nutmeg. Stir the flour mixture and the nuts into apple mixture. Turn into a well-greased nine-inch square pan. Bake forty-five minutes, or until done.
5. Meanwhile, to prepare sauce, brown the butter slightly in a small saucepan. Stir in the sugar, heavy cream and salt. Simmer until mixture is butterscotch-colored.
6. Serve sauce warm over the cake and top with whipped cream.
   Yield: Nine servings.

Apple Pie Cake   *North Dakota*

½ cup shortening
1 cup sugar
1 egg
1 teaspoon baking soda
2 tablespoons hot water
1 cup flour
½ teaspoon cinnamon
¼ teaspoon nutmeg
¼ teaspoon salt
½ cup chopped walnuts
2½ cups peeled, cored and diced apples
   Whipped cream.

1. Preheat the oven to 350 degrees.
2. Cream the shortening and sugar together until light and fluffy. Beat in the egg.
3. Dissolve the baking soda in the water. Sift together the flour, cinnamon, nutmeg and salt and stir with the dissolved baking soda into the batter.
4. Fold in the walnuts and apples. Turn into a

greased nine-inch pie plate. Bake forty-five minutes. Serve with whipped cream.

Yield: Six servings.

Prune Cake   *South Dakota*

Cake layers:
 1 cup granulated sugar
10 tablespoons butter
 3 eggs
 3 tablespoons sour cream
 2 cups flour
½ teaspoon nutmeg
 1 teaspoon cinnamon
 1 teaspoon baking soda
 2 cups cooked, drained, pitted and quartered prunes.
Filling:
 1 cup sour cream
 1 cup granulated sugar
 5 egg yolks
½ cup chopped walnuts.
Icing:
¾ cup light brown sugar
¼ cup butter
 6 tablespoons heavy cream
1½ cups confectioners' sugar.

1. Preheat the oven to 350 degrees.

2. To prepare cake layers, cream the granulated sugar and butter together until very light and fluffy. Beat in the eggs, one at a time, very well. Stir in the sour cream.

3. Sift together the flour, nutmeg, cinnamon and baking soda and fold into the batter. Fold in the prunes and turn into two greased and floured nine-inch layer pans. Bake about thirty-five minutes, or until done. Cool in the pans ten minutes before turning onto a rack to finish cooling.

4. To prepare filling, place the sour cream, granulated sugar and egg yolks in the top of a double boiler and heat, but do not boil, over hot water, stirring occasionally, until mixture thickens. Do this slowly. It takes about twenty-five minutes. When thickened, stir in the walnuts. Cool and chill.

5. To prepare icing, place the brown sugar, butter and cream in a small saucepan and bring to a rolling boil. Remove from the heat and stir in the confectioners' sugar.

6. Spread the filling between the layers and frost with the icing.

Yield: Ten servings.

Sandbakkelse   *North Dakota*

 1 cup butter
 1 cup sugar
 1 egg
 2 cups flour
½ cup very finely chopped blanched almonds
¼ teaspoon almond extract.

1. Preheat the oven to 350 degrees.

2. Cream the butter and sugar together until very light and fluffy. Beat in the egg.

3. Stir in the flour and almonds. Add the almond extract and mix.

4. Press the mixture into well-greased and floured sandbakkelse pans (see note), cutting off evenly with the top edge. Bake thirty-five to forty minutes, or until done. Leave upside down in the tins until cooled slightly. Squeeze tins to release cakes. Finish cooling on a rack.

Yield: About eighteen.

Note: Sandbakkelse pans are available in most fancy-housewares departments or by mail from Maid of Scandinavia, 3245 Raleigh Avenue, Minneapolis, Minnesota 55416.

Fruit and Nut Loaf   *Idaho*

 4 eggs, separated
 1 cup sugar
 1 cup flour
 1 teaspoon ground cloves
½ teaspoon nutmeg
 1 teaspoon baking powder

½ teaspoon salt
¼ cup cognac
½ teaspoon vanilla
2 cups pecans, left whole
2 cups Brazil nuts, left whole
2 cups dates, left whole
1½ cups candied cherries, left whole
1 cup walnuts, left whole.

1. Preheat the oven to 300 degrees.

2. Beat the egg yolks and sugar together until thick and very pale. Sift together three-quarters cup of the flour, the cloves, nutmeg, baking powder and salt.

3. Fold the dry ingredients alternately with the cognac and vanilla into the egg yolk mixture.

4. Combine the pecans, Brazil nuts, dates, cherries and walnuts. Add remaining flour and toss to coat.

5. Stir the coated fruits and nuts into the batter. Beat the egg whites until stiff but not dry and work with the hands into the fruit mixture.

6. Turn into two well-greased and floured 9-by-5-by-3-inch loaf pans. Bake about one and one-quarter hours, or until the cake tops are lightly browned and cakes are done. Cool in the pans fifteen to twenty minutes before turning out onto a rack to finish cooling.

Yield: Two loaves; twenty servings.

Rhubarb Cake   *South Dakota*

1½ cups light brown sugar
½ cup soft shortening
½ teaspoon salt
1 teaspoon baking soda
1 teaspoon vanilla
1½ cups cut-up raw rhubarb
1 cup buttermilk
1 egg, lightly beaten
2 cups flour
⅓ cup granulated sugar
1 teaspoon cinnamon.

1. Preheat the oven to 350 degrees.

2. In a bowl, combine the brown sugar, shortening, salt, baking soda, vanilla and rhubarb.

3. Combine the buttermilk and egg and add alternately with the flour to the rhubarb mixture.

4. Turn into a well-greased 9-by-13-inch baking pan. Combine the granulated sugar and cinnamon and sprinkle over the surface of the batter. Bake thirty to thirty-five minutes, or until done. Cool in the pan.

Yield: Eighteen to two dozen pieces.

Old-Fashioned Christmas Pork Cake
South Dakota

1¼ pounds fresh pork fat with no lean, finely ground
2 cups boiling water
1 pound raisins
1 pound currants
2 eggs
3 cups sugar
1 cup unsulphured molasses
1 teaspoon baking soda
6 cups flour
1 tablespoon salt
1 teaspoon cinnamon
1 teaspoon ground cloves
1 cup chopped walnuts
⅓ cup dark rum or cognac.

1. Day before, place the ground fat in a bowl and pour the boiling water over fat. Cover and let stand overnight. Next day, rinse the raisins and currants and let stand.

2. Preheat the oven to 300 degrees.

3. Beat the eggs until thick. Gradually beat in the sugar and continue to beat until mixture is thick. Combine the molasses and baking soda and stir into egg mixture.

4. Stir in the fat-water mixture. Sift together the flour, salt, cinnamon and cloves and fold in. Stir in the raisins, currants and walnuts.

5. Divide the mixture among four well-greased and floured 8½-by-4½-by-2½-inch loaf pans.

Bake about one hour, or until done. Brush with rum or cognac while warm. Cool in the pans.

Yield: Four loaves; two dozen servings.

Connie's Dutch Apple Cake   *Nebraska*

2 cups flour
2 teaspoons baking powder
½ teaspoon salt
¼ cup butter
1 egg, lightly beaten
¾ cup milk
5 medium-size apples, peeled, cored and cut into eighths
¼ cup currants
¼ cup sugar
1 teaspoon cinnamon.

1. Preheat the oven to 350 degrees.
2. Sift together the flour, baking powder and salt into a bowl. With two knives, a pastry blender or the finger tips, work the butter into the flour as though making pastry.
3. Combine the egg and milk and stir into the flour mixture. Turn into a greased 9-by-13-inch baking dish. Press the thin edges of the apple pieces into the dough in rows.
4. Combine the remaining ingredients and sprinkle over the apples. Bake thirty to forty minutes, or until done.

Yield: Eight to ten servings.

Note: Serve with butter as a hot bread or with lemon sauce as a pudding.

Scripture Cake   *Montana*

1½ cups butter	Psalms 55:21
2 cups sugar	Jeremiah 6:20
6 eggs	Isaiah 10:14
4½ cups flour	I Kings 4:22
⅛ teaspoon salt	Luke 14:34
2 teaspoons baking powder	I Corinthians 5:6
½ teaspoon nutmeg	

2 teaspoons ground allspice	
	II Chronicles 9:9
4 teaspoons cinnamon	
2 teaspoons ground cloves	
½ cup milk	Judges 4:19
2 tablespoons honey	Judges 14:18
2 cups raisins	II Samuel 16:1
2 cups figs, chopped	Song of Solomon 2:13
2 cups blanched almonds, slivered.	Numbers 17:8

1. Preheat the oven to 325 degrees.
2. Cream together the butter and sugar until very light and fluffy. Beat in the eggs, one at a time, very well.
3. Sift together the flour, salt, baking powder, nutmeg, allspice, cinnamon and cloves and add alternately with the milk to the batter.
4. Stir in the honey.
5. Fold in the raisins, figs and almonds. Mix well.
6. Turn into two greased 9-by-5-by-3-inch loaf pans. Bake about sixty minutes, or until loaves test done. Let cool thirty minutes in the pans before turning out onto a rack to finish cooling.

Yield: Two loaves; sixteen servings.

O-Apple Cake   *South Dakota*

1 cup sugar
½ cup butter
1 egg
1¾ cups flour
1 teaspoon cinnamon
1 teaspoon baking soda
⅛ teaspoon salt
½ cup cold black coffee
1 cup diced peeled and cored apple.

1. Preheat the oven to 350 degrees.
2. Cream the sugar and butter together until very light and fluffy. Beat in the egg.
3. Sift together the flour, cinnamon, baking

soda and salt and add alternately with the coffee to the batter. Fold in the apple and turn into a greased nine-inch square baking dish. Bake forty minutes, or until cake tests done. Cool slightly in the pan and serve warm.

Yield: Nine servings.

Quick Coffeecake   *Wyoming*

  1 cup chopped dates
  1 cup buttermilk
  2 cups light brown sugar
2⅓ cups flour
  ½ cup butter
  1 teaspoon baking soda
  1 teaspoon cinnamon
  ½ teaspoon salt
  1 egg, lightly beaten
  ¼ cup chopped nuts.

1. Preheat the oven to 325 degrees.
2. Combine the dates and buttermilk and set aside.
3. Place the brown sugar and two cups of the flour in a bowl and, with two knives, cut in the butter to make a crumbly mixture. Remove three-quarters cup of the mixture and reserve.
4. Sift together the remaining flour, the baking soda, cinnamon and salt and add to the brown sugar mixture in bowl.
5. Add the egg to buttermilk and dates and stir into the dry ingredients until just moistened. Pour into a well-greased and floured 9-by-13-inch baking pan. Combine the reserved brown sugar mixture with the nuts and sprinkle over batter.
6. Bake forty-five minutes, or until cake tests done. Serve hot.

Yield: One dozen to eighteen servings.

Beth's Oatmeal Cake   *Nebraska*

Cake:
  1 cup quick-cooking (dry) oatmeal
1½ cups hot water

  ½ cup shortening
  1 cup dark brown sugar
  1 cup granulated sugar
  2 eggs
1⅓ cups flour
  ½ teaspoon salt
  1 teaspoon baking soda
  1 teaspoon vanilla
  1 cup chopped nuts.
Topping:
  6 tablespoons shortening
  ¾ cup dark brown sugar
  ¼ cup evaporated milk
  1 cup flaked coconut.

1. Preheat the oven to 350 degrees.
2. To prepare cake, combine the oatmeal and water and set aside to cool.
3. Cream together the shortening, brown sugar and granulated sugar until light and fluffy. Beat in the eggs, one at a time, very well.
4. Sift together the flour, salt and baking soda and fold with the vanilla into the creamed mixture. Fold in the nuts.
5. Fold in the cooled oatmeal mixture and pour into a well-greased and floured 9-by-13-inch baking pan. Bake forty minutes, or until cake tests done. Cool.
6. To prepare topping, combine all ingredients. Spread over the cooled cake. Broil under a preheated broiler until brown and bubbly.

Yield: Eighteen servings.

Whole Wheat Chiffon Cake   *Utah*

  1 cup sifted whole wheat flour, chaff discarded before measuring
  ¾ cup sugar
1½ teaspoons baking powder
  ½ teaspoon salt
  ¼ cup oil
  2 egg yolks
  6 tablespoons cold water
  1 teaspoon grated lemon rind
  1 teaspoon vanilla

½ cup egg whites (about four)
¼ teaspoon cream of tartar.

1. Preheat the oven to 350 degrees.
2. Sift together the flour, sugar, baking powder and salt into a mixing bowl. Make a well in the center and add the oil, egg yolks, water, lemon rind and vanilla. Beat until smooth.
3. Beat the egg whites with the cream of tartar until stiff but not dry. Gently fold into the egg yolk mixture.
4. Turn into an ungreased nine-inch angel food pan and bake thirty-five minutes, or until cake tests done. Cool upside down in the pan. When cold, loosen with a spatula to remove from the pan.
Yield: One dozen servings.

Jellyroll   *Utah*

4 eggs, broken and warmed slightly without drying
1 teaspoon baking powder
¼ teaspoon salt
⅔ cup granulated sugar
1 teaspoon vanilla
⅔ cup cake flour
    Confectioners' sugar
1 cup preserves.

1. Preheat the oven to 400 degrees.
2. Beat the eggs with the baking powder and salt until thick and very pale. Gradually beat in the granulated sugar and continue to beat until thick. Beat in the vanilla.
3. Sift the flour twice and fold into the egg mixture. Spread in a 10-by-15-inch jellyroll pan that has been greased, lined with wax paper and greased again.
4. Bake twelve to fifteen minutes, or until golden. Turn out onto a towel sprinkled with confectioners' sugar. Peel off the paper. Roll up from the long side, enclosing the towel. Cool on a rack.

5. When cake is cool, unroll, spread with the preserves and reroll without towel. Serve in slices.
Yield: Ten servings.

This is a variety of devil's food cake found in many Western states, but the origin of its name is cloaked in mystery.

Brownstone Front   *Idaho*

1 cup sour cream
2 eggs
1 teaspoon vanilla
1½ cups cake flour
1 teaspoon baking soda
½ teaspoon salt
2½ tablespoons cocoa powder
1 cup sugar.

1. Preheat the oven to 375 degrees.
2. Beat the sour cream and eggs together well. Stir in the vanilla.
3. Sift together the flour, baking soda, salt, cocoa powder and sugar. Add dry ingredients to sour cream mixture and beat well.
4. Turn into two greased and floured nine-inch layer pans. Bake twenty-five to thirty minutes, or until done.
Yield: Two layers; one dozen servings.
Note: The cake is usually served plain but it can be filled and frosted with any plain or chocolate frosting.

Whipped Cream Cake   *Nebraska*

2¼ cups cake flour
3 teaspoons baking powder
1½ cups sugar
3 eggs, well beaten
1½ cups heavy cream, whipped
1½ teaspoons vanilla.

1. Preheat the oven to 350 degrees.

2. Sift together the flour, baking powder and sugar. Combine the eggs with the whipped cream and vanilla. Fold dry ingredients into cream mixture.

3. Turn into two nine-inch layer pans that have been greased and lined with wax paper on the bottom. Bake forty minutes, or until cake tests done.

Yield: Two layers; eight servings.

Note: Layers can be filled and frosted if desired.

Devil's Food Cake   *North Dakota*

Cake:
½ cup butter
1½ cups sugar
 2 ounces (two squares) unsweetened chocolate, melted and cooled
 3 eggs, separated
 2 cups cake flour
 1 teaspoon baking soda
⅛ teaspoon salt
 1 cup milk
 1 teaspoon vanilla.
Frosting:
 2 cups sugar
½ cup butter
½ cup milk
 2 ounces (two squares) unsweetened chocolate
 1 teaspoon vanilla.

1. Preheat the oven to 375 degrees.

2. To prepare cake, cream the butter and sugar together until very light and fluffy. Beat in the chocolate and egg yolks.

3. Sift together the flour, baking soda and salt and add alternately with the milk to the batter, beginning and ending with flour mixture. Beat the egg whites until stiff but not dry and fold into batter. Fold in the vanilla.

4. Turn into two greased and floured nine-inch layer pans and bake thirty minutes, or until done. Cool on a rack.

5. To prepare frosting, combine the sugar, butter, milk and chocolate in a saucepan and heat slowly while stirring to dissolve sugar and melt chocolate.

6. Stop stirring once mixture comes to a boil and boil vigorously two minutes. Cool. Add the vanilla and beat until frosting reaches desired consistency. Use to fill and frost the cooled layers.

Yield: Ten servings.

Note: The cake can also be baked in a loaf pan at 350 degrees for fifty to sixty minutes.

Vinarterta   *North Dakota*

Layers:
 1 cup butter
 1 cup sugar
 2 eggs
 1 teaspoon vanilla
 4 cups flour
 2 teaspoons baking powder
½ teaspoon salt
¼ cup milk.
Filling:
 2 pounds prunes
 1 cup sugar
¼ teaspoon salt
 1 teaspoon vanilla.

1. To prepare layers, cream the butter and sugar together until very light and fluffy. Beat in the eggs, one at a time. Beat in the vanilla.

2. Sift together the flour, baking powder and salt and add alternately with the milk to the batter, mixing at low speed on an electric mixer or stirring with a wooden spoon. The dough will be soft.

3. Turn dough out onto a piece of wax paper, wrap and chill several hours until firm enough to roll. This step may be hastened if the package is put into the freezer, but care must be taken that the dough does not freeze.

4. While dough is chilling, prepare filling. Cook the prunes in water to cover about twenty

minutes, or until tender. Drain prunes, reserving one-quarter cup of the liquid. Cool.

5. Pit the prunes and place fruit and reserved juice in the container of an electric blender or pass through a good chopper. Add the sugar and salt to prunes in blender and blend until smooth or stir into ground fruit.

6. Transfer the prune mixture to a saucepan and heat, stirring, until hot. Cool. Add the vanilla.

7. Preheat the oven to 350 degrees.

8. Divide the chilled dough into eight equal portions. Leave the remainder of dough in the refrigerator and roll out one portion at a time on a lightly floured pastry cloth into a circle about one-eighth-inch thick and eight to nine inches in diameter. A flan ring makes a good cutter. Place round on a baking sheet and bake ten minutes, or until lightly browned at the edges. Cool on a rack.

9. Repeat with the remaining dough portions. Scraps collected and chilled will produce two more rounds, giving a total of ten layers.

10. When layers and filling are cool, put filling between the layers, pressing down on each layer lightly with palm of hand. Wrap cake in wax paper or cloth and allow to mellow several hours.

Yield: Ten to one dozen servings.

Note: This cake freezes well.

Cranberry Coffeecake   North Dakota

Cake:
2 tablespoons butter
1 cup sugar
1 teaspoon vanilla
2 cups flour
3 teaspoons baking powder
½ teaspoon salt
1 cup milk
2 cups cranberries.
Sauce:
½ cup butter
1 cup sugar
½ cup light cream.

1. Preheat the oven to 375 degrees.

2. To prepare cake, cream the butter and sugar together and beat in the vanilla. Sift together the flour, baking powder and salt and add alternately with the milk to the batter.

3. Fold in the cranberries and turn into a greased and floured 9-by-13-inch baking pan. Bake thirty-five minutes, or until done.

4. Meanwhile, place the sauce ingredients in a small saucepan and stir over medium heat until mixture boils.

5. Boil three minutes and pour over hot coffee-cake straight from the oven. Serve warm.

Yield: Ten to one dozen servings.

Boiled Raisin Whole Wheat Cake

Utah

1½ cups raisins
2½ cups water
1 teaspoon baking soda
½ cup shortening
2 cups light brown sugar
2 eggs
1 teaspoon vanilla
3½ cups whole wheat flour, sifted before measuring and chaff discarded
½ teaspoon salt
½ teaspoon ground cloves
1 teaspoon cinnamon
2 teaspoons baking powder
½ cup chopped nuts.

1. Preheat the oven to 350 degrees.

2. Place the raisins and water in a small saucepan and bring to a boil. Boil two minutes. Stir in the baking soda. Set aside.

3. Cream the shortening and brown sugar together until very light and fluffy. Beat in the eggs, one at a time. Beat in the vanilla.

4. Sift together the flour, salt, cloves, cinnamon and baking powder. Stir alternately with the raisin mixture into the creamed mixture. Stir in the nuts.

5. Pour into a greased 9-by-13-inch baking pan

and bake forty to forty-five minutes, or until cake tests done.

Yield: One dozen servings.

Note: This cake can be frosted with any of the three frostings that follow or served with sauce as a pudding.

Grandma's Elegant Easy Frosting
South Dakota

½ cup sugar
⅛ teaspoon salt
1½ tablespoons cornstarch
 1 ounce (one square) unsweetened chocolate
½ cup boiling water
1½ tablespoons butter
½ teaspoon vanilla.

1. Place the sugar, salt and cornstarch in a saucepan and mix well. Add the chocolate and water. Cook, stirring, over low heat until chocolate melts and mixture thickens.

2. Stir in the butter and vanilla. Cool.

Yield: Enough to fill and frost two nine-inch layers.

Mabel's Chocolate Frosting   *South Dakota*

½ cup granulated sugar
½ cup flour
¼ cup cocoa powder
⅓ cup cold milk
 2 cups milk, scalded
 1 cup soft butter
 1 cup confectioners' sugar
 2 teaspoons vanilla.

1. Combine the granulated sugar, flour and cocoa powder in a small saucepan.

2. Stir in the cold milk and mix well. Gradually stir in the hot milk. Bring to a boil, stirring, and cook, stirring, about fifteen minutes.

3. Cool and chill.

4. Cream the butter with the confectioners'

sugar. Beat in the vanilla and then the chilled cocoa mixture.

Yield: Enough to fill and frost four nine-inch layers.

Old-Fashioned Caramel Frosting
Nebraska

 2 cups sugar
¼ teaspoon salt
¼ cup flour
 1 cup milk
¼ cup butter
 1 teaspoon vanilla.

1. Melt one-half cup of the sugar in a small heavy skillet and cook until lightly golden.

2. Meanwhile, combine remaining sugar, the salt, flour and milk in a saucepan. Bring to a boil, stirring. Pour golden sugar into boiling mixture, stirring to prevent boiling over.

3. Boil until mixture reaches soft ball stage or registers 238 degrees on a candy thermometer. Remove from the heat and stir in the butter and vanilla. Cool mixture to lukewarm and beat until it is a spreading consistency.

Yield: Enough to fill and frost two nine-inch layers.

Rose Hip Pudding   *Wyoming*

⅔ cup dried rose hips (see note)
 4 cups water
½ cup sugar
 3 tablespoons cornstarch
 Whipped cream
 Slivered blanched almonds.

1. Cover the rose hips with the water in a saucepan. Bring to a boil and simmer until tender, about two hours.

2. Strain and reserve liquid. Sieve hips to get three tablespoons puree; discard remainder.

3. Mix the sugar and cornstarch together in a

small saucepan. Gradually add the reserved liquid, bring to a boil and cook, stirring, ten minutes. Fold in the puree. Pour into a serving dish. Cover and cool. Chill.

4. Serve topped with whipped cream and slivered almonds.

Yield: Four servings.

Note: A few stores specializing in Scandinavian imports have dried rose hips. People in Wyoming collect and dry their own.

Date Pudding   *Utah*

Pudding:
 1 cup granulated sugar
 1 cup milk
 2 cups flour
 2 tablespoons butter
 ½ teaspoon salt
 2 teaspoons baking soda
 2 cups dates, chopped
 1 cup nuts, chopped.
Topping:
 2 cups light brown sugar
 ¼ cup butter
 4 cups boiling water.

1. Preheat the oven to 350 degrees.
2. Mix the pudding ingredients together and pour into a greased deep baking dish.
3. Mix the topping ingredients together and pour over pudding. Bake about forty-five minutes.

Yield: Six servings.

Apple Bread Pudding   *North Dakota*

 8 to ten slices stale white bread, finely diced
 4 tart apples peeled, cored and sliced
 ¾ cup plus two tablespoons sugar
 ¾ teaspoon cinnamon
 3 eggs
 4 cups milk
 Whipped cream.

1. Preheat the oven to 300 degrees.
2. Place a layer of bread pieces in the bottom of a well-greased two-quart casserole or baking dish. Top with a layer of apple slices.
3. Combine one-quarter cup of the sugar with one-half teaspoon of the cinnamon and sprinkle half over the apples. Make alternate layers of bread pieces and apple slices sprinkled with sugar-cinnamon mixture until dish is filled to within about one and one-half inches of the top.
4. Beat the eggs with one-half cup of the remaining sugar. Beat in the milk and pour over the bread and apples. Combine remaining sugar and cinnamon and sprinkle over the top.
5. Bake one and one-half hours. Serve warm with whipped cream.

Yield: Six servings.

Apple Cobbler   *North Dakota*

 2 cups thinly sliced peeled and cored apples
 ½ cup light brown sugar
 ¼ teaspoon almond extract
 ½ teaspoon cinnamon
 ½ teaspoon nutmeg
 1½ cups flour
 3 teaspoons baking powder
 3 tablespoons granulated sugar
 ½ teaspoon salt
 ⅓ cup shortening
 ½ cup milk
 1 egg, well beaten.

1. Preheat the oven to 400 degrees.
2. Arrange the apples in the bottom of a greased eight-inch square baking pan. Combine the brown sugar, almond extract, cinnamon and nutmeg and sprinkle over apples. Place pan in oven.
3. Sift together the flour, baking powder, one tablespoon of the granulated sugar and the salt.
4. With the finger tips or a pastry blender, blend the shortening into the flour mixture until it resembles coarse crumbs.

5. Add the milk and egg and mix just enough to moisten.

6. Spread dough over hot apples. Sprinkle with remaining sugar and bake thirty-five to forty minutes.

Yield: Six to eight servings.

Apple Crunch   *North Dakota*

2 cups light brown sugar
2 cups old-fashioned (dry) oatmeal
3 cups plus six tablespoons flour
2 cups shortening
6 cups sliced peeled apples (about eight
   large)
1½ teaspoons cinnamon
2 cups granulated sugar
   Whipped cream or ice cream.

1. Preheat the oven to 375 degrees.
2. Combine the brown sugar, oatmeal and three cups of the flour. With the finger tips or a pastry blender, work in the shortening as though making pastry.
3. Press half the mixture into the bottom of a well-greased 10-by-15-inch roasting or baking pan. Combine the apples with the remaining flour, one teaspoon of the cinnamon and the granulated sugar and put on top.
4. Add and press down remaining oatmeal mixture. Sprinkle with remaining cinnamon. Bake forty to fifty minutes. Serve warm with whipped cream or ice cream.

Yield: One dozen servings.

Baked Carrot Pudding   *Utah*

Pudding:
 ½ cup shortening
 ½ cup granulated sugar
 1 egg
1¼ cups flour
 ½ teaspoon baking soda
 1 teaspoon baking powder

 1 teaspoon salt
 ½ teaspoon cinnamon
 ½ teaspoon nutmeg
 ½ cup cold water
 1 cup grated carrots
 1 cup raisins.
Sauce:
 ½ cup butter
1½ cups confectioners' sugar
 ⅛ teaspoon salt
 1 teaspoon grated orange rind
   Orange juice.

1. Preheat the oven to 350 degrees.
2. To prepare pudding, cream the shortening and granulated sugar together until light and fluffy. Beat in the egg. Sift together the flour, baking soda, baking powder, salt, cinnamon and nutmeg.
3. Fold the dry ingredients alternately with the water into the creamed mixture. Stir in the carrots and raisins.
4. Turn into a well-greased baking dish and bake forty-five to sixty minutes, or until lightly browned and set.
5. To prepare sauce, cream the butter and gradually beat in the confectioners' sugar very well. Beat in the salt, orange rind and enough orange juice to make a soft consistency. Chill. Serve as hard sauce with warm pudding.

Yield: Four servings.

Rhubarb Bread Pudding   *Utah*

2 cups cut-up rhubarb
2 cups soft bread crumbs or cake crumbs
1 cup milk
¾ cup sugar if bread crumbs are used,
   one-half cup if cake crumbs are used
1 teaspoon lemon extract
3 tablespoons butter
   Whipped cream.

1. Preheat the oven to 375 degrees.
2. Combine the rhubarb, crumbs, milk and

sugar and pour into a well-greased baking dish. Sprinkle with the lemon extract and dot with the butter.

3. Bake one hour. Serve with whipped cream.
Yield: Four servings.

Old-Fashioned Tapioca Pudding

Wyoming

1 cup large pearl tapioca
6 eggs, separated
4 cups milk
1 cup plus one tablespoon sugar
⅛ teaspoon salt
1 tablespoon butter
1 teaspoon vanilla.

1. Cover the tapioca with warm water and let soak at least one hour. Place tapioca and water in a saucepan, bring to a boil, cover and simmer gently until lumps become transparent, two to three hours.

2. Preheat the oven to 325 degrees.

3. Mix the egg yolks with the milk, one cup of the sugar, the salt and butter and place in a heavy saucepan. Heat, stirring, until custard mixture thickens slightly and coats the back of the spoon. Do not allow to boil. Stir in the vanilla.

4. Add tapioca to custard.

5. Beat the egg whites until stiff but not dry and beat in the remaining sugar. In a greased baking dish, alternate layers of the tapioca with egg whites, ending with the whites.

6. Bake about fifteen minutes, or until whites are lightly browned. Serve warm or chilled.
Yield: Eight servings.

Steamed Pumpkin-Nut Pudding

Utah

½ cup shortening
¼ cup sugar
2 eggs
2 cups flour
1 teaspoon salt
1 teaspoon cinnamon
½ teaspoon ginger
¼ teaspoon baking soda
1½ teaspoons baking powder
¾ cup pumpkin puree
¼ cup sour cream
1 cup chopped walnuts.

1. Cream the shortening and sugar together until light and fluffy. Beat in the eggs, one at a time.

2. Sift together the flour, salt, cinnamon, ginger, baking soda and baking powder. Mix the pumpkin puree with the sour cream. Stir dry ingredients and pumpkin mixture into the creamed mixture. Stir in the walnuts.

3. Three-quarters fill greased one-and-one-half quart pudding basins, molds or cans. Cover tightly and place on a rack in a kettle with the water coming at least halfway up the sides of the basins, molds or cans. Cover and boil two hours.

4. Unmold the pudding to serve.
Yield: Six to eight servings.

Steamed Carrot Pudding

Utah

Pudding:
2 cups flour
1 teaspoon salt
2 teaspoons cinnamon
2 teaspoons nutmeg
1 teaspoon ground cloves
2 cups light brown sugar
1 cup finely grated or ground suet
1 cup raisins
1 teaspoon baking soda
1½ cups buttermilk
1 cup ground carrots
1 cup ground raw potatoes.
Sauce:
½ cup granulated sugar
1 tablespoon cornstarch
1 cup boiling water
⅛ teaspoon salt

2 tablespoons butter
1 teaspoon grated lemon rind
2 tablespoons lemon juice
¼ teaspoon nutmeg.

1. To prepare pudding, sift the flour with the salt, cinnamon, nutmeg and cloves. Stir in the brown sugar, suet and raisins.

2. Stir the baking soda into the buttermilk and add to the dry ingredients. Mix until moistened. Stir in the carrots and potatoes.

3. Spoon the mixture into well-greased pudding basins, molds or cans, filling them three-quarters full. Cover tightly and place on a rack in a kettle with the water coming at least halfway up the basins, molds or cans.

4. Cover kettle and boil three hours.

5. To prepare sauce, combine the granulated sugar and cornstarch in a small saucepan. Stir in the water and salt and bring to a boil, stirring. Cook until thick and clear. Beat in the remaining ingredients.

6. Unmold the pudding. Serve sauce separately with pudding.

Yield: Ten servings.

Son-of-a-Gun-in-a-Sack *Wyoming*

Pudding:
    2 cups flour
    1 cup soft bread crumbs
    1 cup finely grated or ground suet
    1 teaspoon salt
    1 teaspoon ground cloves
    1 teaspoon cinnamon
    1 teaspoon nutmeg
    2 teaspoons baking soda
    1 cup unsulphured molasses
    1 cup raisins
    1 cup evaporated milk or light cream.
Vanilla sauce:
    ½ cup soft butter
    1¼ cups confectioners' sugar
    1 egg
    1 teaspoon vanilla.

1. To prepare pudding, place the flour, bread crumbs, suet, salt, cloves, cinnamon and nutmeg in a bowl. Add the baking soda to the molasses and stir into the dry ingredients.

2. Stir in the raisins and the milk or cream just enough to moisten.

3. Turn into a flour sack or fine cotton bag. Tie with string, leaving a long end. Place the bag in a kettle of boiling water, tying the long end of the string to the handle. Alternately, the mixture can be put into a greased pudding basin or mold, covered tightly and placed on a rack in a kettle with boiling water extending halfway up the sides of the basin or mold.

4. Cover kettle and boil two hours.

5. To prepare sauce, cream together the butter and confectioners' sugar. Beat in the egg well. Beat in the vanilla and enough hot water to give desired consistency.

6. Turn the pudding out onto a warm plate and serve the sauce separately.

Yield: Eight servings.

Skyr *North Dakota*

8 cups buttermilk
1 to two tablespoons sugar.

1. Let the buttermilk stand overnight out of the refrigerator so that buttermilk becomes quite thick. Strain overnight through a double layer of cheesecloth in a strainer, again out of the refrigerator. Discard the whey.

2. Remove the curd to a bowl and beat with a rotary beater, adding the sugar. Chill.

Yield: About three cups.

Note: Skyr will keep several days in the refrigerator. Serve with cream and sugar and fresh strawberries or blueberries.

Traditionally, this dish is made from scratch, using raw milk and rennet. The version below is a compromise.

Osta Kaka   *South Dakota*

1 pound cottage cheese
3 eggs, lightly beaten
1 cup sugar
2 cups heavy cream
  Preserves.

1. Preheat the oven to 350 degrees.
2. Combine the cottage cheese, eggs, sugar and cream and pour into a greased baking dish. Set on a towel in a pan of hot water. Bake one and one-half hours, or until set. Serve topped with preserves.
Yield: Eight servings.

Kemph   *Nebraska*

3 eggs, lightly beaten
1 teaspoon salt
½ cup milk or light cream
1 cup flour
¼ teaspoon baking powder
2 tablespoons butter
  Stewed apples or cherries.

1. Mix together the eggs, salt, milk or cream, flour and baking powder to make a batter.
2. Heat the butter in a heavy skillet. Pour in the batter and cook quickly while crosscutting the mixture with two knives as it cooks. Mixture will be a mass of cut-up browned bits when done.
3. Serve with stewed fruit.
Yield: Four servings.

Date and Nut Whirls   *Nebraska*

Dough:
1 cup butter

1 cup granulated sugar
1 cup light brown sugar
3 eggs
1 teaspoon vanilla
5 cups flour
1 teaspoon baking soda.
Filling:
1 pound dates, finely chopped
  or ground
1 tablespoon grated orange rind
½ cup granulated sugar
½ cup water
1 cup walnuts, chopped.

1. To prepare dough, cream the butter and sugars together until very light and creamy. Beat in the eggs, one at a time. Beat in the vanilla.
2. Sift the flour with the baking soda and stir into the batter to make a soft dough. Dough may be rolled immediately or chilled for easier handling.
3. To prepare filling, combine the dates, orange rind, granulated sugar and water in a small pan and heat, stirring, until mixture is thick. Cool. Stir in the walnuts.
4. Roll out half the dough on a lightly floured pastry cloth or board into a rectangle about 10 by 16 inches. Spread with half the cooled date mixture and roll from the long side like a jellyroll. Wrap in wax paper and chill several hours or overnight. Repeat with the other half of dough and date mixture.
5. Preheat the oven to 350 degrees.
6. Slice the rolls about one-third-inch thick and place, cut side up, on lightly greased baking sheets. Bake fifteen minutes, or until well browned. Cool on a rack.
Yield: About six dozen.

Note: If preferred, one-half of the dough can be made into rolled filled cookies by only preparing a half quantity of the date mixture, and the other half of the dough can be pushed through a cookie press onto a lightly greased baking sheet and baked about twelve minutes.

Currant Cookies
Utah

1 cup butter
1½ cups sugar
2 eggs
2 tablespoons cognac
3½ cups flour
1½ teaspoons nutmeg
½ cup currants.

1. Beat the butter together with the sugar until very light and creamy. Beat in the eggs, one at a time. Beat in the cognac.
2. Sift together the flour and nutmeg and add the currants. Toss.
3. Stir into the batter. Wrap the dough in wax paper and chill several hours or overnight.
4. Preheat the oven to 350 degrees.
5. Roll out the dough to one-quarter-inch thickness and cut with a three-inch round cookie cutter. Transfer to a lightly greased baking sheet and bake fifteen to twenty minutes, or until slightly browned at the edges. The center of cookie remains pale. Cool on a rack.
Yield: Two dozen three-inch cookies.

Hawkins' Jamestown Buffalo Cookies
North Dakota

½ cup butter
1 cup light brown sugar
1 egg
¼ cup unsulphured molasses
2 cups flour
⅛ teaspoon salt
2 teaspoons baking soda
1 teaspoon ginger
1 teaspoon ground cloves
1 teaspoon cinnamon.

1. Cream the butter and brown sugar together until light and fluffy. Beat in the egg and molasses.
2. Sift together the remaining ingredients and stir into the batter. Wrap the dough in wax paper and chill several hours or overnight.
3. Preheat the oven to 375 degrees.
4. Roll out the dough, one-third at a time, on a lightly floured pastry cloth or board until thin. With homemade paper pattern as a guide, cut dough into buffalo shapes. Place on lightly greased baking sheet.
5. Bake six to eight minutes, or until done. Cool on a rack.
Yield: Four dozen to five dozen.
Note: This is a very "temperamental" cookie that cannot be rolled in hot humid weather. Keep extra dough in the refrigerator at all times.

Berlinerkranser
North Dakota

4 hard-cooked egg yolks, mashed
2 cups sweet butter
4 eggs, separated
1¾ cups confectioners' sugar
5 cups flour
⅛ teaspoon nutmeg
Sugar, preferably colored and coarse grain.

1. Preheat the oven to 350 degrees.
2. Beat the mashed hard-cooked egg yolks and butter together. Beat the raw egg yolks well. Beat the confectioners' sugar and beaten egg yolks into the butter mixture. Sift the flour with the nutmeg and stir into the batter.
3. Roll out the dough to one-quarter-inch thickness and cut with a doughnut cutter into rings.
4. Brush with the egg whites and sprinkle with sugar. Place on lightly greased baking sheet and bake twelve minutes. Cool on a rack.
Yield: Five dozen.

Coconut Cookies
Colorado

2 cups light brown sugar
1 cup shortening
2 eggs

1 teaspoon lemon juice
1 teaspoon vanilla
3¾ cups flour
2 teaspoons baking soda
2 teaspoons cream of tartar
1 cup flaked coconut.

1. Preheat the oven to 350 degrees.
2. Cream the brown sugar and shortening together until very light and fluffy.
3. Beat in the eggs, one at a time. Beat in the lemon juice and vanilla.
4. Sift together the flour, baking soda and cream of tartar. First with a wooden spoon and then with the hands, work the dry ingredients into the batter. Work in the coconut.
5. Form the mixture into one-inch balls. Place on a lightly greased baking sheet and press each ball lightly with a fork. Bake ten to twelve minutes. The cookies are soft when taken from the oven. Cool on a rack.
Yield: About four dozen.

Applesauce Bars   *North Dakota*

½ cup butter
1½ cups granulated sugar
1½ cups applesauce
1 teaspoon cinnamon
¼ teaspoon ground cloves
1 teaspoon salt
2 teaspoons baking soda
2¼ cups flour
1 cup raisins
2 cups confectioners' sugar
Lemon juice.

1. Preheat the oven to 375 degrees.
2. Cream the butter and granulated sugar together until light and fluffy. Stir in the applesauce.
3. Sift together the cinnamon, cloves, salt, baking soda and flour and stir into the batter. Fold in the raisins.
4. Turn the batter into a well-greased 9-by-13-inch baking pan and bake about twenty-five minutes. Moisten the confectioners' sugar with lemon juice and spread over hot baked mixture. Cool in the pan and cut into bars.
Yield: About three dozen.

Fattigman   *North Dakota*

12 egg yolks
½ cup granulated sugar
1 cup heavy cream, whipped
3¾ cups flour, approximately
Fat or oil for deep-frying
Confectioners' sugar.

1. Day before, beat the egg yolks until very pale and thick. This takes about twenty minutes. Gradually add the granulated sugar while continuing to beat about fifteen minutes longer.
2. Fold in the cream and enough flour to make a dough. Wrap in wax paper and refrigerate overnight.
3. Next day, roll dough out fairly thin and cut into strips or diamond shapes. Make a slit in the center of each and pull one end through the hole. Fry until lightly browned, a few at a time, in the fat or oil heated to 360 degrees, turning once. Drain on paper towels. Sprinkle with confectioners' sugar.
Yield: About five dozen, depending on size.

Whole Wheat Applesauce Cookies
Utah

¼ cup shortening
1 cup sugar
1 egg
1 teaspoon baking soda
1 cup applesauce
2 cups less two tablespoons whole wheat flour, sifted before measuring and chaff discarded
½ teaspoon salt
½ teaspoon cinnamon

½ teaspoon nutmeg
½ teaspoon ground cloves
1 cup raisins
½ cup chopped nuts.

1. Preheat the oven to 375 degrees.
2. Cream the shortening and gradually beat in the sugar.
3. Beat in the egg until mixture is light and fluffy. Stir the baking soda into the applesauce and add to the creamed mixture.
4. Sift together the flour, salt, cinnamon, nutmeg and cloves. Add the raisins and nuts and stir mixture into the batter.
5. Drop by teaspoonfuls, two inches apart, onto a greased baking sheet. Bake twenty minutes, or until done and lightly browned. Cool on a rack.
Yield: About three dozen.

Old-Style Ginger Cookies *South Dakota*

1 cup lard
2 cups sugar
2 teaspoons baking soda
2 cups dark molasses
¼ cup water
¾ cup dark rum
8 cups flour
1 tablespoon salt
1 tablespoon ginger.

1. Day before, cream the lard and sugar together until very light and fluffy.
2. Stir the baking soda into the molasses. Add one cup of the molasses mixture, two tablespoons of the water and one-third cup of the rum to the creamed mixture.
3. Sift together the flour, salt and ginger and add alternately with the remaining molasses, water and rum to the batter. Mix well. Chill overnight.
4. Next day, preheat the oven to 350 degrees.
5. Roll out one-quarter of the dough at a time on a lightly floured board or pastry cloth to one-

quarter-inch thickness. Cut with large cookie cutters and place on lightly greased baking sheets.
6. Bake ten minutes, or until done. Cool on a rack. Stored in a plastic bag or jar with a slice of bread, the cookies will keep several weeks.
Yield: About 200, depending on size.

Abigail's Cookies *Idaho*

7 cups flour
5 teaspoons baking powder
1 teaspoon salt
½ pound lard
½ pound butter
2¼ cups sugar
2 teaspoons vanilla
4 eggs, lightly beaten
1 cup milk, approximately.

1. Preheat the oven to 375 degrees.
2. Sift together the flour, baking powder and salt into a large bowl. With the finger tips, a pastry blender or two knives, blend in the lard and butter as though making pastry.
3. Add two cups of the sugar. Combine the vanilla and eggs and stir in with enough milk to make a dough that will roll. Roll out the dough, one-quarter at a time, on a lightly floured board to one-eighth-inch thickness.
4. Cut with cookie cutters and place on lightly greased baking sheets. Sprinkle with remaining sugar. Bake about ten minutes, or until lightly browned at the edges.
Yield: About 200.

Dona's Cookies *South Dakota*

3 cups flour
1 teaspoon cream of tartar
½ teaspoon baking soda
½ teaspoon salt
1 cup shortening
3 eggs, lightly beaten

1 cup sugar
1 teaspoon vanilla.

1. Sift together the flour, cream of tartar, baking soda and salt into a bowl. With two knives, a pastry blender or the finger tips, blend in the shortening until mixture resembles coarse oatmeal.

2. Mix the eggs, sugar and vanilla together and stir into dry ingredients. Gather into a dough and let stand twenty minutes.

3. Preheat the oven to 350 degrees.

4. Roll dough out to one-quarter-inch thickness on a lightly floured board. Cut with cookie cutters and place on greased baking sheets. Bake ten minutes, or until lightly browned.

Yield: About five dozen.

Pepper Cookies   *Idaho*

1 cup butter
1 cup sugar
½ teaspoon vanilla
1¾ cups flour
½ cup cornstarch
2 teaspoons baking powder
½ teaspoon salt
½ teaspoon cardamom
½ teaspoon cinnamon
½ teaspoon freshly ground black pepper
¼ cup heavy cream
⅔ cup finely ground blanched almonds.

1. Preheat the oven to 350 degrees.

2. Cream the butter and sugar together until very light and fluffy. Beat in the vanilla.

3. Sift together the flour, cornstarch, baking powder, salt, cardamom, cinnamon and pepper. Add alternately with the cream, ending with the flour mixture, to the batter. Stir in the almonds.

4. Shape mixture into tiny balls and bake on ungreased baking sheets fifteen minutes, or until done. Cool on a rack.

Yield: About four dozen.

Spritz Cookies   *North Dakota*

½ cup butter
1 cup light brown sugar
1 egg
1 teaspoon baking soda
2 teaspoons warm water
½ teaspoon cream of tartar
2 cups flour
1 teaspoon ginger
1 teaspoon lemon extract.

1. Preheat the oven to 375 degrees.

2. Cream the butter and gradually beat in the brown sugar until mixture is creamy smooth.

3. Beat in the egg. Dissolve the baking soda in the water and add.

4. Sift together the cream of tartar, flour and ginger and stir into batter. Stir in the lemon extract. Push the mixture through a cookie press onto a lightly greased baking sheet. Bake ten minutes, or until done. Cool on a rack.

Yield: Thirty.

Krum Kake I   *North Dakota*

4 extra-large eggs
1 cup sugar
½ cup flour
½ cup cornstarch
1 teaspoon vanilla
1 cup butter, melted and cooled
Shortening.

1. Beat the eggs until light. Gradually beat in the sugar and continue to beat until the mixture is thick and very pale in color.

2. Fold in the flour, cornstarch and vanilla.

3. Fold in the butter.

4. Heat a krum kake iron (see note) slowly. Brush lightly with shortening. Place a rounded teaspoonful of the batter in the center of the iron. Close the iron and cook about forty-five seconds, or until cookie is lightly colored. Turn the iron and cook one-half minute longer, or until cookie

is golden. It requires two or three "cookings" to season iron and adjust heat, especially with a new iron, so do not expect a perfect cookie on the first try.

5. Immediately roll cookie around the lightly greased handle of a wooden spoon and slide onto a rack to cool. Alternately, the cookie can be molded over the underside of a muffin tin or custard cup to make a crisp cup for sherbet or ice cream.

Yield: About three dozen.

Note: Krum kake irons are available in New York City at Lekvar by the Barrel, 1572 First Avenue (10028), and at Nyborg & Nelson, 598 Second Avenue (10022). They are available by mail from Maid of Scandinavia, 3245 Raleigh Avenue, Minneapolis, Minnesota 55416.

Krum Kake II   *North Dakota*

3 eggs, well beaten
1 cup sugar
½ cup heavy cream, whipped
½ cup melted butter
½ teaspoon vanilla
1¾ cups flour
¼ teaspoon salt.

1. Beat the eggs with the sugar until very light and fluffy. Fold in the cream, butter and vanilla. Mix well.

2. Mix the flour with the salt and fold in.

3. Bake krum kake according to directions in previous recipe (steps 4 and 5).

Yield: About three dozen.

Miscellaneous

Pickles, Relishes and Preserves

In making jams and jellies at elevations above 2,000 feet, it is recommended that a candy thermometer be used. Normal temperature for jelling at sea level is 220 degrees Fahrenheit. Lower this temperature two degrees for every 1,000-degree rise in elevation.

Butters and relishes will require shorter cooking times.

Rhubarb Chutney   *Utah*

8 cups sliced rhubarb
6 cups sliced onions
2 cups raisins
7 cups light brown sugar
4 cups cider vinegar
2 tablespoons salt
2 teaspoons cinnamon
2 teaspoons ginger
1 teaspoon ground cloves
⅛ teaspoon cayenne pepper, or to taste.

Combine all ingredients in a heavy kettle. Bring to a boil and simmer gently until fairly thick, about forty-five minutes. Stir often to prevent sticking. Pour into hot sterilized jars. Seal. Store in a cool, dark, dry place.

Yield: Four to five pints.

Aunt Nell's Piccalilli   *Wyoming*

1 gallon green tomatoes, peeled and sliced
  Salt
1 gallon finely chopped cabbage
4 cups finely chopped onions
3 hot green peppers, chopped
¼ cup dry mustard
2 tablespoons ginger
1 tablespoon ground cloves
1 tablespoon mace
1 tablespoon cinnamon
3 pounds sugar
1 gallon boiling cider vinegar, approximately.

1. Sprinkle the tomatoes generously with salt and let stand one hour or longer. Drain off liquid and discard. Chop the tomatoes and place in a large kettle.

2. Add all remaining ingredients except the vinegar. Mix well. Add vinegar barely to cover vegetables. Boil fifteen minutes. Ladle into hot sterilized jars and seal. Store in cool, dark, dry place.

Yield: About eight quarts.

Green Tomato Relish   *South Dakota*

    1 peck (two gallons) green tomatoes, peeled
      and chopped
1½ cups coarse salt
    1 medium-size head cabbage, chopped
    3 quarts cider vinegar
    6 onions, chopped
    3 red sweet peppers, chopped
    2 green peppers, chopped
    7 cups sugar
    2 tablespoons celery seeds
    2 tablespoons mustard seeds
    1 tablespoon cinnamon
    1 tablespoon ground cloves
    1 teaspoon turmeric
    1 clove garlic.

1. Day before, sprinkle the tomatoes with the salt and let stand overnight. Next day, drain well and place in a kettle with the cabbage and vinegar. Bring to a boil and simmer thirty minutes.
2. Add the remaining ingredients and cook until thick, stirring occasionally. Pour into hot sterilized jars and seal. Store in a cool, dark, dry place.
Yield: About four quarts.

Carrot and Cucumber Relish   *Nebraska*

    8 carrots, ground
    6 onions, ground
  12 medium-size cucumbers, peeled and ground
    3 green peppers, ground
    2 small hot red peppers, ground
  ½ cup coarse salt
    4 cups cider vinegar
    4 cups sugar
    1 teaspoon mustard seeds
    1 teaspoon celery seeds.

1. Day before, layer the ground carrots, onions, cucumbers, green peppers and hot peppers in a large crock, sprinkling with the salt as you go. Let stand overnight. Next day, drain well.

2. Combine the remaining ingredients in a saucepan and bring to a boil. Add drained vegetables and simmer fifteen minutes. Pour into hot sterilized jars and seal. Store in a cool, dark, dry place.
Yield: About three quarts.

Corn Relish   *Nebraska*

  10 cups corn kernels (about twelve ears)
  10 cups chopped cabbage
    3 sweet red peppers, chopped
    3 onions, chopped
    8 cups cider vinegar
    1 cup sugar
    3 tablespoons salt
  ¼ cup mustard seeds.

Combine all ingredients in a kettle. Bring to a boil, stirring to prevent scorching, and simmer fifteen minutes. Pour into hot sterilized jars and seal. Store in a cool, dark, dry place.
Yield: Three to four quarts.

Hot Tomato-Apple Butter   *Idaho*

    9 tart apples, peeled, cored and ground
    8 onions, ground
    6 green peppers, ground
    8 small hot green peppers, ground
  16 large, ripe tomatoes, peeled and chopped
    3 cups sugar
2½ cups cider vinegar
    3 tablespoons salt
    2 teaspoons cinnamon
    2 teaspoons ground cloves.

Put all ingredients in a large kettle, bring to a boil and simmer, stirring to prevent sticking, until mixture is dark and thick, about two hours. Pour into hot sterilized jars and seal. Store in a cool, dark, dry place.
Yield: About two quarts.

Spiced Wild Gooseberries   *Wyoming*

2 cups cider vinegar
2½ pounds light brown sugar
1 tablespoon ground allspice
1 tablespoon ground cloves
1 tablespoon nutmeg
1 tablespoon cinnamon
2 teaspoons salt
4 pounds wild gooseberries (see note).

1. Place all ingredients except gooseberries in a kettle and bring to a boil, stirring to dissolve the sugar. Boil five minutes.

2. Add the fruit and cook until fruit is very tender, about thirty minutes. Pour into hot sterilized jars and seal. Store in a cool, dark, dry place.

Yield: About one and one-half quarts.

Note: This relish could also be made with cultivated gooseberries or red currants to serve with poultry and game.

Pickled Cherries (Cherry Olives)
Idaho

8 cups cherries, not too ripe
Cider vinegar
Coriander seeds
Mace
Cayenne pepper
Salt.

1. Wash the fruit, leaving one inch of stem. Put in a crock or jar and cover with vinegar. Let stand in a cool place three weeks. Pour off the vinegar and replace with fresh. Let stand three days longer.

2. Pour off vinegar and measure into a saucepan and for each cup add one-half teaspoon coriander seeds, one-eighth teaspoon mace, cayenne to taste and one-eighth teaspoon salt. Bring to a boil and cool.

3. Put the cherries into clean jars and pour the cooled vinegar mixture over the cherries. Seal.

Store in a cool place at least four weeks before using.

Yield: Two quarts.

Note: These are good with cheese or as a garnish for poultry and game.

Buffalo berry, a wild berry that resembles a currant, got its name from the custom of serving the cooked fruit as a sauce with buffalo.

Buffalo Berry Catchup   *Wyoming*

2 gallons buffalo berries, picked after a heavy frost
2 cups sugar
1½ tablespoons mustard seeds
1½ teaspoons freshly ground black pepper
1½ tablespoons cinnamon
2 onions, finely chopped
4 cups cider vinegar
1½ tablespoons salt
1½ tablespoons whole cloves, tied in a muslin bag.

1. Place the berries in a large kettle with a small quantity of water. Simmer slowly, mashing fruit as it cooks. Add only enough water to prevent scorching and cook until berries are tender.

2. Puree or mash the cooked fruit to give one gallon of pulp. Place the pulp in a large kettle with the remaining ingredients.

3. Bring to a boil, stirring, and cook to reduce volume by about one-half, stirring to prevent sticking.

4. Remove the bag of cloves and turn relish into hot sterilized jars. Seal. Store in a cool, dark, dry place.

Yield: About two quarts.

Note: Serve as relish with wild game.

Uncooked Chili Sauce *Utah*

1 peck (two gallons) ripe tomatoes, chopped and well drained
6 large onions, finely chopped
4 small stalks celery, finely diced
3 cups sugar
½ cup salt
6 cups cider vinegar
1 teaspoon red pepper, or to taste
½ cup mustard seeds
1 teaspoon ground cloves
1 teaspoon ground allspice
1 teaspoon cinnamon.

1. Place the tomatoes, onions and celery in a stone jar or crock or pottery bowl.
2. Combine the remaining ingredients and pour over. Mix. Set aside in a cool, dark, dry place at least ten days before using.
3. The sauce can be stored in quart jars if it is more convenient.

Yield: About one dozen quarts.

Grape Catchup *Utah*

4 cups grapes, peeled and skins reserved
4 cups cider vinegar
6 cups sugar
2 tablespoons cinnamon
2 tablespoons ground cloves.

1. Place the grapes in a saucepan and simmer until tender. Push through a colander or sieve to remove seeds.
2. Return to pan and add the skins, vinegar and sugar. Bring to a boil and simmer thirty minutes. Add the cinnamon and cloves and boil ten minutes longer.
3. Spoon into hot sterilized jars and seal. Store in a cool, dark, dry place.

Yield: About one and one-half quarts.

Yellow Cucumber Pickles (Senfgurken) *Nebraska*

12 large ripe yellow cucumbers, peeled, seeded and cut into long sticks
12 cups water
1½ cups salt
1 gallon cider vinegar
8 cups sugar
¼ cup mustard seeds
¾ cup mixed pickling spices, tied in a muslin bag.

1. Day before, place the cucumber pieces in a crock. Combine the water and salt, stir to dissolve salt and pour mixture over cucumbers. Let stand in a cool place overnight. Next day, drain well.
2. Combine the remaining ingredients in a kettle and bring to a boil. Simmer fifteen minutes. Transfer three to four cups of the liquid to a large heavy skillet or roasting pan. Place a single layer of cucumbers in the liquid so they are just covered. Simmer until clear. Pack in hot sterilized jars. Repeat until all cucumbers are cooked.
3. Fill jars with hot vinegar mixture. Seal. Store in a cool, dark, dry place.

Yield: About ten pints.

Aunt Mary's Pickled Onions *Nebraska*

8 cups small white onions
2 teaspoons salt
4 cups cider vinegar
1 tablespoon mustard seeds
½ cup sugar
2 teaspoons ground cloves
2 teaspoons ground allspice
2 bay leaves.

1. Place the onions in a saucepan and add the salt and enough cold water to cover. Bring to just below the boiling point. Drain off the water and peel onions. Pat dry with a cloth.
2. Combine the vinegar, mustard seeds, sugar,

cloves and allspice in a saucepan and bring to a boil. Simmer ten minutes.

3. Place onions in hot sterilized quart jars and pour hot vinegar mixture over onions. Put a bay leaf in each jar. Seal. Store in a cool, dark, dry place.

Yield: Two quarts.

Kraut Relish South Dakota

1 twenty-nine-ounce can sauerkraut, drained
1 cup sugar
1 teaspoon celery seeds
1 onion, finely grated
½ green pepper, finely chopped
½ red sweet pepper, finely chopped.

Combine all the ingredients in a ceramic or glass bowl and set in the refrigerator overnight or longer. Cover well, since the relish is odoriferous.

Yield: About two cups.

Rhubarb Butter North Dakota

8 cups diced rhubarb
1 cup water
6 cups sugar
1 teaspoon cinnamon
½ teaspoon ground cloves.

1. Place the rhubarb and water in a kettle and simmer gently, stirring to prevent sticking, until rhubarb is very mushy and tender.

2. Add the remaining ingredients and simmer, stirring often, about one hour, or until very thick. Pour into hot sterilized jars and seal. Store in a cool, dark, dry place.

Yield: About four and one-half pints.

Pioneer Wild Plum Butter Nebraska

8 cups wild plums, washed
Sugar
Cinnamon.

1. Place washed plums in a kettle with water barely to cover. Bring to a boil and simmer gently until plums are very tender.

2. Press plums through a colander to remove the seeds. Measure the pulp into a saucepan and add one cup sugar and one-quarter teaspoon cinnamon for each cup pulp.

3. Return to kettle and simmer mixture until very thick. Spoon into hot sterilized jars. Pour two thin layers of melted paraffin over. Cool, cover and store in a cool, dark, dry place.

Yield: About four pints.

Corncob Jelly South Dakota

14 large, freshly shelled red corncobs
Sugar
Powdered or liquid fruit pectin
Red food coloring.

1. Rinse the cobs well to remove all loose bits. Place cobs in a kettle and cover with water. Bring to a boil and simmer thirty minutes or longer, making sure cobs are always covered with water.

2. Strain three cups of the liquid into a saucepan, add an equal amount of sugar, bring to a boil and use the pectin according to manufacturer's instructions. Add food coloring to give a rosy hue. Skim and pour into hot sterilized jelly glasses. Pour two thin layers of melted paraffin over. Cool, cover and store in a cool, dark, dry place.

3. Repeat with remaining three-cup batches corn water.

Yield: About four pints.

Both chokecherries and buffalo berries grow wild in abundance in many Western states. Chokecherries lack pectin and thus will not form jelly alone, although the cherry juice combined with sugar makes a delicious topping for pancakes and hot biscuits.

Chokecherry and Buffalo Berry Jelly
South Dakota

4 cups ripe chokecherries
4 cups barely ripe buffalo berries
   Sugar.

1. Day before, place the cherries and berries in a kettle with just enough water barely to cover. Simmer gently until tender.
2. Strain the juice through a jelly bag overnight.
3. Next day, measure the juice into a saucepan and add one cup sugar for each cup juice. Bring to a boil and boil vigorously until set is reached (two drops come together on side of a spoon or a drop cooled and chilled on a plate sets), about twenty minutes. Pour into hot sterilized jars. Pour two thin layers of melted paraffin over. Cool, cover and store in a dark, cool, dry place.
Yield: Four to five pints.

Crab Apple Jelly
Utah

1 gallon unblemished crab apples, washed, blossom ends removed and apples quartered
   Sugar.

1. Day before, place fruit in a heavy kettle and add water barely to cover. Bring to a boil and simmer gently until fruit is tender.
2. Strain fruit through a jelly bag overnight.
3. Next day, boil juice ten minutes. Measure juice and add one cup sugar for each cup juice. Bring to a boil, stirring to dissolve the sugar, and then boil rapidly until mixture reaches the set stage (the drops run together on the side of a

spoon to give sheet test or a drop cooled and chilled on a plate sets), about twenty minutes. Pour into hot sterilized jelly glasses. Pour two thin layers of melted paraffin over. Cool, cover and store in a cool, dark, dry place.
Yield: About five pints.

Pear Lock
Utah

30 pears, peeled, cored and chopped
   Sugar
1 tablespoon grated orange rind
3 oranges, sectioned and pulp chopped
1 small can crushed pineapple.

1. Day before, measure chopped pears into a bowl and add an equal amount of sugar. Stir and let stand overnight.
2. Next day, transfer to a kettle and add the remaining ingredients. Bring to a boil. Boil ten minutes. Pour into hot sterilized jars. Seal. Store in a cool, dark, dry place.
Yield: About five pints.

Red or Black Currant Jam
Utah

8 cups red or black currants, strings removed and currants crushed
1 cup water
   Sugar.

1. Place the currants and water in a saucepan and simmer gently until currants are very tender. Measure pulp and add one cup sugar for each cup pulp.
2. Bring to a boil, stirring to dissolve sugar, and boil rapidly until jellying point is reached (that is, when preserve sheets off spoon). Pour into hot sterilized jars. Pour two thin layers of melted paraffin over. Cool and store in a cool, dark, dry place.
Yield: About four pints.

Pear and Date Preserve　　　*Utah*

3 oranges, ground
2 lemons, ground
5 pounds pears, peeled, cored and diced
3 pounds sugar
1 pound dates, diced.

1. Day before, place the oranges, lemons and pears in a ceramic or glass bowl and add the sugar. Stir to mix and let stand overnight.

2. Next day, put fruit mixture in a kettle and add dates. Bring to a boil and boil until thick, stirring to prevent sticking. Pour into hot sterilized jars and seal. Store in a cool, dark, dry place.

Yield: About six pints.

Venison Mincemeat　　　*South Dakota*

2 pounds cooked venison, ground
1 pound suet, ground
6 pounds tart apples, peeled, cored and chopped
2 pounds currants
1 pound golden raisins
2 pounds raisins
1 pound finely chopped citron
6 cups light brown sugar
2 teaspoons nutmeg
3 teaspoons ground allspice
3 teaspoons cinnamon
¼ teaspoon ginger
1 teaspoon ground cloves
1 tablespoon salt
　Grated rind of one orange
　Juice of two oranges
8 cups cider.

1. In a large kettle, mix the venison with the suet, apples, currants, raisins and citron. Add the brown sugar, nutmeg, allspice, cinnamon, ginger, cloves and salt.

2. Add the orange rind and orange juice.

3. Stir in the cider. Bring to a boil and simmer thirty minutes. Pack into hot jars. Seal and process pints and quarts at ten pounds pressure for twenty minutes. Cool, check seal and store in a cool, dark, dry place.

Yield: About nine quarts.

Spruce Tip Syrup　　　*Wyoming*

Pick the buds on the spruce in the spring just after the paperlike brown covering has come off. Remember that the new growth is being removed, so do not pick any one tree clean. Cover buds with water and boil fifteen minutes, or until buds are gummy and brown. Strain through a jelly bag overnight. Measure juice and add an equal amount of sugar. Bring to a boil and boil five minutes. Pour into hot sterilized bottles and store in the refrigerator. This syrup is good on sour dough hot cakes.

Rose Hip Syrup　　　*Wyoming*

Remove the bud ends from the rose hips. Cover with water in a kettle and simmer until the fruit is soft. Strain off juice and reserve. Cover remaining pulp with water again and simmer again. Strain juice a second time through a jelly bag and combine with first extraction. Measure juice and for every two cups add one cup sugar. Boil mixture vigorously until set is reached, 220 degrees on a candy thermometer or when syrup sheets off the spoon. Pour into hot sterilized jars and seal. Store in a cool, dark, dry place. This syrup is good on hot cakes.

Note: Fresh, wild rose hips can be gathered in early fall from wild rose bushes in many regions of the country.

Sauces

Game Sauce   *Wyoming*

1 cup red currant jelly
2 tablespoons Dijon or Düsseldorf mustard
¼ teaspoon scraped onion
⅛ teaspoon ground ginger
  Grated rind of one orange
  Grated rind of one lemon
½ cup orange juice
2 tablespoons lemon juice.

1. Combine the jelly and mustard in a small saucepan and mix well. Add the onion, ginger, orange rind and lemon rind.

2. Gradually stir in the orange juice and lemon juice. Cook over low heat until sauce is blended. Use to baste broiling or roasting game and serve hot or cold as a sauce for roast venison.

Yield: About one and one-half cups.

Mormon Gravy   *Utah*

3 tablespoons bacon drippings
4 tablespoons flour
3½ cups potato water or milk
  Salt and freshly ground black pepper to taste.

1. Heat the bacon drippings in a small skillet. Sprinkle with the flour and cook three minutes, stirring constantly.

2. Gradually stir in the potato water or milk and bring to a boil, stirring. Season with salt and pepper.

3. Serve with dumplings, noodles or potatoes.

Yield: About one quart.

Honey Whip Sauce   *Utah*

¼ cup soft butter
½ cup honey
½ cup heavy cream, whipped.

Cream the butter and gradually beat in the honey. Fold in the cream. Use sauce for topping hot cakes, waffles or hot desserts.

Yield: About two cups.

Sorghum Butter   *Wyoming*

1 cup sorghum or unsulphured molasses
⅛ teaspoon salt
3 tablespoons butter
⅛ teaspoon nutmeg
⅛ teaspoon baking soda
2 eggs, lightly beaten.

Combine the sorghum, salt, butter, nutmeg and baking soda in the top of a double boiler and heat. Spoon a little hot mixture onto the eggs. Return all to the pan and cook until thick. Use as a spread for bread or sauce for hot desserts.

Yield: About one and one-half cups.

Rum Sauce   *Wyoming*

2 egg yolks, lightly beaten
½ cup confectioners' sugar
1 cup heavy cream, whipped
2 tablespoons dark rum.

Beat the egg yolks and sugar until thickened and lemon-colored. Fold in the whipped cream and rum. Serve with puddings or plain cake.

Yield: About two cups.

Beverages

Elderberry Wine   *Nebraska*

4 cups elderberry blossoms, removed from
  stems
1 gallon water
4 pounds sugar
2 oranges, ground
1 lemon, ground
2 cakes (two ounces) compressed yeast
1 slice toast.

1. Place the blossoms in a kettle and add the
water. Bring to a boil and simmer ten minutes.
Strain off liquid.

2. Combine the liquid, sugar, oranges and
lemon in the kettle and boil fifteen minutes.
Transfer to a crock and cool.

3. Soften the yeast and spread on the toast
slice. Add to crock and let work five to eight days.
Strain and bottle. Cap loosely for first week; then
seal.

Yield: About one gallon.

Rhubarb Wine   *Nebraska*

4 cups fresh rhubarb juice (see note)
8 cups water
6 cups sugar.

Place all ingredients in a stone jar and let stand
twelve to sixteen days. Strain and bottle.

Yield: About three quarts.

Note: The old-fashioned recipe suggested put-
ting the rhubarb stalks through a clothes wringer
to extract the juice, but a much easier way is to
puree the rhubarb in an electric blender and
squeeze out the juice from the pulp.

Beet Wine   *Idaho*

3 pounds unpeeled beets, washed and sliced
  Cold water
2½ pounds sugar
1 pound raisins
¼ cup lemon juice
1 teaspoon cream of tartar
1 teaspoon active dry yeast
1 tablespoon warm water
¼ slice toast.

1. Place beet slices in a kettle and add one
gallon cold water. Bring to a boil and boil two
hours. Strain juice through a cloth. Measure juice
and make up to one gallon again with water.

2. Add sugar and boil ten minutes.

3. Remove from heat and add the raisins and
lemon juice. Let cool. Add the cream of tartar.
Make a paste with the yeast and warm water,
spread on the toast and add.

4. Cover with muslin and let stand two to four
weeks. Strain and bottle. Cork lightly for first
three days; then seal.

Yield: About one gallon.

Dan's Delight (Chokecherry Wine)
South Dakota

1 gallon chokecherries, coarsely ground
1 pound raisins, coarsely ground
3 pounds sugar
4 cups hot water
  Cold water.

1. Place the cherries and raisins in a stone
crock. Dissolve one pound of the sugar in the hot
water and add to the fruit. Add cold water to
cover fruit by one inch. Mix thoroughly. Cover
with one layer muslin and let stand ten days.

2. Strain off the juice. Add another pound of
sugar to the strained juice and return to the
crock. Mix well and let stand ten days.

3. Strain off juice again, dissolve remaining
sugar in it and return to crock. Mix well and let

stand another twenty-one days. Strain and bottle. Cork lightly for the first three to four days; then seal tightly. The wine gets better the longer it is kept.

Yield: About two quarts.

Candies

Making candies at elevations above 2,000 feet requires careful attention to detail, and it is advisable to obtain exact temperature charts from local extension services to ensure success. In general, temperatures required for each stage should be lowered five to six degrees for every 2,500-foot rise above 2,000 feet.

Honey Taffy   *Utah*

1 cup sugar
2 cups honey
1 cup heavy cream.

Place all ingredients in a heavy saucepan and bring to a boil. Boil gently, stirring only to prevent sticking, until mixture reaches hard ball stage or 264 degrees on a candy thermometer. Pour onto a buttered marble slab or heatproof platter and let cool to lukewarm. Grease the hands and pull the taffy until it turns golden. Cut into pieces.

Yield: About one pound.

Easy No-Cook Fudge   *South Dakota*

3 packages semisweet chocolate bits
1 fifteen-ounce can sweetened condensed milk
1½ teaspoons vanilla
⅛ teaspoon salt
1 cup chopped nuts.

1. Melt the chocolate bits in the top of a double boiler. Remove from heat and stir in the milk, vanilla and salt. Stir until smooth. Add the nuts.

2. Pour mixture into a wax-paper-lined roasting pan. Refrigerate two hours; then cut in squares.

Yield: Two pounds.

Caramels   *Utah*

1 cup granulated sugar
½ cup light brown sugar
½ cup light corn syrup
½ cup heavy cream
1 cup milk
¼ cup butter
1 teaspoon vanilla.

1. Place all ingredients except vanilla in a heavy saucepan and heat, stirring, until sugars are dissolved. Increase heat and boil, stirring until temperature on candy thermometer registers 246 degrees, the firm ball stage.

2. Remove from heat, stir in the vanilla and pour into wax-paper-lined pan to depth of three-quarters inch. Cut when cold.

Yield: About one pound.

Beef Candy   *North Dakota*

2 cups granulated sugar
1 cup light brown sugar
½ cup light corn syrup
3 tablespoons butter
½ cup milk
½ cup firmly packed, finely ground cooked beef
½ cup chopped nuts
1 teaspoon vanilla.

1. Combine the sugars, syrup, butter, milk and beef in a heavy saucepan. Cook slowly to 241 degrees, soft to firm ball stage.

2. Cool to 110 degrees and beat with an elec-

tric mixer until creamy. Add the nuts and vanilla and pour into a greased pan. Cool and cut into squares. Store in the refrigerator.

Yield: About one pound.

Dumplings

Raw Potato Dumplings   *North Dakota*

6½ cups flour
 4 teaspoons baking powder
 3 teaspoons salt
 4 cups grated potatoes
 1 large onion, quartered
 1 ham bone
   Boiling salted water.

1. Sift the flour, baking powder and salt together and stir in the potatoes. Add the onion and ham bone to a large kettle of boiling salted water. Drop potato mixture by spoonfuls into the kettle.

2. Cover and cook one hour, or until dumplings are done. Serve with spareribs or pork.

Yield: Six to eight servings.

Potato Dumplings   *South Dakota*

4 cups cold mashed potatoes
3 cups flour
1 teaspoon salt
1 egg, lightly beaten
  Boiling salted water.

1. Combine the potatoes, flour, salt and egg and mix lightly. Form into a roll, cut off two-inch lengths and make into balls.

2. Drop into rapidly boiling salted water, cover and cook fifteen minutes.

Yield: Fifteen servings.

Bread Dumplings   *South Dakota*

2 eggs
½ cup milk
 1 teaspoon salt
 3 cups flour
½ teaspoon baking powder
 4 slices white bread, crusts removed and bread cubed
   Boiling salted water.

1. Beat the eggs, milk and salt together. Sift the flour with the baking powder and gradually beat into egg mixture.

2. Beat until smooth. The dough should be smooth and stiff enough to hold its shape. Stir in the bread cubes.

3. With wet hands, shape the dough into an oblong roll and roll it in wet, triple-thickness cheesecloth. Tie to secure and drop into a kettle of rapidly boiling salted water. Cover and boil forty-five minutes.

4. Remove cheesecloth package, take off cloth and immediately slice roll one-half-inch thick; otherwise the steam cannot escape and the dumplings will be soggy and hard.

Yield: About one dozen; six servings.

Bohemian Cheese Dumplings with Sour Cream   *North Dakota*

3 tablespoons milk
2 eggs
  Salt to taste
2 cups flour, approximately
1 cup ricotta cheese or pot cheese
1 egg yolk
  Freshly ground black pepper to taste
½ cup chopped scallions, including green part
8 cups water
2 cups sour cream
1 cup toasted, buttered bread cubes.

1. Heat the milk to lukewarm. Combine the eggs, salt and milk in a mixing bowl. Gradually

add the flour, stirring. Add just enough flour to make a soft dough. Gather dough into a ball and set aside.

2. Combine the cheese, egg yolk, salt and pepper. Stir in the scallions.

3. Roll out the dough on a lightly floured board until thin. Cut dough into four-inch squares. Place a spoonful of the cheese mixture in the center of each square and fold the dough over to make filled triangles. Pinch sides firmly to seal.

4. Bring the water to a boil in a kettle and add salt to taste. Drop in the dumplings, a few at a time, and simmer until tender, ten to fifteen minutes. Drain dumplings on paper towels.

5. Preheat the oven to 250 degrees.

6. Arrange dumplings in a buttered baking dish and spoon the sour cream over all. Scatter the bread cubes over the sour cream and bake until heated through but not bubbling. Serve hot.

Yield: Ten or more; four to six servings.

5. Southwest

Appetizers and Soups

Crab and Avocado Cocktail
Southern California

1½ cups picked-over Dungeness
    crab meat
1 ripe avocado, peeled, pitted and cubed
¾ cup diced celery
½ cup homemade mayonnaise
    (page 760)
1 tablespoon lemon juice
Heavy cream
Salt and freshly ground black pepper to
    taste
Butter (Boston) lettuce leaves.

1. Combine the crab, avocado and celery.
2. Mix the mayonnaise with the lemon juice and enough cream to make coating consistency. Pour over the crab mixture, season with salt and pepper, toss and chill. Serve on lettuce leaves.
Yield: Four servings.

Smoked Salmon Appetizers
Southern California

6 ounces smoked salmon, cut into 3-by-½-inch
    strips
1 grapefruit, sectioned and each section halved
    crosswise
1 ripe avocado, peeled, cut in eight sections,
    each section halved crosswise

1 cup sour cream
1 tablespoon chopped chives or scallions,
    including green part
Fresh mint leaves.

1. Wrap each strip of salmon around half a grapefruit section and half an avocado section. Secure each appetizer with a toothpick.
2. In a bowl, combine the sour cream with the chives or scallions.
3. Place the salmon appetizers on a serving tray with the sour cream dip. Garnish with fresh mint leaves.
Yield: Six to eight servings.

Seviche
Southern California

1 pound bay or sea scallops, quartered
¾ cup lime juice
½ cup finely chopped onion
3 mild canned chilies, chopped, or to taste
½ teaspoon salt
3 small tomatoes, peeled, seeded and chopped
½ teaspoon oregano
3 tablespoons olive oil
2 tablespoons chopped cilantro (Chinese
    parsley, see note)

Place the scallops in a glass or ceramic bowl and add the remaining ingredients. Refrigerate at least four hours, stirring occasionally, before serving.

Yield: Four servings.

Note: Cilantro is available in Spanish markets.

Veal Tartar with Lemon

Southern California

1 pound boneless veal round, well trimmed and ground just before using
¼ cup lemon juice
1 scallion, including green part, finely chopped
1 tablespoon capers, drained
¼ teaspoon dry mustard
¼ teaspoon Worcestershire sauce
¼ cup pignoli (pine nuts)
  Salt and freshly ground black pepper to taste
10 to twelve thin slices lemon
  Parsley sprigs.

1. Combine the ground veal, lemon juice, scallion, capers, mustard, Worcestershire, pignoli, salt and pepper in a bowl. Chill two hours.

2. Remove mixture from the refrigerator and blend with two forks. Mound servings the size of walnuts on the lemon slices. Garnish with parsley and serve immediately.

Yield: Four to six servings.

Guacamole I

New Mexico

2 ripe avocados, peeled and finely chopped
1 tomato, peeled and chopped
1 tablespoon finely chopped onion
1 clove garlic, finely chopped
2 tablespoons lemon juice or lime juice
1 tablespoon chopped canned green chilies
1½ teaspoons salt
¼ teaspoon freshly ground black pepper
¼ teaspoon cayenne pepper

1 tablespoon chopped cilantro (Chinese parsley, see note)
  Tostados (crisp fried tortilla pieces).

Mix all the ingredients just before serving as the mixture darkens if held for any time. For a smoother texture, the mixture may be blended, in two or three batches, in an electric blender. Chill and serve with tostados.

Yield About three cups.

Note: Cilantro is available in Spanish markets.

Guacamole II

Arizona

2 ripe avocados
1 clove garlic, finely chopped
  Juice of one lemon, or more to taste
  Salt and freshly ground black pepper to taste
2 teaspoons olive oil
1 or two slices onion, chopped
1 small, ripe tomato
1 teaspoon or more chopped chilies, or to taste
  Tostados (crisp fried tortilla pieces).

1. Peel the avocados and discard the pits. Chop the flesh and add the garlic, lemon juice, salt, pepper, oil and onion.

2. Quarter the tomato and remove the seeds. Cut the tomato into bite-size pieces and stir into the guacamole. Add the chilies. Chill until ready to serve. Serve with tostados.

Yield: Four or more servings.

Chile Cheese Appetizers

Texas

4 tortillas
  Fat for deep-frying
⅓ cup grated Monterey Jack cheese or sharp Cheddar cheese
4 jalapeño chilies.

1. Preheat the oven to 400 degrees.

2. Cut the tortillas into quarters and deep-fry in hot fat until crisp. Spoon about one teaspoonful of the cheese onto each quarter. Slice each chile into four strips and place one strip in the center of each appetizer. Arrange on a flat baking sheet and place in the oven until cheese is just melted.

Yield: Sixteen.

Quesadillas   *Southern California*

¾ pound Monterey Jack cheese or sharp
   Cheddar cheese, cut into 4-by-1-inch sticks
   or grated
1 can mild green chilies, seeds and pith
   removed and chilies finely shredded
12 corn or wheat tortillas.

1. Preheat the oven to 400 degrees.
2. Place a cheese stick or two tablespoons grated cheese and chile pieces to taste in the middle of each tortilla and fold in half. Secure each with a toothpick.
3. Place on a baking sheet and bake until lightly browned, about ten minutes. (Alternately, the filled tortillas can be fried, turning once, in oil in a skillet until crisp and the cheese melted.)

Yield: One dozen servings.

Chile con Queso (Cheese Dip)
                                     New Mexico

2 tablespoons butter
2 tablespoons finely chopped onion
1 clove garlic, finely chopped
2 tomatoes, peeled and diced
1 cup roasted fresh green chilies or one-third
   cup canned chopped chilies
2½ cups grated Monterey Jack cheese or
   sharp Cheddar cheese
   Tostados (crisp fried tortilla pieces).

1. In the top of a double boiler, melt the butter and sauté the onion and garlic in it until transparent.
2. Add the tomatoes, chilies and cheese and heat over hot water, stirring until cheese melts. Serve with tostados as dippers.

Yield: Six servings.

Empanaditas   *Southern California*

½ pound ground lean pork
½ pound ground beef round
2 tablespoons chopped onion
1 clove garlic, finely chopped
⅓ cup tomato puree
1 tablespoon chili powder, or to taste
¼ teaspoon ground cumin seeds
1 tablespoon chopped cilantro (Chinese
   parlsey)
   Salt to taste
   Short crust pastry made from two cups
   flour
   Oil for deep-frying (optional).

1. If baking, preheat oven to 400 degrees.
2. Sauté the pork, beef, onion and garlic in a heavy skillet until all the pink color has left the meat.
3. Add the tomato puree, chili powder, cumin, cilantro and salt. Bring to a simmer and simmer, uncovered, fifteen minutes, stirring occasionally.
4. Roll out the pastry to one-eighth-inch thickness and cut into three-inch circles.
5. Place a tablespoon or two of the meat filling to one side of each round. Moisten the edges with cold water and fold over to seal.
6. Either bake on a lightly greased baking sheet about twenty minutes, or until lightly browned, or deep-fry until golden in the oil heated to 365 degrees. Drain on paper towels.

Yield: About three dozen.

Artichoke Hearts in Batter

Southern California

8 tiny fresh artichokes or one eight-ounce can or one package frozen artichoke hearts, thawed
2 lemon slices
  Salt to taste
1 tablespoon oil
1 clove garlic, optional.
Batter:
1 egg
¼ cup milk
1 cup flour
1 cup ice water
½ teaspoon salt
½ teaspoon sugar
2 tablespoons oil
  Peanut oil
  Hollandaise sauce, made according to any standard recipe except increase the lemon juice by one teaspoon.

1. If fresh artichokes are used, remove outer leaves of each, trim off one-quarter inch from top with scissors and cut off base stem. Stand on a trivet in a steamer. Add two lemon slices, salt to taste, one tablespoon oil and one garlic clove if desired to water in the bottom of the steamer.

2. Once the water boils, cover and let steam ten to fifteen minutes, or until artichokes are tender. Drain, cut and peel until only edible part is left. If canned or frozen hearts are used, drain and cut in half lengthwise.

3. To prepare batter, beat the egg; beat in the milk and then the flour, ice water, salt, sugar and oil. The batter will be thin. Let stand thirty minutes.

4. Pour peanut oil to a depth of one-half inch into a skillet and heat to 375 degrees. Dip the artichoke heart pieces in the batter and quickly transfer to the skillet.

5. Cook until golden brown on all sides. Drain on paper towels. Serve with hollandaise sauce separately.
Yield: About four servings.

Avocado with Prosciutto

Southern California

3 large ripe avocados
¼ cup lemon juice
1 cup homemade French dressing, made with lemon juice
  Boston or Bibb lettuce cups (optional)
¾ pound sliced prosciutto
  Lime wedges.

1. Peel the avocados and slice into the lemon juice. Remove and place in the French dressing to marinate ten minutes.

2. Arrange the avocado slices in lettuce cups or on a platter. Arrange the prosciutto slices over and garnish with lime wedges.
Yield: Six servings.

Jicama Appetizer

Southern California

2 teaspoons salt
¼ teaspoon chili powder, or to taste
¼ jicama root, peeled and cut into small sticks or slices (see note)
1 lime, cut into eight wedges.

Combine the salt and chili powder. The sticks of jicama are rubbed with the lime wedges and dipped in the salt-chili mixture before eating.
Yield: Six servings.
Note: Jicama, a root vegetable grown in South and Central America, is crisp, white and faintly reminiscent of water chestnuts.

Texas Caviar

2 twenty-ounce cans dried black-eyed peas, drained

⅓ cup oil
½ cup red wine vinegar
¼ cup finely grated onion
1 clove garlic, finely chopped
½ teaspoon salt
¼ teaspoon coarsely ground black pepper
½ hot chile pepper, finely chopped
 Salad greens.

1. Place the peas in a ceramic bowl or jar.
2. Shake, or beat, together the oil, vinegar, onion, garlic, salt, black pepper and chile pepper and pour over the peas. Chill in the refrigerator two to ten days.
3. Drain the peas and serve piled on top of salad greens.
Yield: Four to six servings.

Pipian   *Texas*

2 cups pumpkin seeds
3 tablespoons butter, melted
 Salt.

1. Preheat the oven to 325 degrees.
2. Toss the seeds with the butter and spread over a baking sheet. Roast in the oven until lightly browned, about twenty-five minutes.
3. Shake and rub seeds gently to remove the husks. Salt to taste.
Yield: Six servings.

Cheese Appetizers   *Southern California*

Basic mixture:
 2 eight-ounce packages cream cheese
 ¼ cup sweet butter
 2 tablespoons heavy cream.
Cheese dip:
 1 tablespoon capers
 ¼ teaspoon paprika
 ½ teaspoon onion juice
  Radish roses.

Cheese balls:
 2 tablespoons dry sherry or cognac
 ½ cup blanched almonds, roughly chopped.

1. To prepare basic mixture, beat together the cream cheese, butter and cream until light and fluffy. Divide in half.
2. To one half, add the capers, paprika and onion juice. Mix well, place in a serving dish and chill. Serve with radish rose dippers.
3. To the second half of the cheese mixture, add the sherry or cognac and chill. Form into walnut-size balls and roll in the almonds. Chill.
Yield: Eight servings.

Sausage Ball Appetizer   *Texas*

2 pounds hot, spicy, bulk sausage meat
2½ cups homemade tart applesauce
⅓ cup candy "red hots."

1. Form the sausage meat into tiny, inch-diameter balls and fry in a heavy skillet until well browned and cooked.
2. Place the applesauce in a saucepan, add the candies and heat, stirring, until they dissolve. Add the meat balls.
Yield: Ten servings.

Caldo de Camaron (Shrimp Soup)
Southern California

1 pound shrimp, shelled and deveined
4 cups boiling salted water
2 large potatoes, diced
1 small onion, finely chopped
1 one-pound can tomatoes
 Salt and freshly ground black pepper to taste
½ teaspoon oregano
1 clove garlic, finely chopped
1½ tablespoons olive oil
 Chili powder.

1. Add the shrimp to the water and cook two minutes. Add the potatoes, onion, tomatoes, salt, pepper and oregano and cook fifteen minutes, or until potatoes are tender.

2. Meanwhile, sauté the garlic in the oil. Add to the soup. Serve in soup bowls, sprinkled with chili powder.

Yield: Four servings.

Sopa de Albondigas (Meat Ball Soup)
Southern California

2½ cups beef broth
2 medium-size onions, finely chopped
2 cloves garlic, finely chopped
8 sprigs fresh mint, leaves removed and chopped
2 pounds lean ground beef chuck
Salt and freshly ground black pepper to taste
Warm tortillas.

1. Heat the broth with half the onion, half the garlic and half the mint until broth boils; then simmer slowly.

2. Combine the remaining onion, garlic and mint with the beef, salt and pepper and mix well. Form into one-inch balls and drop into the broth. Cover and cook gently forty-five minutes. Serve with tortillas.

Yield: Four servings.

Sopa Seca I (Dry Rice Soup) *New Mexico*

3 tablespoons oil or lard
1 cup uncooked rice
1 medium-size onion, thinly sliced
1 clove garlic, finely chopped
1 cup drained, chopped, peeled and seeded tomatoes, fresh or canned
2 cups chicken broth.

1. Heat the oil or lard and cook the rice in it until golden brown, stirring frequently. Add the onion and garlic and cook, stirring, about one minute.

2. Add the remaining ingredients and blend well. Bring the mixture to a boil and lower the heat until the mixture simmers. Cook, without stirring, until most of the liquid has been absorbed by the rice.

Yield: Four to six servings.

Note: Serve with warmed but not crisp tortillas and a bowl of guacamole as a course between the regular soup and main dish.

Sopa Seca II (Dry Rice Soup) *Texas*

1 onion, chopped
1 clove garlic, finely chopped
½ green pepper, seeded and chopped
3 tablespoons olive oil
1 cup uncooked long grain rice
1 cup Italian plum tomatoes, drained
1½ cups chicken broth
¾ cup drained canned garbanzos (chick-peas).

1. Sauté the onion, garlic and green pepper in the oil in a saucepan until onion is translucent.

2. Add the rice and cook over low heat, stirring occasionally, until rice is golden.

3. Break up the tomatoes by squeezing them with the fingers. Add tomatoes and the broth to rice. Bring to a boil, cover and simmer twenty minutes.

4. Add the garbanzos and cook five minutes longer, or until rice is tender and has absorbed most of the liquid. Allow to stand five to ten minutes before serving.

Yield: Eight servings.

Sopa de Queso (Cheese Soup)
New Mexico

2 tablespoons oil
1 tablespoon flour
1 one-pound can tomatoes, chopped

1 onion, finely chopped
2 teaspoons chili powder
4 cups beef broth
½ pound grated Monterey Jack cheese or
   sharp Cheddar cheese
   Sopaipillas (page 626).

1. Heat the oil in a heavy kettle. Blend in the flour.
2. Add the tomatoes, onion and chili powder and stir.
3. Add the cheese and stir to melt. Simmer one hour. Serve with sopaipillas.
Yield: Six servings.

Pork and Mushroom Soup

Southern California

2 pounds pork bones
2 scallions, including some green part
8 cups water
1 slice gingerroot (optional)
4 dried Chinese mushrooms
  Lukewarm water
  Salt to taste
¼ pound lean boneless pork, cut into thin
  julienne strips
¼ pound snow peas
6 thin slivers lemon peel.

1. Place the bones in a three-quart kettle and add the scallions, eight cups water and the gingerroot if desired. Bring to a boil and simmer one and one-half hours. Soak the mushrooms in lukewarm water.
2. Drain mushrooms and cut into thin strips.
3. Strain the broth and add mushrooms, salt and pork. Simmer twenty minutes. Add the snow peas and simmer two minutes longer. Add the lemon peel and serve.
Yield: Six servings.

Egg Drop Soup   *Southern California*

3 cups chicken broth
2 teaspoons cornstarch
2 tablespoons cold water
1 scallion, including some green part, cut into
  one-quarter-inch pieces
1 egg, well beaten
  Freshly ground pepper (preferably white) to
  taste.

1. Bring the broth to a boil.
2. Blend the cornstarch and water and add to broth slowly, stirring. When thickened, add the scallion.
3. Stirring the soup rapidly, gradually add the beaten egg. Remove from the heat immediately and season with pepper.
Yield: Four servings.

Herbed Fresh Pea Soup

Southern California

4 cups shelled tender peas
½ cup water
6 cups milk, at room temperature
8 sprigs fresh marjoram or one-quarter
  teaspoon dried marjoram
1 sprig thyme or one-eighth teaspoon dried
  thyme
2 mint leaves
1 tablespoon sugar
1½ teaspoon salt
   Pinch summer savory
¼ teaspoon chopped parsley
   Pinch chervil
¼ teaspoon chopped celery leaves
½ fresh basil leaf or pinch dried basil
⅛ teaspoon grated lemon rind.

1. Place the peas and water in a saucepan and heat to just below boiling. Transfer to an electric blender.
2. Add the milk, marjoram, thyme, mint and sugar. Place the remaining ingredients in a mor-

tar and pestle and grind together. Add to the blender and blend until smooth.

3. Press the mixture through a sieve into a saucepan. Heat over hot water until soup reaches serving temperature, but do not boil.

Yield: Four servings.

Curried Avocado Soup   *Arizona*

½ cup finely chopped onion
3 tablespoons butter
1 teaspoon or more curry powder
4 cups chicken broth, fresh or canned
1 cup heavy cream
2 ripe avocados
1 tablespoon lemon juice
   Salt and freshly ground black pepper to taste
   Cayenne pepper to taste
½ cup sour cream.

1. Cook the onion in the butter until wilted. Sprinkle with the curry powder, add the broth and simmer five minutes. Stir in the heavy cream and simmer five minutes longer.

2. Peel each avocado and remove the seed. Put the flesh through a sieve or food mill. Or blend avocado in an electric blender, using one-half to one cup of the broth and onion mixture.

3. Stir the avocado into the soup and stir in the lemon juice. Heat thoroughly, but do not boil. Add salt, black pepper and a little cayenne. Serve in hot soup bowls with a generous dab of the sour cream on top of each serving.

Yield: Six to eight servings.

Fresh Corn Soup   *Southern California*

3 ears corn, kernels removed and cobs
   scraped to get out the milk
½ cup chicken broth or water
1 sprig thyme or one-quarter teaspoon dried
   thyme
½ teaspoon salt

⅛ teaspoon celery seeds, crushed
1 sprig marjoram or one-eighth teaspoon
   dried marjoram
1 leaf basil or one-eighth teaspoon dried basil
8 cups hot milk
1 tablespoon butter
1 tablespoon sugar
   Salt and freshly ground black pepper to
   taste
1 tablespoon dry sherry.

1. Place the kernels and milk from the cobs in a heavy saucepan and add the broth or water. Cook three minutes, taking care not to scorch the corn.

2. Place cooked corn, the thyme, salt, celery seeds, marjoram, basil and hot milk in an electric blender and blend until smooth.

3. Strain into a saucepan and add the butter, sugar, salt and pepper. Heat gently on direct heat or over hot water to boiling, but do not boil.

4. Stir in the sherry and serve.

Yield: Four servings.

Cream of Spinach Soup

Southern California

1 pound spinach leaves
1 cup water
2 sprigs summer savory or one-eighth teaspoon
   dried savory
2 sprigs marjoram or one-eighth teaspoon
   dried marjoram
2 sprigs thyme or one-eighth teaspoon dried
   thyme
3 mint leaves or one-eighth teaspoon dried
   mint
   Salt and freshly ground black pepper to taste
4 cups milk
4 cups light cream
2 tablespoons butter.

1. Place the spinach, water, savory, marjoram, thyme, mint, salt and pepper in a saucepan and boil, covered, three minutes.

2. In an electric blender, blend small amounts of the spinach mixture with some of the milk and cream until all are smooth.

3. Place blended mixture in a saucepan and bring to a boil, but do not allow to boil. Add the butter and check the seasoning.

Yield: Eight servings.

Cold Avocado Soup *Southern California*

¼ cup butter
2 cups coarsely chopped leeks, rinsed well and patted dry
1 cup chopped onions
1 tablespoon curry powder
3 cups cubed raw potatoes
4 cups chicken broth
2 ripe avocados
2 cups heavy cream

Tabasco sauce to taste
Salt and freshly ground black pepper to taste.

1. Melt the butter and cook the leeks and onions in it until onions are wilted. Add the curry powder and stir. Add the potatoes and cook over low heat, stirring, about five minutes.

2. Add the broth and bring to a boil. Simmer, skimming the surface as necessary. Cook twenty minutes or longer, or until the potatoes are tender. Let cool.

3. Place the soup in an electric blender. Peel the avocados, dice them quickly to prevent discoloration and add them to the soup. Blend. It may be necessary to blend the soup in two operations. When blended, pour the soup into a mixing bowl and stir in the cream. Add Tabasco, salt and pepper. Chill.

Yield: Eight or more servings.

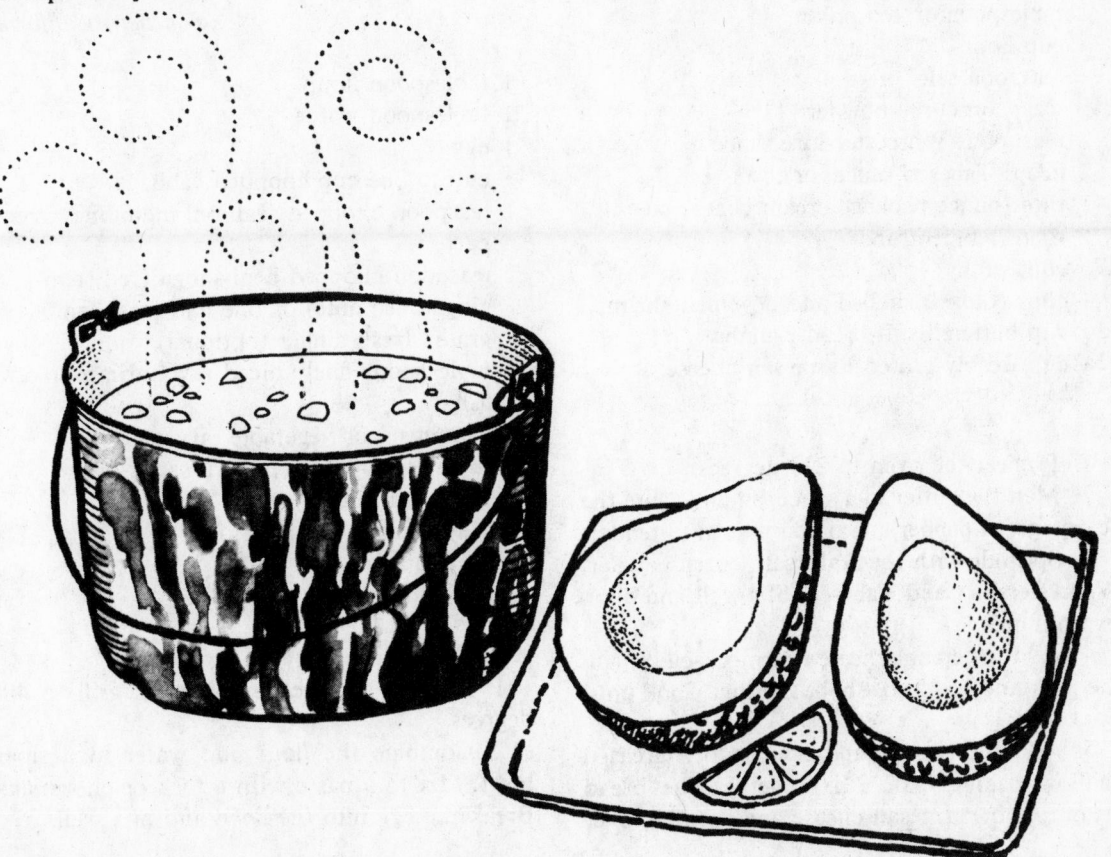

Fish and Shellfish

Shrimp Casserole
Texas

¼ cup butter
1 cup chopped celery
½ cup chopped green pepper
1 tablespoon grated onion
¼ cup flour
¾ teaspoon salt
½ teaspoon curry powder
2 teaspoons Worcestershire sauce
2 drops Tabasco sauce, or to taste
1 three-ounce package cream cheese, at room temperature
1⅔ cups milk
4 cups cooked, shelled and deveined shrimp
⅓ cup buttered soft bread crumbs
¼ cup freshly grated Parmesan cheese.

1. Preheat the oven to 375 degrees.
2. Melt the butter in a saucepan and sauté the celery, green pepper and onion in it until tender.
3. Sprinkle with the flour, salt, curry powder, Worcestershire and Tabasco. Stir well and cook two minutes.
4. Add the cream cheese and mix well. Stir in the milk and bring to a boil, stirring. Cook until thickened.
5. Add the shrimp and pour into a greased shallow baking dish. Mix together the bread crumbs and Parmesan cheese and sprinkle over the top. Bake fifteen minutes, or until hot and lightly browned.
Yield: Six servings.

Okonomiyaki (Japanese Savory Pancakes)
Southern California

1 tablespoon flour
1 tablespoon water
1 egg
½ cup to one cup chopped cabbage
1 teaspoon chopped scallion, including green part
1 teaspoon chopped beni-shoga (red stem ginger, see note) or one-half teaspoon grated fresh ginger (optional)
3 tablespoons finely diced raw shrimp or raw fish
Peanut oil or vegetable oil
Japanese soy sauce, Ikaru sauce or Tonkatsu sauce (see note)
Mayonnaise
Catchup
Hot mustard.

1. Preheat an electric skillet or grill to 400 degrees.
2. Combine the flour and water in a small bowl. Mix to a paste with a fork or chopsticks. Break the egg into the bowl and mix well.

3. Stir the cabbage, scallion, beni-shoga and shrimp or fish into the egg mixture.

4. Rub the hot skillet lightly with absorbent cotton dipped into oil. Spoon or scrape the cabbage batter into the skillet and press down lightly with a pancake turner. The batter should have a round shape like a pancake, five to six inches in diameter.

5. Cook on one side until golden brown, about five minutes. Turn with the pancake turner. Brush the cooked side with soy sauce, Ikaru sauce or Tonkatsu sauce.

6. Cook until golden brown on the other side. Serve with a choice of Japanese sauces, including soy sauce, and with mayonnaise, catchup and hot mustard on the side.

Yield: One serving.

Note: Beni-shoga, Ikaru and Tonkatsu sauce can be bought in Japanese grocery stores such as Katagiri, 224 East 59th Street, New York, New York 10022.

Shrimp with Papaya   *Southern California*

4 ripe papayas
1 cup cooked, shelled and deveined small shrimp
⅔ cup olive oil
⅓ cup red wine vinegar
1 teaspoon salt
¼ teaspoon freshly ground black pepper
   Paprika to taste
1 cup chili sauce
1 cup finely chopped water cress.

1. Cut the papayas in half, carefully discarding all seeds. Peel papayas and cut into slices. Divide the slices and the shrimp equally onto eight plates.

2. Beat the oil with the vinegar. Season with the salt, pepper and paprika. Add the chili sauce and beat until smooth. Add the water cress. Spoon dressing over each serving and serve chilled.

Yield: Eight servings.

Shrimp and Cheese Casserole
Southern California

6 slices day-old white bread, crusts removed and bread cubed
1 pound shrimp, cooked, shelled and deveined
½ pound Monterey Jack cheese or Cheddar cheese, diced
¼ cup butter, melted
3 eggs, beaten
¼ teaspoon dry mustard
   Salt and freshly ground black pepper to taste
   Cayenne pepper to taste
2 cups milk.

1. Arrange layers of bread cubes, shrimp and cheese in a greased casserole and pour the melted butter over all.

2. Combine the eggs, mustard, salt, pepper and cayenne. Stir in the milk and pour this mixture over the casserole contents. If desired, refrigerate overnight.

3. When ready to bake, preheat the oven to 350 degrees.

4. Bake one hour.
Yield: Four servings.

Abalone Santa Barbara
Southern California

⅓ cup flour
½ teaspoon salt
1/8 teaspoon freshly ground black pepper
4 slices abalone, well pounded
1 egg, well beaten
2 tablespoons olive oil
1 tablespoon butter
2 tablespoons lemon juice
1 tablespoon capers.

1. Combine the flour, salt and pepper. Dip the abalone slices into the flour mixture. Dip into the egg and then again into the flour mixture.

2. Heat the oil and butter in a heavy skillet. Add the abalone slices and fry quickly over high heat about two and one-half minutes on each side. (Too long cooking makes the abalone tough.) Sprinkle with the lemon juice and capers before serving.

Yield: Four servings.

Halibut with Orange   *Southern California*

2 pounds halibut fillets, cut into four serving pieces
⅓ cup butter
Salt and freshly ground black pepper to taste
2 tablespoons cognac
1 teaspoon very fine, julienne strips of orange rind
½ cup heavy cream
2 tablespoons chopped parsley
1 orange, cut into very thin slices.

1. Preheat the oven to 350 degrees.
2. Place the fish in a buttered shallow baking dish. Brush with half the butter and season with salt and pepper.
3. Bake twenty minutes, or until fish flakes easily.
4. Heat the remaining butter until it is lightly browned. Stir in the cognac and orange rind. Stir well. Stir in the cream and any liquid from the cooked fish. Bring to a boil and reduce by boiling if too thin. Season with salt and pepper.
5. Add the parsley and pour over the fish. Place the orange slices along length of fillets for garnish.

Yield: Four servings.

Bass with Grapes   *Southern California*

2 one-half-pound bass fillets
Salt to taste
¾ cup sour cream, at room temperature
1 tablespoon freshly snipped dill weed

¼ cup shredded Monterey Jack cheese or Cheddar cheese
3 drops Tabasco sauce, or to taste
1 cup seedless grapes.

1. Preheat the oven to 350 degrees.
2. Place the fillets in a buttered shallow baking dish. Sprinkle with salt.
3. Combine the sour cream, dill, cheese and Tabasco and pour over the fillets. Bake fifteen minutes, or until the fish flakes easily.
4. Scatter the grapes over fish and return to the oven for four minutes.

Yield: Four servings.

Planked Mackerel   *Southern California*

1 three-pound mackerel, cleaned, head removed and fish split
Salt and freshly ground black pepper to taste
½ teaspoon paprika
1 tablespoon lemon juice
1 tablespoon butter
4 cups hot, mashed and seasoned potatoes.

1. Preheat the oven to 450 degrees.
2. Oil a hardwood plank and place the fish on it, skin side down. Season with salt, pepper and paprika. Sprinkle with the lemon juice and dot with the butter.
3. Bake fifteen to twenty minutes, or until the fish flakes easily. Remove the plank from the oven and pipe the mashed potatoes in swirls around the fish.
4. Bake five minutes longer, or until potatoes are lightly browned.

Yield: Four to six servings.

Fish Stew   *Southern California*

2 tablespoons oil
1 green pepper, seeded and chopped
½ cup chopped onion

½ cup chopped celery
1 clove garlic, finely chopped
1 six-ounce can tomato paste
1½ cups water
1 teaspoon salt
¼ teaspoon freshly ground black pepper
1 bay leaf
⅛ teaspoon thyme
2 sole fillets, cut into two-inch pieces
1 pound shrimp, shelled and deveined
2 cups cooked rice.

1. Heat the oil in a saucepan and sauté the green pepper and onion in it until tender. Add the celery and garlic and cook one minute longer.

2. Add the tomato paste, water, salt, pepper, bay leaf and thyme. Bring to a boil and simmer fifteen minutes, stirring occasionally.

3. Add the sole and shrimp and cook six to eight minutes, or until fish is done. Serve over rice.

Yield: Four servings.

Perch with Olives   *Texas*

½ cup butter
4 one-pound perch, split, or two pounds perch fillets
    Freshly ground black pepper to taste
1 tablespoon lime juice
½ cup piñon kernels or slivered blanched almonds
12 stuffed green olives, sliced crosswise.

1. Melt the butter in a heavy skillet. Place the fish, skin side down, in butter. Season with pepper.

2. Sauté until underside is browned. Reduce the heat and add lime juice and nuts to pan. Spoon mixture over the fish, continuing to cook fish until it flakes easily.

3. Scatter the olives over all and spoon the butter mixture over to heat through.

Yield: Four servings.

Salmon Steaks with Grapefruit
Southern California

⅓ cup butter
1 small onion or three shallots, finely chopped
¼ teaspoon ground allspice
½ teaspoon salt
⅛ teaspoon freshly ground black pepper
½ small green pepper, seeds removed and pepper diced
4 one-inch-thick salmon steaks
1 grapefruit, sectioned
½ cup buttered soft bread crumbs.

1. Preheat the oven to 350 degrees.

2. Melt the butter in a small skillet and sauté the onion or shallots in it until tender. Stir in the allspice, salt, black pepper and green pepper.

3. Place the salmon steaks in a buttered shallow baking dish. Spread the onion mixture over each steak. Top with neatly arranged grapefruit sections. Sprinkle the bread crumbs over all. Bake twenty minutes, or until fish flakes easily.

Yield: Four servings.

Artichoke Hearts and Tarragon Crab
Southern California

8 large artichokes
    Boiling salted water
3 Dungeness crabs or four cups fresh crab meat
4 tablespoons butter
3 tablespoons flour
1 cup milk
½ cup dry white wine
¼ cup dry sherry
1 cup heavy cream
    Salt to taste
    Nutmeg to taste
    Cayenne pepper to taste
¼ cup sour cream
¼ cup fresh tarragon leaves, stemmed, or one tablespoon dried tarragon, or to taste

1 tablespoon melted butter
16 tarragon leaves for garnish.

1. Cover the artichokes with boiling salted water and boil one-half hour, or until artichokes are tender. Remove from water and drain upside down in a colander. When cool enough to handle, remove the leaves and carefully discard the "choke" that clings to the heart. Carefully set the hearts aside.

2. Pick the Dungeness crabs or, if crab meat is used, remove bits of shell and cartilage.

3. Melt the butter in a large saucepan. Remove pan from heat and carefully mix the flour into butter until smooth. Return to heat and gradually add the milk, stirring constantly until mixture is thick and smooth. Stirring continuously, add the white wine, sherry and heavy cream. Season with salt, nutmeg and cayenne. Stir in the sour cream and tarragon.

4. Put crab meat into a large skillet. Pour the sauce over and carefully shake the pan to be sure all the crab is covered. Do not use a spoon or fork because the crab must not shred. Heat, but do not boil.

5. Carefully slide the mixture onto a warm platter and surround with artichoke hearts. Brush each artichoke heart with the melted butter and decorate each with a crisscross of the tarragon leaves.

Yield: Eight servings.

Bacalao   *Southern California*

1 pound dried codfish
6 tablespoons oil
1 small onion, cut into thin rings
2 cloves garlic, finely chopped
3 teaspoons chili powder or one green chile, diced
¼ cup water
1 cup peeled, sliced, fresh or canned tomatoes
1 cup buttered soft bread crumbs.

1. Soak the codfish overnight.

2. Next day, preheat the oven to 350 degrees.

3. Drain the fish and place in a buttered shallow baking dish.

4. Heat the oil in a skillet and sauté the onion in it until transparent. Add the garlic and chili powder or chile and cook one minute. Stir in the water. Sprinkle over the fish and add the tomatoes.

5. Top with the bread crumbs and bake twenty-five minutes, or until fish flakes easily.

Yield: Four servings.

Meat, Poultry, Game and Other Main Dishes

Uvalde Chili
Texas

6 tablespoons peanut oil or vegetable oil
3 pounds beef flank or chuck, cut into two-inch cubes
2 or three cloves garlic, finely minced
6 tablespoons flour
6 tablespoons chili powder
1 teaspoon cumin seeds
1 teaspoon oregano
1 teaspoon salt
  Freshly ground black pepper to taste
3 cups fresh or canned beef broth.

1. Heat the oil and add the meat and garlic. Cook, stirring, just until the meat loses its color. Sprinkle with the flour and chili powder.

2. With the fingers, rub the cumin and oregano in the palm of one hand and add to the meat. Add the salt, pepper and broth and bring to a boil. Partly cover and simmer until meat is fork-tender, two hours or longer.

Yield: Six to eight servings.

Texas Chili

5 pounds beef chuck, cut into one-and-one-half-inch cubes
½ cup olive oil
½ cup flour
½ cup chili powder, or to taste
2 teaspoons cumin seeds
2 teaspoons oregano
3 cloves garlic, finely chopped
4 cups beef broth, approximately
1 teaspoon salt
¼ teaspoon freshly ground black pepper.

1. Brown the meat in the oil in a large heavy saucepan. Sprinkle with the flour and chili powder. Cook, stirring, three to five minutes, until meat is coated with flour and chili powder.

2. Place the cumin and oregano in the palm of one hand. Rub the spices between the palms of both hands, letting spices fall over the meat. Add the garlic, four cups broth, the salt and pepper. Bring the mixture to a boil. Cover and simmer very slowly at least four hours. The chili may be cooked over low heat, so that chili barely simmers, for as long as twenty-four hours. More broth may be added during cooking, if necessary.

Yield: Eight to ten servings.

Note: This chili may be frozen after it is cooked. When reheated, it may be necessary to add chili powder to taste to improve the flavor.

Chili con Carne (with Ground Beef)
Texas

3 tablespoons vegetable oil or olive oil
2 cups finely chopped onions
2 cloves garlic, finely minced

1 pound ground round steak
½ pound ground pork
3 tablespoons chili powder, or more to taste
2 cups fresh or canned tomatoes, preferably Italian plum style if canned
2 cups beef broth or water
½ teaspoon celery salt
1 teaspoon cumin seeds
Pinch of oregano
Cayenne pepper to taste (optional)
Salt to taste
2 cups cooked red beans.

1. Heat the oil in a large saucepan and cook the onions and garlic in it until onions are wilted. Add the ground round and pork and cook, breaking up the meat with a wooden spoon. When the meat has lost its red color, stir in the chili powder.

2. Add the tomatoes and half the broth. Reserve the remaining broth to add as the chili cooks. Add the celery salt, cumin, oregano, cayenne and salt and continue cooking, stirring occasionally, one to two hours. Add more broth as necessary.

3. Add the beans or serve separately.
Yield: Four to six servings.

Chili with Hominy and Cheese
Texas

2 tablespoons butter
1 ten-ounce can whole hominy, drained
2 cups Cleto Hernandez's chili (recipe below)
1½ cups grated sharp Cheddar cheese
½ cup finely chopped onion.

1. Preheat the oven to 400 degrees.

2. Melt the butter in a saucepan. Add the drained hominy and cook, stirring, until hominy turns golden.

3. In a buttered one-quart casserole, place a layer of hominy, a layer of chili and a layer of cheese. Continue alternating layers until all ingredients are used, ending with cheese.

4. Bake twenty minutes, or until the casserole is bubbly hot and the cheese is melted. Serve the chopped onion separately.
Yield: Four servings.

Cleto Hernandez's Chili
Texas

1 cup coarsely chopped onions
3 cloves garlic, finely minced
3 tablespoons peanut oil or vegetable oil
1 pound beef round, cut into small cubes or ground
3 tablespoons chili powder
2 tablespoons flour
2 teaspoons cumin seeds
2 cups beef broth
Salt and freshly ground black pepper to taste
Cayenne pepper to taste.

1. Cook the onions and garlic in the oil until onions are wilted. Add the beef and cook, stirring, until meat loses its red color.

2. Stir in the chili powder, flour, cumin and broth and simmer one and one-half hours. Skim off fat and add salt, pepper and cayenne.
Yield: Three or four servings.

Nelson's Chili con Carne
New Mexico

1 pound suet, cut into pieces
4 pounds lean beef round, cut into one-and-one-half-inch cubes
Flour
Salt and freshly ground black pepper to taste
10 cloves garlic, finely chopped
6 medium-size onions, coarsely chopped
3 to five hot jalapeña chilies, chopped
1 two-ounce bottle chili powder
3 tablespoons paprika
2 teaspoons cumin seeds
1¼ cups tomato puree
1 cup water.

1. Place the suet in a skillet and cook over moderate heat to render suet of fat. Discard the rendered suet, but leave the fat in the skillet.

2. Dredge the meat in flour seasoned with salt and pepper. Cook meat, turning the pieces, in the fat until light brown. Add the garlic and stir.

3. Add the onions. When they become translucent, transfer all the mixture to a kettle. Add the remaining ingredients and bring to a boil. Simmer, partially covered, about three hours, or until meat is fork-tender.

Yield: Eight to one dozen servings.

Chili with Rice   *Texas*

3 tablespoons bacon drippings
3 onions, finely chopped
2 green peppers, chopped
4 cloves garlic, finely chopped
3 pounds beef round, cut into one-half-inch cubes
6 tablespoons chili powder
1 teaspoon flour
1 two-pound three-ounce can Italian plum tomatoes
1 tablespoon wine vinegar
1 tablespoon light brown sugar
2½ tablespoons salt
1 tablespoon oregano
1 teaspoon cumin powder
3 bay leaves
3 slices French bread, toasted and broken up
Water, if necessary
½ pound link pork sausage, cooked and sliced
1 cup pitted black olives
2 large cans red kidney beans, drained
2 cups uncooked rice
1 tablespoon lemon juice
4 quarts boiling water
2 tablespoons butter
3 tablespoons heavy cream (optional).

1. Heat the bacon drippings in a large kettle and sauté the onions and green peppers in it until tender. Add the garlic and beef and cook over high heat until meat is browned.

2. Mix the chili powder and flour and add to the kettle along with the tomatoes, vinegar, brown sugar, one tablespoon of the salt, the oregano, cumin, bay leaves and bread. Bring to a boil and simmer, covered, about two hours, or until meat is tender. Add water as necessary if mixture becomes dry.

3. Remove the bay leaves and any surface fat. Add the sausage, olives and beans to mixture. Heat.

4. Meanwhile, wash the rice in a strainer. Add the remaining salt and the lemon juice to the boiling water and gradually sprinkle in the rice. Bring to a boil and boil, uncovered, fifteen minutes. Rice should be barely tender. Drain in a colander.

5. Rinse and dry pot. Place the butter in the pot. When butter has melted, place rice over the butter, cover with a towel and then with the cover and keep warm for at least twenty minutes, shaking occasionally.

6. If desired, add the cream to the chili just before serving. Serve chili over rice or place side by side on plate.

Yield: Six to eight servings.

Texas Spaghetti

4 cups tomato puree
1 eight-ounce can tomato sauce
1 one-pound can tomatoes
¼ teaspoon thyme
¼ teaspoon savory
½ teaspoon sugar
1 cup water
½ pound mushrooms, sliced
2 tablespoons butter
2 pounds round steak, ground
1 onion, chopped
1 clove garlic, finely minced
Salt and freshly ground black pepper to taste
1 tablespoon chili powder

1 tablespoon paprika
1 teaspoon cumin seeds, mashed in a mortar
  and pestle, or one-half teaspoon ground
  cumin
1 pound spaghetti, cooked al dente, drained
1 cup freshly grated Parmesan cheese.

1. Combine the tomato puree, tomato sauce, tomatoes, thyme, savory, sugar and water in a large saucepan and bring to a boil.

2. Cook the mushrooms in the butter until they are wilted. Add the ground meat, onion and garlic and cook, stirring and breaking up the meat with a wooden spoon. When the meat has lost its red color, transfer the meat mixture to the tomato mixture. Add salt, pepper, the chili powder, paprika and cumin. Return to a boil and simmer thirty to forty-five minutes.

3. Serve over the spaghetti. Sprinkle with the cheese.

Yield: Four to six servings.

Hamburgers with Chili   *Arizona*

½ pound pork, ground twice
½ cup minced onion
1½ cloves garlic, finely minced
2 tablespoons olive oil
1 cup tomato puree
½ cup water
3 tablespoons tomato paste
½ teaspoon ground cumin seeds
½ bay leaf
  Salt to taste
1 tablespoon chili powder, or more to taste
2 pounds freshly ground round steak
  Freshly ground black pepper to taste
6 toasted buns
6 pats butter.

1. Cook the pork, onion and one-half clove of the garlic in the oil until meat loses color. Add the tomato puree, water, tomato paste, cumin, bay leaf, salt and chili powder. Simmer, stirring occasionally, about thirty minutes. When finished, the

sauce should have the consistency of thick soup. If necessary, thin with additional tomato puree.

2. Season the ground round with pepper and form into six patties. Broil patties until brown on both sides and pink in the middle.

3. Serve patties on buns, top with butter and spoon chili sauce over.

Yield: Six servings.

Ranch-Style Short Ribs   *Arizona*

2 tablespoons lard or bacon drippings
2 pounds short ribs of beef, cut into two-inch
  lengths
1 large onion, sliced
1 clove garlic, mashed
¼ cup chopped celery
1 cup (one eight-ounce can) tomato sauce
  Juice of one large lemon
1 teaspoon chili powder
1 teaspoon salt
1 tablespoon Worcestershire sauce
2 tablespoons flour.

1. Heat the lard or bacon drippings in a Dutch oven. Brown the meat slowly in it on all sides.

2. Add the onion, garlic, celery, tomato sauce, lemon juice, chili powder, salt and Worcestershire. Simmer, covered, one and one-half hours, or until the meat is tender. Transfer the meat to a hot platter.

3. Skim off excess fat from the drippings in the pan. Mix the flour with a little cold water and add to the juices in the pan. Cook, stirring, until thickened. Pour over the meat.

Yield: Four servings.

Oven-Barbecued Brisket of Beef
New Mexico

1 four-pound to five-pound brisket of beef
¾ cup tomato puree
1 teaspoon Worcestershire sauce
1 teaspoon vinegar

½ teaspoon sugar
2 tablespoons oil
½ teaspoon thyme
½ teaspoon dry mustard
¼ teaspoon liquid smoke (see note)
Salt and freshly ground black pepper to taste.

1. Preheat the oven to 350 degrees.
2. Place the brisket on a large piece of heavy-duty aluminum foil. There should be enough foil to package the beef closely when ready to bake.
3. Combine the remaining ingredients. Bring to a boil.
4. Sprinkle the brisket with salt and pepper and pour the sauce over the meat. Bring up the edges of the foil and seal the meat envelope fashion. Place on a baking sheet and bake two to three hours, or until meat is fork-tender.

Yield: Six or more servings.

Note: Liquid smoke is available at specialty food stores.

Avocado Meat Loaf   *Southern California*

Meat loaf:
1 egg, well beaten
1 pound ground round steak
1 tablespoon finely chopped onion
2 tablespoons celery tops, finely chopped
¼ cup catchup
1½ teaspoons salt
1 cup soft bread crumbs
1 avocado, peeled and roughly mashed
2 tablespoons chopped parsley.
Gravy:
3 tablespoons butter
2 tablespoons finely chopped onion
¼ cup flour
1 cup beef broth
1 tablespoon grated Cheddar cheese
⅛ teaspoon freshly ground black pepper
½ teaspoon Worcestershire sauce
Few drops lime juice or lemon juice
½ avocado, peeled and roughly mashed.

1. Preheat the oven to 400 degrees.
2. Combine all the meat loaf ingredients, mix well and spoon into well-greased twelve-hole muffin tins. Bake twenty minutes. Do not overcook or an acid taste will develop from the avocado.
3. Meanwhile, melt one tablespoon of the butter for the gravy and sauté the onion in the butter slowly until transparent. In a separate small dry skillet, brown the flour, stirring constantly, but do not allow flour to get too brown or to scorch. Add remaining butter, mix well and cool.
4. Add wilted onions to cooled flour mixture. Stir in the broth, cheese, pepper, Worcestershire and lime or lemon juice. Bring to a boil, stirring until thickened.
5. Add the avocado to gravy just before serving. Reheat if necessary, but do not overheat or an acid flavor will develop. Serve gravy over meat loaves.

Yield: Four to six servings.

Meat Balls Stroganoff   *Southern California*

6 to eight slices rye bread with lots of caraway seeds
2 large Bermuda or Spanish onions, finely chopped
½ teaspoon thyme
2 teaspoons salt, or to taste
¼ teaspoon freshly ground black pepper
1 clove garlic, finely chopped
2 eggs, lightly beaten
3 pounds ground sirloin
Oil
3½ cups beef broth
5 bay leaves
1 teaspoon celery seeds
2 tablespoons flour
3 pints sour cream
¾ cup dry sherry.

1. Soak the bread in water and then squeeze as dry as possible. Place the bread and onions in a large bowl.

2. Mix the thyme, salt, pepper and garlic with the eggs and add to the bread mixture. Add the meat and mix well with the hands.

3. Form the mixture into balls about one to one and one-half inches in diameter. Heat oil in a heavy skillet and brown the balls, a few at a time, on all sides. Drain on paper towels.

4. Meanwhile, place the broth, bay leaves and celery seeds in a saucepan. Bring to a boil and boil rapidly six minutes. Remove the bay leaves.

5. Combine the flour and one-quarter cup water. Gradually stir the hot broth into the flour mixture. Return to the pan and heat until broth thickens.

6. Slowly beat the beef broth mixture into the sour cream. Return to the pan and heat slowly, stirring constantly, but do not allow to boil. Set aside to cool to room temperature or hold overnight.

7. Just before serving, reheat sauce very slowly, add meat balls and maintain below boiling until balls are hot. Stir in the sherry. Alternately, the meat balls can be heated in a covered roasting pan in a preheated 350-degree oven fifteen minutes before adding to the hot sauce.

Yield: Nine to one dozen servings.

Dutchie's Meat Balls   *Texas*

1 pound ground beef
1 cup seasoned croutons
1 teaspoon salt
½ teaspoon freshly ground black pepper
¾ cup milk
1 egg, lightly beaten
1 small onion, finely chopped
1 tablespoon sugar
¼ teaspoon nutmeg
⅛ teaspoon ground allspice
¼ cup butter
2 cups beef broth
2 tablespoons chopped parsley.

1. Preheat the oven to 375 degrees.
2. Mix together the beef, croutons, salt and

pepper. Stir in the milk. Add the egg, onion, sugar, nutmeg and allspice. Shape mixture into one-inch balls.

3. Melt the butter in a flameproof one-and-one-half-quart baking dish. Add the meat balls and brown on all sides. Add the broth.

4. Cover the dish and bake thirty minutes, basting meat balls several times with broth. To serve, sprinkle with the parsley.

Yield: Four servings.

Texas Pot Roast

1 four-pound boneless chuck roast
  Salt and freshly ground black pepper to taste
2 tablespoons flour
3 tablespoons oil or rendered suet
1 clove garlic, finely minced
1 teaspoon chili powder
½ teaspoon cumin seeds
3 medium-size whole onions
¾ cup canned Italian plum tomatoes
  Beef broth, water or tomato juice
6 small carrots.

1. Rub the roast with salt, pepper and the flour. In a Dutch oven, brown the meat on all sides in the oil or suet.

2. Pour off most of the fat and add the garlic, chili powder, cumin, onions and tomatoes. Cover closely and cook slowly, adding broth, water or tomato juice as necessary, about two hours.

3. Add the carrots and cover. Cook about one hour longer, or until meat and carrots are tender.

Yield: Eight servings.

Steak Flake   *Texas*

1 tablespoon butter
1 ten-ounce boneless sirloin steak, one inch thick and well trimmed of fat
2 tablespoons finely chopped onion
4 mushrooms, sliced

1 teaspoon Worcestershire sauce
2 tablespoons warm cognac
½ teaspoon gravy coloring and flavoring
Freshly ground black pepper to taste.

1. Heat a heavy skillet until hot enough to sizzle a drop of water. Add the butter and steak and brown one minute.
2. Reduce heat. Add the onion and mushrooms and cook two minutes. Turn. Cook over medium heat six minutes.
3. Add the Worcestershire, cognac and gravy coloring. Remove pan from heat and ignite. Shake pan back and forth. Season with pepper.
Yield: One or two servings.

Ranch Steak   *New Mexico*

⅓ cup flour
1 teaspoon salt
Freshly ground black pepper to taste
1 two-and-one-half-pound sirloin or top round steak, cut one and one-half inches thick
3 tablespoons shortening or oil
1¾ cups fresh or canned beef broth
½ cup water
½ cup barbecue sauce, made according to any preferred recipe
1 teaspoon chili powder
1 green pepper, finely diced
½ cup sliced stuffed olives
Steamed new potatoes and carrots.

1. Combine the flour, salt and pepper and pound into the steak with a mallet or the side of a heavy plate.
2. Heat the shortening or oil in a Dutch oven and brown the meat in it well on both sides. Blend the broth, water, barbecue sauce and chili powder. Pour over the meat. Cover and simmer one hour. Add the green pepper and olives and continue cooking one to one and one-half hours

longer, or until meat is fork-tender. Serve with steamed new potatoes and carrots.
Yield: Four servings.

Gesado (Spanish Stew)   *Southern California*

2½ pounds beef round, cut into cubes
2 tablespoons oil
1 onion, sliced
1 clove garlic, sliced
2 tablespoons flour
1 fifteen-ounce can tomato sauce
1 long green chile, chopped
1 cup dry red wine
1 cup water
1 teaspoon sugar
2 potatoes, diced
Salt and freshly ground black pepper to taste.

1. Brown the meat in the oil heated in a Dutch oven or heavy casserole. Add the onion, garlic and flour. Stir to mix.
2. Stir in the tomato sauce, chile, wine, water and sugar. Bring to a boil, cover and simmer one hour, or until meat is almost tender.
3. Add the potatoes, salt and pepper and cook fifteen minutes longer, or until potatoes are done.
Yield: Four to six servings.

Joe's Barbecued Ribs   *Arizona*

2 teaspoons salt
¼ teaspoon freshly ground black pepper
1 teaspoon paprika
6 pounds spareribs, cut into serving pieces
2 cloves garlic, crushed
¼ cup lemon juice
½ cup dry red wine
1 bay leaf
1 small onion, sliced.
Sauce:
¼ cup bacon drippings
1 cup finely chopped onions

¼ cup chopped celery
½ cup canned tomatoes
½ cup tomato sauce
¼ teaspoon dry mustard
2 tablespoons Worcestershire sauce
1 cup cider vinegar
2 tablespoons light brown sugar
2 canned hot green chilies, seeded and
  chopped
1 teaspoon thyme
½ teaspoon ground cumin.

1. Combine the salt, pepper and paprika and rub into the spareribs. Place in a glass, enamel or ceramic bowl. Combine the garlic, lemon juice, wine, bay leaf and onion and pour over spareribs. Toss to coat.

2. Let stand in the refrigerator six hours or overnight.

3. Preheat the oven to 300 degrees.

4. Combine all the sauce ingredients in a pan and bring to a boil. Simmer two minutes.

5. Drain the ribs and place in a roasting pan. Brush generously with the sauce. Bake one hour. Pour off and discard the fat.

6. Broil the ribs over a charcoal fire or under the broiler, basting frequently with the remaining sauce, until they are dark brown on both sides and cooked.

Yield: Six servings.

Camarillo Sausage and Limas
Southern California

1 pound dried lima beans
  Salt to taste
¼ cup chopped onion
1 green pepper, seeded and diced
  Freshly ground black pepper to taste
1 tablespoon light brown sugar
¼ teaspoon thyme
¼ teaspoon marjoram
⅛ teaspoon summer savory
2 tablespoons chopped parsley

1 pound chorizo (page 587) or pork sausage
1 cup half and half or light cream.

1. Soak the beans overnight in water to cover. Next day, add salt and, with water just covering the beans, bring to a boil. Simmer until barely tender, about twenty-five minutes.

2. Preheat the oven to 350 degrees.

3. Add the onion, green pepper, black pepper, brown sugar, thyme, marjoram, savory and parsley to the beans.

4. Turn the beans into a shallow baking dish.

5. Fry the sausage slowly fifteen minutes and then place on top of the beans. Pour the half and half or cream over all. Bake thirty minutes, or until sausage is cooked.

Yield: Four to six servings.

Bean and Chile Casserole
Arizona

2 cups dried pinto beans
¼ pound salt pork
  Salt
1 four-ounce can diced mild green chilies
3½ cups tomato puree
2 cups chopped onions
1 pound ground round steak
1 pound ground pork
2 cloves garlic, finely minced
1 tablespoon lard or bacon drippings
1 tablespoon chili powder
1 teaspoon ground cumin, or to taste
  Crusty loaf of bread
  Tossed salad.

1. Soak the beans overnight in water to cover.

2. Next day, drain and place in a large kettle with the salt pork and four quarts water. Bring to a boil and cook, partly covered, two hours.

3. Add one tablespoon salt and about half the chilies. Reserve the remaining chilies to add later according to taste. The strength of the chilies varies, and they should be used cautiously.

4. Add the tomato puree and onions. Simmer while preparing the remaining ingredients.

5. Combine the beef, pork and garlic. Cook in the lard or bacon drippings, breaking up meat with a wooden spoon, ten minutes.

6. Add the meat to the beans. Sprinkle with the chili powder, cumin and salt to taste. Stir well and continue cooking one to one and one-half hours, stirring occasionally. Taste, and add more chilies if desired. Serve with a crusty loaf of bread and a tossed salad.

Yield: About eight servings.

Pork Tenderloin en Croute

Southern California

2 fresh pork tenderloins (see note)
3 tablespoons butter
  Salt and freshly ground black pepper to taste
½ teaspoon thyme
  Pastry for a two-crust pie
1 egg, lightly beaten
  Water cress
  Broiled tomato halves.

1. Preheat the oven to 350 degrees.
2. Trim the tenderloins neatly. Melt the butter in a skillet and brown the tenderloins in it lightly on all sides. Sprinkle with salt, pepper and the thyme and let stand while rolling out the pastry.
3. Roll out pastry in a rectangle. The pastry should be less than one-quarter inch thick. Arrange the tenderloins, thick end to thin end, lengthwise on the pastry. Roll up the pastry and seal the edges with water. Tuck in the ends. Place the roll, seam side down, in a flat baking dish. Decorate the top, if desired, with pastry cutouts made from pastry scraps.
4. Beat the egg with one teaspoon water and brush over the top of the roll. Bake forty-five minutes, or until the crust is glazed and brown. Serve garnished with water cress and broiled tomato halves.

Yield: Six servings.

Note: Although fresh pork tenderloins are not commonly available, they may be ordered from many butchers in advance. Some butchers have pork tenderloins available frozen.

Ojai Valley Limas and Pork Chops

Southern California

1 pound dried lima beans
  Salt to taste
2 tablespoons light brown sugar
1 six-ounce can tomato paste
1 onion, finely chopped
¼ teaspoon dry mustard
2 mild green chilies, seeded, deveined and chopped
6 shoulder pork chops.

1. Soak the beans overnight in water to cover. Next day, add salt and bring to a boil in a kettle, with enough water just to cover the beans, until barely tender, about twenty-five minutes.
2. Preheat the oven to 325 degrees.
3. Add the brown sugar, tomato paste, onion, mustard and chilies to the beans and turn into a shallow baking dish.
4. Brown the chops on both sides in a skillet. Place on top of the beans. Bake forty minutes, or until meat is done.

Yield: Six servings.

Gostovich Hungarian Goulash

Southern California

5 tablespoons butter
2 tablespoons oil
2 onions, sliced
2 pounds lean veal or pork shoulder, cut into cubes
  Salt to taste
1 small green pepper, seeded, deveined and sliced into strips
2 tablespoons tomato paste
2 teaspoons sweet Hungarian paprika

1 teaspoon caraway seeds
1 teaspoon marjoram
2 teaspoon cider vinegar
2 cups chicken broth, approximately
3 tablespoons flour
3 tablespoons sour cream.

1. Heat two tablespoons of the butter and the oil in a heavy skillet. Add the onions and cook until they are transparent. Remove onions and reserve.

2. Add the meat to the skillet and brown on all sides. Season the meat with salt and add the green pepper, tomato paste, paprika, caraway seeds, marjoram and cooked onions.

3. Add the vinegar and one cup of the broth. Bring to a boil, cover and simmer gently until the meat is tender, about one and one-half hours. Add more of the broth during cooking as required.

4. In a small saucepan, heat remaining butter and blend in the flour. Gradually add the broth from the cooked meat and bring to a boil, stirring until thickened.

5. Add a little of the hot thickened sauce to the sour cream. Return to the bulk of the sauce and heat, but do not boil. Pour over the meat.

Yield: Four to six servings.

Lamb and Eggplant   *Southern California*

  6 medium-size eggplants
    Boiling water
  3 pounds leg of lamb, ground
  3 tablespoons chopped fresh mint leaves
  ¼ cup cooked rice
  ¼ cup old-fashioned oats
    Tomato sauce (recipe below)
  2 teaspoons salt
  ¼ teaspoon marjoram
  2 tablespoons chopped parsley
  2 eggs
    Lamb bones
  2 teaspoons beef extract (optional)
1½ tablespoons flour.

1. Preheat the oven to 400 degrees.

2. Cut a slice off the stem end of each eggplant.

3. Scoop out some of the pulp, leaving about a three-quarter-inch wall. Steam the eggplants over a large kettle of boiling water eight minutes; do not overcook. Remove, drain and cool.

4. Meanwhile, in a heavy skillet cook the lamb until pink color starts to disappear. Add the mint, rice, oats, one cup tomato sauce, the salt, marjoram, parsley and eggs. Mix well.

5. Stuff the eggplants with the mixture. Set in a shallow baking pan and bake about forty-five minutes, or until tender.

6. Meanwhile, boil the bones with two cups water. Remove the bones and discard. Remove surface fat. Add the beef extract if desired and one to four tablespoons tomato sauce to the broth. Mix the flour with a little water and add to the broth. Stir and cook until it thickens. Serve separately.

Yield: One dozen servings.

Tomato Sauce   *Southern California*

  2 tablespoons olive oil
  ½ cup chopped onion
  1 clove garlic, finely chopped
  ½ green pepper, diced
  1 bay leaf
1¼ cups tomato juice
  ¼ teaspoon salt
  ⅛ teaspoon rosemary
  ⅛ teaspoon thyme
  ¼ teaspoon oregano
  ¼ teaspoon basil
  ¼ cup tomato paste.

1. Heat the oil and sauté the onion and garlic in it until tender. Add the pepper, bay leaf and tomato juice. Simmer fifteen minutes.

2. With a mortar and pestle, grind the salt, rosemary, thyme, oregano and basil together well. Add to the sauce.

3. Add the tomato paste and cook twenty minutes longer.

Yield: About one and one-half cups.

Gostovich Lamb and Vegetable Stew
Southern California

  4 tablespoons oil
1½ pounds breast of lamb, cut into small pieces
    Salt to taste
2½ cups lamb broth, chicken broth or water
  1 large white turnip, peeled and cut into strips
  2 carrots, cut into pennies
  4 onions, thinly sliced
  2 ribs celery, diced
  1 teaspoon fennel seeds, crushed
  1 large potato, diced
  ½ cup string beans, cut into two-inch lengths
  ½ cup fresh peas
  3 large tomatoes, peeled and sliced one-quarter-inch thick
    Freshly ground black pepper to taste
  1 teaspoon lemon juice
  3 tablespoons chopped parsley.

1. Heat two tablespoons of the oil in a heavy skillet and brown the lamb in it on all sides. Season with salt and add the broth or water. Bring to a boil, cover and simmer until the lamb is tender, about one and one-half hours.

2. Remove the meat and reserve. Boil the cooking liquid, uncovered, until it is reduced to about one-half cup. Reserve.

3. Preheat the oven to 350 degrees.

4. Combine the turnip, carrots, onions, celery, fennel seeds, potato, string beans and peas. In a buttered casserole, arrange layers of vegetables, meat and tomato slices. Season each layer of vegetables with salt and pepper.

5. Add the lemon juice, parsley and remaining oil to the reduced broth and pour over. Bring to a boil on top of the stove and then bake, covered, until vegetables are cooked, about thirty-five minutes.

Yield: Four servings.

Indian Zuñi Green Chili Stew
New Mexico

  4 pounds boneless lamb, cut into one and one-half-inch cubes
    Flour
    Salt and freshly ground black pepper
  2 tablespoons peanut oil
  8 juniper berries, crushed
  2 onions, chopped
  2 cans whole hominy with liquid (see note)
    Ground red pepper flakes, chile peppers or chili powder to taste
  2 teaspoons oregano
  ¼ cup chopped parsley
  4 green peppers, cored, seeded and cut into eighths
1½ cups water.

1. Dredge the lamb cubes in flour seasoned with salt and pepper. Heat the oil in a large Dutch oven or heavy casserole and brown the meat in it on all sides.

2. Transfer the meat to another dish and keep warm. Add the juniper berries and onions to the Dutch oven and cook until the onions are golden brown. Return the meat to the Dutch oven and add the remaining ingredients. Simmer one and one-half to two hours, or until the meat is thoroughly tender.

Yield: One dozen or more servings.

Note: Whole hominy is available in many Spanish markets.

Farmers Market Lamb and Cabbage
Southern California

3 pounds lamb shoulder, cut into one-inch cubes

1 head cabbage, cut into one-inch slices and each slice cut into two-inch pieces
3 teaspoons salt
12 white peppercorns, roughly crushed
2 bay leaves
  Water or broth
3 tablespoons chopped parsley
  Boiled potatoes.

1. In a heavy Dutch oven or casserole, place alternate layers of meat and cabbage, sprinkling each layer with salt and peppercorns.

2. Place the bay leaves on top. Add two cups broth or water or enough just to cover. Bring to a boil and skim off any scum.

3. Cover and simmer slowly until meat is tender, about one and one-half hours. Sprinkle with the parsley and serve with boiled potatoes.

Yield: Six servings.

Barbecued Lamb Shanks   *Texas*

2 tablespoons bacon drippings
1 clove garlic
1 cup chopped onions
1½ cups diced potatoes
½ cup diced green pepper
1 cup diced celery
⅓ cup catchup
2 tablespoons light brown sugar
1 teaspoon dry mustard
2 cups beef broth
1 teaspoon salt
⅛ teaspoon cayenne pepper
1 teaspoon chili powder
1 teaspoon Worcestershire sauce
2 slices lemon
8 lamb shanks, uncut.

1. Preheat the oven to 300 degrees.

2. Heat the bacon drippings and cook the garlic and onions in it until transparent.

3. Add the remaining ingredients except the shanks and bring to a boil.

4. Arrange the shanks in an open roasting pan.

Pour the sauce over shanks and bake until lamb is tender, about four hours, basting occasionally. This can all be done ahead of the actual barbecuing.

5. Remove the shanks from the sauce. Pour off and reserve the thin juice from the sauce in the roasting pan, leaving the thick part behind.

6. Place the shanks over white coals on a barbecue grill and baste with the thin liquid. Grill, turning and basting, until shanks are nicely browned.

7. Heat the thick residue in the roasting pan and spoon over the shanks as they are served.

Yield: Eight servings.

Green Chile Burros   *New Mexico*

4 pounds cooked pot roast, shredded or cut into one-half-inch cubes
¼ cup oil
¼ cup flour, approximately
1 teaspoon chili powder
2 small cans green medium hot chilies, seeded, deveined and chopped
1 large onion, chopped
2 cloves garlic, chopped
½ teaspoon oregano
2 cups beef broth
36 large flour tortillas (page 629).

1. Sauté the beef in the oil in a heavy skillet until lightly browned. Sprinkle with one-quarter cup of the flour. Add the chili powder, chilies, onion, garlic, oregano and broth.

2. Heat to boiling and simmer until mixture thickens. If necessary, add a little more flour. The mixture should be quite thick.

3. Heat the tortillas in a skillet or on a griddle. Place three to four tablespoons meat mixture on each. Fold in the sides and roll. Eat like a sandwich.

Yield: About one dozen servings.

Chorizo (Spiced Dried Sausage)

New Mexico

1½ pounds ground beef round
1½ pounds lean ground pork
1 onion, finely chopped
2 cloves garlic, finely chopped
¼ cup wine vinegar
2 tablespoons light brown sugar
1 tablespoon oregano
½ teaspoon coriander
1 tablespoon chopped fresh mint leaves or
  one teaspoon dried mint
3 tablespoons red chili powder
1 tablespoon salt
  Sausage casing (optional).

1. Day before, combine all the sausage ingredients and mix well.

2. Let stand in a cool place or the refrigerator overnight.

3. Next day, stuff into casing if desired, or form into rolls one and one-half inches in diameter and about one foot long and tie in muslin. Hang in shade on a hot day to dry for two days. Remove muslin if used. Slice and fry to cook.

Yield: About three pounds.

Posole (Hominy Stew)

New Mexico

3 pounds pork shoulder, cut into small cubes
6 cups water
6 cups canned hominy
1 small onion, chopped
2 cloves garlic, finely chopped
1 teaspoon oregano
4 red chile pepper pods or three tablespoons
  ground red chile pepper.

1. Place the meat in a kettle and cover with the water. Bring to a boil, cover and simmer until meat is tender, about one and one-half hours.

2. Add the remaining ingredients and simmer for one-half hour longer.

Yield: One dozen servings.

Chicken Mole

Texas

2 three-and-one-half-pound to four-pound
  chickens, cut into quarters
½ cup olive oil
2 tablespoons paprika
2 bay leaves, crumbled
  Salt and freshly ground black pepper to
  taste
1 teaspoon oregano
1 recipe mole sauce (recipe below),
  simmering.

1. Day before, place the chickens in a glass, stainless steel or enamel pan and add the oil, paprika, bay leaves, salt, pepper and oregano.

2. Turn the chicken in the mixture until parts are well coated. Cover and refrigerate overnight. Once in a while turn the chicken in the mixture.

3. Next day, drop the chicken into the simmering mole sauce and cook one hour or longer, or until chicken is fork-tender.

Yield: Eight servings.

Mole Sauce

Texas

½ cup peanut oil
2 cups finely chopped onions
½ cup chopped, long, medium-hot red
  peppers (see note)
2 tablespoons chopped garlic
½ cup finely chopped mushrooms
¾ cup finely chopped green pepper
3 ounces mole powder (see note)
1½ tablespoons flour
2 cups cold water
1 teaspoon oregano
4 bay leaves
2 six-ounce cans tomato paste
5 cups fresh or canned beef broth
1 ounce Mexican chocolate (see note)
  Salt to taste
1 tablespoon cornstarch, blended with a
  little water (optional).

1. Heat the oil in a large casserole or kettle.

2. Add the onions, red peppers, garlic, mushrooms and green pepper. Cook, stirring frequently, until onions are golden brown.

3. Combine the mole powder with the flour and stir into the casserole. While stirring, add the water, oregano, bay leaves, tomato paste and broth. Add the chocolate and stir until it is dissolved. Continue cooking, stirring occasionally, about two hours. Season with salt. If desired the sauce may be thickened with the cornstarch.

Yield: About three quarts.

Note: A small amount of canned jalapeños or chilies serranos may be substituted. These chilies are fiery hot and are available at Casa Moneo, 210 West 14th Street, New York, New York 10011, and Spanish grocery stores.

Mole powder is available in cans at Casa Moneo and Spanish groceries.

El Popular brand of Mexican chocolate is available at Casa Moneo.

Enchiladas Verdes al Estilo de Mi Casa (Chicken and Tortilla Casserole)

Arizona

3 whole chicken breasts
  Chicken broth
12 tortillas, fresh or canned
2 cans tomatillas (Mexican green tomatoes)
2 onions, finely chopped
3 tablespoons oil
1 three-ounce can green mole powder
  Salt to taste
2 cups grated Monterey Jack cheese or Cheddar cheese
2 cups heavy cream, heated.

1. Preheat the oven to 300 degrees.

2. Place the chicken breasts in a large pan and add broth to cover. Bring to a boil and simmer twenty to thirty minutes, or until done. Cool. Remove and discard the skin and bones from the chicken. Reserve the broth. Cut the chicken meat into strips.

3. Meanwhile, place the tortillas in the oven and bake until crisp and slightly browned. Break the tortillas into quarters or eighths.

4. Drain the tomatillas and remove and discard the skins; chop the pulp and add the onions.

5. Heat the oil and add the mole powder. Cook briefly, stirring. Add the green tomato mixture. When it begins to simmer, stir in four cups of the reserved chicken broth. Simmer the sauce until it is slightly thickened and there is no "raw" taste. Season with salt.

6. Increase the oven heat to 350 degrees.

7. Using one or two baking dishes, arrange a layer of tortillas, a layer of chicken and a layer of sauce, in that order. Repeat until all ingredients have been used, ending with the sauce. Dredge the top with the cheese.

8. Bake fifteen to twenty minutes, or until mixture is bubbling and cheese is slightly browned. Pour the warm cream over the casserole and serve immediately.

Yield: Eight to ten servings.

Tamales

Arizona

18 cornhusks, aluminum foil or parchment paper
3 cups yellow corn meal
¼ cup soft butter
¼ cup soft lard
1 teaspoon baking powder
  Salt
1½ cups hot chicken broth
1 cup shredded cooked chicken
1 cup Mexican-style chili sauce
2 cloves garlic, minced
1 tablespoon cumin seeds, crushed
  Freshly ground black pepper to taste
  Chili powder to taste.

1. Soak the cornhusks for two hours in warm water to cover. If husks are not available, cut eighteen pieces of aluminum foil or parchment paper about ten inches square.

2. Place the corn meal in a bowl. Add the

butter, lard, baking powder and one-half teaspoon salt. Blend well.

3. Add the broth, while beating, until a light, soft dough that barely holds together when molded with the fingers is formed.

4. Make a filling by combining the chicken, chili sauce, garlic and cumin. Add pepper, chili powder and salt to taste.

5. If cornhusks are used, drain them. Spread the middle of each husk, foil or parchment paper square with two tablespoons of the corn meal mixture, making a square (4 by 4 inches). Place a spoonful of the chicken filling down the center of each square.

6. Roll each husk or foil square to enclose the filling in the dough and envelop the tamale. Tie securely at both ends with strips of cornhusk or fold the ends of the foil securely.

7. Steam over boiling water in covered pot one hour.

Yield: Eighteen tamales.

Green Enchiladas   *Texas*

    2 small cans whole peeled mild green chilies
    ½ clove garlic
    1 medium-size onion, quartered
    2 medium-size tomatoes, peeled and
        quartered
    ½ cup peanut oil or vegetable oil
    1 cup sour cream
    ½ cup grated sharp Cheddar cheese
    1½ cups shredded stewed chicken
    12 tortillas.

1. Place the chilies, garlic, onion and tomatoes in the container of an electric blender. Blend thoroughly.

2. Heat one tablespoon of the oil in a skillet and add the blended mixture. Cook, stirring frequently, until slightly thickened.

3. Combine the sour cream and cheese and stir well. Add the chicken and blend.

4. Heat the remaining oil in a skillet and dip the tortillas into it briefly, turning once. This is only to soften the tortillas. Do not brown them.

5. Dip the tortillas, one at a time, into the chile mixture so that they are generously coated on both sides. Spoon equal amounts of the sour cream and chicken mixture inside each tortilla. Roll. Cover with remaining hot green chile mixture and serve immediately.

Yield: Six servings.

Chicken Verde   *Texas*

    ½ cup loosely packed fresh coriander (cilantro
        or Chinese parsley)
    2 cups chopped onions
    1 clove garlic, finely minced
    1 ten-ounce can tomatillas (Mexican green
        tomatoes)
    Salt and freshly ground black pepper to
        taste
    2 two-and-one-half-pound chickens, cut into
        serving pieces
    3 tablespoons lard.

1. Combine the coriander, onions, garlic and tomatillas with their packing liquid in the container of an electric blender. Blend well and season with salt and pepper.

2. Brown the chicken parts lightly in the lard and season with salt and pepper. Pour the blended mixture over all and simmer, covered, about one hour, or until tender.

Yield: Four to six servings.

Old-Fashioned Tamale Pie   *Texas*

Filling:
    1 tablespoon peanut oil or bacon drippings
    2 onions, finely chopped
    1 to two cloves garlic, finely minced
    1 green pepper, cored, seeded and chopped
    ¾ pound round steak, ground
    1 tablespoon chili powder, or to taste
    ½ teaspoon ground cumin
    2 cups fresh or canned tomato sauce
    1½ cups corn kernels, scraped from the cob or

one twelve-ounce can whole kernel corn,
drained
1 teaspoon sugar (optional)
Salt and freshly ground black pepper to
taste
1½ cups grated sharp Cheddar cheese
Corn meal crust:
¾ cup yellow corn meal
½ teaspoon salt
2 cups water
2 tablespoons butter.

1. To prepare filling, heat the oil or bacon
drippings in a large skillet and cook the onions,
garlic and green pepper in it until vegetables are
wilted. Add the meat, using a slotted spoon to
break up lumps. Cook until meat loses its red
color. Sprinkle with the chili powder and cumin
and stir in the tomato sauce, corn, sugar, salt and
pepper. Simmer thirty minutes; then remove mixture from the heat. Let cool slightly.
2. Preheat the oven to 375 degrees.
3. Make alternate layers of the filling and the
cheese in a greased one-and-one-half-quart baking dish.
4. To prepare crust, stir the corn meal and salt
into the water. Cook, stirring constantly, until
thickened. Stir in the butter. Spoon mixture over
the casserole and smooth with the back of a
spoon. Bake forty minutes.
Yield: Six servings.

Tamale Peppers   *New Mexico*

 2 cups canned Italian plum tomatoes
½ cup yellow corn meal
Salt and freshly ground black pepper to
taste
 1 tablespoon chili powder, or to taste
½ teaspoon ground cumin
 1 tablespoon olive oil
½ cup finely chopped onion
 1 clove garlic, finely minced
 1 cup chopped cooked ham
 1 cup cooked whole kernel corn

 6 large green peppers, cored and seeded
 1 cup grated sharp Cheddar cheese
Boiling water.

1. Preheat the oven to 350 degrees.
2. Heat the tomatoes in a skillet and add the
corn meal, salt, pepper, chili powder and cumin.
Cook, stirring, about ten minutes.
3. Meanwhile, heat the oil and cook the onion
and garlic in it until onion is wilted. Add to the
tomato mixture along with the ham and corn.
4. Parboil the green peppers three to five
minutes and drain. Fill peppers with the tomato
mixture and top with the cheese. Arrange them
in a baking dish and pour around them boiling
water to the depth of one-half inch. Bake forty-
five minutes to one hour.
Yield: Six servings.

Cream Chicken Enchiladas   *New Mexico*

 1 five-pound fat chicken
Salt to taste
12 peppercorns
 2 ribs celery with leaves
 2 carrots, quartered
 1 onion, studded with four whole cloves
36 tortillas
Fat for deep-frying
 4 cups chopped onions
 2 green peppers, cored, seeded and chopped
 4 cups Italian plum tomatoes
 2 cups fresh or canned tomato sauce
 1 four-ounce can whole medium-hot green
chilies, chopped
 1 clove garlic, finely minced
¼ cup butter
¼ cup flour
 2 cups milk
 1 cup heavy cream
¾ pound grated sharp Cheddar cheese.

1. Place the chicken in a kettle and add water
to cover. Add salt, the peppercorns, celery, carrots and whole onion. Bring to a boil, partly cover

and simmer two hours or longer, or until chicken is fork-tender. Remove from heat and let cool.

2. When cool, skim off one-half cup of chicken fat and reserve. Remove chicken and remove the meat from the bones. Set meat aside and return the chicken skin and bones to the kettle. Return the chicken broth to a boil and simmer thirty minutes longer.

3. Preheat the oven to 350 degrees.

4. Cut the tortillas in half and fry them lightly in deep fat. Drain.

5. Heat the reserved chicken fat and cook the chopped onions and green peppers in it until tender. Add the tomatoes, tomato sauce, green chilies and garlic. Cook twenty minutes. Add salt to taste.

6. Meanwhile, melt the butter in a large saucepan and stir in the flour, using a wire whisk. When blended, add the milk and cream, stirring vigorously with the whisk. Add one cup of the broth from the kettle and continue stirring until mixture comes to a boil. Simmer, stirring occasionally, fifteen minutes. Cool slightly and add the tomato mixture.

7. In a large Dutch oven or other utensil, make alternate layers of chicken, tortillas, sauce and cheese. Reserve some of the cheese to put on top of the casserole. When layers are finished, sprinkle with remaining cheese and bake one hour or longer, or until piping hot, lightly browned and bubbling.

Yield: One dozen or more servings.

Tacos   *New Mexico*

1 pound ground beef round or lean pork
1 small onion, finely chopped
1 clove garlic, finely chopped
2 large tomatoes, peeled and chopped
2 teaspoons oregano
  Shortening
8 corn tortillas (page 629)
2 cups shredded sharp Cheddar cheese
1 small head lettuce, finely shredded
1 recipe taco sauce (recipe below).

1. Preheat the oven to 400 degrees.

2. Fry the meat in a skillet until well browned and cooked. Add the onion, garlic, tomatoes and oregano and cook five minutes longer.

3. Melt shortening to a depth of one-quarter inch in a skillet and heat. Dip the tortillas in the shortening just to soften. Do not allow to become crisp.

4. Fold tortillas in half. Fill with meat mixture and the cheese and place on a baking tray. Heat in the oven five minutes, or until crisp. Top with the lettuce and serve with taco sauce.

Yield: Four servings.

Taco Sauce   *New Mexico*

1 eight-ounce can tomato sauce
1 clove garlic, finely chopped
½ teaspoon cider vinegar
½ teaspoon oregano
½ teaspoon ground cumin
3 teaspoons chili powder, or to taste.

Combine all ingredients
Yield: About one cup.

Stacked Enchiladas   *New Mexico*

  Shortening
12 corn tortillas (page 629)
1½ cups grated Cheddar cheese
6 tablespoons finely chopped onion
1 recipe chile sauce (next recipe)
6 fried eggs.

1. Preheat the oven to 400 degrees.

2. Melt shortening to a depth of one-quarter inch in a skillet and heat. Dip the tortillas into the shortening, but do not allow to get crisp.

3. Sprinkle six of the tortillas with half the cheese and half the onion. Spoon half the chile sauce over. Place another fried tortilla on top of each. Spoon remaining chile sauce over and then top with remaining onion and cheese.

4. Bake five minutes, or until cheese melts. Top each with one fried egg.

Yield: Six servings.

Chile Sauce   *New Mexico*

    2 tablespoons shortening
    1 tablespoon flour
    1 eight-ounce can tomato sauce
    6 tablespoons red chili powder, or to taste
 1½ cups water
      Salt to taste.

1. Melt the shortening, stir in the flour and heat over medium heat, stirring until flour turns brown. Do not allow to burn.

2. Mix together the tomato sauce, chili powder, water and salt and add to the browned flour. Cook, stirring, ten minutes.

Yield: About two cups.

Mission Enchiladas   *Southern California*

    2 pounds dried red chile peppers
    3 cloves garlic
    1 teaspoon oregano
  ⅛ teaspoon cumin seeds
 1½ cups olive oil
    6 tablespoons flour
   12 corn tortillas (page 629)
 1½ pounds Monterey Jack cheese or Cheddar
      cheese, grated
    2 onions, finely chopped
    2 cups ripe olives, sliced.

1. Wash the chile peppers very well. Remove the seeds and veins. Wash peppers again.

2. Cover the chilies with cold water and bring to a boil. Drain off the water and wash again. Grind the peppers and force through a sieve. Mash the garlic and add with the oregano and cumin to the chilies.

3. Add two cups water and set aside.

4. Heat one-half cup of the oil in a skillet and add the flour. Stir and heat until flour is browned. Gradually add to the chile mixture. Simmer twenty minutes.

5. Heat remaining oil in another skillet and fry the tortillas in it until soft and hot on both sides. Dip tortillas into the chile sauce. Place tortillas on a warm platter.

6. Preheat the oven to 350 degrees.

7. Divide half the cheese among the tortillas; top with a little onion and a few bits of olive. Roll the tortillas and place in a greased baking dish.

8. Sprinkle remaining cheese, onions and olives over tortillas and pour remaining chile sauce over all. Bake thirty minutes.

Yield: One dozen servings.

Texas Tamales

Tamale wrappers:
36 cornhusks (see note).
Filling:
    2 pounds lean pork shoulder, cut into
      three-inch cubes
      Salt to taste
   12 peppercorns, crushed
    1 hot red pepper pod or one-half teaspoon
      dried red pepper flakes
  ¼ cup chili powder
  ¼ cup paprika
    1 tablespoon oregano
    1 tablespoon cumin seeds
    1 teaspoon cayenne pepper
      Freshly ground black pepper
    5 cloves garlic, finely minced.
Tamale paste:
3½ cups tamalina (see note) or three cups
      white corn meal
    1 cup lard, at room temperature
    1 tablespoon salt
      Chicken broth or beef broth
    2 teaspoons chili powder.

1. Cover the husks with boiling water and let stand at least one hour.

2. To prepare filling, place the meat in a kettle

and add water to cover, salt, the peppercorns and pepper pod. Bring to a boil and simmer until pork is fork-tender, about one and one-half hours. Drain, but reserve the pork broth.

3. Put the pork through a meat grinder; then place in a mixing bowl and add the spices, garlic and one cup of the reserved broth. Cover and let stand until ready to use.

4. To prepare paste, place the tamalina or corn meal in a mixing bowl and cut in the lard with a pastry blender. Add the salt.

5. Add enough chicken or beef broth to the remaining reserved pork broth to make about three cups. Add the chili powder and stir.

6. If tamalina is used, the broth should be warm. If corn meal is used, the broth should be boiling. Add the broth gradually. Use just enough to make a thoroughly workable but not too wet paste.

7. Drain the cornhusks well. Spread a square of paste about one-eighth-inch thick in the center of each husk. With the fingers, roll a tablespoon or two of the filling into a cigarette shape and place in the center of the paste. Roll the husk rather loosely, cigarette style, so that the paste encloses filling. Tie ends together with thin strips of cornhusks.

8. Place the tamales on a rack in a steamer and steam over boiling water about one hour. Make certain that all the water does not evaporate during the steaming. Add more water as necessary. As an alternative, the tamales may be boiled in chicken broth to cover, but the steaming method is generally preferred.

Yield: Three dozen tamales.

Note: Serve hot with tamale sauce, Tabasco sauce and lemon wedges if desired. Cornhusks and tamalina are frequently available at Casa Moneo, 210 West 14th Street, New York, New York 10011, and other Spanish groceries. If you cannot get cornhusks, substitute six-inch squares of aluminum foil or parchment paper. Husks are preferable, however, because they add flavor.

Empanadas
Arizona

2 tablespoons olive oil
1 medium-size onion, finely chopped
1 medium-size green pepper, seeded and finely chopped
1 medium-size tomato, chopped
¼ pound ground beef chuck
½ cup chopped pimento-stuffed green olives
1 hard-cooked egg, chopped
¼ cup raisins
½ teaspoon freshly ground black pepper
1 tablespoon sugar
3¼ cups plus one tablespoon flour
¼ teaspoon salt
6 tablespoons butter
¾ cup water
Fat for deep-frying.

1. Heat the oil in a saucepan. Add the onion, green pepper, tomato and beef and cook until onion wilts. Add the olives, egg, raisins, black pepper and sugar. Blend.

2. Blend all but one tablespoon of the flour with the salt. Melt one tablespoon of the butter and reserve. With pastry blender or two knives, cut remaining butter into flour mixture. Add the water and mix well. Let stand ten minutes.

3. Roll out pastry to one-eighth-inch thickness or less. Brush with reserved melted butter and sprinkle with reserved flour.

4. Fold half the dough and roll again to one-eighth-inch thickness or less. Cut into thirty-two two-inch rounds. Arrange a teaspoon of filling on sixteen of the rounds. Top with remaining rounds and seal with fork tines. Prick tops. Repeat with second half of pastry.

5. Fry the turnovers in deep fat heated to 375 degrees five to seven minutes, or until golden brown on both sides. Drain on paper towels.

Yield: Thirty-two empanadas; eight servings.

Orange Walnut Chicken

Southern California

1½ teaspoons salt
1 tablespoon curry powder
1 two-and-one-half-pound to three-pound chicken, cut into serving pieces
⅓ cup melted butter
2 teaspoons julienne strips of orange rind
¾ cup orange juice
1 cup chopped fresh pineapple or tidbits with juice
⅓ cup walnut halves
⅓ cup raisins
¼ teaspoon cinnamon
2 oranges, peeled and sliced
1 tablespoon flour
2 tablespoons water
1 teaspoon soy sauce.

1. Preheat the oven to 400 degrees.
2. Mix the salt with the curry powder and use to sprinkle the chicken pieces. Rub into the flesh. Dip the pieces into the butter and place, skin side down, in a shallow baking pan.
3. Bake ten minutes, turn the pieces and bake ten minutes longer.
4. Meanwhile, combine the orange rind, orange juice, pineapple, walnuts, raisins and cinnamon in a saucepan. Bring to a boil.
5. Reduce the oven heat to 350 degrees. Pour boiling mixture over chicken and bake thirty minutes longer, or until chicken is done.
6. Pour the pan juices into a saucepan. Arrange the chicken in a serving dish, garnish with the orange slices and keep warm.
7. Combine the flour, water and soy sauce and stir into the pan juices. Bring to a boil, stirring, and cook two minutes. Pour over garnished chicken.

Yield: Four servings.

Chicken with Artichokes

Southern California

3 tablespoons butter
1 three-and-one-half-pound chicken, cut into serving pieces
1 tablespoon finely chopped shallot or scallion, including green part
½ tablespoon flour
1 tablespoon tomato paste
1 cup chicken broth
¾ cup dry white wine
¼ cup finely chopped parsley
1 sprig fresh rosemary or one-half teaspoon dried rosemary
Salt and freshly ground black pepper to taste
6 small artichokes, trimmed, cut in half and "choke" removed, or one package frozen artichokes.

1. Preheat the oven to 350 degrees.
2. Heat the butter in an ovenproof skillet and brown the chicken in it on all sides. Remove the chicken to a warm place. Add the shallot or scallion to skillet. Cook, stirring, one minute. Sprinkle with the flour and cook, stirring, one minute longer.
3. Add the tomato paste, stir it around in the skillet and add the broth and wine. Simmer five minutes. Return the chicken to the skillet and sprinkle with the parsley, rosemary, salt and pepper. If fresh artichokes are used, add them now. If frozen artichokes are used, add them for the last fifteen minutes of cooking.
4. Cover the skillet and bake thirty to forty-five minutes.

Yield: Four servings.

Chicken au Chou

Texas

1 three-and-one-half-pound to four-pound broiler chicken, left whole
Salt and freshly ground black pepper

1 onion, chopped
6 slices bacon
1 head cabbage, separated into leaves.

1. Prepare a charcoal fire and let stand until coals are covered with white ash.
2. Sprinkle the inside of the chicken with salt and pepper and add the onion. Cover the chicken with the bacon and wrap in the cabbage leaves. Tie securely with string and place on the grill about one foot from the coals. Cover with a hood and cook, turning occasionally, about three hours.
Yield: Two servings.

Chicken Castillia   *Texas*

¼ cup butter
1 cup finely chopped onions
1 clove garlic, finely minced
½ cup finely chopped green pepper
1½ cups chopped peeled ripe tomatoes or canned Italian plum tomatoes
2 tablespoons chopped parsley
3 tablespoons currants or raisins
2 cups strongly flavored chicken broth
1 cup dry white wine
    Salt and freshly ground black pepper to taste
3 cups cubed cooked chicken
    Tabasco sauce to taste
1 cup blanched almonds
    Cooked rice.

1. Melt the butter and add the onions, garlic and green pepper. Cook until onions are wilted, but do not brown.
2. Cook the tomatoes, stirring frequently until they thicken slightly. Add them to the vegetable mixture. Add the parsley, currants or raisins, broth and wine. Season with salt and pepper and simmer twenty minutes.
3. Add the chicken and Tabasco and simmer

ten minutes longer. Stir in the almonds. Serve piping hot with rice.
Yield: Four to six servings.

Chicken Almond   *Texas*

6 tablespoons peanut oil
1 cup blanched, split almonds
2 cloves garlic, finely chopped
2 teaspoons salt
4 cups raw chicken (white meat only), cut into one-half-inch cubes
2 nine-ounce packages frozen Italian green beans, slightly thawed
2 cups celery, cut into one-eighth-inch slices
1 cup scallions, including green part, cut into one-quarter-inch slices
1 cup water chestnuts, drained and sliced
1 cup bamboo shoots, drained
¼ pound mushrooms, sliced
4 cups boiling chicken broth
7 tablespoons cornstarch
⅓ cup soy sauce
2 tablespoons water
    Cooked rice.

1. In a large skillet, heat three tablespoons of the oil.
2. Add the almonds and sauté until golden; drain and reserve.
3. Add remaining oil to the skillet with the garlic and salt. Cook, stirring, until garlic turns golden. Add the chicken cubes and cook until they turn white, about five minutes.
4. Add the beans and celery, cover skillet and cook ten to twelve minutes over medium heat. Vegetables should be crisp.
5. Add the scallions, water chestnuts, bamboo shoots and mushrooms. While stirring, add the broth.
6. Mix the cornstarch with the soy sauce and water. Pour into the skillet and cook, stirring, just until mixture thickens.
7. Add half the almonds and stir in. Sprinkle

finished dish with remaining almonds and serve over rice.

Yield: One dozen servings.

Pollo en Salsa (Chicken in Sauce)

Arizona

2 three-and-one-half-pound to four-pound chickens
  Salt and freshly ground black pepper to taste
¼ cup oil
4 carrots, diced
2 scallions, including green part, sliced
3 ribs celery, diced
1 onion, chopped
2 cloves garlic, chopped
1 bay leaf
1 sprig fresh thyme or one-eighth teaspoon dried thyme
¼ cup chopped parsley
1 cup dry red wine
¼ cup butter
¾ pound mushrooms, sliced
1 large red sweet pepper, seeded and cut into strips
1½ cups pitted ripe olives
3 tablespoons flour
1¼ cups chicken broth.

1. Preheat the oven to 400 degrees.
2. Season the chickens inside and outside with salt and pepper and truss for roasting. Rub each chicken with two tablespoons of the oil and place, breast side up, in a roasting pan.
3. Roast twenty minutes, or until lightly browned. Reduce the oven heat to 325 degrees.
4. Scatter the carrots, scallions, celery, onion, garlic, bay leaf, thyme and parsley around the chickens. Pour in one-half cup of the wine.
5. Roast, basting occasionally with the pan liquids, one and one-half hours, or until chickens are cooked.
6. Remove vegetables and liquid to an electric blender and blend until smooth.

7. Melt the butter in a skillet and cook the mushrooms in it three minutes. Add the red sweet pepper and olives and heat through.
8. Place pepper, olives and mushrooms on warm platter. Place chickens on top.
9. Stir the flour into the liquid remaining in the skillet and add blended vegetables, broth and remaining wine. Bring to a boil and simmer three minutes. Serve separately.

Yield: Six to eight servings.

Chicken with Pumpkin Seed Sauce

New Mexico

1 two-and-one-half-pound to three-pound chicken, cut into serving pieces
  Salt and freshly ground black pepper
2 tablespoons oil
½ cup pumpkin seeds (pipians or pepitas)
¼ cup blanched almonds
¼ teaspoon cumin seeds
1 clove garlic, finely chopped
3 canned green chilies, seeded and chopped
¼ cup chopped parsley
1 cup chicken broth.

1. Season the chicken pieces with salt and pepper and brown on all sides in the oil. Pour off extra oil.
2. Toast the pumpkin seeds, almonds and cumin in a hot dry skillet over low heat, shaking often, until almonds are golden.
3. Grind the toasted mixture in an electric blender or mortar and pestle. Add the garlic, chilies and parsley and mix well. Gradually stir in the broth. Pour into a saucepan. Bring to a boil and pour over the chicken. Cover and simmer forty minutes, or until the chicken is done.

Yield: Four servings.

Arroz con Pollo Nuevo Mexicano (Chicken with Rice, New Mexican Style)
New Mexico

1 cup olive oil
2 two-and-one-half-pound to three-pound chickens, cut into serving pieces
1 cup uncooked rice
2 cloves garlic, finely chopped
2 cups chicken broth or water
2 cups beer
2 teaspoons ground cumin
2 teaspoons leaf saffron
Salt and freshly ground black pepper to taste
3 cups cooked peas or two ten-ounce packages frozen peas, cooked.

1. Heat one-half cup of the oil in a skillet and brown the chicken pieces in it on all sides. Drain chicken and reserve.
2. Add remaining oil to skillet and add the rice. Cook, stirring, until rice is transparent and golden. Stir in the garlic.
3. Set the chicken on top of the rice.
4. Pour in the broth or water and the beer. Stir in the cumin, saffron, salt and pepper. Bring to a boil and simmer, covered, until rice is tender and liquid absorbed.
5. Stir in the peas and reheat.
Yield: Six servings.

Huevos Campechanos (Eggs Campeche Style)
Texas

4 fresh or canned tortillas
¼ cup lard, peanut oil or vegetable oil for shallow frying
4 tablespoons hot refried beans (page 605)
4 hard-cooked eggs
1 cup or more hot ranchero sauce (page 649)
8 slices freshly roasted or canned green chilies
Chopped or whole fresh coriander leaves

(cilantro or Chinese parsley) for garnish (optional)
Xnipek (page 650) (optional).

1. Fry the tortillas in hot lard or oil, turning once. Drain.
2. Smear one tablespoon of hot refried beans in the center of each of four warm plates. Top each with a tortilla.
3. Split the eggs in half lengthwise and place two egg halves, split side down, near the center of each tortilla. Spoon one-quarter cup or so hot ranchero sauce over each egg and garnish each serving with two green chile slices. Garnish with coriander leaves if desired. Serve with cold xnipek on the side if desired.
Yield: Four servings.

Huevos Motulenos (Eggs with Ham and Cheese)
Texas

4 fresh or canned tortillas
¼ cup lard, peanut oil or vegetable oil for shallow frying
4 tablespoons hot refried beans (page 605)
4 teaspoons freshly grated anejo cheese or Parmesan cheese
4 eggs
2 tablespoons bacon drippings or butter
1 cup or more hot ranchero sauce (page 649)
¼ cup chopped white onion
½ cup chopped baked ham
½ cup cubed or shredded sharp Cheddar cheese
¼ cup cooked green peas
Chopped or whole fresh coriander leaves (cilantro or Chinese parsley)
Xnipek (page 650) (optional).

1. Fry the tortillas in hot lard or oil, turning once. Drain.
2. Smear one tablespoon of hot refried beans in the center of each of four warm plates. Sprinkle with the cheese and top with hot tortillas.
3. Meanwhile, fry the eggs sunny side up or

over light in bacon drippings or butter. Arrange the eggs on the tortillas and top each with one-quarter cup or so of the hot ranchero sauce. Sprinkle with equal amounts of the onion, ham, cheese and peas. Garnish with coriander leaves and serve immediately, with cold xnipek on the side if desired.

Yield: Four servings.

Huevos Rancheros (Ranch-Style Eggs)
Texas

4 eggs
2 tablespoons bacon drippings or butter
4 fresh or canned tortillas
¼ cup lard, peanut oil or vegetable oil for shallow frying
1 cup or more hot ranchero sauce (page 649)
Chopped or whole fresh coriander leaves (cilantro or Chinese parsley) for garnish (optional)
Xnipek (page 650) (optional).

1. Fry the eggs sunny side up or over lightly in bacon drippings or butter.
2. Meanwhile, fry the tortillas in hot lard or oil, turning once. Drain.
3. Place one tortilla on each of four hot plates, top with one egg and spoon one-quarter cup or so of the hot ranchero sauce over each. Garnish with coriander leaves if desired. Serve with cold xnipek on the side if desired.

Yield: Four servings.

Eggs Rancheros
Southern California

4 cups chile sauce (recipe below)
1 teaspoon sugar
2 teaspoons vinegar
½ teaspoon oregano
½ cup water
6 eggs
6 tortillas

Oil
Refried beans (page 605).

1. Place the chile sauce, sugar, vinegar, oregano and water in a large skillet. Bring to a boil and cook five minutes.
2. Break the eggs into the sauce and poach.
3. Fry the tortillas until crisp, one at a time, in oil to the depth of one-half inch. Drain on paper towels.
4. Dip the tortillas into the sauce, place on individual serving plates, top with the eggs and serve the beans on the side.

Yield: Six servings.

Chile Sauce
Southern California

12 whole dried mild California chilies or anchos (see note)
3½ cups hot water
¼ cup tomato sauce
2 tablespoons tomato paste
1 clove garlic, finely chopped
1 small onion, finely chopped
3 tablespoons oil
1½ teaspoons salt
¼ teaspoon ground cumin.

1. Preheat the oven to 400 degrees.
2. Place the chilies or anchos on a baking sheet and bake three minutes. Toss three times during the baking.
3. When chilies are cool enough to handle, remove and discard the pith, seeds and stems. Rinse chilies well. Cover the chilies with the hot water and let stand forty-five minutes.
4. Blend the chilies, with a small amount of the water, in an electric blender until smooth.
5. Mix blended chilies with the remaining ingredients including rest of water and simmer ten minutes.

Yield: About one quart.

Note: California chilies or anchos are available in New York City at Casa Moneo, 210 West 14th

Street (10011), and Aphrodisia, 28 Carmine Street (10014), and Spanish grocery stores.

Egg-Filled Tortillas   *Texas*

24 hot prepared tortillas (page 629) (see note)
 1 recipe hot pepita or pumpkin seed sauce
    (page 650)
10 hard-cooked eggs, finely chopped
 1 recipe hot tomato sauce (page 609).

1. Dip the tortillas one by one in the pepita sauce. Add a little chopped egg and roll the tortillas. Line them in an ovenproof dish to keep warm.
2. When all the tortillas are stuffed, pour the pepita sauce over them and add a ring of tomato sauce.
Yield: Six to one dozen servings.
Note: Canned tortillas may be used, but homemade tortillas are far superior.

Kid Stew (Guisado de Cabrito)   *Texas*

¼ cup lard
 2 pounds kid (young goat), cut into cubes
1½ cups water
   Salt and freshly ground black pepper to
   taste
 2 tomatoes, peeled and chopped
 2 dried mild chilies, seeded and crumbled
 1 clove garlic, finely chopped
½ teaspoon ground cumin
⅛ teaspoon oregano.

1. Heat the lard in a heavy skillet and brown the kid in it.
2. Pour off excess fat. Add the water, salt, pepper, tomatoes, chilies, garlic, cumin and oregano. Bring to a boil, cover and simmer two to three hours, or until kid is tender.
Yield: Four servings.

Carne con Vinagre (Meat with Vinegar)
New Mexico

2 pounds lean pork shoulder or beef round
8 cups water
1 tablespoon chili powder
1 teaspoon salt
2 bay leaves
2 cloves garlic, crushed
1 teaspoon oregano
1 teaspoon dried mint or one tablespoon
   chopped fresh mint leaves
½ cup oil
½ cup cider vinegar
4 small scallions, including green part,
   chopped.

1. Day before, place the meat, water, chili powder, salt, bay leaves, garlic, oregano and mint in a deep saucepan. Bring to a boil, cover and simmer one to one and one-half hours, or until meat is tender.
2. Let meat cool in the broth. When cool, slice meat and reserve one-half cup broth. (Use remaining broth for making soup.)
3. Mix together the oil, vinegar, reserved broth and the scallions in a deep bowl. Add the meat and let stand refrigerated overnight. Serve cold.
Yield: Four servings.

Menudo à la California (Tripe California Style)   *Southern California*

6 pounds honeycomb tripe, well washed
   Lightly salted water
4 cups chile sauce (page 598)
1 eight-ounce can tomato sauce
2 teaspoons oregano
1 onion, finely chopped
1 clove garlic, finely chopped
2 tablespoons oil.

1. Place the tripe in a large kettle and cover with lightly salted water. Bring to a boil, cover and simmer until tender, about one hour.

2. Remove tripe from the water, reserving two cups of the liquid. Cut the tripe into strips, three inches long by one inch wide.

3. Combine the chile sauce, tomato sauce and oregano in a four-quart kettle. Sauté the onion and garlic in the oil. Add to the chile sauce mixture. Boil two minutes. Add the tripe and reserved liquid and cook slowly thirty minutes.

Yield: One dozen servings.

Morcilla (Blood Pudding)   *New Mexico*

¼ cup lard
4 cups hog's blood (see note)
1 small onion, chopped
1 clove garlic, chopped
1 cup raisins, plumped in hot water and drained
½ cup shelled piñon nuts (optional)
1 teaspoon oregano
1 tablespoon chopped fresh mint leaves or one teaspoon dried mint
2 teaspoons salt.

1. Heat the lard in a skillet. Add the blood and fry until it loses all pinkness. Add the onion, garlic and raisins and cook thirty minutes.

2. Add the remaining ingredients and cook thirty minutes longer.

Yield: Four to six servings.

Note: Kid's blood may be substituted for hog's blood.

Pipian de Lengua (Tongue Fricassee)
Southern California

½ cup pumpkin seeds
3 tablespoons lard
1 clove garlic, finely chopped
2 cups water the tongue was cooked in or fresh water
1 teaspoon salt
1 teaspoon coriander seeds

2 teaspoons chili powder
3 pounds beef tongue, cooked and sliced.

1. Preheat the oven to 325 degrees.

2. Spread the pumpkin seeds over a baking sheet and roast about twenty minutes, stirring several times.

3. Remove the skins and grind seeds in an electric blender or with a pestle and mortar until powdered.

4. Melt the lard in a skillet. Add the powdered seeds and remaining ingredients except the tongue. Stir and bring to a boil. Add the tongue and simmer slowly twenty minutes.

Yield: Six to eight servings.

Texas Liver

1 cup tomatoes
1 cup chicken broth
1 tablespoon tarragon vinegar
1 cup thinly sliced onion rings
1 clove garlic, finely minced
½ cup sliced green pepper
½ cup sliced mushrooms
1 tablespoon oil
1 bay leaf
¼ teaspoon thyme
Salt and freshly ground black pepper to taste
2 tablespoons butter
1 pound calf's liver, cut into one-inch cubes
Cooked rice.

1. Combine the tomatoes, broth and vinegar in a saucepan and bring to a boil.

2. Cook the onion rings, garlic, green pepper and mushrooms in the oil until onions are wilted. Add the vegetables to the tomato sauce. Season with the bay leaf, thyme, salt and pepper. Bring to a boil and simmer fifteen minutes.

3. Melt the butter in a skillet and quickly sauté the liver in it, stirring over high heat, about one

minute. Add the liver to the tomato sauce. Cover and simmer five minutes. Serve with rice.

Yield: Four to six servings.

Escabeche-Tongue Salad
Southern California

1 smoked beef tongue
1 onion, thinly sliced
1 cup pitted ripe olives
½ cup oil
½ cup cider vinegar
½ teaspoon oregano
Salt and freshly ground black pepper to taste.

1. Place the tongue in a kettle, cover with water, bring to a boil and simmer gently until tender, about two hours.
2. Allow tongue to cool in the liquid. When cold, skin and slice thinly.
3. Combine the remaining ingredients, add tongue and mix well. Chill three hours, stirring often.

Yield: Eight servings.

Roast Wild Ducks with Burgundy-Olive Sauce
Texas

4 wild ducks
Salt and freshly ground black pepper to taste
1 cup chopped celery
8 slices onion
1 cup melted butter
Paprika to taste
Sauce:
½ cup chopped mushrooms
6 scallions, chopped
½ cup melted butter
4 tablespoons flour
1 cup beef stock, heated
2 tablespoons tomato paste
1¼ cups Burgundy wine or other red wine

Freshly ground black pepper to taste
¾ cup unstuffed green olives, chopped.

1. Preheat the oven to 275 degrees.
2. Clean the ducks well and salt and pepper insides. Stuff the cavity of each duck with ¼ cup of the celery and 2 slices of the onion. Truss the ducks and place side by side, breast up, in a roasting pan just large enough to hold them. Pour the one cup melted butter over the birds and sprinkle lightly with paprika, salt, and pepper. Pour about one-half inch water around the ducks.
3. Bake, basting occasionally, about three hours, or until birds are tender.
4. Thirty minutes before ducks are done, prepare the sauce. Sauté the mushrooms and scallions in the butter for about three minutes. Blend the flour with about four tablespoons of the beef stock and add to the butter mixture. Stir in the remaining stock and the tomato paste, mixing well. Add the wine a little at a time, stirring after each addition. When the sauce is bubbling hot, add pepper and the olives. Pour sauce into heated sauceboat.
5. When ducks are done, remove to a serving platter and serve with the prepared sauce.

Yield: About eight servings.

Wild Duck Gumbo
Texas

1 wild duck, cleaned
Salt and freshly ground black pepper to taste
1 medium-size onion
2 cloves garlic, left whole
1 rib celery
3 tablespoons vegetable oil or peanut oil
2 large green peppers, cored, seeded and cut into one-inch cubes
1 large onion, coarsely chopped
1 clove garlic, finely minced
3 tablespoons gumbo filé powder
2 tablespoons flour

¾ cup canned tomatoes
½ teaspoon chili powder
½ teaspoon paprika
¼ teaspoon ground cumin
2½ cups okra, cut into one-half-inch lengths
1 cup cooked rice.

1. Remove most of the skin from the duck and cut the duck into serving pieces. Put the pieces in a kettle with the duck giblets and add water to cover, salt, pepper, the whole onion, whole garlic and celery. Bring to a boil, simmer two hours.

2. Heat the oil in a large saucepan and add the green peppers and chopped onion. Cook until onion is wilted. Sprinkle with salt, pepper, the minced garlic, gumbo filé and flour. Cook, stirring, two minutes. Add the tomatoes. Stir in four cups of the broth in which duck cooked. Add the chili powder, paprika and cumin.

3. Add the duck pieces and simmer five minutes. Add the okra and simmer twenty-five to thirty minutes longer, or until okra is tender. Add the rice and serve. This gumbo is traditionally served with additional rice on the side.

Yield: Four servings.

Roast Mallard Ducks   *Texas*

4 mallard ducks, dressed and trussed
Salt and freshly ground black pepper
4 sprigs fresh thyme or one teaspoon dried thyme
2 bay leaves, broken in half
1¾ cups chicken broth, fresh or canned.

1. Preheat the oven to 425 degrees.
2. Sprinkle the ducks inside and outside with salt and pepper. Add one sprig of the fresh thyme or one-quarter teaspoon of the dried thyme and half a bay leaf to the interior of each duck. Place in a roasting pan and roast thirty minutes, basting frequently with the natural fat that comes from the ducks.
3. Reduce the oven heat to 375 degrees. Pour off fat from the roasting pan and add the broth. Continue roasting and basting forty-five minutes longer.

Yield: Four to eight servings.

Vegetables, Main Dish Accompaniments and Salads

Breaded Artichoke Hearts

Southern California

6 small artichokes
  Boiling salted water
½ lemon
  Oil
½ cup soft bread crumbs
3 tablespoons freshly grated Parmesan cheese
2 eggs, lightly beaten.

1. Trim each artichoke so that only the edible portion of the leaves remains, but leave the choke intact. Place artichokes in a skillet with boiling salted water to cover.

2. Add the lemon and one tablespoon oil and cook, covered, twenty minutes, or until the bottoms are tender. Drain.

3. Halve the artichokes and remove each "choke."

4. Combine the bread crumbs and cheese. Dip each artichoke half into the beaten eggs and then into the crumb mixture. Heat oil to a depth of one-quarter inch in a skillet and sauté the artichoke hearts in it until golden. Drain on paper towels.

Yield: Four servings.

Stuffed Artichokes

Southern California

6 large artichokes
  Boiling salted water
2 cloves garlic
½ lemon
2 tablespoons oil
¼ cup butter
1 small onion, chopped
½ pound mushrooms, sliced
¼ teaspoon crushed rosemary or one teaspoon chopped fresh rosemary
¼ teaspoon dried thyme or one teaspoon chopped fresh thyme
¼ teaspoon dried marjoram or one teaspoon chopped fresh marjoram
2 tablespoons flour
1 cup chicken broth
1 cup finely diced cooked chicken
  Salt and freshly ground black pepper to taste
⅓ cup buttered soft bread crumbs.

1. Cut one inch off tops of artichokes. Add enough boiling salted water to cover artichokes. Add one clove garlic, the lemon half and the oil.

2. Bring to a boil, cover and simmer until tender, about thirty minutes. Drain upside down.

3. Preheat the oven to 375 degrees.

4. When artichokes are cool enough to handle, separate the leaves and cut out each choke with

a teaspoon. Heat the butter in a skillet and sauté the onion in it until tender.

5. Chop the remaining garlic clove finely. Add with the mushrooms to the skillet and cook three minutes. Add the rosemary, thyme, marjoram and flour and stir to mix.

6. Gradually stir in the broth and bring to a boil, stirring. Add the chicken, salt and pepper. Heat to bubbling.

7. Fill the cavity of the artichokes with the chicken mixture, sprinkle with the bread crumbs and place in a shallow baking dish with one-half inch hot water in the bottom. Cover and bake twenty-five minutes, or until heated through.

Yield: Six servings.

Green Corn Pudding   *Southern California*

12 ears ripe corn
 5 eggs, separated
 2 tablespoons bacon drippings or lard
 4 cups milk
 2 tablespoons sugar
 ½ teaspoon salt.

1. Preheat the oven to 250 degrees.
2. Cut the corn kernels off the cobs; then scrape cobs to remove milk. Place kernels and corn milk in a bowl. Beat the egg yolks until thick and lemon-colored and add to the corn.
3. Add the drippings or lard and mix well. Beat in the milk.
4. Beat the egg whites until stiff but not dry; then beat in the sugar and salt. Fold into the corn mixture. Pour into a baking dish, cover and bake one hour, or until set. Remove cover and brown pudding briefly under the broiler.

Yield: Eight servings.

Curried Corn with Chilies   *Arizona*

½ cup butter
 1 clove garlic, finely minced
 1 medium-size onion, chopped

6 to eight ears corn
 1 tablespoon curry powder
   Salt and freshly ground black pepper to taste
 1 cup heavy cream
 3 tablespoons or more chopped canned mild green chilies.

1. Melt the butter in a heavy skillet and add the garlic and onion. Cook until the onion is translucent.
2. Using a sharp knife, cut the corn kernels off the cobs; then scrape cobs to remove the corn milk. Add kernels and corn milk to the skillet.
3. Sprinkle with the curry powder, salt and pepper and add the cream. Partially cover and simmer twenty to thirty minutes over very low heat. Stir in the chilies, cook three minutes longer and serve.

Yield: Six servings.

Cucumbers and Mushrooms   *Arizona*

2 cucumbers, European seedless variety if available
   Salt
 3 tablespoons butter
 1 small onion, thinly sliced
 ½ pound mushrooms, sliced
 ⅛ teaspoon freshly ground black pepper
 2 tablespoons freshly snipped dill weed
 ½ cup chicken broth
 ½ cup sour cream.

1. Peel the cucumbers, halve and remove the seeds if any. Sprinkle lightly with salt and let stand fifteen minutes. Rinse and dry.
2. Cut into one and one-half-inch lengths.
3. Melt the butter in a heavy skillet and add the cucumbers, onion and mushrooms. Sauté, stirring, five minutes. Add one-quarter teaspoon salt, the pepper, dill and broth.
4. Cook three minutes. With a slotted spoon, remove vegetables to a warm dish. Reduce liquid in skillet by boiling to one-quarter to one-third

cup. Stir in the sour cream. Heat, but do not boil. Pour over vegetables.

Yield: Four servings.

Kidney Bean Casserole   *Arizona*

¼ cup butter
1 large onion, finely chopped
2 cloves garlic, finely chopped
1 green pepper, finely chopped
1 tablespoon flour
1 tablespoon chili powder
2 cups canned Italian plum tomatoes, drained
2 twenty-ounce cans cooked kidney beans, drained
1 teaspoon salt
½ teaspoon freshly ground black pepper
1 teaspoon chopped fresh thyme or one-half teaspoon dried thyme
3 tablespoons chopped parsley
¼ cup shredded sharp Cheddar cheese.

1. Preheat the oven to 350 degrees.
2. Heat the butter in a skillet and add the onion, garlic and green pepper. Cook until onion is wilted. Add the flour and chili powder and stir until blended. Stir in the tomatoes and bring to a boil.
3. Add the kidney beans, salt, black pepper, thyme and parsley. Pour the mixture into a two-quart casserole. Bake forty minutes. Sprinkle with the cheese and bake five minutes longer.

Yield: Six servings.

Pinto Beans   *Texas*

1 pound dried pinto beans or dried kidney beans, washed well with cold running water
7 cups cold water
1 teaspoon salt.

1. There are two ways to prepare the beans. One is to soak them overnight in the water. The other is to bring the beans and water to a boil in a saucepan and boil two minutes. Remove from heat, cover and then let stand one hour before cooking.
2. Add the salt to the soaked beans and liquid. Bring to a boil. Cover and simmer thirty-five to forty-five minutes, or until beans are tender. To evaporate excess liquid, cook beans uncovered for last ten minutes, pouring off some of the excess if necessary. If there is not too much excess liquid, some of the beans can be crushed to absorb the liquid.

Yield: Eight servings.

Refried Beans   *Texas*

¼ cup bacon drippings or lard
2 cups cooked pinto beans or kidney beans (recipe above).

Heat the bacon drippings or lard in a skillet and add the beans. Cook, stirring and mashing the beans, until they are fairly dry.

Yield: Four to six servings.

Frijoles (Mexican Beans)   *Texas*

2 cups dried pink beans, dried pinto beans or dried kidney beans
5½ cups lukewarm water, approximately
1 onion
½ bay leaf
Salt to taste
½ cup bacon drippings or lard.

1. Rinse the beans, but do not soak them. Place in a saucepan and add five and one-half cups water, the onion and bay leaf. Cover and simmer, stirring occasionally, until beans are wrinkled.
2. Add the salt and continue cooking until beans are thoroughly tender. If necessary as the beans cook, add more water, a little at a time.

When the beans are nearly done, mash a few to thicken. Continue cooking, stirring frequently, until done. Add the bacon drippings or lard and cook ten minutes longer, or until beans have desired thickness.

Yield: Four to six servings.

Red Beans   *Texas*

1 pound dried pinto beans or other dried red
  or pink beans
3 slices bacon
2 cups chopped onions
2 cloves garlic, finely minced
1 teaspoon cumin seeds
  Salt to taste.

1. Soak the beans overnight in water to cover. Or, to use a quick method, cover the beans with water, bring to a boil and simmer two minutes. Remove from the heat and let stand one hour before proceeding with recipe.
2. Cut the bacon into small bits and cook in a kettle large enough to hold the beans. When cooked, add the onions and garlic and cook, stirring, until onions are wilted.
3. Drain the beans and add them to the kettle. Crush the cumin seeds or rub them between the palms of the hands. Add to kettle. Add salt. Add water to cover the beans to the depth of one inch and bring to a boil. Simmer at least two hours, or until beans are thoroughly tender, adding more water during cooking if necessary.

Yield: Six to eight servings.

California String Beans
Southern California

2 pounds string beans
3 tablespoons olive oil
1 onion, finely chopped
2 mild green chilies, chopped
1 small clove garlic, chopped
2 tomatoes, peeled and chopped

Salt and freshly ground black pepper to taste
1 teaspoon vinegar
  Boiling water.

1. Wash the beans, string if necessary and cut into uniform two-inch pieces.
2. Heat the oil in a heavy skillet and add the beans. Mix well. Add the onion, chilies, garlic, tomatoes, salt, pepper and vinegar.
3. Add one tablespoon boiling water and simmer, covered, until beans are tender. Add another tablespoon water if necessary.

Yield: Eight servings.

Chick-Peas with Chilies   *New Mexico*

3 tablespoons oil
1 onion, finely chopped
1 clove garlic, finely chopped
¼ teaspoon oregano
1 tomato, peeled and chopped
2 canned green chilies, chopped
2 teaspoons red chili powder
1 large can chick-peas (garbanzos), drained
  Salt to taste.

1. Heat the oil in a skillet and sauté the onion, garlic, oregano, tomato, chilies and chili powder in it over low heat about ten minutes.
2. Add the chick-peas and salt. Simmer twenty minutes.

Yield: Four servings.

Eggplant Casserole   *Texas*

1 medium-size eggplant, peeled and sliced
  into one-quarter-inch slices
  Salt
4 large ripe tomatoes, peeled and sliced
1 large sweet onion, sliced
  Freshly ground black pepper
3 tablespoons butter
⅓ cup buttered soft bread crumbs
¼ cup shredded mozzarella cheese.

1. Preheat the oven to 350 degrees.

2. Sprinkle the eggplant slices with salt and let stand twenty minutes. Rinse and dry.

3. Place a layer of eggplant slices, then a layer of tomato slices and then a layer of onion slices in a buttered baking dish. Season with salt and pepper and dot with the butter. Continue the layers until all vegetables are used.

4. Mix the bread crumbs with the cheese and sprinkle on top. Bake forty minutes, or until eggplant is tender.

Yield: Four servings.

Lucy's Quelites (Spinach with Beans)

New Mexico

4 slices bacon
1 small onion, chopped
1 clove garlic, finely chopped
1½ to two pounds fresh spinach, washed, drained and chopped, or two packages frozen chopped spinach
½ cup water
½ cup drained cooked pinto beans
1 tablespoon chopped canned or fresh hot chilies
Salt to taste.

1. Cook the bacon until crisp, remove from the drippings and set aside.

2. Sauté the onion and garlic in the drippings until tender. Add the spinach and water, cover and cook until spinach is cooked.

3. Crumble the reserved bacon and add to spinach. Add the beans, chilies and salt. Heat, stirring gently.

Yield: Eight servings.

Spinach and Artichokes

Southern California

2 pounds spinach
1 package frozen artichoke hearts

4 slices bacon
½ cup finely chopped onion
1 tablespoon flour
1 clove garlic, finely minced
3 scallions, including green part, trimmed and chopped
½ cup heavy cream
Salt and freshly ground black pepper to taste
Cayenne pepper to taste
¼ cup toasted soft bread crumbs
Butter.

1. Trim off any tough stems on the spinach and wash the leaves in several changes of cold water. Shake to remove excess moisture and put the spinach in a kettle. No additional water is needed. The spinach will cook in the water that clings to the leaves. Cover the kettle and bring to a boil. Stir the leaves around when they wilt and continue cooking briefly until just tender. Set aside.

2. Cook the artichoke hearts according to package directions. Set aside.

3. Meanwhile, in a large saucepan cook the bacon until crisp. Remove the bacon, crumble it and reserve.

4. Preheat the oven to 400 degrees.

5. Pour off all but one tablespoon of the fat from the saucepan and add the onion and flour to the saucepan. Cook, stirring, but do not brown. Add the garlic and scallions and stir in the cream. When the mixture is thickened and smooth, drain the spinach well in a colander. Drain the artichokes. Add both vegetables and reserved bacon to the sauce and season with salt, pepper and a touch of cayenne. Pour into a buttered baking dish. Sprinkle with the bread crumbs, dot with butter and bake until thoroughly hot and nicely browned, about fifteen minutes.

Yield: Six to eight servings.

Texas Mustard Greens

2 pounds tender mustard greens
1 ham hock or one-third pound salt pork
1 onion
2 cups water, approximately
  Salt to taste
1 teaspoon sugar (optional).

1. Wash the mustard greens in several changes of water. If there are tough stems, break them off and discard.

2. Place the greens in a kettle and add the ham hock or salt pork. Add the onion, water and salt. There should be enough water barely to cover the greens. Bring to a boil and simmer two hours.

3. When ready to serve, drain and sprinkle with sugar if desired. Toss and serve hot. Many people enjoy mustard greens sprinkled lightly with vinegar and chopped onion.

Yield: Four to six servings.

Mushroom Pie   *Arizona*

1 unbaked nine-inch pie shell
1 egg white, lightly beaten
¼ cup butter
4 scallions, including green part, chopped
1 pound mushrooms, sliced
1 teaspoon lemon juice
  Salt and freshly ground black pepper to taste
2 tablespoons chopped parsley
1 tablespoon flour
¾ cup grated Swiss cheese
1 cup light cream or half and half, scalded
3 eggs, lightly beaten
⅛ teaspoon nutmeg.

1. Preheat the oven to 450 degrees.

2. Brush the pie shell with the egg white and bake ten minutes, or until pastry is set but not browned. Cool.

3. Reduce the oven heat to 350 degrees.

4. Meanwhile, melt the butter in a skillet and

sauté the scallions and mushrooms in it until just tender, about three minutes.

5. Sprinkle with the lemon juice, salt, pepper, parsley and flour and cook until mixture thickens. Spread in bottom of pie shell. Sprinkle with the cheese.

6. Beat the cream or half and half into the eggs. Add the nutmeg and pour over the cheese. Bake thirty-five minutes, or until set, golden and puffed. Let cool slightly before cutting.

Yield: Six servings.

Mushrooms in Sour Cream

Southern California

¼ cup butter
¼ cup finely chopped shallots
1 pound button mushrooms
2 tablespoons cognac
  Salt and freshly ground black pepper to taste
1 tablespoon freshly snipped dill weed
1 cup sour cream.

1. Melt the butter in a skillet and sauté the shallots in it until transparent. Add the mushrooms and cook five minutes over high heat, stirring constantly.

2. Sprinkle with the cognac, salt, pepper and dill. Stir in the sour cream and heat, stirring, but do not boil.

Yield: Four servings.

Nopales or Nopalitos   *Southern California*

2 pounds young tender cactus pads (see note)
1 small onion
2 tablespoons bacon drippings
2 tablespoons grated onion
1 tomato, peeled and chopped
  Salt and freshly ground black pepper to taste
1 teaspoon oregano.

1. Holding cactus pads in kitchen tongs, remove any thorns and cut pads into pieces the size of string beans.

2. Place fresh nopalitos in a small saucepan with the whole onion and enough water to cover. Bring to a boil and simmer until tender, about twenty-five minutes. Remove the onion and drain off the water. If canned nopalitos are used, no initial cooking is needed.

3. Heat the bacon drippings, add the grated onion and sauté. Add the nopalitos, tomato, salt, pepper and oregano. Simmer three minutes.

Yield: Six servings

Note: Cactus pads are nopales or new leaves; if not available fresh, they can be bought canned (nopalitos) at stores specializing in Spanish foods, such as Casa Moneo, 210 West 14th Street, New York, New York 10011.

Smothered Okra   *Texas*

2 cups coarsely chopped green peppers
  Salt to taste
2 tablespoons vegetable oil or peanut oil
1 clove garlic, finely minced
½ cup coarsely chopped onion
3 cups okra, cut into one-half-inch lengths
  Freshly ground black pepper to taste.

1. Place the green peppers in a saucepan and add water to cover. Add salt and bring to a boil. Cook one minute and drain.

2. Heat the oil in a skillet and add the garlic and onion. When the onion is wilted, add the okra. Sprinkle with salt and black pepper. Cook, stirring, ten minutes and add the drained green peppers. Cover and cook briefly. The vegetables should be tender, but they should retain a somewhat crisp texture.

Yield: Six servings.

Chilies Rellenos (Stuffed Long Peppers)
New Mexico

12 long whole canned green chilies
½ pound melting cheese, such as Monterey
  Jack, Fontina, Muenster or Danish Esrom
4 eggs, separated
¼ cup flour
  Salt and freshly ground black pepper to
  taste
  Oil for deep-frying
  New Mexico tomato sauce (recipe below).

1. Lay the chilies on a flat surface.

2. Cut the cheese into long thin strips about two and one-half to three inches long and one-half inch square. The size of the cheese will depend on the size and length of the peppers. Carefully insert one piece of cheese inside each pepper. Some people seal peppers with toothpicks, but it is not necessary.

3. In a mixing bowl, combine the egg yolks and flour. Beat to blend. Add salt and pepper.

4. Beat the egg whites until stiff but not dry and fold them into yolks. Spoon mixture into a flat pan or pie plate.

5. Heat oil to 365 degrees. Dip peppers, one at a time, into egg batter and add them to the oil. Cook until golden brown on one side, turn and cook on the other. Drain. Serve with the tomato sauce.

Yield: Six servings.

New Mexico Tomato Sauce

1 cup finely chopped onions
1 teaspoon finely chopped green pepper
3 tablespoons oil
1 clove garlic, finely minced
1 teaspoon or more chili powder
2 cups tomato puree
2 cups fresh or canned beef broth or chicken
  broth
1 bay leaf

1 teaspoon oregano, crushed in a mortar
Salt to taste.

1. In a one-and-one-half-quart saucepan, cook the onions and green pepper in the oil until wilted. Add the garlic and chili powder and stir.
2. Add the remaining ingredients, bring to a boil and simmer thirty minutes, stirring occasionally.

Yield: About four cups.

Chilies Rellenos Casserole   *New Mexico*

1 four-ounce can whole medium-hot green chilies
½ pound sharp Cheddar cheese, cut into finger lengths
2 eggs
2 cups milk
½ cup flour
1 teaspoon salt.

1. Preheat the oven to 350 degrees.
2. Cut each chile in half. Place a layer of chilies over the bottom of a small buttered casserole. Add a layer of the cheese, then more chilies and cheese.
3. Beat the eggs and add the milk. Beat in the flour and salt. Or, if desired, briefly whisk this mixture in an electric blender. Pour this liquid over the cheese and bake thirty-five to forty minutes.

Yield: Six servings.

Hazel's Rice Casserole   *Texas*

⅓ cup bacon drippings
¾ cup uncooked long grain rice
1 large onion, chopped
¼ cup chopped green pepper
1 clove garlic, finely chopped
1 two-pound-thirteen-ounce can Italian plum tomatoes
1 medium-size hot red pepper, chopped

Salt to taste
⅓ cup grated Monterey Jack cheese or sharp Cheddar cheese.

1. Preheat the oven to 400 degrees.
2. Heat the bacon drippings in a heavy skillet and add the rice. Cook, stirring, until rice starts to color. Add the onion and, when rice starts to brown, add the remaining ingredients except the cheese.
3. Cover and cook slowly until rice is tender, about twenty minutes. Turn into a greased baking dish, sprinkle with the cheese and bake until cheese melts, about fifteen minutes.

Yield: Four servings.

California Green Rice   *Southern California*

3 tablespoons oil
2 tablespoons butter
1 onion, finely chopped
1 clove garlic, finely chopped
2 cups uncooked rice
3½ cups boiling chicken broth or water
4 mild fresh or canned chilies, seeded and chopped
¼ cup finely chopped Italian parsley
½ cup finely chopped celery leaves
½ cup chopped sorrel or spinach leaves, ribs and stems removed
½ cup chopped broccoli or beet leaves
½ cup chopped Swiss chard leaves
2 teaspoons salt.

1. Heat the oil and butter in a heavy casserole or kettle. Add the onion and garlic and sauté slowly until transparent. Add the rice and cook, stirring occasionally, until golden.
2. Add the remaining ingredients, bring to a boil, cover and cook slowly until rice is tender, about twenty-five minutes.

Yield: Six servings.

Texas Rice

1 cup uncooked rice
2 tablespoons butter
½ cup finely chopped onion
½ cup finely chopped green pepper
1 cup canned tomatoes, preferably Italian
   plum style
   Salt to taste
2 teaspoons chili powder
½ teaspoon ground cumin seeds
1½ cups chicken broth.

1. Cook the rice in the butter, stirring frequently. When rice starts to turn golden, add the onion and green pepper. Continue to cook until onion wilts; then add the remaining ingredients. Cover and bring to a boil.

2. Reduce the heat and simmer thirty minutes without raising the cover. Let stand until ready to use. The dish may stand for thirty minutes before serving.

Yield: Four servings.

Rice with Mushrooms   *Texas*

1 onion, chopped
1 clove garlic, finely minced
½ pound mushrooms, thinly sliced
¼ cup olive oil
1 cup uncooked long grain rice
1 cup Italian plum tomatoes, drained
1½ cups chicken broth.

1. In a saucepan with a tight-fitting lid, cook the onion, garlic and mushrooms in the oil until mushrooms are wilted. Continue cooking until most of mushroom liquid evaporates.

2. Add the rice and continue cooking, while stirring, three minutes.

3. Break up the tomatoes by squeezing them through the fingers. Add to rice mixture. Add the broth.

4. Bring the mixture to a boil, cover and sim-

mer twenty minutes. Let stand ten minutes before serving.

Yield: Six servings.

Mexican Rice   *Texas*

½ cup ground pork
3 tablespoons peanut oil
2 chorizos (Spanish sausage, see note), or four
   cooked link sausages
¼ cup chopped onion
2 tablespoons chopped green pepper
1 clove garlic, finely minced
2 cups uncooked rice
4 cups boiling chicken broth
½ teaspoon leaf saffron, crumbled
   Salt to taste.

1. Cook the pork in the oil until pork loses color.

2. Slice the chorizos and add them. Add the onion, pepper and garlic and continue cooking about ten minutes, stirring.

3. Add the rice, broth, saffron and salt and simmer until rice is tender. Cover and let stand until ready to serve.

Yield: Eight servings.

Note: Chorizos are available in Spanish markets or see page 587.

Noodles with Sour Cream
Southern California

1 eight-ounce package medium-size egg
   noodles
   Boiling salted water
4 tablespoons butter, at room temperature
½ cup chopped scallions, including green part
¼ cup finely minced green pepper
   Salt and freshly ground black pepper to
   taste
½ cup fresh or canned chicken broth

1 cup sour cream
¼ cup freshly grated Parmesan cheese.

1. Cook the noodles in boiling salted water until tender but not overcooked. Drain noodles and run hot water over them. Drain again.

2. Melt the butter in a heavy saucepan and add noodles, stirring gently with a plastic spatula until they are coated with butter. Add the scallions, green pepper, salt, black pepper, broth and sour cream. Stir gently. Just before serving, sprinkle with the cheese.

Yield: Six servings.

Noodles with Oriental Mushrooms
Southern California

1 cup dried Chinese or Japanese mushrooms
6 tablespoons butter
1 eight-ounce package broad noodles.

1. Soak the mushrooms in warm water to cover. When they are softened, drain and cut into thin slices.

2. Heat two tablespoons of the butter and toss the mushroom slices in it briefly. Do not let the butter brown.

3. Meanwhile, cook the noodles according to package directions. Pour into a hot serving dish and toss with the remaining butter and the mushroom slices.

Yield: Four to six servings.

Hominy Mexicaine   *Texas*

6 slices bacon, cut into thin strips
1 twenty-ounce can whole hominy (about two and one-half cups)
1 cup finely chopped onions
1 tablespoon flour
1 tablespoon chili powder, or to taste
2 cups fresh or canned tomatoes, preferably Italian plum style if canned

Salt and freshly ground black pepper to taste
¼ pound grated sharp Cheddar cheese.

1. Preheat the oven to 350 degrees.

2. In a heavy casserole or saucepan, brown the bacon over moderate heat, stirring. When bacon is crisp, transfer it to paper towels to drain; reserve. Pour off all but two tablespoons of fat from the casserole.

3. Add the hominy and onions to the casserole and cook, stirring, until golden brown. Sprinkle with the flour and chili powder and stir in the tomatoes. Season with salt and pepper and stir in the reserved bacon.

4. Pour the mixture into a greased one-and-one-half-quart casserole and top with the cheese. Bake thirty minutes.

Yield: Six servings.

Hominy Casserole   *Texas*

3 twenty-ounce cans whole hominy
1½ cups tomato sauce
1 tablespoon chili powder
2 cups shredded sharp cheese
  Toasted tortillas.

1. Preheat the oven to 350 degrees.

2. Drain the hominy. Blend together the tomato sauce and chili powder. Make layers of hominy, tomato sauce and cheese in a buttered casserole, ending with the cheese. Sprinkle with crumbled tortillas and bake fifteen to twenty minutes.

Yield: Six servings.

Grits Soufflé   *New Mexico*

6 cups water
  Salt to taste
1½ cups grits
¼ cup butter
1 cup grated sharp Cheddar cheese

Freshly ground black pepper to taste
¼ cup chopped mild chilies or one-quarter
teaspoon cayenne pepper
4 egg yolks, lightly beaten
4 egg whites, stiffly beaten.

1. Bring the water to a boil and add salt. Gradually add the grits, stirring continuously with a wire whisk or wooden spoon. Stir well until mixture returns to a boil or mixture may lump. Cover and cook over low heat thirty to forty minutes, stirring frequently. If instant grits are used, use the same quantity of grits, but cook according to package directions.

2. Preheat the oven to 350 degrees.

3. Remove the pan from the heat and stir in the butter, cheese, pepper and chilies or cayenne. Let cool to room temperature.

4. Add the egg yolks. Fold in the egg whites and pour into a buttered two-quart casserole. Bake forty to forty-five minutes, or until well puffed and browned.

Yield: Eight servings.

Grits and Cheddar Casserole   *Texas*

4 cups water
1 teaspoon salt
1 cup uncooked quick grits
½ cup butter
¾ pound sharp Cheddar cheese, grated
Freshly ground black pepper
2 tablespoons Worcestershire sauce
1 or two cloves garlic, finely minced
Tabasco sauce to taste (see note)
2 egg whites.

1. Bring the water to a boil and add salt. When water is boiling vigorously, add the grits slowly. Return to a boil and cook over direct heat, stirring occasionally, for two and one-half minutes. While still hot, stir in the remaining ingredients except egg whites. Let cool.

2. Meanwhile, preheat the oven to 400 degrees.

3. Beat the egg whites until stiff and fold them into grits mixture. Pour into a buttered one-and-one-half-quart casserole or soufflé dish and bake about twenty minutes, or until puffed and lightly browned on top. Serve immediately, with meat or poultry.

Yield: Eight or more servings.

Note: One tablespoon or more chopped mild chilies (Ortega or El Paso brands) may be substituted for the Tabasco.

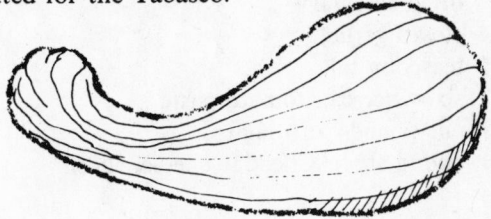

Orange Sprouts   *Southern California*

4 cups Brussels sprouts or two packages
frozen
Boiling salted water
3 tablespoons butter
1 tablespoon flour
¼ teaspoon salt
½ cup milk
1 egg yolk
1 teaspoon grated orange rind
¼ cup orange juice
2 tablespoons lemon juice
2 oranges, peeled and cut into bite-size pieces,
drained.

1. Trim the sprouts and cook in boiling salted water or according to package directions until crisp-tender. Drain.

2. Melt one tablespoon of the butter and blend in the flour. Stir in the salt and milk and bring to a boil, stirring until thickened. Remove from the heat.

3. Stir in the egg yolk, remaining butter, the orange rind, orange juice and lemon juice.

4. Combine the sprouts, orange pieces and sauce.

Yield: Six to eight servings.

Zucchini Torre

Southern California

Peanut oil
1½ pounds one-inch-thick slices zucchini (4 cups)
3 cilantro (coriander leaves or Chinese parsley, see note)
3 fresh or canned mild or hot chilies
1 sprig rosemary or one-eighth teaspoon dried rosemary
4 cloves garlic
1 teaspoon salt
1 six-ounce can tomato paste
1 one-pound can tomatoes
½ pound sharp Cheddar cheese, sliced.

1. Preheat the oven to 400 degrees.
2. Pour the oil to the depth of one-quarter inch into a skillet and heat to 450 degrees. Fry the sliced zucchini in the oil until tender and transparent on both sides. Drain on paper towels.
3. Grind together the cilantro, chilies, rosemary, garlic and salt in a mortar. Combine the tomato paste and tomatoes in a saucepan and add the herb mixture. Cook, stirring, five minutes.
4. Spread the cooked zucchini in the bottom of an earthenware casserole measuring approximately 12 by 15 inches. Pour the sauce over zucchini and top with the cheese. Cover with aluminum foil or casserole cover. Bake forty-five minutes.

Yield: Six to eight servings.

Note: Cilantro is available in Chinese and Spanish markets.

Squash Casserole

Arizona

5 cups sliced yellow squash
1 large onion, finely chopped
Boiling salted water
2 eggs, lightly beaten
½ cup milk
2 tablespoons butter

Salt and freshly ground black pepper to taste
½ cup grated sharp Cheddar cheese.

1. Preheat the oven to 350 degrees.
2. Place the squash and onion in a saucepan and add the water to a depth of one-half inch. Cover and cook, stirring several times, until squash is just tender. Drain well and mash with a potato masher.
3. Stir in the eggs, milk, butter, salt and pepper and pour into a greased baking dish. Sprinkle with the cheese. Bake until set, about twenty-five minutes.

Yield: Six servings.

Zucchini and Cheese Casserole

Texas

1 onion, finely chopped
1 green pepper, cored, seeded and diced
1 clove garlic, finely minced
1 cup finely minced celery
3 tablespoons butter
6 medium-size zucchini, thinly sliced
Salt and freshly ground black pepper to taste
½ teaspoon oregano
Cayenne pepper to taste
2 cups Italian plum tomatoes
1 cup grated sharp Cheddar cheese.

1. Preheat the oven to 400 degrees.
2. In a casserole, cook the onion, green pepper, garlic and celery in the butter until crisp-tender. Add the zucchini, salt, black pepper, oregano and cayenne and simmer on top of the stove until most of the liquid evaporates. Cover and bake ten minutes.
3. Uncover, add the tomatoes and bake fifteen minutes longer. Sprinkle with the cheese and bake, uncovered, until cheese melts.

Yield: Eight servings.

Calabacitas (Green Summer Squash)

New Mexico

3 tablespoons oil
4 medium-size zucchini, sliced or cubed
2 small hot canned chilies, chopped
1 clove garlic, finely chopped
1 tablespoon finely chopped onion
1 cup corn kernels, scraped from the cobs
  Salt to taste
1 cup milk.

1. Heat the oil in a skillet and sauté the zucchini, chilies, garlic and onion in it until tender, about ten minutes.

2. Add the corn, salt and milk and simmer ten minutes.

Yield: Six servings.

Rice-Stuffed Tomatoes   *Southern California*

4 large ripe tomatoes
1 onion, finely chopped
½ cup olive oil
½ cup uncooked rice
1 tablespoon chopped parsley
1 tablespoon freshly snipped dill weed
1 tablespoon finely chopped currants
1 tablespoon pignoli (pine nuts, see note)
  Salt and freshly ground black pepper to taste
½ cup chicken broth or water.

1. Preheat the oven to 350 degrees.

2. Cut about a one-half-inch slice from the top of each tomato. Using a small spoon, scoop out the inside pulp of the tomatoes and chop the pulp coarsely.

3. Cook the onion in two tablespoons of the oil until onion is translucent. Add the rice and tomato pulp. Cook, stirring constantly, about seven minutes. Add the parsley, dill, currants, pignoli, salt and pepper.

4. Stuff the tomatoes with the rice mixture and place in a greased baking dish. Pour the remaining oil and the broth or water over them and bake until rice is tender, thirty to forty minutes. Serve cold.

Yield: Four servings.

Note: Pignoli are available in Greek and Italian markets.

Texas Stuffed Baked Tomatoes

8 large ripe tomatoes
2 carrots, finely chopped
1 green pepper, finely chopped
1 onion, finely chopped
5 tender ribs celery, finely chopped
3 cups chopped raw spinach
1 cup finely chopped parsley
3 tablespoons melted butter
1 egg, lightly beaten
1 cup soft bread crumbs
½ cup milk
  Salt and freshly ground black pepper to taste
½ teaspoon nutmeg.

1. Preheat the oven to 350 degrees.

2. Do not peel the tomatoes, but, for each, remove the core and scoop out most of the seeds and pulp to form a shell.

3. Combine the remaining ingredients and use to fill the tomato cavities.

4. Arrange the tomatoes in a baking dish and pour hot water around them to the depth of one-quarter inch. Bake fifteen minutes, or until tomatoes are heated through and the stuffing begins to brown. Serve immediately.

Yield: Eight servings.

Note: If desired, the filling may be sprinkled with additional hot melted butter when the tomatoes are removed from the oven.

Vegetable Pot   *Southern California*

¼ cup butter
3 carrots, sliced diagonally

1 green pepper, seeded and sliced into strips
1 red sweet pepper, seeded and sliced into strips
4 ribs celery, sliced diagonally
6 scallions, including green part, sliced
1 cup frenched young green beans
2 cauliflower flowerets, thinly sliced
⅓ cup sliced mushrooms
  Salt and freshly ground black pepper to taste
¼ cup beef broth
¼ cup chopped parsley.

1. Melt the butter in a large sauté pan or skillet. Add all the vegetables, salt and pepper and cook, stirring, over high heat about five minutes.

2. Add the broth, cover tightly and cook slowly five minutes longer. Sprinkle with the parsley.

Yield: Six servings.

California Avocado Salad

Southern California

1 avocado
2 pounds zucchini
1 three-ounce package cream cheese, at room temperature
2 canned green chilies, chopped
¼ cup California salad dressing (recipe below)
  Lettuce (romaine, Bibb or Butter).

1. Peel and dice the avocado. Cut the zucchini into slices one-quarter-inch thick and steam-cook two minutes.

2. Break the cream cheese into small pieces and put on top of hot zucchini.

3. Combine the chilies with the avocado and the salad dressing. Mix together carefully avocado mixture with zucchini and cheese so cheese and avocado soften, but not so vigorously as to break up zucchini. Refrigerate one hour. Serve on individual beds of lettuce.

Yield: Six servings.

California Salad Dressing

Southern California

1 tablespoon sugar
1 teaspoon salt
½ teaspoon freshly ground black pepper
1 teaspoon grated onion
1 clove garlic, finely chopped
¼ teaspoon celery salt
¼ teaspoon paprika
¼ teaspoon dry mustard
1 tablespoon oregano
3 tablespoons catchup
2 tablespoons soy sauce
¼ cup dry red wine or wine vinegar
¾ cup oil.

1. Combine the sugar, salt, pepper, onion, garlic, celery salt, paprika, mustard and oregano.

2. Add the catchup and soy sauce. Refrigerate one hour or more to blend.

3. Beat in the wine or vinegar and oil.

Yield: About one cup.

Cactus Salad

Texas

1 seven-and-one-quarter-ounce can cactus (see note)
1 clove garlic, finely minced
1 tablespoon coarsely chopped red onion
  Juice of one-half lime or lemon
2 tablespoons peanut oil
  Salt and freshly ground black pepper to taste
  Tabasco sauce to taste.

1. Rinse the cactus pieces under cold running water and drain well.

2. Combine the cactus and remaining ingredients. Serve chilled.

Yield: About four servings.

Note: Cactus is available at Casa Moneo, 210 West 14th Street, New York, New York 10011, and Spanish grocery stores.

Farmers Market Caesar Salad

Southern California

¾ cup olive oil
2 cloves garlic, crushed
1 cup stale French bread cubes
3 heads romaine lettuce, washed and dried
   Salt and freshly ground black pepper to
   taste
1 egg, cooked for one minute in boiling water
1 large lemon, halved
1 tablespoon Worcestershire sauce
8 anchovy fillets, chopped
⅓ cup freshly grated Romano cheese or
   Parmesan cheese.

1. Day before, combine the oil and garlic and let stand overnight.
2. Next day, remove garlic and discard. Heat one-quarter cup of the oil in a skillet and brown the bread cubes in it on all sides. Drain and reserve.
3. Place the lettuce in a salad bowl. Add the remaining oil, salt and pepper and toss. Break and add the contents of the egg. Toss again.
4. Squeeze the lemon halves over the salad. Add the Worcestershire, anchovies and cheese. Toss. Add the bread cubes and toss again.
Yield: Eight to ten servings.

Kidson's Bronze Lettuce Salad

Southern California

1 clove garlic, crushed
½ cup slivered cooked beets
2 tablespoons beet pickling juice
1 tablespoon chopped chives
2 teaspoons chopped parsley
2 teaspoons chopped chervil
½ teaspoon chopped fresh thyme or
   one-eighth teaspoon dried thyme
3 tomatoes, peeled and quartered
8 cups red leaf or bronze lettuce, washed,
   dried, chilled and torn apart

6 tablespoons olive oil
2 tablespoons wine vinegar
½ teaspoon sugar
   Salt and freshly ground black pepper to
   taste.

1. Rub a salad bowl with the garlic clove.
2. Add the beets, juice, chives, parsley, chervil, thyme, tomatoes and lettuce. Beat together the oil, vinegar, sugar and seasonings.
3. Pour over the salad and toss.
Yield: Six servings.

Chick-Pea Salad

New Mexico

2 cups cooked or canned chick-peas
   (garbanzos)
1 clove garlic, finely minced
¼ cup chopped scallions, including green part
1 ripe tomato, cut into bite-size wedges
¼ cup finely chopped parsley
2 tablespoons wine vinegar
½ cup olive oil
   Salt and freshly ground black pepper to
   taste.

1. Drain the chick-peas well. Pour them into a salad bowl. Add the garlic, scallions, tomato and parsley.
2. Sprinkle with the vinegar and toss. Sprinkle with the oil, salt and pepper. Toss again.
Yield: Four to six servings.

Kidney Bean Salad

Texas

2 twenty-ounce cans kidney beans, rinsed and
   drained
1 cup chopped celery
1 cup finely chopped carrots
½ cup finely chopped onion or scallions,
   including green part
2 tablespoons sweet relish
4 large red radishes, sliced
1 hard-cooked egg, chopped

Salt and freshly ground black pepper to taste
Homemade mayonnaise (page 760).

Combine all the ingredients, adding just enough mayonnaise to moisten.
Yield: Eight servings.

Bean, Carrot and Cabbage Salad

Arizona

2 cups cold cooked pinto beans
½ cup coarsely shredded carrot
½ cup shredded cabbage
1 small onion, grated
¼ cup sweet pickle relish
Salt to taste
⅓ cup homemade French or Italian dressing.

Combine all the ingredients and mix well. Chill.
Yield: Four servings.

Hot Bean Salad

Arizona

3 tablespoons diced salt pork
⅓ cup chopped onion
3 cups cold cooked pinto beans
½ teaspoon dry mustard
¼ cup cider vinegar
¼ cup water
Salt and freshly ground black pepper to taste.

1. Cook the salt pork until crisp. Add the onion and cook until transparent.
2. Add the remaining ingredients and bring to a boil. Let simmer very gently until beans have absorbed the liquid.
Yield: Four servings.

Marinated Green Bean Salad

Texas

1 pound green beans
  Boiling salted water
¼ cup wine vinegar
2 tablespoons olive oil
1 small onion, thinly sliced
½ teaspoon salt
¼ teaspoon freshly ground black pepper
1 clove garlic, finely chopped
½ pound mushrooms, sliced
2 tablespoons chopped parsley
¼ teaspoon oregano
½ teaspoon thyme.

1. Place the beans in a saucepan. Cover with boiling salted water and boil, covered, five minutes. Drain well.
2. Combine the vinegar, oil, onion, salt, pepper and garlic in a saucepan and bring to a boil. Add the mushrooms and simmer five minutes.
3. Add the beans. Bring to a boil and simmer three minutes longer. Add the parsley, oregano and thyme. Chill.
Yield: Six servings.

Cold Rice Salad

Texas

4½ cups boiling water
  2 teaspoons salt
  2 cups uncooked long grain rice
  ¼ cup olive oil
  ¾ cup lemon juice
  ¼ cup chopped parsley
  ¼ cup chopped celery
  ¼ cup chopped red sweet pepper
  ¼ cup chopped fresh basil or freshly snipped dill weed
  ¼ cup sliced pitted ripe olives
    Salt and freshly ground black pepper to taste
  2 tomatoes, peeled and sliced
  2 hard-cooked eggs, sliced.

1. Combine the boiling water and salt and add

the rice. Cover and simmer until the rice is just tender and liquid is absorbed, about twenty-five minutes.

2. Immediately pour the oil and lemon juice over the hot rice; toss and cool.

3. Add the parsley, celery, red pepper, basil or dill, olives, salt and black pepper to cooled rice. Cool. Garnish with the tomato and egg slices.

Yield: Eight servings.

Spinach and Anchovy Salad
Southern California

3 cups spinach leaves, well rinsed in cold water
½ clove garlic, finely minced
1 teaspoon Dijon or Düsseldorf mustard
   Salt and freshly ground black pepper to taste
3 anchovies, finely chopped
2 teaspoons wine vinegar
¼ cup olive oil.

1. Cut or tear the spinach into bite-size pieces and shake the moisture from the leaves.

2. Combine the remaining ingredients in a salad bowl and mix well with a wire whisk or fork. Add the spinach pieces and toss well.

Yield: Six servings.

Frozen Tomato Salad
Southern California

2 cups tomatoes, preferably home-canned
   Homemade mayonnaise (see page 760)
2 tablespoons lemon juice
1 teaspoon chopped fresh basil or one-half teaspoon dried basil
1 tablespoon finely chopped chives or scallion, including green part
2 teaspoons Worcestershire sauce
   Tabasco sauce to taste
   Salt and freshly ground black pepper to taste
⅓ cup water

1 envelope unflavored gelatin
   Horseradish.

1. Place the tomatoes in an electric blender and blend thoroughly.

2. Add one and one-quarter cups of the mayonnaise and blend until thoroughly mixed. Pour the mixture into a mixing bowl and add the lemon juice, basil, chives, Worcestershire, Tabasco, salt and pepper.

3. Combine the water and gelatin. Heat, stirring, over boiling water until gelatin dissolves. Stir this into the tomato mixture. Pour the mixture into freezer trays and freeze. As the mixture freezes, beat it occasionally.

4. When frozen, scoop it out with an ice cream scoop into individual servings. Keep frozen until ready to serve. Serve with mayonnaise or with mayonnaise mixed with horseradish.

Yield: Six or more servings.

Sliced Tomato Salad
Southern California

6 large beefsteak tomatoes, peeled and thickly sliced
   Salt and freshly ground black pepper
¼ cup finely chopped scallions, including green part
2 tablespoons chopped fresh basil leaves or two teaspoons dried basil
¼ cup wine vinegar
¾ cup olive oil
1 clove garlic, finely chopped
1 teaspoon Worcestershire sauce
½ teaspoon sugar.

1. Arrange layers of the tomato slices in a serving dish, sprinkling each layer with salt and pepper to taste, scallions and basil.

2. Combine the vinegar, oil, garlic, Worcestershire, sugar, two teaspoons salt and one-half teaspoon pepper by beating or shaking in a jar. Pour over the tomatoes and chill well.

Yield: Eight servings.

Texas Salad

1 cup cooked lima beans, fresh or frozen
1 cup cooked string beans, cut into one-inch lengths
1 cup cooked field peas, speckled beans or black-eyed peas
½ cup thinly sliced water chestnuts
1 medium-size red onion, chopped or cut into thin rings
¼ cup wine vinegar
½ to one clove garlic, finely minced
¾ cup plus two tablespoons olive oil
  Salt and freshly ground black pepper to taste
24 cherry tomatoes, approximately
¼ cup chopped parsley.

1. The vegetables for this dish should be freshly cooked and not overcooked. They should be tender but still somewhat crisp. Combine the lima beans, string beans, field peas, water chestnuts and onion.

2. Combine the vinegar, garlic, oil, salt and pepper. Beat with a wire whisk until well blended and pour the sauce over the vegetables. Refrigerate several hours or overnight.

3. When ready to serve, toss lightly but thoroughly. Garnish with the cherry tomatoes and sprinkle with the parsley.
  Yield: Six to eight servings.

Tomato Aspic   *Arizona*

2 cups tomato juice
1 six-ounce can tomato paste
1 onion, finely chopped
1 tablespoon chopped green pepper
1 bay leaf
1 rib celery with leaves, diced
1 teaspoon salt
2 envelopes unflavored gelatin
½ cup cold water

2 tablespoons tarragon vinegar
2 sprigs sweet basil
¼ cup lemon juice
½ teaspoon grated lemon rind
  Coarsely ground black pepper to taste
  Salad greens.

1. Day before, place the tomato juice, tomato paste, onion, green pepper, bay leaf, celery and salt in a saucepan and bring to a boil. Simmer ten minutes.

2. Soften the gelatin in the water. Add to the hot tomato mixture and stir well. Add the remaining ingredients except salad greens.

3. Remove the bay leaf and basil sprigs and pour mixture into a mold. Chill overnight. Next day, unmold onto a bed of greens.
  Yield: Six servings.

Mexican Salad   *Texas*

8 cups finely shredded iceberg lettuce
1 cucumber, scored with a fork and diced
6 ribs celery with leaves, chopped
2 tomatoes, peeled and chopped
2 cloves garlic, finely chopped
3 stalks fennel, chopped
1 bunch scallions, including green part, chopped
1 green pepper, seeded and diced
1 bunch radishes, sliced
12 to fifteen sprigs parsley, finely chopped
1 can anchovy fillets, chopped
1 large red onion, cut into rings
1 cup pitted ripe olives
  Salt and freshly ground black pepper to taste
  Oil to taste
  Cider vinegar to taste.

Combine all ingredients in a large bowl. Toss gently.
  Yield: Eight servings.

Dutchie's Tossed Salad
Texas

1 large head romaine lettuce, in bite-size pieces
1 cup raw cauliflower, roughly chopped
1 cup chopped celery
1 cup finely chopped carrots
6 red radishes, sliced
1 cup seasoned croutons
6 stuffed green olives
6 cherry tomatoes
    Homemade Italian dressing.

    1. Combine all ingredients except dressing in a salad bowl.
    2. Toss with the dressing just before serving.
Yield: Six servings.

Fresh Mushroom Salad
Southern California

½ pound mushrooms, cleaned and sliced
¼ cup lemon juice
2 tablespoons chopped parsley
1 scallion, including green part, finely chopped
3 tablespoons olive oil
1 teaspoon dry vermouth
1 teaspoon dry red wine
    Coarse salt and freshly ground black pepper to taste
⅛ teaspoon thyme
⅛ teaspoon marjoram
⅛ teaspoon rubbed rosemary
    As much dry mustard as will cling to the tip of a fork, or to taste
    Boston (Butter) lettuce leaves.

    1. Place the mushrooms, lemon juice, parsley and scallion in a bowl. Place the remaining ingredients except the lettuce in a jar. Shake to mix.
    2. Pour the dressing over the mushrooms and serve on lettuce leaves.
Yield: Four to six servings.

Banana Salad Platter
Southern California

7 large ripe bananas
1 cup sour cream
2 tablespoons dark rum
2 tablespoons light brown sugar
1 tablespoon finely chopped preserved ginger
¼ teaspoon salt
2 teaspoons lime juice
    Romaine lettuce leaves
6 large ripe peaches, peeled, halved and pitted
4 cups strawberries or raspberries.

    1. Mash one of the bananas with a fork and gradually blend in the sour cream, rum, brown sugar, ginger, salt and lime juice. Chill well.
    2. Arrange the lettuce leaves on a serving platter or individual plates. For each serving, top lettuce with a banana sliced lengthwise, two peach halves and berries. Spoon the chilled dressing over all.
Yield: Six servings.

Farmers Market Mayonnaise Dressing
Southern California

¼ teaspoon capers
½ teaspoon chopped water cress
½ teaspoon chopped parsley
1 anchovy fillet
2 egg yolks
½ teaspoon salt
1 teaspoon Worcestershire sauce
1 teaspoon dry mustard, mixed to a paste with a little water
1 tablespoon vinegar
1 tablespoon lemon juice
½ cup olive oil
1 cup vegetable oil
1 tablespoon boiling water.

    1. Combine the capers, water cress, parsley and anchovy in a mortar and grind to a paste with a pestle. Force through a sieve.

2. With an electric mixer, beat together the egg yolks, salt, Worcestershire and mustard.

3. Add half the vinegar and the lemon juice to the yolk mixture and beat well.

4. While still beating, gradually add the olive oil mixed with the vegetable oil until no more oil can be absorbed. Add remaining vinegar and beat in some more oil.

5. Add the boiling water a drop at a time. Stir in the strained caper mixture.

Yield: About one and three-quarter cups.

Southern California French Dressing

1 tablespoon lemon juice
1 tablespoon Worcestershire sauce
¼ teaspoon Tabasco sauce
¼ cup olive oil
1 clove garlic, finely chopped
Salt and freshly ground black pepper to taste
Cayenne pepper to taste.

Combine the lemon juice, Worcestershire and Tabasco. Beat in the oil and add the remaining ingredients.

Yield: About one-third cup.

Sesame Lime Dressing for Fruit Salad
Arizona

1 egg yolk
1 teaspoon salt
1 tablespoon sugar
¼ teaspoon ground ginger
¼ cup lime juice
¾ cup oil
2 teaspoons toasted sesame seeds.

1. Place the egg yolk, salt, sugar, ginger and lime juice in an electric blender. Blend on low speed.

2. Gradually add the oil while blending.

3. Stir in the seeds. Chill.

Yield: About one cup dressing.

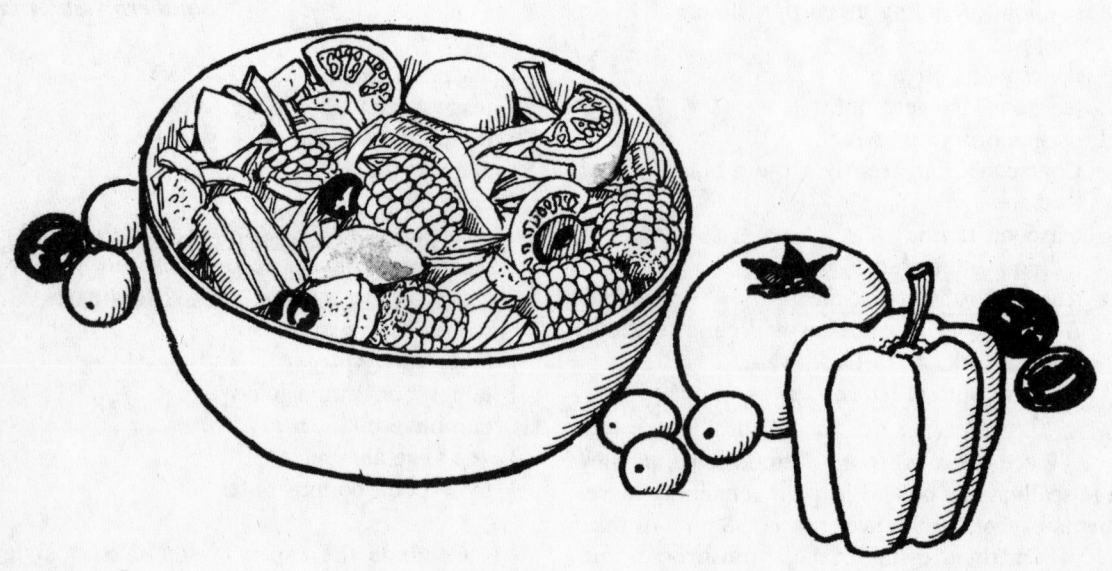

Breads

Walnut-Fig Bread

Southern California

1 cup dried figs
½ cup dry sherry
½ cup boiling water
3 cups flour
1½ teaspoons salt
3 teaspoons baking powder
⅔ cup sugar
1 egg, lightly beaten
¼ cup soft butter
½ cup chopped walnuts
½ teaspoon maple flavoring.

1. Remove the stems from the figs and dice figs finely. Place in a bowl and pour the sherry and water over. Set aside to cool.

2. Sift the flour, salt, baking powder and sugar into a bowl. Stir in the cooled fig mixture, the egg, butter, walnuts and flavoring. Mix well. Turn into a greased 9-by-5-by-3-inch loaf pan. Let stand twenty minutes.

3. Meanwhile, preheat the oven to 350 degrees.

4. Bake one hour, or until done. Let stand in pan ten minutes before turning out onto a rack to cool.

Yield: One loaf.

Wheat Germ Rolls   *Southern California*

2 packages active dry yeast
⅓ cup lukewarm water
1½ cups milk, scalded
½ cup butter
½ cup sugar
2 eggs, lightly beaten
4½ cups stone-ground whole wheat flour
1 cup plus two tablespoons wheat germ
1 tablespoon salt
  Oil, if necessary.

1. Dissolve the yeast in the water and set aside in a warm place until mixture bubbles.

2. In a large bowl, place the milk and add the butter and sugar. Stir to dissolve the sugar and let cool to lukewarm.

3. Add the yeast mixture, the eggs and three cups of the flour. Beat six minutes with an electric mixer on medium speed.

4. Clean the sides of the bowl, cover and let rise in a warm place until doubled in bulk, about one and one-quarter hours.

5. Add one cup of the wheat germ, the salt and enough of the remaining flour to make a kneadable dough. Turn the dough onto a lightly floured board and knead very well, using only flour remaining from the measured amount.

6. If the dough starts to stick, oil the heel of the hand before continuing. The kneading, at least 300 strokes, is the secret to success with this recipe. The dough should be smooth and satiny.

7. Roll out the dough to one-inch thickness and cut into two-and-one-half-inch rounds. Fit into greased muffin tins. Sprinkle a little of the remaining wheat germ over each round, cover and let rise in a warm place until doubled in size, about twenty minutes.

8. Meanwhile, preheat the oven to 350 degrees.

9. Bake twenty-five minutes, or until done. Cool on a rack.

Yield: Two dozen.

Two-Bite-Size Muffins   *Texas*

Muffins:
1 cup sugar
½ cup butter
2 eggs
1 cup buttermilk
1 teaspoon baking soda
1 cup ground raisins
1 cup pecans, chopped
1 tablespoon grated orange rind.
Frosting:
¾ cup orange juice
1 cup sugar.

1. Preheat the oven to 450 degrees.

2. To prepare muffins, cream the sugar and butter together until light. Beat in the eggs. Add the buttermilk, baking soda, raisins, pecans and orange rind and stir to moisten thoroughly.

3. Place one-half teaspoon batter in each of 120 greased tiny petits fours molds. Bake twelve minutes, or until done.

4. Combine the orange juice with the sugar and brush on muffins while still hot.

Yield: One hundred and twenty tiny muffins.

Avocado Pecan Bread   *Texas*

2 cups flour
½ teaspoon baking soda
½ teaspoon baking powder
¼ teaspoon salt
¾ cup sugar
1 egg, lightly beaten
½ cup buttermilk or sour milk
½ cup chopped pecans
1 cup mashed avocado (usually one medium-size avocado).

1. Preheat the oven to 350 degrees.

2. Sift together the flour, baking soda, baking powder, salt and sugar.

3. Combine the remaining ingredients and add to dry mixture; mix. Pour into a greased 9-by-5-by-3-inch loaf pan. Bake one hour. Remove loaf to a rack for cooling.

Yield: One loaf.

Orange Nut Bread   *Southern California*

4 oranges
2 cups sugar
3 cups flour
2½ teaspoons baking powder
⅛ teaspoon salt
2 eggs, lightly beaten
3 tablespoons melted butter, cooled
1 cup milk
¾ cup chopped walnuts.

1. With a swivel-blade potato peeler, remove the orange part of the orange skin from the oranges. Chop into fine slivers and place in a small saucepan. Cover with water and bring to a boil. Simmer until tender, about ten minutes.

2. Drain. Add one cup of the sugar and one-quarter cup water and boil the mixture until it is clear and fairly thick. Cool.

3. Preheat the oven to 350 degrees.

4. Sift the flour, baking powder, salt and remaining sugar into a bowl.

5. Stir in the eggs, butter, milk, cooled orange mixture and the walnuts until blended.

6. Pour into a greased 9-by-5-by-3-inch loaf pan. Bake about one hour, or until loaf tests done. Cool on a rack.

Yield: One loaf.

Lemon Bread   *Southern California*

2¾ cups flour
 ½ teaspoon baking soda
 3 teaspoons baking powder
 ½ teaspoon salt
 ⅓ cup shortening
 1 cup sugar
 ½ cup wheat germ
 3 to four tablespoons grated lemon rind
 2 eggs, lightly beaten
 ½ cup lemon juice
 ½ cup water.

1. Preheat the oven to 350 degrees.
2. Sift the flour, baking soda, baking powder and salt into a bowl. With the finger tips or a pastry blender, work the shortening in as though making pastry.
3. Stir in the sugar, wheat germ, lemon rind and eggs. Mix the lemon juice with the water and stir in. Mix to moisten the dry ingredients. Turn into a greased 9-by-5-by-3-inch loaf pan and bake one hour, or until done.

Yield: One loaf.

Walnut Cheddar Loaf   *Southern California*

2½ cups flour
 2 tablespoons sugar
 2 teaspoons baking powder
 1¼ teaspoons salt
 ½ teaspoon dry mustard
 ½ teaspoon baking soda
    Dash of cayenne pepper
 ¼ cup shortening
 1 cup grated sharp Cheddar cheese

½ teaspoon Worcestershire sauce
 1 egg, lightly beaten
 1 cup buttermilk
 1 cup chopped walnuts.

1. Preheat the oven to 350 degrees.
2. Sift together the flour, sugar, baking powder, salt, mustard, baking soda and cayenne.
3. With a pastry blender or the finger tips, work in the shortening as though making pastry. Stir in the cheese.
4. Combine the Worcestershire, egg and buttermilk and stir into the flour mixture until just moistened. Mix in the walnuts.
5. Turn the batter into a greased 8½-by-4½-by-2½-inch loaf pan. Smooth top with a spatula and bake about fifty-five minutes.
6. When done, turn out onto a rack. Serve warm or cold. The bread can be reheated if wrapped in aluminum foil.

Yield: One loaf.

Walnut Brown Bread   *Southern California*

1¼ cups regular flour
 2 teaspoons baking powder
 ¾ teaspoon baking soda
 1¼ teaspoons salt
 1¼ cups graham flour or whole wheat flour
 1 cup chopped walnuts
 1 egg, lightly beaten
 ⅓ cup light brown sugar
 ½ cup light molasses
 ¾ cup buttermilk
 3 tablespoons melted shortening.

1. Preheat the oven to 350 degrees.
2. Sift together the regular flour, baking powder, baking soda and salt into a bowl. Stir in the graham or whole wheat flour and walnuts.
3. Beat the egg while adding the brown sugar, molasses, buttermilk and shortening. Stir into the dry mixture until moistened. Spoon into three greased one-pound cans. Bake forty-five minutes,

or until done. Let stand ten minutes and then turn out. Serve warm.

Yield: Three round loaves.

Note: Alternately, the mixture can be baked in a 9-by-5-by-3-inch loaf pan fifty minutes or steamed in the three cans for one hour.

Cinnamon Walnut Quick Bread
Southern California

1½ cups coarsely chopped walnuts
1 tablespoon melted butter
1 cup sugar
2 teaspoons cinnamon
3 cups flour
4½ teaspoons baking powder
1½ teaspoons salt
¼ cup shortening
1 egg, lightly beaten
1¼ cups milk.

1. Preheat the oven to 350 degrees.
2. Place the walnuts in a bowl, add the butter and toss. Stir in one-quarter cup of the sugar and the cinnamon.
3. Sift the flour, baking powder and salt into a bowl. Cut in the shortening. Stir in remaining sugar. Combine the egg and milk and stir into the dry ingredients until they are just moistened.
4. Reserve one-quarter cup of the walnut mixture and stir rest into batter. Mix lightly and turn into a greased 9-by-5-by-3-inch loaf pan. Sprinkle with reserved nut mixture. Let stand fifteen minutes.
5. Bake about one hour, or until done. Leave in pan ten minutes. Cool on a rack.

Yield: One loaf.

Lucy's Buñeolos   *New Mexico*

4 cups flour
1 teaspoon salt
1 teaspoon baking powder
2 tablespoons sugar

2 tablespoons lard
1½ cups water or milk, approximately
    Fat or oil for deep-frying
    Sugar-cinnamon mixture (optional).

1. Sift together the flour, salt, baking powder and sugar. With the finger tips, work in the lard. Mix to a soft dough with the water or milk.
2. Turn out onto a lightly floured board and knead until smooth and satiny, about eight minutes.
3. Divide dough into about thirty-six balls and roll each one out to a round four inches in diameter. Fry one or two at a time in the fat or oil heated to 370 degrees on a deep-fat thermometer. Drain on paper towels. Sprinkle with sugar-cinnamon mixture if desired.

Yield: About three dozen.

Sopaipillas (Puffy Fried Bread)
New Mexico

4 cups flour
3 teaspoons baking powder
1 teaspoon salt
2 teaspoons sugar
3 tablespoons lard
¾ cup water, approximately
    Fat for deep-frying
    Butter.

1. Sift together the flour, baking powder, salt and sugar. Cut in the lard and then add enough water to make a dough that is dry but just pliable enough to roll.
2. Let the dough stand covered with a cloth for twenty minutes.
3. Roll out the dough to one-quarter-inch thickness on a floured board. Cut into three-inch squares or diamond-shaped pieces. Fry, a few at a time, in one to two inches of deep fat heated to 370 to 380 degrees. Turn at once so pieces puff

evenly and then turn back to brown both sides. Drain on paper towels. Serve with butter.

Yield: About four dozen.

New Mexican Corn Bread

1 eight-and-one-half-ounce can cream-style corn
1 cup yellow corn meal
2 eggs
1 teaspoon salt
½ teaspoon baking soda
¾ cup milk
⅓ cup melted lard or butter or oil
1 four-ounce can mild diced chilies (optional)
½ cup grated sharp Cheddar cheese
2 tablespoons butter.

1. Preheat the oven to 400 degrees.
2. Combine the corn, corn meal, eggs, salt, baking soda, milk, lard, or butter or oil, chilies if desired and half the cheese in a mixing bowl. Beat well.
3. Meanwhile, put the butter in a one-and-one-half-quart casserole (preferably a glazed, Mexican earthenware casserole) or a nine-inch skillet. Place the casserole or skillet in the oven until butter is hot but not brown.
4. Immediately pour in the corn bread mixture. Sprinkle the top with the remaining cheese and bake forty minutes or longer.

Yield: Eight servings.

Texas Corn Bread

¼ cup bacon drippings or butter
1 cup yellow corn meal
  Salt to taste
1 egg
½ cup flour
2 teaspoons baking powder
¼ cup milk
¼ cup water.

1. Preheat the oven to 350 degrees.
2. Pour the bacon drippings or butter into a heavy black iron skillet nine inches in diameter.
3. Combine the remaining ingredients and mix well. If necessary, add a little water to make a smooth paste.
4. Heat the drippings in the skillet and pour the batter into the hot skillet. Bake twenty-five to thirty minutes, or until corn bread is golden brown on top and cooked in the center.

Yield: Six servings.

Mexican Corn Bread   *Texas*

1 recipe for Texas corn bread (recipe above)
1 tablespoon chili powder
¼ cup finely chopped onion
¼ cup chopped green pepper
¼ cup chopped pimentos.

Follow the recipe for Texas corn bread exactly, but add the chili powder to the dry ingredients. When the batter is made, stir in the remaining ingredients.

Yield: Six servings.

Bacon 'n' Corn Bread   *Texas*

¾ pound lean bacon
1 cup yellow corn meal
1 cup flour
2 tablespoons sugar
½ teaspoon salt
2 teaspoons baking powder
1½ cups grated sharp Cheddar cheese
1 egg, lightly beaten
1 cup milk.

1. Preheat the oven to 450 degrees.
2. Dice one-quarter pound of the bacon and cook in a small skillet until crisp. Drain bacon bits on paper towel. Allow drippings to cool.
3. Place the corn meal, flour, sugar, salt, baking powder and one-half cup of the cheese in a

bowl. Stir in the cooled drippings, bacon bits, egg and milk. Turn into a greased 8-by-8-by-2-inch pan.

4. Sprinkle with the remaining cheese. Make a lattice pattern on top with the remaining bacon. Bake twenty-five to thirty minutes. Serve hot.

Yield: Six servings.

Arizona Christmas Bread

Bread:
 2 packages active dry yeast
 ½ cup lukewarm water
 1 cup milk, scalded
 ¼ cup butter
 1 teaspoon salt
   Granulated sugar
 6 cups flour, approximately
 ½ teaspoon nutmeg
 ½ teaspoon mace
 ¼ teaspoon ground cloves
 2 eggs, beaten
 ½ cup raisins
 ½ cup glacé cherries, quartered
 ½ cup chopped nuts
   Melted butter.
Frosting:
 ¼ cup butter
 2 cups confectioners' sugar
 ½ teaspoon vanilla
   Milk, cream or cold black coffee.

1. To prepare bread, combine the yeast and water. Set aside.

2. Place the milk in a large bowl and add the butter, salt and one-half cup granulated sugar. Stir to dissolve sugar. Let cool to lukewarm.

3. Sift one-half cup of the flour with the nutmeg, mace and cloves.

4. When the milk mixture is lukewarm, stir in the dissolved yeast and the spice mixture and beat well. Stir in the eggs, raisins, cherries and nuts and enough of the remaining flour to make a soft dough.

5. Turn onto a lightly floured board and knead

until smooth. Place in a greased bowl, cover and let rise in a warm place until doubled in bulk, about one and one-quarter hours. Punch down.

6. Shape into two loaves and place in two greased 9-by-5-by-3-inch loaf pans. Cover and let rise until doubled in bulk, about forty-five minutes.

7. Preheat the oven to 375 degrees.

8. Brush loaves with melted butter and sprinkle generously with granulated sugar. Bake forty minutes, or until done. Cool on a rack.

9. To prepare frosting, cream the butter and gradually beat in the confectioners' sugar and vanilla. Beat in enough milk, cream or coffee to make spreading consistency. Use to frost cooled loaves.

Yield: Two loaves.

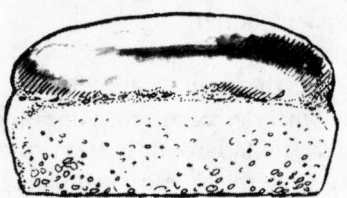

Ranch House Sour Cream Pancakes
Southern California

 4 eggs
1½ cups sour cream
 ½ cup milk
 ½ cup regular flour
 ⅛ cup wheat germ
 ¼ cup whole wheat flour
 ¼ cup old-fashioned rolled oats
 1 teaspoon baking soda
 ½ teaspoon salt.

1. Place all the ingredients in a bowl and beat with a wooden spoon until well mixed.

2. Cook one-quarter-cup amounts on a hot greased griddle until bubbles form on the top of each; turn and brown the other side.

Yield: One dozen to sixteen.

Tortillas, the Mexican version of crepes or thin pancakes, are made with corn meal or masa.

Tortillas New Mexico

1 cup sifted flour
½ cup yellow corn meal
¼ teaspoon salt
1 egg
1½ cups cold water.

1. Combine the flour and corn meal in a mixing bowl and add the salt and egg. Beat with a rotary beater while gradually adding the water.
2. Spoon portions of the mixture onto a hot ungreased griddle. Turn each tortilla when the edges start to curl slightly. Do not brown. Cook on the other side without browning.
Yield: One dozen.

Virginia's Wheat Flour Tortillas
Southern California

4 cups flour
2 teaspoons baking powder
1½ teaspoons salt
4 tablespoons lard
2 cups water.

1. Combine the flour, baking powder and salt in a bowl. Cut in the lard. Mix to a dough with the water.
2. Knead the dough until smooth. Let rest, covered, ten minutes.
3. Form dough into balls three inches in diameter and roll each out into a flat shaped cake about one-eighth inch thick. Cook on a hot greased griddle until spotted with brown; turn and brown the other side.
Yield: One dozen.

Tortillas Texas

2 cups masa harina (see note)
1⅓ cups to one and one-half cups warm water
1 teaspoon salt.

1. Mix the ingredients to form a soft, workable dough. Mix well and thoroughly with the fingers.
2. Open the two "faces" of a tortilla press and cover with a single rectangle of household plastic or wax paper.
3. Tear off enough tortilla dough to make a ball the size of a small egg. Work the dough with the fingers into a small, round, flat shape, like a biscuit, and place it in the center of one face of the tortilla press. Fold the plastic sheet over the dough and then bring the other half of the press forward to cover the first. Press down lightly to make a thin pancake four to five inches across. Very gently pull the plastic off the top of the tortilla; then hold the pancake in one hand while gently pulling the plastic from the other half.
4. Cook the tortilla quickly on one side on an ungreased griddle until the edges begin to curl, about two minutes. Turn with a spatula and cook on the other side about two minutes. The tortilla is ready to eat without long cooking.
Yield: About one dozen.
Note: Masa harina is available where Mexican and Spanish products are sold.
To keep the tortillas warm, dampen a kitchen towel and cover with paper towels. Add a hot tortilla and fold over. Add another paper towel and tortilla and fold. Continue until all are folded. Enclose them in the kitchen towel, dampen it and wrap in aluminum foil. Let stand in a 150-degree oven until ready to serve.

Pies, Cakes, Desserts and Cookies

Apricot Pie
Southern California

Graham crust:
16 graham crackers, crushed
 1 tablespoon sugar
½ teaspoon cinnamon
¼ cup melted butter.
Filling:
 3 eggs, separated
 1 cup sugar
1½ cups apricot pulp, made by skinning and
   pitting ripe fruit and blending in an electric
   blender
¼ teaspoon grated lemon rind
⅛ teaspoon salt
 1 envelope unflavored gelatin
¼ cup cold water
 6 ripe apricots, peeled and halved
   Whipped cream.

1. Preheat the oven to 375 degrees.
2. To prepare crust, combine the graham cracker crumbs, sugar, cinnamon and melted butter and mix well. Press into the bottom and sides of a nine-inch pie plate.
3. Bake eight minutes. Cool.
4. To prepare filling, beat the egg yolks with one-half cup of the sugar until light and fluffy. Add the apricot pulp, lemon rind and salt and place in the top of a double boiler.
5. Heat, stirring, until mixture thickens. Soak the gelatin in the water and add to the hot mix-ture. Stir to melt gelatin. Cool until mixture starts to set.
6. Beat the egg whites until soft peaks form. Gradually beat in the remaining sugar and fold into the cooled apricot mixture.
7. Pour into the cooled shell and chill. Garnish with the apricot halves and whipped cream.
   Yield: Six servings.

California Citrus Chiffon Pie
Southern California

1⅔ cups graham cracker crumbs
1½ cups plus two tablespoons sugar
¼ cup melted butter
   Soft butter
 2 medium-size lemons
 1 medium-size orange
½ medium-size grapefruit
 1 envelope unflavored gelatin
¼ cup cold water
 4 eggs, separated
¼ teaspoon salt
 1 cup heavy cream, whipped
 1 teaspoon vanilla.

1. Mix the graham cracker crumbs with one-quarter cup of the sugar. Add the melted butter and mix lightly with a fork. Mix well. Butter a nine-inch pie plate; then press crumbs over the

bottom and sides of the plate. A spoon may be used for this, but the heel of the hand does a better job.

2. Grate the rind of the lemons, orange and grapefruit half on a fine grater and set aside. Mix one tablespoon of the grated lemon rind thoroughly with two tablespoons of the remaining sugar and set aside. Squeeze the lemons, orange and grapefruit half and strain the juices.

3. Soften the gelatin in the water and let stand.

4. Beat the egg yolks in a bowl until lemon-colored. Add one-half cup of the remaining sugar, the salt and fruit juices. Put the mixture in the top of a double boiler and stir constantly while cooking until thick.

5. Add the gelatin to the hot mixture and stir until dissolved. Stir in the grated fruit rinds. Scrape into a large mixing bowl and set aside to cool.

6. When the mixture begins to set and is the consistency of egg whites, beat the egg whites and gradually add one-half cup of the remaining sugar. Continue beating until whites are thick and glossy. Carefully fold whites into cooled mixture. Blend thoroughly; then fill graham cracker shell and chill.

7. Shortly before serving, top with the whipped cream sweetened with the remaining sugar and the vanilla. Garnish the cream with the reserved sugared lemon rind.

Yield: Eight servings.

Sesame Date Pie   *Southern California*

Pastry:
1½ cups flour
¼ teaspoon salt
¼ cup shortening
1 tablespoon butter
1 tablespoon sesame seeds, lightly toasted
3 tablespoons cold water, approximately.
Filling:
1 envelope unflavored gelatin
¼ cup cold water
1 cup less two tablespoons milk
2 eggs, separated
6 tablespoons sugar
¼ teaspoon salt
1 teaspoon vanilla
2 tablespoons rum or cognac
¾ cup heavy cream, whipped
1 cup pitted fresh dates, finely chopped
    Whole dates.

1. To prepare pastry, place the flour, salt, shortening and butter in a bowl. With a pastry blender or the finger tips, blend the fat into the flour until mixture resembles coarse oatmeal.

2. Using a fork, stir in the sesame seeds and water to make a dough. Wrap the dough in wax paper and chill briefly, about fifteen minutes.

3. Roll out the pastry on a lightly floured board or pastry cloth and fit into a nine-inch pie plate. Decorate the edge and chill shell fifteen minutes.

4. Meanwhile, preheat the oven to 425 degrees.

5. Prick pie shell with a fork. Bake twenty to twenty-five minutes, or until baked and golden. Cool.

6. To prepare filling, soak the gelatin in the water in the top of a double boiler. Beat the milk with the egg yolks and add with four tablespoons of the sugar and the salt.

7. Heat mixture over hot water until gelatin and sugar are dissolved and mixture coats the back of the spoon. Remove from heat. Stir in the vanilla and the rum or cognac. Chill, stirring occasionally, until mixture starts to thicken.

8. Fold in the whipped cream and chopped dates.

9. Beat the egg whites until frothy. Gradually beat in the remaining sugar. Beat until mixture is stiff. Fold into date mixture. Pile into pie shell. Chill well. Garnish with whole dates before serving.

Yield: Six servings.

Rum Walnut Pie   *Southern California*

Pie crust:
  ⅔ cup graham cracker crumbs
  2 tablespoons sugar
  ½ cup grated or very finely chopped (in electric blender) walnuts
  ¼ cup melted butter.
Filling:
  ½ cup sugar
  1 envelope plus one teaspoon unflavored gelatin
  ¼ teaspoon salt
  1¼ cups milk or light cream
  3 eggs, separated
  3 tablespoons dark rum
  ½ cup heavy cream, whipped
  2 tablespoons cocoa powder
  3 tablespoons hot water
  ½ cup finely chopped walnuts
    Whipped cream and walnut halves for garnish (optional).

1. Preheat the oven to 350 degrees.
2. To prepare pie crust, combine the graham cracker crumbs, sugar, walnuts and melted butter. Mix well and press over the bottom and sides of a nine-inch pie plate to form a crust.
3. Bake ten minutes. Cool and chill.
4. To prepare filling, combine one-quarter cup of the sugar, the gelatin and salt in the top of a double boiler. Stir in the milk or cream. Beat the egg yolks lightly and stir in.
5. Heat over simmering water until the mixture thickens and just coats the back of the spoon. Remove from the heat and stir in the rum.
6. Cool and chill until mixture starts to thicken.
7. Beat the egg whites until stiff and gradually beat in the remaining sugar. Fold into the chilling filling. Fold in the whipped cream. Turn one cup of mixture into the chilled crust.
8. Mix the cocoa powder with the water, cool slightly and fold into remaining pie filling along with the chopped walnuts. Chill in bowl until filling starts to set. Spoon over the white filling in the pie shell and chill until firm, at least four hours.
9. If desired, garnish with whipped cream and walnut halves before serving.
  Yield: Six servings.

Chocolate Raisin Pie   *Southern California*

  1½ cups chopped raisins (see note)
  1 cup heavy cream
  2 ounces (one-half bar) German sweet chocolate
  ¼ cup butter
  2 eggs, lightly beaten
  1 teaspoon vanilla
  ⅛ teaspoon cinnamon
  ½ teaspoon instant coffee powder
  ⅛ teaspoon salt
  ¾ cup sugar
  3 tablespoons cornstarch
  1 unbaked nine-inch pie shell, chilled
    Whipped cream.

1. Preheat the oven to 375 degrees.
2. Combine the raisins, heavy cream, chocolate and butter in the top of a double boiler and heat over hot water, stirring to melt the chocolate.
3. Combine the eggs, vanilla, cinnamon, instant coffee, salt, sugar and cornstarch. Mix well and add to chocolate mixture.
4. Pour into the pie shell and bake forty minutes, or until set. Cool.
5. Serve at room temperature, garnished with whipped cream.
  Yield: Eight servings.
  Note: To chop raisins, freeze them and then chop a few at a time in an electric blender.

Fruited Cheese Pie   *Southern California*

  3 cups peeled, diced ripe nectarines, peaches, pears, apples, pitted cherries or diced plums
  ⅓ cup plus one-quarter cup sugar

2 tablespoons flour
2 teaspoons grated lime rind
⅛ teaspoon cinnamon
1 or two drops of red food coloring (optional)
2 three-ounce packages cream cheese, softened
2 tablespoons lime juice
½ teaspoon salt
½ cup heavy cream
3 eggs, separated
1 unbaked nine-inch pie shell, chilled, or eight to ten pastry-lined three-inch to four-inch tart tins.

1. Preheat the oven to 375 degrees.
2. Place the fruit, one-third cup of the sugar, one tablespoon of the flour, one teaspoon of the lime rind, the cinnamon and food coloring if desired in a small saucepan. Heat, stirring gently until sugar is dissolved. Simmer until fruit is barely tender, about five minutes. Cool.
3. In a bowl, beat together the cream cheese, lime juice, remaining flour, remaining sugar, remaining lime rind, the salt, cream and egg yolks.
4. Beat the egg whites until stiff but not dry and fold into the cheese mixture.
5. Place the fruit mixture in the bottom of the pie shell or tart shells and top with the cream cheese mixture. Bake pie forty-five minutes, tarts about twenty-five minutes, or until lightly browned and set. Cool. Serve at room temperature.
Yield: Six to ten servings.

Walnut Tarts   *Southern California*

½ cup butter
¾ cup light brown sugar
½ cup maple syrup
3 eggs, lightly beaten
¼ cup heavy cream
1 cup chopped walnuts
½ teaspoon vanilla
8 three-inch tart pans lined with pastry and well chilled

Whipped cream
Walnut halves.

1. Preheat the oven to 375 degrees.
2. In a saucepan, heat the butter, brown sugar and syrup. Cool slightly.
3. Combine the eggs, heavy cream, chopped walnuts and vanilla. Gradually stir in the butter-syrup mixture.
4. Pour into the lined tart pans. Bake twenty-five minutes, or until golden and set. Cool on a rack.
5. Top with whipped cream and walnut halves as desired.
Yield: Eight.

Frozen Lemon Pie   *Southern California*

3 egg yolks
½ cup sugar
¼ cup lemon juice
2 teaspoons grated lemon rind
1 cup heavy cream, whipped
⅔ cup crushed vanilla wafers.

1. Place the egg yolks, sugar, lemon juice and lemon rind in the top of a double boiler or in a heavy saucepan. Heat, stirring, until the mixture thickens. Do not allow to boil.
2. Cool to room temperature.
3. Fold in the whipped cream.
4. Sprinkle a nine-inch (preferably metal) pie plate with half the crushed wafers. Pour in the lemon mixture. Sprinkle with remaining wafer crumbs and freeze until solid. Cut into wedges.
Yield: Six servings.

Apricot Torte   *Southern California*

2 cups peeled, pitted, chopped apricots
1 cup sugar
1 tablespoon lemon juice
1 cup heavy cream, whipped
1 cup coarse macaroon crumbs.

1. Place the apricots in a bowl and stir in the sugar and lemon juice. Fold in the cream.

2. Sprinkle a nine-inch metal pie plate with half the macaroon crumbs. Pour in the apricot mixture. Top with remaining crumbs and freeze until firm.

Yield: Six servings.

Cheesecake with Almond Crust
New Mexico

¾ of one package zwieback
½ cup toasted almonds
¼ cup butter, melted
1 eight-ounce package and one three-ounce package cream cheese, at room temperature
2 eggs
1 cup sugar
1 teaspoon vanilla
1 cup sour cream.

1. Preheat the oven to 325 degrees.

2. Crush, grind or blend the zwieback and almonds. Place in a mixing bowl and add the butter. Spread mixture over bottom and sides of a nine-inch pie plate and pat well to make a crust.

3. Cream the cheese with an electric mixer and add the eggs, one at a time, beating. Add one-half cup of the sugar and one-half teaspoon of the vanilla. When well blended, spoon the filling into the prepared crust. Bake twenty minutes. Reduce the oven heat to 275 degrees and bake five minutes longer.

4. Blend the sour cream with the remaining sugar and vanilla and spread over the pie. Serve warm or chilled.

Yield: Six servings.

Bourbon Nut Cake
Texas

1 cup butter
2 cups sugar
6 eggs
4 cups plus two tablespoons flour
1 teaspoon baking powder
1 cup bourbon
1½ pounds raisins
1 pound pecans, walnuts or other nuts, roughly chopped.

1. Preheat the oven to 250 degrees.

2. Cream together the butter and sugar. Beat in the eggs, one at a time. Reserve one cup of the flour and combine remainder with the baking powder. Fold the mixture into the batter. Stir in the bourbon.

3. Toss the raisins and nuts with the reserved flour. Sprinkle them over batter and fold in.

4. Pour the mixture into two greased and floured 9-by-5-by-3-inch loaf pans. Bake until loaves test done, one and one-half to two hours.

Yield: Two loaves; sixteen servings.

Apricot Cake
Southern California

1 eight-ounce package cream cheese, at room temperature
½ cup butter
1¼ cups sugar
2 eggs
1 teaspoon vanilla
2 cups flour
1 teaspoon baking powder
1 teaspoon baking soda
¼ teaspoon salt
¼ cup milk
1 twelve-ounce jar apricot preserves.

1. Preheat the oven to 350 degrees.

2. Cream the cheese, butter and sugar together until light and fluffy. Beat in the eggs, one at a time. Beat in the vanilla.

3. Sift together the flour, baking powder, baking soda and salt and stir into the batter alternately with the milk.

4. Spread half the batter in a well-greased 9-by-13-inch baking pan. Carefully spread the preserves over the batter. Top with remaining batter.

Bake about forty-five minutes, or until cake tests done.

Yield: About sixteen servings.

Orange Cake   *Southern California*

½ cup butter
1 cup light brown sugar
2 large eggs
2 cups flour
1 teaspoon baking soda
¼ teaspoon salt
¼ teaspoon lemon extract
½ teaspoon vanilla
1 cup milk or half plain yogurt and half milk
1 large orange
¼ cup blanched almonds
½ cup raisins
½ cup dates
½ cup granulated sugar
¼ cup brandy.

1. Preheat the oven to 350 degrees.
2. Grease and flour a 9-by-2-inch spring mold cake pan. (It has a removable center with a center hole.)
3. Cream the butter and brown sugar together very well. Beat in the eggs, one at a time. Sift together the flour, baking soda and salt.
4. Add the lemon extract and vanilla to the milk or milk and yogurt and stir into batter alternately with the flour mixture.
5. Halve the orange and squeeze, reserving one-half cup juice. Grind orange rind shells together with the almonds, raisins and dates. Stir into the cake batter. Pour the batter into prepared cake pan and bake forty minutes, or until done.
6. Heat the reserved orange juice with the granulated sugar and brandy until sugar dissolves. While the cake is still hot, prick it with a toothpick and spoon the hot orange-brandy sauce over all. When the juice has been absorbed, unmold the cake onto a serving plate.

Yield: Ten to one dozen servings.

Oatmeal Cake   *Southern California*

Cake:
1 cup old-fashioned oats
1½ cups boiling water
½ cup butter
1 cup light brown sugar
1 cup granulated sugar
2 eggs
1 teaspoon vanilla
1 teaspoon baking soda
½ teaspoon salt
1 teaspoon cinnamon
1½ cups flour.
Topping:
2 tablespoons butter
½ cup light brown sugar
⅓ cup evaporated milk or light cream
1 cup shredded coconut
½ cup chopped walnuts.

1. Preheat the oven to 350 degrees.
2. To prepare cake, place the oats in a bowl and pour the water over. Set aside to cool.
3. Cream the butter and sugars together until very light and fluffy. Beat in the eggs, one at a time.
4. Stir in the vanilla, baking soda, salt, cinnamon and cooled oatmeal mixture. Stir in the flour and turn the mixture into a lightly greased 9-by-13-inch baking pan. Bake forty minutes, or until done.
5. Mix the topping ingredients together. Spread on the hot cake and return to the oven for three minutes. Serve warm.

Yield: About eighteen servings.

Walnut Cake   *Southern California*

Cake:
½ cup shortening
1 cup sugar
1 egg
2 egg yolks

1 teaspoon vanilla
2 cups flour
½ teaspoon salt
2 teaspoons baking powder
1 cup milk
1 cup chopped walnuts.
Frosting:
1 cup sugar
1 cup water
⅛ teaspoon cream of tartar
2 egg whites
1 teaspoon lemon juice
1 teaspoon vanilla
2 tablespoons chopped walnuts.

1. Preheat the oven to 350 degrees for layers or to 375 degrees for cupcakes.

2. To prepare cake batter, cream the shortening together with the sugar until light and fluffy. Beat in the egg and the egg yolks very well. Beat in the vanilla.

3. Sift together the flour, salt and baking powder and stir into the batter alternately with the milk.

4. Stir in the walnuts and turn into two greased and floured eight-inch layer pans or fifteen greased and floured muffin tins.

5. Bake layers twenty-five to thirty minutes or cupcakes twelve to fifteen minutes. Cool on a rack.

6. To prepare frosting, place the sugar, water and cream of tartar in a saucepan and bring to a boil, stirring until sugar is dissolved. Continue boiling, without stirring, until syrup registers 238 to 240 degrees on a candy thermometer or forms a soft ball when dropped into water.

7. Beat the egg whites until they form peaks and gradually beat in the hot syrup. Beat in the lemon juice and vanilla and continue beating until mixture is thick enough to spread. Use to fill and frost the layers or to frost the cupcakes. Sprinkle with the walnuts.

Yield: One layer cake, eight servings; or fifteen cupcakes.

Citrus Cake *Southern California*

Cake:
2¼ cups cake flour
1½ cups granulated sugar
3 teaspoons baking powder
1 teaspoon salt
½ cup oil
4 egg yolks
2 tablespoons grated orange rind
¾ cup orange juice
2 tablespoons lemon juice
1 cup egg whites (about ten)
½ teaspoon cream of tartar.
Filling:
1 cup granulated sugar
¼ cup flour
1 tablespoon grated orange rind
1 cup orange juice
2 eggs, beaten
2 tablespoons lemon juice
¼ cup butter.
Frosting:
½ cup granulated sugar
2 egg whites
½ cup shortening
1 cup confectioners' sugar
1 tablespoon grated orange rind
½ teaspoon vanilla
⅛ teaspoon salt.

1. Preheat the oven to 350 degrees.

2. To prepare cake, sift the flour, granulated sugar, baking powder and salt into a large bowl. Make a well in the center and pour in the oil, egg yolks, orange rind, orange juice and lemon juice. Beat with a wooden spoon until smooth.

3. Beat the egg whites until frothy, add the cream of tartar and beat until mixture holds stiff peaks. Pour the flour mixture over the whites and gently fold in with a rubber spatula.

4. Pour into three nine-inch layer pans that have been greased and lined on the bottom with greased wax paper. Bake thirty to thirty-five minutes, or until done. Let cool in pans ten minutes. Finish cooling on a rack.

5. Meanwhile, to prepare filling, combine the granulated sugar and flour in a saucepan. Gradually stir in the orange rind and orange juice. Blend in the eggs and lemon juice.

6. Bring to a boil, stirring constantly. Boil two to three minutes. Stir in the butter and allow to cool thoroughly.

7. To prepare frosting, place the granulated sugar and egg whites in the top of a double boiler over simmering water and heat to lukewarm, stirring constantly.

8. Pour into a small mixing bowl and beat with an electric mixer at high speed until a stiff meringue forms. In another bowl, cream the shortening and confectioners' sugar together until light and fluffy. Add the orange rind, vanilla and salt to creamed mixture and beat well. Add one-half cup of the meringue and beat at medium speed five minutes. Add remaining meringue and beat until fluffy.

9. Spread all but one-half cup of the filling between the layers. Frost sides and outside edge of the top with the frosting. Place reserved filling in the middle of the top.

Yield: One dozen servings.

Orange Butter Cake   *Southern California*

Cake:
　1 cup butter
1¾ cups granulated sugar
　3 egg yolks
　3 cups flour
　1 teaspoon baking powder
　1 teaspoon salt
　1 teaspoon baking soda
　1 cup buttermilk
　3 tablespoons grated orange rind
　1 cup walnuts, finely chopped
　6 egg whites, beaten until stiff but not dry.
Topping:
　1 tablespoon grated orange rind
　2 tablespoons orange juice
1¼ cups confectioners' sugar
　2 teaspoons finely chopped walnuts.

1. Preheat the oven to 350 degrees.

2. To prepare cake, cream the butter and granulated sugar together until light and fluffy. Beat in the egg yolks.

3. Sift together the flour, baking powder, salt and baking soda and add to the butter alternately with the buttermilk.

4. Stir the orange rind and walnuts into the batter. With a rubber spatula, fold in the beaten egg whites. Pour into a well-greased and floured ten-inch bundt cake pan. Bake one hour, or until done.

5. Let cool in the pan five minutes before turning out onto a rack.

6. To prepare topping, beat the orange rind, orange juice and confectioners' sugar together. Drizzle over the cooled cake. Sprinkle with the walnuts.

Yield: One dozen servings.

Harvest Torte   *New Mexico*

4 cups diced unpeeled tart apples
1 cup sugar
½ cup sifted flour
2 teaspoons baking powder
1 egg, lightly beaten
1 tablespoon melted butter
1 teaspoon vanilla
½ cup coarsely chopped walnuts or pecans
½ cup dates, chopped
　Sweetened whipped cream or vanilla ice cream.

1. Preheat the oven to 400 degrees.

2. Place the apples in a mixing bowl. Sift together the sugar, flour and baking powder and pour the mixture over the apples. Add the eggs, butter, vanilla, nuts and dates. Stir thoroughly, but do not beat. Pour the mixture into an oiled 8-by-8-by-2-inch baking pan and bake forty minutes, or until apples are tender when pierced with a fork.

3. Serve hot or cold, with whipped cream or vanilla ice cream.

Yield: Six servings.

Walnut Soufflé   *Southern California*

    1 cup walnut halves
 1½ tablespoons butter
    2 tablespoons cornstarch
  ¾ cup milk
    3 egg yolks, lightly beaten
  ½ teaspoon maple flavoring or two
      tablespoons instant coffee powder
    4 egg whites
  ¼ teaspoon salt
  ⅛ teaspoon cream of tartar
      Sugar
      Whipped cream.

1. Preheat the oven to 350 degrees.
2. Spread the walnut halves over a baking sheet and bake ten to fifteen minutes, stirring frequently, until the walnuts are golden. Do not allow them to burn. Chop the walnuts in an electric blender. There should be three-quarters cup.
3. Butter a one-quart soufflé dish and sprinkle it with one or two tablespoons of the finely chopped nuts.
4. Prepare a collar for the dish from a double thickness of wax paper. Butter the inside of the collar and sprinkle it with walnuts; then tie it in place. The collar should extend several inches above the dish.
5. Melt the butter in a small saucepan. Remove from the heat and stir in the cornstarch, using a wire whisk. Gradually blend in the milk. Bring to a boil, stirring constantly until mixture thickens. Continue to cook the thick sauce over very low heat, while beating with whisk, two minutes.
6. Using the whisk, beat the hot sauce into the egg yolks. Add the maple flavoring or the instant coffee.
7. Beat the egg whites with the salt and cream of tartar until stiff. Gradually beat in one-half cup

sugar to form a meringue. Stir one-quarter of the meringue into the egg yolk mixture. Fold in the walnuts.
8. Fold in the remaining meringue gently but well. Pour mixture into the prepared soufflé dish. Sprinkle top lightly with sugar, if desired, and place in a shallow pan with one inch of hot water in the bottom. Bake fifty to fifty-five minutes, or until well puffed and set. Serve at once, with whipped cream.

Yield: Four to six servings.

Orange Walnut Soufflés
                            Southern California

    2 envelopes unflavored gelatin
    1 cup sugar
    3 tablespoons grated orange peel
  ¼ cup orange juice
  ¼ teaspoon salt
    4 eggs, separated
 2¼ cups milk
    1 teaspoon vanilla
    2 cups heavy cream
  ½ cup finely chopped walnuts.

1. Combine the gelatin, one-half cup of the sugar, the orange peel and juice and salt in a two-and-one-half-quart saucepan.
2. Beat the egg yolks with the milk. Add to gelatin mixture. Stir over low heat until gelatin dissolves and mixture thickens slightly, about ten to twelve minutes.
3. Remove from heat and add the vanilla. Chill, stirring occasionally, until mixture mounds slightly when dropped from spoon.
4. Meanwhile, prepare collars on dessert glasses or demitasse cups by binding a double strip of aluminum foil firmly around top of each glass or cup, extending one inch above top rim of glass or cup.
5. Beat the egg whites until stiff but not dry. Add remaining sugar gradually. Beat until very stiff.
6. Fold in gelatin mixture. Whip the cream

and fold in with the walnuts. Spoon into prepared dessert glasses. Chill until firm.

7. Remove collars. Garnish with additional chopped walnuts, if desired.

Yield: Eight to one dozen servings.

Grandmother's Date Soufflé
Southern California

Soufflé:
¼ cup butter
¼ cup sugar
4 large eggs, separated
¼ cup flour
1 cup milk
½ teaspoon salt
2 cups fresh pitted dates, chopped
1 teaspoon grated lemon rind.
Sauce:
½ cup sugar
1 cup orange juice
1 tablespoon grated orange rind
¼ cup lemon juice
1 tablespoon cornstarch
1 tablespoon butter
1 egg yolk.

1. Preheat the oven to 350 degrees.
2. To prepare soufflé, cream the butter and sugar together until light and fluffy. Beat in the egg yolks. Stir in the flour.
3. Gradually stir in the milk. Beat the egg whites together with the salt until stiff but not dry. Fold into milk mixture.
4. Fold in the dates and lemon rind. Pour into a greased one-and-one-half-quart soufflé dish or casserole and bake one hour, or until done.
5. Meanwhile, combine all the sauce ingredients except the egg yolk in a saucepan. Bring to a boil, stirring. Cook two minutes. Stir a little hot mixture into the yolk. Return to the saucepan and heat, but do not boil. Serve warm with the soufflé.

Yield: Six servings.

Grapefruit Sherbet
Southern California

2 cups plus two tablespoons sugar
1 cup water
2 egg whites
1 tablespoon grated grapefruit rind
1¾ cups fresh grapefruit juice
¼ cup lemon juice.

1. Place one cup of the sugar and the water in a heavy saucepan. Bring to a boil, stirring until the sugar is dissolved. Boil five minutes. Cool slightly.
2. In a large bowl, beat the egg whites to soft peak stage. Gradually beat in the remaining sugar until mixture holds stiff peaks.
3. Continue beating while adding the syrup in a steady stream.
4. Beat in the rind and juices. Pour into ice cube trays or shallow metal pans and freeze until mixture forms a mush and starts to freeze around the edges.
5. Turn into a bowl and beat until smooth. Return to pans and freeze until firm.

Yield: About one and one-half quarts; six servings.

Orange Water Ice
Southern California

3 cups water
2 cups sugar
2 tablespoons grated orange rind
2 cups strained fresh orange juice
Mint sprigs (optional).

1. Combine the water and sugar in a saucepan and bring to a boil. Simmer five minutes and cool.
2. Add the orange rind and orange juice.
3. Pour the mixture into freezer trays and freeze. Shortly before serving time, shave the mixture by scraping the surface with a heavy spoon. Spoon into sherbet glasses and return to the freezer until ready to serve. Garnish with mint sprigs if desired.

Yield: Eight to one dozen servings.

Bavarian Fruit Ice Cream

Southern California

3 cups regular milk
3 cups sugar
1½ cups heavy cream
1 thirteen-and-one-half-ounce can evaporated milk
3 lemons, squeezed (three-quarters cup juice)
3 oranges, squeezed (one and one-half cups juice)
4 bananas, mashed
1½ cups undrained crushed pineapple.

1. Heat the regular milk and dissolve the sugar in it. Add the cream and the evaporated milk. Freeze in an ice cream freezer, according to manufacturer's instructions, until partly frozen.

2. Add the fruit juices, bananas and pineapple and continue to freeze until firm. Remove dasher and pack in ice and coarse salt for two hours to ripen.
Yield: About four quarts.

Flan

New Mexico

1½ cups sugar
8 eggs, lightly beaten
4 cups milk
1 stick cinnamon
1 teaspoon vanilla.

1. Preheat the oven to 300 degrees.

2. Place one-half cup of the sugar in a heavy skillet. Melt and cook until sugar is caramel-colored. Pour into a buttered shallow two-quart casserole so mixture covers the bottom. Cool.

3. Gradually beat the remaining sugar into the eggs.

4. Scald the milk with the cinnamon stick, remove stick and add hot milk to the egg mixture. Strain this over the caramel. Add the vanilla.

5. Set in a pan of boiling water and bake one hour, or until set. Cool and chill.
Yield: Six to eight servings.

Lucy's Milk Pudding

New Mexico

4 cups milk
1¾ cups granulated sugar
¼ cup light brown sugar
Almond extract to taste.

1. Place the milk and sugars in a very heavy saucepan. Bring to a boil, stirring just until sugars dissolve.

2. Reduce the heat and allow mixture to simmer gently for five hours, or until it is thickened and light caramel in color. Let cool slightly. Add extract and chill well.
Yield: Six servings.

Apple Pudding

Southern California

1 cup diced, peeled and cored apple
¼ cup butter, melted
3 cups one-half-inch white bread cubes
½ cup sugar
2 cups milk, scalded
1 teaspoon grated lemon rind
½ cup diced dates
¼ teaspoon salt
1 teaspoon vanilla
3 eggs, separated
¼ teaspoon nutmeg.

1. Preheat the oven to 350 degrees.

2. Toss the apple with the butter and cook in a skillet until the apple is barely tender.

3. Combine with the bread cubes, sugar, milk, lemon rind, dates, salt and vanilla. Beat in the egg yolks.

4. Beat the egg whites until stiff but not dry and fold into the bread mixture. Pour into a greased two-quart casserole, sprinkle with the

nutmeg, set in a pan of hot water and bake forty-five minutes, or until set. Serve hot or cold.

Yield: Six servings.

Strawberry-Grapefruit Mousse

Southern California

1½ cups sugar
2 cups strawberries, washed, hulled and finely diced
3 tablespoons cornstarch
2¼ cups water
⅛ teaspoon salt
2 envelopes unflavored gelatin
   Grated rind from one large grapefruit
1 cup freshly squeezed grapefruit juice
   Few drops red food coloring
1 cup heavy cream, whipped.

1. Sprinkle one-half cup of the sugar over the strawberries and set aside at least thirty minutes.

2. Mix the remaining sugar and the cornstarch in a saucepan. Stir in two cups of the water and the salt. Soften the gelatin in the remaining water and set aside.

3. Bring the cornstarch mixture to a boil, stirring constantly, and cook two minutes. Stir in the softened gelatin until dissolved.

4. Stir in the grapefruit rind and juice and enough food coloring to make the mixture a healthy pink. Stir in the strawberry-sugar mixture and any liquid that has formed.

5. Chill the mixture until it starts to thicken. Fold in the whipped cream and pour into a lightly oiled six-cup mold or spoon into individual soufflé dishes fitted with lightly oiled aluminum foil collars extending one inch above the dishes.

6. Chill several hours or overnight.

Yield: Six servings.

Oranges Flambé   *Southern California*

4 large oranges
2 pints orange sherbet
¼ cup cognac, warmed.

1. Cut a slice off the top of each orange and a small sliver off the bottom so that oranges stand upright.

2. Scoop all the pulp from the inside of each, leaving a shell. Freeze the shells.

3. Fill the frozen shells with the sherbet. Make a small indentation in the top of each mound of sherbet. Freeze.

4. When ready to serve, pour a tablespoon of cognac into each indentation. Ignite.

Yield: Four servings.

Crisp Sugar Cookies   *Southern California*

1 cup butter
  Sugar
2 eggs
1 teaspoon vanilla
3 tablespoons sour cream
½ teaspoon lemon extract
3 cups flour
½ teaspoon baking soda
½ teaspoon salt
  Colored sprinkles (optional).

1. Cream the butter well. Gradually beat in one and one-half cups sugar and continue to beat until the mixture is light and fluffy. Beat in the eggs.

2. Beat in the vanilla, sour cream and lemon extract.

3. Sift together the flour, baking soda and salt and stir into the batter. Wrap in wax paper and chill until firm enough to roll.

4. Preheat the oven to 400 degrees.

5. Roll out the chilled dough to one-eighth-inch thickness. Cut into shapes with cookie cutters and place on ungreased baking sheets.

Sprinkle with sugar or colored sprinkles if desired. Bake ten minutes.

Yield: Four dozen to six dozen, depending on size.

Fig Bar Cookies   *Southern California*

First layer:
½ cup butter
½ cup light brown sugar
1 cup flour.
Second layer:
2 eggs, lightly beaten
1 cup light brown sugar
2 tablespoons flour
½ teaspoon salt
1 teaspoon baking powder
½ cup shredded coconut
½ cup chopped walnuts
¾ cup chopped figs
1 teaspoon grated lemon rind.

1. Preheat the oven to 375 degrees.
2. Place the ingredients for the first layer in a bowl and, with the finger tips or a pastry blender, work the butter into the dry ingredients to make a soft dough. With floured hands, pat dough into an even layer in the bottom of an 8-by-12-inch (two-quart Pyrex) baking dish.
3. Bake ten minutes and remove from the oven. Layer will be soft. Leave in dish and cool on a rack to room temperature.
4. To prepare second layer, blend together the eggs and brown sugar. Stir in the remaining ingredients and spread over the cooled first layer. Bake thirty minutes, or until done. Cool in the pan. Cut into bars when cool.
Yield: Two dozen.

Apricot Bars   *Southern California*

½ cup butter
¼ cup granulated sugar
1⅓ cups flour

½ teaspoon baking powder
¼ teaspoon salt
1 cup light brown sugar
2 eggs, beaten
½ teaspoon vanilla
½ cup chopped walnuts
1 cup thick apricot pulp (blend peeled, pitted ripe fruit in an electric blender or force through a sieve)
Confectioners' sugar.

1. Preheat the oven to 350 degrees.
2. Mix the butter, granulated sugar and one cup of the flour together until crumbly. Pack into a greased 8-by-8-by-2-inch baking pan. Bake twenty-five minutes, or until lightly browned.
3. Sift together the remaining flour, the baking powder and salt. Beat the brown sugar into the eggs and stir in the flour mixture.
4. Add the vanilla, walnuts and apricot pulp and spread over the baked layer. Bake thirty minutes, or until done. Cool in the pan. Cut into bars and coat with confectioners' sugar.
Yield: About two dozen.

Biscochitos (Aniseed Cookies)

New Mexico

2 cups lard
1 cup sugar
2 egg yolks
2 teaspoons aniseed
6 cups flour
1 teaspoon salt
3 teaspoons baking powder
½ cup orange juice or water
Cinnamon-sugar mixture.

1. Preheat the oven to 350 degrees.
2. Cream the lard and sugar together until fluffy. Beat in the egg yolks and aniseed.
3. Sift together the flour, salt and baking powder and add to the creamed mixture alternately with the orange juice or water.

4. Knead the mixture to make a pliable dough that can be rolled.

5. Roll out dough to one-eighth-inch thickness and cut with cookie cutters into fancy shapes. Place on baking sheets and sprinkle with cinnamon-sugar. Bake eight to ten minutes, or until lightly browned.

Yield: About six dozen, depending on size.

Date Chocolate Bars   *Southern California*

1½ cups chopped dates
¾ cup light brown sugar
½ cup butter
½ cup water
8 ounces semi-sweet chocolate bits
1½ cups flour, sifted
1 teaspoon baking soda
½ teaspoon salt
2 eggs, lightly beaten
½ cup orange juice, strained
½ cup milk
½ cup walnuts, chopped.

1. Preheat the oven to 350 degrees.
2. Combine the dates, brown sugar, butter and water in a small pan and cook, stirring occasionally, until mixture is thick and smooth. Remove from the heat and stir in the chocolate bits. Cool.
3. Stir in the remaining ingredients. Pack into a greased 15½-by-10½-by-1-inch jelly roll pan. Bake twenty to twenty-five minutes, or until done. Cool in the pan. Cut into bars when cool.

Yield: Two dozen to three dozen bars, depending on size.

Orange Cookies   *Southern California*

2½ cups flour
½ teaspoon salt
½ cup sugar
½ cup shortening
2 egg yolks, well beaten

2 tablespoons orange juice
1 tablespoon grated lemon rind
1 egg white, lightly beaten
¼ cup finely chopped blanched almonds.

1. Preheat the oven to 350 degrees.
2. Sift the flour, salt and six tablespoons of the sugar into a bowl. With two knives, a pastry blender or the finger tips, work the shortening into the dry ingredients as though making pastry.
3. With a fork, stir in the egg yolks, orange juice and lemon rind. Gather into a ball of dough. Roll out to one-quarter-inch thickness on a lightly floured board. Cut with a cookie cutter and place on a greased baking sheet.
4. Brush with the egg white. Combine the remaining sugar and the almonds and sprinkle over all.
5. Bake ten minutes, or until lightly browned around the edges.

Yield: About three dozen.

Raisin Bars   *Southern California*

Bars:
1 cup plus two tablespoons flour
1¼ cups granulated sugar
⅓ cup butter
2 eggs, lightly beaten
½ teaspoon baking powder
¼ teaspoon salt
1 tablespoon grated orange rind
2 tablespoons orange juice
¾ cup chopped raisins (see note)
½ cup flaked coconut.
Glaze:
1½ teaspoons orange juice
1½ teaspoons lemon juice
1½ teaspoons soft butter
¾ to one cup confectioners' sugar.

1. Preheat the oven to 350 degrees.
2. To prepare bars, place one cup of the flour and one-quarter cup of the granulated sugar in a

bowl. With a pastry blender or the finger tips, work in the butter until mixture is crumbly.

3. Press into the bottom of a greased nine-inch square baking pan. Bake fifteen minutes, or until lightly browned.

4. Meanwhile, combine the eggs with the remaining flour, remaining granulated sugar, the baking powder and salt. Stir until smooth.

5. Stir in the orange rind, orange juice, raisins and coconut. Pour over hot baked layer and bake twenty to twenty-five minutes longer, or until lightly browned. Cool in the pan.

6. To prepare glaze, combine the orange juice, lemon juice, butter and enough confectioners' sugar to make a thin frosting. Spread over the cooled mixture and cut into bars.

Yield: One dozen.

Note: To chop raisins, freeze them and then put into a lightly oiled electric blender container one-half cup at a time and blend two seconds. Remove at once. Repeat until all are chopped.

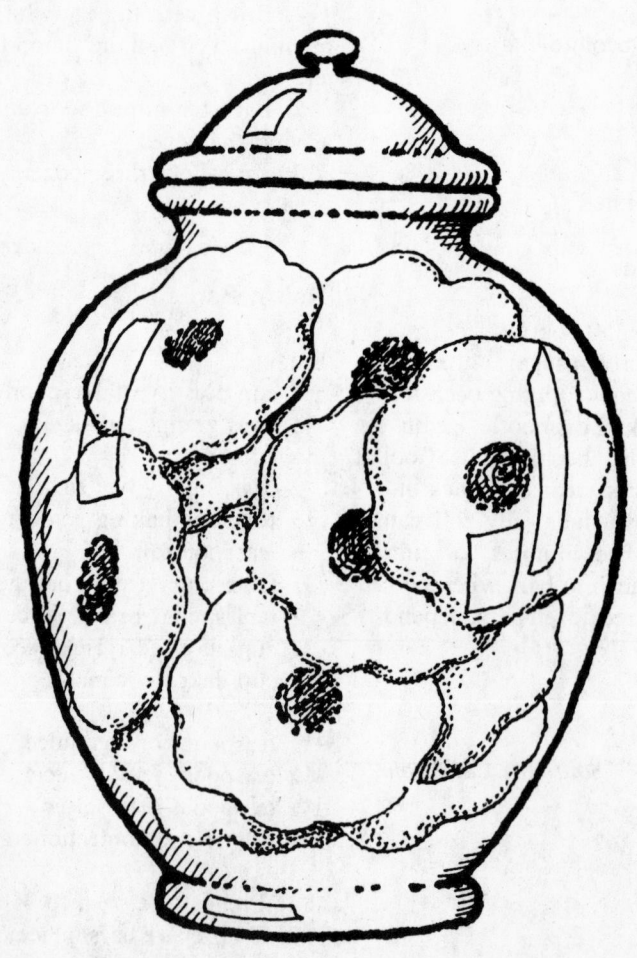

Miscellaneous

Pickles, Relishes and Preserves

Pickled Peppers   *Southern California*

8 cups large firm red sweet peppers, seeds and
     membranes removed and peppers cut into
     strips to fit pint canning jars
4 teaspoons salt
4 teaspoons mustard seeds
3 cups white vinegar
3 cups water.

1. Pack the pepper strips into four pint canning jars. Add one teaspoon of the salt and one
teaspoon of the mustard seeds to each jar.
2. Combine the vinegar and water, heat to
boiling and pour over the pepper strips. Adjust
the caps and process ten minutes in a boiling
water bath. Cool, check seal, and store in a cool,
dark, dry place.
     Yield: Four pints.

Sweet Carrot Pickles   *Southern California*

3 bunches carrots, cut into one-quarter-inch
     sticks to fit pint canning jars
4 teaspoons mustard seeds
1½ cups sugar
1½ cups white vinegar

1½ cups water
1 teaspoon salt.

1. Steam the carrot sticks over rapidly boiling
water three minutes. Immediately plunge into ice
water. Drain.
2. Pack the sticks into four pint canning jars.
Add one teaspoon mustard seeds to each jar.
3. Combine the sugar, vinegar, water and salt
in a saucepan and bring to a boil. Pour over the
carrot sticks. Adjust the caps and process ten
minutes in a boiling water bath. Cool, check seal,
and store in a cool, dark, dry place.
     Yield: Four pints.

Pickled Beans   *Southern California*

2 pounds young, uniform-size green beans
4 cloves garlic
8 sprigs fresh dill weed or four teaspoons
     dill seeds
4 teaspoons salt
2½ cups white vinegar
2½ cups water.

1. Cut the beans to fit pint canning jars. Steam
the beans over rapidly boiling water three
minutes. Remove beans and plunge into ice water. Drain well.
2. Pack the beans into four pint jars. Place one

clove of garlic and two sprigs of dill or one tea-spoon seeds next to the glass in each jar.

3. Add one teaspoon salt to each jar.

4. Combine the vinegar and water in a sauce-pan and bring to a boil. Pour over the beans, adjust the caps and process ten minutes in a boil-ing water bath. Cool, check seal and store in a cool, dark, dry place.

Yield: Four pints.

Mustard Pickles   *Southern California*

8 cups cucumbers, cut into cubes or
  one-half-inch slices
4 cups small white onions
4 cups green tomatoes, cubed
2 red sweet peppers, seeded and diced
1 green pepper, seeded and diced
2 heads cauliflower, broken into flowerets
1 cup salt
8 cups water
¼ cup dry mustard, or to taste
1 tablespoon turmeric
4 cups sugar
1 cup flour
8 cups cider vinegar.

1. Day before, place the prepared vegetables in a large crock or ceramic bowl. Dissolve the salt in the water and pour over the vegetables. Let stand overnight in the refrigerator to crisp.

2. Next day, transfer to a large kettle and bring the vegetables in the brine to a boil. Do not cook. Drain.

3. Mix together the mustard, turmeric, sugar and flour in a saucepan and gradually stir in the vinegar.

4. Bring to a boil, stirring, and cook until thickened.

5. Pour over the hot drained vegetables and immediately pack into hot sterilized jars, leaving one-quarter-inch head space. Adjust caps and process ten minutes in a boiling water bath. Cool, check seal and store in a cool, dark, dry place.

Yield: About six quarts.

Lazy Wife Dills   *Arizona*

16 to twenty-four cucumbers, each five inches
  to six inches long
4 slices onion
1 teaspoon celery seeds
4 teaspoons pickling spices
4 large sprigs fresh dill weed or four
  tablespoons dill seeds
4 cups sugar
½ cup salt
4 cups white vinegar
2 cups water.

1. Wash the cucumbers. Cut each cucumber lengthwise into strips. There should be enough cucumbers to fill four one-quart jars.

2. Pack the cucumbers into four sterilized one-quart jars and add to each jar one onion slice, one-quarter teaspoon celery seeds, one teaspoon pickling spices and one dill sprig or one table-spoon dill seeds.

3. Dissolve the sugar and salt in the vinegar and water. Bring to a boil and pour over the pickles. Seal and process in a hot water bath ten minutes. Cool, check seal and store in a cool, dark, dry place. Do not use for at least one month.

Yield: Four quarts.

Pickled Okra   *Texas*

2 pounds fresh, tender young okra pods
5 hot red pepper pods
5 cloves garlic, peeled
4 cups white vinegar
1 cup water
6 tablespoons salt
1 bay leaf
1 tablespoon celery seeds.

1. Wash the okra and pack it into five scalded half-pint jars. Add one hot pepper and one garlic clove to each jar.

2. Combine the remaining ingredients and

bring to a boil. Pour the liquid over the okra and seal. Store in a cool, dark, dry place. Let stand one month before using. Serve cold.

Yield: Five pints.

Garden Relish   *Southern California*

4 cups finely chopped green cabbage (about one pound)
¾ cup finely chopped green pepper
¾ cup finely chopped carrot
½ cup finely chopped onion
1 cup Southern California French dressing (page 622).

1. Combine the cabbage, pepper, carrot and onion in a large bowl.

2. Pour the French dressing over the vegetables and toss until they are well coated.

3. Chill, covered, in the refrigerator for at least three hours before serving.

Yield: About five cups.

Lone Star Tomato Relish   *Texas*

8 cups tomatoes, peeled and coarsely chopped
4 cups chopped onions
6 hot green peppers, chopped
3 large green peppers, seeded and chopped
1 tablespoon salt
1 teaspoon freshly ground black pepper
2 cups cider vinegar
2 cups sugar.

Combine all the ingredients in a kettle and cook to the desired consistency. (This relish tends to be watery.) Pour into hot sterilized jars and seal. Store in a cool, dark, dry place.

Yield: About seven pints.

Grapefruit Marmalade   *Arizona*

1 grapefruit
1 orange
1 lemon
  Sugar.

1. Wash the fruit. Cut each into halves, remove the seeds and slice fruit into very thin small pieces.

2. Measure the fruit and juice and add three times the amount of water. Soak the fruit twelve hours.

3. Bring the mixture to a boil and simmer, uncovered, twenty minutes. Cover and allow to stand again twelve hours.

4. Measure the mixture into a wide-mouthed kettle and bring to a boil. Add one cup sugar for each cup fruit and water. Stir to dissolve the sugar.

5. Boil the mixture rapidly, uncovered, stirring occasionally and skimming if necessary. After ten minutes, test by placing a small amount of jelly in a spoon, cooling jelly slightly and letting it drop back into the pan from the side of the spoon. As the syrup thickens, two large drops will form along the edge of the spoon. When these two drops converge and fall as one, the marmalade is ready to pour. Tests for set should be made every two or three minutes while the marmalade continues to boil.

6. As soon as the marmalade is ready, pour it immediately into sterilized jelly glasses to within one-quarter inch of the top. Immediately pour a thin layer of melted paraffin over the surface if the marmalade is to be stored for any length of time without refrigeration.

7. When the marmalade is cool, cover the glasses and store in a cool, dark, dry place.

Yield: Eighteen six-ounce glasses.

Lemon Marmalade   *Arizona*

12 large or eighteen medium-size lemons,
   washed
   Sugar.

1. Put the washed lemons through a food chopper. Measure the resulting pulp and add three times as much water. Set aside overnight in a pottery or ceramic bowl.
2. Transfer the mixture to a kettle and bring to a boil. Simmer gently twenty minutes. Let stand overnight in the bowl.
3. Measure the mixture into a large kettle and add one cup sugar for each cup lemon mixture. Bring to a boil, stirring until the sugar dissolves. Boil rapidly, stirring to prevent sticking, until the marmalade sheets from the spoon, a drop chilled on a plate leaves a track when pushed by the finger or the mixture registers 220 degrees on candy thermometer.
4. Let cool in the kettle about twenty minutes and then ladle into hot sterilized jelly jars. Pour two thin layers of melted paraffin over and allow to cool. Cap and store in a cool, dry, dark place.

Yield: About twenty six-ounce jelly jars.

Dorothy's Strawberry Preserves
Southern California

12 cups strawberries, including some underripe
   fruit
 2 tablespoons lemon juice
   Sugar.

1. Place the berries and lemon juice in an enameled pan and simmer over very low heat until juice is extracted from berries.
2. Strain off the juice and measure back into the kettle. Reserve the fruit.
3. For every cup of juice, add three cups sugar. Heat, stirring until sugar dissolves, and then boil rapidly, stirring occasionally, until liquid reaches the jell stage—that is when the syrup sheets off the edge of the spoon—about five minutes.
4. Add the reserved berries to the syrup and

cook two minutes longer. Pour into a shallow pan and let stand overnight. Spoon into hot sterilized clean jars. Let set a few hours; then pour two thin layers of melted paraffin over. Store in a cool, dark, dry place.

Yield: About four pints.

Fig Preserves   *Southern California*

10 pounds underripe green figs with stems
 1 tablespoon lime
 3 gallons plus three quarts water
 7 pounds sugar
 6 lemons, thinly sliced.

1. Peel the figs except for a small area around the stem. Place in an enameled, ceramic or glass crock.
2. Dissolve the lime in three gallons of the water and pour over figs. Let soak forty-five minutes. Drain and rinse thoroughly in several changes of cold water.
3. Place the sugar in a kettle and add the remaining water. Bring to a boil, stirring until sugar dissolves. Add the figs and cook one and one-half hours.
4. Add the lemon slices and cook ten minutes longer. Pack into hot sterilized canning jars. Adjust the caps and process in a boiling water bath ten minutes. Cool, check seal and store in a cool, dark, dry place.

Yield: About ten pints.

Quince Paste or Cheese
Southern California

4 pounds quince
4 pounds sugar.

1. Wash and core the fruit, remove seeds, quarter fruit and cover with water. Bring to a boil and simmer until fruit is soft.
2. Pass through a food mill into a kettle. Add the sugar and cook, stirring frequently, until mixture is thick and dark red.

3. Pour into loaf pans or layer pans and let cool. Remove from the pans, wrap in cheesecloth and set in the sun to dry. Store wrapped in wax paper. Serve like guava paste with cream cheese for dessert.

Yield: About six pounds.

Sauces

Hazel's Ginger Marinade for Chicken
Southern California

½ cup soy sauce
2 tablespoons dry sherry
1 clove garlic, mashed
½ teaspoon sugar
1 tablespoon finely chopped fresh ginger.

Combine ingredients and pour over chicken pieces; toss. Allow to marinate one hour or longer, tossing frequently. Chicken can be rolled in flour or dipped in batter and fried.

Yield: About one-half cup.

Basting Sauce for Barbecues   *Texas*

2 cups water
2 cups cider vinegar
6 cloves garlic, peeled
½ teaspoon cayenne pepper
1 tablespoon paprika
1 teaspoon freshly ground black pepper
2 teaspoons salt
1 teaspoon dry mustard
1 cup bacon drippings or melted butter.

Combine all ingredients in a saucepan and simmer fifteen minutes. Use to baste meat, poultry or game when it is barbecued. Before barbecuing, however, rub the meat or whatever with salt, freshly ground black pepper and a cut clove of garlic.

Yield: About five cups.

Barbecue Sauce   *Texas*

1 six-ounce can tomato paste
¼ cup wine vinegar
¼ cup cider vinegar
½ cup dry red wine
1 onion, chopped
1 clove garlic, crushed
1 bay leaf
1½ teaspoons salt
½ teaspoon freshly ground black pepper
2 tablespoons Worcestershire sauce
  Tabasco sauce to taste
½ cup olive oil
2 tablespoons sugar
6 whole cloves
½ teaspoon dry mustard
⅛ teaspoon chili powder
⅛ teaspoon thyme.

Place all the ingredients in a large saucepan or kettle. Mix well. Bring to a boil, cover and simmer one hour.

Yield: About two cups.

Ranchero Sauce   *Texas*

½ pound salt pork or three tablespoons peanut oil or vegetable oil
¾ cup finely chopped onions
¾ cup finely chopped green peppers
1 or two cloves garlic, finely chopped
1 teaspoon oregano
2 large or three medium-size ripe tomatoes, peeled, seeded and diced
½ cup tomato puree
1 or two hot green chilies, finely chopped, or canned medium-hot green chilies to taste, chopped
  Salt and freshly ground black pepper to taste.

1. Cut the salt pork into one-quarter-inch cubes. Cook in a skillet, stirring, until rendered of fat and crisp.

2. Add the onions, green peppers and garlic and cook until vegetables are wilted. Add the oregano and tomatoes and cook, stirring, about ten minutes. Add the remaining ingredients and simmer, stirring occasionally, ten minutes longer.

Yield: About three cups.

Xnipek   *Texas*

½ cup finely chopped white onion
1 large ripe tomato, peeled, seeded and sliced into small cubes
¼ cup or more chopped fresh or canned mild green chilies
2 tablespoons chopped fresh coriander leaves (cilantro or Chinese parsley) (optional)
½ teaspoon sugar
¼ cup wine vinegar, or to taste
2 tablespoons water
   Salt and freshly ground black pepper to taste.

Combine all ingredients. Taste for seasoning and, if desired, add more vinegar and salt to taste. Chill well before serving. The sauce will keep for a day or so in the refrigerator.

Yield: About two cups.

Pepita or Pumpkin Seed Sauce

Texas

3 cups shelled, toasted pepitas or pumpkin seeds (see note)
4 small serrano chilies or mild chilies to taste (see note), rinsed and seeded
3 cups hot water or chicken broth.

1. Put the pepitas in the container of an electric blender and pulverize. They should be as finely ground as possible. Add the chilies. As the pepitas and chilies are ground, empty into a saucepan.

2. Rinse out the blender container with the water or broth. Gradually add this to the ground

mixture, heating and stirring constantly or the sauce will separate. Keep just below simmer point a few minutes until the sauce is well blended.

Yield: About three cups.

Note: Pepitas are available in many health food and specialty food stores. Serrano chilies are available in Spanish markets. About one-half teaspoon of an herb called epazote is generally added to this recipe in Mexico, but the herb is rarely available here.

The sauce is used with meats and poultry and for soft tortilla dishes.

Tomato Sauce   *Texas*

2 cups chopped onions
¼ cup lard
1 quart tomatoes, peeled, seeded and chopped, or four cups canned Italian plum tomatoes
   Salt and freshly ground black pepper to taste
½ teaspoon sugar.

1. Cook the onions in the lard, stirring, about five minutes.

2. Add the remaining ingredients and simmer, stirring frequently, until thickened to the desired consistency. If desired, sieve the sauce.

Yield: Two and one-half cups to three cups.

Hot Sauce   *Texas*

1 tablespoon red pepper flakes
½ cup finely chopped onion
1 tablespoon olive oil
1 teaspoon finely chopped garlic
5 chopped serrano chilies (see note)
⅓ cup mole sauce.

1. Combine the pepper flakes, onion and oil and cook, stirring, about five minutes.

2. Add the remaining ingredients and simmer fifteen minutes, stirring frequently.

Yield: About one cup.

Note: Serrano chilies are available in Spanish markets.

Salsa Cruda (Cold Crude Sauce)
New Mexico

1 onion, finely minced
1 clove garlic, finely minced
2 ripe tomatoes, peeled, or two cups Italian
   plum tomatoes, finely chopped
1 four-ounce can whole medium-hot green
   chilies, chopped
½ teaspoon ground coriander
   Pinch of oregano
   Salt to taste
   Cider vinegar or olive oil to taste.

Combine all ingredients and refrigerate until ready to use. Serve with meat or poultry.

Yield: About three cups.

Note: Chopped fresh coriander leaves (cilantro or Chinese parsley), added to taste, about two tablespoons, when available, are delicious in this dish.

Beverages

New Mexican Chocolate

½ cup sugar
¼ cup cocoa powder or two ounces (two
   squares) unsweetened chocolate
1 teaspoon cinnamon
⅛ teaspoon salt
4 cups milk, scalded.

1. Combine the sugar, cocoa powder or chocolate, cinnamon and salt in a saucepan. Stir in the milk.

2. While beating to form a froth, cook the chocolate mixture until cocoa no longer tastes raw or chocolate is melted.

Yield: Four servings.

Margharita
Texas

1½ ounces tequila
1 ounce Cointreau or Triple Sec
1 ounce freshly squeezed lime juice or lemon
   juice (reserve lime or lemon)
   Salt.

1. Combine the tequila, Cointreau or Triple Sec and lime or lemon juice in a cocktail shaker.

2. Use the squeezed lime or lemon to rub the rim of a cocktail glass. Immediately dip the rim of the glass into a container of salt. Shake the glass slightly to remove any excess salt.

3. Add ice to tequila mixture and shake well. Strain into the salt-rimmed glass and serve.

Yield: One cocktail.

Sangrita
Arizona

⅓ cup orange juice
⅓ cup tomato juice
   Juice of one-half lemon
½ teaspoon Worcestershire sauce
1 tablespoon grenadine syrup
   Tabasco sauce to taste
   Salt and freshly ground black pepper to
   taste
3 one-ounce jiggers tequila (see note).

Combine all the ingredients in a cocktail shaker and add ice cubes. Shake well and strain into cocktail glasses.

Yield: Two or more servings.

Note: The tequila in this drink may be and frequently is served on the side. To serve this way, shake all ingredients except tequila with ice. Strain into two glasses and serve tequila in very small glasses on the side.

Tequila Punch Arizona

2 "juice" oranges
1 large, sweet grapefruit
2 tangerines (optional)
   Grand Marnier or Cointreau to taste
   Tequila.

1. Squeeze the oranges, grapefruit and tangerines and stir juices together. The quantities will depend on the size and juiciness of the fruit. Blend the fruit juice with Grand Marnier or Cointreau.

2. To serve, measure out two parts of the fruit mixture to one part tequila. Add ice and stir until well chilled.

Yield: Four to six small servings.

Sangria New Mexico

1 bottle dry red Spanish wine, preferably Rioja
   Sugar to taste
1½ ounces cognac
1 ounce Cointreau or Curaçao
¼ cup orange juice (optional)
   Ice cubes
   Lemon slices
   Peach slices
   Club soda to taste.

Place the wine, sugar, cognac, Cointreau or Curaçao, orange juice and ice in a pitcher and macerate with a wooden spoon. Add remaining ingredients and serve cold.

Yield: About one quart.

Candies

Candied Walnuts Southern California

1½ cups sugar
¼ cup honey
½ cup water
½ teaspoon vanilla
3 cups walnut halves.

1. Place the sugar, honey and water in a heavy saucepan and bring to a boil, stirring until the sugar dissolves.

2. Boil, without stirring, until the syrup registers 238 to 240 degrees on a candy thermometer or makes a soft ball when dropped into cold water.

3. Stir in the vanilla and walnuts and stir until syrup becomes creamy and thick. Pour onto a greased marble slab or oiled wax paper on a baking sheet. Let cool. Break up.

Yield: About one pound.

Mexican Whisky Candy Texas

2½ cups sugar
¼ cup light corn syrup
   Small pinch of baking soda
1 tablespoon butter
1 cup evaporated milk
2 tablespoons bourbon
2½ to three cups pecan halves.

1. Combine the sugar, syrup, baking soda, butter and evaporated milk. Cook slowly to the firm ball stage, or until candy thermometer registers 242 degrees.

2. Remove the candy from the heat and add the bourbon. Stir in the pecan halves and beat until candy thickens and looks creamy. Drop by spoonfuls onto wax paper and let cool.

Yield: Three dozen pieces (two pounds).

Toffee
Texas

1 cup sugar
1 cup butter
3 tablespoons water
1 teaspoon vanilla
4 seven-eighth-ounce milk chocolate bars
¾ cup finely chopped pecans.

1. Combine the sugar, butter and water in a heavy pan. Bring to a boil, stirring until sugar is dissolved, and then boil, stirring to prevent burning, until mixture reaches 300 degrees on a candy thermometer, the hard crack stage. Remove from heat and stir in the vanilla. Pour into a buttered nine-inch square pan.
2. Layer the chocolate bars over the surface and spread them evenly as they melt. Sprinkle with the pecans. Cool thoroughly and break into pieces.
Yield: About one and one-half pounds.

Five Minute Fudge
Texas

½ cup butter
2 ounces (two squares) unsweetened chocolate
¼ cup milk
1 teaspoon vanilla
1 pound confectioners' sugar, approximately
1 cup chopped nuts.

1. Place the butter, chocolate and milk in the top of a double boiler and heat over hot water until chocolate and butter melt.
2. Add the vanilla. Beat in the confectioners' sugar gradually by hand, adding just enough to make the mixture smooth and creamy but not crumbly. Stir in the nuts.
3. Press the mixture into a greased eight-inch square pan. Cut into squares when set.
Yield: Two dozen pieces.

Walnut Fudge
Southern California

2 cups sugar
½ cup sour cream
⅓ cup light corn syrup
2 tablespoons butter
¼ teaspoon salt
2 teaspoons vanilla
¼ cup quartered candied cherries
1 cup coarsely chopped walnuts.

1. Place the sugar, sour cream, syrup, butter and salt in a heavy saucepan. Bring to a boil slowly, stirring until the sugar dissolves. Boil, without stirring, until mixture registers 236 degrees on a candy thermometer or a little of the mixture dropped into cold water forms a soft ball.
2. Remove from the heat and let cool fifteen minutes. Add the vanilla and beat until mixture loses its gloss, about eight minutes. Stir in the cherries and walnuts and pour into a greased nine-inch square pan. Cool and then cut into squares.
Yield: About one and one-half pounds.

Perfect Divinity
Southern California

2 cups sugar
½ cup light corn syrup
½ cup hot water
¼ teaspoon salt
2 egg whites, stiffly beaten
1 teaspoon vanilla
½ cup chopped walnuts.

1. Place the sugar, syrup, water and salt in a heavy two-quart saucepan. Cook, stirring, until the sugar dissolves.
2. Wash the sides of the pan with a brush dipped in water to remove any sugar crystals. Boil, without stirring, until mixture registers 250 degrees on a candy thermometer or a little dropped into cold water forms a hard ball.
3. While beating the egg whites about five minutes with an electric mixer at high speed,

gradually pour in the hot syrup. Add the vanilla and beat until soft peaks are formed and the mixture begins to lose its gloss.

4. Stir in the walnuts. Drop by teaspoonfuls onto a baking sheet covered with buttered wax paper, twirling the top of each as you lift spoon.

Yield: About one and one-half pounds.

Candy Date Loaf   *Southern California*

3 cups sugar
1 cup milk
½ pound dates, pitted and chopped
1 cup chopped walnuts
2 tablespoons butter.

1. Combine the sugar, milk and dates in a heavy saucepan. Bring to a boil, stirring until sugar dissolves. Boil until a little of the mixture forms a soft ball when dropped into cold water or mixture registers 238 degrees on a candy thermometer.

2. Remove from heat and stir in walnuts and butter. Pour into a wet cloth that has been wrung out and mold into a long thin roll or loaf. Place in a cool place to harden. Slice to serve.

Yield: About one and one-half pounds.

Molasses Taffy   *Texas*

1 cup unsulphured molasses
½ cup water
1½ cups dark brown sugar
1½ tablespoons cider vinegar
¼ teaspoon salt
5 tablespoons butter
⅛ teaspoon baking soda
Confectioners' sugar.

1. Place the molasses, water, brown sugar, vinegar, salt and butter in a heavy saucepan. Bring to a boil, stirring until sugar dissolves.

2. Boil, without stirring, until the mixture registers 250 to 268 degrees on a candy thermometer or forms a hard ball when a little is dropped into cold water. Stir in the baking soda and pour onto a buttered marble slab or heatproof platter.

3. When taffy is cool enough to handle, pull it with both hands to a spread of about eighteen inches. Fold the taffy back on itself and continue pulling, twisting slightly, until ridges of twists retain their shape, about fifteen minutes.

4. Form into a long rope on a surface sprinkled with confectioners' sugar. Cut into bite-size pieces.

Yield: About one pound.

6. Northwest

Appetizers and Soups

Lois' Clam Fritter Appetizer   *Oregon*

  2 cups flour
1½ teaspoons baking powder
  1 teaspoon salt
  ⅛ teaspoon freshly ground black pepper
  ⅛ teaspoon mace
  2 eggs, beaten
  1 cup milk
  2 teaspoons grated onion
  1 tablespoon melted butter
  2 cups clams, drained
    Fat or oil for deep-frying.

1. Sift together the flour, baking powder, salt, pepper and mace. Add the eggs, milk, onion, butter and clams and mix well.

2. Heat the fat or oil to 375 degrees. Drop the clam mixture by teaspoonfuls into the fat and fry until golden. Drain on paper towels.

Yield: Eight to one dozen servings.

Clam Puff Balls   *Oregon*

1 cup finely chopped clams with liquor
½ cup butter
1 tablespoon freshly snipped dill weed
¼ teaspoon salt
1 cup flour
4 eggs.

1. Preheat the oven to 450 degrees.

2. Drain the clams and measure the liquid. Add water to make one cup. Heat the cup of liquid, the butter, dill and salt in a small saucepan to boiling.

3. Stir in the flour all at once and cook, stirring, until mixture leaves the sides of the pan. Remove from the heat.

4. Beat in the eggs, one at a time, very well. Stir in the clams. Drop by teaspoonfuls onto a greased baking sheet. Bake ten minutes, reduce oven heat to 350 degrees and bake ten minutes longer, or until done.

Yield: About five dozen.

Tillamook Cheese and Clam Appetizers
Oregon

1 onion, chopped
3 tablespoons butter
⅓ cup light cream
2 cups chopped clams with liquor or two
    seven-ounce cans minced clams, undrained
2 eggs, beaten
½ cup soft bread crumbs
1 cup grated Tillamook cheese (see note).

1. Preheat the oven to 400 degrees.

2. Sauté the onion in the butter until tender but not browned. Stir in the cream, clams and eggs.

3. Pour into six greased individual shells or ramekins. Combine the bread crumbs and cheese and sprinkle over top. Bake twenty minutes, or until bubbly hot and browned.

Yield: Six servings.

Note: Cheddar cheese may be substituted for the Tillamook cheese.

Clams Casino   *Northern California*

20 clams
½ cup butter, at room temperature
 1 tablespoon finely minced pimento
 1 tablespoon finely minced green pepper
 1 tablespoon finely minced celery
¼ cup fine bread crumbs
 1 teaspoon anchovy paste
   Bacon.

1. Have the clams opened and leave them on the half shell.

2. Preheat the oven to 425 degrees.

3. Combine the butter, pimento, green pepper, celery, bread crumbs and anchovy paste and work to a paste. Using small spatula, spread the mixture over the opened clams.

4. Cut bacon into twenty pieces, each large enough to nearly cover one clam. Place the bacon on the clams and bake eight to ten minutes, or until bacon is done.

Yield: Four or five servings.

Crab Meat Appetizer   *Northern California*

2 tablespoons butter
2 tablespoons flour
¾ cup milk or half and half
  Salt and freshly ground black pepper to taste
6 slices white bread
½ pound lump crab meat, picked over to remove bits of shell and cartilage
  Tabasco sauce to taste
1 teaspoon lemon juice

½ teaspoon Worcestershire sauce
 1 tablespoon finely chopped chives or scallion
12 anchovy fillets
¼ cup soft bread crumbs
¼ cup freshly grated Parmesan cheese
12 small sprigs parsley
12 thin crescent-shaped slices lemon.

1. Preheat the oven to 400 degrees.

2. Melt the butter in a saucepan and stir in the flour. Add the milk or half and half, stirring rapidly with a wire whisk. Add salt and pepper and simmer about five minutes. This is the sauce.

3. Meanwhile, trim the crusts off the bread and cut each slice in half diagonally to make triangles. Broil lightly on both sides.

4. Stir the crab into the sauce. Add Tabasco, the lemon juice, Worcestershire and chives.

5. Spread the crab mixture over each triangle and top each with an anchovy fillet. Combine the bread crumbs and cheese and sprinkle on top. Place on a baking sheet. Place in the oven and leave just long enough to heat through. Top each canapé with a parsley sprig and a lemon slice. Serve piping hot.

Yield: One dozen.

Cold Anise Chicken Appetizers
                                    Hawaii

16 chicken wings
 2 scallions, including green part, cut into one-inch lengths
½ cup soy sauce
 1 cup water
½ cup dry sherry
 1 teaspoon aniseed or two pieces star anise, crushed
 4 whole cloves
 1 teaspoon sesame oil (see note)
¼ cup light brown sugar.

1. Cut off and discard the small tips of the chicken wings. Cut each wing in half.

2. Place wings in a saucepan and add remain-

ing ingredients. Cover, bring to a boil and simmer one-half hour. Uncover and cook fifteen minutes longer, basting the wings as they cook. Let stand until cool; then refrigerate until ready to serve. Serve cold as an appetizer.

Yield: Eight or more servings.

Note: Sesame oil is available in Chinese markets.

Filipino Seasoned Pork Appetizer

Hawaii

    2 pounds pork fillet or lean boned loin of
       pork
    3 to four cloves garlic, chopped, or to taste
  ⅓ cup cider vinegar
  1½ teaspoons salt
  ⅛ teaspoon freshly ground black pepper
    2 bay leaves
      Pork fat or oil, if necessary.

1. Slice the pork into bite-size pieces. Place in a skillet. Add the garlic, vinegar, salt, pepper, bay leaves and enough water barely to cover meat.

2. Bring to a boil and simmer, uncovered, until the water has evaporated. Continue cooking to brown the meat, adding a little pork fat or oil if necessary.

Yield: Eight servings.

Chinese Pork Balls   *Northern California*

Pork balls:
    3 five-ounce to six-ounce cans water
       chestnuts, drained and finely chopped
  1½ cups finely chopped scallions, including
       green part
    3 pounds ground lean pork
    2 teaspoons salt
    3 tablespoons imported soy sauce
    4 eggs, lightly beaten
  1½ cups fine dry bread crumbs
    1 tablespoon finely chopped fresh, or
       crystallized, ginger

      Cornstarch
      Oil for deep-frying.
Sauce:
    2 cups unsweetened pineapple juice
    1 cup cider vinegar
  ¼ cup imported soy sauce
  ⅔ cup sugar
  1½ cups beef broth bouillon
    2 tablespoons finely chopped fresh, or
       crystallized, ginger
  ½ cup cornstarch
    1 cup water.

1. To prepare pork balls, place the water chestnuts, scallions, pork, salt, soy sauce and eggs in a large bowl. With the hands, work the ingredients together to mix.

2. Add the bread crumbs and ginger and, again with the hands, mix well. Chill mixture for one hour.

3. With the hands, shape the mixture into balls three-quarters inch to one inch in diameter. Roll the balls in cornstarch. Heat oil to 370 degrees.

4. Carefully drop the balls, one at a time (about a dozen at one cooking), into the oil, watching that the foaming does not come dangerously near the top of the pan (the oil should not extend above the halfway mark on the pan).

5. Fry the balls about one to two minutes, or until balls are golden brown and rise to the top of the oil. Break one open to make sure it is cooked through; there should be no pink color left. Drain on paper towels. Reheat oil in between batches. Continue with batches of ten to twelve balls at a time until all are cooked.

6. Meanwhile, prepare the sauce. Place the pineapple juice, vinegar, soy sauce, sugar, bouillon and ginger in a saucepan and bring to a boil.

7. Mix the cornstarch with the water and, using a wire whisk or a wooden spoon, stir the cornstarch mixture into the boiling mixture.

8. Cook, stirring, three minutes. Then place over very low heat or over hot water to keep hot while frying the meat balls.

9. Place the balls in a chafing dish and stir in enough sauce to coat all the balls.

Yield: About 100.

Note: The balls can be covered with aluminum foil and refrigerated overnight. To serve, heat, covered, in a preheated 400-degree oven about twenty to twenty-five minutes. Reheat the sauce while stirring. Proceed as above.

Teriyaki Appetizer   *Hawaii*

½ cup soy sauce
2 tablespoons dry sherry
1 tablespoon finely chopped fresh gingerroot
2 teaspoons sugar
2 scallions, including green part, chopped
2 pounds round steak, cut into strips one-quarter inch thick and one and one-half inches long.

1. Combine the soy sauce, sherry, gingerroot, sugar and scallions. Add the meat and marinate thirty minutes.
2. Thread the pieces of meat on bamboo skewers and broil three minutes.
Yield: About one dozen servings.

Smoked Salmon Rolls   *Washington*

1 cup flour
⅛ teaspoon salt
⅓ cup shortening
  Ice water
6 ounces smoked salmon
1 teaspoon grated fresh horseradish or drained prepared horseradish
2 tablespoons lemon juice
1 teaspoon finely grated onion
1 tablespoon chopped parsley
2 tablespoons mayonnaise, approximately.

1. Place the flour and salt in a bowl and, with a pastry blender or the finger tips, blend in the shortening. Mix to a dough with a tablespoon or two of the ice water. Chill the dough twenty minutes.

2. Meanwhile, flake the salmon in a bowl and combine with remaining ingredients, using just enough mayonnaise to bind.
3. Preheat the oven to 425 degrees.
4. Roll out the pastry to a nine-inch circle. Spread with the salmon mixture.
5. Cut into thirty-two wedges and roll each one, starting at the wide end. Place on a baking sheet. Prick the top of each roll. Bake fifteen minutes, or until pastry is golden and done. Serve hot or cold.
Yield: Thirty-two.

Whitebait Appetizer   *Northern California*

1 pound whitebait
1 egg, lightly beaten
1 tablespoon milk
  Flour or cracker meal
  Oil
  Salt and freshly ground black pepper to taste
  Citrus mayonnaise (see note in "Mayonnaise," page 760).

1. Remove the head and veins of each fish. Rinse the fish and dry on paper towels.
2. Combine the egg and milk and dip the fish into the mixture and then into the flour or cracker meal to coat.
3. Pour oil into a heavy skillet to a depth of one-eighth inch and heat. Fry the fish, a few at a time, in the oil until golden brown on both sides.
4. Drain on paper towels. Season with salt and pepper. Serve with citrus mayonnaise.
Yield: Four servings.

Curried Mushroom Turnovers   *Hawaii*

Pastry:
3 three-ounce packages cream cheese, at room temperature
½ cup butter, at room temperature
1½ cups flour.

Filling:
3 tablespoons butter
1 cup finely chopped onions
½ pound mushrooms, finely chopped
1 teaspoon curry powder
½ teaspoon salt
  Freshly ground black pepper to taste
2 tablespoons flour
¼ cup heavy cream.

1. To prepare pastry, mix the cream cheese and butter together thoroughly. Add the flour and work with the fingers or a pastry blender until smooth. Chill well, at least thirty minutes.

2. Preheat the oven to 450 degrees.

3. To prepare filling, heat the butter in a skillet. Add the onions and brown lightly. Add the mushrooms and cook, stirring often, about three minutes.

4. Add the curry powder, salt and pepper and sprinkle with the flour. Stir in the cream and cook gently until thickened.

5. Roll the dough to one-eighth-inch thickness on a lightly floured surface and cut into rounds with a three-inch biscuit cutter. Place one teaspoon of mushroom filling on each round and fold the dough over the filling. Press the edges together with a fork. Prick top crusts to allow for the escape of steam.

6. Place turnovers on an ungreased baking sheet and bake until lightly browned, about fifteen minutes.

Yield: About two dozen.

Parmesan Wafers   *Northern California*

6 pieces Norwegian flat bread
1 tablespoon soft butter
3 tablespoons freshly grated Parmesan cheese
2 teaspoons chopped fresh tarragon leaves or one-half teaspoon dried tarragon
  Water cress sprigs.

1. Preheat the oven to 450 degrees.

2. With a sharp knife, separate each piece of flat bread into two rectangles. Spread with the butter. Place on a baking sheet.

3. Sprinkle with the cheese and tarragon and bake five minutes, or until lightly browned. Serve overlapping on a round serving platter with a center garnish of water cress.

Yield: Four to six servings.

Chuck's Roasted Sweet Peppers
Northern California

4 red sweet peppers
2 cloves garlic, finely chopped
  Salt and freshly ground black pepper to taste
¼ cup olive oil.

1. Day before or early in the day, preheat the oven to 400 degrees and place the peppers on the oven shelf. Let roast thirty minutes, or until the skins puff up and the peppers look slightly charred.

2. With potholders or asbestos gloves, hold the hot peppers and gently peel off the skin, saving all the juice that is released. Remove and discard the seeds. Slice the peppers into thin strips and arrange in a baking dish with the juice.

3. Sprinkle with the garlic, salt, pepper and oil and refrigerate, covered, until serving time.

4. Preheat the oven to 400 degrees.

5. Bake pepper strips, uncovered, twenty minutes, or until bubbling hot.

Yield: Four servings.

Seasoned Filberts   *Oregon*

⅓ cup butter
1 clove garlic, crushed
1 teaspoon salt
1 teaspoon Worcestershire sauce
¼ teaspoon Tabasco sauce
4 cups shelled filberts.

1. Preheat the oven to 400 degrees.

2. Melt the butter in a saucepan, add the garlic and cook briefly. Remove garlic and discard.

3. Add the remaining ingredients to the butter. Mix. Turn onto a jellyroll pan and bake fifteen to twenty minutes, stirring occasionally. Serve warm.

Yield: Four cups.

Schramsberg Zucchini Blossom Fritters
Northern California

2 eggs, separated
⅔ cup milk
1 tablespoon olive oil
1 tablespoon lemon juice
½ teaspoon salt
  Flour
2 tablespoons butter
¼ cup chopped onion
2 tablespoons freshly grated Parmesan cheese
2 tablespoons brandy
24 large zucchini blossoms, picked in the morning while flower is full.
  Fat or vegetable oil for deep-frying.

1. Beat the egg yolks until light and lemon-colored. Add the milk, olive oil, lemon juice, salt and two-thirds cup flour.

2. Heat the butter in a small skillet and sauté the onion in it until tender. Puree in an electric blender and add to the batter.

3. Stir the cheese and brandy into the batter and set aside for an hour or longer.

4. Beat the egg whites until stiff but not dry and fold into batter.

5. Wash the blossoms and drain by shaking each flower and placing on paper towel.

6. Heat the fat or vegetable oil to 360 degrees.

7. Dust a few flowers at a time with flour, dip into the batter and fry in the fat or oil, turning, until flowers are golden.

8. Drain on paper towels and serve at once.

Yield: Four to six servings.

Egg Rolls
Northern California

Wrappers:
1 large egg, beaten
1 cup lukewarm water
1 cup plus two tablespoons flour
¼ cup cornstarch
½ teaspoon salt
½ teaspoon sugar.
Filling:
1 cup chopped cooked chicken or shrimp
½ cup chopped bean sprouts
½ cup chopped water chestnuts
½ cup chopped bamboo shoots
¼ cup chopped scallions, including green part
¼ cup chopped green pepper
1 teaspoon chopped fresh gingerroot
¼ cup ground almonds
1 teaspoon sugar
1 tablespoon soy sauce
1 egg, lightly beaten
  Fat or oil for deep-frying.

1. To prepare wrappers, combine the egg and water. Gradually beat in the remaining ingredients until mixture is smooth.

2. Heat a ten-inch skillet, brush lightly with oil and then pour into the skillet and spread enough of the batter to make a five-inch square, paper-thin pancake.

3. Cook until set on one side. Remove from the skillet. Repeat until all the batter is used.

4. To prepare filling, mix together the chicken or shrimp, bean sprouts, water chestnuts, bamboo shoots, scallions, green pepper, gingerroot, almonds, sugar and soy sauce. Place a small amount down the center of each pancake. Fold the edges in and roll like a jellyroll.

5. Seal the rolls with the egg and set aside thirty minutes or longer.

6. Heat a bath of deep fat or oil to 360 degrees. Fry the rolls, a few at a time, in the fat until golden, about eight minutes. Drain on paper towels. Slice rolls and serve hot.

Yield: About ten rolls or servings.

Tempura　　　　　　　　　　　*Hawaii*

24 medium-size shrimp
　Flour
½ cup cornstarch
2 tablespoons baking powder
1 teaspoon baking soda
1 egg, lightly beaten
　Salt to taste
1½ cups water, approximately
　Fat for deep-frying
　Soy mustard sauce (recipe below).

1. Shell the shrimp, but leave the last tail segment intact. Run a sharp knife lightly over the upper rim of each shrimp and rinse under cold running water to remove the intestinal vein. Drain and pat dry.

2. Place two cups flour, the cornstarch, baking powder and baking soda in a mixing bowl. Stir in the egg and salt. Add the water, stirring with chopsticks or a fork to make a fairly thin coating batter. When finished, the batter should be a little lumpy.

3. Pour fat to a depth of one inch into a skillet and heat to 375 degrees. Dredge the shrimp lightly in flour, then in the batter. Drop shrimp, one at a time, into the hot fat and cook, turning once or twice, until golden brown. Serve hot with soy mustard sauce.

Yield: Two dozen.

Soy Mustard Sauce　　　　　　*Hawaii*

1 tablespoon dry mustard
⅓ cup soy sauce, preferably imported
½ teaspoon sugar
2 tablespoons mirin (Japanese wine) or water.

1. Place the mustard in a small bowl and add enough water to make a thin paste. Let stand ten minutes.

2. Add the remaining ingredients. Serve as a dip for tempura.

Yield: About one-half cup.

West Coast Sushi　　*Northern California*

Filling I:
　2 eggs, lightly beaten
　4 teaspoons saki (rice wine)
　1 tablespoon sugar
　½ teaspoon salt
　¼ cup oil
　1 three-ounce flounder or sole fillet, cut lengthwise into one-quarter-inch strips
　　Flour
　½ cup well-drained cooked spinach.
Filling II:
　6 medium-size to large shrimp, shelled and deveined
　2 eggs
　2 tablespoons saki (rice wine)
　1 tablespoon sugar
　¼ teaspoon salt
　2 tablespoons oil.
Rice:
2½ cups water
　½ cup white vinegar
　1 tablespoon sugar
　1 teaspoon salt
　2 cups uncooked rice.
Seaweed:
　2 sheets seaweed (see note).
Sauce:
　　Imported soy sauce
　　Fresh ginger slices.

1. To prepare filling I, mix the eggs, saki, sugar and salt together. Heat two tablespoons of the oil in a small skillet, add the eggs and scramble lightly. Remove from the heat and set aside.

2. Heat remaining oil in a second skillet. Dust the fish pieces lightly with flour and sauté in the oil until fish flakes easily, about three minutes. Set aside. Set spinach aside.

3. To prepare filling II, chop the shrimp very finely. Blend with the eggs, saki, sugar and salt. Heat the oil in a skillet, add shrimp mixture and cook until shrimp turn pink, about four minutes. Set aside.

4. To prepare rice, combine the water, vinegar,

sugar and salt and bring to a boil. Add the rice and return to a boil. Simmer, covered, fifteen minutes. Turn heat off, but keep cover on six minutes.

5. To assemble sushi, soften the seaweed sheets in warm water two to three minutes.

6. Place one seaweed sheet on a bamboo mat or clean towel. Spread half the hot rice evenly over the surface, leaving one and one-quarter-inch border of seaweed.

7. Place half of the filling chosen down the center of the rice. If it is filling I, place the egg first, spinach on top of egg and then fish on top of spinach.

8. Roll like a jellyroll into a cylinder, using the bamboo mat or towel as a guide. Slice into eight three-quarter-inch slices. Repeat with remaining rice and second half of filling on second sheet of seaweed.

9. To be eaten, the slices are picked up with the fingers and dipped in soy sauce lightly flavored with ginger.

Yield: Eight servings.

Note: Seaweed sheets are available in stores where Oriental foods are sold.

If both fillings are prepared, double the amount of rice and seaweed sheets.

Marin County Shrimp Appetizer
Northern California

1 large sweet onion, sliced and separated into rings
2½ pounds large shrimp, cooked, shelled and deveined
4 oranges, peeled and thinly sliced
1½ cups oil
⅔ cup lemon juice
1 cup wine vinegar
⅓ cup catchup
2 tablespoons sugar
 Salt and freshly ground black pepper to taste
1 teaspoon celery seeds
1 teaspoon mustard seeds

½ teaspoon crushed red pepper flakes
2 cloves garlic, finely chopped
2 tablespoons chopped parsley or freshly snipped dill weed
 Lettuce leaves.

1. Combine the onion rings, shrimp and orange slices in a large ceramic or glass bowl.

2. Mix together the oil, lemon juice, vinegar, catchup, sugar, salt, pepper, celery seeds, mustard seeds, red pepper flakes, garlic and parsley or dill. Pour over the shrimp mixture. Cover and marinate in the refrigerator twenty-four to forty-eight hours, stirring occasionally.

3. Drain shrimp well before serving on lettuce leaves as an appetizer.

Yield: Six servings.

Hawaiian Sea "Anemones"

½ pound shrimp
2 or three scallions
5 water chestnuts, chopped
1 teaspoon dry sherry
1 teaspoon salt
1½ teaspoons cornstarch
¼ bunch bean thread (Oriental vermicelli)
 Oil for deep-frying.

1. Using a pair of kitchen shears, cut along the upper rim of each shrimp. Pull or peel the shell off each shrimp and rinse shrimp under cold running water to remove the small black vein. Drain well on paper towels. Chop the shrimp and place in a mixing bowl.

2. Trim off the root end of the scallions. Cut off the green part. Chop the white part and add it to the shrimp. Add the water chestnuts, sherry, salt and cornstarch and blend well.

3. Cut the bean thread into one-inch lengths. Shape the shrimp mixture into about twelve balls and roll each ball in the bean threads.

4. Heat the oil to 370 degrees. When it is hot, deep-fry the shrimp balls in it. If the oil is prop-

erly heated, the bean thread will puff up and turn white and crisp when cooked.

Yield: About one dozen.

Charcoal Broiled Shrimp

Northern California

2 pounds jumbo shrimp
3 quarts boiling water
2 slices onion
1 slice lemon
⅛ teaspoon oregano
⅛ cup olive oil
2 tablespoons melted butter
2 tablespoons Worcestershire sauce
6 tablespoons catchup
¼ cup lemon juice
¼ cup beer
¼ teaspoon salt
¼ teaspoon freshly ground black pepper
3 drops Tabasco sauce, or to taste
2 cloves garlic, finely chopped.

1. Put the shrimp in the water, add the onion slices, lemon slice and oregano and cook three minutes. Drain shrimp; shell and devein.

2. Combine the remaining ingredients and pour over the hot deveined and shelled shrimp. (The shrimp should be just covered with the mixture.) Let marinate in the refrigerator three to four hours.

3. Cook the shrimp over hot charcoals in a small grill or hibachi or under the broiler until tender, about five minutes. Serve immediately.

Yield: Four servings.

Mushroom and Clam Soup

Oregon

¼ cup butter
2 tablespoons chopped scallions, including green part
1 pound mushrooms, sliced
¼ cup flour
4 cups clam juice

Salt and freshly ground black pepper to taste
⅛ teaspoon nutmeg
1½ cups light cream.

1. Melt the butter in a saucepan. Sauté the scallion in it until tender. Add the mushrooms and cook three minutes longer.

2. Sprinkle with the flour and cook one minute. Stir in the clam juice, salt, pepper and nutmeg. Bring to a boil and simmer five minutes.

3. Add the cream and reheat, but do not boil.

Yield: Six servings.

Quick Clam Chowder

Washington

6 slices bacon
6 to eight scallions, including green part, chopped
1 green pepper, chopped
2 large potatoes, diced
4 cups finely chopped clams with liquor
¼ cup chopped parsley
4 cups half and half, scalded
3 tablespoons butter
Salt and freshly ground black pepper to taste.

1. Cook the bacon in a kettle until crisp. Add the scallions and green pepper and cook until tender. Add the potatoes.

2. Drain the clams. Measure the liquid and make up to three cups with water. Add to potato mixture and simmer until potatoes are tender.

3. Add clams; cook three minutes. Add the parsley, half and half, butter, salt and pepper and heat, but do not boil.

Yield: Ten servings.

Sea Hag Clam Chowder

Oregon

⅓ cup plus one-half pound butter
6 ribs celery, chopped
2 large onions, chopped

1 gallon boiling water or mixture clam broth
and water
12 cups diced potatoes
8 cups chopped clams
1 pound bacon, cooked until crisp, then
crumbled
½ cup flour
Cold water
Salt and freshly ground black pepper to
taste
8 cups hot milk, approximately.

1. For the clam chowder base, melt one-third cup of the butter in a large heavy kettle and sauté the celery and onions in it until tender. Add the boiling water or broth mixture and the potatoes. Cook gently fifteen minutes, or until potatoes are barely tender.

2. Add the clams and bacon and cook five minutes longer, or until clams are tender.

3. Mix the flour with enough cold water to make a thin smooth paste. Add some of hot chowder base to it while stirring. Return to the kettle and cook, stirring, until mixture thickens.

4. Season with salt and pepper.

5. To serve, add enough hot milk to give the desired consistency. Place a pat of butter in each soup bowl and ladle the chowder into bowls.

Yield: About two dozen servings.

Note: Oregon chowder, because of the addition of flour, is often considerably thicker than its New England counterpart.

Clam and Corn Chowder *Oregon*

½ cup diced bacon
1 small onion, finely chopped
2 cups shucked clams, chopped if large
Clam broth or water, if necessary
1 cup diced potatoes
¼ cup chopped celery leaves
1 teaspoon salt
1 cup fresh corn kernels
3 tablespoons butter
½ teaspoon sugar

2 tablespoons water
2 cups milk, scalded
⅛ teaspoon freshly ground black pepper
1 tablespoon flour.

1. Cook the bacon until crisp, remove bits and reserve. Sauté the onion in the fat remaining.

2. Drain the clams and measure the liquid. If necessary, make up to one cup with broth or water.

3. Add liquid, the potatoes, celery leaves and salt to onion and cook ten minutes.

4. Meanwhile, briefly sauté the corn kernels in two tablespoons of the butter. Add the sugar and two tablespoons water. Cover and simmer two minutes.

5. Add the corn, clams, milk and pepper to the potato mixture. Cook about five minutes, or until clams are tender. Knead the flour and remaining butter together and whisk into the soup. Cook until mixture thickens slightly.

6. Serve sprinkled with reserved bacon bits.
Yield: Six servings.

Portuguese Bean Soup *Hawaii*

2 cups dried kidney beans
Salt
1 ham bone with some meat on
Freshly ground black pepper to taste
¼ cup olive oil
1 clove garlic, finely chopped
1 onion, finely chopped
¾ cup diced carrots
1½ cups shredded cabbage
1 cup diced potatoes
2 cups water cress, roughly chopped (see note).

1. Day before, rinse the beans. Cover with water and let soak overnight. Next day, drain beans and place in a kettle with two teaspoons salt, the ham bone, pepper and enough water barely to cover. Bring to a boil, cover and simmer until barely tender, about thirty minutes.

2. Remove the bone and cut off the meat. Dice the meat.

3. Heat the oil in a skillet and sauté the garlic and onion in it until tender. Add the meat and cook five minutes longer. Add the carrots and cook three minutes.

4. Add the carrot mixture to the kettle of beans. Add the cabbage, potatoes, half the water cress and one and three-quarter quarts water. Simmer until vegetables are tender.

5. Season to taste with salt and pepper and add the remaining water cress just before serving.

Yield: Eight to ten servings.

Note: Spinach may be substituted for the water cress.

Miso-Shiru (Bean Paste Soup)

Northern California

3 cups strongly flavored chicken broth
2½ tablespoons miso paste (fermented bean curd paste)
1 fresh tofu (fresh bean curd), cubed
2 stalks negi (scallion), chopped
½ white radish, sliced paper-thin.

1. Heat the broth to boiling. Add the remaining ingredients.

2. Remove from heat when the tofu is cooked —that is, when the bean curd comes to the surface.

Yield: Four to six servings.

Note: Unusual ingredients can be bought in Japanese grocery stores such as Katagiri, 224 59th Street, New York, New York 10022.

San Juan Island Oyster Stew *Washington*

1 clove garlic, crushed
3 tablespoons butter
1 tablespoon Worcestershire sauce
1 cup oysters, cut if large, with liquor
4 cups milk, scalded
Salt and freshly ground black pepper.

1. Rub the inside of a kettle with the garlic clove.

2. Heat the butter and Worcestershire in the kettle. Add oysters and their liquor. Cook slowly until edges curl and oysters puff up, about three minutes.

3. Add the milk, salt and pepper and reheat, but do not boil.

Yield: Four servings.

Olympia Oysters Poulette *Washington*

1 pint Olympia oysters with liquor
2 tablespoons finely chopped shallots or scallions
½ cup dry white wine
1 cup plus two tablespoons heavy cream
2 egg yolks
Salt and freshly ground black pepper to taste
¼ teaspoon cayenne pepper
Juice of one-half lemon
French bread croutons (see note).

1. Drain the oyster liquor into a saucepan. Reserve the oysters.

2. Add the shallots or scallions and wine to the oyster liquor. Cook over medium heat until the liquid is reduced almost by half.

3. Add one cup of the cream and simmer five minutes.

4. Blend the egg yolks with the remaining cream and spoon a little of the hot sauce into the egg yolk mixture, stirring. Return all to the saucepan and add the oysters. Add salt, pepper and the cayenne. Stir and heat thoroughly, but do not boil or the yolks may curdle. Add the lemon juice and, if desired, more salt and pepper to taste.

5. Place French bread croutons as desired in hot soup bowls and spoon the soup over croutons.

Yield: Six servings.

Note: To prepare French bread croutons, cut one-half-inch slices of French bread into one-quarter-inch cubes. For each cup of cubes, melt two tablespoons butter in a skillet. Add the cubes to the butter and cook, tossing frequently, over medium heat until cubes are golden.

Winter Melon and Ham Soup   *Hawaii*

    4 dried Chinese mushrooms
 ¼ cup warm water
    1 pound winter melon, peeled and cut into
      slices, ¼ inch by 1 inch by 1 inch
    4 cups chicken broth
    1 teaspoon salt
 ¼ teaspoon monosodium glutamate (optional)
 ¼ cup dry cured ham slices, ¼ inch by 1 inch
      by 1 inch.

1. Soak the mushrooms in the water ten minutes. Cut each mushroom into two to four pieces.

2. Add the melon slices to the broth and bring to a boil over high heat. Add the mushrooms, salt and monosodium glutamate if desired. Cover and cook over medium heat ten minutes.

3. Add the ham slices and bring to a boil. Serve hot.

Yield: Four servings.

Cellophane Noodle and Meat Ball Soup
Hawaii

    1 ounce dried cellophane noodles
      Warm water
 ¼ pound pork or beef steak, ground
    1 tablespoon soy sauce
    1 tablespoon dry sherry
    4 cups water
    3 cups chicken broth
    1 teaspoon salt
 ¼ teaspoon monosodium glutamate (optional)
    1 scallion, including green part, chopped.

1. Soak the noodles in warm water twenty minutes. Cut noodles into two-inch lengths and drain.

2. Mix the meat with the soy sauce and sherry. Form into eight balls.

3. Bring the four cups water to a boil. Then drop the meat balls in gently, one by one. Cook five minutes. Drain the meat balls and discard the water.

4. Heat the broth in a saucepan with the salt and monosodium glutamate if desired. Add the meat balls and noodles and cook five minutes. Sprinkle the scallion over soup before serving.

Yield: Four servings.

Korean Dumpling Soup   *Hawaii*

    1 pound top round or boneless sirloin
    2 scallions, including green part, chopped
 ¼ cup sesame seeds, browned in a heavy
      skillet and pulverized in an electric
      blender or with a mortar and pestle
    6 tablespoons soy sauce
 ⅛ teaspoon freshly ground black pepper
    8 cups boiling water
    2 teaspoons oil
 ¼ cup finely chopped fresh, or dried and
      soaked, mushrooms
    1 clove garlic, finely chopped
    1 cup fresh bean sprouts, cooked in boiling
      water three minutes, then drained and
      chopped
 1½ cups chopped bok choy (Chinese cabbage),
      cooked in boiling water three minutes,
      then drained very well
      Salt to taste
    3 cups flour
    1 cup cold water
    3 tablespoons pignoli (pine nuts)
    1 egg, separated.

1. Cut one-quarter pound of the beef into thin one-inch squares and place in a skillet. Add one of the scallions, half the sesame seeds, two tablespoons of the soy sauce and the pepper. Mix well.

2. Cook the mixture until the meat is lightly browned. Add the boiling water, bring to a boil

and simmer gently until the meat is tender, about ten minutes. Set this soup aside.

3. Meanwhile, grind the remaining meat. Mix with the oil, mushrooms, garlic, bean sprouts, bok choy and remaining scallion, sesame seeds and soy sauce. Season with salt.

4. Combine the flour and cold water to make a stiff dough. Knead five minutes. Cover and let stand five minutes. Roll the dough into a rectangle and cut forty to forty-eight squares. Roll each square in turn into a round three inches in diameter.

5. Place one teaspoon of the filling to one side of the center of each round. Add two pignoli, moisten the edges with water and fold over into a crescent shape. Seal firmly.

6. Reheat soup to boiling. Drop the dumplings into the boiling soup. Cook two minutes after they rise to the surface.

7. Beat the egg yolk lightly and pour into a hot, oiled Teflon-lined skillet to make an egg pancake. Turn to cook other side.

8. Beat the egg white lightly and pour into a hot, oiled Teflon-lined skillet to make a small pancake. Turn to cook other side.

9. Chop yellow and white egg pancakes and use to garnish the dumpling soup, served in individual bowls.

Yield: Six servings.

Saimin   *Hawaii*

2 pounds pork bones
8 cups cold water
½ cup dried shrimp, if available
  Salt to taste
1 teaspoon monosodium glutamate (optional)
¼ pound lean boneless pork, cut into thin julienne strips
¾ cup raw shrimp, cut into bite-size pieces
½ pound very thin noodles
  Boiling salted water
⅓ cup chopped scallions, including green part.

1. Place the bones in a three-quart kettle and add the cold water and dried shrimp. Simmer one and one-half hours.

2. Strain broth and add salt, monosodium glutamate, if desired, pork and raw shrimp. Simmer twenty minutes. Cook the noodles until tender in boiling salted water and add. Serve sprinkled with the scallions.

Yield: Six servings.

Pork and Abalone Soup
Northern California

½ pound lean boneless pork, cut into thin julienne strips
2 bamboo shoots, cut into thin julienne strips
2 stalks celery, finely sliced
2 scallions, including green part, trimmed and finely sliced
6 cups water
2 cups canned abalone with the abalone liquor
  Salt and freshly ground black pepper to taste
1 teaspoon monosodium glutamate (optional)
4 thin slivers lemon peel.

1. Place the pork, bamboo shoots, celery and scallions in a saucepan with the water. Bring to a boil and let simmer seven minutes.

2. Cut the abalone into thin strips and add to the saucepan along with the abalone liquor. Season with salt and pepper and add monosodium glutamate, if desired. Bring to a boil again and let simmer another seven minutes. Add the lemon peel and serve.

Yield: Four servings.

Shrimp Chowder

Oregon

¼ cup butter
2 large sweet onions, sliced
1 cup boiling water
4 potatoes, diced
1½ teaspoons salt
½ teaspoon freshly ground black pepper
6 cups milk
½ pound grated mild Cheddar cheese (two cups)
2 pounds shrimp, shelled and deveined
3 tablespoons chopped parsley.

1. Heat the butter in the saucepan and sauté the onions in it until tender. Add the water, potatoes, salt and pepper.
2. Cover and simmer twenty minutes, or until potatoes are tender.
3. Combine the milk and cheese in another saucepan. Heat, stirring, until cheese melts, but do not let boil.
4. Add the shrimp to potato mixture and cook until shrimp are pink, about five minutes. Add cheese mixture and heat, but do not boil. Stir in the parsley.
Yield: Six servings.

Pacific Fish Stew

Oregon

3 tablespoons oil
1 onion, finely chopped
1 clove garlic, finely chopped
½ cup chopped parsley
1 one-pound-twelve-ounce can Italian plum tomatoes
2 six-ounce cans tomato paste
⅛ teaspoon rosemary, crushed
½ teaspoon salt
¼ teaspoon freshly ground black pepper
2 cracked crabs
12 shucked clams with liquor

½ pound shrimp, shelled and deveined
¾ pound halibut fillet, cut into four pieces
½ cup dry sherry.

1. Heat the oil in a kettle and sauté the onion and garlic in it until tender. Add the parsley, tomatoes, tomato paste, rosemary, salt and pepper. Bring to a boil and simmer two hours.
2. Add the crabs, clams, shrimp and halibut to sauce. Simmer fifteen minutes, or until fish flakes easily. Stir in the sherry.
Yield: Four to six servings.

Fish Chowder

Oregon

¼ cup chopped bacon
¼ cup finely chopped onion
2 cups hot water
1 cup diced potatoes
1 pound ocean perch, halibut or cod fillets, cut into bite-size pieces
2 cups half and half, scalded
¾ teaspoon salt
⅛ teaspoon freshly ground black pepper
2 tablespoons butter
2 tablespoons chopped parsley
½ cup croutons.

1. Cook the bacon until crisp. Add the onion and cook until tender.
2. Add the water and potatoes and cook gently ten minutes. Add the fish and simmer gently five minutes. Add the half and half, salt, pepper and butter. Reheat but do not cook.
3. Garnish with the parsley and serve with the croutons.
Yield: Six servings.

Salmon Chowder I

Alaska

3 cups milk
1 pound cooked fresh salmon, bones and skin removed, or canned salmon, drained (reserve liquid)
¼ cup chopped onion
¼ cup chopped celery
¼ cup butter
3 tablespoons flour
1 cup tomato juice
1½ teaspoons salt
2 tablespoons chopped parsley
Hot crisp crackers.

1. Place the milk in a saucepan (replace part of milk with reserved liquid from canned salmon if used) and heat to simmering.
2. Flake the salmon coarsely.
3. Sauté the onion and celery in the butter over low heat ten minutes, or until tender. Stir in the flour.
4. Add hot milk and cook, stirring, until mixture is thickened. Stir in the tomato juice and salt.
5. Add the salmon. Heat, but do not boil. Sprinkle each serving with the parsley. Serve with hot crisp crackers.
Yield: Six servings.

Salmon Chowder II

Washington

4 slices bacon
¼ cup chopped onion
2 cups boiling water or fish stock

1 cup diced potatoes
1 pound salmon fillet, cubed
2 cups hot milk
1 teaspoon salt
⅛ teaspoon freshly ground black pepper
2 tablespoons chopped parsley.

1. Cook the bacon until crisp in a large skillet. Remove bacon, crumble and reserve. In the fat remaining in the skillet, sauté the onion until tender.
2. Add the water or stock and the potatoes. Cook gently ten minutes. Add the salmon and cook ten minutes longer.
3. Add the milk, salt, pepper, parsley and reserved bacon and reheat.
Yield: Four servings.

Cold Raspberry Soup

Washington

4 cups raspberries
½ cup sugar
1½ cups chilled dry white wine
1 cup water.

1. Reserve one-half cup of the raspberries for garnish. Force the remaining through a food mill or blend in an electric blender until smooth.
2. Combine with the sugar, wine and water and chill well. Serve in chilled bowls, topped with the reserved whole berries.
Yield: Four servings.

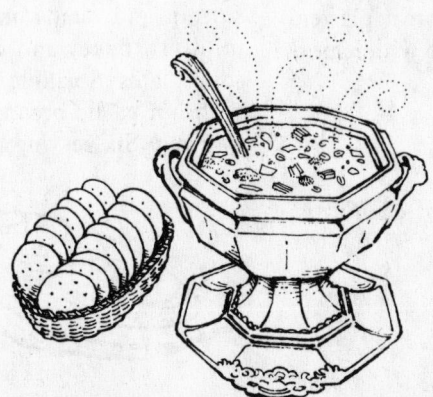

Fish and Shellfish

Abalone with Vermouth

Northern California

2 tablespoons flour
  Salt and freshly ground black pepper to taste
12 large slices abalone, well pounded
6 tablespoons butter
½ cup dry vermouth
2 tablespoons chopped parsley
  Lemon wedges
  Tartar sauce (page 760).

1. Combine the flour, salt and pepper. Wash the abalone slices under cold running water and dry thoroughly with paper towels. Dredge lightly with flour mixture.

2. Heat the butter and vermouth in a skillet. When mixture begins to sizzle, add abalone slices, two at a time, and brown on both sides. Do not cook longer than one minute on each side or abalone will become tough. Repeat the process until all pieces are cooked. Serve on a platter. Sprinkle with the parsley and garnish with lemon wedges. Serve with tartar sauce.

Yield: Six servings.

Cioppino

Northern California

½ cup olive oil
2 onions, finely chopped
2 cloves garlic, finely chopped
1 one-pound-twelve-ounce can Italian plum tomatoes
2 eight-ounce cans tomato sauce
  Salt and freshly ground black pepper to taste
1 teaspoon basil
½ teaspoon oregano
1 pound halibut fillets, cut into serving pieces
2 Dungeness crabs, cleaned and cracked, including crab butter
1 pound shrimp, shelled and deveined
12 small clams (optional)
¼ cup chopped parsley
  Hot garlic bread.

1. Heat the oil in a large kettle and sauté the onions and garlic in it until tender. Add the tomatoes, tomato sauce, salt, pepper, basil and oregano. Bring to a boil and simmer twenty minutes.

2. Add the halibut, crabs and crab butter, shrimp and clams and simmer ten minutes, or until fish flakes and clams open. Serve in large soup plates. Sprinkle with the parsley and serve with hot garlic bread.

Yield: Six servings.

Agate Beach Clam Fritters

Oregon

3 potatoes, peeled and grated
  Salted water
3 eggs, well beaten
¼ cup flour, approximately
1 small onion, grated
½ teaspoon salt
⅛ teaspoon freshly ground black pepper
2 cups ground clams
⅓ cup chopped parsley
12 slices bacon
  Butter.

1. Day before, cover the potatoes with salted water and let soak overnight. Next morning, drain and dry potatoes roughly on paper towel.
2. Mix potatoes with the eggs, enough flour to make mixture hold together, the onion, salt, pepper, clams and parsley.
3. Cook the bacon until crisp on a griddle. Remove and reserve.
4. Heat the bacon drippings on the griddle. Drop the clam mixture into the drippings and cook until lightly browned. Turn and brown other side. Serve topped with butter and with reserved bacon strips.
Yield: Six servings.

Clam Fritters

Washington

2 cups chopped fresh razor clams
4 large soda crackers, crushed
2 eggs, lightly beaten
  Salt and freshly ground black pepper to taste
  Parsley sprigs
  Tartar sauce (page 760).

1. Mix together the clams, crackers, eggs, salt and pepper.
2. Grease a griddle well with shortening and heat to hot. Drop clam mixture onto hot griddle and fry over medium heat until browned. Turn and brown second side.

3. Garnish with parsley sprigs and serve with tartar sauce.
Yield: Four servings.

Orcas Island Clam and Corn Casserole

Washington

1¼ cups crumbled saltine crackers
1 cup milk
2 eggs, well beaten
½ cup chopped clams with liquor
1 cup whole kernel corn
2 tablespoons grated onion
1 tablespoon chopped green pepper
½ teaspoon Worcestershire sauce
⅛ teaspoon freshly ground black pepper
½ cup grated sharp Cheddar cheese.

1. Preheat the oven to 350 degrees.
2. Combine the crackers, milk and eggs. Stir in the clams, corn, onion, green pepper, Worcestershire and pepper. Pour into a greased casserole and bake until set, about forty-five minutes.
3. Sprinkle the top with the cheese and bake five minutes longer.
Yield: Four servings.

Clam Casserole

Washington

12 saltine crackers, crumbled
1 cup milk
¼ cup melted butter
1 cup chopped clams
2 scallions, including green part, finely chopped
2 eggs, lightly beaten.

1. Preheat the oven to 325 degrees.
2. Combine all the ingredients and pour into a greased baking dish. Bake thirty to forty minutes, or until set and lightly browned.
Yield: Two servings.

Port Angeles Clam Cakes
Washington

4 cups clams, well drained
2 tablespoons grated onion
2 eggs, lightly beaten
½ cup cracker crumbs
  Salt to taste
  Melted butter.

1. Combine all ingredients except the butter and shape into patties one and one-half inches in diameter and three-quarters-inch thick.
2. Brush tops with butter and broil or pan-fry in butter until crisp on both sides.
Yield: Six to eight servings.

Clam Loaf
Washington

2 cups clams, drained and chopped
½ pound sausage meat
2 eggs, lightly beaten
1 cup cracker crumbs
1 cup milk
½ clove garlic, finely chopped
  Salt and freshly ground black pepper to taste.

1. Preheat the oven to 350 degrees.
2. Mix together all ingredients and turn into a loaf pan. Bake forty minutes, or until set.
Yield: Four servings.

Broiled Ling Cod with Mustard Sauce
Oregon

2 twelve-ounce ling cod fillets
¾ cup melted butter
  Salt and freshly ground black pepper to taste
¼ cup Dijon or Düsseldorf mustard
2 teaspoons sugar
1 tablespoon dry white wine
1½ tablespoons lemon juice
¼ teaspoon Worcestershire sauce.

1. Brush the fillets with two tablespoons of the butter. Season with salt and pepper and broil in a preheated broiler until fish flakes easily, about fifteen minutes.
2. Meanwhile, combine the remaining butter, the mustard and sugar in a small saucepan. Heat slowly, stirring until mixture is smooth, stir in the wine, lemon juice and Worcestershire and serve over the fish.
Yield: Four servings.

Crab Stew
Northern California

2 pounds lump crab meat, picked over to remove bits of shell and cartilage
½ cup dry sherry
2 tablespoons butter
1 clove garlic, crushed
½ cup finely minced onion
¼ cup finely minced green pepper
1 tablespoon flour
¼ teaspoon chopped rosemary
1 large ripe tomato, peeled and chopped
  Salt and freshly ground black pepper to taste
1 cup light cream, approximately
  Toast or cooked rice.

1. Place the crab meat in a mixing bowl and add the sherry. Refrigerate three to four hours, turning occasionally.
2. Heat the butter and add the garlic, onion and green pepper. Cook, stirring, until onion wilts. Remove and discard the garlic.
3. Sprinkle onion mixture with the flour and add the rosemary, tomato, salt and black pepper. Simmer, stirring, about five minutes. Add the crab meat and one cup cream. Simmer five minutes, adding more cream if the stew seems too thick. Serve on toast or rice.
Yield: Six servings.

Crab Diable   *Northern California*

7 tablespoons butter
4 cups fresh Dungeness crab meat (see note),
   picked over to remove bits of shell and
   cartilage
12 saltine crackers, crumbled
¼ teaspoon nutmeg
¼ teaspoon dry mustard
¼ teaspoon mace
1 teaspoon Worcestershire sauce
   Salt and freshly ground black pepper to
   taste
   Cayenne pepper to taste
2 whole cloves
½ cup dry sherry
2 egg yolks
   Lemon segments.

1. Melt four tablespoons of the butter in the top of a double boiler over boiling water and add the crab meat, crackers, nutmeg, mustard, mace, Worcestershire, salt, pepper, cayenne and cloves. Cook five minutes, stirring frequently, then lower heat.

2. Mix together the sherry and egg yolks and stir into crab mixture, keeping the water below boiling. Mix well and spoon into light small crab shells or ramekins. Dot with remaining butter and put under broiler long enough to brown the surface. Garnish with lemon segments.

Yield: Eight servings.

Note: Canned crab meat can be substituted for the fresh.

Coos Bay Crab Cakes   *Oregon*

1 pound crab meat, picked over to remove
   bits of shell and cartilage
2 eggs, lightly beaten
2 tablespoons mayonnaise
1 teaspoon prepared mustard
½ teaspoon prepared horseradish
¼ teaspoon salt
⅛ teaspoon freshly ground black pepper

1 teaspoon Worcestershire sauce
1 cup crushed cracker crumbs
   Butter.

1. Mix together the crab meat, eggs, mayonnaise, mustard, horseradish, salt, pepper, Worcestershire and one-half cup of the crumbs.

2. Form the mixture into eight cakes. Coat with remaining crumbs.

3. Heat butter to a depth of one-eighth inch in a heavy skillet. Add the crab cakes and fry until lightly browned on both sides.

Yield: Four servings.

Pacific-Style Stuffed Green Peppers
Washington

4 green peppers
   Boiling water
2 slices bacon, diced
2 tablespoons butter
1 onion, finely chopped
¾ cup chopped celery
1 cup soft bread crumbs
1 cup crab meat, picked over to remove bits
   of shell and cartilage, flaked
2 eggs, lightly beaten
   Salt and freshly ground black pepper to
   taste
¼ teaspoon thyme
1 tablespoon chopped chives.

1. Preheat the oven to 350 degrees.

2. Cut a slice from the top of each green pepper and remove seeds and membrane. Cook pepper shells in boiling water five minutes. Drain well.

3. In a skillet, cook the bacon until crisp. Add the butter. Add the onion and celery and sauté until tender. Add the bread crumbs, crab meat, eggs, salt, pepper, thyme and chives and toss to mix.

4. Fill the pepper shells with crab mixture and set in a greased baking dish. Pour hot water to a

depth of one-quarter inch around peppers. Bake twenty minutes.

Yield: Four servings.

Barbecued Newport Crab   *Oregon*

1 crab, back, lungs and sac removed
½ cup barbecue sauce (page 762)
1 cup clam broth
¼ teaspoon curry powder
1 teaspoon catchup
¼ teaspoon Worcestershire sauce.

1. Remove the crab legs and crack. Break the body in half and cut each half into five pieces.
2. In a saucepan, combine the barbecue sauce, broth, curry powder, catchup and Worcestershire. Bring to a boil. Drop in the crab pieces and boil five minutes.

Yield: One serving.

Deviled Western Crab   *Washington*

5 tablespoons butter
1 clove garlic, finely chopped
3 scallions, including green part, chopped
1 green pepper, diced
6 mushrooms, sliced
⅔ cup dry white wine
1 tablespoon dry mustard
3 tablespoons flour
2 cups light cream
  Salt and freshly ground black pepper to taste
⅛ teaspoon cayenne pepper
1 tablespoon chutney
1½ pounds lump crab meat, picked over to remove bits of shell and cartilage
⅓ cup buttered soft bread crumbs
2 tablespoons freshly grated Parmesan cheese.

1. Melt two tablespoons of the butter in a

heavy skillet and sauté the garlic, scallions, green pepper and mushrooms in it until tender.
2. Preheat the oven to 400 degrees.
3. Add the wine and mustard to the skillet and cook to reduce the amount of liquid by one-third.
4. Melt the remaining butter in a saucepan and blend in the flour. Stir in the cream and season with salt, pepper and cayenne. Bring to a boil, stirring, and cook, covered, ten minutes or longer.
5. Stir the vegetable mixture, the chutney and crab meat into the sauce. Spoon the mixture into individual ramekins or a buttered baking dish. Combine the bread crumbs and cheese and sprinkle over the crab mixture. Bake ten minutes, or until bubbly hot. Dish may be browned under the broiler, if desired.

Yield: Six servings.

Marinated Cracked Crab   *Washington*

6 cooked Dungeness crabs
6 lemons
2 cups olive oil
12 cloves (one head) garlic, finely chopped
1 tablespoon chopped parsley
¼ teaspoon Worcestershire sauce.

1. Separate each leg of the crabs with a section of the body meat. Crack the legs with a mallet. Place in a large crock or bowl.
2. Squeeze the juice from four of the lemons. Combine with the oil, garlic, parsley and Worcestershire. Pour over cracked crabs. Chill several hours, stirring occasionally.
3. Cut remaining lemons into wedges. Serve crab garnished with lemon wedges.

Yield: Six servings.

Dungeness Crab and Scallop Stew
          Washington

1 Dungeness crab
1 medium-size onion, finely chopped

1 tablespoon butter
½ bay leaf
⅛ teaspoon saffron
¼ teaspoon salt
¼ teaspoon freshly ground black pepper
1 one-half-inch square piece orange rind
1 one-pound can stewed tomatoes
1 pound sea scallops, quartered
½ green pepper, seeded and diced
Cooked rice.

1. Remove back of the crab. Remove lungs around edge and wash fat out of body cavity. Some of the fat can be reserved to be added to the stew if desired.
2. Remove legs from body, crack and reserve. Remove meat from body and reserve.
3. Sauté the onion in the butter until tender. Add the bay leaf, saffron, salt, black pepper, orange rind and tomatoes.
4. Bring to a boil and add reserved crab legs. Simmer two minutes. Add reserved crab meat and the scallops. Simmer five minutes.
5. Add the green pepper and reserved crab fat and simmer one minute. Serve over rice in soup plates.
Yield: Four servings.

King Crab Sandwich   *Alaska*

6 slices sour dough bread (page 730)
6 teaspoons butter
2 cups chopped cooked king crab meat
½ cup finely chopped celery
1 tablespoon finely chopped scallions, including green part
½ cup mayonnaise, approximately
6 slices mozzarella cheese
6 teaspoons freshly grated Parmesan cheese (optional).

1. Butter each slice of bread with one teaspoon butter. Toast on both sides under the broiler.
2. Combine the crab meat with the celery, scallions and mayonnaise, adding just enough

mayonnaise to bind. Spoon the crab mixture over the toast and top each serving with a slice of the mozzarella cheese. Sprinkle with the Parmesan if desired and place under broiler. Broil just until cheese melts.
Yield: Six servings.

Halibut Creole   *Washington*

1½ pounds halibut fillets
Salt and freshly ground black pepper to taste
2 tomatoes, peeled and thickly sliced
½ green pepper, chopped
2 teaspoons chopped onion
⅓ cup melted butter.

1. Preheat the oven to 400 degrees.
2. Place the halibut in a greased baking dish. Season with salt and pepper. Top with the tomato slices, green pepper and onion.
3. Pour the butter over all and bake twenty to twenty-five minutes, or until fish flakes easily.
Yield: Four servings.

Chilled Halibut Steaks   *Washington*

3 cups water
1 cup dry white wine
6 peppercorns
1 bay leaf
⅛ teaspoon thyme
1 sprig parsley
Salt
2 pounds halibut steaks, cut one-inch thick
⅓ cup olive oil
2 tablespoons lemon juice
Freshly ground black pepper
1 lemon, thinly sliced
2 small white onions, thinly sliced
1 cup sour cream
2 tablespoons mayonnaise
¾ cup peeled and thinly sliced cucumber

1 tablespoon vinegar
1 teaspoon freshly snipped dill weed.

1. In a large skillet, combine the water, wine, peppercorns, bay leaf, thyme, parsley and one teaspoon salt. Bring to a boil.

2. Add the halibut steaks and simmer, covered, about ten minutes, or until the fish flakes easily.

3. Remove halibut from cooking liquid, drain and place in a shallow dish. Combine the oil, lemon juice and salt and pepper to taste and pour over the fish. Top with the lemon slices and onion slices and chill several hours.

4. Combine the remaining ingredients and chill. Serve separately with the fish.

Yield: Four servings.

Anacortes Shell Fish Stew   *Washington*

6 tablespoons butter
2 tablespoons chopped onion
1 rib celery with leaves, chopped
6 mushrooms, sliced
1 cup shucked Olympia oysters or 12 large oysters, shucked with their liquor
½ pound scallops, quartered
½ pound shrimp, shelled and deveined
½ cup picked-over crab meat
1 cup lobster meat, cut into chunks
½ cup dry white wine
Tabasco sauce to taste
1 teaspoon Worcestershire sauce
2½ cups milk
3 tablespoons flour
¼ cup lemon juice
Salt and freshly ground black pepper to taste
Cooked rice.

1. Heat the butter in a large heavy sauté pan.

2. Sauté the onion in the butter until tender. Add the celery and mushrooms and cook three minutes longer.

3. Add the oysters, scallops, shrimp, crab meat and lobster and cook quickly, while stirring, until oysters curl and lobster and shrimp turn pink, about eight minutes.

4. Add the wine, Tabasco and Worcestershire. Stir the milk into the flour gradually to make a smooth mixture. Stir into the sea food mixture. Bring to a boil and simmer two minutes. Add the lemon juice and season with salt and pepper. Serve with rice.

Yield: Four servings.

Hangtown Fry   *Northern California*

1 cup shucked oysters (about eight)
Flour
5 eggs
¾ cup cracker crumbs
Salt and freshly ground black pepper to taste
⅓ cup butter
¼ cup milk or light cream
6 slices bacon, cooked until crisp.

1. Pat the oysters dry on a paper towel and dust lightly with flour. Beat one egg lightly and dip the oysters first into egg and then into cracker crumbs seasoned with salt and pepper.

2. Heat the butter in a heavy skillet and fry the oysters in it quickly on both sides until golden.

3. Beat remaining eggs with the milk or cream, season with salt and pepper and pour over the oysters.

4. Cook until set; turn and brown other side. Serve with the bacon slices on the side.

Yield: Two servings.

Breaded Oysters   *Washington*

18 drained oysters
Flour
1 egg, beaten with two tablespoons milk
Cracker meal
Fat or oil for deep-frying.

1. Roll the oysters in flour. Dip into the egg-milk mixture and then into cracker meal. Place on baking sheet and refrigerate until set.

2. Heat the fat or oil to 350 degrees. Fry oysters, a few at a time, turning once, until golden, about three minutes. Drain on paper towels.

Yield: Three servings.

Note: Drained clams, with necks pounded, may be substituted for the oysters, but fat or oil should be heated to 375 degrees.

Oysters with Almond Butter   *Oregon*

12 ounces small oysters with liquor
½ cup soft butter
½ cup finely ground blanched almonds
 1 clove garlic, finely chopped
 2 teaspoons cognac
 2 tablespoons chopped parsley.

1. Place oysters and liquor in a single layer in a buttered ovenproof baking dish.

2. Cream the butter with the almonds. Stir in the garlic, cognac and parsley and spread over oysters.

3. Broil in preheated broiler until oysters curl.

Yield: Two or three servings.

Olympic Peninsula Oyster Roast
Washington

48 oysters
   Melted butter.

Scrub the oysters very well and place on a grill about four inches from white hot coals. Roast until shells open, about fifteen minutes. Serve in the shells, with melted butter.

Yield: One dozen servings.

Puget Sound Pepper Pan Roast
Washington

½ cup butter
¼ cup finely chopped onion
¼ cup diced green pepper
 4 slices bacon, cooked until crisp and then crumbled
 2 cups shucked Olympia oysters or two dozen large oysters, shucked
½ cup dry white wine
¼ cup lemon juice
   Salt to taste
 2 tablespoons chopped parsley
   Buttered new potatoes, sprinkled with parsley.

1. Preheat the oven to 375 degrees.

2. Heat the butter in a heavy skillet and sauté the onion and green pepper in it until tender. Add the bacon bits and oysters and fry until the oysters curl at the edges, about three minutes for the large ones.

3. Add the wine, lemon juice and salt. Turn into a warmed casserole or individual ramekins and bake until oysters are plump, about eight minutes. Serve with potatoes.

Yield: Four servings.

Salmon with Citrus   *Northern California*

 1 seven-pound salmon
 2 lemons
 1 loaf stale French bread made into crumbs (about four cups crumbs)
½ teaspoon salt
¼ teaspoon freshly ground black pepper
¾ cup chopped walnuts
¼ cup chopped parsley
½ teaspoon sage
¼ cup melted butter
 1 orange
 1 grapefruit.

1. Preheat the oven to 350 degrees or prepare a charcoal fire in a barbecue grill.

2. Clean and wash the salmon, but leave the head and tail on.

3. Grate one lemon to obtain one teaspoon grated lemon rind. Reserve the lemon.

4. Combine the bread crumbs, salt, pepper, walnuts, parsley, sage, butter and grated lemon rind. Stuff the fish with the mixture. Sew the opening closed. Place the fish on a sheet of heavy-duty aluminum foil.

5. Squeeze the juice from the reserved lemon all over the fish. Slice the orange, grapefruit and remaining lemon thinly. Remove seeds.

6. Arrange the citrus slices over the fish. Close the foil with a drugstore wrap and bake about one hour, or until done. Or envelop the package in chicken wire to make turning easier and bake on the grill, turning frequently, until fish flakes easily.

Yield: About one dozen servings.

Salted Salmon   *Washington*

Salmon, cut into pieces that will fit in an earthenware crock or wooden keg
Rock salt.

Clean and scale the salmon pieces and wipe. Layer rock salt and salmon pieces in the crock or keg, using plenty of the salt. When crock or keg is full, add a last layer of salt and weight down with a plate and rock. Store in a cool place at least two weeks before using. Stored in a cool place, salt salmon will keep indefinitely. Salt salmon is used for Hawaiian lomi lomi and other dishes popular in Alaska and the Northwest.

Lomi Salmon   *Hawaii*

1 pound salted King salmon (see above)
5 ripe unpeeled tomatoes, cored
3 scallions, including green part, chopped
Crushed ice.

1. Day before, place the salmon in a bowl and add cold water to cover. Let stand overnight.

2. Next day, carefully remove and discard skin and scales from the salmon. Break the salmon up with the fingers, removing and discarding all bones in the process.

3. In a mixing bowl, work the salmon with the fingers until finely mashed. Break the tomatoes over the salmon and work them together with the fish. Chill thoroughly.

4. When ready to serve, sprinkle with the scallions and serve in individual bowls with bits of crushed ice in each bowl.

Yield: Four or more servings.

Salted Salmon Scallop   *Alaska*

6 potatoes, peeled and thinly sliced
1 onion, finely chopped
1 pound salted salmon fillets (see above)
2 tablespoons freshly snipped dill weed
2 cups milk
3 tablespoons butter.

1. Preheat the oven to 375 degrees.

2. Make layers of the potatoes, onion, salmon and dill in a greased baking dish, beginning and ending with potatoes.

3. Pour the milk over all and dot with the butter. Bake one hour or until potatoes are cooked.

Yield: Four servings.

Bertha's Pickled Salmon   *Alaska*

3 pounds salted salmon (see above)
Vinegar
2 medium-size onions, sliced
5 teaspoons pickling spices
1 teaspoon salt
1 teaspoon sugar
2 medium-size cloves garlic, peeled and sliced.

1. Day before, rinse the salmon and cover with

cold water. Let soak overnight. Next day, drain and cut into bite-size chunks.

2. Put the salmon in a crock and mix with one cup water, one cup vinegar, the onions, pickling spices, salt, sugar and garlic. If there is not sufficient liquid, add more vinegar and water in equal parts. Cover and let stand five days to a week.

Yield: About one and one-half quarts.

Pickled Salmon   *Washington*

    1 four-pound freshly caught salmon
      Rock salt
    1 onion, thinly sliced
    1 cup light brown sugar
    1 cup white vinegar
    6 whole cloves
    3 bay leaves
    3 cloves garlic, peeled and crushed
   12 whole allspice.

1. Have the fish cleaned and the head removed. Wash well. Cut the salmon crosswise into four-inch slices.

2. Add a thin layer of rock salt to the bottom of a stone crock or gallon jar. Add a layer of salmon, a layer of salt, and so on, until all salmon is used, ending with a layer of salt. Let stand five days.

3. Remove the salmon and wash it well. Rinse out container. Put salmon back into container.

4. Combine the remaining ingredients. Pour over salmon. Let stand overnight.

5. Remove salmon and reserve pickling liquid. Slice salmon thin, arrange in jars and pour the pickling liquid over the slices. Seal. Store in refrigerator.

Yield: About four pints.

Wasco Boiled Salmon Heads   *Oregon*

   1 salmon head
   1 cup coarse salt
   3 onions.

Cut the head straight across the eyes and clean well. Make a brine with one gallon water and the salt and soak the head four to six hours. Place head in a kettle and add fresh water to cover. Add onions, bring to a boil and simmer fifteen minutes, or until cooked.

Yield: Three servings.

Note: This is a favorite delicacy of the Warm Springs Indians.

Salmon Cakes   *Washington*

    1 pound cooked fresh or canned salmon
   ¼ cup butter
   ¼ cup finely chopped onion
    2 teaspoons finely minced green pepper
   ½ cup finely minced heart of celery
   ¾ cup soft bread crumbs
   ½ teaspoon rubbed sage
   ¼ cup finely chopped parsley
    2 eggs, lightly beaten
      Salt and freshly ground black pepper to
      taste
      Lemon wedges.

1. Flake the salmon in a mixing bowl.

2. Heat one tablespoon of the butter and add the onion, green pepper and celery. Cook until tender and onion is transparent while stirring. Cool mixture slightly and add to salmon. Add the bread crumbs, sage, parsley, eggs, salt and pepper. Shape into four cakes and chill thirty minutes.

3. Heat the remaining butter in a skillet. Add the salmon cakes and cook on both sides until golden brown and heated through. Serve garnished with lemon wedges.

Yield: Four servings.

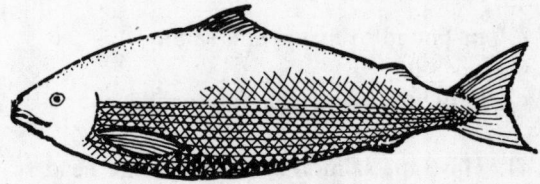

Salmon Pie Nordica

Alaska

2 cups sifted flour
3 teaspoons baking powder
1 teaspoon salt
⅓ cup shortening
2 eggs
½ cup milk
1 one-pound can salmon
1 tablespoon grated onion
1 cup grated Cheddar cheese
   Freshly ground black pepper to taste
½ cup light cream.

1. Preheat the oven to 375 degrees.
2. Sift together the flour, baking powder and salt into a mixing bowl. Using a pastry blender, cut in the shortening until the mixture is the consistency of coarse corn meal. Combine the eggs and milk, stir into the flour mixture and mix just until blended. Turn the dough out onto a lightly floured board and knead about ten strokes.
3. Roll out two-thirds of the dough into an eleven-inch circle. Fit the dough over the bottom and sides of a nine-inch layer cake pan.
4. Drain the salmon, reserve the liquid and flake the fish. Combine flaked salmon with the onion and reserved salmon liquid. Turn the mixture into the prepared pan. Sprinkle with the cheese and pepper. Pour the cream over the filling.
5. Roll out the remaining dough into an eight-inch circle and place on top of filling. Flute the edges to seal. Bake thirty minutes. Serve with sour cream-and-dill sauce (page 761).
Yield: Six servings.

Kippered Salmon

Alaska

1 four-pound to five-pound salmon
   Rock salt
¼ cup light brown sugar (optional).

1. Have the salmon cleaned and the head removed. Cut the fish into fillets, but leave the skin on. Cut each fillet into three pieces.
2. Combine rock salt with enough water to cover the fish when it is added. Dissolve the rock salt in the water, adding just enough salt so that a potato will float when added to the water. Remove the potato.
3. Stir in the brown sugar and, when dissolved, add the fish. Soak forty-five minutes in the brine; then drain. Rinse quickly in and out of cold water. Drain well and let dry slightly in the air.
4. Smoke in a smokehouse or other smoker over alder, hickory, cherry or apple wood. Smoke three to eight hours, depending on smoke conditions, etc.
Yield: Eight to ten servings.

Salmon Loaf

Alaska

1 pound cooked fresh salmon, bones and skin removed, or canned salmon, drained (reserve liquid)
1 cup milk
2 tablespoons butter
2 tablespoons flour
½ teaspoon salt
¼ teaspoon white pepper
2 eggs, beaten
1 tablespoon lemon juice
1 tablespoon Worcestershire sauce
1 tablespoon grated onion
2 cups soft bread crumbs
8 large pimento-stuffed olives, sliced
3 hard-cooked eggs.

1. Preheat the oven to 350 degrees.
2. Flake the salmon and set aside.
3. Place the milk in a saucepan (replace part of milk with reserved liquid from canned salmon if used) and heat to simmering.
4. In another saucepan, melt the butter. Stir in the flour, salt and pepper. Add milk and cook over moderate heat, stirring rapidly, until sauce is smooth and thickened. Pour sauce gradually into the beaten eggs, stirring rapidly.

5. Combine the salmon and sauce. Stir in the lemon juice, Worcestershire, onion and bread crumbs.

6. Grease an 8½-by-4½-by-2½-inch loaf pan and cover bottom with the olives. Spoon in half the salmon mixture and spread evenly to edges. Press the hard-cooked eggs lengthwise into salmon mixture in pan. Cover with remaining salmon mixture and bake forty-five minutes. Remove from oven and turn out onto a warm serving dish.

Yield: Six servings.

Salmon Loaf with Celery Sauce
Washington

Loaf:
1 one-pound can salmon
1½ cups soft bread crumbs
2 tablespoons finely chopped parsley
2 tablespoons butter
¼ cup finely chopped green pepper
½ cup finely chopped onion
⅔ cup heavy cream
1 egg
½ teaspoon Worcestershire sauce
Tabasco sauce to taste
Salt and freshly ground black pepper to taste.
Sauce:
1 cup chopped celery
Salt to taste
¼ cup milk, approximately
½ cup heavy cream
2½ teaspoons butter
2½ tablespoons flour
Freshly ground black pepper to taste
Cayenne pepper to taste
¼ teaspoon grated nutmeg.

1. Preheat the oven to 375 degrees.
2. To prepare loaf, drain liquid from the salmon into a measuring cup and reserve. Place salmon in mixing bowl and, if necessary, remove any bones.

3. Flake salmon and add the bread crumbs and parsley.

4. Melt the butter and cook the green pepper and onion in it until wilted. Add to salmon.

5. Blend the cream with the egg, Worcestershire and Tabasco. Stir with salt and pepper into salmon and blend well.

6. Butter a three-and-one-half-cup or four-cup loaf pan and add salmon mixture. Bake forty minutes, or until set.

7. Prepare the sauce while loaf bakes. Place the celery in a small saucepan and add water barely to cover. Add salt and simmer about five minutes or until celery is crisp-tender.

8. Drain the liquid from celery into measuring cup containing reserved salmon liquid. Add enough milk to make one cup. Combine with the cream. Reserve cooked celery.

9. Melt the butter in a saucepan and stir in the flour. Add the cream mixture, stirring vigorously with a wire whisk. When mixture is thickened and smooth, continue to cook fifteen minutes or longer, stirring vigorously with whisk. Add pepper, cayenne, the nutmeg and reserved celery.

10. Slice the salmon loaf and serve hot with hot celery sauce.

Yield: Four servings.

Agnes' Molded Salmon Loaf
Oregon

1½ pounds salmon fillets
1 rib celery, diced
½ onion, sliced
¼ green pepper, sliced
½ lemon, sliced
Salt to taste
6 peppercorns
Boiling water
Cold water if necessary
1 envelope unflavored gelatin
1 cup finely chopped celery
3 tablespoons finely chopped green pepper
2 tablespoons finely grated onion
2 tablespoons lemon juice

Freshly ground black pepper to taste
Salad greens
Hard-cooked egg slices
Ripe olives.

1. Place the salmon, diced celery, sliced onion, sliced green pepper, lemon slices, salt, peppercorns and boiling water to cover fish in a skillet.

2. Cover the skillet and simmer until the salmon flakes easily, about fifteen minutes. Allow salmon to cool in the liquid.

3. When salmon is cool, strain the cooking liquid and measure one and one-half cups, adding cold water if necessary. Soak the gelatin in one-half cup of the measured liquid and heat to dissolve.

4. Cut salmon into one-quarter-inch cubes. Mix dissolved gelatin with remaining liquid, the salmon cubes, chopped celery, chopped green pepper, grated onion, lemon juice and salt and pepper to taste. Pack mixture into a lightly oiled 9-by-5-by-3-inch loaf pan and chill several hours or overnight.

5. Unmold onto salad greens and garnish with egg slices and olives.

Yield: Six servings.

Salmon Custard   *Alaska*

2 cups cooked salmon, skinned, boned and flaked
1 tablespoon chopped parsley
1 tablespoon chopped pimento
2 cups milk
4 eggs, lightly beaten
1 teaspoon salt
⅛ teaspoon freshly ground black pepper
½ cup soft bread crumbs
1 tablespoon grated onion.

1. Preheat the oven to 350 degrees.

2. Combine the salmon, parsley and pimento and place in the bottom of a well-oiled one-and-one-half-quart ring mold.

3. Mix together the remaining ingredients.

Pour over salmon. Set mold in a pan of boiling water and bake about thirty-five minutes, or until set.

Yield: Four servings.

Bonneville Dam Stuffed Salmon
Oregon

¼ cup butter
1 cup chopped onions
1 cup chopped mushrooms
1 clove garlic, finely minced
1 cup finely grated carrots
2 cups dry bread crumbs
¼ cup chopped parsley
¼ teaspoon marjoram
¼ teaspoon thyme
1½ tablespoons lemon juice
  Salt and freshly ground black pepper
1 six-pound to eight-pound whole salmon, cleaned.

1. Preheat the oven to 350 degrees.

2. Melt the butter in a skillet and sauté the onions in it until tender. Add the mushrooms and garlic and cook two minutes longer. Add the carrots, bread crumbs, parsley, marjoram, thyme, lemon juice, two teaspoons salt and one-quarter teaspoon pepper. Mix well.

3. Season the salmon inside and outside with salt and pepper.

4. Stuff the salmon cavity with the bread crumb mixture. Sew to close. Wrap fish in oiled or buttered aluminum foil, set in a shallow pan and bake about fifteen minutes a pound, or until fish flakes easily.

Yield: Six to eight servings.

Salmon Soufflé   *Washington*

6 tablespoons butter
6 tablespoons flour
1½ cups milk
¼ cup dry white wine

1 teaspoon salt
¼ teaspoon freshly ground black pepper
  Cayenne pepper to taste
1 tablespoon lemon juice
2 tablespoons chopped parsley
1 teaspoon Worcestershire sauce
½ pound skinned, boned, cooked salmon, flaked
4 eggs, separated.

1. Preheat the oven to 325 degrees.

2. Melt the butter and blend in the flour. Gradually stir in the milk and wine. Bring to a boil, stirring until mixture thickens. Add the salt, pepper, cayenne, lemon juice, parsley, Worcestershire and salmon.

3. Beat in the egg yolks. Cool slightly. Beat the egg whites until stiff but not dry and fold in. Turn into a greased two-quart soufflé dish. Set in a pan of hot water. Bake one hour.

Yield: Four servings.

Broiled Salmon Steaks   *Oregon*

½ cup lemon juice
3 tablespoons butter
2 tablespoons grated onion
½ teaspoon salt
⅛ teaspoon freshly ground black pepper
1½ tablespoons light brown sugar
1 teaspoon dry mustard
4 salmon steaks (two pounds)
2 tablespoons chopped parsley.

1. In a saucepan, combine the lemon juice, butter, onion, salt, pepper, brown sugar and mustard. Bring to a boil.

2. Place the salmon steaks in a shallow baking dish. Pour half the lemon juice mixture over all. Broil in preheated broiler about fifteen minutes, basting frequently with remaining lemon juice mixture, until fish flakes easily. Sprinkle with the parsley.

Yield: Four servings.

Salmon Puff-Ups   *Alaska*

1 pound cooked fresh salmon, bones and skin removed, or canned salmon, drained
½ teaspoon salt
⅛ teaspoon freshly ground black pepper
1 teaspoon grated onion
½ cup soft bread crumbs
1 tablespoon lemon juice
3 eggs, separated
6 sprigs parsley.

1. Preheat the oven to 375 degrees. Butter six six-ounce custard cups.

2. Flake the salmon into a bowl. Add the salt, pepper, onion, bread crumbs and lemon juice.

3. Beat the egg yolks and stir into mixture. Beat the egg whites until stiff and fold into mixture.

4. Divide mixture into prepared custard cups. Set cups in shallow pan containing one inch of hot water and bake twenty-five to thirty minutes.

5. Unmold, garnish each with a parsley sprig and serve with a favorite sauce.

Yield: Six servings.

Alaskan Nuggets

1 pound cooked fresh salmon, bones and skin removed, or canned salmon, drained
½ cup mashed potatoes
1 tablespoon minced celery
1 tablespoon minced onion
1 tablespoon butter
½ teaspoon salt
¼ teaspoon freshly ground black pepper
1 teaspoon Worcestershire sauce
½ pound sharp Cheddar cheese, cut into one-half-inch cubes
1 egg, beaten
1 cup dry bread crumbs
  Fat for deep-frying.

1. Flake the salmon. Mash it and mix with potatoes.

2. Sauté the celery and onion in the butter five minutes, or until tender, and mix with salmon. Add the salt, pepper and Worcestershire and shape mixture into balls the size of walnuts.

3. Press a cube of cheese into center of each ball and reshape. Roll balls in the egg, then in the bread crumbs. Deep-fry in fat heated to 365 degrees until nuggets are golden brown on all sides. Drain well on paper towels. Serve with a cheese sauce.

Yield: Four servings.

Salmon with Avocado　　　*Washington*

1 salmon fillet (about two pounds)
　Salt and freshly ground black pepper to
　taste
2 tablespoons butter
3 ripe avocados, peeled and seeded
¼ teaspoon crushed red pepper
3 sprigs parsley
¼ cup chopped onion
¼ cup lemon juice
1 clove garlic, chopped
¼ cup chopped fresh parsley
1 lemon.

1. Preheat the oven to 375 degrees.
2. Place the salmon flat, skin side down, in a baking dish. Sprinkle with salt and black pepper and dot with the butter. Place in the oven and bake exactly twenty minutes. Remove the salmon from the oven and pour off any liquid that has accumulated. Carefully transfer the salmon to a hot serving platter.

3. Meanwhile, combine the avocados, red pepper, parsley sprigs, onion, lemon juice, garlic and salt and pepper. Puree in an electric blender, stirring down with a rubber spatula as necessary. When blended, spoon the mixture over the hot salmon. Sprinkle with the parsley.

4. Trim the lemon and slice thinly. Cut each slice in half. Use to garnish the dish.

Yield: Six to eight servings.

Depoe Bay Broiled Salmon Steaks
Oregon

1 teaspoon rosemary, crushed in a mortar and
　pestle
2 tablespoons white vinegar
3 tablespoons oil
6 salmon steaks, cut one-inch thick (two
　pounds)
　Salt and freshly ground black pepper to taste
　Lemon wedges.

1. Combine the rosemary, vinegar and oil and let stand at room temperature thirty minutes. Strain through cheesecloth.

2. Season the salmon steaks with salt and pepper.

3. Dip the steaks in the oil mixture and broil in a preheated broiler, two inches from the heat, five to eight minutes on each side, or until fish flakes easily. Serve with lemon wedges.

Yield: Six servings.

Barbecued Salmon Indian Style
Oregon

1 seven-pound to twenty-pound Silver, King
　or Chinook salmon
　Salt and freshly ground black pepper
2 green alder stakes (willow can be used)
　Green cedar sticks, six inches to eight
　inches long
　Oregon slaw (page 719).

1. Remove the salmon head and tail. Clean salmon and split lengthwise in two. Season with salt and pepper.

2. Split each green alder stake along three-quarters of its length. Secure the end of the split with a nail.

3. Use one stake for each salmon half. Place each salmon half thick part down toward the stake in between the split alder. Brace the fish, first on one side and then on the other, with the

small cedar sticks so that the fish lies flat. Tie the open end of the alder with wire.

4. Stick the stakes in the ground about eighteen inches from a white-hot pine log fire and cook a total of about forty-five minutes for a seven-pound fish to one and one-half hours for a twenty-pound fish.

5. Fish is turned by reversing the stakes. Cooking is slowed by bending stakes away from fire or hastened by pushing stakes toward fire.

6. When fish flakes easily and the milk has flowed all the way down the fish side and glazed it slightly, remove stakes.

7. Untie wire, twist out the cedar sticks gently, first on one side and then on the other, and let fish drop onto a warm platter. Serve with the slaw.

Yield: Allow three-quarters pound salmon a person.

Port Angeles Fried Scallops   *Washington*

1 cup soft bread crumbs
3 tablespoons freshly grated Parmesan cheese
⅛ teaspoon marjoram
  Salt and freshly ground black pepper to taste
2 pounds scallops
2 eggs, well beaten
2 cups oil
  Tartar sauce (page 760).

1. Mix the bread crumbs with the cheese, marjoram, salt and pepper. Dip the scallops into the eggs and then into the crumb mixture.

2. Heat the oil in a heavy skillet and fry the scallops, in a single layer, about three minutes. Drain on paper towels and serve with tartar sauce.
Yield: Four servings.

Shrimp with Vermouth   *Washington*

2 pounds shrimp, shelled and deveined
⅓ cup olive oil

½ cup dry vermouth
2 cloves garlic, crushed
¾ teaspoon salt
½ teaspoon freshly ground black pepper
3 tablespoons chopped parsley
3 tablespoons lemon juice.

1. Sauté the shrimp in the oil in a heavy skillet until lightly browned. Add the vermouth, garlic, salt and pepper and cook until all liquid has evaporated.

2. Sprinkle with the parsley and lemon juice.
Yield: Four servings.

Shrimp with Garlic   *Northern California*

¼ cup melted butter
1 tablespoon oil
1 teaspoon salt
¼ teaspoon freshly ground black pepper
2 cloves garlic, crushed
1 tablespoon chopped parsley
1½ pounds medium-size shrimp, shelled and deveined
  Lemon wedges.

1. Combine the butter, oil, salt, pepper, garlic and parsley in a bowl. Add the shrimp, toss, cover and refrigerate one hour.

2. Place shrimp in a single layer on a broiler pan. Broil, basting once or twice with the marinade, five minutes or until shrimp turn pink. Serve with lemon wedges.
Yield: Six servings.

Shrimp with Vegetables
Northern California

1 pound shrimp
3 tablespoons soy sauce
1 tablespoon dry sherry
1 teaspoon grated fresh ginger
6 dried Chinese mushrooms
  Lukewarm water

¼ cup peanut oil
6 water chestnuts, thinly sliced
2 tender ribs celery, trimmed and thinly sliced
2 scallions, including green part, cut into one-inch lengths
¼ pound fresh Chinese pea pods (optional)
1½ tablespoons cornstarch
3 tablespoons water.

1. Shell each shrimp and run a knife along the back. Rinse under cold water to remove the intestinal vein. Drain shrimp and dry. Cut each shrimp in half. Place in a bowl and add the soy sauce, sherry and ginger. Let stand one-half hour.

2. Meanwhile, soak the mushrooms in lukewarm water to cover about fifteen minutes. Drain and slice.

3. When ready to cook, heat the oil in a skillet and quickly cook the shrimp, stirring rapidly. Add the mushrooms, water chestnuts, celery, scallions and pea pods if desired and cook, stirring, one to two minutes longer. Blend the cornstarch with the water and gradually stir into the shrimp mixture. Thicken slightly. Serve hot.

Yield: Four servings.

Pickled Shrimp   *Alaska*

1½ cups white cider vinegar
⅓ cup dry sherry
½ cup water
2 tablespoons pickling spices
1 bay leaf
1 stick cinnamon, broken into pieces
½ cup dark brown sugar
4 cups shrimp, cooked and cleaned
1 large onion, sliced and separated into rings.

1. Combine the vinegar, sherry, water, pickling spices, bay leaf, cinnamon stick and brown sugar. Bring to a boil, stirring. Let cool.

2. Arrange a layer of shrimp and a layer of onion rings in the bottom of a stone crock or gallon jar. Add a little pickling liquid. Continue making layers and adding liquid until all ingredients are used. Let stand in refrigerator at least overnight. This will keep in the refrigerator for several weeks.

Yield: About one quart.

Shrimp Victoria   *Northern California*

5 tablespoons butter
1 pound shrimp, shelled and deveined
¼ cup finely minced onion
½ pound small mushrooms, cut into quarters
1 tablespoon flour
   Salt and freshly ground black pepper to taste
1½ cups sour cream
   Cooked rice.

1. Heat four tablespoons of the butter in a saucepan and add the shrimp and onion. Cook, stirring frequently, until onion is wilted and shrimp are pink and white all over.

2. Add the remaining butter and the mushrooms. Cook five minutes and sprinkle with the flour, salt and pepper. Cook, stirring, about one minute. Stir in the sour cream and cook until mixture is thoroughly hot and sauce is smooth. Do not boil. Serve with rice.

Yield: Four servings.

Fried Shrimp Cakes   *Northern California*

2 tablespoons oil
1 pound shrimp
3 scallions, including green part, finely chopped
5 water chestnuts, finely chopped
½ cup soft bread crumbs
½ teaspoon grated lemon rind
2 tablespoons lemon juice
2 eggs, lightly beaten
1 tablespoon finely chopped fresh gingerroot

or one-quarter teaspoon dried powdered ginger
1 teaspoon salt
⅛ teaspoon freshly ground black pepper
¼ cup flour
1 teaspoon ground coriander
⅛ teaspoon cayenne pepper
3 to four tablespoons butter.

1. Heat the oil in a skillet. Add the shrimp and fry, stirring, two minutes. Cool. When shrimp are cool enough to handle, shell, devein and chop finely.

2. Combine the shrimp with the scallions, water chestnuts, bread crumbs, lemon rind, lemon juice, eggs, ginger, salt and pepper. Mix well until mixture holds together. Chill one hour.

3. Shape the chilled mixture into four to six flat cakes. Mix the flour with the coriander and cayenne and use to coat the cakes.

4. Heat the butter in a skillet and add the cakes. Brown on both sides.

Yield: Four servings.

Shrimp Louis   *Northern California*

1 cup mayonnaise
¼ cup chopped scallions, including green part
¼ cup finely chopped green pepper
¼ cup chili sauce
1 teaspoon finely chopped parsley
⅛ teaspoon cayenne pepper
Salt and freshly ground black pepper to taste
¼ cup heavy cream, whipped
Shredded lettuce
1½ pounds shrimp, cooked, shelled, deveined and chilled
2 tomatoes, quartered
2 hard-cooked eggs, sliced.

1. Prepare the Louis dressing. Mixing with a rubber spatula, combine in a bowl the mayon-naise, scallions, green pepper, chili sauce, parsley, cayenne, salt and pepper. Then fold in the cream.

2. Arrange a bed of shredded lettuce on each of four salad plates. Top with the shrimp and spoon the Louis dressing over. Garnish with the tomato wedges and egg slices.

Yield: Four servings.

Note: Crab meat can be used instead of shrimp. The dressing can be varied by the addition of Worcestershire sauce or capers.

Fisherman's Wharf Smelt
Northern California

¼ cup olive oil
2 cloves garlic, finely chopped
2 onions, finely chopped
1 one-pound-twelve-ounce can Italian plum tomatoes
1 six-ounce can tomato paste
1 teaspoon sugar
1½ teaspoons salt
¼ teaspoon freshly ground black pepper
1½ teaspoons oregano
¼ cup chopped parsley
2 pounds pan-ready smelts
1 cup shredded mozzarella cheese
¼ cup freshly grated Parmesan cheese.

1. Preheat the oven to 400 degrees.

2. Heat the oil in a saucepan and sauté the garlic and onions in it until tender. Add the tomatoes, tomato paste, sugar, one teaspoon of the salt, the pepper, oregano and parsley. Bring to a boil and simmer twenty minutes.

3. Pour three-quarters of the sauce into a baking dish large enough to accommodate the smelts in a single layer. Arrange the fish on top of the sauce. Over one end of the fish spoon remaining sauce and over the other the cheeses mixed with the remaining salt.

4. Bake fifteen minutes, or until fish flakes easily.

Yield: Six servings.

Columbia River Smelt *Washington*

½ cup flour
1 teaspoon salt
¼ teaspoon freshly ground black pepper
2 eggs, lightly beaten
2 tablespoons water
2 pounds cleaned smelts
½ cup dry bread crumbs
½ cup oil, approximately
2 tablespoons butter.

1. Combine the flour, salt and pepper. Mix the eggs and water.
2. Dip each smelt first into flour mixture, then into egg mixture and finally into the bread crumbs. Set on a rack to dry for twenty minutes.
3. Heat the oil and butter in a heavy skillet and fry the fish, a few at a time, for two minutes on each side. Drain on paper towels.
Yield: Six servings.

Rex Sole with Lemon Sauce
Northern California

4 Rex sole fillets
1 egg, lightly beaten
Flour
Cracker crumbs
Butter
2 lemons, peeled and thinly sliced
½ cup dry white wine
2 tablespoons chopped parsley.

1. Dip the fillets into the egg, then into flour, then into the egg again and last into cracker crumbs.
2. Heat one-quarter cup butter in a heavy skillet. Add the fillets and fry three minutes on each side. Transfer to a warm platter.
3. Add enough butter to skillet to make two tablespoons. Add the lemon slices and wine. Cook until liquid is reduced by half. Pour over fish and sprinkle with the parsley.
Yield: Four servings.

Schramsberg Petrale Sole with Champagne
Northern California

4 large sole fillets
⅓ cup milk
¼ cup flour
Salt and freshly ground black pepper to taste
¼ cup butter
2 cups hot, cooked, chopped spinach
⅛ teaspoon nutmeg
8 mushrooms, sliced
1 tablespoon chopped parsley
½ cup champagne.

1. Dip the fillets into the milk and dredge in the flour seasoned with salt and pepper.
2. Heat the butter in a heavy skillet, add the fillets and sauté quickly on both sides, a total of about six minutes.
3. Season the spinach with salt, pepper and the nutmeg and spread over a warm platter.
4. Lay fish on top of spinach and keep warm.
5. Add the mushrooms to the skillet and cook three minutes. Add the parsley and champagne and heat briefly, but do not boil. Pour over the fish and serve at once.
Yield: Four servings.

Diamond Lake Trout *Oregon*

6 trout, cleaned with heads left on
Salt
¼ cup melted butter
½ cup soft bread crumbs
¼ teaspoon nutmeg
¼ teaspoon freshly ground black pepper
½ teaspoon thyme
2 teaspoons chopped parsley
½ cup dry white wine.

1. Preheat the oven to 350 degrees.
2. Score one side of each trout with diagonal slashes, just through the skin, about one inch apart. Season all over with salt.

3. Grease a large shallow roasting pan with some of the butter.

4. Combine the bread crumbs with the nutmeg, pepper, thyme and parsley. Spread half the mixture over the bottom of the pan. Arrange trout in a single layer on top of crumbs. Pour wine over all. Brush trout with remaining butter. Sprinkle with remaining crumbs and bake twenty to twenty-five minutes, or until fish flakes easily, basting often.

Yield: Six servings.

Joe's Fried Trout with Walnut Butter
Oregon

½ cup butter
1 clove garlic, finely chopped
¼ cup chopped parsley
¼ cup chopped walnuts
¼ teaspoon salt
4 one-pound trout
  Salt and freshly ground black pepper
  Yellow corn meal
¼ cup melted butter.

1. Cream the butter until light and fluffy.

2. Blend in the garlic, parsley, walnuts and salt and let stand one hour at room temperature.

3. Season the trout with salt and pepper, coat with corn meal and fry in the melted butter in a heavy skillet until brown. Turn and brown the other side. Cook only until fish flakes easily. Drain on paper towels.

4. To serve, top each fish with dollop of nut butter.

Yield: Four servings.

Bok Sui Ngui (Poached Sea Bass, Chinese Style)
Northern California

1 about one-and-one-half-pound sea bass, cleaned (see note)
1 tablespoon dark soy sauce
1 tablespoon light soy sauce
1 teaspoon monosodium glutamate (optional)
1 teaspoon sugar
¼ cup peanut oil or vegetable oil
1 teaspoon sesame oil (optional, see note)
2 cloves garlic, peeled and left whole
4 thin slices fresh ginger, shredded
4 scallions, including green part, trimmed and cut into one-and-one-half-inch lengths
2 pieces cha ga (Chinese canned sweet pickles) or two sweet gherkins, sliced.

1. It is important to have all vegetables chopped and all ingredients ready before starting to prepare this dish.

2. Use a fish cooker or other utensil just large enough to hold the fish. Add enough water to cover the fish. Bring to a boil. Place the fish on the rack of the fish cooker or place the fish in a sling made of cheesecloth. Gently lower the fish into the boiling water and immediately shut off the heat. The water should not boil again. Cover the pot and let the fish stand in the water fifteen to twenty minutes. Fish is done when the eyes are white and pop out of their sockets.

3. While fish is poaching, combine the soy sauces, monosodium glutamate if desired and the sugar in a small mixing bowl.

4. Heat the oils in a saucepan and add the garlic. Cook over low heat until garlic starts to turn brown. Remove and discard garlic. Keep oil warm.

5. Remove the fish and drain it. Place on a serving platter and pour the soy sauce mixture over it.

6. Reheat the oil and add the ginger. When light brown, pour the oil and ginger over the fish. (The oil may splatter, so hold saucepan at arm's length.) Sprinkle fish with the scallions and pickles and serve immediately.

Yield: Two servings.

Note: Porgy may be substituted for the sea bass.

Sesame oil is available at Chinese groceries.

Tempura Fried Fish

Northern California

2 eggs, beaten
¼ cup water
1 cup sifted flour
1 teaspoon salt
18 small fish fillets, such as bluegills, or three large fish fillets, cut into strips

Oil or fat for deep-frying.

1. Combine the eggs, water, flour and salt. Stir briefly to blend. Do not overblend.

2. Dip the fillets, one by one, into the batter; then cook them quickly in oil or fat heated to 365 degrees. Fish should cook to a golden brown in about two minutes. Drain and serve hot.

Yield: About six servings.

Meat, Poultry, Game and Other Main Dishes

Mock Ravioli Casserole
Northern California

1 pound ground beef round
1 onion, chopped
2 cloves garlic, finely chopped
1 tablespoon plus one-quarter cup olive oil
2 cups homemade tomato sauce
¾ cup beef broth
½ teaspoon basil
½ teaspoon oregano
1 teaspoon chopped fresh thyme or one-quarter teaspoon dried thyme
¼ pound mushrooms, sliced
  Salt and freshly ground black pepper
8 ounces bow tie macaroni, cooked al dente, drained
2 packages frozen spinach, cooked and drained
½ cup soft bread crumbs
½ cup chopped parsley
½ cup freshly grated Parmesan cheese
1 teaspoon sage
4 eggs, well beaten.

1. Preheat the oven to 350 degrees.
2. Brown the meat, onion and one clove of the garlic in one tablespoon of the oil until meat loses all its pinkness. Add the tomato sauce, broth, basil, oregano, thyme and mushrooms. Season with salt and pepper to taste. Let simmer ten minutes.

3. Meanwhile, in a large bowl, combine the macaroni, spinach, bread crumbs, parsley, cheese, sage, eggs, one teaspoon salt, the remaining oil and remaining garlic.
4. Place a thin layer of meat sauce in a three-quart casserole.
5. Spread a layer of spinach and macaroni mixture over this, then a layer of meat sauce. Continue alternating layers until all ingredients are used.
6. Bake thirty minutes.
Yield: Ten to one dozen servings.

Pot Roast with Carrot Gravy
Oregon

¼ cup flour
3 teaspoons salt
½ teaspoon freshly ground black pepper
1 four-pound blade, arm or bottom round pot roast
3 tablespoons bacon drippings
1 onion, sliced
1 cup dry red wine
2 bay leaves
1 teaspoon dill seeds
1 cup coarsely grated carrots
¼ cup water, approximately
1 small head cabbage, cut into eight wedges and cooked until crisp-tender.

1. Mix the flour with the salt and pepper. Rub

the pot roast all over with the flour mixture. Reserve any remaining flour mixture.

2. Heat the bacon drippings in a heavy casserole or Dutch oven. Add meat and brown on all sides.

3. Add the onion, wine and bay leaves. Crush the dill seeds roughly and add. Bring to a boil, cover and simmer very slowly two hours.

4. Add the carrots, cover and cook another hour, or until the meat is tender.

5. Mix two tablespoons of the reserved flour mixture with enough water to make a smooth batter. Transfer the meat to a warm platter. While stirring, add the flour batter to the casserole and cook, stirring, until mixture thickens.

6. Garnish meat platter with the cabbage wedges. Serve gravy separately.

Yield: Eight to ten servings.

Vine Maple Roast   *Oregon*

1 four-pound to five-pound sirloin steak, at least one and one-half inches thick
  Fresh cut green vine maple twigs (see note)
  Salt to taste
  Butter to taste.

Sear the steak on both sides over white hot coals in a barbecue grill equipped with a smoking hood. Lift up the grill holding the steak and throw two handfuls of vine maple twigs on the fire. Replace the grill and close the hood. Cook steak until the desired degree of doneness is reached, about ten minutes for rare beef, fifteen minutes for medium. Season steak with salt and spread with butter.

Yield: Four servings.

Note: Vine maple is native to Oregon and the Northwest.

Rock Salt Roast   *Oregon*

1 six-pound to seven-pound standing rib roast
  Freshly ground black pepper to taste

10 cups rock salt
10 cups flour
 5 cups water, approximately.

1. Preheat the oven to 375 degrees.

2. Season the meat with pepper.

3. Insert a meat thermometer into the middle of the thickest part of the lean muscle.

4. In a large bowl or clean pail, mix together the rock salt and flour. Stir in enough water to make a mixture that just clings together.

5. Set the roast on its flat side and mold a one-half-inch layer of rock salt mixture over the arch of bones. If the mixture has a tendency to fall off in large lumps, it is probably too wet. Either add more flour or set the mixture aside for fifteen minutes, stirring occasionally. A too-dry mixture will crumble. Add a little more water.

6. Place the roast, fat side and thermometer up, in an oiled roasting pan.

7. Cover the entire roast with a one-half-inch-thick coating of the rock salt mixture, making sure there are no cracks or holes, especially around the base. Reserve any leftover rock salt mixture.

8. Roast eighteen minutes a pound for rare beef, twenty-two minutes for medium and twenty-five minutes for well done. After the first fifteen minutes of roasting time, check the roast to make sure that the coating is still intact. Repair any cracks or holes, using the reserved rock salt mixture.

9. Double check the degree of doneness on the meat thermometer near the end of the roasting time.

10. Remove roast from the oven, pierce the hard rock salt-flour shell, lift off in sections and discard.

11. Wipe the entire surface of the roast carefully with a damp paper towel to remove all traces of rock salt mixture. Place roast on a warm platter.

Yield: Six servings.

Note: The roast will continue to cook if the hard shell is left on after roast is removed from the oven. One six-and-one-half-pound roast removed after roasting for fifteen minutes a pound reached a rare degree of doneness in twenty-five minutes with the coating left on.

Hawaiian Short Ribs

½ cup flour
3 teaspoons salt
  Freshly ground black pepper
5 pounds meaty short ribs, cut into three-inch pieces
2 tablespoons butter
2 tablespoons oil
2 onions, sliced
¾ cup catchup
¾ cup water
2 tablespoons vinegar
¼ cup imported soy sauce
2 tablespoons Worcestershire sauce
½ cup sugar
1 teaspoon chili powder
  Cooked noodles or rice.

1. Preheat the oven to 300 degrees.
2. Mix the flour with two teaspoons of the salt and pepper to taste. Dredge the ribs in the flour mixture. Heat the butter and oil in a heavy skillet, add the short ribs and brown on all sides.
3. Transfer short ribs to a roasting pan, placing them in a single layer. Sprinkle with the sliced onions.
4. Combine the catchup, water, vinegar, soy sauce, Worcestershire, sugar, chili powder, remaining salt and one teaspoon pepper. Pour over short ribs and onions. Cover and bake three hours, or until ribs are very tender.
5. Carefully skim off every trace of fat. Serve ribs with noodles or rice.
Yield: Five servings.

Ruby's Teriyaki   *Northern California*

Sauce:
2 cups imported soy sauce

½ cup mirin (Japanese wine), dry sherry or dry vermouth
1 cup sugar
1 tablespoon grated fresh gingerroot
¼ cup catchup
½ teaspoon monosodium glutamate (optional)
2 cloves garlic, crushed.

For beef teriyaki:

4 pounds boneless top sirloin, cut into one-quarter-inch slices.
OR
For beef and vegetables on skewers:
3 pounds boneless top sirloin, cut into bite-size chunks
18 small white onions, cooked
4 green peppers, quartered
18 cherry tomatoes
18 button mushrooms.
OR
For chicken teriyaki:
1 two-and-one-half-pound to three-pound chicken, cut into serving pieces.

1. To prepare sauce, combine all the sauce ingredients in a bowl.
2. To prepare beef teriyaki, marinate the meat two hours in the sauce; then place on a rack. Cook over hot coals, turning constantly so that meat does not burn. Baste with sauce as meat cooks.
3. To prepare beef and vegetables on skewers, marinate the meat chunks two hours in the sauce; then alternate on nine bamboo skewers with the onions, green peppers, tomatoes and mushrooms. Grill over hot coals, turning constantly so meat and vegetables do not burn.
4. To prepare chicken teriyaki, marinate the chicken pieces three to four hours in the sauce; then cook over coals on a rack quite a distance above the fire so that chicken does not burn. Baste with the sauce. If desired, the marinated chicken pieces can be oven baked. Place in a single layer in a shallow pan and bake at 350 degrees

for one and one-half hours, turning pieces over halfway through cooking and basting with the sauce.

Yield: About nine to one dozen servings of the two beef teriyaki dishes; four servings of the chicken.

Note: The sauce can also be used on flank steak before broiling and on baked pork chops and spareribs.

Ngo Yuk Fan Kay (Beef Tomato)

Hawaii

4 teaspoons cornstarch
3 tablespoons imported soy sauce
2 teaspoons sugar
  Salt and freshly ground black pepper
½ teaspoon monosodium glutamate (optional)
  Oil
1 pound boneless sirloin tip, sliced one-eighth-inch thick
1 clove garlic, finely chopped
1 sweet onion, sliced
2 green peppers, sliced
2 ribs celery, diced
¼ cup water
3 tomatoes, peeled and cut into wedges
3 scallions, including green part, cut into two-inch lengths.

1. Combine two teaspoons of the cornstarch, the soy sauce, one teaspoon of the sugar, one-eighth teaspoon salt, one-eighth teaspoon pepper, the monosodium glutamate if desired and two tablespoons oil in a bowl. Add the meat and let stand fifteen minutes.

2. Heat oil to a depth of one-eighth inch in a skillet. Add the garlic and cook briefly. Add the meat and cook quickly while stirring. Push meat to the side of the pan. Add more oil if necessary.

3. Add the onion, green peppers and celery and cook a few minutes until crisp-tender. Combine remaining cornstarch with the water. Add remaining sugar and salt and pepper to taste and

add to skillet. Cook, stirring, until sauce becomes clear.

4. Add the tomatoes and scallions, cook thirty seconds, stir and serve.

Yield: Six servings.

Ruby's Sukiyaki

Northern California

2 cakes fresh tofu (fresh bean curd, see note)
1 bunch gobo (burdock roots) (optional)
5 ribs celery, cut in long thin diagonal strips
1 large can bamboo shoots, cut into one-quarter-inch julienne strips
2 bunches scallions, including green part, cut into two-and-one-half-inch lengths with bulbs slit for fast cooking
½ cup imported soy sauce
⅓ cup saki (rice wine) or mirin (Japanese wine)
¼ cup sugar
¼ teaspoon monosodium glutamate (optional)
2 pounds good-quality boneless sirloin or lean eye of the rib beef, cut paper-thin and into bite-size pieces
  Parsley sprigs
1 small piece beef suet.

1. Cut the tofu into bite-size squares and arrange on a platter.

2. Clean the gobo and cut into very thin julienne strips. Soak in water fifteen minutes or longer, or until strips appear white and clean. Place in a saucepan, cover with water and cook until tender. Drain and arrange on platter with tofu.

3. Add the celery, bamboo shoots and scallions to the platter so that they make an attractive arrangement.

4. Combine the soy sauce, one-quarter cup water, the saki or mirin, sugar and monosodium glutamate if desired in a small bowl. Arrange the meat on a platter and garnish with parsley.

5. At the table in a skillet over a burner or in an electric skillet, rub hot pan with the suet to oil bottom and sides.

6. Add meat and toss with chopsticks until most of the pink color has gone.

7. Add half of each of the vegetables, placing them on top of meat in neat sections. Add half of soy sauce mixture. Cook until vegetables are just crisp-tender. Serve vegetables and half the meat.

8. Add remaining vegetables and soy mixture and cook for second helpings.

Yield: Six servings.

Note: Tofu is available in oriental food stores. Fillets of chicken breast or pheasant can be used instead of the beef.

The sukiyaki should be served with hot steamed rice, su-no-mo-no (cucumber salad, page 715), pickled daikon and carrot (page 755) and hot green tea.

California Casserole *Northern California*

1 pound ground round steak
1 tablespoon peanut oil
1 clove garlic, finely minced
  Salt and freshly ground black pepper to taste
1 large onion, finely chopped
1 green pepper, cored, seeded and chopped
1 tablespoon chili powder
1 tablespoon Worcestershire sauce
  Tabasco sauce to taste
1 one-pound can Italian plum tomatoes
1 one-pound can kidney beans
¾ cup uncooked rice
¼ cup chopped stuffed green olives
¾ cup shredded Cheddar cheese.

1. Preheat the oven to 350 degrees.

2. Cook the meat in the oil until meat loses its red color. Add the garlic, salt, pepper, onion, green pepper and chili powder and cook five minutes, or until onion is wilted.

3. Add the Worcestershire, Tabasco, tomatoes, kidney beans and rice and turn into a buttered two-quart casserole. Bake, uncovered,

forty-five minutes. Sprinkle with the olives and cheese and bake fifteen minutes longer, or until cheese is melted.

Yield: Eight servings.

Meg's Stuffed Flank Steak *Oregon*

1 thin flank steak
  Freshly ground black pepper
2 onions
2 tablespoons butter
1 clove garlic, finely chopped
2 cups soft bread crumbs
1 two-ounce can flat anchovy fillets, chopped
2 tablespoons freshly grated Parmesan cheese
1 tablespoon drained capers
2 tablespoons finely chopped celery with leaves
¼ teaspoon thyme
2 tablespoons chopped parsley
6 slices fatty bacon
2 cups beef broth or dry red wine.

1. Preheat the oven to 450 degrees.

2. Spread out the steak and season lightly with pepper.

3. Chop one of the onions finely. Melt the butter in a skillet and sauté the chopped onion and garlic in it until tender. Add the bread crumbs, anchovies, cheese, capers, celery, thyme, parsley and one-quarter teaspoon pepper.

4. Spread mixture over steak. Roll up, tucking in the edges. Secure the roll with string and place the bacon slices overlapping over the top.

5. Slice the remaining onion and place in a baking dish. Pour in the broth or wine and set the roll on the onion slices.

6. Bake three minutes. Turn the oven temperature down to 350 degrees and continue cooking until the meat is tender, about one and one-half hours, basting frequently with the liquid. Add water if liquid evaporates.

Yield: Four to six servings.

Basque Sheepherder's Pasties   *Nevada*

Pastry:
2 cups flour
½ teaspoon salt
⅔ cup shortening
5 tablespoons ice water, approximately.
Filling:
1 pound boneless leg of lamb, finely diced
1 cup finely diced potatoes
½ cup finely chopped onion
1 teaspoon salt
¼ teaspoon freshly ground black pepper
¼ cup water or chicken, lamb or vegetable broth.

1. To prepare pastry, place the flour and salt in a bowl. With the finger tips or a pastry blender, work in the shortening until mixture resembles coarse oatmeal.

2. Add enough of the ice water to make a dough. Gather into a ball, wrap in wax paper and chill twenty minutes.

3. Preheat the oven to 425 degrees.

4. To prepare filling, combine the lamb, potatoes, onion, salt, pepper and the water or broth.

5. Roll out the dough and cut eight four-inch circles. Divide the filling among the circles. Moisten pastry edges with water and draw up edges of pastry around and over the top of the filling. Pinch to seal and then flute to decorate.

6. Place pasties on lightly greased baking sheet and bake ten minutes. Reduce the oven heat to 350 degrees and continue to bake until meat and potatoes are tender, about forty-five minutes longer.

Yield: Eight pasties.

Lamb Curry Baked in Coconuts
Northern California

4 medium-size coconuts
¼ cup butter
1 onion, finely chopped
½ tart apple, peeled, cored and chopped
1 rib celery, chopped
2 pounds lamb shoulder, cut into one-inch cubes
1 tablespoon flour
1½ teaspoons ground ginger
2 teaspoons ground coriander
½ teaspoon ground cumin
½ teaspoon cardamom
½ teaspoon ground cloves
¼ teaspoon cinnamon
1 teaspoon turmeric
Salt to taste
1 cup chicken broth (optional)
1 medium-size green pepper, diced
1 tablespoon lime juice
1 tablespoon chopped fresh mint leaves
1⅓ cups cooked rice, approximately.

1. Pierce two of the eyes of each coconut, drain off the milk and reserve.

2. With coconut held in a vise, saw off the tops with a wood saw or use an electric saw. This usually requires some male assistance, but the coconuts can be prepared a day or two ahead and kept refrigerated.

3. Melt the butter in a heavy skillet. Add the onion, apple and celery and cook until tender but not browned.

4. Add the lamb and cook quickly to seal the outside but not to brown the meat. Sprinkle meat with the flour, ginger, coriander, cumin, cardamom, cloves, cinnamon and turmeric and cook, stirring, three minutes. Add salt.

5. Stir in one cup of the reserved coconut milk (or the broth if desired), bring to a boil, cover and simmer until meat is tender, about thirty minutes.

6. Preheat the oven to 375 degrees.

7. Stir the green pepper, lime juice and mint into the curry mixture.

8. Wrap each coconut in a sheath of aluminum foil extending above the top of the coconut and place in a baking dish.

9. Place the rice in the bottom of each coconut, fill up with the curry mixture, replace the tops, draw the foil over the tops and bake thirty

minutes, or until bubbly hot. Remove the foil before serving.

Yield: Four servings.

Filbert-Stuffed Pork Chops   *Oregon*

2 tablespoons butter
1 tablespoon chopped onion
1 tablespoon chopped green pepper
½ cup chopped celery
½ cup chopped filberts
1 teaspoon grated orange rind
1 cup diced orange pulp
1 cup diced stale white bread cubes
2 tablespoons raisins
  Salt
⅛ teaspoon freshly ground black pepper
⅛ teaspoon nutmeg
4 double, center-cut loin pork chops with pocket cut for stuffing
½ cup beef broth.

1. Preheat the oven to 350 degrees.
2. Heat the butter in a heavy skillet and sauté the onion and green pepper in it until tender. Add the celery and filberts and cook until filberts are lightly toasted.
3. Combine the filbert mixture with the orange rind, orange pulp, bread cubes, raisins, one teaspoon salt, the pepper and nutmeg. Use mixture to stuff the chops. Close with toothpicks.
4. Sprinkle the chops with salt and brown on both sides in the same heavy skillet. Place in a shallow casserole. Add the broth, cover and bake one hour. Remove cover and bake fifteen minutes longer, or until tender. Skim off and discard fat from pan liquid and serve juices over chops.

Yield: Four servings.

Roast Pork with Ginger Marinade

Hawaii

1 five-pound pork roast
5 tablespoons soy sauce
2 teaspoons grated fresh ginger (see note)
8 tablespoons hoisin sauce (see note)
3 tablespoons dry sherry
3 tablespoons honey.

1. Place the pork in a pan. Combine the soy sauce, ginger, hoisin sauce, sherry and honey, add to pan and turn the pork in the mixture. Refrigerate, turning occasionally, two hours or longer.
2. Preheat the oven to 475 degrees.
3. Place the pork, bone side down, in a roasting pan. Reserve the marinade. Roast the pork fifteen minutes and reduce oven heat to 350 degrees. Continue roasting, basting with the marinade, about two and one-half hours, or until thoroughly cooked. Add a little water to the roasting pan as necessary to prevent burning.

Yield: Six to eight servings.

Note: Fresh ginger and hoisin sauce are available in Chinese markets.

Kai's Spareribs   *Hawaii*

2 racks spareribs, preferably small spareribs purchased in a Chinese market
½ cup soy sauce
1 teaspoon freshly ground black pepper
¼ cup dark honey
½ cup dry sherry
½ teaspoon monosodium glutamate (optional).

1. Marinate the spareribs in a mixture of the remaining ingredients. Rub the meat with the mixture so that all parts are coated. Refrigerate one hour.
2. Remove the meat and let it dry one hour.
3. If a home oven is used, preheat it to 350 degrees. If a smoke oven is used, prepare it for smoking.
4. Place spareribs on a rack in a roasting pan and bake one and one-half to two hours. Or place in a smoke oven and let stand one and one-quarter to one and one-half hours.

Yield: Six or more servings.

Spaghetti with Sausages

Northern California

6 tablespoons butter
3 tablespoons olive oil
1 clove garlic, finely minced
2 cups finely chopped onions
1 sprig fresh thyme or one-half teaspoon dried thyme
½ bay leaf
¾ cup finely chopped carrots
2 fresh basil leaves, chopped, or one-half teaspoon dried basil
4 cups peeled, crushed tomatoes
½ teaspoon sugar
  Salt and freshly ground black pepper to taste
6 Italian sweet or hot sausages
1 pound spaghetti
  Freshly grated Parmesan cheese.

1. Melt half the butter in a large saucepan and add the oil. Add the garlic and onions and cook, stirring briefly, until onions are wilted. Add the thyme, bay leaf, carrots, basil, tomatoes, sugar, salt and pepper. Simmer one hour, stirring occasionally to prevent burning.

2. Meanwhile, cook the sausages in a skillet, turning to brown on all sides. Drain off the fat and add the sausages to the sauce for the last thirty minutes of cooking time.

3. Cook the spaghetti according to package directions and drain. Toss immediately with the remaining butter and serve with sauce, sausages and cheese.

Yield: Four to six servings.

Spaghetti with Sausage-and-Zucchini Sauce

Northern California

1½ pounds Italian sausage, half sweet and half hot, cut into one-inch slices
1 onion, finely chopped
½ pound mushrooms, sliced
1 pound (six small) zucchini, cut into one-half-inch bias slices
4 cups Italian plum tomatoes
1 six-ounce can tomato paste
1 teaspoon basil
½ teaspoon thyme
1 teaspoon oregano
  Salt and freshly ground black pepper to taste
1 pound spaghetti, cooked al dente, drained.

1. Cook the sausage in a large skillet until browned and almost cooked. Add the onion and cook until tender.

2. Add the mushrooms and zucchini and cook, stirring, until lightly browned, about eight minutes. Add the tomatoes, tomato paste, basil, thyme, oregano, salt and pepper.

3. Bring to a boil, cover and simmer until the zucchini is tender but not mushy, about twenty-five minutes. Serve over spaghetti.

Yield: Six servings.

Veal Scaloppine

Northern California

½ cup flour
2 teaspoons paprika
2 teaspoons salt
1 teaspoon freshly ground black pepper
3 pounds veal round, pounded thin and cut into serving pieces
½ cup butter, approximately
2 cloves garlic, cut in half
1¼ cups beef broth
2 cups sour cream
1 teaspoon basil
⅛ teaspoon rosemary
1 teaspoon lemon juice
1 teaspoon monosodium glutamate (optional)
½ cup Marsala wine
1 pound chestnuts, scored with cross on flat side and broiled very slowly thirty minutes, then peeled, or one-half pound shelled and peeled filberts
12 halves plump dried apricots, chopped

1 pound noodles, cooked, drained and tossed with croutons.

1. Day before, combine the flour, paprika, salt and pepper. Toss the veal pieces in the flour mixture. Reserve any remaining mixture.

2. Melt the butter in a heavy skillet containing the garlic. Brown the veal pieces on all sides in the butter. Transfer meat to a heavy casserole. Discard the garlic.

3. Sprinkle the skillet with any remaining flour mixture. Cook, stirring, two minutes. Gradually stir in the broth, sour cream, basil, rosemary, lemon juice, monosodium glutamate if desired and Marsala.

4. Halve the chestnuts and add them or the filberts to the veal. Stir in half the apricots and pour the sauce over all.

5. Sprinkle with remaining apricots, cover and let stand refrigerated overnight.

6. Next day, preheat the oven to 350 degrees.

7. Bake the covered veal casserole forty-five minutes. Serve with the noodles.

Yield: Five or six servings.

Osso Buco *Northern California*

12 thick slices veal shanks, preferably from the forelegs
Flour
3 tablespoons olive oil
3 tablespoons butter
¼ cup cognac, warmed
1½ cups beef broth
1 medium-size onion
Salt and freshly ground black pepper to taste
2 teaspoons arrowroot
2 tablespoons cold water
1 lemon.

1. Dredge the veal slices in flour. Heat the oil and butter in a large sauté pan and brown the meat in it on all sides.

2. Remove pan from the heat, pour the cognac over meat, stand back and ignite. When the flame

dies down, check that the marrow in the bones is facing up and add the broth and onion.

3. The pieces of meat should be half submerged. Cover and simmer one and one-quarter hours. Season with salt and pepper and simmer fifteen minutes longer.

4. Arrange the meat in a large hot serving dish. Mix the arrowroot with the water, add the sauce, return to the pan and heat to boiling. Pour over the meat.

5. With a zesteur, strip the yellow rind of the lemon and sprinkle over the dish.

Yield: Six servings.

Tripe Stew *Nevada*

1½ pounds honeycomb tripe
½ teaspoon salt
½ teaspoon sugar
3 onions, sliced
4 ribs celery, diced
3 carrots, sliced
¼ cup chopped parsley
½ teaspoon freshly ground black pepper
Flour
2 teaspoons Worcestershire sauce
1 tablespoon prepared mustard
1 cup light cream.

1. Wash the tripe very well and cut into thin strips.

2. Place the tripe in a heavy kettle and add cold water to cover. Add the salt and sugar. Bring to a boil, cover and simmer two hours.

3. Add the onions, celery, carrots, parsley and pepper and cook, covered, one hour longer, or until tripe is tender. Add more water during cooking if necessary.

4. Pour off the liquid and measure. For each cup liquid, measure one tablespoon flour into a bowl. Add the Worcestershire, mustard and three tablespoons cold water to the flour and mix well. Add some of the hot broth. Return mixture to bulk of broth and pour over the tripe. Bring to a

boil, stirring until mixture thickens. Cook two minutes. Stir in the cream and reheat.

Yield: Six servings.

Fried Chicken with Plum Sauce
Northern California

Fried chicken:
- 1 egg, lightly beaten
- ½ cup milk
- ½ cup flour
- ½ teaspoon salt
- ⅛ teaspoon freshly ground black pepper
- 2 whole chicken breasts, boned, skinned, halved and each half cut into three pieces
  Fat or oil for deep-frying
- ¼ cup crushed blanched toasted almonds.

Plum sauce:
  Prepared Chinese plum sauce (see note)
OR
- 1 sixteen-ounce jar purple plums, pitted
- 2 tablespoons imported soy sauce
- 2 tablespoons vinegar
- 2 tablespoons light brown sugar
- ½ teaspoon dry mustard
- ¼ teaspoon ginger
- 2 teaspoons cornstarch.

1. Combine the egg, milk, flour, salt and pepper to make a batter.

2. Dip the pieces of chicken into the batter and fry, a few at a time, in the fat or oil heated to 375 degrees. Drain on paper towels and coat with the almonds.

3. To prepare homemade plum sauce, place plums and their syrup in an electric blender. Add the remaining ingredients and blend until smooth. Transfer to a saucepan and heat, stirring, until mixture thickens. Let cool to room temperature.

4. Serve plum sauce with chicken.

Yield: Four servings.

Note: Prepared Chinese plum sauce is available in Chinese groceries.

Chicken and Bulghur Casserole
Washington

- 1 two-and-one-half-pound to three-pound chicken, cut into serving pieces
- 3 tablespoons butter
- ¼ cup chopped onion
- 1 clove garlic, finely chopped
- ¼ cup chopped celery with leaves
- ½ teaspoon thyme
- ¼ teaspoon marjoram
  Salt and freshly ground black pepper to taste
- ½ cup no. 1 bulghur
- 1 cup chicken broth
- 1 cup heavy cream.

1. Preheat the oven to 350 degrees.

2. Brown the chicken pieces in the butter in a heavy skillet. Add the onion, garlic and celery and cook until tender, about two minutes longer. Add the thyme, marjoram, salt and pepper.

3. Place the bulghur in the bottom of a one-and-one-half-quart to two-quart casserole. Combine the broth and cream and pour half over the bulghur. Mix well. Season with salt and pepper. Top with the chicken pieces and onion mixture.

4. Add remaining broth and cream to skillet and stir to pick up all the browned-on pieces. Pour over the chicken. Cover and bake forty-five minutes, or until chicken and bulghur are tender.

Yield: Four servings.

Fried Chicken in Teriyaki Sauce
Northern California

- 15 chicken wings, tips removed and discarded or used for soup
- 3 whole chicken breasts, halved and each half cut into three or four pieces
  Flour
  Salt and freshly ground black pepper to taste
  Oil

¼ cup mirin (Japanese wine), dry sherry or dry vermouth
1 cup imported soy sauce
1 eight-ounce can tomato sauce
1 cup sugar.

1. Preheat the oven to 350 degrees.
2. Toss the chicken pieces, a few at a time, in a paper bag containing flour seasoned with salt and pepper.
3. Heat enough oil in the bottom of a large heavy skillet to come to a depth of one-half inch. Add the chicken pieces and fry fairly slowly so that they do not overbrown before they are cooked through.
4. Meanwhile, combine the remaining ingredients in a saucepan and bring to a rolling boil, stirring to dissolve the sugar. Set aside.
5. As the chicken pieces are cooked, drain them on paper towels and then dip into the hot soy sauce mixture and place in a single layer in a shallow baking dish.
6. When all the chicken is in the dish, bake ten minutes.
Yield: Six servings.

Basque Chicken with Rice   *Nevada*

2 tablespoons olive oil
1 two-and-one-half-pound to three-pound chicken, cut into twenty pieces
1 onion, finely chopped
1 clove garlic, finely chopped
4 slices thick lean bacon, diced
1 cup uncooked rice
Salt and freshly ground black pepper to taste
1 tomato, peeled and chopped
¼ teaspoon saffron
2½ cups chicken broth
1 cup cooked peas or lima beans.

1. Heat the oil in a skillet or paella pan. Add the chicken pieces and brown on all sides. Add the onion, garlic and bacon and cook until onion is tender.
2. Add the rice and cook three to five minutes longer. Season with salt and pepper. Add the tomato. Mix the saffron with the broth and add. Bring to a boil and simmer until rice is tender, about twenty minutes.
3. Stir in the peas or limas and reheat.
Yield: Four servings.

Baked Chicken Camp Style   *Nevada*

Flour
Salt and freshly ground black pepper to taste
2 two-and-one-half-pound to three-pound chickens, cut into serving pieces
8 slices bacon
3 onions, thinly sliced
1 cup chopped celery leaves
1 bay leaf, crumbled
½ teaspoon thyme
2 sprigs parsley.

1. Preheat the oven to 325 degrees.
2. Season flour with salt and pepper and coat the chicken pieces with the mixture. Arrange them in a baking dish or roasting pan.
3. Arrange the bacon over chicken. Place the onions and celery leaves over the bacon. Add the bay leaf, thyme, parsley and enough water to come three-quarters of the way up the chicken pieces. Bake, uncovered, two to three hours, or until chicken is very tender.
Yield: Six servings.

California Chicken   *Northern California*

¼ cup flour
1 teaspoon salt
¼ teaspoon freshly ground black pepper
¼ teaspoon paprika
1 two-and-one-half-pound to three-pound frying chicken, cut into serving pieces

3 tablespoons butter
2 tablespoons chopped onion
1¼ cups chicken broth
1 cup crushed pineapple (one eight-and-three-quarter-ounce can)
1½ tablespoons soy sauce
½ cup dates, pitted and halved lengthwise
½ cup chopped green pepper.

1. Mix together the flour, salt, pepper and paprika. Coat the chicken pieces with the mixture, reserving any leftover mixture.

2. Melt the butter in a heavy skillet and brown the chicken pieces in it on all sides. Drain. Sauté the onion until tender in the butter remaining in the pan.

3. Return the chicken pieces to the pan. Add one cup of the broth. Cover and simmer twenty-five minutes, or until the chicken is tender. Remove chicken.

4. Mix the reserved flour mixture with the remaining broth and stir into the pan. Stir in the pineapple and soy sauce. Cook, stirring, until thickened. Add the chicken, dates and green pepper. Reheat.

Yield: Four servings.

Chicken à la Kai   *Hawaii*

1 three-and-one-half-pound chicken
1 small piece fresh ginger (see note)
  Salt to taste
12 peppercorns
2 tablespoons oyster sauce (see note)
1 tablespoon soy sauce
½ teaspoon sesame oil (see note)
1½ tablespoons cornstarch
3 tablespoons cold water.

1. Place the chicken in a kettle and add water to cover. Crush the ginger and add it along with salt and the peppercorns. Cover partly and simmer until chicken is tender, at least thirty minutes.

2. Strain two cups of broth in which chicken cooked into a saucepan and add the oyster sauce, soy sauce and sesame oil. Bring to a boil. Blend the cornstarch with the water and add gradually to the sauce, stirring. Add just enough cornstarch mixture to thicken the sauce slightly.

3. Cut the chicken into serving pieces and serve hot with the sauce.

Yield: Four servings.

Note: Fresh ginger, oyster sauce and sesame oil are available in Chinese groceries.

Chicken Raphael Weill

Northern California

4 small broiling chickens, about one and one-half pounds each, cut into serving pieces
1 lemon, halved or quartered
  Salt and freshly ground black pepper to taste
2 tablespoons flour
¼ pound butter
2 shallots, finely chopped
½ cup dry white wine
1½ cups heavy cream
4 tablespoons strong chicken broth
4 egg yolks
¼ teaspoon nutmeg
⅛ teaspoon cayenne pepper
½ teaspoon chopped chives
½ teaspoon chopped parsley
1 teaspoon lemon juice.

1. Wipe the chicken pieces dry and rub with the lemon. Sprinkle with salt and pepper and dredge lightly with the flour.

2. Heat the butter in a heavy skillet. Add the chicken pieces and cook over low heat until brown on all sides, shaking pan frequently to prevent sticking. Cover and simmer ten minutes.

3. Add the shallots and cook five minutes longer, shaking pan frequently. Add the wine, one-half cup of the cream and the broth. Cover and cook ten minutes, or until chicken is fork-

tender, shaking pan frequently. Do not allow mixture to boil.

4. Meanwhile, beat together the egg yolks and remaining cream. Add salt, pepper, the nutmeg, cayenne, chives and parsley.

5. Just before serving, pour the sauce over chicken in the pan and shake constantly over low heat until the sauce thickens. The sauce must be kept below the boiling point to prevent curdling.

6. Arrange the chicken pieces on a serving platter. Add the lemon juice to sauce and pour over chicken. Serve immediately.

Yield: Eight servings.

Chicken with Peanuts in Hoisin Sauce
Northern California

1 whole chicken breast, one pound or more
1 tablespoon sherry
1 teaspoon cornstarch
¼ teaspoon crushed hot red pepper, or to taste
½ cup plus two tablespoons peanut oil
½ cup fresh, unsalted, shelled, skinless, roasted or unroasted peanuts
4 dried mushrooms
3 water chestnuts, chopped or sliced
1 scallion, including green part, cut into one-inch lengths
½ clove garlic, finely minced
¼ teaspoon monosodium glutamate (optional)
2 tablespoons hoisin sauce (see note).

1. Have the butcher remove the skin and bones of the chicken breast. Or this may be done in the home kitchen, using the fingers and a sharp paring knife.

2. Cut the chicken meat into one-half-inch cubes, more or less. Place the cubes in a small mixing bowl and add the sherry, cornstarch and red pepper. Let stand until ready to use.

3. Heat one-half cup of the oil in a small saucepan and, when oil is hot, add the peanuts. Shaking the pan or stirring with a metal spoon, cook the peanuts briefly, just until golden brown (they

burn quickly). When peanuts are golden brown, drain them in a sieve, then on paper towels.

4. Meanwhile, place the mushrooms in a bowl and cover them with hot water. Let stand at least twenty minutes. When soaked, slice the mushrooms and set aside. Reserve three tablespoons of the soaking liquid.

5. Heat the remaining oil in a skillet and, when oil is quite hot, add the chicken meat. Cook quickly, stirring rapidly, just until chicken becomes white, one to two minutes. Add the sliced mushrooms, water chestnuts, scallion, garlic and monosodium glutamate if desired. Cook, stirring, about ten seconds only. Add the hoisin sauce, reserved mushroom liquid and the peanuts. Mix well and serve.

Yield: Four servings.

Note: Hoisin sauce is available in Chinese groceries. A traditional but not essential ingredient for this dish is fresh coriander (cilantro or Chinese parsley leaves), available in Chinese groceries. The leaves are chopped and sprinkled on the dish, or they are left whole and used as a garnish. In Chinese, cilantro is called hsiang-tsai.

Creamed Chicken and Mushrooms
Northern California

3 tablespoons butter
2 tablespoons finely chopped shallots
4 mushrooms, chopped
3 tablespoons flour
2 tablespoons dry sherry
1 cup chicken broth
⅓ cup heavy cream
   Salt and freshly ground black pepper to taste
⅛ teaspoon nutmeg
2 cups diced cooked chicken.

1. Melt the butter and sauté the shallots in it until tender. Add the mushrooms and cook two minutes longer.

2. Sprinkle with the flour and cook, stirring, two minutes.

3. Stir in the sherry, broth and cream and bring the sauce to a boil, stirring until the sauce thickens. Season with salt, pepper and the nutmeg. Add the chicken.

Yield: About three cups.

Orange Chicken   *Northern California*

1 two-and-one-half-pound to three-pound frying chicken, cut into serving pieces
4 teaspoons grated orange rind
¾ cup orange juice
1½ teaspoons salt
¼ teaspoon freshly ground black pepper
1 teaspoon rosemary
¾ cup flour
1½ teaspoons sweet paprika
½ cup oil or melted shortening, approximately
½ cup orange segments.

1. Place the chicken pieces in a shallow dish. Combine two teaspoons of the rind, the orange juice, one-half teaspoon of the salt, the pepper and rosemary and pour over chicken. Marinate in the refrigerator two to three hours.

2. Drain chicken and reserve marinade. Combine remaining rind, remaining salt, the flour and paprika in a paper bag. Shake the chicken pieces, a couple at a time, in the flour mixture. Reserve remaining flour mixture.

3. Heat the oil or shortening in a heavy skillet, add the chicken pieces and brown on all sides. Cover tightly, reduce heat and cook until chicken is tender, about thirty minutes. Uncover and cook ten minutes to recrisp.

4. Remove chicken to a warm serving platter. Pour off all but three tablespoons drippings from the skillet. Sprinkle with three tablespoons reserved flour mixture and cook two to three minutes.

5. Measure reserved marinade and make up to one and one-half cups by adding water. Stir into cooked flour mixture. Bring to a boil, stirring.

6. Arrange the orange segments over chicken and pour sauce over all.

Yield: Four servings.

Chicken with Luau or Spinach   *Hawaii*

1 coconut
1 cup boiling water
1 four-pound chicken, cut into serving pieces
3 tablespoons butter
Salt to taste
2 pounds luau (young taro leaves) or spinach.

1. Pierce two "eyes" into the coconut and drain the milk from the interior. Crack the coconut and remove the meat. Pare away the brown coating on the meat. Grate the coconut meat, or cut it into cubes and place in an electric blender. Add the water to either the grated coconut or the cubed coconut. If the blender method is used, blend well. In either case, let the mixture stand fifteen minutes; then squeeze it through a double thickness of cheesecloth.

2. Meanwhile, brown the chicken in the butter and add water to cover. Add salt and simmer until chicken is tender. Drain chicken and reserve broth.

3. Preheat the oven to 350 degrees.

4. Trim the taro leaves of their hard stems, including the ribs of the leaves themselves. Cook the leaves or spinach in a little of the reserved chicken broth. Drain and chop.

5. Stir a little coconut cream into the greens and spoon over the bottom of a baking dish. Arrange the chicken pieces over the greens. Add the remaining coconut cream to the remaining chicken broth and spoon this over the chicken.

6. Bake until heated through. Serve immediately.

Yield: Four servings.

Chicken in Pineapples
Hawaii

4 small pineapples
¼ cup butter
1 onion, finely chopped
1 clove garlic, finely chopped
½ tart apple, peeled, cored and diced
1 rib celery, chopped
2 whole chicken breasts, skinned, boned and cut into two-inch cubes
¾ teaspoon salt
1 tablespoon flour
2 teaspoons curry powder
¾ cup coconut milk (to prepare, see "Chicken with Luau or Spinach," step 1, recipe above)
1 tablespoon chopped crystallized ginger
2 tablespoons pineapple juice from fresh pineapple, or canned
⅔ cup diced fresh or canned pineapple
½ cup sliced outer green ribs celery
1⅓ cups cooked rice.

1. Cut the tops off the pineapples and reserve.
2. With a sharp knife, cut out the flesh and core from each pineapple, leaving about one inch pineapple flesh around the outer edge. Wrap each pineapple in aluminum foil, extending foil above top of pineapple and leaving open. Set pineapples in a baking dish.
3. Preheat the oven to 375 degrees.
4. Melt the butter and sauté the onion, garlic, apple and chopped celery in it until tender but not browned. Add the chicken and cook, stirring, until it turns white.
5. Sprinkle with the salt, flour and curry powder and cook three minutes longer. Stir in the coconut milk, ginger, pineapple juice and pineapple and cook until the chicken is tender, about ten minutes. Stir in the celery slices.
6. Place the rice in the bottom of each pineapple and spoon in the curry mixture. Draw up the foil to cover each pineapple and bake twenty-five minutes, or until curry mixture is bubbly hot. Serve with the reserved pineapple tops in place.
Yield: Four servings.

Aunt May's Chicken Fricassee
Oregon

1 three-pound to three-and-one-half-pound chicken, cut into serving pieces
2 leeks
2 sprigs parsley
1 bay leaf
1 sprig thyme or one-half teaspoon dried thyme
2 whole cloves
¼ teaspoon mace
1 carrot, diced
1 onion, sliced
1 quart boiling water
1 teaspoon salt
½ teaspoon freshly ground black pepper
¼ cup butter
¼ cup flour
¼ pound mushrooms, sliced
2 egg yolks, lightly beaten
½ cup heavy cream
2 tablespoons lemon juice
2 tablespoons chopped parsley.

1. Place the chicken pieces in a heavy casserole or Dutch oven. Tie together the leeks, parsley sprigs, bay leaf and thyme sprig if used and add to casserole.
2. Add dried thyme if used, the cloves, mace, carrot, onion, boiling water, salt and pepper. Cover and bring to a boil. Simmer forty minutes. Remove chicken to a serving dish and keep warm.
3. Remove tied bundle from broth. Boil broth vigorously, uncovered, until three cups remain and broth has good flavor.
4. Melt the butter in a saucepan and blend in the flour. Gradually stir in the chicken broth and mushrooms. Bring to a boil, stirring, and simmer ten minutes.
5. Combine the egg yolks and cream and stir in the lemon juice. Stir into the sauce. Pour over the chicken and sprinkle with the chopped parsley.
Yield: Four servings.

Roast Oregon Turkey with Sausage Dressing

1 twelve-pound to fourteen-pound oven-ready
   turkey
   Salt
1 pound sausage meat
8 cups stale white bread cubes
2 cups diced celery
1 onion, finely chopped
2 teaspoons grated orange rind
½ teaspoon grated lemon rind
   Freshly ground black pepper
1 teaspoon thyme
½ teaspoon marjoram
½ teaspoon sage
¼ cup chopped parsley
¼ cup orange juice
½ cup butter, melted.

1. Wash and dry turkey and season inside cavity with two teaspoons salt.

2. Preheat the oven to 325 degrees.

3. In a skillet, cook the sausage meat, breaking up the lumps as it cooks, until lightly browned.

4. Using a slotted spoon, transfer the meat to a large bowl and mix with the bread cubes and celery. Drain off and reserve all but two tablespoons of the sausage fat from the skillet. Add the onion to the skillet and sauté until tender.

5. Add the onion, orange rind, lemon rind, salt and pepper to taste, the thyme, marjoram, sage, parsley and orange juice to the bread mixture. Stir in one-quarter cup of the reserved sausage fat. Use mixture to stuff neck and body cavity of turkey. Close with skewers and string.

6. Truss the turkey, rub with some of the butter and place, breast side down, on a rack in a shallow roasting pan. Roast two and one-half hours, basting often with remaining butter.

7. Turn breast side up and roast, basting frequently with butter and pan drippings, one and one-half to two hours longer or until bird tests done (that is when no pink liquid comes from thigh joint when pricked; internal temperature of thigh joint is 180 degrees). Cover with aluminum foil if turkey overbrowns. Let turkey set in a warm place twenty to thirty minutes before carving.

Yield: Fourteen servings.

Note: To prepare giblet gravy, simmer turkey giblets until tender in a saucepan containing one onion, sliced; one rib celery with leaves, sliced; salt and freshly ground black pepper to taste and water to cover. Strain liquid and add drippings from pan in which turkey was roasted. Blend one-quarter cup flour with one-quarter cup water and stir in some of the prepared liquid. Return to bulk of liquid, bring to a boil and simmer until mixture thickens.

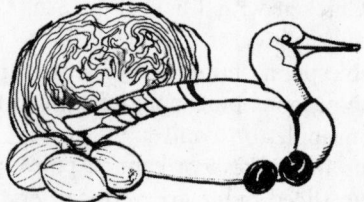

Pheasant in Cream   *Oregon*

¼ cup diced salt pork
1 young pheasant, cut into serving pieces
3 tablespoons flour
   Salt and freshly ground black pepper to taste
1 small onion, finely chopped
1½ cups light cream
½ teaspoon thyme.

1. Cook the salt pork in a skillet until golden brown. Remove the pieces and reserve.

2. Dust the pheasant pieces with flour seasoned with salt and pepper. Brown on all sides in the fat remaining in the skillet.

3. Add the onion and cook three minutes longer. Add the cream, thyme, salt and pepper. Bring to a boil, cover and simmer ten minutes, or until pheasant is tender. Place pheasant on a warm platter and reduce sauce by boiling until slightly thickened. Add reserved salt pork pieces to sauce and pour over the pheasant.

Yield: Two servings.

Scalloped Pheasant or Sage Chicken
Nevada

1 cooked cut-up pheasant or sage chicken
1 tablespoon butter
1 tablespoon flour
Milk if necessary
Salt and freshly ground black pepper to taste
1 cup buttered soft bread crumbs
½ teaspoon thyme.

1. Allow the pheasant or sage chicken to cool in the liquid in which it was cooked until pheasant can be handled.
2. Preheat the oven to 350 degrees.
3. Remove pheasant meat from bones and dice it. Reserve cooking liquid.
4. Melt the butter and blend in the flour. Gradually stir in one cup of the cooking liquid (add milk to make one cup if necessary). Cook, stirring, until mixture thickens. Season with salt and pepper.
5. Combine the bread crumbs and thyme. In a greased small baking dish, make alternate layers meat, gravy and crumbs, ending with crumbs. Bake, uncovered, fifteen minutes, or until heated through.
Yield: Two servings.

Chinese Roast Duck   *Northern California*

1 four-pound to five-pound duckling, cleaned and drawn
2 tablespoons honey
1 teaspoon red food coloring (optional)
2 teaspoons sugar
½ teaspoon salt
¼ cup mein seen diung (yellow bean paste, see note)
¼ cup hoi seen diung (black bean paste, see note)
2 tablespoons gin
Rind of one-half orange, finely shredded
2 scallions, including green part, or one-half leek, cut into two-inch lengths
1 clove garlic, finely chopped
2 tablespoons dark soy sauce (see note)
Duck sauce or plum sauce (see note).

1. There are two ways to prepare this duck, on a barbecue grill or roasted in the oven. Generally speaking, the oven method is preferable.
2. Add enough water to a large kettle to halfway cover the duck when added. Bring the water to a boil and add the honey. Using large tongs or a sling made of cheesecloth, dip the duck first on one side, then the other, into the kettle. Repeat several times, making certain the duck's back in particular is well scalded. If a reddish color is desired in the duck skin, add the food coloring to the water.
3. Drain the duck. Place it on a rack and let drain in a place where air freely circulates. Let stand one hour.
4. Combine the remaining ingredients and spoon the mixture into the cavity of the duck. Let stand two hours longer. Do not refrigerate. Keep at room temperature.
5. If the duck is to be cooked in the oven, preheat the oven to 400 degrees. If the duck is to be cooked over coals, roast it, turning frequently, until done.
6. If the oven method is used, place the duck, breast side up, on a rack in a roasting pan and roast thirty minutes. Pour off the fat as it accumulates. Reduce the oven heat to 350 degrees and continue roasting thirty to forty minutes, depending on the size of the duck.
7. To serve the duck Chinese style, disjoint duck, split body into halves and cut through flesh and bones into one-inch pieces, using a cleaver. Serve with duck sauce or plum sauce as a dip.
Yield: Four servings.
Note: Mein seen diung, hoi seen diung, dark soy sauce, duck sauce and plum sauce are available at Chinese groceries.

Game Sausage   *Alaska*

10 pounds moose, venison, elk or other game
 1 pound ham
 1 pound fat bacon or fresh pork fat
 2 tablespoons salt
¼ cup freshly ground black pepper
 2 tablespoons sugar
 2 teaspoons coriander
 1 tablespoon mustard seeds
 3 cloves garlic, finely chopped
   Sausage casing
   Boiling water.

1. Day before, grind together the game meat, ham and bacon or pork fat. Add the salt, pepper, sugar, coriander, mustard seeds and garlic and work with the hands to mix well.

2. Let set in refrigerator overnight. Next day, stuff into casing and drop into kettle of boiling water. Cook gently until sausage floats.

3. Remove and let dry. Sausage can be smoked for three days in cold smoke or used without smoking by frying or boiling.

Yield: About twelve pounds.

Fried Ptarmigan   *Alaska*

 4 ptarmigan, cleaned and split lengthwise in half
 1 white turnip, peeled and diced
 1 carrot, diced
 1 small onion, sliced
½ rib celery with leaves, diced
⅛ teaspoon mace
 4 whole cloves
 6 peppercorns
 2 cups water
½ pound sausage meat
   Flour
 1 egg, lightly beaten
 2 cups soft bread crumbs
   Fat or oil for deep-frying
 1 tablespoon butter

 1 small tomato, peeled and chopped
   Salt to taste.

1. Remove the end joint of the wings and legs. Wash ptarmigan well.

2. In the bottom of a heavy sauté pan, place the turnip, carrot, onion, celery, mace, cloves, peppercorns and water. Set the ptarmigan halves on top. Bring to a boil, cover tightly and cook gently one hour.

3. Remove bird halves and use one or two tablespoons of the sausage meat to stuff each half-body cavity, smoothing the sausage meat flat with the rib cage. Flour the bird halves and dip into the egg and then into bread crumbs. Fry until golden in the fat or oil heated to 370 degrees. Drain on paper towels.

4. Strain the cooking liquid from the sauté pan. Melt the butter and stir in one tablespoon flour. Gradually stir in the strained liquid. Add the tomato, bring to a boil and cook one minute or until sauce thickens. Season with salt. Serve separately with the bird halves.

Yield: Four to six servings.

Note: Grouse or small wild duck can be prepared the same way.

Reindeer Burgers   *Alaska*

 1 pound ground reindeer meat or other game
 1 teaspoon salt
1½ teaspoons prepared horseradish, drained
 2 teaspoons prepared mustard
1½ teaspoons Worcestershire sauce
 3 tablespoons catchup
 1 small onion, finely chopped
½ cup soft bread crumbs
¼ cup evaporated milk.

Combine all the ingredients and shape into patties. Broil about six minutes on each side.

Yield: Four servings.

Rabbit with Herbs
Washington

2 plump rabbits, fresh or frozen, cut into
  serving pieces
3 cloves garlic
6 tablespoons butter
1 tablespoon celery salt
1 tablespoon chopped fresh tarragon or two
  teaspoons dried tarragon
1 tablespoon chopped fresh thyme or two
  teaspoons dried thyme
  Salt and freshly ground black pepper to
  taste
½ cup dry white wine.

1. Preheat the oven to 550 degrees.
2. Carefully pick over the rabbit pieces and
arrange them on a flat surface. Cut the garlic into
thin slivers. Using a small paring knife, insert
these slivers into the rabbit meat.
3. Melt the butter over low heat and add the
celery salt, tarragon and thyme. Dip rabbit pieces
into the butter mixture and arrange them in one
layer in a metal baking pan. Sprinkle with salt
and pepper. Bake ten minutes, basting frequently.
4. Cover pan closely with aluminum foil and
reduce the oven heat to 350 degrees. Continue
cooking and basting until rabbit pieces are tender,
about thirty minutes longer.
5. Uncover baking pan and add the wine.
Transfer rabbit pieces to a warm platter or serving dish. Place baking pan on top of the stove and
bring liquid to a boil, stirring. Pour the sauce over
the rabbit pieces.
Yield: Eight servings.

Roast Venison
Alaska

1 six-pound to eight-pound leg of venison
3 tablespoons salt, approximately
¼ cup coarsely ground black pepper,
  approximately
5 tablespoons flour, approximately
30 cloves garlic, peeled.

1. Preheat the oven to 500 degrees.
2. Place the venison in a large roasting pan.
Sprinkle the meat with the salt until meat is white
on top.
3. Sprinkle with the pepper until black on top.
Sprinkle with the flour until white again on top.
4. Scatter half the garlic cloves over and
around the meat and place in the oven. Bake
forty-five minutes; then reduce the oven heat to
325 degrees. Continue baking one hour longer.
5. Serve venison thinly sliced, with the remaining raw cloves of garlic and with garlic bread.
Yield: Eight to one dozen servings.

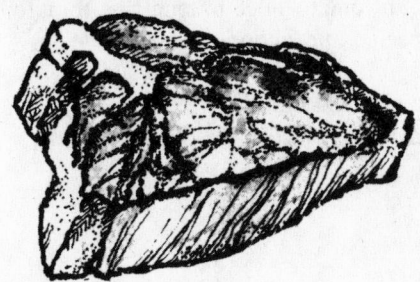

Herbed Game Loaf
Oregon

½ cup soft bread crumbs
½ cup milk
1 pound ground venison or moose meat
1 egg, lightly beaten
2 tablespoons grated onion
2 tablespoons finely chopped parsley
¼ teaspoon freshly ground black pepper
1 clove garlic, finely chopped
1 teaspoon salt
¼ teaspoon oregano
¼ teaspoon crushed rosemary
¼ teaspoon basil.

1. Preheat the oven to 350 degrees.
2. Soak the bread crumbs in the milk. Add the
remaining ingredients and mix well. Turn into a
loaf pan and bake one hour. The loaf can be
served hot or cold.
Yield: Four servings.

Game Stew   *Nevada*

1½ pounds game meat, such as venison, hare
    or elk
    Flour
    Salt and freshly ground black pepper to
    taste
  3 tablespoons bacon drippings
  1 onion, chopped
2½ cups boiling water
  1 tablespoon cider vinegar or lemon juice
  ½ clove garlic, crushed
  1 bay leaf
  ¼ cup tomato juice or one ripe tomato,
    peeled and chopped
  ½ cup diced celery
  ½ cup diced onion
  2 carrots, sliced
  2 white turnips, diced
  2 potatoes, cubed.

1. Cut the game into one-inch cubes. Season flour with salt and pepper and use to coat game cubes. Melt the bacon drippings, add meat and brown on all sides. Add the onion and cook two minutes longer.

2. Add the boiling water, vinegar or lemon juice, the garlic, bay leaf and tomato juice or tomato. Bring to a boil, cover and simmer two hours, or until game is tender.

3. Add the remaining ingredients, season with salt and pepper and simmer, covered, about twenty minutes longer, or until vegetables are cooked.

Yield: Four servings.

Vegetables, Main Dish Accompaniments and Salads

Sweet 'n' Sour Bean Salad
Northern California

1 sixteen-ounce can diagonal-cut green beans
½ cup cider vinegar
½ cup sugar
1 teaspoon celery seeds
¼ teaspoon dry mustard
1 eight-ounce can diagonal-cut wax beans, drained
1 medium-size onion, sliced and separated into rings
1 tablespoon chopped green pepper
1 tablespoon chopped red sweet pepper
Boston lettuce cups.

1. Drain the green beans and place liquid in a saucepan. Add the vinegar, sugar, celery seeds and mustard to the pan. Bring to a boil.

2. Put the green beans, wax beans, onion rings, green pepper and red pepper in a two-quart bowl or container and pour boiling vinegar mixture over.

3. Cover and chill. Drain; then serve in Boston lettuce cups.

Yield: About six servings.

Meg's Apples 'n' Beans
Washington

1 pound dried kidney beans
½ pound pork sausages
2 cups sliced peeled and cored apples
½ cup light brown sugar
4 small onions, thinly sliced
2 cloves garlic, finely chopped
1½ cups tomato juice
3 teaspoons salt
½ teaspoon freshly ground black pepper
½ teaspoon chili powder.

1. Day before, wash the beans. Cover with water and let stand overnight.

2. Next morning, bring to a boil and simmer, covered, one hour, or until beans are tender. Drain beans and put in casserole.

3. Preheat the oven to 275 degrees.

4. In a saucepan, combine all remaining ingredients. Bring to a boil. Add to beans and mix well.

5. Bake two to six hours.

Yield: Eight servings.

Lima Bean Casserole
Washington

1 pound dried lima beans
¼ pound salt pork, diced
Salt to taste
¼ cup oil
1 cup finely chopped onions

1 clove garlic, finely chopped
1 cup chopped green pepper
1 tablespoon cornstarch
1 tablespoon chili powder
1 cup pitted ripe olives, diced
1 cup grated sharp Cheddar cheese.

1. Day before, pick over the beans, wash, cover with water and let stand overnight. Next morning, place in a kettle with enough extra water to cover beans. Add the salt pork and salt.

2. Bring to a boil, cover and simmer until tender, about forty minutes. Drain beans, reserving bean liquid. Place beans in a casserole.

3. Preheat the oven to 300 degrees.

4. Heat the oil in a skillet and sauté the onions, garlic and green pepper in it until tender.

5. Mix together the cornstarch and chili powder with three tablespoons cold water and add to the skillet. Add contents of skillet to the casserole. Add the olives and three-quarters cup of the cheese. Add salt and one and one-half cups reserved bean liquid. Toss to mix.

6. Top with remaining cheese and bake one hour.

Yield: Six servings.

Split Peas with Ham　　　*Washington*

1 pound green or yellow split peas
¼ cup butter
½ cup finely chopped onion
1½ cups diced ham
4 cups chicken broth or ham broth
　Salt and freshly ground black pepper
1 teaspoon caraway seeds
1 bay leaf.

1. Wash and drain the split peas.

2. Heat the butter in a heavy skillet and sauté the onion in it until tender. Add the peas and cook, stirring, until peas are lightly browned.

3. Add the ham and cook three minutes longer.

4. Add the remaining ingredients, bring to a boil, cover and simmer forty-five minutes, or until peas are tender but not mushy.

Yield: Eight servings.

Lentil Casserole　　　*Washington*

1 pound lentils, washed
1 onion, studded with four whole cloves
1 bay leaf
5 cups water
2 teaspoons salt
½ cup catchup
¼ cup unsulphured molasses
2 tablespoons light brown sugar
1 teaspoon dry mustard
½ teaspoon Worcestershire sauce
2 tablespoons chopped onion
4 slices bacon.

1. Place the lentils, onion studded with cloves, the bay leaf, water and salt in a heavy casserole. Bring to a boil, cover and simmer thirty minutes.

2. Preheat the oven to 350 degrees.

3. Stir in the catchup, molasses, brown sugar, mustard, Worcestershire and chopped onion. Top with the bacon. Bake, covered, forty-five minutes. Uncover and bake fifteen minutes longer.

Yield: Ten to twelve servings.

Beet and Kraut Salad　　　*Oregon*

2 envelopes unflavored gelatin
½ cup cold water
2 cups boiling chicken broth or water
　Salt to taste
1 teaspoon sugar
1 sixteen-ounce can shoestring beets, drained
1 sixteen-ounce can sauerkraut
1 unpeeled apple, cored and chopped
2 tablespoons fresh horseradish or drained prepared horseradish
　Salad greens.

1. Soak the gelatin in the cold water. Add the boiling broth or water and stir to dissolve.

2. Add salt, the sugar, beets, sauerkraut, apple and horseradish and mix well. Turn into a lightly oiled two-quart mold. Chill well. Unmold onto salad greens.

Yield: Six servings.

Note: This is a good accompaniment to boiled beef or cold meats.

Broccoli Stalks   *Northern California*

Thick stalks from one bunch broccoli (see note)
Boiling salted water
3 tablespoons oil
1 tablespoon chopped scallion, including green part
Salt to taste
1 tablespoon imported soy sauce
1 cup chicken broth
1 tablespoon cornstarch
6 water chestnuts, sliced.

1. Peel the broccoli stems with a potato peeler and cut into uniform-size julienne strips. Drop into boiling salted water and boil one minute. Drain well.

2. Heat the oil in a heavy skillet. Add the broccoli stems and scallion and cook quickly, stirring constantly, until crisp-tender. Season with salt.

3. Add the soy sauce and half the broth. Mix the cornstarch with remaining broth and add to skillet. Cook, stirring, until mixture thickens. Add the water chestnuts.

Yield: Four servings.

Note: The broccoli flowers can be cooked as a vegetable or used in a salad.

Carrots and Cucumbers

Northern California

2 cucumbers, peeled, halved and seeded
Boiling salted water

1 bunch carrots, cut into two-inch pieces
2 tablespoons butter
¼ cup water
Salt and freshly ground black pepper to taste
1 teaspoon sugar
1 tablespoon chopped parsley.

1. Cut the cucumber halves into two-inch lengths and blanch in the boiling salted water one minute. Drain.

2. In a small heavy pan, combine the carrots, butter, water, salt, pepper and sugar. Cover and simmer about ten minutes, or until the carrots are crisp-tender.

3. Add the cucumbers and stir. Cook, uncovered, stirring occasionally, until extra liquid has been evaporated and vegetables are just tender. Sprinkle with the parsley.

Yield: Four servings.

Ruby's Su-No-Mo-No

Northern California

3 cucumbers or two cucumbers and three ribs celery or three white radishes
1 tablespoon salt
½ cup lemon juice
1 teaspoon imported soy sauce
½ teaspoon monosodium glutamate (optional)
1 cup flaked crab meat, thinly sliced canned abalone or cooked and cleaned shrimp, diced.

1. Score the cucumbers with a fork to leave some dark green skin for color. Cut cucumbers in half and remove seeds.

2. Slice each cucumber half in thin diagonal slices. If using celery or white radishes, clean and slice diagonally. Place all vegetables in a bowl and sprinkle with the salt. Let stand two hours.

3. Squeeze the water out of a handful of the vegetables at a time, repeating until all are squeezed. Rinse slices in ice cold water and

squeeze out excess water. Place slices in a bowl. Add the remaining ingredients and toss.

Yield: Four to six servings.

Note: The sea food can be omitted and two tablespoons toasted sesame seeds added.

Eggplant with Macadamia Nuts

Hawaii

3 medium-size to small eggplants
⅓ cup oil
1 onion, chopped
1 clove garlic, chopped
  Salt and freshly ground black pepper to taste
1 tomato, peeled and chopped
1 teaspoon Worcestershire sauce
2 eggs, lightly beaten
⅔ cup chopped macadamia nuts
½ cup buttered soft bread crumbs.

1. Halve each eggplant and scoop out the pulp, leaving a one-quarter-inch-thick shell. Dice the pulp finely.
2. Preheat the oven to 375 degrees.
3. Heat the oil in a skillet and cook the onion and garlic in it until tender. Add the eggplant pulp and cook slowly until lightly browned and almost tender.
4. Season with salt and pepper, add the tomato and Worcestershire and simmer three minutes. Stir in the eggs and nuts and use to stuff the eggplant shells. Top with the bread crumbs.
5. Set in an oiled shallow roasting pan. Bake twenty-five minutes, or until shells are tender.

Yield: Six servings.

Vegetable Quiche

Northern California

1 medium-size eggplant, peeled and sliced into one-half-inch slices
  Salt
  Flour
  Olive oil

1 onion, finely chopped
¼ cup chopped parsley
1 teaspoon chopped fresh thyme or one-half teaspoon dried thyme
  Freshly ground black pepper
2 large beefsteak tomatoes, peeled and thickly sliced
½ pound mozzarella cheese, sliced
1 cup heavy cream
1½ cups half and half
4 eggs, lightly beaten
3 egg yolks, lightly beaten
⅛ teaspoon nutmeg.

1. Preheat the oven to 375 degrees.
2. Sprinkle the eggplant slices on both sides with salt and let stand ten to fifteen minutes. Rinse. Wipe dry with paper towels.
3. Dredge slices lightly in flour and sauté in oil until lightly browned and barely tender.
4. Transfer eggplant slices to a lightly buttered 9-by-13-inch baking pan or casserole. Sprinkle with the onion, parsley, thyme and salt and pepper to taste.
5. Top each slice with a slice of tomato and then a slice of mozzarella.
6. Beat together the remaining ingredients, season with salt and pepper to taste and pour over the slices. Bake twenty minutes, reduce the oven heat to 300 degrees and bake until set, about twenty minutes longer.

Yield: Six servings.

Spinach with Coconut Cream

Hawaii

2 pounds spinach
1 teaspoon salt
¼ teaspoon freshly ground black pepper
⅛ teaspoon nutmeg
1 cup boiling coconut cream (see note)
2 tablespoons grated fresh horseradish or drained prepared horseradish.

1. Wash the spinach very well. Place in a large kettle with just the water clinging to the leaves.

Cook, stirring once or twice, until wilted. Drain very well, pressing out excess moisture. Chop spinach.

2. Mix spinach with the remaining ingredients.

Yield: Six servings.

Note: Coconut cream is available canned in specialty food stores.

Malfatti   *Northern California*

2 pounds fresh spinach or two packages
  frozen spinach
½ loaf dry, crusty Italian bread
  Hot water
1 onion, finely chopped
1 clove garlic, finely chopped
2 tablespoons olive oil
1 cup dry bread crumbs
½ cup chopped parsley
  Freshly grated Parmesan cheese
1 teaspoon salt
¼ teaspoon freshly ground black pepper
1 teaspoon basil
4 eggs, lightly beaten
  Boiling salted water
3 cups hot homemade tomato sauce.

1. Wash the fresh spinach very well and cook just in the water clinging to the leaves. Or cook the frozen spinach according to package directions. Drain spinach very well, squeezing out as much water as possible, and chop.

2. Soak the bread in hot water and then squeeze dry.

3. Sauté the onion and garlic in the oil until tender. Mix together the onion mixture, spinach and bread and put through the finest blade of a meat grinder.

4. Add the bread crumbs, parsley, one cup cheese, the salt, pepper and basil. Stir in the eggs. With lightly floured hands, shape the mixture into links like pork sausage.

5. Drop the links, a few at a time, into a kettle of boiling salted water. Reduce heat to a simmer

and cook until the malfatti float to the surface. Remove with a slotted spoon, drain and place in a greased baking dish.

6. Spoon the tomato sauce over links, sprinkle with Parmesan cheese and broil to reheat.

Yield: One dozen servings.

Note: This dish can be completely made a day ahead and then reheated.

Spinach Salad   *Northern California*

8 cups washed and well-drained spinach
  leaves
½ pound bacon, cooked crisp and then
  crumbled
2 hard-cooked eggs, roughly chopped
5 scallions, including green part, chopped
¾ cup homemade garlic croutons
½ cup mayonnaise
2 teaspoons Düsseldorf mustard
¼ cup lemon juice
½ cup olive oil
1 tablespoon tarragon vinegar
⅛ teaspoon sugar
  Salt and freshly ground black pepper to
  taste.

1. Tear the spinach leaves into bite-size bits and put in a salad bowl.

2. Arrange the bacon bits, eggs, scallions and croutons in wedges over spinach.

3. Combine all remaining ingredients and mix well. At the table, or just before serving, pour dressing over salad and toss.

Yield: Four servings.

Asparagus Vinaigrette
Northern California

2 pounds fresh young asparagus spears,
  cooked and well drained
3 tablespoons wine vinegar
2 tablespoons lemon juice
¼ cup vegetable oil

2 tablespoons olive oil
½ teaspoon sugar
  Salt and freshly ground black pepper to taste
1 hard-cooked egg, roughly chopped
2 sweet gherkins, finely chopped.

1. Arrange the asparagus spears in one layer in a shallow baking dish.

2. In a jar or small container with a tight-fitting lid, combine the vinegar, lemon juice, vegetable and olive oils, sugar, salt and pepper and shake to mix well. Pour dressing over asparagus and refrigerate for at least an hour.

3. Arrange the asparagus on a serving platter. Sprinkle with the egg and pickle.

Yield: Six servings.

Vinegar Greens   *Alaska*

1 bunch turnip or collard greens or kale or one pound spinach or other greens
  Boiling salted water
3 slices bacon, cubed
3 tablespoons chopped onion
1 tablespoon cider vinegar
2 teaspoons sugar
1 egg, well beaten.

1. Clean the greens well, chop roughly and cook until tender in boiling salted water. Drain very well and chop.

2. Cook the bacon until crisp. Add the onion and cook until tender.

3. Add the vinegar and sugar to egg. Add onion and bacon mixture to the egg mixture and pour over hot greens.

Yield: Four servings.

Sour Cabbage   *Hawaii*

8 cups boiled water, cooled
1 tablespoon cider vinegar
½ cup rock salt
1 large head cabbage, roughly sliced
  Boiling water.

1. Mix together the cooled water, vinegar and rock salt. Stir to dissolve rock salt.

2. Plunge the cabbage into boiling water, remove from heat and let stand a minute or two until cabbage turns bright green. Drain cabbage and cool.

3. Add cooled cabbage to brine, top with a weight to keep cabbage submerged and let stand at room temperature four days to ferment. Remove fermented cabbage from liquid and pack into jars. Store in the refrigerator.

Yield: About one quart.

Apple Slaw   *Washington*

5 cups finely shredded green cabbage
1 cup finely shredded red cabbage
2 unpeeled red apples, cored and diced
⅓ cup finely chopped sweet red onion
½ cup diced green pepper
1½ teaspoons plus one tablespoon sugar
½ cup dry white wine
⅓ cup lemon juice
1 teaspoon salt
¼ teaspoon freshly ground black pepper
3 tablespoons oil
4 hard-cooked egg yolks, mashed
½ cup heavy cream, whipped
2 tablespoons Dijon or Düsseldorf mustard, or to taste
1 cup chopped walnuts.

1. Place the green cabbage, red cabbage, apples, onion and green pepper in a large bowl. Sprinkle with one and one-half teaspoons of the sugar and pour the wine over all. Chill.

2. Meanwhile, combine the lemon juice, remaining sugar, the salt, black pepper, oil and egg yolks. Mix well.

3. Stir in the whipped cream and mustard. Pour over the chilled greens, add the walnuts and toss. Chill.

Yield: Ten servings.

Agnes' Oregon Slaw

1 medium-sized head green cabbage, finely shredded
2 large unpeeled Red Delicious apples, cored and diced
1 green pepper, seeded and diced
⅓ cup mayonnaise
½ cup sour cream
2 tablespoons wine vinegar
2 tablespoons sugar
½ teaspoon salt
½ cup light cream or half and half
⅛ teaspoon freshly ground black pepper.

1. Place the cabbage, apples and green pepper in a salad bowl.

2. In another bowl, beat together the mayonnaise and sour cream until well mixed. Gradually beat in the remaining ingredients.

3. Pour over the cabbage mixture, toss well and refrigerate at least three hours. Check the seasoning and add more salt and pepper if necessary before serving.

Yield: Six servings.

Caesar Salad   *Northern California*

1 head romaine lettuce
½ bunch arugula (see note)
3 slices cold crisp buttered toast
1 clove garlic
1½ tablespoons lemon juice
6 tablespoons olive oil
1 teaspoon Dijon or Düsseldorf mustard
1 two-ounce can anchovies, drained and cut into pieces
1 egg, boiled for exactly sixty seconds
2 tablespoons freshly grated Parmesan cheese
Freshly ground black pepper to taste.

1. Remove the core from the romaine and cut or tear the leaves into bite-size pieces. Drop the lettuce into a basin of cold water.

2. Cut off and discard the root ends of the arugula and cut the leaves in half. Add them to the basin of water. Drain the greens and shake in a salad basket to remove most of the water.

3. Rub the toast with the garlic. Cut the toast into bite-size cubes and set aside.

4. Put the lemon juice in a large salad bowl and stir in the oil and mustard, using a wire whisk.

5. Add the romaine and arugula. Add the anchovies, toast cubes, the lightly cooked egg, the cheese and pepper. Toss gently and serve immediately.

Yield: Four to six servings.

Note: Arugula is a salad green sold in Italian produce markets.

Agnes' Wilted Lettuce   *Oregon*

2 large heads Boston lettuce, washed and well drained
½ pound lean bacon
1 tablespoon finely chopped onion
¼ cup cider vinegar
¼ teaspoon dry mustard
2 teaspoons sugar
1½ cups light cream.

1. Tear the lettuce into bite-size pieces and place in a salad bowl.

2. Cook the bacon in a skillet until crisp. Remove bacon, crumble and reserve. Sauté the onion in the fat remaining in the skillet until tender.

3. Add the vinegar, mustard, sugar and cream to the skillet and bring to a boil, stirring. Add the bacon bits to the lettuce just before serving and pour the dressing over all. Toss and serve.

Yield: Eight servings.

"Alfalfa" (Wilted Lettuce)   *Oregon*

3 slices bacon, diced
1 small onion, finely chopped
1½ tablespoons flour

½ cup sour cream
¼ cup cider vinegar
4 cups salad greens, shredded.

1. Cook the bacon until it is crisp, remove the bits and reserve. Add the onion to the bacon drippings and sauté until tender.
2. Stir in the flour, sour cream and bacon bits. Cook until smooth. Just before serving, stir in the vinegar and pour over the greens in a salad bowl. Toss.
Yield: Four servings.

Baked Leek Omelet   *Oregon*

2 bunches leeks
6 eggs, lightly beaten
  Salt and freshly ground black pepper to taste
1 cup grated Cheddar cheese
2 tablespoons cracker crumbs or dry bread crumbs.

1. Preheat the oven to 325 degrees.
2. Wash the leeks thoroughly and cut into one-half-inch pieces. Steam the pieces in a colander over boiling water five minutes. Drain very well.
3. Add leeks to the eggs. Season with salt and pepper and stir in the cheese and crumbs. Pour into a buttered shallow baking dish and bake thirty minutes, or until set.
Yield: Four servings.

Lotus Root Salad   *Hawaii*

1 lotus root
6 tablespoons white vinegar
¼ teaspoon salt
¼ teaspoon monosodium glutamate (optional)
1 tablespoon sugar.

1. Slice the lotus root on the bias with a knife or sharp cleaver. Place in a saucepan and cover with water to a depth of one inch.
2. Add two tablespoons of the vinegar, bring to a boil and simmer until crisp-tender, about eight minutes. Drain the slices and place in a mixing bowl.
3. Combine the remaining ingredients and bring to a boil. Pour the hot mixture over the lotus root and let stand one hour or longer. Chill slightly.
Yield: Four to six servings.

Mushroom Goulash   *Alaska*

2 tablespoons bacon drippings
1 onion, finely chopped
3 cups sliced mushrooms
½ cup fresh corn kernels
1½ cups peeled chopped tomatoes
1 bay leaf
  Salt and freshly ground black pepper to taste
½ cup sour cream.

1. Heat the bacon drippings in a skillet, add the onion and sauté until tender. Add the mushrooms and corn and cook five minutes.
2. Add the tomatoes, bay leaf, salt and pepper and simmer three minutes. Just before serving, stir the sour cream into mixture.
Yield: Six servings.

Mushroom Pie   *Washington*

1 pound wild or cultivated mushrooms
¼ cup butter
3 scallions, including green part, finely chopped
3 tablespoons flour
1 cup heavy cream
½ cup chicken broth
  Salt and freshly ground black pepper to taste
2 teaspoons lemon juice
2 tablespoons chopped parsley
  Pastry made from one cup flour.

1. Preheat the oven to 425 degrees.

2. Wipe the mushrooms, slice them and sauté in the butter in a heavy skillet. Add the scallions and cook two minutes longer.

3. Sprinkle with the flour and gradually stir in the cream and broth. Season with salt and pepper. Bring to a boil and simmer until mixture thickens. Stir in the lemon juice and parsley and pour into a nine-inch deep-dish pie plate or individual ramekins. Top with the rolled-out pastry.

4. Bake until pastry is golden, about thirty minutes for large pie or about twenty minutes for ramekins.

Yield: Six servings.

Cabbage and Mushroom Casserole

Oregon

4 cups shredded cabbage
　Boiling salted water
6 tablespoons butter
½ teaspoon salt
¼ teaspoon freshly ground black pepper
1 teaspoon dill seeds
2 cups sliced mushrooms
½ cup chopped onion
1 cup tomato sauce, preferably homemade
1 cup sour cream
1 cup buttered soft bread crumbs.

1. Preheat the oven to 375 degrees.

2. Blanch the cabbage two minutes in boiling salted water to cover. Drain well.

3. Stir in three tablespoons of the butter, the salt, pepper and dill.

4. Melt remaining butter in a skillet and sauté the mushrooms and onion in it until tender. Add to cabbage.

5. Stir in the tomato sauce and sour cream. Spoon mixture into a one-and-one-half-quart casserole. Top with the bread crumbs and bake twenty-five minutes.

Yield: Six servings.

Norah's Vegetable Medley　　*Washington*

4 slices bacon, cubed
3 tablespoons oil
1 onion, sliced
1 clove garlic, finely chopped
4 large baking potatoes, cut into
　three-quarter-inch cubes
½ pound green beans, cut into two-inch
　lengths
3 zucchini, thickly sliced
3 tomatoes, peeled and chopped
1½ teaspoons salt
¼ teaspoon freshly ground black pepper
½ teaspoon basil
½ teaspoon thyme
3 tablespoons chopped parsley.

1. Cook the bacon in a heavy skillet until crisp. Remove bacon bits and reserve. Add the oil to skillet and heat.

2. Add the onion and garlic and sauté until tender. Add the potatoes, beans, zucchini, tomatoes, salt, pepper, basil, thyme and parsley. Bring to a boil and, stirring often, simmer, covered, twenty minutes, or until vegetables are tender. Sprinkle with reserved bacon bits.

Yield: Six servings.

Sour Cream Potato Salad　　*Oregon*

4 cups hot cooked and diced potatoes
¼ cup homemade French dressing (page 622)
1 cup chopped celery
2 tablespoons chopped scallions, including
　green part
¼ cup chopped sweet red pepper
2 tablespoons chopped dill pickle or sweet
　pickle
3 hard-cooked eggs, sliced
1 tablespoon Düsseldorf mustard
1 tablespoon cider vinegar
1 teaspoon salt
¼ teaspoon freshly ground black pepper
1 cup sour cream.

1. Place the potatoes in a bowl, pour the dressing over and toss. Refrigerate several hours.

2. Add the celery, scallions, red pepper, pickle and eggs to potatoes. Combine remaining ingredients and stir into the salad. Chill at least one hour before serving.

Yield: Four to six servings.

Lemon Potatoes   *Washington*

2 pounds baking potatoes, cut into two-inch cubes
   Boiling salted water
1 teaspoon grated lemon rind
¼ cup melted butter
¼ cup chopped parsley
3 tablespoons chopped chives or scallions, including green part
¼ teaspoon nutmeg
   Salt and freshly ground black pepper to taste
¼ cup lemon juice.

1. Preheat the oven to 450 degrees.

2. Cover the potato pieces with boiling salted water. Bring to a boil and simmer four minutes. Drain.

3. Toss potatoes with the lemon rind, butter, parsley, chives or scallions, nutmeg, salt and pepper. Turn into a greased casserole and bake twenty-five minutes, or until potatoes are tender. Pour the lemon juice over all.

Yield: Six servings.

Stuffed Potatoes   *Oregon*

3 large baking potatoes
2 tablespoons butter
   Salt and freshly ground black pepper to taste
1 cup shredded sharp Cheddar cheese
½ cup sour cream
2 tablespoons chopped chives

4 slices bacon, cooked until crisp, then crumbled.

1. Preheat the oven to 400 degrees.

2. Scrub and prick the potatoes and bake until tender, about one hour.

3. Put the butter into a mixing bowl. Cut each potato in half and carefully scoop out the center onto the butter. Reserve potato shells. Mash potatoes well and beat until fluffy.

4. Fold in the cheese, sour cream, chives and bacon bits and pile mixture back into the potato shells. Bake fifteen to twenty minutes.

Yield: Six servings.

Potato Bake   *Washington*

6 cups cooked cubed potatoes
¼ cup melted butter
1 cup sour cream
1 cup cottage cheese
1 clove garlic, finely chopped
¼ cup chopped scallions, including green part
¾ teaspoon salt
⅛ teaspoon freshly ground black pepper.

1. Preheat the oven to 350 degrees.

2. Combine all the ingredients and mix well. Turn into a greased casserole or baking dish and bake thirty minutes, or until bubbly hot.

Yield: Six servings.

Sheepherder's Potatoes   *Oregon*

2 large baking potatoes
¼ cup bacon drippings or shortening
½ small onion, finely chopped
   Salt and freshly ground black pepper
2 tablespoons chopped parsley
¼ teaspoon thyme
2 eggs, lightly beaten.

1. Peel the potatoes and slice thinly, using a cabbage slaw slicer. Heat the bacon drippings or

shortening in a heavy skillet. Add the potatoes and cook slowly, covered, until potatoes are almost cooked, about fifteen minutes.

2. Remove cover, add the onion and cook over medium heat, turning the potatoes as they brown. Once potatoes are cooked and browned, season with salt and pepper.

3. Sprinkle with the parsley and thyme. Pour the eggs over the potatoes and stir to distribute eggs evenly. The heat of the pan and potatoes cooks the eggs quickly. Serve at once.

Yield: Four servings.

Potato Gnocchi   *Northern California*

6 large potatoes, scrubbed
  Cold salted water
½ cup butter
3 eggs, lightly beaten
2 teaspoons baking powder
4 cups flour
  Salt and freshly ground white pepper to taste
  Boiling salted water
2 cloves garlic, finely minced
½ cup freshly grated Parmesan cheese.

1. Cover the potatoes with cold salted water, bring to a boil, cover and simmer until tender, about thirty minutes.

2. Preheat the oven to 350 degrees.

3. Peel and rice the potatoes while hot and mix with one-quarter cup butter, the eggs, baking powder, flour, salt and pepper. Mix and knead until dough is smooth.

4. Shape the dough into finger-thick rolls, cut into one-inch pieces and shape into crescents. Drop a few at a time, into a large kettle of boiling salted water. Simmer gently until they rise to the surface and are done, about six minutes. Drain well. Place in a greased 9-by-13-inch baking dish.

5. Sauté the garlic in the remaining butter and pour over the gnocchi. Sprinkle with the cheese. Bake eight minutes.

Yield: One dozen servings.

Sweet Potato Patties (Bitso Bitso)   *Hawaii*

2 cups grated sweet potatoes
¼ cup sugar
¼ cup flour
  Oil or lard.

1. Combine the sweet potatoes, sugar and flour. Shape mixture into six patties, each two inches in diameter and one-half-inch thick.

2. Heat oil or lard to a depth of one-quarter inch in a skillet. Add the patties and fry, first on one side and then on the other.

Yield: Six servings.

Tomato Pudding   *Washington*

1 twenty-ounce can tomato puree, or three cups canned tomatoes, forced through a sieve or food mill, or three cups peeled chopped fresh tomatoes, forced through a food mill
½ cup boiling water
1 cup light brown sugar
½ teaspoon salt
⅛ teaspoon freshly ground black pepper
2 cups soft white bread cubes (about one-inch cubes)
¼ cup melted butter.

1. Preheat the oven to 375 degrees.

2. In a saucepan, combine the tomato puree with the water, brown sugar, salt and pepper. Bring to a boil and simmer ten minutes.

3. Place the bread cubes in a greased casserole and pour the butter over cubes. Pour the tomato mixture over all. Bake, covered, forty minutes.

Yield: Six servings.

Zucchini Toss   *Oregon*

4 cups thinly sliced zucchini
3 tablespoons oil

1 clove garlic, finely chopped
Salt and freshly ground black pepper to
taste
½ teaspoon oregano
¼ teaspoon basil
⅓ cup toasted croutons
1 cup shredded Tillamook cheese or sharp
Cheddar cheese.

1. Sauté the zucchini in the oil with the garlic until barely tender. Do not overcook.
2. Add the remaining ingredients, toss and serve.
Yield: Four servings.

Zucchini in Batter   *Northern California*

2 small zucchini, sliced into one-quarter-inch
slices
2 eggs
¾ cup light cream
¼ cup freshly grated Parmesan cheese
Salt and freshly ground black pepper to
taste
¼ cup melted butter
1 cup flour
Oil

1. Place the zucchini between paper towels to dry surface.
2. Place the eggs, cream, cheese, salt, pepper, two tablespoons of the butter and the flour into an electric blender.
3. Blend until smooth, and let stand thirty minutes or longer if convenient.
4. Heat oil to a depth of one-half inch in a heavy skillet and add remaining butter.
5. Dip the zucchini slices into the batter (it should be thick enough to coat) and drip, a few at a time, into the hot oil. Cook over medium heat until brown; then turn and cook the other side. Test to make sure that the zucchini is tender; then drain on paper towels.
Yield: Four to six servings.

Schramsberg Zucchini Casserole
Northern California

2 pounds small zucchini or mixed summer
squash varieties
¼ cup chopped scallions, including green part
6 tablespoons butter, melted
6 tomatoes, peeled, seeded and chopped
2 tablespoons olive oil
1 clove garlic, finely chopped
1 green pepper, seeded and diced
Salt and freshly ground black pepper to
taste
½ cup freshly grated Parmesan cheese
2 tablespoons chopped parsley.

1. Scrub the squash and cut into one-half-inch-thick slices. Cover with cold water, bring to a boil and drain at once.
2. Sauté the scallions in one tablespoon of the butter in a heavy casserole. Cover with the tomatoes and sprinkle with the oil, garlic and green pepper. Season with salt and black pepper.
3. Cover and simmer five minutes.
4. Preheat the oven to 350 degrees.
5. Spread the drained squash over the tomato mixture. Drizzle half the remaining butter over all. Cover and simmer ten minutes. Sprinkle with the cheese and parsley.
6. Pour remaining butter over all, cover and bake about fifteen minutes, or until squash is barely tender.
Yield: Four to six servings.

Dilled Zucchini   *Northern California*

2 pounds zucchini, sliced one-quarter-inch
thick
1 bunch scallions, including some of the
green part, finely chopped
3 tablespoons freshly snipped dill weed
¼ cup melted butter
1 teaspoon salt
¼ teaspoon freshly ground black pepper.

1. Preheat the oven to 350 degrees.

2. Toss all the ingredients together and turn into a buttered casserole. Cover and bake forty-five minutes to one hour, or until zucchini is tender.

Yield: Four servings.

Chestnut Casserole   *Northern California*

2 tablespoons butter
1½ tablespoons flour
3 cups chicken broth
3 cups shelled chestnuts (see note)
4 slices bacon, cooked until crisp, then crumbled
  Salt and freshly ground black pepper to taste.

1. Preheat the oven to 325 degrees.

2. Melt the butter in a heavy casserole. Blend in the flour and gradually stir in the broth. Add the chestnuts, bacon bits, salt and pepper.

3. Cover and bake, stirring occasionally, three hours, or until chestnuts are tender.

Yield: Six servings.

Note: To shell chestnuts, make a cross slit on the flat side of each chestnut. Fry in one tablespoon butter in a heavy skillet five minutes, tossing frequently. Bake five minutes in oven set at 375 degrees. Shell and skin chestnuts as soon as they can be handled.

This dish is good with baked ham or roast turkey.

Oregon Fried Wheat

2 tablespoons oil
1 onion, finely chopped
½ cup uncooked rice
1 cup no. 1 bulghur
1¾ cups chicken broth
3 tablespoons imported soy sauce
6 scallions, including green part, finely chopped.

1. Heat the oil in a skillet and sauté the onion in it until tender. Add the rice and cook, stirring, until rice looks transparent.

2. Add the bulghur, broth and soy sauce. Bring to a boil, cover and simmer thirty minutes, or until liquid is absorbed.

3. Stir in the scallions.

Yield: Four servings.

Wild Rice with Filberts   *Oregon*

1 cup uncooked wild rice, washed and drained
  Boiling water
¼ cup butter
½ cup filberts
½ cup chopped celery
¼ pound mushrooms, sliced
2 tablespoons chopped onion
½ teaspoon salt
⅛ teaspoon freshly ground black pepper
¼ teaspoon sage
2 cups chicken broth.

1. Cover the wild rice with boiling water. Let stand ten minutes. Drain.

2. Heat the butter in a heavy skillet and sauté the filberts in it until lightly browned. Remove and reserve.

3. Add the celery, mushrooms and onion to the skillet and sauté until tender. Stir in the salt, pepper, sage, broth and drained rice. Bring to a boil and simmer, covered, fifty minutes, or until liquid is absorbed. Stir in filberts.

Yield: Six servings.

Risotto Milanese   *Northern California*

4 scallions, including green part, finely chopped
2 tablespoons butter
1 cup uncooked imported Italian rice (see note)
1½ cups chicken broth

1 cup dry vermouth or dry white wine
¼ teaspoon powdered saffron
 Salt and freshly ground black pepper to taste
4 mushrooms, thinly sliced
½ cup freshly grated Parmesan cheese.

1. In a heavy saucepan, sauté the scallions in the butter until transparent. Add the rice and cook, stirring often, until it is transparent.

2. Heat together the broth, vermouth or wine and the saffron and pour one-quarter of mixture over the rice, stirring and keeping the heat low.

3. When the liquid is absorbed, add another quarter of the mixture in the same way. Repeat the process with remaining liquid. This will take about thirty minutes in total. Season with salt and pepper.

4. Add the mushrooms and cheese and mix well.

Yield: Four to six servings.

Note: Italian rice for risotto is available in Italian groceries. In New York City, these include Manganaro's, 488 Ninth Avenue (10018); P. Carnevale & Son, 645 Ninth Avenue (10036); and Molinari Brothers, 776 Ninth Avenue (10019).

Chicken Spaghetti Salad   *Washington*

3 whole chicken breasts
 Salt and freshly ground black pepper
1 rib celery with leaves, diced
1 sprig parsley
½ bay leaf, crumbled
½ onion, sliced
8 ounces thin spaghetti, cooked al dente, drained
1 cup French dressing (page 622)
½ cup chopped celery
1 hard-cooked egg, chopped
 Mayonnaise, preferably homemade (page 760)
3 tablespoons chopped Italian parsley.

1. Place the chicken breasts in a large skillet. Season with salt and pepper and add the diced celery, parsley sprig, bay leaf, onion and enough water to cover. Bring to a boil and simmer fifteen minutes, or until tender.

2. Remove chicken breasts; skin, bone and dice. Remove one cup broth and reserve. Pour remaining broth over diced chicken pieces and chill several hours or overnight.

3. Add the cup reserved broth and the French dressing to the hot drained spaghetti. Toss and chill several hours or overnight.

4. To serve, drain the chicken pieces and combine with the chopped celery, egg and enough mayonnaise to moisten. Drain the spaghetti and add with the chopped parsley to the chicken mixture. Toss and season with salt and pepper, adding more mayonnaise if necessary.

Yield: Six servings.

Ham and Apricot Salad

Northern California

1½ cups cooked ham, cut into julienne strips
1 cup chopped celery
1 tablespoon chopped scallions, including green part
1 cup peeled, pitted and coarsely chopped fresh apricots
¼ cup sour cream
¼ cup mayonnaise
½ teaspoon Dijon mustard
1½ tablespoons lemon juice
 Salad greens.

1. Combine the ham, celery, scallions and apricots. Blend together the sour cream, mayonnaise, mustard and lemon juice.

2. Arrange ham mixture on salad greens and serve dressing separately.

Yield: Four servings.

Green Goddess Dressing

Northern California

8 anchovy fillets, finely chopped
2 scallions, including green part, finely chopped
¼ cup finely chopped parsley
1½ tablespoons finely chopped fresh tarragon or one-half teaspoon dried tarragon
2 cups mayonnaise
2 tablespoons tarragon vinegar
3 tablespoons finely chopped chives.

Combine the anchovies, scallions, parsley and tarragon and mix well. Fold into the mayonnaise. Stir in the vinegar and chives.

Yield: About two and one-half cups.

Note: This dressing, created at the Palace Hotel, San Francisco, is used on romaine lettuce and sea food salads.

Celery Seed Dressing   *Washington*

¾ teaspoon salt
1 teaspoon dry mustard
3 drops Tabasco sauce
1 teaspoon celery seeds, roughly crushed
2 tablespoons honey
¼ cup white vinegar
1 cup oil
1 teaspoon grated onion.

1. Combine the salt, mustard, Tabasco and celery seeds in a bowl.

2. Add the remaining ingredients and beat until thick.

Yield: About one and one-half cups.

Note: This dressing is delicious over fruit and sea food salads.

Breads

Apple Nut Bread

Washington

2 cups thick peeled and cored
   apple slices (Jonathans or Golden
   Delicious)
2 tablespoons boiling water
1⅛ teaspoons salt
2 cups flour
   Sugar
3 teaspoons baking powder
½ teaspoon baking soda
½ teaspoon cinnamon
½ cup pecans, chopped
2 tablespoons oil
1 egg, lightly beaten.

1. Preheat the oven to 350 degrees.
2. Place the apple slices in a small heavy sauce-pan with the water and one-eighth teaspoon of the salt. Heat gently until apples are tender but not mushy. Pass through a food mill. Set aside to cool.
3. Sift together the flour, remaining salt, three-quarters cup sugar, the baking powder, baking soda and cinnamon. Stir in the pecans.
4. Mix one cup cooled applesauce with the oil and egg. Stir into dry ingredients and mix just enough to moisten. Turn into a greased 9-by-5-by-3-inch loaf pan, sprinkle top surface with a little sugar and bake one hour, or until done.
Yield: One loaf.

Apricot Nut Bread   *Northern California*

1 tablespoon butter
1 cup dried apricots, diced
1 cup raisins
1 cup boiling water
2 cups flour
1 cup sugar
1 teaspoon baking soda
1 teaspoon baking powder
1 cup chopped walnuts.

1. Preheat the oven to 325 degrees.
2. Place the butter, apricots and raisins in a mixing bowl. Pour the boiling water over all and let cool.
3. Sift together the flour, sugar, baking soda and baking powder and stir into the cooled mixture. Stir in the walnuts.
4. Turn into a greased 8½-by-4½-by-2½-inch loaf pan. Bake one hour. Cool on a rack.
Yield: One loaf.

Sesame Bread Sticks   *Northern California*

7 cups flour, approximately
1 tablespoon salt
2 packages active dry yeast
1 tablespoon butter
2½ cups very hot water
1 egg white

1 tablespoon cold water
Sesame seeds
Coarse salt.

1. In the large bowl of an electric mixer, place two and one-half cups of the flour, the salt, yeast and butter.

2. While beating at medium speed, gradually stir in the very hot water. Beat two minutes. Add another cup of the flour and beat at high speed two minutes.

3. With a wooden spoon, beat in enough of the remaining flour to make a soft dough (the dough will be sticky). Place the dough in a greased bowl, cover and let rise in warm place until doubled in bulk, about one hour.

4. Punch dough down. Divide into four pieces.

5. Form each piece of dough into a roll eighteen inches long. Cut each roll into eighteen pieces. Form each piece into a roll about six inches long. Place on a greased baking sheet.

6. Cover and let rise in a warm place until doubled in bulk, about thirty minutes.

7. Preheat the oven to 400 degrees.

8. Combine the egg white and cold water and use to brush over bread sticks. Sprinkle with sesame seeds and coarse salt.

9. Bake twenty minutes, or until golden brown. Cool on a rack.

Yield: Six dozen.

Note: Caraway seeds may be substituted for sesame seeds.

Ham in Rye   *Washington*

1 package active dry yeast
¼ cup lukewarm water
2 tablespoons butter
2 teaspoons salt
2 tablespoons sugar
2 cups milk, scalded
1½ tablespoons caraway seeds
3 cups rye flour
3½ cups regular flour, approximately

1 three-pound canned ham, at room temperature
Yellow corn meal
1 egg white, lightly beaten
1 tablespoon water.

1. Dissolve the yeast in the lukewarm water.

2. Place the butter, salt and sugar in a bowl. Pour the milk over all. Stir to melt the butter. Let cool to lukewarm.

3. Stir the dissolved yeast into the cooled milk mixture. Stir in the caraway seeds, rye flour and enough of the regular flour to make a fairly stiff dough.

4. Turn onto a lightly floured board and knead until smooth and elastic, about ten minutes.

5. Place the dough in a clean greased bowl. Lightly grease the top of the dough, cover the bowl and let dough rise in a warm place until doubled in bulk, about one hour. Place the ham on a platter, cover and let warm in the same place as the bread dough for one hour.

6. Punch the dough down, cover and let stand five minutes.

7. Mark the dough in thirds. On a lightly floured board, press or roll out the center third to give a rectangle big enough to set the ham on and draw up the sides. The two thirds of dough on either end should be still attached and quite thick.

8. Place the ham on the thin center piece of dough, draw up the thin sides of the dough around the ham, then overlap the two thick ends over the top of the ham, pinching together to seal. Shape the dough-covered ham into a neat round and place on a greased ten-inch pie plate sprinkled with corn meal.

9. Cover with clear plastic wrap or a cloth and let rise in a warm place until doubled in bulk, about forty-five minutes.

10. Preheat the oven to 425 degrees.

11. Mix the egg white with the tablespoon water and use to brush the loaf. Bake ten minutes, reduce the oven heat to 375 degrees and bake fifty minutes longer, or until done. Serve hot, or cool on a rack and serve at room temperature.

Yield: Six to eight servings.

Sour Dough White Bread
Northern California

Starter:
1 package active dry yeast
2 cups warm water
2 cups flour.

Bread:
10 to eleven cups flour
4 cups warm water
1 cup starter
¼ cup sugar
2 packages active dry yeast
4 teaspoons salt.

1. Combine the starter ingredients in a large glass or ceramic bowl and mix until well blended. Let stand, uncovered, in a warm place at least forty-eight hours. Stir occasionally and add more warm water if mixture starts to dry out.

2. Starter is then ready to use. After the amount needed for a recipe is removed, the remainder should be replenished by adding equal quantities of warm water and flour and allowing the bowl to stand in a warm place until mixture bubbles well, at least eight hours.

3. Store, loosely covered, in the refrigerator and use and replenish at least once every two weeks.

4. To prepare bread, mix four cups of the flour with the water, starter and sugar. Beat until smooth and then cover with clear plastic wrap. Let stand in a warm place at least eighteen hours, stirring occasionally. The longer the mixture stands, the sourer the flavor.

5. Combine the yeast with the salt and two cups of the remaining flour and add to the bowl. Beat until well blended and then add enough of the remaining flour to give a moderately stiff dough. If the bread is to be shaped into free-standing loaves or rolls to be placed on a baking sheet, the dough should be slightly stiffer than dough that is to be baked in a loaf pan or casserole.

6. Turn the dough onto a lightly floured board and knead until smooth and satiny, ten to fifteen minutes. Divide the dough into three pieces, shape into rounds and place in three greased two-quart round glass casseroles, three 9-by-5-by-3-inch loaf pans or shape into eighteen to twenty-four dinner rolls or three long Italian loaves.

7. Score the tops of the loaves with slashes or in a lattice pattern. Cover and let rise in a warm place until doubled in bulk, about one and one-half hours for loaves and forty-five minutes for rolls.

8. Preheat the oven to 400 degrees.

9. Place a pan of boiling water in the bottom of the oven. Brush the top of the risen loaves or rolls with cold water. Bake forty to forty-five minutes for loaves and twenty-five to thirty minutes for rolls, brushing with water a couple of times during the baking.

10. Remove loaves from pans to cool.

Yield: Three loaves or eighteen to twenty-four rolls.

Sour Dough Pie Crust
Alaska

2 cups flour
½ teaspoon salt
¼ teaspoon baking soda
⅔ cup shortening
⅔ cup sour dough starter, approximately (recipe above).

1. Sift the flour, salt and baking soda into a bowl. With the finger tips or a pastry blender, blend in the shortening until the mixture resembles coarse oatmeal.

2. Stir in enough sour dough starter to make a dough. Cover the dough and let rise in a warm place thirty minutes. Roll out and use like ordinary pastry for pies and tarts.

Yield: Enough pastry for a two-crust pie.

Sour Dough Cinnamon Rolls   *Alaska*

¾ cup butter
½ cup plus one-third cup granulated sugar
1 teaspoon salt
1 cup milk, scalded
1½ teaspoons baking soda
2 cups sour dough starter (page 730)
5 cups flour, approximately
1 teaspoon cinnamon
½ cup raisins
½ cup light brown sugar
¼ cup honey.

1. Add one-quarter cup of the butter, one-half cup of the granulated sugar and the salt to the milk. Stir to melt butter. Let cool to room temperature. Dissolve the baking soda in a little warm water.

2. When milk mixture is cool, add the sour dough starter and the dissolved baking soda.

3. Stir in enough flour to make a soft dough. Knead on a lightly floured board until smooth. Place in a clean greased bowl, cover and let rise in a warm place until doubled in bulk.

4. Punch dough down. Roll out into a rectangle. Spread with one-quarter cup of the remaining butter. Combine remaining granulated sugar with the cinnamon and sprinkle over.

5. Sprinkle the raisins over granulated sugar. Roll rectangle from the long end like a jellyroll and cut into one-inch slices.

6. Heat remaining butter, the brown sugar and honey in a saucepan. Pour into a 9-by-5-by-3-inch loaf pan. Set the rolls, cut side up, in the butter-brown sugar mixture.

7. Cover and let rise in a warm place until doubled in bulk.

8. Preheat the oven to 375 degrees.

9. Bake fifteen to twenty minutes, or until done. Immediately turn out onto a serving plate.
Yield: Two dozen.

Sour Dough Hot Cakes   *Alaska*

2 cups flour
2 cups warm water
Sour dough starter (page 730)
2 eggs, lightly beaten
1 teaspoon baking soda
1 teaspoon salt
1 tablespoon sugar
2 tablespoons oil.

1. Night before, add the flour and water to the starter and set in a warm place.

2. Next day, remove one-half cup of the starter and put in a jar for replenishing. To the remaining starter, add the remaining ingredients.

3. Bake in large cakes on a hot greased griddle.
Yield: About one dozen.

Sour Dough French Bread   *Alaska*

½ cup milk, scalded
2 tablespoons sugar
½ teaspoon salt
1 tablespoon shortening
1 cup sour dough starter (page 730)
2¼ cups flour, approximately
Yellow corn meal.

1. Combine the milk, sugar, salt and shortening and stir to melt shortening. Let cool to lukewarm.

2. Add the sour dough starter and enough flour to make a medium-stiff dough. Turn onto a lightly floured board and knead until smooth.

3. Shape into a loaf and place on a greased baking sheet that has been dusted with corn meal. Cover loaf and let rise until doubled in bulk.

4. Preheat the oven to 400 degrees.

5. Make diagonal slashes over surface of bread and brush with water. Bake forty minutes, or until done, brushing with water twice during baking.
Yield: One loaf
Note: When using part of your sour dough

starter, do not forget to replenish the remainder (page 730).

dle and bake about two and one-half minutes on each side.

Yield: About six servings.

Gold Rush Style Sour Dough Pancakes
Nevada

For starter:
  1 cup warm water
  1 package active dry yeast
  1 cup flour
  3 teaspoons sugar.
For replenishing:
  1 cup warm water
  1 cup flour
  1 teaspoon sugar.
For pancakes:
  1 teaspoon baking soda
  1 teaspoon salt
  1 egg.

1. To prepare starter, place one-half cup of the water in a warm crock or glass jar. Add the yeast and dissolve. Stir in one-half cup of the flour and one teaspoon of the sugar. Cover with a cloth and set in a warm place for twenty-four hours.

2. Add one-quarter cup of the remaining water, one-quarter cup of the remaining flour and one teaspoon of the remaining sugar to jar, cover with cloth and set in a warm place for twenty-four hours.

3. Add remaining water, flour and sugar for starter, cover and set in a warm place for twenty-four hours.

4. Remove all the starter except two tablespoons or so to a mixing bowl. Add the warm water, flour and sugar to jar for replenishing starter. Let jar stand in a warm place at least three hours before refrigerating for future use. Warm up at least three hours before using again.

5. To prepare pancakes, add to the starter in the mixing bowl the baking soda, salt and egg and beat well. Check consistency. It should be a fairly thick griddlecake batter consistency. Add warm water if necessary. Spoon onto a hot greased grid-

Cottage Cheese Biscuits
Northern California

  2 cups flour
  4 teaspoons baking powder
  1½ teaspoons salt
  ¼ cup butter
  1 cup cottage cheese
  1 tablespoon chopped chives
  ⅔ cup milk, approximately.

1. Preheat the oven to 450 degrees.

2. Sift the flour, baking powder and one teaspoon of the salt into a bowl. With a pastry blender or the finger tips, work in the butter until mixture resembles coarse oatmeal.

3. Mix the cottage cheese with remaining salt and the chives and stir into flour mixture. Using a fork add enough milk to make a soft dough.

4. Turn out onto a floured board and knead thirty seconds. Pat out to one-half-inch thickness and cut with a floured two-inch biscuit cutter. Place on a greased baking sheet and bake twelve to fifteen minutes, or until done.

Yield: Two dozen.

Prune Nut Bread   *Northern California*

  3 cups flour
  1 cup sugar
  4 teaspoons baking powder
  1½ teaspoons salt
  ½ teaspoon cinnamon
  1 egg, lightly beaten
  1½ cups milk
  ¼ cup shortening
  1½ cups pitted prunes, cut into small pieces
  ½ cup walnuts.

1. Preheat the oven to 350 degrees.

2. Sift together the flour, sugar, baking powder, salt and cinnamon into a bowl. Add the egg, milk and shortening and stir until smooth.

3. Fold in the prunes and walnuts. Turn into a greased 9-by-5-by-3-inch loaf pan. Bake fifty to sixty minutes, or until bread tests done.

4. Let bread stand in pan ten minutes before turning out onto a rack to cool.

Yield: One loaf.

Stone-Ground Wheat Bread   *Oregon*

2 packages active dry yeast
⅔ cup lukewarm water
½ cup light brown sugar
1 tablespoon salt
2 cups milk, scalded
7 cups stone-ground wheat flour,
    approximately (see note)
3 tablespoons melted shortening.

1. Dissolve the yeast in the water, add one teaspoon of the brown sugar and set aside.

2. Add remaining brown sugar and the salt to hot milk and let cool to lukewarm. Stir yeast into cooled mixture.

3. Stir in three cups of the flour, the shortening and then enough extra flour to make a medium-soft dough.

4. Turn out onto a lightly floured board and knead until smooth, about ten minutes. Place in a greased bowl, cover and let rise in a warm place until doubled in bulk, about one and one-half hours.

5. Punch dough down and shape into two loaves. Place each in a greased 9-by-5-by-3-inch loaf pan. Cover and let rise in a warm place until doubled in bulk, about one hour.

6. Preheat the oven to 400 degrees.

7. Bake forty minutes, or until bread tests done. Cool on a rack.

Yield: Two loaves.

Note: Stone-ground wheat flour is available in specialty and health food stores.

Poi Muffins   *Hawaii*

1⅓ cups flour
½ teaspoon salt
1 tablespoon sugar
4 teaspoons baking powder
⅔ cup poi (see note)
1 egg, lightly beaten
3 tablespoons melted butter
⅓ cup milk.

1. Preheat the oven to 400 degrees.

2. Sift the flour, salt, sugar and baking powder into a bowl. Blend the poi with the egg, butter and milk and stir into dry ingredients until only just moistened.

3. Spoon into greased muffin tins. Bake twenty-five minutes, or until done.

Yield: One dozen.

Note: Poi, a starchy staple made from taro root, is available canned in specialty food stores on the mainland.

Mollie's Salmon Muffins   *Washington*

2 cups flour
3 teaspoons baking powder
1 teaspoon salt
2 teaspoons sugar
¼ cup shortening
1 cup milk
1 egg
1 seven-and-three-quarter-ounce can salmon,
    skinned, boned and flaked.

1. Preheat the oven to 400 degrees.

2. Sift together the flour, baking powder, salt and sugar. With a pastry blender or the finger tips, blend in the shortening until mixture resembles coarse oatmeal.

3. Combine the milk and egg and stir into the dry ingredients just enough to moisten. Fold in the salmon. Fill greased muffin tins two-thirds full. Bake twenty minutes, or until done.

Yield: One dozen.

Guava Muffins

Hawaii

2 cups flour
3 tablespoons sugar
½ teaspoon salt
3 teaspoons baking powder
1 cup milk
2 eggs, lightly beaten
3 tablespoons melted shortening
½ cup cooked or canned guava pulp (see note).

1. Preheat the oven to 400 degrees.
2. Sift together the flour, sugar, salt and baking powder. Combine the milk and eggs and stir into dry ingredients.
3. Stir in the shortening and guava pulp until ingredients are just mixed. Fill greased muffin tins two-thirds full. Bake twenty minutes, or until done.

Yield: Sixteen.

Note: Guava shells are available in specialty food stores and can be blended in an electric blender to give pulp.

Orange Bread

Northern California

Peel of three oranges
Lightly salted boiling water
2 cups sugar
2 tablespoons water
4 cups flour
3 teaspoons baking powder
1 cup milk
2 eggs, lightly beaten
¼ teaspoon salt
¾ cup chopped walnuts.

1. Preheat the oven to 350 degrees.
2. With a sharp-edged spoon, scrape as much of the white pith off the orange peel as possible. With scissors, cut peel into strips.
3. Add peel to lightly salted boiling water and simmer until tender, about ten minutes. Drain.
4. Add one cup of the sugar and the two table-spoons water to the peel. Boil until clear, about one minute. Cool. Sift the flour with the baking powder.
5. When peel mixture is cool, add the remaining sugar, the milk, eggs, salt and the flour mixture. Mix. Fold in the walnuts.
6. Turn into two greased 9-by-5-by-3-inch loaf pans that have the bottoms lined with oiled paper. Bake about fifty minutes, or until loaves test done.

Yield: Two loaves.

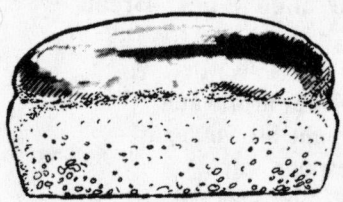

Fresh Pineapple Loaf

Hawaii

¼ cup butter
¾ cup light brown sugar
2 eggs
1¾ cups flour
2 teaspoons baking powder
½ teaspoon salt
¼ teaspoon baking soda
¾ cup coarsely chopped macadamia nuts
1 cup finely shredded fresh pineapple with natural juices.

1. Preheat the oven to 350 degrees.
2. Cream the butter and brown sugar together until light and fluffy. Beat in the eggs, one at a time.
3. Sift together the flour, baking powder, salt and baking soda. Stir in the nuts. Stir half the flour mixture into the creamed mixture. Fold in the pineapple. Fold in remaining flour mixture.
4. Turn into a greased 9-by-5-by-3-inch loaf pan and bake one hour, or until done.

Yield: One loaf.

David's Pancake

Hawaii

½ cup flour
½ cup milk
2 eggs, lightly beaten
Pinch of nutmeg
4 tablespoons butter
2 tablespoons confectioners' sugar
Juice of half a lemon
Jelly, jam or marmalade.

1. Preheat the oven to 425 degrees.
2. In a mixing bowl, combine the flour, milk, eggs and nutmeg. Beat lightly. Leave the batter a little lumpy.
3. Melt the butter in a twelve-inch skillet with heatproof handle. When butter is very hot, pour in batter. Bake in oven fifteen to twenty minutes, or until golden brown.
4. Sprinkle with the confectioners' sugar and return briefly to the oven. Sprinkle with lemon juice; then serve with jelly, jam or marmalade.

Yield: Two to four servings.

Bread Crumb Hot Cakes

Washington

2 cups buttermilk
1 cup soft bread crumbs
2 eggs, separated
1 teaspoon baking soda
1¼ teaspoons baking powder
1 teaspoon salt
1 tablespoon sugar
1½ cups flour
Cooked sausages
Baked apple slices.

1. Night before, pour the buttermilk over the bread crumbs and hold in the refrigerator.
2. Next morning, add the egg yolks, baking soda, baking powder, salt, sugar and flour. Beat the egg whites until stiff but not dry and fold into batter.
3. Cook slowly, one-quarter cup for each cake, on a hot greased griddle. Serve with sausages and apple slices.

Yield: Four servings.

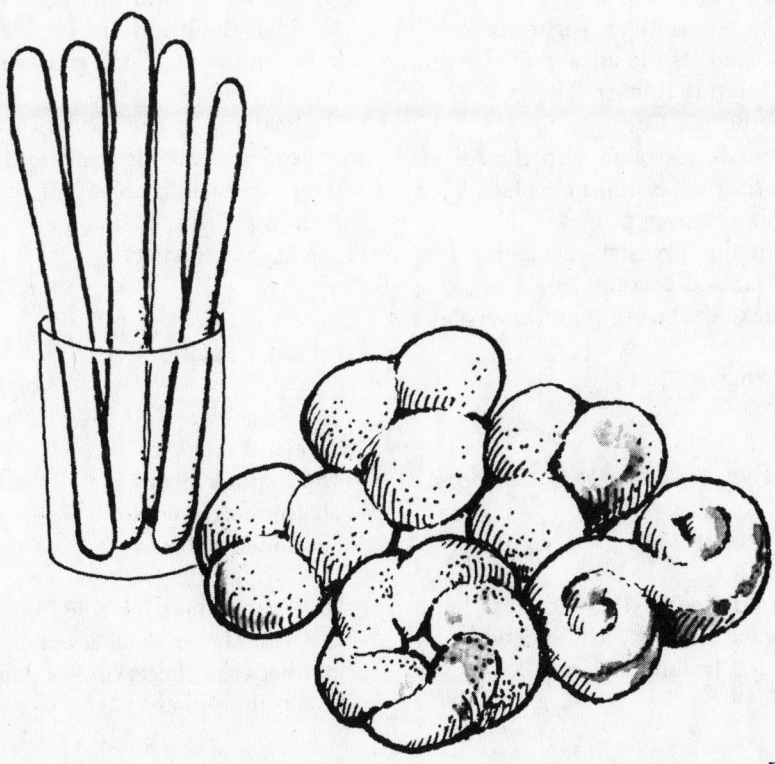

Pies, Cakes, Desserts and Cookies

Prune Pie
Northern California

2 cups orange juice
⅓ cup sugar
1 tablespoon cornstarch
2 tablespoons butter
  Pastry for a two-crust nine-inch pie
2 cups pitted prunes.

1. Preheat the oven to 400 degrees.
2. Combine the orange juice, sugar and cornstarch in a saucepan. Bring to a boil, stirring constantly until mixture thickens. Remove from heat and add the butter. Cool.
3. Line a nine-inch pie plate with the rolled-out pastry. Place the prunes in the pie plate. Pour cooled orange mixture over prunes.
4. Roll out remaining pastry to make a top. Place over pie. Seal and decorate edges, make a steam hole and bake thirty-five minutes, or until done.
Yield: Six servings.

Fresh Apricot Pie
Northern California

3 eggs, separated
1 cup sugar
1½ cups apricot pulp (peeled, pitted fresh apricots blended in an electric blender)
¼ teaspoon grated lemon rind
⅛ teaspoon salt
1 envelope unflavored gelatin
¼ cup cold water
1 nine-inch graham cracker crust (recipe below)
  Fresh apricot slices.

1. In the top of a double boiler, beat the egg yolks with one-half cup of the sugar. Stir in the apricot pulp, lemon rind and salt. Cook, stirring, over hot water until mixture thickens.
2. Soak the gelatin in the water and stir into the hot mixture. Cool and chill until mixture starts to thicken.
3. Beat the egg whites with remaining sugar until stiff but not dry and fold into thickening mixture. Pour into crust and chill. Garnish with the apricot slices.
Yield: Six servings.

Graham Cracker Crust
Northern California

15 graham crackers
1 tablespoon sugar
½ teaspoon cinnamon
¼ cup melted butter.

1. Preheat the oven to 375 degrees.
2. Crumble the crackers in an electric blender or put between sheets of wax paper and crumble with a rolling pin.

3. Add the remaining ingredients to the crumbs and press against the sides and bottom of a buttered nine-inch pie plate.

4. Bake eight minutes. Cool.

Yield: One nine-inch pie shell.

Cranberry-Filbert Tart   *Oregon*

1 cup butter
1 cup granulated sugar
3 egg yolks
1 cup finely chopped toasted filberts
1¼ cups flour
½ teaspoon salt
3 cups cranberries
½ cup light brown sugar
1 tablespoon grated orange rind
⅓ cup orange juice
  Whole filberts.

1. Cream together the butter and granulated sugar until light and fluffy.

2. Beat in the egg yolks. Stir in the chopped filberts, flour and one-quarter teaspoon of the salt. Mix well. Wrap in wax paper and chill two hours or longer.

3. Meanwhile, combine the cranberries, brown sugar, orange rind, orange juice and remaining salt in a saucepan. Bring to a boil and simmer, uncovered, fifteen minutes, or until thick as jam. Cool.

4. Preheat the oven to 375 degrees.

5. Reserve one-half cup chilled dough and pat remaining dough against bottom and sides of a nine-inch tart pan, pie plate or layer pan. Spread cooled cranberry mixture over.

6. Roll out reserved pastry and cut into strips. Form strips into a lattice over fruit. Place a whole filbert in each square formed. Bake forty minutes, or until pastry is done. Serve warm or at room temperature.

Yield: Six servings.

Apple and Apricot Pie   *Washington*

½ cup dried apricots, diced
½ cup water
4 cups diced peeled apples
  Sugar
¼ cup flour
¼ teaspoon nutmeg
¼ teaspoon cinnamon
⅛ teaspoon salt
  Pastry for two-crust nine-inch pie
2 tablespoons butter
⅓ cup finely chopped filberts
  Milk
  Whipped cream.

1. Preheat the oven to 400 degrees.

2. Place the apricots and water in a saucepan and bring to a boil. Cover and simmer five minutes, or until fruit is tender and water absorbed.

3. Add the apples to apricots. Mix together one and one-quarter cups sugar, the flour, nutmeg, cinnamon and salt and stir into fruit mixture.

4. Roll out half the pastry and use to line a nine-inch pie plate. Spoon in the fruit mixture. Dot with the butter and sprinkle with the filberts.

5. Roll out remaining pastry and cut into strips. Make a lattice top over fruit. Brush pastry with milk and sprinkle with sugar. Bake forty minutes, or until pastry is golden. Cool pie to room temperature. Serve with whipped cream.

Yield: Six servings.

Marie's Apple Custard Pie   *Washington*

½ cup sugar
¼ cup water
3 large apples, peeled, cored and cut into eighths
½ cup raisins
  Boiling water
1 unbaked nine-inch pie shell, chilled
¼ teaspoon salt
½ teaspoon cinnamon

1 egg, lightly beaten
½ teaspoon vanilla
½ cup milk, scalded.

1. Preheat the oven to 425 degrees.
2. Combine one-quarter cup of the sugar and the one-quarter cup water in a saucepan and bring to a boil. Add the apples, cover and simmer five minutes.
3. Cover the raisins with boiling water and let stand one minute. Drain well.
4. With a slotted spoon, remove apple slices from syrup and arrange in the pie shell. Sprinkle with raisins.
5. Mix two tablespoons of the remaining sugar with the salt and cinnamon and sprinkle over fruit. Bake fifteen minutes.
6. Beat the egg with remaining sugar and the vanilla. Add the milk. Pour over apple-raisin mixture. Reduce oven heat to 325 degrees and bake until custard is set, about twenty minutes longer.
Yield: Six servings.

Mincemeat-Pumpkin Pie   *Oregon*

1½ cups mincemeat
 1 unbaked nine-inch pie shell, chilled
 1 cup mashed cooked pumpkin
½ cup sugar
½ teaspoon cinnamon
 2 eggs, lightly beaten
¼ teaspoon salt
¼ teaspoon nutmeg
½ cup milk.

1. Preheat the oven to 425 degrees.
2. Place the mincemeat in the bottom of the pie shell.
3. Using a rotary beater, combine the remaining ingredients. Pour over mincemeat. Bake thirty-five to forty minutes, or until set. Serve slightly warm or at room temperature.
Yield: Six servings.

Crumb-Topped Plum Pies   *Washington*

 4 cups sliced pitted purple prune plums
2/3 cup granulated sugar
 2 tablespoons cornstarch
¼ teaspoon salt
 1 teaspoon grated orange rind
 6 four-inch tart pans, lined with unbaked pastry and well chilled, or one unbaked nine-inch pie shell, chilled
¾ cup flour
½ cup light brown sugar
½ teaspoon cinnamon
¼ teaspoon nutmeg
¼ cup butter.

1. Preheat the oven to 400 degrees.
2. Combine the plum slices, granulated sugar, cornstarch, salt and orange rind. Divide among the tart pans or place in pie shell.
3. Combine the flour, brown sugar, cinnamon and nutmeg in a bowl. With a pastry blender or the finger tips, blend in the butter until mixture resembles coarse crumbs. Sprinkle over tarts or shell. Bake tarts thirty to thirty-five minutes or pie forty-five minutes.
Yield: Six servings.

Purple Prune Plum Pie   *Washington*

 4 cups purple prune plums (about three pounds)
 1 cup sugar
1½ teaspoons grated lemon rind
1½ teaspoons grated orange rind
 3 tablespoons flour
½ teaspoon cinnamon
½ teaspoon nutmeg
½ cup coarsely chopped walnuts
   Pastry for a two-crust nine-inch pie
 1 tablespoon fine dry bread crumbs
 2 tablespoons butter
   Whipped cream.

1. Preheat the oven to 400 degrees.

2. Pit and quarter the plums and place in a bowl. Combine the sugar, lemon rind, orange rind, flour and spices and stir together with the walnuts into the plums.

3. Roll out two-thirds of the pastry and use to line a nine-inch pie pan. Sprinkle the bottom with the bread crumbs. Fill with the plum mixture. Dot with the butter.

4. Roll out remaining pastry and use to cover pie. Seal well, decorate edges and make a steam hole.

5. Bake about fifty minutes. (Strips of aluminum foil can be placed around the edges of the pan to prevent boil-over. Remove foil strips before serving.)

6. Serve pie with whipped cream.

Yield: Six to eight servings.

Note: Unbaked plum pies freeze well. Slash crust of frozen pie and bake, unthawed, one and one-quarter hours, or until done.

Mock Cherry Pie   *Alaska*

1 cup Alaskan high bush cranberries
½ cup raisins, finely chopped
1 cup sugar
1 tablespoon flour
1 cup boiling water
1 teaspoon vanilla
  Pastry for a two-crust nine-inch pie.

1. Preheat the oven to 425 degrees.

2. Combine the cranberries, raisins, sugar, flour, water and vanilla.

3. Roll out half the pastry and use to line a nine-inch pie plate. Pour in the cranberry filling. Roll out remaining pastry and use to cover pie. Seal well, decorate edges and make a steam hole.

4. Bake forty minutes, or until pastry is golden and berries are tender.

Yield: Six servings.

Note: Alaskan high bush cranberries are not true cranberries. They have large flat seeds.

Pioneer McGinties   *Oregon*

1 pound dried apples
1½ cups light brown sugar
⅛ teaspoon salt
1 tablespoon cinnamon
  Pastry made with three cups flour
2 tablespoons butter.

1. Day before, rinse the apples and cover with water. Let soak overnight. Next day, simmer in soaking water until tender, adding more water if necessary.

2. Blend the apples in an electric blender or force through a food mill or colander. Place in a saucepan with the brown sugar, salt and cinnamon.

3. Cook slowly until very thick, stirring to prevent scorching. Cool.

4. Preheat the oven to 425 degrees.

5. Line a 9-by-13-inch baking pan with rolled-out pastry. Spoon in the cooled apple mixture. Dot with the butter. Top with remaining pastry. Seal well, decorate edges and make steam holes.

6. Bake ten minutes, reduce oven heat to 350 degrees and bake twenty-five minutes longer, or until pastry is done.

Yield: One dozen servings.

Depoe Bay Blackberry Tarts   *Oregon*

8 cups wild blackberries
1½ cups sugar
3 tablespoons cornstarch
½ cup water
12 baked three-inch tart shells
  Whipped cream.

1. Crush four cups of the berries and place in a saucepan with the sugar, cornstarch and water. Bring to a boil and cook, stirring, until mixture thickens.

2. Stir in the remaining berries left whole.

Spoon into the tart shells and chill. Serve topped with whipped cream.

Yield: One dozen.

Wild Gooseberry Tart   *Nevada*

4 cups wild or cultivated gooseberries
1 cup sugar, or to taste according to tartness
    of berries
⅓ cup water
1 tablespoon flour
1 unbaked nine-inch pie shell
1 egg white, lightly beaten
2 egg yolks
¼ cup heavy cream
¼ cup sour cream
¼ teaspoon cinnamon.

1. Combine the gooseberries, sugar and water in a saucepan and heat to boiling. Simmer gently until berries are barely tender.
2. Sprinkle the flour on top and stir in well. Allow to cool.
3. Preheat the oven to 425 degrees.
4. Prick the pie shell and bake ten minutes, or until set but not browned. Reduce the oven temperature to 350 degrees.
5. Brush the inside of partly baked pie shell with the egg white. Add cooled berry mixture.
6. Mix together the egg yolks, heavy cream, sour cream and cinnamon and pour over berries. Bake twenty minutes, or until done.

Yield: Six servings.

Fresh Strawberry Tart   *Oregon*

8 cups strawberries
1 baked nine-inch pie shell
¾ cup sugar
¼ cup cornstarch
⅓ cup water
2 teaspoons lemon juice
    Whipped cream.

1. Arrange half the berries in the pie shell.
2. Crush the remaining berries and mix with the sugar, cornstarch and water in a saucepan. Bring to a boil and cook, stirring, until mixture thickens.
3. Add the lemon juice and spoon mixture over berries in the pie shell. Chill. Serve decorated with whipped cream.

Yield: Six servings.

Fresh Coconut Upside-Down Cake
                                                 Hawaii

½ cup butter
1 cup light brown sugar
1½ cups grated fresh coconut
¼ cup shortening
½ cup granulated sugar
1 egg
1 cup cake flour
1¼ teaspoons baking powder
⅛ teaspoon salt
⅓ cup milk
½ teaspoon vanilla
    Whipped cream.

1. Preheat the oven to 350 degrees.
2. Melt the butter and brown sugar in an eight-inch square baking pan. Sprinkle the coconut over to make an even layer.
3. Cream together the shortening and granulated sugar until light and fluffy. Beat in the egg. Sift together the flour, baking powder and salt. Combine the milk and vanilla. Add dry ingredients to batter alternately with milk mixture.
4. Pour batter over coconut and bake forty-five minutes, or until done. Invert onto a serving plate and serve warm, with whipped cream.

Yield: Eight servings.

Rub-Up Fruit Cake   *Oregon*

3 cups flour
1 cup butter

1 teaspoon baking powder
½ teaspoon nutmeg
½ teaspoon cinnamon
½ teaspoon ground cloves
1 pound raisins
2 pounds dates, pitted and cut in half
½ pound shelled walnuts
2 pounds mixed candied fruit
½ pound candied cherries
½ teaspoon baking soda
2 tablespoons boiling water
6 eggs
1½ cups sugar
2 cups dry white wine.

1. Preheat the oven to 275 degrees.
2. Place the flour in a bowl. With a pastry blender or the finger tips, work the butter into flour.
3. Add the baking powder, nutmeg, cinnamon and cloves. Combine the raisins, dates, walnuts, candied fruit and candied cherries and add to flour mixture. Toss to coat.
4. Dissolve the baking soda in the water. Beat the eggs until thick; then beat in the sugar, dissolved baking soda and one cup of the wine.
5. Fold in flour-and-fruit mixture. Turn into three 8½-by-4½-by-2½-inch loaf pans that have been greased, then lined with unglazed brown paper or parchment paper. Bake about two hours, or until cakes test done (a straw inserted into center of cake will come out clean).
6. Pour remaining cup of wine over hot cakes. Let cool in the pans.
Yield: Three cakes.

Quick Orange-Ginger Cake
Northern California

1½ cups flour
1 teaspoon baking powder
¼ teaspoon salt
2 teaspoons cinnamon
1 teaspoon ginger

½ teaspoon ground cloves
½ teaspoon ground allspice
½ teaspoon nutmeg
⅓ cup melted lard or shortening
½ cup light molasses
¼ cup sugar
1 egg
1 teaspoon baking soda
½ cup boiling water
1 tablespoon grated orange rind
⅓ cup chopped walnuts.

1. Preheat the oven to 325 degrees.
2. Sift the flour, baking powder, salt, cinnamon, ginger, cloves, allspice and nutmeg into a bowl.
3. Combine the lard or shortening with the molasses and sugar. Beat in the egg. Pour into dry ingredients and mix until moistened. Dissolve the baking soda in the water and stir into batter. Beat thirty seconds.
4. Stir in the orange rind and walnuts and turn into a one-and-one-half-quart ring mold, greased and floured on the bottom only. Bake thirty minutes or until done. Cool in the pan twenty minutes; then turn out onto a rack. Serve warm.
Yield: Eight servings.

Pioneer Chocolate-Potato Cake
Nevada

¾ cup butter
2 cups sugar
4 eggs, separated
2 cups flour
2 teaspoons baking powder
1 teaspoon nutmeg
1 teaspoon ground cloves
1 teaspoon cinnamon
2 tablespoons cocoa powder
½ teaspoon salt
½ teaspoon baking soda
1 cup plus two tablespoons buttermilk
1 cup cold mashed potatoes
1 teaspoon vanilla.

1. Preheat the oven to 350 degrees.

2. Cream the butter and sugar together until very fluffy and light. Beat in the egg yolks, one at a time, very well.

3. Sift together the flour, baking powder, nutmeg, cloves, cinnamon, cocoa powder, salt and baking soda. Blend together the buttermilk and potatoes.

4. Stir the dry ingredients into the creamed mixture alternately with the buttermilk mixture. Stir in the vanilla.

5. Beat the egg whites until stiff but not dry and fold in. Turn mixture into two greased eight-inch square baking pans and bake forty-five minutes, or until done.

Yield: Two cakes.

Sour Cream Coffeecake

Northern California

6 tablespoons butter
¾ cup plus two tablespoons granulated sugar
1 egg
1¼ teaspoons vanilla
1½ cups flour
1¼ teaspoons baking powder
¼ teaspoon baking soda
¼ teaspoon salt
¾ cup sour cream
½ cup chopped walnuts
1 teaspoon cinnamon
1 cup confectioners' sugar
1 tablespoon milk.

1. Preheat the oven to 350 degrees.

2. Cream together the butter and three-quarters cup of the granulated sugar until light and fluffy. Beat in the egg and one teaspoon of the vanilla.

3. Sift the flour with the baking powder, baking soda and salt. Add alternately with the sour cream to the creamed mixture. Spoon half the mixture into a greased two-quart mold.

4. Sprinkle with half the walnuts. Mix remaining granulated sugar with the cinnamon and sprinkle over the nuts. Top with remaining batter. Bake about forty-five minutes, or until done.

5. Let stand in pan fifteen minutes before turning out onto a rack to cool.

6. Combine the confectioners' sugar, milk and remaining vanilla and drizzle over cake. Sprinkle with remaining nuts.

Yield: Ten servings.

Rhubarb and Strawberry Roll *Oregon*

1½ cups plus one tablespoon sugar
1 cup water
2 cups flour
½ teaspoon salt
2½ teaspoons baking powder
⅓ cup butter
½ cup milk
1 cup diced rhubarb
1 cup halved strawberries
1 tablespoon cinnamon
Whipped cream.

1. Preheat the oven to 400 degrees.

2. In a saucepan, combine one cup of the sugar with the water. Bring to a boil and boil five minutes. Pour into a 6-by-10-inch or 8-by-8-inch baking dish.

3. Sift together the flour, salt, one tablespoon of the remaining sugar and the baking powder into a bowl. With a pastry blender or the finger tips, work the butter into the dry ingredients until mixture resembles coarse oatmeal.

4. Stir in the milk just until ingredients are moistened. Turn onto a lightly floured board and knead thirty seconds.

5. Roll into a 15-by-8-inch rectangle. Spread with the fruit. Combine remaining sugar with the cinnamon and sprinkle over fruit. Starting at the long end, roll like a jellyroll. Cut into ten or twelve pieces and place, cut side up, in the syrup in the baking dish.

6. Bake twenty-five to thirty minutes, or until done. Serve hot, with whipped cream.

Yield: Five or six servings.

Note: Whole raspberries may be substituted for the strawberries.

Rhubarb Cake Pudding   *Washington*

2 cups sugar
¼ cup flour
2 tablespoons melted butter
2 cups milk
¼ teaspoon salt
4 eggs, separated
2 cups cooked rhubarb, without added sugar.

1. Preheat the oven to 325 degrees.
2. Combine the sugar and flour in a bowl. Mix together the butter, milk and salt and stir into flour mixture.
3. Lightly beat the egg yolks and stir into batter with the rhubarb.
4. Beat the egg whites until stiff but not dry and fold in. Pour into a greased shallow baking dish. Set in a pan of boiling water and bake until set, about forty-five minutes.
Yield: Four servings.

Peach Preserve Cake   *Oregon*

Cake layers:
¾ cup butter
1 cup sugar
3 eggs, separated
2 cups flour
⅛ teaspoon salt
1 teaspoon baking soda
½ cup buttermilk
1 cup (twelve-ounce jar) peach or apricot
   preserves.
Filling and frosting:
2 cup sugar
1 cup milk
  Shredded coconut
1 small orange, ground and drained of extra
   juice

1 cup chopped nuts
1 cup crushed pineapple, drained.

1. Preheat the oven to 350 degrees.
2. To prepare cake layers, cream the butter and sugar together until very light and fluffy. Beat in the egg yolks, one at a time.
3. Sift together the flour and salt. Stir the baking soda into the buttermilk. Beginning and ending with flour mixture, stir the flour mixture into batter alternately with buttermilk mixture.
4. Fold in the preserves.
5. Beat the egg whites until stiff but not dry and fold into the batter. Spoon into two greased nine-inch layer pans lined on the bottom with wax paper.
6. Bake thirty-five to forty-five minutes, or until cake layers test done. Cool on a rack.
7. To prepare filling and frosting, place the sugar and milk in a heavy saucepan and bring to a boil, stirring until the sugar is dissolved.
8. Boil, stirring to prevent sticking, only until mixture reaches 260 degrees on a candy thermometer. Cool slightly and then beat until creamy.
9. As mixture thickens, quickly stir in one cup coconut, the orange, nuts and pineapple. Use to fill and frost the cooled cake layers. Sprinkle top and sides with extra coconut.
Yield: Ten servings.

Blueberry Upside-Down Squares
Alaska

1½ cups blueberries
½ cup light brown sugar
1 tablespoon butter
¼ cup shortening
½ cup granulated sugar
1 egg, beaten
1 teaspoon grated orange rind
1¼ cups cake flour
¼ teaspoon salt
1½ teaspoons baking powder

⅓ cup orange juice
Whipped cream.

1. Preheat the oven to 350 degrees.
2. Combine the blueberries, brown sugar and butter in a saucepan. Bring to a boil and simmer five minutes. Turn into a greased eight-inch square baking pan.
3. Cream the shortening and granulated sugar together until light and fluffy. Beat in the egg and orange rind.
4. Sift together the flour, salt and baking powder and add to batter alternately with the orange juice. Spoon batter over berries. Bake forty-five minutes, or until done. Invert onto a plate. Cut into squares and serve warm, with whipped cream.
Yield: Six servings.

Sweet Beef Balls   *Washington*

1 tablespoon butter
1 cup cooked ground beef
1 cup raisins, ground
1 medium-size apple, peeled, cored and ground
1 cup light brown sugar
½ cup chopped walnuts
2 teaspoons cognac
1½ cups graham cracker crumbs
Confectioners' sugar.

1. Melt the butter in a saucepan and add the beef, raisins and apple. Add the brown sugar and cook over low heat, stirring, until mixture becomes quite thick. Add the walnuts and cognac and let cool.
2. Work in the graham cracker crumbs and form mixture into one-inch balls. Roll in confectioners' sugar and store in a covered container in the refrigerator.
Yield: About thirty.

Beef 'n' Fruit Bars   *Washington*

1 cup ground cooked beef
1 cup chopped peeled apple
½ cup raisins
½ cup light brown sugar
¼ cup currant jelly
1 tablespoon cider vinegar
¼ teaspoon salt
¼ teaspoon cinnamon
⅛ teaspoon ground cloves
⅛ teaspoon nutmeg
⅛ teaspoon mace
1 envelope unflavored gelatin
¼ cup water
½ cup chopped nuts
Confectioners' sugar.

1. Combine the beef, apple, raisins, brown sugar, jelly, vinegar, salt, cinnamon, cloves, nutmeg and mace in a saucepan. Heat, stirring frequently, over gentle heat until apple is cooked, about fifteen minutes.
2. Soften the gelatin in the water and add to hot mixture. Stir in the nuts and pour mixture into a greased eight-inch square pan.
3. Chill in the refrigerator until firm.
4. Cut into pieces measuring one inch by about one and one-half inches. Coat with confectioners' sugar. Store in the refrigerator.
Yield: Four dozen.

Gugelhopf with Filberts   *Oregon*

1 package active dry yeast
¼ cup lukewarm water
½ cup milk, scalded and cooled to lukewarm
2⅔ cups flour
1 cup raisins
Boiling water
⅔ cup butter
½ cup granulated sugar
4 eggs
1 tablespoon dark rum
¾ teaspoon salt

2 teaspoons grated lemon rind
¼ cup graham cracker crumbs
⅓ cup chopped toasted filberts
   Confectioners' sugar.

1. Dissolve the yeast in the lukewarm water. Combine with the milk. Beat in one cup of the flour.

2. Cover bowl and let mixture rise in a warm place until doubled in bulk, about one hour.

3. Cover the raisins with boiling water. Let stand five minutes and drain.

4. Cream the butter and granulated sugar together until light and fluffy. Beat in the eggs, one at a time, very well.

5. Beat in the rum and the salt.

6. Stir in the raised yeast mixture and remaining flour. Beat until smooth. Stir in the lemon rind and raisins.

7. Beat the batter, with an electric mixer if desired, until very smooth and elastic, at least ten minutes.

8. Generously grease a two-quart bundt pan or heavy cake pan. Sprinkle with the graham cracker crumbs. Arrange some of the filberts in bottom of pan. Carefully pour in half the batter. Sprinkle with remaining filberts and pour in remaining batter. Cover and let rise in a warm place until doubled in bulk, about one hour.

9. Preheat the oven to 350 degrees.

10. Bake one hour, or until cake tests done. Let cool in pan fifteen minutes before turning out onto a rack to finish cooling. Sprinkle with confectioners' sugar.

Yield: One dozen servings.

Dutch Plum Kuchen   *Washington*

Kuchen dough:
½ cup soft butter
¼ cup plus two tablespoons sugar
1 cup milk, scalded
1 package active dry yeast
¼ cup lukewarm water
¼ teaspoon powdered mace

¾ teaspoon salt
2 eggs, well beaten
4 cups flour, approximately.
Topping:
4 tablespoons soft butter
6 tablespoons dry bread crumbs
40 fresh purple prune plums, pitted and cut into quarters
1 cup sugar
1 teaspoon cinnamon
4 tablespoons melted butter
2 egg yolks
2 tablespoons heavy cream.

1. To prepare dough, place the butter and one-quarter cup of the sugar in a large bowl and pour in the milk. Allow to cool to lukewarm.

2. Dissolve the yeast and the remaining sugar in the water. Stir into milk mixture. Stir in the mace, salt and eggs.

3. Gradually beat in the flour to make a soft dough. Turn onto a lightly floured board and knead until smooth, about five minutes. Form into a ball, place in a greased bowl and grease the top of the dough. Cover with a cloth and let stand in a warm place until doubled in bulk, about one hour.

4. Knead again, return to bowl, cover and allow to rise a second time until doubled in bulk. Divide dough in half. Fit half the dough into a well-greased ten-inch round or square pan.

5. To prepare topping, spread dough in pan with two tablespoons of the soft butter. Sprinkle with three tablespoons of the bread crumbs. Cover and let stand fifteen minutes.

6. Arrange half the plums in an attractive pattern over the dough. Sprinkle with one-half cup of the sugar mixed with one-half teaspoon of the cinnamon. Combine two tablespoons of the melted butter, one of the egg yolks and one tablespoon of the cream. Drizzle over plums.

7. Repeat with remaining dough and topping ingredients for a second kuchen.

8. Preheat the oven to 350 degrees.

9. Let the kuchens stand in a warm place fifteen minutes, or until the dough is light. Bake

fifty minutes, or until crust is brown and plums are soft. Serve hot.

Yield: Two kuchens; eight servings each.

Note: To freeze one of the kuchens, chill quickly in the pan in which it was baked, wrap in freezer wrap or aluminum foil, and freeze. To serve, heat, without thawing, in a 350-degree oven.

Butter Twists   *Washington*

  1 package active dry yeast
¼ cup warm water
3½ cups flour
1½ teaspoons salt
  1 cup butter
  2 eggs, lightly beaten
½ cup sour cream
  1 teaspoon vanilla
1½ cups sugar
  1 tablespoon vanilla sugar concentrate or one teaspoon bits of the inside of a vanilla bean.

1. Dissolve the yeast in the water.
2. Mix together the flour and salt. With the finger tips or a pastry blender, work in the butter as though making pastry.
3. Stir in the eggs, sour cream, vanilla and softened yeast. Chill dough at least two hours. (It can be held two to three days.)
4. Preheat the oven to 375 degrees.
5. Divide dough in half. Mix the sugar with the vanilla sugar concentrate or vanilla bean bits. Use half the mixture for each dough half.
6. Roll out half the dough on a lightly floured board to a rectangle 16 by 8 inches. Sprinkle with the sugar mixture.
7. Fold one end of dough to the center, fold opposite end over to make three layers and pinch to seal. Repeat rolling, sprinkling and folding twice more.
8. Roll out to one-quarter-inch thickness. Cut into 4-by-1-inch strips. Give each strip two twists and place on an ungreased baking sheet.

9. Repeat with remaining dough and sugar mixture.
10. Bake fifteen minutes, or until golden. Cool on a rack.

Yield: About five dozen.

Oregon Farmhouse Coffeecakes

Basic dough:
4½ cups flour, approximately
  2 packages active dry yeast
½ teaspoon nutmeg
½ cup milk
½ cup water
½ cup sugar
¼ cup oil
  2 teaspoons salt
  2 teaspoons grated lemon rind
  2 eggs.
Mincemeat coffeecake:
  1 cup mincemeat
1½ cups sugar
1½ teaspoons nutmeg
¾ cup melted butter.
OR
Lemon loaves:
  2 teaspoons grated lemon rind
  2 tablespoons lemon juice
1¼ cups sugar
½ cup chopped pecans
⅓ cup melted butter
¼ cup flour
  2 tablespoons butter.

1. To prepare basic coffeecake dough, place two cups of the flour, the yeast and nutmeg in the bowl of an electric mixer.
2. Heat together the milk, water, sugar, oil and salt to lukewarm, stirring to dissolve the sugar.
3. While beating at medium speed, add the lemon rind and the milk mixture to the flour mixture. Beat two minutes. Beat in the eggs. Add another cup of the remaining flour and beat one minute.
4. Remove bowl from mixing machine and,

with a wooden spoon, beat in enough remaining flour to make a medium-stiff dough. Turn onto a lightly floured board and knead until smooth and satiny, about eight minutes.

5. Place the dough in a clean greased bowl, turn to grease all sides, cover and let rise in a warm place until doubled in bulk, about one hour.

6. The one recipe of the basic dough will make one mincemeat coffeecake or two lemon loaves.

7. To prepare mincemeat coffeecake, punch down the dough and divide into thirds. Cover and let rest ten minutes.

8. Divide each third into sixteen pieces and roll each piece into a ball. Spread half the mincemeat over the bottom of a well-buttered ten-inch tube pan. Combine the sugar and nutmeg.

9. Dip half the balls into the melted butter and then into the sugar mixture and arrange neatly over the mincemcat.

10. Spread the remaining mincemeat over the balls. Dip the remaining balls into melted butter and then into sugar mixture and arrange neatly over mincemeat. Cover and let rise in a warm place until doubled in bulk, about one hour.

11. Preheat the oven to 375 degrees.

12. Bake forty to forty-five minutes, or until done. Let cool in the pan two minutes and then invert onto a serving plate. Serve warm.

OR

13. To prepare lemon loaves, punch down dough, divide in half, cover and let rest ten minutes. Mix together the lemon rind, lemon juice, one cup of the sugar and the pecans. Use half the lemon mixture and half the melted butter for each dough half.

14. Roll one-half of the dough into a 10-by-16-inch rectangle; then cut into four rectangles. Brush one rectangle with the melted butter and sprinkle with the lemon mixture. Top with a second rectangle and repeat with melted butter and the lemon mixture. Repeat with remaining rectangles.

15. Cut the stack lengthwise into four strips. With cut stack side of each strip up, fit strips side by side in a well-greased or Teflon-coated 9-by-5-by-3-inch loaf pan.

16. Roll out and make stacks with second half of dough to fit a second loaf pan.

17. Combine remaining sugar and the flour. Blend in the two tablespoons butter and sprinkle the mixture over the tops of the two loaves. Cover and let rise in a warm place until doubled in bulk, about thirty minutes.

18. Preheat the oven to 400 degrees.

19. Bake thirty to thirty-five minutes, or until done. Cool on a rack.

Yield: One round mincemeat coffeecake or two lemon loaves.

Apricot Noodle Ring   *Northern California*

1½ cups broad noodles, cooked al dente, drained
 2 eggs, lightly beaten
 1 tablespoon melted butter
 ¼ teaspoon salt
 1 cup California-style cottage cheese
 ½ cup sour cream
 ¼ cup grated Cheddar cheese
 ½ cup raisins
 8 poached fresh or canned apricots, diced
 ¼ cup slivered almonds
 ½ teaspoon cinnamon
 ½ cup sugar.

1. Preheat the oven to 375 degrees.

2. Mix all ingredients together. Turn into a buttered two-quart casserole and bake forty-five minutes.

Yield: Six to eight servings.

Apple-Oatmeal Pudding   *Oregon*

 2 cups milk
 3 tablespoons light brown sugar
 1 tablespoon butter
 ¼ teaspoon salt
 ¼ teaspoon cinnamon

1 cup rolled oats
1 cup diced peeled apple
½ cup raisins
  Whipped cream.

1. Preheat the oven to 350 degrees.
2. Combine the milk, brown sugar, butter, salt and cinnamon in a saucepan. Heat just to boiling. Stir in the oats, apple and raisins. Heat until bubbles appear at pan edges.
3. Turn into a buttered one and one-half-quart casserole and bake thirty minutes. Serve hot, with whipped cream.
Yield: Four servings.

Apricot Fritters   *Northern California*

1 cup plus one tablespoon flour
1 cup hot milk
½ cup cognac or dark rum
1 tablespoon melted butter
  Granulated sugar
2 eggs
⅛ teaspoon salt
½ cup chopped candied fruits
2 tablespoons kirsch
12 large apricots
  Fat or oil for deep-frying
  Confectioners' sugar.

1. In an electric blender, combine the flour, milk, cognac or rum, butter, one tablespoon granulated sugar, the eggs and salt. Blend until smooth and then let stand two hours before proceeding.
2. Sprinkle the candied fruits with the kirsch and set aside.
3. Make a small slit in the side of each apricot and remove the pit. Stuff apricots with fruit-kirsch mixture. Roll in granulated sugar.
4. Dip the stuffed apricots into the batter and fry, a few at a time, in a fry basket in fat or oil heated to 370 degrees.
5. Drain on paper towels, dust with confectioners' sugar and serve hot.
Yield: Four servings.

Baked Apple Pudding   *Washington*

6 large apples, peeled, cored and thickly sliced
½ cup water
1 cup graham cracker crumbs
¼ teaspoon cinnamon
1 tablespoon butter, melted
3 eggs, separated
1½ cups sweetened condensed milk
2 tablespoons grated lemon rind
2 tablespoons lemon juice.

1. Preheat the oven to 350 degrees.
2. Place the apples and water in a saucepan and cook until apples are tender.
3. Combine the graham cracker crumbs, cinnamon and butter. Reserve three tablespoons mixture and spread remainder in the bottom of a greased one-and-one-half-quart baking dish.
4. Beat the egg yolks until thick. Stir in the condensed milk, lemon rind and lemon juice. Drain the cooked apples. Measure two cups apples and stir into the egg yolk mixture.
5. Beat the egg whites until stiff but not dry and fold in. Pour mixture into the baking dish. Sprinkle with reserved crumbs and bake fifty minutes, or until set and browned.
Yield: Six servings.

Molasses Dumplings   *Washington*

1 cup unsulphured molasses
1 teaspoon grated lemon rind
¼ cup lemon juice
2 tablespoons butter
2 cups flour
4 teaspoons baking powder
⅛ teaspoon salt
  Whipped cream.

1. Combine the molasses, lemon rind, lemon juice, butter and one-half cup water in a saucepan. Bring to a boil and boil five minutes.
2. Place the flour, baking powder and salt in a

bowl and stir in enough water to make a soft dough. Spoon dough into boiling syrup and cook, covered, twelve to fifteen minutes, or until dumplings are cooked. Serve with whipped cream.

Yield: Four servings.

Baked Pears   *Oregon*

¼ cup lime juice
¼ cup honey
⅓ cup light rum
4 pears, peeled, halved and cored
  Chopped almonds
  Sour cream.

1. Preheat the oven to 325 degrees.
2. Combine the lime juice, honey and rum and spoon some into the cavity of each pear half. Place pear halves in a baking dish. Bake one hour, basting frequently with the remaining rum mixture, until pears are tender.
3. Turn pears over and sprinkle with almonds. Serve with sour cream.

Yield: Four servings.

Citrus Sherbet   *Northern California*

3 cups sugar
1 cup water
¾ cup lemon juice
1½ cups orange juice
3 bananas, mashed
1 teaspoon grated lemon rind
1 tablespoon grated orange rind
1 cup heavy cream, whipped
3 egg whites, beaten until stiff but not dry.

1. Combine the sugar and water in a saucepan. Bring to a boil, stirring until sugar dissolves. Boil five minutes. Let cool.
2. Add the lemon juice, orange juice, bananas, lemon rind and orange rind to the syrup. Fold in the cream and egg whites. Freeze until firm.

Yield: Six to eight servings.

Banana Meringue Dessert   *Hawaii*

3 egg whites
¾ cup granulated sugar
½ teaspoon vanilla
¼ teaspoon vinegar
1 cup mashed ripe bananas
¼ teaspoon salt
1½ tablespoons lemon juice
1 cup heavy cream, whipped
¼ cup confectioners' sugar.

1. Preheat the oven to 275 degrees.
2. Beat the egg whites until stiff. Gradually beat in the granulated sugar. Beat in the vanilla and vinegar.
3. Cut two pieces of parchment paper the size of a freezing tray. Place the pieces of paper on a dampened baking sheet and spread the meringue over the pieces of paper. Bake forty-five minutes. Remove paper and cool meringue.
4. Combine the remaining ingredients. Place one sheet of meringue in a freezing tray, trimming meringue if necessary. Cover with banana filling and top with second meringue layer. Freeze three hours. Slice and serve.

Yield: Six servings.

Fruit Ice   *Hawaii*

2 ripe papayas, peeled and diced
4 ripe bananas, diced
1 six-ounce can frozen orange juice
  concentrate
1 six-ounce can water
¼ cup lemon juice
1 cup sugar.

Combine all ingredients in an electric blender and blend until smooth. Pour into freezing trays. Freeze, stirring and blending once during freezing to break up ice crystals, until firm.

Yield: One dozen servings.

Note: Other fruits can be substituted.

Filbert Rice Mold · *Oregon*

3½ cups cold cooked rice
1¾ cups confectioners' sugar
2 tablespoons vanilla
2 envelopes unflavored gelatin
⅔ cup cold water
2½ cups heavy cream, whipped
1 cup toasted, finely chopped filberts
4 cups fresh raspberries.

1. Mix together the rice, confectioners' sugar and vanilla. Soften the gelatin in the water and dissolve over low heat.
2. Stir gelatin into rice mixture. Cool, stirring occasionally, until mixture starts to set or thicken.
3. Fold in the cream and filberts and spoon into a two-quart mold. Chill until firm. Turn out and serve garnished with the raspberries.

Yield: Ten servings.

Frozen Apricot Dessert

Northern California

2 cups chopped peeled and pitted fresh apricots
1 cup sugar
1 tablespoon lemon juice
1 cup heavy cream, whipped
1 cup coarse macaroon crumbs.

1. Combine the apricots, sugar and lemon juice. Fold in the cream.
2. Sprinkle the bottom of a one-quart freezer tray with half the macaroon crumbs. Pour in the apricot mixture. Top with remaining crumbs and freeze until firm.

Yield: Six servings.

Jim's Apple and Sour Cream Dessert

Washington

3 tablespoons butter
1 cup granulated sugar
2 tablespoons lemon juice
4 large apples, peeled, cored and thickly sliced
4 eggs, separated
1½ teaspoons grated lemon rind
1 tablespoon dark rum
½ cup sour cream
Confectioners' sugar
1 cup heavy cream, whipped.

1. Preheat the oven to 350 degrees.
2. Heat the butter in a large skillet. Add two-thirds cup of the granulated sugar, the lemon juice and apples. Cook, uncovered, turning slices until they are glazed and liquid has evaporated.
3. Arrange half the apple slices in an oven-proof ten-inch skillet. Reserve remaining slices.
4. Beat the egg yolks until thick. Stir in the lemon rind, rum and sour cream.
5. Beat the egg whites with remaining granulated sugar until stiff but not dry and fold into yolk mixture. Spoon over apples in skillet and arrange remaining apple slices over the top. Bake twenty-five minutes, or until well puffed and golden. Sprinkle with confectioners' sugar and serve warm, with whipped cream.

Yield: Six servings.

Filbert Mousse · *Oregon*

4 ounces (four squares) semisweet chocolate
1 tablespoon instant coffee powder
3 tablespoons plus one-third cup water
1½ envelopes unflavored gelatin
5 eggs, separated
½ cup sugar
1½ cups milk, scalded
1 teaspoon vanilla
1½ cups ground toasted filberts

1½ cups heavy cream, whipped
Chopped toasted filberts (optional).

1. Combine the chocolate, instant coffee and three tablespoons of the water in a small saucepan and heat gently to melt chocolate.
2. Soften the gelatin in remaining water.
3. Beat the egg yolks and sugar together until light and fluffy. Gradually stir in the milk and pour mixture into the top of a double boiler. Cook over hot water until mixture thickens and coats the back of the spoon.
4. Add gelatin and stir until dissolved. Stir in the vanilla, ground filberts and melted chocolate mixture. Chill until the mixture starts to set.
5. Beat the egg whites until stiff but not dry and fold into gelatin mixture. Pour into a five-cup soufflé dish which has an oiled four-inch collar tied around or into eight individual glasses.
6. Chill until set. Remove collar from soufflé dish if used. Sprinkle mousse with a few chopped toasted filberts if desired.
Yield: Eight servings.

Peach Surprise   *Oregon*

3 cups sour cream
½ teaspoon nutmeg
1 teaspoon vanilla
¼ cup Grand Marnier or Cointreau
1 cup light brown sugar
2 cups peach slices, sweetened to taste and flavored with Grand Marnier to taste.

1. Preheat the broiler.
2. Combine the sour cream, nutmeg, vanilla and Grand Marnier. Beat lightly until blended and pour into a nine-inch pie plate. Sprinkle with the brown sugar and run under the broiler. Broil just until sugar caramelizes. Do not burn.
3. Chill. Serve with peach slices.
Yield: Six to eight servings.

Rogue River Refrigerator Cookies   *Oregon*

4 cups flour
1 teaspoon baking powder
¼ teaspoon baking soda
1 teaspoon salt
⅔ cups shortening
⅔ cup butter
1 cup light brown sugar
⅔ cup granulated sugar
2 eggs, well beaten
1½ teaspoons vanilla.

1. Day before, sift together the flour, baking powder, baking soda and salt.
2. Cream together the shortening, butter, brown sugar and granulated sugar until very light and fluffy. Add the eggs and vanilla.
3. Fold in the dry ingredients. Shape into a roll two to three inches in diameter, wrap in wax paper and chill overnight or longer.
4. Next day, preheat the oven to 400 degrees.
5. Cut the dough roll into thin slices and place on a lightly greased baking sheet. Bake cookies five to eight minutes.
Yield: Six dozen.
Note: For chocolate cookies, add four ounces (four squares) unsweetened chocolate, melted and cooled, to the creamed shortening, butter and sugars mixture.

Holiday Cookies   *Washington*

1¼ cups honey
2 cups light brown sugar
7 cups flour
½ teaspoon baking soda
¼ teaspoon ground cloves
¼ teaspoon nutmeg
1 teaspoon cinnamon
2 eggs, well beaten
½ pound almonds, blanched and slivered
⅓ cup chopped candied orange peel
¾ cup chopped moist citron

½ cup chopped glazed cherries
1 cup confectioners' sugar
1 teaspoon light corn syrup.

1. Place the honey, brown sugar and one-quarter cup water in a small saucepan, bring to a boil and boil five minutes. Let cool.

2. Sift together twice the flour, baking soda, cloves, nutmeg and cinnamon.

3. Add the eggs to the cooled honey mixture. Add all but one cup flour mixture, reserving that for dredging fruits.

4. Mix the almonds, orange peel, citron and cherries with reserved flour mixture and stir into the batter. With the hands, knead the mixture well.

5. Wrap in wax paper and then aluminum foil and store in the refrigerator three to four days to ripen.

6. Preheat the oven to 350 degrees.

7. Divide dough into four portions. Roll out one portion to one-quarter-inch thickness on a lightly floured board. Cut into 3-by-2-inch rectangles. Place on a lightly greased baking sheet and bake twelve to fifteen minutes, or until lightly browned. Cool on a rack. Repeat process with remaining portions of dough.

8. Combine the confectioners' sugar with the syrup and enough water to give a coating consistency. Use to ice cooled cookies. Store in an airtight container at least one month before serving.
Yield: About ten dozen.

Jane's Spritz Cookies   *Oregon*

½ cup butter
¼ cup shortening
½ cup sugar
1 egg yolk
½ teaspoon almond extract
2 cups cake flour
¼ teaspoon salt
  Candied cherries, nuts or raisins.

1. Preheat the oven to 375 degrees.

2. Cream the butter, shortening and sugar together until very light and fluffy. Beat in the egg yolk and almond extract.

3. Sift together the flour and salt and stir into the creamed mixture.

4. Force through a cookie press onto a lightly greased baking sheet. If dough is too soft to hold its shape, chill in refrigerator until firm.

5. Decorate cookies with a piece of cherry, nut or a raisin and bake eight to ten minutes, or until lightly browned.

6. Cool on a rack.
Yield: About three dozen.
Note: For chocolate cookies, add one and one-half ounces (one and one-half squares) unsweetened chocolate, melted and cooled, and two tablespoons milk to the creamed butter, shortening and sugar mixture.

Italian Biscotti   *Northern California*

½ cup butter
¾ cup sugar
3 eggs
½ teaspoon vanilla
3 cups flour
3 teaspoons baking powder
½ teaspoon salt
1 tablespoon aniseed
2 tablespoons grated lemon rind
2 tablespoons grated orange rind
1 cup chopped blanched almonds.

1. Preheat the oven to 350 degrees.

2. Cream the butter and sugar together until light and fluffy. Beat in the eggs, one at a time, very well. Add the vanilla.

3. Sift together the flour, baking powder and salt and stir into the batter. Stir in the remaining ingredients and blend well.

4. Divide dough into three parts and shape each into a long roll one and one-half inches in diameter.

5. Place each roll on a separate baking sheet, flatten the top slightly and bake fifteen minutes.

6. Remove from the oven and cut each roll into three-quarter-inch slices and lay, cut side down, on the baking sheet. Return to the oven and bake fifteen minutes longer.

7. Cool on a rack.

Yield: About four dozen.

Soft Molasses Cookies   *Washington*

1 cup butter, melted
1½ cups unsulphured molasses
¼ cup sugar
½ teaspoon salt
1½ teaspoons cinnamon
½ teaspoon ground ginger
½ teaspoon ground cloves
2 teaspoons baking soda
1 tablespoon warm water
2 eggs, lightly beaten
6 cups flour, approximately.

1. Combine the butter, molasses, sugar, salt, cinnamon, ginger and cloves.

2. Dissolve the baking soda in the water. Stir the eggs and the dissolved baking soda into the batter.

3. Stir in enough flour to make a dough. Wrap in wax paper and chill several hours, or until firm enough to roll.

4. Preheat the oven to 375 degrees.

5. Roll out dough, one-quarter at a time, to one-eighth-inch thickness. Cut into two-inch rounds and place on lightly greased baking sheet.

6. Bake fifteen minutes, or until done. Cool on a rack.

Yield: About seven dozen.

Cinnamon Stars   *Oregon*

3 egg whites
Dash salt
Sifted confectioners' sugar
½ teaspoon cinnamon
½ teaspoon grated lemon rind

½ pound very finely ground unblanched almonds.

1. Preheat the oven to 325 degrees.

2. Beat the egg whites with salt until almost stiff. Gradually add one cup confectioners' sugar and whip until mixture is very stiff. Blend in the cinnamon and lemon rind. Reserve one-quarter of meringue mixture.

3. Fold the almonds into remainder of meringue.

4. Spread a board or pastry cloth with confectioners' sugar and pat or roll almond dough to one-third-inch thickness. Cut with star, or other, cookie cutter.

5. Using a wide spatula, place cookies on greased baking sheet. Spread tops of cookies with reserved meringue and bake about one-half hour, or until lightly browned.

Yield: About twenty.

Chinese Almond Cookies
Northern California

1⅓ cups shortening
1 cup sugar
1 egg, well beaten
1 teaspoon almond extract
3 cups flour
1 teaspoon baking soda
½ teaspoon salt
Blanched almonds, halved.

1. Preheat the oven to 350 degrees.

2. Cream the shortening and sugar together until very light and fluffy. Beat in the egg and almond extract. Sift together the flour, baking soda and salt and stir into the creamed mixture.

3. Form into balls one inch in diameter and place on greased baking sheets. With the thumb, make a depression in the middle of each ball and set an almond half in each. Bake twenty minutes, or until lightly browned.

Yield: About fifty-four.

Pumpkin Cookies
Washington

1½ cups sugar
½ cup shortening
1 egg
1⅓ cups mashed cooked pumpkin
1¾ cups flour
4 teaspoons baking powder
¼ teaspoon nutmeg
¼ teaspoon ground cloves
½ teaspoon ginger
½ teaspoon cinnamon
½ cup raisins
½ cup chopped walnuts
1 cup whole bran.

1. Preheat the oven to 375 degrees.
2. Cream together the sugar and shortening until light and fluffy. Beat in the egg; then beat in the pumpkin.
3. Sift together flour, baking powder, nutmeg, cloves, ginger and cinnamon; add to batter.
4. Stir in the raisins, walnuts and bran. Drop by tablespoonfuls two inches apart onto greased baking sheets. Bake eighteen to twenty minutes, or until golden.
Yield: About four dozen.

Filbert Brownies
Oregon

2 ounces (two squares) unsweetened chocolate
½ cup butter
2 eggs
1 cup sugar
1 teaspoon vanilla
¾ cup flour
½ teaspoon baking powder
¼ teaspoon salt
1 cup toasted chopped filberts.

1. Preheat the oven to 350 degrees.
2. Melt the chocolate and butter together over hot water. Cool.
3. Beat together the eggs and sugar until light. Beat in the cooled chocolate mixture and the vanilla.
4. Sift together the flour, baking powder and salt and stir into chocolate mixture. Fold in the filberts.
5. Spread mixture in a greased eight-inch square baking pan. Bake thirty to thirty-five minutes. Cool ten minutes and then cut into squares.
Yield: About sixteen.

Miscellaneous

Pickles, Relishes and Preserves

Chinese Cabbage Pickle

Northern California

3 pounds bok choy (Chinese cabbage)
3 tablespoons salt
1 hot pepper, sliced
1 strip dashi knobu (seaweed flavoring, see note)
Imported soy sauce.

1. Cut the cabbage lengthwise into six stalks. Wash well and dry. Place a layer of cabbage in a wooden tub or ceramic bowl and sprinkle with salt. Place next layer cabbage crosswise over the first and sprinkle with salt. Repeat layers until all cabbage is used.

2. Place pepper slices at intervals in layers.

3. Wash the dashi knobu, break into three strips and insert into layers of cabbage. Place a cover and heavy object on top of cabbage to weight it down and leave at room temperature about three days, or until water rises from cabbage and submerges all ingredients.

4. To serve, rinse off stalks and cut into one-inch slices. Dip into soy sauce.

Yield: About one quart.

Note: Dashi knobu is available in Oriental stores.

Pickled Daikon and Carrot

Northern California

½ pound daikon (white radishes), peeled and finely shredded
1 carrot, shredded
1 tablespoon salt
1 cup water
1 tablespoon white vinegar
1 teaspoon sugar
¼ teaspoon monosodium glutamate (optional).

1. Place the daikon, carrot, salt and water in a bowl and let stand thirty minutes.

2. Drain vegetables and squeeze as dry as possible. Place in a clean bowl, add the remaining ingredients and mix well. Serve at room temperature.

Yield: Six servings

Zucchini Pickles

Northern California

8 onions, thinly sliced
1 gallon zucchini, sliced one-quarter-inch thick
3 green peppers, finely shredded
½ cup salt

5 cups cider vinegar
5 cups sugar
1½ teaspoons turmeric
2 tablespoons mustard seeds
1½ teaspoons celery seeds
1 stick cinnamon, quartered.

1. Place the onions, zucchini and green peppers in layers in a ceramic crock or bowl, sprinkling each layer with salt. Weight down vegetables and let stand in the refrigerator four hours.

2. Drain vegetables. Rinse and drain well.

3. In a large kettle, combine the remaining ingredients, bring to a boil and boil ten minutes. Add vegetables and return to boiling point, but do not cook. Turn into hot sterilized jars and seal. Store in a cool, dark, dry place.

Yield: About eight pints.

Brandied Apricots   *Northern California*

6 pounds apricots
  Whole cloves
3 cups cider vinegar
3 sticks cinnamon, broken up
10 cups sugar
6 tablespoons cognac.

1. Wash the fruit and stud each apricot with two cloves.

2. Place the vinegar, cinnamon sticks and sugar in a heavy skillet. Heat, stirring to dissolve the sugar. Add half the fruit and simmer until tender but not mushy.

3. Pack fruit and a piece of cinnamon stick into hot sterilized jars. Add remaining apricots to skillet and repeat process.

4. Heat syrup to boiling and pour over the apricots. Add one tablespoon cognac to each jar.

Yield: About six quarts.

Cranberry Catchup   *Alaska*

1 pound onions
4 pounds high bush cranberries (see note)
2 cups water
2 cups cider vinegar
4 cups sugar
1 tablespoon ground cloves
1 tablespoon cinnamon
1 tablespoon ground allspice
1 tablespoon salt
1 tablespoon celery seeds
1 teaspoon freshly ground black pepper.

1. Place the onions, cranberries and water in a kettle and cook over medium heat until very soft. Force through a sieve, discard seeds and place pulp back in the kettle.

2. Add the remaining ingredients, bring to a boil and cook, stirring occasionally, until mixture is thick. Pour into hot sterilized jars and seal. Store in a cool, dark, dry place.

Yield: About three pints.

Note: Alaskan high bush cranberries are not true cranberries. High bush cranberries have large flat seeds.

Prune Catchup   *Northern California*

6 pounds prunes
4 cups sugar
1 tablespoon cinnamon
2 teaspoons ground cloves
2 teaspoons ground allspice
¾ cup cider vinegar.

1. Cover the prunes with water and bring to a boil. Simmer, covered, until very tender, about two and one-half hours. Pit the prunes and put through an electric blender or food mill.

2. Place pulp in a heavy saucepan and add the remaining ingredients. Bring to a boil and cook, stirring until mixture is thick. Pour into hot sterilized jars and seal. Store in a cool, dark, dry place.

Yield: About four pints.

Note: Prune catchup is good with game or poultry.

Apricot Chutney   *Northern California*

1¾ cups cider vinegar
1⅔ cups sugar
24 large, firm apricots, pitted and chopped
7 red sweet peppers, seeded and chopped
3 onions, chopped
1 clove garlic, finely chopped
1 teaspoon salt
1 cup raisins
1 whole orange, chopped
1 whole lemon, chopped
¼ pound crystallized ginger, chopped
1 cup almonds, blanched and slivered
1 teaspoon ground ginger.

1. Boil one and one-quarter cups of the vinegar with the sugar five minutes in a large kettle. Add the apricots, peppers, onions, garlic, salt, raisins, orange, lemon and crystallized ginger. Cook thirty minutes, stirring frequently.

2. Add the almonds, powdered ginger and remaining vinegar. Cook thirty minutes longer, stirring to prevent sticking.

3. Ladle into hot sterilized jars and seal. Store in a cool, dark, dry place.

Yield: About three pints.

Note: Apricot chutney is excellent with meats and curries.

Medford Pear Chutney   *Oregon*

7 to eight cups peeled, cored and diced Bartlett pears
1 pound light brown sugar
2 cups cider vinegar
1 onion, chopped
1 cup raisins
2 ounces crystallized ginger, chopped
1 clove garlic, finely chopped

Cayenne pepper to taste
2 teaspoons salt
1 teaspoon cinnamon
½ teaspoon ground cloves
2 teaspoons mustard seeds.

Combine all the ingredients in a heavy kettle. Bring to a boil and simmer gently until mixture is thick, about one hour. Pour into hot sterilized jars and seal. Store in a cool, dark, dry place.

Yield: About two and one-half pints.

Purple Plum Chutney   *Washington*

6 cups pitted purple prune plums, cut into eighths (about four pounds)
8 cups firm tart apples, peeled, cored and coarsely chopped (about two pounds)
4 cups coarsely chopped sweet Spanish onions
1½ cups white vinegar
1½ cups raisins
2 cups dark brown sugar
2 cups granulated sugar
1½ teaspoons ground allspice
1½ teaspoons ground ginger
1 teaspoon ground cloves
4 teaspoons salt
2 cloves garlic, finely chopped
6 drops Tabasco sauce, or to taste.

1. Place the plums, apples, onions and vinegar in a large heavy kettle. Bring to a boil and simmer, uncovered, one hour.

2. Add the remaining ingredients, bring to a boil and simmer until mixture thickens and is the consistency of cold fruit preserves. Turn into hot sterilized jars and adjust covers. Cool and store in a cool, dark, dry place.

Yield: About four and one-half pints.

Rhubarb and Berry Relish   *Alaska*

4 cups diced rhubarb, ground
2 cups cranberries, blueberries or lingonberries,
   ground
   Sugar.

Combine the rhubarb and berries and measure. Add an equal amount of sugar and stir to dissolve. Serve with poultry and game.

Yield: About one and one-half quarts.

Singari Daikon   *Northern California*

4 ounces dried daikon (white radish, see note)
1 cup julienne strips carrots
1 tablespoon finely chopped fresh ginger
2 tablespoons imported soy sauce
1 small piece dashi knobu (kelp or seaweed
   flavoring, see note)
3 tablespoons cider vinegar
1 tablespoon sugar.

1. Combine all the ingredients in a large ceramic bowl. Weight down with a plate and heavy object and leave at room temperature about five days, or until liquid rises to top.

2. Refrigerate seven days. Serve as side dish with plain boiled rice.

Yield: About one and one-half cups.

Note: Daikon and dashi knobu are available in Oriental food stores.

Pineapple Chutney   *Hawaii*

4 cups chopped fresh pineapple
1½ cups cider vinegar
1½ cups light brown sugar
1 fifteen-ounce package raisins
1 tablespoon salt
2 tablespoons finely chopped fresh ginger
2 tablespoons finely chopped garlic
3 hot peppers, seeded and chopped
1 cup chopped unsalted macadamia nuts.

1. In a kettle, combine all the ingredients except the nuts. Bring to a boil and simmer, stirring to prevent sticking, until mixture is very thick, about forty-five minutes.

2. Stir in the nuts and ladle into hot sterilized jars. Pour two thin layers of melted paraffin over. Cool and store in a cool, dark, dry place.

Yield: About four pints.

Elderberry Chutney   *Oregon*

6 cups elderberries
2 small onions, finely chopped
1 teaspoon whole cloves
1 teaspoon ginger
¾ cup light brown sugar
1 tablespoon salt
1 cup raisins
   Cayenne pepper to taste
⅛ teaspoon nutmeg
1 teaspoon mustard seeds
1¼ cups cider vinegar.

1. Wash the berries and remove stems. Crush berries and place in a heavy kettle.

2. Add the remaining ingredients and bring to a boil. Cook, stirring to prevent sticking, until thick and clear. Pour into hot sterilized jars and seal. Store in a cool, dark, dry place.

Yield: About two pints.

Horseradish Relish   *Washington*

12 cups peeled, chopped tomatoes
¾ cup freshly grated horseradish
1 hot red pepper, seeded and chopped
1 cup chopped celery
1 cup chopped onions
¾ cup light brown sugar
1½ cups cider vinegar
2 tablespoons salt
1 teaspoon ground allspice
½ teaspoon cinnamon
½ teaspoon ground cloves

3 tablespoons mustard seeds
1 tablespoon dill seeds.

1. Place the tomatoes in a colander and let drain two to three hours. Use liquid in stew or soup, or discard.
2. Place tomatoes in a heavy kettle. Add the horseradish, red pepper, celery and onions.
3. Combine the remaining ingredients in another saucepan and bring to a boil. Pour over the tomato mixture. Bring to a boil and simmer until thick.
4. Ladle into hot sterilized jars and seal. Store in a cool, dark, dry place.

Yield: About two quarts.

Pineapple Marmalade   *Hawaii*

1 large, ripe pineapple
2 lemons, shredded and seeds removed
4 cups water
Sugar.

1. Day before, carefully peel the pineapple to remove all dark spots. Pare away and discard the core. Shred remaining pineapple flesh. There should be approximately four cups.
2. Add the lemons and water. Let stand overnight.
3. Next day, bring fruit mixture to a boil and cook twenty minutes.
4. Measure fruit and juice and for each cup add one cup sugar. Cook in small quantities (six cups is generally enough for one kettle) over high heat until syrup thickens and sheets from spoon in two streams. This should require about thirty to forty minutes at a fast boil. Remove marmalade from stove and pour into hot sterilized jars. Pour two thin layers of melted paraffin over. Store in a cool, dark, dry place.

Yield: Six to eight eight-ounce jars.

Orange Marmalade   *Northern California*

4 large oranges
2 lemons
1½ cups water
⅛ teaspoon baking soda
5 cups sugar
½ bottle liquid fruit pectin.

1. Remove the rind in strips from the oranges and lemons.
2. Place one-third of the strips in the container of an electric blender. Add one-half cup of the water, cover and blend on high speed seven to ten seconds. Pour into a saucepan.
3. Repeat the process twice, using the remaining fruit rinds and water. Combine all the blended mixture in the saucepan.
4. Add the baking soda. Bring the mixture to a boil and simmer twenty minutes.
5. Scoop the pulp and juice from the oranges and lemons and add to the saucepan. Cook ten minutes longer. Add the sugar, bring to a full rolling boil and boil one minute.
6. Remove from the heat and add the pectin. To keep fruit rinds from floating, let marmalade cool ten minutes before bottling.
7. Pour into hot sterilized jelly glasses. Pour two thin layers of melted paraffin over. Store in a cool, dark, dry place.

Yield: Six to seven six-ounce glasses.

Rhubarb Marmalade   *Washington*

2 quarts diced rhubarb
2 fifteen-ounce packages raisins
2 oranges, quartered and ground
2 quarts water
4 ounces crystallized ginger, chopped
10 cups sugar.

Place all the ingredients in a heavy kettle. Bring to a boil and simmer, stirring occasionally, until thick. Pour into hot sterilized jars. Pour two thin layers of melted paraffin over. Cool and store in a cool, dark, dry place.

Yield: About five pints.

Cloudberry Jam   *Alaska*

8 cups crushed cloudberries
6 cups sugar.

1. Place the berries in a heavy kettle and heat gently to boiling. Simmer one minute. Stir in the sugar until it dissolves.

2. Cook, stirring, until mixture thickens. Pour into hot sterilized jars. Pour two thin layers of melted paraffin over. Cool and store in a cool, dark, dry place.

Yield: About four pints.

Note: Lingonberries or blueberries can be substituted for the cloudberries.

Cranberry-Apple Butter   *Alaska*

1 pound dried apples
8 cups water
8 cups high bush cranberries (see note, page 756)
6 cups sugar
1 teaspoon cinnamon
¼ teaspoon salt
½ teaspoon ground cloves
Grated rind and juice of one lemon.

1. Soak the apples in the water one hour. Add the cranberries and cook gently until soft.

2. Force the pulp through a food mill or sieve. Discard seeds and place pulp in a heavy kettle. Add the sugar, cinnamon, salt and cloves. Bring to a boil and cook until clear. Stir in the lemon rind and juice. Pour into hot sterilized jars and seal. Store in a cool, dark, dry place.

Yield: About four pints.

Sauces

Tartar Sauce   *Washington*

2 cups mayonnaise, preferably homemade (see below)
1 scallion, finely chopped
½ dill pickle, chopped
1 rib celery, chopped
1 tablespoon chopped chives
2 teaspoons lemon juice
  Tabasco sauce to taste
  Worcestershire sauce to taste.

Mix all ingredients together and chill well.
Yield: About two and one-half cups.

Mayonnaise   *Northern California*

2 egg yolks, beaten until thick and lemon-colored
½ teaspoon salt
1 teaspoon dry mustard
⅛ teaspoon cayenne pepper
¼ cup wine vinegar
1 cup olive oil
1 cup vegetable oil.

1. Combine the egg yolks, salt, mustard and cayenne. Beat in half the vinegar.

2. Combine the olive oil and vegetable oil and add to the yolk mixture, drop by drop, while beating. As the mixture thickens, add the oil in larger quantities. Do not overbeat.

3. Slowly add remaining vinegar. Chill.

Yield: About two cups.

Note: To prepare citrus mayonnaise, substitute one-quarter cup lemon juice or lime juice for the vinegar and stir in one teaspoon each grated lemon rind and orange rind.

Hollandaise Sauce   *Northern California*

8 egg yolks
6 tablespoons hot water
4 tablespoons lemon juice
  Salt and freshly ground black pepper to taste
1 cup butter.

1. In a saucepan, beat the egg yolks with a wire whisk until they are thick and pale. Add the water, lemon juice, salt and pepper and beat vigorously.
2. In another saucepan, heat the butter just to bubbling. Pour it slowly into the egg yolk mixture, beating rapidly.
3. Place the sauce over very low heat and cook, stirring constantly, until sauce is properly thickened. Do not overcook or sauce will curdle. (To restore slightly curdled sauce, add two tablespoons cold light cream and beat quickly, off the heat.)
  Yield: About one and one-half cups.

Sweet and Sour Sauce   *Washington*

1 tablespoon oil
1 clove garlic, crushed
⅔ cup sugar
¼ cup catchup
⅔ cup pineapple juice
½ cup vinegar
2 tablespoons soy sauce
2 tablespoons cornstarch.

1. Heat the oil in a saucepan and sauté the garlic in it until lightly browned. Remove the garlic and discard.
2. Mix together the sugar, catchup, one-third cup of the pineapple juice, the vinegar and soy sauce. Stir into the oil in the saucepan. Bring to a boil.
3. Mix the cornstarch with the remaining pineapple juice and stir into the boiling liquid until mixture thickens and becomes transparent.
  Yield: About three and one-half cups.

Sour Cream-and-Dill Sauce   *Alaska*

1 cup sour cream
¼ teaspoon salt
3 to four tablespoons chopped fresh dill weed
¼ cup thinly sliced and then chopped peeled
  cucumber.

Combine all ingredients and serve cold or warm. To warm, heat in the top of a double boiler over very hot water until warmed through.
  Yield: About one and one-quarter cups.

Orange Glaze and Sauce for Ham
Northern California

¾ cup red currant jelly
⅛ teaspoon nutmeg
2 teaspoons grated orange rind
½ cup orange juice
3 tablespoons lemon juice
½ cup cider
  Red food coloring
1 tablespoon cornstarch
¼ cup water
2 oranges, peeled and diced.

1. In a saucepan, combine the jelly, nutmeg, orange rind, one tablespoon of the orange juice, one tablespoon of the lemon juice and one tablespoon of the cider.
2. Bring to a boil, stirring, and boil five minutes. Add food coloring as desired. Cool one-half cup of this mixture and use to glaze a ham.
3. To mixture remaining in saucepan, add remaining juices and cider. Mix the cornstarch with the water and add. Bring to a boil, stirring. Cook until thick and clear. Stir in the orange pieces.
  Yield: One-half cup glaze and two cups sauce.

Cucumber Sauce   *Washington*

1 cucumber
  Salt

1 cup sour cream
1 teaspoon finely chopped scallion, including green part
Freshly ground black pepper to taste
2 teaspoons freshly snipped dill weed.

1. Peel and halve the cucumber and remove the seeds. Slice cucumber very thinly. Sprinkle with salt and let stand one hour.
2. Rinse cucumber slices and squeeze out most excess moisture. Combine cucumber slices with the sour cream, scallion, pepper and dill weed. Chill. Serve with cold poached salmon.
Yield: About two cups.

Mustard and Caper Sauce   *Alaska*

1 teaspoon sugar
1 teaspoon dry mustard
½ teaspoon salt
2 egg yolks
½ cup oil
3 tablespoons lemon juice
3 tablespoons drained capers, chopped
1 tablespoon grated onion.

1. Combine the sugar, mustard and salt. Beat into the egg yolks. Gradually beat in the oil, one-quarter teaspoon at a time, until mixture is thick and creamy.
2. Beat in the lemon juice, capers and onion.
Yield: About one cup.
Note: This sauce is good served with hot roasts or game.

Hot Mustard Sauce   *Alaska*

1 cup dry mustard
2 teaspoons salt
2 tablespoons sugar
2 egg yolks
2 tablespoons Worcestershire sauce
1 tablespoon freshly grated horseradish
2 cups cider vinegar, approximately.

Combine all the ingredients in the container of an electric blender and blend thoroughly, using enough vinegar to give desired consistency. Spoon into a jar, cover and store in the refrigerator.
Yield: About two and one-half cups.

Pacific Coast Barbecue Sauce   *Oregon*

2 cups catchup
½ cup oil
¼ cup lemon juice
¼ cup Worcestershire sauce
2 large cloves garlic, crushed
Salt and freshly ground black pepper to taste
¼ cup light brown sugar
1 teaspoon dry mustard
½ teaspoon ground rosemary
½ cup water.

Combine all the ingredients in a saucepan. Bring to a boil and simmer five minutes. Use for basting fish, poultry, ribs and chops.
Yield: About three cups.

Candies

Candied Lemon or Orange Peel
Northern California

Peel of four lemons or three oranges
2 cups sugar.

1. Cut the peel into strips one-third-inch wide and about three inches long. Cover the peel with water and simmer fifteen minutes. Drain, add more water and cook peel until tender. Drain.
2. Mix one and two-thirds cup sugar with one-half cup water and heat, stirring, to 238 degrees on a candy thermometer. Add the peel. Simmer until syrup is absorbed.

3. Roll the peel in remaining sugar. Spread on a rack to dry.

Yield: About thirty strips.

Toffee   *Alaska*

2 cups sugar
2 cups butter
¼ cup water
2 cups blanched almonds, halved.

1. Combine the sugar, butter and water and cook over low heat, stirring constantly, until melted and blended. Add the almonds, turn heat high and cook, stirring constantly, until mixture is light brown or until almonds take on a well-toasted look.

2. Immediately remove the mixture from the heat and pour quickly onto a buttered cookie sheet or marble slab. Spread and let cool. Before the mixture is firmly set, slice it with a sharp knife into squares.

Yield: Three dozen to four dozen.

Dressings (Stuffings)

Potato Dressing   *Washington*

½ cup butter
3 baking potatoes, peeled and thinly sliced
1 onion, finely chopped
3 cups toasted white bread cubes
1 teaspoon sage
2 tablespoons chopped parsley
  Salt and freshly ground black pepper to taste
½ teaspoon thyme
⅓ cup beef broth.

1. Heat the butter in a heavy skillet and slowly sauté the potatoes and onion in it until tender and lightly browned, stirring often to prevent sticking.

2. Combine the remaining ingredients in a large bowl. Add potato-and-onion mixture and toss to mix. Use to stuff poultry.

Yield: About five cups, enough to stuff an eight-pound turkey.

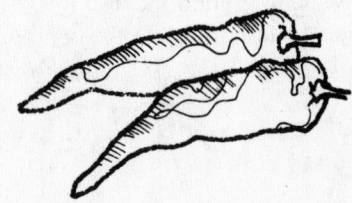

Macadamia Nut Stuffing   *Hawaii*

2 quarts soft bread cubes
½ cup butter
1 cup chopped onions
½ clove garlic, finely chopped
½ cup chopped celery
½ cup chopped celery leaves
1 teaspoon sage
½ teaspoon thyme
½ teaspoon crumbled bay leaf
1½ teaspoons salt
½ teaspoon freshly ground black pepper
1 egg, beaten
2 tablespoons cognac
1 cup macadamia nuts, chopped
¼ cup chicken broth.

1. Put the bread cubes in a large bowl.

2. Heat the butter in a skillet and sauté the onions and garlic in it until tender. Add the celery and celery leaves and cook two minutes longer. Add to bread cubes.

3. Add the remaining ingredients and toss to mix. Use to stuff chickens and turkey.

Yield: About ten cups, enough to stuff a twelve-pound to fourteen-pound turkey.

Note: To prepare Oregon filbert stuffing, substitute chopped filberts for the macadamia nuts.

Ham Dressing or Coating

Oregon

1 onion, finely chopped
¾ pound pecans, finely chopped
1 tablespoon dry mustard
3 large dill pickles, finely chopped
    Freshly ground black pepper to taste
1 teaspoon ground cloves
    Salt to taste

1 egg, lightly beaten.

Combine all the ingredients and pat over surface of a ready-to-eat ham. Bake fifteen minutes a pound in preheated 325-degree oven. Or the mixture can be baked separately in a covered baking dish while ham is baking.

Yield: Enough coating or dressing accompaniment for a five-pound boneless ham or a ten-pound bone-in ham.

Index

abalone
  Santa Barbara, 571
  soup, pork and, 669
  with vermouth, 672
Abigail's
  biscuit-topped haddock pie, 36
  cookies, 544
Addie's squash rolls, 398
adobe bread, 395
aebleskiver (Danish doughnuts), 407
Agate Beach clam fritters, 673
Agnes'
  molded salmon loaf, 683
  Oregon slaw, 719
  wilted lettuce, 719
aguacate (avocado sauce), 303
Alaskan nuggets, 685
"alfalfa," 719
Alison's shortbread, 439
almond
  butter
    cookies, 439
    oysters with, 679
  chicken, 595
  cookies, Chinese, 753
  crust, cheesecake with, 634
  gingersnaps, Swedish, 445
  peach jam, 292
  soup, 184
  strips, 403
  and wild rice stuffing, roast young
    capon with, 357
amber pie, 409
Anacortes shellfish stew, 678
anadama bread, 102
anchovies
  mushrooms with, stuffed, 81
  trout with, 474
anchovy
  salad dressing, 389
  and spinach salad, 619
  -stuffed cherry tomatoes, 8

angel food
  cake
    prize Northeastern, 117
    Southern, 277
  pie, Grandmother's, 410
anise chicken appetizers, 658
aniseed cookies (biscochitos), 642
Anne's hamburgers, 344
Annie's pumpkin chiffon pie, 413
appetizers, 3–11, 167–77, 315–18,
  469–70, 561–65, 657–65
  anchovy-stuffed cherry tomatoes, 8
  anise chicken, cold, 658
  artichoke hearts in batter, 564
  avocado with prosciutto, 564
  benne seed wafers, 176
  caviar mousse, 4
  cheese
    balls, 175
    crisps, 469
    -olive, 316
    Southwestern, 565
    straws, 176
    -stuffed mushrooms, 9
    wafers, 316
  cherry tomatoes, stuffed, 174
  chicken wings, oven-barbecued, 318
  chile
    cheese, 562
    con queso (cheese dip), 563
  clam
    fritter, Lois', 657
    puff balls, 657
  clams
    baked stuffed, 5
    Casino, 658
  conch
    seviche, 167
    vinaigrette, 167
  cottage cheese spread, 317
  crab
    and avocado cocktail, 561

appetizers (cont'd)
  meat
    deviled I (Maryland), 168
    deviled II (Maryland), 168
    Northwestern, 658
    puffs, 169
    sauté, 168
    and shrimp, baked, 5
  crevettes Paula, 7
  cucumber and shad roe, 169
  curried
    flan, 10
    mushroom turnovers, 660
  deer liver pâté, 3
  egg rolls, 662
  eggs sardou, 174
  empanaditas, 563
  felafel, 8
  Filipino seasoned pork, 659
  grits balls, deep-fried, 176
  guacamole
    I (New Mexico), 562
    II (Arizona), 562
  ham
    biscuits, 174
    and egg canapés, 173
  herb dip for raw vegetables, 175
  jicama, 564
  liver
    paste, Holiday Folk Fair Danish,
      317
    pâté, Danish, 317
  lobster canapés, 6
  mackerel, pickled, 6
  mushroom quiche, 10
  oyster, 169
  oysters
    with cocktail sauce, 169
    in cream, 6
  Parmesan wafers, 661
  pâté maison, 3
  Pat's favorite dip, 175

appetizers (cont'd)
  pickled
    lake herring, 315
    perch, 315
    venison heart, 4
  pipian, 565
  quesadillas, 563
  quiche à la Roma, 8
  roasted sweet peppers, Chuck's, 661
  red snapper
    chilled, 172
    escabeche of, 173
  rullepolse (spiced meat roll), 469
  sardines, marinated Maine, 6
  sauerkraut balls, 318
  sausage ball, 565
  scallops mayonnaise, 7
  sea "anemones," Hawaiian, 664
  sea food and Southern cocktail
      sauce, 172
  seasoned filberts, 661
  seviche, 561
  shrimp
    charcoal broiled, 665
    cocktail with celery-tomato
        sauce, 170
    Creole, chilled Gulf Coast, 171
    with hot sauce, 170
    with Lamaze sauce, 170
    Marin County, 664
    paste, 172
    pickled, 170
    remoulade, 171
  shrimps Wilder, 171
  smelts in aspic, 470
  smoked
    fish, 315
    salmon, 561
      rolls, 660
  soufflé roll with ham and spinach
      filling, 7
  sushi, West Coast, 663
  sweetbreads and oyster, 4
  tempura, shrimp, 663
  teriyaki, 660
  Texas caviar, 564
  three drops, 10
  Tillamook cheese and clam, 657
  tiropetes (cheese pastries), 9
  tomato freeze with avocado
      topping, 175
  veal tartar with lemon, 562
  whitebait, 660
  zucchini, 8
    blossom fritters, Schramsberg,
        662
apple
  and apricot pie, 737
  and blackberry jelly, 291
  -blueberry conserve, 153
  bread pudding, 537

apple (cont'd)
  butter, 453
  cake
    Dutch, Connie's, 531
    Mountain/Northern Plains, 528
    Passover, 123
    pie, 528
    raw, 528
    upside-down, 123
  cheese pie, glazed, 414
  -cherry pie, 525
  chutney, 152
  cobbler, 537
  coffecake
    German, 400
    Northeastern, 125
  -cranberry butter, 760
  crisp, 137
  crunch, 538
  custard pie, Marie's, 737
  -ginger custard, 130
  kraut
    and pork, 352
    and pork steaks, 353
  nut bread, 728
  -oatmeal pudding, 747
  and pear preserves, 453
  pie
    cheese, glazed, 414
    cider, 415
    Dutch, sack, 107
    Greta's, 414
    pudding, 431
    with sour cream, 106
    squash-, 106
    Tewksbury, 107
    winy raisin-, 107
  and potato salad, hot, 92
  preserves, quick, 292
  pudding, 640
    baked, 748
  red cabbage and, 373
  slaw, 718
  snow with custard sauce, 134
  and sour cream dessert, Jim's, 750
  stack pie, 271
  strudel, 525
  -stuffed buffalo ribs, 491
  toast, 407
  -tomato butter, 548
  and tomato relish, 451
apples
  cider, 136
  and dumplings (schnitz un knepp),
      51
  fried, 291
  maple, 137
  'n' beans, Meg's, 713
  onions and, fried, 81

applesauce
  bars, 543
  cake, 423
  cookies, whole wheat, 543
  fruitcake, 278
  squares, filled, 145
apricot
  -apple
    pie, 737
    stuffing, pork chops with, 58
  bars, 642
  cake, 634
  chutney, 757
  dessert, frozen, 750
  fritters, 748
  glaze, 120
  and ham salad, 726
  lattice cake, 124
  noodle ring, 747
  nut bread, 728
  pie, 630
    fresh, 736
  or prune filling for kolaches, 402
  and prune upside-down cake,
      Slovak, 418
  -stuffed pork chops, 351
  stuffing, wild goose with, 484
  torte, 633
apricots, brandied, 756
Arizona Christmas bread, 628
Armenian squash dolma, 349
arroz con pollo Nuevo Mexicano
    (chicken with rice, New Mexican
    style), 597
artichoke
  hearts
    in batter, 564
    breaded, 603
    and tarragon crab, 573
  pickles, whole, 296
  relish, 300
  and sea food casserole, 198
artichokes
  chicken with, 594
  and spinach
    Asphodel style, 250
    Southwestern, 607
  stuffed, 603
asparagus
  baked, with cheese sauce, 73
  pudding, 369
  salad, 94
  soup, chilled, 20
  vinaigrette, 717
aspic, tomato, 620
assorted greens, 245
Audrey's pickle chips, 447
Aunt Mary's
  kolaches, 401
  pickled onions, 550
Aunt May's chicken fricassee, 707

Aunt Nell's piccalilli, 547
Aunt Willie's stuffed tomatoes, 382
Austrian butter horns, 436
avocado
  and crab cocktail, 561
  guacamole
    I (New Mexico), 562
    II (Arizona), 562
  meat loaf, 579
  pecan bread, 624
  with prosciutto, 564
  salad, California, 616
  salmon with, 686
  sauce (aguacate), 303
  soup
    cold, 569
    curried, 568
  topping, tomato freeze with, 175

bacalao, 574
bacon
  and cheese spoon bread, 259
  cooked dressing, 254
  corn pudding with, 78
  dressing, dandelion greens and, 94
  'n' corn bread, 627
baked
  apple pudding, 748
  asparagus with cheese sauce, 73
  bean soup, 21
  beans
    home-, 74
    Northeastern
      I (Massachusetts), 74
      II (Massachusetts), 74
    Sister Josephine's Shaker, 73
  bluefish with rosemary, 32
  bourbon spiced sweet potatoes, 248
  cabbage, 504
  carrot pudding, 538
  catfish, 185
  chicken, 65
    camp style, 703
  ciscoes, 333
  clams, 24
    stuffed, 5
  custard, 427
  gefilte fish, 42
  haddock, 37
  lamb, 54
    ring with mashed potatoes, 53
  leek omelet, 720
  lobster, 27
  mushrooms, 506
  pears, 749
  pickerel, 333
  pike, 332
  pork
    chops with rice, 352
    steaks, 56

baked *(cont'd)*
  red snapper, 203
  shrimp
    and crab, 5
    with feta cheese, 31
  striped bass, 32
  stuffed
    clams, 5
    trout, 476
  trout, 475
    Oklahoma, 331
  walleyed pike, 333
  wild duck breasts en casserole, 365
  wild rice with carrots, 378
  zucchini
    and eggplant, 87
    Northeastern, 88
balls
  beef, sweet, 744
  cheese, 175
  chocolate, 443
  fish
    Midwestern, 336
    Sister Lisset's Shaker, 43
  grits, deep-fried, 176
  popcorn, 462
  rum (rum kegeln), 444
  sauerkraut, 318
banana
  bread
    Mountain/Northern Plains, 522
    Northeastern, 99
    Southern, 262
  chiffon cake, 421
  drops, sugar-coated, 444
  fruitcake, 418
  ice cream, homemade, 427
  meringue dessert, 749
  muffins, 393
  pudding, 281
  salad platter, 621
bananas
  à la Turtle Cay, 287
  flambées, 287
barbecue sauce
  Hornersville, 455
  hot, 303
  Lion's Club, 456
  Mississippi, 303
  Pacific Coast, 762
  Pendennis Club, 304
  Southwestern, 649
barbecued
  beef roast, 340
  chicken
    Midwestern, 358
    Southern, 223
    wings, oven-, 318
  lamb shanks, 586
  meat balls, 345
  Newport crab, 676

barbecued *(cont'd)*
  salmon Indian style, 686
  spareribs
    Joe's, 581
    Midwestern, 354
  venison, 362
barley
  and beef soup, 16
  soup
    Midwestern, 323
    Mountain/Northern Plains, 472
bars
  applesauce, 543
  apricot, 642
  beef 'n' fruit, 744
  date chocolate, 643
  maple walnut, 146
  molasses fruit and nut, 147
  raisin, 643
basic roux for gravies, 457
Basque
  chicken with rice, 703
  sheepherder's pasties, 698
bass
  with grapes, 572
  sea, poached Chinese style (bok sui
    ngui), 691
  striped
    baked, 32
    clam-stuffed, baked, 185
    with minced clam stuffing, 32
basting sauce for barbecues, 649
batter
  bread, 256
  -fried chicken, 219
  frying
    for vegetables, 564
    zucchini in, 724
Bavarian
  cream, peppermint stick, 284
  dumplings (semmel knodel), 466
  fruit ice cream, 640
beach plum jelly without pectin, 155
bean
  cakes, hominy and, 243
  carrot and cabbage salad, 618
  and chile casserole, 582
  paste soup (miso-shiru), 667
  pot
    Connecticut, 56
    stew, Monday's, 45
  salad
    hot, 618
    marinated, 93
    twenty-four-hour, 385
  soup
    for a crowd, five, 326
    Mountain, 471
beanhole beans, 371

beans
  apples 'n', Meg's, 713
  baked: see baked beans
  beef 'n', 340
  brown, meat balls with, 48
  green: see green beans
  kidney: see kidney beans
  pease porridge hot, 75
  porridge, 76
  salad, sweet 'n', 713
  samp 'n', 75
  spinach with (Lucy's quelites), 607
  string: see green beans
  white, salad of, 75
bear steak, 494
beaten biscuits, 261
beef, 44–51, 208–11, 338–47, 477–79,
    575–81, 693–97
  balls, sweet, 744
  and barley soup, 16
  bean pot stew, Monday's, 45
  boiled
    horseradish and dill gravies
      for, Holiday Folk Fair, 458
    with stappa (mashed rutabagas),
      342
  brisket of, oven-barbecued, 578
  burgers, potato and, 344; see also
    hamburgers
  burros, green chile, 586
  California casserole, 697
  candy, 556
  chili: see chili
  chipped
    corn with, 375
    rarebit, 233
  corned: see corned beef
  cubes with biscuits, 477
  fillet of, roast, 340
  gesado (Spanish stew), 581
  ground: see ground beef; also
    hamburgers, meat balls, meat
      loaf
  hamburgers
    Anne's, 343
    camping, 344
  hot-ta-meat pies, 209
  how to corn, 342
  meat balls
    barbecued, 345
    with brown beans, 48
    in cream, Norwegian, 478
    Dutchie's, 580
    Greek, 47
    Midwestern
      I (Iowa), 344
      II (Minnesota), 344
      III (Iowa), 345
    Northeastern, 45
    Stroganoff, 579
  meat loaf

beef (cont'd)
  avocado, 579
  cheese and, 343
  Dakota, 478
  fruit-stuffed, 48
  with mushroom tomato sauce,
    Paula's surprise, 47
  with parsley, 346
  meat patties (fleischkuechle), 478
  mock ravioli casserole, 693
  mold, jellied, 479
  'n' beans, 340
  'n' fruit bars, 744
  ngo yuk fan kay (beef tomato), 696
  -over, Grandmother's, 478
  pot roast
    with carrot gravy, 693
    spicy New England, 45
    Texas, 580
  pudding, 44
  rock salt roast, 694
  round roast, Cuban, 209
  sauerbraten, 341
  short ribs
    Hawaiian, 695
    ranch-style, 578
  steak: see steak
  sukiyaki, Ruby's, 696
  tenderloin casserole, Charlie's Café
    peppered, 343
  teriyaki, Ruby's, 695
  tongue fricassee (pipian de lengua),
    600
  vegetable soup, 319
  vine maple roast, 694
  and wild rice casserole, 346
beer
  and buffalo pie, 493
  cheese soup, 472
  cheesecake with, 127
  and cucumber soup, chilled, 20
  soup, 327
beet
  borscht, spring, 323
  and kraut salad, 714
  pickles, best ever, 448
  relish, 151
  wine, 555
beets
  honey fruited, 503
  tangy, 370
benne seed wafers, 176
Berlinerkranser (Christmas wreaths),
    439
Berlinerkranser, 542
Bermuda pork chops, 212
berry and rhubarb relish, 758
Bertha's pickled salmon, 680
best ever beet pickles, 448
Beth's oatmeal cake, 532

beverages, 158–59, 306–9, 459–60,
    555–56, 651–52
  beet wine, 555
  blackberry syrup, 307
  buttermilk shake, 459
  café brûlot, 307
  chocolate, New Mexican, 651
  cocktail
    Margharita, 651
    salty dog, 308
    sangrita, 651
    Sazerac, 308
    Tarpon Isle rum, 308
  Dan's delight (chokeberry wine),
    555
  dandelion wine, 460
  eggnog
    Joe's, 459
    John's, 306
    Southern, 306
  elderberry blossom wine
    Mountain/Northern Plains, 555
    Southern, 307
  fisherman's swizzle, 158
  hot buttered rum, 159
  lemonade, Fourth of July, 459
  mint julep, 308
  punch
    Edenton, 307
    hot grape, 460
    Jefferson Davis, 460
    milk, 307
    tequila, 652
  rhubarb wine, 555
  sangria, 652
  scuppernong nectar, 308
  slemp, 159
  Wassail bowl, 159
Bibb lettuce salad, 252
biscochitos (aniseed cookies), 642
biscotti, Italian, 752
biscuits
  beaten, 261
  cheese, 261
  clam, 97
  cottage cheese, 732
  ham, 174
  jam, 437
  potato, 97
  sour cream puff, 477
  Southern
    Mississippi, 261
    South Carolina, 260
  sweet potato, 261
  tea, 441
  water cress, 391
  whole wheat, 522
bisque
  crawfish, 177
  shrimp, 178
bitso bitso (sweet potato patties), 723

bitter orange marmalade, 294
black bean soup, 180
black beans
    with rum, 237
    savory (frijoles negros), 237
black bear Stroganoff, 494
black bottom pie, 267
black-eyed pea soup, 180
black-eyed peas
    and hog jawl (jowl), Mrs. Jackson
        Porter Dick's, 215
    and rice (Hopping John), 239
    Southern, 238
    Texas caviar, 564
black walnut pie, 264
blackberry
    and apple jelly, 291
    syrup, 307
    tarts, Depoe Bay, 739
blender hollandaise, 157
blintzes
    cheese, 139
    Passover, 139
blitz torte, 527
blod polse (blood sausage), 356
blood
    pudding (morcilla), 600
    sausage (blod polse), 356
blue ribbon maple syrup fudge, 160
blueberry
    -apple conserve, 153
    buckle, fresh, 138
    cobbler, Down-East, 138
    gingerbread, Edna's, 121
    muffins, 98
    nut bread, 99
    pie
        deep-dish, 108
        Northeastern, 107
        velvet custard, 108
    and rhubarb relish, 758
    roll, 138
    shortcake, 129
    upside-down squares, 743
bluefish
    baked
        with rosemary, 32
        stuffed (oyster), 33
    Boston, Florentine, 33
bog, chicken, 228
Bohemian
    cheese dumplings with sour cream,
        557
    oukrop, 471
    spareribs, 480
boil, fish, 335
boiled
    and baked country ham, 216
    beef
        horseradish and dill gravies for,
            Holiday Folk Fair, 458

boiled (cont'd)
    with stappa (mashed rutabagas),
        342
    dinner, Vermont, 49
    raisin whole wheat cake, 535
    salad dressing
        Mountain/Northern Plains, 512
        Southern, 253
    salmon heads, Wasco, 681
    spareribs, 212
bok choy pickle (Chinese cabbage),
    755
bok sui ngui (poached sea bass,
    Chinese style), 691
bologna gravy, 355
bonbons, lemon, 444
Bonneville Dam stuffed salmon, 684
borscht
    chilled, 324
    spring beet, 323
Bosnian casserole, Paula's, 351
Boston
    bluefish Florentine, 33
    cream pie, 122
    tripe, 64
bouillabaisse, Martha's Vineyard
    Stonewall, 41
bourbon
    "brandied" peaches, 153
    date pudding, 282
    jelly, 295
    nut cake, 634
    pie, 269
    spiced sweet potatoes, baked, 248
braised
    frogs' legs with sherry, 229
    lettuce with rosemary, 79
    pheasant, 489
    quail, 231
        with sherry, 366
    stuffed pork chops, 353
brandied
    apricots, 756
    peaches, 452
Brandywine River salad, 91
bread and butter pickles
    Midwestern, 448
    New York, 149
    Winchester Center, 149
bread crumb hot cakes, 735
bread dumplings, 557
bread pudding
    apple, 537
    Ozark's, 432
    rhubarb, 538
    royal, 432
bread sticks, sesame, 728
breaded
    artichoke hearts, 603
    oysters, 678

breads, 96–105, 255–63, 390–407,
    513–23, 623–29, 728–35
    high-altitude baking, note on, 513
breads, quick
    apple nut, 728
    apricot nut, 728
    avocado pecan, 624
    banana
        Mountain/Northern Plains, 522
        Northeastern, 99
        Southern, 262
    batter, 256
    biscuits: see biscuits
    blueberry nut, 99
    brown
        Northeastern I (Massachusetts),
            98
        Northeastern II (Maine), 98
    buñeolos, Lucy's, 626
    cinnamon walnut quick, 626
    corn
        bacon 'n', 627
        buttermilk, Southern, 257
        crackling, 256
        dumplings, mixed greens with,
            245
        harvest, 391
        hot water (hoe cake), 255
            deep-fried, 257
            Midwestern, 390
        lacy, 259
        Mexican, 627
        molasses, 259
        New Mexican, 627
        Southern
            Arkansas, 220
            South Carolina, 255
        stuffing
            chicken with, 219
            cranberry, 161
        Texas, 627
        Vivian's, 255
        waterground, Philipsburg, 96
    crullers: see crullers
    doughnuts: see doughnuts
    flat
        Ethel's, 516
        Mylah's, 516
    fruit, 392
    hot cakes: see hot cakes
    johnnycakes, 96
    lemon, 625
    muffins: see muffins
    oatmeal bran, 99
    orange
        Northwestern, 734
        nut, 624
    Osage squaw, 390
    pancakes: see pancakes
    Passover crispy sticks, 105
    pineapple loaf, fresh, 734

breads, quick *(cont'd)*
popovers: *see* popovers
prune nut, 732
puffs: *see* puffs
rolls: *see* rolls
salt-rising, 517
scones: *see* scones
sopapillas (puffy fried bread), 626
spoon, 256
bacon and cheese, 259
steamed Indian, 390
sweet potato, 260
waffles: *see* waffles
walnut
brown, 625
Cheddar loaf, 625
-fig, 623
breads, yeast
adobe, 395
almond strips, 403
anadama, 102
apple, 104
buffalo, Jamestown, 513
casserole, 395
challah, Rebecca's, 99
Christmas
Arizona, 628
Czech, 520
see also julekage
coffeecake
apple
German, 400
Northeastern, 125
Maggie Murphy's aunt's, 125
Mountain/Northern Plains, 519
Northeastern, 124
quick, 126
ring, Jennie's, 104
sour cream, 125
Valborg's, 404
Danish, filled, 399
dumplings: *see* dumplings
ham in rye, 729
julekage (Christmas bread), 400
kause seed, 516
kolaches, Aunt Mary's, 40
kuchen
I (North Dakota), 518
II (Nebraska), 518
marmalade, and fruit loaves, 402
Norwegian dark, 396
potato, 103
pumpkin
Midwestern, 392
Northeastern, 103
ranch, 514
rolls: *see* rolls
rye
Finnish sour (ruisleipa), 397
Grandmother Rezac's, 513
Northeastern, 103

breads, yeast *(cont'd)*
orange, 517
sour dough: *see* sour dough
Swedish, 397
saffron, 402
Sally Lunn, 263
sausage, 395
sesame bread sticks, 728
sour dough
French, 731
pie crust, 730
rye, 396
white
Northeastern, 102
Northwestern, 730
stone-ground wheat, 733
Swedish limpa, 403
tea loaf, rich, 104
twist loaf, Ukrainian, 399
whole wheat, easy 100 per cent,
515
yeast recipe, large, 394
breasts of chicken
cold, 69
stuffed, 222
breasts of grouse
with ham, 486
in Madeira sauce, 487
breasts of pheasant, fried, 489
bridal pudding, 283
brisket of beef, oven-barbecued, 578
brittle, peanut, 461
broccoli
with ham and cheese, 372
and onion casserole, 77
ring, 372
Sicilian, 76
stalks, 715
brochette, oysters en, 194
broiled
ling cod with mustard sauce, 674
live Maine lobster, 29
red snapper, 201
salmon steaks, 686
Depoe Bay, 686
scrod, 35
shad roe, 39
soft-shelled crabs, 189
tomatoes, 251
venison steaks, 497
walleyed pike fillets, 332
broth, liver dumplings in
(leberkloesse), 322
brown beans, meat balls with, 48
brown bread
Northeastern
I (Massachusetts), 98
II (Maine), 98
wainut, 625
brown sugar muffins, 393
brownie drops, 144

brownies
cream cheese, 147
filbert, 754
fudge, 445
our Aunt Harriet's favorite, 290
Passover, 148
brownstone front, 533
Brunswick stew
old-fashioned, Michigan style, 357
Southern, 228
Brussels sprouts, orange, 613
Buckeye maple syrup cake, 424
buckwheat griddlecakes, 406
buffalo
and beer pie, 493
birds, 491
buffaloaf, 493
meat balls in wine sauce, 492
ribs, apple-stuffed, 491
steak, deviled, 492
steaks with wild rice dressing, 492
buffalo berry
catchup, 549
and chokecherry jelly, 552
buffalo bread, Jamestown, 513
buffalo cookies, Hawkins'
Jamestown, 542
buffalo fish chowder, 327
buffaloaf, 493
bulghur or cracked wheat
and chicken casserole, 702
cole slaw with, 510
fried wheat, Oregon, 725
tomato, 509
bullhead, baked, 476
bundt cake, 119
buñeolos, Lucy's, 626
burgers
meat and potato, 344
reindeer, 710
wild, 364
see also hamburgers
Burgundy-olive sauce, roast wild
ducks with, 601
burros, green chile, 586
butter
almond, oysters with, 679
apple, 453
cake, 275
cranberry-apple, 760
fingers, 288
-fried corn, 240
lemon, old-fashioned, 305
rhubarb, 551
sauce, 369
for apple pie pudding, 431
tomato, 452
apple, hot, 548
twists, 746
walnut, Joe's fried trout with, 691
butterflied leg of lamb, crumbed, 53

buttergebachtness, 440
buttermilk
  corn bread, Southern, 257
  dessert, 429
  -glazed pineapple carrot cake, 420
  pancakes, 407
  shake, 459
  sherbet, 429
  soup, cold, 329
butternut squash, spiced, 89
butterscotch
  candy, 461
  chocolate pie, 268

cabbage
  baked, 504
  bean and carrot salad, 618
  casserole
    Midwestern, 373
    Southern, 239
  chicken au chou, 594
  Chinese, pickle, 755
  cream, 373
  dressing for roast pheasant, 488
  -filled peppers, 82
  fried, 504
  golden, 77
  and lamb, Farmers Market, 585
  and mushroom casserole, 721
  Pennsylvania Dutch, 77
  and pepper relish, 449
  and potato, 504
  red: see red cabbage
  rolls, 480
  salad, 384
    Greta's, 385
  slaw, 509
  sour, 718
cactus
  pads (nopales or nopalitos), 608
  salad, 616
Caesar salad
  Farmers Market, 617
  Northwestern, 719
café brûlot, 307
Cajun jambalaya, 228
cake fillings: see fillings, cake
cake frostings and icings: see frostings
  and icings
cakes, 115–30, 273–80, 417–27,
  528–36, 634–38, 740–47
  angel food
    prize Northeastern, 117
    Southern, 277
  apple
    Dutch, Connie's, 531
    Mountain/Northern Plains, 528
    Passover, 123
    pie, 528
    raw, 528

cakes (cont'd)
  upside-down, 123
  applesauce, 423
  apricot
    lattice, 124
    Southwestern, 634
  banana chiffon, 421
  blueberry
    gingerbread, Edna's, 121
    upside-down squares, 743
  Boston cream pie, 122
  bourbon nut, 634
  brownstone front, 533
  bundt, 119
  butter, Southern, 275
  buttermilk glazed pineapple carrot,
    420
  cheesecake
    with beer, 127
    cottage cheese, 128
    deluxe, 127
    Evelyn's, 126
    no-crust, 426
    Passover, 126
  chocolate
    French, 116
    Greta's, 422
    -potato, pioneer, 741
  Christmas, 122
    pork, old-fashioned, 530
  citrus, 636
  coconut upside-down, fresh, 740
  coffeecake
    apple, 125
    cranberry, 535
    Maggie Murphy's aunt's, 125
    Northeastern, 124
    Oregon farmhouse, 746
    quick
      Mountain/Northern Plains,
        532
      Northeastern, 126
    sour cream
      Northeastern, 125
      Northwestern, 742
  devil's food, 534
  1870 mahogany, 423
  fruit
    and nut loaf, 529
    rub-up, 740
  fruitcake
    applesauce, 278
    banana, 418
    Dymple's, 419
    Northeastern, 121
    past perfect, 278
    white, 278
  gingerbread, blue, Edna's, 121
  golden, 417
  gugelhopf with filberts, 744
  honey chocolate, 115

cakes (cont'd)
  jam, 276
  jellyroll, 533
  Lady Baltimore, 280
  lane
    filling, 279
    layers, 279
  lemon, 276
  maple
    sugar, 119
    syrup, Buckeye, 424
  Mrs. D's Moravian sugar, 280
  molasses, 425
  o-apple, 531
  oatmeal
    Beth's, 532
    Midwestern, 423
    Southwestern, 635
  old-fashioned cream, 124
  orange
    à l', 274
    butter, 637
    -ginger, quick, 741
    glazed, Julia's, 123
    Southern, 273
    Southwestern, 635
  peach preserve, 743
  pecan cherry, 276
  persimmon upside-down, 425
  plum kuchen, Dutch, 745
  poppy seed, 426
  poundcake
    Midwestern, 417
    Southern
      I (South Carolina), 275
      II (South Carolina), 275
  prune
    and apricot upside-down cake,
      Slovak, 418
    Mountain/Northern Plains, 529
  pumpkin, 115
  red velvet, 422
  rhubarb, 530
    pudding, 743
    and strawberry roll, 742
  sandbakkelse, 529
  sausage, Dymple's, 420
  Scripture, 531
  Serbian torte, 426
  shortcake
    blueberry, 129
    Fourth of July, 129
  sorghum, Grandmother's, 425
  spice, 119
  spongecake
    Northeastern, 118
    Passover, 118
    zuppa inglese, 117
  sugar plum, 277
  torte: see torte
  velvet lunch, 121

cakes *(cont'd)*
  vinaterta, 534
  walnut, 635
  whipped cream, 533
  white, with choice of frostings, 420
  whole wheat
    boiled raisin, 535
    chiffon, 532
  zuppa inglese, 117
calabacitas (green summer squash),
  615
caldo de camaron (shrimp soup), 565
calf's liver, Texas, 600
California
  avocado salad, 616
  casserole, 697
  chicken, 703
  citrus chiffon pie, 630
  green rice, 610
  salad dressing, 616
  string beans, 606
calves' testicles: *see* Rocky Mountain
  (or prairie) oysters
Camarillo sausage and limas, 582
canapés
  ham and egg, 173
  lobster, 6
  see also appetizers
candied
  carrots for Passover, 78
  grapefruit peel, 161
  lemon or orange peel, 762
  orange
    pecans, 310
    peel, 160
    walnuts, 652
candies, 159–61, 309–11, 461–63,
  556–57, 652–54, 762–63
  beef, 556
  butterscotch, 461
  candied
    grapefruit peel, 161
    lemon or orange peel, 762
    orange
      pecans, 310
      peel, 160
      walnuts, 652
  candy date loaf, 654
  caramel popcorn, 159
  caramels
    Mountain/Northern Plains, 556
    Peggy's, 462
    Southern, 310
  chocolate, Southern, 309
  crystallized
    grapes, 311
    rose petals, 463
  fruit, for Passover, 160
  fudge
    easy no-cook, 556
    five-minute, 653

candies *(cont'd)*
    maple syrup, blue ribbon, 160
    peanut butter, 461
    Southern, 309
    walnut, 653
  Grandmother's Thanksgiving
    special, 462
  hard, homemade, 161
  high-altitude candy-making, note
    on, 556
  honey taffy, 556
  lollipops, homemade, 161
  molasses taffy, 654
  peanut brittle, 461
  peppermint taffy, 461
  perfect divinity, 653
  popcorn balls, 462
  pralines, 309
  salami sweetmeat (uncooked), 462
  sugar-glazed nuts, 310
  toffee
    Northwestern, 763
    Southwestern, 653
candy date loaf, 654
Canlis salad, 90
cantaloupe
  and orange jam, 292
  -peach preserve, 453
Cape Cod
  clam chowder, 11
  cranberry pie, 109
  deep-dish clam pie, 23
  lobster
    roll, 28
    soup, 12
caper and mustard sauce, 762
capers
  cole slaw with, 252
  pork chops with, 351
  whitefish with, 333
capon
  cranberry sausage stuffing for, 464
  roast young, with wild rice and
    almond stuffing, 357
caramel popcorn, 159
caramels
  Peggy's, 462
  Southern, 310
caraway seeds, chicken with, 358
carbonnades à la flamande, elk, 498
carne con vinagre (meat with
  vinegar), 599
carrot
  bean and cabbage salad, 618
  cookies, 141
  and cucumber relish, 548
  gravy, pot roast with, 693
  loaf, 503
  marmalade, New England, 154
  pickled daikon and, 755
  pickles

carrot *(cont'd)*
  Peggy's, 448
  sweet, 645
  pie, spiced, 271
  pineapple cake, buttermilk glazed,
    420
  pudding
    baked, 538
    steamed, 539
carrots
  candied, for Passover, 78
  with celery, 374
  crystal, 374
  and cucumbers, 715
  pickled garden, 295
  wild rice with, baked, 378
casserole bread, 395
casserole pudding, a (cazuela), 133
casseroles
  artichoke and sea food, 198
  bean and chile, 582
  broccoli and onion, 77
  cabbage
    Midwestern, 373
    and mushroom, 721
    Southern, 239
  California, 697
  cheese grits, 234
  chestnut, 725
  chicken
    and bulghur, 702
    and tortilla (enchiladas verde al
      estilo de mi casa), 588
    and wild rice, 357
  chilies rellenos, 610
  clam
    and corn, Oreas Island, 673
    Northwestern, 673
  corn
    Midwestern, 375
    Mountain/Northern Plains, 501
  eggplant
    and chicken liver, 66
    and macaroni, Helen's, 52
    Midwestern, 376
    Southwestern, 606
  green bean, 236
  grits and Cheddar, 613
  hominy, 612
  hunt and polo eggplant, 242
  kidney bean, 605
  lentil, 714
  lima bean, 713
  mashed potato, 83
  mock ravioli, 693
  Paula's Bosnian, 351
  pecan squash, 250
  peppered tenderloin, Charlie's Café,
    343
  potato, 381
  rice

casseroles *(cont'd)*
    and green bean, 370
    Hazel's, 610
    and parsley, 378
    shrimp, 570
    squash
        and cheese, 88
        Southwestern, 614
    veal and eggplant, 347
    vegetable
        Mountain/Northern Plains, 501
        summer, Libby's, 87
    wild duck breasts en, baked, 365
    wild rice
        and beef, 346
        Midwestern, 379
        and olive, 378
    zucchini and cheese, 614
Castillia, chicken, 595
catchup
    buffalo berry, 549
    cranberry, 756
    gooseberry, 452
    grape, 550
    prune, 756
catfish
    baked, 185
    or bullhead, baked, 476
    gumbo, 186
cauliflower slaw, 252
caviar
    mousse, 4
    Texas, 564
cazuela (a casserole pudding), 133
celery
    carrots with, 374
    in cheese sauce, 239
    chowder, 182
    with egg and lemon sauce, 240
    fried, 501
    sauce, salmon loaf with, 683
    seed dressing
        Midwestern, 388
        Northwestern, 727
cellophane noodle and meat ball soup,
    668
challah, Rebecca's, 99
charcoal broiled shrimp, 665
Charles Street Indian pudding, 134
Charleston breakfast shrimp, 201
Charlie's Café peppered tenderloin
    casserole, 343
Chartres Street trout, 206
Cheddar cheese
    balls, 175
    chili with hominy and, 576
    chilies rellenos (stuffed long
        peppers), 609
        casserole, 610
    crackus, 234
    custard, 234

Cheddar cheese *(cont'd)*
    green rice, 509
    and grits casserole, 613
    and leek omelet, baked, 720
    and rice soufflé, 377
    sauce, baked asparagus with, 73
    scalloped rutabagas or yellow
        turnips, 84
    and shrimp casserole, 571
    soup, 22
    straws, 176
    wafers, 316
    walnut loaf, 625
    Welsh rabbit, 234
    and zucchini casserole, 614
cheese and cheese dishes
    appetizers, 565
    apple pie, glazed, 414
    and bacon spoon bread, 259
    balls, 175
    biscuits, 261
        cottage cheese, 732
    blintzes, 139
        Passover, 139
    broccoli with ham and, 372
    chile appetizers, 562
    chili with hominy and, 576
    chilies rellenos (stuffed long
        peppers), 609
        casserole, 610
    and clam appetizers, 657
    crackus, 234
    crisps, 469
    custard, 234
    dip (chile con queso), 563
    dumplings with sour cream,
        Bohemian, 557
    eggs with ham and (huevos
        motulenos), 597
    grits casserole, 234
    and meat loaf, 343
    -olive appetizers, 316
    pastries (tiropetes), 9
    pie, fruited, 632
    potato bake, 508
    quesadillas, 563
    and rice soufflé, 377
    sauce
        Northeastern, 73
        Southern, 239
    scalloped rutabagas or yellow
        turnips, 84
    soup
        Northeastern, 22
        Southwestern (sopa de queso),
        566
    squash and, casserole, 88
    straws, 176
    -stuffed
        mushrooms, 9
        squash, 250

cheese and cheese dishes *(cont'd)*
    wafers, 316
    zucchini
        casserole, 614
        custard, 249
cheesecake
    with almond crust, 634
    with beer, 127
    cottage cheese, 128
    deluxe, 127
    Evelyn's, 126
    no-crust, 426
    Passover, 126
Cherokee hickory nut pie, 414
cherries, pickled (cherry olives), 549
cherry
    -apple pie, 525
    olives (pickled cherries), 549
    pecan cake, 276
    pie, crumb-topped, 416
    and rum sauce, 305
    soup, 327
cherry tomatoes, stuffed, 174
Chesapeake Bay fish stew, 205
chess
    pie
        rum and rhubarb, 273
        Southern
            I (Kentucky), 265
            II (Kentucky), 266
    tarts, 266
chestnut casserole, 725
chicken, 65–70, 217–29, 357–62,
    482–83, 587–89, 594–97, 702–7
    à la Kai, 704
    à la king, 360
    almond, 595
    anise appetizers, cold, 658
    arroz con pollo Nuevo Mexicano
        (rice with, Mexican style), 597
    with artichokes, 594
    au chou, 594
    baked, 65
        camp style, 703
    barbecued
        Midwestern, 358
        Southern, 223
    Basque, with rice, 703
    batter-fried, 219
    bog, 228
    breasts
        cold, 69
        stuffed, 222
    Brunswick stew
        old-fashioned, Michigan style,
        357
        Southern, 228
    and bulghur casserole, 702
    California, 703
    capon: *see* capon
    with caraway seeds, 358

chicken (cont'd)
  Castillia, 595
  corn bread, 361
    stuffing with, 219
  and corn pudding, Iowa, 360
  crab
    bake, 223
    -stuffed, 70
  creamed, and mushrooms, 705
  and dumplings, 482
  eggplant with, 68
  enchiladas, cream, 590
  fricassee, Aunt Mary's, 707
  fried
    Iowa, 358
    with plum sauce, 702
    round steak with cream gravy, 338
    in teriyaki sauce, 702
    see also Southern fried in this entry
  green enchiladas, 589
  gumbo, 225
  jambalaya, 226
  legs, stuffed, 359
  liver
    and eggplant casserole, 66
    soup, 473
  livers
    with sage, 65
    wild rice with, 379
  loaf
    Midwestern, 360
    Southern, 224
  with luau or spinach, 706
  marinade for, Hazel's ginger, 649
  mole, 587
  'n' dumplings, 220
  with noodle balls, 482
  Olivette, 220
  orange, 706
    walnut, 594
  paprika, 68
  parsley-stuffed, 67
  with peanuts in hoisin sauce, 705
  pie
    elegant, 66
    Hancock Shaker Village Sister
        Clymena's, 67
    Mom's Arkansas, 221
  in pineapples, 707
  pot pie, Pennsylvania, 65
  poulet Floride, 224
  pressed
    Midwestern, 361
    Southern, 224
  pudding, 221
  with pumpkin seed sauce, 596
  Raphael Weill, 704
  salad, fruited, Peggy's, 386
  in sauce (pollo en salsa), 596

chicken (cont'd)
  scalloped Iowa, 359
  Seven Hearths, 223
  soup
    corn and, 17
    cream of, 17
    with noodles, 322
  Southern fried
    I (Mississippi), 217
    II (Tennessee), 218
    III (Alabama), 218
  spaghetti, 226
    salad, 726
  stew, dumplings for, 465
  stuffings
    corn bread, 219
    dressing, 465
    fruit, Midwestern, 465
    potato, 162
    rice, 464
  tamales, 588
  teriyaki, 695
  and tongue mold, 362
  tortilla casserole (enchiladas verdes
      al estilo de mi casa), 588
  verde, 589
  with wild rice casserole, 357
  wings
    gumbo-style, 225
    oven-barbecued, 318
  and zucchini, 68
chick-pea salad, 617
chick-peas with chilies, 606
chiffon
  cake
    banana, 421
    whole wheat, 532
  pie
    citrus, California, 630
    cranberry pumpkin, 109
    lemon, 270
    orange, 110
      liqueur, 270
    pumpkin, Annie's, 413
  tart, orange liqueur, 270
chile
  and bean casserole, 582
  cheese appetizers, 562
  con queso (cheese dip), 563
  green, burros, 586
  sauce
    New Mexico, 592
    Southern California, 598
chili
  Cleto Hernandez's, 576
  con carne
    with ground beef, 575
    Nelson's, 576
  hamburgers with, 578
  with hominy and cheese, 576
  with rice, 577

chili (cont'd)
  sauce
    Fulling Mill Farm, 152
    Southern, 300
    uncooked, 550
  soup, 318
  stew, Indian Zuñi green, 585
  Texas, 575
  Uvalde, 575
chilies
  chick-peas with, 606
  curried corn with, 604
  rellenos (stuffed long peppers), 609
    casserole, 610
chilled
  borscht, 324
  Gulf Coast shrimp Creole, 171
  halibut steaks, 677
  red snapper appetizer, 172
Chilmark scallops, 31
Chinese
  almond cookies, 753
  cabbage pickle, 755
  pork balls, 659
  roast duck, 709
chipped beef
  corn with, 375
  rarebit, 233
chitterlings, 214
chocolate
  balls, 443
  butterscotch pie, 268
  cake
    French, 116
    Greta's, 422
    seven-layer, for Passover, 116
  candy, 309
  date bars, 643
  frosting
    Greta's, 422
    Mabel's, 536
    Midwestern, 421
    Northeastern, 117
  homemade ice cream, 427
  honey cake, 115
  "macaroons," 442
  New Mexican, 651
  pie
    French silk, 411
    Northeastern, 112
  -potato cake, pioneer, 741
  pudding
    Northeastern, 132
    pecan, 282
  puff balls, 433
  raisin pie, 632
  rum
    dessert, 430
    pie, 268
  sauce
    Northeastern, 132

chocolate *(cont'd)*
    Southern, 284
    surprise cookies, 141
    walnut mousse, 136
chokecherry
    and buffalo berry jelly, 552
    or Juneberry pie, 527
    wine (Dan's delight), 555
chorizo (spiced dried sausage), 587
chowder, fish
    buffalo fish, 327
    clam
        Cape Cod, 11
        and corn, 666
        Maryland, 179
        old-fashioned, 11
        quick, 665
        Sea Hag, 665
    conch, 176
    haddock, Down-East, 11
    Mountain, 470
    Northwestern, 670
    Rhode Island, 15
    salmon
        I (Alaska), 671
        II (Washington), 671
    shrimp, 670
    whiting, Montauk, 14
chowder, vegetable
    celery, 182
    corn
        Midwestern, 325
        Northeastern, 17
    egg, 22
    Yankee bean, 21
Christmas
    Berlinerkranser, 542
    bread
        Arizona, 628
        Czech, 520
        julekage
            Midwestern, 400
            Mountain/Northern Plains,
                521
    cake, 122
    cookies
        Finnish, 440
        Veronica's, 143
    crullers (Swedish klenater), 405
    pork cake, old-fashioned, 530
    pudding, 132
    wreaths (Berlinerkransar), 439
Chuck's roasted sweet peppers, 661
church supper scalloped potatoes, 507
chutney: *see* pickles, relishes,
    preserves and condiments
cider
    apple pie, 415
    apples, 136

cinnamon
    rolls
        plain and fancy, 405
        sour dough, 731
        whole wheat, 519
    stars, 753
    walnut quick bread, 626
cioppino, 672
ciscoes, baked, 333
citrus
    cake, 636
    chiffon pie, California, 630
    salmon with, 679
    sherbet, 749
clam
    bake, Rhode Island steamer, 26
    biscuits, 97
    cakes
        Massachusetts, 25
        Port Angeles, 674
        Rhode Island, 27
    casserole, 673
    chowder
        Cape Cod, 11
        corn and, 666
        old-fashioned, 11
        quick, 665
        Sea Hag, 665
    fritter appetizer, 657
    fritters
        Agate Beach, 673
        Northeastern, 26
        Washington, 673
    loaf, 674
    and mushroom soup, 665
    pie
        Cape Cod deep-dish, 23
        Massachusetts, 24
        New York, 23
    puff balls, 657
    salad, 89
    sauce, spaghetti with, 25
    soufflé, 24
    -stuffed baked rock fish (striped
        bass), 185
    stuffing, striped bass with minced,
        32
    and Tillamook cheese appetizers,
        657
    and tomato broth, hot, 19
clams
    baked, 24
        stuffed, 5
    Casino, 658
    fried
        Maryland, 186
        Northeastern, 26
Cleto Hernandez's chili, 576
cloudberry jam, 760

cobblers and crisps
    apple cobbler, 537
    apple crisp, 137
    blueberry cobbler, Down-East, 138
    peach cobbler, 272
cocktail
    crab and avocado, 561
    meat balls, 469
    sauce
        celery-tomato, for shrimp, 170
        Midwestern, for sea foods, 455
        Southern, for sea food, 172
    shrimp, with celery-tomato sauce,
        170
cocktails
    Margharita, 651
    salty dog, 308
    sangrita, 651
    Sazerac, 308
    Tarpon Isle rum, 308
coconut
    cake with apricot glaze for
        Passover, 120
    cookies, Mountain/Northern Plains,
        542
    cream, spinach with, 716
    frosting, 120
    squares, 146
    upside-down cake, fresh, 740
cod
    bacalao, 574
    balls, 336
    creamed, 35
    ling, with mustard sauce, broiled,
        674
    maître d'hôtel, fresh, 34
    pie, 34
coffee walnut soufflés, 135
coffeecake
    apple
        German, 400
        Northeastern, 125
    cranberry, 535
    Maggie Murphy's aunt's, 125
    Mountain/Northern Plains, 519
    Northeastern, 124
    quick
        Mountain/Northern Plains, 532
        Northeastern, 126
    ring, Jennie's, 104
    sour cream
        Northeastern, 125
        Northwestern, 742
    Valborg's, 404
cognac pie, 112
cold
    anise chicken appetizers, 658
    avocado soup, 569
    buttermilk soup, 329
    chicken breasts, 69

cold *(cont'd)*
  curried vegetables, 87
  pickled duck, 365
  raspberry soup, 671
  rice salad, 618
  vegetable soup, 321
cole slaw
  with bulghur, 510
  with capers, 252
  with cooked dressing, 94
  dressing, 253
  Midwestern, 384
  Southern, 252
  whipped cream, 385
  see also slaw
collard greens, mustard, turnip, and, 244
Columbia River smelt, 690
conch
  chowder, 176
  salad, raw, 186
  seviche, 167
  vinaigrette, 167
Connecticut bean pot, 56
Connie's Dutch apple cake, 531
conserves: *see* pickles, relishes, preserves, and condiments
cooked bacon dressing, 254
cookies, 140–48, 288–90, 435–46, 541–46, 641–44, 751–54
  Abigail's, 544
  almond
    butter, 439
    gingersnaps, Swedish, 445
  applesauce
    bars, 543
    whole wheat, 543
  Berlinerkranser, 542
  biscochitos (aniseed), 642
  biscotti, Italian, 752
  brownie drops, 144
  brownies
    cream cheese, 147
    filbert, 754
    fudge, 445
    our Aunt Harriet's favorite, 290
    Passover, 148
  buffalo, Hawkins' Jamestown, 542
  butter
    fingers, 288
    horns, Austrian, 436
  buttergebachtness, 440
  carrot, 141
  Chinese almond, 753
  chocolate
    balls, 443
    "macaroons," 442
    surprise, 141
  Christmas
    Berlinerkranser, 542
    Finnish, 440

cookies *(cont'd)*
  St. Nicholoos, 144
  Veronica's, 143
  wreaths (Berlinerkranser), 439
  cinnamon stars, 753
  coconut
    Mountain/Northern Plains, 542
    squares, Peggy's, 146
  currant
    Mountain/Northern Plains, 542
    Northeastern, 142
  Danish
    cones with whipped cream, 145
    pastry, 437
  date
    chocolate bars, 643
    and nut whirls, 541
  Dona's, 544
  fattigman
    Midwestern Scandinavian, 438
    Mountain/Northern Plains, 543
  fig bar, 642
  filled applesauce squares, 145
  Frazer's cheaters (nut squares), 146
  fruit bars, 446
  ginger, old-style, 544
  gingerbread men, 142
  hermits, 289
  holiday, 751
  Isabella's, 142
  jam biscuits, 437
  jan hagel, 147
  krum kake
    I (North Dakota), 545
    II (North Dakota), 546
  lemon bonbons, 444
  linzer, Hungarian, 435
  lizzies, 144
  makova zavin (Czech poppy seed roll), 435
  maple
    lace wafers, 145
    walnut bars, 146
  molasses
    fruit and nut bars, 147
    soft, 753
  orange
    oatmeal, 142
    Southwestern, 643
  Peggy's filled, 441
  pepper, 545
  persimmon, 445
  pfirsiche ("peaches"), 443
  prune-filled, Rose's, 441
  pumpkin, 754
  raisin bars, 643
  refrigerator, 438
    Rogue River, 751
  rocks
    Midwestern, 442
    Northeastern, 141

cookies *(cont'd)*
  rose water, 438
  rum kegeln (rum balls), 444
  St. Nicholoos, 144
  shellbark hickory kisses, 143
  shortbread
    Alison's, 439
    Finnish, 439
    rolls, Mary Lu's pecan, 443
  snickerdoodles, 289
  sour cream, old-fashioned, 140
  spice, 435
  spritz, 545
    Jane's 752
  sugar
    -coated banana drops, 444
    crisp, 641
    Southern, 289
  tea biscuits, 441
  walnut strips, Serbian, 436
cooler
  raspberry, 139
  strawberry, 183
Coos Bay crab cakes, 675
corn
  bread
    bacon 'n', 627
    buttermilk, Southern, 257
    chicken, 361
    crackling, 256
    dumplings, mixed greens with, 245
    harvest, 391
    hot water (hoe cake), 255
      deep-fried, 257
      Midwestern, 390
    lacy, 259
    Mexican, 627
    molasses, 259
    New Mexican, 628
    Southern
      Arkansas, 220
      South Carolina, 255
    stuffing
      chicken with, 219
      cranberry, 161
    Texas, 627
    Vivian's, 255
    waterground, Philipsburg, 96
  butter-fried, 240
  casserole
    and clam, Oreas Island, 673
    Midwestern, 375
    Mountain/Northern Plains, 501
  and chicken soup, 17
  with chipped beef, 375
  chowder
    Midwestern, 325
    Northeastern, 17
  and clam chowder, 666

corn *(cont'd)*
  curried, with chilies, 604
  fritters, 375
  meal
    muffins, 262
      cranberry, 98
    mush, fried, 257
    sticks, 257
  oysters, 240
  and pepper relish, 450
  pudding
    with bacon, 78
    chicken and, Iowa, 360
    green, 604
    Midwestern, 374
    Northeastern, 78
  relish, 548
  scalloped, Midwestern, 375
  soup
    cream of, 181
    fresh, 568
    Midwestern, 324
  stewed, Francille's, 240
  spider corncake, 96
corncob jelly, 551
corned beef
  hash, 50
  in a pot, 342
  red flannel hash, 50
  Reuben sandwich, 50
  and slaw salad, 387
  Vermont boiled dinner, 49
cottage cheese
  biscuits, 732
  cheesecake
    Evelyn's, 126
    Passover, 126
  filling for kolaches, 401
  and lima bean loaf, 371
  pumpkin pie with, 109
  spread, 317
country ham: *see* ham, country
court bouillon, 173
cow or field pea soup, 182
crab
  artichoke hearts and tarragon, 573
  and avocado cocktail, 561
  bake, 27
  barbecued Newport, 676
  cakes
    Coos Bay, 675
    I (Maryland), 186
    II (Maryland), 187
  chicken bake, 223
  deviled Western, 676
  diable, 675
  gumbo, 188
  marinated cracked, 676
  meat
    appetizer, 658
    deviled Northeastern

crab *(cont'd)*
    I (Maryland), 168
    II (Maryland), 168
  imperial, 189
  puffs, hot, 169
  sandwich, king, 677
  sauce, poached pollock with, 33
  sauté, 168
  she-
    and lobster soup, 178
    soup, 178
  shrimp and, baked, 5
  soup, South River Club, 179
  stew
    Northeastern, 27
    Northwestern, 674
    Southern, 187
  stone, steamed, 188
  -stuffed
    chicken, 70
    flounder, whole, Herb's, 35
crab apple
  jelly, 552
  pickles, 449
crabs
  hard-shelled, steamed, 189
  soft-shelled
    broiled, 189
    deep-fried, 187
cracked crab, marinated, 676
cracked wheat or bulghur
  cole slaw with, 510
  tomato, 509
cracker pudding, 134
crackling
  bread cakes, 258
  corn bread, 256
crackus, 234
cranberries, sweets and, scalloped, 86
cranberry
  -apple butter, 760
  catchup, 756
  corn bread stuffing, 161
  corn meal muffins, 98
  -filbert tart, 737
  and horseradish sauce, 304
  pie
    Cape Cod, 109
    -pumpkin chiffon, 109
  pork chops, 57
  pudding, steamed, 130
  relish, uncooked, 151
  salad, molded, 317
  sauce, 152
  sausage stuffing, 464
  sherbet, 139
crawfish
  à la Nage, 190
  bisque, 177
  étouffée, 190
  steamed Florida lobster, 191

crayfish: *see* crawfish
cream
  cabbage, 373
  cake, old-fashioned, 124
  cheese
    appetizers, 565
    brownies, 147
    pie, fruited, 632
  cheesecake
    with almond crust, 634
    beer, 127
  chicken enchiladas, 590
  coconut, spinach with, 716
  dressing, 512
  gravy
    chicken fried round steak with, 338
    rabbit in, 490
    sausage with biscuits and, 213
  mushrooms with, 80
  pheasant with, 708
cream of
  chicken soup, 17
  corn soup, 181
  peanut soup, 184
  spinach soup
    Southern, 182
    Southwestern, 568
  tomato soup, 326
creamed
  chicken and mushrooms, 705
  cod, 35
  kohlrabi, 503
  lobster, 29
  oysters, 195
  potato salad, 511
  potatoes, 508
  shad roe with sherry, 331
  veal, 60
Creole
  chicken, 226
  gumbo, Pontchartrain, 205
  halibut, 677
  red snapper, 202
  shrimp
    chilled Gulf Coast, 171
    Southern, 200
  tripe, 211
crevettes Paula, 7
crisp
  rutabaga salad, 93
  sugar cookies, 641
  watermelon pickles, 296
crisps, cheese, 469
croquettes, ham, with egg sauce, 217
crown roast of lamb, eggplant-stuffed, 52
crullers, Christmas (Swedish klenater), 405

crumb-topped
  cherry pie, 416
  plum pies, 738
crumbed butterflied leg of lamb, 53
crunch, apple, 538
crusts, pie
  Dona's favorite, 524
  hot water, 408
  lard, 524
  Lou's, 524
  no-fail, 408
  regular, 408
crystal carrots, 374
crystallized
  grapes, 311
  rose petals, 463
Cuban
  round roast, 209
  sausages, 213
cucumber
  and beer soup, chilled, 20
  and carrot relish, 548
  marmalade, 154
  pickles, yellow (senfgurken), 550
  salad, 385; see also su-no-mo-no
  sauce, 761
  and shad roe, 169
  in sour cream, 85
cucumbers
  in butter and dill, 295
  and carrots, 715
  and mushrooms, 604
  slippery Jims, 376
  in sour cream, 385
currant
  cookies
    Mountain/Northern Plains, 542
    Northeastern, 142
  jam, red or black, 552
  sauce, 500
curried
  avocado soup, 568
  corn with chilies, 604
  flan appetizer, 10
  mushroom turnovers, 660
  vegetables, cold, 87
curry
  honey sauce, Midwestern, 456
  and honey sauce, Shreveport Club, 305
  lamb, baked in coconuts, 698
  sauce for venison or elk fondue, 497
custard
  apple pie, Marie's, 737
  sauce flavored with Pernod, 306
custards
  baked, 427
  cheese, 234
  fried cream or, 262
  ginger-apple, 130

custards (cont'd)
  rice, with lemon sauce, Mrs.
    Mescal Johnston's, 281
  salmon, 684
  sauce, apple snow with, 134
  spinach, 85
  tomato, Shaker, 86
  zucchini cheese, 249
Czech
  Christmas bread, 520
  gravies for dumplings, 457
    basic roux, 457
    dill pickle, 457
    mushroom, 458
    onion, 457
    tomato, 457
  poppy seed roll cookies (makova zavin), 435

daikon (white radish)
  and carrot, pickled, 755
  Singari, 758
Dakota
  beef loaf, 478
  rolls, 515
damson jam, 294
dandelion
  flowers, sautéed, 79
  green salad, 509
  greens and bacon dressing, 94
  stems, 78
Danish
  cones with whipped cream, 145
  doughnuts (aebleskiver), 407
  filled, 399
  liver
    paste, Holiday Folk Fair, 317
    pâté, 317
  pastry, 437
  raspberry pie, 416
Dan's delight (chokecherry wine), 555
dark chocolate cake, 117
dark bread, Norwegian, 396
date
  bourbon pudding, 282
  chocolate bars, 643
  loaf, candy, 654
  and nut whirls, 541
  and pear preserve, 553
  pudding
    Midwestern, 434
    Mountain/Northern Plains, 537
  sesame pie, 631
  soufflé, Grandmother's, 639
David's pancake, 734
deep-dish
  blueberry pie, 108
  clam pie, Cape Cod, 23
  mushroom pies, 506

deep-fried
  frogs' legs, 229
  grits balls, 176
  hot water corn bread, 257
  mushrooms, 80
  soft-shelled crabs, 187
  spareribs, 212
deer liver pâté, 3
deluxe cheesecake, 127
Depoe Bay
  blackberry tarts, 739
  broiled salmon steaks, 686
dessert sauces: see sauces, dessert
desserts, 130–40, 281–88, 427–35,
    536–41, 638–41, 747–51
  apple
    crunch, 538
    and sour cream, Jim's, 750
  apricot
    fritters, 748
    noodle ring, 747
  banana meringue, 749
  bananas
    à la Turtle Cay, 287
    flambées, 287
  buckle, fresh blueberry, 138
  buttermilk, 429
  cakes: see cakes
  cider apples, 136
  cobblers and crisps
    apple cobbler, 537
    apple crisp, 137
    blueberry cobbler, Down-East, 138
    peach cobbler, 272
  cookies: see cookies
  cooler, raspberry, 139
  custards: see custards
  farmer in the dell, 140
  filbert rice mold, 750
  flan
    Southern, 282
    Southwestern, 640
  floating island, 429
  frozen
    apricot, 750
    raspberry, 428
  ice, water: see water ice
  ice cream: see ice cream
  kemph, 541
  "lemmon syllabub," 284
  lemon fluff, 282
  maple apples, 137
  Minetry McCoy's miracle, 286
  molasses dumplings, 748
  mousse: see mousse
  oranges
    en surprise, 287
    flambé, 641
    stuffed frozen, 287
  osta kaka, 541

desserts *(cont'd)*
  peach surprise, 751
  pears, baked, 749
  peppermint stick Bavarian cream,
      284
  pies: *see* pies, dessert
  porridge, Swedish, 427
  puddings: *see* puddings
  rice custard with lemon sauce, Mrs.
      Mescal Johnston's, 281
  roll-up cakes
    blueberry, 137
    peach, 272
  rum chocolate, 430
  sauces: *see* sauces, dessert
  sherbet: *see* sherbet
  shortcakes: *see* shortcake
  skyr, 540
  snow on the mountain, 283
  son-of-a-gun-in-a-sack, 540
  soufflés: *see* soufflés, dessert
  sponge, Hancock Village steamed
      ginger, 135
  sweet potato pone, 281
  trifle, 285
    pudding, 286
    royal, 285
  wild grape dumplings, 430
deviled
  buffalo steak, 492
  crab meat
    Northeastern
      I (Maryland), 168
      II (Maryland), 168
    Western, 676
  oysters, 192
  steak, 44
Diamond Lake trout, 690
dill
  gravy
    for boiled beef, Holiday
        Folk Fair, 458
    koprova omacka, 456
  lamb with, 55
  pickle gravy, 457
  potato soup, 471
dilled
  lamb stew, 349
  potato salad, 511
  rice for shrimp, 249
  zucchini, 724
dills
  lazy wife, 646
  special, 447
dips
  cheese (chile con queso), 563
  guacamole
    I (New Mexico), 562
    II (Arizona), 562
  herb, for raw vegetables, 175
  Pat's favorite, 175

dirty rice (jambalaya), 249
divinity, perfect, 653
dolma, Armenian squash, 349
dolphin fillets Norsaga, 190
Dona's
  cookies, 544
  favorite pie crust, 524
Dorothy's strawberry preserves, 648
doughnuts
  aebleskiver (Danish), 407
  potato, 522
  sour cream
    Midwestern, 406
    Mountain/Northern Plains, 521
  see also crullers
doves
  Halidon Hill potted, 232
  Pontchartrain, 232
  Wyatt Earp, 366
Down-East
  blueberry cobbler, 138
  haddock chowder, 11
dressings: *see* stuffings
dressings, salad: *see* salad dressings
dried beans, peas, and lentils
  beanhole beans, 371
  black beans
    with rum, 237
    savory (frijoles negros), 237
  black-eyed peas and hog jawl
      (jowl), Mrs. Jackson Porter
      Dick's, 239
    and rice (Hopping John), 239
    soup, 180
    Texas caviar, 564
  kidney beans
    frijoles (Mexican), 605
    Mrs. Sylvester's baked, 371
    soup, Portuguese, 666
    Southwestern, 605
    see also kidney beans
  lentil
    casserole, 714
    soup, 323
  lima beans
    bake, 502
    and cottage cheese loaf, 371
    Grandmother's, bake, 372
    see also lima beans
  pinto beans
    and chile casserole, 582
    frijoles (Mexican), 605
    red beans, 606
    Southwestern, 605
      refried, 605
    see also pinto beans
  red beans
    Idaho baked, 502
    with rice, Southern
      I (Louisiana), 238
      II (Louisiana), 238

dried beans, peas, and lentils *(cont'd)*
    Southwestern, 606
  soup, for a crowd, five, 326
drops, sugar-coated banana, 444
dry rice soup (sopa seca)
  I (New Mexico), 566
  II (Texas), 566
duchess soup, 328
duck
  pickled, cold, 365
  potato dressing for roast, 463
  pressed, 230
  roast, Chinese, 709
  stuffings for
    fruit, Northeastern, 162
    potato dressing, 463
    wild rice, 463
  Wichita, 364
  wild
    breasts
      en casserole, baked, 365
      grilled, 365
    country captain, 231
    gumbo, 601
    Mountain/Northern Plains
      I (Wyoming), 483
      II (Wyoming), 484
    pecan-stuffed, 483
ducks
  mallard, roast, 602
  wild
    with Madeira, 230
    roast, with Burgundy-olive sauce,
        601
dumpling soup, Korean, 668
dumplings, 163, 465, 557
  and apples (schnitz un knepp), 51
  Bavarian (semmel knodel), 466
  bread, 557
  cheese, with sour cream, Bohemian,
      557
  chicken
    and, 482
    'n', 220
  for chicken stew, 465
  corn bread, mixed greens with, 245
  gravies for, Czech
    basic roux, 457
    dill pickle, 457
    mushroom, 458
    onion, 457
    tomato, 457
  lima bean with, soup, 327
  liver, in broth (leberkloesse), 322
  matzoh balls
    marrow bone, 163
    Northeastern, 163
  molasses, 748
  potato
    Mountain/Northern Plains, 557
    raw, 557

dumplings *(cont'd)*
  for soup
    Midwestern (kleppa), 465
    Northeastern, 163
    see also matzoh balls
  vegetable soup with, 320
  wild grape, 430
  yeast fruit, 520
Dungeness crab
  diable, 675
  marinated cracked, 676
  and scallop stew, 676
Dutch
  apple
    cake, Connie's, 531
    sack pie, 107
  plum kuchen, 745
Dutchie's
  meat balls, 580
  tossed salad, 621
Dymple's
  fruitcake, 419
  sausage cake, 420

easy
  hollandaise sauce, 174
  no-cook fudge, 556
  100 per cent whole wheat bread,
    515
  pickled watermelon rind, 297
  pickles, 497
Edna's blueberry gingerbread, 121
egg
  chowder, 22
  dressing, minute, 388
  drop soup, 567
  drops, sour cream soup with, 328
  -filled tortillas, 599
  and ham canapés, 173
  rolls, 662
  sauce, ham croquettes with, 217
eggnog
  Joe's, 459
  John's, 306
  pudding, fruit, 284
  sauce, 131
  Southern, 306
eggplant
  casserole
    Midwestern, 376
    Southwestern, 606
  with chicken, 68
  and chicken liver casserole, 66
  Clara's, 241
  and lamb
    Southwestern, 584
    Syrian style, 349
  and macadamia nuts, 716
  and macaroni casserole, Helen's, 52
  soufflé, 241

eggplant *(cont'd)*
  stuffed
    crown roast of lamb, 52
    Southern, 242
  and veal casserole, 347
  and zucchini, baked, 87
eggs
  Campeche style (huevos
    campechanos), 597
  with ham and cheese (huevos
    motulenos), 597
  ranch-style (huevos rancheros)
    Southern California, 598
    Texas, 598
  sardou, 174
1870 mahogany cake, 423
'89er lemon pie, 409
elderberry
  blossom wine, 307
  chutney, 758
elegant chicken pie, 66
elk
  carbonnades à la flamande, 498
  fondue, venison or, 497
  heart, pickled, 499
  steak and kidney pie, 499
empanadas, 593
empanaditas, 563
enchiladas
  cream chicken, 590
  green, 589
  Mission, 592
  stacked, 591
  verdes al estilo de mi casa (chicken
    and tortilla casserole), 588
end-of-the-garden sauce, 456
Ernie's mustard pickles, 149
escabeche
  of red snapper, 173
  -tongue salad, 601
escarole soup, 18
Ethel's flat bread, 516
Evelyn's cheesecake, 126

farmer in the dell, 140
Farmers Market
  Caesar salad, 617
  lamb and cabbage, 585
  mayonnaise dressing, 621
farmhouse coffeecakes, Oregon, 746
fat cakes (kuechlie), 394
fattigman
  Midwestern Scandinavian, 438
  Mountain/Northern Plains, 543
fennel, mushrooms with, 81
festsuppe, 321
feta cheese
  pastries (tiropetes), 9
  shrimp with, baked fresh, 31
field or cow pea soup, 182

fig
  bar cookies, 642
  preserves
    Southern, 291
    Southwestern, 648
  -walnut bread, 623
filbert
  brownies, 754
  -cranberry tart, 737
  mousse, 750
  rice mold, 750
  -stuffed pork chops, 699
  stuffing, for turkey, 763
filberts
  gugelhopf with, 744
  seasoned, 661
  wild rice with, 725
filet mignon, flamed, 339
Filipino seasoned pork appetizers, 659
filled
  applesauce squares, 145
  cookies, Peggy's, 441
  Danish, 399
fillets
  ciscoes, baked, 333
  dolphin, Norsaga, 190
  pickerel, baked, 333
  pike
    baked, 332
    broiled walleyed, 332
  sole
    with champagne, 690
    Rex, with lemon sauce, 690
    with white wine, 334
fillings
  for kolaches
    cottage cheese, 401
    poppy seed, 402
    prune or apricot, 402
  ham and spinach, 7
  for ravioli
    spinach and ricotta, 348
    veal, 348
    see also stuffings
fillings, cake and dessert
  custard, for zuppa inglese, 117
  lane, 279
Finnish
  Christmas cookies, 440
  shortbread, 439
  sour rye bread (ruisleipa), 397
fish, 32–43, 185–207, 330–38, 474–76,
    570–74, 672–92
  balls
    Midwestern, 336
    Sister Lisset's Shaker, 43
  boil, 335
  cakes: *see* fishcakes
  chowder
    Mountain, 470
    Northwestern, 670

fish *(cont'd)*
  Rhode Island, 15
  see also chowder, fish
  court bouillon, 173
  sauce for poached, 303
  smoked, appetizer, 315
  soufflé, 336
  steaks Atlantic Avenue style, 38
  stew
    Chesapeake Bay, 204
    Louisiana, 203
    New England, 41
    New York, 40
    Pacific, 670
    pine bark, 203
    Southern California, 572
    see also stew, fish
  tempura fried, 692
  *see also under names of specific fish
    and shellfish*
fishcakes, salmon, 336
fisherman's swizzle, 158
Fisherman's Wharf smelt, 689
five bean soup for a crowd, 326
five-minute fudge, 653
flamed filet, 339
flans
  dessert
    Southern, 282
    Southwestern, 640
  main-dish
    smoked haddock, 36
flat bread
  Ethel's, 516
  Mylah's, 516
fleischkuechle (meat patties), 478
float away oatmeal muffins, 392
floating island, 429
Florida lobster, steamed, 191
flounder, crab-stuffed whole, Herb's,
  35
foamy sauce, 131
fondue, venison or elk, 497
Fourth of July
  boiled salmon, peas and egg sauce,
    38
  lemonade, 459
  potato salad, 511
  shortcake, 129
fowl, dressing for, 465
fra diavolo, fresh tuna, 39
Francille's stewed corn, 240
Frazer's cheaters (nut squares), 146
French
  bread, sour dough, 731
  chocolate cake, 116
  dressing, Southern California, 622
  potato salad, 247
  silk chocolate pie, 411

fresh
  apricot pie, 736
  blueberry buckle, 138
  coconut upside-down cake, 740
  mushroom salad, 621
  pineapple loaf, 734
  quail with grits and gravy, 231
  strawberry tart, 740
  tuna fra diavolo, 39
  vegetable soup, 472
fricassee, Aunt May's chicken, 707
fried
  apples, 291
  cabbage, 504
  celery, 501
  chicken
    with plum sauce, 702
    in teriyaki sauce, 702
    see also Southern fried chicken
  clams
    Maryland, 186
    Northeastern, 26
  corn meal mush, 257
  cream or custard, 262
  fresh peach turnovers, 271
  fruit turnovers, 271
  hominy grits, 243
  okra, 246
  onions and apples, 81
  oysters
    Northeastern, 30
    Southern, 194
  pheasant breasts, 489
  plantains, 247
  ptarmigan, 710
  pumpkin blossoms, 380
  ravioli, 348
  scallops, Port Angeles, 687
  shrimp cakes, 688
  squirrel, 367
frijoles negros (savory black beans),
  237
fritters
  apricot, 748
  clam
    Agate Beach, 673
    appetizer, Lois', 657
    Northeastern, 26
    Washington, 673
  corn, 375
  tomato, 86
  wild mushroom, 506
  zucchini blossom, Schramsberg, 662
frogs' legs
  braised, with sherry, 229
  deep-fried, 229
  omelet, 232
  pan-fried, 368
fromage de tête (head cheese), 213
  vinaigrette, 214

frostings and icings
  caramel, old-fashioned, 536
  chocolate
    Greta's, 422
    Mabel's, 536
    Midwestern, 421
    Northeastern, 117
  Christmas bread, Arizona, 628
  citrus, for citrus cake, 636
  coconut, 120
  devil's food cake, 534
  1870 mahogany cake, 423
  fudge, 424
  Grandma's elegant easy, 536
  maple, 119
    syrup cake, Buckeye, 424
  $100, 421
  poppy seed cake, 426
  red velvet, 422
  royal, 143
  sorghum cake, Grandmother's, 425
  thin sugar, 401
  white
    for Lady Baltimore cake, 280
    for walnut cake, 635
frozen
  apricot dessert, 750
  lemon pie, 633
  pumpkin pie, 413
  raspberry dessert, 428
  tomato salad, 619
fruit
  bars, 446
  bread, 392
  cake, rub-up, 740; *see also* fruitcake
  candy for Passover, 160
  dressing for poultry, 465
  dumplings, yeast, 520
  ice, 749
  ice cream, Bavarian, 640
  'n' beef bars, 744
  and nut
    bars, molasses, 147
    loaf, 529
  salad
    dressing, 389
    sesame lime dressing for, 622
  soups
    peach, chilled, 183
    strawberry cooler, 183
  -stuffed meat loaf, 48
  stuffing, 162
  turnovers, fried, 271
fruitcake
  applesauce, 278
  banana, 418
  Dymple's, 419
  Northeastern, 121
  past perfect, 278
  white, 278

fruited
 cheese pie, 632
 chicken salad, Peggy's, 386
 eggnog pudding, 284
fudge
 brownies, 445
 easy no-cook, 556
 five-minute, 653
 frosting, 424
 maple syrup, blue ribbon, 160
 peanut butter, 461
 perfect divinity, 653
 Southern, 309
 walnut, 653
Fulling Mill Farm chili sauce, 152

galakto boureka, 114
galatoise polonaise, 57
game and game birds, 229–33,
 362–68, 483–500, 601–2, 708–12
 loaf, herbed, 711
 marinade for, 499
 sauce
  herbed, 363
  Mountain/Northern Plains, 554
  Northeastern, 158
  pepper, 500
 sausage, 710
 stew, 712
 see also under names of specific
  game and game birds
garbanzos: see chick-peas
garden relish, Southern California,
 647
garlic, shrimp with, 687
gefilte fish, 42
 baked, 42
George's spanakopita (spinach-onion
 pie), 84
German
 apple coffeecake, 400
 rolled steak, 339
ginger
 -apple custard, 130
 cookies
  Moravian, 289
  old-style, 544
 -lemon-peach conserve, 153
 marinade for chicken, Hazel's, 649
  roast pork with, 699
 -melon ice, 288
 -orange cake, 741
 sponge, Hancock Village steamed,
  135
gingerbread men, 142
glazed
 apple cheese pie, 414
 Vermont ham, 51
 yellow turnips, 84

glazes
 apricot, 120
 orange, for ham, 761
 strawberry, 127
gnocchi, potato, 723
Gold Rush style sour dough
 pancakes, 732
golden
 cabbage, 77
 cake, 417
goose
 roast, 71
 snow, stuffed, 484
 stuffings for
  apricot, 484
  fruit, Northeastern, 162
  oyster, 162
 wild
  with apricot stuffing, 484
  roast stuffed, 485
  with stuffing, 485
gooseberries, spiced wild, 549
gooseberry
 catchup, 452
 tart, wild, 740
Gostovich
 Hungarian goulash, 583
 lamb and vegetable stew, 585
goulash
 Gostovich Hungarian pork or veal,
  583
 Mountain/Northern Plains pork,
  481
 mushroom, 720
graham cracker
 crust, 736
 pie, 411
graham muffins, 393
grand hot cakes, 259
Grandma's
 elegant easy frosting, 536
 squash bake, 503
Grandmother Rezac's rye bread, 513
Grandmother's
 angel food pie, 410
 beef-over, 478
 date soufflé, 639
 lima bean bake, 372
 sorghum cake, 425
 squash pie, 413
 Thanksgiving special candy, 462
 tomato soup, 326
grape
 catchup, 550
 punch, hot, 460
grapefruit
 marmalade, 647
 peel, candied, 161
 sherbet, 639
 -strawberry mousse, 641

grapes
 bass with, 572
 crystallized, 311
gravad lax (pickled salmon), 330
gravy
 avocado, for meat loaf, 579
 bologna, 355
 carrot, pot roast with, 693
 chicken cream, 219
 cream
  for rabbit, 490
  for sausage and biscuits, 213
  for steak, chicken fried round,
   338
 Czech, for dumplings, 457
 dill (koprova omacka), 456
 dill pickle, 457
 horseradish and dill, for boiled
  beef, Holiday Folk Fair, 458
 Mormon, 554
 mushroom, 458
 onion, 457
 red eye, for ham steak, 216
 roux, basic, 457
 tomato
  Mae's, 457
  Midwestern, 457
  Southern, 304
Greek
 meat balls, 47
 salad, 89
green bean
 casserole, 236
 and rice casserole, 370
 salad
  marinated, 618
  sweet 'n' sour, 713
green beans
 with brown butter sauce, 237
 California, 606
 with herb sauce, 85
 with mint, Sandra's, 85
 Missouri country-style, 370
 pickled
  Southern, 296
  Southwestern, 645
 pioneer leatherbritches, 370
 snibbled, 369
 Southern style, 237
 and tomatoes au gratin, 236
green chile burros, 586
green corn pudding, 604
green enchiladas, 589
green goddess dressing, 727
green pepper
 and cabbage relish, 449
 jelly, 294
green peppers
 cabbage-filled, 82
 Pacific-style stuffed, 675

green peppers *(cont'd)*
  pork-stuffed, 212
  roasted Italian, 82
  round steak with, 339
  see also red peppers
green relish, 300
green rice
  California, 610
  Mountain/Northern Plains, 509
  ring, 248
green summer squash (calabacitas),
  615
green tomato
  mincemeat, 150
  pickle, 451
  pie
    Midwestern, 417
    Peggy's, 525
  relish
    Midwestern, 454
    Mountain/Northern Plains, 548
    Southern, 299
greens
  assorted, 245
  mixed, with corn bread dumplings,
    245
  mustard, turnip, and collard, 244
  pokeweed or pokeberry, 505
  Texas mustard, 608
  turnip
    mustard or dandelion, 505
    Southern-style, 244
  vinegar, 718
Greta's
  apple pie, 414
  cabbage salad, 385
  chocolate cake, 422
griddlecakes, buckwheat, 406
  see also hotcakes, pancakes
grilled
  duck breasts, 365
  pig with a blanket, 354
grits
  balls, deep-fried, 176
  and Cheddar casserole, 613
  cheese casserole, 234
  hominy: *see* hominy
  quail with gravy and, fresh, 231
  soufflé
    Southern, 244
    Southwestern, 612
grouper, Out Island, 191
ground beef
  beef-over, Grandmother's, 478
  Hazel's tallerine, 346
  meat and potato burgers, 344
  one-dish supper, 345
  patties (fleischkuechle), 478
  piccadillo, 208
  tamale pie, 208
    with hominy grits, 209

ground beef *(cont'd)*
  and wild rice casserole, 346
  see also meat balls; meat loaf
grouse breasts
  with ham, 486
  in Madeira sauce, 487
Gruyère
  and squash casserole, 88
  veal scallops with, 61
  see also Swiss cheese
guacamole
  I (New Mexico), 562
  II (Arizona), 562
guava
  muffins, 734
  pecan pie, 264
gugelhopf with filberts, 744
guisado de cabrito (kid stew), 599
gumbo
  catfish, 186
  chicken, 225
  crab, 188
  Creole, Pontchartrain, 205
  shrimp, 199
  -style chicken wings, 225
  wild duck, 601

haddock
  baked, 37
  balls, 336
  chowder, Down-East, 11
  flan, smoked, 36
  pie, Abigail's biscuit-topped, 36
  soufflé, 336
halibut
  Creole, 677
  with orange, 572
  steaks, 677
Halidon Hall potted doves, 232
ham
  and apricot salad, 726
  biscuits, 174
  broccoli with cheese and, 372
  country
    boiled and baked, 216
    Smithfield or Smithfield-style
      Virginia, 215
    Southern Maryland stuffed, 216
  croquettes with egg sauce, 217
  dressing or coating, 764
  and egg canapés, 173
  eggs with cheese and, 597
  grouse breasts with, 486
  hocks, 217
  loaf, 355
  mousse, 51
  -okra soup, 183
  orange glaze and sauce for, 761
  in rye, 729
  schnitz un knepp, 51

ham *(cont'd)*
  Smithfield or Smithfield-style
    Virginia, 215
  and spinach filling, 7
  split peas with, 714
  steak and red eye gravy, 216
  and veal
    manicotti with, 63
    picnic loaf, 63
  Vermont, glazed, 51
  and winter melon soup, 668
hamburgers
  Anne's, 343
  camping, 344
  with chili, 578
Hancock Shaker Village
  India relish, 151
  salt pork-and-milk gravy, 43
  Sister Clymena's chicken pie, 67
  steamed ginger sponge, 135
Hangtown fry, 678
hard
  candies, homemade, 161
  sauce, 131
hard-shelled crabs, steamed, 189
harvest
  corn bread, 391
  torte, 637
hasenpfeffer, 490
hash
  -brown potatoes, 382
  corned beef, 50
  red flannel, 50
Hawaiian
  sea "anemones," 664
  short ribs, 695
Hawkins' Jamestown buffalo cookies,
  542
Hazel's
  ginger marinade for chicken, 649
  rice casserole, 610
  tallerine, 346
head cheese (fromage de tête)
  Midwestern, 354
  Southern, 213
  vinaigrette, 214
heart
  elk's, pickled, 499
  venison, pickled, 4
heart of palm (swamp cabbage), 246
  au gratin, 246
Helen's eggplant and macaroni
  casserole, 52
herb
  dip for raw vegetables, 175
  and lime sauce vinaigrette, 302
  sauce
    string beans with, 85
    for venison or elk fondue, 497

herbed
  fresh pea soup, 567
  game
    loaf, 711
    sauce, 363
herbs, rabbit with, 711
Herb's crab-stuffed whole flounder, 35
hermits, 289
herring
  pickled
    lake, 315
    salt (inlagd sill), 330
  salad, Mama's, 476
hickory nut pie, Cherokee, 414
high altitude
  baking, notes on, 513, 524
  candy-making, note on, 556
  cooking, note on, 547
high bush cranberry
  -apple butter, 760
  pie (mock cherry), 739
hocks, ham, 217
hoe cake (hot water corn bread), 255
hoe cakes, lacy, 258
hog jawl (jowl), Mrs. Porter Dick's
  black-eyed peas and, 215
holiday cookies, 751
Holiday Folk Fair
  Danish liver paste, 317
  horseradish and dill gravies for
    boiled beef, 458
  potato pancakes, 382
  Ukrainian borscht, 319
hollandaise
  blender, 157
  easy, 174
  Northwestern, 761
  Southern, 301
home-baked beans, 74
homemade
  hominy, 242
  ice cream, 427
  lollipops or hard candies, 161
  noodles, 376
hominy
  baked, and tomatoes, 244
  and bean cakes, 243
  casserole, 612
  chili with cheese and, 576
  grits
    fried, 243
    tamale pie with, 209
  homemade, 242
  Mexicaine, 612
  with sausage, quick big, 235
  stew (posole), 587
  see also grits
honey
  chocolate cake, 115
  curry sauce, Midwestern, 456

honey (cont'd)
  and curry sauce, Shreveport Club,
    305
  dressing, 93
  fruited beets, 503
  raisin pie, 110
  soufflé, 135
  taffy, 556
Hopping John or black-eyed peas and
  rice, 239
Hornersville barbecue sauce, 455
horns, Austrian butter, 436
horseradish
  and cranberry sauce, 304
  creamed, Veronica's, 79
  gravy for boiled beef, Holiday Folk
    Fair, 458
  and port wine sauce, 304
  relish, 758
hot
  apple and potato salad, 92
  barbecue sauce, 303
  bean salad, 618
  buttered rum, 159
  cakes: see hotcakes
  chicken salad, 361
  crab meat puffs, 169
  grape punch, 460
  mustard sauce, 762
  oysters à la Louisiane, 193
  potato salad, 247
  sauce, 650
  slaw, 386
  tomato-apple butter, 548
  water
    corn bread (hoe cake), 255
      deep-fried, 257
      Midwestern, 390
    pie crust, 408
hot cakes
  bread crumb, 735
  grand, 259
  sour dough, 731
hot-ta-meat pies, 209
how to corn beef, 342
huevos (eggs)
  campechanos (Campeche style), 597
  motulenos (with ham and cheese),
    597
  rancheros (ranch-style), 598
Hungarian
  goulash, Gostovich, 583
  linzer cookies, 435
hunt and polo eggplant casserole, 242
hush puppies, 258
  River Road, 258

ice, water: see water ice

ice cream
  Bavarian fruit, 640
  cooked custard, 288
  homemade, 427
    cooked, Mary Alice's, 428
  lemon, 428
  vanilla, 428
icings: see frostings and icings
Idaho baked beans, 502
imperial, crab meat, 189
Indian
  bread, steamed, 390
  pudding
    Charles Street, 134
    Northeastern, 133
  Zuñi green chili stew, 585
inlagd sill (pickled salt herring), 330
Iowa
  chicken and corn pudding, 360
  fried chicken, 358
  scalloped chicken, 359
Isabella's cookies, 142
Italian biscotti, 752

Jackson Lake trout shish kebab, 475
jam
  biscuits, 437
  cake, 276
jams: see pickles, relishes, preserves
  and condiments
jambalaya, 206
  Cajun, 228
  chicken, 226
Jamestown buffalo bread, 513
jan hagel, 147
Jane's spritz cookies, 752
Japanese savory pancakes
  (okonomiyaki), 570
Jeff Davis pie, 267
Jefferson Davis punch, 460
jelled veal, 62
jellied
  beef mold, 479
  meat loaf (ky-va), 479
  pork (souse), 215
  veal loaf (sylta), 349
jellies: see pickles, relishes, preserves
  and condiments
Jennie's coffeecake ring, 104
jerky, oven method (dried venison),
  498
jicama appetizer, 564
Jim's apple and sour cream dessert,
  750
Joe's
  barbecued ribs, 581
  eggnog, 459
Johnny Reb, oysters, 192
johnnycakes, 96
John's eggnog, 306

julekage (Christmas bread)
  Midwestern, 400
  Mountain/Northern Plains, 521
julep, mint, 308
Julia's glazed orange cake, 123
Juneberry pie, 527

Kai's spareribs, 699
kale, 373
  and oatmeal, 505
  soup, 473
kause seed bread, 516
kemph, 541
Kentucky lemon pie, 269
Key West old lime sour, 301
kid stew (guisado de cabrito), 599
kidney bean
  casserole, 605
  porridge, 76
  soup, Portuguese, 666
  salad, 617
kidney beans
  apples 'n', Meg's, 713
  frijoles (Mexican), 605
  Mrs. Sylvester's baked, 371
  refried, 605
  Southwestern pinto beans or, 605
Kidson's bronze lettuce salad, 617
king crab sandwich, 677
kippered salmon, 682
klenater, Swedish (Christmas
      crullers), 405
kleppas (soup dumplings), 465
kohlrabi
  cabbage, 505
  creamed, 503
kolaches, Aunt Mary's, 401
  cottage cheese filling for, 401
  poppy seed filling for, 402
  prune or apricot filling for, 402
koprova omacka (dill gravy), 456
Korean dumpling soup, 668
kraut
  apple, pork steaks and, 353
  and beet salad, 714
  pork and apple, 352
  relish, 551
krum kake
  I (North Dakota), 545
  II (North Dakota), 546
kuchen
  Midwestern
    I (North Dakota), 518
    II (Nebraska), 518
  plum, Dutch, 745
kuechlie (fat cakes), 394
kugel for Passover, potato, 83
ky-va (jellied meat loaf), 479

lacy
  corn bread, 259
  hoe cakes, 258
Lady Baltimore cake, 280
lake
  herring, pickled, 315
  trout, planked, 332
Lamaze sauce, shrimp with, 170
lamb, 52–55, 349–50, 480–81, 584–86,
      698–99
  Basque sheepherder's pasties, 698
  and cabbage, Farmers Market, 585
  crown roast, eggplant stuffed, 52
  curry baked in coconuts, 698
  with dill, 55
  and eggplant
    Southwestern, 584
    Syrian style, 349
  leg of
    butterflied, crumbed, 53
    with saffron-and-caper sauce, 54
    in sour cream sauce, 350
    on a spit, 53
  loaf, 350
  ragout, Nicole's, 55
  riblets, parsleyed, 482
  ring with mashed potatoes, 53
  shanks
    barbecued, 586
    with potatoes, lemon, 481
  squash dolma, Armenian, 349
  stew
    dilled, 349
    green chili, Indian Zuñi, 585
    vegetable and, Gostovich, 585
lane cake
  filling, 279
  layers, 279
lard pie crust, 524
large yeast bread recipe, 394
Latvian pumpkin pickle, 449
lazy wife dills, 646
leberkloesse (liver dumplings in
      broth), 322
leek omelet, baked, 720
leeks and rice, 82
lefsa, 394
leg of lamb
  butterflied, crumbed, 53
  with saffron-and-caper sauce, 54
  in sour cream sauce, 350
  on a spit, 53
"lemmon syllabub," 284
lemon
  bonbons, 444
  bread, 625
  butter, old-fashioned, 305
  cake, 276
  chiffon pie, 270
  coffeecake loaves, Oregon
      farmhouse, 746

lemon (cont'd)
  and egg sauce, celery with, 240
  '89er pie, 409
  fluff, 282
  ice cream, 428
  marmalade, 648
  mousse, 429
  nutmeg custard pie, 408
  or orange peel, candied, 762
  -peach-ginger conserve, 153
  pie
    frozen, 633
    pioneer, 110
  pie-cake, Peg's, 526
  potatoes, 722
  relish, 450
  sauce
    for rice custard, 281
    Rex sole with, 690
    warm, 458
  shanks with potatoes, 481
  water ice, 140
lemonade, Fourth of July, 459
lemons, stuffed oranges and, 297
lentil
  casserole, 714
  soup, 323
lettuce
  braised, with rosemary, 79
  salad, Kidson's bronze, 617
  wilted
    Agnes', 719
    "alfalfa," Northwestern, 719
    leaf, Mountain/Northern Plains,
      510
    Midwestern, 373
    Northeastern, 80
Libby's summer vegetable casserole,
      87
light rolls, 263
lima bean
  bake
    Grandmother's, 372
    Mountain/Northern Plains, 502
  casserole, 713
  and cottage cheese loaf, 371
  with dumplings soup, 327
lima beans
  Camarillo sausage and, 582
  and pork chops, Ojai Valley, 583
lime
  chutney, 298
  and herb sauce vinaigrette, 302
  marmalade, 154
  meringue pie, 269
  sesame dressing for fruit salad, 622
  sour, Key West old, 301
limpa, Swedish, 403
limping Susan, 246
ling cod with mustard sauce, broiled,
      674

lingonberries, rice pudding with, 431
lingonberry and rhubarb relish, 758
linzer cookies, Hungarian, 435
Lion's Club barbecue sauce, 456
liver
    calf's, Texas, 600
    dumplings in broth (leberkloesse),
        322
    pancakes, 356
    paste, Holiday Folk Fair Danish,
        317
    pâté
        Danish, 317
        deer, 3
livers, chicken, with sage, 65
lizzies
    Midwestern, 419
    Northeastern, 144
loaf
    beef, Dakota, 478
    candy date, 654
    carrot, 503
    chicken
        Midwestern, 360
        Southern, 224
    clam, 674
    game, herbed, 711
    ham, 355
    lamb, 350
    lima bean and cottage cheese, 371
    pheasant, 489
    pineapple, fresh, 734
    salmon, 682
        with celery sauce, 683
        molded, Agnes', 683
    veal, jellied (sylta), 349
    walnut Cheddar, 625
    see also meat loaf
lobster
    Alexander, 28
    baked, 27
    broiled
        live Maine, 29
        stuffed, 30
    cocktail dressing, 303
    creamed, 29
    Florida, steamed, 191
    roll, Cape Cod, 28
    sauce, 458
    and she-crab soup, 178
    soup, Cape Cod, 12
    and steak on a skewer, 338
    steamed, 28
    thermidor, 28
Lois' clam fritter appetizer, 657
lollipops, homemade, 161
lomi salmon, 680
Lone Star tomato relish, 647
Lorraine, veal, 60
lotus root salad, 720
Louis, shrimp, 689

Louisiana
    fish stew, 203
    red bean soup, 180
    sauce remoulade, 302
Lou's pie crust, 524
luau or spinach, chicken with, 706
Lucy's
    buñeolos, 626
    milk pudding, 640
    quelites (spinach with beans), 607
lutefisk, 335
    pudding, 335

macadamia nut stuffing, for turkey,
    763
macadamia nuts, eggplant with, 716
macaroni
    deluxe, 376
    and eggplant casserole, Helen's, 52
    with mushrooms, 377
"macaroons," chocolate, 442
mackerel
    how to cook salt, 192
    how to salt, 191
    pickled, 6
    planked, 572
Mackinaw trout, baked, 475
Madeira sauce, breasts of grouse in,
    487
Mae's tomato gravy, 457
Maggy Murphy's aunt's coffeecake,
    125
mahogany cake, 1870, 423
Maine sardine salad, 91
maître d'hôtel, fresh cod, 34
makova zavin (Czech poppy seed roll
    cookies), 435
malfatti, 717
mallard ducks, roast, 602
Maltese baked rice, Papa's, 46
Mama's herring salad, 476
mango chutney, 299
manicotti with veal and ham, 63
maple
    apples, 137
    frosting, 119
    lace wafers, 145
    nut ice cream, 427
    pecan pie, 111
    sugar cake, 119
    syrup cake, Buckeye, 424
    walnut bars, 146
Margharita, 651
Marie's apple custard pie, 737
Marin County shrimp appetizer, 664
marinade
    for chicken, Hazel's ginger, 649
    for game, 499
    roast pork with ginger, 699
marinara sauce with sausage, 157

marinated
    bean salad, 93
    cracked crab, 676
    green bean salad, 618
    sardines, Maine, 6
marmalade bread and fruit loaves,
    402
marmalades: see pickles, relishes,
    preserves and condiments
Martha's Vineyard Stonewall
    bouillabaisse, 41
Mary Alice's homemade cooked ice
    cream, 428
Mary Lu's pecan shortbread rolls, 443
Maryland
    clam chowder, 179
    fried clams, 186
mashed potato casserole, 83
matzoh balls
    marrow bone, 163
    Northeastern, 163
mayhaw jelly, 293
mayonnaise
    dressing, Farmers Market, 621
    mustard, 302
    Northeastern, 95
    Northwestern, 760
meat
    ball soup (sopa de albondigas), 566
        cellophane noodle and, 668
    balls
        barbecued, 345
        with brown beans, 48
        buffalo, in wine sauce, 492
        cocktail, 469
        in cream, Norwegian, 478
        Dutchie's, 580
        Greek, 47
        Midwestern
            I (Iowa), 344
            II (Minnesota), 344
            III (Iowa), 345
        Northeastern, 45
        Stroganoff, 579
        venison, 497
    loaf
        avocado, 579
        beef, Dakota, 478
        buffaloaf, 493
        cheese and, 343
        fruit-stuffed, 48
        jellied, 479
        with mushroom tomato sauce,
            Paula's surprise, 47
    veal
        and ham picnic, 63
    sour cream
        Mountain/Northern Plains,
            481
        Northeastern, 63
    and potato burgers, 344

meat *(cont'd)*
  roll, spiced (rullepolse), 469
  sauce, polenta ring with, 46
  with vinegar (carne con vinagre), 599
  see also under names of specific meats
Medford pear chutney, 757
medley, Norah's vegetable, 721
Meg's
  apples 'n' beans, 713
  stuffed flank steak, 697
melon
  -ginger ice, 288
  -peach conserve, 293
menudo à la California (tripe California style), 599
meringue, 270
  dessert, banana, 749
  pie, lime, 269
meunière, trout
  Mountain/Northern Plains, 475
  Southern, 206
Mexicaine, hominy, 612
Mexican
  corn bread, 627
  rice, 611
  salad, 620
  whisky candy, 652
Michigan-style old-fashioned Brunswick stew, 357
Midsummer Eve soup of fresh green peas, 18
milk pudding, Lucy's, 640
mince pies, 113
mincemeat
  coffeecake, Oregon farmhouse, 746
  green tomato, 150
  Midwestern, 455
  -pumpkin pie, 738
  venison
    Mountain/Northern Plains, 553
    Northeastern, 150
    Vermont, 150
Minetry McCoy's miracle, 286
mining camp potatoes, 508
mint
  julep, 308
  string beans with, Sandra's, 85
minute egg dressing, 388
miso-shiru (bean paste soup), 667
Mrs. D's Moravian sugar cake, 280
Mrs. Jackson Porter Dick's black-eyed peas and hog jawl (jowl), 215
Mrs. Mescal Johnston's rice custard with lemon sauce, 281
Mrs. Sylvester's baked kidney beans, 371
Mission enchiladas, 592
Mississippi steak sauce, 304

Missouri country-style green beans, 370
mixed greens with corn bread dumplings, 245
mixed-up relish, 450
mock
  cherry pie, 739
  ravioli casserole, 693
molasses
  cake, 425
  cookies, soft, 753
  dumplings, 748
  fruit and nut bars, 147
  nut pie, 264
  taffy, 654
mold
  filbert rice, 750
  tongue and chicken, 362
molded
  cranberry salad, 387
  salmon loaf, Agnes', 683
mole
  chicken, 587
  sauce, 587
Mollie's salmon muffins, 733
Mom Abram's mustard pickle, 449
Mom's Arkansas chicken pie, 221
Monday's bean pot stew, 45
Montauk whiting chowder, 14
Monterey Jack cheese
  chile appetizers, 562
  chilies rellenos (stuffed long peppers), 610
  dip (chile con queso), 563
  enchiladas, Mission, 592
  quesadillas, 563
  and shrimp casserole, 571
  soup (sopa de queso), 566
Moravian ginger cookies, 289
morcilla (blood pudding), 600
Mormon gravy, 554
mousse
  dessert
    chocolate walnut, 136
    filbert, 750
    lemon, 429
    orange, 136
    strawberry-grapefruit, 641
  main-dish
    caviar, 4
    ham, 51
muffins
  banana, 393
  blueberry, 98
  brown sugar, 393
  corn meal, 262
  cranberry corn meal, 98
  graham, 393
  guava, 734
  oatmeal, float away, 392
  poi, 733

muffins *(cont'd)*
  salmon, Mollie's, 733
  two-bite-size, 624
mulberry pie, 416
mushroom
  and cabbage casserole, 721
  and clam soup, 665
  goulash, 720
  gravy, 458
  omelet, baked Christmas, 233
  pie
    Northwestern, 720
    Southwestern, 608
  pies, deep-dish, 506
  and pork soup, 567
  quiche, 10
  salad, fresh, 621
  soup, 19
  stew, 507
  turnovers, curried, 660
mushrooms
  au beurre, 380
  au gratin, 245
  baked, 506
  cheese-stuffed, 9
  chicken and, creamed, 705
  and cucumbers, 604
  deep-fried, 80
  with fennel, 81
  Oriental, noodles with, 612
  rice with, 611
  in sour cream, 608
  stuffed, 80
    with anchovies, 81
mussels, steamed, 30
mustard
  and caper sauce, 762
  mayonnaise, 302
  pickle, Mom Abram's, 449
  pickles
    Ernie's, 149
    Southwestern, 646
  pork chops, 56
  sauce
    broiled ling cod with, 674
    hot, 762
    potatoes with, 83
  soy sauce, 663
mustard greens
  Texas, 608
  turnip greens
    and collard greens, 244
    and dandelion greens, 505
Mylah's flat bread, 516

Nelson's chili con carne, 576
New England
  carrot marmalade, 154
  fish stew, 41

New Mexican
  chocolate, 651
  corn bread, 627
  tomato sauce, 609
ngo yuk fan kay (beef tomato), 696
Nicole's lamb ragout, 55
no-crust cheesecake, 426
no-fail
  pie crust, 408
  Welsh rabbit, 234
noodle
  balls, chicken with, 482
  ring, apricot, 747
noodles
  chicken soup with, 322
  homemade, 376
  with Oriental mushrooms, 612
  with sour cream, 611
nopales or nopalitos, 608
Norah's vegetable medley, 721
Norwegian
  dark bread, 396
  meat balls in cream, 478
nut
  apple bread, 728
  apricot bread, 728
  bourbon cake, 634
  bread, blueberry, 99
  and date whirls, 541
  orange bread, 624
  Passover torte, 128
  squares (Frazer's cheaters), 146
nuts, sugar-glazed, 310

o-apple cake, 531
oat scones, 522
oatmeal
  -apple pudding, 747
  -bran bread, 99
  cake
    Beth's, 532
    Midwestern, 423
    Southwestern, 635
  cookies, orange, 142
  muffins, 392
Oklahoma baked trout, 331
okonomiyaki (Japanese savory
  pancakes), 570
okra
  fried, 246
  ham soup, 183
  limping Susan, 246
  pickled, 646
  smothered, 609
old-fashioned
  Brunswick stew, Michigan style,
    357
  Christmas pork cake, 530
  clam chowder, 11

old-fashioned (cont'd)
  cream cake, 124
  lemon butter, 305
  raisin pie, 412
  sour cream cookies, 140
  tapioca pudding, 539
old-style ginger cookies, 544
olive
  -cheese appetizers, 316
  and wild rice casserole, 378
olives, perch with, 573
Olivette, chicken, 220
Olympia oysters poulette, 667
Olympic Peninsula oyster roast, 679
omelets
  Christmas mushroom, baked, 233
  frogs' legs, 232
  leek, baked, 720
  sour cream, 356
  Sunday brunch, 355
one-dish supper, 345
$100 frosting, 421
onion
  and broccoli casserole, 77
  -cheese tart, 316
  gravy, 457
  relish, 152
  -sour cream pie
    Midwestern, 380
    Northeastern, 82
  -spinach pie, 84
Onion Gulch potatoes, 507
onions
  and apples, fried, 81
  delicious, 380
orange
  bread, 734
  butter cake, 637
  cake
    à l', 274
    glazed, Julia's, 123
    Southern, 273
    Southwestern, 635
  and cantaloupe jam, 292
  chicken, 706
  chiffon pie, 110
  cookies, 643
  -ginger cake, quick, 741
  glazed sweet potatoes, 247
  halibut with, 572
  or lemon peel, candied, 762
  liqueur chiffon tart, 270
  marmalade, 759
  mousse, 136
  nut bread, 624
  -oatmeal cookies, 142
  peel, candied, 160
  pudding, 431
  rye bread, 517
  sauce and glaze for ham, 761

orange (cont'd)
  Seville (bitter), marmalade, 294
  sprouts, 613
  walnut
    chicken, 594
    soufflés, 638
  water ice, 639
oranges
  en surprise, 287
  flambé, 641
  stuffed
    frozen, 287
    lemons and, 297
Oreas Island clam and corn casserole,
  673
Oregon
  farmhouse coffeecakes, 746
  fried wheat, 725
  slaw, Agnes', 719
Oriental mushrooms, noodles with,
  612
Osage squaw bread, 390
Osgood pie, 410
osso buco, 701
osta kaka, 541
oukrop, Bohemian, 471
our Aunt Harriet's favorite brownies,
  290
Out Island grouper, 191
oven-barbecued
  brisket of beef, 578
  chicken wings, 318
  venison, spicy, 496
oven method jerky (dried venison),
  498
oxtail
  soup, 320
  stew, 64
oyster
  appetizer, 169
  Hangtown fry, 678
  pie, 196
  roast
    Olympic Peninsula, 679
    Puget Sound pepper pan, 679
    for 24, 196
  stew, 12
    San Juan Island, 667
  stuffing for lobster, 30
  and sweetbreads appetizer, 4
oyster plant: see salsify
oysters
  à la Louisiane, hot, 193
  with almond butter, 679
  Bienville, 193
  breaded, 678
  Casino, 193
  with cocktail sauce, 169
  corn, 240
  in cream, 6

oysters *(cont'd)*
  creamed, 195
  deviled, 192
  en brochette, 194
  fried
    Northeastern, 30
    Southern, 194
  Johnny Reb, 192
  Olympia, poulette, 667
  prairie: *see* prairie oysters
  Rockefeller, 194
  scalloped, Southern, 195
  turkey and, in patty shells, 70
Ozark's bread pudding, 432

Pacific Coast barbecue sauce, 762
Pacific fish stew, 670
Pacific-style stuffed green peppers, 675
paluski, Polish, 393
pan-fried frogs' legs, 368
pancake, David's, 735
pancakes
  with bread, 406
  buttermilk, 407
  Japanese savory, 570
  liver, 356
  potato, Holiday Folk Fair, 382
  sour cream, ranch house, 628
  sour dough, 523
    Gold Rush style, 732
  tortillas
    New Mexico, 629
    Texas, 629
    wheat flour, Virginia's, 629
Papa's Maltese baked rice, 46
papaya
  sauce, 305
  shrimp with, 571
paprika
  chicken, 68
  schnitzel, 61
Parker House rolls, 100
Parmesan cheese
  broccoli with ham and, 372
  crisps, 469
  -stuffed mushrooms, 9
  wafers, 661
parsley
  and rice casserole, 378
  -stuffed chickens, 67
parsleyed lamb riblets, 482
parsnip soup, 18
Passover
  apple cake, 123
  brownies, 148
  candied carrots for, 78
  candy, fruit, 160
  cheese blintzes, 139
  cheesecake, 126

Passover *(cont'd)*
  coconut cake with apricot glaze, 120
  crispy sticks, 105
  nut torte, 128
  potato kugel, 83
  seven-layer chocolate cake, 116
  spongecake, 118
past perfect fruitcake, 278
pasta, 49; *see also under names of specific types of pasta*
pasties, Basque sheepherder's, 698
pastry
  for pies, 273
    rich, 316
  see also pies: crust
pâté
  deer liver, 3
  maison, 3
  pork, Danish, 317
Pat's favorite dip, 175
patties
  meat (fleischkuechle), 478
  sweet potato (bitso bitso), 723
patty shells, turkey and oysters in, 70
Paula's
  Bosnian casserole, 351
  surprise meat loaf with mushroom tomato sauce, 47
pea soup, herbed fresh, 567
peach
  almond jam, 292
  -cantaloupe preserve, 453
  chutney, 298
  cobbler, 272
  conserve, 292
  -lemon-ginger conserve, 153
  -melon conserve, 293
  pie
    fresh, 272
    sour cream, 113
  preserve cake, 743
  roll-ups, 272
  soup, chilled, 183
  surprise, 751
  turnovers, fried fresh, 271
peaches
  bourbon "brandied," 153
  brandied, 452
"peaches" (pfirsiche), 443
peanut
  brittle, 461
  pie, 265
  -pumpkin pudding, 133
  soup, cream of, 184
peanut butter fudge, 461
peanuts, chicken with, in hoisin sauce, 705
pear
  and apple preserves, 453

pear *(cont'd)*
  chutney, Medford, 757
  and date preserve, 553
  lock, 552
  relish, 298
  soup, 473
pears, baked, 749
peas, black-eyed: *see* black-eyed peas
pease porridge hot, 75
pecan
  avocado bread, 624
  cherry cake, 276
  maple pie, 111
  pudding, 432
  shortbread rolls, Mary Lu's, 443
  squash casserole, 250
  -stuffed wild duck, 483
  tarts, 526
Peggy's
  caramels, 462
  carrot pickles, 448
  coconut squares, 146
  filled cookies, 441
  fruited chicken salad, 386
  green tomato pie, 525
  pumpkin chip preserves, 452
  tomato dressing, 387
  wild sandplum jelly, 454
Peg's lemon pie-cake, 526
Pendennis Club barbecue sauce, 304
Pennsylvania
  chicken pot pie, 65
  Dutch cabbage, 77
pepita or pumpkin seed sauce, 650
pepper
  cookies, 545
  pot, Philadelphia, 15
  sauce for game, 500
peppered tenderloin casserole, Charlie's Café, 343
peppermint
  stick Bavarian cream, 284
  taffy, 461
peppers, green: *see* green peppers
peppers, red: *see* red peppers
perch
  appetizer, pickled, 315
  with olives, 573
perfect divinity, 653
Pernod, custard sauce flavored with, 306
persimmon
  cookies, 445
  pudding, 432
  upside-down cake, 425
pesto alla romano, 156
pesto genovese for spaghetti, 156
pfirsiche ("peaches"), 443
pheasant
  braised, 489

pheasant *(cont'd)*
  cacciatore, 71
  in cream, 708
  fried breasts, 489
  loaf, 489
  roast
    cabbage dressing for, 488
    with sour cream sauce, 488
    stuffed, 487
    young, 488
  scalloped, or sage chicken, 709
  in sour cream, 489
Philadelphia pepper pot, 15
Philipsburg waterground corn bread,
  96
piccadillo, 208
piccalilli, 151
  Aunt Nell's, 547
pickle
  Chinese cabbage, 755
  chips, Audrey's, 447
  and frank hot potato salad, 510
  see also pickles, relishes, preserves
    and condiments
pickled
  beans, 645
  cherries (cherry olives), 549
  daikon and carrot, 755
  duck, cold, 365
  elk's heart, 499
  garden carrots, 295
  green beans, 296
  lake herring, 315
  mackerel, 6
  okra, 646
  onions, Aunt Mary's, 550
  peppers, 645
  perch appetizer, 315
  salmon
    Bertha's, 680
    gravad lax, 330
    Washington, 681
  salt herring (inlagd sill), 330
  shrimp
    Northwestern, 688
    Southern, 170
  venison heart, 4
  white radish and carrot (daikon),
    755
pickles, relishes, preserves and
    condiments, 149–56, 291–300,
    447–55, 547–53, 645–51, 755–60
  apple butter, 453
  apples, fried, 291
  barbecue sauce, 649
  basting sauce for barbecues, 649
  brandied
    apricots, 756
    peaches, 452
  "brandied" peaches, bourbon, 153

pickles, relishes, preserves and
    condiments *(cont'd)*
  catchup
    buffalo berry, 549
    cranberry, 756
    gooseberry, 452
    grape, 550
    prune, 756
  chili sauce
    Fulling Mill Farm, 152
    uncooked, 550
  chutney
    apple, 152
    apricot, 757
    elderberry, 758
    lime, 298
    mango, 299
    Medford pear, 757
    peach, 298
    pineapple, 758
    purple plum, 757
    rhubarb, 547
  conserves: *see* preserves *in this
    entry*
  cranberry
    -apple butter, 760
    sauce, 760
  cucumbers in butter and dill, 295
  high-altitude cooking, note on, 547
  hot sauce, 650
  jams
    cantaloupe and orange, 292
    cloudberry, 760
    damson, 294
    peach almond, 292
    red or black currant, 552
  jellies
    beach plum, without pectin, 155
  blackberry and apple, 291
    bourbon, 295
    chokecherry and buffalo berry,
      552
    corncob, 551
    crab apple, 552
    mayhaw, 293
    pepper, green, 294
    rose, 454
    wild sandplum, Peggy's, 454
  marinade for chicken, Hazel's
    ginger, 649
  marmalades
    carrot, New England, 154
    cucumber, 154
    grapefruit, 647
    lemon, 648
    lime, 154
    orange, 759
    pineapple, 759
    quince, 155
    rhubarb

pickles, relishes, preserves and
    condiments *(cont'd)*
  Midwestern, 453
  Northwestern, 759
  Seville (bitter) orange, 294
  tomato
    Midwestern, 454
    Northeastern, 155
  mincemeat
    green tomato, 150
    Midwestern, 455
    venison
      Mountain/Northern Plains,
        553
      Vermont, 150
  pepita or pumpkin seed sauce, 650
  piccalilli, 151
  pickle
    Chinese cabbage, 755
    chips, Audrey's, 447
    green tomato, 451
    mustard, Mom Abram's, 449
  pickled
    cherries (cherry olives), 549
    daikon and carrot, 755
    garden carrots, 295
    green beans, 296
    okra, 646
    onions, Aunt Mary's, 550
    peppers, 645
    watermelon rind, easy, 297
  pickles
    artichoke, whole, 296
    beet, best ever, 448
    bread and butter
      Midwestern, 448
      New York, 149
      Winchester, 149
    carrot, Peggy's, 448
    crab apple, 449
    cucumber
      quick, 295
      yellow (senfgurken), 550
    dills
      lazy wife, 646
      special, 447
    easy, 447
    mustard
      Ernie's, 149
      Southwestern, 646
    pumpkin, Latvian, 449
    ripe tomato, 300
    sweet carrot, 645
    watermelon, crisp, 296
    zucchini, 755
  pear lock, 552
  preserves
    apple
      -blueberry conserves, 153
      quick, 292

pickles, relishes, preserves and
    condiments (cont'd)
  cantaloupe-peach, 453
  cranberry conserves, whole, 153
  fig
    Southern, 291
    Southwestern, 648
  lemon-peach-ginger conserves,
    153
  peach
    conserve, 292
    -melon, 293
  pear
    and apple, 453
    and date, 553
  pumpkin, 453
    chip, Peggy's, 452
  strawberry, Dorothy's, 648
  Surinam, 293
ranchero, 649
relishes
  artichoke, 300
  beet, 151
  cabbage and pepper, 449
  carrot and cucumber, 548
  corn
    Mountain/Northern Plains,
      548
    and pepper, 450
  cranberry, uncooked, 151
  garden, Southern California, 647
  green, 300
  green tomato
    Midwestern, 454
    Mountain/Northern Plains,
      548
    Southern, 299
  horseradish, 758
  India, Hancock Shaker Village,
    151
  kraut, 551
  lemon, 450
  mixed-up, 450
  onion, 150
  pear, 298
  piccalilli, 151
    Aunt Nell's, 547
  rhubarb and berry, 758
  Singari daikon (white radish),
    758
  spiced wild gooseberries, 549
  sweet, 451
  tomato
    and apple, 451
    Lone Star, 647
rhubarb butter, 551
salsa cruda (cold crude sauce), 651
stuffed oranges and lemons, 297
tomato-apple butter, hot, 548
wild plum butter, pioneer, 551
xnipek, 650

picnic potato salad, 91
pie plant or rhubarb cream pie, 415
pies, dessert, 106–14, 264–73, 408–17,
    524–27, 630–33, 736–40
  amber, 409
  angel food, Grandmother's, 410
  apple
    cheese, glazed, 414
    cider, 415
    custard, Marie's, 737
    Dutch, sack, 107
    Greta's, 414
    with sour cream, 106
    squash-, 106
    stack, 271
    Tewksbury, 107
    -winy raisin, 107
  apricot, 630
    fresh, 736
  black bottom, 267
  black walnut, 264
  blueberry
    deep-dish, 108
    Northeastern, 107
    velvet custard, 108
  Boston cream, 122
    bourbon, 269
  carrot, spiced, 271
  cherry
    -apple, 525
    crumb-topped, 416
  chess
    I (Kentucky), 265
    II (Kentucky), 266
    rum and rhubarb, 273
    tarts, 266
  chocolate
    butterscotch, 268
    French silk, 411
    raisin, 632
    rum, 268
  citrus chiffon, California, 630
  cognac, 112
  cranberry
    Cape Cod, 109
    pumpkin chiffon, 109
  crust
    Dona's favorite, 524
    graham cracker, 736
    hot water, 408
    lard, 524
    Lou's, 524
    no-fail, 408
    regular, 408
    sour dough, 730
  fruited cheese, 632
  graham cracker, 411
    crust, 411
  green tomato
    Midwestern, 417
    Peggy's, 525

pies, dessert (cont'd)
  hickory nut, Cherokee, 414
  high-altitude baking, note on, 524
  honey raisin, 110
  Jeff Davis, 267
  Juneberry, 527
  lemon
    chiffon, 270
    '89er, 409
    frozen, 633
    Kentucky, 269
    nutmeg custard, 408
    pie-cake, Peg's, 526
    pioneer, 110
  lime meringue, 269
  mince, 113
  mincemeat-pumpkin, 738
  mock cherry, 739
  molasses nut, 264
  mulberry, 416
  orange
    chiffon, 110
    liqueur chiffon, 270
  Osgood, 410
  pastry for, 273
  peach, fresh, 272
  pecan
    guava, 264
    maple, 111
    Southern, 265
  pine nut, Yankee, 111
  pioneer McGinties, 739
  plum, crumb-topped, 738
  poorman's, 411
  prune, 736
  purple prune plum, 738
  pumpkin
    chiffon, Annie's, 413
    frozen, 413
    St. Louis, 412
  raisin
    old-fashioned, 412
    sour cream, 526
  raspberry, Danish, 416
  rhubarb
    or pie plant cream, 415
    and strawberry custard, 415
  rum, 268
    cream, Retha's, 410
    walnut, 632
  rutabaga, 111
  St. Genevieve angel, 411
  sesame date, 631
  shoofly, 113
  sour cream
    Northeastern, 113
    peach, 113
    raisin and walnut, 111
    Southern, 267
    squash, Grandmother's, 413
  strawberry, 412

pies, dessert *(cont'd)*
 sweet potato, 266
 tarts: *see* tarts
 vinegar, 409
 walnut, 265
 yam, sliced, 266
pies, main-course or
  accompaniment
 buffalo and beer, 493
 chicken
  elegant, 66
  Hancock Shaker Village's Sister
   Clymena's, 67
  Mom's Arkansas, 221
  pot, Pennsylvania, 65
 clam
  Cape Cod deep-dish, 23
  Massachusetts, 24
  New York, 23
 codfish, 34
 elk steak and kidney, 499
 haddock, Abigail's biscuit-topped,
   36
 hot-ta-meat, 209
 mushroom
  deep-dish, 506
  Northwestern, 720
  Southwestern, 608
 onion sour cream
  Midwestern, 380
  Northeastern, 82
 oyster, 196
 pastry, rich, 316
 salmon, Nordica, 682
 spinach-onion, 84
 tamale, 208
  with hominy grits, 209
  old-fashioned, 589
 tarts: *see* tarts
pig with a blanket, grilled, 354
pike
 baked, 332
  Minnesota, 332
  walleyed, 333
 broiled walleyed, fillets, 332
pine bark stew, 203
pine nut pie, Yankee, 111
pineapple
 -carrot cake, buttermilk glazed, 420
 chutney, 758
 marmalade, 759
pineapples, chicken in, 707
 pinto bean
 salad
  carrot, cabbage and, 618
  hot, 618
pinto beans
 and chile casserole, 582
 frijoles (Mexican), 605
 red beans, 606
 refried, 605

pinto beans *(cont'd)*
 Southwestern, 605
 spinach with (Lucy's quelites), 607
pioneer
 chocolate-potato cake, 741
 leatherbritches, 370
 lemon pie, 110
 McGinties, 739
 potatoes, 381
 popcorn pudding, 433
 sausage, 355
 wild plum butter, 551
pipian, 565
 de lengua (tongue fricassee), 600
plaintains, fried, 247
planked
 lake trout, 332
 mackerel, 572
plum
 chutney, purple, 757
 kuchen, Dutch, 745
 pie, crumb-topped, 738
 pudding, 131
 purple prune, pie, 738
 sauce, fried chicken with, 702
 wild, butter, 551
poached
 fish, sauce for, 303
 sea bass, Chinese style (bok sui
   ngui) 691
 trout in wine, 474
poi muffins, 733
pokeweed or pokeberry greens, 505
polenta ring with meat sauce, 46
Polish paluski, 393
pollo en salsa (chicken in sauce), 596
pollock
 Florentine, 33
 poached, with crab sauce, 33
pompano
 baked en papillote, 196
 Grenoble style, 197
 meunière, 197
Pontchartrain
 Creole gumbo, 205
 doves, 232
poorman's pie, 411
popcorn
 balls, 462
 pudding, pioneer, 433
popovers
 Midwestern, 391
 quahog, 97
poppy seed
 cake, 426
 dressing
  Northeastern, 95
  Shreveport, 253
 filling for kolaches, 402
 roll cookies, Czech (makova zavin),
   435

pork, 55–59, 211–17, 351–56, 480–81,
  581–84, 699–700
 and abalone soup, 669
 appetizer, Filipino seasoned, 659
 balls, Chinese, 659
 blood sausage, 356
 cabbage rolls, 480
 chops
  with apricot-apple stuffing, 58
  apricot-stuffed, 351
  baked, 56
  Bermudiana, 212
  with capers, 351
  cranberry, 57
  filbert-stuffed, 699
  kraut and apple, 352
  mustard, 56
  Ojai Valley limas and, 583
  and potato casserole, 352
  with rice, baked, 352
  sauce for, 158
  with spinach, 58
  stuffed, braised, 353
 galatoise polonaise, 57
 goulash
  Gostovich Hungarian, 583
  Mountain/Northern Plains, 481
 ham: *see* ham
 hamburgers with chili, 578
 head cheese: *see* head cheese
 jellied (souse), 215
 liver pancakes, 356
 loin, roast marinated, 211
 and mushroom soup, 567
 pig with a blanket, grilled, 354
 roast
  with ginger marinade, 699
  with herbs, 58
 sausage: *see* sausage
 scrapple, 55
 spareribs: *see* spareribs
 steaks and apple kraut, 353
 -stuffed peppers, 212
 tenderloin en croute, 583
porridge
 pease, hot, 75
 Swedish, 427
Port Angeles
 clam cakes, 674
 fried scallops, 687
port wine and horseradish sauce, 304
Portuguese bean soup, 666
posole (hominy stew), 587
pot pie, chicken, Pennsylvania, 65
pot roast
 with carrot gravy, 693
 sauerbraten, 341
 spicy New England, 45
 Texas, 580
potage d'haricots rouge (Louisiana
  red bean soup), 180

potatis korv, Swedish (potato
   sausage), 480
potato
   bake, 722
   biscuits, 97
   bread, 103
   and cabbage, 504
   casserole, 381
   -cheese bake, 508
   -chocolate cake, pioneer, 741
   -dill soup, 471
   doughnuts, 522
   dressing
      for roast duck, 463
      for turkey, 763
   dumplings
      Mountain/Northern Plains, 557
      raw, 557
   gnocchi, 723
   kugel for Passover, 83
   lefsa, 394
   mashed, casserole, 83
   and meat burgers, 344
   pancakes, Holiday Folk Fair, 382
   and pork chops casserole, 352
   puffs, 382
   salad
      apple and, hot, 92
      creamed, 511
      dilled, 511
      Fourth of July, 511
      French, 247
      hot, 247
      Northeastern
         I (New Jersey), 92
         II (Massachusetts), 92
      pickle and frank hot, 510
      picnic, 91
      sour cream
         hot, 510
         Midwestern, 386
         Northwestern, 721
   sausage (potatis korv, Swedish), 480
   soup
      with rivals, 325
      and turnip, 325
   stuffing or filling, 162
   turnip puree, 381
      and turnip soup, 325
potatoes
   hash brown, 382
   lemon, 722
   lemon shanks with, 481
   mining camp, 508
   with mustard sauce, 83
   Onion Gulch, 507
   pioneer, 381
   scalloped
      and carrots, 508
      church supper, 507
   sheepherder's, 722

potatoes (cont'd)
   skillet, 382
   stuffed, 722
   sweet: see sweet potatoes
potted doves, Halidon Hall, 232
poulet Floride, 224
poultry, 65–71, 217–29, 357–62,
   482–83, 594–97, 702–8; see also
   under names of specific types of
   poultry
poundcake
   Midwestern, 417
   Southern
      I (South Carolina), 275
      II (South Carolina), 275
Prairie (or Rocky Mountain) oysters,
   481
pralines, 309
pressed
   chicken
      Midwestern, 361
      Southern, 224
   duck, 230
prize angel food cake, 117
prosciutto, avocado with, 564
prune
   or apricot filling for kolaches, 402
   and apricot upside-down cake,
      Slovak, 418
   cake, 529
   catchup, 756
   -filled cookies, Rose's, 441
   nut bread, 732
   pie, 736
ptarmigan, fried, 710
pudding, 130–34, 281–83, 432–34,
   536–40, 640–41
   apple
      baked, 748
      -oatmeal, 747
      pie, 431
   asparagus, 369
   banana, 281
   beef, 44
   bourbon date, 282
   bread
      apple, 537
      Ozark's, 432
      rhubarb, 538
      royal, 432
   bridal, 283
   carrot, baked, 538
   casserole (cazuela), 133
   chicken, 221
   chocolate
      Northeastern, 132
      pecan, 282
      puff balls, 433
   Christmas, 132
   corn
      with bacon, 78

pudding (cont'd)
   green, 604
   Iowa chicken and, 360
   Midwestern, 374
   Southern, 78
   cracker, 134
   date
      Midwestern, 434
      Mountain/Northern Plains, 537
   fruited eggnog, 284
   Indian
      Charles Street, 134
      Northeastern, 133
   lutefisk, 335
   milk, Lucy's, 640
   orange, 431
   peanut-pumpkin, 133
   pecan, 432
   persimmon, 432
   plum, 131
   popcorn, pioneer, 433
   raisin-suet, 433
   rhubarb cake, 743
   rice, with lingonberries, 431
   rose hip, 536
   son-of-a-gun-in-a-sack, 540
   steamed
      carrot, 539
      cranberry, 130
      Midwestern, 434
      pumpkin-nut, 539
   tapioca, old-fashioned, 539
   tomato
      Northwestern, 723
      Southern, 251
puffballs, 506
puffs
   American Indian corn, 391
   hot crab meat, 169
   potato, 382
puff-ups, salmon, 685
puffy fried bread (sopaipillas), 626
Puget Sound pepper pan roast, 679
pumpkin
   blossoms, fried, 380
   bread
      Midwestern, 392
      Northeastern, 103
   chip preserves, 452
   cookies, 754
   nut pudding, steamed, 539
   pickle, Latvian, 449
   pie
      chiffon, Annie's, 413
      with cottage cheese, 109
      cranberry, chiffon, 109
      frozen, 413
      St. Louis, 412
   preserves, 453
   rolls, 101
   seed sauce

pumpkin *(cont'd)*
    chicken with, 596
    pepita or, 650
    soup
        Northeastern, 19
        Southern, 182
punch
    Edenton, 307
    hot grape, 460
    Jefferson Davis, 460
    milk, 307
    tequila, 652
purple plum chutney, 757
purple prune plum pie, 738

quahog popovers, 97
quail
    braised, 231
        with sherry, 366
    with grits and gravy, fresh, 231
    smothered, 366
quesadillas, 563
quiche
    à la Roma, 8
    mushroom, 10
    vegetable, 716
quick
    apple preserves, 292
    big hominy with sausage, 235
    clam chowder, 665
    coffeecake
        Mountain/Northern Plains, 532
        Northeastern, 126
    and easy sauce, 456
    mixer rolls, 398
    orange-ginger cake, 741
quince marmalade, 155

rabbit
    à la crème, 367
    in cream gravy, 490
    hasenpfeffer, 490
    with herbs, 711
ragout
    lamb, Nicole's, 55
    venison, 495
raisin
    -apple pie, winy, 107
    bars, 643
    -chocolate, 632
    honey pie, 110
    pie, old-fashioned, 412
    sour cream and walnut pie, 111
    -suet pudding, 433
    whole wheat cake, boiled, 535
ranch
    bread, 514
    house sour cream pancakes, 628
    steak, 581

ranch *(cont'd)*
  -style
    eggs (huevos rancheros)
        Southern California, 598
        Texas, 598
    short ribs, 578
ranchero sauce, 649
Raphael Weill chicken, 704
rarebit, chipped beef, 233
raspberry
    cooler, 139
    dessert, frozen, 428
    pie, Danish, 416
    soup, cold, 671
ravioli
    à la romana, 49
    casserole, mock, 693
    fried, 348
    spinach and ricotta filling for, 348
    veal filling for, 348
raw
    apple cake, 528
    conch salad, 186
    potato dumplings, 557
Rebecca's challah, 99
red bean
    salad, 512
    soup, Louisiana, 180
red beans
    Idaho baked, 502
    with rice
        I (Louisiana), 238
        II (Louisiana), 238
        Southwestern, 606
red cabbage and apple, 374
red eye gravy, ham steak and, 216
red flannel hash, 50
red or black currant jam, 552
red pepper and corn relish, 450
red peppers
    pickled, 645
    roasted sweet, Chuck's, 661
    see also green peppers
red snapper
    appetizer, chilled, 172
    baked, 203
    broiled, 201
    Creole, 202
    escabeche of, 173
    Florida Keys, 202
    Grenobloise, 201
red velvet cake, 422
    frosting, 422
refrigerator cookies, 438
    Rogue River, 751
refried beans: *see* kidney beans
regular pie crust, 408
reindeer burgers, 710
relishes: *see* pickles, relishes,
    preserves and condiments

remoulade
    sauce, Louisiana, 302
    shrimp, 171
Retha's rum cream pie, 410
Reuben sandwich, 50
Rex sole with lemon sauce, 690
Rhode Island
    clam cakes, 27
    fish chowder, 15
    steamer clambake, 26
rhubarb
    and berry relish, 758
    bread pudding, 538
    butter, 551
    cake, 530
        pudding, 743
    chutney, 547
    marmalade
        Midwestern, 453
        Northwestern, 759
    or pie plant cream pie, 415
    and rum chess pie, 273
    and strawberry
        custard pie, 415
        roll, 742
    wine, 555
riblets, lamb, parsleyed, 482
rice and rice dishes
    arroz con pollo Nuevo Mexicano
        (chicken with, New Mexican
        style), 597
    Basque chicken with, 703
    black-eyed peas and (Hopping
        John), 239
    casserole, Hazel's, 610
    and cheese soufflé, 377
    chili with, 577
    custard, with lemon sauce, Mrs.
        Mescal Johnston's, 281
    dilled, for shrimp, 249
    dirty (jambalaya), 249
    dressing, 464
    filbert mold, 750
    green
        California, 610
        Mountain/Northern Plains, 509
    and green bean casserole, 370
    leeks and, 82
    Maltese baked, Papa's, 46
    Mexican, 611
    with mushrooms, 611
    and parsley casserole, 378
    pork chops with, baked, 352
    pudding with lingonberries, 431
    ring, green, 248
    risotto
        milanese, 725
        tomato, fresh, 86
    salad, cold, 618
    scallion, 377
    soup, dry (sopa seca)

rice and rice dishes *(cont'd)*
    I (New Mexico), 566
    II (Texas), 566
  steamboat, 248
  -stuffed tomatoes, 615
  stuffing, for chicken, 464
  Texas, 611
  wild: *see* wild rice
rich
  pie pastry, 316
  tea loaf, 104
ricotta and spinach filling for
  ravioli, 348
ripe tomato pickle, 300
risotto
  milanese, 725
  tomato, fresh, 86
rivals, potato soup with, 325
rivel soup, 22
River Road hush puppies, 258
roast
  barbecued beef, 340
  duck, Chinese, 709
  fillet of beef, 340
  goose, 71
  mallard ducks, 602
  marinated pork loin, 211
  Oregon turkey with sausage
    dressing, 708
  pheasant with sour cream sauce,
    488
  pork with ginger marinade, 699
  saddle or leg of venison, 363
  stuffed wild goose, 485
  veal with plums, 59
  venison, 494
    leg of, 711
  wild turkey, 486
  young capon with wild rice and
    almond stuffing, 357
  young pheasant, 488
roasted
  Italian peppers, 82
  sweet peppers, Chuck's, 661
rock fish (striped bass),
  clam-stuffed baked, 185
rock salt roast, 694
rocks
  Midwestern, 442
  Northeastern, 141
Rocky Mountain (or prairie) oysters,
  481
roe, broiled shad, 39
Rogue River refrigerator cookies, 751
rollatine, veal, 61
rolled steak, German, 339
rolls
  cinnamon, plain and fancy, 405
  Dakota, 515
  flaky, 100
  light, 263

rolls *(cont'd)*
  Parker House, 100
  pumpkin, 101
  quick mixer, 398
  refrigerator, 399
  sour dough cinnamon, 731
  squash, Addie's, 398
  wheat germ, 623
  whole wheat, 514
    cinnamon, 519
roll-up cakes
  blueberry, 137
  jellyroll, 533
  peach, 272
  rhubarb and strawberry, 742
rose
  hip
    pudding, 536
    syrup, 553
  jelly, 454
  petals, crystallized, 463
  water cookies, 438
Rose's prune-filled cookies, 441
rosemary, braised lettuce with, 79
round
  roast, Cuban, 209
  steak
    with cream gravy, chicken
      fried, 338
    with green peppers, 339
    rolled, German, 339
roux for gravies, 457
royal
  bread pudding, 432
  icing, 143
rub-up fruit cake, 740
Ruby's
  sukiyaki, 696
  su-no-mo-no, 715
  teriyaki, 695
ruisleipa (Finnish sour rye bread), 397
rum
  balls (rum kegeln), 444
  and cherry sauce, 305
  -chocolate dessert, 430
  cocktail, Tarpon Isle, 308
  cream pie, Retha's, 410
  hot buttered, 159
  kegeln, 444
  pie, 268
  and rhubarb chess pie, 273
  sauce
    cherry and, 305
    Mountain/Northern Plains, 554
    Southern, 306
  walnut pie, 632
Russian salad dressing, 388
rutabaga
  pie, 111
  salad, crisp, 93

rutabagas
  boiled beef with mashed (stappa),
    342
  cheese scalloped, 84
  rye bread
    Finnish sour (ruisleipa), 397
    Grandmother's Rezac's, 513
    ham in, 729
    Northeastern, 103
    orange, 517
    sour dough, 396
    Swedish, 397

sablefish appetizer, smoked, 315
saffron bread, 402
sage
  chicken
    livers with, 65
    scalloped pheasant or, 709
saimin, 669
St. Genevieve angel pie, 411
St. Louis pumpkin pie, 412
St. Nicholoos cookies, 144
salad dressings, 93–95, 253–54,
  388–89, 512, 727
  anchovy, 389
  bacon, cooked, 254
  boiled
    Mountain/Northern Plains, 512
    Southern, 253
  California, 616
  celery seed
    Midwestern, 388
    Northwestern, 727
  cole slaw, 253
  cooked, 94
  cream, 512
  egg, minute, 388
  French, Southern California, 622
  fruit, 389
  green goddess, 727
  honey, 93
  mayonnaise
    Farmers Market, 621
    Northeastern, 95
  poppy seed
    Northeastern, 95
    Shreveport, 253
  Russian, 388
  sesame lime, for fruit salad, 622
  sour cream
    Midwestern, 388
    Mountain/Northern Plains, 512
  tomato, Peggy's, 387
salade de champignons, 90
salads, 90–95, 252–54, 384–88,
  509–12, 616–22, 717–20
  asparagus, 94
  avocado, California, 616

salads (cont'd)
banana, platter, 621
bean
carrot and cabbage, 618
hot, 618
sweet 'n' sour, 713
twenty-four-hour, 385
beet and kraut, 714
Bibb lettuce, 252
Brandywine River, 91
cabbage, 384
Greta's, 385
slaw, 509
cactus, 616
Caesar
Farmers Market, 617
Northwestern, 719
Canlis, 90
cauliflower slaw, 252
salade de champignons, 90
chicken
fruited, Peggy's, 386
hot, 361
spaghetti, 726
chick-pea, 617
clam, 89
cole slaw
with capers, 252
with cooked dressing, 94
dressing, 253
Midwestern, 384
Southern, 252
whipped cream, 385
corned beef and slaw, 387
cucumber, 385; see also
su-no-mo-no
dandelion green, 509
dandelion greens and basic
dressing, 94
Greek, 89
ham and apricot, 726
hot slaw, 386
kidney bean, 617
Kidson's bronze lettuce salad, 617
lotus root, 720
marinated
bean, 93
green bean, 618
Mexican, 620
molded cranberry, 387
mushroom, fresh, 621
potato
apple and, hot, 92
creamed, 511
dilled, 511
Fourth of July, 511
French, 247
hot, 247
Northeastern
I (New Jersey), 92

salads (cont'd)
II (Massachusetts), 92
pickle and frank hot, 510
picnic, 91
sour cream
hot, 510
Midwestern, 386
Northwestern, 721
rice, cold, 618
sardine, Maine, 91
sauerkraut, 387
spinach
and anchovy, 619
Midwestern, 386
Northeastern, 93
Stella's Pensacola gazpachy, 252
sweet 'n' sour bean, 713
Texas, 620
tomato
aspic, 620
frozen, 619
sliced, 619
tossed
Dutchie's, 621
with honey dressing, 93
salami sweetmeat (uncooked), 462
Sally Lunn, 263
salmon
Alaskan nuggets, 685
with avocado, 686
barbecued, Indian style, 686
boiled, peas and egg sauce, Fourth
of July, 38
cakes
Midwestern, 336
Washington, 681
chowder
I (Alaska), 671
II (Washington), 671
with citrus, 679
custard, 684
gravad lax, 330
heads, Wasco boiled, 681
kippered, 682
loaf, 682
with celery sauce, 683
molded, Agnes', 683
lomi, 680
muffins, Mollie's, 733
pickled
Bertha's, 680
gravad lax, 330
Washington, 681
pie Nordica, 682
puff-ups, 685
salted, 680
scallop, 680
smoked
appetizers, 561
rolls, 660

salmon (cont'd)
soufflé, 684
steaks
broiled, 685
Depoe Bay broiled, 686
stuffed, Bonneville Dam, 684
salsa cruda (cold crude sauce), 651
salsify or vegetable oyster soup, 324
salt
herring, pickled (inlagd sill), 330
pork-and-milk gravy, Hancock
Shaker Village, 43
-rising bread, 517
salted salmon, 680
scallop, 680
salty dog cocktail, 308
samp 'n' beans, 75
San Juan Island oyster stew, 667
sandbakkelse, 529
sandplum jelly, Peggy's wild, 454
Sandra's
string beans with mint, 85
tomato sauce, 156
sandwiches
king crab, 677
Reuben, 50
sangria, 652
sangrita, 651
Sarah's oando, 243
sardine salad, Maine, 91
sardines, marinated Maine, 6
sauces, dessert
butter, for apple pie pudding, 431
chocolate
Midwestern, 459
Northeastern, 132
Southern, 284
custard, 134
flavored with Pernod, 306
eggnog, 131
foamy, 131
hard, 131
honey whip, 554
lemon
Midwestern, 458
Southern, 281
orange, 459
for Grandmother's date soufflé,
639
papaya, 305
rum
and cherry, 305
Mountain/Northern Plains, 554
Southern, 306
sorghum butter, 554
vanilla, for son-of-a-gun-in-a-sack,
540
white sugar, 434
sauces for fish, poultry, meat and
vegetables, 156–58, 300–6,

455–59, 554, 649–50, 760–62
aguacate (avocado), 303
barbecue
 Hornersville, 455
 hot, 303
 Lion's Club, 456
 Mississippi, 303
 Pacific Coast, 762
 Pendennis Club, 304
 Southwestern, 649
Burgundy-olive, for roast wild
  ducks, 601
butter, 369
celery, for salmon loaf, 683
celery-tomato cocktail, for shrimp,
  170
cheese, 73
 for celery, 239
chile
 New Mexico, 592
 Southern California, 598
chili
 Fulling Mill Farm, 152
 Southern, 300
 uncooked, 550
clam, 25
cocktail, for sea foods, 455
crab, 33
cranberry
 and horseradish, 304
 Northeastern, 152
crude, cold (salsa cruda), 651
cucumber, 761
currant, 500
curry, for venison or elk fondue,
  497
egg, for ham croquettes, 217
end-of-the-garden, 456
game
 herbed, 363
 Mountain/Northern Plains, 554
 Northeastern, 158
gravy: see gravy
herb, for venison or elk fondue, 497
hollandaise
 blender, 157
 easy, 174
 Northwestern, 761
 Southern, 301
honey
 curry, Midwestern, 456
 and curry, Shreveport Club, 305
hot
 for shrimp, 170
 Southwestern, 650
Key West old lime sour, 301
koprova omacka (dill gravy), 456
Lamaze, 170
lemon and egg, for celery, 240
lobster

sauces for fish, poultry, meat and
  vegetables (cont'd)
 Midwestern, 458
 or shrimp cocktail dressing, 303
mayonnaise
 mustard, 302
 Northeastern, 95
 Northwestern, 760
meat, Northeastern, 46
mushroom tomato, 47
mustard
 and caper, 762
 hot, 762
orange glaze and, for ham, 761
papaya, 305
peas and egg, 38
pepita or pumpkin seed, 650
pepper, for game, 500
pesto alla romano, 156
pesto genovese for spaghetti, 156
plum, for fried chicken, 702
for poached fish, 303
for pork chops, 158
port wine and horseradish, 304
quick and easy, 456
ranchero, 649
remoulade, Louisiana, 302
sour cream
 -and-dill, 761
 -and-mustard, 58
Southern cocktail, for sea food, 172
soy mustard, 663
steak, 304
sweet and sour, 761
taco, 591
tartar
 Louisiana, 302
 Maryland, 187
 Northeastern, 157
 Northwestern, 760
tomato
 marinara, with sausage, 157
 Mississippi, 227
 New Mexico, 609
 Northeastern, 52
 Sandra's, 156
 Southern, 301
 Southern California, 584
 Texas, 650
 for venison or elk fondue, 497
vinaigrette, lime and herb, 302
sauerbraten, 341
sauerkraut
 apple, pork steaks and, 353
 balls, 318
 pork and apple, 352
 salad, 387
 with spareribs, 353
sausage
 ball appetizer, 565
 blood (blod polse), 356

sausage (cont'd)
 bread, 395
 Camarillo, and limas, 582
 -cranberry stuffing, 464
 with cream gravy and biscuits, 213
 dressing, roast Oregon turkey with,
  708
 game, 710
 marinara sauce with, 157
 pioneer, 355
 quick big hominy with, 235
 spiced dried (chorizo), 587
 -and-zucchini sauce, 700
sausages
 Cuban, 213
 spaghetti with, 700
sautéed dandelion flowers, 79
savory
 soufflé roll, 7
  ham and spinach filling, 7
 veal cutlet, 347
scallion rice, 377
scallop
 stew, 12
  Dungeness crab and, 676
scalloped
 carrots and potatoes, 508
 chicken, Iowa, 359
 corn, 375
 pheasant or sage chicken, 709
 potatoes, church supper, 507
 sweets and cranberries, 86
scallops
 Chilmark, 31
 fried, Port Angeles, 687
 mayonnaise, 7
scallops of veal with cheese, 61;
  see also scaloppine, veal
scaloppine, veal
 Midwestern, 347
 Northwestern, 700
Scandinavian cookies (fattigman), 438
schnitz un knepp (apples and
  dumplings), 51
schnitzel, paprika cream, 61
Schramsberg
 Petrale sole with champagne, 690
 zucchini
  blossom fritters, 662
  casserole, 724
scones, oat, 522
scrapple, 55
Scripture cake, 531
scrod, broiled, 35
scuppernong nectar, 308
sea "anemones," Hawaiian, 664
sea bass, poached, Chinese style (bok
  sui ngui), 691
sea food
 casserole, artichoke and, 198
 with eggs, 197

sea food (cont'd)
and Southern cocktail sauce, 172
Sea Hag clam chowder, 665
seasoned filberts, 661
semmel knodel (Bavarian dumplings), 466
senfgurken (yellow cucumber pickles), 550
Serbian
torte, 426
walnut strips, 436
sesame
bread sticks, 728
date pie, 631
lime dressing for fruit salad, 622
Seven Hearths chicken, 223
seven-layer chocolate cake for Passover, 116
seviche, 561
Seville (bitter) orange marmalade, 294
shad
roe
broiled, 39
creamed, with sherry, 331
cucumber and, 169
stuffed with mousse and roe, 198
shake, buttermilk, 459
Shaker tomato custard, 86
shanks
lamb
barbecued, 586
or veal with potatoes, lemon, 481
veal, à la grecque, 62
she-crab
and lobster soup, 178
soup, 178
sheepherder's potatoes, 722
shellbark hickory kisses, 143
shellfish, 23–31, 185–96, 334–35, 570–72, 672–79, 687–89
stew, Anacortes, 678
see also under names of specific shellfish
sherbet
buttermilk, 429
citrus, 749
cranberry, 139
grapefruit, 639
see also water ice
sherry
braised quail with, 366
creamed shad roe with, 331
shish kebab, Jackson Lake trout, 475
shish kebabs, venison, 496
shoofly pie, 113
short ribs
Hawaiian, 695
ranch-style, 578
shortbread
Alison's, 439
Finnish, 439

shortbread (cont'd)
rolls, Mary Lu's pecan, 443
shortcake
blueberry, 129
Fourth of July, 129
shoulder veal roast, 59
Shreveport
Club honey and curry sauce, 305
poppy seed dressing, 253
shrimp
à la Mann, 334
à la Perea, 31
à la Turque, 199
appetizer, Marin County, 664
baked fresh, with feta cheese, 31
bisque, 178
cakes, fried, 688
casserole, 570
charcoal broiled, 665
Charleston breakfast, 201
and cheese casserole, 571
chowder, 670
cocktail
with celery-tomato sauce, 170
dressing, lobster or, 303
and crab, baked, 5
Creole
chilled Gulf Coast, 171
Southern, 200
crevettes Paula, 7
dilled rice for, 249
with garlic, 687
gumbo, 199
with Lamaze sauce, 170
Louis, 689
with papaya, 571
paste, 172
pickled
Northwestern, 688
Southern, 170
remoulade, 171
soup (caldo de camaron), 565
in sour cream, 200
steamed live, 200
tempura, 663
with vegetables, 687
with vermouth, 687
Victoria, 688
shrimps Wilder, 171
Sicilian broccoli, 76
Singari daikon (white radish), 758
Sister Josephine's Shaker baked beans, 73
Sister Lisset's fish balls, 43
Hancock Shaker Village
salt-port-and-milk gravy for, 43
skewered steak and lobster, 338
skillet potatoes, 382
skyr, 540

slaw
apple, 718
cabbage, 509
and corned beef salad, 387
Oregon, Agnes', 719
see also cole slaw
slemp, 159
sliced
tomato salad, 619
yam pie, 266
slippery Jims, 376
Slovak prune and apricot upside-down cake, 418
smelt
Columbia River, 689
Fisherman's Wharf, 689
Smithfield or Smithfield-style Virginia ham, 215
smoked
fish appetizer, 315
haddock flan, 36
salmon
appetizer, 561
rolls, 660
smothered
okra, 609
quail, 366
snapper-soup-more-or-less-in-the-style-of-Bookbinder's, 14
snapping turtle
how to cook for soups, 13
how to prepare for soup, 13
and vegetable soup, 14
snibbled beans, 369
snickerdoodles, 289
snow goose, stuffed, 484
snow on the mountain, 283
soft molasses cookies, 753
soft-shelled crabs, deep-fried, 187
sole
Rex, with lemon sauce, 690
Schramsberg Petrale, with champagne, 690
with white wine, 334
sopa (soup)
de albondigas (meat ball), 566
de queso (cheese), 566
seca (dry rice)
I (New Mexico), 566
II (Texas), 566
sopaipillas (puffy fried bread), 626
sorghum cake, Grandmother's, 425
soufflés
dessert
coffee walnut, 135
date, Grandmother's, 639
honey, 135
orange walnut, 638
walnut, 638
main-dish
cheese and rice, 377

soufflés *(cont'd)*
    clam, 24
    eggplant, 241
    fish, 336
    grits
        Southern, 244
        Southwestern, 612
    roll with ham and spinach filling,
        7
    salmon, 684
soup dumplings
    Midwestern (kleppas), 465
    Northeastern, 163
    see also matzoh balls
soups, 11–22, 176–84, 318–29,
        470–73, 565–69, 665–71
    almond, 184
    baked bean, 21
    barley
        Midwestern, 323
        Mountain/Northern Plains, 472
    bean, 471
        Portuguese, 666
    beef and barley, 16
    beer, 327
        cheese, 472
    bisque
        crawfish, 177
        shrimp, 178
    black bean, 180
    black-eyed pea, 180
    Bohemian oukrop, 471
    borscht
        Holiday Folk Fair Ukrainian,
            319
        spring beet, 323
    caldo de camaron (shrimp), 565
    cellophane noodle and meat ball,
        668
    cheese, 22
    chicken
        and corn, 17
        with noodles, 322
    chicken liver, 473
    chili, 318
    chowder
        celery, 182
        corn
            Midwestern, 325
            Northeastern, 17
        egg, 22
        Yankee bean, 21
        see also soups: fish chowder
    clam and tomato broth, hot, 19
    cold
        asparagus, chilled, 20
        avocado, 569
        beer and cucumber, chilled, 20
        borscht, 324
        buttermilk, 329
        cherry, 327

soups *(cont'd)*
        peach, chilled, 183
        raspberry, 671
        strawberry cooler, 183
        vegetable, 321
    corn, 324
        fresh, 568
    crab
        she-, 178
            and lobster, 178
        South River Club, 179
    cream of
        chicken, 17
        corn, 181
        peanut, 184
        spinach
            Southern, 182
            Southwestern, 568
        tomato, 326
    curried avocado, 568
    duchess, 328
    dumpling, Korean, 668
    dumplings for, 163
    egg drop, 567
    escarole, 18
    festsuppe, 321
    field or cow pea, 182
    fish chowder
        buffalo fish, 327
        clam
            Cape Cod, 11
            and corn, 666
            Maryland, 179
            old-fashioned, 11
            quick, 665
            Sea Hag, 665
        conch, 176
        fish, Rhode Island, 15
        haddock, Down-East, 11
        Mountain, 470
        Northwestern, 670
        salmon
            I (Alaska), 671
            II (Washington), 671
        shrimp, 670
        whiting, Mountain, 14
    fish stew
        oyster, 12
            San Juan Island, 667
        Pacific, 670
        scallop, 12
    five bean, for a crowd, 326
    green peas, Midsummer Eve fresh,
        18
    herbed fresh pea, 567
    kale, 473
    lentil, 323
    lima bean with dumplings, 327
    liver dumplings in broth
        (leberkloesse), 322
    lobster, Cape Cod, 12

soups *(cont'd)*
    miso-shiru, 667
    mushroom, 19
        and clam, 665
    okra ham, 183
    Olympia oyster poulette, 667
    parsnip, 18
    pear, 473
    pepper pot, Philadelphia, 15
    pork
        and abalone, 669
        and mushroom, 567
    potato
        dill, 471
        with rivals, 325
    pumpkin
        Northeastern, 19
        Southern, 182
    red bean, Louisiana (potage d'
        haricots rouges), 180
    rivel, 22
    saimin, 669
    salsify or vegetable oyster, 324
    snapper-more-or-less-
        in-the-style-of-Bookbinder's, 14
    snapping turtle and vegetable, 14
    sopa
        de albondigas (meat ball), 566
        de queso (cheese), 566
        seca (dry rice)
            I (New Mexico), 566
            II (Texas), 566
    sour cream, with egg drops, 328
    split pea, 21
        yellow, 471
    stock pot, 16
    tomato
        fresh, 19
        Grandmother's, 326
        Southern, 181
    turkey, 322
    turnip and potato, 325
    vegetable
        beef, 319
        with dumplings, 320
        fresh, 472
        Midwestern, 320
    water cress, 20
    winter melon and ham, 668
sour cabbage, 718
sour cream
    and apple dessert, Jim's, 750
    apple pie with, 106
    cheese dumplings with, Bohemian,
        557
    coffeecake
        Northeastern, 125
        Northwestern, 742
    cookies, old-fashioned, 140
    cucumber in, 85
    cucumbers in, 385

sour cream *(cont'd)*
  -and-dill sauce, 761
  doughnuts
    Midwestern, 406
    Mountain/Northern Plains, 521
  dressing for salad
    Midwestern, 388
    Mountain/Northern Plains, 512
  meat loaf, veal
    Mountain/Northern Plains, 481
    Northeastern, 63
  mushrooms in, 608
  and mustard sauce, 58
  noodles with, 611
  omelet, 356
  onion pie
    Midwestern, 380
    Northeastern, 82
  pancakes, ranch house, 628
  pastry turnovers, 114
  peach pie, 113
  pheasant in, 489
  pie
    Northeastern, 113
    Southern, 267
  potato salad
    hot, 510
    Midwestern, 386
    Northwestern, 721
  puff biscuits, 477
  raisin
    pie, 526
    and walnut pie, 111
  sauce
    leg of lamb in, 350
    roast pheasant with, 488
  shrimp in, 200
  soup with egg drops, 328
  veal meat loaf, 63
  venison with, 495
sour dough
  cinnamon rolls, 731
  French bread, 731
  hot cakes, 731
  pancakes, 523
    Gold Rush style, 732
  pie crust, 730
  rye, 396
  white bread
    Northeastern, 102
    Northwestern, 730
souse (jellied pork), 215
South River Club crab soup, 179
Southern buttermilk corn bread, 257
Southern California
  French dressing, 622
  garden relish, 647
Southern fried chicken
  I (Mississippi), 217
  II (Tennessee), 218
  III (Alabama), 218

Southern Maryland stuffed ham, 216
Southern-style
  biscuits, 260
  turnip greens, 244
soy mustard sauce, 663
spaghetti
  chicken, 226
  with clam sauce, 25
  salad, chicken, 726
  with sausage-and-zucchini sauce,
    700
  with sausages, 700
  Texas, 577
spanakopita, George's (spinach-onion
    pie), 84
Spanish stew (gesado), 581
spareribs
  barbecued
    Joe's, 581
    Midwestern, 354
  Bohemian, 480
  boiled, 212
  deep-fried, 212
  Kai's, 699
  sauerkraut with, 353
special dills, 447
spice
  cake, 119
  cookies, 435
spiced
  butternut squash, 89
  carrot pie, 271
  meat roll (rullepolse), 469
spicy, oven-barbecued venison, 496
spider corncake, 96
spinach
  and anchovy salad, 619
  and artichokes
    Asphodel style, 250
    Southwestern, 607
  with beans (Lucy's quelites), 607
  with coconut cream, 716
  custard, 85
  and ham filling, 7
  or luau, chicken with, 706
  malfatti, 717
  onion pie, 84
  pork chops with, 58
  and ricotta filling for ravioli, 348
  salad
    Midwestern, 386
    Northeastern, 93
    Northwestern, 717
  soup, cream of
    Southern, 182
    Southwestern, 568
spit-roasted
  leg of lamb, 53
  saddle of venison, 229

split pea soup, 21
  yellow, 471
split peas with ham, 714
sponge, Hancock Village steamed
    ginger, 135
spongecake
  Northeastern, 118
  Passover, 118
  zuppa inglese, 117
spoon bread, 256
  bacon and cheese, 259
spreads, canapé
  cottage cheese, 317
  see also appetizers
spring beet borscht, 323
spritz cookies, 545
  Jane's, 752
spruce tip syrup, 553
squash
  -apple pie, 106
  bake
    Grandma's, 503
    Midwestern, 381
  butternut, spiced, 89
  dolma, Armenian, 349
  pecan casserole, 250
  pie, Grandmother's, 413
  rolls, Addie's, 398
  summer, green (calabacitas), 615
  yellow
    casserole, 614
    and cheese casserole, 88
    cheese-stuffed, 250
squirrel, fried, 367
stacked enchiladas, 591
stappa (mashed rutabagas), boiled
    beef with, 342
stars, cinnamon, 753
steak
  bear, 494
  buffalo
    deviled, 492
    with wild rice stuffing, 492
  deviled, 44
  filet mignon, flamed, 339
  flake, 580
  flank, Meg's stuffed, 697
  and lobster on a skewer, 338
  ranch, 581
  round
    chicken fried, with cream gravy,
      338
    with green peppers, 339
    rolled German, 339
  in a sack, 477
  sauce, Mississippi, 304
  venison, broiled, 497
steamboat rice, 248
steamed
  carrot pudding, 539
  cranberry pudding, 130

steamed (cont'd)
Florida lobster, 191
hard-shelled crabs, 189
Indian bread, 390
live shrimp, 200
lobster, 28
mussels, 30
pudding, 434
pumpkin-nut pudding, 539
stone crab, 118
steamer clambake, Rhode Island, 26
Stella's Pensacola gazpachy salad, 252
stew, fish
bouillabaisse, Martha's Vineyard
Stonewall, 41
Chesapeake Bay, 204
crab
Dungeness, and scallop, 676
Northeastern, 27
Northwestern, 674
Southern, 187
Louisiana, 203
New England, 41
New York, 40
oyster, 12
San Juan Island, 667
pine bark, 203
scallop, 12
shellfish, 678
Southern California, 572
stew, meat, poultry, and vegetable
bean pot, Monday's, 45
Brunswick
old-fashioned, Michigan style,
357
Southern, 228
game, 712
hominy (posole), 587
kid (guisado de cabrito), 599
lamb
dilled, 349
green chili, Indian Zuñi, 585
vegetable and, Gostovich, 585
mushroom, 507
oxtail, 64
Spanish (gesado), 581
tripe, 701
stewed tomatoes, 507
stock pot soup, 16
stone crab, steamed, 188
stone-ground wheat bread, 733
strawberry
cooler, 183
glaze, 127
-grapefruit mousse, 641
pie, 412
preserves, Dorothy's, 648
and rhubarb
custard pie, 415
roll, 742
tart, fresh, 740

straws, cheese, 176
string beans: see green beans
striped bass
baked, 32
clam-stuffed baked, 185
with minced clam stuffing, 32
Stroganoff
black bear, 494
meatballs, 579
strudel, apple, 525
stuffed
artichokes, 603
baked tomatoes, Texas, 615
cherry tomatoes, 174
chicken
breasts, 222
legs, 359
country ham, Southern Maryland,
216
eggplant, 242
flank steak, Meg's, 697
green peppers, Pacific-style, 675
long peppers (chilies rellenos), 609
casserole, 610
mushrooms, 80
with anchovies, 81
oranges and lemons, 297
potatoes, 722
roast pheasant, 487
salmon, Bonneville Dam, 684
snow goose, 484
tomatoes, Aunt Willie's, 382
trout, baked, 476
venison slices, 496
whitefish, 334
stuffings and garnishes for meat,
poultry, fish and vegetables,
161–62, 357, 463–65, 763–64
apple, for buffalo ribs, 491
apricot
for pork chops, 351
for wild goose, 484
apricot-apple, for pork chops, 58
cabbage dressing, for roast
pheasant, 488
corn bread, for chicken, 219
cranberry
-corn bread, for turkey, 161
sausage, for turkey or capon, 464
dressing for fowl, 465
filbert, Oregon, for turkey, 763
fruit
Midwestern, for poultry, 465
Northeastern, for goose or duck,
162
ham dressing or coating, 76
macadamia nut, for turkey, 763
oyster
for lobster, 30
for turkey or goose, 162
potato

stuffings and garnishes (cont'd)
for chicken, 162
dressing
for roast duck, 463
for turkey, 763
rice
for chicken, 464
dressing, 464
sausage dressing, roast Oregon
turkey with, 708
wild rice
and almond, for roast young
capon, 357
for buffalo steaks, 492
for wild or domestic fowl, 463
suet-raisin pudding, 433
sugar
-coated banana drops, 444
cookies, 209
-glazed nuts, 310
plum cake, 277
sukiyaki, Ruby's, 696
summer squash: see squash, summer
Sunday brunch omelet, 355
su-no-mo-no, Ruby's, 715
Surinam preserves, 293
sushi, West Coast, 663
swamp cabbage: see heart of palm
Swedish
almond gingersnaps, 445
klenater (Christmas crullers), 405
limpa, 403
porridge, 427
potatis korv (potato sausage), 480
rye bread, 397
sweet
beef balls, 744
carrot pickles, 645
'n' sour bean salad, 713
relish, 451
sweet potato
biscuits, 261
patties (bitso bitso), 723
pie, 266
pone, 281
spoon bread, 260
sweet potatoes
bourbon spiced, baked, 248
and cranberries, scalloped, 86
orange-glazed, 247
sweetbreads and oyster appetizer, 4
sweetmeat, salami (uncooked), 462
Swiss cheese
balls, 175
beer soup, 472
potato bake, 508
and squash casserole, 88
veal scallops with, 61
Swiss veal, 62
sylta (jellied veal loaf), 349
Syrian-style lamb and eggplant, 349

syrup
blackberry, 307
rose hip, 553
spruce tip, 553

taco sauce, 591
tacos, 591
taffy
honey, 556
molasses, 654
peppermint, 461
tamale
peppers, 590
pie, 208
with hominy grits, 209
old-fashioned, 589
tamales, 588
Texas, 592
tangy beets, 370
tapioca pudding, old-fashioned, 539
Tarpon Isle rum cocktail, 308
tarragon crab, artichoke hearts and,
573
tartar sauce
Louisiana, 302
Maryland, 187
Northwestern, 760
tarts
blackberry, Depoe Bay, 739
cranberry-filbert, 737
onion cheese, 316
pecan, 526
strawberry, fresh, 740
walnut, 633
wild gooseberry, 740
tea
biscuits, 441
loaf, rich, 104
tempura
fried fish, 692
shrimp, 663
tenderloin (beef) casserole, Charlie's
Café peppered, 343
tenderloin en croute, pork, 583
tequila punch, 652
teriyaki
appetizer, 660
Ruby's, 695
sauce, fried chicken in, 702
testicles, calves': see Rocky Mountain
(or prairie) oysters
Tewksbury apple pie, 107
Texas
caviar, 564
chili, 575
corn bread, 627
liver, 600
mustard greens, 608
pot roast, 580
rice, 611

Texas (cont'd)
salad, 620
spaghetti, 577
stuffed baked tomatoes, 615
tamales, 592
thermidor, lobster, 29
thin sugar frosting, 401
three drops, 10
Tillamook cheese and clam appetizers,
657
tiropetes (cheese pastries), 9
toast, apple, 407
toffee
Northwestern, 763
Southwestern, 653
tomato
apple butter, hot, 548
and apple relish, 451
aspic, 620
bulghur or cracked wheat, 509
butter, 452
and clam broth, hot, 19
custard, Shaker, 86
dressing, Peggy's, 387
freeze with avocado topping, 175
fritters, 86
gravy
Mae's, 457
Midwestern, 457
Southern, 304
marmalade
Midwestern, 454
Northeastern, 155
pudding
Northwestern, 723
Southern, 251
relish
green
Midwestern, 454
Mountain/Northern Plains,
548
Southern, 299
Lone Star, 647
ripe, pickle, 300
risotto, fresh, 86
salad
frozen, 619
sliced, 619
sauce
marinara, with sausage, 157
Mississippi, 227
New Mexico, 609
Northeastern, 52
Sandra's, 156
Southern, 301
Southern California, 584
Texas, 650
for venison or elk fondue, 497
soup
cream of, 326
fresh, 19

tomato (cont'd)
Grandmother's, 326
Southern, 181
tomatoes
broiled, 251
cherry, stuffed, 174
and green beans au gratin, 236
hominy and, baked, 244
rice-stuffed, 615
stewed, 507
stuffed
Aunt Willie's, 383
baked, Texas, 615
tongue
and chicken mold, 362
-escabeche salad, 601
fricassee (pipian de lengua), 600
torte
apricot, 633
blitz, 527
harvest, 637
Passover nut, 128
Serbian, 426
tortillas
egg-filled, 599
New Mexico, 629
Texas, 629
wheat flour, Virginia's, 629
tossed salad
Dutchie's, 621
with honey dressing, 93
trifle, 285
pudding, 286
royal, 285
tripe
Boston, 64
California style (menudo à la
California), 599
Creole, 211
stew, 701
trout
amandine, 207
with anchovies, 474
baked, 475
stuffed, 476
Chartres Street, 206
chowder, Mountain, 470
Diamond Lake, 690
fried, with walnut butter,
Joe's, 691
lake, planked, 332
Mackinaw, baked, 475
meunière
Mountain/Northern Plains, 475
Southern, 206
Oklahoma, baked, 331
poached in wine, 474
shish kebab, Jackson Lake, 475
tuna
fra diavolo, fresh, 39
-stuffed peppers à la sarda, 40

turkey
  and oysters in patty shells, 70
  roast Oregon, with sausage
      dressing, 708
  soup, 322
  stuffings for
    cranberry
        -corn bread, 161
        sausage, 464
    filbert, Oregon, 763
    macadamia nut, 763
    oyster, 162
    potato, 763
    wild rice, 463
  wild, roast, 486
turnip
  potato puree, 381
  and potato soup, 325
turnip greens
  mustard greens
      and collard greens, 244
      or dandelion greens, 505
  Southern-style, 244
turnips, yellow
  cheese scalloped, 84
  glazed, 84
turnovers
  curried mushroom, 660
  fruit, fried, 271
  peach, fried fresh, 271
  sour cream pastry, 114
turtle, how to cook for soups, 13; see
    also snapping turtle
twenty-four-hour bean salad, 385
twist loaf, Ukrainian, 399
twists, butter, 746
two-bite-size muffins, 624
tzimmes, carrot, 78

Ukrainian
    borscht, Holiday Folk Fair, 319
    twist loaf, 399
uncooked
    chili sauce, 550
    cranberry relish, 151
upside-down cakes
    apple, 123
    coconut, fresh, 740
    persimmon, 425
    prune and apricot, Slovak, 418
    squares, blueberry, 743
Uvalde chili, 575

Valborg's coffeecake, 404
vanilla
    ice cream, 428
    sauce, for son-of-a-gun-in-a-sack,
        540

veal, 59–64, 347–49, 481, 700–1
  creamed, 60
  cutlet, savory, 347
  and eggplant casserole, 347
  filling for ravioli, 348
  goulash, Gostovich Hungarian, 583
  and ham
      manicotti with, 63
      picnic loaf, 63
  jelled, 62
  lemon shanks with potatoes, 481
  loaf, jellied (sylta), 349
  Lorraine, 60
  osso buco, 701
  paprika cream schnitzel, 61
  roast, with plums, 59
  rollatine, 61
  scallops with cheese, 61
  scaloppine
      Midwestern, 347
      Northwestern, 700
  schnitzel, paprika cream, 61
  shanks à la grecque, 62
  shoulder roast, 59
  sour cream meat loaf
      Mountain/Northern Plains, 481
      Northeastern, 63
  Swiss, 62
  tartar with lemon, 562
vegetable
  bake, 384
  beef soup, 319
  casserole
      Libby's summer, 87
      Mountain/Northern Plains, 501
  and lamb stew, Gostovich, 585
  medley, Norah's, 721
  oyster soup, salsify or, 324
  platter, Yette's garden, 88
  pot, 615
  quiche, 716
  soup
      cold, 321
      with dumplings, 320
      fresh, 472
      Midwestern, 320
vegetables, 73–95, 236–51, 369–84,
    501–9, 603–16, 713–25
  curried, cold, 87
  shrimp with, 687
  see also under names of specific
      vegetables
velvet lunch cake, 121
venison
  barbecued, 363
  braten, 363
  broiled steaks, 497
  fondue, elk or, 497
  heart, pickled, 4
  jerky, oven method, 498
  leg or saddle of, 363

venison (cont'd)
  meat balls, 497
  mincemeat
      Mountain/Northern Plains, 553
      Northeastern, 150
  ragout, 495
  roast, 494
      leg of, 711
  saddle of, spit-roasted, 229
  shish kebabs, 496
  with sour cream, 495
  spicy, oven-barbecued, 496
  stuffed slices, 496
  supreme, 72
  wild burgers, 364
Vermont
  boiled dinner, 49
  ham, glazed, 51
  mincemeat, 150
vermouth
  abalone with, 672
  shrimp with, 687
Veronica's
  Christmas cookies, 143
  creamed horseradish, 79
vinaigrette
  asparagus, 717
  lime and herb sauce, 302
vinaterta, 534
vine maple roast, 694
vinegar
  greens, 718
  pie, 409
Virginia ham, Smithfield or
    Smithfield-style, 215; see also
    ham, country
Virginia's wheat flour tortillas, 629

wafers
  benne seed, 176
  cheese, 316
  Parmesan, 661
waffles, 260
walleyed pike
  baked, 333
  fillets, broiled, 333
walnut
  brown bread, 625
  butter, Joe's fried trout with, 691
  cake, 635
  Cheddar loaf, 625
  chocolate mousse, 136
  cinnamon quick bread, 626
  and date whirls, 541
  -fig bread, 623
  fudge, 653
  orange chicken, 594
  pie, 265
  pumpkin pudding, steamed, 539
  rum pie, 632

walnut *(cont'd)*
  soufflé, 638
  soufflés, coffee, 135
  strips, Serbian, 436
  tarts, 633
walnuts, candied, 652
warm lemon sauce, 458
Wasco boiled salmon heads, 681
Wassail bowl, 159
water cress
  biscuits, 391
  soup, 20
water ice
  fruit, 749
  ginger-melon, 288
  lemon, 140
  orange, 639
  see also sherbet
watermelon
  pickles, crisp, 296
  rind, easy pickled, 297
Welsh rabbit, no-fail, 234
wheat
  bread, stone-ground, 733
  flour tortillas, Virginia's, 629
  germ rolls, 623
  Oregon fried, 725
whipped cream
  cake, 533
  cole slaw, 385
whisky candy, Mexican, 652
white bean salad, 75
white cake with choice of frostings, 420
white fruitcake, 278
white radish (daikon) and carrot, pickled, 755
white sugar sauce, 434
white wine, sole with, 334
whitebait appetizer, 660
whitefish
  appetizer, smoked, 315
  balls, 336
  with capers, 333
  soufflé, 336
  stuffed, 334
whiting chowder, Montauk, 14
whole artichoke pickles, 296
whole wheat
  applesauce cookies, 543
  biscuits, 522
  boiled raisin cake, 535
  bread, easy 100 per cent, 515

whole wheat *(cont'd)*
  chiffon cake, 532
  rolls, 514
    cinnamon, 519
Wichita duck, 364
wild burgers, 364
wild duck
  breasts
    en casserole, baked, 365
    grilled, 365
  country captain, 231
  gumbo, 601
  Mountain/Northern Plains
    I (Wyoming), 483
    II (Wyoming), 484
  pecan-stuffed, 483
wild ducks
  with Madeira, 230
  roast, with Burgundy-olive sauce, 601
wild goose
  with apricot stuffing, 484
  roast stuffed, 485
  with stuffing, 485
wild gooseberries, spiced, 549
wild gooseberry tart, 740
wild grape dumplings, 430
wild mushroom fritters, 506
wild plum butter, pioneer, 551
wild rice
  and almond stuffing, roast young capon with, 357
  and beef casserole, 346
  with carrots, baked, 378
  and chicken casserole, 357
  with chicken livers, 379
  dressing, buffalo steaks with, 492
  with filberts, 725
  Midwestern
    I (Minnesota), 379
    II (Minnesota), 380
  and olive casserole, 378
  stuffing for wild or domestic fowl, 463
wild sandplum jelly, Peggy's, 454
wild turkey, roast, 486
wilted
  leaf lettuce, 510
  lettuce
    Agnes', 719
    "alfalfa," 719
    Midwestern, 373

wilted lettuce *(cont'd)*
  Northeastern, 80
Winchester Center bread and butter pickles, 149
wine
  beet, 555
  elderberry blossom
    Mountain/Northern Plains, 555
    Southern, 307
  rhubarb, 555
  trout poached in, 474
winter melon and ham soup, 668
winy apple-raisin pie, 107
Wyatt Earp, doves, 366

xnipek, 650

yam pie, sliced, 266
Yankee
  bean chowder, 21
  pine nut pie, 111
yeast
  breads: *see* breads, yeast
  fruit dumplings, 520
  large recipe for bread, 394
yellow cucumber pickles (senfgurken), 550
yellow split pea soup, 471
yellow squash: *see* squash: yellow
yellow turnips: see turnips, yellow
Yette's garden platter, 88

zucchini
  appetizer, 8
  baked, 88
  in batter, 724
  blossom fritters, Schramsberg, 662
  calabacitas, 615
  and cheese
    casserole, 614
    custard, 249
  chicken and, 68
  dilled, 724
  eggplant and baked, 87
  pickles, 755
  -and-sausage sauce, spaghetti with, 700
  Schramsberg, casserole, 724
  squash bake, 381
  torre, 614
  toss, 723
zuppa inglese, 117